Solaris 8 System Administrator's Reference

Janice Winsor

Sun Microsystems Press
A Prentice Hall Title

Printed in the United States of America
Editorial/production supervisor: Wil Mara
Cover design director: Jerry Votta
Cover designer: Kavish & Kavish Digital Publishing & Design
Manufacturing manager: Alexis R. Heydt
Marketing manager: Bryan Gambrel
Acquisitions editor: Gregory G. Doench
Sun Microsystems Press
Marketing manager: Michael Llwyd Alread
Publisher: Rachel Borden
10 9 8 7 6 5 4 3
ISBN 0-13-027701-0
Sun Microsystems Press
A Prentice Hall Title

PREFACE

The *Solaris 8 System Administrator's Reference* is your complete guide to all of the manual pages in Section 1M, "Maintenance Commands," of the online reference documentation.

All documentation references within this guide are to the official Solaris documentation and to RFCs. To access Sun Microsystems, Inc., documentation online, see

http://docs.sun.com.

Audience

This book is for any administrator of the Solaris system software who needs to refer to any of the Section 1M Maintenance Commands in the online manual pages for quick reference or for more detailed information.

Conventions Used in This Book

The following table shows the typographic conventions used in this book.

Typeface or Symbol	Description
courier	Indicates a command, file name, object name, method, argument, JavaScript keyword, HTML tag, file content, or code excerpt.
courier italics	Indicates a variable that you should replace with a valid value.

Typeface or Symbol	Description
courier	Indicates text that you type.
italics	Indicates definitions, emphasis, or a book title.

Note — In this document, the term IA (Intel Architecture) is used instead of x86 to refer to the Intel 32-bit processor architecture, which includes the Pentium, Pentium Pro, Pentium II, Pentium II Xeon, Celeron, Pentium III Xeon processors and comparible microprocessor chips made by AMD and Cyrix.

Icons

Within this guide, any material that is new or revised in the Solaris 8 release is marked with a "New" icon in the margin.

In addition, the list of commands in the "Introduction" chapter and in the Intro manual page in Chapter I are marked with asterisks to show commands that are changed or revised in this release and show the New icon in the margin for new commands.

How This Book Is Organized

The "Introduction" chapter provides a quick reference to the contents of this book by functional grouping. The commands are grouped alphabetically within their installation package categories and list the number for the first page of each command. Within the "Core Solaris (Usr)" category, the commands are grouped by function.

The rest of the book is a dictionary-style alphabetic reference to the commands.

The Subject Index contains page references for commands both by name and by subject.

ACKNOWLEDGMENTS

Sun Microsystems Press would like to acknowledge the following people for their contributions to this book.

Bill Calkins, Sr. Consultant, Pyramid Design Inc., for acting as a technical reference and providing some of the more complex examples.

Burk P. Holzgen, Pyramid Consulting, for answering questions and providing some of the more complex examples.

Peter Gregory, author of *Solaris Security* published by Sun Microsystems Press and Prentice Hall and principal of the HartGregory Group, for acting as a technical reference and providing some of the more complex examples.

Larissa Brown and Bill Lane of Sun Microsystems, Inc., for enabling me to participate in the Solaris 8 Beta program.

Leanne Berger, Tina Bracksher, Kevin Brown, Jennifer Cardoza, David Comay, Liz Hruniewich, Michael Hutchings, Thomas Johnson, Mara Roccaforte, Ann Marie Rubin, Ken Silvers, Matt Simmons, Ghee Seng Teo, Karen Vergakes, and Susan Weber of Sun Microsystems, Inc., for answering my questions about the Solaris 8 Beta release.

Maria Santiago of Sun Microsystems, Inc., for enabling me to participate in the SEAS 3.0 Beta program and for answering questions about the products in the Solaris 8 Admin Pack.

Gordon Marler, AT&T Wireless Services, WLTG, for information about the `clear_locks` command.

Linda Gallops, SQA Product Engineering, Sun Microsystems, Inc., for technical help.

Mary Lautner, Program Manager, Solaris Software Group, Sun Microsystems, Inc., for providing useful information about the Solaris 8 release.

Janice Gelb, Sun Microsystems, Inc., for information about terminology.

Gary Parker, Sun Microsystems, Inc., for technical help.

The author would like to acknowledge the following people for their contributions to this book.

Rachel Borden of Sun Microsystems Press and Greg Doench of Prentice Hall for their unfailing support and friendship.

Mary Lou Nohr for editing this manuscript with her usual skill and tact.

Camille Trentacoste for book and template designs and for her help in implementing additional design elements.

Her husband, Maris, for his love and support.

CONTENTS

D

N

Introduction

The *Solaris 8™ System Administrator's Reference* is your complete alphabetic reference to all of the manual pages in Section 1M of the online reference documentation for the Solaris 8 release.

This chapter provides a quick reference to the contents of this book by functional grouping. The commands are grouped alphabetically within their installation package categories and list the number for the first page of each command. Within the "Core Solaris (Usr)" category, the commands are grouped by function. Commands that have been revised in the Solaris 8 release are marked with an asterisk (*). Commands that are new in the Solaris 8 release are marked with a New icon in the margin.

AnswerBook2 Documentation Server (SUNWab2u)

Authentication Management Infrastructure (SUNWami)

Automated Security Enhancement Tools (SUNWast)

Core Solaris (Usr) (64-bit) (SUNWcsxu)

Core Solaris Libraries (32-bit SUNWcsl) (64-bit SUNWcslx)

Core Solaris (Shared Libs) (SUNWcsl)

Core Solaris (Usr) (SUNWcsu)

Archiving Commands

Auditing Commands

Date and Time-Zone Commands

Disk Management Commands

DNS Commands

File Management Commands

New!

Installation Commands

New!

Kernel Module Commands

Mail Commands

Miscellaneous Commands

New!

Networking Commands

New!

NIS+ Commands

Service Access Facility (SAF) Commands

Shell Programming Commands

Streams Commands

System Management Commands

New!

Network Time Protocol v3, NTP Daemon, and Utilities (xntpd 3.4y) (SUNWntpu)

Networking UUCP Utilities (Usr) (SUNWbnuu)

NIS Server for Solaris (Usr) (SUNWypu)

PGX32 (Raptor GFX) X Window System Support) (TSIpgxw)

Platform Support, OS Functionality (Root) (SUNWos86u)

Solstice Enterprise Agents 1.0.3 Simple Network Management Protocol (SUNWsasnm)

Solstice Enterprise Agents 1.0.3 SNMP Daemon (SUNWmibii)

Solstice Launcher (SUNWsadml)

SPARCstorage Array Utility (SUNWssaop)

Sun Enterprise Network Array Firmware and Utilities (SUNWluxop)

SunSoft Print Client (Usr) (SUNWpcu)

A

ab2admin — Command-Line Interface for AnswerBook2 Administration

Synopsis

```
/usr/lib/ab2/bin/ab2admin [-h][-H command][-o command [arguments]]
```

Description

Use the `ab2admin` command-line interface to administer AnswerBook2 collections and documents on a specified AnswerBook2 server. You can perform the following tasks with the `ab2admin` command.

- Scan for locally installed collections and update the server database.
- Obtain a listing of collections and books.
- Stop the server.
- Start the server.
- Restart the server.
- Turn on or off the server log files.
- Rotate the log files.
- Configure the server to resolve links to books located on other AnswerBook2 servers.
- Control server access by adding or deleting users to the pool of administrative users.
- Enable or disable access control.

21

ab2admin can connect to any AnswerBook2 server, either local or remote. Certain functions such as stop, start, and restart apply only to the local AnswerBook2 server. If the AnswerBook2 server is protected by a password, then you must provide a user ID and password to initiate an administration task.

To run ab2admin interactively, type ab2admin from the command line and then enter commands as prompted. You can also execute the command entirely from the command line with the -o option.

The ab2admin command is run automatically as part of the installation of the SUNWab2u AnswerBook2 package.

Options

-h   Display help.

New! -H [command] Display help and help for a specified command.

-o subcommand [arguments]

The supported subcommands are listed below.

New! access_off [-m server] [-p server-port-number]

Disable the server access log file.

access_on [-m server] [-p server-port-number]

Enable the server access log file.

add_admin -u user-id [-m server] [-p server-port-number]

Add user to the authorized list of server administrators.

add_coll -d path [-m server] [-p server-port-number]

Add AnswerBook1 or AnswerBook2 collections into the specified AnswerBook2 server database.

add_server -M alternate-server
-P alternate-server-port-number [-m server]
[-p server-port-number]

Add alternate server to the specified server.

auth_off [-m server] [-p server-port-number]

Disable the server administration verification.

auth_on [-m server] [-p server-port-number]

Enable the server administration verification.

New! autostart_no [-m server] [-p server-port-number]

Stop AnswerBook2 server from starting automatically when system is (re)booted.

New! autostart_yes [-m server] [-p server-port-number]

Automatically start AnswerBook2 server when system is (re)booted.

browser [-m *server*][-p *server-port-number*] **New!**

Launch a Web browser for accessing AnswerBook2 Administration pages.

change_password -u *admin-id* [-m *server*] [-p *server-port-number*]

Change authorized administrator's password.

del_admin -u *user-id* [-m *server*][-p *server-port-number*]

Delete the user from the list of authorized server administrators.

del_coll -t *collection-title* [-m *server*] [-p] *server-port-number*]

Remove AnswerBook1 or AnswerBook2 collections from the specified server's database.

del_server -M *alternate-server* -P *alternate-server-port-number* [-m *server*] [-p *server-port-number*]

Delete alternate server from list of servers known to the specified server.

error_off [-m *server*][-p *server-port-number*]

Disable the server error log file.

error_on [-m *server*][-p *server-port-number*]

Enable the server error log file.

help [*command*] **New!**

List information about all commands or about a specified command.

list [-m *server*][-p *server-port-number*]

List AnswerBook1 and AnswerBook2 collections available on the specified server. The listing includes the books contained within collections.

list_server [-m *server*][-p *server-port-number*] **New!**

List all alternate servers defined for the specified server.

menu Display a condensed list of command options. **New!**

modify_server_name -s *new-server-name* [-m *server*] [-p *server-port-number*]

Modify the server's name.

modify_server_port -a*new-server-port-number* [-m *server*] [-p *server-port-number*]

Modify the server's port number.

```
restart
```
Restart local AnswerBook2 server. Requires root access.

```
rotate_access [-m server][-p server-port-number]
```
Save and reset the server access log file.

```
rotate_error [-m server][-p server-port-number]
```
Save and reset the server error log file.

```
scan [-m server][-p server-port-number]
```
Scan for locally installed collections (AnswerBook1 or AnswerBook2) and update the collections on specified server's database.

```
start
```
Start local AnswerBook2 server. Requires root access.

```
start -D
```
Start local AnswerBook2 server in debug mode. Requires root access.

```
stop
```
Stop local AnswerBook2 server. Requires root access.

```
view_access [-m server][-p server-port-number]
```
View the contents of the server access log file.

```
view_config [-m server][-p server-port-number]
```
View the configuration settings of the server.

```
view_error [-m server][-p server-port-number]
```
View the contents of the server error log file.

New! **Note** — The install and uninstall subcommands have been removed from the ab2admin command in the Solaris 8 release. Instead, use the pkgadd and pkgrm commands to install and uninstall AnswerBook2.

Usage

quit	Exit interactive mode.
bye	Exit interactive mode.
exit	Exit interactive mode.
New! ? [command]	Get help in interactive mode.
New! h [command]	Get help in interactive mode.

Examples

The following example lists AnswerBook2 collections on the local system paperbark. As the example shows, you must define an AnswerBook2 administrator ID and assign a password before you can perform any administrative functions.

> **Note** — The administrator ID does not need to match a user's system login ID. The administrator ID is used only by the ab2admin command for performing document-related administrative functions on a specific server.

```
paperbark% alias ab2admin /usr/lib/ab2/bin/ab2admin
paperbark% ab2admin -o list
```

You are trying to access the AnswerBook2 administration functions on this document server. Access to these functions is controlled by AnswerBook2-specific administrator ids and passwords.

At the present time, AnswerBook2 administrative access control is turned on; however, there is no defined AnswerBook2 administrator ID and password on this system.

To define an AnswerBook2 administrator ID and password, perform the following steps:

1. Log in as root on the AnswerBook2 server machine.
2. Run the following command: /usr/lib/ab2/bin/ab2admin -o add_admin -u ID
   Where: ID is the login ID for the administrator and can consist of any number of characters and numbers.
3. The AnswerBook2 software will prompt you to enter and verify the password for the specified login ID.

```
paperbark% su
# /usr/lib/ab2/bin/ab2admin -o add_admin -u winsor
```

Please enter password for winsor :
Please reenter the same password :
Administrative user created successfully
```
# exit
paperbark% ab2admin -o list
```

To do any administration, a password is required.
Please enter administrative ID : **winsor**
Please enter administrative password :

```
Collection Listing
  AnswerBook2 Collection:
    "KCMS Collection"
    "OpenBoot Collection"
    "Solaris 8 Common Desktop Environment Developer Collection"
    "Solaris 8 Installation Collection"
    "Solaris 8 Software Developer Collection"
    "Solaris 8 System Administrator Collection"
    "Solaris 8 User Collection"
    "AnswerBook2 Version 1.4.1 Help Collection - Japanese"
    "AnswerBook2 Version 1.4.1 Help Collection"
    "AnswerBook2 ???? - zh"
```

```
"AnswerBook2 ??? ?? - ko"
"AnswerBook2 ?????? - zh_TW"
"Answerbook2 Version 1.4.1-Hilfe-Kollektion"
"Colección de Ayuda AnswerBook2 Version 1.4.1"
"Collection d'Aide AnswerBook2 Version 1.4.1"
"Collezione sulla guida di AnswerBook2 Version 1.4.1"
"Hjälpsamling för Answerbook2 Version 1.4.1"
```

paperbark%

If you do not want to define an administrative user, you can turn off access control, as shown in the following example.

Warning — If you turn off access control, any user who can access your documentation server can modify the server.

paperbark% **ab2admin -o auth_off**

```
To do any administration, a password is required.
Please enter administrative ID : winsor
Please enter administrative password :
```

```
Administrative access control turned off.
This will allow any user to administer the AnswerBook2 server software.
paperbark%
```

The following example lists collections available on the local server paperbark using port 8888.

castle% **ab2admin -o list -m paperbark -p 8888**

To use ab2admin in interactive mode for the same operation as the previous example, type ab2admin and press Return. The ab2admin>> prompt is displayed, and you can then type interactive commands without specifying the -o option.

castle% **ab2admin**
ab2admin >> **list -m paperbark -p 8888**

```
To do any administration, a password is required.
Please enter administrative ID : winsor
Please enter administrative password :
```

```
Collection Listing
  AnswerBook2 Collection:
    "KCMS Collection"
    "OpenBoot Collection"
    "Solaris 8 Common Desktop Environment Developer Collection"
    "Solaris 8 Installation Collection"
    "Solaris 8 Software Developer Collection"
    "Solaris 8 System Administrator Collection"
    "Solaris 8 User Collection"
    "AnswerBook2 Version 1.4.1 Help Collection - Japanese"
    "AnswerBook2 Version 1.4.1 Help Collection"
```

```
"AnswerBook2 ???? - zh"
"AnswerBook2 ??? ?? - ko"
"AnswerBook2 ?????? - zh_TW"
"Answerbook2 Version 1.4.1-Hilfe-Kollektion"
"Colección de Ayuda AnswerBook2 Version 1.4.1"
"Collection d'Aide AnswerBook2 Version 1.4.1"
"Collezione sulla guida di AnswerBook2 Version 1.4.1"
"Hjälpsamling för Answerbook2 Version 1.4.1"
```

```
ab2admin >>
```

The following example installs an AnswerBook2 collection introduced to the system with pkgadd(1M) that did not get updated to the server database.

```
# ab2admin -o add_coll -d /opt/answerbooks/english/solaris_2.8/
    SUNWabsdk/collinfo
```

> **Note** — -d path must include the collinfo file. Refer to "Using AnswerBook2 to View Online Information" in your information library for more information.

The following example inspects how a Solaris 8 AnswerBook2 collection is defined.

```
paperbark% cat /opt/answerbooks/english/solaris_8/
    SUNWabsdk/collinfo
dwCollections {
  coll.45.13 dwCollection
}
s
dwSetParam coll.45.13 {
  location /opt/answerbooks/english/soslaris_8/SUNWabsdk
  title "Solaris 8 Software Developer Collection"
  type EbtCollection
}
paperbark%
```

Files

/var/log/ab2/catalog/local.socat

Catalog file.

/var/log/ab2/catalog/remote.socat

Catalog file.

/var/log/ab2/catalog/delegate.socat

Catalog file.

/var/log/ab2/catalog/libcat.socat

Catalog file.

/var/log/ab2/logs/access_8888.log

Default access log file.

```
/var/log/ab2/logs/errors_8888.log
```
> Default error log file.

```
/usr/lib/ab2/dweb/data/config/ab2_collections.template
```
> AnswerBook2 collection database.

```
/var/log/ab2/catalog/ab1_cardcatalog
```
> AnswerBook1 collection database.

```
/usr/lib/ab2/dweb/data/config/admin_passwd
```
> File containing *username:password*.

Attributes

See `attributes(5)` for descriptions of the following attributes.

Attribute Type	Attribute Value
Availability	SUNWab2u

See Also

`pkgadd(1M)`, `pkgrm(1M)`, `attributes(5)`

ab2cd — Run AnswerBook2 Server from the Documentation CD

Synopsis

New!

```
/cdrom/cdrom0/ab2cd [-h][stop][-s][-d path-to-CD-mountpoint]
   [-p port-number][-s][-v]
```

Description

Use the `ab2cd` command to run an AnswerBook2 server directly from the Documentation CD by creating necessary space in the `/tmp/.ab2` directory to store configuration files and other necessary data. `ab2cd` requires root access to the system on which the Solaris Documentation CD is mounted.

Options

-d *path-to-CD-mountpoint*
> Specify a mount point for the CD other than `/cdrom`.

-h
> Display a usage statement and a brief list of options.

New! -p [*port-number*]
> Specify a port number to use for the server. Default is 8888.

-s Scan for AnswerBook1 and AnswerBook2 collections installed on the system and add them to the database of the AnswerBook2 server running from the CD.

stop Stop AnswerBook2 server running from the CD and remove any files in the /tmp/.ab2 directory.

-v Display the version number of the ab2cd script. **New!**

Usage

ab2cd expects /cdrom as the default mount point. To override this default, use the -d option.

Using the /cdrom/cdrom0/ab2cd stop option shuts down the server running from the Documentation CD and cleans up any files in /tmp/.ab2.

By default, ab2cd tries to launch a Web browser (preferably Netscape Navigator) **New!** with the appropriate URL to display the user's Library Page. If Netscape is not found in the user's path, ab2cd looks for other browsers.

For an Answerbook2 server to read multibyte characters correctly, the iconv command must be installed on the system. If it is not, the ab2cd command starts the server but the user won't be able to view Asian book titles or other information correctly.

Examples

The following example runs the AnswerBook2 server from the CD, and then, if there is a Web browser in the root path, asks you if you want to launch a Web browser with the URL for the Library Page.

> **Note** — The default root path does not include a path to a Web browser. If no browser is found in the path, the ab2cd command displays a message telling you to start the Web browser and gives you the URL to use. To enable the ab2cd command to launch the Netscape browser, first add /usr/dt/bin to the root path.

```
paperbark% su
# /cdrom/cdrom0/ab2cd
. . . . . . . . . . . . . . . . . . . . . . . . . . . . . . . . . . . . . . . . . . . . . . . . . . . . . . .


Scanning for collections and attempting to start AnswerBook2 server from
   CD.

Please wait ...

Adding AnswerBook2 Help collection in C locale
Adding AnswerBook2 Help collection in de locale
Adding AnswerBook2 Help collection in es locale
Adding AnswerBook2 Help collection in fr locale
Adding AnswerBook2 Help collection in it locale
Adding AnswerBook2 Help collection in ja locale
Adding AnswerBook2 Help collection in ko locale
Adding AnswerBook2 Help collection in sv locale
Adding AnswerBook2 Help collection in zh locale
Adding AnswerBook2 Help collection in zh_TW locale
```

```
Solaris 8 System Administrator Collection
Solaris 8 User Collection
Solaris 8 Software Developer Collection
KCMS Collection
Solaris 8 Common Desktop Environment Developer Collection
Solaris 8 Installation Collection
OpenBoot Collection
sort: can't read /tmp/ab1_sort.1887: No such file or directory

Starting AnswerBook2 server from CD ...
Started http-8888 service on port 8888 (as daemon)


To read documents from the CD, open a browser with the URL:
http://paperbark:8888

Do you want to start Netscape now? [y,n] y


Starting browser with URL http://paperbark:8888 ....

After you are finished reading documents from the CD, stop the server
   using:
/cdrom/cdrom0/ab2cd stop

#
```

The following example adds any locally installed collections to the server's database. Also, no browser is defined in the user's path.

```
# /cdrom/cdrom0/ab2cd -s
.......................................................


Scanning for collections and attempting to start AnswerBook2 server from
   CD.

Please wait ...

Adding AnswerBook2 Help collection in C locale
Adding AnswerBook2 Help collection in de locale
Adding AnswerBook2 Help collection in es locale
Adding AnswerBook2 Help collection in fr locale
Adding AnswerBook2 Help collection in it locale
Adding AnswerBook2 Help collection in ja locale
Adding AnswerBook2 Help collection in ko locale
Adding AnswerBook2 Help collection in sv locale
Adding AnswerBook2 Help collection in zh locale
Adding AnswerBook2 Help collection in zh_TW locale

Solaris 8 System Administrator Collection
Solaris 8 User Collection
Solaris 8 Software Developer Collection
KCMS Collection
```

```
Solaris 8 Common Desktop Environment Developer Collection
Solaris 8 Installation Collection
OpenBoot Collection

Detecting local collections ...

Duplicate SUNWakcs.

Duplicate SUNWdtad.

Duplicate SUNWinab.

Duplicate SUNWopen.

Duplicate SUNWaadm.

Duplicate SUNWabe.

Duplicate SUNWabsdk.
sort: can't read /tmp/ab1_sort.3178: No such file or directory

Starting AnswerBook2 server from CD ...
Started http-8888 service on port 8888 (as daemon)


To read documents from the CD, open a browser with the URL:
http://paperbark:8888


After you are finished reading documents from the CD, stop the server
   using:
/cdrom/cdrom0/ab2cd stop

#
```

The following example launches ab2cd successfully and locates the ab2cd script in a specific place. However, support for all locales is not provided.

```
example# ab2cd -d /home/myuser/CDROM

Warning : AnswerBook2 requires the following iconv packages to be
   installed
prior to running ab2cd:
SUNWciu8 SUNWhiu8 SUNWjiu8 SUNWkiu8 SUNWuiu8

If you continue running ab2cd, multiple-byte characters might not
   display correctly and collections with non-English titles will not be
   viewable with this server.
Do you want to continue? [y,n] y
```

Scanning for collections and attempting to start AnswerBook2 server from
   CD.

Please wait ...

Adding AnswerBook2 Help collection in C locale
Skipping AnswerBook2 Help collection in de locale
Skipping AnswerBook2 Help collection in es locale
Skipping AnswerBook2 Help collection in fr locale
Skipping AnswerBook2 Help collection in it locale
Skipping AnswerBook2 Help collection in ja locale
Skipping AnswerBook2 Help collection in ko locale
Skipping AnswerBook2 Help collection in sv locale
Skipping AnswerBook2 Help collection in zh locale
Skipping AnswerBook2 Help collection in zh_TW locale

Solaris 8 System Administrator Collection
Solaris 8 User Collection
Solaris 8 Software Developer Collection
KCMS Collection
Solaris 8 Common Desktop Environment Developer Collection
Skipping Solaris 8 Installation Collection - de collection
Skipping Solaris 8 Userbook Collection - de collection
Skipping Solaris 8 Installation Collection - de collection
Solaris Common Desktop Environment Developer Collection
.
.
.
Skipping Solaris 8 Installation Collection - sv collection
Solaris XGL 3.3 AnswerBook

Starting AnswerBook2 server from CD ...
Started http-8888 service on port 8888

To read documents from the CD, open a browser with the URL:
http://ow:8888

Do you want to start Netscape now? [y,n] **n**

After you are finished reading documents from the CD, stop the server
   using:
/home/myuser/CDROM/ab2cd stop

   The following example stops the AnswerBook2 server running from the CD and
cleans up any files in the /tmp directory.
/cdrom/cdrom0/ab2cd stop
....

Stopping AnswerBook2 server from ab2cd ...

If you have shut down your regular AnswerBook2 server in order to run
/cdrom/cdrom0/ab2cd, use "ab2admin -o start" to restart your regular
AnswerBook2 server.
\#

Files

/tmp/.ab2/*   Configuration files and other necessary data.

Attributes

See attributes(5) for descriptions of the following attributes.

Attribute Type	Attribute Value
Availability	Solaris Documentation CD

See Also

answerbook2(1), ab2admin(1M), attributes(5)

---

ab2regsvr — Register an AnswerBook2 Document Server with the Federated Naming Service

Synopsis

/usr/lib/ab2/bin/ab2regsvr [-d][-h][-l][-r] *server-url*

Description

Use the ab2regsvr command to set up the appropriate namespace for the AnswerBook2
document server, depending on which naming service has been selected by the system
administrator. The naming service can be nis, nisplus, or files.

Registering an AnswerBook2 document server with FNS enables a system
administrator to specify the default AnswerBook2 server that users access when they
select the CDE desktop icon or OpenWindows root menu. The server's URL does not
have to be entered into a Web browser.

To register the server with nis, you must be logged in as root on the NIS master
server. To register with nisplus, you must have administrative privileges; you can
register either from the nisplus master or an nisplus client. To register for files, you
must be logged in as root on the system; this command is system specific and is not seen
on other systems.

Options

-d	Delete the AnswerBook2 entry in FNS.
-h	Display a usage statement and a brief list of options.
-l	List currently registered AnswerBook2 document servers.
-r	Replace the currently defined URL for AnswerBook2 with a new URL.

Operands

server-url	Fully qualified URL for users to access the registered server.

Examples

The following example registers a server named imaserver located at port 8888.

```
# ab2regsvr http://imaserver.eng.sun.com:8888/
```

Attributes

See attributes(5) for descriptions of the following attributes.

Attribute Type	Attribute Value
Availability	SUNWab2u

See Also

fnlookup(1), attributes(5), fns(5)

---

accept, reject — Accept or Reject Print Requests

Synopsis

```
/usr/sbin/accept destination...
/usr/sbin/reject [-r "reason"] destination...
```

Description

Use the accept and reject commands on a print server system to turn on or off a print queue that stores requests to be printed. These commands have no meaning on a client system. If you invoke accept or reject on a client system, a warning message is displayed and the command exits.

A printer must accept print requests before you can enable it by using the enable command.

Use lpstat -a to check if destinations are accepting or rejecting print requests.

Note — accept and reject affect queuing only on the print server's spooling system. Requests made from a client system remain queued in the client system's queuing mechanism until they are cancelled or accepted by the print server's spooling system.

Options

The following option is supported for reject.

-r "*reason*"   Assign a reason for rejection of print requests for *destination*. Enclose reason in quotes if it contains blanks. *reason* is reported by lpstat -a. By default, *reason* is unknown reason for existing destinations, and new printer for destinations added to the system but not yet accepting requests.

Operands

destination   The name of the destination accepting or rejecting print requests. Destination specifies the name of a printer or class of printers (see lpadmin(1M)). Specify *destination* using atomic name, for example, accept seachild. See printers.conf(4) for information regarding the naming conventions for atomic names.

Examples

The following example enables the printer seachild to accept print requests.

```
seachild% su
# accept seachild
destination "seachild" now accepting requests
#
```

Exit Status

0   Successful completion.

non-zero   An error occurred.

Files

/var/spool/lp/*

   LP print queue.

Attributes

See attributes(5) for descriptions of the following attributes.

Attribute Type	Attribute Value
Availability	SUNWpcu
CSI	Enabled

Note — accept is CSI enabled except for the destination names.

See Also

enable(1), lp(1), lpstat(1), lpadmin(1M), lpsched(1M), printers.conf(4), attributes(5)

---

acct — Overview of Accounting and Miscellaneous Accounting Commands

Synopsis

```
/usr/lib/acct/acctdisk
/usr/lib/acct/acctdusg [-u filename][-p filename]
/usr/lib/acct/accton [filename]
/usr/lib/acct/acctwtmp reason filename
/usr/lib/acct/closewtmp
/usr/lib/acct/utmp2wtmp
```

Description

Accounting software is structured as a set of commands (consisting of both C programs and shell procedures) that enable you to collect and record data about user connect time, CPU time charged to processes, and disk usage. The SUNWaccr and SUNWaccu packages install the accounting commands in the /usr/lib/acct directories. Accounting data is collected and stored in /var/adm/pacct. You can use the accounting data to generate reports and charge fees for system use.

acctsh(1M) describes the set of shell procedures built on top of the C programs.

New! Connect-time accounting is handled by various commands that write records into /var/adm/wtmpx, as described in utmpx(4) (changed from utmp in the Solaris 8 release). The programs described in acctcon(1M) convert this file into session and charging records, which are then summarized by acctmerg(1M).

Process accounting is performed by the system kernel. When a process terminates, one record per process is written to a file (normally /var/adm/pacct). The programs in acctprc(1M) summarize this data for charging purposes; acctcms(1M) summarizes command use. You can examine current process data by using acctcom(1).

You can merge process accounting records and connect time accounting records (or any accounting records in the tacct format described in acct(3HEAD)) and summarized into total accounting records with acctmerg (see tacct format in acct(3HEAD)). Use prtacct (see acctsh(1M)) to format any or all accounting records.

acctdisk	Read lines that contain user ID, login name, and number of disk blocks and convert them to total accounting records that can be merged with other accounting records. Return an error if the input file is corrupt or improperly formatted.

/usr/lib/acct/acctdusg [-u *filename*] [-p *filename*]

> Gather all disk accounting information. acctdusg can process a maximum of 3,000 users with each invocation. Read standard input (usually from find / -print), and compute disk resource consumption (including indirect blocks) by *login*.

accton [*filename*]

> Without arguments, turn process accounting off. If you specify *filename*, it must be the name of an existing file to which the kernel appends process accounting records (see acct(2) and acct(3HEAD)).

acctwtmp *reason filename*   *New!*

> The startup command (see acctsh(1M)) adds a boot record to /var/adm/wtmpx showing the system name and login name. You can also use acctwtmp to write a utmpx(4) record (changed from utmp in the Solaris 8 release) to *filename*. The record contains the current time and a string of characters that describe the reason. A record type of ACCOUNTING is assigned (see utmpx(4)). *reason* must be a string of 11 or fewer characters, numbers, $, or spaces. For example, the following are suggestions for use in reboot and shutdown procedures.

> acctwtmp "acctg on" /var/adm/wtmpx   *New!*

> acctwtmp "acctg off" /var/adm/wtmpx

closewtmp   For each user currently logged on, put a false DEAD_PROCESS record in *New!*
             the /var/adm/wtmpx file. runacct (see runacct(1M)) uses this false
             DEAD_PROCESS record so that the connect accounting procedures can
             track the time used by users logged on before runacct was invoked.

utmp2wtmp   For each user currently logged on, runacct uses utmp2wtmp to create   *New!*
             an entry in the file /var/adm/wtmpx that is created by runacct.
             Entries in /var/adm/wtmpx enable subsequent invocations of
             runacct to account for connect times of users currently logged in.

Options

-u *filename*   Put records in *filename* records consisting of those file names for
                which acctdusg charges no one (a potential source for finding users
                trying to avoid disk charges).

-p *filename*   Specify a password file, *filename*. This option is not needed if the
                password file is /etc/passwd.

Examples

If necessary, install the SUNWaccr and SUNWaccu packages by using the pkgadd or admintool command.

The following example installs /etc/init.d/acct as the startup script for run level 2 and as the stop script for run level 0.

```
# ln /etc/init.d/acct /etc/rc2.d/S22acct
# ln /etc/init.d/acct /etc/rc0.d/K22acct
#
```

The following example modifies the admcrontab file to start the ckpacct, runacct, and monacct programs automatically.

```
# crontab -e adm
0 * * * * /usr/lib/acct/ckpacct
30 2 * * * /usr/lib/acct/runacct 2> /var/adm/acct/nite/fd2log
30 7 1 * * /usr/lib/acct/monacct
```

The following example modifies the root crontab file to start the dodisk program automatically.

```
# crontab -e
30 22 * * 4 /usr/lib/acct/dodisk
```

Edit /etc/acct/holidays to include national and local holidays. The following example shows the default /etc/acct/holidays file.

```
paperbark% more /etc/acct/holidays
* @(#)holidays  January 1, 1999
*
* Prime/Non-prime Table for UNIX Accounting System
*
* Curr   Prime    Non-Prime
* Year   Start    Start
*
  1999   0800     1800
*
* only the first column (month/day) is significant.
*
* month/day       Company
*                 Holiday
*
1/1               New Years Day
7/4               Indep. Day
12/25             Christmas
paperbark%
```

The following example starts accounting. You can also start accounting by rebooting the system.

```
# /etc/init.d/acct start
```

Environment Variables

If any of the LC_* variables (LC_TYPE, LC_MESSAGES, LC_TIME, LC_COLLATE, LC_NUMERIC, and LC_MONETARY) (see environ(5)) are not set in the environment, the operational behavior of acct for each corresponding locale category is determined by the value of the LANG environment variable. If LC_ALL is set, its contents override both the LANG and the other LC_* variables. If none of the above variables is set in the environment, the C (U.S. style) locale determines how acct behaves.

LC_CTYPE　　　　Determine how acct handles characters. When LC_CTYPE is set to a valid value, acct can display and handle text and file names containing valid characters for that locale. acct can display and handle Extended Unix Code (EUC) characters where any character can be 1, 2, or 3 bytes wide. acct can also handle EUC characters of 1, 2, or more column widths. In the C locale, only characters from ISO 8859-1 are valid.

LC_TIME　　　　　Determine how acct handles date and time formats. In the C locale, date and time handling follows the U.S. rules.

Files

/etc/passwd　　Used for login name to user ID conversions.

/usr/lib/acct Holds all accounting commands listed in subclass 1M of this manual.

/var/adm/pacct

　　　　　　　　Current process accounting file.

/var/adm/wtmpx　　　　　　　　　　　　　　　　　　　　　　　　　　*New!*

　　　　　　　　History of user access and administration information. wtmpx is an extended database file that replaces the obsolete wtmp database file.

Attributes

See attributes(5) for descriptions of the following attributes.

Attribute Type	Attribute Value
Availability	SUNWaccu

See Also

acctcom(1), acctcms(1M), acctcon(1M), acctmerg(1M), acctprc(1M),　*New!*
acctsh(1M), fwtmp(1M), runacct(1M), acct(2), acct(3HEAD), passwd(4),
utmpx(4), attributes(5), environ(5)
　　System Administration Guide, Volume II

acctcms — Command Summary from Process Accounting Records

Synopsis

/usr/lib/acct/acctcms [-a[-o][-p]] [-c] [-j] [-n] [-s] [-t] *filename*...

Description

acctcms reads one or more file names, normally in the form described in acct(3HEAD). It adds all records for processes that executed identically named commands, sorts them, and writes them to the standard output, normally using an internal summary format.

Note — Unpredictable output results if you use the -t option on new-style internal summary format files or if you do not use it with old-style internal summary format files.

Options

-a   Print output in ASCII instead of in the internal summary format. The output includes command name, number of times executed, total kcore-minutes, total CPU minutes, total real minutes, mean size (in kilobytes), mean CPU minutes per invocation, hog factor, characters transferred, and blocks read and written, as in acctcom(1). Output is normally sorted by total kcore-minutes.

You can use the following options only with the -a option.

-o   Output a (non-prime) offshift-time-only command summary.

-p   Output a prime-time-only command summary.

Using -o and -p together produces a combination prime-time and non-prime-time report. All the output summaries are total usage except number of times executed, CPU minutes, and real minutes, which are split into prime and non-prime.

-c   Sort by total CPU time instead of total kcore-minutes.

-j   Combine all commands invoked only once under ***other.

-n   Sort by number of command invocations.

-s   Report any file names encountered hereafter in internal summary format.

-t   Process all records as total accounting records. The default internal summary format splits each field into prime- and non-prime-time parts. This option combines the prime- and non-prime-time parts into a single field that is the total of both and provides upward compatibility with old-style acctcms internal, summary-format records.

Examples

The following example shows a typical sequence for performing daily command accounting and for maintaining a running total.

```
castle% acctcms /var/adm/pacct > today
castle% cp total previoustotal
castle% acctcms -s today previoustotal > total
castle% acctcms -a -s today
```

			TOTAL COMMAND SUMMARY				
COMMAND	NUMBER	TOTAL	TOTAL	TOTAL	MEAN	MEAN	HOG

NAME	CHARS CMDS BLOCKS TRNSFD READ	KCOREMIN	CPU-MIN	REAL-MIN	SIZE-K	CPU-MIN	FACTOR
TOTALS	381 529579616	502.81 2210	0.44	101.08	1148.41	0.00	0.00
wtmpfix	1 526385152	216.15 16	0.27	0.46	792.24	0.27	0.59
dtdbcach	1 670208	62.53 79	0.02	0.02	3473.78	0.02	0.74
dtgreet	1 483264	40.19 166	0.01	1.60	4230.74	0.01	0.01
dwhttpd	1 64424	13.14 300	0.00	0.07	3754.67	0.00	0.05
dtpad	1 133568	13.06 13	0.00	0.04	3405.91	0.00	0.09
acctcms	4 248942	10.12 15	0.01	0.01	979.35	0.00	0.82
sh	54 78527	8.42 115	0.01	2.17	885.89	0.00	0.00
dtsessio	3 740	8.24 2	0.00	0.01	1977.92	0.00	0.33

(Additional lines deleted from this example)

Attributes

See attributes(5) for descriptions of the following attributes.

Attribute Type	**Attribute Value**
Availability	SUNWaccu

See Also

acctcom(1), acct(1M), acctcon(1M), acctmerg(1M), acctprc(1M), acctsh(1M), **New!**
fwtmp(1M), runacct(1M), acct(2), acct(3HEAD), utmpx(4), attributes(5)

acctcon, acctcon1, acctcon2 — Connect-Time Accounting

Synopsis

```
/usr/lib/acct/acctcon [-l lineuse][-o reboot]
/usr/lib/acct/acctcon1 [-p][-t][-l lineuse][-o reboot]
/usr/lib/acct/acctcon2
```

Description

Use the acctcon commands to convert a sequence of login/logoff records to total accounting records (see the tacct format in acct(3HEAD)). The login/logoff records are read from standard input.

acctcon is a combination of the acctcon1 and acctcon2 commands. Use acctcon1 to convert login/logoff records from the fixed /var/adm/wtmpx file to ASCII output. Use acctcon2 to read the ASCII records produced by acctcon1 and convert them to tacct records. You can use acctcon1 with any or all of the options.

New!

> **Note —** The file /var/adm/wtmpx (changed from wtmp in the Solaris 8 release) is usually the source of the login/logoff records. However, because the file may contain corrupted records or system date changes, you should first fix it by using the wtmpfix (see fwtmp(1M)) command with the /var/adm/wtmpx file as an argument. You can then redirect the fixed version of the /var/adm/wtmpx file to acctcon. The tacct records are written to standard output.

The acctcon, acctcon1, and acctcon2 commands can process the following maximums during a single invocation. If the actual number of any one of these items exceeds the maximum, the command does not succeed.

- 6,000 distinct sessions.
- 1,000 distinct terminal lines.
- 2,000 distinct login names.

Options

-p   Print input only, showing line name, login name, and time (in both numeric and date/time formats).

-t   Use the last time found from acctcon1 input instead of the current time, thus ensuring reasonable and repeatable numbers for noncurrent files. The acctcon1 command maintains a list of lines on which users are logged in. When it reaches the end of its input, acctcon1 produces a session record for each line that still seems to be active. acctcon1 ordinarily assumes that its input is a current file so that it uses the current time as the ending time for each session still in progress.

-l *lineuse*   Create a *lineuse* file containing a summary of line usage that shows the line name, number of minutes used, percentage of total elapsed time used, number of sessions charged, number of logins, and number of logoffs. This file helps track line usage, identify bad lines, and find software and hardware oddities. Hangup, termination of login(1), and termination of the login shell each generate logoff records, so that the number of logoffs is often three to four times the number of sessions. See init(1M) and utmpx(4).

-o *reboot*   Fill *reboot* with an overall record for the accounting period, giving starting time, ending time, number of reboots, and number of date changes.

Examples

The following example uses the wtmpfix file to fix the /var/adm/wtmpx file and redirects the output to /tmp/tmpwtmpx.

```
paperbark% /usr/lib/acct/wtmpfix /var/adm/wtmpx > /tmp/tmpwtmpx

checking offset 351665
checking offset 351666
checking offset 351667
checking offset 351670
checking offset 351671
checking offset 351672
...(Additional lines deleted from this example)
paperbark%
```

The following example shows a typical use of the acctcon command, using the fixed /tmp/tmpwtmpx file as input, and shows the contents of the lineuse and reboots files created by acctcon.

```
paperbark% /usr/lib/acct/acctcon -l lineuse -o reboots <
    /tmp/tmpwtmpx > ctacct
paperbark% more lineuse
TOTAL DURATION IS 50275 MINUTES
LINE          MINUTES  PERCENT  # SESS  # ON  # OFF
console       5718     11       28      28    108
pts/7         0        0        0       0     9
TOTALS        5718     --       28      28    117
paperbark% more reboots
from Wed Sep  8 12:18:43 1999
to   Wed Oct 13 10:13:15 1999
43       system boot
34       run-level 3
23       run-level 0
2        run-level 6
2        acctg on
1        acctcon
paperbark%
```

The following example shows a typical use of the acctcon1 command.

```
paperbark% /usr/lib/acct/acctcon1 -l lineuse -o reboots <
    /tmp/tmpwtmpx | sort +1n +2 > ctmp
The old time is: Thu Jan  1 08:00:00 1970
the new time is: Tue Sep 21 13:14:26 1999
The old time is: Tue Sep 21 13:14:26 1999
the new time is: Tue Sep 21 13:14:30 1999
The old time is: Tue Sep 21 13:14:30 1999
the new time is: Tue Sep 21 13:14:40 1999
...(Additional lines deleted from this example)
paperbark%
```

The following example shows a typical use of the acctcon2 command and shows the contents of the ctmp file created by acctcon2.

```
paperbark% /usr/lib/acct/acctcon2 < ctmp > ctacct
paperbark% more ctmp
0   0     root    81      0       939104584   Tue Oct  5 14:23:04 1999
0   1001  winsor  12714   50400   939627987   Mon Oct 11 15:46:27 1999
0   1001  winsor  13310   0       938145574   Fri Sep 24 11:59:34 1999
```

```
0   1001   winsor   14575   50400   939715806   Tue Oct 12 16:10:06 1999
0   1001   winsor   17980   0       939609907   Mon Oct 11 10:45:07 1999
0   1001   winsor   18877   0       939084046   Tue Oct  5 08:40:46 1999
```
. . .(*Additional lines deleted from this example*)
```
paperbark%
```

Files

/var/adm/wtmpx

> History of user access and administration information.The wtmpx database file supersedes the obsolete wtmp database file.

Attributes

See attributes(5) for descriptions of the following attributes.

Attribute Type	Attribute Value
Availability	SUNWaccu

See Also

acctcom(1), login(1), acct(1M), acctcms(1M), acctmerg(1M), acctprc(1M), acctsh(1M), fwtmp(1M), init(1M), runacct(1M), acct(2), acct(3HEAD), utmpx(4), attributes(5)
System Administration Guide, Volume II

acctdisk — Convert Accounting Data to Total Accounting Records

Synopsis

/usr/lib/acct/acctdisk

Description

See acct(1M).

acctdusg — Compute Disk Resource Consumption by Login

Synopsis

/usr/lib/acct/acctdusg [-u *filename*][-p *filename*]

Description

    See acct(1M).

---

acctmerg — Merge or Add Total Accounting Files

Synopsis

    /usr/lib/acct/acctmerg [-a][-i][-p][-t][-u][-v][*filename*]...

Description

    Use the acctmerg command to read standard input and up to nine additional files, all in the tacct format (see acct(3HEAD)) or an ASCII version thereof. acctmerg merges these inputs by adding records whose keys (normally user ID and name) are identical and expects the inputs to be sorted on those keys.

Options

    -a   Produce output in ASCII version of tacct.

    -i   Specify that input files are in ASCII version of tacct.

    -p   Print input with no processing.

    -t   Produce a single record that totals all input.

    -u   Summarize by user ID instead of by user ID and name.

    -v   Produce output in verbose ASCII format with more precise notation for floating-point numbers.

Examples

    The following example shows a sequence that is useful for making repairs to any files kept in the acctmerg format.

    castle% **acctmerg -v < *filename1* > *filename2***
    Edit filename2 as desired.
    castle% **acctmerg -i < *filename2* > *filename1***

Attributes

    See attributes(5) for descriptions of the following attributes.

Attribute Type	Attribute Value
Availability	SUNWaccu

See Also

acctcom(1), acct(1M), acctcms(1M), acctcon(1M), acctprc(1M), acctsh(1M), *New!*
fwtmp(1M), runacct(1M), acct(2), acct(3HEAD), utmpx(4), attributes(5)
    System Administration Guide, Volume II

accton — Append Process Accounting Records to an Existing File

Synopsis

/usr/lib/acct/accton [*filename*]

Description

See acct(1M).

acctprc, acctprc1, acctprc2 — Process Accounting

Synopsis

/usr/lib/acct/acctprc
/usr/lib/acct/acctprc1 [*ctmp*]
/usr/lib/acct/acctprc2

Description

Use the acctprc command to read the standard input in the form described by acct(3HEAD) and to convert it to total accounting records (see the tacct record in acct(3HEAD)). acctprc divides CPU time into prime time and non-prime time and determines mean memory size (in memory segment units). It then summarizes the tacct records according to user IDs and adds login names corresponding to the user IDs. The summarized records are then written to the standard output.

acctprc1 reads input in the form described by acct(3HEAD), adds login names corresponding to user IDs then writes for each process an ASCII line giving user ID, login name, prime CPU time (ticks), non-prime CPU time (ticks), and mean memory size (in memory segment units). If you specify *ctmp*, it is expected to contain a list of login sessions sorted by user ID and login name. If you do not supply this file, acctprc1 obtains login names from the password file just as acctprc does. The information in *ctmp* helps it distinguish between different login names sharing the same user ID.

From the standard input, acctprc2 reads records in the form written by acctprc1, summarizes them according to user ID and name, then writes the sorted summaries to the standard output as total accounting records.

The acctprc, acctprc1, and acctprc2 commands can process the following maximum values during a single invocation. If at some point the actual number of any of these items exceeds the maximum, the command does not succeed.

- 6,000 distinct sessions.
- 1,000 distinct terminal lines.
- 2,000 distinct login names.

Notes

Although it is possible for acctprc1 to distinguish among login names that share user IDs for commands run normally, it is difficult for acctprc1 to do so for those commands run from cron(1M). You can convert more precisely by using the acctwtmp program in acct(1M). acctprc does not distinguish among users with identical user IDs.

A memory segment of the mean memory size is a unit of measure for the number of bytes in a logical memory segment on a particular processor.

Examples

The following example shows a typical use of the acctprc command.

```
paperbark% /usr/lib/acct/acctprc < /var/adm/pacct > ptacct
paperbark% file ptacct
ptacct:         data
paperbark% ls -l ptacct
-rw-r--r--  1 winsor   staff       304 Oct 13 15:21 ptacct
paperbark%
```

The following example shows a typical use of the acctprc1 command.

```
paperbark% /usr/lib/acct/acctprc1 ctmp < /var/adm/pacct
0       root    3       0       65
0       root    0       0       0
0       root    1       0       88
```
(*Additional lines deleted from this example*)
```
1       daemon  1       0       126
1       daemon  3       0       372
1       daemon  21      0       470
1       daemon  7       0       95
0       root    2       0       101
0       root    1       0       54
0       root    2       0       60
```
(*Additional lines deleted from this example*)
```
1001    winsor  1       0       190
1001    winsor  1       0       193
1001    winsor  1       0       226
1001    winsor  1       0       207
```
(*Additional lines deleted from this example*)
```
paperbark%
```

The following example show a typical use of the acctprc2 command.

```
paperbark% acctprc2 > ptacct
```

Files

```
/etc/passwd   System password file.
```

Attributes

See attributes(5) for descriptions of the following attributes.

Attribute Type	Attribute Value
Availability	SUNWaccu

See Also

New!

acctcom(1), acct(1M), acctcms(1M), acctcon(1M), acctmerg(1M), acctsh(1M), cron(1M), fwtmp(1M), runacct(1M), acct(2), acct(3HEAD), utmpx(4), attributes(5)

acctsh, chargefee, ckpacct, dodisk, lastlogin, monacct, nulladm, prctmp, prdaily, prtacct, shutacct, startup, turnacct — Shell Procedures for Accounting

Synopsis

```
/usr/lib/acct/chargefee login-name number
/usr/lib/acct/ckpacct [blocks]
/usr/lib/acct/dodisk [-o][filename...]
/usr/lib/acct/lastlogin
/usr/lib/acct/monacct number
/usr/lib/acct/nulladm filename...
/usr/lib/acct/prctmp filename
/usr/lib/acct/prdaily [-c][-l][mmdd]
/usr/lib/acct/prtacct filename ["heading"]
/usr/lib/acct/shutacct ["reason"]
/usr/lib/acct/startup
/usr/lib/acct/turnacct on | off | switch
```

Description

Note — See runacct(1M) for the main daily accounting shell script, which daily accumulates connect, process, fee, and disk accounting. It also creates summaries of command usage.

chargefee *login-name number*

If you provide special user services on a request basis, such as restoring files or remote printing, you may want to bill users by running chargefee. chargefee records charges in the /var/adm/fee file and merges new entries into the total accounting records each time the runacct(1M) command is executed.

ckpacct [*blocks*]

> Initiated by cron(1M) to periodically check the size of /var/adm/pacct. If the size exceeds *blocks*, 500 by default, invoke turnacct with argument *switch*. If the number of free disk blocks in the /var file system falls below 500, automatically turn off the collection of process accounting records by using the off argument to turnacct. When at least 500 blocks are restored, activate the accounting again on the next invocation of ckpacct. This feature is sensitive to the frequency at which ckpacct is executed, usually by cron.

dodisk [-o][*filename...*]

> Invoked by cron to perform the disk accounting functions. The following example modifies the root crontab file to start the dodisk command automatically.
>
> ```
> # crontab -e
> 30 22 * * 4 /usr/lib/acct/dodisk
> ```
> For a complete example of how to set up accounting, see "Examples" on page 996.
>
> Information gathered by running dodisk is stored in /var/adm/acct/nite/disktacct. The information in this file is overwritten the next time you run dodisk. Therefore, you should avoid running dodisk twice in the same day.

lastlogin   Invoked by runacct(1M) to update /var/adm/acct/sum/loginlog, which shows the last date on which each person logged in.

monacct *number*

> Invoke once each month or each accounting period. *number* indicates which month or period it is. If you do not specify *number*, the default is the current month (01-12). This default is useful if monacct is executed by cron(1M) on the first day of each month. monacct creates a report based on data stored in /var/adm/acct/fiscal that has been updated daily by runacct. After creating the report, monacct cleans up the summary files in /var/adm/acct/sum to prepare them for new runacct data.

nulladm *filename...*

> Create *filename* with mode 664, and ensure that owner and group are adm. nulladm is called by various accounting shell procedures.

prctmp *filename*

> Print the session record file (normally /var/adm/acct/nite/ctmp created by acctcon1 (see acctcon(1M)).

prdaily [-c][-l][*mmdd*]

> Invoke by runacct(1M) to format a report of the previous day's accounting data. The report resides in /var/adm/acct/sum/rprt/*mmdd* where *mmdd* is the month and day of

the report. You can print the current daily accounting reports by typing `prdaily`. Print accounting reports for previous days by using the *mmdd* option and specifying the exact report date desired.

`prtacct` *filename* [`"heading"`]

Use to format and print any total accounting (`tacct`) file.

`shutacct` [`"reason"`]

When the `shutdown` command is used, `shutacct` is invoked automatically to turn off process accounting and append a *reason* record to `/var/adm/wtmpx` (changed from `wtmp` in the Solaris 8 release).

`startup`

Invoke when the system is brought to a multiuser state to turn on process accounting.

`turnacct on | off | switch`

Provide an interface to `accton` (see `acct`(1M)) to turn on or off process accounting. The `switch` argument moves the current `/var/adm/pacct` to the next free name in `/var/adm/pacctincr` (where *incr* is a number starting with 1 and incrementing by 1 for each additional `pacct` file), then turns on accounting again. This procedure is called by `ckpacct` and thus can be taken care of by `cron` and used to keep `pacct` to a reasonable size. `shutacct` uses `turnacct` to stop process accounting. `startup` uses `turnacct` to start process accounting.

Options

`-c`

Print a report of exceptional resource usage by command. You can use this option only on the accounting data for the current day.

`-l`

Print a report of exceptional usage by login ID for the specified date. Previous daily reports are cleaned up and are, therefore, inaccessible after each invocation of `monacct`.

`-o`

Use `acctdusg` (see `acct`(1M)) to do a slower version of disk accounting by login directory.

Operands

filename...

Specify one or more file-system names where disk accounting is done. If you specify *filename...*, disk accounting is done only on these file systems. With the `-o` option, *filename...* should be mount points of mounted file systems. If you omit the `-o` option, *filename...* should be the special file names of mountable file systems.

Files

`/usr/lib/acct`

Holds all accounting commands listed in section 1M.

`/usr/lib/acct/ptecms.awk`

> Contains, by command name, the limits for exceptional usage.

`/usr/lib/acct/ptelus.awk`

> Contains, by login ID, the limits for exceptional usage.

`/var/adm/acct/fiscal`

> Fiscal reports directory.

`/var/adm/acct/nite`

> Working directory.

`/var/adm/acct/sum`

> Summary directory contains information for `monacct`.

`/var/adm/acct/sum/loginlog`

> File updated by last login.

`/var/adm/fee`   Accumulator for fees.

`/var/adm/pacct`

> Current file for per-process accounting.

`/var/adm/pacct`*incr*

> Used if `pacct` gets large and during execution of daily accounting procedure.

`/var/adm/wtmpx`

New!

> History of user access and administration information. The `wtmpx` database file supersedes the obsolete `wtmp` database file.

Attributes

See `attributes`(5) for descriptions of the following attributes.

Attribute Type	Attribute Value
Availability	SUNWaccu

See Also

`acctcom(1)`, `acct(1M)`, `acctcms(1M)`, `acctcon(1M)`, `acctmerg(1M)`, `acctprc(1M)`, `cron(1M)`, `fwtmp(1M)`, `runacct(1M)`, `acct(2)`, `acct(3HEAD)`, `utmpx(4)`, `attributes(5)`

New!

acctwtmp — Write a utmpx Record to a File

Synopsis

```
/usr/lib/acct/acctwtmp reason filename
```

Description

See acct(1M).

adbgen — Generate adb Script

Synopsis

```
/usr/lib/adb/adbgen [-m model] filename.adb...
```

Description

Use the adbgen command to write adb(1) macros that do not contain hard-coded dependencies on structure member offsets. The input to adbgen is a file named *filename*.adb that contains the following elements.

- Header information.
- A null line.
- The name of a structure.
- An adb script.

adbgen deals with one structure only per file; all member names are assumed to be in this structure. The output of adbgen is an adb script in *filename*. adbgen generates a C program that determines structure member offsets and sizes, which in turn generate the adb script.

The header lines up to the null line are copied verbatim into the generated C program. Typically, these are #include statements, which include the headers containing the relevant structure declarations.

The adb script part can contain any valid adb commands (see adb(1)) and can also contain adbgen requests, each enclosed in braces ({}). The following list describes the request types.

- Print a structure member. The request form is {*member, format*}. *member* is a member name of the structure given earlier, and *format* is any valid adb format request or any of the adbgen format specifiers listed below, such as {POINTER}. For example, to print the p_pid field of the proc structure as a decimal number, write {p_pid,d}.
- Print the appropriate adb format character for the given adbgen format specifier. This action takes the data model into consideration. The request form is {*format specifier*}. The following adbgen format specifiers are valid.

{POINTER}	Pointer value in hexadecimal.
{LONGDEC}	Long value in decimal.
{ULONGDEC}	Unsigned long value in decimal.
{ULONGHEX}	Unsigned long value in hexadecimal.
{LONGOCT}	Long value in octal.
{ULONGOCT}	Unsigned long value in octal.

- Reference a structure member. The request form is {*member,base}. member is the member name whose value you want, and base is an adb register name that contains the base address of the structure. For example, to get the p_pid field of the proc structure, get the proc structure address in an adb register, say, <f, and write {*p_pid,<f}.
- Tell adbgen that the offset is valid. The request form is {OFFSETOK}. This form is useful after you invoke another adb script that moves the adb dot.
- Get the size of the structure. The request form is {SIZEOF}. adbgen replaces this request with the size of the structure. This form is useful in incrementing a pointer to step through an array of structures.
- Calculate an arbitrary C expression. The request form is {EXPR,expression}. adbgen replaces this request with the value of the expression. This form is useful when more than one structure is involved in the script.
- Get the offset to the end of the structure. The request form is {END}. This form is useful at the end of the structure to get adb to align the dot for printing the next structure member.

adbgen tracks the movement of the adb dot and generates adb code to move forward or backward as needed before printing any structure member in a script. adbgen's model of the behavior of adb's dot is simple: it assumes that the first line of the script is of the form struct_address/adb text and that subsequent lines are of the form +/adb text. The adb dot then moves in a sane fashion. adbgen does not check the script to ensure that these limitations are met. adbgen also checks the size of the structure member against the size of the adb format code and warns if they are not equal.

Options

-m model   Specify the data type model to be used by adbgen for the macro. This model affects the outcome of the {format specifier} requests and the offsets and sizes of data types. model can be ilp32 for 32-bit programs or lp64 for 64-bit programs. If you do not specify the -m option, the default data type model is ilp32.

Operands

filename.adb   Input file that contains header information followed by a null line, the name of the structure, and finally an adb script.

Examples

Suppose you have an include file x.h, that contains the following data.

```
struct x {
        char *x_cp;
        char x_c;
        int x_i;
};
```

An adbgen file called script.adb to print the file x.h would look like the following example.

```
#include "x.h"
x ./"x_cp"16t"x_c"8t"x_i"n{x_cp,{POINTER}}{x_c,C}{x_i,D}
```

When you run adbgen using the following command

% **/usr/lib/adb/adbgen script.adb**

the output file script contains the following information.

```
./"x_cp"16t"x_c"8t"x_i"nXC3+D
```

For a macro generated for a 64-bit program using the lp64 data model as follows,

% **/usr/lib/adb/adbgen/ -m lp64 script.adb**

the output file script would contain

```
./"x_cp"16t"x_c"8t"x_i"nJC3+D
```

To invoke the script, type the following command.

```
castle% adb program
x$<script
```

Files

/usr/platform/*platform-name*/lib/adb/*

> Platform-specific adb scripts for debugging the 32-bit kernel.

/usr/platform/*platform-name*/lib/adb/sparcv9/*

> Platform-specific adb scripts for debugging the 64-bit SPARC V9 kernel.

/usr/lib/adb/*

> adb scripts for debugging the 32-bit kernel.

/usr/lib/adb/sparcv9/*

> adb scripts for debugging the 64-bit SPARC V9 kernel.

Note — You can find *platform-name* with the -i option of uname(1).

Attributes

See attributes(5) for descriptions of the following attributes.

Attribute Type	Attribute Value
Availability	SUNWesu

See Also

adb(1), uname(1), kadb(1M), attributes(5)

Diagnostics

Warnings are given about structure member sizes not equal to adb format items and about badly formatted requests. The C compiler complains if you reference a structure member that does not exist. It also complains about an ampersand before array names; you can ignore these complaints.

Bugs

adb syntax is ugly; there should be a higher-level interface for generating scripts.

Structure members that are bit fields cannot be handled because C does not give the address of a bit field. The address is needed to determine the offset.

add_drv — Add a New Device Driver to the System

Synopsis

```
/usr/sbin/add_drv [-b basedir][-c class-name][-i 'identify-name...']
    [- m 'permission','...'][-n][-f][-v] device-driver
```

Description

Use the add_drv command to inform the system about newly installed device drivers.

Each device on the system has a name associated with it. This name is represented by the name property for the device. Similarly, the device can also have a list of driver names associated with it. This list is represented by the compatible property for the device.

The system determines which devices are managed by the driver being added by examining the contents of the name property and the compatible property (if it exists) on each device. If the value in the name property does not match the driver being added, each entry in the compatible property is tried, in order, until either a match occurs or there are no more entries in the compatible property.

Note — In some cases, adding a new driver may require a reconfiguration boot. Aliases may require quoting (with double quotes) if they contain numbers.

You can add a driver for a device already being managed by a different driver when the driver being added appears in the device's compatible list before the current driver. In such cases, you must do a reconfiguration boot (boot -r) (see boot(1M) and kernel(1M)). After the reconfiguration boot, device nodes in /devices, entries in /dev, and references to these files may no longer be valid (see the -v option). If a reconfiguration boot is required to complete the driver installation, add_drv fails unless you specify the -f option.

You should not run add_drv when installing a STREAMS module. See the *STREAMS Programming Guide* for details.

Options

-b *basedir*   Install the driver on the system with a root directory of *basedir* instead of installing on the system executing add_drv. You typically use this option in package postinstallation scripts when the package is not being installed on the system executing the pkgadd command. The system using *basedir* as its root directory must reboot to complete the driver installation.

-c *class-name* Specify that the driver being added to the system export the class *class-name*.

-f   Force addition of the driver even if a reconfiguration boot is required. See the -v option. Normally, if a reconfiguration boot is required to complete the configuration of the driver into the system, add_drv does not add the driver.

-i '*identify-name*'

          Specify a white-space-separated list of aliases for the driver *device-driver*.

-m '*permission*'

          Specify the file-system permissions for device nodes created by the system on behalf of *device-driver*.

-n   Do not try to load and attach *device-driver*; just modify the system configuration files for the *device-driver*.

-v   Provide additional information regarding the success or failure of a driver's configuration into the system.

Examples

The following example adds the SUNW,example driver to the system with an alias name of SUNW,alias. It assumes the driver has already been copied to /usr/kernel/drv.

```
# add_drv -m '* 0666 bin bin','a 0644 root sys' -i 'SUNW,alias'
    SUNW,example
```

Every minor node created by the system for the SUNW,example driver has the permission 0666 and must be owned by user bin in the group bin, except for the minor device a, which is owned by root, group sys, and has a permission of 0644.

The following example adds the driver to the client /export/root/sun1. The driver is installed and loaded when the client machine, sun1, is rebooted. This example produces the same result as the first, except the changes are on the diskless client, sun1, and the client must be rebooted to complete the driver installation.

add_drv -m '* 0666 bin bin','a 0644 root sys' -i 'SUNW,alias' -b
   /export/root/sun1 SUNW,example

The following example adds a new driver for a device that is already managed by an existing driver. Consider a device that is currently managed by the driver dumb_framebuffer. The name and compatible properties for this device are as follows.

name="display" compatible="whizzy_framebuffer", "dumb_framebuffer"

If you use add_drv without any options to add the whizzy_framebuffer driver, the following message is displayed.

add_drv whizzy_framebuffer
Error: Could not install driver (whizzy_framebuffer)
Device managed by another driver.
#

If you specify the -v option, an error message is also displayed, as shown in the following example.

add_drv -v whizzy_framebuffer
Error: Could not install driver (whizzy_framebuffer)
Device managed by another driver.
Driver installation failed because the following entries in /devices
   would be affected:
/devices/iommu@f,e0000000/sbus@f,e0001000/display[:*](Devicecurrently
   managed by driver "dumb_framebuffer")
The following entries in /dev would be affected:
/dev/fbs/dumb_framebuffer0
#

If you specify both the -v and -f options, as shown in the following example, the driver is added.

add_drv -vf whizzy_framebuffer
#

You must perform a reconfiguration boot (boot -r) to complete the installation of this driver.

The following entries in /devices are affected.

/devices/iommu@f,e0000000/sbus@f,e0001000/display[:*](Devicecurrently
   managed by driver "dumb_framebuffer"

The following entries in /dev are affected.

/dev/fbs/dumb_framebuffer0

The above example is currently relevant only to devices exporting a generic device name.

Exit Status

0   Success.

1   Failure.

Files

/kernel/drv   Boot device drivers.

/usr/kernel/drv

Other drivers that could potentially be shared among platforms.

/platform/`uname -i`/kernel/drv

Platform-dependent drivers.

/etc/driver_aliases

Driver aliases file.

/etc/driver_classes

Driver classes file.

/etc/minor_perm

Minor node permissions.

/etc/name_to_major

Major number binding.

Attributes

See attributes(5) for descriptions of the following attributes.

Attribute Type	Attribute Value
Availability	SUNWcsu

See Also

boot(1M), devlinks(1M), disks(1M), drvconfig(1M), kernel(1M),
modinfo(1M), ports(1M), rem_drv(1M), tapes(1M), driver.conf(4),
system(4), attributes(5), ddi_create_minor_node(9F)
   Writing Device Drivers

Bugs

add_drv tries to use a full path name for *device-driver*. However, the kernel does not
use the full path name; it uses only the final component and searches the internal driver
search path for the driver. This behavior can lead to the kernel loading a different driver
than expected.

For this reason, it is not recommended that you use add_drv with a full path name.
See kernel(1M) for more information on the driver search path.

add_install_client — Script to Add or Remove Clients for Network Installation

Synopsis

```
cdrom-mnt-pt/Solaris_8/Tools/add_install_client [-i IP-address]
    [-e Ethernet-address][-s server-name : path][-c server-name :
    path][-n [server] : name-service [(netmask)][-p server-name : path]
    hostname platform-group
```

Description

See install_scripts(1M).

add_to_install_server — Script to Copy Packages from Additional Solaris Copackaged CDs to an Existing Net Install Server

New!

Synopsis

```
cdrom-mnt-pt/Sol_8_sparc_2/Solaris_8/Tools/add_to_install_server[-s]
    [-p product-image-path] install-server-path
```

Description

See install_scripts(1M).

addbadsec — Map Out Defective Disk Blocks

Synopsis

```
addbadsec [-p][-a blkno [blkno...]][-f filename] raw-device
```

Description

Use addbadsec to map out bad disk blocks on IA systems. Normally, these blocks are identified during surface analysis. Occasionally, the disk subsystem reports unrecoverable data errors indicating a bad block. You can feed a block number reported in this way directly into addbadsec, and the block is remapped. addbadsec first tries hardware remapping. This feature is supported on SCSI drives and takes place at the disk hardware level. If the target is an IDE drive, then software remapping is used. For software remapping to succeed, the partition must contain an alternate slice and there must be room in this slice to perform the mapping.

Bad blocks lead to data loss. Remapping a defective block does not repair a damaged file. If a bad block occurs to a disk-resident file-system structure such as a superblock, you may have to recover the entire slice from a backup.

Note — The format(1M) command is available to format, label, analyze, and repair SCSI disks. This command is included with the addbadsec, diskscan(1M), fdisk(1M), and fmthard(1M) commands available for IA. To format an IDE disk, use the DOS format command; however, to label, analyze, or repair IDE disks on IA systems, use the Solaris format(1M) command.

Options

-a   Add the specified blocks to the hardware or software map. If you specify more than one block number, quote the entire list and separate block numbers with white space.

-f   Add the specified blocks to the hardware or software map. List the bad blocks, one per line, in the specified file.

-p   Print the current software map. The output shows the defective block and the assigned alternate. You cannot use this option to print the hardware map.

Operands

raw-device   The address of the disk drive.

Files

The raw device should be /dev/rdsk/c?[t?]d?p0.

Attributes

See attributes(5) for descriptions of the following attributes.

Attribute Type	Attribute Value
Architecture	IA
Availability	SUNWcsu

See Also

disks(1M), diskscan(1M), fdisk(1M), fmthard(1M), format(1M), attributes(5)

admintool — System Administration with a Graphical User Interface

Synopsis

```
/usr/bin/admintool
```

Description

> **Note** — admintool modifies files only on the local system; that is, the system on which you are running admintool. admintool does not modify or update global networked databases such as NIS or NIS+.
>
> admintool is not the tool for a distributed environment. It is used for local administration.

admintool is a graphical user interface that enables you to accomplish several system administration tasks on a local system. You can run admintool as root or by using your user name if you are a member of the sysadmin group (GID 14). Members of the sysadmin group can use admintool to create, delete, and modify local system files. Nonmembers have read-only permissions (where applicable).
Help is available through the Help button.

> **Warning** — If you use admintool to add a host, and your local system and your site uses a network nameservice such as NIS or NIS+, admintool host operations may not have the desired effect. The reason is that information in the network nameservice takes precedence over the information in the local /etc/hosts file, which is where admintool updates information.

Usage

admintool enables you to do the following tasks.

- Add, delete, or modify user accounts. admintool makes the appropriate changes to the system's /etc/passwd file (see passwd(4)).
- Add, delete, or modify groups. admintool makes the appropriate changes to the system's /etc/group file (see group(4)).
- Add, delete, or modify hosts. admintool makes the appropriate changes to the system's /etc/hosts file (see hosts(4)).
- Add or delete access to a printer or modify a system's printer access. admintool makes the appropriate changes to the system's /etc/lp directory.
- Enable or disable serial port services. admintool sets up the software services necessary to use a modem or terminal attached to a system's serial port.
- Add or remove software. admintool adds software from a product CD or on a hard disk to an installed system or removes software from an installed system.

Exit Status

admintool terminates with exit status 0.

Attributes

See `attributes`(5) for descriptions of the following attributes.

Attribute Type	Attribute Value
Availability	SUNWadmap

See Also

`group(4)`, `hosts(4)`, `passwd(4)`, `attributes(5)`

New! afbconfig, SUNWafb_config — Configure the AFB Graphics Accelerator

Synopsis

```
/usr/sbin/afbconfig [-dev device-filename][-res video-mode [now | try]
    [noconfirm | nocheck]][-file machine | system][-deflinear true |
    false][-defoverlay true | false][-overlayorder first | last]
    [expvis enable | disable] [-sov enable | disable] [-maxwinds n]
    [-extovl enable | disable] [-g gamma-correction-value][-gfile
    gamma-correction-file][-linearorder first | last][-propt][-prconf]
    [-defaults]
/usr/sbin/afbconfig [-propt] [-prconf]
/usr/sbin/afbconfig [-help] [-res ?]
```

Description

The `afbconfig` command is new in the Solaris 8 release. Use it to configure the AFB Graphics Accelerator and some of the X11 window system defaults for AFB.

The following form of `afbconfig` stores the specified options in the OWconfig file.

```
/usr/sbin/afbconfig [-dev device-filename][-res video-mode [now | try]
    [noconfirm | nocheck]][-file machine | system][-deflinear true |
    false][-defoverlay true | false][-overlayorder first | last][expvis
    enable | disable] [-sov enable | disable] [-maxwinds n] [-extovl
    enable | disable] [-g gamma-correction-value][-gfile
    gamma-correction-file][-propt][-prconf][-defaults]
```

Use the options to initialize the AFB device the next time the window system is run on that device. When you update options in the OWconfig file, the settings persist across window system sessions and system reboots.

The following forms of the `afbconfig` command invoke only the -prconf, -propt, -help, and -res ? options. None of these options update the OWconfig file.

```
/usr/sbin/afbconfig [-propt] [-prconf]
/usr/sbin/afbconfig [-help] [-res ?]
```

Additionally, the following invocation of `afbconfig` ignores all other options.

```
/usr/sbin/afbconfig [-help] [-res ?]
```

You can specify options for only one AFB device at a time. To specify options for multiple AFB devices, invoke the afbconfig command for each device you want to configure.

You can specify only AFB-specific options for afbconfig. You still specify the normal window system options for default depth, visual class, and so forth as device modifiers on the openwin command line.

You can also specify the OWconfig file that is to be updated. By default, the machine-specific file in the /etc/openwin directory tree is updated. You can use the -file option to specify an alternate file to use. For example, you can update the system-global OWconfig file in the /usr/openwin directory tree instead.

Both of the standard OWconfig files can be written only by root. Consequently, the afbconfig program, which is owned by the root user, always runs with setuid root permission.

Option Defaults

If you do not specify an option on the command line, the corresponding OWconfig option is not updated; it retains its previous value. When the window system is run, if an AFB option has never been specified by way of afbconfig, a default value is used. The option defaults are shown below.

```
-dev           /dev/fbs/afb0

-file          machine

-res           none

-deflinear     false

-defoverlay    false

-linearorder   last

-overlayorder last

-expvis        enabled

-sov           enabled

-maxwids       32

-extovl        enabled

-g             2.22
```

The default of none for the -res option means that, when the window system is run, the screen resolution is the video mode currently programmed in the device.

This default provides compatibility for users who are accustomed to specifying the device resolution through the PROM. On some devices (for example, GX) the PROM is the only way of specifying the video mode, which means that the PROM ultimately determines the default AFB video mode.

Options

-defaults   Reset all option values to their default values.

-deflinear true | false

AFB possesses two types of visuals: linear and nonlinear. Linear visuals are gamma corrected and nonlinear visuals are not. Two visuals have both linear and nonlinear versions: 24-bit TrueColor and 8-bit StaticGray.

If `true`, the default visual is set to the linear visual that satisfies other specified default visual selection options (specifically, the `Xsun(1)` `defdepth` and `defclass` options described in the *OpenWindows Reference Manual*).

If `false` or if no linear visual satisfies the other default visual selection options, the nonlinear visual specified by these other options are chosen as the default. You cannot use this option when the `-defoverlay` option is present because AFB doesn't possess a linear overlay visual.

`-defoverlay true | false`

> The AFB provides an 8-bit PseudoColor visual whose pixels are disjoint from the rest of the AFB visuals. This visual is called the overlay visual. Windows created in this visual do not damage windows created in other visuals. The converse, however, is not true. Windows created in other visuals damage overlay windows.
>
> The number of colors available to the windows created with this visual depends on the settings for the `-extovl` option. If the `-extovl` is enabled, extended overlay with 256 opaque color values is available. See `-extovl`. If `-extovl` is disabled, extended overlay is not available and the visual has 256 `-maxwids` number of opaque color values. See `-maxwids`.
>
> If `-defoverlay` is `true`, the overlay visual is made the default visual. If `-defoverlay` is `false`, the nonoverlay visual that satisfies the other default visual selection options, such as `def`, `depth`, and `defclass`, are chosen as the default visual. See the *OpenWindows Reference Manual*.
>
> Whenever the `defoverlay true` option is used, the default depth and class specified on the `openwin` command line must be 8-bit PseudoColor. If not, a warning message is printed and the `-defoverlay` option is treated as `false`.
>
> You cannot use the `-defoverlay` option when you specify the `-deflinear` option because AFB doesn't possess a linear overlay visual.

`-dev device-filename`

> Specify the AFB special file. The default is `/dev/fbs/afb0`.

`-expvis enable | disable`

> If enabled, activate OpenGL Visual Expansion. Multiple instances of selected visual groups (8-bit PseudoColor, 24-bit TrueColor, and so forth) are in the screen visual list.

`-extovl enable | disable`

> If enabled, make extended overlay available. The overlay visuals have 256 opaque colors. The SOV visuals have 255 opaque colors and 1 transparent color.
>
> This option also enables hardware-supported transparency, thus provides better performance for windows using the SOV visuals.

`-file machine | system`

> Specify which OWconfig file to update. If you specify machine, use the machine-specific OWconfig file in the /etc/openwin directory tree. If you specify system, use the global OWconfig file in the /usr/openwin directory tree. If the specified file does not exist, create it.

`-g gamma-correction-value`

> Change the gamma correction value. All linear visuals provide gamma correction. By default, gamma-correction-value is 2.22. Any value less than 0 is illegal. Apply the gamma correction value to the linear visual, which then has an effective gamma value of 1.0, which is the value returned by XSolarisGetVisualGamma(3). See XSolarisGetVisualGamma(3) for a description of that function.
>
> This option can be used while the window system is running. Changing the gamma correction value affects all the windows being displayed using the linear visuals.

`-gfile gamma-correction-file`

> Load the gamma correction table from the specified gamma-correction-file file. You should format this file to provide 256 gamma correction values for R, G, and B channels on each line. Each of these values should be in hexadecimal format and separated by at least one space.
>
> An example of a gamma-correction-file follows.

```
0x00  0x00  0x00
0x01  0x01  0x01
0x02  0x02  0x02
. . .
. . .
0xff  0xff  0xff
```

> Using this option, you can load the gamma correction table while the window system is running. The new gamma correction affects all the windows being displayed using the linear visuals. When gamma correction is being done with a user-specified table, the gamma correction value is undefined. By default, the window system assumes a gamma correction value of 2.22 and loads the gamma table it creates corresponding to this value.

`-help`

> Print a list of the afbconfig command-line options, along with a brief explanation of each.

-linearorder first | last

If first, linear visuals come before their nonlinear counterparts on the X11 screen visual list for the AFB screen. If last, the nonlinear visuals come before the linear ones.

-maxwids *n* Specify the maximum number of AFB X channel pixel values that are reserved for use as window ID s (WIDs). The remainder of the pixel values in overlay colormaps are used for normal X11 opaque color pixels. The reserved WIDs are allocated on a first-come first-serve basis by 3D graphics windows (such as XGL), MBX windows, and windows that have a nondefault visual. The X channel codes 0 to $(255 - n)$ are opaque color pixels. The X channel codes $(255 - n + 1)$ to 255 are reserved for use as WIDs. Legal values are 1, 2, 4, 8, 16, 32, and 64.

This option is available only if -extovl is disabled.

-overlayorder first | last

If first, the depth 8 PseudoColor Overlay visual comes before the non-overlay visual on the X11 screen visual list for the AFB screen. If last, the non-overlay visual comes before the overlay one.

-propt Print the current values of all AFB options in the OWconfig file specified by the -file option for the device specified by the -dev option. Print the values of options as they will be in the OWconfig file after the call to afbconfig completes.

The following display is typical.

```
--- OpenWindows Configuration for /dev/fbs/afb0 ---
OWconfig: machine
Video Mode: 1280x1024x76
Default Visual: Non-Linear Normal Visual
Visual Ordering: Linear Visuals are last
Overlay Visuals are last
OpenGL Visual Expansion: enabled
Server Overlay Visuals: enabled
Extended Overlay: enabled
Underlay WIDs: 64 (not configurable)
Overlay WIDs: 4 (not configurable)
Gamma Correction Value: 2.220
Gamma Correction Table: Available
```

-prconf Print the AFB hardware configuration.

The following display is typical.

```
--- Hardware Configuration for /dev/fbs/afb0 ---
Type: double-buffered AFB with Z-buffer
Board: rev 0 (Horizontal)
Number of Floats: 6
PROM Information: @(#)afb.fth x.xx xx/xx/xx
AFB ID: 0x101df06d
```

```
DAC: Brooktree 9070, version 1 (Pac2)
3DRAM: Mitsubishi 130a, version x
EDID Data: Available - EDID version 1 revision x
Monitor Sense ID: 4   (Sun 37x29cm RGB color monitor)
Monitor possible resolutions: 1024x768x77, 1024x800x84, 1
1152x900x76, 1280x1024x67, 1280x1024x76, 960x680xx108s
Current resolution setting: 1280x1024x76
```

-sov enable | disable

> If enabled, advertise the root window's SERVER_OVERLAY_VISUALS
> property. Export SOV visuals and this property can retrieve their
> transparent types, values, and layers. If disabled, the
> SERVER_OVERLAY_VISUALS property is not defined and SOV visuals
> are not exported.

-res *video-mode* [now | try [noconfirm | nocheck]]

> Specify the video mode used to drive the monitor connected to the
> specified AFB device.
>
> The format of these built-in video modes is *widthxheightxrate*,
> where *width* is the screen width in pixels, *height* is the screen height
> in pixels, and *rate* is the vertical frequency of the screen refresh.
>
> The s suffix of 960x680x112s and 960x680x108s signifies stereo video
> modes. The i suffix of 640x480x60i and 768x575x50i signifies
> interlaced video timing. If absent, noninterlaced timing is used.
>
> As a convenience, -res also accepts formats with an at sign (@) in
> front of the refresh rate instead of *n*, (1280x1024@76). Some
> *video-mode*s supported by AFB may not be supported by the monitor.
> You can display the list of *video-mode*s supported by the AFB device
> and the monitor by running afbconfig with the -res ? option.
>
> The following list shows all possible video-modes supported on AFB.

```
1024x768x60
1024x768x70
1024x768x75
1024x768x77
1024x800x84
1152x900x66
1152x900x76
1280x800x76
1280x1024x60
1280x1024x67
1280x1024x76
960x680x112s      (Stereo)
960x680x108s      (Stereo)
640x480x60
640x480x60i       (Interlaced)
768x575x50i       (Interlaced)
```

For convenience, some of the *video-modes* supported on the AFB have symbolic names. Instead of the form *widthxheightxrate*, you can supply one of these names as the argument to the -res option. The symbolic name none means that when the window system is run, the screen resolution is the video mode that is currently programmed in the device.

The following list shows the symbolic names for video modes that are supported on AFB.

Name	Corresponding Video Mode
svga	1024x768x60
1152	1152x900x76
1280	1280x1024x76
stereo	960x680x112s
ntsc	640x480x60i
pal	768x575x50i
none	Use the video mode currently programmed in the device

The -res option also accepts additional, optional arguments immediately following the video mode specification. You can specify any or all of the following arguments.

noconfirm   Bypass confirmation messages and program the requested video mode anyway. This option is useful when afbconfig is run from a shell script.

Because it is possible to put the system into an unusable state with the -res option if there is any ambiguity in the monitor sense codes, afbconfig, by default, prints a warning message and prompts to find out if it is OK to continue.

nocheck   Suspend the normal error checking based on the monitor sense code. Accept the video mode specified by the user regardless of whether it is appropriate for the currently attached monitor. (This option is useful if a different monitor is to be connected to the AFB device.) Use of this option implies noconfirm as well.

now   Update the video mode in the OWconfig file, and immediately program the AFB device to display this video mode. This option is useful for changing the video mode before starting the window system.

It is not advisable to use this argument with afbconfig while the configured device is being used (for example, while running the window system); unpredictable results may occur. To run afbconfig with the now argument, first bring the window system down. If you use the now argument within a window system session, the video mode is changed immediately, but the width and height of the affected screen don't change until the window system is exited and reentered. In addition, the system may not recognize changes in stereo mode. Consequently, this usage is strongly discouraged.

try

Program the specified video mode on a trial basis. You are asked to confirm the video mode by typing y within 10 seconds. Or, you can terminate the trial before 10 seconds are up by typing any character. Any character other than y or Return is considered a no. The previous video mode is restored, and afbconfig does not change the video mode in the OWconfig file (other options specified still take effect). If you press Return, you are prompted for a yes or no answer on whether to keep the new video mode. This option implies the now argument (see the warning note on the now argument).

Examples

The following example switches the monitor type to a resolution of 1280 x1024 at 76 Hz.

example% **/usr/sbin/afbconfig -res 1280x1024x76**

Attributes

See attributes(5) for descriptions of the following attributes.

Attribute Type	Attribute Value
Availability	SUNWafbcf

See Also

mmap(2), attributes(5)
   OpenWindows Reference Manual

aliasadm — Manipulate the NIS+ Aliases Map

Synopsis

```
/usr/bin/aliasadm -a alias expansion [options comments] [optional-flags]
/usr/bin/aliasadm -c alias expansion [options comments] [optional-flags]
/usr/bin/aliasadm -d alias [optional-flags]
/usr/bin/aliasadm -e alias [optional-flags]
/usr/bin/aliasadm -l alias [optional-flags]
/usr/bin/aliasadm -m alias [optional-flags]
/usr/bin/aliasadm [-I] [-D domainname] [-f filename] [-M mapname]
```

Description

Use the `aliasadm` command to create, modify, and delete aliases in the NIS+ alias map. Mail aliases must be unique within the domain. To use the `aliasadm` command, you must be root, a member of the NIS+ group that owns the `Aliases` database, or the person who created the database. Alternatively, if you have Solstice AdminSuite, you can use the Database Manager to edit the `aliases` database.

The alias map is an NIS+ table object with four columns.

`alias`	The name of the alias as a null-terminated string.
`expansion`	The value of the alias as it would appear in a sendmail `/etc/aliases` file.
`options`	A list of options applicable to this alias. The only option currently supported is CANON. With this option, if the user has requested an inverse alias lookup and there is more than one alias with this expansion, this alias is given preference.
`comments`	An arbitrary string containing comments about this alias. The sendmail(1M) command reads this map in addition to the NIS aliases map and the local `/etc/aliases` database.

Options

`-a`	Add an alias.
`-c`	Change an alias.
`-d`	Delete an alias.
`-D domainname`	Edit the map in domain `domainname` instead of the current domain.
`-e`	Edit the alias map.
`-f filename`	When editing or listing the database, use `filename` instead of invoking the editor.
`-I`	Initialize the NIS+ aliases database.
`-l`	List the alias map.

-m   Print or match an alias.

-M *mapname*   Edit *mapname* instead of *mail_aliases*.

Examples

The following example lists the contents of the aliases table for a newly created NIS+ server in alphabetical order by alias.

```
# aliasadm -l
paperbark# # aliasadm -l
MAILER-DAEMON: postmaster
Postmaster: root
nobody: /dev/null
#
```

If you have a large aliases table, listing the entire contents can take a while. You can pipe the output through grep if you are searching for a specific entry.

The following example lists an individual entry in the NIS+ mail_aliases table.

```
# aliasadm -m ignatz
ignatz: ignatz@castle  # Alias for Iggy Ignatz
#
```

The aliasadm -m option matches only the complete alias name. If you want partial matches, pipe the aliasadm -l command through grep.

Files

/etc/aliases   Mail aliases for the local host in ASCII format.

Attributes

See attributes(5) for descriptions of the following attributes.

Attribute Type	Attribute Value
Availability	SUNWnisu

See Also

sendmail(1M), attributes(5)

allocate — Device Allocation

Synopsis

```
/usr/sbin/allocate [-s][-U uname] device
/usr/sbin/allocate [-s][-U uname] -g dev-type
/usr/sbin/allocate [-s][-U uname] -F device
```

Description

Use the `allocate` command to manage the ownership of devices. `allocate` ensures that each device is used by only one qualified user at a time.

Use the `device` argument to specify the device to be manipulated. To preserve the integrity of the device's owner, the allocate operation is executed on all the device special files associated with that device.

Use the `dev-type` argument to specify the device type to be operated on. You can use the `dev-type` argument only with the `-g` option.

The default allocate operation allocates the device special files associated with device to the UID of the current process.

If you specify the `-F` option, the device cleaning program is executed when allocation is performed. This cleaning program is found in `/etc/security/lib`. The name of this program is found in the `device_allocate`(4) entry for the device in the `dev-exec` field.

Note — The functionality described in this manual page is available only if the Basic Security Module (BSM) has been enabled. See `bsmconv`(1M) for more information.

Options

`-F` *device*	Reallocate the device allocated to another user. This option is often used with `-U` to reallocate a specific device to a specific user. Only superuser is permitted to use this option.
`-g` *dev-type*	Allocate a nonallocated device with a device type matching *dev-type*.
`-s`	Suppress any diagnostic output.
`-U` *uname*	Use the user ID *uname* instead of the user ID of the current process when performing the allocate operation. Only superuser is permitted to use this option.

Exit Status

`allocate` returns a non-zero exit status in the event of an error.

Files

`/etc/security/device_allocate`

> File that contains mandatory access control information about each physical device.

`/etc/security/device_maps`

> File that contains access control information about each physical device.

`/etc/security/dev/*`

> Directory that contains security device files.

`/etc/security/lib/*`

> Directory that contains security executables.

Attributes

See attributes(5) for descriptions of the following attributes.

Attribute Type	Attribute Value
Availability	SUNWcsu

See Also

bsmconv(1M), device_allocate(4), device_maps(4), attributes(5)

---

amiserv — AMI Keyserver

New!

Synopsis

/usr/lib/security/amiserv

Description

The Authentication Management Infrastructure (AMI) is new in the Solaris 8 release. AMI is a public-key-based authentication/privacy system that includes a set of security-related APIs and commands. You can use these APIs to tailor a public key infrastructure (PKI) suitable for your site's authentication and privacy requirements.

The AMI keyserver, amiserv, is a per-host daemon that performs cryptographic operations with private keys. The daemon is initiated at system startup by the /etc/rc2.d/S95amiserv run control script. The private key operations performed by the keyserver include digital signature and decryption operations.

amiserv also acts as a repository for user and host keystores. When users require access to their keystore, they retrieve it from amiserv and not from the (possibly insecure) naming service.

Users register their keystore with amiserv by executing the amilogin(1) command, which uses the entered password to cryptographically validate the keystore and decrypt the private key (see amikeystore(1)). The validated keystore is then sent to amiserv via a UNIX RPC call. The keystore remains with amiserv until the user runs the amilogout(1) command or amiserv is restarted. The amilogout command removes the user's keystore from amiserv.

> **Note** — The user's keystore is not automatically removed from amiserv when a user runs logout(1).

amiserv stores all keystores that have been registered with it in memory in an obscured form. Keystores that have been permanently registered with amiserv (by the amilogin command with the -p option) are also stored internally on the local file system. This file is read by amiserv on startup to initialize itself with a set of permanent host and user keystores.

> **Note** — You must be root to run amiserv.

Exit Status

0	Successful completion.
1	An error occurred.

Attributes

See `attributes`(5) for descriptions of the following attributes.

Attribute Type	Attribute Value
Availability	SUNWami

See Also

`amikeystore`(1), `amilogin`(1), `amilogout`(1), `attributes`(5)

answerbook2_admin — AnswerBook2 GUI Administration Tool

Synopsis

`/usr/dt/bin/answerbook2_admin [-h]`

Description

Use the `answerbook2_admin` command to open the default Web browser showing the administration interface for the local AnswerBook2 server. The AnswerBook2 administration tool based on the Web browser provides the same functionality as the `ab2admin`(1M) command-line administration tool.

   This functionality is also accessible through the AnswerBook2 Admin option within the System_Admin subset of the Application Manager function on the CDE front panel Applications menu.

Note — Once a Web browser is open and you have access to the AnswerBook2 Administration tool, use its online Help system to find out more about administering the AnswerBook2 server.

Options

-h	Display a usage statement.

Usage

At startup time, `answerbook2_admin` starts up the default Web browser (for example, Netscape or HotJava) and displays the URL specified for administering the local AnswerBook2 server (`http://localhost:8888`). If the user has set up administration access control, the Web browser prompts for a valid administrator login and password for this document server before displaying the administration tool.

Files

/usr/lib/ab2/dweb/data/config/admin_passwd

File containing *username:password*.

Attributes

See attributes(5) for descriptions of the following attributes.

Attribute Type	Attribute Value
Availability	SUNWab2m

See Also

ab2admin(1M), attributes(5)

arp — Address Resolution Display and Control

Synopsis

```
/usr/sbin/arp hostname
/usr/sbin/arp -a
/usr/sbin/arp -d hostname
/usr/sbin/arp -f filename
/usr/sbin/arp -s hostname ether-address [temp][pub][trail]
```

Description

Use the arp command to display and modify the Internet-to-Ethernet address
translation tables used by the address resolution protocol (see arp(7P)). You can specify
hostname either by name or by number, using Internet dot notation.

arp is useful as a diagnostic tool to resolve point-to-point connectivity problems. If
the ARP table of a host system contains an incorrect entry, the system is unreachable
because outgoing packets contain the wrong Ethernet address.

Options

-a   Display all of the current ARP entries. The following flags are used in
the table.

P   Publish; include IP address for the machine and the
addresses that have explicitly been added with the -s option.
ARP responds to ARP requests for this address.

S   Static; not learned for the ARP protocol.

U   Unresolved; waiting for ARP response.

M   Mapping; used only for the multicast entry for 224.0.0.0

-d	Delete an entry for the host called *hostname*. Only superuser can use this option.
-f	Read the file named *filename* and set multiple entries in the ARP tables. Entries in the file should be of the following form.

hostname ether-address [temp] [pub] [trail]

(See option -s for argument definitions.)

-s	Create an ARP entry for the host called *hostname* with the Ethernet address *ether-address*. Specify the Ethernet address as six hexadecimal bytes separated by colons. The entry is permanent unless you specify the word temp in the command. If you specify the word pub, the entry is published. For example, this system responds to ARP requests for *hostname* even though the hostname is not its own. The word trail indicates that trailer encapsulations can be sent to this host. You can use arp - s for a limited form of proxy ARP when a host on one of the directly attached networks is not physically present on the subnet. Another system can then be configured with arp -s to respond to ARP requests. This option is useful in certain SLIP or PPP configurations.

Operands

hostname	Specify the host either by name or by number, using Internet dot notation.
ether-address	

Specify the Ethernet address as six hexadecimal bytes separated by colons.

Examples

The following example uses arp -a to display the ARP table.

arp -a

```
Net to Media Table: IPv4
Device    IP Address                 Mask        Flags  Phys Addr
------  ------------------   ----------------  -----  ----------------
hme0    G3                         255.255.255.255        00:05:02:35:aa:1c
hme0    castle                     255.255.255.255        08:00:20:18:69:71
hme0    paperbark                  255.255.255.255 SP     08:00:20:7d:79:d4
hme0    224.0.0.0                  240.0.0.0       SM     01:00:5e:00:00:00
#
```

The S flag means static, the P flag means publish, the M flag means mapping.

The following example lists the ARP entry for the system paperbark.

arp paperbark
```
paperbark (172.16.8.22) at 8:0:20:7d:79:d4 permanent published
#
```

The following example deletes the ARP entry for the system paperbark.

```
# arp -d paperbark
paperbark (172.16.8.22) deleted
#
```

The following example recreates the paperbark entry in the ARP table as permanent published.

```
# arp -s paperbark 8:0:20:7d:79:d4 pub
# arp paperbark
paperbark (172.16.8.22) at 8:0:20:7d:79:d4 permanent published
#
```

Attributes

See attributes(5) for descriptions of the following attributes.

Attribute Type	Attribute Value
Availability	SUNWcsu

See Also

ifconfig(1M), attributes(5), arp(7P)

aset — Monitor or Restrict Access to System Files and Directories

Synopsis

```
/usr/aset/aset [-p][-d aset-dir][-l sec-level][-n user@host]
   [-u userlist-file]
```

Description

The Automated Security Enhancement Tool (ASET) is a set of administrative commands that enable you to monitor and control system security by automatically performing tasks that you would otherwise do manually. You can use it to check the settings of system files, including attributes such as permissions and ownership and the contents of the system files. It warns the users of potential security problems and, where appropriate, sets the system files automatically according to the specified security level.

You can set ASET to operate at one of three security levels either by specifying the -l option at the command line or by setting the ASETSECLEVEL environment variable to low, med, or high. All the functionality operates according to the value of the security level.

- At the low level, ASET ensures that attributes of system files are set to standard release values. ASET performs several checks and reports potential security weaknesses. At this level, ASET takes no action and does not affect system services.

- At the med level, ASET provides adequate security control for most environments. ASET modifies some of the system file settings and parameters, restricting system access to reduce the risks from security attacks. ASET reports security weaknesses and any modifications it makes to restrict access. At this level, ASET does not affect system services, and all of the system applications and commands maintain all of their original functionality.
- At the high level, ASET provides a highly secure system. ASET adjusts many system files and parameter settings to minimize access permissions. Most system applications and commands continue to function normally, but at this level, security considerations take precedence over other system behavior. The majority of system applications and commands maintain their functionality, although there may be a few that exhibit behaviors that are not familiar in normal system environment.

Refer to the *System Administrator's Manual, Volume I* for more exact definitions of what aset does at each of these levels. The asetenv(4) file and the master files (see asetmasters(4)) determine to a large extent what aset performs at each level, and experienced administrators can use these files to redefine the definitions of the levels to suit their particular needs. These files are provided by default to fit most security-conscious environments, and, in most cases, the files provide adequate security safeguards without modification. They are, however, designed so that they can be easily edited by experienced administrators with specific needs.

You can periodically activate aset at the specified security level with default definitions by using the -p option. aset is automatically activated at a frequency specified by the administrator, starting from a designated future time (see asetenv(4)). Without the -p option, aset operates only once, immediately.

Options

-d *aset-dir*   Specify a working directory other than /usr/aset for ASET. /usr/aset is the default working directory where ASET is installed, and it is the root directory of all ASET commands and data files. If you use another directory as the ASET working directory, you can define it either with the -d option or by setting the ASETDIR environment variable before invoking aset. If you specify the command-line option, it overwrites the environment variable.

-l *sec-level*   Specify a security level (low, med, or high). The default level is low. You can also specify the level by setting the ASETSECLEVEL environment variable before invoking aset. If you specify the command-line option, it overwrites the environment variable.

-n *user@host*   Notify *user* at system *host*. Send the output of aset to *user* by e-mail. If you do not specify this option, send the output to the standard output. Note that this output is not the reports of ASET, but instead is an execution log that includes any error messages. This output is typically fairly brief. The actual reports of ASET are found in the /usr/aset/reports/latest directory. See the -d option.

-p   Schedule aset to be executed periodically by adding an entry for aset
                                in the /etc/crontab file. Use the PERIODIC_SCHEDULE environment
                                variable in the /usr/aset/asetenv file to define the time for
                                execution. See crontab(1) and asetenv(4). If a crontab(1) entry for
                                aset already exists, produce a warning in the execution log.

-u *userlist-file*

                                Specify a file containing a list of users. aset performs environment
                                checks (for example, UMASK and PATH variables) on these users. By
                                default, aset checks only for root. *userlist-file* is an ASCII text
                                file. Each entry in the file is a line that contains only one user name
                                (login name).

Usage

The following paragraphs discuss the tasks ASET performs. Execute the first task,
tune, only once per installation of ASET. Execute the other tasks periodically at the
specified frequency.

tune Task

Use the tune task to tighten system file permissions. ASET provides three configurable
files—tune.low, tune.med, and tune.high—that define the available ASET security
levels. In standard releases, system files or directories have permissions defined to
maximize open information sharing. In a more security-conscious environment, you
may want to redefine these permission settings to more restrictive values. aset enables
you to reset these permissions, based on the specified security level. Generally, at the
low level, the permissions are set to what they should be as released. At the medium
level the permissions are tightened to ensure reasonable security that is adequate for
most environments. At the high level, they are further tightened to very restrictive
access. See asetmasters(4).

cklist Task

Use the cklist task to examine system files and to compare each one with a description
of that file listed in a master file. The /usr/aset/masters/cklist.level is created the
first time ASET runs the cklist task. See asetenv(4). Any discrepancies found are
reported in the cklist.rpt file. The following information is compared for directories
and files.

- Owner and group.
- Permission bits.
- Size and checksum (if file).
- Number of links.
- Last modification time.

The lists of directories to check are defined in asetenv(4), based on the specified
security level, and are configurable with the CKLISTPATH_LOW, CKLISTPATH_MED, and
CKLISTPATH_HIGH environment variables. Typically, the lower-level lists are subsets of
the higher-level lists.

usrgrp Task

Use the usrgrp task to check the consistency and integrity of user accounts and groups as defined in the passwd and group databases and to report any potential problems in the usergrp.rpt file. This task checks for the following violations.

- passwd file entries not in the correct format.
- User accounts without a password.
- Duplicate user names.
- Duplicate user IDs. Duplicate user IDs are reported unless allowed by the uid_alias file. See asetmasters(4)).
- Invalid login directories.
- If C2 is enabled, check C2 hidden passwd format.

Potential problems for the group file include the following.

- Group file entries not in the right format.
- Duplicate group names.
- Duplicate group IDs.
- Null group passwords.

aset checks the local passwd file. If the YPCHECK environment variable is set to true, aset also checks the NIS passwd files. See asetenv(4). Problems in the NIS passwd file are reported only and are not corrected automatically. The checking is done for all three security levels except where noted.

sysconf Task

Use the sysconf task to check various system configuration tables, most of which are in the /etc directory. aset checks and makes appropriate corrections for each system table at all three levels, except where noted. All problems are reported in the sysconf.rpt file. The following discussion assumes familiarity with the various system tables. See the manual pages for these tables for further details.

The operations for each system table are shown below.

/etc/hosts.equiv

> The default file contains a single + line, thus making every known host a trusted host: not advised for system security. aset performs the following operations.

> Low   Warn administrators about the + line.

> Medium   Warn administrators about the + line.

> High   Warn about and delete the + entry.

/etc/inetd.conf

> Check the following entries for system daemons for possible weaknesses.

> tftp(1) does not do any authentication. Ensure that in.tftpd(1M) is started in the right directory on the server and is not running on clients. At the low level, aset warns if the mentioned condition is not true. At the medium and high levels, aset warns, and changes (if necessary), the in.tftpd entry to include the -s /tftpboot option after ensuring the directory /tftpboot exists.

ps(1) and netstat(1M) provide valuable information to potential system crackers. Disable these commands when aset is executed at a high security level.

rexd is known to have poor authentication mechanism. Disable rexd for medium and high security levels by commenting out the entry. If rexd is activated with the -c (secure RPC) option, do not disable it.

/etc/aliases   The decode alias of UUCP is a potential security weakness. Disable the alias for medium and high security levels by commenting out the entry.

/etc/default/login

Check the CONSOLE= line to enable root login only at a specific terminal depending on the security level.

Low	Take no action.
Medium	Take no action.
High	Add the following line to the file.

CONSOLE=/dev/console

/etc/vfstab   Check for world-readable or writeable device files for mounted file systems.

/etc/dfs/dfstab

Check for file systems that are exported without any restrictions.

/etc/ftpusers At high security level, ensure that root is in /etc/ftpusers (and create the entry if necessary), thus disallowing ftp(1) to be used as root.

/var/adm/utmpx

Make this files not world-writeable for the high level. (Some applications may not run properly with this setting.) Note that the utmpx database file in Solaris 8 supersedes the obsolete utmp database file of previous releases.

/.rhosts   The use of an .rhosts file for the entire system is not advised. Warn for the low level and move the file to /.rhosts.bak for levels medium and high.

env task

The env task checks how the PATH and UMASK environment variables are set for root and users specified with the -u *userlist-file* option by parsing the /.profile, /.login, and /.cshrc files. It checks the PATH variable to ensure that it does not contain . as a directory, which makes an easy target for Trojan horse attacks. It also checks that the directories in the PATH variable are not world-writeable. It checks the UMASK variable to ensure files are not created as readable or writeable by world. Any problems found by these checks are reported in the env.rpt file.

eeprom task

Newer versions of the EEPROM enable you to specify a secure parameter. See eeprom(1M). aset recommends that the administrator set the parameter to command for the medium level and to full for the high level. aset gives warnings in the eeprom.rpt file if it detects the parameter is not set adequately.

firewall task

The firewall task ensures that the system can be safely used as a network relay. At the high security level, aset takes proper measures so that the system can be safely used as a firewall in a network. These measures mainly involve disabling IP packet forwarding and making routing information invisible. Firewalling provides protection against external access to the network. Any changes made by this task are reported in the firewall.rpt file.

Environment Variables

ASETDIR	Specify the ASET working directory. Default is /usr/aset.
ASETSECLEVEL	Specify the ASET security level. Default is low.
TASKS	Specify the tasks to be executed by aset. Default is all tasks.

Files

/usr/aset/reports

Directory of ASET reports.

Attributes

See attributes(5) for descriptions of the following attributes.

Attribute Type	**Attribute Value**
Availability	SUNWast

See Also

crontab(1), ftp(1), ps(1), tftp(1), eeprom(1M), in.tftpd(1M), netstat(1M), asetenv(4), asetmasters(4), attributes(5)
System Administration Guide, Volume I

aset.restore — Restore System Files Affected by ASET

Synopsis

/usr/aset/aset.restore [-d *aset-dir*]

Description

Use the `aset.restore` command to restore system files that are affected by the Automated Security Enhancement Tool (ASET) to their pre-ASET content. When ASET is executed for the first time, it saves and archives the original system files in the `/usr/aset/archives` directory. The `aset.restore` command reinstates these files. It also deschedules ASET if it is currently scheduled for periodic execution. See `asetenv`(4).

If you have made changes to system files after running ASET, these changes are lost when you run `aset.restore`. If you want to be absolutely sure that you keep the existing system state, back up your system before using `aset.restore`.

Use `aset.restore` under the following circumstances.

- You want to remove ASET permanently and restore the original system (if you want to deactivate ASET, you can remove it from scheduling).
- You are unfamiliar with ASET and want to experiment with it. You can use `aset.restore` to restore the original system state.
- When some major system functionality is not working properly and you suspect that ASET is causing the problem; you may want to restore the system to see if the problem persists without ASET.

`aset.restore` requires root privileges to execute.

Options

-d *aset-dir*   Specify that the working directory for ASET is located under *aset-dir*. By default, this directory is `/usr/aset`.

Files

`/usr/aset/archives`

Archive of system files before `aset` is executed.

Attributes

See `attributes`(5) for descriptions of the following attributes.

Attribute Type	Attribute Value
Availability	SUNWast

See Also

`aset(1M)`, `asetenv(4)`, `attributes(5)`
System Administration Guide, Volume I

aspppd, aspppls — Asynchronous PPP Link Manager

Synopsis

```
/usr/sbin/aspppd [-d debug-level]
/usr/sbin/aspppls
```

Description

The aspppd link manager is a user-level daemon that automates the process of
connecting to a remote host for Point-to-Point Protocol (PPP) service. It works with the
IP-Dialup driver (ipdcm) and PPP streams module (ppp(7M)) to provide IP network
services over an analog modem using dialed, voice-grade telephone lines. This
automated process starts whenever any activity that generates IP traffic takes place
(for example, a user logging in to a remote system). When a remote host tries to
establish a connection, the link manager on the local host completes the connection.

aspppd can initiate the connection process either by sending an IP datagram to a
(disconnected) peer host or by receiving a notification that a peer host wants to establish
a connection.

The aspppls command is invoked as a login shell that starts PPP after you dial up
and log in. Its function is similar to the /usr/lib/uucp/uccico command. When you
configure a system as a dial-in server, you must specify aspppls as the login shell in the
/etc/passwd file in the entries for every nomadic computer allowed to dial in to the local
host.

aspppls is invoked by the serial port monitor when a peer machine logs into a
PPP-enabled account. It enables the aspppd link manager to accept the incoming call.

Options

-d debug-level

> Specify the debug level as a number between 0 and 9. Higher
> numbers give more detailed debugging information. Write the output
> to the log file /etc/log/asppp.log.

Usage

If the configuration file /etc/asppp.cf is present, the link manager is invoked at boot
time. After parsing the configuration file and building a path object for each peer host,
it sleeps until one of the following events occurs.

- An IP datagram is routed to one of the ipd or ipdptp interfaces (see ppp(7M)). The
  link manager consults the UUCP database, dials the modem, logs into the peer
  host, establishes the PPP data link, brings up IP, and forwards the IP datagram
  that initiated the process.

- It is notified by the login service that a peer host is trying to make a connection.
  The link manager opens the file descriptor supplied by the login service,
  establishes the PPP data link, and brings up IP.

If the link manager determines that there has been no IP traffic for the period
specified by the inactivity_timeout keyword, it disconnects the link by bringing down
IP and PPP and closing the connection to the peer host.

You can reinitialize the link manager by sending it the -HUP signal (with kill(1), for example), which disconnects all open PPP links and rereads the configuration file.

Path

A path object contains the state of a connection with a peer host. Information such as system names, interface names, timeout values, and other attributes are kept in the path object. A path exists for each potential peer host. You define paths in the configuration file.

Interfaces

The link manager supports two types of IP layer interfaces: the point-to-multipoint interface (ipd) and the point-to-point interface (ipdptp) (see ppp(7M)).

- The point-to-multipoint interface logically connects the host machine to a network containing one or more peer hosts. IP traffic to or from any of the peer hosts is routed through the point-to-multipoint interface. When an ipd interface is configured, only one IP address, that of the host, is assigned. In other words, it behaves similarly to an Ethernet interface, although the broadcast capability is not supported. This type of interface is well suited for a dial-in PPP server.

- The point-to-point interface logically connects the host machine with one peer host. Only IP traffic to or from the peer host is routed through this interface. When an ipdptp interface is configured, two IP addresses are assigned. This type of interface is well suited to support a remote or nomadic machine.

An interface must be fully configured and enabled (that is, up) before an IP datagram is routed to it. A point-to-multipoint interface must also be fully configured and enabled before the link manager can associate an incoming connection with it. You do not, however, need to configure and enable a point-to-point interface before an incoming connection is assigned to it. A point-to-point interface that is "plumbed," but otherwise not configured or enabled (that is, down), can be used to accept an incoming connection if the path associated with the potential connection contains a dynamic interface specification (for example, interface ipdptp*). In this case, the link manager selects a disabled (down) interface, configures the host and peer addresses, brings the interface up, and assigns it for the duration of the connection.

Routing

You should pay special attention to routing issues that can arise if a host has more than one interface configured and enabled. By definition, a host with more than one enabled interface is a router, and the routing daemon (typically, in.routed) advertises the routes provided by the PPP interfaces. This behavior is normally acceptable for a dial-in server but can cause network disruptions if not administered properly.

To prevent routing information packets (RIP) from flowing over point-to-point interfaces, specify the norip keyword followed by the interface name in the /etc/gateways file. The following entries, for example, prevent RIP from being sent over ipdptp0 and ipdptp1.

```
norip     ipdptp0
norip     ipdptp1
```

See in.routed(1M) for further information.

Authentication

You can configure the link manager to support either the Password Authentication Protocol (PAP) or the Challenge Handshake Authentication Protocol (CHAP) as specified in RFC1334. Both protocols can be configured simultaneously, in which case, CHAP has precedence. A single host can participate as an authenticator (the local host requests that the peer host authenticate itself) or an authenticatee (the local host has been asked by the peer host to authenticate itself) or as both. It is also possible for a host to be an authenticator for one protocol and an authenticatee for the other protocol.

- PAP is a simple protocol similar to a standard login/password type of authentication. The PAP authenticator sends a message to its peer, requesting that the peer authenticate itself. The peer responds with an authenticate request packet that contains an ID and a password (both in plaintext). The ID and password are matched against a local copy, and if they match, the connection is established. If they don't match, the connection is dropped.

- CHAP does not pass any plaintext authentication data across the link. The CHAP authenticator sends a challenge packet to the peer that contains a random string. The peer then takes the string in the challenge packet and computes a response string that is a function of the challenge string and a shared secret key. The peer then sends a response packet back to the authenticator. The authenticator computes a string based on the original challenge string and the shared secret key and matches that result with the received response. If they match, the connection is established. Otherwise, the connection is dropped.

Configuration File

The primary purpose of the /etc/asppp.cf configuration file is to define each path used by the link manager to establish and maintain communication with a peer system.

The file consists of a sequence of tokens separated by white space (blanks, Tabs, and newlines). No record boundaries or any other constraints are put on the placement of the tokens. If a token begins with a pound sign (#), all characters between the pound sign and the next newline (\n) are ignored (that is, they are treated as a comment). Alphanumeric tokens are case insensitive and are translated by the lexical analyzer into lower case before further processing.

A string is a single token that does not contain embedded white space. You can use the standard ANSI C \ escape sequence to embed special characters (see an ANSI C manual for a list of escaped special characters). Use \s for the space character. If a pound sign appears at the beginning of a string, you must escape it (\#) to prevent it from being interpreted as a comment. A null (\0) truncates the string.

Groups of tokens are assembled into units known as paths (essentially a human-readable form of the path object). A path begins with the keyword path and ends at the token found before any subsequent path (or defaults) keyword or at the last token in the file. The tokens that make up a path are further partitioned into small groups consisting mostly of keyword/value pairs that define the attributes of the current path. If a particular keyword/value pair is not listed for a path, the default value is assumed.

The token sequences that begin with the substrings ipcp_ or lcp_ refer to PPP initial configuration options as specified in RFC1332, *The PPP Internet Protocol Control Protocol (IPCP)*. See the RFC for a more complete definition of these options.

The following is an alphabetic list of the token sequences that can be contained in a configuration file. Required sequences are noted.

Keywords

chap_name *string*

> Specify one or more octets representing the identification of this host. Do not terminate the name with null or CR/LF. Send the name to the authenticator in a response packet. Put this key/value pair in the authenticatee's configuration file.

chap_peer_secret *string*

> Specify one or more octets, preferably at least 16, that contain the secret key that is used with the challenge value to generate the string to match with the response received from the peer. Put this key/value pair in the authenticator's configuration file.

chap_peer_name *string*

> Specify one or more octets representing the identification of the peer transmitting the packet. Do not terminate the name with null or CR/LF. The name is received from the peer in a response packet. Put this key/value pair in the authenticator's configuration file.

chap_secret *string*

> Specify one or more octets, preferably at least 16, that contain the secret key that is used with the received challenge value to generate the response sent to the authenticator. Put this key/value pair in the authenticatee's configuration file.

debug_level *number*

> Specify a debug level. *number* is a value between 0 and 9. Higher numbers give more detailed debugging information. Write the output to the /etc/log/asppp.log file. The value set by the debug_level keyword overrides the -d command line option.
>
> | | |
> |---|---|
> | 0 | Errors only. |
> | 1 | Minimal information. |
> | 4 | Some UUCP chat-script information. |
> | 5 | All UUCP chat-script information. |
> | 7 | Maximum UUCP information. |
> | 8 | PPP message traces. |
> | 9 | Raw IP packets. |

defaults   Specify that all following token sequences up the next path keyword, or the end-of-file, set default attributes that affect subsequently defined paths.

default_route

> When the IP layer corresponding to the current path is fully operational, add the peer IP address to the route table as the default destination. The route is removed when the IP layer is brought down.

Note that the `default_route` keyword is installed only by
point-to-point interfaces.

`ifconfig` *parameters*

(Required) Pass the `ifconfig` keyword and associated parameters to
the shell for evaluation and execution. Use it to define an interface.
See the `ifconfig`(1M) manual page for more information.

`inactivity_timeout` *seconds*

Specify in *seconds* the maximum number of seconds that the
connection associated with the current path can remain idle before it
is terminated. You can specify `0` to indicate no timeout. The default is
120 seconds.

`interface` (`ipd`*n* | `ipdptp`*n* | `ipdptp*`)

(Required) Associate a specific point-to-multipoint or point-to-point
interface as denoted by the nonnegative integer *n* with the current
path. The third form, `ipdptp*`, indicates that the interface associated
with the path is a dynamic interface that is selected at connect time
from a pool of previously configured, inactive (down) point-to-point
interfaces.

`ipcp_async_map` *hex-number*

Specify the async control character map for the current path.
hex-number is the natural (that is, big-endian) form representation of
the four octets that make up the map. The default value is `ffffffff`.

`ipcp_compression` (`vj` | `off`)

Indicate whether IP compression is enabled. If enabled (`vj`), use the
Van Jacobson compression algorithm. The default is compression (`vj`).

`lcp_compression` (`on` | `off`)

Indicate whether PPP address, control, and protocol field compression
are enabled. If enabled, both the address and control field
compression and the protocol field compression options are set. The
default is compression (`on`).

`lcp_mru` *number*

Specify a desired maximum receive unit packet size in octets. The
default is `1500`.

`negotiate_address` (`on` | `off`)

Indicate whether local IP address assignment is obtained through
negotiation and assigned dynamically. If enabled, the local address is
obtained from the remote end of the PPP link. If so obtained, you can
use any local address other than `0.0.0.0` to initially configure the
interface. The default is to not negotiate (`off`).

`pap_id` *string*

Specify one or more octets that represent the host name that is sent to
the authenticator. To indicate a zero length string, do not include the

keyword. Put this key/value pair in the authenticatee's configuration file.

pap_password *string*

Specify one or more octets that indicate the password that is sent to the authenticator for this host. To indicate a zero-length string, do not include the keyword. Put this key/value pair in the authenticatee's configuration file.

pap_peer_id *string*

Specify one or more octets that indicate the name of the peer to be authenticated. To indicate a zero-length string, do not include the keyword. Put this key/value pair in the authenticator's configuration file.

pap_peer_password *string*

Specify one or more octets that indicate the password to be used for authentication. To indicate a zero-length string, do not include the keyword. Put this key/value pair in the authenticator's configuration file.

path   (Required) Group all following token sequences as attributes of this (current) path. Terminate the collection of attributes that make up the current path by the occurrence of a subsequent path or defaults keyword or by the end-of-file.

peer_ip_address *IP-address*

(Required for point-to-multipoint paths) Associate the IP-address with the current path. Ignore the value if the path specifies a point-to-point interface. *IP-address* can be in dotted decimal, hexadecimal, or symbolic (that is, host-name) format.

peer_system_name *name*

(Required) Associate the peer system name with the current path. Use the name to look up modem and peer-specific information for outbound connections in the UUCP /etc/uucp/Systems file. For incoming connections, determine the appropriate path by matching *name* with the login name that was used to obtain the connection (that is, an entry in the /etc/passwd file specifies *name* in the username field).

require_authentication (off | pap [chap] | chap [pap])

Indicate that the local host is the authenticator and that the peer is required to authenticate itself. If you specify either pap or chap, the peer must participate in the authentication protocol or the connection is terminated. If you specify both pap and chap, then the local host tries to negotiate chap, and if that fails, the connection is terminated. The local host does not try to negotiate pap. The default does not require authentication (off).

If pap is required, then you should specify the pap_peer_id and pap_peer_password keywords and values for the associated path. If you do not specify them, set the corresponding values to the null string. If chap is required, then you must specify the chap_peer_name and chap_peer_secret keywords and values for the associated path.

version *n*   Specify that the contents of the configuration file correspond to format version *n*. If this keyword is present, it must be the first keyword in the file. If absent, the version is assumed to be 1. This document contains the definition of the version 1 format for the configuration file.

will_do_authentication (off | pap [chap] | chap [pap])

Indicate that the local host is a potential authenticatee and is willing to participate in the specified authentication protocol. If both pap and chap are present, then the local host is willing to participate in either authentication protocol. The default does not participate in authentication (off).

If pap is available, then you should specify the pap_id and pap_password keywords and values for the associated path. If they are not specified, the corresponding values are set to the null string. If chap is available, then you must specify the chap_name and chap_secret keywords and values for the associated path.

Examples

The following example shows a remote machine that is likely to be nomadic or a home machine with a single modem.

```
#
# Dial in to two servers
#
ifconfig ipdptp0 plumb nomad1 dialin1 private up
path
                    interface ipdptp0
                    peer_system_name Pdialin1
                    will_do_authentication pap
                    ap_id nomad1
                    pap_password secret
ifconfig ipdptp1 plumb nomad1 dialin2 private up
path
                    interface ipdptp1
                    peer_system_name Pdialin2
                    lcp_mru 1006
```

The following example shows a dial-in server supporting a point-to-multipoint interface. Several modems can be attached to this server. The network addressed by the ipd interface is advertised by the router, and all traffic destined for that network is routed through this host. For that reason, it is unwise to support multiple dial-in servers with point-to-multipoint interfaces to the same network.

```
#
# A point-to-multipoint dial in server
```

```
#
ifconfig ipd0 plumb dialin1 netmask + up
defaults
        interface ipd0
        inactivity_timeout 900 # 15 minutes
        require_authentication chap pap
        chap_peer_name nomadc path
        peer_system_name Pnomad1
        chap_peer_secret abcd
        pap_peer_id nomad1
        pap_peer_password secret
        peer_ip_address nomad1
path
        peer_system_name Pnomad2
        chap_peer_secret a\sspace
        peer_ip_address nomad2
path
        peer_system_name Pnomad3
        inactivity_timeout 0 # No timeout for this host
        chap_peer_secret \#123;.
        peer_ip_address nomad3
path
        peer_system_name Pnomad4
        chap_peer_secret My\sSecret#Word
        peer_ip_address nomad4
```

The following example is for another dial-in server that supports dynamic
point-to-point interfaces. Usually the server has one modem for each interface. One
advantage of using dynamic interfaces is that (host) routes are advertised only when an
interface is up. Therefore, multiple dial-in servers can be supported.

```
#
# A dynamic point-to-point dial in server
#
ifconfig ipdptp0 plumb dialin2 client1 down
ifconfig ipdptp1 plumb dialin2 client2 down
ifconfig ipdptp2 plumb dialin2 client3 down
defaults
        interface ipdptp*
        inactivity_timeout 900
        debug_level 5
path
        peer_system_name Pnomad1
path
        peer_system_name Pnomad2
path
        peer_system_name Pnomad3
path
        peer_system_name Pnomad4
```

Files

/etc/asppp.cf

> Configuration file.

/etc/log/asppp.log

> Message log file.

/etc/uucp/Devices

> File that contains information for all the devices that can be used to establish a link to a remote computer.

/etc/uucp/Dialers

> File that contains dialing instructions for many commonly used modems.

/etc/uucp/Sysfiles

> File that enables you to assign different files to be used by uucp and cu as Systems, Devices, and Dialers files.

/etc/uucp/Systems

> File that contains the information needed by the uucico daemon to establish a communication link to a remote computer. It is the first file you need to edit to configure UUCP.

/tmp/.asppp.fifo

> Communication path between aspppd and aspppls.

/usr/sbin/aspppd

> Link manager.

/usr/sbin/aspppls

> Login service.

Attributes

See attributes(5) for descriptions of the following attributes.

Attribute Type	Attribute Value
Availability	SUNWapppu

See Also

kill(1), ifconfig(1M), in.routed(1M), attributes(5), ppp(7M)
TCP/IP and Data Communications Administration Guide

aspppls — Asynchronous PPP Link Manager

Synopsis
```
/usr/sbin/aspppls
```

Description
See aspppd(1M).

audit — Control the Behavior of the Audit Daemon

Synopsis
```
/usr/sbin/audit -n | -s | -t
```

Description
When the Basic Security Module is enabled (see bsmconv(1M) for more information), you can use the suite of auditing commands to detect potential security breaches. Auditing can reveal suspicious or abnormal patterns of system use and provide a way to trace suspect actions back to a specific user. Auditing can serve as a deterrent: if users know that their actions are likely to be audited, they may be less likely to attempt malicious activities.

Successful auditing depends on two other security features.

- Identification.
- Authentication.

At login, after a user supplies a user name and password, a unique audit ID is associated with the user's process. The audit ID is inherited by every process started during the login session. Even if a user changes identity (see the su(1M) command), all actions performed are tracked with the same audit ID.

Auditing makes it possible for you to perform the following tasks.

- Monitor security-relevant events that take place on the system.
- Record the events in an audit trail.
- Detect misuse or unauthorized activity (by analyzing the audit trail).

During system configuration, the system administrator selects the activities to monitor. The administrator can also fine-tune the degree of auditing that is done for individual users.

After audit data is collected, audit-reduction and interpretation tools enable you to examine interesting parts of the audit trail. For example, you can choose to look at audit records for individual users or groups, look at all records for a certain type of event on a specific day, or select records that were generated at a certain time of day.

Note — The `audit` command does not modify a process's preselection mask. It affects only which audit directories are used for audit data storage and specifies the minimum size free.

You start `audit` by enabling the `auditd` daemon. See `auditd`(1M).

When auditing is enabled, use the `audit` command as the administrative interface for maintaining an audit trail. You can perform the following tasks with the `audit` command.

- Notify the audit daemon to read the contents of the `audit_control`(4) file and to reinitialize the current audit directory to the first directory listed in the `audit_control` file.
  - If `auditd` receives the signal `SIGUSR1`, it closes the current audit file and opens another.
  - If `SIGHUP` is received, `auditd` closes the current audit trail, rereads the `audit_control` file, and opens a new trail.
  - If `SIGTERM` is received, `auditd` closes the audit trail and terminates auditing.
- Open a new audit file in the current audit directory specified in the `audit_control` file as last read by the audit daemon.
- Signal the audit daemon to close the audit trail and disable auditing.

Each time the audit daemon opens a new audit trail file, it updates the file `audit_data`(4) to include the correct name.

Options

`-n`	Signal audit daemon to close the current audit file, and to open a new audit file in the current audit directory.
`-s`	Signal audit daemon to read the audit control file. The audit daemon stores the information internally.
`-t`	Signal audit daemon to close the current audit trail file, disable auditing, and die.

Diagnostics

`0`	Success.
`>0`	Failure.

Files

`/etc/security/audit_user`

> An access-restricted database that stores per-user auditing preselection data.

`/etc/security/audit_control`

> File that contains audit control information used by `auditd`(1M).

Attributes

See attributes(5) for descriptions of the following attributes.

Attribute Type	Attribute Value
Availability	SUNWcsu

See Also

bsmconv(1M), praudit(1M), audit(2), audit_control(4), audit_user(4), attributes(5)

auditconfig — Configure Auditing

Synopsis

/usr/sbin/auditconfig *option*...

Description

Use the auditconfig command-line interface to get and set kernel audit parameters.

Note — The functionality described in this manual page is available only if the Basic Security Module (BSM) has been enabled. See bsmconv(1M) for more information.

Options

-chkconf   Check the configuration of kernel audit event to class mappings. If the runtime class mask of a kernel audit event does not match the configured class mask, report a mismatch.

-conf   Configure kernel audit event to class mappings. Runtime class mappings are changed to match those in the audit event to class database file.

-getfsize   Return the maximum audit file size in bytes and the current size of the audit file in bytes.

-setfsize *size*

      Set the maximum size of an audit file to *size* bytes. When the size limit is reached, close the audit file and start another.

-getcond   Display the kernel audit condition. The condition displayed is the literal string auditing, which means auditing is enabled and turned on (the kernel audit module is constructing and queuing audit records) or noaudit, which means auditing is enabled but turned off (the kernel audit module is not constructing and queuing audit records), or disabled, which means that the audit module has not been enabled. See auditon(2) and auditd(1M) for further information.

-setcond [auditing|noaudit]

Set the kernel audit condition to the condition specified where auditing enables auditing or noaudit disables auditing.

-getclass *event*

Display the preselection mask associated with the specified kernel audit event. *event* is the kernel event number or event name.

-setclass *event audit-flag* [,*audit-flag*...]

Map the kernel event *event* to the classes specified by *audit-flag*. *event* is an event number or name. An *audit-flag* is a two-character string representing an audit class. See audit_control(4) for further information.

-lsevent   Display the currently configured (runtime) kernel and user-level audit event information.

-getpinfo *pid*

Display the audit ID, preselection mask, terminal ID, and audit session ID for the specified process.

-setpmask *pid flags*

Set the preselection mask of the specified process. *flags* is the ASCII representation of the flags similar to that in *audit_control*(4).

-setsmask *asid flags*

Set the preselection mask of all processes with the specified audit session ID.

-setumask *auid flags*

Set the preselection mask of all processes with the specified audit ID.

-lspolicy   Display the kernel audit policies with a description of each policy.

-getpolicy Display the kernel audit policy.

-setpolicy[+|-]*policy-flag*[,*policy-flag*...]

Set the kernel audit policy. *policy-flag* is a literal string that denotes an audit policy. A prefix of + adds the specified policies to the current audit policies. A prefix of – removes the specified policies from the current audit policies. The following list shows the valid policy flag strings. You can also list the current, valid, audit policy-flag strings with auditconfig -lspolicy.

arge   Include the execv(2) system call environment arguments to the audit record. This information is not included by default.

argv   Include the execv(2) system call parameter arguments to the audit record. This information is not included by default.

cnt   Do not suspend processes when audit resources are
            exhausted. Instead, drop audit records and keep a count of
            the number of records dropped. By default, processes are
            suspended until audit resources become available.

group   Include the supplementary group token in audit records.
            By default, the group token is not included.

path   Add secondary path tokens to audit record. These are
            typically the path names of dynamically linked shared
            libraries or command interpreters for shell scripts. By
            default, they are not included.

trail   Include the trailer token in every audit record. By default,
            the trailer token is not included.

seq   Include the sequence token as part of every audit record.
            By default, the sequence token is not included. The
            sequence token attaches a sequence number to every audit
            record.

Examples

The following example uses the -getcond option to show that auditing is enabled.

```
# auditconfig -getcond
audit condition = auditing
#
```

The following example uses the -getpinfo option to show information about the auditd daemon process.

```
# ps -ef | grep auditd
    root   296    1  0 13:03:45 ?          0:00 /usr/sbin/auditd
    root   517  492  0 13:25:13 pts/6      0:00 grep auditd
# auditconfig -getpinfo 296
audit id = root(0)
process preselection mask = no(0x0,0x0)
terminal id (maj,min,host) = 0,0,unknown(0.0.0.0)
audit session id = 0
#
```

The following example uses the -setclass option to map audit event number 10 to the fr audit class.

```
# auditconfig -setclass 10 fr
#
```

The following example uses the -setpolicy option to turn on inclusion of exec arguments in exec audit records. You can use the -setpolicy option to change the default Solaris BSM audit policies.

```
# auditconfig -setpolicy +argv
```

Exit Status

0   Successful completion.

1   An error occurred.

Files

/etc/security/audit_event

> An ASCII system file that stores event definitions and specifies the event to class mappings.

/etc/security/audit_class

> An ASCII system file that stores class definitions.

Attributes

See attributes(5) for descriptions of the following attributes.

Attribute Type	Attribute Value
Availability	SUNWcsu

See Also

auditd(1M), bsmconv(1M), praudit(1M), auditon(2), execv(2), audit_class(4), audit_control(4), audit_event(4), attributes(5)

---

auditd — Control the Generation and Location of Audit Trail Files

Synopsis

/usr/sbin/auditd

Description

The auditd audit daemon controls the generation and location of audit trail files. When the Basic Security Module is enabled, the audit_control file is read at system startup and the auditd daemon is automatically started. See bsmconv(1M) for information on how to enable the Basic Security Module.

    The /etc/security/audit_startup file is an executable script that is invoked as part of the startup sequence just before the execution of the audit daemon (see audit_startup(1M). A default audit_startup script, shown below, automatically configures the event to class mappings and sets the audit policies during the BSM (Basic Security Module) package installation. You can edit the audit_startup file to define your own auditing policies.

```
#!/bin/sh
auditconfig -conf
```

```
auditconfig -setpolicy none
auditconfig -setpolicy +cnt
```

auditd reads the audit_control(4) file to get a list of directories into which audit files can be written and the percentage limit for how much space to reserve on each file system before changing to the next directory.

Use the audit(1M) command to send signals to the auditd daemon. See audit(1M).

Each time the audit daemon opens a new audit trail file, it updates the file audit_data(4) to include the correct name.

Auditing Conditions

The audit daemon invokes the audit_warn(1M) command to warn you of the following specific auditing conditions.

audit_warn soft *pathname*

> The file system on which *pathname* resides has exceeded the minimum free space limit defined in audit_control(4). A new audit trail has been opened on another file system.

audit_warn allsoft

> All available file systems have been filled beyond the minimum free space limit. A new audit trail has been opened anyway.

audit_warn hard *pathname*

> The file system on which *pathname* resides has filled or for some reason become unavailable. A new audit trail has been opened on another file system.

audit_warn allhard *count*

> All available file systems have been filled or for some reason become unavailable. The audit daemon repeats this call to audit_warn every 20 seconds until space becomes available. *count* is the number of times that audit_warn has been called since the problem arose.

audit_warn ebusy

> An audit daemon is already running.

audit_warn tmpfile

> The file /etc/security/audit/audit_tmp exists, indicating a fatal error.

audit_warn nostart

> The internal system audit condition is AUC_FCHDONE. Auditing cannot be started without rebooting the system.

audit_warn auditoff

> The internal system audit condition has been changed to not be AUC_AUDITING by someone other than the audit daemon. The audit daemon exits.

```
audit_warn postsigterm
```

An error occurred during the orderly shutdown of the auditing
system.

```
audit_warn getacdir
```

There is a problem getting the directory list from
/etc/security/audit/audit_control. The audit daemon hangs in
a sleep loop until this file is fixed.

Examples

The following example shows the contents of the default audit_control file.

```
# more audit_control
#
# Copyright (c) 1988 by Sun Microsystems, Inc.
#
#ident  @(#)audit_control.txt  1.3     97/06/20 SMI
#
dir:/var/audit
flags:
minfree:20
naflags:lo
#
```

The following example shows the contents of the audit_data file.

```
# more /etc/security/audit_data
296:/var/audit/19991018050345.not_terminated.paperbark
#
```

Files

```
/etc/security/audit_user
```

An access-restricted database that stores per-user auditing
preselection data.

```
/etc/security/audit_control
```

File that contains audit control information used by auditd(1M).

Attributes

See attributes(5) for descriptions of the following attributes.

Attribute Type	Attribute Value
Availability	SUNWcsu

See Also

audit(1M), audit_warn(1M), bsmconv(1M), praudit(1M), auditon(2),
auditsvc(2), audit.log(4), audit_control(4), audit_data(4), attributes(5)

auditreduce — Merge and Select Audit Records from Audit Trail Files

Synopsis

```
/usr/sbin/auditreduce [options][audit-trail-file...]
```

Description

Use the `auditreduce` command to choose sets of records to examine. For example, you can select all records from the past 24 hours to generate a daily report; you can select all records generated by a specific user to examine that user's activities; or you can select all records resulting from a specific event type to see how often that type occurs. Use `auditreduce` to merge audit records from one or more input audit files or to perform a postselection of audit records.

Audit records from one or more input audit trail files are merged into a single output file. The records in an audit trail file are assumed to be sorted in chronological order (oldest first), and this order is maintained by `auditreduce` in the output file.

Unless instructed otherwise, `auditreduce` merges the entire audit trail, which consists of all the audit trail files in the directory structure `audit_root_dir/*/files` (see `audit_control`(4) for details of the structure of the audit root). Unless you specify the `-R` or `-S` option, `audit_root_dir` defaults to `/etc/security/audit`. By using the file selection options, you can select some subset of these files, files from another directory, or files named explicitly on the command line.

The `select` function enables you to select audit records according to numerous criteria relating to the record's content (see `audit.log`(4) for details of record content). A record must meet all of the record-selection-option criteria to be selected.

Note — The functionality described in this manual page is available only if the Basic Security Module (BSM) has been enabled. See `bsmconv`(1M) for more information.

The Solaris 8 release adds new options to the `auditreduce` command. See "Options." *New!*

Audit Trail File-Name Format

Any audit trail file not named on the command line must conform to the audit trail file-name format. Files produced by the audit system already have this format. Output file names produced by `auditreduce` are in the audit trail file-name format shown below.

```
start-time.end-time.suffix
```

start-time is the 14-character timestamp of when the file was opened, *end-time* is the 14-character timestamp of when the file was closed, and *suffix* is the name of the machine that generated the audit trail file, or some other meaningful suffix (such as `all` if the file contains a combined group of records from many machines). *end-time* can be the literal string `not_terminated`, to signify that the file is still being written to by the audit system. Timestamps are of the form *yyyymmddhhmmss* (year, month, day, hour, minute, second). The timestamps are in Greenwich Mean Time (GMT).

Options

File-Selection Options

The file-selection options indicate files that are to be processed and certain types of special treatment.

-A	Select all of the records from the input files regardless of their timestamp. This option effectively disables the a, b, and d options and is useful in preventing the loss of records if you use the -D option to delete the input files after they are processed. Note, however, that if a record is not selected because of another option, then -A does not override that case.
-C	Process only complete files. Files whose file-name end-time timestamp is not_terminated are not processed (such a file is currently being written to by the audit system). This option is useful in preventing the loss of records if you use -D to delete the input files after they are processed. It does not apply to files specified on the command line.
-D *suffix*	Delete input files after they are processed. The files are deleted only if the entire run is successful. If auditreduce detects an error while reading a file, then that file is not deleted. If you specify -D, then -A, -C, and -O are also implied. Give *suffix* to the -O option. This option helps prevent the loss of audit records by ensuring that all of the records are written, only complete files are processed, and the records are written to a file before being deleted. Note that if you specify both -D and -O on the command line, the order of specification is significant. The suffix associated with the latter specification is in effect.
-M *machine*	Enable selection of records from files with *machine* as the file-name suffix. If you do not specify -M, process all files regardless of suffix. You can also use -M to enable selection of records from files that contain combined records from many machines and have a common suffix (such as all).
-N	Select objects in *newmode*. This option is off by default to retain backward compatibility. In the existing *oldmode*, the -e, -f, -g, -r, or -u options select not only actions taken with those IDs but also certain objects owned by those IDs. When the system is running in *newmode*, only actions are selected. To select objects in *newmode*, you must use the -o option.
-O *suffix*	Direct output stream to a file in the current *audit-root-dir* with the indicated suffix. *suffix* can contain a full path name, in which case the last component is taken as the suffix, ahead of which the timestamps are placed, ahead of which the remainder of the path name is placed. If you do not specify the -O option, send the output to the standard output. When auditreduce puts timestamps in *filename*, it uses the times of the first and last records in the merge as the start time and end time.

New!

-Q	Suppress notification about errors with input files.
-R *pathname*	Specify the path name of an alternate audit root directory *audit-root-dir* to be *pathname*. Instead of using /etc/security/audit/*/*files* by default, examine *pathname*/*/*files* instead.
-S *server*	Read audit trail files from a specific location (server directory). *server* is normally interpreted as the name of a subdirectory of the audit root; therefore, auditreduce looks in *audit-root-dir/server/files* for the audit trail files. But if server contains any / characters, it is the name of a specific directory not necessarily contained in the audit root. In this case, consult *server/files*. This option enables you to easily manipulate archived files without requiring that they be physically located in a directory structure like that of /etc/security/audit.
-V	Display the name of each file as it is opened and the total number of records written to the output stream.

Record Selection Options

Use the record selection options listed below to indicate which records are written to the output file produced by auditreduce.

Note — You cannot specify multiple arguments of the same type.

-a *date-time*	Choose records that occurred at or after *date-time*. The *date-time* argument is described under "Option Arguments" on page 106. *date-time* is in local time. You can use the -a and -b options together to form a range.
-b *date-time*	Choose records that occurred before *date-time*.
-c *audit-classes*	Choose records with events that are mapped to the audit classes specified by *audit-classes*. Audit class names are defined in audit_class(4). The *audit-classes* can be a comma-separated list of audit flags like those described in audit_control(4). Using the audit flags, you can choose records according to success and failure criteria.
-d *date-time*	Choose records that occurred on a specific day (a 24-hour period beginning at 00:00:00 of the day specified and ending at 23:59:59). The day specified is in local time. Ignore the time portion of the argument if supplied. Choose any records with timestamps during that day. If any hours, minutes, or seconds are given in *date-time*, ignore them. You cannot use -d with -a or -b.
-e *effective-user*	Choose records with the specified *effective-user*.

`-f effective-group`

    Choose records with the specified `effective-group`.

`-g real-group`   Choose records with the specified `real-group`.

`-j subject-ID`   Choose records with the specified `subject-ID`, where `subject-ID` is a process ID.

`-m event`   Choose records with the specified `event`. The event is the literal string or the event number.

`-o object-type=objectID-value`

    Choose records by object type. A match occurs when the record contains the information describing the specified `object-type` and the object ID equals the value specified by `objectID-value`. The following object types and values are allowed.

    `file=pathname`

        Choose records containing file-system objects with the specified path name, where `pathname` is a comma-separated list of regular expressions. If a regular expression is preceded by a tilde (~), exclude files matching the expression from the output. For example, the following option chooses all files in /usr or /etc except those in /usr/openwin.

        `file="~/usr/openwin,/usr,/etc"`

        The order of the regular expressions is important because auditreduce processes them from left to right and stops when a file is known to be either chosen or excluded. Thus, the following option chooses all files in /usr and all files in /etc.

        `file=/usr, /etc, ~/usr/openwin`

        Files in /usr/openwin are not excluded because the regular expression /usr is matched first. Surround the path name with quotes to prevent the shell from expanding any tildes.

New!   `filegroup=group`

        Select records containing file-system objects owned by `group`.

New!   `fileowner=user`

        Select records containing file-system objects owned by `user`.

    `msgqid=ID`   Choose records containing message queue objects with the specified ID where `ID` is a message queue ID.

msgqgroup=*group*   *New!*

        Select records containing message queue objects owned or created by *group*.

pid=*ID*   Choose records containing process objects with the specified ID where *ID* is a process ID. Note that processes are objects when they are receivers of signals.

procgroup=*group*   *New!*

        Select records containing process objects with the real or effective *group*.

procowner=*user*   *New!*

        Select records containing process objects with the real or effective *user*.

semid=*ID*   Choose records containing semaphore objects with the specified ID where *ID* is a semaphore ID.

semgroup=*group*   *New!*

        Select records containing semaphore objects owned or created by *group*.

semowner=*user*   *New!*

        Select records containing semaphore objects owned or created by *user*.

shmid=ID   Choose records containing shared memory objects with the specified ID where *ID* is a shared memory ID.

shgroup=*group*   *New!*

        Select records containing shared memory objects owned or created by *group*.

showner=*user*   *New!*

        Select records containing shared memory objects owned or created by *user*.

sock=*port-number*|*machine*

        Choose records containing socket objects with the specified *port-number* or the specified machine, where *machine* is a machine name as defined in hosts(4).

-r *real-user* Choose records with the specified *real-user*.

-u*audit-user* Choose records with the specified *audit-user*. When one or more file-name arguments appear on the command line, process only the named files.

Files specified in this way need not conform to the audit trail file-name format. However, you cannot use -M, -S, and -R when processing named files. If the file name is -, then take the input from the standard input.

Option Arguments

audit-trail-file

An audit trail file as defined in audit.log(4). An audit trail file not named on the command line must conform to the audit trail file-name format. Audit trail files produced as output of auditreduce use the following format.

start-time.end-time.suffix

start-time is the 14-character timestamp denoting when the file was opened. end-time is the 14-character timestamp denoting when the file was closed. end-time can also be the literal string not_terminated, signifying that the file is still being written to by the audit daemon or that the file was not closed properly (a system crash or abrupt halt occurred). suffix is the name of the machine that generated the audit trail file (or some other meaningful suffix. For example, all would be a good suffix if the audit trail file contains a combined group of records from many machines).

date-time   The date-time argument to -a, -b, and -d can be of two forms. An absolute date-time takes the following form

yyyymmdd [hh [mm [ss]]]

where yyyy specifies a year (with 1970 as the earliest value), mm is the month (01-12), dd is the day (01-31), hh is the hour (00-23), mm is the minute (00-59), and ss is the seconds (00-59). The default is 00 for hh, mm, and ss.

You can also specify an offset such as +n d|h|m|s where n is a number of units and the tags d, h, m, and s stands for days, hours, minutes, and seconds. An offset is relative to the starting time. Thus, you can use this form only with the -b option.

event   The literal string or ordinal event number as found in audit_event(4). If event is not found in the audit_event file, it is considered invalid.

group   The literal string or ordinal group ID number as found in group(4). If group is not found in the group file, it is considered invalid. group can be negative.

pathname   A regular expression describing a path name.

user   The literal user name or ordinal user ID number as found in passwd(4). If the user name is not found in the passwd file, it is considered invalid. user can be negative.

Examples

The following example pipes the output of auditreduce through the praudit(1M) command to display audit records in human-readable form.

```
# auditreduce | praudit
file,Mon 18 Oct 1999 12:35:33 PM WST, + 0 msec,
header,36,2,system booted,na,Mon 18 Oct 1999 12:35:33 PM WST, +
   330000749 msec
text,booting kernel
header,86,2,su,,Mon 18 Oct 1999 12:57:30 PM WST, + 800005198 msec
subject,winsor,root,staff,winsor,staff,491,377,0 0 paperbark
text,success for user root
return,success,0
header,36,2,system booted,na,Mon 18 Oct 1999 01:02:47 PM WST, +
   329999144 msec
text,booting kernel
header,86,2,su,,Mon 18 Oct 1999 01:05:55 PM WST, + 919999045 msec
subject,winsor,root,staff,winsor,staff,492,376,0 0 paperbark
text,success for user root
return,success,0
header,36,2,system booted,na,Mon 18 Oct 1999 04:04:27 PM WST, +
   339999508 msec
text,booting kernel
header,86,2,su,,Mon 18 Oct 1999 04:08:56 PM WST, + 440004800 msec
subject,winsor,root,staff,winsor,staff,494,376,0 0 paperbark
text,success for user root
return,success,0
file,Mon 18 Oct 1999 04:08:56 PM WST, + 0 msec,
```

The following example views the audit data for February 16, 2000, for user bcalkins.

```
# auditreduce -d 20000216 -u bcalkins | praudit
file,Wed 31 Dec 1969 07:00 PM EST, + 0 msec
file,Wed 16 Feb 2000 11:41 AM EST, + 0 msec
#
```

If you are combining all the audit trail files into one large file, then deleting the original files could be desirable to prevent the records from appearing twice, as shown in the following example.

```
# auditreduce -V -d /etc/security/audit/combined/all
auditreduce: command line error - invalid date/time format - not all
   digits (/etc/security/audit/combined/all).
#
```

The following example prints what user winsor did on October 18, 1999. The output is piped through the praudit command to display it in a human-readable form to the standard output.

```
# auditreduce -d 19991018 -u winsor | praudit
file,Mon 18 Oct 1999 12:57:30 PM WST, + 0 msec,
header,86,2,su,,Mon 18 Oct 1999 12:57:30 PM WST, + 800005198 msec
subject,winsor,root,staff,winsor,staff,491,377,0 0 paperbark
text,success for user root
return,success,0
header,86,2,su,,Mon 18 Oct 1999 01:05:55 PM WST, + 919999045 msec
```

```
subject,winsor,root,staff,winsor,staff,492,376,0 0 paperbark
text,success for user root
return,success,0
header,86,2,su,,Mon 18 Oct 1999 04:08:56 PM WST, + 440004800 msec
subject,winsor,root,staff,winsor,staff,494,376,0 0 paperbark
text,success for user root
return,success,0
file,Mon 18 Oct 1999 04:08:56 PM WST, + 0 msec,
#
```

The above example may produce a large volume of data if user winsor has been busy. To restrict the output, the following example uses the -c option to select records from a specified class.

```
# auditreduce -d 19991018 -u winsor -c lo | praudit
file,Mon 18 Oct 1999 12:57:30 PM WST, + 0 msec,
header,86,2,su,,Mon 18 Oct 1999 12:57:30 PM WST, + 800005198 msec
subject,winsor,root,staff,winsor,staff,491,377,0 0 paperbark
text,success for user root
return,success,0
header,86,2,su,,Mon 18 Oct 1999 01:05:55 PM WST, + 919999045 msec
subject,winsor,root,staff,winsor,staff,492,376,0 0 paperbark
text,success for user root
return,success,0
header,86,2,su,,Mon 18 Oct 1999 04:08:56 PM WST, + 440004800 msec
subject,winsor,root,staff,winsor,staff,494,376,0 0 paperbark
text,success for user root
return,success,0
file,Mon 18 Oct 1999 04:08:56 PM WST, + 0 msec,
#
```

The following example shows milner's login/logout activity for April 13, 14, and 15. The results are saved to a file in the current working directory. Note that the name of the output file has milnerlo as the suffix, with the appropriate timestamp prefixes. Note that the long form of the name is used for the -c option.

```
% auditreduce -a 19880413 -b +3d -u milner -c login_logout -o milnerlo
```

To follow milner's movement about the file system on April 13, 14, and 15, you could view the chdir record types. Note that to get the same time range as the above example, you needed to specify the -b *time* as the day after our range because 19880416 defaults to midnight of that day, and records before that fall on 0415, the end-day of the range.

```
% auditreduce -a 19880413 -b 19880416 -u milner -m AUE_CHDIR | praudit
```

In the following example, the audit records are being collected in summary form (the login/logout records only). The records are written to a summary file in a directory different from the normal audit root to prevent the selected records from existing twice in the audit root.

```
% auditreduce -d 19880330 -c lo -o /etc/security/audit_summary/logins
```

If activity for user ID 9944 has been observed but that user is not known to the system administrator, then the following example searches the entire audit trail for any records generated by that user. auditreduce queries the system about the current validity of ID 9944 and prints a warning message if it is not currently active.

% **auditreduce -o /etc/security/audit_suspect/user9944 -u 9944**

Files

/etc/security/audit/*server*/files/*

> Location where audit trails are stored.

Attributes

See attributes(5) for descriptions of the following attributes.

Attribute Type	Attribute Value
Availability	SUNWcsu

See Also

bsmconv(1M),praudit(1M),audit.log(4),audit_class(4),audit_control(4), group(4), hosts(4), passwd(4), attributes(5)

Diagnostics

auditreduce prints error messages for command-line errors and then exits. If fatal errors occur during the run, auditreduce prints an explanatory message and exits. In this case, the output file may be in an inconsistent state (no trailer or partially written record) and auditreduce prints a warning message before exiting. Successful invocation returns 0 and unsuccessful invocation returns 1.

Because auditreduce may be processing a large number of input files, it is possible to exceed the machinewide limit on open files. If this happens, auditreduce prints a message to that effect, gives information on how many file there are, and exits.

If auditreduce prints a record's timestamp in a diagnostic message, that time is in local time. However, when file names are displayed, their timestamps are in GMT.

Bugs

Conjunction, disjunction, negation, and grouping of record selection options should be allowed.

audit_startup — Audit Subsystem Initialization Script

Synopsis

/etc/security/audit_startup

Description

Use the audit_startup script to initialize the audit subsystem before the audit daemon is started. You can configure this script, which currently consists of a series of auditconfig(1M) commands to set the system default policy and download the initial event to class mapping.

> **Note —** The functionality described in this manual page is available only if the Basic Security Module (BSM) has been enabled. See bsmconv(1M) for more information.

See Also

auditconfig(1M), auditd(1M), bsmconv(1M), attributes(5)

auditstat — Display Kernel Audit Statistics

Synopsis

/usr/sbin/auditstat [-c *count*][-h *numlines*][-i *interval*][-n][-v]

Description

Use the auditstat command to display kernel audit statistics, as shown in the following example.

```
# auditstat
gen nona kern  aud  ctl  enq wrtn wblk rblk drop  tot  mem
  2    1    0    1    0    2    2    0    2    0    0   48
#
```

> **Note —** The functionality described in this manual page is available only if the Basic Security Module (BSM) has been enabled. See bsmconv(1M) for more information.

The following list describes, in alphabetical order, the fields in the auditstat output.

aud	The total number of audit records processed by the audit(2) system call.
ctl	This field is obsolete.
drop	The total number of audit records that have been dropped. Records are dropped according to the kernel audit policy. See auditon(2), AUDIT_CNT policy, for details.
enq	The total number of audit records put on the kernel audit queue.
gen	The total number of audit records that have been constructed (not the number written).
kern	The total number of audit records produced by user processes (as a result of system calls).
mem	The total number of kilobytes of memory currently in use by the kernel audit module.

nona	The total number of nonattributable audit records that have been constructed. These are audit records that are not attributable to any particular user.
rblk	The total number of times that auditsvc(2) has blocked, waiting to process audit data.
tot	The total number of kilobytes of audit data written to the audit trail.
wblk	The total number of times that user processes blocked on the audit queue at the high watermark.
wrtn	The total number of audit records written. The difference between enq and wrtn is the number of outstanding audit records on the audit queue that have not been written.

Options

-c count	Display the statistics a total of *count* times. If *count* is equal to zero, statistics are displayed indefinitely. You must specify a time interval.
-h numlines	Display a header for every *numlines* of statistics printed. The default is to display the header every 20 lines. If *numlines* is equal to 0, never display the header.
-i interval	Display the statistics every interval where *interval* is the number of seconds to sleep between each collection.
-n	Display the number of kernel audit events currently configured.
-v	Display the version number of the kernel audit module software.

Exit Status

0	Success.
1	Failure.

Attributes

See attributes(5) for descriptions of the following attributes.

Attribute Type	Attribute Value
Availability	SUNWcsu

See Also

auditconfig(1M), praudit(1M), bsmconv(1M), audit(2), auditon(2), auditsvc(2), attributes(5)

audit_warn — Audit Daemon Warning Script

Synopsis

/etc/security/audit_warn [*option* [*arguments*]]

Description

The audit_warn script processes warning or error messages from the audit daemon. When a problem is encountered, the audit daemon, auditd(1M) calls audit_warn with the appropriate arguments. The *option* argument specifies the error type.

You can specify a list of mail recipients to be notified when an audit_warn situation arises, by defining a mail alias called audit_warn in aliases(4). The users that make up the audit_warn alias are typically the audit and root users.

Note — The functionality described in this manual page is available only if the Basic Security Module (BSM) has been enabled. See bsmconv(1M) for more information.

Options

allhard *count*

> Indicate that the hard limit for all file systems has been exceeded *count* times. The default action for this option is to send mail to the audit_warn alias only if the count is 1 and to write a message to the machine console every time. It is recommended that mail not be sent every time because you could saturate the file system that contains the mail spool directory.

allsoft

> Indicate that the soft limit for all file systems has been exceeded. The default action for this option is to send mail to the audit_warn alias and to write a message to the machine console.

auditoff

> Indicate that someone other than the audit daemon changed the system audit state to something other than AUC_AUDITING. The audit daemon has exited in this case. The default action for this option is to send mail to the audit_warn alias and to write a message to the machine console.

ebusy

> Indicate that the audit daemon is already running. The default action for this option is to send mail to the audit_warn alias and to write a message to the machine console.

getacdir *count*

> Indicate that there is a problem getting the directory list from audit_control(4). The audit daemon hangs in a sleep loop until the file is fixed. The default action for this option is to send mail to the audit_warn alias only if count is 1 and to write a message to the machine console every time. It is recommended that mail not be sent

every time because you could saturate the file system that contains the mail spool directory.

hard*filename*

Indicate that the hard limit for the file has been exceeded. The default action for this option is to send mail to the audit_warn alias and to write a message to the machine console.

nostart   Indicate that auditing could not be started. The default action for this option is to send mail to the audit_warn alias and to write a message to the machine console. Some administrators may prefer to modify audit_warn to reboot the system when this error occurs.

postsigterm   Indicate that an error occurred during the orderly shutdown of the audit daemon. The default action for this option is to send mail to the audit_warn alias and to write a message to the machine console.

soft*filename*

Indicate that the soft limit for *filename* has been exceeded. The default action for this option is to send mail to the audit_warn alias and to write a message to the machine console.

tmpfile   Indicate that the temporary audit file already exists, indicating a fatal error. The default action for this option is to send mail to the audit_warn alias and to write a message to the machine console.

Attributes

See attributes(5) for descriptions of the following attributes.

Attribute Type	**Attribute Value**
Availability	SUNWcsr

See Also

audit(1M), auditd(1M), bsmconv(1M), aliases(4), audit.log(4), audit_control(4), attributes(5)

automount — Install Automatic Mount Points

Synopsis

/usr/sbin/automount [-t *duration*] [-v]

Description

The automount command installs autofs mount points and associates an automount map with each mount point. The automount command is run automatically at boot time by the `/etc/rc2.d/S74autofs` script. If you make changes to the automounting maps, you may want to run the command manually to update the automounter.

The `autofs` file-system monitors try to access directories within the file system and notify the `automountd`(1M) daemon. The daemon uses the map to locate a file system, which it then mounts at the point of reference within the `autofs` file system. You can assign a map to an `autofs` mount by using an entry in the `/etc/auto_master` map or by using a direct map.

If the file system is not accessed within an appropriate interval (five minutes by default), the `automountd` daemon unmounts the file system.

The file `/etc/auto_master` determines the locations of all `autofs` mount points. By default, this file contains the following four entries.

```
#
# Master map for automounter
#
+auto_master
/net    -hosts -nosuid
/home   auto_home
/xfn    -xfn
```

The `+auto_master` entry is a reference to an external NIS or NIS+ master map. If such a map exists, then its entries are read as if they occurred in place of the `+auto_master` entry. The remaining entries in the master file specify a directory on which an `autofs` mount is made followed by the automounter map to be associated with it. You can supply optional mount options as an optional third field in the each entry. These options are used for any entries in the map that do not specify mount options explicitly. You usually run the `automount` command without arguments. It compares the entries in `/etc/auto_master` with the current list of `autofs` mounts in `/etc/mnttab` and adds, removes, or updates `autofs` mounts to bring `/etc/mnttab` up to date with the `/etc/auto_master` file.

At boot time `automount` installs all `autofs` mounts from the master map. You can subsequently run it to install `autofs` mounts for new entries in the master map or the direct map or to perform unmounts for entries that have been removed from these maps.

Notes

`autofs` mount points must not be hierarchically related. `automount` does not allow an `autofs` mount point to be created within another `autofs` mount.

Because each direct map entry results in a new `autofs` mount, such maps should be kept short.

You can modify entries in both direct and indirect maps at any time. The new information is used when `automountd` next uses the map entry to do a mount.

New entries added to a master map or direct map are not useful until the `automount` command is run to install them as new `autofs` mount points. New entries added to an indirect map can be used immediately.

Starting with the Solaris 2.6 release, a listing (see `ls`(1)) of the `autofs` directory associated with an indirect map shows all potential mountable entries. The attributes associated with the potential mountable entries are temporary. The real file-system attributes are only shown once the file system has been mounted.

You can assign default mount options to an entire map when you specify them as an optional third field in the master map. These options apply only to map entries that have no mount options. Note that map entities with options override the default options because, at this time, the options do not concatenate. The concatenation feature is planned for a future release.

The Network Information Service (NIS) was formerly known as Sun Yellow Pages (YP). The functionality of the two remains the same.

Options

-t *duration*   Specify a duration, in seconds, that a file system is to remain mounted when not in use. The default is 10 minutes.

-v   Notify of autofs mounts, unmounts, or other non-essential information.

Usage

Map Entry Format

A simple map entry (mapping) takes the following form

```
key [-mount-options] location...
```

where *key* is the full path name of the directory to mount when used in a direct map, or the simple name of a subdirectory in an indirect map. *mount-options* is a comma-separated list of mount options, and *location* specifies a file system from which the directory can be mounted. In the case of a simple NFS mount, the options that can be used are as specified in mount_nfs(1M), and *location* takes the following form

```
host:pathname
```

where *host* is the name of the host from which to mount the file system, and *pathname* is the absolute path name of the directory to mount.

Options to other file systems are documented on the other mount_* reference manual pages, for example, mount_cachefs(1M).

Replicated File Systems

You can specify multiple location fields for replicated NFS file systems, in which case automount and the kernel each try to use that information to increase availability. If the read-only flag is set in the map entry, automount mounts a list of locations that the kernel can use, sorted by several criteria. When a server does not respond, the kernel switches to an alternate server. The sort ordering of automount determines how the next server is chosen. If the read-only flag is not set, automount mounts the best single location, chosen by the same sort ordering, and new servers are chosen only when an unmount has been possible and a remount is done. Servers on the same local subnet are given the strongest preference, and servers on the local net are given the second strongest preference. Among servers equally far away, response times determine the order if no weighting factors (see below) are used.

If the list includes server locations using both the NFS Version 2 Protocol and the NFS Version 3 Protocol, automount chooses only a subset of the server locations on the list, so that all entries are the same protocol. It chooses servers with the NFS Version 3 Protocol as long as an NFS Version 2 Protocol server on a local subnet is not ignored. See the *NFS Administration Guide* for additional details.

If each location in the list shares the same path name, then a single location can be used with a comma-separated list of host names.

```
hostname,hostname...:pathname
```

You can weight requests for a server by appending the weighting factor as an integer in parentheses to the server name. Servers without a weighting are assumed to have a value of zero (most likely to be selected). Progressively higher values decrease the chance of being selected. In the following example, hosts `alpha` and `bravo` have the highest priority. Host `delta` has the lowest.

```
man -ro alpha,bravo,charlie(1),delta(4):/usr/man
```

Server proximity takes priority in the selection process. In the example above, if the server `delta` is on the same network segment as the client but the others are on different network segments, then the weighting value is ignored and `delta` is selected. The weighting has effect only when selecting between servers with the same network proximity.

In cases where each server has a different export point, the weighting can still be applied. For example,

```
man -ro alpha:/usr/man bravo,charlie(1):/usr/share/man
    delta(3):/export/man
```

You can continue a mapping across input lines by escaping the newline with a backslash (\). Comments begin with a number sign (#) and end at the subsequent newline.

Map Key Substitution

The ampersand (&) character is expanded to the value of the key field for the entry in which it occurs. In the following example, the & expands to `jane`.

```
jane sparcserver:/home/&
```

Wildcard Key

The asterisk (*) character, when supplied as the key field, is recognized as the catch-all entry. Such an entry matches any key not previously matched. For instance, if the following entry appeared in the indirect map for `/config`

```
* &:/export/config/&
```

it would allow automatic mounts in `/config` of any remote file system whose location could be specified as

```
hostname:/export/config/hostname
```

Variable Substitution

You can use client-specific variables within an automount map. For example, if `$HOST` appeared within a map, `automount` would expand it to its current value for the client's host name. The following variables are supported.

ARCH	The application architecture name. The architecture name is derived from the output of `uname -m`, for example, `sun4` on a sun4u system.
CPU	The processor type output of `uname -p`. For example, `sparc`.
HOST	The host-name output of `uname -n`. For example, `castle`.
OSNAME	The OS name output of `uname -s`. For example, `SunOS`.
OSREL	The OS release name output of `uname -r`. For example `2.5, 2.5.1, 2.6, 5.7, 5.8`.

OSVERS   The OS version output of uname -v. For example, Beta.

NATISA   The native instruction set architecture output of isainfo -n. For example, sparcv9.

If you need to protect a reference from affixed characters, surround the variable name with curly braces ({}).

Multiple Mounts

A multiple mount entry takes the following form.

```
key [-mount-options][[mountpoint][-mount-options] location...]...
```

The initial [mountpoint] is optional for the first mount and mandatory for all subsequent mounts. The optional mountpoint is taken as a path name relative to the directory named by key. If you omit mountpoint in the first occurrence, a mount point of / (root) is implied.

Given the following entry in the indirect map for /src, all offsets must exist on the server under beta. automount automatically mounts /src/beta, /src/beta/1.0, and /src/beta/1.0/man, as needed, from either svr1 or svr2, whichever host is nearest and responds first.

```
beta -ro \
        /            svr1,svr2:/export/src/beta\
        /1.0         svr1,svr2:/export/src/beta/1.0\
        /1.0/man     svr1,svr2:/export/src/beta/1.0/man
```

The backslash at the end of each line tells the automounter to consider the entire entry as one line, and it makes the entry easier to read. The last entry line does not have a backslash because it ends the sequence.

Other File-System Types

The automounter assumes NFS mounts as a default file-system type. You can describe other file-system types with the fstype mount option. You can combine other mount options specific to this file-system type with the fstype option. The location field must contain information specific to the file-system type. If the location field begins with a slash, you must prepend a colon character. The following example mounts a CD file system.

```
cdrom -fstype=hsfs,ro :/dev/sr0
```

The following example performs an autofs mount.

```
src -fstype=autofs auto_src
```

Note — Use the above procedure only if you are not using Volume Manager.

Mounts using CacheFS are most useful when applied to an entire map as map defaults. The following entry in the master map describes cached home directory mounts. It assumes the default location of the cache directory, /cache.

```
/home auto_home -fstype=cachefs,backfstype=nfs
```

See "Notes" on page 114 for information on option inheritance.

Indirect Maps

An indirect map enables you to specify mappings for the subdirectories you want to mount under the directory indicated on the command line. In an indirect map, each key consists of a simple name that refers to one or more file systems that are to be mounted as needed. The auto_home map is a good example of an indirect map that mounts a resource from a single server.

Direct Maps

Entries in a direct map are associated directly with autofs mount points. Each key is the full path name of an autofs mount point. The direct map as a whole is not associated with any single directory.

Included Maps

You can include the contents of another map within a map with an entry of the form +*mapname*.

If *mapname* begins with a slash, it is assumed to be the path name of a local file. Otherwise, the location of the map is determined by the policy of the nameservice switch according to the entry for the automounter in /etc/nsswitch.conf, such as

automount: files nis

If the nameservice is files, then the name is assumed to be that of a local file in /etc. If the key being searched for is not found in the included map, the search continues with the next entry.

Special Maps

Three special maps are available.

-hosts
-xfn
-null

The -hosts map is used with the /net directory and assumes that the map key is the host name of an NFS server. The automountd daemon dynamically constructs a map entry from the server's list of exported file systems. For example, a reference to /net/hermes/usr would initiate an automatic mount of all exported file systems from hermes that are mountable by the client. References to a directory under /net/hermes refers to the corresponding directory relative to hermes root.

The -xfn map is used to mount the initial context of the Federated Naming Service (FNS) namespace under the /xfn directory. For more information on FNS, see fns(5), fns_initial_context(5), fns_policies(5), and the *Federated Naming Service Guide*.

The -null map, when indicated on the command line, cancels a previous map for the directory indicated. This map is most useful in the /etc/auto_master for cancelling entries that would otherwise be inherited from the +auto_master include entry. For -null entries to be effective, they must be inserted before the included map entry.

Executable Maps

Local maps that have the execute bit set in their file permissions are executed by the automounter and provided with a key to be looked up as an argument. The executable map is expected to return the content of an automounter map entry on its standard output or no output if the entry cannot be determined. You cannot make a direct map executable.

Configuration and the auto_master Map

When initiated without arguments, automount consults the master map for a list of autofs mount points and their maps. It mounts any autofs mounts that are not already mounted and unmounts autofs mounts that have been removed from the master map or direct map.

The master map is assumed to be called auto_master, and its location is determined by the nameservice switch policy. Normally, the master map is located initially as a local file /etc/auto_master.

Browsing

Starting with the Solaris 2.6 release, browsing of indirect maps is supported. This feature enables all of the potential mount points to be visible, regardless of whether they are mounted. You can add the -nobrowse option to any indirect autofs map to disable browsing, as shown in the following example.

```
/net  -hosts  -nosuid,nobrowse
/home auto_home
```

In this case, any host names would be visible in /net only after they are mounted, but all potential mount points would be visible under /home. The -browse option enables browsability of autofs file systems. It is the default for all indirect maps.

Exit Status

0	Successful completion.
1	An error occurred.

Files

/etc/auto_master

   Master automount map.

/etc/auto_home

   Map to support automounted home directories.

/etc/nsswitch.conf

   The nameservice switch configuration file.

Attributes

See attributes(5) for descriptions of the following attributes.

Attribute Type	Attribute Value
Availability	SUNWcsu

See Also

isainfo(1), ls(1), uname(1), automountd(1M), mount(1M), mount_cachefs(1M), mount_nfs(1M), attributes(5), fns(5), fns_initial_context(5), fns_policies(5), nfssec(5)
   NFS Administration Guide

automountd — Mount/Unmount Daemon for autofs

Synopsis

/usr/lib/fs/autofs/automountd [-Tvn][-D *name=value*]

Description

The automountd daemon controls automounting activities. It is an RPC server that answers file-system mount and unmount requests from the autofs file system. automountd uses local files or nameservice maps to locate file systems to be mounted. These maps are described with the automount(1M) command.

The automountd daemon is automatically invoked in run level 2 from the /etc/rc2.d/S74autofs run control script.

Options

-T	Expand each RPC call and display it on the standard output.
-v	Log status messages to the console.
-n	Turn off browsing for all autofs mount points. This option overrides the -browse autofs map option on the local host.
-D*name=value*	Assign *value* to the indicated automount map-substitution variable. You cannot use these assignments to substitute variables in the master map auto_master.

Usage

See largefile(5) for the description of the behavior of automountd when encountering files greater than or equal to 2 Gbytes ($2**31$ bytes).

Files

/etc/auto_master

Master map for automounter.

Attributes

See attributes(5) for descriptions of the following attributes.

Attribute Type	Attribute Value
Availability	SUNWcsu

See Also

automount(1M), attributes(5), largefile(5)

autopush — Configure Lists of Automatically Pushed STREAMS Modules

Synopsis

```
/usr/sbin/autopush -f filename
/usr/sbin/autopush -g -M major -m minor
/usr/sbin/autopush -r -M major -m minor
```

Description

In the SunOS 4.x release, the `streamtab` structure enabled a driver to specify that certain STREAMS modules be pushed when the device was opened. In the Solaris 8 operating environment, you use the `autopush` command to specify when a STREAMS module is pushed. If required, you can run `autopush` at driver installation. The `/etc/inittab` file contains an entry that automatically runs `autopush` at bootup.

The `autopush` command configures the list of modules to be automatically pushed onto the stream when a device is opened. You can also use it to remove a previous setting or get information on a setting. The `autopush` command configures the list of modules for a STREAMS device. It automatically pushes a prespecified list of modules from the `/etc/iu.ap` autopush configuration file onto the stream when the STREAMS device is opened and the device is not already open.

The following example shows an `/etc/iu.ap` configuration file.

```
# /dev/console and /dev/contty autopush setup
#
#       major   minor lastminor  modules

        wc      0       0         ldterm ttcompat
        zs      0       1         ldterm ttcompat
        ptsl    0       15        ldterm ttcompat
```

The first line configures a single minor device whose major name is `wc` and whose minor numbers start and end at 0, creating only one minor number. The `ldterm` and `ttcompat` modules are automatically pushed. The second line configures the `zs` driver whose minor device numbers are 0 and 1, and automatically pushes the same modules. The last line configures the `ptsl` driver whose minor device numbers are from 0 to 15, and automatically pushes the same modules.

Options

-f *filename*   Set up the autopush configuration for each driver according to the information stored in *filename*. An autopush file consists of lines of four or more fields, separated by spaces, as shown below.

major minor last-minor module1 module2... module8   **New!**
[*anchor*]

The first field is a string that specifies the major device name, as listed in the `/kernel/drv` directory. The next two fields are integers that specify the minor device number and *last-minor* device

number. The fields following represent the names of modules. If
minor is -1, then all minor devices of a major driver specified by
major are configured and the value for *last-minor* is ignored. If
last-minor is 0, then only a single minor device is configured. To
configure a range of minor devices for a particular major, *minor* must
be less than *last-minor*.

New!

The remaining fields list the names of modules to be automatically
pushed onto the stream when opened, along with the position of an
optional anchor. The maximum number of modules that can be
pushed is eight. The modules are pushed in the order you specify
them. The optional special character sequence [*anchor*] puts a
STREAMS anchor on the stream at the module previously specified
in the list. Specifying more than one anchor or putting an anchor first
in the list results in an error.

A non-zero exit status indicates that one or more of the lines in the
specified file failed to complete successfully.

-g   Get the current configuration setting of a particular major and minor
            device number specified with the -M and -m options and display the
            autopush modules associated with it. Return the starting minor
            device number if the request corresponds to a setting of a range (as
            described with the -f option).

-M *major* Specify the major device number.

-m *minor* Specify the minor device number.

-r   Remove the previous configuration setting of the particular major
            and minor device number specified with the -M and -m options. If the
            values of *major* and *minor* correspond to a previously established
            setting of a range of minor devices, where *minor* matches the first
            minor device number in the range, remove the configuration for the
            entire range.

Examples

The following example gets the current configuration settings for the major device 29
and minor device 0 and displays the autopush modules associated with them for the
character-special device /dev/term/a.

```
# autopush -g -M 29 -m 0
    Major     Minor  Lastminor        Modules
       29         0         63        ldterm ttcompat
#
```

New! Exit Status

0   Successful completion.

non-zero   An error occurred.

Files

/etc/iu.ap   Contains a prespecified list of modules that can be pushed onto the streams device if the STREAM is not already open.

Attributes

See attributes(5) for descriptions of the following attributes.

Attribute Type	Attribute Value
Availability	SUNWcsu

See Also

bdconfig(1M), ttymon(1M), attributes(5), sad(7D), streamio(7I), ldterm(7M), ttcompat(7M)

  STREAMS Programming Guide

B

bdconfig — Configure the Buttons and Dials Stream

Synopsis

```
/usr/sbin/bdconfig [startup][off][on][term][status][verbose]
```

Description

Use the bdconfig command to configure the autopush facility and define to the system what serial device to use for the buttons and dials (bd) stream.

bdconfig just configures the AUTOPUSH facility. It does not actually manipulate the serial port or stream in any way. Only the first open of a dismantled stream sees the effects of a previously run bdconfig.

Options

If you specify no options, then an interactive mode is assumed. In this mode, the current status is presented along with the usage line, as shown below, and a series of interactive questions is asked.

```
paperbark% bdconfig
Usage: bdconfig [startup] [off] [on] [<term>] [status] [verbose]
bdconfig: status is/was: OFF, serial device set to: /dev/term/b

    Do you want to alter the configuration? (y/n):
```

Root privilege is required to change the configuration. The status option does not require root privilege. bdconfig can be installed as a setuid root program.

You can specify the following noninteractive options in any order.

off
: Reconfigure the configured term for TTY use.

on
: Reconfigure the configured term for bd use. If term has not been previously specified, ask interactive questions.

startup
: Configure as was last configured before the system went down. This option is used by the startup script and precludes the use of the on, off, and term options. This option implies noninteractive mode.

status
: Emit the current configuration in terms of the words used as options: off, on, /dev/term/a, /dev/term/b, and so forth. This option implies noninteractive mode.

term
: Specify the serial device for bd use. The on option is the default unless you specify the off option.

verbose
: Describe what bdconfig finds and what it is doing.

Exit Status

0
: Success.

1
: General error.

2
: Argument error.

Attributes

See attributes(5) for descriptions of the following attributes.

Attribute Type	Attribute Value
Availability	SUNWdialh

See Also

autopush(1M), attributes(5), x_buttontest(6), x_dialtest(6), bd(7M), sad(7D), streamio(7I)

Diagnostics

The bdconfig command is silent unless you use the verbose option, interactive modes, or issue bdconfig with no arguments.

Bugs

The interface does not support more than one dialbox and one buttonbox, both of which must be on the same serial device.

There should be a library routine to read, parse, and validate records in the iu.ap file, so that bdconfig could return to the appropriate record in iu.ap as the default configuration.

boot — Start the System Kernel or a Stand-alone Program

Synopsis

SPARC Platform

```
boot [OBP names][file][-afV][-D default-file][boot-flags][--]
     [client-program-args]
b [device [(c, u, p)]][-afV][-D default-file][boot-flags][--]
     [client-program-args]
```

IA Platform

```
b [file][-f][boot-args]
i
```

Description

Booting (or bootstrapping) a system is the process of loading and executing a stand-alone program. Typically, the stand-alone program is the operating system kernel (see kernel(1M)), but you can boot any stand-alone program. For example, on a SPARC-based system, you can boot the diagnostic monitor as a stand-alone program.

At boot time, the OpenBoot PROM (OBP), internal, hard-coded software, checks the computer memory, peripherals, and I/O channels to verify that they are working. Then, the stand-alone program is loaded.

If the stand-alone program is identified as a dynamically linked executable, boot loads the interpreter (linker/loader) as indicated by the executable format and then transfers control to the interpreter. If the stand-alone is statically linked, boot jumps directly to the stand-alone.

You initiate the default boot sequence either by turning on the computer or by typing boot at the ok PROM prompt. The default SPARC-based boot sequence is summarized below.

- OBP executes the primary boot.
- OBP loads and starts the ufsboot secondary boot program.
- OBP loads and starts the kernel.
- The kernel reads the /etc/system file.
- The kernel is initialized.
- The kernel runs /sbin/init to bring the system to the initdefault state specified in /etc/inittab. See inittab(4).
- init executes the run control (rc) scripts.

The following sections describe how the bootstrap procedure differs for SPARC-based and IA-based systems.

SPARC Bootstrap Procedure

The bootstrap procedure on most SPARC-based systems consists of the following basic phases.

- After the system is turned on, the system firmware (in PROM) executes power-on self-test (POST). The form and scope of these tests depends on the version of the system firmware.

- After the tests have been completed successfully, the firmware tries to autoboot if the appropriate flag has been set in the nonvolatile storage area used by the firmware. You can manipulate the name of the file to load and the device to load it from. You can set autoboot flags and file names by using the eeprom(1M) command from the shell or by using PROM commands from the ok prompt after halting the system.
- The second-level program is either ufsboot (when booting from a disk) or inetboot (when booting across the network). When booting from disk, the bootstrapping process consists of two conceptually distinct phases: primary boot and secondary boot. The PROM assumes that the primary bootblock resides in blocks 1 to 15 of the local disk. When booting over the network, the PROM makes a reverse ARP request and when it receives a reply, the PROM broadcasts a TFTP request to fetch inetboot over the network from any server that responds and executes it. inetboot also makes another reverse ARP request, then uses the bootparams protocol (see bootparams(4)) to locate its root file system. It then fetches the kernel across the network by using the NFS protocol and then executes it.
- If the path name to the stand-alone is relative (does not begin with a slash), the second-level boot looks for the stand-alone in a platform-dependent search path. This path is guaranteed to contain /platform/*platform-name*. Many SPARC platforms next search the platform-specific path entry /platform/*hardware-class-name*. See filesystem(5). If the path name is absolute, boot uses the specified path. The boot program then loads the stand-alone at the appropriate address and transfers control.
- If you do not specify the file name on the command line or specify it otherwise—for example, by the boot_file NVRAM variable—boot chooses an appropriate default file to load based on the software that is installed on the system, the capabilities of the hardware and firmware, and on a user-configurable policy file.

OpenBoot PROM boot Command Behavior

The OpenBoot boot command takes arguments of the following form at the ok prompt.

boot [*device-specifier*] [*arguments*]

The default boot command has no arguments.

boot

If you specify no *device-specifier* on the boot command line, OpenBoot typically uses the boot_device or diag_device nvram variable. If you specify no optional arguments on the command line, OpenBoot typically uses the boot_file or diag_file nvram variable as default boot arguments. (If the system is in diagnostics mode, OpenBoot uses diag_device and diag_file instead of boot_device and boot_file.)

arguments can include more than one string. All argument strings are passed to the secondary booter; they are not interpreted by OpenBoot.

If you specify any arguments on the boot command line, then neither the boot_file nor the diag_file nvram variable is used. The contents of the nvram variables are not merged with command-line arguments. For example, the command

```
ok boot -s
```

ignores the settings in both `boot_file` and `diag_file`; it interprets the string `-s` as arguments. `boot` does not use the contents of `boot_file` or `diag_file`.
   The commands

```
ok boot net
```

and

```
ok boot cdrom
```

have no arguments; they use the settings in `boot_file` or `diag_file`, if they are set, as default file name and arguments and pass them to `boot`. Accordingly, if `boot_file` is set to the 64-bit kernel file name and you try to boot the installation CD with `boot cdrom`, `boot` fails if the installation CD contains only a 32-bit kernel.
   Because the contents of `boot_file` or `diag_file` may be ignored depending on the form of the `boot` command used, reliance on the `boot_file` is discouraged for most production systems. To change the OS policy, change the `policy` file. A significant exception is the case when a production system has both 32-bit and 64-bit packages installed, but the production system requires use of the 32-bit OS.
   In most cases, it is best to allow the `boot` command to choose an appropriate default based on the system type, system hardware and firmware, and on what is installed on the root file system. It is accepted practice to augment the `boot` command's policy by modifying the `policy` file; however, changing `boot_file` or `diag_file` may generate unexpected results in certain circumstances.
   This behavior is found on most OpenBoot 2.x- and 3.x-based systems. Note that differences may occur on some platforms.

IA Bootstrap Procedure

On IA-based systems, the bootstrapping process consists of two conceptually distinct phases: primary boot and secondary boot.
   The primary boot is implemented in the BIOS ROM on the system board and in BIOS extensions in ROMs on peripheral boards. It is distinguished by its ability to control the installed peripheral devices and to provide I/O services through software interrupts. It begins the booting process by loading the first physical sector from a diskette or hard disk, or—if supported by the system BIOS—from a CD-ROM. The primary boot is implemented in IA real-mode code.
   The secondary boot is loaded by the primary boot. It is implemented in 32-bit, paged, protected mode code. It also loads and uses peripheral-specific BIOS extensions written in IA real-mode code. The secondary boot, called `boot.bin`, is capable of reading and booting from a UFS file system on a hard disk or a CD or by way of a LAN using the NFS protocol.
   The secondary boot is responsible for running the Configuration Assistant program, which determines the installed devices in the system (possibly with help from the user). The secondary boot then reads the script in `/etc/bootrc`, which controls the booting process. This file contains boot interpreter commands, which are defined below, and can be modified to change defaults or to adapt to a specific system.
   The standard `/etc/bootrc` script prompts the user to enter a b character to boot with specified options, an i character to invoke the interpreter interactively, or any other character to boot the default kernel. Once the kernel is loaded, it starts the operating system, loads the necessary modules, mounts the necessary file systems (see `vfstab(4)`), and runs `/sbin/init` to bring the system to the `initdefault` state specified in `/etc/inittab`. See `inittab(4)`.

Options

SPARC Platform

OBP names   Specify the OpenBoot PROM designations. For example, on Desktop SPARC-based systems, the designation `/sbus/esp@0,800000/sd@3,0:a` specifies a SCSI disk (`sd`) at target `3, lun0` on the SCSI bus, with the `esp` host adapter plugged into slot `0`.

file   Name of a stand-alone program to boot. If you do not specify a *filename* either on the `boot` command line or in the `boot_file` NVRAM variable, choose an appropriate default file name. On most systems, the default file name is the 32-bit kernel. On systems capable of supporting both the 32-bit and 64-bit kernels, the 64-bit kernel is chosen in preference to the 32-bit kernel. `boot` chooses an appropriate default file to boot, based on the software that is installed on the system, the capabilities of the hardware and firmware, and on a user-configurable policy file.

`-a`   Prompt for the name of the stand-alone. Then, pass the `-a` flag to the stand-alone program.

`-f`   When booting an Autoclient system, force the `boot` program to bypass the client's local cache and read all files over the network from the client's file server. Ignore this flag for all non-Autoclient systems. Then, pass the `-f` flag to the stand-alone program.

`-V`   Display verbose debugging information.

`-D` *default-file*

Explicitly specify the *default-file*. On some systems, `boot` chooses a dynamic default file, used when none is otherwise specified. This option enables you to explicitly set the *default-file* and can be useful when booting kadb(1M) because, by default, kadb loads the *default-file* as exported by the `boot` program.

boot-flags   Pass all *boot-flags* to *file*. *boot-flags* are not interpreted by `boot`. See the `kernel`(1M) and `kadb`(1M) manual pages for information about the options available with the default stand-alone program.

client-program-args

Pass all *client-program-args* to *file*. `boot` does not interpret them.

IA Platform

`b`   Boot with specified options

file   Name of a stand-alone program to boot. The default is to boot `/platform/`*platform-name*`/kernel/unix` from the root partition, but you can specify another program on the command line.

-f   When booting an Autoclient system, force the boot program to bypass the client's local cache and read all files over the network from the client's file server. Ignore this flag for all non-Autoclient systems. Then, pass the -f flag to the stand-alone program.

boot-args   The boot program passes all *boot-args* to *file*. The arguments are not interpreted by boot. See kernel(1M) and kadb(1M) for information about the options available with the kernel.

i   Invoke the interpreter interactively.

IA Boot Sequence Details

After a PC-compatible system is turned on, the system firmware in the BIOS ROM executes a power-on self-test (POST), runs BIOS extensions in peripheral board ROMs, and invokes software interrupt INT 19h, Bootstrap. The INT 19h handler typically performs the standard PC-compatible boot, which consists of trying to read the first physical sector from the first diskette drive or, if that fails, from the first hard disk. The processor then jumps to the first byte of the sector image in memory.

IA Primary Boot

The first sector on a diskette contains the master boot block. The boot block is responsible for loading the image of the boot loader strap.com, which then loads the secondary boot, boot.bin. A similar sequence occurs for CD-ROM boot, but the master boot block location and contents are dictated by the El Torito specification. The El Torito boot also leads to strap.com, which in turn loads boot.bin.

The first sector on a hard disk contains the master boot block, which contains the master boot program and the FDISK table, named for the PC program that maintains it. The master boot finds the active partition in the FDISK table, loads its first sector, and jumps to its first byte in memory. This completes the standard PC-compatible hard disk boot sequence.

An IA FDISK partition for the Solaris software begins with a one-cylinder boot slice, which contains the partition boot program (pboot) in the first sector, the standard Solaris disk label and volume table of contents (VTOC) in the second and third sectors, and the bootblk program in the fourth and subsequent sectors. When the FDISK partition for the Solaris software is the active partition, the master boot program (mboot) reads the partition boot program in the first sector into memory and jumps to it. It in turn reads the bootblk program into memory and jumps to it.

Regardless of the type of the active partition, if the drive contains multiple FDISK partitions, the user is given the opportunity to reboot another partition.

bootblk or strap.com (depending on the active partition type) reads boot.bin from the file system in the Solaris root slice and jumps to its first byte in memory.

IA Secondary Boot

The secondary boot, boot.bin, switches the processor to 32-bit, paged, protected mode, and performs some limited system initialization. It runs the Configuration Assistant program, which either autoboots the system or presents a list of possible boot devices, depending on the state of the auto-boot? variable (see eeprom(1M)).

Disk target devices (including CD-ROM drives) are expected to contain UFS file systems. Network devices first issue Reverse Address Resolution Protocol (RARP) requests to discover the system's IP address and then issue a bootparams RPC to find out which server provides the root file system. The root file system is then mounted, using NFS. After a successful root mount, `boot.bin` invokes a command interpreter, which interprets `/etc/bootrc`.

Secondary Boot Programming Language for IA Platforms

The wide range of hardware that must be supported on IA-based systems demands great flexibility in the booting process. This flexibility is achieved in part by making the secondary boot programmable. The secondary boot contains an interpreter that accepts a simple command language similar to `sh` and `csh`. The primary differences are that pipelines, loops, standard output, and output redirection are not supported.

IA Lexical Structure

The boot interpreter splits input lines into words separated by blanks and Tabs. The metacharacters are dollar sign ($), single quote ('), double quote ("), number sign (#), newline, and backslash (\). You can escape the special meaning of metacharacters by preceding them with a backslash. A newline preceded by a backslash is treated as a blank. A number sign introduces a comment, which continues to the next newline.

A string enclosed in a pair of single-quote or double-quote characters forms all or part of a single word. White space and newline characters within a quoted string become part of the word. You can quote characters within a quoted string by preceding them with a backslash character; thus, a single-quote character can appear in a single-quoted string if preceded by a backslash. Two backslashes produce a single backslash, and a newline preceded by a backslash produces a newline in the string.

IA Variables

The boot interpreter maintains a set of variables, each of which has a string value. The first character of a variable name must be a letter, and subsequent characters can be letters, digits, or underscores. The `set` command creates a variable, assigns a value to it, or displays the values of variables. The `unset` command deletes a variable.

Variable substitution is performed when the interpreter encounters a dollar sign that is not preceded by a backslash. The variable name following the dollar sign is replaced by the value of the variable, and parsing continues at the beginning of the value. Variable substitution is performed in double-quoted strings, but not in single-quoted strings. A variable name can be enclosed in braces to separate it from following characters.

IA Commands

A command is a sequence of words terminated by a newline character. The first word is the name of the command, and subsequent words are arguments to the command. All commands are built-in commands. Stand-alone programs are executed with the `run` command.

IA Conditional Execution of Commands

You can conditionally execute commands by surrounding them with the `if`, `elseif`, `else`, and `endif` commands.

```
if expr1
...
elseif expr2
...
elseif expr3
...
else
```

```
...
endif
```

You can embed an `if` block in other `if` blocks.

IA Expressions

The `set`, `if`, and `elseif` commands evaluate arithmetic expressions with the syntax and semantics of the C programming language. The `||`, `&&`, `|`, `^`, `&`, `==`, `!=`, `<`, `>`, `<=`, `>=`, `>>`, `<<`, `+`, `-`, `*`, `/`, `%`, `~`, and `!` operators are accepted, as are `(`, `)`, and comma. Signed 32-bit integer arithmetic is performed.

Expressions are parsed after the full command line has been formed. Each token in an expression must be a separate argument word, so blanks must separate all tokens on the command line.

Before an arithmetic operation is performed on an operand word, the word is converted from a string to a signed 32-bit integer value. After an optional leading sign, a leading `0` produces octal conversion, and a leading `0x` or `0X` produces hexadecimal conversion. Otherwise, decimal conversion is performed. A string that is not a legal integer is converted to `0`.

Several built-in functions for string manipulation are provided. Built-in function names begin with a dot. String arguments to these functions are not converted to integers. To treat an operator, for example, `-`, as a string, you must precede it with a backslash, and that backslash must be quoted with another backslash. Also, be aware that a null string can produce a blank argument, and thus an expression syntax error. For example, the following expression is the safe way to test whether the variable `usrarg` starts with a `-`, even if it could be null.

```
if .strneq ( ${usrarg}X , \- , 1 )
```

IA I/O

The boot interpreter takes its input from the system console or from one or more files. The `source` command reads a file into memory and begins parsing it. The `console` command takes its input from the system console. Reaching end-of-file resumes parsing of the previous input source. Control-D entered at the beginning of console line is treated as end-of-file.

The `echo` command writes its arguments to the display. The `read` command reads the system console and assigns word values to its argument variables.

IA Debugging

The `verbose` command turns verbose mode on and off. In verbose mode, the interpreter displays lines from the current source file and displays the command as actually executed after variable substitution.

The `singlestep` command turns single-step mode on and off. In single-step mode, the interpreter displays `step ?` before processing the next command and waits for keyboard input, which is discarded. Processing proceeds when you press Enter. This sequence enables slow execution in verbose mode.

IA Initialization

When the interpreter is first invoked by `boot`, it begins execution of a compiled-in initialization string. This string typically consists of `"source /etc/bootrc\n"` to run the `boot` script in the root file system.

IA Communication with Stand-Alone Programs

The boot command passes information to stand-alone programs through arguments to the run command. A stand-alone program can pass information back to boot by setting a boot interpreter variable using the var_ops() boot service function. It can also pass information to the kernel, using the setprop() boot service function. The whoami property is set to the name of the stand-alone program.

IA Built-in Commands

console   Interpret input from the console until Control-D.

echo *arg1*...   Display the arguments separated by blanks, and terminate with a newline.

echo -n *arg1*...

                Display the arguments separated by blanks, but do not terminate with a newline.

getprop *propname varname*

                Assign the value of property *propname* to the variable *varname*. A property value of length 0 produces a null string. If the property does not exist, do not set the variable.

getproplen *propname varname*

                Assign the length in hexadecimal of the value of property *propname* to the variable *varname*. Property value lengths include the terminating null. If the property does not exist, set the variable to 0xFFFFFFFF (-1).

if *expr*   If the expression *expr* is true, execute instructions to the next elseif, else, or endif. If *expr* is false, do not execute the instructions.

elseif *expr*   If the preceding if and elseif commands all failed and *expr* is true, execute instructions to the next elseif, else, or endif. Otherwise, do not execute the instructions.

else   If the preceding if and elseif commands all failed, execute instructions to the next elseif, else, or endif. Otherwise, do not execute the instructions.

endif   Revert to the execution mode of the surrounding block.

help   Display a help screen that contains summaries of all available boot shell commands.

read *name1*...

                Read a line from the console, break it into words, and assign them as values to the variables *name1*, and so forth.

readt *time*...

                Same as read, but time out after *time* seconds.

```
run name arg1...
```
>   Load and transfer control to the stand-alone program *name*, passing it
>   *arg1* and further arguments.

`set`   Display all the current variables and their values.

`set` *name*   Set the value of the variable *name* to the null string.

`set` *name word*   Set the value of the variable *name* to *word*.

`set` *name expr*   Set the value of the variable *name* to the value of *expr*. *expr* must
                     consist of more than one word. The value is encoded in unsigned
                     hexadecimal, so that -1 is represented by 0xFFFFFFFF.

`setcolor`   Set the text-mode display attributes. Allowable colors are black,
                     blue, green, cyan, red, magenta, brown, white, gray, lt_blue,
                     lt_green, lt_cyan, lt_red, lt_magenta, yellow, and hi_white.

`setprop` *propname word*

>   Set the value of the property *propname* to *word*.

`singlestep` | `singlestep on`

>   Turn on singlestep mode, in which the interpreter displays step ?
>   and waits for keyboard input before it processes each command. Press
>   Enter to execute the next command.

`singlestep off`

>   Turn off singlestep mode.

`source` *name*   Read the file *name* into memory and begin to interpret it. At
                     end-of-file, return to the previous source of input.

`unset` *name*   Delete the variable *name*.

`verbose` | `verbose on`

>   Turn on verbose mode, which displays lines from source files and
>   commands to be executed.

`verbose off`   Turn off verbose mode.

IA Built-in Functions

The following built-in functions are accepted within expressions.

`.strcmp(`*string1*`, `*string2*`)`

>   Return an integer value that is less than, equal to, or greater than
>   zero, as *string1* is lexicographically less than, equal to, or greater
>   than *string2*.

`.strncmp(`*string1*`, `*string2*`, `*n*`)`

>   Return an integer value that is less than, equal to, or greater than
>   zero, as *string1* is lexicographically less than, equal to, or greater
>   than *string2*. At most, compare *n* characters.

`.streq (`*string1*`, `*string2*`)`

>   Return true if *string1* is equal to *string2*, and false otherwise.

```
.strneq (string1, string2, n)
```

>   Return true if *string1* is equal to *string2*, and false otherwise. At
>   most, compare *n* characters.

```
.strfind (string, addr, n)
```

>   Scan *n* locations in memory starting at *addr*, looking for the
>   beginning of *string*. The string in memory need not be
>   null-terminated. Return true if *string* is found, and false
>   otherwise. You can use .strfind to search for strings in the ROM
>   BIOS and BIOS extensions that identify different systems and
>   peripheral boards.

64-bit SPARC Platform

Booting UltraSPARC Systems

Certain platforms may need a firmware upgrade to run the 64-bit kernel. See the *Sun Hardware Platform Guide* for details. If the 64-bit kernel packages are installed and boot detects that the platform needs a firmware upgrade to run 64-bit, boot displays a message on the console and chooses the 32-bit kernel as the default file instead.

On systems containing 200 MHz or lower UltraSPARC-1 processors, it is possible for a user to run a 64-bit program designed to exploit a problem that could cause a processor to stall. Because 64-bit programs cannot run on the 32-bit kernel, the 32-bit kernel is chosen as the default file on these systems.

The code sequence that exploits the problem is very unusual and is not likely to be generated by a compiler. Assembler code had to be specifically written to demonstrate the problem. It is highly unlikely that a legitimate handwritten assembler routine would use this code sequence.

Users willing to assume the risk that a user might accidentally or deliberately run a program that was designed to cause a processor to stall may choose to run the 64-bit kernel by modifying the boot policy file. Edit /platform/*platform-name*/boot.conf so that it contains an uncommented line with the variable named ALLOW_64BIT_KERNEL_ON_UltraSPARC_1_CPU set to the value true as shown in the following example.

```
ALLOW_64BIT_KERNEL_ON_UltraSPARC_1_CPU=true
```

For more information, see the *Sun Hardware Platform Guide*.

IA Platform Only

Because the – key on national language keyboards has been moved, you must use an alternate key to supply arguments to the boot command on an IA-based system using these keyboards. Use the – on the numeric keypad. The specific language keyboard and the alternate key to be used in place of the – during bootup are shown below.

Keyboard	Substitute Key
Italy	'
Spain	'
Sweden	+
France	?

Keyboard	Substitute Key
Germany	?

For example, b -r on Swedish keyboards would be typed as b +r even though the screen displays b -r.

Examples

SPARC Platform
The following examples boot the default kernel in single-user interactive mode.
```
ok boot -as
ok boot disk3 -as
```

32-bit SPARC Platform
The following example boots kadb, specifying the 32-bit kernel as the default file.
```
ok boot kadb -D kernel/unix
```

The following examples specify the kernel file name to boot the 32-bit kernel explicitly.
```
ok boot kernel/unix -as
ok boot disk3 kernel/unix -as
```

64-bit SPARC Platform
The following examples specify the 64-bit kernel explicitly to boot in single-user interactive mode.
```
ok boot kernel/sparcv9/unix -a
ok boot disk3 kernel/sparcv9/unix -as
```

Refer to "Booting UltraSPARC Systems" on page 136 before booting the 64-bit kernel, using an explicit file name.

IA Platform
The following example boots the default kernel in single-user interactive mode.
```
> b -as b kernel/unix -as
```

Files

/platform/*platform-name*/ufsboot

  Second-level program to boot from a disk or CD.

/etc/inittab Table in which the initdefault state is specified.

/sbin/init Program that brings the system to the initdefault state.

/platform/*platform-name*/boot.conf
/platform/*hardware-class-name*/boot.conf

  Primary and alternate path names for the boot policy file. Note that the policy file is not implemented on all platforms.

32-bit SPARC and IA Platforms

/platform/*platform-name*/kernel/unix

> Default program to boot system.

64-bit SPARC Platform Only

/platform/*platform-name*/kernel/sparcv9/unix

> Default program to boot system. See "Booting UltraSPARC Systems" on page 136.

IA Platform Only

/etc/bootrc   Script that controls the booting process.

/platform/*platform-name*/boot/solaris/boot.bin

> Second-level boot program used on IA systems in place of ufsboot.

/platform/*platform-name*/boot

> Directory containing boot-related files.

Note — You can find *platform-name* by using the -i option of uname(1). You can find *hardware-class-name* by using the -m option of uname(1).

See Also

uname(1), eeprom(1M), init(1M), installboot(1M), kadb(1M), kernel(1M), shutdown(1M), uadmin(2), bootparams(4), inittab(4), vfstab(4), filesystem(5)
System Administration Guide, Volume I
Sun Hardware Platform Guide

Warning — The boot command is unable to determine which files can be used as bootable programs. If the booting of a file that is not bootable is requested, the boot command loads it and branches to it. What happens after that is unpredictable.

---

bootparamd — Boot Parameter Server

Synopsis

/usr/sbin/rpc.bootparamd [-d]

Description

See rpc.bootparamd(1M).

bsmconv, bsmunconv — Enable or Disable the Basic Security Module (BSM)

Synopsis

```
/etc/security/bsmconv [rootdir...]
/etc/security/bsmunconv [rootdir...]
```

Description

The basic security module (BSD) is Sun Microsystem's implementation of C2 security. It provides an auditing capability with self-contained audit records that contain all the relevant information about an event. For example, an audit record describing a file event contains the absolute path name and a time- and date-stamp of the opening or closing of the file.

BSD provides the following auditing features.

- The audit ID assigned to a user's processes stays the same even when the user ID changes.
- Each session has an audit session ID.
- Full path names are saved in audit records.

Because each audit record contains an additional user identification attribute—the audit ID—and full path names are recorded in audit records, you can look at individual audit records and get meaningful information without having to look back through the audit trail.

Use the bsmconv command as root to enable BSM. The optional *rootdir* argument is a list of one or more root directories of diskless clients that have already been configured by way of the Host Manager; see admintool(1M).

> **Note —** The bsmconv command adds a line to /etc/system that disables the ability to abort the system by using the Stop-A keyboard sequence. If you want to retain that ability, you must comment out the following line in the /etc/system file after you run the bsmconv command.
>
> ```
> set abort_enable = 0
> ```

BSM is included in the full Solaris release and is part of the release media. You do not need to install BSM separately because you can now enable BSM with the bsmconv command and disable it with the bsmunconv command. All of the BSM software is included in the initial system installation, provided you install the following packages.

- SUNWcar—Core architecture
- SUNWcsr—Core (root)
- SUNWcsu—Core (user)
- SUNWhea—Header files
- SUNWman—Online manual pages

Enabling BSM

Use the following procedure to enable BSM.

1. Become superuser.
2. Type **telinit 1** and press Return to bring the system to single-user mode.
3. Type **/etc/security/bsmconv** and press Return to start BSM.
4. Type **y** and press Return to enable BSM.
5. Type **telinit 6** and press Return to reboot the system as a multiuser BSM system.

Disabling BSM

If you no longer require BSM, you can disable it by running bsmunconv. Use the bsmunconv command as root to disable BSD and remove the BSD entry from the /etc/system file. The optional *rootdir* argument is a list of one or more root directories of diskless clients that have already been configured by way of the Host Manager; see admintool(1M).

1. Become superuser.
2. Type **telinit 1** and press Return to bring the system to single-user mode.
3. Type **/etc/security/bsmunconv** and press Return to start BSM.
4. Type **y** and press Return to disable BSM.
5. Type **telinit 6** and press Return to reboot the system as a multiuser BSM system.

To enable or disable BSM on a diskless client, a server, or a stand-alone system, log on as superuser to the system being converted and use the bsmconv or bsmunconv commands without any options.

To enable or disable BSM on a diskless client from that client's server, log on to the server as superuser and use bsmconv, specifying the root directory of each diskless client you want to affect. For example, the following command enables BSM on the two systems named client1 and client2.

```
# /etc/security/bsmconv /export/root/client1 /export/root/client2
```

The following command enables BSM only on the system called castle. You no longer need to enable BSM on both the server and its diskless clients.

```
# /etc/security/bsmconv
```

After you run bsmconv, you can configure the system by editing the files in /etc/security. Each diskless client has its own copy of configuration files in its root directory. You may want to edit these files before rebooting each client.

Following the completion of either command, reboot the affected system(s) to properly initialize the auditing subsystem.

Examples

The following example uses the bsmconv command to enable the basic security model and uses the telinit 6 command to reboot the system.

```
# /etc/security/bsmconv
This script is used to enable the Basic Security Module (BSM).
Shall we continue with the conversion now? [y/n] y
bsmconv: INFO: checking startup file.
bsmconv: INFO: move aside /etc/rc2.d/S92volmgt.
```

```
bsmconv: INFO: turning on audit module.
bsmconv: INFO: initializing device allocation files.

The Basic Security Module is ready.
If there were any errors, please fix them now.
Configure BSM by editing files located in /etc/security.
Reboot this system now to come up with BSM enabled.
# telinit 6
```

The following example uses the bsmunconv command to disable the basic security model.

```
# /etc/security/bsmunconv
This script is used to disable the Basic Security Module (BSM).
Shall we continue the reversion to a non-BSM system now? [y/n] y
bsmunconv: INFO: moving aside /etc/security/audit_startup.
bsmunconv: INFO: restore /etc/rc2.d/S92volmgt.
bsmunconv: INFO: removing c2audit:audit_load from /etc/system.

The Basic Security Module has been disabled.
Reboot this system now to come up without BSM.
# telinit 6
```

Attributes

See attributes(5) for descriptions of the following attributes.

Attribute Type	Attribute Value
Availability	SUNWcsr

See Also

admintool(1M), auditd(1M), audit_startup(1M), audit.log(4), audit_control(4), attributes(5)

busstat — Report Bus-Related Performance Statistics

New!

Synopsis

```
/bin/busstat -e device-inst | -h | -l
/bin/busstat [-a][-n][-w device-inst [,pic0=event,picn=event]]...
   [-r device-inst]...[interval [count]]
```

Description

The busstat command is new in the Solaris 8 release. It provides access to the bus-related performance counters in the system. These performance counters measure statistics like hardware clock cycles and bus statistics, including DMA and cache coherency transactions on a multiprocessor system. Current supported hardware includes the SPARCsystem devices SBus, AC, and PCI. Currently, no IA devices are supported.

You can program each bus device that supports these counters to count a number of events from a specified list. Each device supports one or more Performance Instrumentation Counters (PIC) that are capable of counting events independently of each other.

You can select separate events for each PIC on each instance of these devices. busstat summarizes the counts over the last *interval* seconds, repeating forever. If you specify a *count*, the statistics are repeated *count* times.

Only superuser can program these counters. Non-root users have the option of reading the counters that have been programmed by a root user.

The default value for the *interval* argument is 1 second, and the default *count* is unlimited.

The devices that export these counters are highly platform dependent and the data may be difficult to interpret without an in-depth understanding of the operation of the components that are being measured and of the system they reside in.

Options

-a   Display absolute counter values. The default is delta values.

-e *device-inst*

Display the list of events that the specified device supports for each pic. Valid arguments for *device-inst* are SPARCsystem devices sbus, ac, and pci.

Specify *device-inst* as device (name) followed by an optional instance number. If you specify an instance number, display the events for that instance. If you specify no instance number, display the events for the first instance of the specified device.

-h   Print a usage message.

-l   List the devices in the system that support performance counters.

-n   Do not display a title in the output. The default is to display titles.

-r *device-inst*

Read and display all pic values for the specified device

Specify *device-inst* as device (name) followed by instance number if specifying an instance number of a device whose counters are to be read and displayed. If all instances of this device are to be read, use device (name) without an instance number. All pic values are sampled when the -r option is used.

-w *device-inst* [,pic0=event][,picn=event]

Program (write) the specified devices to count the specified events. Write access to the counters is restricted to root users only. Non-root users can use the -r option.

Specify *device-inst* as device (name) followed by an optional instance number if specifying an instance number of a device to program these events on. If all instances of this device are to be programmed the same, then use device without an instance number. Specify an event to be counted for a specified pic by providing a comma-separated list of *pic n=event* values.

The -e option displays all valid event names for each device. Any devices that are programmed are sampled every *interval* seconds and repeated *count* times. It is recommended that you specify *interval* small enough to ensure that counter wraparound is detected. The rate at which counters wrap around varies from device to device. If a user is programming events using the -w option and busstat detects that another user has changed the events that are being counted, the tool terminates because the programmed devices are now being controlled by another user. Only one user can be programming a device instance at any one time. You can sample extra devices with the -r option. Using multiple instances of the -w option with the same *device-inst* specifying a different list of events for the pics gives the effect of multiplexing for that device. busstat switches between the list of events for that device every *interval* seconds. *event* can be a string representing the event name or a number representing the bit pattern to be programmed into the Performance Control Register (PCR). This usage assumes you have explicit knowledge of the meaning of the control register bits for a device. You can specify the number in hexadecimal, decimal, or octal, using the usual conventions of strtol(3C).

Exit Status

0	Successful completion.
1	An error occurred.
2	Another user is writing to the same devices.

Examples

SPARC Devices Only

The following example uses the -l option to display the devices available on the system paperbark. In this example, only sbus0 is available.

```
paperbark% busstat -l
Busstat Device(s):
sbus0
paperbark%
```

The following example uses the -e option to display the list of devices supported for each pic.

```
paperbark% busstat -e sbus
pic0
dvma_stream_rd
dvma_stream_wr
dvma_const_rd
dvma_const_wr
dvma_tlb_misses
dvma_stream_buf_mis
```

```
dvma_cycles
dvma_bytes_xfr
interrupts
upa_inter_nack
pio_reads
pio_writes
sbus_reruns
pio_cycles

pic1
dvma_stream_rd
dvma_stream_wr
dvma_const_rd
dvma_const_wr
dvma_tlb_misses
dvma_stream_buf_mis
dvma_cycles
dvma_bytes_xfr
interrupts
upa_inter_nack
pio_reads
pio_writes
sbus_reruns
pio_cycles
paperbark%
```

The following example reads and displays the values for each pic using the default interval.

```
# busstat -r sbus
time dev    event0              pic0        event1              pic1
1    sbus0  0xf                 0           0xf00               0
2    sbus0  0xf                 0           0xf00               0
3    sbus0  0xf                 0           0xf00               0
4    sbus0  0xf                 0           0xf00               0
5    sbus0  0xf                 0           0xf00               0
6    sbus0  0xf                 0           0xf00               0
7    sbus0  0xf                 0           0xf00               0
8    sbus0  0xf                 0           0xf00               0
9    sbus0  0xf                 0           0xf00               0
10   sbus0  0xf                 0           0xf00               0
11   sbus0  0xf                 0           0xf00               0
12   sbus0  0xf                 0           0xf00               0
13   sbus0  0xf                 0           0xf00               0
```
. . . *(Additional lines deleted from this example)*

In the following example, ac0 refers to the Address Controller, instance 0. The counters are programmed to count Memory Bank stalls on an Ultra Enterprise system at 10 second intervals and display the values in absolute form instead of displaying deltas.

```
# busstat -a -w ac0,pic0=mem_bank0_stall,pic1=mem_bank1_stall 10
time   dev   event0          pic0    event1          pic1
10     ac0   mem_bank0_stall 1234    mem_bank1_stall 5678
20     ac0   mem_bank0_stall 5678    mem_bank1_stall 12345
```

```
30    ac0   mem_bank0_stall  12345   mem_bank1_stall    56789
```
... (*Additional lines deleted from this example*)

Use the -e option for a complete list of the supported events for a device.

The following example programs and monitors the counters on all instances of the address controller. ac refers to all ac instances. This example programs all instances of the Address Controller counters to count_clock cycles and mem_bank0_rds at 2-second intervals, 100 times, displaying the values as deltas.

```
# busstat -w ac,pic0=clock_cycles,pic1=mem_bank0_rds 2 100
time  dev   event0        pic0         event1         pic1
2     ac0   clock_cycles  167242902    mem_bank0_rds  3144
2     ac1   clock_cycles  167254476    mem_bank0_rds  1392
4     ac0   clock_cycles  168025190    mem_bank0_rds  40302
4     ac1   clock_cycles  168024056    mem_bank0_rds  40580
```
... (*Additional lines deleted from this example*)

The following example monitors the events that are being counted on the sbus1 device, 100 times at 1-second intervals. It suggests that a root user has changed the events that sbus1 was counting to be dvma_tlb_misses and interrupts instead of pio_cycles.

```
% busstat -r sbus0 1 100

time  dev    event0            pic0   event1       pic1
1     sbus1  pio_cycles        2321   pio_cycles   2321
2     sbus1  pio_cycles        48     pio_cycles   48
3     sbus1  pio_cycles        49     pio_cycles   49
4     sbus1  pio_cycles        2281   pio_cycle    2281
5     sbus1  dvma_tlb_misses   0      interrupts   0
6     sbus1  dvma_tlb_misses   6      interrupts   2
7     sbus1  dvma_tlb_misses   8      interrupts   11
```
... (*Additional lines deleted from this example*)

The following example programs ac0 to alternate between counting (clock cycles, mem_bank0_rds) and (addr_pkts, data_pkts) at 2-second intervals while also monitoring what ac1 is counting.

It shows the expected output of the above busstat command.

Another root user on the machine has changed the events that this user programmed, and busstat detects the change and terminates the command with a message.

```
# busstat -w ac0,pic0=clock_cycles,pic1=mem_bank0_rds
  -w ac0,pic0=addr_pkts,pic1=data_pkts -r ac1 2

time  dev   event0        pic0        event1         pic1
2     ac0   addr_pkts     12866       data_pkts      17015
2     ac1   rio_pkts      385         rio_pkts       385
4     ac0   clock_cycles  168018914   mem_bank0_rds  2865
4     ac1   rio_pkts      506         rio_pkts       506
6     ac0   addr_pkts     144236      data_pkts      149223
6     ac1   rio_pkts      522         rio_pkts       522
8     ac0   clock_cycles  168021245   mem_bank0_rds  2564
8     ac1   rio_pkts      387         rio_pkts       387
```

```
10     ac0    addr_pkts       144292          data_pkts       159645
10     ac1    rio_pkts        506             rio_pkts        506
12     ac0    clock_cycles    168020364       mem_bank0_rds   2665
12     ac1    rio_pkts        522             rio_pkts        522
busstat: events changed (possibly by another busstat).
#
```

Attributes

See attributes(5) for descriptions of the following attributes.

Attribute Type	Attribute Value
Availability	SUNWcsu

See Also

iostat(1M), mpstat(1M), vmstat(1M), strtol(3C), attributes(5)

C

cachefslog — Cache File-System Logging

Synopsis

```
/usr/sbin/cachefslog [-f logfile | -h] cachefs-mount-point
```

Description

CacheFS statistics enable you to determine an appropriate cache size and to observe the performance of the cache. Use the `cachefslog` command to display where CacheFS statistics are being logged, to set where CacheFS statistics are being logged, or to halt logging for a cache specified by `cachefs-mount-point`. The `cachefs-mount-point` argument is a mount point of a cache file system. All file systems cached under the same cache as `cachefs-mount-point` are logged.

Options

You must be superuser to use the `-f` and `-h` options.

`-f logfile`   Specify the log file to be used.

`-h`   Halt logging.

Operands

`cachefs-mount-point`

A mount point of a cache file system.

Usage

See `largefile(5)` for the description of the behavior of `cachefslog` when encountering files greater than or equal to 2 Gbytes (2**31 bytes).

Examples

The following example checks if the directory `/export/home/winsor` is being logged.

```
castle% cachefslog /Docs
not logged: /export/home/winsor
castle%
```

The following example changes the log file of `/export/home/winsor/Docs` to `/var/tmp/winsorlog`.

```
# cachefslog -f /var/tmp/winsorlog /export/home/winsor/Docs
/var/tmp/winsorlog: /export/home/winsor/Docs
#
```

The following example verifies the change of the previous example.

```
castle% cachefslog /export/home/winsor/Docs
/var/tmp/winsorlog: /export/home/winsor/Docs
castle%
```

The following example halts logging for the `/export/home/winsor` directory.

```
# cachefslog -h /export/home/winsor/Docs
not logged: /export/home/winsor/Docs
#
```

Exit Status

0	Success.
non-zero	An error has occurred.

Attributes

See `attributes(5)` for descriptions of the following attributes.

Attribute Type	Attribute Value
Availability	SUNWcsu

See Also

`cachefsstat(1M)`, `cachefswssize(1M)`, `cfsadmin(1M)`, `attributes(5)`, `largefile(5)`

Diagnostics

`Invalid path`   It is illegal to specify a path within a cache file system.

cachefspack — Pack Files and File Systems in the Cache

Synopsis

```
/usr/lib/fs/cachefs/cachefspack [-h][-i | -p | -u][-f packing-list]
   [-U cache-directory][file...]
```

Description

Use the cachefspack command to set up and maintain files in the cache. This command affords greater control over the cache, ensuring that the specified files are in the cache whenever possible.

Options

-f *packing-list*

Specify a file containing a list of files and directories to be packed. You can also specify options within subdirectories and files. The format and rules governing *packing-list* are described on the packingrules(4) manual page. Directories are packed recursively. Symbolic links that match a regular expression on a LIST command are followed. Symbolic links encountered while recursively processing directories are not followed.

-h   Print a brief help summary of all the options.

-i   View information about the packed files.

-p   Pack the file or files specified by *file*. (the default behavior).

-u   Unpack the file or files specified by *file*.

-U *cache-directory*

Unpack all files in the specified cache directory.

Operands

file   A path name of a file to be packed or unpacked.

Usage

See largefile(5) for the description of the behavior of cachefspack when encountering files greater than or equal to 2 Gbytes (2**31 bytes).

Examples

The following example packs the file projects in the cache.

```
castle% cachefspack -p projects
castle%
```

The following example packs the files projects, updates, and master_plan in the cache.

```
castle% cachefspack -p projects updates master_plan
castle%
```

The following example unpacks the file projects from the cache.

```
castle% cachefspack -u projects
castle%
```

The following example unpacks the files projects, updates, and master_plan from the cache.

```
castle% cachefspack -u projects updates master_plan
castle%
```

The following example unpacks all files in the cache directory cache1.

```
castle% cachefspack -U /cache/cache1
castle%
```

The following example uses a packing list to specify files to be packed in the cache. The lists.pkg file has the following contents.

```
IGNORE SCCS BASE /src/junk LIST *.c LIST *.h
```

The following command packs all files in the directory /src/junk with .c and .h extensions that do not contained the string SCCS in the file's path name.

```
castle% cachefspack -f lists.pkg
castle%
```

Exit Status

0	Successful completion.
>0	An error occurred.

Attributes

See attributes(5) for descriptions of the following attributes.

Attribute Type	Attribute Value
Availability	SUNWcsu

See Also

cfsadmin(1M), mount_cachefs(1M), packingrules(4), attributes(5), largefile(5)

cachefsstat — Cache File-System Statistics

Synopsis

/usr/lib/cachefs/cachefsstat [-z][*path*...]

Description

Use the cachefsstat command to display statistical information about the cache file system mounted on *path*. The statistical information includes cache hits and misses, consistency checking, and modification operations. If you do not specify *path*, all mounted cache file systems are used.

You can also use cachefsstat to reinitialize this information (see -z option).

The statistical information has the following format.

cache hit-rate consistency-checks modifies

hit-rate   The percentage of cache hits over the total number of attempts, followed by the actual numbers of hits and misses.

consistency-checks

                 The number of consistency checks performed, followed by the number that passed and the number that failed.

modifies   The number of modify operations, including writes, creates, and so on.

Options

-z   Zero (reinitialize) statistics. Execute cachefsstat -z before executing cachefsstat again to gather statistics on the cache performance. Only superuser can use this option. The statistics printed reflect those just before the statistics are reinitialized.

Usage

See largefile(5) for the description of the behavior of cachefsstat when encountering files greater than or equal to 2 Gbytes (2**31 bytes).

Examples

The following example shows the output of the cachefsstat command.

```
castle% cachefsstat /export/home/winsor cache
hit rate: 73% (1234 hits, 450 misses)
consistency checks: 700 (650 pass, 50 fail)
modifies: 321
```

Exit Status

0   Success.

non-zero   An error has occurred.

Attributes

See attributes(5) for descriptions of the following attributes.

Attribute Type	Attribute Value
Availability	SUNWcsu

See Also

cachefslog(1M), cachefswssize(1M), cfsadmin(1M), attributes(5), largefile(5)

cachefswssize — Determine Working Set Size for Cache File System

Synopsis

/usr/lib/fs/cachefs/cachefswssize *logfile*

Description

Use the cachefswssize command to display the workspace size determined from *logfile*. The output includes the amount of cache space needed for each file system that was mounted under the cache, as well as a total.

Usage

See largefile(5) for the description of the behavior of cachefswssize when encountering files greater than or equal to 2 Gbytes (2**31 bytes).

Examples

The following example shows output of the cachefswssize command.

```
castle% cachefswssize /var/tmp/winsorlog
/export/home/winsor
                          end size:            10688k
                    high water size:           10704k

/foo
                          end size:              128k
                    high water size:             128k

/usr/dist
                          end size:             1472k
                    high water size:            1472k
```

```
total for cache
                        initial size:          110960k
                             end size:           12288k
                      high water size:           12304k
castle%
```

Exit Status

0   Success.

non-zero   An error has occurred.

Attributes

See attributes(5) for descriptions of the following attributes.

Attribute Type	Attribute Value
Availability	SUNWcsu

See Also

cachefslog(1M), cachefsstat(1M), cfsadmin(1M), attributes(5), largefile(5)

Diagnostics

```
problems were encountered writing log file
```

> Problems were encountered when the kernel was writing the log file. The most common problem is running out of disk space.

```
invalid log file
```

> The log file is not a valid log file or was created with a newer version of the Solaris Operating Environment than the one where cachefswssize is running.

captoinfo — Convert a termcap Description into a terminfo Description

Synopsis

/bin/captoinfo [-1][-v...][-V][-w width] filename...

Description

Use the captoinfo command to convert termcap entries into terminfo entries. For example, you may need to use it to enable the function keys on a Wyse® terminal to work properly. captoinfo looks in filename for termcap descriptions. For each one found, it writes an equivalent terminfo description to standard output, along with any comments found. A description that is expressed as relative to another description (as specified in the termcap tc = field) is reduced to the minimum superset before being displayed.

If you specify no file name, then the environment variable TERMCAP is used for the file name or entry. If TERMCAP is a full path name to a file, only the terminal whose name is specified in the environment variable TERM is extracted from that file. If the environment variable TERMCAP is not set, then the file /usr/share/lib/termcap is read.

Note — You should use captoinfo to convert termcap entries to terminfo entries because the termcap database may not be supplied in future releases.

Options

-1   Display the fields one to a line. Otherwise, print the fields several to a line, with a maximum width of 60 characters.

-v   Display tracing information on the standard error as the program runs. Specifying additional -v options displays more detailed information.

-V   Display the version of the program in use on the standard error and then exit.

-w *width*   Change the output to *width* characters.

Examples

The following example uses the captoinfo command to display the output of the TERM environment variable, dtterm, to standard output. On the system paperbark, the TERMINFO environment variable is not set.

```
paperbark% captoinfo
captoinfo: obsolete 2 character name 'dt' removed.
        synonyms are: 'dtterm|CDE terminal emulator'
dtterm|CDE terminal emulator,
        am, mir, msgr, xenl, xon,
        cols#80, lines#24,
        bel=^G, civis=\E[?25l, clear=\E[H\E[J, cnorm=\E[?25h,
        cr=\r, csr=\E[%i%p1%d;%p2%dr, cub=\E[%p1%dD, cub1=\b,
        cud=\E[%p1%dB, cud1=\n, cuf=\E[%p1%dC, cuf1=\E[C,
        cup=\E[%i%p1%d;%p2%dH, cuu=\E[%p1%dA, cuu1=\E[A,
        dch=\E[%p1%dP, dch1=\E[P, dl=\E[%p1%dM, dl1=\E[M,
        ed=\E[J, el=\E[K, flash=\E[?5h\E[?5l$<200>, home=\E[H,
        ht=\t, hts=\EH, ich=\E[%p1%d@, il=\E[%p1%dL, il1=\E[L,
        ind=\n, is2=\E\sF\E>\E[?1l\E[?7h\E[?45l, kbs=\b,
        kcub1=\E[D, kcud1=\E[B, kcuf1=\E[C, kcuu1=\E[A,
        kf1=\E[11~, kf2=\E[12~, kf3=\E[13~, kf4=\E[14~,
        kf5=\E[15~, kf6=\E[17~, kf7=\E[18~, kf8=\E[19~,
        kf9=\E[20~, rc=\E8, ri=\EM, rmacs=^O, rmir=\E[4l,
        rmso=\E[22;27m, rmul=\E[24m, sc=\E7, smacs=^N,
        smir=\E[4h, smso=\E[2;7m, smul=\E[4m, tbc=\E[3g,
paperbark%
```

The following example uses the captoinfo command to configure a Data General®
terminal.

1. Become superuser.
2. Enter the following information in a new file named /tmp/new.dg to contain the
   termcap and terminfo information.

```
dgansi|dg-ansi|DG ansi terminal mode::co#80:li#24:cl=\E[;H\E[2J:
:bs:am:cm=\E[%i%d;%dH:nd=\E [C:up=\E[A:do=\E[B::ce=\E[K:ho=\E[H:nl=\E[B:
cr=^M:te=\E[;H\E[2J:
```

3. Type **cp /usr/share/lib/termcap /usr/share/lib/termcap.save** and press
   Return to make a copy of the termcap file.
4. Type **cat /tmp/new.dg >> /usr/share/lib/termcap** and press Return to append
   the new terminal description.
5. Type **tail /usr/share/lib/termcap** and press Return to check the end of the
   termcap file to verify that it is complete.
6. Type **captoinfo /tmp/new.dg > /tmp/dg.ansi** and press Return.
7. Type **tic /tmp/dg.ansi** and press Return. This step and the previous one are
   needed to make vi work properly. Note: A warning message may be displayed, but
   you can ignore it.
8. Type **ls -l /usr/share/lib/terminfo/d/dgansi** and press Return to confirm
   that the previous two steps worked properly. The result should look like the
   following.

```
-rw-r--r--  1 root  798  Nov 12 13:32 /usr/share/lib/terminfo/d/dgansi
```

9. Modify the /etc/ttytab file for the ports that have the Data General terminals
   attached.

The terminal type is dgansi. The following example shows the ttytype record.

```
ttya     "/usr/etc/getty std.9600"     dgansi    on local secure
```

10. Type **kill -1 1** and press Return to reset the ports.
11. Reconfigure the Data General Terminals to be in ansi mode.
12. Power the terminals off and back on to confirm the mode change.

Files

/usr/share/lib/terminfo/?/*

Compiled terminal description database.

/usr/share/lib/termcap

BSD compiled terminal description database.

Attributes

See `attributes`(5) for descriptions of the following attributes.

Attribute Type	Attribute Value
Availability	SUNWcsu

See Also

`infocmp(1M), curses(3X), terminfo(4), attributes(5)`

---

cfgadm — Configuration Administration

Synopsis

New!

```
/usr/sbin/cfgadm [-f][-y | -n][-v][-o hardware-options] -c function
    ap-id
/usr/sbin/cfgadm [-f][-y | -n][-v][-o hardware-options]
    -x hardware-function ap-id
/usr/sbin/cfgadm [-v][-a][-s listing-options][-o hardware-options]
    [-l [ap-id | ap-type]]
/usr/sbin/cfgadm [-v][-o hardware-options] -t ap-id ap-id]
/usr/sbin/cfgadm [-v][-o hardware-options] -h [ap-id | ap-type]
```

Note — In the Solaris 8 Operating Environment the optional [*ap-id*]
argument is no longer valid.

Description

Use the `cfgadm` command to administer operations, including the following, on
dynamically reconfigurable hardware resources.

- Displaying status (-1).
- Initiating testing (-t).
- Invoking configuration state changes (-c).
- Invoking hardware-specific functions (-x).
- Obtaining configuration administration help messages (-h).

You perform configuration administration at attachment points, which are places
where you can dynamically configure hardware resources during continued operation of
the Solaris Operating Environment.

Configuration administration makes a distinction between hardware resources that
are physically present in the machine and hardware resources that are configured and
visible to the Solaris Operating Environment. Configuration administration functions
are hardware-specific and are performed by calling hardware-specific libraries.

Configuration administration operates on an attachment point. Hardware resources
located at attachment points may or may not be physically replaceable during system
operation but are dynamically reconfigurable by way of the configuration
administration interfaces.

An attachment point defines two unique elements, which are distinct from the hardware resources that exist beyond the attachment point. The two elements of an attachment point are a *receptacle* and an *occupant*. Physical insertion or removal of hardware resources occurs at attachment points and results in a receptacle gaining or losing an occupant.

Configuration administration supports the physical insertion and removal operations as well as other configuration administration functions at an attachment point.

Attachment points have associated state and condition information. The configuration administration interfaces provide control for transitioning attachment point states.

A receptacle can exist in one of three states.

- Empty. A receptacle must provide the empty state, which is the normal state of a receptacle when the attachment point has no occupants.

- Disconnected. A receptacle can provide the disconnected state if it has the capability of isolating its occupants from normal system access. Typically, the disconnected state is used for various hardware-specific testing before the occupant's resources are brought into full use by the system or as a step in preparing an occupant for physical removal or reconfiguration. A receptacle in the disconnected state isolates its occupant from the system as much as its hardware allows but may provide access for testing and setup. A receptacle must provide the connected state, which allows normal access to hardware resources contained on any occupants.

- Connected. The connected state is the normal state of a receptacle that contains an occupant and that is not currently undergoing configuration administration operations.

An occupant can exist in one of two states.

- Configured. The hardware resources of an occupant in the configured state are represented by normal Solaris data structures; thus, some or all of those hardware resources may be in use by the Solaris Operating Environment.

- Unconfigured. The hardware resources contained on an occupant in the unconfigured state are not represented by normal Solaris data structures (such as device tree nodes) and are thus not available for use by the Solaris Operating Environment. Operations allowed on an unconfigured occupant are limited to configuration administration operations.

An occupant is required to provide both the configured and unconfigured states. An attachment point can be in one of the following five conditions.

- Unknown.
- OK.
- Failing.
- Failed.
- Unusable.

An attachment point can enter the system in any condition, depending on results of power-on tests and nonvolatile record keeping.

An attachment point with an occupant in the configured state is in one of four conditions.

- Unknown.
- OK.
- Failing.
- Failed.

If the condition is not `failing` or `failed`, then an attachment point can change to `failing` during the course of operation if a hardware-dependent recoverable error threshold is exceeded. If the condition is not `failed`, an attachment point can change to `failed` during operation as a result of an unrecoverable error.

An attachment point with an occupant in the `unconfigured` state can be in any of the defined conditions. The condition of an attachment point with an `unconfigured` occupant may decay from `ok` to `unknown` after a machine-dependent time threshold. Initiating a test function changes the attachment point's condition to `ok`, `failing`, or `failed` depending on the outcome of the test. An attachment point that does not provide a test function may leave the attachment point in the `unknown` condition. If a test is interrupted, the attachment point's condition may be set to the previous condition, `unknown`, or `failed`. You can retest an attachment point in the `unknown`, `ok`, `failing`, or `failed` conditions.

An attachment point may exist in the unusable condition for a variety of reasons, such as inadequate power or cooling for the receptacle, an occupant that is unidentifiable, unsupported, incorrectly configured, and so on. The system can never use an attachment point in the `unusable` condition. The attachment point typically remains in this condition until the physical cause is remedied.

An attachment point also maintains busy information that indicates when a state change is in progress or the condition is being reevaluated.

Attachment points are referred to by hardware-specific identifiers (*ap-id*) that are related to the type and location of the attachment points in the system device hierarchy. An *ap-id* cannot be ambiguous; it must identify a single attachment point. Two types of *ap-id* specifications are supported.

- A physical *ap-id* contains a fully specified path name.
- A logical *ap-id* contains a shorthand notation to identify an attachment point in a more user-friendly way.

For example, a receptacle representing a system's backplane slot number 7 might have a physical *ap-id* of `/central/fhc/sysctrl:slot7`, whereas the logical *ap-id* might be `system:slot7`. Another example, the third receptacle on the second PCI I/O bus on a system might have a logical *ap-id* of `pci2:plug3`.

In the Solaris 8 release, you can also create attachment points dynamically. A dynamic attachment point is named relative to a base attachment point that is present in the system. *ap-id*s for dynamic attachment points consist of a base component followed by two colons (`::`) and a dynamic component. The base component is the base attachment point *ap-id*. The dynamic component is hardware-specific and is generated by the corresponding hardware-specific library.

For example, consider a base attachment point that represents a SCSI Host Bus Adapter (HBA) with the physical *ap-id* `/devices/sbus@1f,0/SUNW,fas@e,8800000:scsi` and logical *ap-id* `c0`. A disk attached to this SCSI HBA could be represented by a dynamic attachment point with logical *ap-id* `c0::dsk/c0t0d0`, where `c0` is the base component and `dsk/c0t0d0` is the hardware-specific dynamic component. Similarly, the physical *ap-id* for this dynamic attachment point would be

`/devices/sbus@1f,0/SUNW,fas@e,8800000:scsi::dsk/c0t0d0`

The cfgadm command parses an *ap-id* and uses the name portion to locate and dynamically load the hardware-specific library that supports that type of attachment point. The hardware-specific libraries are located by searching the device tree for node of type DDI_NT_ATTACHMENT_POINT. The node name is used to search for a hardware-specific library, named lib$\{*name*\}.so.1, first in the following sequence.

1. /usr/platform/${machine}/lib/cfgadm/

2. /usr/platform/${arch}/lib/cfgadm/

3. /usr/lib/cfgadm/

Failing that, the same search is conducted using the driver name. The *ap-id* is passed on to the hardware-specific library to perform operations. The hardware-specific library validates that the *ap-id* is complete and identifies a single attachment point to operate on.

An *ap-type* is a partial form of an *ap-id* that can be ambiguous and not specify a particular attachment point. The *ap-type* is used by the list function to allow listing of all attachment points of the same type and by the help operation to request help on attachment points of that type. It consists of the name portion of an *ap-id*; you can omit the instance, the colon separator, and the specific attachment point identifier. For example, an *ap-type* of pci would show all attachment points whose node names or driver names contain pci.

The cfgadm command parses an *ap-type* and uses the name portion to locate and dynamically load the hardware-specific libraries that support attachment points of that type. The *ap-type* is passed to the hardware-specific library to perform listing operations.

> **Note —** The use of *ap-type*s is discouraged. The select suboption to the -s option, new in the Solaris 8 release, provides a more general and flexible mechanism for selecting attachment points. **New!**

The cfgadm command interacts primarily with hardware-dependent functions contained in hardware-specific libraries, and thus its behavior is hardware-dependent.

For each configuration administration operation, a service interruption may be required. Should the completion of the requested function require a noticeable service interruption to interactive users, a prompt is output on the standard error output for confirmation on the standard input before the function is started. You can override confirmation with the -y or -n options to always answer either yes or no. Supply hardware-specific options, such as test level, as suboptions with the -o option.

Operations that change the state of the system configuration are audited by the system log daemon syslogd(1M).

The arguments for this command conform to the getopt(3C) and getsubopt(3C) syntax convention.

Notes

Hardware resources enter the unconfigured pool in a hardware-specific manner. This entry can occur at various times such as at system initialization or as a result of an unconfigure operation. An occupant that is in the unconfigured state is not available for use by the system until specific intervention occurs, either as an operator-initiated command or by an automatic configuring mechanism.

You can use the listing option of the cfgadm command to provide parsable input for another command, for example, within a shell script. You can use the -s option to select the fields required and suppress the column headings. The following fields always produce parsable output: ap_id, physid, r_state, o_state, condition, busy, status_time_p, and type. Parsable output never has white space characters embedded in the field value.

The following shell script fragment finds the first good, unconfigured occupant of type CPU.

```
found=
cfgadm -l -s "noheadings,cols=ap-id:r_state:condition:type" | \
while read ap_id r_state cond type
do
    if ["$r_state" = unconfigured -a "$cond" = ok -a "$type" = CPU]
                        then
        if [-z "$found"]
                                    then
                                    found=$ap-id
                                    fi
                    fi
    done
    if [-n "$found"]
    then
                        echo "Found CPU $found"
    fi
    [...]
done
```

The format of the parsable time field (status_time_p) is *YYYYMMDDhhmmss*, giving the year, month, day, hour, minute, and second in a form suitable for string comparison.

Refer to the hardware-specific documentation for details of System Configuration Administration support.

Options

-a   Specify that the -l option must also list dynamic attachment points.

-c *function*   Perform the state change function on the attachment point specified by *ap-id*.

Specify function as insert, remove, disconnect, connect, configure, or unconfigure. These functions result in state transitions at the attachment point by calling hardware-specific library routines.

insert   Perform operations that enable you to manually insert an occupant or to activate a hardware-supplied mechanism that performs the physical insertion. insert can have hardware-specific side effects that temporarily suspend activity in portions of the system. In such cases, the hardware-specific library generates appropriate warning messages and informs you of any special considerations or procedures unique to that hardware. This function can fail and set the receptacle condition to unusable because of various hardware-specific errors.

remove   Perform operations that enable you to manually
                    remove an occupant or to activate a
                    hardware-supplied mechanism to perform the
                    physical removal. remove can have hardware-specific
                    side effects that temporarily suspend activity in
                    portions of the system. In such cases, the
                    hardware-specific library generates appropriate
                    warning messages and informs you of any special
                    considerations or procedures unique to that hardware.
                    This function can fail and set the receptacle condition
                    to unusable because of various hardware-specific
                    errors.

disconnect   Perform hardware-specific operations to put a
                    receptacle in the disconnected state, which can
                    prevent an occupant from operating in a normal
                    fashion through the receptacle.

connect   Perform hardware-specific operations to put the
                    receptacle in the connected state, which enables an
                    occupant to operate in a normal fashion through the
                    receptacle.

configure   Perform hardware-specific operations that enable an
                    occupant's hardware resources to be usable by the
                    Solaris Operating Environment.

                    Occupants that are configured are part of the system
                    configuration and are available for manipulation by
                    Solaris device-manipulation maintenance commands
                    (for example, psradm(1M), mount(1M),
                    ifconfig(1M)).

unconfigure   Perform hardware-specific operations that logically
                    remove an occupant's hardware resources from the
                    system. The occupant must currently be configured
                    and its hardware resources must not be in use by the
                    Solaris Operating Environment.

State transition functions can fail because of the condition of the
attachment point or other hardware-dependent considerations. All
state change functions in the direction of adding resources, (insert,
connect, and configure) are passed on to the hardware-specific
library when the attachment point is in the ok or unknown condition.
All other conditions require the use of the -f option to enable these
functions to be passed on to the hardware-specific library. Attachment
point condition does not prevent a hardware-specific library being
called for removal functions related to the removal (remove,
disconnect, and unconfigure) of hardware resources from the
system. Hardware-specific libraries can reject state change functions
if the attachment point is in the unknown condition.

The condition of an attachment point is not necessarily changed by the state change functions; however, errors during state change operations can change the attachment point condition. You can try to override a condition and force a state change that would otherwise fail by specifying the force option (-f). Hardware-specific safety and integrity checks can prevent the force option from having any effect.

-f   Force the specified action to occur. Typically, this action is a hardware-dependent override of a safety feature. Forcing a state change operation can enable use of the hardware resources of occupant that is not in the ok or unknown conditions, at the discretion of any hardware-dependent safety checks.

-h [ap-id | ap-type...]

Print the help message text. If you specify *ap-id* or *ap-type*, call the help routine of the hardware-specific library for the attachment point indicated by the argument.

-l [ap-id | ap-type...]

List the state and condition of attachment points. If you specify *ap-id* or *ap-type*, limit the listing call to the attachment points indicated by the argument. If you specify *ap-id*, limit the listing to those particular attachment points. Invoking cfgadm without one of the action options is equivalent to -l without an *ap-id* or an *ap-type* argument. The format of the display is controlled by the -v and -s options.

-n   Suppress any interactive confirmation and assume that the answer is no. If you specify neither -n nor -y, obtain interactive confirmation through the standard error output and the standard input. If either of these standard channels does not correspond to a terminal (as determined by isatty(3C)), then assume the -n option.

-o *hardware-options*

Supply hardware-specific options to the main command option. The format and content of the hardware option string is completely hardware-specific. The option string *hardware-options* conforms to the getsubopt(3C) syntax convention.

New!   -s *listing-options*

Supply listing options to the list (-l) command. *listing-options* conforms to the getsubopt(3C) syntax convention. Use the suboptions to specify the attachment-point selection criteria (select=*select-string*), the type of matching desired (match=*match-type*), order of listing (sort=*field-spec*), the data that is displayed (cols=*field-spec* and cols2=*field-spec*), the column delimiter (delim=*string*), and whether to suppress column headings (noheadings).

When you specify the `select` suboption, list only attachment points that match the specified criteria. The `select` suboption has the following syntax

`cfgadm -s select=`*class*`(`*value1*`):`*type*`(`*value2*`)...`

where an *attr* is one of *ap-id*, *class*, or *type*. *ap-id* refers to the logical *ap-id* field, *class* refers to attachment point class, and *type* refers to the type field. *value1*, *value2*, and so forth are the corresponding values to be matched. You can specify the type of match by the `match` suboptions as follows.

`cfgadm -s match=`*match-type*`,select=`*attr1*`(`*value1*`)...`

You can quote arguments to the `select` suboption to protect them from the shell.

A *field-spec* is one or more data fields concatenated using : (colon) as in *data-field*:*data-field*:*data-field*. A *data-field* is one of *ap-id*, *physid*, *r-state*, *o-state*, *condition*, *type*, *busy*, *status-time*, *status-time-p*, and *info*. The *ap-id* field output is the logical name for the attachment point, and the *physid* field contains the physical name. The *r-state* field can be empty, disconnected, or connected. The *o-state* field can be configured or unconfigured. The *busy* field can be either y if the attachment point is busy or n if it is not. The *type* and *info* fields are hardware-specific. The *status-time-p* field is a parsable version of the status-time field. If an attachment point has an associated class, the class field lists the class name.

The order of the fields in *field-spec* is significant. For the `sort` suboption, the first field is the primary sort key. For the `cols` and `cols2` suboptions, the fields are printed in the order requested. You can reverse the order of sorting on a data field by putting a dash (-) before the data-field name within the *field-sec* for the `sort` suboption. The default value for `sort` is *ap-id*. The default values for `cols` and `cols2` depend on whether you specify the -v option. Without it, `cols` is *ap-id*:*r-state*:*o-state*:*condition* and `cols2` is not set. With -v, `cols` is *ap-id*:*r-state*:*o-state*:*condition*:*info* and `cols2` is status-time:type:busy:physid:. The default value for `delim` is a single space. The value of `delim` can be a string of arbitrary length. The delimiter cannot include comma characters; see `getsubopt`(3C). You can use these listing options to create parsable output.

-t   Perform a test of one or more attachment points. Use the `test` function to reevaluate the condition of the attachment point. Without a `test` level specifier in *hardware-options*, use the fastest test that identifies hard faults.

More comprehensive tests are hardware-specific, and you choose them by specifying *hardware-options*.

The result of the test is used to update the condition of the specified occupant to `ok` if no faults are found, `failing` if recoverable faults are found, or `failed` if any unrecoverable faults are found.

If a test is interrupted, you can restore the attachment point's condition to its previous value or set it to `unknown` if no errors were found, set it to `failing` if only recoverable errors were found, or set it to `failed` if any unrecoverable errors were found. The attachment point should be set to `ok` only on normal completion of testing with no errors.

`-v` Execute in verbose mode. For the `-c`, `-t`, and `-x` options, output a message giving the results of each attempted operation. For the `-h` option, output detailed help information. For the `-l` option, output full information for each attachment point.

`-x hardware-function`

Perform hardware-specific functions. Private hardware-specific functions should not normally change the state of a receptacle or occupant. Attachment point conditions can change as the result of errors encountered during private hardware-specific functions. The format and content of the `hardware-function` string is completely hardware-specific. The option string `hardware-function` conforms to the `getsubopt`(3C) syntax convention.

`-y` Suppress any interactive confirmation and assume that the answer is yes.

Usage

The required privileges to use this command are hardware-dependent. Typically, a default system configuration restricts all but the list option to the superuser.

Examples

The following example lists current configurable hardware information.

```
# cfgadm
Ap_Id            Receptacle      Occupant        Cond
cw(1.375000i) cw(1.375000i) cw(1.375000i) cw(1.375000i)
 1 1 1 1.
system:slot0     connected       configured      ok
system:slot1     connected       configured      ok
system:slot2     connected       configured      ok
system:slot3     connected       unconfigured    unknown
system:slot4     connected       configured      failing
system:slot5     connected       configured      ok
system:slot6     disconnected    unconfigured    unusable
system:slot7     empty           unconfigured    ok
#
```

The following example displays information about attachment points on a system. `c0` and `c1` represent two SCSI controllers. The other `Ap_Id`s such as `ac0:bank1` and `sysctrl0:slot0` represent other types of system components.

```
# cfgadm -l
Ap_Id                    Receptacle     Occupant       Condition
ac0:bank0                connected      configured     ok
ac0:bank1                connected      configured     ok
c0                       connected      configured     unknown
c1                       connected      configured     unknown
sysctrl0:slot0           connected      configured     ok
sysctrl0:slot1           connected      configured     ok
#
```

> **Note** — cfgadm -l displays information about SCSI HBAs but not SCSI
> devices. Use the cfgadm -al command to display information about SCSI
> devices such as disk and tapes.

The following example displays information about a system's SCSI controllers and
their attached devices.

```
# cfgadm -al
Ap_Id                    Receptacle     Occupant       Condition
ac0:bank0                connected      configured     ok
ac0:bank1                connected      configured     ok
c0                       connected      configured     unknown
c0::dsk/c0t0d0           connected      configured     unknown
c0::rmt/0                connected      configured     unknown
c1                       connected      configured     unknown
c1::dsk/c1t10d0          connected      configured     unknown
c1::dsk/c1t4d0           connected      configured     unknown
c2                       connected      unconfigured   unknown
sysctrl0:slot0           connected      configured     ok
sysctrl0:slot1           connected      configured     ok
#
```

The following example configures a SCSI controller and then uses the cfgadm -al
command to verify that the controller is configured.

```
# cfgadm -c configure c1
# cfgadm -al
Ap_Id                    Receptacle     Occupant       Condition
c0                       connected      configured     unknown
c0::dsk/c0t0d0           connected      configured     unknown
c0::rmt/0                connected      configured     unknown
c1                       connected      configured     unknown
c1::dsk/c1t10d0          connected      configured     unknown
c1::dsk/c1t4d0           connected      configured     unknown
#
```

The following example identifies an unconfigured device (c1t4d0), configures it, and
verifies that the device is configured.

```
# cfgadm -al
Ap_Id                    Receptacle     Occupant       Condition
c0                       connected      configured     unknown
c0::dsk/c0t0d0           connected      configured     unknown
c0::rmt/0                connected      configured     unknown
c1                       connected      configured     unknown
```

```
c1::dsk/c1t10d0                       connected    configured   unknown
c1::dsk/c1t4d0                        connected    unconfigured unknown
# cfgadm -c configure c1::dsk/c1t4d0
# cfgadm -al
Ap_Id                                 Receptacle   Occupant     Condition
c0                                    connected    configured   unknown
c0::dsk/c0t0d0                        connected    configured   unknown
c0::rmt/0                             connected    configured   unknown
c1                                    connected    configured   unknown
c1::dsk/c1t10d0                       connected    configured   unknown
c1::dsk/c1t4d0                        connected    configured   unknown
#
```

The following example disconnects SCSI controller c1. Be careful when disconnecting a SCSI device, especially when dealing with controllers for disks containing critical file systems such as root, usr, var, and the swap partition. The dynamic reconfiguration software cannot detect all cases that may hang the system. Use the following command with caution.

```
# cfgadm -al
Ap_Id                                 Receptacle   Occupant     Condition
c0                                    connected    configured   unknown
c0::dsk/c0t0d0                        connected    configured   unknown
c0::rmt/0                             connected    configured   unknown
c1                                    connected    configured   unknown
c1::dsk/c1t10d0                       connected    configured   unknown
c1::dsk/c1t4d0                        connected    configured   unknown
# cfgadm -c disconnect c1
WARNING: Disconnecting critical partitions may cause system hang.
Continue (yes/no)? y
# cfgadm -al
Ap_Id                                 Receptacle   Occupant     Condition
c0                                    connected    configured   unknown
c0::dsk/c0t0d0                        connected    configured   unknown
c0::rmt/0                             connected    configured   unknown
c1                                    disconnected configured   unknown
c1::dsk/c1t10d0                       disconnected configured   unknown
c1::dsk/c1t4d0                        disconnected configured   unknown
#
```

The controller and all the devices attached to it are disconnected from the system.

The following example verifies that the c1 controller is disconnected, connects it, and verifies the connection.

```
# cfgadm -al
Ap_Id                                 Receptacle   Occupant     Condition
c0                                    connected    configured   unknown
c0::dsk/c0t0d0                        connected    configured   unknown
c0::rmt/0                             connected    configured   unknown
c1                                    disconnected configured   unknown
c1::dsk/c1t10d0                       disconnected configured   unknown
c1::dsk/c1t4d0                        disconnected configured   unknown
# cfgadm -c connect c1
# cfgadm -al
```

```
Ap_Id                              Receptacle   Occupant     Condition
c0                                 connected    configured   unknown
c0::dsk/c0t0d0                     connected    configured   unknown
c0::rmt/0                          connected    configured   unknown
c1                                 connected    configured   unknown
c1::dsk/c1t10d0                    connected    configured   unknown
c1::dsk/c1t4d0                     connected    configured   unknown
#
```

The following example removes SCSI disk c1t4d0 from a SCSI controller.

```
# cfgadm -al
Ap_Id                              Receptacle   Occupant     Condition
c0                                 connected    configured   unknown
c0::dsk/c0t0d0                     connected    configured   unknown
c0::rmt/0                          connected    configured   unknown
c1                                 connected    configured   unknown
c1::dsk/c1t10d0                    connected    configured   unknown
c1::dsk/c1t4d0                     connected    configured   unknown
# cfgadm -x remove_device c1::dsk/c1t4d0
Removing SCSI device: /devices/sbus@1f,0/SUNW,fas@1,8800000/sd@4,0
This operation will suspend activity on SCSI bus: c1
Continue (yes/no)? y
SCSI bus quiesced successfully.
It is now safe to proceed with hotplug operation.
Enter y if operation is complete or n to abort (yes/no)?
```

I/O activity on the SCSI bus is suspended while the hot-plug operation is in progress. Power off the device to be removed and remove it. When the operation is complete, type **y**. Then, verify that the device has been removed.

```
# cfgadm -al
Ap_Id                              Receptacle   Occupant     Condition
c0                                 connected    configured   unknown
c0::dsk/c0t0d0                     connected    configured   unknown
c0::rmt/0                          connected    configured   unknown
c1                                 connected    configured   unknown
c1::dsk/c1t10d0                    connected    configured   unknown
#
```

Environment Variables

See environ(5) for descriptions of the following environment variables that affect the execution of cfgadm: LC_TIME, LC_MESSAGES, NLSPATH, and TZ.

LC_MESSAGES	Determine how cfgadm displays column headings and error messages. Listing output data is not affected by the setting of this variable.
LC_TIME	Determine how cfgadm displays human-readable status-changed time (status_time).
TZ	Specify the time zone used when converting the status-changed time. This variable applies to both the human-readable (status_time) and parsable (status_time_p) formats.

Exit Status

0	Successful completion.
1	An error occurred.
2	Configuration administration not supported on specified target.
3	Usage error.

Attributes

See attributes(5) for descriptions of the following attributes.

Attribute Type	Attribute Value
Availability	SUNWcsu

See Also

New!

cfgadm_scsi(1M), ifconfig(1M), mount(1M), prtdiag(1M), psradm(1M), syslogd(1M), config_admin(3CFGADM), getopt(3C), getsubopt(3C), isatty(3C), attributes(5), environ(5)

Diagnostics

Diagnostic messages are displayed on the standard error output. Other than options and usage errors, you may see the following messages.

cfgadm: Configuration administration not supported on *ap-id*

cfgadm: No library found for *ap-id*

cfgadm: *ap-id* is ambiguous

cfgadm: operation: Insufficient privileges

cfgadm: Attachment point is busy, try again

New!

cfgadm: No attachment points with specified attributes found

cfgadm: System is busy, try again

cfgadm: operation: Operation requires a service interruption

cfgadm: operation: Data error: *error-text*

cfgadm: operation: Hardware specific failure: *error-text*

See config_admin(3CFGADM) for additional details regarding error messages.

cfgadm_ac — EXX00 Memory System Administration   `New!`

Synopsis

```
/usr/sbin/cfgadm [-c configure] [-t] [-o disable-at-boot | enable-at-boot]
   ac#:bank#...
/usr/sbin/cfgadm [-c unconfigure] [-o disable-at-boot |
   enable-at-boot] ac#:bank#...
/usr/sbin/cfgadm [-o quick | normal | extended] -t ac#:bank#...
/usr/sbin/cfgadm -x relocate-test ac#:bank#...
/usr/sbin/cfgadm [-l] -o disable-at-boot | enable-at-boot ac#:bank#...
```

Description

The `cfgadm_ac` command is new in the Solaris 8 release. As part of the Dynamic Reconfiguration of CPU/Memory boards using `cfgadm_sysctrl`(1M), the `ac` hardware-specific library `/usr/platform/sun4u/lib/cfgadm/cfgadm_ac.so.1` provides the functionality for configuring and unconfiguring memory banks on E6X00, E5X00, E4X00, and E3X00 systems.

Memory banks appear as attachment points in the device tree. For each CPU/Memory board, two attachment points are published, one for each bank on the board, `bank0` and `bank1`. If the bank is unpopulated, the receptacle state is `empty`. If the bank is populated, the receptacle state is `connected`. The receptacle state of a memory bank can never be `disconnected`. The occupant state of a connected memory bank can be `configured` or `unconfigured`. If the occupant state is `configured`, the memory is in use by the Solaris Operating Environment; if `unconfigured`, it is not.

> **Note** — Refer to the *Sun Enterprise 6x00, 5x00, 4x00, and 3x00 Systems Dynamic Reconfiguration User's Guide* for additional details regarding dynamic reconfiguration of EXX00 system CPU/Memory boards.

Options

Refer to `cfgadm`(1M) for complete descriptions of the command options.

`-c configure | unconfigure`

> Change the occupant state. The `configure` argument ensures that the memory is initialized and adds the memory to the Solaris memory pool. The `unconfigure` argument removes the memory from use by the Solaris Operating Environment. When a CPU/Memory board is to be removed from a system, you must unconfigure both banks of memory.
>
> `cfgadm` refuses the `configure` operation if the memory on the board is marked `disabled-at-boot` (see info field), unless you specify either the `-f` (force) option or the enable at boot option, (`-o enable-at-boot`). The `configure` operation takes a short time proportional to the size of memory that must be initialized.

cfgadm refuses the unconfigure operation if there is not enough uncommitted memory in the system (VM viability error) or if the bank to be unconfigured has memory that can't be removed (nonrelocatable pages error). The presence of nonrelocatable pages is indicated by the word permanent in the info listing field. Removing memory from use by the Solaris Operating Environment can take a significant time because of factors such as system load and how much paging to secondary storage is required. You can cancel the unconfigure operation at any time and return the memory to the fully configured state by interrupting the command invocation with a signal. The unconfigure operation self-cancels if no memory can be removed within a timeout period. You can change the default timeout period of 60 seconds with the -o timeout=# option, with a value of 0 disabling the timeout.

-f   Force override of the block on configuring a memory bank marked as disabled at boot in the nonvolatile disabled-memory-list variable. See *Platform Notes: Sun Enterprise 6x00/5x00/4x00/3x00 Systems*.

-l   The list option is supported as described in cfgadm(1M).

The *type* field is always memory.

The *info* field has the following information for empty banks.

slot# empty

The slot# indicates the system slot into which the CPU/Memory board is inserted. For example, for slot 11 the attachment point for use with cfgadm to manipulate the associated board is sysctrl0:slot11. The info field has the following information for connected banks.

slot# *size*Mb|*size*Gb [(*size*Mb|*size*Gb used)] *base* 0x###
    [interleaved #-way][disabled at boot][permanent]

Show the size of the bank in megabytes or gigabytes as appropriate. If the memory is less than completely used, report the used size. Show the physical base address in hexadecimal. If the memory bank is interleaved with some other bank, report the interleave factor. If the memory on the board is disabled at boot by the nonvolatile disabled-memory-list variable, then report it. If the bank has memory that cannot be removed, report it as permanent.

-o disable-at-boot | enable-at-boot

Modify the state of the nonvolatile disabled-memory-list variable. You can use these options with a -c option or with the explicit or implied listing command, -l, if no command is required. Use -o enable-at-boot with the configure command to override the block on configuring memory on a board in the disabled memory list.

-o normal | quick | extended

Use with the -t option to specify test level.

The `normal` test level ensures that each memory cell stores both a 0 and a 1 and checks that all cells are separately addressable. The `quick` test level tests only the 0s and 1s and typically misses address line problems. The `extended` test uses patterns to test for adjacent cell interference problems. The default test level is `normal`. See `-t`.

`-o timeout-#`   Use this option with the `unconfigure` command to set the self-cancelling timeout. The default value is `60` and the unit is seconds. A value of `0` means no timeout.

`-t`   Test an unconfigured bank of memory. Specify the test level using the `-o quick | normal | extended` option.

   `cfgadm` exits with a `0` (success) if the test was able to run on the memory bank. The result of the test is available in the condition for the attachment point.

`-x relocate-test`

   For all pages of memory in use on the specified memory bank, try a `relocation` operation as used in the `unconfigure` command. The success of this operation does not guarantee that the bank can be unconfigured. Failure indicates that it probably cannot be unconfigured. This option is for test purposes only.

Operands

`ac#:bank#`   Publish the attachment points for memory banks by instances of the address controller (`ac`) driver (`ac#`). One instance of the `ac` driver is created for each system board, but only those instances associated with CPU/Memory boards publish the two bank attachment points, `bank0` and `bank1`.

   This form conforms to the logical *ap-id* specification given in `cfgadm`(1M). The corresponding physical *ap-id*s are listed in the "Files" section.

   The `ac` driver instance numbering has no relation to the slot number for the corresponding board. The full, physical-attachment-point identifier has the slot number incorporated into it as twice the slot number in hexadecimal directly following the `fhc@` part.

Files

`/devices/fhc@*,f8800000/ac@0,1000000:bank?`

   Attachment points.

`/usr/platform/sun4u/lib/cfgadm/cfgadm_ac.so.1`

   Hardware-specific library file.

Attributes

See attributes(5) for descriptions of the following attributes.

Attribute Type	Attribute Value
Availability	SUNWkvm.u

See Also

cfgadm(1M), cfgadm_sysctrl(1M), config_admin(3), attributes(5)

Sun Enterprise 6x00, 5x00, 4x00, and 3x00 Systems Dynamic Reconfiguration User's Guide

Platform Notes: Sun Enterprise 6x00/5x00/4x00/3x00 Systems

New! cfgadm_pci — Configuration Administration Command for PCI Hot Plug

Synopsis

```
/usr/sbin/cfgadm [-f][-y | -n][-v][-o hardware-options] -c function
   ap-id [ap-id]
/usr/sbin/cfgadm [-f][-y | -n][-v][-o hardware-options]
   -x hardware-function ap-id [ap-id]
/usr/sbin/cfgadm[-v][-slisting-options][-ohardware-options][-l[ap-id
   |ap-type]]
/usr/sbin/cfgadm [-v][-o hardware-options] -t ap-id [ap-id]
/usr/sbin/cfgadm [-v][-o hardware-function] -h [ap-id| ap-type]
```

Description

The PCI hardware-specific commands for cfgadm are new in the Solaris 8 release. The PCI hardware-specific library /usr/lib/cfgadm/pci.so.1 provides support for hot-plugging pci adapter cards into pci hot-pluggable slots in a system that is hot-plug capable, through cfgadm(1M). See cfgadm(1M).

For PCI Hot Plug, each hot-plug slot on a specific PCI bus is represented by an attachment point of that specific PCI bus.

An attachment point consist of two parts: a receptacle and an occupant. The receptacle under PCI hot plug is usually referred to as the physical hot-pluggable slot; and the occupant is usually referred to as the PCI adapter card that plugs into the slot.

Attachment points are named through *ap-id*s. There are two types of *ap-id*s: logical and physical. The physical *ap-id* is based on the physical path name, that is, /devices/pci@1/hpc0_slot3, whereas the logical *ap-id* is a shorter and more user-friendly name. For PCI hot-pluggable slots, the logical *ap-id* is usually the corresponding hot-plug controller driver name plus the logical slot number, that is, pci0:hpc0slot1; pci nexus driver, with hot-plug controller driver named hpc and slot number 1. The *ap-type* for Hot Plug PCI is pci.

See the *System Administration Guide, Volume I* for a detailed description of the hot-plug procedure.

Options

-c *function*   The following functions are supported for PCI hot-pluggable slots.

     configure   Configure the PCI device in the slot to be used by the Solaris Operating Environment.

     connect   Connect the slot to PCI bus.

     disconnect   Disconnect the slot from the PCI bus.

     insert   Perform operations required to allow manual insertion of a PCI device.

     remove   Perform operations required to allow manual removal of a PCI device.

     unconfigure   Logically remove the PCI device's resources from the system.

-f   Not supported.

-h *ap-id* | *ap-type*

    Print PCI hot-plug-specific help message.

-l [ap-id | ap-type]

    List the values of PCI Hot Plug spots.

-n   Suppress any interactive confirmation and assume that the answer is no. If you specify neither -n nor -y, obtain interactive confirmation through the standard error output and the standard input. If either of these standard channels does not correspond to a terminal (as determined by isatty(3C)), then assume the -n option.

-o *hardware-options*

    No hardware-specific options are currently defined.

-s *listing-options*

    Same as the generic cfgadm(1M).

-t *ap-id*   This option is supported only on a platform that supports testing capability on the slot.

-v   Execute in verbose mode.

    When you use -v with -l option, output information about the attachment point. For PCI Hot Plug, the info field is the slot's system label. This string is obtained from the slot-name property of the slot's bus node. The occupant Type field describes the contents of the slot. The possible values are listed below.

     null   The slot is empty.

     subclass,board

               The card in the slot is either a single-function or multifunction device.

subclass is a string representing the subclass code of the device, for example, SCSI, ethernet, pci-isa, and so forth. If the card is a multifunctional device, print MULT.

board is a string representing the board type of the device, for example, HP for PCI Hot Plug adapter, HS for Hot Swap Board, NHS for Non-Hot Swap cPCI Board, BHS for Basic Hot Swap cPCI Board, FHS for Full Hot Swap cPCI Board.

-x *hardware-function*

Perform hardware-specific function. These hardware-specific functions should not normally change the state of a receptacle or occupant.

The following *hardware-function*s are supported.

enable_slot | disable_slot

Change the state of the slot and preserve the state of slot across reboot. Not all platforms support this feature.

enable_slot enables the addition of hardware to this slot for hot-plugging and at boot time.

disable_slot disables the addition of hardware to this slot for hot-plugging and at boot time.

enable_autoconfig | disable_autoconfig

Change the ability to autoconfigure the occupant of the slot. Only platforms that support autoconfiguration support this feature.

enable_autoconfig enables the ability to autoconfigure the slot.

disable_autoconfig disables the ability to autoconfigure the slot.

led=[*led-sub-arg*],mode=[*mode-sub-arg*]

Without subarguments, print a list of the current LED settings. With subarguments, set the mode of a specific LED for a slot.

Specify *led-sub-arg* as fault, power, att, or active.

Specify *mode-sub-arg* as on, off, or blink.

Changing the state of the LED does not change the state of the receptacle or occupant. Normally, the LEDs are controlled by the hot-plug controller, and no user intervention is necessary. Use this command for testing purposes.

Caution: Changing the state of the LED can misrepresent the state of occupant or receptacle.

The following command prints the values of LEDs.

```
# cfgadm -x led pci0:hpc0_slot1 Ap_Id Led
  pci0:hpc0_slot1 power=on,fault=off,
  active=off,attn=off
```

The following command turns on the Fault LED.

```
# cfgadm -x led=fault,mode=on
  pci0:hpc0_slot1
```

The following command turns off the Power LED.

```
# cfgadm -x led=power,mode=off
  pci0:hpc0_slot0
```

The following command sets the active LED to blink to indicate the location of the slot.

```
# cfgadm -x led=active,mode=on
  pci0:hpc0_slot3
```

-y   Suppress any interactive confirmation and assume that the answer is yes.

Examples

The following command prints the values of each slot.

```
paperbark% cfgadm -l
Ap_Id             Type       Receptacle    Occupant        Condition
pci1:hpc0_slot0   unknown    empty         unconfigured    unknown
pci1:hpc0_slot1   unknown    empty         unconfigured    unknown
pci1:hpc0_slot2   unknown    empty         unconfigured    unknown
pci1:hpc0_slot3   HP/SCSI    connected     configured      ok
pci1:hpc0_slot4   unknown    empty         unconfigured    unknown
paperbark%
```

The following command prints PCI hot-plug-specific commands.

```
paperbark% cfgadm -h pci
Usage:
      cfgadm [-f] [-y|-n] [-v] [-o hardware_opts] -c function ap_id
    [ap_id...]
      cfgadm [-f] [-y|-n] [-v] [-o hardware_opts] -x function ap_id
    [ap_id...]
        cfgadm [-v] [-s listing_options] [-o hardware_opts] [-a] [-l
    [ap_id|ap_type...]]
          cfgadm [-v] [-o hardware_opts] -t ap_id [ap_id...]
          cfgadm [-v] [-o hardware_opts] -h [ap_id|ap_type...]
paperbark%
```

Files

/usr/lib/cfgadm/libpci.so.1

Hardware-specific library for PCI hot-plugging.

Attributes

See attributes(5) for descriptions of the following attributes.

Attribute Type	Attribute Value
Availability	SUNWkvm.u

See Also

cfgadm(1M), config_admin(3CFGADM), libcfgadm(4), attributes(5)
System Administration Guide, Volume I

New! **cfgadm_scsi** — SCSI Hardware-Specific Commands for cfgadm

Synopsis

```
/usr/sbin/cfgadm [-f][-y | -n][-v][-o hardware-option] -c function
    ap-id...
/usr/sbin/cfgadm [-f][-y | -n][-v][-o hardware-option]
    -x hardware-function ap-id...
/usr/sbin/cfgadm [-v][-a][-s listing-option][-o hardware-option]
    [-l [ap-id |ap-type...]]
/usr/sbin/cfgadm [-v][-o hardware-option] -t ap-id...
/usr/sbin/cfgadm [-v][-o hardware-option] -h [ap-id...]
```

Description

The SCSI hardware-specific commands for cfgadm are new in the Solaris 8 release. The SCSI hardware-specific library /usr/lib/cfgadm/scsi.so.1 provides the functionality for SCSI hot-plugging through the cfgadm(1M) command. cfgadm operates on attachment points, which are locations in the system where hardware resources can be dynamically reconfigured. Refer to cfgadm(1M) for information regarding attachment points.

For SCSI hot-plugging, each SCSI controller is represented by an attachment point in the device tree. In addition, each SCSI device is represented by a dynamic attachment point. Attachment points are named through *ap-id*s. Two types of *ap-id*s are defined: logical and physical. The physical *ap-id* is based on the physical path name, whereas the logical *ap-id* is a shorter more user-friendly name. For SCSI controllers, the logical *ap-id* is usually the corresponding disk controller number. For example, a typical logical *ap-id* would be c0.

SCSI devices are named relative to the controller *ap-id*. Thus, if a disk device is attached to controller c0, its *ap-id* can look like the following example, where dsk/c0t0d0 identifies the specific device.

```
c0::dsk/c0t0d0
```

In general, the device identifier is derived from the corresponding logical link for the device in /dev. For example, a SCSI tape drive logical *ap-id* could be c0::rmt/0. Here, c0 is the logical *ap-id* for the SCSI controller, and rmt/0 is derived from the logical link for the tape drive in `/dev/rmt`. If an identifier cannot be derived from the link in `/dev`, a unique identifier is assigned to it. For example, if the tape device has no link in `/dev`, it can be assigned an *ap-id* of the form `c0::st3` where `st3` is a unique, internally generated identifier.

A simple listing of attachment points in the system includes attachment points at SCSI controllers but not SCSI devices. Use the `-a` flag to the list option (`-l`) to list SCSI devices as well, as shown in the following example.

```
# cfgadm -l
Ap_Id              Type         Receptacle    Occupant       Condition
c0                 scsi-bus     connected     configured     unknown
sysctrl0:slot0     cpu/mem      connected     configured     ok
sysctrl0:slot1     sbus-upa     connected     configured     ok
#
```

To list SCSI devices in addition to SCSI controllers, also specify the `-a` option.

```
# cfgadm -al

Ap_Id              Type         Receptacle    Occupant       Condition
c0                 scsi-bus     connected     configured     unknown
c0::dsk/c0t14d0    disk         connected     configured     unknown
c0::dsk/c0t11d0    disk         connected     configured     unknown
c0::dsk/c0t8d0     disk         connected     configured     unknown
c0::dsk/c0t0d0     disk         connected     configured     unknown
c0::rmt/0          tape         connected     configured     unknown
sysctrl0:slot0     cpu/mem      connected     configured     ok
sysctrl0:slot1     sbus-upa     connected     configured     ok
#
```

Refer to `cfgadm(1M)` for more information about listing attachment points. The receptacle and occupant state for attachment points at the SCSI controller have the following meanings.

empty	Not applicable.
disconnected	Bus quiesced (I/O activity on bus is suspended).
connected	Bus active.
configured	One or more devices on the bus is configured.
unconfigured	No device on the bus is configured.

The corresponding states for individual SCSI devices have the following meanings.

empty	Not applicable.
disconnected	Bus to which the device is attached is quiesced.
connected	Bus to which device is attached is active.
configured	Device is configured.
unconfigured	Device is not configured.

Options

cfgadm defines several types of operations besides listing (-1). These operations include testing, (-t), invoking configuration state changes, (-c), invoking hardware-specific functions (-x), and obtaining configuration administration help messages (-h).

-a   Specify that the -1 option must also list dynamic attachment points.

-c *function*   The following generic commands are defined for the SCSI hardware-specific library.

For SCSI controller attachment points, the following configuration state change operations are supported.

connect   Unquiesce the SCSI bus.

disconnect   Quiesce the bus (suspend I/O activity on bus).

                           Incorrect use of this command can hang the system.

configure   Configure new devices on SCSI bus.

unconfigure   Unconfigure all devices connected to bus.

The following generic commands are defined for SCSI devices.

configure   Configure a specific device.

unconfigure   Unconfigure a specific device.

-f   When used with the disconnect command, force a quiesce of the SCSI bus if supported by hardware. Incorrect use of this command can hang the system.

-h *ap-id*   Obtain SCSI-specific help by using the help option with any SCSI attachment point.

-n   Suppress any interactive confirmation and assume that the answer is no. If you specify neither -n nor -y, obtain interactive confirmation through the standard error output and the standard input. If either of these standard channels does not correspond to a terminal (as determined by isatty(3C)), then assume the -n option.

-o *hardware-option*

No hardware-specific options are currently defined.

-s *listing-option*

List attachment points of class scsi by using the select suboption. Refer to the cfgadm(1M) manual page for additional information.

-t *ap-id*   No test commands are available at present.

-v   Execute in verbose mode.

-x *hardware-function*

Some of the following commands can be used only with SCSI controllers and some only with SCSI devices.

In the following, *controller-ap-id* refers to an *ap-id* for a SCSI controller, for example, c0. *device-ap-id* refers to an *ap-id* for a SCSI device, for example: c0::dsk/c0dt3d0.

The following hardware-specific functions are defined.

insert_device *controller-ap-id*

> Add a new device to the SCSI controller, *controller-ap-id*. This command is intended for interactive use only.

remove_device *device-ap-id*

> Remove device *device-ap-id*. This command is intended for interactive use only.

replace_device *device-ap-id*

> Remove device *device-ap-id* and replace it with another device of the same kind. This command is intended for interactive use only.

reset_device *device-ap-id*

> Reset *device-ap-id*.

reset_bus *controller-ap-id*

> Reset bus *controller-ap-id* without resetting any devices attached to the bus.

reset_all *controller-ap-id*

> Reset bus *controller-ap-id* and all devices on the bus.

-y

> Suppress any interactive confirmation and assume that the answer is yes.

Note — The disconnect (quiesce) operation is not supported on controllers that control disks containing critical partitions such as root (/), /usr, swap, or /var. Do not try the disconnect operation on such controllers. Incorrect usage can hang a system and require a reboot.

Hot-plugging operations are not supported by all SCSI controllers.

Examples

The following example configures a disk attached to controller c0.

```
# cfgadm -c configure c0::dsk/c0t3d0
```

The following example unconfigures a disk attached to controller c0.

```
# cfgadm -c unconfigure c0::dsk/c0t3d0
```

The following example adds a new device to controller c0.

```
# cfgadm -x insert_device c0
Adding device to SCSI HBA: /devices/sbus@1f,0/SUNW,fas@e,8800000
This operation will suspend activity on SCSI bus c0
Continue (yes/no)? y
SCSI bus quiesced successfully.
```

```
It is now safe to proceed with hotplug operation.
Enter y if operation is complete or n to abort (yes/no)? y
#
```

The following example replaces a device attached to controller c0.

```
# cfgadm -x replace_drive c0::dsk/c0t3d0
Replacing SCSI device: /devices/sbus@1f,0/SUNW,fas@e,8800000/sd@3,0
This operation will suspend activity on SCSI bus: c0
Continue (yes/no)? y
SCSI bus quiesced successfully.
It is now safe to proceed with hotplug operation.
Enter y if operation is complete or n to abort (yes/no)? y
#
```

The following example illustrates the warning that cfgadm displays when encountering a mounted file system while unconfiguring a disk.

```
# cfgadm -c unconfigure c1::dsk/c1t0d0
cfgadm: Component system is busy, try again: failed to offline:
/devices/pci@1f,4000/scsi@3,1/sd@1,0
        Resource                    Information
------------------      --------------------------
/dev/dsk/c1t0d0s0    mounted filesystem "/mnt"
#
```

Files

/usr/lib/cfgadm/scsi.so.1

Hardware-specific library for generic SCSI hot-plugging.

Attributes

See attributes(5) for descriptions of the following attributes.

Attribute Type	Attribute Value
Availability	SUNWcsl (32 bit)
	SUNWcslx (64 bit)

See Also

cfgadm(1M), luxadm(1M), config_admin(3), libcfgadm(3LIB), attributes(5)

cfgadm_sysctrl — EXX00 System Board Administration

New!

Synopsis

```
/usr/sbin/cfgadm -c function [-f][-o disable-at-boot |
   enable-at-boot][-n | -y] sysctrl0:slot#...
/usr/sbin/cfgadm -x quiesce-test sysctrl0:slot#
/usr/sbin/cfgadm -x insert-test | remove-test sysctrl0:slot#...
/usr/sbin/cfgadm -x set-condition-test=# sysctrl0:slot#...
/usr/sbin/cfgadm [-l] -o disable-at-boot | enable-at-boot
   sysctrl0:slot#...
```

Description

The EXX00 system board administration functionality of the cfgadm command is new in the Solaris 8 release. The sysctrl hardware-specific library /usr/platform/sun4u/lib/cfgadm/sysctrl.so.1 provides dynamic reconfiguration functionality for configuring and disconnecting system boards on E6X00, E5X00, E4X00, and E3X00 systems. You can insert both I/O and CPU boards into a slot on a running system that is configured for the Solaris Operating Environment without rebooting. You can also disconnect and remove both types of boards from a running system without rebooting.

System slots appear as attachment points in the device tree, one attachment point for each actual slot in the system chassis. If a board is not in a slot, the receptacle state is empty. If a board is powered off and ready to remove, the receptacle state is disconnected. If a board is powered on and is connected to the system bus, the receptacle state is connected.

The occupant state is unconfigured when the receptacle state is empty or disconnected. The occupant state is either unconfigured or configured when the receptacle state is connected.

In the configured state, the devices on a board are available for use by the Solaris Operating Environment. In the unconfigured state, the devices on the board are not available.

Inserting a board changes the receptacle state from empty to disconnected. Removing a board changes the receptacle state from disconnected to empty.

Warning — Removing a board that is in the connected state crashes the operating system and can result in permanent damage to the system.

Refer to the *Sun Enterprise 6x00, 5x00, 4x00 and 3x00 Systems Dynamic Reconfiguration User's Guide* for additional details regarding dynamic reconfiguration of EXX00 system CPU/Memory boards.

Options

Refer to cfgadm(1M) for a more complete description of options.

-c *function*   Perform the state change *function*. Specify function as connect, disconnect, configure, or unconfigure.

        configure   Change the occupant state to configure.

If the receptacle state is `disconnected`, the `configure` function first tries to connect the receptacle. The `configure` function walks the OBP device tree created as part of the `connect` function and creates the Solaris device tree nodes, attaching devices as required. For CPU/Memory boards, add CPUs to the CPU list in the powered-off state. These are visible to the `psrinfo`(1M) and `psradm`(1M) commands. Two memory attachment points are published for CPU/memory boards. Use `mount`(1M) and `ifconfig`(1M) to use I/O devices on the new board. To use CPUs, use `psradm -n` to bring the new processors on-line. Use `cfgadm_ac`(1M) to test and configure the memory banks.

connect   Change the receptacle state to `connected`.

Changing the receptacle state requires that the system bus be frozen while the bus signals are connected and the board tested. Freeze the bus by running a quiesce operation to stop all process activity and suspend all drivers. Because the quiesce operation and the subsequent resume can be time consuming and are not supported by all drivers, the `-x quiesce` test is provided. While the system bus is frozen, the board being connected is tested by firmware. This operation takes a short time for I/O boards and a significant time for CPU/Memory boards because of CPU external cache testing. This function does not provide memory testing. You are prompted for confirmation before proceeding with the quiesce. Use the `-y` or `-n` option to override the prompt. The `connect` operation is refused if the board is marked as `disabled-at-boot`, unless you specify either the `-f` (force) or `-o enable-at-boot` option. See `-l`.

disconnect   Change the receptacle state to disconnected.

If the occupant state is `configure`, the `disconnect` function first tries to unconfigure the occupant. The `disconnect` operation does not require a quiesce operation and operates quickly. The board is powered off, ready for removal.

unconfigure   Change the occupant state to `unconfigured`.

Devices on the board are made invisible to the Solaris Operating Environment during this process. The I/O devices on an I/O board are removed from the Solaris device tree. Any device that is still in use stops the unconfigure process and is reported as in use. The unconfigure operation must be retried after the device is made nonbusy. For CPU/Memory boards, the memory must have been changed to the unconfigured state before issuing the board unconfigure operation. The CPUs on the board are taken off-line, powered off, and removed from the Solaris CPU list. CPUs that have processes bound to them cannot be taken off-line. See psradm(1M), psrinfo(1M), pbind(1M), and p_online(2) for more information on taking CPUs off-line.

-f   Force a block on connecting a board marked as disabled-at-boot in the nonvolatile disabled-board-list variable. See *Platform Notes: Sun Enterprise 6x00/5x00/4x00/3x00 Systems.*

-l   List options. Supported as described in cfgadm(1M).

The type field can be one of cpu/mem, mem, dual-sbus, sbus-upa, dual-pci, soc+sbus, soc+upa, disk, or unknown.

The hardware-specific info field is set as follows: [disabled at boot][non-detachable][100 MHz capable].

For sbus-upa and soc+upa type boards, the following additional information appears first: [single buffered ffb|double buffered ffb|no ffb installed] For disk-type boards, the following additional information appears first: {target: # | no disk} {target: # | no disk}.

-n   Suppress any interactive confirmation and assume that the answer is no. If you specify neither -n nor -y, obtain interactive confirmation through the standard error output and the standard input. If either of these standard channels does not correspond to a terminal (as determined by isatty(3C)), then assume the -n option.

-o disable-at-boot | enable-at-boot

Modify the state of the nonvolatile disabled-board-list variable. Use the -o option with the -c *function* or -l options.

Use -o enable-at-boot with the -c connect to override a block on connecting a disabled-at-boot board.

-x insert-test | remove-test

Perform a test.

Specify remove-test to change the driver state for the specified slot from disconnected to empty without the need for physically removing the board during automated test sequences.

Specify `insert-test` to change the driver state of a slot made to appear empty by using the `remove-test` command to the `disconnected` state as if it had been inserted.

`-x quiesce-test sysctrl0:slot1`

Perform a test.

Allow the quiesce operation required for board-connect operations to be exercised. The execution of this test confirms that, with the current software and hardware configuration, it is possible to quiesce the system. If a device or process cannot be quiesced, print its name in an error message. You can use any valid board attachment point with this command, but because all systems have a slot1, the given form is recommended.

`-x set-condition-test=#`

Perform a test.

Allow the condition of a system board attachment point to be set for testing the policy logic for state change commands. Give the new setting as a number indicating one of the following condition values.

0	Unknown.
1	OK.
2	Failing.
3	Failed.
4	Unusable.

`-y` Suppress any interactive confirmation and assume that the answer is yes.

Operands

`sysctrl0:slot#`

The attachment points for boards on EXX00 systems are published by instance 0 of the `sysctrl` driver (`sysctrl0`). The names of the attachment points are numbered from `slot0` through `slot15`. Specify # as a number between 0 and 15, indicating the slot number. This form conforms to the logical *ap-id* specification given in `cfgadm`(1M). The corresponding physical *ap-id*s are listed in the "Files" section.

Files

`/usr/platform/sun4u/lib/cfgadm/sysctrl.so.1`

Hardware-specific library.

`/devices/central@1f,0/fhc@0,f8800000/clockboard@0,900000:slot*`

Attachment points.

Attributes

See attributes(5) for descriptions of the following attributes.

Attribute Type	Attribute Value
Availability	SUNWkvm.u

See Also

cfgadm(1M), cfgadm_ac(1M), ifconfig(1M), mount(1M), pbind(1M), psradm(1M), psrinfo(1M), config_admin(3), attributes(5)

Sun Enterprise 6x00, 5x00, 4x00 and 3x00 Systems Dynamic Reconfiguration User's Guide

Platform Notes: Sun Enterprise 6x00/5x00/4x00/3x00 Systems

Refer to the *Sun Enterprise 6x00, 5x00, 4x00 and 3x00 Systems Dynamic Reconfiguration User's Guide* for additional details regarding dynamic reconfiguration of EXX00 system CPU/Memory boards.

---

cfsadmin — Administer Disk Space for Cache File System

Synopsis

```
/usr/lib/fs/cachefs/cfsadmin -c [-o cacheFS-parameters] cache-directory
/usr/lib/fs/cachefs/cfsadmin -d [cache-ID | all] cache-directory
/usr/lib/fs/cachefs/cfsadmin -l cache-directory
/usr/lib/fs/cachefs/cfsadmin -s [mntpt1... | all]
/usr/lib/fs/cachefs/cfsadmin -u [-o cacheFS-parameters] cache-directory
```

Description

You can use the Cache File System (CacheFS) to improve performance of remote file systems or slow devices such as CD-ROM drives. When a file system is cached, the data read from the remote file system or CD-ROM is stored in a cache on the local system.

The cfsadmin command enables you to perform the following CacheFS functions.

- Create a cache.
- Delete cached file systems.
- List cache contents and statistics.
- Adjust resource parameters when the file system is unmounted.

For each form of the command except -s, you must specify a cache directory, that is, the directory under which the cache is actually stored. A path name on the client system (called the front file system) identifies the cache directory. For the -s form of the command, you must specify a mount point.

You can specify a cache ID when you mount a file system with CacheFS, or you can let the system generate one for you. The -l option includes the cache ID in its listing of information. You must know the cache ID to delete a cached file system.

Options

-c   Create a cache under the directory specified by *cache-directory*. This directory must not exist before you create the cache.

-d   Remove the file system whose cache ID you specify and release its resources, or remove all file systems in the cache by specifying all. After deleting a file system from the cache, you must run the fsck_cachefs(1M) command to correct the resource counts for the cache.

-l   List file systems stored in the specified cache, as well as statistics about them. Each cached file system is listed by cache ID. The statistics document resource use and cache resource parameters.

-o *cacheFS-parameters*

         cacheFS-parameters are described in "CacheFS Resource Parameters" on page 186

-s   Request a consistency check on the specified file system (or all cachefs-mounted file systems). The -s option works only if the cache file system was mounted with demandconst enabled (see mount_cachefs(1M)). Check each file in the specified cache file system for consistency with its corresponding file on the server (the back file system). Note that the consistency check is performed file by file as files are accessed. If no files are accessed, no checks are performed. Use of this option does not result in a sudden "storm" of consistency checks.

-u   Update resource parameters of the specified cache directory. You can increase only parameter values. To decrease the values, you must remove the cache and recreate it. All file systems in the cache directory must be unmounted when you use this option. Changes take effect the next time you mount any file system in the specified cache directory. The -u option with no -o option sets all parameters to their default values.

CacheFS Resource Parameters

You can specify the following CacheFS resource parameters as arguments to the -o option. Separate multiple parameters with commas.

maxblocks=*n*   Maximum amount of storage space that CacheFS can use, expressed as a percentage of the total number of blocks in the front file system. If CacheFS does not have exclusive use of the front file system, there is no guarantee that all the space the maxblocks parameter allows is available. The default is 90.

minblocks=*n*   Minimum amount of storage space, expressed as a percentage of the total number of blocks in the front file system that CacheFS is always allowed to use without limitation by its internal control mechanisms. If CacheFS does not have exclusive use of the front file system, there is no guarantee that all the space the minblocks parameter tries to reserve is available. The default is 0.

threshblocks=*n*

A percentage of the total blocks in the front file system beyond which CacheFS cannot claim resources once its block usage has reached the level specified by minblocks. The default is 85.

maxfiles=*n*   Maximum number of files that CacheFS can use, expressed as a percentage of the total number of inodes in the front file system. If CacheFS does not have exclusive use of the front file system, there is no guarantee that all the inodes the maxfiles parameter allows are available. The default is 90.

minfiles=*n*   Minimum number of files, expressed as a percentage of the total number of inodes in the front file system, that CacheFS is always allowed to use without limitation by its internal control mechanisms. If CacheFS does not have exclusive use of the front file system, there is no guarantee that all the inodes the minfiles parameter tries to reserve are available. The default is 0.

threshfiles=*n*

A percentage of the total inodes in the front file system beyond which CacheFS cannot claim inodes once its usage has reached the level specified by minfiles. The default is 85.

maxfilesize=*n*

Largest file size, expressed in megabytes, that CacheFS is allowed to cache. The default is 3.

Note — You cannot decrease the block or inode allotment for a cache. To decrease the size of a cache, you must remove it and create it again with different parameters.

Operands

cache-directory

The directory under which the cache is actually stored.

mntpt1   The directory where the CacheFS is mounted.

Usage
See largefile(5) for the description of the behavior of cfsadmin when encountering files greater than or equal to 2 Gbytes (2**31 bytes).

Examples
The following example creates a cache directory named /cache.

```
# cfsadmin -c /cache
#
```

The following example creates a cache specifying maxblocks, minblocks, and threshblocks. It creates a cache named /cache1 that can claim a maximum of 60 percent of the blocks in the front file system, can use 40 percent of the front file system blocks without interference by CacheFS internal control mechanisms, and has a threshold value of 50 percent. The threshold value indicates that after CacheFS reaches its guaranteed minimum, it cannot claim more space if 50 percent of the blocks in the front file system are already used.

```
# cfsadmin -c -o maxblocks=60,minblocks=40, threshblocks=50 /cache1
#
```

The following example changes the `maxfilesize` parameter for the cache directory `/cache2` to 2 megabytes.

```
# cfsadmin -u -o maxfilesize=2 /cache2
#
```

The following example lists the contents of a cache directory named `/cache3` and provides statistics about resource utilization.

```
# cfsadmin -l /cache3
cfsadmin: list cache FS information
   maxblocks       90%
   minblocks        0%
   threshblocks    85%
   maxfiles        90%
   minfiles         0%
   threshfiles     85%
   maxfilesize      3MB
  castle:_docs-cachemount:_docs
#
```

The following example removes all cached file systems from the cache directory `/cache3`.

```
# cfsadmin -d all /cache3
```

The following example checks for consistency all file systems mounted with `demandconst` enabled. No errors are reported if no `demandconst` file systems were found.

```
# cfsadmin -s all
#
```

Exit Status

0	Successful completion.
1	An error occurred.

Attributes

See `attributes`(5) for descriptions of the following attributes.

Attribute Type	Attribute Value
Availability	SUNWcsu

See Also

cachefslog(1M), cachefsstat(1M), cachefswssize(1M), fsck_cachefs(1M),
mount_cachefs(1M), attributes(5), largefile(5)

cg14config — Configure the SX/CG14 Graphics Accelerator Device

Synopsis

/usr/platform/*platform-name*/sbin/cg14config [-d *device*]
  [-r *resolution*][-g *gammavalue*][-G *gammafile*][-u *degammavalue*]
  [-U *degammafile*]

Description

Use the cg14config command to set the state of the selected cgfourteen device. You
can find *platform-name* with the -i option of uname(1).

cg14config is supported only on Desktop SPARCsystems with the SX graphics
option.

The interface, output, and command location are uncommitted and subject to change
in future releases.

Options

-d *device*   Use *device* as the cgfourteen device to configure. Default is
                  /dev/fb.

-r *resolution*

                  Use *resolution* as the desired screen resolution. Resolution is
                  specified in terms of screen width and height (in pixels) and vertical
                  refresh (in HZ). The following resolutions are available.

                  1024x768@60
                  1024x768@66
                  1024x768@70
                  1152x900@66
                  1152x900@76
                  1280x1024@66
                  1280x1024@76
                  1600x1280@66
                  1920x1080@72

The default is the value read from the monitor sense codes. Note that some or all of the resolutions above may not be supported by any given monitor. If a programmed resolution is outside of the range of allowable values for a monitor, unpredictable results can occur, including damage to the monitor. Thus, you should be careful when programming the resolution. See *OpenBoot Command Reference* for a description of how to reset the console device to the default value if it becomes unusable from programming an unsupported resolution.

The -r option is not available when the window system is running.

-g *gammavalue* Load each entry of the gamma lookup table with entry^(1/*gammavalue*). The gamma lookup table has 256 entries. Default *gammavalue* is 2.2.

-G *filename* Initialize the gamma lookup table with the contents of *filename*. The format of *filename* is 256 triplets (red, green, blue) of nonnegative integers separated by newline characters. The integers must be in the range 0 to 1023.

-u *degammavalue*

Load each entry of the degamma lookup table with entry^(*degammavalue*). The degamma lookup table has 256 entries. Default *degammavalue* is 2.2.

-U *filename* Initialize the degamma lookup table with the contents of *filename*. The format of *filename* is 256 entries of nonnegative integers separated by newline characters. The integers must be in the range 0 to 255, inclusive.

Exit Status

cg14config returns 0 on success and one of the following positive integers on failure.

1	Selected device is not a cgfourteen device.
2	Requested action failed.
3	Unsupported resolution.
4	Gamma or degamma value out of range.

Files

/platform/*platform-name*/kernel/drv/cgfourteen

cgfourteen device driver.

Attributes

See attributes(5) for descriptions of the following attributes.

Attribute Type	Attribute Value
Availability	SUNWkvm

See Also

uname(1), init(1M), mmap(2), attributes(5)
Platform Notes: SPARCstation 10SX System Configuration Guide
OpenBoot Command Reference

---

chargefee — Shell Procedures for Accounting

Synopsis

/usr/lib/acct/chargefee *login-name number*

Description

See acctsh(1M).

---

check-hostname — Check if sendmail Can Determine the Fully Qualified Host Name

Synopsis

/usr/lib/mail/sh/check-hostname

Description

The check-hostname command is a migration aid for sendmail(1M). This command tries to determine the local host's fully qualified host name (FQHN) in a manner similar to sendmail(1M). If check-hostname can determine the FQHN of the local host, it reports success. Otherwise, check-hostname reports how to reconfigure the system so that the FQHN can be properly determined.

Examples

The following example shows that check-hostname cannot determine the fully qualified host name for the system paperbark.

```
paperbark% /usr/lib/mail/sh/check-hostname
hosts: Not found.
Hostname paperbark could not be fully qualified.
We recommend listing files first for hosts in /etc/nsswitch.conf
and then changing the /etc/hosts entry:

172.16.8.22 paperbark

to:

172.16.8.22 paperbark paperbark.pick.some.domain
paperbark%
```

Files

/etc/hosts   Host-name database.

/etc/nsswitch.conf

                  Configuration file for nameservice switch.

/etc/resolv.conf

                  Configuration file for name server routines.

Attributes

See attributes(5) for descriptions of the following attributes.

Attribute Type	Attribute Value
Availability	SUNWsndmu

See Also

sendmail(1M), hosts(4), attributes(5)

---

check-permissions — Check Permissions on Mail Rerouting Files

Synopsis

/usr/lib/mail/sh/check-permissions [*login*]

Description

The check-permissions command is a migration aid for sendmail(1M). Use it to check the /etc/mail/sendmail.cf file for all configured alias files and to check the alias files for :include: files. It also checks for certain .forward files. For each file that check-permissions checks, it verifies that none of the parent directories are group- or world-writeable. It reports on any directories that are overly permissive. Otherwise, it reports that no unsafe directories were found.

The command-line arguments determine which .forward files are checked. If you specify no argument, the current user's home directory is checked for the presence of a .forward file. If any arguments are given, they are assumed to be valid logins and the home directory of each one is checked.

If you specify the special argument ALL, the passwd entry in the /etc/nsswitch.conf file is checked, and all password entries that can be obtained through the switch file are checked. In large domains, this can be time-consuming.

Operands

login   Specify a valid user name that is used to check the home directory.

ALL   Check the home directory of all users.

Examples

The following example uses the check-permissions command on the system paperbark and it finds no unsafe directories.

```
paperbark% /usr/lib/mail/sh/check-permissions
No unsafe directories found.
paperbark%
```

Files

/etc/mail/sendmail.cf

Environment definitions for sendmail.

/etc/mail/aliases

ASCII mail aliases file.

Attributes

See attributes(5) for descriptions of the following attributes.

Attribute Type	Attribute Value
Availability	SUNWsndmu

See Also

getent(1M), sendmail(1M), aliases(4), attributes(5)

check — Script to Validate the Rules in a JumpStart rules File

Synopsis

cdrom-mnt-pt/sol_8_sparc/s0/Solaris_8/Tools/jumpstart_sample/check
    [-p install-dir-path][-r rulesfile]

Description

See install_scripts(1M).

chown — Change Owner

Synopsis

    /usr/ucb/chown [-f][-R] owner [group] filename...

Description

Use the chown command to change the owner of a file or files. The owner can be either a decimal user ID (UID) or a login name found in the password file. You can also specify an optional group, which can be either a decimal group ID (GID) or a group name found in the GID file.

Only superuser can change owner IDs.

Options

-f	Do not report errors.
-R	Recursively descend into directories, setting the ownership of all files in each directory encountered. When symbolic links are encountered, change their ownership but do not traverse them.

Examples

In the following example, even though winsor owns the file, she cannot change the ownership of the file named list. Superuser changes the owner to user ray.

```
paperbark% ls -l list
-rw-r--r--   1 winsor     staff          104 Oct  7 13:26 list
paperbark% /usr/ucb/chown ray list
chown: list: Not owner
paperbark% whoami
winsor
paperbark% su
# chown ray list
# ls -l list
-rw-r--r--   1 ray        staff          104 Oct  7 13:26 list
#
```

Files

    /etc/passwd   Password file.

Attributes

See attributes(5) for descriptions of the following attributes.

Attribute Type	Attribute Value
Availability	SUNWcsu

See Also

chgrp(1), chown(2), group(4), passwd(4), attributes(5)

chroot — Change Root Directory for a Command

Synopsis

/usr/sbin/chroot *newroot command*

Description

Use the chroot command to execute *command* relative to *newroot*. The meaning of any initial slashes (/) in the path names is changed to *newroot* for *command* and any of its child processes. On execution, the initial working directory is *newroot*.

Notice that redirecting the output of command to a file creates the file x relative to the original root of the command, not the new one.

chroot *newroot command* > x

The new root path name is always relative to the current root. Even if a chroot is currently in effect, the *newroot* argument is relative to the current root of the running process.

Only superuser can run this command.

Note — Exercise extreme caution when referencing device files in the new root file system.

References by routines such as ttyname(3C) to standard input, standard output, and standard error find that the device associated with the file descriptor is unknown after chroot is run.

Examples

The following example uses the chroot command to provide an easy way to extract tar files (see tar(1)) written with absolute file names to a different location. The present implementation of tar does not have a feature that enables you to restore a tar file created with an absolute path to a relative path. You can, however, trick tar into believing that a path that is not / is / by using the chroot command. The test.tar file for this example was made from /export/home/bill/temp.

```
castle% tar tvf test.tar
/export/home/bill/temp/file1
/export/home/bill/temp/file2
castle%
```

The following commands extract these files into /chroot/export/home/bill/temp.

Note — You need to put the tar command in /chroot; otherwise, the system won't be able to find it. Remember, you're changing the path to /. During this command, /usr/bin/tar is not a valid path.

```
# mkdir /chroot
# cp /usr/sbin/static/tar /chroot
# chroot /chroot tar xvf test.tar
#
```

The following procedure backs out a patch when booted from a CD-ROM.

Note — This procedure works only if the patch was installed without using the `installpatch -d` option. Otherwise, there will be no backout patch.

1. Print the `/etc/vfstab` file.
2. Halt the system.
3. At the `ok` prompt, type **boot cdrom -s** and press Return.
4. Mount all partitions that are needed for this patch. For example, for a kernel jumbo patch, you should mount the `/`, `/usr`, `/opt`, `/var`, and `/export` file systems. Use the printout of the `/etc/vfstab` file as a reference.

   ```
   # mount /dev/dsk/c0t3d0s0 /a
   # mount /dev/dsk/c0t3d0s4 /a/var
   # mount /dev/dsk/c0t3d0s3 /a/usr
   # mount /dev/dsk/c0ted0s5 /a/opt
   # mount /dev/dsk/c0t3d0s7 /a/export
   ```

   Some of the partitions might be part of the root (`/`) file system and do not need to be mounted manually. Again, refer to the `vfstab` file for a list of the file systems that you need to mount manually. If you didn't print the `vfstab` file, you can always just look in `/a/etc/vfstab`.

5. Type **chroot /a/var/sadm/patch/101945-32/backoutpatch 101945-32** and press Return to back out the old jumbo kernel patch.

Exit Status

The exit status of `chroot` is the return value of *command*.

Attributes

See `attributes(5)` for descriptions of the following attributes.

Attribute Type	Attribute Value
Availability	SUNWcsu

See Also

cd(1), tar(1), chroot(2), ttyname(3C), attributes(5)

ckpacct — Accounting Command to Periodically Check the Size of /var/adm/pacct

Synopsis
    /usr/lib/acct/ckpacct [blocks]

Description
    See acctsh(1M).

clear_locks — Clear Locks Held on Behalf of an NFS Client

Synopsis
    /usr/sbin/clear_locks [-s] hostname

Description
Use the clear_locks command to remove all file, record, and share locks created by *hostname* and held on the current host, regardless of which process created or owns the locks.

Only superuser can run this command.

Warning — Use this command to repair only the rare case of a client crashing and failing to clear held locks. If you clear locks held by an active client, applications can fail in an unexpected manner.

If you run clear_locks on the NFS server, it clears any type of file locks set by an NFS client on files that are local to this server and that are exported with NFS. You would most likely use clear_locks on a server if the client sets the locks and immediately panics or if something happens that permanently locks the files.

If you run clear_locks -s on a client system, it clears all locks held by the client on the NFS server that you specify with the *hostname* argument.

Options

    -s   Remove all locks created by the current system and held by the server
                    hostname.

Operands

    hostname   Name of host server.

Exit Status

0	Successful operation.
1	Not root.
2	Usage error.
3	Unable to contact server (RPC).

Attributes

See attributes(5) for descriptions of the following attributes.

Attribute Type	Attribute Value
Availability	SUNWcsu

See Also

fcntl(2), attributes(5)

New! clinfo — Display Cluster Information

Synopsis

/usr/sbin/clinfo [-nh]

Description

The clinfo command is new in the Solaris 8 release. Use it to display cluster configuration information about the node from which you execute the command.

Without arguments, clinfo returns an exit status of 0 if the node is configured and booted as part of a cluster. Otherwise, clinfo returns an exit status of 1.

Options

-h	Print the highest node number in the cluster configuration. This value is not necessarily the same as the number of nodes in the cluster because not all nodes need to be defined. For example, it is possible to have a cluster with two nodes numbered 1 and 5. In this case, the highest node number is 5, but only two nodes are defined in the cluster configuration.
-n	Print the number of the node from which you execute clinfo.

Exit Status

0	Successful completion.
1	An error occurred, usually because the node is not configured or is booted as part of a cluster.

Attributes

See `attributes`(5) for descriptions of the following attributes.

Attribute Type	**Attribute Value**
Availability	SUNWcsu

See Also

`attributes`(5)

---

closewtmp — Put a False Dead Process Record in the /var/adm/wtmpx File

Synopsis

`/usr/lib/acct/closewtmp`

Description

See `acct`(1M).

---

clri, dcopy — Clear Inode

Synopsis

```
/usr/sbin/clri [-F FSType][-V] special i-number
/usr/sbin/dcopy [-F FSType][-V] special i-number
```

Description

Use the `clri` command to clear a bad inode that `fsck` is unable to fix. `clri` writes zeros on the inodes with the decimal `i-number` on the file system stored on `special`. After `clri` is run, any blocks in the affected file show up as missing in an `fsck`(1M) of `special` and any data is lost. You cannot clear an inode on a mounted file system.

Read and write permission are required on the specified file system device. The inode becomes allocatable.

Note — The primary purpose of this command is to remove a file that, for some reason, appears in no directory. If you use clri to clear an inode that does appear in a directory, take care to track down the entry and remove it. Otherwise, when the inode is reallocated to some new file, the old entry still points to that file. At that point, removing the old entry destroys the new file. The new entry again points to an unallocated inode, so you are likely to repeat the whole cycle again.

---

dcopy is a symbolic link to clri.
This command may not be supported for all *FSTypes*.

Options

-F *FSType*   Specify the *FSType* on which to operate. You should either specify the FSType here or clri should be able to be determine it from /etc/vfstab by matching *special* with an entry in the table, or by consulting /etc/default/fs.

-V   Echo the complete command line but do not execute the command. clri generates the command line by using the specified options and adding to them information derived from /etc/vfstab. Use this option to verify and validate the command line.

Example

The following example uses the clri command to remove a file that cannot be deleted with the rm file1 command because of corruption.

```
# cd /data
# ls -li
total 16
      4 -rw-r--r--    1 root     other           0 Jan  7 15:53 file1
      3 drwx------    2 root     root         8192 Jan  3 10:41 lost+found
# cd /
# umount /data
# clri /dev/dsk/c0t3d0s6 4
clearing 4
#
```

Usage

See largefile(5) for the description of the behavior of clri and dcopy when encountering files greater than or equal to 2 Gbytes (2**31 bytes).

Files

/etc/default/fs

                Default local file system type.

/etc/vfstab   List of default parameters for each file system.

Attributes

See attributes(5) for descriptions of the following attributes.

Attribute Type	Attribute Value
Availability	SUNWcsu

See Also

fsck(1M), vfstab(4), attributes(5), largefile(5)

oomsat   Diff Server

Synopsis

/usr/sbin/in.comsat

Description

See in.comsat(1M).

consadm — Specify or Display Devices Used as Auxiliary   New! Console Devices

Synopsis

```
/usr/sbin/consadm
/usr/sbin/consadm [-a device...][-p]
/usr/sbin/consadm [-d device...][-p]
/usr/sbin/consadm [-p]
```

Description

The consadm command is new in the Solaris 8 release. Use it to specify the hardware device or devices to be used as auxiliary console devices or to display the current device. Only superuser can make or display auxiliary console device selections.

Auxiliary console devices receive copies of console messages and can be used as the console during single-user mode. In particular, they receive kernel messages and messages directed to /dev/sysmsg. On Solaris- or IA-based systems, you can also use them for interaction with the bootstrap.

Note — Auxiliary console devices are not usable for kadb or firmware I/O, do not receive panic messages, and do not receive output directed to /dev/console.

By default, specifying a display device to be used as an auxiliary console device selects that device for the time the system remains up. If you need the selection to persist across reboots, you can specify the -p option.

consadm runs a daemon in the background, monitoring auxiliary console devices. Any devices that are disconnected (hang up, lose carrier) are removed from the auxiliary console device list, though not from the persistent list. While auxiliary console devices may have been removed from the device list receiving copies of console messages, those messages always continue to be displayed by the default console device.

The daemon does not run if it finds there are no auxiliary devices configured to monitor. Likewise, after the last auxiliary console is removed, the daemon shuts itself down. Therefore, the daemon persists only as long as auxiliary console devices remain active.

Options

-a *device*   Add *device* to the list of auxiliary console devices. Specify *device* as the path name to the device or devices to be added to the auxiliary console device list.

-d *device*   Remove *device* from the list of auxiliary console devices. Specify *device* as the path name to the device or devices to be removed from the auxiliary console device list.

-p   Print the list of auxiliary consoles that are auxiliary across reboots. When invoked with the -a or -d options, tell the application to make the change persist across reboot.

Examples

The following example adds /dev/term/a to the list of devices that receive console messages.

```
# consadm -a /dev/term/a
```

The following example removes /dev/term/a from the list of devices that receive console messages and from the persistent list.

```
# consadm -d -p /dev/term/a
```

The following example prints the name or names of the devices currently selected as auxiliary console devices.

```
# consadm
```

Environment Variables

See environ(5) for descriptions of the following environment variables that affect the execution of consadm: LC_CTYPE, LC_MESSAGES, and NLSPATH.

Exit Status

0   Successful completion.

>0   An error occurred.

Attributes

See attributes(5) for descriptions of the following attributes.

Attribute Type	Attribute Value
Availability	SUNWcsu
Stability level	Evolving

See Also

eeprom(1M), kadb(1M), syslogd(1M), attributes(5), environ(5), sysmsg(7d), console(7d)

---

conv_lp — Convert LP Configuration

Synopsis

/usr/lib/print/conv_lp [-d *dir*][-f *file*]

Description

When you install or upgrade the Solaris 8 release, existing printer configuration information is automatically converted. You can use the conv_lp command to convert the printer configuration information for a system running SunOS 5.5.1. The conv_lp command reads LP printer configuration information from a directory and converts it to an output file for use with print client software.

If you are not using a nameservice, you should create a master /etc/printers.conf file that includes the existing printers at your site. You can then copy the master file to all of the print clients.

Note — If you are using the NIS or NIS+ nameservice to configure printer information, do not use an /etc/printers.conf file on your print client. A print client looks first in the /etc/printers.conf file to locate a printer. However, the /etc/printers.conf file might conflict with printer information in the NIS or NIS+ maps with unexpected results. To avoid this problem, remove the /etc/printers.conf file on print clients that use NIS or NIS+ for printer information.

Options

-d *dir*	Specify the root (/) directory from which LP configuration information is read. The default is root (/).
-f *file*	Specify the output file to which conv_lp writes the converted LP configuration information. The default is /etc/printers.conf.

Examples

The following example converts LP configuration information from directory root (/) to the /etc/printers.conf file.

```
paperbark% /usr/lib/print/conv_lp
paperbark%
```

The following example converts LP configuration information from directory /export/root/client to file /export/root/client/etc/printers.conf.

```
paperbark% conv_lp -d /export/root/client -f
      /export/root/client/etc/printers.conf
```

Exit Status

0	Successful completion.
non-zero	An error occurred.

Files

/etc/printers.conf

System printer configuration database.

Attributes

See attributes(5) for descriptions of the following attributes.

Attribute Type	Attribute Value
Availability	SUNWpcu

See Also

lpset(1M), printers.conf(4), attributes(5)

conv_lpd — Convert LPD Configuration

Synopsis

/usr/lib/print/conv_lpd [-c printers | -c printcap][-n] *file*

Description

When you install or upgrade the Solaris 8 release, existing printer configuration information is automatically converted. You can use the conv_lpd command to convert the printer configuration information for a system running SunOS 4.1. The conv_lpd command converts LPD printer configuration information in a printcap configuration format to entries in an /etc/printers.conf file (see printers.conf(4)). Alternatively, if the printer configuration information is in `printers.conf` format, the `conv_lpd` command converts it to `printcap` format.

If you are not using a nameservice, you should create a master `/etc/printers.conf` file that includes the existing printers at your site. You can then copy the master file to all of the print clients.

> **Note** — If you are using the NIS or NIS+ nameservice to configure printer information, do not use an `/etc/printers.conf` file on your print client. A print client looks first in the `/etc/printers.conf` file to locate a printer. However, the `/etc/printers.conf` file might conflict with printer information in the NIS or NIS+ maps with unexpected results. To avoid this problem, remove the `/etc/printers.conf` file on print clients that use NIS or NIS+ for printer information.

Options

`-c printers | -c printcap`

Specify the type of output file produced by the conversion. `-c printers` converts to a `printers.conf` file. `-c printcap` converts to a `printcap` file. `-c printers` is the default.

`-n` Preserve the namelist during the conversion.

Operands

`file` The file to be converted.

Examples

The following example converts a `printcap` file to a `printers.conf` file.

First, copy a `printcap` file from a SunOS 4.1 system into the `/etc` directory of a system running the Solaris 8 release. Then, become superuser on the Solaris 8 system and issue the following command to convert the `printcap` file to the `printers.conf` format.

```
# /usr/lib/print/conv_lpd
#
```

The following example converts a `printcap` file to a `printers.conf` file and preserves the namelist.

```
# /usr/lib/print/conv_lpd -c printers -n /etc/printcap
```

The following example converts a `printers.conf` file to a `printcap` file and preserves the namelist.

```
# /usr/lib/print/conv_lpd -c printcap -n /etc/printers.conf

seachild:\
        :rm=seachild:\
        :rp=seachild:\
        :description=PostScript Printer:
_default:\
        :use=seachild:
#
```

Exit Status

0	Successful completion.
non-zero	An error occurred.

Files

/etc/printers.conf

System printer configuration database.

/etc/printcap

SunOS 4.x printer capability database.

Attributes

See attributes(5) for descriptions of the following attributes.

Attribute Type	**Attribute Value**
Availability	SUNWpcu

See Also

lpset(1M), printers.conf(4), attributes(5)

New! **coreadm** — Core File Administration

Synopsis

```
/bin/coreadm [-g pattern][-i pattern][-d option...][-e option...]
/bin/coreadm [-p pattern][pid...]
/bin/coreadm -u
```

Description

The coreadm command is new in the Solaris 8 release. It provides more flexible core file naming conventions and better core file retention than previous releases. Use coreadm to specify the name and location of core files produced by abnormally terminating processes. See core(4).

Only superuser can execute the first form shown in the synopsis to configure system-wide core-file options, including a global, core-file-name pattern and a per-process core-file-name pattern for the init(1M) process. All such settings are saved in the /etc/coreadm.conf coreadm configuration file for setting on reboot. See init(1M).

Nonprivileged users can execute the second form to specify the file-name pattern to be used by the operating system when generating a per-process core file.

Only superuser can execute the third form to update all system-wide core-file options based on the contents of /etc/coreadm.conf. Normally, this option is used only on reboot by the startup script /etc/init.d/coreadm.

A core-file-name pattern is a normal file-system path name with embedded variables, specified with a leading % character, that are expanded from values in effect when a core file is generated by the operating system. The following list describes these variables.

%p	Process ID.
%u	Effective user-ID.
%g	Effective group-ID.
%f	Executable file name.
%n	System node name (uname -n).
%m	Machine name (uname -m).
%t	Decimal value of time(2).
%%	Literal %.

For example, the following core-file-name pattern would result for command foo with process ID 1234 in the /var/core/core.foo.1234 core file.

```
/var/core/core.%f.%p
```

The coreadm command with no arguments reports the current system configuration, as shown in the following example.

```
paperbark% coreadm
     global core file pattern:
       init core file pattern: core
            global core dumps: disabled
       per-process core dumps: enabled
      global setid core dumps: disabled
 per-process setid core dumps: disabled
     global core dump logging: disabled
paperbark%
```

The coreadm command with only a list of process IDs reports each process's per-process core-file-name pattern, as shown in the following example.

```
# coreadm 278 5678
278: core.%f.%p
5678: /export/home/winsor/cores/%f.%p.%t
#
```

Only the owner of a process or the superuser can interrogate a process.

When a process is dumping core, the operating system generates two possible core files.

- A per-process core file that defaults to core and is enabled by default. If enabled, the per-process core-file path produces a core file when the process terminates abnormally. The per-process path is inherited by a new process from its parent process. When generated, a per-process core file is owned by the process with read/write permissions for the process. Only the owning process can view this file.
- A global core file that defaults to core and is disabled by default. If enabled, the global core-file path creates an additional core file with the same content as the per-process core file. The additional core file is produced by using the global

core-file path. When generated, a global core file is owned by superuser and is created with mode 600 under the credentials of the process. Nonprivileged users cannot view this file.

Based on the system options in effect, both files, one or the other, or no file is generated. When a process terminates abnormally, it produces a `core` file in the current directory as in previous Solaris releases. If the global core-file path is enabled and set to `/corefiles/core`, for example, then each process that expires produces two `core` files, one in the current working directory and one in the `/corefiles` directory.

By default, the Solaris Operating Environment core paths and core-file retention remain the same.

- A setuid process does not produce core files using either the global or per-process path.
- The global core-file path is disabled.
- The per-process core-file path is enabled.
- The per-process core-file path is set to `core`.

Enabling setuid Programs to Produce Core Files

You can use the `coreadm` command to enable or disable setuid programs to produce core files for all system processes or on a per-process basis by setting the following paths.

- A global core-file path enables all setuid programs on a system to produce core files.
- A per-process core-file path enables specific processes to produce core files.

By default, both flags are disabled. For security reasons, the global core-file path must be a full path name starting with a leading `/`. If superuser disables per-process core files, individual users cannot obtain core files.

Global core files are owned by superuser with read/write permissions for superuser only. Ordinary users cannot access them even if the process that produced the global core file was owned by an ordinary user.

A process that is or ever has been setuid or setgid since its last `exec(2)`, including a process that began life with superuser privileges and gave up that privilege by way of `setuid(2)`, presents security issues with respect to dumping core, because the process can contain sensitive information in its address space to which the current nonprivileged owner of the process should not have access. If setid core files are enabled, they are created mode 600 and are owned by superuser.

Options

`-d` *option*...	Disable the specified core-file option. See the `-e` option for descriptions of possible options. You can specify multiple `-e` and `-d` options on the command line. Only superuser can use this option.
`-e` *option*...	Enable the specified core-file option. Specify *option* as one of the following:

`global`	Allow core dumps using global core pattern.
`process`	Allow core dumps using per-process core pattern.
`global-setid`	Allow setid core dumps using global core pattern.
`proc-setid`	Allow setid core dumps using per-process core pattern.

log   Generate a syslog(3C) message when generation of
                   a global core file is attempted.

You can specify multiple -e and -d options on the command line. Only
superuser can use this option.

-g *pattern*   Set the global core-file-name pattern to *pattern*. The pattern must
                   start with a / and can contain any of the special % variables described
                   in "Description" on page 206. Only superuser can use this option.

-i *pattern*   Set the per-process core-file-name pattern for init(1M) to *pattern*.
                   This option is the same as coreadm -p pattern 1 except that the
                   setting persists across reboots. Only superuser can use this option.

-p *pattern*   Set the per-process core-file-name pattern to *pattern* for each of the
                   specified process-IDs. The pattern can contain any of the special %
                   variables and need not begin with /. If it does not begin with /, the file
                   is evaluated relative to the current directory in effect when the
                   process generates a core file.

                   A nonprivileged user can apply the -p option only to processes owned
                   by that user. The superuser can apply it to any process. The
                   per-process core-file-name pattern is inherited by future child
                   processes of the affected processes. See fork(2).

-u   Update system-wide core-file options from the contents of the
                   configuration file /etc/coreadm.conf. If the configuration file is
                   missing or contains invalid values, substitute default values.
                   Following the update, resynchronize the configuration file with the
                   system core-file configuration. Only superuser can use this option.

Operands

pid   Process ID.

Exit Status

0   Successful completion.

1   A fatal error occurred while either obtaining or modifying the system
                   core-file configuration.

2   Invalid command-line options were specified.

Examples

When executed from a user's $HOME/.profile or $HOME/.login, the following
command sets the core-file-name pattern for all processes run during the login session.

```
paperbark% coreadm -p core.$f.%p $$
```

$$ is the process ID of the currently running shell. The per-process core-file-name
pattern is inherited by all child processes.

The following example dumps all of the user's core dumps into the `corefiles` subdirectory of the home directory, discriminated by the system node name. This example is useful for users who use many different machines but have a shared home directory.

```
paperbark% coreadm -p $HOME/corefiles/%n.%f.%p $$
paperbark%
```

You can use the $$ symbols as an argument to `coreadm` to display the core-file settings of the current process, as shown in the following example.

```
paperbark% coreadm $$
507:    /export/home/winsor/corefiles/%n.%f.%p
paperbark%
```

The following example sets a per-process file-name pattern and saves this setting across a system reboot.

```
# coreadm -i $HOME/corefiles/%f.%p
#
```

The following example sets a global file-name pattern and saves this setting across a system reboot.

```
# coreadm -g /var/corefiles/%f.%p
#
```

Files

`/etc/init.d/coreadm`

> Startup script that restores the core file configuration that was in effect before reboot.

`/etc/coreadm.conf`

> ASCII file that stores the parameters for system core file configuration.

Attributes

See `attributes`(5) for descriptions of the following attributes.

Attribute Type	Attribute Value
Availability	SUNWcsu

See Also

`gcore(1)`, `init(1M)`, `exec(2)`, `fork(2)`, `setuid(2)`, `time(2)`, `syslog(3C)`, `core(4)`, `attributes(5)`

cpustat — Monitor System Behavior by Using CPU Performance Counters

New!

Synopsis

```
cpustat -c eventspec [-c eventspec]... [-ntD] [interval [count]]
cpustat -h
```

Description

The cpustat command is new in the Solaris 8 release. Use it to monitor the overall behavior of the CPUs in the system by using the CPU performance counters.

If you specify *interval*, cpustat samples activity every *interval* seconds, repeating forever. If you specify *count*, the statistics are repeated *count* times. If you specify neither operand, an interval of five seconds is used, and there is no limit to the number of samples that are taken.

Options

-c *eventspec*	Specify a set of events for the CPU performance counters to monitor. You can determine the syntax of these event specifications by using the -h option to generate the usage message. You can determine the semantics of these event specifications by reading the CPU manufacturer's documentation for the events. See cpc_strtoevent(3CPC) for a description of the syntax.
	You can specify multiple -c options, in which case the command cycles between the different event settings on each sample.
-D	Enable debug mode.
-h	Print an extensive help message on how to use the command and how to program the processor-dependent counters.
-n	Omit all header output (useful if cpustat is the beginning of a pipeline).
-t	Print an additional column of processor cycle counts, if available on the current architecture.

Usage

You can use the cputrack(1) command to monitor the behavior of individual applications with little or no interference from other activities on the system.

You must be superuser to run the cpustat command because there is an intrinsic conflict between the use of the CPU performance counters system-wide by cpustat and the use of the CPU performance counters to monitor an individual process (for example, by cputrack).

Once any instance of this command has started, no further per-process or per-LWP use of the counters is allowed until the last instance of the command terminates.

The times printed by the command correspond to the wall clock time when the hardware counters were actually sampled, instead of when the program told the kernel to sample them. The time is derived from the same timebase as gethrtime(3C).

The processor cycle counts enabled by the -t option always apply to both user and system modes, regardless of the settings applied to the performance counter registers.

The output of cpustat is designed to be readily parsable by nawk(1) and perl(1), thereby enabling you to compose performance tools by embedding cpustat in scripts. Alternatively, you can construct tools directly by using the same APIs on which cpustat is built, using the facilities of libcpc(3LIB). See cpc(3CPC).

The cpustat command monitors only the CPUs that are accessible to it in the current processor set. Thus, you can run several instances of the command on the CPUs in different processor sets. See psrset(1M) for more information about processor sets.

Because cpustat uses LWPs bound to CPUs, you may have to terminate the command before you can change the configuration of the relevant processor.

Warning — By running the cpustat command, superuser forcibly invalidates all existing performance counter contexts, which may, in turn, prematurely exit with unspecified errors for all invocations of the cputrack command and other users of performance counter contexts.

Examples

The following example shows the output of the cpustat command monitoring two events.

```
# cpustat -c pic0=1,pic1=1
    time cpu event      pic0      pic1
   5.009  0  tick    1227757   1227757
  10.009  0  tick    4426193   4426193
  15.009  0  tick    2070354   2070354
  20.009  0  tick    1054092   1054092
  25.009  0  tick    9372747   9372747
  30.009  0  tick   27303493  27303493
  35.009  0  tick    7987741   7987741
  40.009  0  tick    1597473   1597473
  45.009  0  tick    1273163   1273163
  50.009  0  tick    1166195   1166195
  55.009  0  tick    2104287   2104287
^C#
```

Attributes

See attributes(5) for descriptions of the following attributes.

Attribute Type	Attribute Value
Availability	SUNWcpcu
Interface stability	Evolving

See Also

cputrack(1), nawk(1), perl(1), iostat(1M), prstat(1M), psrset(1M), vmstat(1M), cpc(3CPC), cpc_strtoevent(3CPC), gethrtime(3C), libcpc(3LIB), attributes(5)

Sun Microelectronics UltraSPARC I & II User's Manual, January 1997, STP1031
http://www.sun.com/sparc
Intel Architecture Software Developer's Manual, Volume 3

System Programmers Guide, 243192
http://developer.intel.com

crash — Examine System Images

Synopsis
/usr/sbin/crash [-d *dumpfile*][-n *namelist*][-w *output-file*]

Description
Use the crash command to examine the system memory image of a running or a crashed system by formatting and printing control structures, tables, and other information.

Notes
The crash command may not be present in versions after the Solaris 8 release. The functionality of the crash command for examining system crash dumps is superseded by the new mdb(1) command. The crash command's interface was structured around implementation details, such as slots, that have no relation to the Solaris Operating Environment implementation. To enable transition, the Solaris 8 release contains documentation that explains the mdb syntax that is equivalent to each crash subcommand.

New!

You should examine kernel core dumps on the same platform on which they were created.

The kmausers and mblkusers commands require you to set KFM_AUDIT in kmem_flags. To do so, add the following line to the /etc/system file and then reboot the system.

set kmem_flags=1

kmem auditing is quite expensive in both memory consumption and CPU time because it records a complete stack trace for every allocation.

Options

-d *dumpfile* Specify *dumpfile* as the file containing the system memory image. The default *dumpfile* is /dev/mem. The system image can also be the path name of a dump file generated by the savecore(1M) command.

-n *namelist* Specify the text file *namelist*, which contains the symbol table information needed for symbolic access to the system memory image to be examined. The default *namelist* is /dev/ksyms. Note that it is recommended that you analyze crash dumps on a system having the same kernel architecture as the system from which the dump was taken.

-w output-file

> Specify the name of a file to receive the output from the session initiated by the crash command. The default *output-file* is the standard output.

Usage

Input during a crash session is of the following form.

function [argument...]

where *function* is one of the crash functions described in "Functions" on page 215 and *arguments* are qualifying data that indicate which items of the system image to print.
    The default for process-related items is the current process for a running system or the process that was running at the time of the crash for a crashed system. Similarly, the default for thread-related items is the current thread for a running system or the thread that was running at the time of the crash for a crash system. If the contents of a table are being dumped, the default is all active table entries.

Function Options

The following function options are available to crash functions wherever they are semantically valid. Valid function options are shown in "Functions" on page 215.

-e	Display every entry in a table.
-f	Display the full structure.
-p	Interpret all address arguments in the command line as physical addresses. If the addresses specified are not physical addresses, results are inconsistent.
-s *process*	Specify a process slot other than the default.
-w *filename*	Redirect the output of a function to *filename*.

You can pipe output from crash functions to another program in the following way.

function [argument...] ! shell-command

You cannot use the -w redirection option with this feature.
    Depending on the context of the function, numeric arguments are assumed to be in a specific radix. Counts are assumed to be decimal. Addresses are always hexadecimal. Table address arguments larger than the size of the function table are interpreted as hexadecimal addresses; those smaller are assumed to be decimal slots in the table. You can override default bases on all arguments. The C conventions for designating the bases of numbers are recognized. A number that is usually interpreted as decimal is interpreted as hexadecimal if it is preceded by 0x and as octal if it is preceded by 0. Decimal override is designated by 0d, and binary by 0b.
    Aliases for functions can be any uniquely identifiable initial substring of the function name. Traditional aliases of one letter, such as b for buffer, remain valid.
    Many functions accept different forms of entry for the same argument. Requests for table information accept a table entry number, a physical address, a virtual address, a symbol, a range, or an expression. You can specify a range of slot numbers in the form *a-b* where *a* and *b* are decimal numbers. An expression consists of two operands and an operator. An operand can be an address, a symbol, or a number; the operator can be +, -, *, /, &, or |. Precede an operand that is a number with a radix prefix if it is not a decimal

number (0 for octal, 0x for hexadecimal, 0b for binary). The expression must be enclosed in parentheses. Other functions accept any of these argument forms that are meaningful.

```
table-entry = slot number | address | symbol | range | expression
start-addr = address | symbol | expression
```

Functions

`? [-w filename]`

> List available functions.

`!command`   Escape to the shell and execute `command`.

`base [-w filename] number...`

> Print `number` in binary, octal, decimal, and hexadecimal. Precede a number in a radix other than decimal with a prefix that indicates its radix as follows: 0x, hexadecimal; 0, octal; and 0b, binary.

```
buffer [-w filename][-format] bufferslot
buffer [-w filename][-format][-p] start-addr
```

> Alias: b
>
> Print the contents of a buffer in the designated format. The following format designations are recognized: -b, byte; -c, character; -d, decimal; -x, hexadecimal; -o, octal; -i, inode. If you specify no format, use the previous format. The default format at the beginning of a crash session is hexadecimal.

`bufhdr [-f][-w filename][[-p] table-entry...]`

> Alias: buf
>
> Print system buffer headers.

`callout [-l][-w filename]`

> Alias: c
>
> Print the callout table. If you specify the -l option, also display the contents of the locks pertaining to the callout structure.

`class [-w filename][table-entry...]`

> Print information about process scheduler classes.

`help [-w filename] function...`

> Print a description of the named function, including syntax and aliases.

`kmalog [-w filename][slab | fail]`   *New!*

> Display events in a kernel memory allocator transaction log in time-reverse order with the most recent event displayed first. For each event, display the time relative to the most recent event in T-minus notation (for example, T-0.000151879), the *bufctl*, the

buffer address, the kmem cache name, and the stack trace at the time of the event.

Without arguments, display the kmem transaction log, which is present only if KMF_AUDIT is set in kmem_flags. See "Notes" on page 213 for information about how to set KMF_AUDIT in kmem_flags.

kmalog fail displays the allocation failure log, which is always present. This option can be useful in debugging drivers that don't cope correctly with allocation failure.

kmalog slab displays the slab create log, which is always present. This option can be useful in locating memory leaks.

kmastat [-w *filename*]

Print kernel memory allocator statistics.

kmausers [-e][-f][-w *filename*][*cachename...*]

Print the information about the medium and large users of the kernel memory allocator that have current memory allocations. The output consists of one entry for each unique stack trace, specifying the total amount of memory and number of allocations that were made with that stack trace.

This function is available only if the kernel has the KMF_AUDIT flag set in kmem_flags.

If you specify one or more cache names (for example, kmem_alloc_256), restrict the scan of memory usage to those caches. By default, include all caches.

If you specify the -e option, include the small users of the allocator. The small users are allocations that total less than 1024 bytes of memory or for which there are less than 10 allocations with the same stack trace.

If you use the -f option, print the stack traces for each individual allocation.

lck [-e][-w *filename*][[-p] *lock-addr...*]

Alias: l

Print record locking information. If you use the -e option or specify lock address arguments, print the record lock list. If you specify no arguments, print information on locks relative to UFS inodes.

mblk [-e][-f][-w *filename*][[-p] *table-entry...*]

Print allocated streams message block and data block headers.

mount [-f][-w *filename*][[-p] *table-entry...*]

Alias: m, vfs

Print information about mounted *filename* systems.

nm [-w *filename*] *symbol...*

Print value and type for the given symbol.

od [-p] [-w *filename*] [-*format*] [-*mode*] [s *process*] *start-addr* [*count*]

> Alias: rd

> Print *count* values starting at *start-addr* in one of the following formats: character (-c), decimal (-d), hexadecimal (-x), octal (-o), ASCII (-a), or hexadecimal/character (-h), and one of the following modes: long (-l), short (-t), or byte (-b). The default mode for character and ASCII formats is byte; the default mode for decimal, hexadecimal, and octal formats is long. The format -h prints both hexadecimal and character representations of the addresses dumped; you do not need to specify *mode*. When you omit *format* or *mode*, use the previous value. At the start of a crash session, the format is hexadecimal and the mode is long. If you enter no count, the default is 1.

proc [-e] [-f] [-l] [-w *filename*] [[p] [-a] *table-entry*... | #*procid*...]
proc [-e] [-f] [-l] [-w *filename*] [-r]

> Alias: p

> Print the process table. You can specify process table information in two ways. First, you can enter any mixture of table entries and process IDs. Precede each process ID with #. Alternatively, you can specify process table information for runnable processes with the runnable option -r. If you specify the -l option, also display all relevant locking information.

snode [-e] [-f] [-l] [-w *filename*] [[p] *table-entry*...]

> Print information about open special file names. If you specify the -l option, also display all relevant locking information.

strstat [-w *filename*]

> Print STREAMS statistics.

tsdptbl [-w *filename*] [*table-entry*...]

> Print the timesharing dispatcher parameter table. See ts_dptbl(4).

uinode [-d] [-e] [-f] [-l] [-r] [w *filename*] [[-p] *table-entry*...]

> Alias: ui

> Print the UFS inode table. The -d option lists the address and i-number of all UFS inodes in use and on the free list. If you specify the -l option, also display all relevant locking information. The -r option displays all free UFS inodes.

var [-w *filename*]

> Alias: v

> Print the tunable system parameters.

vfs [-e] [-w *filename*] [[-p] *address*...]

> Alias: m, mount

Print information about mounted *filename* systems.

vfssw [-f][-w *filename*][[-p] *table-entry*...]

Alias: fs

Print information about configured *filename* system types.

vnode [-w *filename*][-l][-p] *vnode-addr*...

Print information about vnodes.

vtop [-w *filename*][-s *process*] *start-addr*...

Print the physical address translation of the virtual address *start-addr*.

Examples

The following example uses the new kmalog function to display the slab create log.

```
# crash
dumpfile = /dev/mem, namelist = /dev/ksyms, outfile = stdout
> kmalog slab

T-0.000000000  bc=b6cc8  addr=70a00000  ufs_inode_cache
        kmem_slab_create+0x2e8
        kmem_cache_alloc+0x17c
        ufs_alloc_inode+0xc
        ufs_iget+0x1cc
        ufs_dirlook+0x414
        ufs_lookup+0x11c
        lookuppnvp+0x270
        lookuppn+0x11c
        lookupname+0x9c
        vn_open+0xec
        copen+0x84

T-9777.996850752  bc=b6d28  addr=70a02000  kmem_alloc_2048
        kmem_slab_create+0x2e8
        kmem_cache_alloc+0x17c
        kmem_alloc+0x30
        bio_getfreeblk+0x28
        getblk_common+0x2ac
        bread_common+0x80
        hs_findisovol+0x140
        hs_mountfs+0x140
        hsfs_mount+0x1e8
        domount+0x540
        mount+0xd8
        syscall_ap+0x6c
...(Additional lines deleted from this example)
> quit
#
```

Using crash or adb to its full potential requires a detailed knowledge of the kernel and is beyond the scope of this book. However, the following is a brief example.

```
paperbark% su
# /usr/sbin/crash
dumpfile = /dev/mem, namelist = /dev/ksyms, outfile = stdout
> status
system name:     SunOS
release:         5.8
node name:       paperbark
version:         Beta_Refresh
machine name:    sun4u
time of crash:   Wed Jan 19 15:57:41 2000
age of system:   6 min.
panicstr:
panic registers:
        pc: 0        sp: 0
> size buf proc queue
120
1832
124
> quit
#
```

Usage

See largefile(5) for the description of the behavior of crash when encountering files greater than or equal to 2 Gbytes (2**31 bytes).

Exit Status

0	Successful completion.
1	An error has occurred.

Files

/dev/mem	System image of currently running system.
/dev/ksyms	System namelist.

Attributes

See attributes(5) for descriptions of the following attributes.

Attribute Type	Attribute Value
Availability	SUNWcsu (32-bit)
	SUNWcsxu (64-bit)

See Also

adb(1), mdb(1), kadb(1M), savecore(1M), soconfig(1M), rt_dptbl(4), ts_dptbl(4), attributes(5), largefile(5)

cron — Clock Daemon

Synopsis

`/usr/sbin/cron`

Description

The `cron` (chronograph) command starts the `cron` system daemon that executes commands at specified dates and times. `cron` is started at system boot time through the `/etc/rc2.d/s75cron` run control script. The file `/etc/cron.d/FIFO` is used (among other things) as a lock file to prevent the execution of more than one instance of `cron`.

`cron` is not a user command and should never be executed directly. `cron` operations are scheduled and executed from `crontab` files in the directory `/var/spool/cron/crontabs`. Users can submit their own `crontab` file by using the `crontab(1)` command. Commands that are to be executed only once can be submitted with the `at(1)` command.

`cron` examines `crontab` or at command files only during its own process initialization phase and when the `crontab` or at command is run. This procedure reduces the overhead of checking for new or changed files at regularly scheduled intervals.

`cron` captures the output of the job's standard output and standard error streams, and, if it is not empty, mails the output to the user. If the job does not produce output, no mail is sent to the user (unless the job is an `at(1)` job and the `-m` option was specified when the job was submitted).

Setting cron Defaults

To keep a log of all actions taken by `cron`, `CRONLOG=YES` (by default) must be specified in the `/etc/default/cron` file. If `CRONLOG=NO` is specified, no logging is done. Keeping the log is a user configurable option because `cron` usually creates huge log files.

You can set the `PATH` for user `cron` jobs with `PATH=` in `/etc/default/cron`. You can set the `PATH` for root `cron` jobs with `SUPATH=` in `/etc/default/cron`. You should carefully consider the security implications of setting `PATH` and `SUPATH`.

The default `/etc/default/cron` file contains only the entry `CRONLOG=YES`. The following example of an `/etc/default/cron` file enables logging and sets the default `PATH` used by non-root jobs to `/usr/bin:/usr/ucb:`.

```
# more /etc/default/cron
CRONLOG=YES
PATH=/usr/bin:/usr/ucb:
#
```

Root jobs continue to use `/usr/sbin:/usr/bin`.

The `/etc/cron.d/logchecker` script is run by `cron` to check for log files that exceed the system `ulimit`. If found, the log file is moved to `/var/cron/olog`.

Files

/etc/cron.d   Main cron directory.

/etc/cron.d/FIFO

> Used as a lock file.

/etc/default/cron

> Contains cron default settings.

/var/cron/log cron

> History information.

/var/spool/cron

> Spool area.

/etc/cron.d/logchecker

> Moves log file to /var/cron/olog if log file exceeds system ulimit.

/etc/cron.d/queuedefs

> Queue description file for at, batch, and cron.

Attributes

See attributes(5) for descriptions of the following attributes.

Attribute Type	Attribute Value
Availability	SUNWcsu

See Also

at(1), crontab(1), sh(1), queuedefs(4), attributes(5)

Diagnostics

A history of all actions taken by cron is stored in /var/cron/log and (possibly) /var/cron/olog.

cvcd — Virtual Console Daemon

Description

The cvcd daemon is a server process that resides on an Enterprise 10000 domain. cvcd accepts connections from netcon_server on a System Service Processor (SSP) to create a Network Console Window on that SSP. The Network Console Window is able to read data from, and possibly send data to, the domain. This process takes place by way of the SSP netcon command. See netcon_server(1M) and netcon(1M) in the *Sun Enterprise 10000 SSP Reference Manual*.

When you execute the netcon command in an SSP Window, netcon_server connects with the cvcd daemon running on the domain specified in the SSP's SUNW_HOSTNAME environment variable and the window becomes a Host Console Window.

The console session ends when you exit the session, netcon_server terminates, or a network failure occurs. If cvcd dies, netcon automatically switches to the alternate communications path to send and receive console data. The alternate communications path is implemented as JTAG and communicates through the control board.

cvcd is normally started up at system boot time. Each domain supports only one cvcd process at a time.

Warning — cvcd uses the file /etc/ssphostname, one copy of which resides on each domain. If the SSP has been renamed, you must edit all /etc/ssphostname files to reflect that change.

Attributes

See attributes(5) for descriptions of the following attributes.

Attribute Type	Attribute Value
Architecture	Sun Enterprise 100000 servers only
Availability	SUNWcvc.u

See Also

services(4), attributes(5), cvc(7D), cvcredir(7D)

netcon(1M) and netcon_server(1M) in the *Sun Enterprise 10000 SSP Reference Manual*.

Sun Enterprise 10000 SSP User's Guide

D

dcopy — Clear Inode

Synopsis

    /usr/sbin/dcopy [-F FSType][-V] special i-number

Description

See clri(1M).

dd — Convert and Copy a File

Synopsis

    /usr/bin/dd if=input-file of=output-file [operand=value...]

Description

Use the dd command to copy and convert files. The main advantage of the dd command is that it quickly converts and copies files with different data formats, such as differences in block size or record length. The most common use of this command is to transfer a complete file system or partition from a hard disk to a tape. You can also use it to copy files from one disk to another.

223

dd copies the specified input file to the specified output with possible conversions. The standard input and output are used by default. You can specify the input and output block sizes to take advantage of raw physical I/O. Specify sizes in bytes; end a number with k, b, or w to specify multiplication by 1024, 512, or 2. Separate numbers with x to indicate multiplication.

dd reads the input one block at a time, using the specified input block size; it then processes the block of data actually returned, which could be smaller than the requested block size. dd applies any specified conversions and writes the resulting data to the output in blocks of the specified output block size.

cbs is used only if you specify ascii, asciib, unblock, ebcdic, ebcdicb, ibm, ibmb, or block conversion. In the first two cases, cbs characters are copied into the conversion buffer, any specified character mapping is done, trailing blanks are trimmed, and a newline is added before the line is sent to output. In the last three cases, characters up to newline are read into the conversion buffer, and blanks are added to make up an output record of size cbs. ASCII files are presumed to contain newline characters. If cbs is unspecified or 0, the ascii, asciib, ebcdic, ebcdicb, ibm, and ibmb options convert the character set without changing the input file's block structure; the unblock and block options become a simple file copy.

After completion, dd reports the number of whole and partial input and output blocks.

Notes

Do not use dd to copy files between file systems that have different block sizes.

Using a blocked device to copy a file adds extra nulls to the file to pad the final block to the block boundary.

When dd reads from a pipe, using the ibs=*X* and obs=*Y* operands, the output always is blocked in chunks of size *Y*. When bs=*Z* is used, the output blocks are whatever was available to be read from the pipe at the time.

When dd is used to copy files to a tape device, the file size must be a multiple of the device sector size (for example, 512 kilobytes). To copy files of arbitrary size to a tape device, use tar(1) or cpio(1).

For SIGINT, dd writes status information to standard error before exiting. It takes the standard action for all other signals.

Operands

if=*file*	Specify the input path; standard input is the default.
of=*file*	Specify the output path; standard output is the default. If you do not also specify the seek=*expr* conversion, truncate the output file before the copy begins unless you specify conv=*notrunc*. If you specify seek=*expr* but not conv=*notrunc*, the effect of the copy is to preserve the blocks in the output file over which dd seeks, but not to preserve any other portion of the output file. (If the size of the seek plus the size of the input file is less than the previous size of the output file, the output file is shortened by the copy.)
ibs=*n*	Specify the input block size in *n* bytes (default is 512).
obs=*n*	Specify the output block size in *n* bytes (default is 512).

`bs=n`	Set both input and output block sizes to `n` bytes, superseding `ibs=` and `obs=`. If you specify no conversion other than `sync`, `noerror`, or `notrunc`, copy each input block to the output as a single block without aggregating short blocks.
`cbs=n`	Specify the conversion block size for block and unblock in bytes by `n` (default is 0). If you omit `cbs=` or specify a value of 0, using `block` or `unblock` produces unspecified results.

Use this option only if you specify ASCII or EBCDIC conversion. For the `ascii` and `asciib` operands, handle the input as described for the `unblock` operand, except convert characters to ASCII before deleting the trailing space characters. For the `ebcdic`, `ebcdicb`, `ibm`, and `ibmb` operands, handle the input as described for the `block` operand, except convert the characters to EBCDIC or IBM EBCDIC after adding the trailing space characters.

`files=n`	Copy and concatenate `n` input files before terminating (makes sense only where input is a magnetic tape or similar device).
`skip=n`	Skip `n` input blocks (using the specified input block size) before starting to copy. On seekable files, the implementation reads the blocks or seeks past them; on nonseekable files, the blocks are read and the data is discarded.
`iseek=n`	Seek `n` blocks from beginning of input file before copying (appropriate for disk files, where `skip` can be incredibly slow).
`oseek=n`	Seek `n` blocks from beginning of output file before copying.
`seek=n`	Skip `n` blocks (using the specified output block size) from beginning of output file before copying. On nonseekable files, read existing blocks and space from the current end-of-file to the specified offset, if any, filled with null bytes; on seekable files, the implementation seeks to the specified offset or reads the blocks as described for nonseekable files.
`count=n`	Copy only `n` input blocks.

`conv=value[,value...]`

Where values are comma-separated symbols from the following list.

`ascii`	Convert EBCDIC to ASCII.
`asciib`	Convert EBCDIC to ASCII, using BSD-compatible character translations.
`ebcdic`	Convert ASCII to EBCDIC. If converting fixed-length ASCII records without newlines, you must first set up a pipeline with `dd conv=unblock`.
`ebcdicb`	Convert ASCII to EBCDIC, using BSD-compatible character translations. If converting fixed-length ASCII records without newlines, you must first set up a pipeline with `dd conv=unblock`.

ibm	Slightly different map of ASCII to EBCDIC. If converting fixed-length ASCII records without newlines, you must first set up a pipeline with dd conv=unblock.
ibmb	Slightly different map of ASCII to EBCDIC, using BSD-compatible character translations. If converting fixed-length ASCII records without newlines, you must first set up a pipeline with dd conv=unblock.

The ascii (or asciib), ebcdic (or ebcdicb), and ibm (or ibmb) values are mutually exclusive.

block	Treat the input as a sequence of newline-terminated or end-of-file-terminated variable-length records independent of the input block boundaries. Convert each record to a fixed length specified by the conversion block size. Remove any newline character from the input line. Append space characters to lines that are shorter than their conversion block size to fill the block. Truncate lines that are longer than the conversion block size to the largest number of characters that fit into that size. Report the number of truncated lines.
unblock	Convert fixed-length records to variable length. Read a number of bytes equal to the conversion block size (or the number of bytes remaining in the input; if less than the conversion block size), delete all trailing space characters and append a newline character.

The block and unblock values are mutually exclusive.

lcase	Map uppercase characters specified by the LC_CTYPE keyword tolower to the corresponding lowercase character. Do not modify characters for which no mapping is specified.
ucase	Map lowercase characters specified by the LC_CTYPE keyword toupper to the corresponding uppercase character. Do not modify characters for which no mapping is specified.

The lcase and ucase symbols are mutually exclusive.

swab	Swap every pair of input bytes. If the current input record is an odd number of bytes, ignore the last byte in the input record.
noerror	Do not stop processing on an input error. When an input error occurs, write a diagnostic message on standard error followed by the current input and output block counts in the same format as used at completion. If you specify the sync conversion, replace the missing input with null bytes and process normally; otherwise, omit the input block from the output.

notrunc   Do not truncate the output file. Preserve blocks in the
            output file not explicitly written by this invocation of dd.
            (See also the `of=file` operand.)

sync   Pad every input block to the size of the `ibs=` buffer,
            appending null bytes. (If you also specify either `block` or
            `unblock`, append space characters instead of null bytes.)

If you specify operands other than `conv=` more than once, the last specified
`operand=value` is used.

For the `bs=`, `cbs=`, `ibs=`, and `obs=` operands, the application must supply an
expression specifying a size in bytes. The expression, `expr`, can be in one of the following
forms.

- A positive decimal number.
- A positive decimal number followed by k, specifying multiplication by 1024.
- A positive decimal number followed by b, specifying multiplication by 512.
- Two or more positive decimal numbers (with or without k or b) separated by x,
  specifying the product of the indicated values.

All of the operands are processed before any input is read.

Usage

See `largefile`(5) for the description of the behavior of dd when encountering files
greater than or equal to 2 Gbytes (2**31 bytes).

Examples

The following example uses the dd command to duplicate tapes. This procedure requires
two tape drives, from tape drive 0 to tape drive 1, using a common, historical-device-
naming convention.

```
paperbark% dd if=/dev/rmt/0h of=/dev/rmt/1h
```

The following example strips the first 10 bytes from standard input.

```
paperbark% dd ibs=10 skip=1
```

The following example reads an EBCDIC tape blocked in ten 80-byte EBCDIC card
images per block into the ASCII file x.

```
paperbark% dd if=/dev/tape of=x ibs=800 cbs=80 conv=ascii,lcase
```

The following example uses `conv=sync` when writing to a tape.

```
paperbark% tar cvf - . | compress | dd obs=1024k of=/dev/rmt/0 conv=sync
```

The following example uses the dd command with `tar` to create an archive on a
remote tape drive by piping the output to a tape drive called `/dev/rmt0` on a remote
system named `castle`.

```
paperbark% tar cf - files | rsh castle dd of=/dev/rmt/0 obs=128
```

The following example reads a `tar` tape from a Silicon Graphics system. SGI swaps
every pair of bytes, making a `tar` tape otherwise unreadable on a Solaris system.

```
paperbark% dd if=/dev/nrst0 conv=swab | tar xvf -
```

Environment Variables

See environ(5) for descriptions of the following environment variables that affect the execution of dd: LC_CTYPE, LC_MESSAGES, and NLSPATH.

Exit Status

0   The input file was copied successfully.

>0   An error occurred.

If an input error is detected and you have not specified the noerror conversion, any partial output block is written to the output file, a diagnostic message is written, and the copy operation is discontinued. If some other error is detected, a diagnostic message is written and the copy operation is discontinued.

Attributes

See attributes(5) for descriptions of the following attributes.

Attribute Type	Attribute Value
Availability	SUNWcsu

See Also

cp(1), sed(1), tr(1), attributes(5), environ(5), largefile(5)

Diagnostics

f+p records in(out)

Numbers of full and partial blocks read (written).

deallocate — Device Deallocation

Synopsis

```
/usr/sbin/deallocate [-s] device
/usr/sbin/deallocate [-s][-F] device
/usr/sbin/deallocate [-s] -I
```

Description

Devices that a user allocates are not automatically deallocated when the process terminates or when the user logs out. Use the deallocate command to deallocate a device allocated to the invoking user. *device* can be a device defined in device_allocate(4) or one of the device special files associated with the device. deallocate resets the ownership and the permission on all device special files associated with device, disabling the user's access to that device. Superuser can use this command to remove access to the device by another user.

When deallocation or forced deallocation is performed, the appropriate device cleaning program is executed, based on the contents of device_allocate(4). These cleaning programs are normally stored in /etc/security/lib.

> **Note** — The functionality for the deallocate command is available only if the Basic Security Module (BSM) has been enabled. See bsmconv(1M) for more information.

Options

-s	Suppress any diagnostic output.
-F *device*	Force deallocation of the device associated with the file specified by *device*. Only superuser is permitted to use this option.
-I	Force deallocation of all allocatable devices. Only superuser is permitted to use this option. Use this option only at system initialization.

Operands

device	Deallocate the device associated with the device special file specified by *device*.

Examples

In the following example, superuser deallocates a tape drive that the user did not deallocate.

```
# deallocate -F /dev/rmt0
```

The following example forces deallocation of all allocatable devices. You should use this option only at system initialization.

```
# deallocate -I
```

Diagnostics

deallocate returns a non-zero exit status in the event of an error.

Files

/etc/security/device_allocate

Mandatory access control information about each physical device.

/etc/security/device_maps

Access control information about each physical device.

/etc/security/dev/*

Devices directory.

/etc/security/lib/*

Executable shell script directory.

Attributes

See attributes(5) for descriptions of the following attributes.

Attribute Type	Attribute Value
Availability	SUNWcsu

See Also

allocate(1M), bsmconv(1M), device_allocate(4), device_maps(4), attributes(5)

devattr — Display Device Attributes

Synopsis

/bin/devattr [-v] *device* [*attribute*...]

Description

Use the devattr command to display the values for a device's attributes. The display can be presented in two formats. Used without the -v option, only the attribute values are shown. Used with the -v option, the attributes are shown in an *attribute=value* format. When you specify no attributes on the command line, all attributes for the specified device are displayed in alphabetical order by attribute name. If you specify attributes on the command line, only those attributes are shown, displayed in command-line order.

Options

-v   Display attribute values in an *attribute=value* format.

Operands

device   Define the device whose attributes should be displayed. *device* can be the path name of the device or the device alias.

attribute   Define which attribute or attributes should be shown. Default is to show all attributes for a device. See the putdev(1M) manual page for a complete listing and description of available attributes.

Examples

The following example lists the attributes for disk c0t0d0s0.

```
paperbark% devattr /dev/dsk/c0t0d0s0
dpart100
/dev/dsk/c0t0d0s0
299440
/dev/rdsk/c0t0d0s0
```

```
Disk Partition
fs
ufs
/
false
dpart
paperbark%
```

The following example lists the attributes for the same disk as the previous example and uses the -v option to display the output in *attribute=value* format.

```
paperbark% devattr -v /dev/dsk/c0t0d0s0
alias='dpart100'
bdevice='/dev/dsk/c0t0d0s0'
capacity='299440'
cdevice='/dev/rdsk/c0t0d0s0'
desc='Disk Partition'
dparttype='fs'
fstype='ufs'
mountpt='/'
removable='false'
type='dpart'
paperbark%
```

Exit Status

0	Successful completion.
1	Command syntax was incorrect, invalid option was used, or an internal error occurred.
2	Device table could not be opened for reading.
3	Requested device could not be found in the device table.
4	Requested attribute was not defined for the specified device.

Files

/etc/device.tab

Attributes

See attributes(5) for descriptions of the following attributes.

Attribute Type	Attribute Value
Availability	SUNWcsu

See Also

getdev(1M), putdev(1M), attributes(5)

devconfig — Configure Device Attributes

Synopsis

```
/usr/sbin/devconfig
```

Description

Use the devconfig interactive editor on IA systems to edit device driver hardware configuration files and the OpenWindows configuration file.

Devices that are not self-identifying require correct information in the hardware configuration file so that the device can be recognized. devconfig eases the task of maintaining correct device information in the configuration files.

Prototype configuration information files stored in /usr/lib/devconfig check user input to ensure that the values provided for each attribute are of the correct type and fall within legal bounds. See device.cfinfo(4) for a description of the format of configuration information files. You can set the location for the cfinfo files with the devconfigHOME environment variable.

After changes are made to a hardware configuration file that has a driver associated with it, an attempt is made to reload the driver to verify the attributes. Some drivers may not be unloadable. In this case, you must initiate a system reboot before the new attributes can take effect. If necessary, devconfig also updates the OpenWindows configuration file, OWconfig (see the *OpenWindows Desktop Reference Manual*). devconfig makes a backup copy of a modified file in a .bak file. In addition, the first version of OWconfig is saved in OWconfig.save because the original version of OWconfig contains helpful prototype information that you may want to refer to in case you need to edit OWconfig manually.

If the default location for configuration files is not writeable (as is the case during installation) devconfig writes the updated files in the same location relative to the directory /tmp/root. No attempt is made to reload the driver in this case.

devconfig is controlled by a simple menu system. Use the Up/Down arrow keys to move the cursor to different items in a menu. Use the Left/Right arrow keys to move the cursor to different items in a field. Press Enter to select an item. (The Enter key may be labeled Return on some keyboards.) See the online help for more guidance.

Operation

devconfig first displays a list of configured devices in the system. Selecting a configured device enables you to view its attributes or unconfigure it.

> **Note** — You cannot use the devconfig command to add or unconfigure self-identifying devices, and self-identifying devices are not displayed in the list of devices.

When you add a new device, devconfig displays the supported device categories. After you choose a device category, devconfig displays the devices supported in that category. After you have selected the device to be added, devconfig displays the list of the device attributes. Once you have chosen the proper values for the attributes and applied them by using the Apply button, the device is added to the list of configured devices. You can cancel an operation by using the Cancel button.

Files

/kernel/drv/*.conf

        Hardware configuration files.

/usr/lib/devconfig/*.cfinfo

        Configuration information files.

/usr/openwin/server/etc/OWconfig

        Network OpenWindows configuration file.

/etc/openwin/server/etc/OWconfig

        Local OpenWindows configuration file.

Attributes

See attributes(5) for descriptions of the following attributes.

Attribute Type	Attribute Value
Architecture	IA
Availability	SUNWo86u

See Also

drvconfig(1M), prtconf(1M), device.cfinfo(4), attributes(5)
OpenWindows Desktop Reference Manual

---

devfree — Release Devices from Exclusive Use

Synopsis

/bin/devfree *key* [*device*...]

Description

Use the devfree command to release devices from exclusive use. You request exclusivity with the devreserv command.

When you invoke devfree with only the *key* argument, it releases all devices that have been reserved for that key. When called with *key* and *device* arguments, devfree releases the specified devices that have been reserved with that key.

Note — As of this writing, the devfree and devreserv commands do not work.

The commands devreserv and devfree manage the availability of devices on a system. These commands do not place any constraints on the access to the device. They serve only as a centralized bookkeeping point for those who want to use them. Processes that do not use `devreserv` can concurrently use a device with a process that has reserved that device.

Operands

`key`	Designate the unique key on which the device was reserved.
`device`	Define device that this command releases from exclusive use. `device` can be the path name of the device or the device alias.

Exit Status

0	Successful completion.
1	Command syntax was incorrect, an invalid option was used, or an internal error occurred.
2	Device table or device reservation table could not be opened for reading.
3	Reservation release could not be completely fulfilled because one or more of the devices was not reserved or was not reserved on the specified key.

Files

`/etc/device.tab`

        Device table.

`/etc/devlkfile`

        Device lock file.

Attributes

See `attributes`(5) for descriptions of the following attributes.

Attribute Type	Attribute Value
Availability	SUNWcsu

See Also

`devreserv`(1M), `attributes`(5)

devfsadm — Administration Command for /dev and /devices *New!*

Synopsis

```
/usr/sbin/devfsadm [-C] [-c device-class] [-i driver-name] [-n]
    [-r root-dir] [-s] [-t table-file] [-v]
/usr/lib/devfsadm/devfsadmd
```

Description

The `devfsadm` command is new in the Solaris 8 release. `devfsadm` maintains the /dev and /devices namespaces. Because the `devfsadm` daemon, `devfsadmd`(1M), automatically detects device configuration changes generated by any reconfiguration event, you do not need to run this command interactively.

The `devfsadm` command replaces the previous suite of `devfs` administration commands including `drvconfig`(1M)—which managed the physical device entries in the /devices directories—and the five link generators, `disks`(1M), `tapes`(1M), `ports`(1M), `audlinks`(1M), and `devlinks`(1M)—which managed the logical device entries in the /dev directory. These commands were not aware of hot-pluggable devices, nor were they flexible enough for devices with multiple instances. For compatibility, these commands are symbolic links to the `devfsadm` command.

The default operation is to try to load every driver in the system and attach to all possible device instances. `devfsadm` then creates device special files in /devices and logical links in /dev.

The `devfsadmd`(1M) daemon is started by the /etc/rc* scripts during system startup and handles both reconfiguration boot processing and /dev and /devices updating in response to dynamic reconfiguration event notifications from the kernel.

In addition to managing /dev and /devices, `devfsadm` also maintains the `path_to_inst`(4) database.

Note — This manual page documentation does not constitute an API. /etc/minor_perm, /etc/name_to_major, /etc/driver_classes, and /devices may not exist or may have different contents or interpretations in a future release. The existence of this notice does not imply that any other documentation that lacks this notice constitutes an API.

Options

`-c device-class`

        Restrict operations to devices of class *device-class*. The Solaris Operating Environment defines the following values for *device-class*: disk, tape, port, audio, and pseudo. You can use this option more than once to specify multiple device classes.

`-C`

        Invoke cleanup routines that are not normally invoked to remove dangling logical links. If you also specify `-c`, clean up only for the listed devices' classes.

`-i driver-name`

        Configure only the devices for the named driver, *driver-name*.

-n	Do not try to load drivers or add new nodes to the kernel device tree.
-r *root-dir*	Look for the /dev and /devices directory trees under *root-dir*, not directly under root (/). Make no other use or assumptions about *root-dir*.
-s	Suppress any changes to /dev or /devices. This option is useful with the -v option for debugging.
-t *table-file*	
	Read an alternate devlink.tab file. devfsadm normally reads /etc/devlink.tab.
-v	Print changes to /dev and /devices in verbose mode.

Exit Status

0	Successful completion.
1	An error occurred.

Files

/devices	Device nodes directory.
/dev	Logical symbolic links to /devices.
/usr/lib/devfsadm/devfsadmd	
	devfsadm daemon.
/etc/init.d/devfsadm	
	Daemon start/stop script.
/etc/rcS.d/S50devfsadm	
	Link to init.d script.
/etc/rc0.d/K83devfsadm	
	Link to init.d script.
/dev/.devfsadm_dev.lock	
	Update lock file.
/dev/.devfsadm_daemon.lock	
	Daemon lock file.

Attributes

See attributes(5) for descriptions of the following attributes.

Attribute Type	Attribute Value
Availability	SUNWcsu

See Also

add_drv(1M), devfseventd(1M), devlinks(1M), disks(1M), drvconfig(1M), modinfo(1M), modload(1M), modunload(1M), ports(1M), rev_drv(1M), tapes(1M), path_to_inst(4), attributes(5)

---

devfseventd — Kernel Event Notification Daemon for devfsadmd

New!

Synopsis

/usr/lib/devfsadm/devfseventd

Description

The devfseventd daemon is new in the Solaris 8 release. It provides kernel event notification services to the devfsadmd(1M) daemon.

    devfsadmd uses devfseventd to receive notifications when device nodes are added or removed from the kernel device tree or when a new version of path_to_inst(4) needs to be flushed to disk.

    The /etc/rcS.d/S50devfsadm script starts devfseventd.

Note — This manual page documentation does not constitute an API. devfseventd and /etc/path_to_inst may not exist or may have different contents or interpretations in a future release. The existence of this notice does not imply that any other documentation that lacks this notice constitutes an API.

Exit Status

0	Successful completion.
non-zero	An error occurred.

Files

/usr/lib/devfsadm/devfseventd

        devfsevent daemon.

/etc/init.d/devfsadm

        Daemon start and stop script.

/etc/rcS.d/S50devfsadm

        Link to init.d script.

/etc/rc0.d/K83devfsadm

        Link to init.d script.

/dev/.devfseventd_daemon.lock
> Update lock file.

Attributes

See attributes(5) for descriptions of the following attributes.

Attribute Type	Attribute Value
Availability	SUNWcsu

See Also

devfsadm(1M), devfsadmd(1M), path_to_inst(4), attributes(5)

---

devinfo — Print Device-Specific Information

Synopsis

/usr/sbin/devinfo -i *device*
/usr/sbin/devinfo -p *device*

Description

Use the devinfo command to print device-specific information about disk devices on standard output. Only superuser can use this command.

Options

-i   Print the following device information.

- Device name.
- Software version (not supported and prints as 0).
- Drive ID number (not supported and prints as 0).
- Device blocks per cylinder.
- Device bytes per block.
- Number of device partitions with a block size greater than 0.

-p   Print the following device partition information.

- Device name.
- Device major and minor numbers (in hexadecimal).
- Partition start block.
- Number of blocks allocated to the partition.

- Partition flag.
- Partition tag.

Various other commands use the devinfo command to obtain device-specific information for the making of file systems and determining partition information. If the device cannot be opened, an error message is reported.

Operands

device   Device name.

Examples

The following example uses the -i option to print information about /dev/rdsk/c0t0d0s0.

```
# devinfo -i /dev/rdsk/c0t0d0s0
/dev/rdsk/c0t0d0s0       0        0       1520     512      5
#
```

The following example uses the -p option to print information about the same disk.

```
# devinfo -p /dev/rdsk/c0t0d0s0
/dev/rdsk/c0t0d0s0      20        0        0      299440   0      2
#
```

Exit Status

0   Successful operation.

2   Operation failed.

Attributes

See attributes(5) for descriptions of the following attributes.

Attribute Type	Attribute Value
Availability	SUNWcsu

See Also

prtvtoc(1M), attributes(5)

devlinks — Add /dev Entries for Miscellaneous Devices and Pseudodevices

Synopsis

/usr/sbin/devlinks [-d] [-r rootdir] [-t table-file]

Description

New! The devfsadm(1M) command, new in the Solaris 8 release, is now the preferred command for administering /dev and /devices. The newfsadm command in the Solaris 8 release is a symbolic link to the devfsadm(1M) command. See devfsadm(1M).

devnm — Device Name

Synopsis

```
/usr/sbin/devnm name [name...]
```

Description

Use the devnm command to identify the special file associated with the mounted file system where the argument *name* resides. You can specify one or more *name* arguments.

Examples

The following example shows the special files for the mount points /usr and /export/home/winsor.

```
paperbark% devnm /usr /export/home/winsor
/dev/dsk/c0t0d0s6 /usr
/dev/dsk/c0t0d0s7 /export/home/winsor
paperbark%
```

Files

```
/dev/dsk/*
```

```
/etc/mnttab
```

Attributes

See attributes(5) for descriptions of the following attributes.

Attribute Type	Attribute Value
Availability	SUNWcsu

See Also

mnttab(4), attributes(5)

devreserv — Reserve Devices for Exclusive Use

Synopsis
```
/bin/devreserv [key [device-list...]]
```

Description
Use the devreserv command to reserve devices for exclusive use. When the device is no longer required, use devfree to release it.

devreserv reserves at most one device per device-list. Each list is searched in linear order until the first available device is found. If a device cannot be reserved from each list, the entire reservation fails.

When you invoke devreserv without arguments, it lists the devices that are currently reserved and shows to which key it was reserved. When you invoke devreserv with only the key argument, it lists the devices that are currently reserved to that key.

> **Note** — As of this writing, the devfree and devreserve commands do not work.
>
> The devreserv and devfree commands manage the availability of devices on a system. Their use is on a participatory basis, and they do not place any constraints on the actual access to the device. They serve as a centralized bookkeeping point for those who want to use them. Devices that have been reserved cannot be used by processes that use the device reservation functions until the reservation has been canceled. However, processes that do not use device reservation may use a device that has been reserved because such a process would not have checked for its reservation status.

Operands
key   Designate a unique key on which the device is reserved. The key must be a positive integer.

device-list   Define a list of devices that devreserv searches to find an available device. Format the list as a single argument to the shell.

Examples
The following example reserves a diskette and a cartridge tape.
```
$ key=$$
$ echo "The current Process ID is equal to: $key"
The Current Process ID is equal to: 10658
$ devreserv $key diskette1 ctape1
```

The following example lists all devices currently reserved.
```
$ devreserv
disk1      2423
diskette1   10658
```

```
ctape1     10658
$
```

The following example lists all devices currently reserved to a particular key.

```
$ devreserv $key
diskette1
ctape1
$
```

Exit Status

0	Successful completion.
1	Command syntax was incorrect, an invalid option was used, or an internal error occurred.
2	Device table or device reservation table could not be opened for reading.
3	Device reservation request could not be fulfilled.

Files

/etc/device.tab

Device table.

/etc/devlkfile

Device lock file.

Attributes

See attributes(5) for descriptions of the following attributes.

Attribute Type	Attribute Value
Availability	SUNWcsu

See Also

devfree(1M), attributes(5)

df — Display Number of Free Disk Blocks and Files

Synopsis

```
/usr/bin/df [-F FSType] [-abegklntV] [-o FSTypespecific-options]
    [block-device | directory | file | resource...]
/usr/xpg4/bin/df [-F FSType] [-abegklnPtV] [-o FSType-specific-options]
    [block-device | directory | file | resource...]
```

Description

Use the df command to display the amount of disk space occupied by mounted or unmounted file systems, the amount of used available space, and the amount of the file system's total capacity that has been used. Specify file system by device or by referring to a file or directory on the specified file system.

Used without operands or options, df reports on all mounted file systems.

Note — df may not be supported for all FSTypes.

If you run df on a networked mount point that the automounter has not yet mounted, the file system size is reported as zero. As soon as the automounter mounts the file system, the sizes are reported correctly.

Note — If UFS logging is enabled on a file system, the disk space used for the log is reflected in the df report. The log is allocated from free blocks on the file system, and it is sized approximately as 1 Mbyte per 1 Gbyte of file system, up to a maximum of 64 Mbytes.

Options

-a	Report on all file systems including ones whose entries in /etc/mnttab (see mnttab(4)) have the ignore option set.
-b	Print the total number of kilobytes free.
-e	Print only the number of files free.
-F FSType	Specify the FSType on which to operate. The -F option is intended for use with unmounted file systems. Specify the FSType here, or df should be able to determine it from /etc/vfstab (see vfstab(4)) by matching the directory, block-device, or resource with an entry in the table, or by consulting /etc/default/fs. See default_fs(4).
-g	Print the entire statvfs(2) structure. Use this option only for mounted file systems. You cannot use it with the -o option. This option overrides the -b, -e, -k, -n, -P, and -t options.
-k	Print the allocation in kilobytes as one line of information for each specified file system. This information includes the file-system name, the total space allocated in the file system, the amount of space allocated to existing files, the total amount of space available for the creation of new files by unprivileged users, and the percentage of normally available space that is currently allocated to all files on the file system. This option overrides the -b, -e, -n, and -t options.
-l	Report on local file systems only. Use this option only for mounted file systems. You cannot use it with the -o option.
-n	Print only the FSType name. Invoked with no operands, print a list of mounted file-system types. Use this option only for mounted file systems. You cannot use it with the -o option.

-o *FSType-specific-options*

Specify *FSType-specific-options* as a comma-separated list with no intervening spaces. See the manual page for the FSType-specific command for details.

-P   Same as -k except print the allocation in 512-byte units. (/usr/xpg4/bin/df only.)

-t   Print full listings with totals. This option overrides the -b, -e, and -n options.

-V   Echo the complete set of file-system-specific command lines, but do not execute them. Generate the command line by using the specified options and operands and adding to them information derived from /etc/mnttab, /etc/vfstab, or /etc/default/fs. You can use this option to verify and validate the command line.

Operands

df interprets operands according to the following precedence: *block-device*, *directory*, *file*.

block-device A block special device (for example, /dev/dsk/c1d0s7); the corresponding file system need not be mounted.

directory   A valid directory name. df reports on the file system that contains directory.

file   A valid file name. df reports on the file system that contains file.

resource   An NFS resource name.

Usage

See largefile(5) for the description of the behavior of df when encountering files greater than or equal to 2 Gbytes (2**31 bytes).

Examples

The following example writes portable information about the /usr file system.

```
paperbark% /usr/xpg4/bin/df -P /usr
Filesystem            512-blocks      Used    Available Capacity
    Mounted on
/dev/dsk/c0t0d0s6      2113486       1437708     548970    73%    /usr
paperbark%
```

The following example writes portable information about the /usr file system when /usr/src is part of the /usr file system.

```
paperbark% /usr/xpg4/bin/df -P /usr/src
Filesystem            512-blocks      Used    Available Capacity
    Mounted on
/dev/dsk/c0t0d0s6      2113486       1437708     548970    73%    /usr
paperbark%
```

The following example displays inode usage on all UFS file systems.

```
paperbark% /usr/xpg4/bin/df -F ufs -o i
Filesystem           iused    ifree   %iused   Mounted on
/dev/dsk/c0t0d0s0      6838    67210     9%     /
/dev/dsk/c0t0d0s6     33044   231916    12%     /usr
/dev/dsk/c0t0d0s7      2756   321916     1%     /export/home
paperbark%
```

Environment Variables

SYSV3   Override the default behavior of df and provide compatibility with
               INTERACTIVE UNIX System and SCO UNIX installation scripts.
               Because the SYSV3 variable is provided for compatibility only, you
               should not use it in new scripts. When set, any header that normally
               displays files now displays nodes.

See environ(5) for descriptions of the following environment variables that affect the
execution of df : LC_CTYPE, LC_MESSAGES, and NLSPATH.

Exit Status

0   Successful completion.

>0   An error occurred.

Files

/dev/dsk/*   Disk devices.

/etc/default/fs

               Default local file-system type. Default values can be set for the flags
               in /etc/default/fs. For example, LOCAL=ufs, where LOCAL is the
               default partition for a command if no FSType is specified.

/etc/mnttab   Mount table.

/etc/vfstab   List of default parameters for each file system.

Attributes

See attributes(5) for descriptions of the following attributes.

/usr/bin/df

Attribute Type	Attribute Value
Availability	SUNWcsu

/usr/xpg4/bin/df

Attribute Type	Attribute Value
Availability	SUNWxcu4

See Also

find(1), df_ufs(1M), mount(1M), statvfs(2), default_fs(4), mnttab(4), vfstab(4), attributes(5), environ(5), largefile(5), XPG4(5)

df_ufs — Report Free Disk Space on UFS File Systems

Synopsis

/bin/df -F ufs [*generic-options*][-o i][*directory* | *special*]

Description

Use the df command with the -F ufs option to display the amount of disk space occupied by UFS file systems, the amount of used and available space, and how much of the file system's total capacity has been used.

The amount of space reported as used and available is less than the amount of space in the file system because the system reserves a fraction of the space in the file system to allow its file-system allocation routines to work well. The amount reserved is typically about 10 percent; you can adjust this percentage with tunefs(1M). When all the space on the file system except for this reserve is in use, only superuser can allocate new files and data blocks to existing files. When the file system is overallocated in this way, df may report that the file system is more than 100 percent used.

If you specify neither *directory* nor *special*, df displays information for all mounted UFS file systems.

Note — df calculates its results differently for mounted and unmounted file systems. For unmounted systems, the numbers reflect the 10 percent reservation mentioned above; this reservation is not reflected in df output for mounted file systems. For this reason, the available space reported by the generic command may differ from the available space reported by this module.

Options

generic-options

        Specify options supported by the generic df command. See df(1M) for a description of these options.

-o i   Report the number of used and free inodes. You cannot use this option with *generic-options*.

Files

/etc/mnttab   List of file systems currently mounted.

Attributes

See attributes(5) for descriptions of the following attributes.

Attribute Type	Attribute Value
Availability	SUNWcsu, SUNWxcu4

See Also

df(1M), tunefs(1M), fs_ufs(4), mnttab(4), attributes(5)

dfmounts — Display Mounted Resource Information

Synopsis

/usr/sbin/dfmounts[-FFSType][-h][-ospecific-options][restriction...]

Description

Use the dfmounts command to show the local resources shared through a distributed file system FSType along with a list of clients that have the resource mounted. If you do not specify a restriction, dfmounts shows file systems that are currently shared on any NFS server. specific-options as well as the availability and semantics of restriction are specific to particular distributed file-system types.

If you enter dfmounts without arguments, all remote resources currently mounted on the local system are displayed, regardless of file-system type.

dfmounts Output

The output of dfmounts consists of an optional header line, which you can suppress with the -h option, followed by a list of lines containing white-space-separated fields. Each resource has the following fields.

resource server pathname clients...

resource	The resource name that must be given to the mount(1M) command.
server	The system from which the resource was mounted.
pathname	The path name that must be given to the share(1M) command.
clients	A comma-separated list of systems that have mounted the resource. Clients are listed in the form domain., domain.system, or system, depending on the file-system type.

A field value can be null. Each null field is indicated by a dash (-) unless the remainder of the fields on the line are also null; in that case, the dash may be omitted. Fields with white space are enclosed in quotation marks (" ").

Options

-F *FSType*   Specify file-system type. Default to the first entry in
/etc/dfs/fstypes. Note that nfs is currently the only valid *FSType*.

-h   Suppress header line in output.

-o *specific-options*

Specify options specific to the file system provided by the -F option.
Note that no options are currently supported.

Examples

The following example shows the resources that are shared from the system castle. In
this example, a cacheFS file system is shared to the client named paperbark.

```
# dfmounts
RESOURCE      SERVER PATHNAME                   CLIENTS
   -          castle /export/home/winsor/Docs paperbark
#
```

Files

/etc/dfs/fstypes

File system types.

Attributes

See attributes(5) for descriptions of the following attributes.

Attribute Type	Attribute Value
Availability	SUNWcsu

See Also

dfshares(1M), mount(1M), share(1M), unshare(1M), attributes(5)

dfmounts_nfs — Display Mounted NFS Resource Information

Synopsis

/usr/sbin/dfmounts [-F nfs][-h][*server...*]

Description

Use the dfmounts -F nfs command to show the local resources shared through NFS,
along with the list of clients that have mounted the resource. You can omit the -F option
if NFS is the only file-system type listed in the file /etc/dfs/fstypes.

dfmounts without options displays all remote resources mounted on the local system,
regardless of file-system type.

The output of dfmounts consists of an optional header line, which you can suppress with the -h option, followed by a list of lines containing white-space-separated fields. Each resource has the following fields.

```
resource server pathname clients...
```

resource	Does not apply to NFS. Printed as a dash (-).
server	The system from which the resource was mounted.
pathname	The path name that must be given to the share(1M) command.
clients	A comma-separated list of systems that have mounted the resource.

Options

-F nfs	Specify the nfs FSType.
-h	Suppress header line in output.

Operands

server	Display information about the resources mounted from each server, where *server* can be any system on the network. If you specify no server, assume the server is the local system.

Files

/etc/dfs/fstypes

List of the default file-system types for remote file systems.

Attributes

See attributes(5) for descriptions of the following attributes.

Attribute Type	Attribute Value
Availability	SUNWcsu

See Also

mount(1M), share(1M), unshare(1M), attributes(5)

dfshares — List Available Resources from Remote or Local Systems

Synopsis

/usr/sbin/dfshares [-F *FSType*] [-h] [-o *specific-options*] [*server...*]

Description

Use the dfshares command to display information about resources available to the host through a distributed file system of type *FSType*. *specific-options* as well as the semantics of server are specific to particular distributed file systems.

If you enter dfshares without arguments, all resources currently shared on the local system are displayed, regardless of file-system type.

The output of dfshares consists of an optional header line, which you can suppress with the -h option, followed by a list of lines containing white-space-separated fields. Each resource has the following fields.

resource server access transport

resource	The resource name that must be given to the mount(1M) command.
server	The name of the system that is making the resource available.
access	The access permissions granted to the client systems, either ro (for read-only) or rw (for read/write). If dfshares cannot determine access permissions, a dash (-) is displayed.
transport	The transport provider over which the resource is shared.

A field value can be null. Each null field is indicated by a dash (-) unless the remainder of the fields on the line are also null; in that case, you can omit the dash.

Options

-F *FSType*	Specify file-system type. Default is the first entry in /etc/dfs/fstypes.
-h	Suppress header line in output.
-o *specific-options*	
	Specify options specific to the file system provided by the -F option.

Examples

The following example uses the dfshares command without options to display all resources shared from the system named castle.

```
# dfshares
RESOURCE                                        SERVER ACCESS    TRANSPORT
     castle:/export/home/opt                    castle  -          -
     castle:/export/home/winsor/Docs            castle  -          -
#
```

Files

/etc/dfs/fstypes

List of the default file-system types for remote file systems.

Attributes

See attributes(5) for descriptions of the following attributes.

Attribute Type	Attribute Value
Availability	SUNWcsu

See Also

dfmounts(1M), mount(1M), share(1M), unshare(1M), attributes(5)

dfshares_nfs — List Available NF3 Resources from Remote Systems

Synopsis

/usr/sbin/dfshares [-F nfs][-h][server...]

Description

Use the dfshares command to display information about resources available to the host through NFS. You can omit the -F option if nfs is the first file-system type listed in the /etc/dfs/fstypes file.

The query may be restricted to the output of resources available from one or more servers.

dfshares without arguments displays all resources shared on the local system, regardless of file-system type.

Specifying *server* displays information about the resources shared by each server. *server* can be any system on the network. If you specify no server, then *server* is assumed to be the local system.

The output of dfshares consists of an optional header line, which you can suppress with the -h option, followed by a list of lines containing white-space-separated fields. Each resource has the following fields.

resource server access transport

resource	The resource name that must be given to the mount(1M) command.
server	The name of the system that is making the resource available.
access	The access permissions granted to the client systems; however, dfshares cannot determine this information for an NFS resource and populates the field with a dash (-).
transport	The transport provider over which the resource is shared; however, dfshares cannot determine this information for an NFS resource and populates the field with a dash (-).

A field value can be null. Each null field is indicated by a dash (-) unless the remainder of the fields on the line are also null; in that case, you can omit the dash.

Options

`-F nfs`	Specify the NFS file-system type.
`-h`	Suppress header line in output.

Examples

The following example, issued from the system `castle`, displays NFS resources that are shared from the system `paperbark`.

```
# dfshares -F nfs paperbark
RESOURCE                                        SERVER ACCESS      TRANSPORT
 paperbark:/export/home/winsor/adminsuite    paperbark  -           -
 #
```

Files

`/etc/dfs/fstypes`

List of the default file-system types for remote file systems.

Attributes

See `attributes`(5) for descriptions of the following attributes.

Attribute Type	Attribute Value
Availability	`SUNWcsu`

See Also

`mount`(1M), `share`(1M), `unshare`(1M), `attributes`(5)

---

dhcpagent — Daemon for Client DHCP

Synopsis

`/sbin/dhcpagent [-a][-dn][-f][-v]`

Description

Dynamic Host Configuration Protocol (DHCP) is a standard developed to enable host systems in a TCI/IP network to be automatically configured for the network as they boot. The `dhcpagent` daemon implements the client half of DHCP for workstations with a local disk.

DHCP manages IP address assignments through leasing, which enables IP addresses to be reclaimed when not in use and reassigned to other clients. This process enables a site to use a smaller pool of IP addresses than would be needed if all clients were assigned a permanent address.

The `dhcpagent` daemon obtains configuration parameters for the client (local) system's network interfaces from a DHCP server. These parameters can include a lease on an IP address, which gives the client system use of the address for the period of the lease, which can be infinite. If the client wants to use the IP address for a period longer than the lease, it must negotiate an extension by using DHCP. For this reason, you must run dhcpagent as a daemon terminating only when the client powers down.

The dhcpagent daemon is controlled through ifconfig(1M) in much the same way that the init(1M) daemon is controlled by telinit(1M). You can invoke dhcpagent as a user process (requiring root privileges), but you do not need to do so because ifconfig(1M) starts it automatically.

When started, dhcpagent enters a passive state while awaiting instructions to be passed to it by ifconfig(1M). When it receives a command to configure an interface, it starts the DHCP protocol. Once DHCP is complete, dhcpagent can be queried for the values of the various network parameters. In addition, if DHCP was used to obtain a lease on an address for an interface, the interface is configured and brought up. When a lease is obtained, it is automatically renewed as necessary. If the lease cannot be renewed, dhcpagent takes the interface down at the end of the lease. If the configured interface has a different IP address, subnet mask, or broadcast address from those obtained from DHCP, the interface is abandoned from DHCP control.

In addition, to DHCP, you can configure dhcpagent to support BOOTP. See RFC 951, *Bootstrap Protocol*. Configuration parameters obtained from a BOOTP server are treated identically to those received from a DHCP server except that the IP address received from a BOOTP server always has an indefinite lease.

The DHCP protocol also acts as a mechanism to configure other information needed by the client, such as name, domain, and addresses of routers. The agent does not directly configure the workstation with this information but instead acts as a database that can be interrogated by other programs, in particular, by dhcpinfo(1). This approach is more flexible; it may eventually allow third-party software access to the data through a published API, and it gives system administrators more control over client configuration by enabling editing of startup scripts to customize various aspects of the client and its software in a specific order.

On clients with a single interface, customizing startup scripts is quite straightforward. Clients with multiple interfaces may, however, present difficulties, as there exists the possibility that some information arriving on different interfaces may need to be merged, or indeed that the information may be inconsistent. Furthermore, the configuration of the interfaces is asynchronous, so requests may arrive while some or all of the interfaces are still unconfigured. The agent resolves these problems by permitting one interface, referred to as the primary, to be designated as special in that, in the absence of any other information, it is the only interface to be regarded as authoritative for global parameters. If a request for the value of the parameter is received and the parameter is not contained in the repository for the primary interface, the request fails. dhcpinfo(1) enables this behavior to be overridden by insisting that the global data sought be associated with a particular interface. (See dhcpinfo(1) for details.)

Messages

With the Solaris 8 release, handling of messages has been revised. Instead of the four categories: errors, warnings, log, and debug, dhcpagent now writes informational and error messages in the following five categories.

critical   Critical messages indicate severe conditions that prevent proper operation.

errors   Error messages are important; sometimes they report unrecoverable events because of resource exhaustion and other unexpected failure of system calls. Ignoring errors can lead to degraded functionality.

`warnings`   Warnings indicate less severe problems and, in most cases, describe unusual or incorrect datagrams received from servers or requests for services that cannot be provided.

`informational` Informational messages provide key pieces of information that can be useful for debugging a DHCP configuration. Informational messages are generally controlled with the -v option. However, certain critical pieces of information, such as the IP address obtained, are always provided.

`debug`   Debugging messages, which can be generated at two different levels, are chiefly useful to persons having access to source code. They can also be useful in debugging difficult DHCP configuration problems. Debugging messages are generated only when the -d option is used.

When you run `dhcpagent` without the -f option, all messages are sent to the system logger `syslog(3C)` at the appropriate matching priority and with a facility identifier `LOG_DAEMON`. When you run `dhcpagent` with the -f option, all messages are directed to standard error.

New!

Note — Configurations where more than one interface is attached to the same physical network are currently unsupported. This configuration precludes the use of virtual interfaces.

Options

New!

-a   Instruct the agent to take over control of the interface. This option is intended primarily for use in boot scripts. Use this option with diskless DHCP clients. For diskless DHCP, DHCP has already been performed on the network interface providing the operating system image before running `dhcpagent`.

-d*n*   Set debug level to *n*. If debug is turned on, also enable log messages.

-f   Run in the foreground instead of as a daemon process.

-v   Provide verbose debugging output.

Files

New!

`dhcpagent` files have been revised and expanded in the Solaris 8 release. The `interface.dhc` file has been renamed `if.dhc`, and the `/etc/default/dhcpagent` file contains default values for tunable parameters.

`/etc/dhcp/if.dhc`

Contains the configuration for the interface. The existence of this file does not imply that the configuration is correct, because the lease may have expired.

`/etc/default/dhcpagent`

Contains default values for tunable parameters. To qualify all values with the interface they apply to, prepend the interface name and a dot (`.`) to the interface parameter name. The parameters include the following.

RELEASE_ON_SIGTERM

Perform a RELEASE instead of a DROP on managed interfaces when the agent terminates.

OFFER_WAIT — Specify how long to wait between checking for valid offers after sending a DISCOVER.

ARP_WAIT — Specify how long to wait for clients to respond to an ARP request before concluding that the address in the ARP request is unused.

IGNORE_FAILED_ARP

Specify whether the agent should assume an address is available in the unlikely event that ARP cannot be performed on that address.

CLIENT_ID — Indicate the value to be used to uniquely identify the client to the server.

PARAM_REQUEST_LIST

Specify a list of comma-separated integer values of options for which the client would like values.

Attributes

See attributes(5) for descriptions of the following attributes.

Attribute Type	Attribute Value
Availability	SUNWcsr
Interface Stability	Evolving

See Also

dhcpinfo(1), ifconfig(1M), init(1M), syslog(3), attributes(5)

Croft, B. and Gilmore, J., RFC 951, *Bootstrap Protocol (BOOTP) Network Working Group*, September 1985.

Droms, R., *Dynamic Host Configuration Protocol*, RFC 2131, Bucknell University, March 1997.

New!

dhcpconfig — DHCP Service Configuration Command

Synopsis

/usr/sbin/dhcpconfig

Description

General Description

The dhcpconfig command is a Korn shell (ksh) front end to the DHCP table administration commands dhtadm(1M) and pntadm(1M). dhcpconfig enables and configures the DHCP server service on the system on which it is run. This command automatically gathers information from existing file systems to provide a useful initial configuration. Therefore, before running dhcpconfig, be sure that the files are correct.

   To make configuration changes after the initial configuration, you must make changes to the system files and rerun dhcpconfig to pick up the changes.

   dhcpconfig displays the following menu.

```
# dhcpconfig
***         DHCP Configuration         ***
Would you like to:
1)     Configure DHCP Service
2)     Configure BOOTP Relay Agent
3)     Unconfigure DHCP or Relay Service
4)     Exit
Choice:
```

After choosing one of the menu items at the Choice line, you are prompted to answer a series of questions concerning your choice, with recommended defaults. The menu choices are explained in more detail below.

1. Configure DHCP Service—Configure the DHCP service, including setting startup options, such as OFFER timeout, dhcptab rescan interval, and enabling BOOTP compatibility mode, as well as bootstrapping dhcptab configuration data and producing the appropriate dhcp network tables.

2. Configure BOOTP Relay Agent—In this mode, no DHCP service databases are required. You are prompted for a list of BOOTP or DHCP servers to which the relay agent is to forward BOOTP/DHCP requests.

3. Unconfigure DHCP or Relay Service—Restore the DHCP service to an uninitialized state. Use this option with extreme caution because it removes the DHCP tables for the BOOTP/DHCP service. Be especially careful if the resource type you are using is nisplus because other DHCP servers may be using this information.

Note — You can run dhcpconfig over and over again. Parameters are merged with existing parameters. Thus, you can use dhcpconfig to synchronize the dhcptab configuration table with the server machine's settings.

How DHCP Tables Are Bootstrapped

dhcpconfig scans various configuration files on a Solaris system for information it can use to populate the dhcptab configuration table. The following table lists the information and source used for this information.

Information	Source
Time zone	System date, time zone settings.
DNS parameters	nsswitch.conf, /etc/resolve.conf.
NIS parameters	System domainname, nsswitch.conf, NIS.
NIS+ parameters	System domainname, nsswitch.conf, NIS+.
Default router	System routing tables, user prompt.
Subnet mask	Network interface, netmasks table in nameservice.
Broadcast address	Network interface, user prompt.

> **Note** — If you have not set these parameters on the server, do so before running dhcpconfig. Otherwise, you need to rerun dhcpconfig to pick up any changes and merge them with your dhcptab configuration table.

Serving BOOTP Clients

If you want to configure the DHCP service to serve BOOTP clients, you need to add the appropriate DHCP daemon startup options, as well as allocate IP addresses for your BOOTP clients.

Run dhcpconfig and select menu choice 1) Configure DHCP Service. Descend into the DHCP server daemon option setup section, answering Yes when prompted for enabling BOOTP compatibility mode.

You next are prompted for whether or not you would like the DHCP server to automatically allocate BOOTP-only IP addresses. If you answer Yes, be sure to enter the Select Networks For BOOTP/DHCP Support section, and add additional IP addresses to the appropriate DHCP network tables. You later are asked whether you would like some (or all) of these addresses reserved for BOOTP clients. BOOTP IP addresses for automatic allocation are treated separately from DHCP addresses to prevent competition between BOOTP and DHCP clients for the same pool of addresses.

Attributes

See attributes(5) for descriptions of the following attributes.

Attribute Type	Attribute Value
Availability	SUNWdhcsu

See Also

dhcpmgr(1M), dhtadm(1M), in.dhcpd(1M), pntadm(1M), dhcp(4), dhcp_network(4), dhcptab(4), nsswitch.conf(4), resolv.conf(4), attributes(5)

New! dhcpmgr — Graphical Interface for Managing DHCP Services

Synopsis

/usr/sadm/admin/bin/dhcpmgr

Description

The dhcpmgr command is new in the Solaris 8 release. dhcpmgr is a graphical user interface that enables you to manage the DHCP service on the local system. It performs the functions of the dhcpconfig, dhtadm, and pntadm commands. You must be root to use dhcpmgr. The dhcpmgr help, available from the Help menu, contains detailed information about using the tool.

Usage

You can perform the following tasks using dhcpmgr.

Configure DHCP service

Configure the system as a DHCP server.

Configure BOOTP relay service

Configure the system as a BOOTP relay.

Manage DHCP or BOOTP relay service

Start, stop, enable, disable, or unconfigure the DHCP or BOOTP relay service, or change its execution options.

Manage DHCP addresses

Add, modify, or delete IP addresses leased by the DHCP service.

Manage DHCP macros

Add, modify, or delete macros used to supply configuration parameters to DHCP clients.

Manage DHCP options

Add, modify, or delete options used to define parameters deliverable through DHCP.

Examples

When you type /usr/sadm/admin/bin/dhtadm&, the following window is displayed.

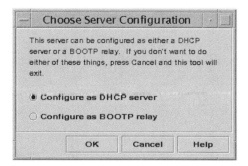

When you choose your server configuration and click on the OK button, the DHCP Configuration Wizard window is displayed.

Click on the arrow buttons at the bottom of the window to choose the step you want to perform. To enter information into one of the text fields, double-click in the text field, type the text, and then press Enter.

The Review step displays the following window containing review information.

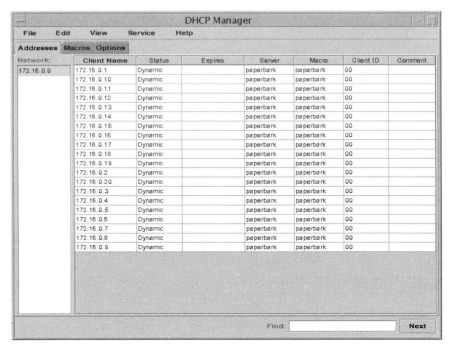

You can view IP addresses, Macros, and Options by clicking on the appropriate tab.

Exit Status

0	Successful completion.

Attributes

See attributes(5) for descriptions of the following attributes.

Attribute Type	Attribute Value
Availability	SUNWdhcm

See Also

dhcpconfig(1M), dhtadm(1M), in.dhcpd(1M), pntadm(1M), dhcp-network(4),
dhcptab(4), attributes(5)

TCP/IP and Data Communications Administration Guide

dhtadm — DHCP Configuration Table Management Command

Synopsis

```
/usr/sbin/dhtadm -C [-r resource] [-p path]
/usr/sbin/dhtadm -A -s symbol-name -d definition [-r resource] [-p path]
/usr/sbin/dhtadm -A -m macro-name -d definition [-r resource] [-p path]
/usr/sbin/dhtadm -M -s symbol-name -d definition [-r resource] [-p path]
/usr/sbin/dhtadm -M -m macro-name -n new-name [-r resource] [-p path]
/usr/sbin/dhtadm -M -s symbol-name -d definition [-r resource] [-p path]
/usr/sbin/dhtadm -M -m macro-name -d definition [-r resource] [-p path]
/usr/sbin/dhtadm -M -m macro-name -e symbol=value [-r resource] [-p v]
/usr/sbin/dhtadm -D -s symbol-name [-r resource] [-p path]
/usr/sbin/dhtadm -D -m macro-name [-r resource] [-p path]
/usr/sbin/dhtadm -P [-r resource] [-p path]
/usr/sbin/dhtadm -R [-r resource] [-p path]
```

Description

Use the dhtadm command to manage the DHCP service configuration table, dhcptab. For a description of the table format, see dhcptab(4). You must specify one of the -C, -A, -M, -D, or -R options.

Depending on the resource type (-r option), you must have the proper file permissions or NIS+ credentials.

Options

-A   Add a symbol or macro definition to the dhcptab table by specifying one of the following required suboptions.

        -d definition

                Specify a macro or symbol definition.

        -m macro-name

                Specify the name of the macro to be added.

        -s symbol-name

                Specify the name of the symbol to be added.

-C   Create the DHCP service configuration table, dhcptab.

-D   Delete a symbol or macro definition by using one of the following required suboptions.

        -m macro-name

                Specify a macro to delete.

        -s symbol-name

                Specify the name of the symbol to delete.

-M   Modify an existing symbol or macro definition by specifying one of the
                   following required suboptions.

    -d *definition*

        Specify a macro (-m) or symbol (-s) definition.

    -e *symbol=value*

        Edit a symbol/value pair within a macro. To add a
        symbol that does not have an associate value, enter

        symbol=NULL_VALUE_

        To delete a symbol definition from a macro, enter

        symbol=

    -m *macro-name*

        The -n, -d, or -e suboptions are legal companions for
        this macro.

    -n *new-name*   Specify a new macro name.

    -s *symbol-name*

        Specify a symbol. The -d suboption is a legal
        companion.

-p *path*   Override the /etc/default/dhcp configuration value for resource
                   path. The resource path for the files resource is an absolute UNIX
                   path name and a fully specified nisplus directory (including the
                   tailing period) for the NIS+ resource. See dhcp(4) for more details.

-P   Display the dhcptab table.

-r *resource*   Override the /etc/default/dhcp configuration value for *resource*
                   type. Currently supported resource types are files or nisplus. See
                   dhcp(4).

-R   Remove the dhcptab table.

Examples

The following example creates the DHCP service configuration table, dhcptab.

```
# dhtadm -C
```

The following example adds a Vendor option symbol definition for a new symbol
called MySym to the dhcptab table in the files resource in the /var/mydhcp directory.

```
# dhtadm -A -s MySym -d 'Vendor=SUNW.PCW.LAN,20,IP,1,0' -r files -p
    /var/mydhcp
```

The following command adds the aruba macro definition to the dhcptab table. Note
that symbol/value pairs are bracketed with colons (:).

```
# dhtadm -A -mv aruba -d ':Timeserv=10.0.0.10
    10.0.0.11:DNSserv=10.0.0.1:'
```

The following example modifies the Locale macro definition, setting the value of the UTCOffst symbol to 18000 seconds. Note that any macro definition that includes the definition of the Locale macro inherits this change.

```
# dhtadm -M -m Locale -e 'UTCOffst=18000'
```

The following example deletes the Timeserv symbol from the aruba macro. Note that any macro definition that includes the definition of the aruba macro inherits this change.

```
# dhtadm -M -m aruba -e 'Timeserv='
```

The following command adds the Hostname symbol to the aruba macro. Note that the Hostname symbol takes no value and thus requires the special value _NULL_VALUE_. Note also that any macro definition that includes the definition of the aruba macro inherits this change.

```
# dhtadm -M -m aruba -e 'Hostname=_NULL_VALUE_'
```

The following example renames the Locale macro to MyLocale. Note that any include statements in macro definitions that include the Locale macro also need to be changed.

```
# dhtadm -M -m Locale -n MyLocale
```

The following example deletes the MySym symbol definition. Note that any macro definitions that use MySym need to be modified.

```
# dhtadm -D -s MySym
```

The following example removes the dhcptab table in the nisplus directory specified.

```
# dhtadm -R -r nisplus -p Test.Nis.Plus.
```

Exit Status

0	Successful completion.
1	Object already exists.
2	Object does not exist.
3	Noncritical error.
4	Critical error.

Files

/var/dhcp/dhcptab

    File or NIS+ table.

/etc/default/dhcp

    DHCP service configuration file.

/etc/inet/hosts

    File or NIS+ table.

Attributes

See attributes(5) for descriptions of the following attributes.

Attribute Type	Attribute Value
Availability	SUNWdhcsu

See Also

New!

dhcpconfig(1M), dhcpmgr(1M), dhcp(4), dhcp_network(4), dhcptab(4), hosts(4), attributes(5)

Alexander, S., and R. Droms, *DHCP Options and BOOTP Vendor Extensions*, RFC 1533, Lachman Technology, Inc., Bucknell University, October 1993.

Droms, R., *Interoperation Between DHCP and BOOTP*, RFC 1534, Bucknell University, October 1993.

Droms, R., *Dynamic Host Configuration Protocol*, RFC 1541, Bucknell University, October 1993.

Wimer, W., *Clarifications and Extensions for the Bootstrap Protocol*, RFC 1542, Carnegie Mellon University, October 1993.

disks — Create /dev Entries for Hard Disks Attached to the System

Synopsis

/usr/sbin/disks [-C][-r *rootdir*]

Description

New!

The devfsadm(1M) command, new in the Solaris 8 release, is now the preferred command for administering /dev and /devices. The disks command in the Solaris 8 release is a symbolic link to the devfsadm(1M) command.

diskscan — Perform Surface Analysis

Synopsis

diskscan [-W][-n][-y] *raw-device*

Description

Use diskscan on IA systems to perform surface analysis on a portion of a hard disk. The disk portion can be a raw partition or slice identified by its raw device name. By default, the specified portion of the disk is read (nondestructive) and errors are reported on standard error. In addition, a progress report is printed on standard out. You should save the list of bad blocks in a file and later feed them into addbadsec(1M) to remap them.

> **Note** — The format(1M) command is available to format, label, analyze, and repair SCSI disks. This command is included with the diskscan, addbadsec(1M), fdisk(1M), and fmthard(1M) commands available for IA systems. To format an IDE disk, use the DOS format command; however, to label, analyze, or repair IDE disks on IA systems, use the Solaris format(1M) command.

Options

-n   Suppress linefeeds when printing progress information on standard out.

-W   Perform write and read surface analysis. This type of surface analysis is destructive and should be invoked with caution.

-y   Suppress the warning regarding destruction of existing data that is issued when you use the -W option.

Operands

raw-device   The address of the disk drive.

Files

The raw device should be /dev/rdsk/c?[t?]dv[ps]?. See disks(1M) for an explanation of SCSI and IDE device-naming conventions.

Attributes

See attributes(5) for descriptions of the following attributes.

Attribute Type	Attribute Value
Architecture	IA
Availability	SUNWcsu

See Also

addbadsec(1M), disks(1M), fdisk(1M), fmthard(1M), format(1M), attributes(5)

dispadmin — Process Scheduler Administration

Synopsis

```
/usr/sbin/dispadmin -l
/usr/sbin/dispadmin -c class -g [-r res]
/usr/sbin/dispadmin -c class -s file
```

Description

Use the dispadmin command to display or change process scheduler parameters while the system is running.

dispadmin does limited checking on the values supplied in file to verify that they are within their required bounds. The checking, however, does not try to analyze the effect that the new values have on the performance of the system. Inappropriate values can have a negative effect on system performance. (See *System Administration Guide, Volume I.*)

Options

-l   List the scheduler classes currently configured in the system.

-c class   Specify the class whose parameters are to be displayed or changed. Valid class values are RT for the real-time class, TS for the timesharing class, and IA for the interactive class. The timesharing and interactive classes share the same scheduler, so changes to the scheduling parameters of one change those of the other.

-g   Get the parameters for the specified class and write them to the standard output. Parameters for the real-time class are described in rt_dptbl(4). Parameters for the timesharing and interactive classes are described in ts_dptbl(4).

-r res   When using the -g option you can also use the -r option to specify a resolution to be used for outputting the time quantum values. If you specify no resolution, time quantum values are in milliseconds. res must be a positive integer between 1 and 1000000000 inclusive, and the resolution used is the reciprocal of res in seconds. For example, a res value of 10 yields time quantum values expressed in tenths of a second; a res value of 1000000 yields time quantum values expressed in microseconds. If the time quantum cannot be expressed as an integer in the specified resolution, it is rounded up to the next integral multiple of the specified resolution.

-s file   Set scheduler parameters for the specified class, using the values in file. These values overwrite the current values in memory, and they become the parameters that control scheduling of processes in the specified class. The values in file must be in the format output by the -g option. Moreover, the values must describe a table that is the same size (has same number of priority levels) as the table being overwritten. You must be superuser to use the -s option.

Note — The -g and -s options are mutually exclusive. You cannot retrieve the table at the same time you are overwriting it.

Examples

The following example lists the scheduler classes currently configured on the system paperbark.

```
paperbark% dispadmin -l
CONFIGURED CLASSES
==================

SYS      (System Class)
TS       (Time Sharing)
IA       (Interactive)
paperbark%
```

The following example retrieves the current scheduler parameters for the real-time class from kernel memory and writes them to the standard output. Time quantum values are in microseconds.

```
paperbark% dispadmin -c RT -g -r 100000
# Real Time Dispatcher Configuration
RES=100000

# TIME QUANTUM                          PRIORITY
# (rt_quantum)                           LEVEL
     100000                    #            0
     100000                    #            1
     100000                    #            2
     100000                    #            3
     100000                    #            4
     100000                    #            5
     100000                    #            6
     100000                    #            7
     100000                    #            8
     100000                    #            9
      80000                    #           10
      80000                    #           11
      80000                    #           12
... (Additional lines deleted from this example)
```

If you create a file named rt.config that contains scheduling parameters, the following example overwrites the current scheduler parameters for the real-time class with the values specified in rt.config.

```
# displadmin -c RT -s rt.config
#
```

The following example retrieves the current scheduler parameters for the time-sharing class from kernel memory and writes them to the standard output. Time quantum values are in nanoseconds.

```
# dispadmin -c TS -g -r 1000000000
# Time Sharing Dispatcher Configuration
```

```
RES=1000000000
```

# ts_quantum	ts_tqexp	ts_slpret	ts_maxwait	ts_lwait	PRIORITY	LEVEL
200000000	0	50	0	50	#	0
200000000	0	50	0	50	#	1
200000000	0	50	0	50	#	2
200000000	0	50	0	50	#	3
200000000	0	50	0	50	#	4
200000000	0	50	0	50	#	5
200000000	0	50	0	50	#	6
200000000	0	50	0	50	#	7
200000000	0	50	0	50	#	8
200000000	0	50	0	50	#	9
160000000	0	51	0	51	#	10
160000000	1	51	0	51	#	11
160000000	2	51	0	51	#	12

. . . (*Additional lines deleted from this example*)

If you create a file named ts.config that contains scheduling parameters for the timesharing class, the following example overwrites the current scheduler parameters for the timesharing class with the values specified in ts.config.

```
# dispadmin -c TS -s ts.config
#
```

Attributes

See attributes(5) for descriptions of the following attributes.

Attribute Type	Attribute Value
Availability	SUNWcsu

See Also

priocntl(1), priocntl(2), rt_dptbl(4), ts_dptbl(4), attributes(5)
System Administration Guide, Volume I, System Interface Guide

Diagnostics

dispadmin prints an appropriate diagnostic message if it fails to overwrite the current scheduler parameters because of permissions or a problem with the specified input file.

dmesg — Collect System Diagnostic Messages to Form Error Log

Synopsis

```
/usr/bin/dmesg [-]
/usr/sbin/dmesg [-]
```

Description

> **Note** — dmesg is made obsolete by syslogd(1M) for maintenance of the
> system error log.

dmesg looks in a system buffer for recently printed diagnostic messages and prints
them on the standard output. The messages are those printed or logged by the system
when errors occur. If you specify the – option, then dmesg computes (incrementally) the
new messages since the last time it was run and places these on the standard output.

Files

/var/adm/msgbuf

> Scratch file for memory of – option.

Attributes

See attributes(5) for descriptions of the following attributes.

Attribute Type	Attribute Value
Availability	SUNWesu (32-bit)
	SUNWesxu (64-bit)

See Also

syslogd(1M), attributes(5)

dmi_cmd — DMI Command-Line Interface Command

Synopsis

```
/usr/sbin/dmi_cmd -AL -c compId -g groupId [-dp][-a attrId]
   [-m max-count][-r req-mode][-s hostname]
/usr/sbin/dmi_cmd -CD -c compId [-s hostname]
/usr/sbin/dmi_cmd -CI mif-file [-s hostname]
/usr/sbin/dmi_cmd -CL [-dp][-c compId][-m max-count][-r req-mode]
   [-s hostname]
/usr/sbin/dmi_cmd -GD -c compId -g groupId [-s hostname]
/usr/sbin/dmi_cmd -GI schema-file -c compId [-s hostname]
/usr/sbin/dmi_cmd -GL -c compId -g groupId [-dp][-m max-count]
   [-r req-mode][-s hostname]
/usr/sbin/dmi_cmd -GM -c compId [-m max-count][-s hostname]
/usr/sbin/dmi_cmd -h
/usr/sbin/dmi_cmd -ND -c compId -l language-string [-s hostname]
/usr/sbin/dmi_cmd -NI schema-file -c compId [-s hostname]
/usr/sbin/dmi_cmd -NL -c compId [-s hostname]
/usr/sbin/dmi_cmd -V [-s hostname]
```

```
/usr/sbin/dmi_cmd -W config-file [-s hostname]
/usr/sbin/dmi_cmd -X [-s hostname]
```

Description

The Desktop Management Interface (DMI) is part of the Solstice Enterprise Agents (SEA), based on the new extensible agent technology or master/subagent technology. SEA is for component developers and system and network managers who want to develop custom Simple Network Management Protocol (SNMP) or DMI subagents to instrument different components, subsystems, and applications within a device to enable management from an SNMP management console.

The dmi_cmd command provides the following capabilities.

- Obtain version information about the DMI Service Provider.
- Set the configuration to describe the language required by the management application.
- Obtain configuration information describing the current language in use for the session.
- Install components into the database.
- List components in a system to determine what is installed.
- Delete an existing component from the database.
- Install group schemas to an existing component in the database.
- List class names for all groups in a component.
- List the groups within a component.
- Delete a group from a component.
- Install a language schema for an existing component in the database.
- List the set of language mappings installed for a specified component.
- Delete a specific language mapping for a component.
- List the properties for one or more attributes in a group

Options

-a attrId	Specify an attribute by its ID (positive integer). The default value is 0.
-AL	List the attributes for the specified component.
-c compId	Specify a component by its ID (positive integer). The default value is 0.
-CD	Delete the specified component.
-CI mif-file	Install the component described in mif-file.
-CL	List component information.
-d	Display descriptions.
-g groupId	Specify a group by its ID (positive integer). The default value is 0.
-GD	Delete a group for the specified component.
-GI schema-file	Install the group schema specified in schema-file.

-GL	List the groups for the specified component.
-GM	List the class names for the specified component.
-h	Print the command-line usage.
-l *language-string*	
	Specify a language mapping.
-m *max-count*	Specify the maximum number of components to display.
-ND	Delete a language mapping for the specified component.
-NI *schema-file*	
	Install the language schema specified in *schema-file*.
-NL	List the language mappings for a specified component.
-p	Display the pragma string.
-r *req-mode*	Specify the request mode. The valid values are shown below.

	1 DMI_UNIQUE	Access the specified item (or table row).
	2 DMI_FIRST	Access the first item.
	3 DMI_NEXT	Access the next item. The default request mode is 1 DMI_UNIQUE.

-s *hostname*	Specify the host system on which dmispd is running. The default host is the local host.
-V	Print version information about the DMI service provider.
-W *config-file*	
	Set the configuration specified in *config-file* to dmispd.
-X	Retrieve configuration information describing the current language in use.

Examples

The following example prints the version information about the DMI service provider.

```
# dmi_cmd -V
Connecting to dmispd on the localhost...

dmispd version: Dmi2.0
description:    This is a DMI2.0 based on ONC RPC

#
```

The following example lists the ID, name, storage, access mode, data type, and maximum size of all attributes in group 1 of component 1 in the dmispd running on local host by using default request mode (DMI_UNIQUE). No description is displayed and no limitation is set for max count.

```
# dmi_cmd -AL -g 1 -c 1
Connecting to dmispd on the localhost...

12 attrs listed for group 1 of comp 1
```

```
Attr Id:          1
Name:             Manufacturer
Storage:          MIF_COMMON
Access:           MIF_READ_ONLY
Type:             MIF_DISPLAYSTRING
maxSize:          64

Attr Id:          2
Name:             Product
Storage:          MIF_COMMON
Access:           MIF_READ_ONLY
Type:             MIF_DISPLAYSTRING
maxSize:          64

Attr Id:          3
Name:             Version
Storage:          MIF_COMMON
Access:           MIF_READ_ONLY
Type:             MIF_DISPLAYSTRING
maxSize:          64

Attr Id:          4
Name:             Serial Number
Storage:          MIF_SPECIFIC
Access:           MIF_READ_ONLY
Type:             MIF_DISPLAYSTRING
maxSize:          64

Attr Id:          5
Name:             Installation
Storage:          MIF_SPECIFIC
Access:           MIF_READ_ONLY
Type:             MIF_DATE
maxSize:          28

Attr Id:          6
Name:             Verify
Storage:          MIF_SPECIFIC
Access:           MIF_READ_ONLY
Type:             MIF_INTEGER
maxSize:          4

Attr Id:          7
Name:             ComponentId
Storage:          MIF_SPECIFIC
Access:           MIF_READ_ONLY
Type:             MIF_INTEGER
maxSize:          4

Attr Id:          8
Name:             ComponentName
Storage:          MIF_SPECIFIC
Access:           MIF_READ_ONLY
```

```
Type:             MIF_DISPLAYSTRING
maxSize:          256

Attr Id:          9
Name:             ComponentDesc
Storage:          MIF_SPECIFIC
Access:           MIF_READ_ONLY
Type:             MIF_DISPLAYSTRING
maxSize:          256

Attr Id:          10
Name:             GroupId
Storage:          MIF_SPECIFIC
Access:           MIF_READ_ONLY
Type:             MIF_INTEGER
maxSize:          4

Attr Id:          11
Name:             GroupName
Storage:          MIF_SPECIFIC
Access:           MIF_READ_ONLY
Type:             MIF_DISPLAYSTRING
maxSize:          256

Attr Id:          12
Name:             LanguageName
Storage:          MIF_SPECIFIC
Access:           MIF_READ_ONLY
Type:             MIF_DISPLAYSTRING
maxSize:          256

#
```

The following example uninstalls component 5 in dmispd running on the local host.

```
# dmi_cmd -CD -c 5
Connecting to dmispd on the localhost...
comp 5 is uninstalled.
#
```

The following example installs namedir.mif in dmispd running on the local host. The file namedir.mif is located in the directory specified in the configuration file.

```
# dmi_cmd -CI namedir.mif
Connecting to dmispd on the localhost...
"namedir.mif" is installed as comp 21.
#
```

The following example displays the version of dmispd running on the solaris8 server.

```
# dmi_cmd -s solaris8 -V

Connecting to dmispd on the localhost...
```

```
dmispd version:    Dmi2.0

description:       This is a DMI2.0 based on ONC RPC
#
```

Exit Status

0	Successful completion.
-1	An error occurred.

Attributes

See attributes(5) for descriptions of the following attributes.

Attribute Type	**Attribute Value**
Availability	SUNWsadmi

See Also

dmiget(1M), dmispd(1M), attributes(5)

dmiget — DMI Command-Line Retrieval Command

Synopsis

```
/usr/sbin/dmiget -c compId [-a attrId][-g groupId][-s hostname]
/usr/sbin/dmiget -h
```

Description

Use the dmiget command to retrieve the table information of a specific component in the DMI Service Provider.

Options

-a *attrId*	Display the attribute information for the component specified with the -c argument.
-c *compId*	Display all the table information for the specified component.
-g *groupId*	Display all the attribute information in the group specified with *groupId* for the component specified with the -c argument.
-h	Print the command-line usage.
-s *hostname*	Specify the host system on which dmispd is running. The default host is the local host.

Examples

The following example displays the table information in group 2 of component 3.

```
# dmiget -c 3 -g 2
Connecting to dmispd on the localhost...

For group 2 of component 3:
Id: 10,          10
Id: 20,          developer1
Id: 30,          SunSoft
Id: 40,          Solaris 2.6
Id: 10,          20
Id: 20,          developer2
Id: 30,          SunSoft
Id: 40,          Solaris 2.6
Id: 10,          30
Id: 20,          developer3
Id: 30,          SunSoft
Id: 40,          Solaris 2.6
#
```

The following example displays the table information for component 3.

```
# dmiget -c 3
Connecting to dmispd on the localhost...
For group 1 of component 3:
Id: 1,           SunSoft
Id: 2,           DMTF Demonstration
Id: 3,           Version 1.0
Id: 4,           1.00000
Id: 5,           1994 06 03 09 00 00
Id: 6,           0
Id: 7,           0
Id: 8,
Id: 9,
Id: 10,          0
Id: 11,
Id: 12,
#
```

The following example displays table information for group 42 of component 3.

```
# dmiget -c 3 -g 42
Id: 1,           Circus
Id: 2,           4.0a
Id: 1,           Disk Blaster
Id: 2,           2.0c
Id: 1,           Oleo
Id: 2,           3.0
Id: 1,           Presenter
Id: 2,           1.2
#
```

The following example displays the table information for attribute 20 in group 2 of component 3 on server snowbell.

```
# dmiget -c 3 -g 2 -a 20 -s snowbell
Connecting to dmispd on the snowbell...
For group 2 of component 3:
Id: 20,                    developer1
Id: 20,                    developer2
Id: 20,                    developer3
#
```

Exit Status

0   Successful completion.

-1   An error occurred.

Attributes

See attributes(5) for descriptions of the following attributes.

Attribute Type	**Attribute Value**
Availability	SUNWsadmi

See Also

dmi_cmd(1M), dmispd(1M), attributes(5)

dminfo — Report Information About a Device Entry in a Device Maps File

Synopsis

```
/usr/sbin/dminfo [-v][-a][-f pathname]
/usr/sbin/dminfo [-v][-a][-f pathname] -n dev-name...
/usr/sbin/dminfo [-v][-a][-f pathname] -d dev-path...
/usr/sbin/dminfo [-v][-a][-f pathname] -t dev-type...
/usr/sbin/dminfo [-v][-f pathname] -u dm -entry
```

Description

Use the dminfo command to report and update information about the device_maps(4) file.

Note — The dminfo functionality is available only if the Basic Security Module (BSM) has been enabled. See bsmconv(1M) for more information.

At the time this section was written, the dminfo command did not work. See Bug ID 4122379, Subject: dminfo doesn't work.

Options

`-v`	Print the requested entry or entries, one line per entry, on the standard output. If you specify no entries, print all.
`-a`	Succeed if any of the requested entries are found. If used with `-v`, print all entries that match the requested case(s).
`-f` *pathname*	Use a *device_maps* file with *pathname* instead of `/etc/security/device_maps`.
`-n` *dev-name*	Search `device_maps(4)` for a *device_name* field matching *dev-name*. You cannot use this option with `-d`, `-t`, or `-u`.
`-d` *dev-path*	Search `device_maps(4)` for a device special path name in the *device_list* field matching the *dev-path* argument. You cannot use this option with `-d`, `-t`, or `-u`.
`-t` *dev-type*	Search `device_maps(4)` for a *device_type* field matching the given *dev-type*. You cannot use this option with `-d`, `-n`, or `-u`.
`-u` *dm-entry*	Add entries to the `device_maps(4)` file. The *dm-entry* must be a complete `device_maps(4)` file entry. Specify the *dm-entry* with the same fields as in the `device_maps` file. Use colons (:) as a field separator and white space as the *device_list* subfield separators. If any fields are missing or if the *dm-entry* would be a duplicate, do not make the *dm-entry*. Only superuser can update the default device maps file.

Diagnostics

0	Success.
1	The request failed.
2	Incorrect syntax.

Files

`/etc/security/device_maps`

Access control information about each physical device.

Attributes

See `attributes(5)` for descriptions of the following attributes.

Attribute Type	Attribute Value
Availability	SUNWcsu

See Also

`bsmconv(1M)`, `device_maps(4)`, `attributes(5)`

dmispd — Sun Solstice Enterprise DMI Service Provider

Synopsis

    /usr/lib/dmi/dmispd [-h][-c config-dir][-d debuglevel]

Description

The DMI Service Provider, dmispd, is the core of the DMI solution. Management applications and component instrumentations communicate with each other through the Service Provider. The Service Provider coordinates and arbitrates requests from the management application to the specified component instrumentations. The Service Provider handles runtime management of the Component Interface (CI) and the Management Interface (MI), including component installation, registration at the MI and CI level, request serialization and synchronization, event handling for CI, and general flow control and housekeeping.

Options

    -c config-dir

Specify the full path of the directory containing the dmispd.conf configuration file. The default directory is /etc/dmi/conf.

    -d debug-level

Specify a debug level from 0 to 5. The default is 0, providing no debug information. If you omit this option, dmispd is run as a daemon process.

    -h   Print the command-line usage.

Exit Status

    0   Successful completion.
    1   An error occurred.

Files

    /etc/dmi/conf/dmispd.conf

DMI Service Provider configuration file.

Attributes

See attributes(5) for descriptions of the following attributes.

Attribute Type	Attribute Value
Availability	SUNWsadmi

See Also

snmpXdmid(1M), attributes(5)

---

dodisk — Shell Procedure Invoked by cron to Perform Disk Accounting Functions

Synopsis

/usr/lib/acct/dodisk [-o][*filename*...]

Description

See acctsh(1M).

---

domainname — Display or Set Name of the Current Domain

Synopsis

/bin/domainname [*name-of-domain*]

Description

Without an argument, use the domainname command to display the name of the current domain, which typically encompasses a group of hosts or passwd entries under the same administration.

The domain name is usually set during boot time through the domainname command in the /etc/init.d/inetinit file. If the new domain name is not saved in the /etc/defaultdomain file, the system reverts to the old domain after rebooting.

The domain name can also be set by various components of the Solaris Operating Environment to resolve names for types such as passwd, hosts, and aliases. By default, various naming services such as NIS, NIS+, the Internet Domain Name Service (DNS), and sendmail(1M) use the value returned by domainname to resolve names. The domainname is normally a valid Internet domain name.

The domainname for various naming services can also be set by other means. For example, ypinit can be used to specify a different domain for all NIS calls. The file /etc/resolv.conf can be used to specify a different domain for DNS lookups. For sendmail, the domainname can be specified through the sendmail_vars entry in the /etc/nsswitch.conf file or through the /etc/mail/sendmail.cf file.

Only superuser can set the name of the domain by specifying the new domain name as an argument.

Files

/etc/defaultdomain

> File that stores the system's NIS domain name.

/etc/init.d/inetinit

> Startup script that initiates the second phase of TCP/IP configuration.

/etc/mail/sendmail.cf

> Configuration file for sendmail.

/etc/nsswitch.conf

> Nameservice switch configuration file.

/etc/resolv.conf

> List of nameservers for BIND clients to query.

Attributes

See attributes(5) for descriptions of the following attributes.

Attribute Type	Attribute Value
Availability	SUNWcsu

See Also

nis+(1), nischown(1), nispasswd(1), hostconfig(1M), named(1M), nisaddcred(1M), sendmail(1M), sysunconfig(1M), ypinit(1M), aliases(4), hosts(4), nsswitch.conf(4), passwd(4), attributes(5)

New! **dr_daemon** — Enterprise 10000 Dynamic Reconfiguration Daemon

Synopsis

dr_daemon [-a]

Description

The dr_daemon command is new in the Solaris 8 release. It is a Remote Procedure Call (RPC) program that provides the interface to the Sun Enterprise 10000 Dynamic Reconfiguration (DR) driver, dr(7). See dr(7). The Hostview and DR applications provide the user interface to DR. See hostview(1M) in the *Sun Enterprise 10000 SSP Reference Manual* and dr(1M) in the *Sun Enterprise 10000 Dynamic Reconfiguration Reference Manual*.

Options

-a   Disable communications with the Alternate Pathing (AP) daemon. See `ap_daemon`(1M) in the *Sun Enterprise Server Alternate Pathing Reference Manual*.

Configuration Information

The `/platform/SUNW,Ultra-Enterprise-10000/lib/dr_daemon` RPC program name is DRPROG, its RPC program number is `300326`, and its underlying protocol is TCP. It is invoked as an inetd server by the TCP transport. The UID required for access to the daemon is ssp. This UID can be a non-login UID. The entry for the daemon in the `/etc/inetd.conf` file is

```
00326/4 tli rpc/tcp wait root
       /platform/SUNW,Ultra-Enterprise-10000/lib/dr_daemon
```

The daemon's only clients are Hostview and DR. Hostview provides a GUI interface; dr(1M) is a command-line interface for nonwindowing environments. The DR daemon uses syslog(3) to report status and error messages. These error messages are logged with the LOG_DAEMON facility and the LOG_ERR and LOG_NOTICE priorities. dr_daemon communicates by way of RPC with the Alternate Pathing (AP) daemon to notify the AP software when controllers are attached to and detached from the system, or to gather information about the system configuration. See `ap_daemon`(1M) in the *Sun Enterprise Server Alternate Pathing Reference Manual*.

Attributes

See attributes(5) for descriptions of the following attributes.

Attribute Type	Attribute Value
Availability	SUNWdrru

See Also

add_drv(1M), devlinks(1M), drv_config(1M), disks(1M), inetd(1M), ports(1M), prtconf(1M), tapes(1M), syslog(3), attributes(5), dr(7)
    dr(1M) in the *Sun Enterprise 10000 Dynamic Reconfiguration Reference Manual*
    hostview(1M) and hpost(1M) in the *Sun Enterprise 10000 SSP Reference Manual*
    ap(1M) and ap_daemon(1M) in the *Sun Enterprise Server Alternate Pathing Reference Manual*
    Sun Enterprise Server Alternate Pathing User's Guide

drvconfig — Configure the /devices Directory

Synopsis

```
/usr/sbin/drvconfig [-bn] [-a alias-name] [-c class-name]
    [-i driver-name] [-m major-num] [-r rootdir]
```

Description

New!   The devfsadm(1M) command, new in the Solaris 8 release, is now the preferred command for administering /dev and /devices. The drvconfig command in the Solaris 8 release is a symbolic link to the devfsadm(1M) command.

du — Summarize Disk Usage

Synopsis

New!
```
/usr/bin/du [-adkLr][-s | -o][file...]
/usr/xpg4/bin/du [-a | -s][-krx][file...]
```

Description

Use the du command to write to standard output the size of the file space allocated to, and the size of the file space allocated to each subdirectory of the file hierarchy rooted in each of the specified files. The size of the file space allocated to a file of type directory is defined as the sum total of space allocated to all files in the file hierarchy rooted in the directory plus the space allocated to the directory itself.

Files with multiple links are counted and written for only one entry. The directory entry that is selected in the report is unspecified. By default, file sizes are written in 512-byte units, rounded up to the next 512-byte unit.

/usr/xpg4/bin/du

When du cannot obtain file attributes or read directories (see stat(2)), it reports an error condition and the final exit status is affected.

Note — A file with two or more links is counted only once. If, however, there are links between files in different directories where the directories are on separate branches of the file system hierarchy, du counts the excess files more than once.

Files containing holes result in an incorrect block count.

Options

The following options are supported for /usr/bin/du and /usr/xpg4/bin/du.

-a	In addition to the default output, report the size of each file not of type *directory* in the file hierarchy rooted in the specified file. Regardless of the presence of the -a option, non-directories given as file operands are always listed.
-k	Write the files sizes in units of 1024 bytes instead of the default 512-byte units.
-s	Instead of the default output, report only the total sum for each of the specified files.

The following options are supported for `/usr/bin/du` only.

`-d`	Do not cross file-system boundaries. For example, `du -d /` reports usage only on the root partition.
`-L`	Process symbolic links by using the file or directory that the symbolic link references instead of the link itself. This option is new in the Solaris 8 release.
`-o`	Do not add child directories' usage to a parent's total. Without this option, the usage listed for a particular directory is the space taken by the files in that directory, as well as the files in all directories beneath it. This option does nothing if you specify `-s`.
`-r`	Generate messages about directories that cannot be read, files that cannot be opened, and so forth, instead of being silent (the default).

The following options are supported for `/usr/xpg4/bin/du` only.

`-r`	By default, generate messages about directories that cannot be read, files that cannot be opened, and so forth.
`-x`	When evaluating file sizes, evaluate only those files that have the same device as the file specified by the *file* operand.

Operands

file	The path name of a file whose size is to be written. If you specify no file, use the current directory.

Output

The output from `du` consists of the amount of the space allocated to a file and the name of the file. The following example displays the output in 512-byte blocks.

```
paperbark% du /export/home/winsor/Docs
7452    /export/home/winsor/Docs
paperbark%
```

The following example uses the `-k` option to display the output for the same directory in 1024-byte blocks.

```
paperbark% du -k /export/home/winsor/Docs
3726    /export/home/winsor/Docs
paperbark%
```

Usage

See `largefile(5)` for the description of the behavior of `du` when encountering files greater than or equal to 2 Gbytes (2**31 bytes).

Environment Variables

See `environ(5)` for descriptions of the following environment variables that affect the execution of `du`: `LC_CTYPE`, `LC_MESSAGES`, and `NLSPATH`.

Exit Status

0	Successful completion.
>0	An error occurred.

Attributes

See attributes(5) for descriptions of the following attributes.

/usr/bin/du

Attribute Type	Attribute Value
Availability	SUNWcsu
CSI	Enabled

/usr/xpg4/bin/du

Attribute Type	Attribute Value
Availability	SUNWxcu4
CSI	Enabled

See Also

ls(1), stat(2), attributes(5), environ(5), largefile(5), XPG4(5)
System Administration Guide, Volume I

---

dumpadm — Configure Operating System Crash Dump

Synopsis

```
/usr/sbin/dumpadm [-nuy][-c content-type][-d dump-device]
     [-m min k | min m | min%][-s savecore-dir][-r root-dir]
```

Description

Use the administrative dumpadm command to manage the configuration of the operating system crash dump facility. A crash dump is a disk copy of the physical memory of the computer at the time of a fatal system error. When a fatal operating system error occurs, a message describing the error is printed to the console. The operating system then generates a crash dump by writing the contents of physical memory to a predetermined dump device, which is typically a local disk partition. You can configure the dump device with the dumpadm command. Once the crash dump has been written to the dump device, the system reboots.

Fatal operating system errors can be caused by bugs in the operating system, its associated device drivers and loadable modules, or by faulty hardware. Whatever the cause, the crash dump itself provides invaluable information to aid in diagnosing the problem. As such, it is vital that the crash dump be retrieved and given to your support provider. Following an operating system crash, the savecore(1M) command is executed automatically during boot to retrieve the crash dump from the dump device and write it in your file system to a pair of files named unix.*X* and vmcore.*X*, where *X* is an integer identifying the dump. Together, these data files form the saved crash dump. You can also configure the directory in which the crash dump is saved on reboot with dumpadm.

By default, the dump device is configured to be an appropriate swap partition. Swap partitions are disk partitions reserved as virtual memory backing store for the operating system, and thus no permanent information resides there to be overwritten by the dump. See swap(1M). To view the current dump configuration, execute dumpadm with no arguments. The following example shows the default dump configuration for the system paperbark.

```
# dumpadm
      Dump content: kernel pages
       Dump device: /dev/dsk/c0t0d0s1 (swap)
Savecore directory: /var/crash/paperbark
  Savecore enabled: yes
#
```

When you specify one or more options, dumpadm verifies that your changes are valid and, if so, reconfigures the crash dump parameters and displays the resulting configuration. You must be root to view or change dump parameters.

Dump Device Selection

When you specify dumpadm -d swap, using the special swap token as the argument to the -d option, dumpadm tries to configure the most appropriate swap device as the dump device. dumpadm configures the largest swap block device as the dump device; if no block devices are available for swap, the largest swap entry is configured as the dump device. If no swap entries are present or none can be configured as the dump device, a warning message is displayed. Although you can configure local and remote swap files as the dump device, this is not recommended.

Dump Device/Swap Device Interaction

When the dump device is also a swap device and the swap device is deleted by the administrator using the swap -d command, the swap command automatically invokes dumpadm -d swap to try to configure another appropriate swap device as the dump device. If no swap devices remain or none can be configured as the dump device, the crash dump is disabled and a warning message is displayed. Similarly, if the crash dump is disabled and you add a new swap device using the swap -d command, dumpadm -d swap is invoked to reenable the crash dump using the new swap device.

Once dumpadm -d swap has been issued, the new dump device is stored in the configuration file for subsequent reboots. If a larger or more appropriate swap device is added by the administrator, the dump device is not changed; the administrator must reexecute dumpadm -d swap to reselect the most appropriate device from the new list of swap devices.

Minimum Free Space

If you use the dumpadm -m option to create a minfree file based on a percentage of the total size of the file system containing the savecore directory, this value is not automatically recomputed if the file system subsequently changes size. In this case, the administrator must reexecute dumpadm -m to recompute the minfree value. If no such file exists in the savecore directory, savecore defaults to a free space threshold of one megabyte. If you do not want a free space threshold, you can create a `minfree` file containing size 0.

Security Issues

If, on reboot, the specified `savecore` directory is not present, it is created before the execution of `savecore` with permissions `0700` (read, write, execute by owner only) and the owner is `root`. It is recommended that you also create alternate `savecore` directories with similar permissions because the operating system crash dump files themselves can contain security information.

Options

    `-c content-type`

            Modify the dump configuration so that the crash dump consists of the specified dump content. The content should be one of the following.

            `kernel`   Kernel memory pages only.

            `all`   All memory pages.

    `-d dump-device`

            Modify the dump configuration to use the specified dump device. The dump device can be one of the following.

            `dump-device` A specific dump device specified as an absolute path name, such as `/dev/dsk/cNtNdNsN`.

            `swap`   If you specify the special token `swap` as the dump device, `dumpadm` examines the active swap entries and chooses the most appropriate entry to configure as the dump device. See `swap(1M)`. Refer to "Dump Device Selection" on page 285 for details of the algorithm used to select an appropriate swap entry. When the system is first installed, `dumpadm` uses `swap` to determine the initial dump device setting.

    `-m min k | min m | min%`

            Create a `minfree` file in the current `savecore` directory indicating that `savecore` should maintain at least the specified amount of free space in the file system where the `savecore` directory is located. The `min` argument can be one of the following.

            `k`   A positive integer suffixed with the unit `k` specifying kilobytes.

            `m`   A positive integer suffixed with the unit `m` specifying megabytes.

            `%`   A `%` symbol, which means to compute the `minfree` value as the specified percentage of the total current size of the file system containing the `savecore` directory. The `savecore` command consults the `minfree` file, if present, before writing the dump files. If the size of these files would decrease the

	amount of free disk space below the minfree threshold, write no dump files and log an error message. You should immediately clean up the savecore directory to provide adequate free space and then reexecute the savecore command manually. You can also specify an alternate directory on the savecore command line.
-n	Modify the dump configuration to not run savecore automatically on reboot. This system configuration is not recommended; if the dump device is a swap partition, the dump data is overwritten as the system begins to swap. If savecore is not executed shortly after boot, crash dump retrieval may not be possible.
-r *root-dir*	Specify an alternate root directory relative to which dumpadm should create files. If you specify no -r argument, use the default root directory /.
-s *savecore-dir*	
	Modify the dump configuration to use the specified directory to save files written by savecore. The directory should be an absolute path and exist on the system. If on reboot the directory does not exist, it is created before savecore is executed. See "Security Issues" on page 286 for a discussion of security issues relating to access to the savecore directory. The default savecore directory is /var/crash/*hostname* where *hostname* is the output of the uname -n command.
-u	Forcibly update the kernel dump configuration based on the contents of /etc/dumpadm.conf. Normally, this option is used only on reboot by the startup script /etc/init.d/savecore, when the dumpadm settings from the previous boot must be restored. Your dump configuration is saved in the configuration file for this purpose. If the configuration file is missing or contains invalid values for any dump properties, the default values are substituted. Following the update, the configuration file is resynchronized with the kernel dump configuration.
-y	Modify the dump configuration to automatically run savecore on reboot. This is the default for this dump setting.

Examples

The following example reconfigures the dump device to a dedicated dump device.

```
# dumpadm -d /dev/dsk/c0t2d0s2
Dump content: kernel pages
Dump device: /dev/dsk/c0t2d0s2 (dedicated)
Savecore directory: /var/crash/paperbark
Savecore enabled: yes
#
```

Exit Status

0	Dump configuration is valid and the specified modifications, if any, were made successfully.
1	A fatal error occurred in either obtaining or modifying the dump configuration.
2	Invalid command line options were specified.

Files

/dev/dump   Special device dump file.

/etc/init.d/savecore

     Startup script that configures a savecore file.

/etc/dumpadm.conf

     ASCII file containing configuration parameters for a system crash dump.

savecore-directory/minfree

     File specifying the minimum free space to leave in the file system where the savecore directory is located.

Attributes

See attributes(5) for descriptions of the following attributes.

Attribute Type	**Attribute Value**
Availability	SUNWcsr

See Also

uname(1), savecore(1M), swap(1M), attributes(5)

E

edquota — Edit User Quotas for UFS File System

Synopsis

```
/usr/sbin/edquota [-p proto-user] username...
/usr/sbin/edquota -t
```

Description

You can set up quotas to set hard and soft limits on the amount of disk space and number of inodes available to users. These quotas are automatically activated each time a file system is mounted. Only superuser can edit quotas.

Use the edquota editor to assign limits to specific users and groups. You can specify one or more users on the command line. For each user, edquota invokes the vi(1) editor or the editor specified by the EDITOR environment variable, creates a temporary file with an ASCII representation of the current disk quotas for that user for each mounted UFS file system that has a quotas file, and opens the file with the editor.

If you specify no options, the temporary file created has one or more lines of the following form.

```
fs / blocks (soft = 0, hard = 0) inodes (soft = 0, hard = 0)
```

A block is considered to be a 1024-byte (1-kilobyte) block.

You can then edit the file to modify or add new quotas. When you leave the editor, edquota reads the temporary file and modifies the binary quota files to reflect the changes made.

If you are setting quotas for a user for the first time, you must run quotacheck(1M) before you turn quotas on; if not, the quota limit remains 0 and no changes made with edquota take effect.

For quotas to be established on a file system, the root directory of the file system must contain a file, owned by root, called quotas. (See quotaon(1M).) The quotas are not enforced until you turn them on by using the quotaon command.

When you have established a quota for one user by using the edquota command, you can then use the optional -p *proto-user* argument as a prototype to set quotas for one or more *username* to the same values as those of *proto-user*. You can specify *proto-user* and *username* as a numeric UID. You can specify unassigned UIDs; you cannot specify unassigned names. In this way, you can establish default quotas for users who are later assigned a UID.

Note — You cannot assign quotas to users with a UID greater than 67108864.

Options

-p   Duplicate the quotas of the *proto-user* specified for each *username* specified. This mechanism is normally used to initialize quotas for groups of users.

-t   Edit the soft time limits for each file system. If the time limits are zero, use the default time limits in /usr/include/sys/fs/ufs_quota.h. The temporary file created has one or more lines of the following form.

fs *mount-point blocks* time limit = *number tmunit, files* time limit = *number tmunit*

tmunit can be one of month, week, day, hour, min, or sec; characters appended to these keywords are ignored, so you can write months or minutes if you prefer. You can modify the *number* and *tmunit* fields to set desired values. Time limits are printed in the greatest possible time unit so that the value is greater than or equal to 1. default printed after the *tmunit* indicates that the value shown is 0 (the default).

Operands

username   The name or UID of a user.

Examples

The following example uses the edquota command to edit quotas for user winsor. Initially, the /quota file does not exist and edquota displays a message and exits. When the /quota file exists, edquota opens an editor for you to use to set the quotas.

```
# edquota winsor
/etc/mnttab: no UFS filesystems with quotas file
# touch /quotas
# edquota winsor

fs / blocks (soft = 0, hard = 0) inodes (soft = 0, hard = 0)
```

With the `vi` editor, the following changes were made to the quota line, the `quotacheck` file is run, and then quotas are turned on.

```
fs / blocks (soft = 50, hard = 60) inodes (soft = 90, hard = 100)
ZZ
# quotacheck /
# quotaon /
#
```

Usage

See `largefile(5)` for the description of the behavior of `edquota` when encountering files greater than or equal to 2 Gbytes (2**31 bytes).

Files

quotas	Quota file at the file system root.
/etc/mnttab	Table of mounted file systems.

Attributes

See `attributes(5)` for descriptions of the following attributes.

Attribute Type	Attribute Value
Availability	SUNWcsu

See Also

`vi(1)`, `quota(1M)`, `quotacheck(1M)`, `quotaon(1M)`, `repquota(1M)`, `attributes(5)`, `largefile(5)`, `quotactl(7I)`

---

eeprom — EEPROM Display and Load Command

Synopsis

SPARC Platform

`/usr/platform/platform-name/sbin/eeprom [-][-f device]`
`    [parameter[=value]]`

IA Platform

`/usr/platform/platform-name/sbin/eeprom [-][-f device][-I]`
`    [mmu-modlist][parameter[=value]][acpi-user-options]`

New!

Description

Use the `eeprom` command to display or set boot configuration parameters stored in the NVRAM. `eeprom` also detects and reports any corrupted EEPROM settings. If you specify no value, the current value of the parameter is displayed. If you specify a value, the parameter is set to the new value.

eeprom processes parameters in the specified order. A dash (-) option specifies that parameters and values are to be read from the standard input (one *parameter* or *parameter=value* per line).

Only superuser can alter the EEPROM contents.

eeprom verifies the EEPROM checksums and complains if they are incorrect.

platform-name is the name of the platform implementation; you can find it with the -i option of uname(1).

SPARC Platform

SPARC- based systems implement firmware password protection with eeprom, using the security-mode, security-password, and security-#badlogins properties.

IA Platform

EEPROM storage is simulated with a file residing in the platform-specific boot area. The /platform/*platform-name*/boot/solaris/bootenv.rc file simulates EEPROM storage.

Because IA-based systems typically implement password protection in the system BIOS, there is no support for password protection in the eeprom program. Although it is possible to set the security-mode, security-password, and security-#badlogins properties, these properties have no special meaning or behavior on IA-based systems.

Options

-f *device*   Use *device* as the EEPROM device.

IA Platform Only

-I   Initialize boot properties on an IA-based system. Only init(1M) run-level initialization scripts should use this option.

Operands

IA Platform Only

New!

acpi-user-options

A configuration variable that controls the use of ACPI. A value of 0x0 tries to use ACPI if it is available on the system. A value of 0x2 disables the use of ACPI. The default value is 0x0.

mmu-modlist   A colon-separated list of candidate modules that implement memory management. If *mmu-modlist* is defined, it overrides the default list derived from the memory configuration on IA-based systems. Instead, use the first module in the list that is found in /platform/*platform-name*/kernel/mmu.

NVRAM Configuration Parameters

Not all OpenBoot systems support all parameters. Defaults may vary depending on the system and the PROM revision.

auto-boot?   If `true`, boot automatically after power-on or reset. Default is `true`.

ansi-terminal?

Configuration variable used to control the behavior of the terminal emulator. The value `false` makes the terminal emulator stop interpreting ANSI escape sequences, instead of just echoing them to the output device. Default value: `true`.

boot-command

Command executed if `auto-boot?` is `true`. Default value is `boot`.

boot-device   Device from which to boot. `boot-device` can contain 0 or more device specifiers separated by spaces. Each device specifier can be either a PROM device alias or a PROM device path. The boot PROM tries to open each successive device specifier in the list, beginning with the first device specifier. The first device specifier that opens successfully is used as the device to boot from. Default is `disk net`.

boot-file   File to boot (an empty string lets the secondary booter choose default). Default is an empty string.

boot-from   Boot device and file (OpenBoot PROM version 1.x only). Default is `vmunix`.

boot-from-diag

Diagnostic boot device and file (OpenBoot PROM version 1.x only). Default is `le()unix`.

com*X*-noprobe   Where *X* is the number of the serial port, prevents device probe on serial port *X*.

diag-device   Diagnostic boot source device. Default is `net`.

diag-file   File from which to boot in diagnostic mode. Default is an empty string.

diag-level   Diagnostics level. Values include `off`, `min`, `max`, and `menus`. There may be additional platform-specific values. When set to `off`, POST is not called. If POST is called, the value is made available as an argument to, and is interpreted by, POST. The default value is platform dependent.

diag-switch?

If `true`, run in diagnostic mode. Default is `true`.

fcode-debug?   If `true`, include name parameter for plug-in device FCodes. Default is `false`.

hardware-revision

System version information.

`input-device`

Input device used at power-on (usually `keyboard`, `ttya`, or `ttyb`). Default is `keyboard`.

`keyboard-click?`

If `true`, enable keyboard click. Default is `false`.

`keymap`   Keymap for custom keyboard.

`last-hardware-update`

System update information.

`load-base`   Default load address for client programs. Default value is `16384`.

`local-mac-address?`

If `true`, network drivers use their own MAC address, not system's. Default is `false`.

`mfg-mode`   Manufacturing mode argument for POST. Possible values include `off` or `chamber`. The value is passed as an argument to POST. Default is `off`.

`mfg-switch?`   If `true`, repeat system self-tests until interrupted with STOP-A. Default is `false`.

`nvramrc`   Contents of NVRAMRC. Default is `empty`.

`oem-banner`   Custom OEM banner (enabled by setting `oem-banner?` to `true`). Default is an empty string.

`oem-banner?`   If `true`, use custom OEM banner. Default is `false`.

`oem-logo`   Byte array custom OEM logo (enabled by setting `oem-logo?` to `true`). Displayed in hexadecimal.

`oem-logo?`   If `true`, use custom OEM logo (else, use Sun logo). Default is `false`.

`output-device` Output device used at power-on (usually `screen`, `ttya`, or `ttyb`). Default is `screen`.

`sbus-probe-list`

Which SBus slots are probed and in what order. Default is `0123`.

`screen-#columns`

Number of on-screen columns (characters/line). Default is `80`.

`screen-#rows`

Number of on-screen rows (lines). Default is `34`.

`scsi-initiator-id`

SCSI bus address of host adapter, range 0-7. Default is `7`.

`sd-targets`   Map SCSI disk units (OpenBoot PROM version 1.x only). Default is `31204567`, which means that unit 0 maps to target 3, unit 1 maps to target 1, and so on.

security-#badlogins

>   Number of incorrect security password attempts. This property has
>   no special meaning or behavior on IA-based systems.

security-mode

>   Firmware security level (options: none, command, or full). If set to
>   command or full, system prompts for PROM security password.
>   Default is none.
>
>   This property has no special meaning or behavior on IA-based
>   systems.

security-password

>   Firmware security password (never displayed). Can be set only when
>   security mode is set to command or full.
>
>   # **eeprom security-password=**
>   Changing PROM password:
>   New password:
>   Retype new password:
>
>   This property has no special meaning or behavior on IA-based
>   systems.

selftest-#megs

>   Megabytes of RAM to test. Ignored if diag-switch? is true. Default
>   is 1.

skip-vme-loopback?

>   If true, POST does not do VMEbus loopback tests. Default is false.

st-targets   Map SCSI tape units (OpenBoot PROM version 1.x only). Default is
>   45670123, which means that unit 0 maps to target 4, unit 1 maps to
>   target 5, and so on.

sunmon-compat?

>   If true, display Restricted Monitor prompt (>). Default is false.

testarea   One-byte scratch field, available for read/write test. Default is 0.

tpe-link-test?

>   Enable 10baseT link test for built-in twisted pair Ethernet. Default is
>   true.

ttya-mode   TTYA (baud rate, #bits, parity, #stop, handshake). Default is
>   9600,8,n,1,-.
>
>   Fields, in left-to-right order, are
>
>   baud rate   110, 300, 1200, 4800, 9600...
>
>   data bits   5, 6, 7, 8
>
>   parity   n (none), e (even), o (odd), m (mark), s (space)
>
>   stop bits   1, 1.5, 2

	handshake	– (none), h (hardware:rts/cts), s (software: xon/xoff)

ttyb-mode   TTYB (baud rate, #bits, parity, #stop, handshake). Default is `9600,8,n,1,-`.

Fields, in left-to-right order, are

baud rate	`110, 300, 1200, 4800, 9600...`
data bits	`5, 6, 7, 8`
stop bits	`1, 1.5, 2`
parity	n (none), e (even), o (odd), m (mark), s (space)
handshake	– (none), h (hardware:rts/cts), s (software: xon/xoff)

ttya-ignore-cd

> If `true`, operating system ignores carrier-detect on TTYA. Default is true.

ttyb-ignore-cd

> If `true`, operating system ignores carrier-detect on TTYB. Default is true.

ttya-rts-dtr-off

> If `true`, operating system does not assert DTR and RTS on TTYA. Default is `false`.

ttyb-rts-dtr-off

> If `true`, operating system does not assert DTR and RTS on TTYB. Default is `false`.

use-nvramrc?

> If `true`, execute commands in NVRAMRC during system start-up. Default is `false`.

version2?   If `true`, hybrid (1.x/2.x) PROM comes up in version 2.x. Default is true.

watchdog-reboot?

> If `true`, reboot after watchdog reset. Default is `false`.

Examples

The following example uses the `eeprom` command without arguments to display the current settings.

```
paperbark% eeprom
tpe-link-test?=true
scsi-initiator-id=7
keyboard-click?=false
keymap: data not available.
ttyb-rts-dtr-off=false
ttyb-ignore-cd=false
ttya-rts-dtr-off=false
ttya-ignore-cd=false
```

```
ttyb-mode=9600,8,n,1,-
ttya-mode=9600,8,n,1,-
sbus-probe-list=0123
mfg-mode=off
diag-level=max
#power-cycles=202
system-board-serial#=5012967004264
system-board-date: data not available.
fcode-debug?=false
output-device=screen
input-device=keyboard
load-base=16384
boot-command=boot
auto-boot?=true
watchdog-reboot?=false
diag-file: data not available.
diag-device=net
boot-file: data not available.
boot-device=disk
local-mac-address?=false
ansi-terminal?=true
screen-#columns=80
screen-#rows=34
silent-mode?=false
use-nvramrc?=false
nvramrc: data not available.
security-mode=none
security-password: data not available.
security-#badlogins=0
oem-logo: data not available.
oem-logo?=false
oem-banner: data not available.
oem-banner?=false
hardware-revision: data not available.
last-hardware-update: data not available.
diag-switch?=false
paperbark%
```

The following example changes the number of megabytes of RAM that the system tests from 1 to 2.

```
# eeprom selftest-#megs
selftest-#megs=1
# eeprom selftest-#megs=2
selftest-#megs=2
#
```

The following example sets the method for setting the auto-boot? parameter to true. You may need to enclose the command in double quotation marks to prevent the shell from interpreting the question mark.

```
# eeprom "auto-boot?"=true
#
```

Alternatively, you can precede the question mark with an escape character ($\backslash$) to prevent the shell from interpreting the question mark.

Files

/dev/openprom

>Device file.

/usr/platform/*platform-name*/sbin/eeprom

>Platform-specific version of eeprom. Use uname -i to obtain *platform-name*.

Attributes

See attributes(5) for descriptions of the following attributes.

Attribute Type	Attribute Value
Availability	SUNWcsu

See Also

passwd(1), sh(1), uname(1), init(1M), attributes(5)
OpenBoot 3.x Command Reference Manual
ONC+ Developer's Guide

F

fbconfig — Frame Buffer Configuration Command

Synopsis

```
/usr/sbin/fbconfig [-list | -help]
/usr/sbin/fbconfig [-dev device-filename] [-prconf] [-propt] [-res]
/usr/sbin/fbconfig[-devdevice-filename] [-resresolution-specification]
    device-specific-options
```

Description

The fbconfig command is new in the Solaris 8 release. Use this generic command-line interface to query and configure frame buffer attributes.

The following form of fbconfig is the interface for the device-independent operations performed by fbconfig.

```
fbconfig [-list | -help]
```

The following form of fbconfig is the interface for configuring a frame buffer.

```
fbconfig [-dev device-filename] [-prconf] [-propt] [-res]
```

If you omit the -dev option, the default frame buffer (/dev/fb or /dev/fb0) is assumed. In the absence of specific options, the response depends on the device-specific configuration program and how it responds to no options.

299

Options

-dev *device-filename*

Specify the FFB special file. The default is /dev/fbs/ffb0.

-help   Print the fbconfig command usage summary. This option is the default.

-list   Print the list of installed frame buffers and associated device-specific configuration routines.

-prconf   Print the current hardware configuration.

-propt   Print the current software configuration.

-res   Print a list of the resolutions supported by the hardware.

Operands

device-specific-options

Specify in the format shown by the -help option or the corresponding device-specific manual page.

Examples

The following example lists the installed frame buffers and associated device-specific configuration routines.

```
paperbark% fbconfig -list
Device Filename                   Specific Config Program
---------------                   -----------------------
/dev/fbs/ffb0                     SUNWffb_config
/dev/fbs/ffb1                     SUNWffb_config
/dev/fbs/m640                     SUNWm64_config
/dev/fbs/cgsix0                   not configurable
paperbark%
```

The following example uses the -prconf option to list the current hardware configuration.

```
# fbconfig -prconf

--- Hardware Configuration for /dev/fb ---
Type: double-buffered FFB1 with Z-buffer
Board: rev 1
PROM Information: Not Available
FBC: version 0x1
DAC: Brooktree 9068, version 4 (Pac1)
3DRAM: Mitsubishi 1308, version 5
EDID Data: Not Available
Monitor Sense ID: 6   (Sun monitor)
Monitor possible resolutions: 1024x768x77, 1024x800x84, 1152x900x66,
        1152x900x76, 1280x1024x67, 1280x1024x76, 960x680x112s,
    960x680x108s
Current resolution setting: 1152x900x76
#
```

Attributes

See attributes(5) for descriptions of the following attributes.

Attribute Type	Attribute Value
Availability	SUNWfbc

See Also

afbconfig(1M), ffbconfig(1M), attributes(5)

---

fdetach — Detach a Name from a STREAMS-Based File Descriptor

Synopsis

/bin/fdetach *path*

Description

Use the fdetach command to detach a STREAMS-based file descriptor from a name in the file system. Use the *path* operand to specify the path name of the object in the file system namespace. See fattach(3C).

The user must be the owner of the file or a user with the appropriate privileges. All subsequent operations on *path* operate on the underlying file system entry and not on the STREAMS file. The permissions and status of the entry are restored to the state they were in before the STREAMS file was attached to the entry.

Operands

path   Specify in the file-system namespace the path name of the object that was previously attached.

Attributes

See attributes(5) for descriptions of the following attributes.

Attribute Type	Attribute Value
Availability	SUNWcsu

See Also

fattach(3C), fdetach(3C), attributes(5), streamio(7I)
   STREAMS Programming Guide

fdisk — Create or Modify Fixed-Disk Partition Table

Synopsis

```
/usr/sbin/fdisk [-o offset][-s size][-P fill-patt][-S geom-file]
    [-w | r | d | n | I | B | t | T | g | G | R][-F fdisk-file][[-v]
    -W {fdisk-file | -}][-h][-b masterboot][-A id : act : bhead : bsect :
    bcyl : ehead : esect : ecyl : rsect : numsect][-D id : act : bhead:
    bsect : bcyl : ehead: esect : ecyl : rsect : numsect] rdevice
```

Description

Many IA (Intel Architecture)-based systems come preinstalled with other operating systems such as MS-DOS, Microsoft Windows, Microsoft Windows NT, OS/2, or another third-party's implementation of UNIX.

The preinstalled operating system often uses the entire disk on the system (on one fdisk partition) and contains data that you don't want to lose. Installing the Solaris Operating Environment on that fdisk partition erases the existing operating system and its associated user data and replaces it with the Solaris 8 Operating Environment. If you want to keep an existing operating system on the system and use the Solaris Operating Environment as well, you need to create multiple fdisk partitions on the disk.

Use the fdisk command to create and modify the partition table and to install the master boot (IA only) record that is put in the first sector of the fixed disk. This table is used by the first-stage bootstrap (or firmware) to identify parts of the disk reserved for different operating systems and to identify the partition containing the second stage bootstrap (the active Solaris partition). You must use the *rdevice* argument to specify the raw device associated with the fixed disk, for example, /dev/rdsk/c0t0d0p0.

You can operate the fdisk command in three different modes.

- In interactive mode the command displays the partition table as it exists on the disk and then presents a menu enabling you to modify the table. The menu, questions, warnings, and error messages are intended to be self-explanatory. In interactive mode, if there is no partition table on the disk, you are given the options of creating a default partitioning or specifying the initial table values. The default partitioning allocates the entire disk for the Solaris system and makes the Solaris system partition active. In either case, when the initial table is created, fdisk also writes out the first-stage bootstrap (IA only) code along with the partition table.

- The second mode of operation is used for automated entry addition, entry deletion, or replacement of the entire fdisk table. This mode can add or delete an entry described on the command line. In this mode, the entire fdisk table can be read in from a file replacing the original table. fdisk can also be used to create this file. A command-line option replaces any fdisk table with the default of the whole disk for the Solaris system.

- The third mode of operation is used for disk diagnostics. In this mode, you can fill a section of the disk with a user-specified pattern, and sections of the disk can also be read or written.

Menu Options

The fdisk command provides the following menu options for interactive mode.

Create a partition

> Create a new partition. The maximum number of partitions is four. The command asks for the type of the partition (SOLARIS, MS-DOS, UNIX, or other). It then asks for the size of the partition as a percentage of the disk. You can also enter the letter c and then you are asked for the starting cylinder number and size of the partition in cylinders. If you do not enter a c, fdisk determines the starting cylinder number where the partition fits. In either case, if the
>
> partition would overlap an existing partition or does not fit, fdisk displays a message and returns to the original menu.

Change Active (Boot from) partition

> Specify the partition where the first-stage bootstrap looks for the second-stage bootstrap, otherwise known as the active partition.

Delete a partition

> Delete a previously created partition. Note that this option destroys all data in that partition.

Use the following options to include your modifications to the partition table at this time or to cancel the session without modifying the table.

Exit
> Write the new version of the table created during this session to the fixed disk and exit the command.

Cancel
> Exit without modifying the partition table.

Options

-A *id:act:bhead:bsect:bcyl:ehead:esect:ecyl:rsect:numsect*

> Add a partition as described by the argument (see the -F option for the format). Use of this option zeros out the VTOC on the Solaris partition if the fdisk table changes.

-b *master-boot*

> (IA only) Specify the *master-boot* file as the master boot command. The default master boot command is /usr/platform/*platform-name*/lib/fs/ufs/mboot. You can find the platform name by using the -i option of uname(1).

-B
> Default to one Solaris partition that uses the whole disk.

-d
> Turn on verbose debug mode and print the state on standard error as you use the command. Do not use the output from this option with -F.

-D *id:act:bhead:bsect:bcyl:ehead:esect:ecyl:rsect:numsect*

> Delete a partition as described by the argument (see the -F option for the format). The argument must be an exact match or the entry is not

deleted. Use of this option zeros out the VTOC on the Solaris partition if the fdisk table changes.

-F *fdisk-file* Use *fdisk-file* to initialize the table. Use of this option zeros out the VTOC on the Solaris partition if the fdisk table changes.

The *fdisk-file* contains up to four specification lines. Each line is delimited by a newline character (\n). If the first character of a line is an asterisk (*), treat the line as a comment. Each line is composed of entries that are position-dependent, separated by white space or colons, with the following format.

id act bhead bsect bcyl ehead esect ecyl rsect numsect

where the entries have the following values.

id	Specify the type of partition. You can find the correct numeric values in the /usr/include/sys/dktp/fdisk.h file.
act	Specify the active partition flag; 0 means not active and 128 means active.
bhead	Specify the head where the partition starts. If you set this field to 0, fdisk correctly fills in the value from other information.
bsect	Specify the sector where the partition starts. If you set this field to 0, fdisk correctly fills in the value from other information.
bcyl	Specify the cylinder where the partition starts. If you set this field to 0, fdisk correctly fills in the value from other information.
ehead	Specify the head where the partition ends. If you set this field to 0, fdisk correctly fills in the value from other information.
esect	Specify the sector where the partition ends. If you set this field to 0, fdisk correctly fills in the value from other information.
ecyl	Specify the cylinder where the partition ends. If you set this field to 0, fdisk correctly fills in the value from other information.
rsect	Specify the relative sector from the beginning of the disk where the partition starts. You must specify this value, which is used by fdisk to fill in other fields.
numsect	Specify the size, in sectors, of this disk partition. You must specify this value, which is used by fdisk to fill in other fields.

-g   Get the label geometry for disk, and display on standard output (see the -s option for the format).

-G	Get the physical geometry for disk, and display on standard output (see the -S option for the format).
-h	Issue verbose message listing all options, and supply an explanation for each.
-I	Generate a file image of what would go on a disk without using the device. Note that you must use -S with this option.
-n	Don't update fdisk table unless explicitly specified by another option. If you use no other options, write only the master boot record to the disk. In addition, if you specify the -n option, do not start up in interactive mode.
-o *offset*	Block offset from start of disk. Use this option with -P, -r, and -w. When you do not use this option, zero is assumed.
-P *fill-patt*	Fill disk with pattern *fill-patt*. *fill-patt* can be decimal or hexadecimal and is used as *number* for constant long-word pattern. If *fill-patt* is #, then pattern is block # for each block. Pattern is put in each block as long words and fills each block (see -o and -s).
-r	Read from disk and write to standard output. See -o and -s, which specify the starting point and size of the operation.
-R	Treat disk as read-only. This option is for testing purposes.
-s *size*	Specify the number of blocks to perform operation on (see -o).
-S *geom-file*	Set the label geometry to the content of *geom-file*. The *geom-file* contains one specification per line. Each line is delimited by a newline character (\n). If the first character of a line is an asterisk (*), treat the line as a comment. Each line is composed of entries that are position dependent, separated by white space, with the following format.

PCYL NCYL ACYL BCYL NHEADS NSECTORS SECTSIZ

where the entries have the following values.

PCYL	The number of physical cylinders for the drive.
NCYL	The number of usable cylinders for the drive.
ACYL	The number of alternate cylinders for the drive.
BCYL	The number of offset cylinders for the drive (should be 0).
NHEADS	The number of heads for this drive.
NSECTORS	The number of sectors per track.
SECTSIZ	The size in bytes of a sector.

-t	Adjust incorrect slice table entries so that they do not cross partition table boundaries.
-T	Remove incorrect slice table entries that span partition table boundaries.

-v	(IA only) Output the HBA (virtual) geometry dimensions. You must use this option in conjunction with the -W option. This option works for platforms that support virtual geometry.
-w	Write to disk and read from standard input. See -o and -s, which specify the starting point and size of the operation.
-W	Output the disk table to standard output.

-W *fdisk-file*

Create *fdisk-file* from disk table. You can use this option with the -F option.

Files

/dev/rdsk/c0t0d0p0

Raw device associated with the fixed disk.

IA Only

/usr/platform/*platform-name*/lib/fs/ufs/mboot

Default master boot command.

Attributes

See attributes(5) for descriptions of the following attributes.

Attribute Type	Attribute Value
Architecture	IA, PowerPC Edition
Availability	SUNWcsu

See Also

uname(1), fmthard(1M), prtvtoc(1M) attributes(5)

Diagnostics

Most messages are self-explanatory. The following messages may appear immediately after the command is started.

Fdisk: cannot open *device*

The device name argument is not valid.

Fdisk: unable to get device parameters for device *device*

The configuration of the fixed disk has a problem, or the fixed disk driver has an error.

Fdisk: error reading partition table

An error occurred when trying initially to read the fixed disk. This problem could be with the fixed disk controller or driver or with the configuration of the fixed disk.

```
Fdisk: error writing boot record
```
An error occurred when trying to write the new partition table to the fixed disk. This problem could be with the fixed disk controller, the disk itself, the driver, or the configuration of the fixed disk.

ff — List File Names and Statistics for a File System

Synopsis
```
/usr/sbin/ff [-F FSType] [-V] [generic-options] [-o specific-options]
    special...
```

Description
Use ff to print the path names and inode numbers of files in the file system that resides on the special device *special*. You can print other information about the files by using options described below. You can use selection criteria to instruct ff to print information only for certain files. If you specify no selection criteria, information for all files considered is printed (the default); you can use the -i option to limit files to those whose inodes are specified.

Output is sorted in ascending inode number order. The ff command produces the following default line.

```
pathname i-number
```

The command can provide the following maximum information.

```
pathname i-number size uid
```

Note — This command may not be supported for all *FSType*s.

The -a, -m, and -c flags examine the st_atime, st_mtime, and st_ctime fields of the stat structure. (See stat(2).)

Options
-F *FSType*	Specify the *FSType* on which to operate. Either specify the *FSType* here or ff should be able to determine it from /etc/vfstab by matching *special* with an entry in the table or by consulting /etc/default/fs.
-V	Echo the complete command line, but do not execute the command. Generate the command line by using the specified options and arguments and adding to them information derived from /etc/vfstab. You can use this option to verify and validate the command line.

generic-options

Options that are supported by most *FSType*-specific modules of the command. The following options are available.

-I	Do not print the inode number after each path name.
-l	Generate a supplementary list of all path names for multiply linked files.
-p *prefix*	Add the specified prefix to each generated path name. The default is dot (.).
-s	Print the file size, in bytes, after each path name.
-u	Print the owner's login name after each path name.
-a *-n*	Select the file if it has been accessed in *n* days.
-m *-n*	Select the file if it has been written or created in *n* days.
-c *-n*	Select the file if its status has been changed in *n* days.
-n *file*	Select the file if it has been modified more recently than the argument *file*.
-i *inode-list*	Generate names for only those inodes specified in *inode-list*. *inode-list* is a list of numbers separated by commas (with no intervening spaces).

-o

Specify *FSType-specific* options in a comma-separated (without spaces) list of suboptions and keyword-attribute pairs for interpretation by the *FSType*-specific module of the command.

Operands

special   A special device.

Examples

The following example shows part of the listing for the special device /dev/rdsk/c0t0d0s0.

```
# ff /dev/rdsk/c0t0d0s0
/dev/rdsk/c0t0d0s0:
3          /lost+found/ .
5696       /usr/ .
11392      /export/ .
22784      /var/ .
34182      /etc/ .
34191      /opt/ .
35         /bin
39911      /dev/ .
36         /devices/ .
22831      /kernel/ .
40         /lib
68386      /mnt/ .
41         /proc/ .
```

```
5732      /sbin/.
22832     /tmp/.
57021     /platform/.
11698     /net/.
45806     /home/.
11699     /xfn/.
118       /.cpr_config
11712     /vol/.
28758     /cdrom/.
28772     /.dt/.
314       /.dtprofile
28778     /TT_DB/.
490       /.cshrc
336       /.Xauthority
68861     /nis+files/.
507       /quotas
11395     /var/sadm/pkg/SUNWulcfx/install/.
17090     /var/sadm/pkg/SUNWulcfx/save/.
6         /var/sadm/pkg/SUNWulcfx/pkginfo
22788     /var/sadm/pkg/SUNWtxplt/install/.
28485     /var/sadm/pkg/SUNWtxplt/save/.
8         /var/sadm/pkg/SUNWtxplt/pkginfo
9         /var/sadm/pkg/SUNWtiu8/install/copyright
```
...(*Additional lines deleted from this example*)

Usage

See largefile(5) for the description of the behavior of ff when encountering files greater than or equal to 2 Gbytes (2**31 bytes).

Files

/etc/default/fs

> Default local file-system type. You can set default values for the following flag in /etc/default/fs. For example, LOCAL=ufs.
>
> LOCAL   The default partition for a command if no *FSType* is specified.

/etc/vfstab   List of default parameters for each file system.

Attributes

See attributes(5) for descriptions of the following attributes.

Attribute Type	Attribute Value
Availability	SUNWcsu

See Also

find(1), ncheck(1M), stat(2), vfstab(4), attributes(5), largefile(5)
Manual pages for the FSType-specific modules of ff.

ff_ufs — List File Names and Statistics for a UFS File System

Synopsis

```
/usr/sbin/ff -F ufs [generic-options][-o a,m,s] special...
```

Description

Use the ff command to print the path names and inode numbers of files in the file system that resides on the special device *special*. ff is described in ff(1M); UFS-specific options are described below.

Options

-o   Specify UFS file-system specific options. The following options are available.

a   Print the . and .. directory entries.

m   Print mode information. You must specify this option in conjunction with the -i *inode-list* option (see ff(1M)).

s   Print only special files and files with setuser-ID mode.

Attributes

See attributes(5) for descriptions of the following attributes.

Attribute Type	Attribute Value
Availability	SUNWcsu

See Also

find(1), ff(1M), ncheck(1M), attributes(5)

ffbconfig — Configure the FFB Graphics Accelerator

Synopsis

```
/usr/sbin/ffbconfig [-dev device-filename][-res video-mode
  [now | try][noconfirm | nocheck]][-file | machine | system]
  [-deflinear | true | false][-defoverlay | true | false]
  [-linearorder | first | last][-overlayorder | first | last]
  [-expvis | enable | disable][-sov | enable | disable][-maxwids n]
  [-extovl | enable | disable] [-g gammacorrection-value]
  [-gfile gamma-correction-file][-propt][-prconf][-defaults]
```

```
/usr/sbin/ffbconfig [-propt][-prconf]
/usr/sbin/ffbconfig [-help][-res ?]
```

Description

Use the ffbconfig command to configure the FFB Graphics Accelerator and some of the X11 window system defaults for FFB.

The first form of ffbconfig stores the specified options in the OWconfig file. These options initialize the FFB device the next time the window system is run on that device. Updating options in the OWconfig file provides persistence of these options across window system sessions and system reboots.

The second and third forms of ffbconfig, which invoke only the -prconf, -propt, -help, and -res ? options do not update the OWconfig file. Additionally, for the third form all other options are ignored.

You can specify options for only one FFB device at a time. To specify options for multiple FFB devices, invoke ffbconfig for each FFB device.

Only FFB-specific options can be specified through ffbconfig. The normal window system options for specifying default depth, default visual class, and so forth, are still specified as device modifiers on the openwin command line. See the *OpenWindows Desktop Reference Manual* for details.

You can also specify the OWconfig file that is to be updated. By default, the machine-specific file in the /etc/openwin directory tree is updated. You can use the -file option to update the system-global OWconfig file in the /usr/openwin directory tree instead.

Both of these standard OWconfig files can be written only by root. Consequently, the ffbconfig command, which is owned by the root user, always runs with setuid root permission.

Options

-dev *device-filename*

Specify the FFB special file. The default is /dev/fbs/ffb0.

-res video-mode [now | try [noconfirm | nocheck]]

Specify the video mode used to drive the monitor connected to the specified FFB device.

video-mode has the format of *width*x*height*x*rate* where *width* is the screen width in pixels, height is the screen *height* in pixels, and *rate* is the vertical frequency of the screen refresh.

Use the s suffix, as in 960x680x112s and 960x680x108s, to indicate stereo video modes. Use the i suffix, as in 640x480x60i and 768x575x50i, to indicate interlaced video timing. If absent, use noninterlaced timing.

-res also accepts formats with @ (at sign) in front of the refresh rate instead of x. For example, 1280x1024@76.

Some video modes are supported only on certain revisions of FFB. Also, some video modes, supported by FFB, may not be supported by the monitor. You can obtain the list of video modes supported by the FFB device and the monitor by running ffbconfig with the -res ? option.

The following table lists all video modes supported by FFB.

```
1024x768x60
```

```
1024x768x70
```

```
1024x768x75
```

```
1024x768x77
```

```
1024x800x84
```

```
1152x900x66
```

```
1152x900x76
```

```
1280x800x76
```

```
1280x1024x60
```

```
1280x1024x67
```

```
1280x1024x76
```

```
960x680x112s
```
(stereo)

```
960x680x108s
```
(stereo)

```
640x480x60
```

```
640x480x60i
```
(interlaced)

```
768x575x50i
```
(interlaced)

```
1440x900x76
```
(hi-res)

```
1600x1000x66
```
(hi-res)

```
1600x1000x76i
```
(hi-res)

```
1600x1280x76
```
(hi-res)

For convenience, some video modes have symbolic names defined for them. Instead of the form *widthxheightxrate*, you can supply one of these names as the argument to -res. The meaning of the symbolic name none is that when the window system is run, the screen resolution is the video mode that is currently programmed in the device.

svga	1024x768x60
1152	1152x900x76
1280	1280x1024x76
stereo	960x680x112s
ntsc	640x480x60i
pal	768x575x50i
none	Video mode currently programmed in device.

The -res option also accepts additional, optional arguments immediately following the video mode specification. Any or all of these can be present.

now
Specify that the FFB device is immediately programmed to display this video mode in addition to updating the video mode in the OWconfig file. This option is useful for changing the video mode before starting the window system.

It is not advisable to use this suboption with ffbconfig while the configured device is being used (for example, while running the window system); unpredictable results can occur. To run ffbconfig with the now suboption, first bring the window system down. If you use the now suboption within a window system session, the video mode is changed immediately but the width and height of the affected screen don't change until the window system is exited and reentered. In addition, the system may not recognize changes in stereo mode. Consequently, this usage is strongly discouraged.

noconfirm
Bypass confirmation and warning messages and program the requested video mode anyway.

Using the -res option, it is possible to put the system into an unusable state where there is no video output. This state can happen if there is ambiguity in the monitor sense codes for the particular code read. To reduce the chance of this state happening, the default behavior of ffbconfig is to print a warning message to this effect and to prompt to find out if it is okay to continue. This option is useful when ffbconfig is being run from a shell script.

nocheck
Suspend normal error checking based on the monitor sense code. The specified video mode is accepted regardless of whether it is appropriate for the currently attached monitor. This option is useful if a different monitor is to be connected to the FFB device. Note that the use of this option implies noconfirm as well.

try
Program the specified video mode on a trial basis. You are asked to confirm the video mode by typing y within 10 seconds. You can also terminate the trial before 10 seconds are up by typing any character. Any character other than y or Return is considered a no and the previous video mode is restored and ffbconfig does not change the video mode in the OWconfig file. Other specified options still take effect. If you press Return, you are prompted for a yes or no answer on whether to keep the new video

mode. This option implies the now suboption (see the warning note in the now suboption).

`-file machine |system`

Specify which OWconfig file to update. If machine, use the machine-specific OWconfig file in the /etc/openwin directory tree. If system, use the global OWconfig file in the /usr/openwin directory tree. If the file does not exist, create it.

`-deflinear true | false`

FFB possesses two types of visuals: linear and nonlinear. Linear visuals are gamma corrected and nonlinear visuals are not. Two visuals have both linear and nonlinear versions: 24-bit TrueColor and 8-bit StaticGray.

-deflinear true sets the default visual to the linear visual that satisfies other specified default visual selection options. Specifically, the default visual selection options are those set by the Xsun (1) defdepth and defclass options. See the *OpenWindows Desktop Reference Manual* for details.

-deflinear false (or if there is no linear visual that satisfies the other default visual selection options) sets the default visual to the nonlinear visual as the default.

You cannot use this option when the -defoverlay option is present because FFB does not possess a linear overlay visual.

`-defoverlay true | false`

FFB provides an 8-bit PseudoColor visual, called the overlay visual, whose pixels are disjoint from the rest of the FFB visuals. Windows created in this visual do not damage windows created in other visuals. The converse, however, is not true. Windows created in other visuals can damage overlay windows. This visual has 256 maxwids of opaque color values. See -maxwids.

If -defoverlay is true, set the overlay visual as the default visual. If -defoverlay is false, choose the nonoverlay visual that satisfies the other default visual selection options, such as defdepth and defclass as the default visual. See the *OpenWindows Desktop Reference Manual* for details.

Whenever you use -defoverlay true, the default depth and class chosen on the openwin command line must be 8-bit PseudoColor. If not, a warning message is printed and the -defoverlay option is treated as false. You cannot use this option when the -deflinear option is present because FFB doesn't possess a linear overlay visual.

`-linearorder first | last`

If first, put linear visuals before their nonlinear counterparts on the X11 screen visual list for the FFB screen. If last, put the nonlinear visuals before the linear ones.

`-overlayorder first | last`

If `first`, put the depth 8 PseudoColor Overlay visual before the nonoverlay visual on the X11 screen visual list for the FFB screen. If `last`, put the nonoverlay visual before the overlay one.

`-expvis enable | disable`

If enabled, activate OpenGL Visual Expansion. Multiple instances of selected visual groups (8-bit PseudoColor, 24-bit TrueColor, and so forth) can be found in the screen visual list.

`-sov enable | disable`

Advertise the root window's SERVER_OVERLAY_VISUALS property. Export SOV visuals. You can retrieve their transparent types, values, and layers through this property. If you specify `-sov disable`, do not define the SERVER_OVERLAY_VISUALS property and do not export SOV visuals.

`-maxwids n`   Specify the maximum number of FFB X channel pixel values that are reserved for use as window IDs (WIDs). Use the remainder of the pixel values in overlay colormaps for normal X11 opaque color pixels. 3D graphics windows (such as XGL), MBX windows, and windows that have a nondefault visual allocate the reserved WIDs on a first-come first-served basis. The X channel codes 0 to (255 − n) are opaque color pixels. The X channel codes (255 − n + 1) to 255 are reserved for use as WIDs. Legal values on FFB, FFB2 are 1, 2, 4, 8, 16, and 32. Legal values on FFB2+ are 1, 2, 4, 8, 16, 32, and 64.

`-extovl enable | disable`

This option is available only on FFB2+. If enabled, extended overlay is available. The overlay visuals have 256 opaque colors. The SOV visuals have 255 opaque colors and 1 transparent color. This option enables hardware-supported transparency, which provides better performance for windows using the SOV visuals.

`-g gamma-correction value`

This option is available only on FFB2+. Change the gamma correction value. All linear visuals provide gamma correction. By default, the gamma correction value is 2.22. Any value less than zero is illegal. You can use this option while the window system is running. Changing the gamma correction value affects all the windows being displayed with the linear visuals.

`-gfile gamma-correction file`

This option is available only on FFB2+. Load gamma correction table from the specified file. Format this file to provide the gamma correction values for R, G, and B channels on each line. Provide 256 triplet values, each in hexadecimal format and separated by at least 1 space. Following is an example of this file.

```
0x00  0x00  0x00
0x01  0x01  0x01
0x02  0x02  0x02

. . .

. . .

0xff  0xff  0xff
```

With this option, the gamma correction table can be loaded while the window system is running. The new gamma correction affects all the windows being displayed through the linear visuals. Note, when gamma correction is being done through a user-specified table, the gamma correction value is undefined. By default, the window system assumes a gamma correction value of 2.22 and loads the gamma table it creates corresponding to this value.

-defaults   Reset all option values to their default values.

-propt   Print the current values of all FFB options in the OWconfig file specified by the -file option for the device specified by the -dev option. Print the values of options as they are in the OWconfig file after the call to ffbconfig completes. The following is a typical display when the -propt option is used.

```
--- OpenWindows Configuration for /dev/fbs/ffb0 ---
OWconfig: machine
Video Mode: NONE
Default Visual: Non-Linear Normal Visual
Visual Ordering: Linear Visuals are last
                Overlay Visuals are last
OpenGL Visuals: disabled
SOV: disabled
Allocated WIDs: 32


   -prconf   Prints the FFB hardware configuration.   The fol-
             lowing  is  a  typical  display  using  the -prconf
             option:

--- Hardware Configuration for /dev/fbs/ffb0 ---
Type: double-buffered FFB2 with Z-buffer
Board: rev x
PROM Information: @(#)ffb2.fth x.x xx/xx/xx
FBC: version x
DAC: Brooktree 9068, version x
3DRAM: Mitsubishi 1309, version x
EDID Data: Available - EDID version 1 revision x
Monitor Sense ID: 4  (Sun 37x29cm RGB color monitor)
Monitor possible resolutions: 1024x768x60, 1024x768x70,
                    1024x768x75, 1152x900x66, 1152x900x76,
                    1280x1024x67, 1280x1024x76, 960x680x112s,
                    640x480x60
Current resolution setting: 1280x1024x76
```

-help   Print a list of the ffbconfig command-line options, along with a brief explanation of each.

Defaults

For a given invocation of ffbconfig, if an option does not appear on the command line, the corresponding OWconfig option is not updated; it retains its previous value.

When the window system is run, if an FFB option has never been specified with ffbconfig, a default value is used. The option defaults are listed in the following table.

Option	Default
-dev	/dev/fbs/ffb0
-file	machine
-res	none
-deflinear	false
-defoverlay	false
-linearorder	last
-overlayorder	last
-expvis	enabled
-sov	enabled
-maxwids	32

The default of none for the -res option means that when the window system is run, the screen resolution is the video mode that is currently programmed in the device.

This setting provides compatibility for users who are accustomed to specifying the device resolution through the PROM. On some devices (for example, GX), specifying the device resolution through the PROM is the only way of specifying the video mode, which means that the PROM ultimately determines the default FFB video mode.

Examples

The following example switches the monitor type to the resolution of 1280 by1024 at 76 Hz.

paperbark% **/usr/sbin/ffbconfig -res 1280x1024x76**

Files

/dev/fbs/ffb0

Device special file.

Attributes

See attributes(5) for descriptions of the following attributes.

Attribute Type	Attribute Value
Availability	SUNWffbcf

See Also

mmap(2), attributes(5), fbio(7I), ffb(7D)
OpenWindows Desktop Reference Manual

---

fingerd — Remote User Information Server

Synopsis

/usr/sbin/in.fingerd

Description

See in.fingerd(1M).

---

firmware — Bootable Firmware Programs and Firmware Commands

Description

Between the time most computers are turned on and the boot command is loaded to bootstrap the machine, the computer is in an operating state known as the firmware state. In the firmware state, a small command in non-volatile memory is running on the machine, and you can perform certain system operations usually unavailable from single- or multiuser operating states.

The two basic kinds of firmware operations are running firmware commands and running bootable commands.

Running firmware commands includes commands for displaying the Equipped Device Table, performing a system memory dump, displaying the firmware version, creating a floppy key, and so forth. These commands are executed by the firmware command.

Running bootable commands includes the operating system and other bootable commands (for example, a command to fill the Equipped Device Table). These commands are located in the /stand file system. When a bootable command is requested from firmware, the firmware command loads and executes the command, passing control of the system to the bootable command.

Some firmware commands enable you to request the configuration of a new bootable operating system from firmware by specifying the name of a configuration file (usually /stand/system) as the name of the command to boot; see system(4).

OpenBoot Firmware

The OpenBoot firmware is stored in the boot PROM (programmable read-only memory) so that it is executed immediately after you turn on your system. The primary task of the OpenBoot firmware is to boot the operating system from either a mass storage device or from a network. The firmware also provides extensive features for testing hardware and software interactively.

The OpenBoot architecture provides a significant increase in functionality over the boot PROMs in earlier Sun systems. Although this architecture was first implemented on SPARC systems, its design is processor independent. The OpenBoot firmware includes the following features.

- Plug-in device drivers. A plug-in device driver is usually loaded from a plug-in device such as an SBus card. The plug-in device driver can be used to boot the operating system from that device or to display text on the device before the operating system has activated its own drivers. This feature enables the input and output devices supported by a particular system to evolve without changing the system PROM.

- FCode interpreter. Plug-in drivers are written in a machine-independent interpreted language called FCode. Each OpenBoot system PROM contains an FCode interpreter. Thus, the same device and driver can be used on machines with different CPU instruction sets.

- Device tree. The device tree is an OpenBoot data structure describing the devices (permanently installed and plug-in) attached to a system. Both the user and the operating system can determine the hardware configuration of the system by inspecting the device tree.

- Programmable user interface. The OpenBoot user interface is based on the interactive programming language Forth. You can combine sequences of user commands to form complete programs. This capability provides power for debugging hardware and software.

See the hardware guide that accompanies your computer for descriptions of the firmware commands and commands available with your machine.

Warning — The firmware command typically does not know if a requested command is bootable or not; requesting a command that is not bootable from firmware can lead to unpredictable results.

Attributes

See `attributes`(5) for descriptions of the following attributes.

Attribute Type	Attribute Value
Architecture	SPARC

See Also

`system(4)`, `attributes(5)`
Writing FCode 2.x Programs
OpenBoot 2.x Command Reference Manual

fmthard — Populate VTOC on Hard Disks

Synopsis

SPARC Platform

```
/usr/sbin/fmthard -d data | -n volume-name | -s datafile [-i]
    /dev/rdsk/c?[t?]d?s2
```

IA Platform

```
/usr/sbin/fmthard -d data | -n volume-name | -s datafile [-i]
    [-p pboot][-b bootblk] /dev/rdsk/c?[t?]d?s2
```

Description

Use the fmthard command to update the VTOC (Volume Table of Contents) on hard disks and, on IA systems, to add boot information to the Solaris fdisk partition. You must specify one or more of the options -s datafile, -d data, or -n volume-name to request modifications to the disk label. To print disk label content, see prtvtoc(1M). The /dev/rdsk/c?[t?]d?s2 file must be the character special file of the device where the new VTOC is to be installed. On IA systems, you must run fdisk(1M) on the drive before running fmthard.

If you are using an IA system, note that the term partition in this page refers to slices within the IA fdisk partition on IA machines. Do not confuse the partitions created by fmthard with the partitions created by fdisk.

Note — Take special care when overwriting an existing VTOC because incorrect entries could result in current data being inaccessible. As a precaution, save the old VTOC.

fmthard cannot write a disk label on an unlabeled disk. Use format(1M) for this purpose.

Options

-d data
: Specify a string representing the information for a particular partition in the current VTOC. The string must be of the format

    part:tag:flag:start:size

    where part is the partition number, tag is the ID TAG of the partition, flag is the set of permission flags, start is the starting sector number of the partition, and size is the number of sectors in the partition. See the description of the datafile below for more information on these fields.

-i
: Create the desired VTOC table and print the information to standard output instead of modifying the VTOC on the disk.

-n volume-name
: Assign the disk a volume-name up to 8 characters long.

-s *datafile*   Populate the VTOC according to a user-created *datafile*. If
                 datafile is -, read from standard input. The *datafile* format is
                 described below. This option sets all of the disk partition timestamp
                 fields to zero.

Every VTOC generated by fmthard also has a partition 2, by convention, that
corresponds to the whole disk. If the input in *datafile* does not specify an entry for
partition 2, a default partition 2 entry is created automatically in VTOC with the *tag*
V_BACKUP and *size* equal to the full size of the disk.

datafile contains one specification line for each partition, starting with partition 0.
Delimit each line with a newline character (\n). If the first character of a line is an
asterisk (*), treat the line as a comment. Each line is composed of entries that are
position-dependent, separated by white space, with the following format.

partition tag flag starting-sector size-in-sectors

where the entries have the following values.

partition   The partition (or slice) number. Currently, for Solaris SPARC
                 platforms, a disk can have up to 8 partitions, 0-7. Even though the
                 partition field has 4 bits, only 3 bits are currently used. For IA, all 4
                 bits are used to allow slices 0-15. Each Solaris fdisk partition can
                 have up to 16 slices.

tag   The partition tag: a decimal number. The following are reserved
                 codes: 0 (V_UNASSIGNED), 1 (V_BOOT), 2 (V_ROOT), 3 (V_SWAP),
                 4 (V_USR), 5 (V_BACKUP), 6 (V_STAND), 7 (V_VAR), and 8 (V_HOME).

flag   The flag enables you to flag a partition as unmountable or read only,
                 the masks are V_UNMNT 0x01 and V_RONLY 0x10. For mountable
                 partitions, use 0x00.

starting_sector

                 The sector number (decimal) on which the partition starts.

size_in_sectors

                 The number (decimal) of sectors occupied by the partition.

Note — You can save the output of a prtvtoc command to a file, edit the
file, and use it as the *datafile* argument to the -s option.

IA Options

The functionality provided by the following two IA options is also provided by
installboot(1M). Because the functionality described here may be removed in future
versions of fmthard, you should use installboot to install boot records. The following
options currently apply to fmthard.

-p *pboot*   Override the default partition boot file,
                 /usr/platform/*platform-name*/lib/fs/ufs/pboot.The partition
                 boot file is platform dependent, where you can determine
                 platform-name with the -i option to uname(1).

-b *bootblk*   Override the default bootblk file,
/usr/platform/*platform-name*/lib/fs/ufs/bootblk. The boot
block file is platform dependent, where you can determine
platform-name with the -i option to uname(1).

Attributes

See attributes(5) for descriptions of the following attributes.

Attribute Type	Attribute Value
Availability	SUNWcsu

See Also

uname(1), format(1M), prtvtoc(1M), attributes(5)

IA Only

fdisk(1M), installboot(1M)

fncheck — Check for Consistency Between FNS Data and NIS+ Data

Synopsis

/usr/sbin/fncheck [-r][-s][-u][-t *type*][*domainname*]

Description

Use the fncheck command to check for inconsistencies between Federated Name
Service (FNS) user name or host name contexts and the contents of the corresponding
NIS+ passwd.org_dir or hosts.org_dir tables in the NIS+ domain *domainname*. If
you omit *domainname*, the domain name of the current machine is used. By default (in
the absence of the -r and -s options), the following inconsistencies are displayed.

- Items that appear only in the FNS context but do not appear in the NIS+ table.
- Items that appear only in the NIS+ table but do not appear in the FNS context.

Options

-r   Display items that appear only in the FNS context but do not appear
            in the corresponding NIS+ table.

-s   Display items that appear in the NIS+ table but do not appear in the
            corresponding FNS context.

-u	Update the FNS context based on information in the corresponding NIS+ table. If you also specify the -r option, remove items that appear only in the FNS context from the FNS context. If you also specify the -s option, add items that appear only in the NIS+ table to the FNS context. If you specify neither -r nor -s, add and remove items from the FNS context to make it consistent with the corresponding NIS+ table.
-t *type*	Specify the type of context to check. *type* can be either hostname or username. If you omit this option, check both hostname and username contexts. If *type* is hostname, check the FNS hostname context against the NIS+ hosts.org_dir table. If *type* is username, check the FNS username context against the NIS+ passwd.org_dir table.

Usage

Although you can use fncheck to add users and hosts to the username and hostname contexts as you add new users and hosts to NIS+, that is not its intended purpose. fncheck is an expensive operation because it makes complete comparisons of the NIS+ table and the corresponding FNS context. When you add or remove a user or host from NIS+ using AdminSuite (see solstice(1M)), that action automatically updates the appropriate FNS contexts.

Attributes

See attributes(5) for descriptions of the following attributes.

Attribute Type	Attribute Value
Availability	SUNWfns

See Also

nis(1), admintool(1M), fncreate(1M), fndestroy(1M), attributes(5), fns(5), fns_policies(5)

fncopy — Copy FNS Contexts, Possibly from One Naming Service to Another

Synopsis

/usr/sbin/fncopy [-f *filename*] [-i *old-naming-service*]
    [-o *new-naming-service*] *old-fns-context new-fns-context*

Description

Use the fncopy command to recursively copy the Federated Name Service (FNS) context, *old-fns-context*, and attributes to a new FNS context, *new-fns-context*. If you specify -i and -o options with the respective naming service, the *old-fns-context* is resolved, using *old-naming-service* as the underlying naming service, and *new-fns-context* is created, using *new-naming-service* as the underlying naming service. In the absence of -i and -o options, use the default naming service (see fnselect(1M)).

When you use the -f option, *filename* specifies a file containing a list of contexts in the *old-fns-context* to be copied to the *new-fns-context*.

If the FNS context *new-fns-context* already exists in the target naming service, *new-naming-service*, this command copies only the contexts and bindings that do not exist in the target naming service. This command does not overwrite any of the existing FNS contexts in the target naming service.

This command follows links and copies FNS contexts and binding to the *new-fns-context* namespace.

Options

-f *filename*   Specify a file name that contains a list of FNS contexts to be copied.

-i *old-naming-service*

Specify the source naming service; currently only nis is supported.

-o *new-naming-service*

Specify the target naming service; currently only nisplus is supported.

Operands

old-fns-context

The current FNS context.

new-fns-context

The new FNS context.

Examples

The following example copies the FNS printer context .../fednaming.eng.sun.com/service/printer and its subcontexts and bindings to the FNS printer context .../sun.com/orgunit/ssi.eng/service/printer.

paperbark% **fncopy.../fed-naming.eng.sun.com/service/printer \
   .../sun.com/orgunit/ssi.eng/service/printer**

The following example copies the NIS FNS users' contexts specified in the /etc/ssi-users-list file to NIS+ FNS users' context of the orgunit ssi.eng.

paperbark% **fncopy -i nis -o nisplus -f /etc/ssi-users-list \
   thisorgunit/user org/ssi.eng/user**

Exit Status

0   Operation was successful.

1   Operation failed.

Attributes

See attributes(5) for descriptions of the following attributes.

Attribute Type	Attribute Value
Availability	SUNWfns

See Also

fnbind(1), fnunbind(1), fncreate(1M), fncreate_fs(1M),
fncreate_printer(1M), fndestroy(1M), attributes(5), fns(5)

fncreate — Create an FNS Context

Synopsis

```
/usr/sbin/fncreate -t context-type [-Dosv][-f input-file]
   [-r reference-type] composite-name
```

Description

Use the fncreate command to create a Federated Naming Service (FNS) context of type
context-type. Valid values for *context-type* are org, hostname, host, username,
user, service, fs, site, nsid, or generic. The fncreate command takes as the last
argument a composite name, *composite-name*, that you use to specify the context to be
created. In addition to creating the named context, fncreate creates subcontexts of the
named context using FNS Policies of which types of contexts should be bound in those
contexts. See fns_policies(5).

fncreate discovers which naming service is in use and creates contexts in the
appropriate naming service. When you are initially setting up FNS, by default fncreate
creates contexts for NIS+. You can change this default by using fnselect(1M) to
explicitly select a naming service.

When using FNS for an NIS+ environment, fncreate creates NIS+ tables and
directories in the NIS+ hierarchy. See fns_nis+(5) for more information on the
necessary NIS+ credentials and the use of the environment variable NIS_GROUP when
using fncreate and other FNS commands.

When using FNS for an NIS environment, fncreate creates NIS maps, and you must
execute the command as superuser on the NIS master of the FNS-related maps. See
fns_nis(5) for more information specific to the use of FNS in an NIS environment.

When using FNS for an environment that uses /etc files for its naming information,
fncreate creates files in the /var/fn directory. See fns_files(5) for more information
specific to the use of FNS for files.

Options

-D   Display information about the creation of a context and corresponding
NIS+ directories and tables, NIS maps, or files entries as each context
is created.

-f *input-file*

> Create a context for every user or host listed in *input-file*. This
> option is applicable only when used with the -t *username* or
> -t *hostname* options. The format of the file is one atomic user name or
> host name per line. Use this option to create contexts for a subset of
> the users/hosts found in the corresponding passwd or hosts database
> of the naming service (that is, for NIS+, these are the passwd.org_dir
> or hosts.org_dir tables, respectively). If you omit this option, create
> a context for every user/host found in the corresponding passwd or
> hosts database.

-o

> Create only the context named by *composite-name*. Create no
> subcontexts. When you omit this option, create subcontexts according
> to the FNS Policies for the type of the new object.

-r *reference-type*

> Use *reference-type* as the reference type of the generic context
> being created. You can use this option only with the -t generic
> option.

-s

> Create the context and bind it in to supersede any existing binding
> associated with *composite-name*. If you omit this option, fncreate
> fails if *composite-name* is already bound.

-t *context-type*

> The following are valid entries for *context-type*.

> > fs
> >
> > > Create a file-system context for a user or host and
> > > bind the reference of the context to
> > > *composite-name*. The composite name must be the
> > > name of a host or a user, with either fs/ or _fs/
> > > appended to it. If the suffix of *composite-name* is
> > > fs/, also bind the file-system context to the
> > > composite name and replace the suffix with _fs/,
> > > and the reverse.
> > >
> > > Typically, you do not need to explicitly create a
> > > file-system context because it is created by default as
> > > a subcontext of a user or host context.
> > >
> > > The file-system context of a user is the user's home
> > > directory as stored in the passwd database of the
> > > naming service (that is, in NIS+ table
> > > passwd.org_dir, passwd NIS map, or /etc/passwd
> > > file). The file-system context of a host is the set of
> > > NFS file systems that the host exports.
> > >
> > > Use the fncreate_fs(1M) command to create
> > > file-system contexts for organizations and sites, or to
> > > create file-system contexts other than the defaults
> > > for users and hosts.

generic   Create a generic context in which slash-separated left-to-right names can be bound, and bind the reference of the context to *composite-name*. You can use the -r option to specify the reference type to be associated with the context. If you omit the -r option, use the reference type of the parent context if the parent context is a generic context; otherwise, the reference type is onc_fn_generic.

host   Create a host context for a specific host and its service and fs subcontexts, and bind the reference of the context to *composite-name*. The following example creates a host context and service and fs subcontexts for host castle.

```
% fncreate -t host org/sales/host/castle/
```

hostname   Create a hostname context in which atomic host names can be bound, and bind the reference of the context to *composite-name*. If the suffix of *composite-name* is host/, also bind the hostname context created to the composite name and replace the suffix with _host/, and the reverse (that is, if you supply a composite name with a _host/ suffix, create a binding for host/). Also create a host context for every host entry in the corresponding hosts database of the naming service (hosts.org_dir NIS+ table, hosts NIS map, or /etc/hosts file), unless you specify either the -o or -f option. The following example creates host contexts for all hosts in the sales organization.

```
% fncreate -t hostname org/sales/host/
```

Typically, you do not need to explicitly create a hostname context because it is created by default as a subcontext under org.

nsid   Create a context in which namespace identifiers can be bound. This context has a flat namespace in which only atomic names can be bound. An example of such a context is site/east/. This context can have the following bindings: site/east/host, site/east/user, and site/east/service.

org   Create organization context and default subcontexts for an existing NIS+ domain, NIS domain, or /etc files environment.

For NIS+, *composite-name* is of the form *org*/*domain*/ where *domain* is an NIS+ domain. An empty domain name indicates the creation of the organization context for the root NIS+ domain;

otherwise, the domain name names the corresponding NIS+ domain. *domain* can be either the fully qualified, dot-terminated NIS+ domain name or the NIS+ domain name named relative to the NIS+ root domain.

The following example creates the root organization context and its subcontexts for the NIS+ root domain `Wiz.Com.`.

```
% fncreate -t org org//
```

You can achieve the same result by using the following command.

```
% fncreate -t org org/Wiz.COM./
```

Typically, this is the first FNS context created.

To create the organization context for a subdomain of `Wiz.COM.`, execute either of the following commands.

```
% fncreate -t org org/sales/
```

or

```
% fncreate -t org org/sales.Wiz.COM./
```

Note that if the corresponding NIS+ domain does not exist, fncreate fails. See `nissetup`(1M) for setting up an NIS+ domain.

A `ctx_dir` directory is created under the directory of the named organization.

For NIS or an `/etc` files environment, *domain* should be null (empty) because NIS and `/etc` files do not support a hierarchy namespace of domains. The following example creates the organization context for the NIS or `/etc` files environment.

```
% fncreate -t org org//
```

For NIS+, NIS, and `/etc` files, creating the organization context also creates the organization's immediate subcontexts host, user, and service and their subcontexts. This setup includes a context for every host entry in the corresponding hosts database of the naming service (that is, `hosts.org_dir` NIS+ table, `hosts` NIS map, or `/etc/hosts` file), and a context for every user entry in the `passwd` database of the naming service (that is, `passwd.org_dir` NIS+ table, `passwd` NIS map, or `/etc/passwd` file) unless you specify the -o option. Bindings for these subcontexts are recorded under the organization context.

service Create a `service` context in which slash-separated left-to-right service names can be bound, and bind the reference of the context to *composite-name*. If the suffix of *composite-name* is `service/`, also bind the service context to the composite name and replace the suffix with `service/`, and the reverse.

Typically, you do not need to explicitly create a service context because it is created by default as a subcontext under `org`, `host`, or `user` contexts.

site Create a site context in which dot-separated right-to-left site names can be bound. Also create a `service` subcontext and bind the reference of the context to *composite-name*. If the suffix of *composite-name* is `site/`, also bind the hostname context to the composite name and replace the suffix with `_site/`, and the reverse. Typically, you create a site context at the same level as the `org` context and use it as a geographical namespace that complements the organizational namespace of an enterprise.

username Create a username context in which atomic user names can be bound and bind the reference of the context to *composite-name*. If the suffix of *composite-name* is `user/`, also bind the username context to the composite name and replace the suffix with `_user/`, and the reverse. Also create a user context for every user entry in the corresponding `passwd` database of the naming service (that is, `passwd.org_dir` NIS+ table, `passwd` NIS map, or `/etc/passwd` file) unless you specify either the `-o` or `-f` option. The following example creates username contexts for all users in the `sales` organization.

```
% fncreate -t username org/sales/user/
```

Typically, you do not need to explicitly create a username context because it is created by default as a subcontext under `org`.

user Create a user context for a specific user and its `service` and `fs` subcontexts, and bind the reference of the context to *composite-name*. The following example creates a user context and `service` and `fs` subcontexts for user `jsmith`.

```
% fncreate -t user org/sales/user/jsmith/
```

-v Display information about the creation of a context as each context is created.

Operands

```
composite-name
```
     An FNS named object.

Examples

The following example creates a host context in the root organization and a user context in a suborganization.

```
paperbark% fncreate -t org org//
```

The above command automatically invokes the following commands.

```
fncreate -t service org//service/
fncreate -t hostname org//host/
fncreate -t username org//user/
```

The following example creates a context and subcontexts for host paperbark.

```
paperbark% fncreate -t host org//host/paperbark/
```

The above command automatically invokes the following commands.

```
fncreate -t service org//host/paperbark/service/
fncreate -t fs org//host/paperbark/fs/
```

The following example creates a context and subcontexts associated with a suborganization dct.

```
paperbark% fncreate -t org orvg/dct/
```

The above command automatically invokes the following commands.

```
fncreate -t service org/dct/service/
fncreate -t hostname org/dct/host/
fncreate -t username org/dct/user/
```

The following example creates a context and subcontexts for user ray.

```
paperbark% fncreate -t user org/dct/user/ray/
```

The above command automatically invokes the following commands.

```
fncreate -t service org/dct/user/ray/service/
fncreate -t fs org/dct/user/ray/fs/
```

The following examples create service contexts.

```
paperbark% fncreate -t service org/dct/service/fax
paperbark% fncreate -t service org/dct/service/fax/classA
```

Exit Status

0	Operation was successful.
1	Operation failed.

Attributes

See attributes(5) for descriptions of the following attributes.

Attribute Type	Attribute Value
Availability	SUNWfns

See Also

nis(1), fncheck(1M), fncreate_fs(1M), fndestroy(1M), fnselect(1M),
nissetup(1M), xfn(3N), attributes(5), fns(5), fns_files(5), fns_nis(5),
fns_nis+(5), fns_policies(5), fns_references(5)

---

fncreate_fs — Create FNS File-System Contexts

Synopsis

```
/usr/sbin/fncreate_fs [-r][-v] -f input-file composite-name
/usr/sbin/fncreate_fs [-r][-v] composite-name [mount-options]
  [mount-location...]
```

Description

Use the fncreate_fs command to create or update the FNS file-system context named
by composite-name. Provide a description of the context's bindings in input-file if you
use the first form of the command, or specify the description of the context's binding on
the command line if you use the second form.

Notes

The fncreate_fs command affects only the FNS file-system namespace. It does not
have any effect on the servers that export the files and directories from which the
namespace is constructed. Destroying an FNS context does not remove any files on any
server.

FNS policies specify that file-system contexts are bound after the namespace
identifier fs in composite names (see fns_policies(5)). Therefore, composite-name
must contain an fs. You can use the alias _fs in place of fs.

The context named by the components of composite-name preceding fs must exist
before the call to fncreate_fs, because fncreate_fs creates only file-system contexts.

Default file-system contexts for hosts and users are generally created by the
command fncreate(1M). These defaults may be overridden with fncreate_fs.
Overriding a host's default file-system context is unlikely to make sense.

The input file format is similar to the format of indirect automount maps (see
automount(1M)), with the following differences.

- The name field may be hierarchical and may be dot (.).
- Maps or special maps are not included.
- Entries can have neither options nor locations.
- The characters * and & have no special meaning.

The process executing the fncreate_fs command may need certain credentials to update information in the underlying naming service. See fns_nis(5), fns_nis+(5), and fns_files(5) for more information.

Options

-r   Replace the bindings in the context named by *composite-name* with only those specified in the input. This action is equivalent to destroying the context (and, recursively, its subcontexts) and then running fncreate_fs without this option. Use this option with care.

-v   Display verbose information about the contexts being created and modified.

-f *input-file*

Read input from *input-file*. If *input-file* is a dash (-), read from standard input instead.

Operands

composite-name

An FNS named object.

Usage

The fncreate_fs command populates the file-system portions of the FNS namespace. The automounter (see automount(1M)) then mounts the FNS namespace under /xfn. The directory with the FNS name org/engineering/fs, for example, can be found on the file system as /xfn/org/engineering/fs.

The format of the input to fncreate_fs is similar, but not identical, to the format of indirect automount maps. See "Notes" on page 331.

Input File Format

The input file supplies the names and values to be bound in the context of *composite-name*. The format of the input file is a sequence of lines of the following format.

name [-options][location...]

For each such entry, a reference to the location(s) and the corresponding options is bound to the name *composite-name/name*. The *name* field can be a simple atomic name, a slash-separated hierarchical name, or dot (.). If it is ., then the reference is bound directly to *composite-name*. The *name* field must not begin with a slash.

The *location* field specifies the host or hosts that serve the files for *composite-name/name*. In the case of a simple NFS mount, *location* takes the form

host:path

where *host* is the name of the host from which to mount the file system and *path* is the path name of the directory to mount.

The *options* field is a comma-separated list of the mount options to use when mounting the location bound to *composite-name/name*. These options also apply to any subcontexts of *composite-name*/*name* that do not specify their own mount options. If you specify *options* but not *location*, the options apply to subcontexts only.

If you specify neither *options* nor *location*, then no reference is bound to *composite-name*/*name*. Any existing reference is unbound.

You can continue a single logical line across multiple input lines by escaping the newline with a backslash (\). Comments begin with a pound sign (#) that is either at the beginning of a line or is prefixed by white space and ends at the end of the line.

Command-Line Input

If you specify no *input-file* on the command line, then the *mount-options* and *mount-location* fields given on the command line are bound directly to *composite-name*. This syntax is equivalent to providing a one-line input file with a . in the *name* field.

Multiple Locations

You can specify multiple *location* fields for NFS file systems that are exported from multiple, functionally equivalent locations. If several locations in the list share the same path name, you can combine them in a comma-separated list of host names.

host1,*host2*,...:*path*

You can weight the hosts by appending the weighting factor to the host name as a nonnegative integer in parentheses. The lower the number, the more desirable the server. The default weighting factor is 0 (most desirable). The following example gives hosts alpha and bravo the default weighting factor of 0 as the most desirable and the host delta as the least.

alpha,bravo,charlie(1),delta(2):/usr/man

See "Usage" on page 115 of automount(1M) for additional information on how the automounter interprets the location field.

Variable Substitution

You can use variable names prefixed by a dollar sign ($) with the *options* or *location* fields. For example, you can specify the location in the following way.

svr1:/export/$CPU

The automounter substitutes client-specific values for these variables when mounting the corresponding file systems. In the above example, $CPU is replaced by the output of uname -p; for example, sparc. See "Usage" on page 115 of automount(1M) for additional information on how the automounter treats variable substitution.

Alternate Input Format

For additional compatibility with automount maps (see automount(1M)), the following input format is accepted.

```
name [options][location...]
        \ /offset1 [options1] location1... \
        \ /offset2 [options2] location2... \
        ...
```

where each *offset* field is a slash-separated hierarchy. This syntax is interpreted as being equivalent to the following.

```
name [options][location...^]
name/offset1 [options1] location1...
name/offset2 [options2] location2...
...
```

The first line is omitted if you omit both *options* and *location*.

This format is for compatibility only; it provides no additional functionality. Its use is deprecated.

Examples

The following examples create a file-system context for the engineering organization. It specifies that org/engineering/fs/src is a read-only NFS mount from server svr1, and that org/engineering/fs/dist is a read-only NFS mount from either svr2 or svr3.

```
paperbark% cat input1 src -ro svr1:/export/src dist -ro
    svr2,svr3:/export/dist
paperbark% fncreate_fs -f input1 org/engineering/fs
```

Once this step is done, you can create the src/cmd context for the engineering organization in several equivalent ways. You could create it by using the composite name org/engineering/fs, as shown below.

```
paperbark% cat input2 src/cmd svr1:/export/cmd
paperbark% fncreate_fs -f input2 org/engineering/fs
```

Equivalently, you could create the src/cmd context for the engineering organization by using the composite name org/engineering/fs/src, as shown below.

```
paperbark% cat input3 cmd svr1:/export/cmd
paperbark% fncreate_fs -f input3 org/engineering/fs/src
```

You can achieve the same results in the following way.

```
paperbark% fncreate_fs org/engineering/fs/src/cmd
    svr1:/export/cmd
```

Note — cmd is mounted read-only because it is a subcontext of src and does not have mount options of its own.

In the first example of this section, the -ro mount option was specified for each entry in the input file. Instead, you could have specified it only once, as shown below.

```
paperbark% cat input4 . -ro src svr1:/export/src dist
    svr2,svr3:/export/dist
paperbark% fncreate_fs -f input4 org/engineering/fs
```

The -ro option here applies to all bindings in the context org/engineering/fs and any of its subcontexts. In particular, it also applies to the cmd context from the above examples.

The following command changes the NFS server for the src context.

```
paperbark% fncreate_fs org/engineering/fs/src svr4:/export/src
```

If you used the -r option, the cmd subcontext would have been destroyed as well, as shown in the following example.

```
paperbark% fncreate_fs -r org/engineering/fs/src svr4:/export/src
```

Only the FNS context is destroyed. The /export/cmd directory on svr1 is not affected.

The file-system contexts of users and hosts are not usually created by fncreate_fs (see "Notes" on page 331). You can, however, override the defaults set by fncreate. For example, the following command sets Jane's file system to be an NFS mount from svr1.

```
paperbark% fncreate_fs user/jane/fs svr1:/export/home/jane
```

Exit Status

0	Operation was successful.
1	Operation failed.

Attributes

See attributes(5) for descriptions of the following attributes.

Attribute Type	**Attribute Value**
Availability	SUNWfns

See Also

fnbind(1), fnlist(1), fnlookup(1), fnunbind(1), nis+(1), automount(1M), fncreate(1M), fndestroy(1M), attributes(5), fns(5), fns_files(5), fns_nis(5), fns_nis+(5), fns_policies(5)

fncreate_printer — Create New Printers in the FNS Namespace

Synopsis

```
/bin/fncreate_printer [-sv] composite-name printer-name printer-addr
    [printer-addr...]
/bin/fncreate_printer [-sv] [-f filename] composite-name
```

Description

Use the fncreate_printer command to create a new printer context for an org, user, host, or site object. *composite-name* is the Federated Naming Service (FNS) name of the object. fncreate_printer uses *printer-name* to name the new printer and bind it to an FNS reference constructed from the set of *printer-addr*s. You can also use fncreate_printer to add new *printer-addr*s for an existing *printer-name*.

The command also supports creating a set of printers as listed in the file *filename*.

The new printer context is created with the FNS name *composite-name*/service/printer/*printer-name*. If the intermediate service or printer names do not exist, their FNS contexts are also created by this command. Normally, these intermediate contexts would be created by an administrative script that uses fncreate(1M) and is run at the time a new FNS organization is set up. The reference bound to the FNS printer name is of type onc_printers and is constructed from the set of *printer-addr*s. A *printer-addr* is of the form *address-type=address*. See printers.conf(4) for the format of *printer-addr* and also the examples below for currently supported address types and address strings.

An FNS printer name is accepted as a valid printer name by lp(1), lpstat(1), cancel(1), lpmove(1M), lpr(1B), lpq(1B), and lprm(1B).

The *printer-name* argument can be a slash-separated name. In this case, before creating the printer context denoted by the leaf name, the fncreate_printer command creates printer context(s) for the intermediate node(s) if they do not already exist.

fncreate_printer creates entries in the naming service determined by fnselect(1M). See fnselect(1M) for more information on the default naming service and on selecting a naming service. Furthermore, the process executing the fncreate_printer command may require certain credentials to update information in the underlying namespace. See fns_nis+(5), fns_nis(5), and fns_files(5) for more information.

Options

-s	Supersede an existing address with the new address with the same address type, if any, for *composite-name*/service/printer /*printer-name*. If you omit this option, append the *printer-addr* to an existing reference or create a new reference using *printer-addr* for the printer.
-v	Display information about individual printer contexts as they are created.
-f *filename*	Use *filename* to obtain a list of printers for which to create contexts. If you omit this option, use /etc/printers.conf as the input file, in which case you should use the -s option to supersede the entries already present in this file.

Operands

filename	The file that contains a list of printers to be created. This file uses the same format as /etc/printers.conf. See printers.conf(4) for more information.
printer-name	The name of the new printer context created.
printer-addr	An address to be associated with the printer context name.
composite-name	
	The FNS name for the org, host, user, or site object for which the new printer contexts are created.

Examples

The following examples create a set of printer contexts under an organization, a printer context for a user, and a printer context associated with a hierarchical printer name for a site.

The following example creates a printer context for every entry listed in the `/etc/printers.conf` file on the system where the command is executed. The printer contexts thus created are bound under the organization's printer context, `org/marketing/service/printer`. The `-s` option is required to force the creation of the printer contexts in the underlying namespace because the default `/etc/printers.conf` file is being used.

example% **fncreate_printer -s org/marketing**

The following example creates a printer named `ps` for user `jsmith` and associates it with the `killtree` printer served by the print server `paperwaster`.

example% **fncreate_printer -s usr/jsmith ps**
    bsdaddr=paperwaster,killtree

The user can print to this printer by using the following command.

example% **lp -d *thisuser*/service/printer/ps *filename***

The following example creates a printer with the hierarchical name `color/fast` under a site. It associates the printer named `site/bldg14/northwing/service/printer/color/fast` with the laser printer on server `paperwaster`. If the intermediate printer context `site/bldg14/northwing/service/printer/color` does not exist, it is also created and associated with the same printer. If the printer name `site/bldg14/northwing/service/printer/color/fast` already exists and has an address of type `bsdaddr` associated with it, this command fails.

example% **fncreate_printer site/bldg14/northwing color/fast**
    bsdaddr=paperwaster,laser

Exit Status

0	Successful operation.
1	Operation failed.

Attributes

See `attributes`(5) for descriptions of the following attributes.

Attribute Type	Attribute Value
Availability	SUNWfns

See Also

cancel(1), lp(1), lpstat(1), lpq(1B), lpr(1B), lprm(1B), fncreate(1M), fnselect(1M), lpmove(1M), printers(4), printers.conf(4), attributes(5), fns(5), fns_files(5), fns_nis(5), fns_nis+(5)

fndestroy — Destroy an FNS Context

Synopsis

    /usr/sbin/fndestroy composite-name

Description

Use the fndestroy command to remove the Federated Naming Service (FNS) context bound to composite-name. The context is not removed if there are subcontexts associated with composite-name.

Examples

The following example destroys the context named by user/jsmith/ and removes the binding of jsmith from the context user/.

    example% **fndestroy user/jsmith/**

This command fails if the context user/jsmith/ contains subcontexts or if the invoker does not have the NIS+ credentials required to delete the NIS+ tables that store the user's bindings. See fns(5).

Attributes

See attributes(5) for descriptions of the following attributes.

Attribute Type	Attribute Value
Availability	SUNWfns

See Also

fnlist(1), fnlookup(1), fnunbind(1), fncreate(1M), attributes(5), fns(5), fns_policies(5)

fnselect — Select a Specific Naming Service to Use for the FNS Initial Context

Synopsis

    /usr/sbin/fnselect [-D]
    /usr/sbin/fnselect naming-service

Description

Use the fnselect command to set the specified naming service to be used to construct the bindings in the Federated Naming Service (FNS) Initial Context. This setting affects

the entire machine as well as applications that make subsequent calls to
fn_ctx_handle_from_initial(3N). Only an administrator who has root privilege on
the system can change this setting.

Options

D   Display the actual naming service used to generate the FNS Initial
                                Context.

Operands

naming-service

                    naming-service can have the following possible values.

                    default   Use the FNS default algorithm to determine the target
                                 naming service.

                    nisplus   Use NIS+ as the target naming service.

                    nis   Use NIS as the target naming service.

                    files   Use /etc files as the target naming service.

Usage

When you specify the default option, FNS determines the underlying naming service
by using the following algorithm.

- First, it checks for NIS+ with FNS installed.
- If the result is true, then FNS assumes nisplus as the underlying naming
  service.
- Otherwise, it checks whether the system is an NIS client.
- If true, FNS assumes nis as the underlying naming service.
- Otherwise, FNS assumes /etc files.

fnselect without any arguments displays the service currently selected for the
Initial Context (one of default, nisplus, nis, or files).

When you specify the -D option and the current setting is default, fnselect uses
the algorithm that is used by FNS and display the actual naming service used for the
FNS Initial Context.

Examples

The following example specifies NIS+ as the underlying naming service for the FNS
Initial Context.

```
# fnselect nisplus
#
```

The following example prints the naming service currently being used to generate
the FNS Initial Context.

```
castle% fnselect
default
castle%
```

Exit Status

0	Operation was successful.
1	Operation failed.

Attributes

See attributes(5) for descriptions of the following attributes.

Attribute Type	Attribute Value
Availability	SUNWfns

See Also

fnbind(1), fnlist(1), fnlookup(1), fnunbind(1), fncreate(1M),
fncreate_fs(1M), fncreate_printer(1M), fndestroy(1M),
fn_ctx_handle_from_initial(3N), attributes(5), fns(5),
fns_initial_context(5)

fnsypd — Update FNS Context on an NIS Master Server

Synopsis

/usr/sbin/fnsypd

Description

The fnsypd daemon is a Remote Procedure Call (RPC) service that accepts requests
from NIS clients to update and modify Federated Naming Service (FNS) contexts. This
daemon runs on an NIS master server with FNS on top of it. The fnsypd daemon
requires the Secure Key Infrastructure (SKI) mechanism for authentication. The SKI
mechanism is part of the SUNWski package. If SUNWski is not installed, authentication
cannot be performed and users receive "permission denied" error messages. The
SUNWski manual pages are located at /opt/SUNWski/man.

fnsypd enables users and hosts to modify only their respective FNS contexts.
Organization, site, hostname, and username contexts cannot be modified with fnsypd.

Exit Status

0	Successful completion.
1	An error occurred.

Attributes

See `attributes(5)` for descriptions of the following attributes.

Attribute Type	Attribute Value
Availability	SUNWfns

See Also

`nis(1)`, `attributes(5)`, `fns(5)`, `fns_policies(5)`

format — Partition and Maintain Disks

Synopsis

```
/usr/sbin/format [-f command-file] [-l log-file] [-x data-file]
    [-d disk-name] [-t disk-type] [-p partition-name]
    [-s] [-m] [-M] [-e] [disk-list]
```

Description

Use the `format` command to prepare hard disk drives for use on a Solaris system. The `format` command enables you to format, label, repair, and analyze hard disks.

Disk drives are partitioned and labeled as part of the Solaris installation process. You may need to use the `format` command in the following circumstances.

- To display slice (partition) information.
- To divide a disk into slices.
- To add a disk drive to an existing system.
- To format a disk drive.
- To repair a disk drive.

Unlike previous disk maintenance commands, `format` runs under SunOS. Because of limitations to what can be done to the system disk while the system is running, `format` is also supported within the memory-resident system environment. For most applications, however, it is more convenient to run `format` under SunOS.

`format` first uses the disk list defined in `data-file` if you specify the `-x` option. `format` then checks for the FORMAT_PATH environment variable, a colon-separated list of file names or directories. In the case of a directory, `format` searches for a file named `format.dat` in that directory; a file name should be an absolute path name and is used without change. `format` adds all disk and partition definitions in each specified file to the working set. Multiple identical definitions are silently ignored. If FORMAT_PATH is not set, the path defaults to `/etc/format.dat`.

`disk-list` is a list of disks in the form `c?t?d?` or `/dev/rdsk/c?t?d?s?`. Shell wildcard specifications are supported with the latter form. For example, specifying `/dev/rdsk/c2*` works on all drives connected to controller c2 only. If you specify no `disk-list`, `format` lists all the disks present in the system.

`format` provides a help facility you can use whenever `format` is expecting input. You can request help about what information is expected by typing a question mark (?);

format prints a brief description of what type of input is needed. If you enter a ? at the menu prompt, a list of available commands is displayed.

Note — For SCSI disks, formatting is done with both Primary and Grown defect lists by default. However, if only Primary list is extracted in the Defect menu before formatting, formatting is done with Primary list only.

Options

-d *disk-name*

Specify which disk should be made current when entering the command. Specify the disk by its logical name (for instance, -d c0t1d0). You can also specify a single disk in the *disk-list* operand.

-e

Enable SCSI expert menu. Note that this option is not recommended for casual use.

-f *command-file*

Take command input from *command-file* instead of the standard input. The file must contain commands that appear just as they would if they had been entered from the keyboard. With this option, format does not display continue? prompts; you do not need to specify y(es) or n(o) answers in *command-file*. In noninteractive mode, format does not initially expect the input of a disk selection number. You must specify the current working disk with the -d *disk-name* option when you invoke format or specify disk and the disk selection number in *command-file*.

-l *log-file*   Log a transcript of the format session to the specified *log-file*, including the standard input, the standard output, and the standard error.

-m

Enable extended messages. Provide more detailed information in the event of an error.

-M

Enable extended and diagnostic messages. Provide extensive information on the state of a SCSI device's mode pages during formatting.

-p *partition-name*

Specify the partition table for the disk that is current on entry into the command. Specify the table by its name as defined in *data-file*.

You can use this option only if a disk is being made current and its type is either specified or available from the disk label.

-s

Suppress all of the standard output. Error messages are still displayed. You generally use this option in conjunction with the -f option.

-t *disk-type*   Specify the type of disk that is current on entry into the command. You specify a disk's type by name in *data-file*. You can use this option only if a disk is being made current as described above.

-x *data-file*   Use the list of disks contained in *data-file*.

Usage

The format command's main menu items enable you to do the following tasks.

analyze	Run read, write, and compare tests.
backup	Search for backup labels.
cache	Enable, disable, and query the state of the write cache and read cache. This menu item appears only when you invoke format with the -e option and is supported only on SCSI devices. Note that not all SCSI devices support changing or saving the state of the cache. The cache menu item is new in the Solaris 8 release.
current	Display the device name, the disk geometry, and the path name to the disk device.
defect	Retrieve and print defect lists.
disk	Choose the disk that is used in subsequent operations (known as the current disk.)
fdisk	Run the fdisk(1M) command to create a fdisk partition for Solaris software (IA-based systems only).
format	Format and verify the current disk.
inquiry	Display the vendor, product name, and revision level of the current drive.
label	Write a new label to the current disk.
partition	Create and modify slices.
quit	Exit the format menu.
repair	Repair a specific block on the disk.
save	Save new disk and slice information.
type	Select (define) a disk type.
verify	Read and display labels. Print information such as the number of cylinders, alternate cylinders, heads, sectors, and the partition table.
volname	Label the disk with a new eight-character volume name.

New!

Warning — When you choose the format function to format the Maxtor 207MB disk, the following message is displayed.

```
Mode sense page(4) reports rpm value as 0, adjusting it to 3600
```

This is a drive bug that may also occur with older third-party drives. The message is not an error; the drive still functions correctly.

Examples

The following example uses the `format` command to display current information about disk 1 and to show vendor information about that disk.

```
# format
Searching for disks...done


AVAILABLE DISK SELECTIONS:
       0. c0t0d0 <SUN2.1G cyl 2733 alt 2 hd 19 sec 80>
          /sbus@1f,0/SUNW,fas@e,8800000/sd@0,0
       1. c0t1d0 <SUN2.1G cyl 2733 alt 2 hd 19 sec 80>
          /sbus@1f,0/SUNW,fas@e,8800000/sd@1,0
Specify disk (enter its number): 1
selecting c0t1d0
[disk formatted]


FORMAT MENU:
        disk       - select a disk
        type       - select (define) a disk type
        partition  - select (define) a partition table
        current    - describe the current disk
        format     - format and analyze the disk
        repair     - repair a defective sector
        label      - write label to the disk
        analyze    - surface analysis
        defect     - defect list management
        backup     - search for backup labels
        verify     - read and display labels
        save       - save new disk/partition definitions
        inquiry    - show vendor, product and revision
        volname    - set 8-character volume name
        !<cmd>     - execute <cmd>, then return
        quit
format> current
Current Disk = c0t1d0
<SUN2.1G cyl 2733 alt 2 hd 19 sec 80>
/sbus@1f,0/SUNW,fas@e,8800000/sd@1,0

format> inquiry
Vendor:    SEAGATE
Product:   ST32550W SUN2.1G
Revision:  0418
format> quit
#
```

The following example invokes `format` with the `-e` option to display the new `cache` menu item and uses its options to enable writing to the cache.

```
# format -e
Searching for disks...done
```

```
AVAILABLE DISK SELECTIONS:
       0. c0t0d0 <SUN2.1G cyl 2733 alt 2 hd 19 sec 80>
          /sbus@1f,0/SUNW,fas@e,8800000/sd@0,0
       1. c0t1d0 <SUN2.1G cyl 2733 alt 2 hd 19 sec 80>
          /sbus@1f,0/SUNW,fas@e,8800000/sd@1,0
Specify disk (enter its number): 0
selecting c0t0d0
[disk formatted]
Warning: Current Disk has mounted partitions.


FORMAT MENU:
       disk       - select a disk
       type       - select (define) a disk type
       partition  - select (define) a partition table
       current    - describe the current disk
       format     - format and analyze the disk
       repair     - repair a defective sector
       label      - write label to the disk
       analyze    - surface analysis
       defect     - defect list management
       backup     - search for backup labels
       verify     - read and display labels
       save       - save new disk/partition definitions
       inquiry    - show vendor, product and revision
       scsi       - independent SCSI mode selects
       cache      - enable, disable or query SCSI disk cache
       volname    - set 8-character volume name
       !<cmd>     - execute <cmd>, then return
       quit
format> cache


CACHE MENU:
       write_cache - display or modify write cache settings
       read_cache  - display or modify read cache settings
       !<cmd>      - execute <cmd>, then return
       quit
cache> write_cache
WRITE_CACHE MENU:
       display    - display current setting of write cache
       enable     - enable write cache
       disable    - disable write cache
       !<cmd>     - execute <cmd>, then return
       quit
write_cache> display
Write Cache is disabled
write_cache> enable
write_cache> display
Write Cache is enabled
write_cache> quit
cache> quit
format> quit
#
```

Environment Variables

FORMAT_PATH   A colon-separated list of file names or directories of disk and partition definitions. If a directory is specified, format searches for the file format.dat in that directory.

Files

/etc/format.dat

Default data file.

Attributes

See attributes(5) for descriptions of the following attributes.

Attribute Type	Attribute Value
Availability	SUNWcsu

See Also

fmthard(1M), prtvtoc(1M), format.dat(4), attributes(5), ipi(7D), sd(7D)
Disk Management in *System Administration Guide, Volume I*

IA Platform Only
fdisk(1M)

fsck — Check and Repair File Systems

Synopsis

```
/usr/sbin/fsck [-F FSType][-m][-V][special...]
/usr/sbin/fsck [-F FSType][-n | N | y | Y][-V]
   [-o FSType-specific-options][special...]
```

Description

File systems rely on an internal set of tables to keep track of inodes and used and available blocks. When these internal tables are not properly synchronized with data on a disk, inconsistencies result and file systems need to be repaired.

File systems can be damaged or become inconsistent because of abrupt termination of the operating system in the following ways.

- Power failure.
- Accidental unplugging of the system.
- Turning off the system without proper shutdown procedure.
- A software error in the kernel.

File-system corruption, though serious, is not common. When a system is booted, the fsck command is run to automatically check file-system consistency. Most of the time, fsck repairs problems it encounters.

The fsck command puts files and directories that are allocated but unreferenced in the lost+found directory in that file system. The inode number of each file is assigned as a name. If the lost+found directory does not exist, fsck creates it. If there is not enough space in the lost+found directory, fsck increases its size.

You may need to interactively check file systems when they cannot be mounted or if they develop problems while in use.

Use the fsck command to audit and interactively repair inconsistent file-system conditions. If the file system is inconsistent, the default action for each correction is to wait for you to respond yes or no. If you do not have write permission, fsck defaults to a no action. Some corrective actions result in loss of data. You can determine the amount and severity of data loss from the diagnostic output.

You specify *FSType-specific-options* in a comma-separated (with no intervening spaces) list of options or keyword-attribute pairs for interpretation by the *FSType*-specific module of the command.

Note — fsck may not be supported for all *FSType*s.

special represents the character special device on which the file system resides, for example, /dev/rdsk/c1t0d0s7.

Note — Use the character special device, not the block special device. fsck does work on a block device if it is mounted.

If you do not specify a *special* device, fsck checks the file systems listed in /etc/vfstab file. Those entries in /etc/vfstab that have a character special device entry in the fsckdev field and have a non-zero numeric entry in the fsckpass field are checked. Specifying -F *FSType* limits the file systems to be checked to those of the type indicated.

If you specify *special* but don't use the -F option, the file-system type is determined by a search for a matching entry in /etc/vfstab. If no entry is found, the default local file-system type specified in /etc/default/fs is used.

If a file-system type supports parallel checking, for example, ufs, some file systems eligible for checking can be checked in parallel. Consult the file system-specific manual page (for example, fsck_ufs(1M)) for more information.

Warning — The operating system buffers file system data. If you run fsck on a mounted file system, the operating system's buffers can become out of date with the disk. For this reason, you should unmount the file system when you use fsck. If this is not possible, take care that the system is quiescent and that it is rebooted immediately after you run fsck. Quite often, however, this approach is not sufficient. Running fsck on a file system modifies the file system and can result in a panic.

Options

-F *FSType*	Specify the file-system type on which to operate. Supported *FSTypes* are cachefs, s5fs, ufs, and udfs.
-m	Check, but do not repair. This option checks that the file system is suitable for mounting, returning the appropriate exit status. If the file system is ready for mounting, fsck displays a message such as

```
ufs fsck: sanity check: /dev/rdsk/c0t3d0s1 okay
```

-n|N   Assume a no response to all questions asked by fsck; do not open the file system for writing.

-V   Echo the expanded command line but do not execute the command. You can use this option to verify and to validate the command line.

-y|Y   Assume a yes response to all questions asked by fsck.

-o *specific-options*

The specific options can be any combination of the following separated by commas (with no intervening spaces).

b=*n*   Use block *n* as the superblock for the file system. Block 32 is always one of the alternate superblocks. Determine the location of other superblocks by running newfs(1M) with the -Nv options.

c   If the file system is in the old (static table) format, convert it to the new (dynamic table) format. If the file system is in the new format, convert it to the old format provided the old format can support the file-system configuration. In interactive mode, fsck lists the direction the conversion is to be made and asks whether the conversion should be done. If you give a negative answer, no further operations are done on the file system. In preen mode, the direction of the conversion is listed and done if possible without user interaction. Conversion in preen mode is best used

when all the file systems are being converted at once. The format of a file system can be determined from the first line of output from fstyp(1M). Note that the c option is seldom used and is included only for compatibility with pre-4.1 releases. There is no guarantee that this option will be included in future releases.

f   Force checking of file systems regardless of the state of their superblock clean flag.

p   Check and fix the file system noninteractively (preen). Exit immediately if there is a problem requiring intervention. This option is required to enable parallel file-system checking.

w   Check writable file systems only.

Exit Status

0   File system is okay and does not need checking.

1   Erroneous parameters are specified.

32   File system is unmounted and needs checking (fsck -m only).

33	File system is already mounted.
34	Cannot stat device.
36	Uncorrectable errors detected—terminate normally.
37	A signal was caught during processing.
39	Uncorrectable errors detected—terminate immediately.
40	For root, same as 0.

Usage

See largefile(5) for the description of the behavior of fsck when encountering files greater than or equal to 2 Gbytes (2**31 bytes).

Note — Running fsck on file systems larger than 2 Gbytes fails if you specify the block interface to the device as fsck /dev/dsk/c?t?d?s? instead of the raw (character special) device fsck /dev/rdsk/c?t?d?s?

Files

/etc/default/fs

Default local file-system type. Default values can be set for the following flag in /etc/default/fs. For example, LOCAL=ufs.

LOCAL   The default partition for a command if you specify no *FSType*.

/etc/vfstab List of default parameters for each file system.

Attributes

See attributes(5) for descriptions of the following attributes.

Attribute Type	**Attribute Value**
Availability	SUNWcsu

See Also

clri(1M), crash(1M), fsck_cachefs(1M), fsck_s5fs(1M), fsck_ufs(1M), fsdb_ufs(1M), fsirand(1M), fstyp(1M), mkfs(1M), mkfs_ufs(1M), mountall(1M), newfs(1M), reboot(1M), fs_ufs(4), vfstab(4), attributes(5), largefile(5)

fsck_cachefs — Check Integrity of Data Cached with CacheFS

Synopsis
```
/usr/sbin/fsck -F cachefs [-m | -o | noclean] cache-directory
```

Description
The CacheFS version of the `fsck` command checks the integrity of a cache directory. By default, it corrects any CacheFS problems it finds. There is no interactive mode. The most likely invocation of `fsck` for CacheFS file systems is at boot time from an entry in the `/etc/vfstab` file (see `vfstab`(4)).

Options

`-m`	Check, but do not repair.
`-o noclean`	Force a check on the cache even if there is no reason to suspect there is a problem.

Examples
The following example forces a check on the cache directory `/cache3`.
```
# fsck -F cachefs -o noclean /cache3
```

Attributes
See `attributes`(5) for descriptions of the following attributes.

Attribute Type	**Attribute Value**
Availability	SUNWcsu

See Also
`cfsadmin(1M), fsck(1M), mount_cachefs(1M), vfstab(4), attributes(5)`

fsck_s5fs — File-System Consistency Check and Interactive Repair

Synopsis
```
/usr/sbin/fsck -F s5fs [generic-options][special...]
/usr/sbin/fsck -F s5fs [generic-options][-o
  specific-options][special...]
```

Description

Use `fsck -F s5fs` to audit and interactively repair inconsistent conditions on System V file systems. You can specify the file system to be checked by giving the name of the block or character special device or by giving the name of its mount point if a matching entry exists in `/etc/vfstab`. If you specify no special device, all s5 file systems specified in the `vfstab` with a `fsckdev` entry are checked.

By default, `fsck` asks for confirmation before making a repair of serious inconsistencies and waits for a yes or no response. If you do not have write permission on the file system, `fsck` defaults to a `-n` (no corrections) action. See `fsck`(1M).

> **Note** — Repairing some file system inconsistencies can result in loss of data. You can determine the amount and severity of data loss from the diagnostic output.

`fsck` automatically corrects innocuous inconsistencies such as unreferenced inodes, missing blocks in the free list, blocks appearing in the free list and in files, or incorrect counts in the superblock. It displays a message for each inconsistency corrected that identifies the nature of the correction on which the file system took place. After successfully correcting a file system, `fsck` prints the number of files on that file system and the number of used and free blocks.

Checks are made for the following inconsistencies.

- Blocks claimed by more than one inode or the free list.
- Blocks claimed by an inode or the free list outside the range of the file system.
- Incorrect link counts.
- Incorrect directory sizes.
- Bad inode format.
- Blocks not accounted for anywhere.
- Directory checks, file pointing to unallocated inode, inode number out of range, absence of . and .. entries in any directory.
- Superblock checks: more blocks for inodes than there are in the file system.
- Bad free block list format.
- Total free block and/or free inode count incorrect.

Orphaned files and directories (allocated but unreferenced) are, with the operator's concurrence, reconnected by placing them in the `lost+found` directory. The name assigned is the inode number. If the `lost+found` directory does not exist, `fsck` creates it.

> **Note** — It is usually faster to check the character special device than the block special device.

Options

See generic `fsck`(1M) for *generic-options* and details for specifying special.

`-o`	Specify s5 file system specific options. These options can be any combination of the following separated by commas (with no intervening spaces).

`D`	Perform more extensive directory checking than normal.
`f` | `F`	Fast check; duplicate blocks and free list check only.

l		After all other output is done, print i-number/path name correspondences for damaged files.
p		Preen the file system by checking and fixing the file system noninteractively. Exit immediately if there is a problem requiring intervention.
q		Produce less verbose output.
s	*cyl:skip*	If the free block list must be rewritten (salvaged) to correct an inconsistency, interleave the blocks so that, to the extent possible within each group of *cyl* consecutive free blocks, the interval between blocks is *skip*. For example, with an interleave of 8:3, in each group of eight consecutive free blocks, the order on the free list would be 1 4 7 2 5 8 3 6. If you specify no *cyl:skip*, take the value either from the superblock, or, if unspecified (either has a value of 0), use 400:7. For obscure historical reasons, interleave specification of 3 and 4 (without colons) are taken to mean 200:5 and 418:7.
S	*cyl:skip*	Same as above except rewrite the free block list unconditionally.
t	*scratchfile*	
T	*scratchfile*	
		If there is insufficient memory and a temporary file is needed to complete file-system checking, use *scratchfile* as the temporary file.
?		Print usage message.

Files

/etc/vfstab   List of default parameters for each file system.

Attributes

See attributes(5) for descriptions of the following attributes.

Attribute Type	**Attribute Value**
Architecture	IA
Availability	SUNWs53

See Also

fsck(1M), attributes(5)

fsck_udfs — File-System Consistency Check and Interactive [New!] Repair

Synopsis
```
/usr/bin/fsck -F udfs [generic-options][special...]
/usr/bin/fsck-Fudfs[generic-options][-ospecific-options][special...]
```

Description
The Universal Disk Format (UDF) file system is included in the Solaris 8 release. UDF is the industry-standard format for storing readable and rewriteable information on the optical media technology called Digital Versatile Disc or Digital Video Disc (DVD). Use the fsck_udfs command, new in the Solaris 8 release, to audit and interactively repair inconsistent conditions on UDF file systems. Specify the file system to be checked by giving the name of the block or character special device or by giving the name of its mount point if a matching entry exists in /etc/vfstab.

special represents the character special device, for example, /dev/rdsk/c0t2d0s0, on which the file system resides. Use the character special device, not the block special device. fsck does not work on a mounted block device.

If you specify no special device, all udfs file systems specified in the vfstab file with a fsckdev entry are checked. If you specify the -p (preen) option, udfs file systems with an fsckpass number greater than 1 are checked in parallel. See fsck(1M).

When correcting serious inconsistencies, by default, fsck asks for confirmation before making a repair and waits for a yes or no response. If you do not have write permission on the file system, fsck defaults to the -n (no corrections) option. See fsck(1M).

Note — Repairing some file system inconsistencies can result in loss of data. You can determine the amount and severity of data loss from the diagnostic output.

---

fsck automatically corrects innocuous inconsistencies. It displays a message for each corrected inconsistency that identifies the nature of the correction that took place on the file system. After successfully correcting a file system, fsck prints the number of files on that file system and the number of used and free blocks.

The following inconsistencies are checked.

- Blocks claimed by more than one file or the free list.
- Blocks claimed by a file or the free list outside the range of the file system.
- Incorrect link counts in file entries.
- Incorrect directory sizes.
- Bad file entry format.
- Blocks not accounted for anywhere.
- Directory checks: file pointing to unallocated file entry and absence of a parent directory entry.
- Descriptor checks, more blocks for files than the file system contains.
- Bad free block list format.
- Total free block count incorrect.

Warning — The operating system buffers file-system data. If you run `fsck` on a mounted file system, the operating system's buffers can become out of date with the disk. For this reason, you should unmount the file system before running `fsck`. If this is not possible, take care to quiesce the system and reboot it immediately after you run `fsck`. Quite often, however, this approach is not sufficient. A panic will probably occur if running `fsck` on a file system modifies the file system.

If the file system is not ummounted before the system is shut down, the file system might become corrupted. In this case, you should complete a file-system check before the next mount operation.

Options

`generic-options`

The following `generic-options` are supported.

`-m`   Check but do not repair. Check to be sure that the file system is suitable for mounting, and return the appropriate exit status. If the file system is ready for mounting, display a message such as the following.

`udfs fsck: sanity check: /dev/rdsk/c0t2d0s0 okay.`

`-n | -N`   Assume a no response to all questions; do not open the file system for writing.

`-V`   Echo the expanded command line, but do not execute the command. You can use this option to verify and to validate the command line.

`-y | -Y`   Assume a yes response to all questions.

`-o specific-options`

Specify `udfs`-file-system-specific options in a comma-separated list with no intervening spaces. The following `specific-options` are available.

`-f`   Force checking of file systems regardless of the logical volume integrity state.

`-p`   Check and fix the file system noninteractively (preen). Exit immediately if there is a problem that requires intervention. This option is required to enable parallel file-system checking.

`-w`   Check writeable file systems only.

Files

`/etc/vtstab`   List of default parameters for each file system.

Attributes

See attributes(5) for descriptions of the following attributes.

Attribute Type	Attribute Value
Availability	SUNWudf

See Also

crash(1M), fsck(1M), fsdb_udfs(1M), fstyp(1M), mkfs(1M), mkfs_udfs(1M), mountall(1M), reboot(1M), vfstab(4), attributes(5)

Diagnostics

not writeable

> You cannot write to the device.

Currently Mounted on

> The device is already mounted and cannot run fsck.

FILE SYSTEM WAS MODIFIED

> File system has been modified to bring it to a consistent state.

Can't read allocation extent

> Cannot read the block containing allocation extent.

Bad tag on alloc extent

> Invalid tag detected when expecting an allocation extent.

Volume sequence tag error

> Invalid tag detected in the volume sequence.

Space bitmap tag error

> Invalid tag detected in the space bitmap.

UNEXPECTED INCONSISTENCY; RUN fsck MANUALLY

> Use fsck in interactive mode.

fsck_ufs — File-System Consistency Check and Interactive Repair

Synopsis

```
/usr/sbin/fsck -F ufs [generic-options][special...]
/usr/sbin/fsck-Fufs[generic-options][-ospecific-options][special...]
```

Description

Use the fsck_ufs command to audit and interactively repair inconsistent conditions on UFS file systems. You can specify the file system to be checked by giving the name of the block or character special device or by giving the name of its mount point if a matching entry exists in /etc/vfstab.

The *special* parameter represents the character special device, for example, /dev/rdsk/c1t0d0s7, on which the file system resides. You should use the character special device, not the block special device. The fsck command does not work on a block device if the block device is mounted, unless the file system is error-locked.

If you specify no special device, all ufs file systems specified in the vfstab with a fsckdev entry are checked. If you specify the -p (preen) option, ufs file systems with an fsckpass number greater than 1 are checked in parallel. See fsck(1M).

When correcting serious inconsistencies, by default, fsck asks for confirmation before making a repair and waits for a yes or no response. If you do not have write permission on the file system, fsck defaults to -n (no corrections). See fsck(1M).

Note — Repairing some file-system inconsistencies can result in loss of data. You can determine the amount and severity of data loss from the diagnostic output.

The fsck command automatically corrects innocuous inconsistencies such as unreferenced inodes, too-large link counts in inodes, missing blocks in the free list, blocks appearing in the free list and also in files, or incorrect counts in the superblock. It displays a message for each inconsistency corrected that identifies the nature of the correction that took place on the file system. After successfully correcting a file system, fsck prints the number of files on that file system, the number of used and free blocks, and the percentage of fragmentation.

Checks are made for the following inconsistencies.

- Blocks claimed by more than one inode or the free list.
- Blocks claimed by an inode or the free list outside the range of the file system.
- Incorrect link counts.
- Incorrect directory sizes.
- Bad inode format.
- Blocks not accounted for anywhere.
- Directory checks, file pointing to unallocated inode, inode number out of range, and absence of . and . . as the first two entries in each directory.
- Superblock checks: more blocks for inodes than there are in the file system.
- Bad free block list format.
- Total free block or free inode count incorrect.

Orphaned files and directories (allocated but unreferenced) are, with the operator's concurrence, reconnected by being placed in the lost+found directory. The name assigned is the inode number. If the lost+found directory does not exist, it is created. If there is insufficient space in the lost+found directory, its size is increased.

Mounting a ufs file system with the -o nolargefiles option fails if the file system has ever contained a large file (a file whose size is greater than or equal to 2 Gbytes). Invoking fsck resets the file-system state if no large files are present in the file system. A successful mount of the file system after an invocation of fsck indicates the absence of large files in the file system. An unsuccessful mount attempt indicates the presence of at least one large file. See mount_ufs(1M).

> **Warning** — The operating system buffers file system data. If you run `fsck`
> on a mounted file system, the operating system's buffers can become out of
> date with the disk. For this reason, you should unmount the file system
> before running `fsck`. If this is not possible, take care to quiesce the system
> and reboot it immediately after you run `fsck`. Quite often, however, this
> approach is not sufficient. A panic will probably occur if running `fsck` on a
> file system modifies the file system.

Notes

It is usually faster to check the character special device than the block special device.
Running `fsck` on file systems larger than 2 Gbytes fails if you use the block interface
to the device

```
fsck /dev/dsk/c?t?d?s?
```

instead of the raw (character special) device

```
fsck /dev/rdsk/c?t?d?s?
```

Options

The `generic-options` are listed below.

-m

Check, but do not repair. Check that the file system is suitable for mounting, returning the appropriate exit status. If the file system is ready for mounting, `fsck` displays a message such as the following.

```
ufs fsck: sanity check: /dev/rdsk/c0t3d0s1 okay
```

-n|N

Assume a no response to all questions asked by `fsck`; do not open the file system for writing.

-V

Echo the expanded command line, but do not execute the command. You can use this option to verify and to validate the command line.

-y|Y

Assume a yes response to all questions asked by `fsck`.

See generic `fsck`(1M) for the details for specifying `special`.

-o `specific-options`

Specify UFS-file-system specific options. These options can be any combination of the following separated by commas (with no intervening spaces).

b=*n*

Use block *n* as the superblock for the file system. Block 32 is always one of the alternate superblocks. Determine the location of other superblocks by running `newfs`(1M) with the -Nv options.

c

If the file system is in the old (static table) format, convert it to the new (dynamic table) format. If the file system is in the new format, convert it to the old format provided the old format can support the file system configuration. In interactive mode, `fsck` lists the direction the conversion is to be made and asks whether the conversion should be done. If you give a negative answer, do no further operations on the file system. In preen mode, the direction of the conversion is listed and done if possible without user interaction. Conversion in preen mode is best used when all the file systems are being converted at once. The format of a file system can be determined from the first line of output from fstyp(1M). Note that the c option is seldom used and is included only for compatibility with pre-4.1 releases. There is no guarantee that this option will be included in future releases.

f   Force checking of file systems regardless of the state of their superblock clean flag.

p   Check and fix the file system noninteractively (preen). Exit immediately if there is a problem requiring intervention. This option is required to enable parallel file-system checking.

w   Check writeable file systems only.

Files

/etc/vfstab   List of default parameters for each file system.

Attributes

See attributes(5) for descriptions of the following attributes.

Attribute Type	Attribute Value
Availability	SUNWcsu

See Also

clri(1M), crash(1M), fsck(1M), fsdb_ufs(1M), fsirand(1M), fstyp(1M), mkfs(1M), mkfs_ufs(1M), mount_ufs(1M), mountall(1M), newfs(1M), reboot(1M), fs_ufs(4), vfstab(4), attributes(5), largefile(5)

fsdb — File-System Debugger

Synopsis

/usr/sbin/fsdb [-F FSType][-V][-o FSType-specific-options] special

Description

Use the fsdb file system debugger to manually repair a file system after a crash. *special* is a special device that specifies the file system to be debugged. fsdb is intended for experienced users only. *FSType* is the file-system type to be debugged. Because different *FSType*s have different structures and hence different debugging capabilities, consult the manual pages for the *FSType*-specific fsdb for a more detailed description of the debugging capabilities.

Note — This command may not be supported for all *FSType*s.

Options

-F *FSType*   Specify the *FSType* on which to operate. You should either specify the *FSType* here or fsdb should be able to determine it from /etc/vfstab by matching *special* with an entry in the table or by consulting /etc/default/fs.

-V   Echo the complete command line, but do not execute the command. Generate the command line by using the specified options and arguments and adding to them information derived from /etc/vfstab. You can use this option to verify and validate the command line.

-o   Specify *FSType*-specific options.

Usage

See largefile(5) for the description of the behavior of fsdb when encountering files greater than or equal to 2 Gbytes (2**31 bytes).

Files

/etc/default/fs

Default local file-system type. Default values can be set for the following flag in /etc/default/fs. For example, LOCAL=ufs.

LOCAL   The default partition for a command if no *FSType* is specified.

/etc/vfstab   List of default parameters for each file system.

Attributes

See attributes(5) for descriptions of the following attributes.

Attribute Type	Attribute Value
Availability	SUNWcsu

See Also

vfstab(4), attributes(5), largefile(5)
Manual pages for the *FSType*-specific modules of fsdb.

New! **fsdb_udfs** — UDFS File-System Debugger

Synopsis

```
/usr/sbin/fsdb -F udfs [generic-option] [-o specific-option] special
```

Description

The fsdb_udfs command is new in the Solaris 8 release. This command is the universal disk format file system (UDFS)-specific module of the fsdb command. Use it to patch up a damaged UDFS file system. fsdb_udfs has conversions to translate block and i-numbers into their corresponding disk addresses. Mnemonic offsets to access different parts of an inode are also included. Mnemonic offsets greatly simplify the process of correcting control block entries or descending the file-system tree.

fsdb contains several error-checking routines to verify inode and block addresses. You can disable these by invoking fsdb with the -o option or by using the o command.

fsdb reads one block at a time, and therefore works with raw as well as block I/O devices. A buffer management routine is used to retain commonly used blocks of data to reduce the number of read system calls. All assignment operations result in an immediate write-through of the corresponding block. To modify any portion of the disk, you must invoke fsdb with the -w option.

Wherever possible, adb-like syntax has been adopted to promote the use of fsdb through familiarity.

Options

-o *specific-option*

> Specify UDFS-file-system-specific options in a comma-separated list with no intervening spaces. The following specific options are supported.

> | | |
> |---|---|
> | o | Override some error conditions. |
> | p=*string* | Set prompt to *string*. |
> | w | Open for write. |
> | ? | Display usage. |

Usage

Numbers are considered hexadecimal by default. You control how data is to be displayed or accepted. The base command displays or sets the input and output base. Once set, all input defaults to this base and all output displays in this base. You can temporarily override the base for input by preceding hexadecimal numbers with 0x, decimal numbers with 0t, or octal numbers with 0. You must precede hexadecimal numbers beginning with a-f or A-F with 0x to distinguish them from commands.

Disk addressing by fsdb is at the byte level. However, fsdb offers many commands to convert a desired inode, directory entry, block, and so forth, to a byte address. After the address has been calculated, fsdb records the result in the current address (dot).

fsdb maintains the following global values.

- Current base (referred to as base).
- Current address (referred to as dot).
- Current inode (referred to as inode).
- Current count (referred to as count).
- Current type (referred to as type)

Most commands use the preset value of dot in their execution. For example, > 2:inode first sets the value of dot (.) to 2, colon (:), signifies the start of a command, and the inode command sets inode to 2. Specify a count after a comma (,). Once set, count remains at this value until a new command is encountered that resets the value back to 1 (the default).

So, if you enter > 2000,400/X, then 400 hex longs are listed from 2000, and when completed, the value of dot is 2000 + 400 * sizeof (long). If you then press Return, the output routine uses the current values of dot, count, and type and displays 400 more hex longs. An asterisk (*) displays the entire block. The following example shows several commands and the use of Return.

```
> 2:ino; 0:dir?d
> 2:ino; 0:db:block?d
```

The two examples are synonymous for getting to the first directory entry of the root of the file system. Once there, subsequently entering Return, plus (+), or minus (–) advances to subsequent entries. Notice that the following two commands are synonymous.

```
> 2:inode; :ls
> :ls /
```

Expressions

The following symbols are recognized by fsdb.

Return	Update the value of dot by the current value of type, and display using the current value of count.
#	Update the value of dot by specifying a numeric expression. Specify numeric expressions using addition, subtraction, multiplication, and division operators (+, –, *, and %). Numeric expressions are evaluated from left to right and can use parentheses. After evaluation, update the value of dot.
, count	Update the count indicator. Update the global value of count to *count*. The value of count remains until a new command is run. A count specifier of * tries to show a block's worth of information. The default for count is 1.
? f	Display in structured style with format specifier f. See "Formatted Output" on page 364.
/ f	Display in unstructured style with format specifier f. See "Formatted Output" on page 364.
.	Display the value of dot.
+e	Increment the value of dot by the expression e. The amount actually incremented depends on the size of type: dot = dot + e * sizeof (type) The default for e is 1.

-e	Decrement the value of dot by the expression e. See +.
*e	Multiply the value of dot by the expression e. Multiplication and division don't use type. In the above calculation of dot, consider the sizeof (type) to be 1.
%e	Divide the value of dot by the expression e. See *.
< name	Restore an address saved in register name. name must be a single letter or digit.
> name	Save an address in register name. name must be a single letter or digit.
= f	Display indicator. If f is a legitimate format specifier (see "Formatted Output" on page 364), then display the value of dot using format specifier f. Otherwise, assignment is assumed. See = [s] [e].
= [s] [e]	Change the value of dot by using an assignment indicator. Change the address pointed to by dot to the value of the expression e or to the ASCII representation of the quoted (") string s. This symbol can be useful for changing directory names or ASCII file information.
=+ e	Change the value of dot by using an incremental assignment. Increment the address pointed to by dot by expression e.
=- e	Change the value of dot by using a decremental assignment. Decrement the contents of the address pointed to by dot by expression e.

Commands

Prefix a with a colon (:). You need to type only enough letters of the command to uniquely distinguish it. You can enter multiple commands on one line by separating them with a space, Tab, or semicolon (;).

To enable viewing a potentially unmounted disk in a reasonable manner, fsdb supports the cd, pwd, ls, and find commands. The functionality of each of these commands basically matches that of its UNIX counterpart. See cd(1), pwd(1), ls(1), and find(1) for details. The *, , , ?, and - wildcard characters are also supported.

The following commands are supported.

:base[=b]	Display or set the base. All input and output is governed by the current base. Without the =b, display the current base. Otherwise, set the current base to b. Base is interpreted according to the old value of base, so to ensure correctness, use the 0, 0t, or 0x prefix when changing the base. The default for base is hexadecimal.
:block	Convert the value of dot to a block address.
:cd [dir]	Change the current directory to directory dir. Also update the current values of inode and dot. If you do not specify dir, change directories to inode 2, root (/).
:directory	If the current inode is a directory, convert the value of dot to a directory slot offset in that directory, and dot now points to this entry.
:file	Set the value of dot as a relative block count from the beginning of the file. Update the value of dot to the first byte of this block.

:find *dir* [-name *n*] | [-inum *i*]

    Find files by name or i-number. Recursively search directory *dir* and below for file names whose i-number matches *i* or whose name matches pattern *n*. Only one of the two options (-name or -inum) can be used at one time. The find -print option is not needed or accepted.

:fill=*p*   Fill an area of disk with pattern *p*. The area of disk is delimited by dot and count.

:inode   Convert the value of dot to an inode address. If successful, also update the current value of inode. As a convenient shorthand, if :inode appears at the beginning of the line, the value of dot is set to the current inode and that inode is displayed in inode format.

:ls [-R] [-l] *pat1 pat2*...

    List directories or files. If you specify no file, assume the current directory. You can use either or both of the options (but, if used, you must specify them before the file-name specifiers). Wild-card characters are available and multiple arguments are acceptable. The long listing shows only the i-number and the name; use the inode command with ?i to get more information.

:override   Toggle the value of override. Some error conditions might be overridden if override is toggled to on.

:prompt   Change the fsdb prompt to *p*. *p* must be enclosed in quotes.

:pwd   Display the current working directory.

:quit   Quit fsdb.

:tag   Convert the value of dot and if this is a valid tag, print the volume structure according to the tag.

:!   Escape to the shell.

Inode Commands

In addition to the above commands, several other commands deal with inode fields and operate directly on the current inode (they still require the colon (:)). You can use the inode commands to more easily display or change the particular fields. The value of dot is used only by the :db and :ib commands. On completion of the command, the value of dot is changed so that it points to that particular field. For example, > :ln=+1 increments the link count of the current inode and sets the value of dot to the address of the link count field.

    The following inode commands are supported.

:at   Access time.

:bs   Block size.

:ct   Creation time.

:gid   Group ID.

:ln   Link number.

:mt   Modification time.

:md	Mode.
:maj	Major device number.
:min	Minor device number.
:nm	This command actually operates on the directory name field. Once poised at the desired directory entry (using the directory command), you can change or display the directory name. For example, > 7:dir:nm="foo" gets the 7th directory entry of the current inode and changes its name to foo. You cannot make directory names larger than the field allows. If you try to make a directory name larger than the field allows, the string is truncated to fit and a warning message is displayed.
:sz	File size.
:uid	User ID.
:uniq	Unique ID.

Formatted Output

Formatted output comes in two styles and many format types. The two styles of formatted output are: structured and unstructured. Structured output displays inodes, directories, and so forth. Unstructured output displays raw data.

Format specifiers are preceded by the slash (/) or question mark (?) character. type is updated as necessary on completion.

The following format specifiers are preceded by the ? character.

?i	Display as inodes in the current base.
?d	Display as directories in the current base.

The following format specifiers are preceded by the / character.

/b	Display as bytes in the current base.
/c	Display as characters.
/o | O	Display as octal shorts or longs.
/d | D	Display as decimal shorts or longs.
/x | X	Display as hexadecimal shorts or longs.

Examples

The following example uses fsdb as a calculator for complex arithmetic. The following command displays 2010 in decimal format.

```
> 2000+400%(20+20)=D
```

The following example displays the i-number 386 in inode format. 386 becomes the current inode.

```
> 386:ino?i
```

The following example changes the link count for the current inode to 4.

> `:ln=4`

The following example increments the link count by 1.

> `:ln=+1`

The following example displays the creation time as a hexadecimal long.

> `:ct=X`

The following example displays the modification time in *time* format.

> `:mt=t`

The following example displays, in ASCII, block 0 of the file associated with the current inode.

> `0:file/c`

The following example displays the first block's directory entries for the root inode of this file system. This command stops prematurely if the EOF is reached.

> `2:ino,*?d`

The following example changes the current inode to that associated with the 5th directory entry (numbered from 0) of the current inode. The first logical block of the file is then displayed in ASCII.

> `5:dir:inode; 0:file,*/c`

The following example changes the i-number for the 7th directory slot in the root directory to 3.

> `2:inode; 7:dir=3`

The following example changes the name field in the directory slot to name.

> `7:dir:nm="name"`

The following example displays the 3rd block of the current inode as directory entries.

> `2:db:block,*?d`

The following example sets the contents of address 2050 to 0xffffffff. 0xffffffff can be truncated, depending on the current type.

> `2050=0xffff`

The following example places the ASCII string this is some text at address 1c92434.

> `1c92434="this is some text"`

Attributes

See attributes(5) for descriptions of the following attributes.

Attribute Type	Attribute Value
Availability	SUNWudf

See Also

clri(1M), fsck_udfs(1M), dir(4), attributes(5)

fsdb_ufs — UFS File-System Debugger

Synopsis

/usr/sbin/fsdb -F ufs [*generic-options*] [*specific-options*] *special*

Description

The fsdb_ufs command is an interactive tool that you can use to patch up a damaged UFS file system. It has conversions to translate block and i-numbers into their corresponding disk addresses. Also included are mnemonic offsets to access different parts of an inode. These features greatly simplify the process of correcting control block entries or descending the file system tree.

fsdb contains several error-checking routines to verify inode and block addresses. You can disable these routines if necessary by invoking fsdb with the –o option or by the use of the o command.

fsdb reads a block at a time and, therefore, works with either raw or block I/O devices. A buffer management routine is used to retain commonly used blocks of data to reduce the number of read system calls. All assignment operations result in an immediate write-through of the corresponding block. Note that you must invoke fsdb with the -o w option to modify any portion of the disk.

Wherever possible, adb-like syntax was adopted to make using fsdb more familiar.

Warning — Because fsdb reads the disk raw, extreme caution is advised in determining accessibility of fsdb on the system. Suggested permissions are 600 and owned by bin.

Note — The old command-line syntax for clearing inodes using the UFS-specific -z *i-number* option is still supported by the new debugger, although it is obsolete and will be removed in a future release. Use of this option results in correct operation, but an error message is printed warning of the impending obsolescence of this option. The equivalent functionality is available from the more flexible clri(1M) command.

Options

-o
Specify UFS-file-system specific options. These options can be any combination of the following separated by commas (with no intervening spaces).

?	Display usage.
o	Override some error conditions.
p='*string*'	Set prompt to *string*.
w	Open for write.

Usage

Numbers are considered hexadecimal by default. However, you can control how data is displayed or accepted. Use the base command to display or set the input/output base. Once set, all input defaults to this base and all output is shown in this base. You can temporarily override the base for input by preceding hexadecimal numbers with 0x, decimal numbers with 0t, or octal numbers with 0. You must precede hexadecimal numbers beginning with a-f or A-F with 0x to distinguish them from commands.

Disk addressing by fsdb is at the byte level. However, fsdb offers many commands to convert a desired inode, directory entry, block, superblock and so forth to a byte address. Once the address has been calculated, fsdb records the result in dot (.).

fsdb maintains several global values.

- The current base (referred to as base).
- The current address (referred to as dot).
- The current inode (referred to as inode).
- The current count (referred to as count).
- The current type (referred to as type).

Most commands use the preset value of dot in their execution. The following example first sets the value of dot to 2. The colon indicates the start of a command, and the inode command sets inode to 2.

```
> 2:inode
```

A count is specified after a comma (,). Once set, count remains at this value until a new command is encountered, which then resets the value to 1 (the default). So, if you type the following command, 400 hex longs are listed from 2000, and when completed, the value of dot is 2000 + 400 * sizeof (long).

```
> 2000,400/X
```

If you then press Return, the output routine uses the current values of dot, count, and type and displays 400 more hex longs. An asterisk (*) displays the entire block.

fsdb maintains end-of-fragment, block, and file. When displaying data as fragments or blocks, an error message is displayed when the end of fragment or block is reached. When displaying data by the db, ib, directory, or file commands, an error message is displayed if the end-of-file is reached. This message is needed mainly to avoid passing the end of a directory or file and getting unknown and unwanted results.

The following examples show several commands and the use of Return.

```
> 2:ino; 0:dir?d
> 2:ino; 0:db:block?d
```

The two examples are synonymous for getting to the first directory entry of the root of the file system. Once there, any subsequent Return (or +, –) advances to subsequent entries. Note that the following two commands are synonymous.

```
> 2:inode; :ls
> :ls /
```

Expressions

The following symbols are recognized by fsdb.

Return	Update the value of dot by the current value of type and display, using the current value of count.
#	Numeric expressions can be composed of +, –, *, and % operators (evaluated left to right) and can use parentheses. Once evaluated, the value of dot is updated.
, count	Count indicator. The global value of count is updated to count. The value of count remains until you run a new command. A count specifier of * tries to show a block's worth of information. The default for count is 1.
? f	Display in structured style with format specifier f. See "Formatted Output" on page 371.
/ f	Display in unstructured style with format specifier f. See "Formatted Output" on page 371.
.	The value of dot.
+e	Increment the value of dot by the expression e. The amount actually incremented depends on the size of type. dot = dot + e * sizeof (type) The default for e is 1.
-e	Decrement the value of dot by the expression e. See +.
*e	Multiply the value of dot by the expression e. Multiplication and division don't use type. In the above calculation of dot, consider the sizeof(type) to be 1.
%e	Divide the value of dot by the expression e. See *.
< name	Restore an address saved in register name. name must be a single letter or digit.
> name	Save an address in register name. name must be a single letter or digit.
= f	Display indicator. If f is a legitimate format specifier, then display the value of dot using the format specifier f. See "Formatted Output" on page 371. Otherwise, assignment is assumed. See =.
= [s][e]	Assignment indicator. Change the contents of the address pointed to by dot to the value of the expression e or to the ASCII representation of the quoted (") string s. This expression can be useful for changing directory names or ASCII file information.

| `=+ e` | Incremental assignment. Increment the contents of the address pointed to by `dot` by expression `e`. |
| `=- e` | Decremental assignment. Decrement the contents of the address pointed to by `dot` by expression `e`. |

Commands

You must prefix a command with a colon (`:`) character. You need to use only enough letters of the command to uniquely distinguish it. You can enter multiple commands on one line by separating them by a space, Tab, or semicolon (`;`).

To enable the viewing of a potentially unmounted disk in a reasonable manner, `fsdb` provides the `cd`, `pwd`, `ls`, and `find` commands. The functionality of these commands substantially matches those of their UNIX counterparts. See individual commands for details. The `*`, `?`, and `[-]` wildcard characters are also available.

`:base=b`	Display or set base. All input and output is governed by the current base. If you omit the `=b`, display the current base.
	Otherwise, set the current base to `b`. Note that this command is interpreted using the old value of base so, to ensure correctness, use the `0`, `0t`, or `0x` prefix when changing the base. The default for base is hexadecimal.
`:block`	Convert the value of `dot` to a block address.
`:cd dir`	Change the current directory to directory `dir`. Also, update the current values of inode and dot. If you specify no `dir`, change directories to inode 2 (`/`).
`:cg`	Convert the value of `dot` to a cylinder group.
`:directory`	When current inode is a directory, convert the value of `dot` to a directory slot offset in that directory, and `dot` now points to this entry.
`:file`	Take the value of `dot` as a relative block count from the beginning of the file. Update the value of `dot` to the first byte of this block.
`:find dir [-name n][-inum i]`	
	Find files by name or i-number. Recursively search directory `dir` and below for file names whose i-number matches `i` or whose name matches pattern `n`. Note that you can use only one of the two options (`-name` or `-inum`) at one time. Also, `-print` is not needed or accepted.
`:fill=p`	Fill an area of disk with pattern `p`. The area of disk is delimited by `dot` and `count`.
`:fragment`	Convert the value of `dot` to a fragment address. The only difference between the `fragment` command and the `block` command is the amount that can be displayed.
`:inode`	Convert the value of `dot` to an inode address. If successful, update the current value of inode as well as the value of `dot`. As a convenient shorthand, if `:inode` is at the beginning of the line, set the value of `dot` to the current inode and display that inode in inode format.

:log_chk	Run through the valid log entries and verify the layout without printing any information.
:log_delta	Count the number of deltas in the log, using the value of dot as an offset into the log. Do no checking to make sure that offset is within the head/tail offsets.
:log_head	Display the header information about the file system logging. This information shows the block allocation for the log and the data structures on the disk.
:log_otodb	Return the physical disk block number, using the value of dot as an offset into the log.
:log_show	Display all deltas between the beginning of the log (BOL) and the end of the log (EOL).
:ls [-R][-l] *pat1 pat2*...	
	List directories or files. If you specify no file, assume the current directory. You can use either or both of the options. If you use them, they must be specified before the file-name specifiers. Wildcard characters are available, and you can specify multiple arguments. The long listing shows only the i-number and the name; use the inode command with ?i to get more information.
:override	Toggle the value of override. Some error conditions may be overridden if override is toggled on.
:prompt *p*	Change the fsdb prompt to *p*. *p* must be surrounded by double quotes (").
:pwd	Display the current working directory.
:quit	Quit fsdb.
:sb	Take the value of dot as a cylinder group number and then convert it to the address of the superblock in that cylinder group. As a shorthand, :sb at the beginning of a line sets the value of dot to the superblock and displays it in superblock format.
:shadow	If the current inode is a shadow inode, then set the value of dot to the beginning of the shadow inode data.
:!	Escape to shell.

Inode Commands

Several additional commands deal with inode fields and operate directly on the current inode (they still require the :). You can use these commands to more easily display or change the particular fields.

The value of dot is only used by the :db and :ib commands. On completion of the command, the value of dot is changed to point to that particular field. For example, > :ln=+1 increments the link count of the current inode and sets the value of dot to the address of the link count field.

:at	Access time.
:bs	Block size.

`:ct`	Creation time.
`:db`	Use the current value of `dot` as a direct block index, where direct blocks number from 0–11. To display the block itself, you need to pipe this result into the `block` or `fragment` command. For example, the following command gets the contents of data block field 1 from the inode and converts it to a block address. It then displays 20 longs in hexadecimal. See "Formatted Output" on page 371.

> `1:db:block,20/X`

`:gid`	Group ID.
`:ib`	Use the current value of `dot` as an indirect block index where indirect blocks number from 0–2. This command gets only the indirect block itself (the block containing the pointers to the actual blocks). Use the `file` command and start at block 12 to get to the actual blocks
`:ln`	Link count.
`:mt`	Modification time.
`:md`	Mode.
`:maj`	Major device number.
`:min`	Minor device number.
`:nm`	Although listed here, this command actually operates on the `directory` name field. Once poised at the desired directory entry (using the `directory` command), this command enables you to change or display the directory name. For example, the following command gets the 7th directory entry of the current inode and changes its name to `foo`.

> `7:dir:nm="foo"`

Note that names cannot be made larger than the field size. If you try to make the name larger than the field size, the string is truncated to fit and a warning message is displayed.

`:si`	Shadow inode.
`:sz`	File size.
`:uid`	User ID.

Formatted Output

Formatted output has many formats and two styles: structured and unstructured. Use structured output to display inodes, directories, superblocks, and the like. Use unstructured format to display raw data.

`?c`	Display as cylinder groups.
`?i`	Display as inodes.
`?d`	Display as directories.
`?s`	Display as superblocks.
`?S`	Display as shadow inode data.

/b	Display as bytes.
/c	Display as characters.
/o /O	Display as octal shorts or longs.
/d /D	Display as decimal shorts or longs.
/ x /X	Display as hexadecimal shorts or longs.

The values displayed by /b and all ? formats are displayed in the current base. Also, type is appropriately updated on completion.

Examples

> **2000+400%(20+20)=D**

Display 2010 in decimal (use of fsdb as a calculator for complex arithmetic).

> **386:ino?i** Display i-number 386 in an inode format. This inode now becomes the current one.

> **:ln=4** Change the link count for the current inode to 4.

> **:ln=+1** Increment the link count by 1.

> **:ct=X** Display the creation time as a hexadecimal long.

> **:mt=t** Display the modification time in time format.

> **0:file/c** Display, in ASCII, block 0 of the file associated with the current inode.

> **2:ino,*?d** Display the first block's worth of directory entries for the root inode of this file system. Stop prematurely if the end-of-file is reached.

> **5:dir:inode; 0:file,*/c**

Change the current inode to that associated with the 5th directory entry (numbered from zero) of the current inode. The first logical block of the file is then displayed in ASCII.

> **:sb** Display the superblock of this file system.

> **1:cg?c** Display cylinder group information and summary for cylinder group 1.

> **2:inode; 7:dir=3**

Change the i-number for the seventh directory slot in the root directory to 3.

> **2:db:block,*?d**

Display the third block of the current inode as directory entries.

> **7:dir:nm="name"**

Change the name field in the directory slot to *name*.

> **3c3:fragment,20:fill=0x20**

Get fragment 3c3 and fill 20 type elements with 0x20.

> **2050=0xffff**

>> Set the contents of address 2050 to 0xffffffff. 0xffffffff may be truncated, depending on the current type.

> **1c92434="some text"**

>> Put the ASCII for the string at 1c92434.

> **2:ino:si:ino;0:shadow,*?S**

>> Display all of the shadow inode data in the shadow inode associated with the root inode of this file system.

Attributes

See attributes(5) for descriptions of the following attributes.

Attribute Type	Attribute Value
Availability	SUNWcsu

See Also

clri(1M), fsck_ufs(1M), dir_ufs(4), fs_ufs(4), attributes(5)

---

fsirand — Install Random Inode Generation Numbers

Synopsis

/usr/lib/fs/ufs/fsirand [-p] *special*

Description

To help increase the security of file systems exported by NFS, use the fsirand command to install random inode generation numbers on all the inodes on device *special* and install a file system ID in the superblock.

Use fsirand only on an unmounted file system that has been checked with fsck(1M) The only exception is that you can use this command on the root file system in single-user mode if you immediately reboot the system afterwards.

Options

-p   Print the generation numbers for all the inodes, but do not change the generation numbers.

Examples

The following example shows part of the output generated by using the -p option to print generation numbers for all the inodes.

```
# fsirand -p /dev/rdsk/c0t1d0s0
fsid: 0 0
ino 0 gen 2d8adbbb
ino 1 gen 4db4fa89
ino 2 gen 44070ae9
ino 3 gen 76ca1a32
ino 4 gen 2f53fdab
ino 5 gen 5976e64b
ino 6 gen 7195314e
ino 7 gen 277f4e2f
ino 8 gen 7a955da7
ino 9 gen 4e77679d
ino 10 gen 18bb617d
...(Additional lines deleted from this example)
```

Usage

See largefile(5) for the description of the behavior of fsirand when encountering files greater than or equal to 2 Gbytes (2**31 bytes).

Attributes

See attributes(5) for descriptions of the following attributes.

Attribute Type	Attribute Value
Availability	SUNWcsu

See Also

fsck(1M), attributes(5), largefile(5)

fstyp — Determine File-System Type

Synopsis

/usr/sbin/fstyp [-v] *special*

Description

Use the fstyp command to determine the file-system type of unmounted file systems by using heuristic programs.

An fstyp module for each file-system type to be checked is executed; each of these modules applies an appropriate heuristic to determine whether the supplied special file is of the type for which it checks. If it is, the command prints on standard output the usual file-system identifier for that type (for example, ufs) and exits with a return code of 0; if none of the modules succeed, the error message unknown_fstyp (no matches) is returned and the exit status is 1. If more than one module succeeds, the error message unknown_fstyp (multiple matches) is returned and the exit status is 2.

Note — The use of heuristics implies that the result of fstyp is not
guaranteed to be accurate.

Options

-v   Display verbose information about the file system's superblock. This
                                information varies across different *FSType*s. See fs_ufs(4),
                                mkfs_ufs(1M), and tunefs(1M) for details.

Examples

The following example shows that the file-system type of /dev/rdsk/c0t1d0s0 is ufs.

```
# fstyp /dev/rdsk/c0t1d0s0
ufs
#
```

The following example shows part of the verbose information about the
/dev/rdsk/c0t1d0s0 file-system superblock.

```
# fstyp -v /dev/rdsk/c0t1d0s0
ufs
magic   11954   format  dynamic time     Wed Nov  3 18:10:46 1999
sblkno  16      cblkno  24      iblkno  32      dblkno  768
sbsize  2048    cgsize  5120    cgoffset 40     cgmask  0xffffffe0
ncg     86      size    2077080 blocks  2012390
bsize   8192    shift   13      mask    0xffffe000
fsize   1024    shift   10      mask    0xfffffc00
frag    8       shift   3       fsbtodb 1
minfree 3%      maxbpg  2048    optim   time
maxcontig 16    rotdelay 0ms    rps     90
csaddr  768     cssize  2048    shift   9       mask    0xfffffe00
ntrak   19      nsect   80      spc     1520    ncyl    2733
cpg     32      bpg     3040    fpg     24320   ipg     5888
nindir  2048    inopb   64      nspf    2
nbfree  251546  ndir    2       nifree  506364  nffree  13
cgrotor 3       fmod    0       ronly   0       logbno  0
fs_reclaim is not set
file-system state is valid, fsclean is 1
blocks available in each rotational position
cylinder number 0:
    position 0:  0    5   10   15   20   25   30   35   40   45   50   55
                60   65   70   75   80   85   90
    position 1:  1    6   11   16   21   26   31   36   41   46   51   56
                61   66   71   76   81   86   91
    position 3:  2    7   12   17   22   27   32   37   42   47   52   57
                62   67   72   77   82   87   92
    position 4:  3    8   13   18   23   28   33   38   43   48   53   58
                63   68   73   78   83   88   93
    position 6:  4    9   14   19   24   29   34   39   44   49   54   59
                64   69   74   79   84   89   94
cs[].cs_(nbfree,ndir,nifree,nffree):
    (2941,2,5884,13) (2946,0,5888,0) (2946,0,5888,0) (2946,0,5888,0)
```

```
(2946,0,5888,0) (2946,0,5888,0) (2946,0,5888,0) (2946,0,5888,0)
(2946,0,5888,0) (2946,0,5888,0) (2946,0,5888,0) (2946,0,5888,0)
(2946,0,5888,0) (2946,0,5888,0) (2946,0,5888,0) (2946,0,5888,0)
(2946,0,5888,0) (2946,0,5888,0) (2946,0,5888,0) (2946,0,5888,0)
(2946,0,5888,0) (2946,0,5888,0) (2946,0,5888,0) (2946,0,5888,0)
(2946,0,5888,0) (2946,0,5888,0) (2946,0,5888,0) (2946,0,5888,0)
```
...(*Additional lines deleted from this example*)

Usage

See largefile(5) for the description of the behavior of fstyp when encountering files greater than or equal to 2 Gbytes (2**31 bytes).

Attributes

See attributes(5) for descriptions of the following attributes.

Attribute Type	Attribute Value
Availability	SUNWcsu

See Also

mkfs_ufs(1M), tunefs(1M), fs_ufs(4), attributes(5), largefile(5), hsfs(7FS), pcfs(7FS)

---

ftpd — File Transfer Protocol Server

Synopsis

/usr/sbin/in.ftpd [-dl][-t *timeout*]

Description

See in.ftpd(1M).

---

fuser — Identify Processes Using a File or File Structure

Synopsis

/usr/sbin/fuser [- [c | f] ku] *files* [[- [c | f] ku] *files*]...

Description

Use the fuser command to display the IDs of the processes that are using the files specified as arguments.

Each process ID is followed by a letter code. These letter codes are interpreted as follows: if the process is using the file as

c	The process is using the file as its current directory.
m	The process is using a file mapped with mmap(2). See mmap(2) for details.
o	The process is using the file as an open file.
r	The process is using the file as its root directory.
t	The process is using the file as its text file.
y	The process is using the file as its controlling terminal.

For block special devices with mounted file systems, all processes using any file on that device are listed. For all types of files (text files, executables, directories, devices, and so forth), only the processes using that file are reported.

If you specify more than one group of files, you can respecify the options for each additional group of files. A lone dash cancels the options currently in force.

The process IDs are printed as a single line on the standard output, separated by spaces and terminated with a single newline. All other output is written on standard error.

Any user can run fuser, but only superuser can terminate another user's process.

Note — Because fuser works with a snapshot of the system image, it may miss processes that begin using a file while fuser is running. Also, processes reported as using a file may have stopped using it while fuser was running. Keep these factors in mind if you plan to use the -k option.

Options

-c	Report on files that are mount points for file systems and any files within that mounted file system.
-f	Print a report for the named file, not for files within a mounted file system.
-k	Send the SIGKILL signal to each process. Because this option spawns kills for each process, the kill messages may not show up immediately (see kill(2)).
-u	Display the user login name in parentheses following the process ID.

Examples

The following example lists the process ID of the files in the /export/home/winsor directory.

```
paperbark% fuser /export/home/winsor/
/export/home/winsor/:      527c    515c    514c    499c    455c
   454c    445c    443c    442c    441c    434c    431c    428c
   425c    417c    415c    414c    413c    412c    410c    403c
   402c    385c    384c    382c    347c    337c    317c
paperbark%
```

The following example lists the three processes that are currently accessing the CD that is in the CD drive.

```
# fuser /cdrom/sol_8_sparc
/cdrom/sol_8_sparc:        637c       627c       425c
paperbark#
```

Environment Variables

See environ(5) for descriptions of the following environment variables that affect the execution of fuser: LANG, LC_ALL LC_CTYPE, LC_MESSAGES, and NLSPATH.

Attributes

See attributes(5) for descriptions of the following attributes.

Attribute Type	Attribute Value
Availability	SUNWcsu

See Also

ps(1), mount(1M), kill(2), mmap(2), signal(3C), attributes(5), environ(5)

fwtmp, wtmpfix — Manipulate Connect Accounting Records

Synopsis

```
/usr/lib/acct/fwtmp [-ic]
/usr/lib/acct/wtmpfix [file...]
```

Description

Use the fwtmp command as part of the accounting software to edit the wtmpx file. fwtmp reads from the standard input and writes to the standard output, converting binary records of the type found in /var/adm/wtmpx to formatted ASCII records. The ASCII version is useful when you need to edit bad records. In the Solaris 8 release, the /var/adm/wtmpx file replaces the obsolete wtmp database file.

wtmpfix examines the standard input or named files in utmpx format, corrects the time/date stamps to make the entries consistent, and writes to the standard output. You can use a dash (-) in place of file to indicate the standard input. If time/date corrections are not performed, acctcon(1M) faults when it encounters certain date change records.

Each time the date is set, a pair of date change records is written to /var/adm/wtmpx. The first record is the old date denoted by the string old time placed in the line field and the flag OLD_TIME placed in the type field of the utmpx structure. The second record specifies the new date and is denoted by the string new time placed in the line field and the flag NEW_TIME placed in the type field. wtmpfix uses these records to synchronize all timestamps in the file.

In addition to correcting time/date stamps, wtmpfix checks the validity of the name field to ensure that it consists solely of alphanumeric characters or spaces. If it encounters a name that is considered invalid, it changes the login name to INVALID and write a diagnostic to the standard error. In this way, wtmpfix reduces the chance that acctcon fails when processing connect accounting records.

Options

ic   Denotes that input is in ASCII form and output is to be written in
                      binary form.

Files

/var/adm/wtmpx

                      History of user access and administration information. wtmpx is an
                      extended database file that replaces the obsolete wtmp database file.

Attributes

See attributes(5) for descriptions of the following attributes.

Attribute Type	Attribute Value
Availability	SUNWaccu

See Also

acctcom(1), ed(1), acct(1M), acctcms(1M), acctcon(1M), acctmerg(1M),
acctprc(1M), acctsh(1M), runacct(1M), acct(2), acct(4), utmpx(4),
attributes(5)
   System Administration Guide, Volume I

G

---

gencc — Create a Front End to the cc Command

Synopsis

```
gencc
```

Description

The gencc command is an interactive command designed to aid in the creation of a front-end to the cc command. The gencc command is obsolete.

---

getdev — List Devices Based on Criteria

Synopsis

```
/bin/getdev [-ae][criteria...][device...]
```

Description

Use the getdev command to generate a list of devices that match certain criteria. The criteria include a list of attributes (given in expressions) and a list of devices. If you specify no criteria, all devices are included in the list.

Devices must satisfy at least one of the criteria in the list unless you specify the -a option. Then, only those devices that match all of the criteria in a list are included.

381

Devices that are defined on the command line and that match the criteria are included in the generated list. However, if you use the -e option, the list becomes a set of devices to be excluded from the list.

Options

-a   Specify that a device must match all criteria to be included in the list generated by this command. The option has no effect if you define no criteria.

-e   Exclude the list of devices that follows on the command line from the list generated by this command. Without -e, include the named devices in the generated list. The option has no effect if no devices are defined.

Operands

criteria   Define the criteria that a device must match to be included in the generated list. *criteria* is specified by expressions.

The *criteria* argument can have four possible expression types.

attribute=value

> Choose all devices that have *attribute* defined and equal to *value*.

attribute!=value

> Choose all devices that have *attribute* defined and not equal to *value*.

attribute:*   Choose all devices that have *attribute* defined.

attribute!:*   Choose all devices that do not have *attribute* defined.

See the putdev(1M) manual page for a complete listing and description of available attributes.

device   Define the devices that should be included in the generated list. This definition can be the path name of the device or the device alias.

Example

The following example uses the getdev command to display all available devices on the system paperbark.

```
paperbark% getdev
disk1
disk2
disk3
dpart100
dpart107
spool
paperbark%
```

Exit Status

0	Successful completion.
1	Command syntax was incorrect, invalid option was used, or an internal error occurred.
2	Device table could not be opened for reading.

Files

/etc/device.tab

Device table.

Attributes

See attributes(5) for descriptions of the following attributes.

Attribute Type	Attribute Value
Availability	SUNWcsu

See Also

devattr(1M), getdgrp(1M), putdev(1M), putdgrp(1M), attributes(5)

---

getdgrp — List Device Groups That Contain Devices That Match Criteria

Synopsis

/usr/sbin/getdgrp [-ael][*criteria*...][*dgroup*...]

Description

Use the getdgrp command to generate a list of device groups that contain devices matching the given criteria. The criteria are given in the form of expressions.

Options

-a	Specify that a device must match all criteria to be included in the list generated by this command. The option has no effect if you define no criteria.
-e	Exclude the list of device groups on the command line from the list generated by this command. Without the -e option, include the named device groups in the generated list. The option has no effect if no devices are defined.

-1
: List all device groups (subject to the -e option and the *dgroup* list) even if they contain no valid device members. This option has no effect if you specify *criteria* on the command line.

Operands

criteria
: Define criteria that a device must match before a device group to which the device belongs can be included in the generated list. Specify *criteria* as an expression or a list of expressions that a device must meet for its group to be included in the list generated by getdgrp. If you specify no criteria, include all device groups in the list.

  Devices must satisfy at least one of the criteria in the list. However, you can use the -a option to perform a "logical and" operation. Then, only those groups containing devices that match all of the criteria in a list are included.

  The *criteria* argument can have four possible expression types.

  attribute=value
  : Choose all devices that have *attribute* defined and equal to *value*.

  attribute!=value
  : Choose all devices that have *attribute* defined and not equal to *value*.

  attribute:*   Choose all devices that have *attribute* defined.

  attribute!:*   Choose all devices that do not have *attribute* defined.

  See the putdev(1M) manual page for a complete listing and description of available attributes.

dgroup
: Define a set of device groups that should be included in or excluded from the generated list. Include device groups that are defined and that contain devices matching the criteria.

  If you specify the -e option, this list defines a set of device groups to be excluded. When you use the -e option and also define *criteria*, the generated list includes device groups containing devices that match the criteria and are not in the command-line list.

Examples

The following example uses the getdgrp command without arguments to display all device groups on the system paperbark.

```
paperbark% getdgrp
disk
dpart
paperbark%
```

Exit Status

0	Successful completion of the task.
1	Command syntax was incorrect, invalid option was used, or an internal error occurred.
2	Device table or device group table could not be opened for reading.

Files

/etc/device.tab

> Device table.

/etc/dgroup.tab

> Device group table.

Attributes

See attributes(5) for descriptions of the following attributes.

Attribute Type	**Attribute Value**
Availability	SUNWcsu

See Also

devattr(1M), getdev(1M), putdev(1M), putdgrp(1M), attributes(5)

---

getent — Get Entries from Administrative Database

Synopsis

/bin/getent database [key...]

Description

Use the getent command to display a list of entries from the administrative database specified by database. The information generally comes from one or more of the sources that are specified for the database in /etc/nsswitch.conf.

database is the name of the database to be examined. The value can be passwd, group, hosts, services, protocols, ethers, networks, or netmasks. For each of these databases, getent uses the appropriate library routines described in getpwnam(3C), getgrnam(3C), gethostbyname(3N), getservbyname(3N), getprotobyname(3N), ethers(3N), and getnetbyname(3N).

Each key must be in a format appropriate for searching on the respective database. For example, it can be a user name or numeric-UID for passwd; host name or IP address for hosts; or service, service/protocol, port, or port/proto for services.

getent prints the database entries that match each of the supplied keys, one per line, in the format of the matching administrative file: passwd(4), group(4), hosts(4), services(4), protocols(4), ethers(3N), networks(4), or netmasks(4). If you specify no *key*, all entries returned by the corresponding enumeration library routine (for example, getpwent or gethostent) are printed.

Examples

The following example uses the getent command to display all of the entries in the hosts database for the system paperbark.

```
paperbark% getent hosts
127.0.0.1          localhost
172.16.8.22        paperbark loghost
172.16.8.22        paperbark loghost
172.16.8.18        seachild
172.16.8.20        mac
172.16.8.21        G3
172.16.8.19        castle
paperbark%
```

The following example displays the entry from the /etc/passwd file for user ray.

```
paperbark% getent passwd ray
ray:x:1002:10::/export/home/ray:/bin/csh
paperbark%
```

Exit Status

0	Successful completion.
1	Command syntax was incorrect, an invalid option was used, or an internal error occurred.
2	At least one of the specified entry names was not found in the database.
3	There is no support for enumeration on this database.

Files

/ctc/nsswitch.conf

Nameservice switch configuration file.

/etc/passwd   Password file.

/etc/group   Group file.

/etc/hosts   Host-name database.

/etc/services

Internet services and aliases.

/etc/protocols

Protocol-name database.

/etc/ethers   Ethernet address to host-name database or domain.

/etc/networks

> Network-name database.

/etc/netmasks

> Network-mask database.

Attributes

See attributes(5) for descriptions of the following attributes.

Attribute Type	Attribute Value
Availability	SUNWcsu

See Also

getpwnam(3C), getgrnam(3C), ethers(3N), gethostbyname(3N),
gethostent(3N),getnetbyname(3N),getprotobyname(3N),getservbyname(3N),
group(4), hosts(4), netmasks(4), networks(4), nsswitch.conf(4),
passwd(4), protocols(4), services(4), attributes(5)

---

gettable — Get DoD Internet Format Host Table from a Host

Synopsis

/usr/sbin/gettable *host*

Description

Use the gettable command to obtain the DoD Internet host table from a host-name
server. The specified *host* is queried for the table. The table is placed in the file
hosts.txt.

gettable operates by opening a TCP connection to the port indicated in the service
specification for host name. A request is then made for all names, and the resultant
information is placed in the output file.

gettable is best used in conjunction with the htable(1M) command, which converts
the DoD Internet host table format to that used by the network library lookup routines.

Note — gettable should allow requests for only part of the database.

Example

The following example uses gettable to get a new version of the Internet host table
from the NIC. nichost is the name of the host with the NIC database. hosts.ver is the
name of the output file.

```
# gettable -v nichost hosts.ver
#
```

Attributes

See attributes(5) for descriptions of the following attributes.

Attribute Type	Attribute Value
Availability	SUNWnisu

See Also

htable(1M), attributes(5)

Harrenstien, Ken, Mary Stahl, and Elizabeth Feinler, *HOSTNAME Server*, RFC 953, Network Information Center, SRI International, Menlo Park, California, October 1985.

getty — Set Terminal Type, Modes, Speed, and Line Discipline

Synopsis

```
/usr/lib/saf/ttymon [-h][-t timeout] line [speed [type [linedisc]]]
/usr/lib/saf/ttymon -c file
```

Description

The getty command sets terminal type, modes, speed, and line discipline.

Note — getty is a symbolic link to /usr/lib/saf/ttymon. It is included for compatibility with previous releases for the few applications that still call getty directly.

Only superuser can execute getty. Initially, getty prints the login prompt, waits for the user's login name, and then invokes the login command. getty tries to adapt the system to the terminal speed by using the options and arguments specified on the command line.

Without optional arguments, getty specifies the following.

- The speed of the interface is set to 300 baud.
- Either parity is allowed.
- Newline characters are converted to Return-line feed.
- Tab expansion is performed on the standard output.
- getty types the login prompt before reading the user's name a character at a time.
- If a null character (or framing error) is received, it is assumed to be the result of the user pressing the Break key. getty tries the next speed in the series.

The series that getty tries is determined by what it finds in /etc/ttydefs.

Options

-h	If the -h flag is not set, force a hangup by setting the speed to 0 before setting the speed to the default or a specified speed.

-t *timeout*	Exit if the open on the line succeeds and no one types anything in *timeout* seconds.
-c *file*	This option is no longer supported. Instead, use /usr/sbin/sttydefs -l to list the contents of the /etc/ttydefs file and perform a validity check on the file.

Operands

line	The name of a TTY line in /dev to which getty is to attach itself. getty uses this string as the name of a file in the /dev directory to open for reading and writing.
speed	A label to a speed and TTY definition in the file /etc/ttydefs. This definition tells getty at what speed to run initially, what the initial TTY settings are, and what speed to try next, (should the user press the Break key to indicate that the speed is inappropriate). The default speed is 300 baud.

type and *linedisc*

These options are obsolete and are ignored.

Files

/etc/ttydefs Terminal line setting information for ttymon.

Attributes

See attributes(5) for descriptions of the following attributes.

Attribute Type	Attribute Value
Availability	SUNWcsr

See Also

login(1), ct(1C), sttydefs(1M), ttymon(1M), ioctl(2), attributes(5), tty(7D)

getvol — Verify Device Accessibility

Synopsis

```
/usr/bin/getvol -n [-l label] device
/usr/bin/getvol [-f | -F][-ow][-l label | -x label] device
```

Description

The getvol command verifies that the specified device is accessible and that a volume of the appropriate medium has been inserted. The command is interactive and displays instructional prompts, describes errors, and shows required label information.

Note — This command uses the device table to determine the characteristics of the device when performing the volume label checking.

Options

-n	Run the command in noninteractive mode. Assume that the volume is already inserted.
-1 *label*	Specify that the label *label* must exist on the inserted volume (can be overridden by the -o option).
-f	Format the volume after insertion, using the format command defined for this device in the device table.
-F	Format the volume after insertion and put a file system on the device. Also uses the format command defined for this device in the device table.
-o	Override a label check.
-w	Write a new label on the device. You are prompted to supply the label text. This option is ineffective if you specify the -n option.
-x *label*	Specify that the label *label* must exist on the device. Use this option in place of the -1 option when the label can only be verified by visual means. Use of the option displays a message asking you to visually verify that the label is indeed *label*.

Operands

device	Specify the device to be verified for accessibility.

Exit Status

0	Successful completion.
1	Command syntax was incorrect, invalid option was used, or an internal error occurred.
3	Device table could not be opened for reading.

Files

/etc/device.tab

Device table.

Attributes

See attributes(5) for descriptions of the following attributes.

Attribute Type	Attribute Value
Availability	SUNWcsu

See Also

attributes(5)

GFXconfig — Configure the PGX32 (Raptor GFX) Graphics Accelerator

Synopsis

```
/usr/sbin/pgxconfig [-dev device-filename][-res videomode
   [try | noconfirm | nocheck]][-file machine | system]
   [-depth 8 | 24][-24only][-defaults]
/usr/sbin/pgxconfig [-propt][-prconf]
/usr/sbin/pgxconfig [-help][-res ?]
/usr/sbin/pgxconfig [-i]
```

Description

See pgxconfig(1M).

groupadd — Add (Create) a New Group Definition on a System

Synopsis

```
/usr/sbin/groupadd [-g gid [-o]] group
```

Description

Use the groupadd command to create a new group definition on the system by adding the appropriate entry to the /etc/group file.

> **Note** — groupadd adds a group definition only to the local system. If a network nameservice such as NIS or NIS+ is being used to supplement the local /etc/group file with additional entries, groupadd cannot change information supplied by the network nameservice. However, groupadd does verify the uniqueness of group name and group ID against the external nameservice.

Options

-g *gid* Assign the group ID *gid* for the new group. This group ID must be a nonnegative decimal integer below MAXUID as defined in /usr/include/sys/param.h. The group ID defaults to the next available (unique) number above the highest number currently assigned. For example, if groups 100, 105, and 200 are assigned as groups, the next default group number is 201. (Group IDs from 0-99 are reserved by SunOS for future applications.)

-o Enable the *gid* to be duplicated (nonunique).

Operands

group A string consisting of characters from the set of lowercase alphabetic characters and numeric characters. Write a warning message if the string exceeds MAXGLEN, which is usually set at eight characters. The group field must contain at least one character; it accepts lowercase or numeric characters or a combination of both and must not contain a colon (:) or newline.

Exit Status

0 Successful completion.

2 Invalid command syntax. A usage message for the groupadd command is displayed.

3 An invalid argument was provided to an option.

4 The *gid* is not unique (when the -o option is not used).

9 The group is not unique.

10 The /etc/group file cannot be updated.

Files

/etc/group Group file.

/usr/include/userdefs.h

User definitions file.

Attributes

See attributes(5) for descriptions of the following attributes.

Attribute Type	Attribute Value
Availability	SUNWcsu

See Also

```
users(1B), groupdel(1M), groupmod(1M), grpck(1M), logins(1M), pwck(1M),
useradd(1M), userdel(1M), usermod(1M), group(4), attributes(5)
```

groupdel — Delete a Group Definition from the System

Synopsis

/usr/sbin/groupdel *group*

Description

Use the groupdel command to delete a group definition from the system. It deletes the appropriate entry from the /etc/group file.

> **Note** — The groupdel command deletes a group definition only from the local /etc/group file. If a network nameservice such as NIS or NIS+ is being used to supplement the local /etc/group file with additional entries, groupdel cannot change information supplied by the network nameservice.

Operands

group   An existing group name to be deleted.

Exit Status

0	Success.
2	Invalid command syntax. A usage message for the groupdel command is displayed.
6	*group* does not exist.
10	Cannot update the /etc/group file.

Files

/etc/group   System file containing group definitions.

Attributes

See attributes(5) for descriptions of the following attributes.

Attribute Type	Attribute Value
Availability	SUNWcsu

See Also

users(1B), groupadd(1M), groupmod(1M), logins(1M), useradd(1M), userdel(1M), usermod(1M), attributes(5)

groupmod — Modify a Group Definition on the System

Synopsis

/usr/sbin/groupmod [-g *gid* [-o]] [-n *name*] *group*

Description

Use the groupmod command to modify the definition of the specified group by modifying the appropriate entry in the /etc/group file.

Note — The groupmod command modifies group definitions only in the /etc/group file. If a network nameservice such as NIS or NIS+ is being used to supplement the local /etc/group file with additional entries, groupmod cannot change information supplied by the network nameservice. The groupmod command does, however, verify the uniqueness of group name and group ID against the external nameservice.

Options

-g *gid*	Specify the new group ID for the group. This group ID must be a nonnegative decimal integer less than MAXUID, as defined in <param.h>. The group ID defaults to the next available (unique) number above 99. (Group IDs from 0-99 are reserved by SunOS for future applications.)
-o	Enable the *gid* to be duplicated (nonunique).
-n *name*	Specify the new name for the group. The *name* argument is a string of no more than eight bytes consisting of characters from the set of lowercase alphabetic and numeric characters. Write a warning message if these restrictions are not met. A future Solaris release may refuse to accept group fields that do not meet these requirements. The *name* argument must contain at least one character and must not include a colon (:) or newline (\n).

Operands

group	An existing group name to be modified.

Exit Status

0	Success.
2	Invalid command syntax. A usage message for the groupmod command is displayed.
3	An invalid argument was provided to an option.
4	*gid* is not unique (when you do not specify the -o option).
6	*group* does not exist.
9	*name* already exists as a group name.
10	Cannot update the /etc/group file.

Files

/etc/group   Group file.

Attributes

See attributes(5) for descriptions of the following attributes.

Attribute Type	**Attribute Value**
Availability	SUNWcsu

See Also

users(1B), groupadd(1M), groupdel(1M), logins(1M), useradd(1M), userdel(1M), usermod(1M), group(4), attributes(5)

grpck — Password and Group File Checkers

Synopsis

/usr/sbin/grpck [*filename*]

Description

See pwck(1M).

gsscred — Add, Remove, and List gsscred Table Entries

Synopsis

```
/usr/sbin/gsscred [-n user [-o oid][-u uid]][-c comment] -m mech -a
/usr/sbin/gsscred [-n user [-o oid]][-u uid][-m mech] -r
/usr/sbin/gsscred [-n user [-o oid]][-u uid][-m mech] -l
```

Description

The gsscred table is used on server machines for lookup of the UID of incoming clients connected using RPCSEC_GSS.

Use the gsscred command to create and maintain a mapping between a security principal name and a local UNIX UID. The format of the user name is assumed to be GSS_C_NT_USER_NAME. You can use the -o option to specify the object identifier of the name type. The OID must be specified in dot-separated notation, for example, 1.2.3.45464.3.1.

When adding users, if you specify no user name, an entry is created in the table for each user from the passwd table. If you specify no comment, the gsscred command inserts a comment that specifies the user name as an ASCII string and that the GSS-API security mechanism that applies to the user name. The security mechanism is in string representation as defined in the /etc/gss/mech file.

The parameters are interpreted by the gsscred command to delete users in the same way they create users. You must specify at least one of the -n, -u, or -m options. If you specify no security mechanism, then all entries are deleted for the user identified by either *uid* or *user*. If you specify only the security mechanism, then all user entries for that security mechanism are deleted.

The parameters are interpreted by the gsscred command to search for users in the same way they create users. If you specify no options, then the entire table is returned. If you specify the user name or UID, then all entries for that user are returned. If you specify a security mechanism, then all user entries for that security mechanism are returned.

Options

-a	Add a table entry.
-c comment	Insert a comment about this table entry.
-l	Search table for entry.
-m mech	Specify the mechanism for which this name is to be translated.
-n user	Specify the optional principal name.
-o oid	Specify the OID indicating the name type of the user.
-r	Remove the entry from the table.
-u uid	Specify the UID for the user if the user is not local.

Examples

The following example creates a gsscred table for the kerberos v5 security mechanism. gsscred obtains user names and UID's from the passwd table to populate the table.

```
# gsscred -m kerberos_v5 -a
```

The following example adds an entry for root/host1 with a specified UID of 0 for the kerberos v5 security mechanism.

```
# gsscred -m kerberos_v5 -n root/host1 -u 0 -a
```

The following example lists all user mappings for the kerberos v5 security mechanism.

```
# gsscred -m kerberos_v5 -l
```

The following example lists all mappings for all security mechanisms for the user winsor.

```
# gsscred -n winsor -l
```

The following example adds a kerberos v5 entry, followed by diffie_hellman_640_0, and then lists by name over all mechanisms.

```
# gsscred -a -m kerberos_v5 -n bcalkins
# gsscred -a -m diffie_hellman_640_0 -n bcalkins
# gsscred -l -n bcalkins
040100092B0604012A021A02040000002800092B0604012A021A0101756E69782E33393
    13737406D706B31372E656E672E73756E2E636F6D00
                        39177    jkabat, diffie_hellman_640_0

    040100092A864886F71201020200000027000A2A864886F712010201016A6B6162617
    44053554E534F46542E454E472E53554E2E434F4D00
                        39177    jkabat, kerberos_v5
#
```

Exit Status

0	Successful completion.
>0	An error occurred.

Attributes

See attributes(5) for descriptions of the following attributes.

Attribute Type	Attribute Value
Availability	SUNWgss

See Also

gssd(1m), attributes(5)

gssd — Generate and Validate GSS-API Tokens for Kernel RPC

Synopsis

```
/usr/lib/gss/gssd
```

Description

gssd is the user mode daemon that operates between the kernel RPC and the Generic Security Service Application Program Interface (GSS-API) to generate and validate GSS-API security tokens. In addition, gssd maps the GSS-API principal names to the local user and group IDs. By default, all groups that the requested user belongs to are be included in the group-list credential. gssd is invoked by the Internet daemon inetd(1m) the first time that the kernel RPC requests GSS-API services.

Exit Status

0	Successful completion.
>0	An error occurred.

Attributes

See attributes(5) for descriptions of the following attributes.

Attribute Type	Attribute Value
Availability	SUNWgssk

See Also

gsscred(1m), attributes(5)
RFC 2078

H

halt, poweroff — Stop the Processor

Synopsis

```
/usr/sbin/halt [-dlnqy]
/usr/sbin/poweroff [-dlnqy]
```

Description

Use the `halt` and `poweroff` commands to write out any pending information to the disks and then stop the processor. `poweroff` removes the machine's power if possible.

`halt` and `poweroff` normally log the system shutdown to the system log daemon, `syslogd`(1M), and put a shutdown record in the `/var/adm/wtmpx` login accounting file (changed from `wtmp` in the Solaris 8 release). These actions are inhibited if you specify the `-n` or `-q` options.

Note — `halt` does not execute the `rc0` scripts as do `shutdown`(1M) and `init`(1M).

`poweroff` is equivalent to `init 5`.

Options

-d   Force a system crash dump before rebooting. See `dumpadm`(1M) for information on configuring system crash dumps. This option is new in the Solaris 8 release.

-l	Suppress sending a message to the system log daemon, syslogd(1M), about who executed halt.
-n	Prevent sync(1M) before stopping.
-q	Quick halt. No graceful shutdown is attempted.
-y	Halt the system even from a dialup terminal.

Files

New!

/var/adm/wtmpx

History of user access and administration information. wtmpx is an extended database file in the Solaris 8 release that replaces the obsolete wtmp database file.

Attributes

See attributes(5) for descriptions of the following attributes.

Attribute Type	Attribute Value
Availability	SUNWcsu

See Also

init(1M), reboot(1M), shutdown(1M), sync(1M), syslogd(1M), attributes(5)

hostconfig — Configure a System's Host Parameters

Synopsis

New!

/usr/bin/hostconfig -p *protocol* [-d] [-h] [-n] [-v] [-i *interface*]
    [-f *hostname*]

Description

Use the hostconfig command to acquire a system's host parameters and set these parameters on a system. The hostconfig command uses the argument to the required -p option to select which protocol to use. Different protocols can set different host parameters. Currently, only one protocol (bootparams) is defined.

> **Note** — At the time this section was written, the hostconfig command did not work on the Solaris 8 release. The examples are from a Solaris 7 system.

Options

-d	Enable debug output.

`-f hostname`	Run the protocol as if this machine were named *hostname*.
`-h`	Echo the received *hostname* to standard output instead of setting *hostname* by using the system name directly.
`-i interface`	Use only the named network interface to run the protocol.
`-n`	Run the network protocol, but do not set the acquired parameters into the system.
`-p protocol`	
	Use *protocol*. Currently only one protocol (`bootparams`) is available. This option is required. Specifying the `-p bootparams` option uses the whoami call of the RPC `bootparams` protocol. This call sets the system *hostname*, *domainname*, and default IP router parameters.
`-v`	Enable verbose output.

Examples

The following example displays the parameters that would be set with the `bootparams` whoami protocol.

```
# hostconfig -p bootparams -n -v# hostconfig -p bootparams -n -v
From [192.9.200.4]: hostname = sparc4
                ypdomain =
                router = 192.9.200.14
#
```

The following example configures the host parameters, using the `bootparams` whoami protocol with a verbose output.

```
# hostconfig -p bootparams -v
From [192.9.200.4]: hostname = sparc4
                ypdomain =
                router = 192.9.200.14
#
```

The following example configures a system's host parameter, less the system name, using the whoami call of the RPC `bootparams` protocol.

```
# hostconfig='hostconfig -p bootparams -h'
```

Attributes

See `attributes`(5) for descriptions of the following attributes.

Attribute Type	Attribute Value
Availability	SUNWcsu

See Also

hostname(1), domainname(1M), route(1M), attributes(5)

htable — Convert DoD Internet Format Host Table

Synopsis

/usr/sbin/htable *filename*

Description

Use the htable command to convert a host table in the format specified by RFC 952 to the format used by the network library routines. htable creates the hosts, networks, and gateways files. The hosts file is used by the gethostbyname(3N) routines in mapping host names to addresses. The networks file is used by the getnetbyname(3N) routines in mapping network names to numbers. The gateways file is used by the routing daemon to identify passive Internet gateways.

If any of the files localhosts, localnetworks, or localgateways are present in the current directory, the file's contents are prepended to the output file without interpretation to enable sites to maintain local aliases and entries that are not normally present in the master database.

htable is best used in conjunction with the gettable(1M) command, which retrieves the DoD Internet host table from a host.

Note — htable does not properly calculate the gateways file.

Files

localhosts　　File that can be used to contain local host aliases and entries not normally present in the master database.

localnetworks

　　　　　　　File that can be used to contain local network aliases and entries not normally present in the master database.

localgateways

　　　　　　　File that can be used to contain local gateway aliases and entries not normally present in the master database.

Attributes

See attributes(5) for descriptions of the following attributes.

Attribute Type	Attribute Value
Availability	SUNWnisu

See Also

gettable(1M), gethostbyname(3N), getnetbyname(3N), attributes(5)

Harrenstien, Ken; Stahl, Mary; and Feinler, Elizabeth, *DoD Internet Host Table Specification*, RFC 952, Network Information Center, SRI International, Menlo Park, California, October 1985.

I

id — Return User Identity

Synopsis

```
/usr/bin/id [user]
/usr/bin/id -a [user]
/usr/xpg4/bin/id [user]
/usr/xpg4/bin/id -G [-n][user]
/usr/xpg4/bin/id -g [-nr][user]
/usr/xpg4/bin/id -u [-nr][user]
```

Description

Use the id command to display user identity information. If you specify no *user* operand, the id command writes the user and group IDs and the corresponding user and group names of the invoking process to standard output. If the effective and real IDs do not match, both are written. If multiple groups are supported by the underlying system, the supplementary group affiliations of the invoking process also are written.

If you specify a *user* operand and the process has the appropriate privileges, the user and group IDs of the selected user are written. In this case, effective IDs are assumed to be identical to real IDs. If the selected user has more than one allowable group membership listed in the group database, these are written in the same manner as the supplementary groups described in the preceding paragraph.

Formats

The following formats are used when the LC_MESSAGES locale category specifies the C locale. In other locales, the strings uid, gid, euid, egid and groups may be replaced with more appropriate strings corresponding to the locale.

```
uid=%u(%s) gid=%u(%s)\n real-user-ID, username, real-group-ID,
    group-name
```

If the effective and real user IDs do not match, the following string is inserted immediately before the \n character in the previous format

```
euid=%u(%s)
```

with the following arguments added at the end of the argument list.

```
effective-user-ID, effective-user-name
```

If the effective and real group IDs do not match, the following string is inserted directly before the \n character in the format string (and after any addition resulting from the effective and real user IDs not matching),

```
egid=%u(%s)
```

with the following arguments added at the end of the argument list.

```
effective-group-ID, effective-group-name
```

If the process has supplementary group affiliations or the selected user is allowed to belong to multiple groups, the following string is added directly before the newline character in the format string

```
groups=%u(%s)
```

The following arguments are added at the end of the argument list

```
supplementary-group-ID, supplementary-group-name
```

The necessary number of the following arguments are added after that for any remaining supplementary group IDs

```
,%u(%s)
```

The necessary number of the following arguments are added at the end of the argument list

```
supplementary-group-ID, supplementary-group-name
```

If any of the user ID, group ID, effective user ID, effective group ID, or supplementary/multiple group IDs cannot be mapped by the system into printable user or group names, the corresponding (%s) and name argument are omitted from the corresponding format string.

New! When you specify any of the options, the output format is as described under "Options."

Options

The following option is supported for /usr/bin/id only.

-a	Report user name, user ID, and all the groups to which the user belongs.

The following options are supported for /usr/xpg4/bin/id only.

-G	Output all different group IDs (effective, real, and supplementary) only, using the format %u\n. If there is more than one distinct group affiliation, output each such affiliation, using the format %u, before the newline character.
-g	Output only the effective group ID, using the format %u\n.
-n	Output the name in the format %s instead of the numeric ID using the format %u.
-r	Output the real ID instead of the effective ID.
-u	Output only the effective user ID, using the format %u\n.

Note — Output produced by the -G option and by the default case could potentially produce very long lines on systems that support large numbers of supplementary groups.

Operands

user	The user (login) name for which information is to be written.

Examples

The following example uses the /usr/bin/id command to display identity information about the current user.

```
paperbark% id
uid=1001(winsor) gid=10(staff)
paperbark%
```

The following example uses the /usr/bin/id command to display identity information about user ray.

```
paperbark% id ray
uid=1002(ray) gid=10(staff)
paperbark%
```

The following example uses the /usr/xpg4/bin/id command with no arguments to display identity information for user root.

```
# /usr/xpg4/bin/id
uid=0(root) gid=1(other)
    groups=0(root),2(bin),3(sys),4(adm),5(uucp),6(mail),7(tty),8(lp),9(nu
    ucp),12(daemon)
#
```

The following example uses the /usr/xpg4/bin/id command with the -g option to display the primary group ID for user winsor.

```
paperbark% /usr/xpg4/bin/id -g winsor
10
paperbark%
```

The following example uses the /usr/xpg4/bin/id command with the -G option to display all group IDs for user winsor.

```
paperbark% /usr/xpg4/bin/id -G winsor
10 14
paperbark%
```

Environment Variables

See environ(5) for descriptions of the following environment variables that affect the execution of id: LC_CTYPE, LC_MESSAGES, and NLSPATH.

Exit Status

| 0 | Successful completion. |
| >0 | An error occurred. |

Attributes

See attributes(5) for descriptions of the following attributes.

/usr/bin/id

Attribute Type	Attribute Value
Availability	SUNWcsu SUNWcar

/usr/xpg4/bin/id

Attribute Type	Attribute Value
Availability	SUNWxcu4

See Also

fold(1), logname(1), who(1), getgid(2), getgroups(2), getuid(2), attributes(5), environ(5), XPG4(5)

ifconfig — Configure Network Interface Parameters

Synopsis

```
/sbin/ifconfig interface [address-family][address [dest-address]]     New!
    [up][down][auto-revarp][netmask mask][broadcast address]
    [metric n][mtu n][tsrc address][tdest address]
    [-auth_algs authentication algorithm][-encr_algs encryption
    algorithm][-enc_auth_algs authentication algorithm]
    [trailers | -trailers][private | -private][arp | -arp]
    [plumb][unplumb]
/usr/sbin/ifconfig interface [address-family][address [dest-address]]  New!
    [up][down][auto-revarp][netmask mask][broadcast address]
    [metric n][mtu n][tsrc address][tdst address][-auth_algs
    authentication algorithm][-encr_algs encryption algorithm]
    [-enc_auth_algs authentication algorithm][trailers | -trailers]
    [private | -private][arp | -arp][plumb][unplumb]
/sbin/ifconfig interface {auto-dhcp | dhcp} [primary][wait seconds] drop  New!
    | extend | inform | ping | release | start | status
/usr/sbin/ifconfig interface {auto-dhcp | dhcp} [primary][wait seconds]  New!
    drop | extend | inform | ping | release | start | status
```

Description

The ifconfig command assigns an address to a network interface, configures network interface parameters, or both. ifconfig is run at boot time by the /etc/rc2.d scripts to define the network address of each interface present on a machine; you can also use it at a later time to redefine an interface's address or other operating parameters. If you specify no option, ifconfig displays the current configuration for a network interface. If you specify an address family, ifconfig reports only the details specific to that address family. Only superuser can modify the configuration of a network interface. You must specify one of the options appearing within braces ({}).

The two versions of ifconfig, /sbin/ifconfig and /usr/sbin/ifconfig, behave differently with respect to nameservices. The order in which names are looked up by /sbin/ifconfig when the system is booting is fixed and cannot be changed. By contrast, changing /etc/nsswitch.conf may affect the behavior of /usr/sbin/ifconfig. The system administrator can configure the source and lookup order in the tables via the nameservice switch. See nsswitch.conf(4) for more information.

> **Note** — When choosing host names, it is recommended that you do not choose the names broadcast, down, private, trailers, up, and the other possible option names. Using any of these names as host names can result in bizarre problems that can be extremely difficult to diagnose.

DHCP Configuration

The third and fourth forms of ifconfig control configuring of the DHCP (Dynamic Host Configuration Protocol) interface. DHCP is available only on interfaces whose address family is inet. In this mode, ifconfig controls operation of dhcpagent(1M), the DHCP client daemon. Once an interface is placed under DHCP control (by using the start operand), you should not use ifconfig in normal operation to modify the address or characteristics of the interface. If the address of an interface under DHCP is changed, the agent implicitly drops the interface from its control, although this does not occur until dhcpagent wakes up to conduct another DHCP operation on the interface.

IPv6

The Internet Protocol version 6 (IPv6) is new in the Solaris 8 release. IPv6 adds increased address space and improves Internet functionality with a simplified header format, support for authentication and privacy, autoconfiguration of address assignments, and new quality-of-service capabilities. The ifconfig command was modified to create the IPv6 stack and support new parameters.

Options

arp Enable the use of the Address Resolution Protocol (ARP) in mapping between network level addresses and link level addresses (default). This option is currently implemented for mapping between TCP/IP addresses and 10 Mb/s Ethernet addresses.

-arp Disable the use of the Address Resolution Protocol ARP.

-auth_algs *authentication algorithm*

For a tunnel, enable IPsec AH with the specified authentication algorithm. The algorithm can be either a number or an algorithm name including any to express no preference. You must specify all IPsec tunnel properties on the same command line. To disable tunnel security, specify an auth_alg of none.

auto-dhcp Use the Dynamic Host Configuration Protocol (DHCP) to automatically acquire an address for this interface. This option has a completely equivalent alias called dhcp.

primary Define the interface as the primary, which means define the interface as the preferred one for the delivery of clientwide configuration data. See dhcpagent(1M) and dhcpinfo(1) for details. Only one interface can be the primary at any given time. If you subsequently choose another interface as the primary, it replaces the previous one. Nominating an interface as the primary one does not have much significance once the client workstation has booted because many applications already have started and been configured with data read from the previous primary interface.

wait *seconds* Wait either until the operation completes or for the interval specified, whichever is the sooner. If you specify no wait interval and the operation is one that cannot complete immediately, ifconfig exits immediately but continues the requested operation. The exit status of ifconfig in this case indicates merely the validity of the request, not whether that request was actually successful. You can use the symbolic value `forever` in place of a numeric.

drop	Remove the specified interface from the control of `dhcpagent`.
extend	Try to extend the lease on the interface's IP address. This option is not required because the agent automatically extends the lease well before it expires.
inform	Obtain network configuration parameters from DHCP without obtaining a lease on an IP address. This option is useful in situations where an IP address is obtained through mechanisms other than DHCP.
ping	Check whether the interface is under DHCP control. An exit status of 0 means yes.
release	Relinquish the IP address on the interface and mark the interface as `down`.
start	Start DHCP on the interface.
status	Display the DHCP configuration status of the interface.

New! appears beside the `inform` entry.

auto-revarp   Use the Reverse Address Resolution Protocol (RARP) to automatically acquire an address for this interface.

broadcast *address*

(`inet` only.) Specify the address to use to represent broadcasts to the network. The default broadcast address is the address with a host part of all 1's. A plus sign (+) for the broadcast value resets the broadcast address to a default appropriate for the (possibly new) address and netmask. Note that the arguments of `ifconfig` are interpreted left to right. Therefore, the following two commands can result in different values being assigned for the broadcast addresses of the interfaces.

```
ifconfig -a netmask + broadcast +
ifconfig -a broadcast + netmask +
```

dhcp	Alias for the `auto-dhcp` option.
down	Mark an interface as down so that the system does not try to transmit messages through it. If possible, reset the interface to disable reception as well. This action does not automatically disable routes using the interface.

-encr_auth_algs *authentication algorithm*   *New!*

For a tunnel, enable IPsec ESP with the specified authentication algorithm. You can specify the algorithm as either a number or a name including `any` to indicate no preference. If you specify an ESP encryption algorithm but no authentication algorithm, the default value for the ESP authentication algorithm is any.

New!   -encr_algs *encryption algorithm*

For a tunnel, enable IPsec ESP with the specified encryption algorithm. The algorithm can be either a number or a name. Note that you must specify all IPsec tunnel properties on the same command line. To disable tunnel security, specify the value of encr_alg as none. If you specify an ESP authentication algorithm but no encryption algorithm, the default value for the ESP encryption algorithm is any.

metric *n*   Set the routing metric of the interface to *n*; if you specify no value, the default is 0. The routing metric is used by the routing protocol. Higher metrics make a route less favorable; metrics are counted as addition hops to the destination network or host.

mtu *n*   Set the maximum transmission unit of the interface to *n*. For many types of networks, the mtu has an upper limit, for example, 1500 for Ethernet.

netmask *mask*   (inet only.) Specify how much of the address to reserve for subdividing networks into subnetworks. The mask includes the network part of the local address and the subnet part, which is taken from the host field of the address. The mask contains 1's for the bit positions in the 32-bit address that are to be used for the network and subnet parts, and 0's for the host part. The mask should contain at least the standard network portion, and the subnet field should be contiguous with the network portion. You can specify the mask in one of four ways.

- A single hexadecimal number with a leading 0x.

- A dot-notation address.

- A plus sign (+) address.

- A pseudo host name/pseudo network name found in the network database networks(4).

If you specify a plus sign for the netmask value, look up the mask in the netmasks(4) database. This lookup finds the longest matching netmask in the database by starting with the interface's IP address as the key and iteratively masking off more and more low order bits of the address. This iterative lookup ensures that you can use the netmasks(4) database to specify the netmasks when variable length subnetmasks are used within a network number.

If you supply a pseudohost name/pseudonetwork name as the netmask value, netmask data may be located in the hosts or networks database. Look up names by first using gethostbyname(3N). If the names are not found there, look them up in getnetbyname(3N). These interfaces can, in turn, use nsswitch.conf(4) to determine what data store(s) to use to fetch the actual value.

`plumb`	Open the device associated with the physical interface name and set up the streams needed for TCP/IP to use the device. Before this is done, the interface does not show up in the output of `ifconfig -a`.
`unplumb`	Destroy any streams associated with this device and close the device. After this command is executed, the device name should not show up in the output of `ifconfig a`.
`private`	Tell the `in.routed` routing daemon not to advertise the interface.
`-private`	Specify unadvertised interfaces.
`trailers`	This option previously encapsulated `inet` packets in a nonstandard way on certain link levels. Drivers supplied with this release no longer use this option. It is provided for compatibility but is ignored.
`-trailers`	Disable the use of a trailer link-level encapsulation.
`tsrc` *address*	Set the source address of a tunnel. This source address is on an outer encapsulating IP header; it must be an address of another interface already configured with `ifconfig`.
`tdst` *address*	Set the destination address of a tunnel. The address should not be the same as the *dest-address* of the tunnel because no packets leave the system over such a tunnel.
`up`	Mark an interface as up. When setting the first address on an interface, the interface is automatically marked as up. Use the `up` option to enable an interface after an `ifconfig down`, which reinitializes the hardware.

Operands

The `interface` operand and the address parameters that affect it are described below.

`interface`	Specify a string of the form, *name physical-unit*, for example, `le0` or `ie1`; or of the form *name physical-unit : logical-unit*, for example, `le0:1`. Five special interface names, `-a`, `-ad`, `-au`, `-adD`, and `-auD`, are reserved and refer to all or a subset of the interfaces in the system. If you specify one of these interface names, apply the commands following it to all of the interfaces that match.

`-a`	Apply the commands to all interfaces in the system.
`-ad`	Apply the commands to all down interfaces in the system.
`-adD`	Like `-ad`, but apply the commands only if the interface is not under DHCP (Dynamic Host Configuration Protocol) control.
`-au`	Apply the commands to all up interfaces in the system.
`-auD`	Like `-au`, but apply the commands only if the interface is not under DHCP control.

address-family

Because an interface can receive transmissions in differing protocols, each of which may require separate naming schemes, interpret the parameters and addresses according to the rules of the address family specified by the *address-family* parameter. The address families currently supported are ether and inet. If you specify no address family, assume inet.

address   For the TCP/IP family (inet), the address is either a host name present in the host-name database (see hosts(4)), in the Network Information Service (NIS) map hosts, or a TCP/IP address expressed in the Internet standard dot notation. Typically, an Internet address specified in dot notation consists of the system's network number and the unique host number. A typical Internet address is 192.9.200.44, where 192.9.200 is the network number and 44 is the host number.

For the ether address family, the address is an Ethernet address represented as *x:x:x: x:x:x* where *x* is a hexadecimal number between 0 and FF.

Some, though not all, of the Ethernet interface cards have their own addresses. To use cards that do not have their own addresses, refer to section 3.2.3(4) of the IEEE 802.3 specification for a definition of the locally administered address space. The use of interface groups should be restricted to those cards with their own addresses (see "Interface Groups" on page 413).

dest-address If you supply the *dest-address* parameter in addition to the address parameter, it specifies the address of the correspondent on the other end of a point-to-point link.

Logical Interfaces

Solaris TCP/IP allows multiple logical interfaces to be associated with a physical network interface. This association enables a single machine to be assigned multiple IP addresses, even though it may have only one network interface. Physical network interfaces have names of the form

driver-name physical-unit-number

and logical interfaces have names of the form

driver-name physical-unit-number:logical-unit-number

A physical interface is configured into the system with the plumb subcommand, for example,

```
ifconfig le0 plumb
```

Logical interfaces do not need to be plumbed. Once a physical interface has been plumbed, you can configure logical interfaces associated with the physical interface by naming them in subsequent ifconfig commands. However, only root can create or delete a logical interface. For example, when executed by root, the following command allocates a logical interface associated with the physical interface le0 and reports its status.

```
ifconfig le0:1
```

When executed by a nonprivileged user, `ifconfig` reports the status of the interface if it already exists, or gives an error message if it does not exist.

You can configure a logical interface with parameters (address, netmask, and so on) different from the physical interface with which it is associated. You can also give logical interfaces that are associated with the same physical interface different parameters. Each logical interface must be associated with a physical interface. So, for example, the logical interface `lc0:1` can only be configured after the physical interface `le0` has been plumbed.

To delete a logical interface, first ensure that the interface has been marked as down, then simply name the interface specifying an address of 0. For example, the following command deletes the logical interface `le0:1`.

```
ifconfig le0:1 0 down
```

Interface Groups

If an interface (logical or physical) shares an IP prefix with another interface, these interfaces are collected into an interface group. IP uses an interface group to rotate source address selection when the source address is unspecified and, in the case of multiple physical interfaces in the same group, to scatter traffic across different IP addresses on a per-IP-destination basis. (See `netstat`(1M) for per-IP destination information.)

You can enable this feature by using ndd(1M).

Examples

If a workstation is not attached to an Ethernet, you should mark the `le0` interface down with the following command.

```
paperbark% ifconfig le0 down
```

The following example prints the addressing information for each interface for the system `paperbark`.

```
paperbark% ifconfig -a
lo0: flags=1000849<UP,LOOPBACK,RUNNING,MULTICAST,IPv4> mtu 8232 index 1
        inet 127.0.0.1 netmask ff000000
hme0: flags=1000843<UP,BROADCAST,RUNNING,MULTICAST,IPv4> mtu 1500 index
  2
        inet 172.16.8.22 netmask ffffff00 broadcast 172.16.8.255
paperbark%
```

The following example resets each interface's broadcast address after the netmasks have been correctly set.

```
# ifconfig -a broadcast +
#
```

The following example changes the Ethernet address for interface `le0`.

```
# ifconfig le0 ether aa:1:2:3:4:5
#
```

New!

The following example begins configuration of an IP-in-IP tunnel by first plumbing it.

```
# ifconfig ip.tun0 plumb
#
```

The next command configures the tunnel as a point-to-point interface, supplying the tunnel source and the tunnel destination.

```
# ifconfig ip.tun0 myaddr mydestaddr tsrc another_myaddr tdst
  a_dest_addr up
#
```

Next, tunnel security properties are configured on one invocation of ifconfig.

```
# ifconfig ip.tun0 encr_auth_algs md5 encr_algs 3des
#
```

The following example uses the any keyword to request a service without any algorithm preferences.

```
# ifconfig ip.tun0 encr_auth_algs any encr_algs any
#
```

Either of the following examples disables all security by specifying none as the value for either auth_algs or encr_algs.

```
# ifconfig ip.tun0 auth_algs none
# ifconfig ip.tun0 encr_algs none
```

Files

/etc/netmasks

Netmask data.

Attributes

See attributes(5) for descriptions of the following attributes.

/usr/sbin/ifconfig

Attribute Type	Attribute Value
Availability	SUNWcsu

/sbin/ifconfig

Attribute Type	Attribute Value
Availability	SUNWcsr

See Also

New!

dhcpinfo(1), dhcpagent(1M), in.routed(1M), ndd(1M), netstat(1M),
ethers(3SOCKET), gethostbyname(3NSL), getnetbyname(3NSL), hosts(4),

```
netmasks(4), networks(4), nsswitch.conf(4), attributes(5), arp(7P),
ipsecah(7P), ipsecesp(7P), tun(7M)
```

Diagnostics

`ifconfig` sends messages that indicate the following conditions.

- The specified interface does not exist.
- The requested address is unknown.
- The user is not privileged and tried to alter an interface's configuration.

in.comsat, comsat — Biff Server

Synopsis

```
/usr/sbin/in.comsat
```

Description

`in.comsat` notifies users when new mail has arrived. The `comsat` server process is invoked as needed by `inetd`(1M), and times out if inactive for a few minutes.

`in.comsat` listens on a datagram port associated with the `biff` service specification (see `services`(4)) for one-line messages of the following form.

user@mailbox-offset

If the specified user is logged in to the system and has used `biff y` to enable notification of mail, the first 7 lines or 560 characters of the message are printed on the user's terminal. Lines that seem to be part of the message header other than the From, To, Date, or Subject lines are not printed when displaying the message.

Note — The message header filtering is prone to error.

Files

`/var/adm/utmpx`

New!

To find out who is logged in and on what terminals. `utmpx` is an extended database file that replaces the obsolete `utmp` database file.

Attributes

See `attributes`(5) for descriptions of the following attributes.

Attribute Type	Attribute Value
Availability	SUNWcsu

See Also
```
inetd(1M),  services(4),  attributes(5)
```

in.dhcpd — Dynamic Host Configuration Protocol Server

Synopsis

New!
```
/usr/lib/inet/in.dhcpd [-dnv][-h relay-hops] [-i interface,...]
    [-l Syslog-local-Facility][-b | automatic | manual]
    [-o DHCP-offer-Time-to-Live] [-t dhcptab-rescan-interval]
```
New!
```
/usr/lib/inet/in.dhcpd [-dv][-h relay-hops][-i interface,...]
    [-l Syslog-local-Facility] -r IP-address | hostname,...
```

Description

The in.dhcpd daemon responds to Dynamic Host Configuration Protocol (DHCP) requests and, optionally, to BOOTP protocol requests. The daemon forks a copy of itself that runs as a background process. It must be run as root. The daemon has two run modes.

- DHCP server (with optional BOOTP compatibility mode). The first synopsis illustrates the options available in the DHCP/BOOTP server mode.
- BOOTP relay agent mode. The second synopsis illustrates the options available when the daemon is run in BOOTP relay agent mode.

The DHCP and BOOTP protocols provide configuration parameters to Internet hosts. This mechanism allocates IP addresses and other host configuration parameters to client systems.

The DHCP/BOOTP server manages two types of databases, the dhcptab database. (See dhcptab(4)) and the dhcp network databases. (See dhcp_network(4)).

dhcptab Database

The dhcptab database contains macro definitions defined in a termcap-like syntax that permits network administrators to define groups of DHCP configuration parameters to be returned to clients. A DHCP/BOOTP server returns the following information.

- Hostname.
- Network broadcast address.
- Network subnet mask or IP maximum transfer unit (MTU) if requested by a client attached to the same network as the server without having to be explicitly configured in the dhcptab.

The dhcptab database is read at startup, on receipt of a SIGHUP signal, or periodically as specified by the -t option. A SIGHUP rereads the dhcptab within an interval from 0-60 seconds (depending on where the dhcp server is in its polling cycle). For busy servers, you can force the dhcptab to be reread by running /etc/init.d/dhcp stop, followed by /etc/init.d/dhcp start.

dhcp Network Databases

The dhcp network databases contain client identifier to IP address mappings. These databases are named after the network they support. For example, 10_0_0_0 is the dhcp network database for the 10.0.0.0 network.

The dhcp network databases are consulted during runtime. A client request received from a network for which no dhcp network database exists is ignored.

Multiple DHCP servers on the same network operate much more efficiently if they share DHCP databases through NIS+ or NFS. Sharing enables DHCP servers to communicate through a common datastore, increasing redundancy and balancing load among cooperating servers.

The hosts database is consulted if the clients request their host name. See hosts(4) and nsswitch.conf(4) for more details.

> **Note** — This command may change in future releases of Solaris software. Scripts, programs, or procedures that use this command might need modification when you upgrade to future Solaris software releases.

Options

-b automatic | manual

Enable BOOTP compatibility mode, which enables the DHCP server to respond to BOOTP clients. The argument specifies whether the DHCP server should automatically allocate permanent-lease IP addresses to requesting BOOTP clients if the clients are not registered in the server's database (automatic) or respond only to BOOTP clients who have been manually registered in the server's databases (manual). This option affects only DHCP server mode.

-d

Keep the daemon as a foreground process and display verbose debugging messages as it processes DHCP or BOOTP datagrams. Display messages on the current TTY. You can use this option in both DHCP/BOOTP server mode and BOOTP relay agent mode.

-h relay-hops

Specify the maximum number of relay agent hops that can occur before the daemon drops the DHCP/BOOTP datagram. The default number of relay agent hops is 4. This option affects both DHCP/BOOTP server mode and BOOTP relay agent mode.

-i interface,...

Choose the network interfaces that the daemon should monitor for DHCP/BOOTP datagrams. Ignore DHCP/BOOTP datagrams on network interfaces not specified in this list. This option is useful only on systems that have multiple network interfaces. If you do not specify this option, listen for DHCP/BOOTP datagrams on all network interfaces. The interface argument is a comma-separated list of interface names. It affects both DHCP/BOOTP server and BOOTP relay agent run modes.

    -l *Syslog-local-Facility*

This option is new in the Solaris 8 release. Turn on DHCP Server or BOOTP relay agent transaction logging. Specify the syslog local facility as an integer from 0 to 7. The DHCP daemon uses this value to tag the transactions. Using a facility separate from the LOG_DAEMON facility enables you to capture these transactions separately from other DHCP daemon events to be able to generate transaction reports. See syslog(3C), for details about local facilities. Transaction records are logged with the following nine space-separated fields.

1. Protocol

   Relay mode: BOOTP.

   Server mode: BOOTP or DHCP based on client type.

2. Type

   Relay mode: RELAY-CLNT, RELAY-SRVR.

   Server mode: ASSIGN, EXTEND, RELEASE, DECLINE, INFORM, NAK ICMP-ECHO.

3. Transaction time: Absolute time in seconds (UNIX time).

4. Lease time

   Relay mode: Always 0.

   Server mode: 0 for ICMP-ECHO events, otherwise absolute time in seconds (UNIX time).

5. Source IP address: Dotted Internet form.

   Relay mode: Relay interface IP on RELAY-CLNT, INADDR_ANY on RELAY-SRVR.

   Server mode: Client IP.

6. Destination IP address: Dotted Internet form.

   Relay mode: Client IP on RELAY-CLNT, Server IP on RELAY-SRVR.

   Server mode: Server IP.

7. Client Identifier: Hex representation (0-9, A-F).

   Relay mode: MAC address.

   Server mode: BOOTP—MAC address; DHCP—client ID.

8. Vendor Class identifier (white space converted to periods (.)).

   Relay mode: Always N/A.

   Server mode: Vendor class ID tokenized by converting white space characters to periods (.).

9. MAC address: Hex representation (0-9, A-F).

    Relay mode: MAC address.

    Server mode: MAC address.

Note that the format of this record is subject to change between releases.

Transactions are logged to the console if daemon is in debug mode (-d).

Logging transactions impact daemon performance.

It is suggested that you manage log-file size periodically using a script run by cron(1M) and sending syslogd(1M) a SIGHUP signal. You could, for example, clone /usr/lib/newsyslog and alter it to match your DHCP logging requirements.

-n   Disable automatic duplicate IP address detection. When you specify this option, the DHCP server does not try to verify that an IP address that it is about to offer a client is not in use. By default, the DHCP server pings an IP address before offering it to a DHCP/BOOTP client to verify that the address is not in use by another machine.

-o *DHCP-offer-Time-To-Live*

           Specify the number of seconds the DHCP server should cache the offers it has extended to discovering DHCP clients. The default is 10 seconds. On slow network media, you can increase this value to compensate for slow network performance. This option affects only DHCP server mode.

-r *IP-address* | *hostname,...*

           Enable BOOTP relay agent mode. The argument specifies a comma-separated list of IP addresses or host names of DHCP or BOOTP servers to which the relay agent is to forward BOOTP requests. When the daemon is started in this mode, ignore any DHCP databases and act simply as a BOOTP relay agent.

           A BOOTP relay agent listens to UDP port 68 and forwards BOOTP request packets received on this port to the destinations specified on the command line. It supports the BROADCAST flag described in RFC 1542. A BOOTP relay agent can run on any system that has knowledge of local routers and, thus, does not have to be an Internet gateway machine.

           Note that the proper entries must be made to the netmasks database so that the DHCP server being served by the BOOTP relay agents can identify the subnet mask of the foreign BOOTP/DHCP client's network. See netmasks(4) for the format and use of this database.

-t *dhcptab-rescan-interval*

           Specify the interval, in minutes, that the DHCP server should use to schedule the automatic rereading of the dhcptab information. Typically, you would use this option if the changes to the dhcptab are

relatively frequent. Once the contents of the dhcptab have stabilized,
turn off this option to avoid needless reinitialization from dhcptab.

-v   Display more verbose messages than in the default mode. Note that
               verbose mode can reduce daemon efficiency because of the time taken
               to display messages. If you also specify the debugging option, display
               messages to the current TTY; otherwise, log messages to the syslogd
               facility. You can use this option in both DHCP/BOOTP server mode
               and BOOTP relay agent mode.

Examples

The following example starts a DHCP server in BOOTP compatibility mode, permitting
the server to automatically allocate permanent IP addresses to BOOTP clients who are
not registered in the server's database; limits the server's attention to incoming
datagrams on network devices le2 and tr0; drops BOOTP packets whose hop count
exceeds 2; configures the DHCP server to cache extended DHCP offers for 15 seconds;
and schedules dhcptab rescans to occur every 10 minutes.

```
# in.dhcpd -i le2,tr0 -h 2 -o 15 -t 10 -b automatic
#
```

The following example starts the daemon in BOOTP relay agent mode, registering
the hosts bladerunner and 10.0.0.5 as relay destinations, with debugging and verbose
modes enabled, and drops BOOTP packets whose hop count exceeds 5.

```
# in.dhcpd -d -v -h 5 -r bladerunner,10.0.0.5
#
```

Files

/var/dhcp/dhcptab

               File or NIS+ table.

/var/dhcp/*NNN_NNN_NNN_NNN*

               Database files(s) or NIS+ table(s) that are named for the network
               they support. For example, 10_0_0_0 is the dhcp network database
               that serves the 10.0.0.0 network. See dhcp_network(4) for more
               details.

/etc/hosts   File or NIS+ hosts table.

/etc/init.d/dhcp

               DHCP startup file.

/etc/default/dhcp

               Configuration file. See dhcp(4) for more details.

Attributes
See attributes(5) for descriptions of the following attributes.

Attribute Type	Attribute Value
Availability	SUNWdhcsu

See Also
cron(1M), dhcp_config(1M), dhcpmgr(1M), htadm(1M), pntadm(1M), syslogd(1M), syslog(3C), dhcp(4), dhcp_network(4), dhcptab(4), ethers(4), hosts(4), netmasks(4), nsswitch.conf(4), attributes(5)

Alexander, S., and Droms, R. *DHCP Options and BOOTP Vendor Extensions*, RFC 2132, Silicon Graphics, Inc., Bucknell University, March 1997.

Droms, R., *Interoperation Between DHCP and BOOTP*, RFC 1534, Bucknell University, October 1993.

Droms, R., *Dynamic Host Configuration Protocol*, RFC 2131, Bucknell University, March 1997.

Wimer, W., *Clarifications and Extensions for the Bootstrap Protocol*, RFC 1542, Carnegie Mellon University, October 1993.

in.fingerd, fingerd — Remote User Information Server

Synopsis
/usr/sbin/in.fingerd

Description
The fingerd daemon provides information about users that are logged in to a system. The fingerd waits for connections on TCP port 79. When connected, it reads a single command line terminated by Return-linefeed, prepends the -s option, and passes the command on to the local finger(1) program. As soon as the output is finished, fingerd closes its connections.

You must invoke fingerd from inetd. See inetd(1M) for more information.

fingerd implements the server side of the Name/Finger protocol specified in RFC 742. The Name/Finger protocol provides a remote interface to programs that display information on system status and individual users. The protocol imposes little structure on the format of the exchange between client and server. The client provides a single command line to the finger server, which returns a printable reply.

Note — Connecting directly to the server from a TIP or an equally narrow-minded TELNET-protocol user program can send meaningless tries at option negotiation to the server. These tries foul up the command-line interpretation. fingerd should be taught to filter out IACs and perhaps even respond negatively (IAC does not) to all option commands received.

Files

/var/adm/utmpx

> User and accounting information.

/etc/passwd   System password file.

/var/adm/lastlog

> Last login times.

$HOME/.Plan   User's plans.

$HOME/.project

> User's projects.

Attributes

See attributes(5) for descriptions of the following attributes.

Attribute Type	Attribute Value
Availability	SUNWcsu

See Also

finger(1), inetd(1M), attributes(5)

Harrenstien, Ken, *NAME/FINGER*, RFC 742, Network Information Center, SRI International, Menlo Park, Calif., December 1977.

in.ftpd, ftpd — File Transfer Protocol Server

Synopsis

in.ftpd [-dl][-t *timeout*]

Description

The in.ftpd daemon is the Internet File Transfer Protocol (FTP) server process. The server uses the TCP protocol and listens at the port specified in the ftp service specification. See services(4).

Note — The in.ftpd command is IPv6 enabled. See ip6(7P).

To deny login for a particular user, add the user's login to the /etc/inet/ftpusers file.

ftpaccess(4) is the configuration file. For backward compatibility, you can set umask and banner as follows. Set the umask used to create files during PUT operations, by adding the following line to /etc/default/ftpd.

UMASK=*nnn*

You can configure the banner returned by `in.ftpd` in the parenthetical portion of its greeting. The default is equivalent to `uname -sr` and is used if no banner is set in `/etc/default/ftpd`. To set the banner, add a line of the following form to `/etc/default/ftpd`.

`BANNER="..."`

Nonempty banner strings are ted to shells for evaluation. You can obtain the default banner by including the following line in `/etc/default/ftpd`.

`BANNER="`uname -s` `uname -r`"`

To suppress printing of a banner, include the following line in `/etc/default/ftpd`.

`BANNER=""`

Notes

The anonymous FTP account is inherently dangerous and should be avoided when possible.

The nameservice caching daemon `/usr/sbin/nscd` may interfere with some of the functionality of anonymous FTP. The sublogin feature does not work unless caching for `passwd` is disabled in `/etc/nscd.conf`.

The server must run as superuser to create sockets with privileged port numbers. It maintains an effective user ID of the logged-in user, reverting to superuser only when binding addresses to sockets. The possible security holes have been extensively scrutinized, but the list of known holes is possibly incomplete.

The `/etc/ftpusers` file, which is now included as part of the Solaris Operating Environment, contains a list of users who cannot access the system; the default list of users in `/etc/ftpusers` includes all of the accounts in `passwd`(4). See `ftpusers`(4).

Options

`-d`	Log debugging information to the system log daemon `syslogd`(1M).
`-l`	Log each FTP session to the system log daemon `syslogd`(1M).
`-t timeout`	Set the inactivity timeout period to `timeout` seconds. The FTP server times out an inactive session after 15 minutes.

Requests

The FTP server currently supports the following FTP requests; case is not distinguished.

ABOR	Abort previous command.
ACCT	Specify account (ignored).
ALLO	Allocate storage (vacuous).
APPE	Append to a file.
CDUP	Change to parent of current working directory.
CWD	Change working directory.
DELE	Delete a file.
EPRT	Specify data connection port.

EPSV	Prepare for server-to-client transfer.
HELP	Give help information.
LIST	Give list files in a directory (`ls -lg`).
LPRT	Specify data connection port.
MKD	Make a directory.
MODE	Specify data transfer mode.
NLST	Give name list of files in directory (`ls`).
NOOP	Do nothing.
PASS	Specify password.
PASV	Prepare for server-to-server transfer.
PORT	Specify data connection port.
PWD	Print the current working directory.
QUIT	Terminate session.
RETR	Retrieve a file.
RMD	Remove a directory.
RNFR	Specify rename-from file name.
RNTO	Specify rename-to file name.
STOR	Store a file.
STOU	Store a file with a unique name.
STRU	Specify data transfer structure.
TYPE	Specify data transfer type.
USER	Specify user name.
XCUP	Change to parent of current working directory.
XCWD	Change working directory.
XMKD	Make a directory.
XPWD	Print the current working directory.
XRMD	Remove a directory.

The remaining FTP requests specified in RFC 959 are recognized but not implemented.

The FTP server aborts an active file transfer only when the ABOR command is preceded by a Telnet "Interrupt Process" (IP) signal and a Telnet "Synch" signal in the command Telnet stream, as described in RFC 959.

in.ftpd interprets file names according to the globbing conventions used by sh(1), which permit the metacharacters * ? [] { } ~ in file names.

in.ftpd authenticates users according to the following four rules.

1. The user name must be in the password database and not have a null password. In this case, the client must provide a password before any file operations can be performed. The PAM framework (see "Security" on page 426) verifies that the correct password was entered.

2. The user name must not appear in the file /etc/inet/ftpusers. If the user name is in this file, FTP access is denied.

3. The user must have a standard shell returned by getusershell(3C).

4. If the user name is anonymous or ftp, an anonymous ftp account must be present *New!* in the passwd and shadow files (user ftp). In this case, the user can log in by specifying any password. By convention, the password is given as the user's e-mail address, such as user@host.Sun.COM.

For anonymous ftp users, in.ftpd takes special measures to restrict the client's access privileges. The server performs a chroot(2) command to the home directory of the ftp user. So that system security is not breached, it is recommended that you construct the ftp subtree with care by using the following suggested directory permissions.

> **Note** — The ftpconfig(1M) command sets these directories up automatically.

~ftp	Make the home directory owned by root and unwriteable by anyone.
~ftp/bin	Make this directory owned by root and unwriteable by anyone. Make this a symbolic link to ~ftp/usr/bin. The ls(1) command must be present in this directory to support the list commands. The ls(1) command should have mode 111.
~ftp/usr/lib	Make this directory owned by root and unwriteable by anyone. Copy the following shared libraries from /usr/lib into this directory. ld.so.1* libc.so.1* libdl.so.1* libmp.so.2* libnsl.so.1* libsocket.so.1* nss_compat.so.1* nss_dns.so.1* nss_files.so.1* nss_nis.so.1* nss_nisplus.so.1* nss_xfn.so.1* straddr.so* straddr.so.2*
~ftp/etc	Make this directory owned by root and unwriteable by anyone. Copies of the passwd(4), group(4), and netconfig(4) files must be present for the ls(1) command to work properly. These files should have mode 444.
~ftp/pub	Make this directory mode 755 and owned by root. Users should then put files that are to be accessible to the anonymous account in this directory.

~ftp/dev   Make this directory owned by root and unwriteable by anyone. First,
                  perform ls -1L on the device files listed below to determine their
                  major and minor numbers, then use mknod to create them in this
                  directory.
                  /dev/zero
                  /dev/tcpo
                  /dev/udp
                  /dev/ticotsord

                  Set the read and write mode on these nodes to 666 so that passive ftp
                  does not fail with permission denied errors.

~ftp/usr/share/lib/zoneinfo

                  Make this directory mode 555 and owned by root. Copy its contents
                  from /usr/share/lib/zoneinfo to enable ls -1 to display
                  timestamps and date stamps correctly.

Security

in.ftpd uses pam(3) for authentication, account management, and session
management. The PAM configuration policy, listed through /etc/pam.conf, specifies
the module to be used for in.ftpd. The following example shows a partial pam.conf file
with entries for the in.ftpd command, using the UNIX authentication, account
management, and session management modules.

```
ftp auth required /usr/lib/security/pam_unix.so.1
ftp account required /usr/lib/security/pam_unix.so.1
ftp session required /usr/lib/security/pam_unix.so.1
```

If the ftp service has no entries, then the entries for the other service are used.
Unlike login, passwd, and other commands, the ftp protocol supports only a single
password. Using multiple modules prevents in.ftpd from working properly.

Examples

The following example sets up anonymous FTP by adding an entry to the /etc/passwd
file. /export/ftp is chosen to be the anonymous FTP area, and the shell is the
nonexistent file /nosuchshell to prevent users from logging in as the ftp user.
    Add the following line to the /etc/passwd file.

ftp:x:30000:30000:Anonymous FTP:/export/ftp:/nosuchshell

Add the following entry to the /etc/shadow file.

ftp:NP:6445::::::

The following shell script sets up the anonymous FTP area. It assumes that names
are resolved using NIS.

```
#!/bin/sh
# Script to set up anonymous ftp area
#
# Verify you are root
/usr/bin/id | grep -w 'uid=0' >/dev/null 2>&1
if [ "$?" != "0" ]; then
```

```
        echo
        exit 1
fi

# Handle the optional command-line argument
case $# in
        # The default location for the anon ftp comes from the passwd
        # file.
        0) ftphome="`getent passwd ftp | cut -d: -f6`"
        ;;
        1) if [ "$1" = "start" ]; then
                        ftphome="`getent passwd ftp | cut -d: -f6`"
        else
                        ftphome=$1
        fi
        ;;
        *) echo "Usage: $0 [anon-ftp-root]"
        exit 1
        ;;
esac

if [ -z "${ftphome}" ]; then
        echo "$0: ftphome must be non-null"
        exit 2
fi

case ${ftphome} in
        /*) # ok
        ;;

        *) echo "$0: ftphome must be an absolute pathname"
        exit 1
        ;;
esac

# This script assumes that ftphome is neither / nor /usr so ...
if [ -z "${ftphome}" -o "${ftphome}" = "/" -o "${ftphome}" = "/usr" ];
  then
        echo "$0: ftphome must be non-null and neither / or /usr"
        exit 2
fi

# If ftphome does not exist but parent does, create ftphome.
if [ ! -d ${ftphome} ]; then
        # lack of -p below is intentional
        mkdir ${ftphome}
fi
chown root ${ftphome}
chmod 555 ${ftphome}

echo Setting up anonymous ftp area ${ftphome}

# Ensure that the /usr directory exists.
if [ ! -d ${ftphome}/usr ]; then
```

```
        mkdir -p ${ftphome}/usr
fi

# Now set the ownership and modes to match the man page.
chown root ${ftphome}/usr
chmod 555 ${ftphome}/usr

# Ensure that the /usr/bin directory exists.
if [ ! -d ${ftphome}/usr/bin ]; then
        mkdir -p ${ftphome}/usr/bin
fi

# Now set the ownership and modes to match the man page.
chown root ${ftphome}/usr/bin
chmod 555 ${ftphome}/usr/bin

# This may not be the right thing to do
# but we need the bin -> usr/bin link.
rm -f ${ftphome}/bin
ln -s usr/bin ${ftphome}/bin

# Ensure that the /usr/lib and /etc directories exist.
if [ ! -d ${ftphome}/usr/lib ]; then
        mkdir -p ${ftphome}/usr/lib
fi
chown root ${ftphome}/usr/lib
chmod 555 ${ftphome}/usr/lib

if [ ! -d ${ftphome}/usr/lib/security ]; then
        mkdir -p ${ftphome}/usr/lib/security
fi
chown root ${ftphome}/usr/lib/security
chmod 555 ${ftphome}/usr/lib/security

if [ ! -d ${ftphome}/etc ]; then
        mkdir -p ${ftphome}/etc
fi
chown root ${ftphome}/etc
chmod 555 ${ftphome}/etc

# A list of all the commands that should be copied to
# ${ftphome}/usr/bin.
# /usr/bin/ls is needed at a minimum.
ftpcmd="
        /usr/bin/ls
"

# ${ftphome}/usr/lib needs to have all the libraries needed by the above
# commands, plus the runtime linker, and some nameservice libraries
# to resolve names. We just take all of them here.

ftplib="`ldd $ftpcmd | nawk '$3 ~ /lib/ { print $3 }' | sort | uniq`"
ftplib="$ftplib /usr/lib/nss_* /usr/lib/straddr* /usr/lib/libmp.so*"
ftplib="$ftplib /usr/lib/libnsl.so.1 /usr/lib/libsocket.so.1
```

```
     /usr/lib/ld.so.1"
ftplib="`echo $ftplib | tr ' ' '\n' | sort | uniq`"

cp ${ftplib} ${ftphome}/usr/lib
chmod 555 ${ftphome}/usr/lib/*

cp /usr/lib/security/* ${ftphome}/usr/lib/security
chmod 555 ${ftphome}/usr/lib/security/*

cp ${ftpcmd} ${ftphome}/usr/bin
chmod 111 ${ftphome}/usr/bin/*

# You also might want to have separate minimal versions of passwd
# and group.
cp /etc/passwd /etc/group /etc/netconfig /etc/pam.conf ${ftphome}/etc
chmod 444 ${ftphome}/etc/*

# Need /etc/default/init for time zone to be correct.
if [ ! -d ${ftphome}/etc/default ]; then
     mkdir ${ftphome}/etc/default
fi
chown root ${ftphome}/etc/default
chmod 555 ${ftphome}/etc/default
cp /etc/default/init ${ftphome}/etc/default
chmod 444 ${ftphome}/etc/default/init

# Copy time zone database.
mkdir -p ${ftphome}/usr/share/lib/zoneinfo
(cd ${ftphome}/usr/share/lib/zoneinfo
     (cd /usr/share/lib/zoneinfo; find . -print |
     cpio -o) 2>/dev/null | cpio -imdu 2>/dev/null
     find . -print | xargs chmod 555
     find . -print | xargs chown root
)

# Ensure that the /dev directory exists.
if [ ! -d ${ftphome}/dev ]; then
     mkdir -p ${ftphome}/dev
fi

# Make device nodes. ticotsord and udp are necessary for
# 'ls' to resolve NIS names.
for device in zero tcp udp ticotsord ticlts
do
     line=`ls -lL /dev/${device} | sed -e 's/,//'`
     major=`echo $line | awk '{print $5}'`
     minor=`echo $line | awk '{print $6}'`
     rm -f ${ftphome}/dev/${device}
     mknod ${ftphome}/dev/${device} c ${major} ${minor}
done

chmod 666 ${ftphome}/dev/*
```

```
## Now set the ownership and modes.
chown root ${ftphome}/dev
chmod 555 ${ftphome}/dev

# Uncomment the below if you want a place for people to store things,
# but be aware of the security implications.
#if [ ! -d ${ftphome}/pub ]; then
# mkdir -p ${ftphome}/pub
#fi
#chown root ${ftphome}/pub
#chmod 1755 ${ftphome}/pub
```

After running this script, edit the files in ~ftp/etc and remove all nonpublic information.

Files

/etc/default/ftpd

        File that is used to configure the FTP banner.

/etc/ftpusers

        File listing users for whom FTP login privileges are disallowed.

Attributes

See attributes(5) for descriptions of the following attributes.

Attribute Type	Attribute Value
Availability	SUNWcsu

See Also

ftp(1), ld.so.1(1), ls(1), sh(1), aset(1M), inetd(1M), mknod(1M), syslogd(1M), chroot(2), getsockopt(3SOCKET), pam(3PAM), ftpusers(4), group(4), inetd.conf(4), netconfig(4), netrc(4), pam.conf(4), passwd(4), services(4), attributes(5), pam_unix(5)

Allman, M., Ostermann, S., and Metz, C., RFC 2428, *FTP Extensions for IPv6 and NATs*, The Internet Society, 1998.

Piscitello, D., RFC 1639, *FTP Operation Over Big Address Records (FOOBAR)*, Network Working Group, June 1994.

Postel, Jon, and Reynolds, Joyce, RFC 959, *File Transfer Protocol (FTP)*, Network Information Center, SRI International, Menlo Park, Calif., October 1985.

Diagnostics

in.ftpd logs various errors to syslogd, with a facility code of daemon.

Info Severity

The following messages are logged only if you specified the -l option.

```
FTPD: connection from host at time
```

> A connection was made to ftpd from the host *host* at the date and time *time*.

```
FTPD: User user timed out after timeout seconds at time
```

> The user *user* was logged out because he had not entered any commands after *timeout* seconds; the logout occurred at the date and time *time*.

Debug Severity

The following messages are logged only if you specified the -d option.

```
FTPD: command: command
```

> A command line containing *command* was read from the FTP client.

```
lost connection
```

> The FTP client dropped the connection.

```
<--- replycode
<--- replycode-
```

> A reply was sent to the FTP client with the reply code *replycode*. The next message logged includes the message associated with the reply. If a - follows the reply code, the reply is continued on later lines.

in.lpd — BSD Print Protocol Adapter

Synopsis

```
/usr/lib/print/in.lpd
```

Description

The in.lpd daemon manages the BSD print spooling system. It implements the network listening service for the BSD print protocol specified in RFC 1179. The BSD print protocol provides a remote interface for systems to interact with a local spooling system. The protocol defines five standard requests from the client to the server: starting queue processing, transferring print jobs, retrieving terse status, retrieving verbose status, and cancelling print jobs.

in.lpd is started from inetd (see inetd(1M)). inetd waits for connections on TCP port 515. On receipt of a connect request, in.lpd is started to service the connection. Once the request has been filled, in.lpd closes the connection and exits.

Exit Status

0   Successful completion.

non-zero   An error occurred.

Files

/etc/printers.conf

System printer configuration database.

printers.conf.byname

NIS version of /etc/printers.conf.

fns.ctx_dir.domain

NIS+ version of /etc/printers.conf.

/usr/lib/print/bsd-adaptor/bsd_*.so*

Spooler translation modules.

Attributes

See attributes(5) for descriptions of the following attributes.

Attribute Type	Attribute Value
Availability	SUNWpcu

See Also

inetd(1M), printers.conf(4), attributes(5)

---

in.named, named — Internet Domain Name Server

Synopsis

```
in.named [-d debuglevel][-q][-r][-p remote |local-port]
  [-w dirname][[-b | -c] bootfile]
```

Description

The in.named daemon is the Internet domain nameserver. in.named spawns the named-xfer process whenever it needs to perform a zone transfer. See named-xfer(1M).

The in.named nameservice is used by hosts on the Internet to provide access to the Internet distributed naming database. See RFC 1034 and RFC 1035 for more information on the Internet domain name system.

With no arguments, in.named reads the default configuration file /etc/named.conf for any initial data and listens for queries. Any additional arguments beyond those shown in the "Synopsis" section are interpreted as the names of boot files. If multiple boot files are specified, only the last is used.

The nameserver reads the boot file to obtain instructions on where to find its initial data.

Options

-w *dirname*   Change the current working directory of in.named to *dirname*.

-b *bootfile*   Use *bootfile* instead of /etc/named.conf. File names can begin with a leading dash.

-c *bootfile*   Use *bootfile* instead of /etc/named.conf. File names can begin with a leading dash.

-d *debug-level*

    Print debugging information. *debug-level* is a number indicating the level of messages printed.

-p *remote/local-port*

    Use different port numbers. The default is the standard port number as returned by getservbyname(3N) for service domain. You can specify up to two port numbers separated by a slash (/). When you specify two ports, the first is used for contacting remote servers and the second is the service port bound by the local instance of in.named. Use this option mostly for debugging.

-r   Turn recursion off in the server. Answers can come only from local (primary or secondary) zones. You can use this option on root servers. Note that this option probably is abandoned in favor of the boot-file directive, option no-recursion.

Usage

/etc/named.conf File Directives

The following simple configuration file /etc/named.conf contains directives to guide the in.named process at startup time.

```
options {
    directory  "/usr/local/adm/named";
    pid-file   "/var/named/named.pid";
    named-xfer "/usr/sbin/named-xfer";
    forwarders         {
            10.0.0.78;
            10.2.0.78;
    };
    transfers-in     10;
    forward only;
    fake-iquery yes;
    pollfd-chunk-size 20;
};
```

```
logging {
    category lame-servers { null; };
    category cname   { null; };
};

zone "." in {
    type hint;
    file "root.cache";
};

zone "cc.berkeley.edu" in {
    type slave;
    file "128.32.137.3";
    masters { 128.32.137.8; };
};

zone "6.32.128.in-addr.arpa" in {
    type slave;
    file "128.32.137.3";
    masters { 128.32.137.8; };
};
zone "0.0.127.in-addr.arpa" in {
    type master;
    file "master/db.127";
};

zone "berkeley.edu" in {
    type master;
    file "berkeley.edu.zone";
};

zone "32.128.in-addr.arpa" in {
    type master;
    file "ucbhosts.rev";
};
```

The configuration file consists of sections and comments. Sections end with a ; and contain statements enclosed in { } that can span multiple lines. The following sections are supported: options, zone, server, logging, acl, include, and key.

Comments Syntax
The following examples show comments syntax in BIND 8.1.

```
/* This is a BIND comment as in C */
// This is a BIND comment as in C++
#  This is a BIND comment as in common UNIX shells and Perl
```

Warning — You cannot use the semicolon character (;) to start a comment.

Options Section

The options syntax is described below.

```
options {
        [directory path_name;]
        [named-xfer path_name;]
        [pid-file path_name;]
        [auth-nxdomain yes_or_no;]
        [fake-iquery yes_or_no;]
        [fetch-glue yes_or_no;]
        [multiple-cnames yes_or_no;]
        [notify yes_or_no;]
        [recursion yes_or_no;]
        [forward ( only | first );]
        [forwarders { [in_addr ; [in_addr ;...]] };]
        [check-names ( master | slave | response )
            ( warn | fail | ignore);]
        [allow-query { address_match_list };]
        [allow-transfer { address_match_list };]
        [listen-on [port ip_port] { address_match_list };]
        [query-source [address ( ip_addr | * )][port ( ip_port | * )] ;]
        [max-transfer-time-in number;]
        [transfer-format ( one-answer | many-answers );]
        [transfers-in number;]
        [transfers-out number;]
        [transfers-per-ns number;]
        [coresize size_spec ;]
        [datasize size_spec ;]
        [files size_spec ;]
        [stacksize size_spec ;]
        [clean-interval number;]
        [interface-interval number;]
        [scan-interval number;]
        [topology { address_match_list };]
};
```

Definitions and Use of Options

The *options* section sets up global options to be used by BIND. You can include this section only once in a configuration file; if more than one occurrence is found, the first occurrence determines the actual options used and a warning is generated. If there is no *options* section, an options block with each option set to its default is used.

Path Names

directory   The working directory of the server. Any nonabsolute path names in the configuration file are taken as relative to this directory. This directory is the default location for most server output files (for example, named.run). If you do not specify a directory, the working directory defaults to ., the directory from which the server was started. Specify the directory as an absolute path.

named-xfer The path name to the *named-xfer* program that the server uses for inbound zone transfers. If not specified, the default is operating-system dependent, for example, `/usr/sbin/named-xfer`.

pid-file The path name of the file into which the server writes its process ID. If not specified, the default is operating system dependent but is usually `/var/run/named.pid` or `/etc/named.pid`. The *pid-file* is used by programs like `ndc` that want to send signals to the running nameserver.

Boolean Options

`auth-nxdomain`

If yes, then the AA bit is always set on NXDOMAIN responses even if the server is not actually authoritative. The default is yes. Do not turn off `auth-nxdomain` unless you are sure you know what you are doing, because some older software does not like that action.

`fake-iquery` If yes, the server simulates the obsolete DNS query type IQUERY. The default is no.

`fetch-glue` If yes (the default), the server fetches glue resource records it does not have when constructing the additional data section of a response. You can use `fetch-glue no` in conjunction with `recursion no` to prevent the server's cache from growing or becoming corrupted (at the cost of requiring more work from the client).

`multiple-cnames`

If yes, then multiple CNAME resource records are allowed for a domain name. The default is no. Allowing multiple CNAME records is against standards and is not recommended. Multiple CNAME support is available because previous versions of BIND allowed multiple CNAME records and these records have been used for load balancing by a number of sites.

`notify` If yes (the default), DNS NOTIFY messages are sent when changes to a zone for which the server is authoritative are made. The use of NOTIFY speeds convergence between the master and its slaves. Slave servers that receive a NOTIFY message and understand it contact the master server for the zone and see if they need to do a zone transfer. If they do, they initiate it immediately. You can also specify the `notify` option in the zone section, in which case it overrides the `options notify` statement.

`recursion` If yes and a DNS query requests recursion, then the server tries to do all the work required to answer the query. If recursion is no, the server returns a referral to the client if it doesn't know the answer. The default is yes. See also `fetch-glue` above.

Forwarding

You can use the forwarding facility to create a large sitewide cache on a few servers, reducing traffic over links to external nameservers. You can also use this facility to enable queries by servers that do not have direct access to the Internet but want to look up exterior names anyway. Forwarding occurs only on those queries for which the server is not authoritative and for which the server does not have the answer in its cache.

forward   Specify a value of `first` (the default) to first query the forwarder. If that doesn't answer the question, then look for the answer itself. Specify a value of `only` to query only the forwarders list. This option is meaningful only if the `forwarders` list is not empty.

forwarders   Specify the IP addresses to be used for forwarding. The default is the empty list (no forwarding). Future versions of BIND 8 will provide a more powerful forwarding system. The syntax described above will continue to be supported.

Name Checking

The server can check domain names based on their expected client contexts. For example, a domain name used as a host name can be checked for compliance with the valid host names defined in the RFCs. Three checking methods are available.

ignore   Do no checking.

warn   Check names against their expected client contexts. Log invalid names and continue processing normally.

fail   Check names against their expected client contexts. Log invalid names and reject the offending data. The server can check nàmes in three areas: master zone files, slave zone files, and in responses to queries the server has initiated. If check-names response `fail` has been specified and answering the client's question would require sending an invalid name to the client, the server sends a REFUSED response code to the client.

The defaults are listed below.

- `check-names master fail`
- `check-names slave warn`
- `check-names response ignore`

You can also specify `check-names` in the zone section, in which case it overrides the `options check-names` statement. When used in a zone section, the area is not specified because it can be deduced from the zone type.

Access Control

You can restrict access to the server according to the IP address of the requesting system. See `address_match_list` for details on how to specify IP address lists.

allow-query   Specify which hosts are allowed to ask ordinary questions. You can also specify `allow-query` in the zone section, in which case it overrides the `options allow-query` statement. If not specified, the default is to allow queries from all hosts.

allow-transfer

> Specify which hosts are allowed to receive zone transfers from the server. You can also specify `allow-transfer` in the zone section, in which case it overrides the `options allow-transfer` statement. If not specified, the default is to allow transfers from all hosts.

Interfaces

You can specify the interfaces and ports from which the server answers queries by using the `listen-on` option. `listen-on` takes an optional port and an `address_match_list`. The server listens on all interfaces allowed by the address match list. If a port is not specified, port 53 is used.

Multiple `listen-on` statements are allowed, as shown in the following example.

```
listen-on { 5.6.7.8; };
listen-on port 1234 { !1.2.3.4; 1.2/16; };
```

> If no `listen-on` is specified, the server listens on port 53 on all interfaces.

Query Address

If the server does not know the answer to a question, it queries other nameservers. `query-source` specifies the address and port used for such queries. If address is * or is omitted, a wildcard IP address (`INADDR_ANY`) is used. If port is * or is omitted, a random unprivileged port is used. The default is

```
query-source address * port *;
```

Note — `query-source` currently applies only to UDP queries; TCP queries always use a wildcard IP address and a random unprivileged port.

Zone Transfers

max-transfer-time-in

> Terminate inbound zone transfers (`named-xfer` processes) running longer than this many minutes. The default is 120 minutes.

transfer-format

> The server supports two zone transfer methods. `one-answer` uses one DNS message per resource record transferred. `many-answers` packs as many resource records as possible into a message. `many-answers` is more efficient but is only known to be understood by BIND 8.1 and patched versions of BIND 4.9.5. The default is `one-answer`. You can override `transfer-format` on a per-server basis by using the server section.

transfers-in   The maximum number of inbound zone transfers that can be running concurrently. The default value is 10. Increasing `transfers-in` can speed up the convergence of slave zones, but it also can increase the load on the local system.

transfers-out

> This option will be used in the future to limit the number of concurrent outbound zone transfers. It is checked for syntax but is otherwise ignored.

transfers-per-ns

> The maximum number of inbound zone transfers (named-xfer processes) that can be concurrently transferring from a given remote nameserver. The default value is 2. Increasing transfers-per-ns can speed up the convergence of slave zones but it also can increase the load on the remote nameserver. You can override transfers-per-ns on a per-server basis by using the transfers statement in the server section.

Resource Limits

The server's usage of many system resources can be limited. Some operating systems do not support some of the limits, and a warning is generated if you set an unsupported limit in the configuration file.

Scaled values are allowed when you specify resource limits. For example, you can use 1G instead of 1073741824 to specify a limit of one gigabyte; unlimited requests unlimited use or the maximum available amount. default uses the limit that was in force when the server was started. See ulimit(1) for a discussion of `ulimit -a ` (ksh only) for defaults.

coresize The maximum size of a core dump. The default is system dependent.

datasize The maximum amount of data memory the server can use. The default is system dependent.

files The maximum number of files that the server can have open concurrently. The default is system dependent.

stacksize The maximum amount of stack memory the server can use. The default is system dependent.

Topology

All other things being equal, when the server chooses a nameserver to query from a list of nameservers, it prefers the one that is topologically closest to itself. The topology statement takes an address_match_list and interprets it in a special way. Each top-level list element is assigned a distance. Nonnegated elements get a distance based on their position in the list, where the closer the match is to the start of the list, the shorter the distance is between it and the server. A negated match is assigned the maximum distance from the server. If there is no match, the address gets a distance that is further than any nonnegated list element and closer than any negated element. For example,

```
topology {
        10/8;
        !1.2.3/24;
```

```
        { 1.2/16; 3/8; };
};
```

prefers servers on network 10 the most, followed by hosts on network 1.2.0.0 (netmask
255.255.0.0) and network 3, with the exception of hosts on network 1.2.3 (netmask
255.255.255.0), which are preferred least of all. The default topology is

```
topology { localhost; localnets; };
```

The Server Section

The server syntax is described below.

```
server ip_addr {
        [bogus yes_or_no;]
        [transfers number;]
        [transfer-format ( one-answer | many-answers );]
        [keys { key_id [key_id...] };]
};
```

   The server statement defines the characteristics to be associated with a remote
nameserver.
   If you discover that a server is giving out bad data, marking it as bogus prevents
further queries to it. The default value is no.
   The server supports two zone transfer methods. The first, one-answer, uses one DNS
message per resource record transferred. The second, many-answers, packs as many
resource records as possible into a message. many-answers is more efficient but is
known to be understood only by BIND 8.1 and patched versions of BIND 4.9.5. You can
specify which method to use for a server with the transfer-format option. If you do not
specify transfer-format, the transfer-format specified by the *options* statement is
used.
   The transfers are used in a future release of the server to limit the number of
concurrent inbound zone transfers from the specified server. It is checked for syntax but
is otherwise ignored.
   The keys statement is intended for future use by the server. It is checked for syntax
but is otherwise ignored.

The Zone Section

The zone syntax is described below.

```
zone domain_name [( in | hs | hesiod | chaos )] {
        type master;
        file path_name;
        [check-names ( warn | fail | ignore );]
        [allow-update { address_match_list };]
        [allow-query { address_match_list };]
        [allow-transfer { address_match_list };]
        [notify yes_or_no;]
        [also-notify { ip_addr; [ip_addr;...] };
};

zone domain_name [( in | hs | hesiod | chaos )] {
        type ( slave | stub );
        [file path_name;]
        masters { ip_addr; [ip_addr;...] };
```

```
        [check-names ( warn | fail | ignore );]
        [allow-update { address_match_list };]
        [allow-query { address_match_list };]
        [allow-transfer { address_match_list };]
        [max-transfer-time-in number;]
        [notify yes_or_no;]
        [also-notify { ip_addr; [ip_addr;...] };
};

zone . [( in | hs | hesiod | chaos )] {
        type hint;
        file path_name;
        [check-names ( warn | fail | ignore );]
};
```

You can optionally follow the zone name with a class. If you do not specify a class, `in` (for Internet) is assumed., which is correct for the vast majority of cases.

`in`	The Internet domain.
`hs`	The MIT Athena Hesiod domain.
`hesiod`	The MIT Athena Hesiod class. The `hesiod` class is used to share information about various system databases such as users, groups, and printers. You can find more information at MIT. The keyword `hs` is a synonym for `hesiod`.
`chaos`	The Chaos class. CHAOSnet, a LAN protocol, was created at MIT in the mid 1970s. It is still seen on some LISP stations and other hardware in the AI community.

The following zone types are defined.

`master`	The master copy of the data in a zone.
`slave`	A replica of a master zone. The masters list specifies one or more IP addresses that the slave contacts to update its copy of the zone. If you specify `file`, then the replica is written to the file. Use of `file` is recommended because it often speeds server startup and eliminates wasted bandwidth.
`stub`	Like a slave zone, except replicate only the NS records of a master zone instead of the entire zone.
`hint`	Specify the initial set of root nameservers using a hint zone. When the server starts up, it uses the root `hints` to find a root nameserver and get the most recent list of root nameservers. Note that previous releases of BIND used the term `primary` for a master zone, `secondary` for a slave zone, and `cache` for a hint zone.

You can optionally follow the zone by a class. If you do not specify a class, class `in` is used.

The following `zone` options are described.

`check-names`	See "Name Checking" on page 437.
`allow-query`	See the description of `allow-query` in "Access Control" on page 437.

allow-update   Specify which hosts are allowed to submit dynamic DNS updates to the server. The default is to deny updates from all hosts.

allow-transfer

See the description of allow-transfer in "Access Control" on page 437.

max-transfer-time-in

See the description of max-transfer-time-in in "Zone Transfers" on page 438.

notify   See the description of notify in "Boolean Options" on page 436.

also-notify   Specify that all of the listed nameservers for the zone (other than the primary master) plus any IP addresses specified with also-notify is the set of systems that receive a DNS NOTIFY message for the zone. also-notify is meaningful only if notify is active for this zone and is not meaningful for subzones. The default is the empty list. The set of machines that receive a DNS NOTIFY message for this zone comprise all the listed nameservers for the zone (other than the primary master) plus any IP addresses specified with also-notify. also-notify is not meaningful for stub zones. The default is the empty list.

The Logging Section
The logging syntax is described below.

```
logging {
      [channel channel_name {
      ( file path_name
      [versions ( number | unlimited )]
      [size size_spec]
      | syslog ( kern | user | mail | daemon | auth | syslog |
      lpr |
      news | uucp | cron | authpriv | ftp |
      local0 | local1 | local2 | local3 |
      local4 | local5 | local6 | local7 )
      | null );
      [severity ( critical | error | warning | notice | info | debug
   [level] | dynamic );][print-category yes_or_no;][print-severity
   yes_or_no;][print-time yes_or_no;] };]
      [category category_name {
      channel_name; [channel_name;...]
      };]
      ...
      };
```

The logging statement configures a wide variety of logging options for the nameserver. Its channel phrase associates output methods, format options, and severity levels with a name that can then be used with the category phrase to select how various classes of messages are logged.

Only one logging statement is used to define how many channels and categories are wanted. If there are multiple logging statements in a configuration, the first defined determines the logging, and warnings are issued for the others. If there is no `logging` statement, the default `logging` configuration is

```
logging {
        category default { default_syslog; default_debug; };
        category panic { default_syslog; default_stderr; };
        category packet { default_debug; };
        category eventlib { default_debug; };
};
```

The Channel Phrase

All log output goes to one or more channels; you can make as many channels as you want.

Every channel definition must include a clause that says whether messages selected for the channel go to a file, to a particular `syslog` facility, or are discarded. It can optionally also limit the message severity level that is accepted by the channel (default is `info`), and it can specify whether to include a named-generated timestamp, the category name, or severity level (default is not to include any).

The word `null` as the destination option for the channel discards all messages sent to it; other options for the channel are meaningless.

The `file` clause can include limitations both on how large the file is allowed to become and how many versions of the file are saved each time the file is opened.

The `size` option for files is simply a hard ceiling on log growth. If the file ever exceeds the size, then `named` just does not write anything more to it until the file is reopened; exceeding the size does not automatically trigger a reopen. The default behavior is to not limit the size of the file.

If you use the `version` logfile option, then `named` retains that many backup versions of the file by renaming them when opening. For example, if you choose to keep three old versions of the file `lamers.log`, then just before it is opened, `lamers.log.1` is renamed to `lamers.log.2`, `lamers.log.0` is renamed to `lamers.log.1`, and `lamers.log` is renamed to `lamers.log.0`. No rolled versions are kept by default. The unlimited keyword is synonymous with 99 in current BIND releases.

The argument for the `syslog()` clause is a `syslog()` facility as described in the `syslog(3)` manual page. The `syslog.conf(4)` manual page describes how `syslogd(1M)` handles messages sent to this facility. If you have a system that uses a very old version of `syslog()` that only uses two arguments to the `openlog()` function, then this clause is silently ignored.

The `severity` clause works like the `priorities` to `syslog()` except that they can also be used if you are writing directly to a file instead of using `syslog()`. Messages that are not at least of the severity level given are not selected for the channel; messages of higher severity levels are accepted.

If you are using `syslog()`, then the `syslog.conf` priorities also determine what eventually passes through. For example, with `syslog.conf`, suppose you define a `channel` facility as `daemon` and severity as `debug` but log only `daemon.warning`. The result is that messages of `info` and `notice` severity are dropped. If the situation were reversed, with `named` writing messages of only `warning` or higher, then `syslogd` would print all messages it received from the channel.

The server can supply extensive debugging information when it is in debugging mode. If the server's global debug level is greater than 0, then debugging mode is active. You can set the global debug level either by starting the server with the `-d` option followed by a positive integer, or by sending the server the `SIGUSR1` signal (for example, by using `ndc trace`). You can set the global debug level to 0 and turn off debugging mode by sending the server the `SIGUSR2` signal (`ndc notrace`). All debugging messages in the server have a debug level, and higher debug levels give more detailed output. Channels that specify a specific debug severity, for example,

```
channel specific_debug_level {
        file "foo";
        severity debug 3;
        };
```

get debugging output of level 3 or less any time the server is in debugging mode, regardless of the global debugging level. Channels with dynamic severity use the server's global level to determine what messages to print.

If print-time has been turned on, then the date and time are logged. You can specify print-time for a syslog() channel, but it is usually pointless because syslog() also prints the date and time. If you request print-category, then the category of the message is logged as well. Finally, if print-severity is on, then the severity level of the message is logged. You can use the print-options in any combination, and they are always printed in the following order: time, category, severity. In the following example, all three print-options are on.

```
28-Apr-1997 15:05:32.863 default: notice: Ready to answer queries.
```

Four predefined channels are used for default logging for in.named as follows. How they are used is described in the next section.

```
channel default_syslog {
        syslog daemon; # Send to syslog's daemon facility.
        severity info; # Send only priority info and higher.
};
channel default_debug {
        file "named.run"; # Write to named.run in the working directory.
        severity dynamic; # Log at the server's current debug level.
};
channel default_stderr { # Write to stderr.
        file "<stderr>"; # This is illustrative only;
        # there's currently
        # no way of specifying an internal file
        # descriptor in the configuration language.
        severity info; # Send only priority info and higher.
};
channel null {
        null; # Toss anything sent to this channel.
};
```

Once you define a channel, you cannot redefine it. Thus, you cannot alter the built-in channels directly, but you can modify the default logging by pointing categories at channels you have defined.

The Category Phase
Because there are many categories, you can send the logs you want to see wherever you want without seeing logs you do not want. If you do not specify a list of channels for a category, then log messages in that category are sent to the default category instead. If do not specify a default category, the following "default default" is used.

```
category default { default_syslog; default_debug; };
```

For example, if you want to log security events to a file but you also want keep the default logging behavior, you would specify the following.

```
channel my_security_channel {
        file "my_security_file";
        severity info;
        };
        category security { my_security_channel; default_syslog;
        default_debug;
};
```

To discard all messages in a category, specify the `null` channel.

```
category lame-servers { null; }; category cname { null; };
```

The following categories are available.

`default`	The catch-all. The things still not classified into categories all end up here. Also, if you do not specify any channels for a category, the `default` category is used instead. If you do not define the `default` category, the following definition is used.

```
category default { default_syslog; default_debug; };
```

`config`	High-level configuration file processing.
`parser`	Low-level configuration file processing.
`queries`	Generate a short log message for every query the server receives.
`lame-servers`	Messages such as `Lame server on....`
`statistics`	Statistics.
`panic`	If the server has to shut itself down because of an internal problem, it logs the problem in this category as well as in the problem's native category. If you do not define the `panic` category, the following definition is used.

```
category panic { default_syslog; default_stderr; };
```

`update`	Dynamic updates.
`ncache`	Negative caching.
`xfer-in`	Zone transfers the server is receiving.
`xfer-out`	Zone transfers the server is sending.
`db`	All database operations.
`eventlib`	Debugging information from the event system. You can specify only one channel for this category and it must be a file channel. If you do not define the `eventlib` category, the following definition is used.

```
category eventlib { default_debug; };
```

`packet`	Dumps of packets received and sent. You can specify only one channel for this category and it must be a file channel. If you do not define the packet category, the following definition is used.

```
category packet { default_debug; };
```

notify	The NOTIFY protocol.
cname	Messages such as... points to a CNAME.
security	Approved/unapproved requests.
os	Operating system problems.
insist	Internal consistency check failures.
maintenance	Periodic maintenance events.
load	Zone loading messages.

response-checks

                Messages arising from response checking, such as the following.
```
Malformed response...
wrong ans. name...
unrelated additional info...
invalid RR type...
bad referral....
```

The Key Section

The key syntax is described below.

```
key key_id {
      algorithm algorithm_id;
      secret secret_string;
};
```

The key section defines a key ID that can be used in a server section to associate an authentication method with a particular nameserver.

You must create a key ID with the key statement before it can be used in a server definition.

The algorithm_id is a string that specifies a security/authentication algorithm. secret_string is the secret to be used by the algorithm.

The key statement is intended for future use by the server. It is checked for syntax but is otherwise ignored.

The Include Section

The include section syntax is described below.

```
include path_name;
```

The include statement inserts the specified file at the point that the include statement is encountered. Because you cannot use the include statement within another statement, a line such as acl internal_hosts { "include internal_hosts.acl" } is not allowed. Use include to break up the configuration into easily managed chunks, as shown in the following example, that could be used at the top of a BIND configuration file to include any ACL or key information.

```
include "/etc/security/keys.bind";
include "/etc/acls.bind";
```

> **Note** — Be careful not to type #include, as you would in a C program, because # is used in this context to start a comment.

The ACL Format

The ACL session syntax is described below.

```
acl name {
        address_match_list
};
```

The acl statement creates a named address match list. It gets its name from a primary use of address match lists: Access Control Lists (ACLs).

> **Note** — You must define an address match list's name with acl before it can be used elsewhere; no forward references are allowed.

The following ACLs are built in.

any	Allow all hosts.
none	Deny all hosts.
localhost	Allow the IP addresses of all interfaces on the system.
localnets	Allow any host on a network for which the system has an interface.

Zone File Format

The zone files are also known as the authoritative master files (data files) for a zone. In the boot file, references were made to these files as part of the specification of any primary directives.

Two classes of entries populate the zone files: directives and resource records. The start of the zone file is likely to contain one or two directives that establish a context that modifies the way subsequent records are interpreted.

Resource records for a zone determine how a zone is managed by establishing zone characteristics. For example, one type of zone record establishes the zone's mailbox information.

The very first record of each zone file should be a Start-of-Authority record (SOA) for a zone. A multiple-line SOA record is presented below. The meaning of the values in this sample become clearer with the help of a list that describes the purpose of each field in the zone record (see the SOA list subitem under the rr-type list item in, "Format of Resource Records in Zone Files" on page 448).

```
@ IN SOA ucbvax.Berkeley.EDU. rwh.ucbvax.Berkeley.EDU. (
1989020501 ;serial
10800 ;refresh
3600 ;retry
3600000 ;expire
86400 ) ;minimum
```

Resource records normally end at the end of a line but may be continued across lines between opening and closing parentheses (as demonstrated in the preceding sample).

Comments are introduced by semicolons. They continue to the end of the line.

Directives in Zone Files

Two control directives help determine how the zone file is processed: $INCLUDE and
$ORIGIN.

The $INCLUDE directive refers to yet another file within which zone characteristics
are described. Such files typically contain groups of resource records, but they can also
contain further directives.

The $ORIGIN directive establishes a current origin that is appended to any domain
values that do not end with a dot (.). The placeholder domain represents the first
resource record field as shown in "Format of Resource Records in Zone Files" on
page 448. These directives have the following format.

```
$INCLUDE filename opt-current-domain $ORIGIN current-domain
```

current-domain

> Specify the value of the current origin that remains in effect for this
> configuration file unless a subsequent $ORIGIN directive overrides it
> for the remaining portion of the file.

filename

> Specify a file, the contents of which are, in effect, incorporated into the
> configuration file at the location of the corresponding $INCLUDE
> directive.

opt-current-domain

> Optionally define a current origin that is applicable only to the
> records residing in the specified file in the corresponding $INCLUDE
> directive. This directive overrides the origin given in a preceding
> $ORIGIN directive, but only for the scope of the included text. See also
> current-domain. Neither the opt-current-domain argument of
> $INCLUDE nor the $ORIGIN directive in the included file can affect the
> current origin in effect for the remaining records in the main
> configuration file (as defined by those $ORIGIN directives that reside
> there).

Format of Resource Records in Zone Files

Resource records have the following format.

```
domain opt-ttl opt-class rr-type rr-data...
```

domain

> Specify the domain being described by the current line and any
> following lines that lack a value for this field. Beware of any domain
> values that you enter without full qualification—the value of the
> current origin is appended to them. Append the value of the current
> origin when domain does not end with a dot.
>
> Replace a domain value specified as the symbol @ with the value of the
> current origin. Use the current domain or any locally overriding
> opt-current-domain value as its replacement. (For a discussion of
> these placeholders, see the earlier discussion of the $ORIGIN and
> $INCLUDE directives.)
>
> A domain value specified as a dot (.) represents the root.

opt-ttl   Specify the number of seconds corresponding to the time-to-live value applicable to the zone characteristic that is defined in the remaining fields. This field is optional. It defaults to 0. Zero is interpreted as the minimum value specified in the SOA record for the zone.

opt-class   Specify the object address type; currently only one type is supported, IN, for objects connected to the Internet.

rr-type rr-data...

Specify values that describe a zone characteristic. Permissible *rr-type* and other field values are listed below. The field values are listed in the order in which they must appear.

A *address*   Specify the host address (in dotted-quad format). DCE or AFS server.

CNAME *canonical-name*

Specify in a domain-name format the canonical name for the alias (domain).

HINFO *cpu-type*

OS-type host information supplied in terms of a CPU type and an OS type.

MX *preference mail-exchanger*

Specify in domain-name format a mail exchanger preceded by a preference value (between 0 and 32767), with lower numeric values representing higher logical preferences.

NS *authoritative-server*

Specify in domain-name format an authoritative nameserver.

NULL   Specify a null zone record.

PTR *domain-pointer*

Specify in domain-name format a domain name pointer.

RP *mailbox txt-referral*

Offer details about how to reach a responsible person for the domain name.

SOA *host-domain maintainer-addr serial-no refresh retry expire ttl*

Establish the start of a zone of authority in terms of the domain of the originating host (*host-domain*), the domain address of the maintainer (*maintainer-addr*), a serial number (*serial-no*), the refresh period in seconds (*refresh*), the retry period in seconds (*retry*), the expiration period in seconds (*expire*), and the minimum time-to-live period in seconds (*ttl*). See RFC 1035.

The serial number should be changed each time the master file is changed. Secondary servers check the serial number at intervals specified by the refresh time in seconds; if the serial number changes, a zone transfer is done to load the new data.

If a master server cannot be contacted when a refresh is due, the retry time specifies the interval at which to try refreshes. If a master server cannot be contacted within the interval given by the expire time, all data from the zone is discarded by secondary servers. The minimum value is the time-to-live used by records in the file with no explicit time-to-live value.

You can specify the serial number as a dotted number. However, it is very unwise to do so because the translation to normal integers is by concatenation instead of multiplication and addition. You could spell out the year, month, day of month, and 0..99 version number and still fit it inside the unsigned 32-bit size of this field. This strategy should work for the forseeable future (but is questionable after the year 4293).

For more detailed information, see RFC 883.

rr-data...   See the description of rr-type.

Consult *Name Server Operations Guide for BIND* for further information about the supported types of resource records.

Exit Status

0   Successful completion.

1   An error occurred.

Files

/etc/named.conf

Name server configuration boot file.

/etc/named.pid

The process ID (on older systems).

/var/tmp/named.run

Debug output.

/var/tmp/named.stats

Nameserver statistics data.

/var/tmp/nameddump.db

        Dump of the nameservers database.

/var/tmp/named.pid

        The process ID (on newer systems).

Attributes

See attributes(5) for descriptions of the following attributes.

Attribute Type	Attribute Value
Availability	SUNWcsu

See Also

kill(1), named-xfer(1M), syslogd(1M), getservbyname(3N), listen(3N), resolver(3N), signal(3C), syslog(3), resolv.conf(4), syslog.conf(4),attributes(5)

    Braden, R. (Editor), *Requirements for Internet Hosts Applications and Support*, RFC 1123, Internet Engineering Task Force—Network Working Group, October 1989.

    Mockapetris, Paul, *Domain System Changes and Observations*, RFC 973, Network Information Center, SRI International, Menlo Park, Calif., January 1986.

    Mockapetris, Paul, *Domain Names—Concepts and Facilities*, RFC 1034, Network Information Center, SRI International, Menlo Park, Calif., November 1987.

    Mockapetris, Paul, *Domain Names—Implementation and Specification*, RFC 1035, Network Information Center, SRI International, Menlo Park, Calif., November 1987.

    Partridge, Craig, *Mail Routing and the Domain System*, RFC 974, Network Information Center, SRI International, Menlo Park, Calif., January 1986.

    Vixie, Paul, Keven J. Dunlap, Michael J. Karels, *Name Server Operations Guide for BIND (public domain)*, Internet Software Consortium, 1995.

Notes

The following signals have the specified effect when sent to the server process using the kill(1) command.

SIGHUP	Read /etc/named.conf and reload the database.
	Also check the serial number on all secondary zones. Normally, the serial numbers are checked only at the intervals specified by the SOA record at the start of each zones definition file.
SIGINT	Dump the current database and cache to /var/tmp/nameddump.db.
SIGIOT	Dump statistical data into /var/tmp/named.stats. Append statistical data to the file.
SIGUSR1	Turn on debugging at the lowest level when received the first time; receipt of each additional SIGUSR1 increments the debug level.
SIGUSR2	Turn off debugging completely.
SIGWINCH	Toggle logging of all incoming queries through the syslog system daemon. See syslogd(1M).

New! in.ndpd — Daemon for IPv6 Autoconfiguration

Synopsis
```
/usr/sbin/in.ndpd [-adt][-f config-file]
```

Description
The in.ndpd daemon is new in the Solaris 8 release. in.ndpd provides both the host and router autoconfiguration components of Neighbor Discovery for IPv6 and Stateless Address Autoconfiguration for IPv6. In particular, in.ndpd implements the following functionality.

- Router discovery.
- Prefix discovery.
- Parameter discovery.
- Address autoconfiguration.

Other aspects of Neighbor Discovery are implemented by ipv6(7P), including the following.

- Address resolution.
- Neighbor unreachability detection.
- Redirect.

The duplicate address detection function is implemented by ifconfig(1M).

If the /etc/inet/ndpd.conf file does not exist or does not set the variable AdvSendAdvertisements to true for a network interface, then in.ndpd makes the node a host for that interface, that is, sending router solicitation messages and then using router advertisement messages it receives to autoconfigure the node.

If AdvSendAdvertisements is set to true for an interface, then in.ndpd performs router functions on that interface, that is, sending router advertisement messages to autoconfigure the attached hosts, but not use any advertisements it receives for autoconfiguration. However, when sending advertisements, in.ndpd uses the advertisements it sends itself to autoconfigure its prefixes. For improved robustness in.ndpd stores any autoconfigured IPv6 addresses and their expiration times in state files, named ndpd_state.interface, that are located in the /var/inet directory. Should in.ndpd fail to find any routers, it uses the state files as a fallback, autoconfiguring those addresses if the recorded addresses have remaining lifetime. This fallback ensures that a host that reboots faster than the routers, for example, after a short power failure, continues using the addresses that it had before the power failure.

Options

-a   Turn off stateless address autoconfiguration. Do not autoconfigure or renumber any addresses.

-d   Turn on large amounts of debugging output on standard output. Run the program in the foreground and keep it attached to the controlling terminal.

-f *config-file*

> Use *config-file* for configuration information instead of the default /etc/inet/ndpd.conf.

-t

> Turn on tracing (printing) of all sent and received packets to standard output. Run the program in the foreground and keep it attached to the controlling terminal.

Files

/etc/inet/ndpd.conf

> Configuration file. Not needed on a host but required on a router to enable in.ndpd to advertise autoconfiguration information to the hosts.

/var/inet/ndpd_state.interface

> Contains the addresses for interface. The existence of an address in this file does not imply that the address is usable, because the address lifetime may have expired.

Attributes

See attributes(5) for descriptions of the following attributes.

Attribute Type	Attribute Value
Availability	SUNWcsu

See Also

ifconfig(1M), ndpd.conf(4), attributes(5), icmpv6(7p), ipv6(7p)

> Narten, T., Nordmark, E., Simpson, W., RFC 2461, *Neighbor Discovery for IP Version 6 (IPv6)*, The Internet Society, December 1998.
> Thomson, S., Narten, T., RFC 2462, *IPv6 Stateless Address Autoconfiguration*, The Internet Society, December 1998.

Diagnostics

Receipt of a SIGHUP signal restarts in.ndpd and rereads /etc/inet/ndpd.conf.

in.rarpd, rarpd — DARPA Reverse Address Resolution Protocol Server

Synopsis

/usr/sbin/in.rarpd [-d] -a
/usr/sbin/in.rarpd [-d] *device unit*

Description

The `in.rarpd` daemon responds to Reverse Address Resolution Protocol (RARP) requests. The daemon forks a copy of itself that runs in background. It must be run as root.

RARP is used by machines at boot time to discover their Internet Protocol (IP) address. The booting machine provides its Ethernet address in an RARP request message. Using the `ethers` and `hosts` databases, `in.rarpd` maps this Ethernet address into the corresponding IP address, which it returns to the booting machine in an RARP reply message. The booting machine must be listed in both databases for `in.rarpd` to locate its IP address. `in.rarpd` issues no reply when it fails to locate an IP address.

`in.rarpd` uses the STREAMS-based Data Link Provider Interface (DLPI) message set to communicate directly with the datalink device driver.

Options

`-a`   Get the list of available network interfaces from IP, using the `SIOCGIFADDR` ioctl, and start an RARP daemon process on each interface returned.

`-d`   Print assorted debugging messages while executing.

Examples

The following example starts an `in.rarpd` for each network interface name returned from `/dev/ip`.

```
# /usr/sbin/in.rarpd -a
#
```

The following example starts an `in.rarpd` on the device `/dev/le` with the device instance number `0`.

```
# /usr/sbin/in.rarpd le 0
#
```

Files

`/etc/ethers`   File or NIS+ map.

`/etc/hosts`   File or NIS+ map.

`/tftpboot`   Directory that, if present, configures the system as a TFTP, `bootparams`, and RARP server.

`/dev/ip`   IP character special device file.

`/dev/arp`   ARP character special device file.

Attributes

See `attributes`(5) for descriptions of the following attributes.

Attribute Type	Attribute Value
Availability	SUNWcsu

See Also

boot(1M), ifconfig(1M), ethers(4), hosts(4), netconfig(4), attributes(5), dlpi(7P)

RFC-903, *A Reverse Address Resolution Protocol*, Network Information Center, SRI International.

UNIX International, *Data Link Provider Interface*, Version 2, May 7, 1991, Sun Microsystems, 800-6915-01.

---

in.rdisc, rdisc — Network Router Discovery Daemon

Synopsis

/usr/sbin/in.rdisc [-a][-f][-s][*send-address*][*receive-address*]
/usr/sbin/in.rdisc -r [-p *preference*][-T *interval*][*send-address*]
  [*receive-address*]

Description

The in.rdisc command implements the ICMP router discovery protocol. Use the first form of the command on hosts and the second form on routers. On a host, in.rdisc is invoked at boot time to populate the network routing tables with default routes. On a router, it is also invoked at boot time to start advertising the router to all the hosts.

Host (First Form)

On a host, in.rdisc listens on the ALL_HOSTS (224.0.0.1) multicast address for ROUTER_ADVERTISE messages from routers. The received messages are handled thus: first, those listed router addresses with which the host does not share a network are ignored. Among the remaining addresses, the ones with the highest preference are selected as default routers, and a default route is entered in the kernel routing table for each one of them.

Optionally, in.rdisc can avoid waiting for routers to announce themselves by sending out a few ROUTER_SOLICITATION messages to the ALL_ROUTERS (224.0.0.2) multicast address when it is started.

A timer is associated with each router address. The address is no longer considered for inclusion in the routing tables if the timer expires before a new advertise message is received from the router. The address is also excluded from consideration if the host receives an advertise message with the preference being maximally negative.

Router (Second Form)

When in.rdisc is started on a router, it uses the SIOCGIFCONF ioctl(2) to find the interfaces configured into the system and it starts listening on the ALL_ROUTERS multicast address on all the interfaces that support multicast. It sends out advertise messages to the ALL_HOSTS multicast address advertising all its IP addresses. A few initial advertise messages are sent out during the first 30 seconds, and after that in.rdisc transmits advertise messages approximately every 600 seconds.

When in.rdisc receives a solicitation message, it sends an advertise message to the host that sent the solicitation message.

When in.rdisc is terminated by a signal, it sends out an advertise message with the preference being maximally negative.

Options

-a   Accept all routers independently of the preference they have in their advertise messages. Normally, in.rdisc accepts (and enters in the kernel routing tables) only the router or routers with the highest preference.

-f   Run in.rdisc forever even if no routers are found. Normally, in.rdisc gives up if it has not received any advertise message after soliciting three times, in which case it exits with a non-zero exit code. If you do not specify -f in the first form, then you must specify -s.

-p *preference*

         Set the preference transmitted in the solicitation messages. The default is zero.

-r   Act as a router instead of a host.

-s   Send three solicitation messages initially to quickly discover the routers when the system is booted. When you specify -s, in.rdisc exits with a non-zero exit code if it can not find any routers. This option can be overridden with the -f option.

-T *interval*   Set the interval between transmitting the advertise messages. The default time is 600 seconds.

Attributes

See attributes(5) for descriptions of the following attributes.

Attribute Type	Attribute Value
Availability	SUNWcsu

See Also

in.routed(1M), ioctl(2), attributes(5), icmp(7P), inet(7P)

Deering, S.E., ed. *ICMP Router Discovery Messages*, RFC 1256, Network Information Center, SRI International, Menlo Park, California, September 1991.

in.rexecd, rexecd — Remote Execution Server

Synopsis

/usr/sbin/in.rexecd

Description

The in.rexecd daemon is the server for the rexec(3N) routine. The server provides remote execution facilities with authentication based on user names and passwords. It is invoked automatically as needed by inetd(1M) and then executes the following protocol.

1. The server reads characters from the socket up to a null (\0) byte. The resultant string is interpreted as an ASCII number, base 10.

2. If the number received in step 1 is non-zero, it is interpreted as the port number of a secondary stream to be used for the standard error. A second connection is then created to the specified port on the client's machine.

3. A null-terminated user name of at most 16 characters is retrieved on the initial socket.

4. A null-terminated password of at most 16 characters is retrieved on the initial socket.

5. A null-terminated command to be passed to a shell is retrieved on the initial socket. The length of the command is limited by the upper bound on the size of the system's argument list.

6. rexecd then validates the user as is done at login time and, if the authentication was successful, changes to the user's home directory and establishes the user and group protections of the user. If any of these steps fail, the connection is aborted and a diagnostic message is returned.

7. A null byte is returned on the connection associated with the standard error, and the command line is passed to the normal login shell of the user. The shell inherits the network connections established by rexecd.

Attributes

See attributes(5) for descriptions of the following attributes.

Attribute Type	**Attribute Value**
Availability	SUNWcsu

See Also

inetd(1M), rexec(3N), attributes(5)

Diagnostics

All diagnostic messages are returned on the connection associated with the standard error, after which any network connections are closed. An error is indicated by a leading byte with a value of 1 (0 is returned in step 7 above on successful completion of all the steps before the command execution).

username too long

> The name is longer than 16 characters.

password too long

> The password is longer than 16 characters.

command too long

> The command line passed exceeds the size of the argument list (as configured into the system).

```
Login incorrect.
```
No password file entry for the user name existed.
```
Password incorrect.
```
The wrong password was supplied.
```
No remote directory.
```
The chdir command to the home directory failed.
```
Try again.
```
A fork by the server failed.
```
/usr/bin/sh:...
```
The user's login shell could not be started.

New! in.ripngd — Network Routing Demon for IPv6

Synopsis

```
/usr/sbin/in.ripngd [-s][-q][-t][-p n][-P][-v][logfile]
```

Description

The in.ripngd daemon is new in the Solaris 8 release. in.ripngd is the IPv6 equivalent of in.routed(1M). It is invoked at boot time by the S69inet run control script to manage the network routing tables. The routing daemon uses the Routing Information Protocol for IPv6.

In normal operation, in.ripngd listens on the udp(7P) socket port 521 for routing information packets. If the host is an internetwork router, it periodically supplies copies of its routing tables to any directly connected hosts and networks.

When in.ripngd is started, it uses the SIOCGLIFCONF ioctl(2) to find those directly connected IPv6 interfaces configured into the system and marked up; the software loopback interface is ignored. If multiple interfaces are present, it is assumed the host will forward packets between networks. in.ripngd then multicasts a request packet on each IPv6 interface and enters a loop, listening for request and response packets from other hosts.

When a request packet is received, in.ripngd formulates a reply based on the information maintained in its internal tables. The response packet contains a list of known routes. With each route is a number specifying the number of bits in the prefix. The prefix is the number of bits in the high-order part of an address that indicate the subnet or network that the route describes. Each route reported also has a "hop count" metric. A count of 16 or greater is considered "infinity." The metric associated with each route returned provides a metric relative to the sender.

The request packets received by in.ripngd update the routing tables if one of the following conditions is satisfied.

- No routing table entry exists for the destination network or host, and the metric indicates the destination is reachable, that is, the hop count is not infinite.

- The source host of the packet is the same as the router in the existing routing table entry. That is, updated information is being received from the same internetwork router through which packets for the destination are being routed.
- The existing entry in the routing table has not been updated for a period of time, defined to be 90 seconds, and the route is at least as cost effective as the current route.
- The new route describes a shorter route to the destination than the one currently stored in the routing tables; this route is determined by comparing the metric of the new route against the one stored in the table.
- When an update is applied, in.ripngd records the change in its internal tables and generates a response packet to all directly connected hosts and networks. To allow possible unstable situations to settle, in.ripngd waits a short period of time (no more than 30 seconds) before modifying the kernel's routing tables.
- In addition to processing incoming packets, in.ripngd also periodically checks the routing table entries. If an entry has not been updated for 3 minutes, the entry's metric is set to infinity and marked for deletion. Deletions are delayed an additional 60 seconds to ensure the invalidation is propagated throughout the Internet.
- Hosts acting as internetwork routers gratuitously supply their routing tables every 30 seconds to all directly connected hosts and networks.

Note

The kernel's routing tables may not correspond to those of in.ripngd for short periods of time while processes that use existing routes exit; the only remedy for this circumstance is to place the routing process in the kernel.

in.ripngd currently does not support all of the functionality of in.routed(1M). Future releases may support more if appropriate.

in.ripngd initially obtains a routing table by examining the interfaces configured on a machine and the gateways file. It then sends a request on all directly connected networks for more routing information. in.ripngd does not recognize or use any routing information already established on the machine before startup. With the exception of interface changes, in.ripngd does not see any routing table changes that have been done by other programs on the machine, for example, routes added, deleted, or flushed by way of the route(1M) command. Therefore, these types of changes should not be done while in.ripngd is running. Instead, shut down in.ripngd, make the changes required, and then restart in.ripngd.

Options

-p *n*	Send and receive the routing packets from other routers, using the UDP port number *n*.
-P	Do not use poison reverse.
-q	Do not supply routing information.
-s	Force supply of routing information regardless of whether in.ripngd is acting as an internetwork router.

`-t`	Print to standard output all packets sent or received. `in.ripngd` does not divorce itself from the controlling terminal. Accordingly, interrupts from the keyboard kill the process.
`-v`	Print to standard output all changes made to the routing tables with a timestamp.

Operands

`logfile`	Any other argument supplied is interpreted as the name of the file in which to log the actions of `in.ripngd`, as specified by this option or by `-t`, instead of being sent to standard output.

Attributes

See `attributes`(5) for descriptions of the following attributes.

Attribute Type	Attribute Value
Availability	SUNWcsu

See Also

in.routed(1M), ioctl(2), attributes(5), udp(7P)

Malkin, G., Minnear, R., RFC 2080, *RIPng for IPv6*, January 1997.

in.rlogind, rlogind — Remote Login Server

Synopsis

/usr/sbin/in.rlogind

Description

The `in.rlogind` daemon is the server for the `rlogin`(1) program. The server provides a remote login facility with authentication based on privileged port numbers.

`in.rlogind` is invoked by `inetd`(1M) when a remote login connection is established, and executes the following protocol.

- The server checks the client's source port. If the port is not in the range 0-1023, the server aborts the connection.
- The server checks the client's source address. If an entry for the client exists in both `/etc/hosts` and `/etc/hosts.equiv`, a user logging in from the client is not prompted for a password. If the address is associated with a host for which no corresponding entry exists in `/etc/hosts`, the user is prompted for a password, regardless of whether an entry for the client is present in `/etc/hosts.equiv` (see hosts(4) and hosts.equiv(4)).

Once the source port and address have been checked, `in.rlogind` allocates a pseudoterminal and manipulates file descriptors so that the slave half of the pseudoterminal becomes the standard input, standard output, and standard error for a login process. The login process is an instance of the login(1) program, invoked with the -r option.

The login process then proceeds with the pam(3) authentication process. If automatic authentication fails, it reprompts the user to log in.

The parent of the login process manipulates the master side of the pseudoterminal, operating as an intermediary between the login process and the client instance of the rlogin program. In normal operation, a packet protocol is invoked to provide Ctrl-S/ Ctrl-Q type facilities and to propagate interrupt signals to the remote programs. The login process propagates the client terminal's baud rate and terminal type, as found in the environment variable, TERM; see environ(4).

Security

in.rlogind uses pam(3) for authentication, account management, and session management. The PAM configuration policy, listed through /etc/pam.conf, specifies the modules to be used for in.rlogind. The following partial pam.conf file shows entries for the rlogin command, using the rhosts and UNIX authentication modules, and the UNIX account, session management, and password management modules.

```
rlogin    auth      sufficient    /usr/lib/security/pam_rhosts_auth.so.1
rlogin    auth      required      /usr/lib/security/pam_unix.so.1
rlogin    account   required      /usr/lib/security/pam_unix.so.1
rlogin    session   required      /usr/lib/security/pam_unix.so.1
```

With this configuration, the server checks the client's source address. If an entry for the client exists in both /etc/hosts and /etc/hosts.equiv, a user logging in from the client is not prompted for a password. If the address is associated with a host for which no corresponding entry exists in /etc/hosts, the user is prompted for a password, regardless of whether an entry for the client is present in /etc/hosts.equiv (see hosts(4) and hosts.equiv(4)).

If there are no entries for the rlogin service, then the entries for the other service are used. If multiple authentication modules are listed, then the user may be prompted for multiple passwords. Removing the pam_rhosts_auth.so.1 entry disables the /etc/hosts.equiv and ~/.rhosts authentication protocol, and the user would always be forced to type the password. The sufficient flag indicates that authentication through the pam_rhosts_auth.so.1 module is sufficient to authenticate the user. Only if this authentication fails is the next authentication module used.

Note — The authentication procedure used here assumes the integrity of each client machine and the connecting medium, which is insecure but useful in an open environment.

A facility to allow all data exchanges to be encrypted should be present.

Attributes

See attributes(5) for descriptions of the following attributes.

Attribute Type	Attribute Value
Availability	SUNWcsu

See Also

login(1), rlogin(1), in.rshd(1M), inetd(1M), pam(3), environ(4),
hosts(4),hosts.equiv(4),pam.conf(4),attributes(5),pam_rhosts_auth(5),
pam_unix(5)

Diagnostics

All diagnostic messages are returned on the connection associated with the standard
error, after which any network connections are closed. An error is indicated by a leading
byte with a value of 1.

Hostname for your address unknown.

> No entry in the host-name database existed for the client's machine.

Try again.   A fork by the server failed.

/usr/bin/sh:...

> The user's login shell could not be started.

in.routed, routed — Network Routing Daemon

Synopsis

/usr/sbin/in.routed [-s][-q][-t][-g][-S][-v][*logfile*]

Description

The in.routed daemon is invoked at boot time by the /etc/rc2.d/S69inet run control
script to manage the network routing tables. The routing daemon uses a variant of the
Xerox NS Routing Information Protocol in maintaining up-to-date kernel routing table
entries.

In normal operation, in.routed listens on udp(7P) socket 520 (decimal) for routing
information packets. If the host is an internetwork router, in.routed periodically
supplies copies of its routing tables to any directly connected hosts and networks.

When in.routed is started, it uses SIOCGIFCONFioctl(2) to find those directly
connected interfaces configured into the system and marked up (the software loopback
interface is ignored). If multiple interfaces are present, it is assumed the host forwards
packets between networks. in.routed then transmits a request packet on each
interface (using a broadcast packet if the interface supports it) and enters a loop,
listening for request and response packets from other hosts.

When a request packet is received, in.routed formulates a reply based on the
information maintained in its internal tables. The response packet contains a list of
known routes, each marked with a hop count metric (a count of 16, or greater, is
considered infinite). The metric associated with each route returned provides a metric
relative to the sender.

request packets received by in.routed update the routing tables if one of the
following conditions is satisfied.

- No routing table entry exists for the destination network or host and the metric
  indicates the destination is reachable (that is, the hop count is not infinite).

- The source host of the packet is the same as the router in the existing routing table entry. That is, updated information is being received from the same internetwork router through which packets for the destination are being routed.
- The existing entry in the routing table has not been updated for some time (defined to be 90 seconds) and the route is at least as cost effective as the current route.
- The new route describes a shorter route to the destination than the one currently stored in the routing tables; the metric of the new route is compared to the one stored in the table to decide the shorter route.

When an update is applied, in.routed records the change in its internal tables and generates a response packet to all directly connected hosts and networks. in.routed waits a short period of time (no more than 30 seconds) before modifying the kernel's routing tables to allow possible unstable situations to settle.

In addition to processing incoming packets, in.routed also periodically checks the routing table entries. If an entry has not been updated for 3 minutes, the entry's metric is set to infinity and marked for deletion. Deletions are delayed an additional 60 seconds to ensure the invalidation is propagated throughout the Internet.

Hosts acting as internetwork routers gratuitously supply their routing tables every 30 seconds to all directly connected hosts and networks.

In addition to the facilities described above, in.routed supports the notion of "distant" passive and active gateways. When in.routed is started up, it reads the file gateways to find gateways that may not be identified, using the SIOCGIFCONF ioctl. Gateways specified in this manner should be marked passive if they are not expected to exchange routing information; gateways marked active should be willing to exchange routing information (that is, they should have a in.routed process running on the machine). Passive gateways are maintained in the routing tables forever. Information regarding their existence is not included in any routing information transmitted. Active gateways are treated equally to network interfaces. Routing information is distributed to the gateway and if no routing information is received for a period of time, the associated route is deleted.

The gateways file contains a series of lines, each in the following format.

```
net | host > filename1 gateway filename2 metric value < passive | active
```

The net or host keyword indicates whether the route is to a network or specific host.

filename1 is the name of the destination network or host. This destination can be a symbolic name located in networks or hosts, or an Internet address specified in dot notation; see inet(3N).

filename2 is the name or address of the gateway to which messages should be forwarded.

value is a metric indicating the hop count to the destination host or network.

The keyword passive or active indicates whether the gateway should be treated as passive or active (as described above).

Notes

The kernel's routing tables may not correspond to those of in.routed for short periods of time while processes that use existing routes exit; the only remedy for this condition is to place the routing process in the kernel.

in.routed should listen to intelligent interfaces, such as an IMP, and to error protocols, such as ICMP, to gather more information.

in.routed initially obtains a routing table by examining the interfaces configured on a machine and the gateways file. It then sends a request on all directly connected networks for more routing information. in.routed does not recognize or use any routing information already established on the machine before startup. With the exception of interface changes, in.routed does not see any routing table changes that have been done by other programs on the machine, for example, routes added, deleted, or flushed by way of the route(1M) command. Therefore, these types of changes should not be done while in.routed is running. Instead, shut down in.routed, make the changes required, and then restart in.routed.

Options

-g   Use on internetwork routers to offer a route to the default destination. You typically use this option on a gateway to the Internet or on a gateway that uses another routing protocol whose routes are not reported to other local routers.

-q   The opposite of the -s option.

-s   Force in.routed to supply routing information whether it is acting as an internetwork router or not.

-S   If in.routed is not acting as an internetwork router, instead of entering the whole routing table in the kernel, enter only a default route for each internetwork router. This action reduces the memory requirements without losing any routing reliability.

-t   Print all packets sent or received on standard output. In addition, in.routed does not divorce itself from the controlling terminal, so interrupts from the keyboard kill the process. Interpret any other argument supplied as the name of the file in which to log in.routed actions. This log contains information about any changes to the routing tables and a history of recent messages sent and received which are related to the changed route.

-v   Create a *logfile* (whose name must be supplied) showing the changes made to the routing tables with a timestamp.

Files

/etc/gateways
            List of distant gateways.

/etc/networks
            Associations of Internet Protocol network numbers with network names.

/etc/hosts   Internet host table.

Attributes

See attributes(5) for descriptions of the following attributes.

Attribute Type	Attribute Value
Availability	SUNWcsu

See Also

route(1M), ioctl(2), inet(3N), attributes(5), inet(7P), udp(7P)

in.rshd, rshd — Remote Shell Server

Synopsis

/usr/sbin/in.rshd *host.port*

Description

The in.rshd daemon is the server for the rsh(1) program. The server provides remote execution facilities with authentication based on privileged port numbers.

in.rshd is invoked by inetd(1M) each time a shell service is requested and executes the following protocol.

1. The server checks the client's source port. If the port is not in the range 0-1023, the server aborts the connection. The client's host address (in hexadecimal) and port number (in decimal) are the arguments passed to in.rshd.

2. The server reads characters from the socket up to a null (\0) byte. The resultant string is interpreted as an ASCII number, base 10.

3. If the number received in step 1 is non-zero, it is interpreted as the port number of a secondary stream to be used for the standard error. A second connection is then created to the specified port on the client's machine. The source port of this second connection is also in the range 0-1023.

4. The server checks the client's source address. If the address is associated with a host for which no corresponding entry exists in the host-name database (see hosts(4)), the server aborts the connection. Refer to "Security" on page 466 for more details.

5. A null-terminated user name of at most 16 characters is retrieved on the initial socket. This user name is interpreted as a user identity to use on the server's machine.

6. A null-terminated user name of at most 16 characters is retrieved on the initial socket. This user name is interpreted as the user identity on the client's machine.

7. A null-terminated command to be passed to a shell is retrieved on the initial socket. The length of the command is limited by the upper bound on the size of the system's argument list.

8. in.rshd then validates the user according to the following steps. The remote user name is looked up in the passwd file and a chdir is performed to the user's home directory. If the lookup fails, the connection is terminated. If the chdir fails, it does a chdir to / (root). If the user is not superuser, (user ID 0), and if the pam_rhosts_auth PAM module is configured for authentication, the file /etc/hosts.equiv is consulted for a list of hosts considered equivalent. If the client's host name is present in this file, the authentication is considered successful. See "Security" on page 466 for a discussion of PAM authentication. If the lookup fails, or the user is superuser, then the file .rhosts in the home

directory of the remote user is checked for the machine name and identity of the user on the client's machine. If this lookup fails, the connection is terminated.

9. A null byte is returned on the connection associated with the standard error, and the command line is passed to the normal login shell of the user. (The PATH variable is set to /usr/bin.) The shell inherits the network connections established by in.rshd.

Note — The authentication procedure used here assumes the integrity of each client machine and the connecting medium, which is insecure but useful in an open environment.

A facility to allow all data exchanges to be encrypted should be present.

Security

in.rshd uses pam(3) for authentication, account management, and session management. The PAM configuration policy, listed through /etc/pam.conf, specifies the modules to be used for in.rshd. The following partial pam.conf file contains entries for the rsh command, using rhosts authentication, UNIX account management, and the session management modules.

```
rsh    auth      required    /usr/lib/security/pam_rhosts_auth.so.1
rsh    account   required    /usr/lib/security/pam_unix.so.1
rsh    session   required    /usr/lib/security/pam_unix.so.1
```

If there are no entries for the rsh service, then the entries for the other service are used. To maintain the authentication requirement for in.rshd, the rsh entry must always be configured with the pam_rhosts_auth.so.1 module. Multiple authentication modules cannot be listed for the rsh service.

Files

/etc/hosts.equiv

File containing host names, host-user pairs, or netgroups that specify trusted users who can gain rlogin access to the host.

Attributes

See attributes(5) for descriptions of the following attributes.

Attribute Type	Attribute Value
Availability	SUNWcsu

See Also

rsh(1), inetd(1M), pam(3), hosts(4), pam.conf(4), attributes(5), pam_rhosts_auth(5), pam_unix(5)

Diagnostics

The following diagnostic messages are returned on the connection associated with standard error, after which any network connections are closed. An error is indicated by a leading byte with a value of 1 in step 9 above (0 is returned above on successful completion of all the steps before command execution).

`locuser too long`

> The name of the user on the client's machine is longer than 16 characters.

`remuser too long`

> The name of the user on the remote machine is longer than 16 characters.

`command too long`

> The command line passed exceeds the size of the argument list (as configured into the system).

`Hostname for your address unknown.`

> No entry in the `host` name database existed for the client's machine.

`Login incorrect.`

> No password file entry for the user name existed.

`Permission denied.`

> The authentication procedure described above failed.

`Can't make pipe.`

> The pipe needed for the standard error was not created.

`Try again.`   A fork by the server failed.

---

in.rwhod, rwhod — System Status Server

Synopsis

`/usr/sbin/in.rwhod [-m [ttl]]`

Description

The in.rwhod daemon is the server that maintains the database used by the rwho(1) and ruptime(1) programs. Its operation is predicated on the ability to broadcast or multicast messages on a network.

in.rwhod operates as both a producer and consumer of status information. As a producer of information, it periodically queries the state of the system and constructs status messages that are broadcast or multicast on a network. As a consumer of information, it listens for other in.rwhod servers' status messages, validating them, then recording them in a collection of files located in the directory /var/spool/rwho.

The rwho server transmits and receives messages at the port indicated in the rwho service specification, see services(4). The messages sent and received are of the following form.

```
struct outmp {
        char   out_line[8]; /* tty name */
        char   out_name[8]; /* user id */
        long   out_time; /* time on */
        };
        struct whod {
        char   wd_vers;
        char   wd_type;
        char   wd_fill[2];
        int wd_sendtime;
        int wd_recvtime;
        char   wd_hostname[32];
        int wd_loadav[3];
        int wd_boottime;
        struct whoent {
        struct outmp we_utmp;
        int we_idle;
        } wd_we[1024 / sizeof (struct whoent)];
};
```

New!   All fields are converted to network byte order before transmission. The load averages are as calculated by the w(1) program and represent load averages over the 5-, 10-, and 15-minute intervals before a server's transmission. The host name included is that returned by the uname(2) system call. The array at the end of the message contains information about the users who are logged in to the sending machine. This information includes the contents of the utmpx(4) entry (changed from utmp in the Solaris 8 release) for each nonidle terminal line and a value indicating the time since a character was last received on the terminal line.

Messages received by the rwho server are discarded unless they originated at an rwho server's port. In addition, if the host's name, as specified in the message, contains any unprintable ASCII characters, the message is discarded. Valid messages received by in.rwhod are placed in files named whod.*hostname* in the directory /var/spool/rwho. These files contain only the most recent message, in the format described above.

New!   Status messages are generated approximately once every three minutes, which is a change from the previous default of 60 seconds in earlier releases.

Note — This service takes up progressively more network bandwidth as the number of hosts on the local net increases. For large networks, the cost becomes prohibitive.

in.rwhod should relay status information between networks. People often interpret the server dying as a machine going down.

Options

     -m [*ttl*]   Use the rwho IP multicast address (224.0.1.3) when transmitting. Receive announcements both on this multicast address and on the IP broadcast address. If you do not specify *ttl*, multicast on all interfaces but with the IP TimeToLive set to 1 (that is, packets are not forwarded by multicast routers.) If you specify *ttl*, transmit packets only on one interface and set the IP TimeToLive to the specified *ttl*.

Files

/var/spool/rwho/rwhod/.*

>   Information about other machines.

Attributes

See attributes(5) for descriptions of the following attributes.

Attribute Type	Attribute Value
Availability	SUNWcsu

See Also

ruptime(1), rwho(1), w(1), uname(2), services(4), utmpx(4), attributes(5) *New!*

>   **Warning** — This service can cause network performance problems when
>   used by several hosts on the network. It is not run at most sites by default.
>   If used, include the -m multicast option.

in.talkd, talkd — Server for Talk Program

Synopsis

/usr/sbin/in.talkd

Description

The talkd daemon is a server used by the talk(1) program. It listens at the UDP port
indicated in the talk service description; see services(4). The actual conversation takes
place on a TCP connection that is established by negotiation between the two machines
involved.

>   **Note** — The protocol is architecture dependent.

Attributes

See attributes(5) for descriptions of the following attributes.

Attribute Type	Attribute Value
Availability	SUNWcsu

See Also

talk(1), inetd(1M), services(4), attributes(5)

in.telnetd, telnetd — DARPA TELNET Protocol Server

Synopsis

    /usr/sbin/in.telnetd

Description

The in.telnetd daemon is a server that supports the DARPA standard TELNET
virtual terminal protocol. in.telnetd is invoked in the Internet server (see inetd(1M)),
normally for requests to connect to the TELNET port as indicated by the /etc/services
file (see services(4)).

in.telnetd operates by allocating a pseudoterminal device for a client, then creating
a login process that has the slave side of the pseudoterminal as its standard input,
output, and error. in.telnetd manipulates the master side of the pseudoterminal,
implementing the TELNET protocol and passing characters between the remote client
and the login process.

When a TELNET session starts up, in.telnetd sends TELNET options to the client
side, indicating a willingness to do remote echo of characters and to suppress go-ahead.
The pseudoterminal allocated to the client is configured to operate in "cooked" mode and
with XTABS, ICRNL, and ONLCR enabled (see termio(7I)).

in.telnetd is willing to do echo, binary, suppress go ahead, and timing mark.
in.telnetd is willing to have the remote client do binary, terminaltype,
terminalsize, logout option, and suppress go ahead.

in.telnetd also allows environment variables to be passed, provided that the client
negotiates this during the initial option negotiation. The DISPLAY environment variable
can be sent this way, either by the TELNET general environment passing methods or by
the XDISPLOC TELNET option. DISPLAY can be passed in the environment option during
the same negotiation where XDISPLOC is used. Note that if you use both methods, you
should use the same value for both. Otherwise, the results may be unpredictable.

These options are specified in Internet standards RFC 1096, RFC 1408, RFC 1571,
and RFC 1572.

The banner printed by in.telnetd is configurable. The default is (more or less)
equivalent to "`uname -sr`" and is used if no banner is set in /etc/default/telnetd.
To set the banner, add a line of the following form to /etc/default/telnetd.

    BANNER="..."

Nonempty banner strings are fed to shells for evaluation. You can obtain the default
banner by

    BANNER="\\r\\n\\r\\n`uname -s` `uname -r`\\r\\n\\r\\n"

and no banner is printed if /etc/default/telnetd contains

    BANNER=""

Security

in.telnetd uses pam(3) for authentication, account management, session management,
and password management. The PAM configuration policy, listed through
/etc/pam.conf, specifies the modules to be used for in.telnetd. The following partial

`pam.conf` file contains entries for the `telnet` command, using the UNIX authentication, account management, session management, and password management modules.

```
telnet    auth      required  /usr/lib/security/pam_unix.so.1
telnet    account   required  /usr/lib/security/pam_unix.so.1
telnet    session   required  /usr/lib/security/pam_unix.so.1
telnet    password  required  /usr/lib/security/pam_unix.so.1
```

If there are no entries for the `telnet` service, then the entries for the `other` service are used. If multiple authentication modules are listed, then the user may be prompted for multiple passwords.

Notes

Some `TELNET` commands are only partially implemented.

Binary mode has no common interpretation except between similar operating systems.

The terminal type name received from the remote client is converted to lower case.

The packet interface to the pseudoterminal should be used for more intelligent flushing of input and output queues.

`in.telnetd` never sends `TELNET go ahead` commands.

Files

`/etc/default/telnetd`

File containing the default `telnetd` banner message.

Attributes

See `attributes`(5) for descriptions of the following attributes.

Attribute Type	Attribute Value
Availability	SUNWcsu

See Also

`telnet(1)`, `inetd(1M)`, `pam(3)`, `pam.conf(4)`, `services(4)`, `attributes(5)`, `pam_unix(5)`, `termio(7I)`

Alexander, S., *TELNET Environment Option*, RFC 1572, Network Information Center, SRI International, Menlo Park, Calif., January 1994.

Borman, Dave, *TELNET Environment Option*, RFC 1408, Network Information Center, SRI International, Menlo Park, Calif., January 1993.

Borman, Dave, *TELNET Environment Option Interoperability Issues*, RFC 1571, Network Information Center, SRI International, Menlo Park, Calif., January 1994.

Crispin, Mark, *TELNET Logout Option*, RFC 727, Network Information Center, SRI International, Menlo Park, Calif., April 1977.

Marcy, G., *TELNET X Display Location Option*, RFC 1096, Network Information Center, SRI International, Menlo Park, Calif., March 1989.

Postel, Jon, and Reynolds, Joyce, *TELNET Protocol Specification*, RFC 854, Network Information Center, SRI International, Menlo Park, Calif., May 1983.

Waitzman, D., *TELNET Window Size Option*, RFC 1073, Network Information Center, SRI International, Menlo Park, Calif., October 1988.

in.tftpd, tftpd — Internet Trivial File Transfer Protocol Server

Synopsis

    /usr/sbin/in.tftpd [-s] [homedir]

Description

The in.tftpd daemon is a server that supports the Internet Trivial File Transfer
Protocol (TFTP). This server is normally started by inetd(1M) and operates at the port
indicated in the tftp Internet service description in the /etc/inetd.conf file. The
default entry for in.tftpd in /etc/inetd.conf is commented out, as shown below.

    #
    # Tftp service is provided primarily for booting. Most sites run this
    # only on machines acting as "boot servers."
    #
    #tftp dgram udp6 wait root usr/sbin/in.tftpd in.tftpd -s /tftpboot
    #

To make in.tftpd operational, delete the comment character from the tftp line. See
inetd.conf(4).

Before responding to a request, the server tries to change its current directory to
homedir; the default directory is /tftpboot.

The use of tftp does not require an account or password on the remote system.
Because of the lack of authentication information, in.tftpd allows only publicly
readable files to be accessed. Files can be written only if they already exist and are
publicly writeable. Note that the concept of "public" extends to include all users on all
hosts that can be reached through the network; this security may not be appropriate on
all systems, and you should consider the implications before enabling this service.

in.tftpd runs with the user ID and group ID set to [GU]ID_NOBODY under the
assumption that no files exist with that owner or group. However, nothing checks this
assumption or enforces this restriction.

Options

    -s [homedir]   Change the root directory to homedir. The directory change to
                   homedir must succeed.

Files

    /etc/inetd.conf

                   Configuration file for inetd.

Attributes

See attributes(5) for descriptions of the following attributes.

Attribute Type	Attribute Value
Availability	SUNWcsu

See Also

tftp(1), inetd(1M), inetd.conf(4), netconfig(4), attributes(5)

Sollins, K.R., *The TFTP Protocol (Revision 2)*, RFC 783, Network Information Center, SRI International, Menlo Park, California, June 1981.

in.tnamed, tnamed — DARPA Trivial Name Server

Synopsis

/usr/sbin/in.tnamed [-v]

Description

The in.tnamed daemon is a server that supports the DARPA Name Server Protocol. The nameserver operates at the port indicated in the "name" service description (see services(4)) and is invoked by inetd(1M) when a request is made to the nameserver.

Note — The protocol implemented by this program is obsolete. Its use should be phased out in favor of the Internet Domain Name Service (DNS) protocol.

Options

-v   Invoke the daemon in verbose mode.

Attributes

See attributes(5) for descriptions of the following attributes.

Attribute Type	Attribute Value
Availability	SUNWcsu

See Also

uucp(1C), inetd(1M), services(4), attributes(5)

Postel, Jon, *Internet Name Server*, IEN 116, SRI International, Menlo Park, California, August 1979.

in.uucpd, uucpd — UUCP Server

Synopsis

```
/usr/sbin/in.uucpd [-n]
```

Description

The in.uucpd daemon is the server that supports UUCP connections over networks.
in.uucpd is invoked by inetd(1M) when a UUCP connection is established (that is,
a connection to the port indicated in the uucp service specification) and executes the
following protocol (see services(4)).

1. The server prompts with login:. The uucico(1M) process at the other end must
   supply a user name.

2. Unless the user name refers to an account without a password, the server then
   prompts with Password:. The uucico process at the other end must supply the
   password for that account.

If the user name is not valid or is valid but refers to an account that does not have
/usr/lib/uucp/uucico as its login shell, or if the password is not the correct password
for that account, the connection is dropped. Otherwise, uucico is run, with the user ID,
group ID, group set, and home directory for that account, with the environment
variables USER and LOGNAME set to the specified user name, and with a -u option
specifying the user name. Unless you specify the -n option, entries are made in
/var/adm/utmpx, /var/adm/wtmpx, and /var/adm/lastlog for the user name. The
utmpx and wtmpx database files in the Solaris 8 release replace the obsolete wtmp and
utmp database files. in.uucpd must be invoked by a user with appropriate privilege
(usually root) to be able to verify that the password is correct.

Security

in.uucpd uses pam(3) for authentication, account management, and session
management. The PAM configuration policy, listed through /etc/pam.conf, specifies
the modules to be used for in.uucpd. The following partial pam.conf file shows the
entries for uucp, using the UNIX authentication, account management, and session
management modules.

```
uucp     auth       required   /usr/lib/security/pam_unix.so.1
uucp     account    required   /usr/lib/security/pam_unix.so.1
uucp     session    required   /usr/lib/security/pam_unix.so.1
```

If the uucp service has no entries, then the entries for the other service are used. If
multiple authentication modules are listed, then the peer may be prompted for multiple
passwords.

Options

-n   Do not make entries in /var/adm/utmpx, /var/adm/wtmpx, and
                /var/adm/lastlog for the user name.

Files

/var/adm/utmpx

New!

> History of user access and administration information. utmpx is an
> extended database file that replaces the obsolete utmp database file.

/var/adm/wt.mpx

New!

> History of user access and administration information. wtmpx is an
> extended database file that replaces the obsolete wtmp database file.

/var/adm/lastlog

> Time of last login.

Attributes

See attributes(5) for descriptions of the following attributes.

Attribute Type	Attribute Value
Availability	SUNWonuu

See Also

inetd(1M), uucico(1M), pam(3), pam.conf(4), services(4), attributes(5),
pam_unix(5)

Diagnostics

All diagnostic messages are returned on the connection, after which the connection is
closed.

user read   An error occurred while reading the user name.

passwd read An error occurred while reading the password.

Login incorrect.

> The user name is invalid or refers to an account with a login shell
> other than /usr/lib/uucp/uucico, or the password is not the correct
> password for the account.

inetd — Internet Services Daemon

Synopsis

/usr/sbin/inetd [-d][-s][-t][-r *count interval*][*configuration-file*]

Description

The inetd daemon is the server process for the Internet standard services that manages
other daemons. It is usually started up at system boot time by the

/etc/rc2.d/S72inetsvc run control script. The *configuration-file* lists the services
that inetd is to provide. If you specify no *configuration-file* on the command line,
inetd reads its configuration information from the file /etc/inetd.conf. The following
example shows the default inetd.conf file.

```
#
#pragma ident      "@(#)inetd.conf     1.38     99/08/27 SMI"     /* SVr4.0 1.5
   */
#
#
# Configuration file for inetd(1M).  See inetd.conf(4).
#
# To re-configure the running inetd process, edit this file, then
# send the inetd process a SIGHUP.
#
# Syntax for socket-based Internet services:
#  <service_name> <socket_type> <proto> <flags> <user> <server_pathname> <args>
#
# Syntax for TLI-based Internet services:
#
#  <service_name> tli <proto> <flags> <user> <server_pathname> <args>
#
# Ftp and telnet are standard Internet services.
#
ftp     stream    tcp6    nowait    root    /usr/sbin/in.ftpd     in.ftpd
telnet  stream    tcp6    nowait    root    /usr/sbin/in.telnetd  in.telnetd
#
# Tnamed serves the obsolete IEN-116 nameserver protocol.
#
name    dgram     udp     wait      root    /usr/sbin/in.tnamed      in.tnamed
#
# Shell, login, exec, comsat and talk are BSD protocols.
#
shell   stream    tcp6    nowait    root    /usr/sbin/in.rshd     in.rshd
login   stream    tcp6    nowait    root    /usr/sbin/in.rlogind  in.rlogind
exec    stream    tcp6    nowait    root    /usr/sbin/in.rexecd   in.rexecd
comsat  dgram     udp     wait      root    /usr/sbin/in.comsat   in.comsat
talk    dgram     udp     wait      root    /usr/sbin/in.talkd    in.talkd
#
# Must run as root (to read /etc/shadow); "-n" turns off logging in utmp/wtmp.
#
uucp    stream    tcp     nowait    root    /usr/sbin/in.uucpd       in.uucpd
#
# Tftp service is provided primarily for booting.  Most sites run this
# only on machines acting as "boot servers."
#
#tftp   dgram   udp6   wait   root   /usr/sbin/in.tftpd    in.tftpd -s tftpboot
#
# Finger, systat and netstat give out user information which may be
# valuable to potential "system crackers."  Many sites choose to disable
# some or all of these services to improve security.
#
finger  stream  tcp6    nowait  nobody     /usr/sbin/in.fingerd      in.fingerd
#systat         stream  tcp    nowait  root    /usr/bin/ps        ps -ef
#netstat        stream  tcp    nowait  root    /usr/bin/netstat   netstat -f inet
#
```

```
# Time service is used for clock synchronization.
#
time      stream      tcp6      nowait      root      internal
time      dgram       udp6      wait        root      internal
#
# Echo, discard, daytime, and chargen are used primarily for testing.
#
echo         stream      tcp6      nowait      root      internal
echo         dgram       udp6      wait        root      internal
discard      stream      tcp6      nowait      root      internal
discard      dgram       udp6      wait        root      internal
daytime      stream      tcp6      nowait      root      internal
daytime      dgram       udp6      wait        root      internal
chargen      stream      tcp6      nowait      root      internal
chargen      dgram       udp6      wait        root      internal
#
#
# RPC services syntax:
#   <rpc_prog>/<vers> <endpoint-type> rpc/<proto> <flags> <user> \
#   <pathname> <args>
#
# <endpoint-type> can be either "tli" or "stream" or "dgram".
# For "stream" and "dgram" assume that the endpoint is a socket descriptor.
# <proto> can be either a nettype or a netid or a "*". The value is
# first treated as a nettype. If it is not a valid nettype then it is
# treated as a netid. The "*" is a short-hand way of saying all the
# transports supported by this system, ie. it equates to the "visible"
# nettype. The syntax for <proto> is:
#       *|<nettype|netid>|<nettype|netid>{[,<nettype|netid>]}
# For example:
# dummy/1     tli  rpc/circuit_v,udp  wait  root      /tmp/test_svc      test_svc
#
# Solstice system and network administration class agent server
100232/10     tli  rpc/udp     wait root /usr/sbin/sadmind      sadmind
#
# Rquotad supports UFS disk quotas for NFS clients
#
rquotad/1     tli  rpc/datagram_v   wait root /usr/lib/nfs/rquotad      rquotad
#
# The rusers service gives out user information.  Sites concerned
# with security may choose to disable it.
#
rusersd/2-3  tli   rpc/datagram_v,circuit_v   wait root
   /usr/lib/netsvc/rusers/rpc.rusersd      rpc.rusersd
#
# The spray server is used primarily for testing.
#
sprayd/1     tli    rpc/datagram_v     wait root
   /usr/lib/netsvc/spray/rpc.sprayd      rpc.sprayd
#
# The rwall server allows others to post messages to users on this machine.
#
walld/1           tli    rpc/datagram_v     wait root
   /usr/lib/netsvc/rwall/rpc.rwalld      rpc.rwalld
#
# Rstatd is used by programs such as perfmeter.
#
```

```
rstatd/2-4     tli   rpc/datagram_v wait root /usr/lib/netsvc/rstat/rpc.rstatd
   rpc.rstatd
#
# The rexd server provides only minimal authentication and is often not run
#
#rexd/1         tli  rpc/tcp wait root /usr/sbin/rpc.rexd     rpc.rexd
#
# rpc.cmsd is a data base daemon which manages calendar data backed
# by files in /var/spool/calendar
#
#
# Sun ToolTalk Database Server
#
100083/1     tli    rpc/tcp wait root /usr/dt/bin/rpc.ttdbserverd
   rpc.ttdbserverd
#
# UFS-aware service daemon
#
#ufsd/1   tli      rpc/*     wait     root     /usr/lib/fs/ufs/ufsd     ufsd -p
#
# Sun KCMS Profile Server
#
100221/1  tli     rpc/tcp  wait root /usr/openwin/bin/kcms_server   kcms_server
#
# Sun Font Server
#
fs       stream     tcp     wait nobody /usr/openwin/lib/fs.auto     fs
#
# CacheFS Daemon
#
100235/1 tli rpc/tcp wait root /usr/lib/fs/cachefs/cachefsd cachefsd
#
# Kerberos V5 Warning Message Daemon
#
100134/1     tli    rpc/ticotsord    wait     root
   /usr/lib/krb5/ktkt_warnd ktkt_warnd
#
# Print Protocol Adaptor - BSD listener
#
printer   stream     tcp6    nowait    root /usr/lib/print/in.lpd    in.lpd
#
# GSS Daemon
#
100234/1     tli    rpc/ticotsord    wait     root    /usr/lib/gss/gssd gssd
dtspc stream tcp nowait root /usr/dt/bin/dtspcd /usr/dt/bin/dtspcd
100068/2-5 dgram rpc/udp wait root /usr/dt/bin/rpc.cmsd rpc.cmsd
reve    dgram    udp     wait    root    /usr/local/games/in.reved in.reved
```

See `inetd.conf`(4) for more information on the format of this file. `inetd` listens for service requests on the TCP or UDP ports associated with each of the services listed in the configuration file. When a request arrives, `inetd` executes the server program associated with the service.

> **Warning** — Do not configure udp services as nowait. Doing so results in a race condition where the inetd program selects on the socket and the server program reads from the socket. Many server programs are forked and performance is severely compromised.

A service can be configured to be single-threaded, in which case inetd waits for the server process to exit before starting a second server process. RPC services can also be started by inetd.

inetd provides a number of simple Internet services internally. These include echo, discard, chargen (character generator), daytime (human-readable time), and time (machine-readable time, in the form of the number of seconds since midnight, January 1, 1900).

inetd rereads its configuration file once when it is started and again whenever it receives a hangup signal, SIGHUP. You can activate new services and delete or modify existing services by editing the configuration file then sending inetd a SIGHUP signal.

> **Note** — For RPC services, inetd listens on all the transports (not only tcp and udp) as specified for each service in the inetd.conf(4) file.

Options

-d Run inetd in the foreground and enable debugging output.

-s Run inetd standalone, outside the Service Access Facility (SAF). If you omit the -s option, try to contact the service access controller (SAC) and exit if SAC is not already running. See sac(1M)

-t Trace the incoming connections for all of its TCP services. Log the client's IP address and TCP port number along with the name of the service, using the syslog(3) command. UDP services cannot be traced. When tracing is enabled, use the syslog code daemon and notice priority level.

-r count interval

 Detect and then suspend broken, connectionless, datagram services servers, for example, UDP, and RPC/CLTS. Without this detection, a buggy server that fails before consuming the service request is continuously restarted and taxes system resources too much. count and interval are decimal numbers that represent the maximum count of invocations per interval of seconds a service can be started before the service is considered broken. Once considered broken, a server is suspended for 10 minutes. After 10 minutes, inetd again enables service, hoping the server behaves correctly.

 If you do not specify the -r option, behave as though you specified -r40 60.

Operands

configuration-file

 List the services inetd is to provide.

Exit Status

inetd does not return an exit status.

Attributes

See attributes(5) for descriptions of the following attributes.

Attribute Type	Attribute Value
Availability	SUNWcsu

See Also

in.ftpd(1M), in.rexecd(1M), in.rshd(1M), in.tftpd(1M), sac(1M), syslog(3), inetd.conf(4), attributes(5)

Postel, Jon, *Echo Protocol*, RFC 862, Network Information Center, SRI International, Menlo Park, CA, May 1983.

Postel, Jon, *Character Generator Protocol*, RFC 864, Network Information Center, SRI International, Menlo Park, CA, May 1983.

Postel, Jon, *Daytime Protocol*, RFC 867, Network Information Center, SRI International, Menlo Park, CA, May 1983.

Postel, Jon, *Discard Protocol*, RFC 863, Network Information Center, SRI International, Menlo Park, CA, May 1983.

Postel, Jon, and Harrenstien, Ken, *Time Protocol*, RFC 868, Network Information Center, SRI International, Menlo Park, CA, May 1983.

infocmp — Compare or Print terminfo Descriptions

Synopsis

/usr/bin/infocmp [-d][-c][-n][-I][-L][-C][-r][-u][-s | d | i | l | c]
    [-v][-V][-1][-w *width*][-A *directory*][-B *directory*][*termname*...]

Description

Use the infocmp command to compare a binary terminfo entry with other terminfo entries, rewrite a terminfo description to take advantage of the use= terminfo field, or print a terminfo description from the binary file (term) in a variety of formats. infocmp displays boolean fields first, then numeric fields, followed by the string fields. If you specify no options and specify zero or one *termname*, the -I option is assumed. If you specify more than one *termname*, the -d option is assumed.

Options

You can use the -d, -c, and -n options for comparisons. infocmp compares the terminfo description of the first terminal *termname* with each of the descriptions given by the entries for the other terminal's *termname*. If a capability is defined for only one of the terminals, the value returned depends on the type of the capability: F for boolean variables, -1 for integer variables, and null for string variables.

-c   Produce a list of each capability that is common between two entries. Ignore capabilities that are not set. You can use this option as a quick check to see if the -u option is worth using.

-d   Produce a list of each capability that is different between two entries. This option is useful to show the difference between two entries, created by different people, for the same or similar terminals.

-n   Produce a list of each capability that is in neither entry. If you specify no *termname*, use the environment variable TERM for both of the term names. You can use this option as a quick check to see if anything was left out of a description.

The -C, -I, and -L options produce a source listing for each terminal named.

-C   Use the termcap names. You can use the source produced by the -C option directly as a termcap entry, but not all of the parameterized strings may be changed to the termcap format. infocmp tries to convert most of the parameterized information, but anything not converted is plainly marked in the output and commented out. You should manually edit items not converted.

-I   Use the terminfo names.

-L   Use the long C variable name listed in term.h.

-r   When using -C, put all capabilities in termcap form.

If you specify no *termname*, the environment variable TERM is used for the terminal name.

All padding information for strings is collected and placed at the beginning of the string where termcap expects it. Mandatory padding (padding information with a trailing /) becomes optional.

All termcap variables no longer supported by terminfo but derivable from other ≈ variables are displayed. Not all terminfo capabilities are translated; only those variables that were part of termcap are normally displayed. Specifying the -r option removes this restriction, allowing all capabilities to be displayed in termcap form.

Note — Because padding is collected at the beginning of the capability, not all capabilities are displayed. Mandatory padding is not supported. Because termcap strings are not as flexible as terminfo strings, it is not always possible to convert a terminfo string capability into an equivalent termcap format. A subsequent conversion of the termcap file back into terminfo format does not necessarily reproduce the original terminfo source.

Some common terminfo parameter sequences, their termcap equivalents, and some terminal types that commonly have such sequences, are listed in the following table.

terminfo	termcap	Representative Terminals
%p1%c	%.	adm
%p1%d	%d	hp, ANSI standard, vt100

terminfo	termcap	Representative Terminals
%p1%'x'%+%c	%+x	concept
%i	%i	ANSI standard, vt100
%p %?%'x'%>%t%p 1%'y'%+%;	%>xy	concept
%p2 is printed before %p1	%r	hp

-u   Produce a terminfo source description of the first terminal *termname* that is relative to the sum of the descriptions given by the entries for the other terminals' *termname*s. Analyze the differences between the first *termname* and the other *termname*s and produce a description with use= fields for the other terminals. In this way, you can retrofit generic terminfo entries into a terminal's description. Or, if two similar terminals exist but were coded at different times or by different people so that each description is a full description, using infocmp shows what can be done to change one description to be relative to the other.

A capability is displayed with an at-sign (@) if it no longer exists in the first *termname* but one of the other *termname* entries contains a value for it. A capability's value is displayed if the value in the first *termname* is not found in any of the other *termname* entries or if the first of the other *termname* entries that has this capability gives a different value for that capability.

The order of the other *termname* entries is significant. Because the terminfo compiler tic does a left-to-right scan of the capabilities, specifying two use= entries that contain differing entries for the same capabilities produces different results, depending on the order in which the entries are given. infocmp flags any such inconsistencies between the other *termname* entries as they are found.

Alternatively, specifying a capability after a use= entry that contains it ignores the second specification. Using infocmp to recreate a description can be a useful check to make sure that everything was specified correctly in the original source description.

Specifying superfluous use= fields does not result in incorrect compiled files but does slow down the compilation time. infocmp flags any superfluous use= fields.

-s   Sorts the fields within each type according to the argument below.

d   Leave fields in the order in which they are stored in the terminfo database.

i   Sort by terminfo name.

l   Sort by the long C variable name.

c   Sort by the termcap name.

If you do not specify the -s option, sort the fields alphabetically by the terminfo name within each type, except in the case of the -C or the -L options, which sort by the termcap name or the long C variable name.

-v   Print tracing information on standard error as the program runs.

-V   Print the version of the program in use on standard error and exit.

-1   Print the fields one to a line. Otherwise, print the fields several to a
            line to a maximum width of 60 characters.

-w *width*   Change the output to *width* characters.

The location of the compiled terminfo database is taken from the environment
variable TERMINFO. If the variable is not defined or the terminal is not found in that
location, the system terminfo database, usually in /usr/share/lib/terminfo, is used.
You can use the -A and -B options to override this location.

-A *directory* Set TERMINFO for the first *termname*.

-B *directory* Set TERMINFO for the other *termname*s. You can use this option to
                compare descriptions for a terminal with the same name located in
                two different databases. This option is useful for comparing
                descriptions for the same terminal created by different people.

Examples

The following example shows the output of the infocmp file with no arguments on the
system paperbark.

```
paperbark% infocmp
#       Reconstructed via infocmp from file:
  /usr/share/lib/terminfo/d/dtterm
dtterm|CDE terminal emulator,
        am, mir, msgr, xenl, xon,
        colors#8, cols#80, it#8, lines#24, lm#0, pairs#8,
        acsc=``aaffggjjkkllmmnnooppqqrrssttuuvvwwxxyyzz{{||}}~~,
        bel=^G, blink=\E[5m, bold=\E[1m, civis=\E[?25l,
        clear=\E[H\E[J, cnorm=\E[?25h, cr=\r,
        csr=\E[%i%p1%d;%p2%dr, cub=\E[%p1%dD, cub1=\b,
        cud=\E[%p1%dB, cud1=\n, cuf=\E[%p1%dC, cuf1=\E[C,
        cup=\E[%i%p1%d;%p2%dH, cuu=\E[%p1%dA, cuu1=\E[A,
        dch=\E[%p1%dP, dch1=\E[P, dim=\E[2m, dl=\E[%p1%dM,
        dl1=\E[M, ech=\E[%p1%dX, ed=\E[J, el=\E[K, el1=\E[1K,
        flash=\E[?5h$<200>\E[?5l, home=\E[H, ht=\t, hts=\EH,
        ich=\E[%p1%d@, il=\E[%p1%dL, il1=\E[L, ind=\ED,
        invis=\E[8m, is2=\E\sF\E>\E[?1l\E[?7h\E[?45l, kbs=\b,
        kcub1=\E[D, kcud1=\E[B, kcuf1=\E[C, kcuu1=\E[A,
        kdch1=\E[3~, kf1=\E[11~, kf10=\E[21~, kf11=\E[23~,
        kf12=\E[24~, kf13=\E[25~, kf14=\E[26~, kf15=\E[28~,
        kf16=\E[29~, kf17=\E[31~, kf18=\E[32~, kf19=\E[33~,
        kf2=\E[12~, kf20=\E[34~, kf3=\E[13~, kf4=\E[14~,
        kf5=\E[15~, kf6=\E[17~, kf7=\E[18~, kf8=\E[19~,
        kf9=\E[20~, kfnd=\E[1~, khlp=\E[28~, kich1=\E[2~,
        knp=\E[6~, kpp=\E[5~, kslt=\E[4~, nel=\EE,
        op=\E[39;49m, rc=\E8, rev=\E[7m, ri=\EM, rmacs=^O,
        rmam=\E[?7l, rmir=\E[4l, rmso=\E[22;27m, rmul=\E[24m,
        sc=\E7, setab=\E[%p1%{40}%+%dm,
        setaf=\E[%p1%{30}%+%dm,
```

```
sgr=\E[0%?%p1%t;2;7%;%?%p2%t;4%;%?%p3%t;7%;%?%p4%t;5%;%?%p5%t;2%;%?%p
6%t;1%;%?%p7%t;8%;m%?%p9%t^N%e^O%;,
       sgr0=\E[0m, smacs=^N, smam=\E[?7h, smir=\E[4h,
       smso=\E[2;7m, smul=\E[4m, tbc=\E[3g,
paperbark%
```

Files

```
/usr/share/lib/terminfo/?/*
```
                    Compiled terminal description database.

Attributes

See `attributes`(5) for descriptions of the following attributes.

Attribute Type	Attribute Value
Availability	SUNWcsu

See Also

```
captoinfo(1M), tic(1M), curses(3X), terminfo(4), attributes(5)
```

init, telinit — Process Control Initialization

Synopsis

```
/sbin/init [0123456abcQqSs]
/etc/telinit [0123456abcQqSs]
```

Description

The `init` command is a general process-spawner. `init` is the parent of all other processes. `init` examines the contents of the `/etc/inittab` file to determine the order for starting up other processes and what to do when one of those processes ends. Use `telinit`, which is linked to `/sbin/init`, to direct the actions of `init`. `telinit` takes a one-character argument and signals `init` to take the appropriate action.

Notes

`init` and `telinit` can be run only by a privileged user.

Do not use the S or s (single user) state indiscriminately in `/etc/inittab`. When modifying this file, it is best to avoid adding the s or S state to any line other than `initdefault`.

If a default state is not specified in the `initdefault` entry in `/etc/inittab`, state 6 is entered. Consequently, the system loops by going to firmware and rebooting continuously.

New! If the `utmpx` file (changed from `utmp` in the Solaris 8 release) cannot be created when booting the system, the system boots to state s regardless of the state specified in the `initdefault` entry in `/etc/inittab`. This circumstance can occur if the `/var` file system is not accessible.

Run Level Defined

At any given time, the system is in one of seven possible run levels. A run level is a software configuration under which only a selected group of processes exists. Processes spawned by `init` for each of these run levels are defined in `/etc/inittab` as shown below.

```
paperbark% more /etc/inittab
ap::sysinit:/sbin/autopush -f /etc/iu.ap
ap::sysinit:/sbin/soconfig -f /etc/sock2path
fs::sysinit:/sbin/rcS sysinit           >/dev/msglog 2<>/dev/msglog
   </dev/console
is:3:initdefault:
p3:s1234:powerfail:/usr/sbin/shutdown -y -i5 -g0 >/dev/msglog 2<>/dev/msglog
sS:s:wait:/sbin/rcS             >/dev/msglog 2<>/dev/msglog </dev/console
s0:0:wait:/sbin/rc0             >/dev/msglog 2<>/dev/msglog </dev/console
s1:1:respawn:/sbin/rc1          >/dev/msglog 2<>/dev/msglog </dev/console
s2:23:wait:/sbin/rc2            >/dev/msglog 2<>/dev/msglog </dev/console
s3:3:wait:/sbin/rc3             >/dev/msglog 2<>/dev/msglog </dev/console
s5:5:wait:/sbin/rc5             >/dev/msglog 2<>/dev/msglog </dev/console
s6:6:wait:/sbin/rc6             >/dev/msglog 2<>/dev/msglog </dev/console
fw:0:wait:/sbin/uadmin 2 0      >/dev/msglog 2<>/dev/msglog </dev/console
of:5:wait:/sbin/uadmin 2 6      >/dev/msglog 2<>/dev/msglog </dev/console
rb:6:wait:/sbin/uadmin 2 1      >/dev/msglog 2<>/dev/msglog </dev/console
sc:234:respawn:/usr/lib/saf/sac -t 300
co:234:respawn:/usr/lib/saf/ttymon -g -h -p "`uname -n` console login: " -T sun
-d /dev/console -l console -m ldterm,ttcompat
paperbark%
```

`init` can be in one of seven run levels, `0-6` and `S` or `s` (`S` and `s` are identical). The run level changes when a privileged user runs `/sbin/init` and sends appropriate signals to the original `init` spawned by the operating system at boot time, saying which run level to invoke.

init and System Booting

When the system is booted, `init` is invoked and the following occurs. First, `init` reads `/etc/default/init` to set environment variables. This file is typically where `TZ` (time zone) and locale-related environments such as `LANG` or `LC_CTYPE` get set. The following example shows the `/etc/default/init` file for the system `paperbark`.

```
paperbark% more /etc/default/init
# @(#)init.dfl 1.5 99/05/26
#
# This file is /etc/default/init.  /etc/TIMEZONE is a symlink to this file.
# This file looks like a shell script, but it is not.  To maintain
# compatibility with old versions of /etc/TIMEZONE, some shell constructs
# (i.e., export commands) are allowed in this file, but are ignored.
#
# Lines of this file should be of the form VAR=value, where VAR is one of
# TZ, LANG, CMASK, or any of the LC_* environment variables.
#
TZ=Australia/West
CMASK=022
```

```
LC_COLLATE=en_US.ISO8859-1
LC_CTYPE=en_US.ISO8859-1
LC_MESSAGES=C
LC_MONETARY=en_US.ISO8859-1
LC_NUMERIC=en_US.ISO8859-1
LC_TIME=en_US.ISO8859-1
paperbark%
```

init then looks in /etc/inittab for the initdefault entry (see inittab(4)). The following table describes what happens if there is no /etc/inittab file.

Exists	init usually uses the run level specified in that entry as the initial run level to enter.
Does not exist	init asks the user to enter a run level from the system console.

	S or s	init goes to the single-user state. In this state, the system console device (/dev/console) is opened for reading and writing, and the command /sbin/su (see su(1M)) is invoked. Use either init or telinit to change the run level of the system. Note that if the shell is terminated (by an end-of-file), init only reinitializes to the single-user state if /etc/inittab does not exist.
	0-6	init enters the corresponding run level. Run levels 0, 5, and 6 are reserved states for shutting the system down. Run levels 2, 3, and 4 are available as multiuser operating states.

If this is the first time since power-up that init has entered a run level other than single-user state, init first scans /etc/inittab for boot and bootwait entries (see inittab(4)). These entries are performed before any other processing of /etc/inittab takes place, provided that the run level entered matches that of the entry. In this way any special initialization of the operating system, such as mounting file systems, can take place before users are allowed on the system. init then scans /etc/inittab and executes all other entries that are to be processed for that run level.

To spawn each process in /etc/inittab, init reads each entry and for each entry that should be respawned, it forks a child process. After it has spawned all of the processes specified by /etc/inittab, init waits for one of its descendant processes to die, for a power-fail signal, or for a signal from another init or telinit process to change the system's run level. When one of these conditions occurs, init reexamines /etc/inittab.

inittab Additions

You can add new entries to /etc/inittab at any time; however, init still waits for one of the above three conditions to occur before reexamining /etc/inittab. To get around this, use the init Q or init q command to wake init to reexamine /etc/inittab immediately.

When init comes up at boot time and whenever the system changes from the single-user state to another run state, init sets the ioctl(2) states of the console to those modes saved in the file /etc/ioctl.syscon. init writes this file whenever the single-user state is entered.

Run-Level Changes

When a run-level change request is made, init sends the warning signal (SIGTERM) to all processes that are undefined in the target run level. init waits five seconds before forcibly terminating these processes by sending a kill signal (SIGKILL).

When init receives a signal telling it that a process it spawned has died, it records the fact and the reason it died in /var/adm/utmpx and /var/adm/wtmpx (changed from utmp and wtmp in the Solaris 8 release) if they exist (see who(1)). A history of the processes spawned is kept in /var/adm/wtmpx.

If init receives a power-fail signal (SIGPWR), it scans /etc/inittab for special entries of the type powerfail and powerwait. These entries are invoked (if the run levels permit) before any further processing takes place. In this way, init can perform various cleanup and recording functions during the power-down of the operating system.

/etc/defaults/init File

You can set default values for the following flags in /etc/default/init. For example, TZ=US/Pacific.

TZ	Either specify the time zone information (see ctime(3C)) or the name of a time zone information file, for example, /usr/share/lib/zoneinfo.
LC_CTYPE	Character characterization information.
LC_MESSAGES	Message translation.
LC_MONETARY	Monetary formatting information.
LC_NUMERIC	Numeric formatting information.
LC_TIME	Time formatting information.
LC_ALL	If set, all other LC_* environmental variables take on this value.
LANG	If LC_ALL is not set and any particular LC_* is also not set, the value of LANG is used for that particular environment variable.

Security

init uses pam(3) for session management. The PAM configuration policy, listed through /etc/pam.conf, specifies the session management module to be used for init. The partial pam.conf file below shows entries for init, using the UNIX session management modules.

```
init session required /usr/lib/security/pam_unix.so.1
```

If there are no entries for the init service, then the entries for the other service are used.

Options

0	Go into firmware.
1	Put the system in system administrator mode. Mount all local file systems. Leave only a small set of essential kernel processes running. This mode is for administrative tasks such as installing optional command packages. All files are accessible and no users are logged in on the system.
2	Put the system in multiuser mode. Spawn all multiuser environment terminal processes and daemons. This state is commonly referred to as the multiuser state.
3	Extend multiuser mode by making local resources available over the network.
4	Available to be defined as an alternative multiuser environment configuration. This option is not necessary for system operation and is usually not used.
5	Shut the system down so that it is safe to remove the power. Have the machine remove power, if possible.
6	Stop the operating system and reboot to the state defined by the initdefault entry in /etc/inittab.
a, b, c	Process only those /etc/inittab entries having the a, b, or c run level set. These pseudostates can be defined to run certain commands but do not change the current run level.
Q, q	Reexamine /etc/inittab.
S, s	Enter single-user mode. This run level is the one that does not require the existence of a properly formatted /etc/inittab file. If this file does not exist, then by default, the only legal run level that init can enter is single-user mode. When in single-user mode, mount the file systems required for basic system operation. When the system comes down to single-user mode, these file systems remain mounted (even if provided by a remote file server) and any other local file systems are also left mounted. During the transition down to single-user mode, kill all processes started by init or init.d scripts that should only be running in multiuser mode. In addition, kill any process that has a utmpx entry (changed from utmp in the Solaris 8 release). This last condition ensures that all port monitors started by the SAC are killed and that all services started by these port monitors, including ttymon login services, are killed.

New!

Files

/etc/inittab Controls process dispatching by init.

New!

/var/adm/utmpx

User access and administration information. utmpx is an extended database file that replaces the obsolete utmp database file.

/var/adm/wtmpx

New!

> History of user access and administration information. wtmpx is an extended database file that replaces the obsolete wtmp database file.

/etc/ioctl.syscon

> ioctl system configuration file.

/dev/console System console device.

/etc/default/init

> Environment variables.

Attributes

See attributes(5) for descriptions of the following attributes.

Attribute Type	Attribute Value
Availability	SUNWcsu

See Also

login(1), sh(1), stty(1), who(1), shutdown(1M), su(1M), ttymon(1M),
ioctl(2), kill(2), ctime(3C), pam(3), inittab(4), pam.conf(4), utmpx(4),
attributes(5), pam_unix(5), termio(7I)

New!

Diagnostics

If init finds that it is respawning an entry from /etc/inittab more than ten times in two minutes, it assumes that there is an error in the command string in the entry and generates an error message on the system console. init then refuses to respawn this entry until either five minutes have elapsed or it receives a signal from a user-spawned init or telinit. This time delay prevents init from eating up system resources when someone makes a typographical error in the inittab file or when a program is removed that is referenced in /etc/inittab.

init.wbem — Start and Stop the CIM Boot Manager

New!

Synopsis

/etc/init.d/init.wbem -start | -stop

Description

The init.wbem command is new in the Solaris 8 release. The init.wbem command is run automatically during installation and each time the system is rebooted by the /etc/rc2.d/S90wbem run control script. This command starts the Common Information Model (CIM) Boot Manager, cimomboot, a process that listens for connection requests from web-based enterprise management (WBEM) clients. When a client requests a connection, the cimomboot program starts the CIM Object Manager. Generally, you do not need to stop the CIM Object Manager. However, if you change an existing provider, you must stop and restart the CIM Object Manager before using the updated provider.

CIM Object Manager

The CIM Object Manager manages CIM objects on a WBEM-enabled system. A CIM object is a computer representation, or model, of a managed resource, such as a printer, disk drive, or CPU. CIM objects are stored internally as Java classes.

When a WBEM client application accesses information about a CIM object, the CIM Object Manager contacts either the appropriate provider for that object or the CIM Object Manager Repository. Providers are classes that communicate with managed objects to access data.

When a WBEM client application requests data from a managed resource that is not available from the CIM Object Manager Repository, the CIM Object Manager forwards the request to the provider for that managed resource. The provider dynamically retrieves the information.

At startup, the CIM Object Manager performs the following functions.

- Listens for RMI connections on RMI port 5987 and for XML/HTTP connections on HTTP port 80.
- Sets up a connection to the CIM Object Manager Repository.
- Waits for incoming requests.

During normal operations, the CIM Object Manager performs the following functions.

- Performs security checks to authenticate user login and authorization to access namespaces.
- Performs syntactical and semantic checking of CIM data operations to ensure that they comply with the latest CIM Specification.
- Routes requests to the appropriate provider or to the CIM Object Manager Repository.
- Delivers data from providers and from the CIM Object Manager Repository to WBEM client applications.

A WBEM client application contacts the CIM Object Manager to establish a connection when it needs to perform WBEM operations, such as creating a CIM class or updating a CIM instance. When a WBEM client application connects to a CIM Object Manager, it gets a reference to the CIM Object Manager, which it then uses to request services and operations.

System Booting

The init.wbem script is installed in the /etc/init.d directory. The init.wbem script is executed at system reboot. It is also executed by /etc/rc2.d/S90wbem start when init state 2 is entered and by /etc/rc0.d/K36wbem stop when init state 0 is entered.

Options

-start	Start the CIM Boot Manager on the local host.
-stop	Stop the CIM Object Manager on the local host.

Attributes

See attributes(5) for descriptions of the following attributes.

Attribute Type	Attribute Value
Availability	SUNWwbcor

See Also

wbemadmin(1M), wbemlogviewer(1M), mofcomp(1M), attributes(5)

install — Install Commands

Synopsis

```
/usr/sbin/install -c dira [-m mode][-u user][-g group][-o][-s] file
/usr/sbin/install -f dirb [-m mode][-u user][-g group][-o][-s] file
/usr/sbin/install -n dirc [-m mode][-u user][-g group][-o][-s] file
/usr/sbin/install -d | -i [-m mode][-u user][-g group][-o][-s] dirx...
/usr/sbin/install [-m mode][-u user][-g group][-o][-s] file [dirx...]
```

Description

The install command is most commonly used in makefiles (see make(1S)) to install a file in specific locations, or to create directories within a file system. Each file is installed by being copied into the appropriate directory.

install uses no special privileges to copy files from one place to another. The implications of the lack of security are as follows.

- You must have permission to read the files to be installed.

- You must have permission to copy into the destination directory.

- You must have permission to change the modes on the final copy of the file if you want to use the -m option.

- You must be superuser if you want to specify the ownership of the installed file with the -u or -g options. If you are not superuser, the installed file is owned by you, regardless of who owns the original.

install prints messages telling you exactly what files it is replacing or creating and where they are going.

If you specify no options or directories (dirx...), install searches a set of default directories (/bin, /usr/bin, /etc, /lib, and /usr/lib, in that order) for a file with the same name as file. When the first occurrence is found, install issues a message saying that it is overwriting that file with file and proceeds to do so. If the file is not found, the program states so and exits.

If you specify one or more directories (dirx...) after file, those directories are searched before the default directories.

Options

-c *dira*	Install *file* in the directory specified by *dira* if *file* does not yet exist. If it is found, issue a message saying that the file already exists, and exit without overwriting it.
-f *dirb*	Force *file* to be installed in given directory, even if *file* already exists. If the file being installed does not already exist, set the mode of the file to 755 and the owner to bin. If the file already exists, use the mode and owner of the already existing file.
-n *dirc*	If *file* is not found in any of the searched directories, put it in the directory specified in *dirc*. Set the mode of the file to 777 and the owner to bin.
-d	Create missing parent directories as required, as in mkdir -p. If the directory already exists, set the owner, group, and mode to the values given on the command line.
-i	Ignore default directory list, searching only through the given directories (*dirx*...).
-m *mode*	Set the mode of the new file to *mode*. Set to 0755 by default.
-u *user*	Set the owner of the new file to *user*. This option is available only to superuser. Set to bin by default.
-g *group*	Set the group ID of the new file to *group*. This option is only available to superuser. Set to bin by default.
-o	If *file* is found, save the found file by copying it to OLDfile in the directory in which it was found. This option is useful when you are installing a frequently used file such as /bin/sh or /lib/saf/ttymon, where you cannot remove the existing file.
-s	Suppress printing of messages other than error messages.

Usage

See largefile(5) for the description of the behavior of install when encountering files greater than or equal to 2 Gbytes ($2^{**}31$ bytes).

Attributes

See attributes(5) for descriptions of the following attributes.

Attribute Type	Attribute Value
Availability	SUNWcsu

See Also

chgrp(1), chmod(1), chown(1), cp(1), mkdir(1), chown(1M), make(1S), attributes(5), largefile(5)

install_scripts — Scripts to Install the Solaris Software

Synopsis

```
cdrom-mnt-pt/Solaris_8/Tools/add_install_client [-i IP-address]
    [-e Ethernet-address][-s server-name : path][-c server-name : path]
    [-n [server] : name-service [(netmask)][-p server-name : path]
    hostname platform-group
cdrom-mnt-pt/Solaris_8/Tools/rm_install_client hostname
cdrom-mnt-pt/Solaris_8/Tools/setup_install_server[-b]install-dir-path
cdrom-mnt-pt/Solaris_8/Tools/modify_install_server[-p]install-dir-path New!
    installer_miniroot_path
cdrom-mnt-pt/Solaris_8/Misc/jumpstart_sample/check
    [-p install-dir-path][-r rulesfile]
cdrom-mnt-pt/Sol_8_sparc_2/Solaris_8/Tools/add_to_install_server [-s] New!
    [-p product-image-path] install-server-path
```

Description

These commands are located on slice 0 of the Solaris CD. (If the Solaris CD has been copied to a local disk, *cdrom-mnt-pt* is the path to the copied Solaris CD.) You can use the install scripts to perform the following installation tasks.

- Use add_install_client and rm_install_client to add or remove clients for network installation (these commands update the bootparams(4) file). You must run the add_install_client command from the install server's Solaris installation image (a mounted Solaris CD or a Solaris CD copied to disk) or the boot server's boot directory (if a boot server is required). The Solaris installation image or the boot directory must be the same Solaris release that you want installed on the client.

- Use setup_install_server to copy the Solaris CD to a disk (to set up an install server) or to copy just the boot software of the Solaris CD to a disk (to set up a boot server). An install server is required to install clients over the network. A boot server is also required for network installations if the install server and clients to be installed are on different subnets (the boot server must be located on the client's subnet).

- Use modify_install_server to replace miniroot on an existing net install   *New!* server with a Solaris Installation CD's Web Start user interface. An existing install image (created with setup_install_server) must exist before you can use the modify_install_server command. The modify_install_server command is new in the Solaris 8 release.

- Use check to validate the rules in a rules file if you are setting up a custom JumpStart installation.

- Use add_to_install_server to copy packages from additional Solaris   *New!* copackaged CDs to an existing Net Install Server. The add_to_install_server command is new in the Solaris 8 release.

Options

add_install_client

`-c` *server-name:path*

> This option is required only to specify a JumpStart directory for a custom JumpStart installation. *server-name* is the host name of the server with a JumpStart directory. *path* is the absolute path to the JumpStart directory.

`-e` *Ethernet-address*

> Specify the Ethernet address of the system to be installed.

`-i` *IP-address*

> Specify the IP address of the client to be installed.

`-n` [*server*]:*name-service*[(*netmask*)]

> Specify which nameservice to use during system configuration. This option sets the ns keyword in the bootparams(4) file.

> | | |
> |---|---|
> | *name-service* | Valid entries are nis, nisplus, and none. |
> | *server* | The name of the server or IP address of the specified nameservice. If the server specified is on a different subnet, then the netmask may be needed to enable the client to contact the server. |
> | *netmask* | A series of four numbers separated by periods, specifying which portion of an IP address is the network part and which is the host part. |

`-p` *server-name:path*

> Specify the location of the user-defined sysidcfg file for preconfiguring system/network information. *server-name* is either a valid host name or IP address. *path* is the absolute path to the file.

`-s` *server-name*:path

> This option is required only using add_install_client is used from a boot server. Specify the name of the server and the absolute path of the Solaris installation image to be used for this installation. *path* is either the path to a mounted Solaris CD or a path to a directory with a copy of the Solaris CD.

New!

add_to_install_server

`-p`

> Specify the location of the CD containing the supplemental products to be copied.

`-s`

> Select from a list of only the products needing installation.

check

New!

-p *install-dir-path*

> Validate the `rules` file by using the `check` script from a specified Solaris installation image instead of the `check` script from the system you are using. *install-dir-path* specifies the path to a Solaris installation image on a local disk or on a mounted Solaris CD.

-r *rulesfile* Specify a rules file other than the one named `rules`. You can use this option to test the validity of a rule before integrating it into the `rules` file. `check` reports whether the rule is valid but does not create the `rules.ok` file needed for a custom JumpStart installation.

modify_install_server

New!

-p

> Preserve the existing image's `miniroot` in *install-dir-path*/`Solaris_8/Tools/Boot.orig`.

setup_install_server

-b

> Set up the server only as a boot server.

Operands

add_install_client

hostname

> The name of the client to be installed.

platform_group

> Vendor-defined grouping of hardware platforms for the purpose of distributing specific software. Examples of valid platform groups follow.

System	Platform Name
IA	i86pc
SPARCstation 1+	sun4c
SPARCstation 5	sun4m
SPARC Ultra-2	sun4u

> Use the `uname(1)` command (option -m) to determine a system's platform group.

add_to_install_server

install-server-path

> The absolute path of the directory on the install server in which the Solaris software is to be copied. The directory must be empty.

modify_install_server

install-dir-path

> The absolute path of the directory in which the Solaris software is to be copied.

installer_miniroot_path

> The absolute path to the `miniroot`.

rm_install_client

hostname

> The name of the client to be removed.

setup_install_server

install-dir-path

> The absolute path of the directory in which the Solaris software is to be copied. The directory must be empty.

Examples

The following example uses the `add_install_client` command with the -e option to add the client `castle` for network installation from a mounted Solaris CD on an install server.

```
# cd /cdrom/cdrom0/s0/Solaris_8/Tools
# ./add_install_client -e 8:0:20:18:69:71 castle sun4m
Adding Ethernet number for castle to /etc/ethers
saving original /etc/dfs/dfstab in /etc/dfs/dfstab.orig
Adding "share -F nfs -o ro,anon=0 /cdrom/sol_8_sparc/s0" to
  /etc/dfs/dfstab
...(Additional lines deleted from this example)
```

The following example uses the `setup_install_server` command to copy the mounted Solaris CD to a directory named /export/install on the local disk. Note that the copying process can take some time. In the following example, copying the files to the Sun Ultra-2 system `paperbark` took more than four hours.

```
# cd /cdrom/cdrom0/s0/Solaris_8/Tools
paperbark# ./setup_install_server /export/install
Verifying target directory...
Calculating the required disk space for the Solaris_8 product
Copying the CD image to disk...
Install Server setup complete
#
```

The following example uses the `add_install_client` command to add clients for network installation from a mounted Solaris CD on an install server. The -c option specifies a server and path to a JumpStart directory that has a `rules` file and a `profile` file for performing a custom JumpStart installation. Also, the Solaris CD has been copied to the /export/install directory.

```
# cd /export/install/Solaris_8/Tools
# ./add_install_client -c install_server:/jumpstart system_1 i86pc
# ./add_install_client -c install_server:/jumpstart system_2 i86pc
```

The following example uses the `rm_install_client` command to remove clients for network installation.

```
# cd /export/install/Solaris_8/Tools
# ./rm_install_client holmes
# ./rm_install_client watson
```

The following example uses the `setup_install_server` command to copy the boot software of a mounted Solaris CD to a directory named `/boot_dir` on a system that is going to be a boot server for a subnet.

```
# cd /cdrom/cdrom0/s0/Solaris_8/Tools
# ./setup_install_server -b /boot_dir
Verifying target directory...
Calculating the required disk space for the Solaris_8 product
Copying the CD image to disk...
Install Server setup complete
#
```

The following example uses the `check` command to validate the syntax of the `rules` file used for a custom JumpStart installation.

```
# cd /cdrom/cdrom0/s0/Solaris_8/Misc/jumpstart_sample
# ./check -p /cdrom/cdrom0/s0
Validating rules...
Validating profile host_class...
Validating profile net924_sun4c...
Validating profile upgrade...
Validating profile IA-class...
Validating profile any_machine...
./check: rules.ok: cannot create
sum: rules.ok No such file or directory
./check: rules.ok: cannot create
#
```

The following example uses the `modify_install_server` command to replace the `miniroot` created by the `setup_install_server` command with the `miniroot` on the Solaris Installation CD.

```
# cd /cdrom/cdrom0/s0
# ./modify_install_server /export/install /cdrom/cdrom0/s1
Setting up installer net image

removing existing miniroot
    Setup complete
#
```

The following example uses the `modify_install_server` command to move the `miniroot` created with the `setup_install_server` command to `Boot.orig` and replaces it with the `miniroot` on the Solaris Installation CD.

```
# cd /cdrom/cdrom0/s0
# ./modify_install_server -p /export/install /cdrom/cdrom0/s1
Setting up installer net image
preserving existing miniroot in
   /export/install/Solaris_8/Tools/Boot.orig
Setup complete
#
```

Exit Status

0	Successful completion.
1	An error has occurred.

Attributes

See attributes(5) for descriptions of the following attributes.

Attribute Type	Attribute Value
Availability	Solaris CD

See Also

uname(1), bootparams(4), attributes(5)
  Solaris Advanced Installation Guide

installboot — Install Bootblocks in a Disk Partition

Synopsis

SPARC Platform
/usr/sbin/installboot *bootblk raw-disk-device*

IA Platform
installboot *pboot bootblk raw-disk-device*

Description

The boot(1M) program, ufsboot, is loaded from disk by the bootblock program that resides in the boot area of a disk partition.

The ufs boot objects are platform dependent and reside in the /usr/platform/*platform-name*/lib/fs/ufs directory. You can find the platform name by using the -i option of uname(1).

Operands

bootblk	The name of the bootblock code.

raw-disk-device

> The name of the disk device onto which the bootblock code is to be installed; the device must be a character device that is readable and writeable. Naming conventions for a SCSI or IPI drive are c?t?d?s? and c?d?s? for an IDE drive.

pboot   The name of the partition boot file.

Examples

SPARC Platform

The following command installs a `ufs` bootblock on slice 0 of target 0 on controller 1 of the platform where the command is being run.

```
# installboot /usr/platform/`uname -i`/lib/fs/ufs/bootblk
  /dev/rdsk/c1t0d0s0
#
```

IA Platform

The following command installs the `ufs` bootblock and partition boot program on slice 2 of target 0 on controller 1 of the platform where the command is being run.

```
# installboot /usr/platform/`uname -i`/lib/fs/ufs/pboot
  /usr/platform/`uname -i`/lib/fs/ufs/bootblk
  /dev/rdsk/c1t0d0s2
```

Files

`/usr/platform/`*platform-name*`/lib/fs/ufs`

> Directory where UFS boot objects reside.

`/platform/`*platform-name*`/ufsboot`

> Second-level program to boot from a disk or CD.

Attributes

See `attributes`(5) for descriptions of the following attributes.

Attribute Type	Attribute Value
Availability	SUNWcsu

See Also

od(1), uname(1), boot(1M), init(1M), kadb(1M), kernel(1M), reboot(1M), rpc.bootparamd(1M), init.d(4), attributes(5)
   Solaris Advanced Installation Guide

SPARC Platform

monitor(1M)

IA Platform

fdisk(1M), fmthard(1M)

> **Warning** — The installboot command fails if the *bootblk*, *pboot* or
> openfirmware files do not exist or if the raw disk device is not a character
> device.

installf — Add a File to the Software Installation Database

Synopsis

```
/usr/sbin/installf [-c class][[-M] -R root-path][-V fs-file] fs-file
   pathname [ftype [major minor][mode owner group]]
/usr/sbin/installf [-c class][[-M] -R root-path][-V fs-file] fs-file
/usr/sbin/installf -f [-c class][[-M] -R root-path][-V fs-file] fs-file
```

Description

Use the installf command as part of creating installation scripts to inform the system
that you are creating or modifying a path name not listed in the pkgmap(4) file. You
should invoke the installf command before making any file modifications.

When you use the second synopsis, the path-name descriptions are read from
standard input. These descriptions are the same as would be given in the first synopsis
but you specify the information in the form of a list. The descriptions should be in the
following form.

pathname [ftype [major minor][mode ownergroup]]

After all files have been appropriately created or modified, invoke installf with the
-f synopsis form to indicate that installation is final. Links are created at this time and,
if attribute information for a path name was not specified during the original invocation
of installf or was not already stored on the system, the current attribute values for the
path name are stored. Otherwise, installf verifies that attribute values match those
given on the command line, making corrections as necessary. In all cases, the current
content information is calculated and stored appropriately.

Notes

When you specify ftype, all applicable fields, as shown below, must be defined.

ftype	Required Fields
p, x, d, f, v, or e	mode owner group
c or b	major minor mode owner group

The installf command creates directories, named pipes, and special devices on the
original invocation. Links are created when you invoke installf with the -f option to
indicate installation is complete.

Specify links as *path1=path2*. *path1* indicates the destination and *path2* indicates
the source file.

Files installed with `installf` are placed in the class none, unless you define a class. Subsequently, the files are removed when the associated package is deleted. If this file should not be deleted at the same time as the package, be certain to assign it to a class that is ignored at removal time. If special action is required for the file before removal, you must define a class with the `-c` option and deliver an appropriate class action script with the package.

When classes are used, `installf` must be used in one of the following forms.

```
installf -c class1...
installf -f -c class1...
installf -c class2...
installf -f -c class2...
```

Options

`-c class`	Class to which installed objects should be associated. Default class is none.
`-f`	Indicate that installation is complete. Use this option with the final invocation of `installf` (for all files of a given class).
`-M`	Instruct `installf` not to use the $root-path/etc/vfstab file for determining the client's mount points. This option assumes the mount points are correct on the server, and it behaves consistently with Solaris 2.5 and earlier releases.
`-R root-path`	Define the full path name of a directory to use as the root-path. Relocate all files, including package system information files, to a directory tree starting in the specified root-path. You can specify the root-path when installing to a client from a server (for example, /export/root/client1).
`-V fs-file`	Specify an alternative fs-file to map the client's file systems. Use this option in situations where the $root-path/etc/vfstab file is nonexistent or unreliable.

Operands

`fs-file`	Name of package instance with which to associate the path name.
`pathname`	Path name that is being created or modified.
`ftype`	A one-character field that indicates the file type. You can specify the following file types.

b	Block special device.
c	Character special device.
d	Directory.
e	A file to be edited on installation or removal.
f	A standard executable or data file.
l	Linked file.
p	Named pipe.

s	Symbolic link.
v	Volatile file (one whose contents are expected to change).
x	An exclusive directory.
major	The major device number. Specify this field only for block or character special devices.
minor	The minor device number. Specify this field only for block or character special devices.
mode	The octal mode of the file (for example, 0664). A question mark (?) means to leave the mode unchanged, implying that the file already exists on the target machine. This field is not used for linked or symbolically linked files.
owner	The owner of the file (for example, bin or root). The field is limited to a length of 14 characters. A question mark (?) indicates that the owner is left unchanged, implying that the file already exists on the target machine. This field is not used for linked or symbolically linked files.
group	The group to which the file belongs (for example, bin or sys). The field is limited to a length of 14 characters. A question mark (?) indicates that the group is left unchanged, implying that the file already exists on the target machine. This field is not used for linked or symbolically linked files.

Examples

The following example shows the use of installf, invoked from an optional preinstall or postinstall script.

```
# create /dev/xt directory
# (needs to be done before drvinstall)
installf $PKGINST /dev/xt d 755 root sys ||
     exit 2
majno=`/usr/sbin/drvinstall -m /etc/master.d/xt
     -d $BASEDIR/data/xt.o -v1.0` ||
     exit 2
i=00
while [$i -lt $limit]
do
    for j in 0 1 2 3 4 5 6 7
    do
        echo /dev/xt$i$j c $majno `expr $i ? 8 + $j`
             644 root sys |
        echo /dev/xt$i$j=/dev/xt/$i$j
    done
    i=`expr $i + 1`
    [$i -le 9] && i="0$i" #add leading zero
done | installf $PKGINST - || exit 2
# finalized installation, create links
installf -f $PKGINST || exit 2
```

Exit Status

| 0 | Successful operation. |
| >0 | An error occurred. |

Attributes

See attributes(5) for descriptions of the following attributes.

Attribute Type	Attribute Value
Availability	SUNWcsu

See Also

pkginfo(1), pkgmk(1), pkgparam(1), pkgproto(1), pkgtrans(1), pkgadd(1M),
pkgask(1M), pkgchk(1M), pkgrm(1M), removef(1M), pkgmap(4), space(4),
attributes(5)

Application Packaging Developer's Guide

Intro, intro — Introduction to Maintenance Commands and Application Programs

Description

This section describes, in alphabetical order, commands that are used chiefly for system maintenance and administration purposes.

Because of command restructuring for the Virtual File System architecture, some manual pages begin with the same name. For example, the mount manual pages are mount(**1M**), mount_cachefs(**1M**), mount_hsfs(**1M**), mount_nfs(**1M**), mount_pcfs(**1M**), mount_s5fs(**1M**), mount_tmpfs(**1M**), mount_udfs(**1M**), mount_ufs(**1M**), and mount_xmemfs(**1M**). In each such case, the first manual page describes the syntax and options for the generic command—in other words, those options that apply to all FSTypes (file-system types). The succeeding pages describe the functionality of the FSType-specific modules of the command. These pages list the command followed by an underscore (_) and the FSType to which they pertain. Note that the generic command provides a common interface to all of the specific FStype commands. You can think of the FSType-specific manual pages as detailing aspects of that command that are specific to a particular FSType.

Command Syntax

Unless otherwise noted, commands described in this section accept options and other arguments according to the following syntax.

name [*option*(s)] [*cmdarg*(s)]

| *name* | The name of an executable file. |

option	Specify *noargletter*(s) or *argletter<>optarg* where <> is optional white space.
noargletter	A single letter representing an option without an argument.
argletter	A single letter representing an option requiring an argument.
optarg	Argument (character string) satisfying preceding *argletter*.
cmdarg	Path name (or other command argument) not beginning with – or – by itself indicating the standard input.

Attributes

See attributes(5) for a discussion of the attributes listed in this section.

See Also

getopt(1), getopt(3C), attributes(5)

Diagnostics

On termination, each command returns 0 for normal termination and non-zero to indicate troubles such as erroneous parameters, bad or inaccessible data, or other inability to cope with the task at hand. The exit status codes are called variously exit code, exit status, or return code and are described only where special conventions are involved. This book describes the codes in the "Exit Status" section for each command.

Note — Unfortunately, not all commands adhere to the standard syntax.

List of Commands

New!

A New icon in the margin next to a command name indicates that the command is new in the Solaris 8 release. An asterisk (*) next to a command name indicates that the command is revised in the Solaris 8 release.

ab2admin(1M) *	Command-line interface for AnswerBook2 administration.
ab2cd(1M) *	Run AnswerBook2 server from the Documentation CD.
ab2regsvr(1M) *	
	Register an AnswerBook2 document server with FNS (Federated Naming Service).
accept(1M) *	Accept or reject print requests.
acct(1M) *	Overview of accounting and miscellaneous accounting commands.
acctcms(1M) *	Command summary from process accounting records.
acctcon(1M) *	Connect-time accounting.
acctcon1(1M) *	See acctcon(1M).
acctcon2(1M)	See acctcon(1M).
acctdisk(1M) *	See acct(1M).
acctdusg(1M) *	See acct(1M).
acctmerg(1M) *	Merge or add total accounting files.

accton(1M)*   See acct(**1M**).

acctprc(1M)*   Process accounting.

acctprc1(1M)* See acctprc(**1M**).

acctprc2(1M)* See acctprc(**1M**).

acctsh(1M)*   Shell procedures for accounting.

acctwtmp(1M)* See acct(**1M**).

adbgen(1M)   Generate adb script.

add_drv(1M)   Add a new device driver to the system.

add_install_client(1M)

         See install_scripts(**1M**).

add_to_install_server(1M)   *New!*

         See install_scripts(**1M**).

addbadsec(1M)

         Map defective disk blocks.

admintool(1M)

         System administration with a graphical user interface.

afbconfig(1M) Configure the AFB graphics accelerator.   *New!*

aliasadm(1M)   Manipulate the NIS+ aliases map.

allocate(1M)   Device allocation.

amiserv(1M)   AMI keyserver.   *New!*

answerbook2_admin(1M)

         Start AnswerBook2 administration tool GUI.

arp(1M)   Address resolution display and control.

aset(1M)*   Monitor or restrict access to system files and directories.

aset.restore(1M)

         Restore system files to their content before ASET is installed.

aspppd(1M)   Asynchronous PPP link manager.

aspppls(1M)   See aspppd(**1M**).

audit(1M)   Control the behavior of the audit daemon.

audit_startup(1M)

         Audit subsystem initialization script.

audit_warn(1M)

         Audit daemon warning script.

auditconfig(1M)

         Configure auditing.

auditd(1)   Audit daemon.

auditreduce(1M)*

     Merge and select audit records from audit trail files.

auditstat(1M)

     Display kernel audit statistics.

automount(1M)*

     Install automatic mount points.

automountd(1M)

     autofs mount/unmount daemon.

autopush(1M)* Configure lists of automatically pushed STREAMS modules.

bdconfig(1M) Configure the bd (buttons and dials) stream.

boot(1M)* Start the system kernel or a standalone program.

bootparamd(1M)

     See rpc.bootparamd(1M).

bsmconv(1M) Enable or disable the Basic Security Module (BSM).

bsmunconv(1M)

     See bsmconv(1M).

New! busstat(1M) Report bus-related performance statistics.

cachefslog(1M)

     Cache File System logging.

cachefspack(1M)

     Pack files and file systems in the cache.

cachefsstat(1M)

     Cache File System statistics.

cachefswssize(1M)

     Determine working set size for cachefs.

captoinfo(1M)

     Convert a termcap description to a terminfo description.

cfgadm(1M)* Configuration administration.

New! cfgadm_ac(1M) EXX00 memory system administration.

New! cfgadm_pci(1M)

     Configuration administration command for PCCI Hot Plug.

New! cfgadm_scsi(1M)

     SCSI hardware-specific commands for cfgadm.

New! cfgadm_sysctrl(1M)

     EXX00 system board administration.

cfsadmin(1M)   Administer disk space used for caching file systems with the Cache File System (CacheFS).

cg14config(1M)

        Configure the cgfourteen device.

chargefee(1M)*

        See acctsh(**1M**).

check-hostname(1M)

        Check whether sendmail can determine the system's fully qualified host name.

check-permissions(1M)

        Check permissions on mail rerouting files.

check(1M)   See install_scripts(**1M**).

chown(1M)   Change owner.

chroot(1M)   Change root directory for a command.

ckpacct(1M)*   See acctsh(**1M**).

clear_locks(1M)

        Clear locks held on behalf of an NFS client.

clinfo(1M)   Display cluster information.   *New!*

closewtmp(1M)*

        See acct(**1M**).

clri(1M)   Clear inode.

comsat(1M)*   See in.comsat(**1M**).

conv_lp(1M)   Convert LP configuration.

conv_lpd(1M)   Convert LPD configuration.

consadm(1M)   Select or display devices used as auxiliary console devices.   *New!*

coreadm(1M)   Core file administration.   *New!*

cpustat(1M)   Monitor system behavior, using CPU performance counters.   *New!*

crash(1M)   Examine system images.

cron(1M)   Clock daemon.

cvcd(1M)   Virtual console daemon.

dcopy(1M)   See clri(**1M**).

dd(1M)   Convert and copy a file.

deallocate(1M)

        Device deallocation.

devattr(1M)*   Display device attributes.

`devconfig(1M)` *

　　　　　　　　Configure device attributes.

`devfree(1M)`　　Release devices from exclusive use.

New!　　`devfsadm(1M)`　Administration command for `/dev` and `/devices`.

New!　　`devfseventd(1M)`

　　　　　　　　Kernel event notification daemon for `devfsadmd`.

`devinfo(1M)`　　Print device-specific information.

`devlinks(1M)` * Add `/dev` entries for miscellaneous devices and pseudodevices.

`devnm(1M)`　　　Device name.

`devreserv(1M)`

　　　　　　　　Reserve devices for exclusive use.

`df(1M)` *　　　Display number of free disk blocks and files.

`df_ufs(1M)`　　Report free disk space on UFS file systems.

`dfmounts(1M)`　Display mounted resource information.

`dfmounts_nfs(1M)`

　　　　　　　　Display mounted NFS resource information.

`dfshares(1M)`　List available resources from remote or local systems.

`dfshares_nfs(1M)`

　　　　　　　　List available NFS resources from remote systems.

`dhcpagent(1M)` *

　　　　　　　　Daemon for client Dynamic Host Configuration Protocol (DHCP).

`dhcpconfig(1M)` *

　　　　　　　　DHCP service configuration command.

New!　　`dhcpmgr(1M)`　Graphical interface for managing DHCP service.

`dhtadm(1M)` *　DHCP configuration table management command.

`disks(1M)` *　Create `/dev` entries for hard disks attached to the system.

`diskscan(1M)`　Perform surface analysis.

`dispadmin(1M)`

　　　　　　　　Process scheduler administration.

`dmesg(1M)`　　　Collect system diagnostic messages to form error log.

`dmi_cmd(1M)`　　DMI command-line interface command.

`dmiget(1M)`　　DMI command-line retrieval command.

`dminfo(1M)`　　Report information about a device entry in a device maps file.

`dmispd(1M)`　　Sun Solstice Enterprise DMI Service Provider.

`dodisk(1M)` *　See `acctsh(1M)`.

domainname(1M)

> Set or display name of the current domain.

dr_daemon(1M) Enterprise 10000 Dynamic Reconfiguration daemon. *New!*

drvconfig(1M)*

> Configure the /devices directory.

du(1M) Summarize disk usage.

dumpadm(1M) Configure operating system crash dump.

edquota(1M) Edit user quotas for UFS file system.

eeprom(1M)* EEPROM display and load command.

fbconfig(1M) Frame buffer configuration command. *New!*

fdetach(1M) Detach a name from a STREAMS-based file descriptor.

fdisk(1M)* Create or modify fixed disk partition table.

ff(1M) List file names and statistics for a file system.

ff_ufs(1M) List file names and statistics for a UFS file system.

ffbconfig(1M) Configure the FFB Graphics Accelerator.

fingerd(1M) See in.fingerd(1M).

firmware(1M) Bootable firmware programs and firmware commands.

fmthard(1M) Populate VTOC on hard disks.

fncheck(1M) Check for consistency between FNS data and NIS+ data.

fncopy(1M) Copy FNS contexts, possibly from one naming service to another naming service.

fncreate(1M) Create an FNS context.

fncreate_fs(1M)

> Create FNS file-system contexts.

fncreate_printer(1M)

> Create new printers in the FNS namespace.

fndestroy(1M)

> Destroy an FNS context.

fnselect(1M) Select a specific naming service to use for the FNS Initial Context.

fnsypd(1M) Update FNS context on an NIS master server.

format(1M)* Disk partitioning and maintenance command.

fsck(1M) Check and repair file systems.

fsck_cachefs(1M)

> Check integrity of data cached with CacheFS.

fsck_s5fs(1M)

> File-system consistency check and interactive repair.

fsck_udfs(1M)

                    File-system consistency check and interactive repair.

fsck_ufs(1M)   File-system consistency check and interactive repair.

fsdb(1M)   File-system debugger.

fsdb_ufs(1M)   UFS file-system debugger.

fsirand(1M)   Install random inode generation numbers.

fstyp(1M)   Determine file-system type.

ftpd(1M)*   See in.ftpd(**1M**).

fuser(1M)   Identify processes, using a file or file structure.

fwtmp(1M)*   Manipulate connect accounting records.

getdev(1M)   List devices based on criteria.

getdgrp(1M)   List device groups that contain devices that match criteria.

getent(1M)   Get entries from administrative database.

gettable(1M)   Get DoD Internet format host table from a host.

getty(1M)   Set terminal type, modes, speed, and line discipline.

getvol(1M)   Verify device accessibility.

GFXconfig(1M)   See pgxconfig(**1M**).

groupadd(1M)   Add (create) a new group definition on the system.

groupdel(1M)   Delete a group definition from the system.

groupmod(1M)   Modify a group definition on the system.

grpck(1M)   See pwck(**1M**).

gsscred(1M)   Add, remove, and list gsscred table entries.

gssd(1M)   Generate and validate GSS-API tokens for kernel RPC.

halt(1M)*   Stop the processor.

hostconfig(1M)

                    Configure a system's host parameters.

htable(1M)   Convert DoD Internet format host table.

id(1M)*   Return user identity.

ifconfig(1M)*

                    Configure network interface parameters.

in.comsat(1M)*

                    biff server.

in.dhcpd(1M)*

                    Dynamic Host Configuration Protocol server.

in.fingerd(1M)

                    Remote user information server.

`in.ftpd(1M)*`	File transfer protocol server.
`in.lpd(1M)`	BSD print protocol adapter.
`in.named(1M)`	Internet domain nameserver.
`in.ndpd(1M)`	Daemon for IPv6 autoconfiguration.
`in.rarpd(1M)`	DARPA Reverse Address Resolution Protocol server.
`in.rdisc(1M)`	Network router discovery daemon.
`in.rexecd(1M)`	
	Remote execution server.
`in.ripngd(1M)`	
	Network routing daemon for IPv6.
`in.rlogind(1M)`	
	Remote login server.
`in.routed(1M)`	
	Network routing daemon.
`in.rshd(1M)`	Remote shell server.
`in.rwhod(1M)*`	
	System status server.
`in.talkd(1M)`	Server for talk program.
`in.telnetd(1M)`	
	DARPA TELNET protocol server.
`in.tftpd(1M)`	Internet Trivial File Transfer Protocol server.
`in.tnamed(1M)`	
	DARPA trivial nameserver.
`in.uucpd(1M)`	UUCP server.
`inetd(1M)`	Internet services daemon.
`infocmp(1M)`	Compare or print `terminfo` descriptions.
`init(1M)*`	Process control initialization.
`init.wbem(1M)`	Start and stop the CIM boot manager.
`install(1M)`	Install commands.
`install_scripts(1M)`	
	Scripts to install the Solaris software.
`installboot(1M)`	
	Install bootblocks in a disk partition.
`installf(1M)`	Add a file to the software installation database.
`intro(1M)*` `Intro(1M)`	Introduction to maintenance commands and application programs.

New!

New!

New!

	iostat(1M)	Report I/O statistics.
New!	ipsecconf(1M)	
		Configure system-wide IPsec policy.
New!	ipseckey(1M)	Manually manipulate an IPsec Security Association Database (SADB).
	kadb(1M)	Kernel debugger.
	kdmconfig(1M)	
		Configure or unconfigure keyboard, display, and mouse options for OpenWindows and internationalization.
	kerbd(1M)	Generate and validate Kerberos tickets for kernel RPC.
	kernel(1M)	UNIX system executable file containing basic operating system services.
	keyserv(1M)	Server for storing private encryption keys.
	killall(1M)	Kill all active processes.
New!	ktkt_warnd(1M)	
		Kerberos warning daemon.
	kstat	Display kernel statistics.
	labelit(1M)	List or provide labels for file systems.
	labelit_hsfs(1M)	
		Provide and print labels for HSFS file systems.
New!	labelit_udfs(1M)	
		Provide and print labels for UDF file systems.
	labelit_ufs(1M)	
		Provide and print labels for UFS file systems.
	lastlogin(1M)*	
		See acctsh(**1M**).
New!	ldap_cachemgr(1M)	
		LDAP daemon to cache server and client information for NIS lookups.
New!	ldapclient(1M)	
		Initialize LDAP client machine or create an LDIF of an LDAP client profile.
New!	ldap_gen_profile(1M)	
		See ldapclient(**1M**).
	link(1M)*	Link and unlink files and directories.
	list_devices(1M)	
		List allocatable devices.
	listdgrp(1M)	List members of a device group.

listen(1M)   Network listener daemon.

llc2_loop(1M)   *New!*

Loopback diagnostics to test the driver, adapter, and network.

lockd(1M)   Network lock daemon.

lockfs(1M)   Change or report file system locks.

lockstat(1M)   Report kernel lock statistics.

lofiadm(1M)   Administer files available as block devices through lofi.   *New!*

logins(1M)   List user and system login information.

lpadmin(1M)   Configure the LP print service.

lpfilter(1M)   Administer filters used with the LP print service.

lpforms(1M)   Administer forms used with the LP print service.

lpget(1M)   Get printing configuration.

lpmove(1M)   Move print requests.

lpsched(1M)   Start the LP print service.

lpset(1M)   Set printing configuration in /etc/printers.conf or FNS.

lpshut(1M)   Stop the LP print service.

lpsystem(1M)   Register remote systems with the print service.

lpusers(1M)   Set printing queue priorities.

luxadm(1M) *   Administration program for the Sun Enterprise Network Array
                (SENA), RSM, and SPARCstorage Array.

m64config(1M)

Configure the M64 Graphics Accelerator.

mail.local(1M)

Store mail in a mailbox.

makedbm(1M) *   Make a dbm file, or get a text file from a dbm file.

makemap(1M)   Create database maps for sendmail.

mibiisa(1M)   Sun SNMP Agent.

mk(1M)   Remake the binary system and commands from source code.

mkfifo(1M)   Make FIFO special file.

mkfile(1M)   Create a file.

mkfs(1M)   Construct a file system.

mkfs_pcfs(1M)   *New!*

Construct a FAT file system.

mkfs_udfs(1M)   *New!*

Construct a UDFS file system.

`mkfs_ufs(1M)`*

> Construct a UFS file system.

`mknod(1M)`   Make a special file.

New! `modify_install_server(1M)`

> See `install_scripts`(**1M**).

`modinfo(1M)`* Display information about loaded kernel modules.

`modload(1M)`   Load a kernel module.

`modunload(1M)`

> Unload a module.

New! `mofcomp(1M)`   Compile MOF files into CIM classes.

`monacct(1M)`* See `acctsh`(**1M**).

`monitor(1M)`   SPARCsystem PROM monitor.

`mount(1M)`* Mount or unmount file systems and remote resources.

`mount_cachefs(1M)`

> Mount CacheFS file systems.

`mount_hsfs(1M)`

> Mount HSFS file systems.

`mount_nfs(1M)`

> Mount remote NFS resources.

`mount_pcfs(1M)`

> Mount PCFS file systems.

`mount_s5fs(1M)`

> Mount s5 file systems.

`mount_tmpfs(1M)`

> Mount TMPFS file systems.

New! `mount_udfs(1M)`

> Mount UDFS file systems.

`mount_ufs(1M)`

> Mount UFS file systems.

New! `mount_xmemfs(1M)`

> Mount XMEMFS file systems.

`mountall(1M)`*

> Mount, unmount multiple file systems.

`mountd(1M)`   Server for NFS mount requests and NFS access checks.

`mpstat(1M)`* Report per-processor statistics.

New! `msgid(1M)`   Generate message IDs.

mvdir(1M)   Move a directory.

named-bootconf(1M)

                 Convert configuration file from BIND 4.8.x or BIND 4.9.x format to a
                 format suitable for BIND 8.1.

named-xfer(1M)

                 Ancillary agent for inbound zone transfers.

named(1M)   See in.named(1M).

ncheck(1M)   Generate a list of path names versus i-numbers.

ncheck_ufs(1M)

                 Generate path names versus i-numbers for UFS file systems.

ndd(1M)   Get and set driver configuration parameters.

netstat(1M)*   Show network status.

newfs(1M)   Construct a new UFS file system.

newkey(1M)   Create a new Diffie-Hellman key pair in the publickey database.

nfsd(1M)   NFS daemon.

nfslogd(1M)   NFS logging daemon.

nfsstat(1M)   NFS statistics.

nis_cachemgr(1M)

                 NIS+ command to cache location information about NIS+ servers.

nisaddcred(1M)

                 Create NIS+ credentials.

nisaddent(1M)

                 Create NIS+ tables from corresponding /etc files or NIS maps.

nisauthconf(1M)

                 Configure NIS+ security.

nisbackup(1M)

                 Backup NIS+ directories.

nisclient(1M)

                 Initialize NIS+ credentials for NIS+ principals.

nisd(1M)   See rpc.nisd(1M).

nisd_resolv(1M)

                 See rpc.nisd_resolv(1M).

nisinit(1M)   NIS+ client and server initialization command.

nislog(1M)   Display the contents of the NIS+ transaction log.

nispasswdd(1M)

                 See rpc.nispasswdd(1M).

nisping(1M)* Send ping to NIS+ servers.

nispopulate(1M)

Populate the NIS+ tables in an NIS+ domain.

nisprefadm(1M)

NIS+ command to set server preferences for NIS+ clients.

nisrestore(1M)

Restore NIS+ directory backup.

nisserver(1M)

Set up NIS+ servers.

nissetup(1M)

Initialize an NIS+ domain.

nisshowcache(1M)

NIS+ command to print the contents of the shared cache file.

nisstat(1M)* Report NIS+ server statistics.

nisupdkeys(1M)

Update the public keys in an NIS+ directory object.

nlsadmin(1M) Network listener service administration.

nscd(1M) Nameservice cache daemon.

nslookup(1M)

Query nameservers interactively.

nstest(1M) DNS test shell.

nsupdate(1M) Update DNS nameservers.

ntpdate(1M) Set the date and time by way of Network Time Protocol (NTP).

ntpq(1M) Standard NTP query program.

ntptrace(1M) Trace a chain of NTP hosts back to their master time source.

nulladm(1M)* See acctsh(1M).

obpsym(1M) Kernel symbolic debugging for OpenBoot firmware.

New! ocfserv(1M) OCF server.

parse_dynamic_clustertoc(1M)

Parse clustertoc file according to dynamic entries.

passmgmt(1M) Password files management.

patchadd(1M) Apply a patch package to a Solaris system.

patchrm(1M) Remove a Solaris patch package and restore previously saved files.

pbind(1M) Control and query bindings of processes to processors.

pcmciad(1M) PCMCIA user daemon.

pfinstall(1M) Test installation profiles.

pgxconfig(1M) Configure the PGX32 (Raptor GFX) graphics accelerator.   *New!*

ping(1M) Send ICMP ECHO_REQUEST packets to network hosts.

pkgadd(1M)* Transfer software packages to the system.

pkgask(1M) Store answers to a request script.

pkgchk(1M)* Check package installation accuracy.

pkgrm(1M)* Remove a package from the system.

pmadm(1M) Port monitor administration.

pmconfig(1M) Configure the power management system.

pntadm(1M)* DHCP network table management command.

ports(1M)* Create /dev entries and inittab entries for serial lines.

powerd(1M) Power manager daemon.

poweroff(1M)*

    See halt(**1M**).

praudit(1M) Print contents of an audit trail file.

prctmp(1M)* See acctsh(**1M**).

prdaily(1M)* See acctsh(**1M**).

printmgr(1M) A graphical user interlace for managing printers in a network.   *New!*

prstat(1M) Report active process statistics.   *New!*

prtacct(1M)* See acctsh(**1M**).

prtconf(1M) Print system configuration.

prtdiag(1M) Display system diagnostic information.

prtvtoc(1M) Report information about a disk geometry and partitioning.

psradm(1M) Change processor operational status.

psrinfo(1M)* Display information about processors.

psrset(1M) Create and manage processor sets.

putdev(1M) Edit device table.

putdgrp(1M) Edit device group table.

pwck(1M) Password/group file checkers.

pwconv(1M) Install and update /etc/shadow with information from /etc/passwd.

quot(1M) Summarize file-system ownership.

quota(1M) Display a user's UFS file-system disk quota and usage.

quotacheck(1M)

    UFS file-system quota consistency checker.

quotaoff(1M) See quotaon(**1M**).

quotaon(1M) Turn UFS file-system quotas on and off.

rarpd(1M)	See in.rarpd(1M).
rdate(1M)	Set system date from a remote host.
rdisc(1M)	See in.rdisc(1M).
re-preinstall(1M)	
	Install the JumpStart software on a system.
reboot(1M)*	Restart the operating system.
reject(1M)*	See accept(1M).
rem_drv(1M)	Remove a device driver from the system.
removef(1M)	Remove a file from software database.
repquota(1M)	Summarize quotas for a UFS file system.
restricted_shell(1M)	
	See rsh(1M).
rexd(1M)	See rpc.rexd(1M).
rexecd(1M)	See in.rexecd(1M).
rlogind(1M)	See in.rlogind(1M).
rm_install_client(1M)	
	See install_scripts(1M).
rmmount(1M)	Removable media mounter for CD-ROM and floppy.
rmt(1M)	Remote magtape protocol module.
roleadd(1M)	Administer a new role account.
rolemod(1M)	Modify an existing role account.
roledel(1M)	Delete the login for a role.
route(1M)	Manually manipulate the routing tables.
routed(1M)	See in.routed(1M).
rpc.bootparamd(1M)	
	Boot parameter server.
rpc.nisd(1M)	NIS+ service daemon.
rpc.nisd_resolv(1M)	
	NIS+ service daemon.
rpc.nispasswdd(1M)	
	NIS+ password update daemon.
rpc.rexd(1M)	RPC-based remote execution server.
rpc.rstatd(1M)	
	Kernel statistics server.

New! roleadd(1M)
New! rolemod(1M)
New! roledel(1M)

rpc.rusersd(1M)

>   Network user nameserver.

rpc.rwalld(1M)

>   Network rwall server.

rpc.sprayd(1M)

>   Spray server.

rpc.yppasswdd(1M)

>   Server for modifying NIS password file.

rpc.ypupdated(1M)

>   Server for changing NIS information.

rpcbind(1M)   Universal addresses to RPC program number mapper.

rpcinfo(1M)   Report RPC information.

rpld(1M)   IA Network Booting RPL (Remote Program Load) Server.

rquotad(1M)   Remote quota server.

rsh(1M)   Restricted shell command interpreter.

rshd(1M)   See in.rshd(**1M**).

rstatd(1M)   See rpc.rstatd(**1M**).

rtc(1M)*   Provide all real-time clock and GMT-lag management.

runacct(1M)*   Run daily accounting.

rusersd(1M)   See rpc.rusersd(**1M**).

rwall(1M)   Write to all users over a network.

rwalld(1M)   See rpc.rwalld(**1M**).

rwhod(1M)*   See in.rwhod(**1M**).

sa1(1M)   See sar(**1M**).

sa2(1M)   See sar(**1M**).

sac(1M)*   Service access controller.

sacadm(1M)   Service access controller administration.

sadc(1M)   See sar(**1M**).

sadmind(1M)*   Distributed system administration daemon.

saf(1M)   Service Access Facility.

sar(1M)   System activity report package.

savecore(1M)   Save a crash dump of the operating system.

sendmail(1M)   Send mail over the Internet.

server_upgrade(1M)

>   Upgrade clients of a heterogeneous OS server.

setmnt(1M)   Establish mount table.

setuname(1M)   Change system information.

setup_install_server(1M)

> See install_scripts(**1M**).

share(1M)   Make local resource available for mounting by remote systems.

share_nfs(1M)

> Make local NFS file systems available for mounting by remote systems.

shareall(1M)   Share, unshare multiple resources.

showmount(1M)

> Show all remote mounts.

showrev(1M) *   Show system and software revision information.

shutacct(1M) *

> See acctsh(**1M**).

shutdown(1M)   Shut down system, change system state.

New!   slpd(1M)   Service location protocol daemon.

New!   smartcard(1M)   Configure and administer a smartcard.

New!   smrsh(1M)   Restricted shell for sendmail.

snmpXdmid(1M)

> Sun Solstice Enterprise SNMP-DMI mapper subagent.

snmpdx(1M)   Sun Solstice Enterprise Master Agent.

snoop(1M) *   Capture and inspect network packets.

soconfig(1M)   Configure transport providers for use by sockets.

soladdapp(1M)

> Add an application to the Solstice application registry.

soldelapp(1M)

> Remove an application from the Solstice application registry.

solstice(1M)   Access system administration tools with a graphical user interface.

spray(1M)   Spray packets.

sprayd(1M)   See rpc.sprayd(**1M**).

ssaadm(1M)   Administration program for SPARCstorage Array and SPARCstorage RSM disk systems.

startup(1M) *   See acctsh(**1M**).

statd(1M)   Network status monitor.

strace(1M)   Print STREAMS trace messages.

strclean(1M)   STREAMS error logger cleanup program.

strerr(1M)   STREAMS error logger daemon.

`sttydefs(1M)` Maintain line settings and hunt sequences for TTY ports.

`su(1M)` Become superuser or another user.

`sulogin(1M)` Access single-user mode.

`suninstall(1M)`

Install the Solaris environment.

`swap(1M)*` Swap administrative interface.

`swmtool(1M)` Install, upgrade, and remove software packages.

`sxconfig(1M)` Configure contiguous memory for the SX video subsystem.

`sync(1M)` Update the superblock.

`syncinit(1M)` Set serial line interface operating parameters.

`syncloop(1M)` Synchronous serial loopback test program.

`syncstat(1M)` Report driver statistics from a synchronous serial link.

`sys-unconfig(1M)`

Undo a system's configuration.

`sysdef(1M)` Output system definition.

`sysidconfig(1M)`

Execute system configuration applications, or define set of system configuration applications.

`sysidnet(1M)*`

See `sysidtool`(**1M**).

`sysidnis(1M)*`

See `sysidtool`(**1M**).

`sysidpm(1M)*` See `sysidtool`(**1M**).

`sysidroot(1M)*`

See `sysidtool`(**1M**).

`sysidsys(1M)*`

See `sysidtool`(**1M**).

`sysidtool(1M)*`

System configuration.

`syslogd(1M)*` Log system messages.

`talkd(1M)` See `in.talkd`(**1M**).

`tapes(1M)*` Create `/dev` entries for tape drives attached to the system.

`taskstat(1M)` Prints ASET tasks status.

`tcxconfig(1M)`

Configure the default linearity of the 24-bit TrueColor Visual for OpenWindows on a system with an S24 frame buffer (TCX).

telinit(1M)* See init(1M).

telnetd(1M) See in.telnetd(1M).

tftpd(1M) See in.tftpd(1M).

tic(1M) terminfo compiler.

tnamed(1M) See in.tnamed(1M).

traceroute(1M)*

Print the route that packets take to network host.

ttyadm(1M) Format and output port monitor-specific information.

ttymon(1M) Port monitor for terminal ports.

tunefs(1M)* Tune up an existing file system.

turnacct(1M)*

See acctsh(1M).

uadmin(1M) Administrative control.

ufsdump(1M)* Incremental file-system dump.

ufsrestore(1M)*

Incremental file-system restore.

umount(1M)* See mount(1M).

umountall(1M)*

See mountall(1M).

unlink(1M)* See link(1M).

unshare(1M) Make local resource unavailable for mounting by remote systems.

unshare_nfs(1M)

Make local NFS file systems unavailable for mounting by remote systems.

unshareall(1M)

See shareall(1M).

useradd(1M)* Administer a new user login or role on the system.

userdel(1M)* Delete a user's login from the system.

usermod(1M)* Modify a user's login information or role on the system.

utmp2wtmp(1M)*

See acct(1M).

utmpd(1M) utmpx monitoring daemon.

uucheck(1M) Check the UUCP directories and permissions file.

uucico(1M) File transport program for the UUCP system.

uucleanup(1M)

UUCP spool directory cleanup.

uucpd(1M)	See in.uucpd(1M).
uusched(1M)	UUCP file transport program scheduler.
Uutry(1M)	Try to contact remote system with debugging on.
uuxqt(1M)	Execute remote command requests.
vmstat(1M)	Report virtual memory statistics.
volcopy(1M)	Make an image copy of file system.
volcopy_ufs(1M)	
	Make an image copy of a UFS file system.
vold(1M)	Volume management daemon to manage CD-ROM and floppy devices.
wall(1M)	Write to all users.
wbemadmin(1M)	*New!*
	Start Sun WBEM user manager.
wbemlogviewer(1M)	*New!*
	Start WBEM log viewer.
whodo(1M)*	Report who is doing what.
wtmpfix(1M)*	See fwtmp(1M).
xntpd(1M)*	Network Time Protocol daemon.
xntpdc(1M)	Special NTP query program. *New!*
ypbind(1M)	NIS binder process.
ypinit(1M)	Set up NIS client.
ypmake(1M)	Rebuild NIS database.
yppasswdd(1M)	
	See rpc.yppasswdd(1M).
yppoll(1M)	Return current version of an NIS map at an NIS server host.
yppush(1M)	Force propagation of changed NIS map.
ypserv(1M)	NIS server and binder processes.
ypset(1M)	Point ypbind at a particular server.
ypstart(1M)	Start and stop NIS services.
ypstop(1M)	See ypstart(1M).
ypupdated(1M)	
	See rpc.ypupdated(1M).
ypxfr(1M)	Transfer NIS map from an NIS server to host.
ypxfr_1perday(1M)	
	See ypxfr(1M).

```
ypxfr_1perhour(1M)
                See ypxfr(1M).
ypxfr_2perday(1M)
                See ypxfr(1M).
ypxfrd(1M)      See ypserv(1M).
zdump(1M)       Time-zone dumper.
zic(1M)         Time-zone compiler.
```

iostat — Report I/O Statistics

Synopsis

```
/usr/bin/iostat [-cdDeEIMnpPtx][-l n][disk...][interval [count]]
```

Description

Use the iostat command to monitor terminal, disk, and tape I/O activity and CPU use. The first line of output is for all time since boot; each subsequent line is for the prior interval only.

To compute this information, the kernel maintains a number of counters. For each disk, the kernel counts reads, writes, bytes read, and bytes written. The kernel also takes hi-res timestamps at queue entry and exit points, which enable it to keep track of the residence time and cumulative residence-length product for each queue. Using these values, iostat produces highly accurate measures of throughput, use, queue lengths, transaction rates, and service time. For terminals collectively, the kernel simply counts the number of input and output characters.

During execution of this kernel status command, the state of the kernel can change. An example would be CPUs going online or offline. iostat reports such changes as <<State change>>.

For more general system statistics, use sar(1), sar(1M), or vmstat(1M).

See *Solaris 1.x to 2.x Transition Guide* for device-naming conventions for disks.

Options

The iostat command's activity class options default to tdc (terminal, disk, and CPU). If you specify any activity class options, the default is completely overridden. Therefore, if you specify only -d, neither terminal nor CPU statistics are reported. The last disk option specified (-d, -D, or -x) is the only one that is used.

    -c   Report the percentage of time the system has spent in user mode, in system mode, waiting for I/O, and idling.

    -d   For each disk, report the number of kilobytes transferred per second, the number of transfers per second, and the average service time in milliseconds.

    -D   For each disk, report the reads per second, writes per second, and percentage disk use.

-e	Display total errors, hard errors, soft errors, and transport errors summary statistics.
-E	Display all device error statistics.
-I	Report the counts in each interval instead of rates (where applicable).
-l *n*	Limit the number of disks included in the report to *n*; the disk limit defaults to 4 for -d and -D, and unlimited for -x. Note that disks explicitly requested (see *disk* below) are not subject to this disk limit.
-M	Display data throughput in megabytes/sec instead of kilobytes/sec.
-n	Display names in descriptive format (for example, c*X*t*Y*d*Z*, rmt/*N*, *server*:/*export*/*path*).
-p	For each disk, report per-partition statistics in addition to per-device statistics.
-P	For each disk, report per-partition statistics only, no per-device statistics.
-t	Report the number of characters read and written to terminals per second.
-x	For each disk, report extended disk statistics. The output is in tabular form.

Operands

disk	Explicitly specify the disks to be reported; in addition to any explicit disks, also report any active disks up to the disk limit (see -l).
count	Print only *count* reports.
interval	Report once each *interval* seconds.

Examples

The following example shows the output of the iostat command with the -xtc options, an interval of five seconds, and an output of two reports.

```
paperbark% iostat -xtc 5 2
                          extended disk statistics    tty       cpu
disk r/s w/s Kr/s  Kw/s  wait actv svc_t %w %b  tin tout us sy wt id
sd0  6.2 0.0 21.5  0.0   0.0  0.1  24.1  0  15   0  84   4 94 2  0
sd1  1.8 0.0 14.3  0.0   0.0  0.1  41.6  0  7
sd2  0.0 0.0 0.0   0.0   0.0  0.0  0.0   0  0
sd3  5.6 0.2 25.7  0.2   0.0  0.1  22.5  0  13
                          extended disk statistics    tty       cpu
disk r/s  w/s Kr/s Kw/s wait actv svc_t %w %b  tin  tout  us  sy wt id
sd0  2.6  3.0 20.7 22.7 0.1  0.2  59.2  6  19   0   84    3   85 11  0
sd1  4.2  1.0 33.5 8.0  0.0  0.2  47.2  2  23
sd2  0.0  0.0 0.0  0.0  0.0  0.0  0.0   0  0
sd3  10.2 1.6 51.4 12.8 0.1  0.3  31.2  3  31
paperbark%
```

The fields have the following meanings.

`disk`	Name of the disk.
`r/s`	Reads per second.
`w/s`	Writes per second.
`Kr/s`	Kilobytes read per second.
`Kw/s`	Kilobytes written per second.
`wait`	Average number of transactions waiting for service (queue length).
`actv`	Average number of transactions actively being serviced (removed from the queue but not yet completed).
`svc_t`	Average service time, in milliseconds.
`%w`	Percent of time there are transactions waiting for service (queue nonempty).
`%b`	Percent of time the disk is busy (transactions in progress).

The following example uses the `-xnp` options.

```
paperbark% iostat -xnp
                              extended disk statistics
r/s w/s kr/s kw/s wait actv wsvc_t asvc_t %w %b device
0.0 0.0 0.0  0.0  0.0  0.0  0.0    0.0    0  0  server:/export/home/bob
0.0 0.2 0.2  1.1  0.0  0.0 13.4   17.1    0  0  c0t0d0
0.0 0.0 0.0  0.2  0.0  0.0 22.3   27.2    0  0  c0t0d0s2
0.0 0.0 0.0  0.0  0.0  0.0  2.4   27.9    0  0  c0t0d0s6

paperbark%
```

The fields have the same meanings as in the previous example, with the following additions.

`wsvc_t`	Average service time in wait queue, in milliseconds.
`asvc_t`	Average service time in active transactions, in milliseconds.

Attributes

See `attributes`(5) for descriptions of the following attributes.

Attribute Type	Attribute Value
Availability	SUNWcsu

See Also

`sar`(1), `sar`(1M), `vmstat`(1M), `attributes`(5)
Solaris 1.x to 2.x Transition Guide
System Administration Guide, Volume I

ipsecconf — Configure Systemwide IPsec Policy

Synopsis

```
/usr/sbin/ipsecconf
/usr/sbin/ipsecconf -a file [-q]
/usr/sbin/ipsecconf -d index
/usr/sbin/ipsecconf -f
/usr/sbin/ipsecconf -l [-n]
```

Description

The `ipsecconf` command is new in the Solaris 8 release. It is part of the IP security Architecture that provides protection for IP datagrams. Protection can include confidentiality, strong integrity of the data, partial sequence integration (replay protection), and data authentication. Only superuser can run this command.

You use the `ipsecconf` command to configure the IPsec policy for a host. Policy entries are not preserved across reboot. Thus, you need to add the policy every time the system reboots. To configure policies early in the boot, you first need to create an `/etc/inet/ipsecinit.conf` file, which is then read from the `inetinit` startup script. IPsec is started by the `/etc/rc2.d/S69inet` script only if an `/etc/inet/ipsecinit.conf` file exists. The Solaris 8 software includes a sample file named `/etc/inet/ipsecinit.sample` that you can use as a template to create your own `ipsecinit.conf` file.

Once the policy is configured, all outbound and inbound datagrams are subject to policy checks as they exit and enter the host. If no entry is found, no policy checks are completed and all the traffic passes through. Datagrams that are being forwarded are not subjected to policy checks that are added with this command. See `ifconfig`(1M) and `tun`(7P) for information on how to protect forwarded packets. Depending on the match of the policy entry, a specific action is taken.

Each entry protects traffic only in one direction, that is, either outbound or inbound. Thus, to protect traffic in both directions, you need to have one entry in each direction.

When you issue the command without any arguments, the policies configured in the system are shown. Each entry is displayed with an index followed by a number. You can use the `-d` option with the index to delete a given policy in the system. The entries are displayed in the order in which they were added, which is not necessarily the order that the traffic match takes place. To view the order in which the traffic match takes place, use the `-l` option.

See "Security Considerations" on page 534.

Options

-a *file*
    Add the IPsec policy to the system as specified by each entry in the file. An IPsec configuration file contains one or more entries that specify the configuration. Once the policy is added, all outbound and inbound datagrams are subject to policy checks. Entries in the files are described in "Operands" on page 528. Policy is latched for TCP/UDP sockets on which a `connect`(3SOCKET) or `accept`(3SOCKET) is issued. So, addition of new policy entries may not affect such endpoints/sockets. Also, an old connection that was not

subject to any policy may be subject to policy checks by the addition of new policy entries, which could disrupt the old communication if the other end is not expecting similar policy. Make sure that there are not any preexisting connections that would be subject to checks by the new policy entries.

Note that the policy latching feature explained above may change in the future. It is not advisable to depend on this feature.

-d *index*   Delete the policy denoted by the index. Obtain the index by viewing the policy configured in the system. Once the entry is deleted, all outbound and inbound datagrams affected by this policy entry are not subjected to policy checks. Be advised that for connections whose policy has been latched, packets continue to go out with the same policy even it has been deleted.

-f   Flush all the policies in the system. Constraints are similar to the -d option with respect to latching.

-l   Display a long listing of the policy entries. When you invoke ipsecconf without any arguments, it shows the complete list of policy entries added by the user since the boot. The -l option displays the current kernel table. The current table can differ from the previous one if, for example, a multiple-home entry was added or policy reordering occurred. In the case of a multiple-home entry, all the addresses are listed explicitly. If a mask was not specified earlier but was instead inferred from the address, it is explicitly listed here. Use this option to view policy entries in the correct order. The outbound and inbound policy entries are listed separately.

-n   Show network addresses, ports, protocols in numbers. You can use the -n option only with the -l option.

-q   Run in quiet mode. Suppress the warning message generated when policies are added.

Operands

Each policy entry contains three parts specified as follows.

{*pattern*} *action* {*properties*}

Every policy entry begins on a new line and can span multiple lines. *pattern* specifies the traffic pattern that should be matched against the outbound and inbound datagrams. If a match is found, a specific *action* determined by the second argument is taken, depending on the *properties* of the policy entry. Pattern and properties are name-value pairs where name and value are separated by space, Tab, or newline. Separate multiple name-value pairs by space, Tab, or newline. The beginning and end of the pattern and properties are marked by curly braces ({ }).

Files can contain multiple policy entries. An unspecified name-value pair in *pattern* is considered a wildcard. Wildcard entries match any corresponding entry in the datagram.

Comment items in the file by using # as the first character. You can put comments either at the beginning or the end of a line.

The complete syntax of a policy entry is shown below.

```
policy ::= {pattern} action {properties}

pattern ::=  pattern_name_value_pair|
             pattern_name_value_pair, pattern

action ::= apply | permit | bypass

properties ::=  prop_name_value_pair|
                prop_name_value_pair, properties

pattern_name_value_pair ::=
    saddr/prefix address|
    smask mask|
    sport part|
    daddr/prefix address|
    dmask mask|
    dport port|
    ulp protocol

address ::= Internet dot notation | String recognized by gethostbyname
    | String recognized by getnetbyname

prefix ::=  number

mask ::= 0xhexdigit[hexdigit] | 0Xhexdigit[hexdigit] |
         Internet dot notation
port ::= number| String recognized by getservbyname

protocol ::=  number| String recognized by getprotobyname

prop_name_value_pair ::=
    auth_algs auth_alg|
    encr_algs encr_alg|
    encr_auth_algs auth_alg|
    sa sa_val|
    dir dir_val

auth_alg ::= md5 | hmac-md5 | sha | sha1 | hmac-sha | hmac-sha1 | number

encr_alg ::= des | des-cbc | 3des | 3des-cbc | number

sa_val ::= shared | unique

dir_val ::= out | in

number ::=  0 | 1 | 2... 9 number
```

Policy entries can contain the following (name-value) pairs in the pattern field. Each (name-value) pair can appear only once in a given policy entry.

saddr/plen   The value that follows is the source address of the datagram with the prefix length. Only plen leading bits of the source address of the packet are matched. plen is optional.

The source address value can be a host name, as described in gethostbyname(3XNET) or a network name, as described in getnetbyname(3XNET), or a host address or network address in the Internet standard dot notation. See inet_addr(3XNET).

If you specify a host name and gethostbyname(3XNET) returns multiple addresses for the host, then policy is added for each of the addresses, with other entries remaining the same.

daddr/plen   The value that follows is the destination address of the datagram with the prefix length. Only plen leading bits of the destination address of the packet are matched. plen is optional.

See saddr for valid values. If multiple source and destination addresses are found, then policy entries covering each (source address-destination address) pair are added to the system.

smask   The value that follows is the source mask. If prefix length is given with saddr, do not use this policy entry. You can represent the value either as a hexadecimal number with a leading 0x or 0X, for example, 0xffff0000, 0Xffff0000 or in the Internet decimal dot notation, for example, 255.255.0.0 and 255.255.255.0. The mask should be contiguous; the behavior is not defined for noncontiguous masks.

smask is considered only when you specify saddr.

dmask   The value that follows is the destination mask. If prefix length is given with daddr, do not use this policy entry. You can represent the value either as a hexadecimal number with a leading 0x or 0X, for example, 0xffff0000, 0Xffff0000 or in the Internet decimal dot notation, for example, 255.255.0.0 and 255.255.255.0. The mask should be contiguous and the behavior is not defined for non-contiguous masks.

dmask is considered only when you specify daddr.

sport   The value that follows is the source port of the datagram. This value can be either a port number or a string searched with a null proto argument, as described in getservbyname(3XNET)

dport   The value that follows is the destination port of the datagram. This value can be either a port number or a string as described in getservbyname(3XNET) searched with null proto argument.

ulp   The value that follows is the Upper Layer Protocol that this entry should be matched against. Specify it as a number or a string as described in getprotobyname(3XNET).

Any unspecified components are considered a wildcard entry. Thus, if pattern is null, all packets match the policy entry. If you specify neither the prefix length nor the mask for the address, a mask is inferred. For example, if a.b.c.d is the address and the following values are used, then

- b, c, and d are zeroes, the mask is 0xff000000.
- Only c and d are zeroes, the mask is 0xffff0000.
- Only d is zero, the mask is 0xffffff00.

- Neither a, b, c, nor d is zero, the mask is 0xffffffff.To avoid ambiguities, it is advisable to explicitly give either the prefix length or the mask.

Policy entries can contain the following (name value) pairs in the properties field. Each (name value) pair may appear only once in a give policy entry.

auth_algs   An acceptable following value implies that IPsec AH header is present in the outbound datagram. The values that follow describe the authentication algorithms that are used while applying the IPsec AH on outbound datagrams and verified to be present on inbound datagrams. See RFC 2402.

This entry can contain either a string or a decimal number.

If auth_algs is not present, the AH header is not present in the outbound datagram, and the same is verified for the inbound datagram.

string   This value should be either MD5 or HMAC-MD5, denoting the HMAC-MD5 algorithm as described in RFC 2403, and SHA1, HMAC-SHA1, SHA, or HMAC-SHA, denoting the HMAC-SHA algorithm described in RFC 2404. The value can also be ANY, which denotes no preference for the algorithm. Default algorithms are chosen on the basis of SAs available at this time for manual SAs and the key negotiating daemon for automatic SAs. Strings are not case sensitive.

number   A number in the range 1-255. This entry is useful when new algorithms can be dynamically loaded.

encr_algs   An acceptable following value implies that IPsec ESP header is present in the outbound datagram. The value that follows describes the encryption algorithms that are used to apply the IPsec ESP protocol to outbound datagrams and verify it to be present on inbound datagrams. See RFC 2406.

This entry can contain either a string or a decimal number. Strings are not case sensitive.

string   Specify either DES or DES-CBC to denote the algorithm described in RFC 2405 or 3DES or 3DES-CBC to denote the used of 3DES in a manner consistent with RFC 2451. The value can be NULL which implies a null encryption pursuant to RFC 2410, which means that the payload is not encrypted.The string can be ANY, which denotes no preference for the algorithm. Default algorithms are chosen depending on the SAs available at this time for manual SAs and on the key negotiating daemon for automatic SAs.

number   A decimal number in the range 1-255. This entry is useful when new algorithms can be dynamically loaded.

encr_auth_algs

> An acceptable value following encr_auth_algs implies that the IPsec ESP header is present in the outbound datagram. The values following encr_auth_algs describe the authentication algorithms that are used while applying the IPsec ESP protocol on outbound datagrams and verified to be present on inbound datagrams. See RFC 2406. This entry can contain either a string or a number. Strings are case insensitive.
>
> > string   Valid values are the same as the ones described for auth_algs above.
> >
> > number   Specify a decimal number in the range 1-255. This entry is useful when new algorithms can be dynamically loaded.

If encr_algs is present and encr_auth_algs is not present in a policy entry, the system uses an ESP SA regardless of whether the SA has an authentication algorithm or not.

If encr_algs is not present and encr_auth_algs is present in a policy entry, null encryption is provided, which is equivalent to encr_algs with NULL, for outbound and inbound datagrams.

If both encr_algs and encr_auth_algs are not present in a policy entry, ESP header is not present for outbound datagrams and the same is verified for inbound datagrams.

If both encr_algs and encr_auth_algs are present in a policy entry, ESP header with integrity checksum is present on outbound datagrams and the same is verified for inbound datagrams.

dir

> The following value determines whether this entry is for outbound or inbound datagrams. A valid value is one of the following strings.
>
> > out   Consider this policy entry only for outbound datagrams.
> >
> > in   Consider this policy entry only for inbound datagrams.

The dir entry is not needed when the action is apply or permit. But if you specify it while the action is apply, the value for dir must be out; while the action is permit, the value for dir must be in. These values are mandatory when the action is bypass.

sa

> The following value determines the attribute of the security association. Value indicates whether to use a unique security association or any existing SA. If there is a policy requirement, SAs are created dynamically on the first outbound datagram, using the key management daemon. Static SAs can be created with ipseckey(1M). The values used here determine whether a new SA is used/obtained. Specify one of the following values.
>
> > unique   Unique association. A new/unused association is obtained/used for packets matching this policy entry. An SA address uses five tuple values for {Source address, Destination address, Source port, Destination Port, Protocol (for example,

TCP/UDP)}. If an SA that was previously used by the same five tuples exists, reuse it. Thus, uniqueness is expressed by the five tuples given above. The security association used by the above five tuples is not used by any other socket. For inbound datagrams, uniqueness is not verified.

shared   Shared association. If an SA already exists for this source-destination pair, then use it. Otherwise, obtain a new SA.

The `sa` entry is mandatory only for outbound policy entries and should not be given for entries whose action is `bypass`. If this entry is not given for inbound entries, for example, when `dir` is in or `action` is `permit`, it is assumed to be shared.

`action` follows the `pattern`, and you should specify it before properties. This field is mandatory and should have one of the following values.

apply   Apply IPsec to the datagram, as described by the properties, if the pattern matches the datagram. If you specify `apply`, match the pattern only on the outbound datagram.

permit   Permit the datagram if the pattern matches the incoming datagram and satisfies the constraints described by the properties. If it does not satisfy the properties, discard the datagram. If you specify `permit`, match the pattern only for inbound datagrams.

bypass   Bypass any policy checks if the pattern matches the datagram. `dir` in the properties decides whether the check is done on outbound or inbound datagrams. Check all the `bypass` entries before checking with any other policy entry in the system. This field has the highest precedence over any other entries. `dir` is the only field that should be present when `action` is `bypass`.

If the file contains multiple policy entries, they are assumed to be listed in the order that they are to be applied. In cases of multiple entries matching the outbound and inbound datagram, the first match is taken. The system reorders the policy entry, that is, adds the new entry before the old entry, only in the following circumstances.

- The level of protection is "stronger" than the old level of protection. Currently, strength is defined as:

AH and ESP > ESP > AH

The standard uses of AH and ESP are what drive this ranking of "stronger." There are flaws with this ranking. ESP can be used either without authentication, which enables cut-and-paste or replay attacks, or without encryption, which makes it equivalent or slightly weaker than AH. Take care to use ESP properly. See `ipsecesp(7P)` for more details.

- If the new entry has `bypass` as action, `bypass` has the highest precedence. You can add it in any order and the system still matches all the `bypass` entries before matching any other entries. This action is useful for key management daemons, which can use this feature to bypass IPsec because it protects its own traffic.

Entries with both AH (`auth_algs` present in the policy entry) and ESP protection (`encr_auth_algs` or `encr_auth_algs` present in the policy entry) are ordered after all the entries with AH and ESP and before any AH-only and ESP-only entries. In all other cases, the specified order is not modified, that is, newer entries are added at the end of all the old entries.

A new entry is considered a duplicate of the old entry if an old entry matches the same traffic pattern as the new entry.

Security Considerations

Be cautious about transmitting a copy of the policy file over the network. If, for example, the policy file comes over the wire from an NFS mounted file system, an adversary can modify the data contained in the file, thus changing the policy configured on the machine to suit his needs.

Policy is latched for TCP/UDP sockets on which a connect(3SOCKET) or accept(3SOCKET) has been issued. Adding new policy entries does not have any effect on them. This feature of latching may change in the future. It is advisable not to depend on it.

Make sure to set up the policies before starting any communications because existing connections can be affected by the addition of new policy entries. Similarly, do not change policies in the middle of a communication.

If your source address is a host that can be looked up over the network and your naming system itself is compromised, then any names used are no longer trustworthy.

Examples

The following example protects outbound TCP traffic with ESP and the DES algorithm.

```
#
# Protect the outbound TCP traffic between hosts spiderweb
# and arachnid with ESP and use DES algorithm.
#
{
        saddr spiderweb
        daddr arachnid
        lp tcp #only TCP datagrams.
} apply {
        encr_algs DES
}
```

This entry specifies that any TCP packet from spiderweb to arachnid should be encrypted with DES and that the SA could be a shared one. Because no prefix len or mask is given, a mask is inferred. To look at the mask, use the ipsecconf command with the -l option. Note that dir is not given in properties, because apply implies that only outbound packets are matched with the pattern.

The above entry does verify whether the inbound traffic is encrypted. Thus, you need the following entry to protect inbound traffic.

The following example verifies whether inbound traffic is encrypted.

```
#
# Protect the TCP traffic on inbound with ESP/DES from arachnid
# to spiderweb
#
{
        saddr arachnid
        daddr spiderweb
```

```
        ulp tcp
} permit {
        encr_algs DES
}
```

sa can be absent for inbound policy entries because the example implies that the entry can be a shared one. Uniqueness is not verified on inbound. Note that in both the above entries, authentication is not specified, which can lead to cut-and-paste attacks. As mentioned previously, although the authentication is not specified, the system still uses an ESP SA with encr_auth_alg specified if it is found in the SA tables.

The following example authenticates all inbound traffic to the telnet port.

```
#
# All the inbound traffic to the telnet port should be
# authenticated.
#
{
        dport telnet # telnet is 23
} permit {
        auth_algs SHA1
        dir in
}
```

This entry specifies that any inbound datagram to telnet port should come in authenticated with the SHA1 algorithm. Otherwise, the datagram should not be permitted. Without this entry, traffic destined to port number 23 can come in clear. Note that dir as given is optional, because permit implies that this policy entry is checked only on inbound. sa is not specified, which implies that it is shared, which can be done only for inbound entries. You need to have an equivalent entry to protect outbound traffic so that the outbound traffic is authenticated as well.

The following example verifies that inbound traffic is null encrypted.

```
#
# Make sure that all inbound traffic from network-B is NULL
# encrypted, but bypass for host-B alone from that network.
# Add the bypass first.
{
        saddr host-B
} bypass {
        dir in
}
# Now add for network-B.
{
        saddr network-B/16
} permit {
        encr_algs NULL
        encr_auth_algs md5
}
```

The first entry specifies that any packet with address host-B should not be checked against any policies. The second entry specifies that all inbound traffic from network-B should be encrypted with a null-encryption algorithm and the MD5 authentication algorithm. NULL encryption implies that ESP header is used without encrypting the datagram. Even though the first entry is bypass, you do not need to put it first because bypass entries have the highest precedence. Thus, any inbound traffic is matched against all bypass entries before any other policy entries.

The following example on hostB specifies that any packet from hostA to hostB should be encrypted with 3DES and SHA1.

```
{
        saddr hostA
        daddr hostB
} permit {
        encr_algs 3DES
        encr_auth_algs SHA1
}
```

If you try to add an entry

```
{
        saddr hostA
        daddr hostB
        dport 23
} permit {
encr_algs DES
}
```

it fails with ioctl:File exists. But, if you change the order and give the second entry first, the entry succeeds because traffic to port number 23 from hostB to hostA is protected with DES and the remainder is protected with 3DES and SHA1.

If you modify the second entry as follows, it does not fail.

```
{
        saddr hostA
        daddr hostB
        dport 23
} permit {
        encr_algs DES
        auth_algs SHA1
}
```

This entry gets ordered first in the list because the entry is protected with AH and ESP, which has precedence before the preceding entry that has only ESP. You can add a bypass entry in any order, and it always has the highest precedence. But, all other entries are subject to the check as explained above.

The following entry expects any traffic originating from 134.56.0.0 to be authenticated.

```
{
        daddr 134.56.0. # Network address
        mask 0xffff0000
} permit { auth_algs any}
```

You cannot add the following entry after the above entry has been added because the previous entry would match the traffic from 134.56.0.0.

```
{
        daddr 134.56.123.0
        dmask 0xffffff00
} permit { encr_algs any}
```

You can, however, add this entry before adding the previous entry, or you can add it with AH and ESP protection and it is reordered and considered before the previous one.

The following example creates entries to bypass traffic from IPsec. The first two entries provide that any datagram leaving the machine with source port 500 or coming into port number 500 not be subjected to IPsec policy checks, regardless of any other policy entry in the system. Thus, the last two entries are considered only for ports other than port number 500.

```
#
# Bypass traffic for port no 500
#
{sport 500} bypass {dir out}
{dport 500} bypass {dir in}
saddr spiderweb} apply { encr_algs any sa unique}
addr spiderweb} permit { encr_algs any}
```

The following example protects outbound traffic.

```
#
# Protect the outbound traffic from all interfaces.
#
{ saddr spiderweb} apply {auth_algs any sa unique}
```

If gethostbyname(spiderweb) yields multiple addresses, multiple policy entries are added for all the source addresses with the same properties.

```
{
        saddr spiderweb
        daddr arachnid
} apply { auth_algs any sa unique}
```

If gethostbyname (spiderweb) and gethostbyname (arachnid) yield multiple addresses, multiple policy entries are added for each (saddr daddr) pair with the same properties. Use ipsecconf -l to view all the policy entries added here.

The following example bypasses unauthenticated traffic.

```
#
# Protect all the outbound traffic with ESP except any traffic
# to network-b which should be authenticated and bypass anything
# to network-c
{daddr network-b/16} apply { auth_algs any }
{} apply { encr_algs any sa shared} # NULL pattern
{daddr network-c/16} bypass {dir out}
```

Note — You can specify bypass anywhere and it takes precedence over all other entries. NULL pattern matches all the traffic.

Files

`/etc/inet/ipsecpolicy.conf`

> File containing IPsec policies configured in the system. Maintained by `ipsecconf` command. Do not manually edit this file.

`/etc/inet/ipsecinit.conf`

> File containing IPsec policies that are configured early in the boot. If present, it is read from `/etc/initd.d/inetinit` after `/usr` is mounted.

`/etc/inet/ipsecinit.sample`

> Sample file that you can use as a template to create an `ipsecinit.conf` file.

Attributes

See `attributes(5)` for descriptions of the following attributes.

Attribute Type	Attribute Value
Availability	SUNWcsu
Stability	Evolving

See Also

`ifconfig(1M)`, `init(1M)`, `ipseckey(1M)`, `accept(3SOCKET)`, `connect(3SOCKET)`, `socket(3SOCKET)`, `attributes(5)`, `ipsecah(7P)`, `ipsecesp(7P)`, `tun(7P)`

Glenn, R., and Kent, S. RFC 2410, *The NULL Encryption Algorithm and Its Use With IPsec,* The Internet Society, 1998.

Kent, S. and Atkinson, R., RFC 2402, *IP Authentication Header,* The Internet Society, 1998.

Kent, S., and Atkinson, R., RFC 2406, *IP Encapsulating Security Payload (ESP),* The Internet Society, 1998.

Madsen, C., and Glenn, R., RFC 2403, *The Use of HMAC-MD5-96 within ESP and AH,* The Internet Society, 1998.

Madsen, C., and Glenn, R., RFC 2404, *The Use of HMAC-SHA-1-96 within ESP and AH,* The Internet Society, 1998.

Madsen, C., and Doraswamy, N., RFC 2405, *The ESP DES-CBC Cipher Algorithm With Explicit IV,* The Internet Society, 1998.

Pereira, R., and Adams, R., RFC 2451, *The ESP CBC-Mode Cipher Algorithms,* The Internet Society, 1998.

Diagnostics

```
Bad "string" on line N.
Duplicate "string" on line N.
```

> `string` reflects one of the names in pattern or properties is wrong. `Bad` indicates a malformed argument, and `Duplicate` indicates that there are multiple arguments of similar type, for example, multiple saddr.

```
Error before or at line N.
```
> Parsing error before or at line N.

```
Non-existent index
```
> The index for delete is not a valid one.

```
ioctl: File exists
```
> A policy entry already exists that matches the traffic of this new entry.

ipseckey — Manually Manipulate an IPsec Security Association Database (SADB)

New!

Synopsis
```
ipseckey [-nvp]
ipseckey [-nvp] -f filename
ipseckey [-nvp][delete | get] SA_TYPE {EXTENSION value...}
ipseckey [-np][monitor | passive_monitor | pmonitor]
ipseckey [-nvp] flush {SA_TYPE}
ipseckey [-nvp] dump {SA_TYPE}
ipseckey [-nvp] save SA_TYPE {filename}
ipseckey [-nvp] -s filename
```

Description

The ipseckey command is new in the Solaris 8 release. It is part of the IP security Architecture that provides protection for IP datagrams. Protection can include confidentiality, strong integrity of the data, partial sequence integration (replay protection), and data authentication. Only superuser can run this command.

Use ipseckey to manually manipulate the security association (SA) databases of the network security services, ipsecah(7P) and ipsecesp(7P). You can also use the ipseckey command to set up security associations between communicating parties when automated key management is not available.

ipseckey uses a PF_KEY socket and the message types SADB_ADD, SADB_DELETE, SADB_GET, SADB_UPDATE, SADB_FLUSH, and SADB_X_PROMISE.

ipseckey handles sensitive cryptographic keying information. Please read "Security Considerations" on page 544 for details on how to use this command securely.

Notes

In spite of its IPsec-specific name, ipseckey is analogous to route(1M) in that it is a command-line interface to a socket-based administration engine, in this case, PF_KEY. PF_KEY was originally developed at the United States Naval Research Laboratory.

To have machines communicate securely with manual keying, SAs need to be added by all communicating parties. If two nodes want to communicate securely, both nodes need the appropriate SAs added.

If you do not use the -n option when saving SAs, the resulting name for an address may not directly map to the address of an SA. In the future, ipseckey may be invoked under additional names as other security protocols become available to PF_KEY.

Options

-f [*filename*]

> Read commands from an input file, *filename*. The lines of the input file are identical to the command-line language. The load command provides similar functionality. The -s option or the save command can generate files readable by the -f option.

-n

> Prevent attempts to print host and network names symbolically when reporting actions. This option is useful, for example, when all nameservers are down or are otherwise unreachable.

-p

> Be paranoid and do not print any keying material even if saving SAs. Print an X instead of an actual hexadecimal digit.

-s [*filename*] The opposite of the -f option. Output a snapshot of all current SA tables in a form readable by the -f option. The output is a series of add commands. If you specify a dash (-) for *filename*, direct the output to the standard output.

-v

> Print the messages being sent into the PF_KEY socket and raw seconds values for lifetimes.

Commands

Although the ipseckey command has only a limited number of general options, it supports a rich command language. You can specify requests to be delivered by means of a programmatic interface specific for manual keying. See pf_key(7P). When you invoke ipseckey with no arguments, it enters an interactive mode that prints a prompt to the standard output and accepts commands from the standard input until the end-of-file is reached. Some commands require an explicit security association (SA) type, and others permit the SA type to be unspecified and to act on all SA types.

add

> Add an SA. Because it involves the transfer of keying material, you cannot invoke this command from the command line. The add command accepts all extension-value pairs described "Extension Value Types" on page 541.

update

> Update SA lifetime, and in the cases of larval SAs (left over from faulty automated key management), keying material and other extensions. Like add, you cannot invoke this command from the command line because keying material could be seen by the ps(1) command. The update command accepts all extension-value pairs but normally is used only for SA lifetime updates.

delete

> Delete a specific SA from a specific SADB. This command requires the spi extension, and the dest extension for IPsec SAs. Other extension-value pairs are superfluous for a delete message.

get

> Look up and display a security association from a specific SADB. Like delete, this command requires only spi and dest for IPsec.

flush	Remove all SAs for a given SA_TYPE, or all SAs for all types.
monitor	Continuously report on any PF_KEY messages. This command uses the SADB_X_PROMISC message to enable messages to be received that a normal PF_KEY socket would not receive. See pf_key(7P).
passive monitor	
	Like monitor, except do not use the SADB_X_PROMISC message.
pmonitor	Synonym for passive_monitor.
dump	Display all SAs for a given SA type, or display all SAs. Because of the large amount of data generated by this command, there is no guarantee that all SA information is successfully delivered or that this command even completes.
save	The command analog of the -s option. It is included as a command to provide a way to snapshot a particular SA type, for example, esp or ah.
help	Print a brief summary of commands.

Security Association Types

all	Specify all known SA types. This type is used only for the flush and dump commands. This command is equivalent to having no SA type for these commands.
ah	Specify the IPsec Authentication Header (AH) SA.
esp	Specify the IPsec Encapsulating Security Payload (ESP) SA.

Extension Value Types

Commands like add, delete, get, and update require that you specify certain extensions and associated values. The extensions are listed here, followed by the commands that use them and the commands that require them. Requirements are currently documented according to the IPsec definitions of an SA. Required extensions may change in the future. You can specify *number* in either hex (0x*nnn*), decimal (*nnn*) or octal (0*nnn*). *string* is a text string. *hexstr* is a long hexadecimal number with a bit-length. Extensions are usually paired with values; however, some extensions require two values after them.

spi *number*	Specify the security parameters index of the SA. This extension is required for the add, delete, get, and update commands.
replay *number*	
	Specify the replay window size. If not specified, the replay window size is assumed to be 0. It is not recommended that manually added SAs have a replay window. This extension is used by the add and update commands.

state *string* | *number*

> Specify the SA state, either by numeric value or by the strings larval,
> mature, dying, or dead. If not specified, the value defaults to mature.
> This extension is used by the add and update commands.

auth_alg *string* | *number*
authalg *string* | *number*

> Specify the authentication algorithm for an SA, either by numeric
> value or by strings indicating an algorithm name. Current
> authentication algorithms include the following.
>
> HMAC-MD5   md5, hmac-md5
>
> HMAC-SH-1   sha, sha-1, hmac-sha1, hmac-sha
>
> Often, algorithm names have several synonyms. This extension is
> required by the add command for certain SA types. It is also used by
> the update command.

encr_alg *string* | *number*
encralg *string* | *number*

> Specify the encryption algorithm for an SA, either by numeric value,
> or by strings indicating an algorithm name. Current encryption
> algorithms include DES (des) and Triple-DES (3des). This extension
> is required by the add command for certain SA types. It is also used by
> the update command.

The next six extensions are lifetime extensions. They are of two varieties, hard and
soft. If a hard lifetime expires, the SA is deleted automatically by the system. If a soft
lifetime expires, an SADB_EXPIRE message is transmitted by the system and its state is
downgraded to dying from mature. See pf_key(7P). The monitor command to key
enables you to view SADB_EXPIRE messages.

soft_bytes *number*
hard_bytes *number*

> Specify the number of bytes that this SA can protect. If you do not
> specify *number*, the default value is 0, which means that the SA does
> not expire. This extension is used by the add and update commands.

soft_addtime *number*
hard_addtime *number*

> Specify the number of seconds that this SA can exist after being
> added or updated from a larval SA. An update of a mature SA does
> not reset the initial time that it was added. If you do not specify
> *number*, the default value is 0, which means the SA does not expire.
> This extension is used by the add and update commands.

```
soft_usetime number
hard_usetime number
```

> Specify the number of seconds this SA can exist after first being used. If you do not specify *number*, the default value is 0, which means the SA does not expire. This extension is used by the add and update commands.

```
srcaddr address
src address
```

> Synonyms that indicate the source address of the SA. If unspecified, the source address either remains unset or is set to a wildcard address if a destination address was supplied. This extension is valid for IPsec SAs. Future SA types may alter this assumption. This extension is used by the add, update, get, and delete commands.

```
dstaddr addr
dst addr
```

> Synonyms that indicate the destination address of the SA. If unspecified, the destination address remains unset. Because IPsec SAs require a specified destination address and spi for identification, this extension, with a specific value, is required for the add, update, get, and delete commands.

```
proxyaddr address
proxy address
```

> Synonyms that indicate the proxy address for the SA. A proxy address is used for an SA that is protecting an inner protocol header. The proxy address is the source address of the inner protocol's header. This extension is used by the add and update commands.

```
authkey hexstring
```

> Specify the authentication key for this SA. The key is expressed as a string of hexadecimal digits, with an optional / at the end, for example, 123/12. Bits are counted from the most significant bits down. For example, to express three 1 bits, the proper syntax is the string e/3. For multikey algorithms, the string is the concatenation of the multiple keys. This extension is used by the add and update commands.

```
encrkey hexstring
```

> Specify the encryption key for this SA. The syntax of the key is the same as for authkey. A concrete example of a multikey encryption algorithm is 3des, which would express itself as a 192-bit key, which is three, 64-bit, parity-included DES keys. This extension is used by the add and update commands.

Keying material is very sensitive and should be generated as randomly as possible. Some algorithms have known weak keys. IPsec algorithms have built-in weak key checks, so that if a weak key is in a newly added SA, the add command fails with an invalid value.

Certificate identities are useful in the context of automated key management because they tie the SA to the public key certificates used in most automated key management protocols. They are less useful for manually added SAs. Unlike other extensions, `srcidtype` takes two values, a type, and an actual value. The type can be one of the following.

`prefix`	An address prefix.
`fqdn`	A fully qualified domain name.
`domain`	Domain name, synonym for `fqdn`.
`user_fqdn`	User identity of the form *user@fqdn*.
`mailbox`	Synonym for `user_fqdn`.

The value is an arbitrary text string, which should identify the certificate.

`srcidtype` *type, value*

> Specify a source certificate identity for this SA. This extension is used by the `add` and `update` commands.

`dstidtype` *type, value*

> Specify a destination certificate identity for this SA. This extension is used by the `add` and `update` commands.

Security Considerations

The `ipseckey` command enables a privileged user to enter cryptographic keying information. If an adversary gains access to such information, the security of IPsec traffic is compromised. Take the following issues into account when using the `ipseckey` command.

1. Is the TTY going over a network (interactive mode)?
   - If it is, then the security of the keying material is the security of the network path for this TTY's traffic. Using `ipseckey` over a clear-text `telnet` or `rlogin` session is risky.
   - Even local windows may be vulnerable to attacks where a concealed program that reads window events is present.
2. Is the file accessed over the network or readable to the world (`-f` option)?
   - A network-mounted file can be sniffed by an adversary as it is being read. A world-readable file with keying material in it is also risky.

If your source address is a host that can be looked up over the network and your naming system itself is compromised, then any names used are no longer trustworthy.

Security weaknesses often lie in misapplication of tools, not in the tools themselves. Administrators are urged to be cautious when using `ipseckey`. The safest mode of operation is probably on a console or other hard-connected TTY.

For further thoughts on this subject, see the afterword by Matt Blaze in Bruce Schneier's *Applied Cryptography: Protocols, Algorithms, and Source Code in C.*

Examples

The following example empties out all SAs.

```
# ipseckey flush
#
```

The following example flushes out only IPsec AH SAs.

```
# ipseckey flush ah
#
```

The following example saves all SAs to the standard output.

```
# ipseckey save all
```

The following example saves ESP SAs to the file /tmp/snapshot.

```
# ipseckey save esp /tmp/snapshot
```

The following example deletes an IPsec SA. You need to specify only the SPI and the destination address.

```
# ipseckey delete esp spi 0x2112 dst 224.0.0.1
```

The following example specifies only the destination address and SPI to get information about an IPsec SA.

```
# ipseckey get ah spi 0x5150 dst mypeer
```

The following example uses the ipseckey interactive mode to add and update IPsec SAs.

```
# ipseckey
ipseckey> add ah spi 0x90125 src me.domain.com dst you.domain.com
   authalg md5 authkey 1234567890abcdef1234567890abcdef
ipseckey> update ah spi 0x90125 dst you.domain.com hard_bytes 16000000
ipseckey> exit
#
```

The following example adds an SA in the opposite direction. SAs are unidirectional. To communicate securely, you need to add a second SA in the opposite direction. The peer machine also needs to add both SAs.

```
# ipseckey
ipseckey> add ah spi 0x2112 src you.domain.com dst me.domain.com authalg
   md5 authkey bde359723576fdea08e56cbe876e24ad hard_bytes 16000000
ipseckey> exit
#
```

The following example monitors PF_KEY messages.

```
# ipseckey monitor
```

The following example shows commands in a file that can be parsed with the -f option. The file can contain comment lines.

```
# This sample file flushes out the ESP table and adds a pair of SAs.
#
flush esp
#
### Watch out! I have keying material in this file. See the
### SECURITY CONSIDERATIONS section in this manual page for why this can be
### dangerous.
#
```

```
add esp spi 0x2112 src me.domain.com dst you.domain.com authalg md5 authkey
   bde359723576fdea08e56cbe876e24ad encralg des encrkey be02938e7def2839
   hard_usetime 28800
add esp spi 0x5150 src you.domain.com dst me.domain.com authalg md5
authkey 930987dbe09743ade09d92b4097d9e93
encralg des encrkey 8bd4a52e10127deb hard_usetime 28800
#
## End of file - This is a gratuitous comment
```

Attributes

See `attributes`(5) for descriptions of the following attributes.

Attribute Type	Attribute Value
Availability	SUNWcsu
Stability	Evolving

See Also

`ps(1)`, `ipsecconf(1M)`, `route(1M)`, `attributes(5)`, `ipsec(7P)`, `ipsecah(7P)`, `ipsecesp(7P)`, `pf_key(7P)`

Schnier, B., *Applied Cryptography: Protocols, Algorithms, and Source Code in C.* Second ed. New York, New York: John Wiley & Sons, 1996.

Diagnostics

`Parse error on line N.`

If an interactive use of `ipseckey` would print usage information, this message prints instead. Usually preceded by another diagnostic.

`Unexpected end of command line.`

An additional argument was expected on the command line.

`Unknown`   A value for a specific extension was unknown.

`Address type N not supported.`

A name-to-address lookup returned an unsupported address family.

`is not a bit specifier`

`bit length N is too big for`

`string is not a hex string`

Keying material was not entered appropriately.

`Can only specify single`

A duplicate extension was entered.

`Don't use extension for <string> for <command>.`

An extension not used by a command was used.

K

kadb — Kernel Debugger

Synopsis

SPARC Platform
```
ok boot device-specifier kadb [-d] [boot-flags]
> b kadb [-d] [boot-flags]
```

IA Platform
```
select (b)oot or (i)nterpreter: b kadb [-d] [boot-flags]
select (b)oot or (i)nterpreter: i kadb [-d] [boot-flags]
```

Description

The kadb command is an interactive kernel debugger with a user interface similar to that of adb(1), the assembly language debugger.

You must load kadb before the standalone program it is to debug. kadb runs with the same environment as the standalone program, so it shares many resources with that program. The debugger is aware of and able to control multiple processors, should they be present in a system.

When you start kadb, it requests the default file name from boot(1M), and if loaded noninteractively (without the -d option), it loads the default file name.

On systems that support both 32-bit and 64-bit operating systems, boot(1M) chooses an appropriate default file name for that system. If loaded interactively (by specifying the -d option), kadb prompts with the default file name, which can be changed before continuing. You can specify the default file name on the boot(1M) command line. See boot(1M) for details.

Before loading the 64-bit kernel explicitly, review the information in boot(1M) for restrictions on running the 64-bit kernel on certain configurations.

Unlike adb(1), kadb runs in the same supervisor virtual address space as the program being debugged, although it maintains a separate context. The debugger runs as a coprocess that cannot be killed (no :k command as in adb) or rerun (no :r command as in adb). kadb has no signal control (no :i, :t, or $i commands as in adb), although the keyboard facilities (Control-C, Control-S, and Control-Q) are simulated.

In the case of the UNIX system kernel, the keyboard abort sequence suspends kernel operations and breaks into the debugger. You can disable this behavior with the kbd(1) command, and the keyboard abort sequence may not be the current default on all systems. See kb(7M) for more information.

Because the kernel is composed of the core image file and the set of loadable modules already in memory, kadb can debug all of these by traversing special data structures. kadb uses this feature to enable it to reference any kernel data structure, even if the data resides in a loadable module. kadb sets the -d option by default so the program being debugged can tell it is being watched. If you do not specify this option, kadb loads and immediately runs the default kernel.

Most adb(1) commands function in kadb as they do in adb. As with adb -k, $p works when debugging kernels. The verbs ? and / are equivalent in kadb, because there is only one address space in use.

SPARC Platform

The keyboard abort sequence is L1-A (Stop-A) for the console and BREAK for a serial line.

Once aborted, kadb responds with the following prompt, where *cpu* is the number of the CPU on which kadb is currently executing.

kadb [*cpu*]:

Warning — On a SPARC-based system, kadb cannot reliably single-step over instructions that change the processor status register.

IA Platform

The keyboard abort sequence is CTRL-ALT-D for the console and BREAK for a serial line.

Once aborted, kadb responds with the following prompt, where *cpu* is the number of the CPU on which kadb is currently executing.

kadb [*cpu*]:

Options

    -d   Stop after loading and display the kadb: prompt followed by the name of the default program to debug. You can either press Return to debug the default program or backspace followed by the name of another program to debug.

Operands

    boot-flags   Specify *boot-flags* as arguments to kadb. Pass the specified *boot-flags* to the program being debugged. See boot(1M) for available *boot-flags*.

SPARC Platform Only

device-specifier

> Specify the device from which to load. See monitor(1M).

Usage

Kernel Macros

As with adb(1), you can use kernel macros with kadb, but they cannot be read from a file at runtime. Use the kadb $M command to list all of the built-in kadb macros.

Commands

kadb reads commands from the standard input and displays responses on the standard output. kadb supports the majority of the adb(1) commands. kadb does not support the adb commands :k, :r, :i, :t, or $i. See adb(1).

Additionally, kadb supports the following commands.

[Perform the same function as : e in adb(1) with only one keystroke and no Return (Enter, on IA-based systems).

]   Perform the same function as : s in adb(1) with only one keystroke and no Return (Enter, on IA-based systems).

:a   Set a hardware access (read or write breakpoint by using the processor hardware facilities. The syntax and action for this command are the same as for the : b command in adb, with the following exceptions.

- Trigger the breakpoint if any bytes from the breakpoint for *length* bytes are being accessed. See $1 below for setting the length of a hardware breakpoint.

- Align breakpoints for the length specified. Any address is valid for length 1. Use addresses divisible by 2 for length 2 (short). Use addresses divisible by 4 for length 4 (int).

- Detection of an access breakpoint occurs after completion of the instruction that caused it.

- Use one of the four of hardware breakpoint registers.

- Because this breakpoint does not modify memory locations, this command works on locations that are not in core at the time the breakpoint is set.

@*fmt*   Use in the same manner as the adb / and ? commands. Specify @ as a physical memory address as opposed to the normal virtual address. Specify *fmt* as any of the formats used with the adb / command. This command is useful for displaying memory that may not be mapped, for example, kernel page tables or buffers used for DMA by device drivers.

function :: call *arg1*, *arg2*, *arg3*,...

> Invoke kernel functions with 0 or more arguments. Using this command results in a a response such as the following.
>
> *retval* = *function*(*arg1*,*arg2*,*arg3*,...);
>
> where *retval* is the return value of the function. This feature can be error prone because functions can have side effects that result in failures if the kernel is continued.

:p

> Set a hardware access (read or write) breakpoint, using the processor hardware facilities when an instruction at the specified address is run. The $l operation has no effect on this type of breakpoint. This breakpoint occurs before the instruction is executed.

:P

> Work as :a, but breakpoint only when an access is made to the address in IA I/O space. See :a.

:w

> Set a write hardware access breakpoint, using the processor hardware facilities.

[*length*]$l

> Set the default data length for an access or write breakpoint. You can set *length* to 1 for byte, 2 for short, and 4 for int word accesses. If you do not specify *length*, 1 for byte is assumed. Once set, this value affects any newly set access or write breakpoints but does not affect ones set before this operation.

$b

> Display two additional columns that adb does not offer. The first is the type column, which indicates soft for a normal breakpoint, access for an access hardware breakpoint, write for a write hardware breakpoint, and inst for an instruction hardware breakpoint. The second is the len column, which indicates the length of the operation to break on for access and write breakpoints.

SPARC Platform

$q

> Give control to the boot PROM, from which you can reboot the system.

cpu:x

> Switch the active CPU to *cpu*. Thereafter, commands such as $r and $c display the registers and stack of the new CPU, *cpu*.

IA Platform

port:i

> Input a byte for display from *port*. *port* is an address-specified I/O port. For example, 330:i inputs from address port 330.

port:i8

> Same as the :i command. See :i.

port:i16

> Input two bytes for display from *port*. *port* is an address-specified I/O port.

port:i32

> Input four bytes for display from *port*. *port* is an address-specified I/O port.

port,*data*:o

> Output a byte to *port*. *port* is an address-specified I/O port. [*address*],[*data*]:o outputs the value *data* to *address* I/O port. For example, 330,80:o outputs 80 to address port 330.

port,data:o8 Same as the :o command. See *port,data*:o.

port,data:o16

Output two bytes to *port*. *port* is an address-specified I/O port.

port,data:o32

Output four bytes to *port*. *port* is an address-specified I/O port.

$q Prompt with the following string.

```
Type y if you really want to reboot.
```

Responding with a y or Y reboots the system. Responding with anything other than a y or Y returns control to kadb. Use this feature when you cannot press the reset switch on your system. Because using $q can result in data loss, use this command only when you would press the reset switch or power off your system.

Online Help Commands

::help Display the formats of kadb commands and extended commands.

::? Same as the ::help command. See ::help.

::morehelp Display additional information about commonly used commands, and provide an explanation of data formats.

Scroll Control Feature

num::more A common problem with using kadb is that scrolling is sometimes too fast and that Control-S and Control-Q are inexact. kadb has a conditional scroll control feature similar to more(1). To enable this feature, specify the number of lines to be displayed followed by ::more. For example, the command 14::more displays 14 (current radix) lines, followed by the --More-- prompt. At this prompt, press Enter or Return to display one more line. Press c, C, or Control-C to interrupt the display. Press any other key to display the next *num* number of specified lines (14 in this example). The ::more command displays the current setting for the number of lines that kadb displays before printing the --More-- prompt. The initial scroll control value of this feature is 0, meaning that scrolling is disabled. Once enabled, you can disable the scroll control feature with the 0::more command.

Deferred Breakpoint Feature

Because the kernel is dynamically loaded, all modules may not be loaded when a breakpoint is set. kadb can set deferred breakpoints that are dynamically inserted when the corresponding module is loaded. You must specify both the module and the location when referring to a deferred breakpoint, as follows.

module_name#*location*:

This syntax is implemented for kadb only and uses existing breakpoint commands (for example, ufs#ufs_open:b or ufs#ufs_open+4,5:b).

If the module has been loaded, kadb tries to find the symbol in the specified module. If kadb finds the symbol, it sets a regular breakpoint. If it does not find the symbol, it generates an error message and returns to the command line without setting a breakpoint.

If kadb fails to find the module on the list of currently loaded modules, it does not resolve the location. Instead, it displays a message and sets a deferred breakpoint.

When the specified module is loaded, kadb tries to resolve the location. If the location can be resolved, the deferred breakpoint is converted to a regular breakpoint. If kadb cannot resolve the location, a message is displayed, and kadb halts execution. In this case, kadb does not convert the deferred breakpoint to a regular breakpoint; it removes it from the breakpoint table. You can then reenter a correct breakpoint. Strict scoping is enforced, so kadb does not look at any module other than the one specified with the location.

The output from the $b command indicates whether the breakpoint is of type deferred (defr) or is another type.

Files

/platform/*platform-name*/kadb

> Primary debugger path.

/platform/*hardware-class-name*/kadb

> Alternative debugger path for some platforms.

/platform/*platform-name*/kernel/unix

> Primary default 32-bit kernel.

/platform/*hardware-class-name*/kernel/unix

> Alternative default 32-bit kernel for some platforms.

> **Note —** You can find *platform-name* by using the -i option of uname(1). You can find *hardware-class-name* by using the -m option of uname(1).

Attributes

See attributes(5) for descriptions of the following attributes.

Attribute Type	Attribute Value
Availability	SUNWcar

See Also

adb(1), more(1), uname(1), boot(1M), kernel(1M), attributes(5), kb(7M)

SPARC Platform Only

kbd(1), monitor(1M), obpsym(1M)

Diagnostics

When there is no current command or format, kadb comments about syntax errors, abnormal termination of commands, and the like.

kdmconfig — Configure or Unconfigure Keyboard, Display, and Mouse Options

Synopsis

```
kdmconfig
kdmconfig [-fv][-s hostname] -c | -t | -u |-d filename
```

Description

Use the `kdmconfig` command on IA-based systems to configure or unconfigure the `/etc/openwin/server/etc/OWconfig` file with the keyboard, display, and mouse information relevant to a client's machine for Solaris software. You can also use `kdmconfig` to set up the display, pointer, and keyboard entries in the `bootparams(4)` database on a server machine or the monitor, keyboard, display, and pointer keywords in a `sysidcfg(4)` file. `kdmconfig` can be run only by superuser. On completion of device selection, `kdmconfig` prompts you to test the configuration by running the window system.

The `kdmconfig` program is normally run during installation and on reboot. You can also run it from the command line after the system has been installed. When configuring a client during an initial installation or a reconfigure reboot, the `sysidconfig(1M)` command invokes `kdmconfig` with the `-c` option. When you execute the `sysunconfig(1M)` command, `kdmconfig` is executed with the `-u` option. Similarly, when you run `kdmconfig` from the command line, use the `-u` option to unconfigure the existing OpenWindows configuration. You can then rerun `kdmconfig` with the `-cf` options to create a new OpenWindows configuration. To edit the existing configuration, run `kdmconfig` from the command line without options. After each reboot, `kdmconfig` is invoked by the system with the `-t` (test mode) option to ensure autoconfiguration capability and to identify possible conflicts between the current configuration and the one recorded in the `OWconfig` file.

Options

`-c`	Run the configuration mode. Use this mode to create or update the `OWconfig` file. When invoked in this way, `kdmconfig` first looks for the relevant configuration information in the `bootparams(4)` databases. Unless you also specify the `-s` option, it also takes into account the information returned from device probe. The `bootparams(4)` databases available to the client are all of the `/etc/bootparams` files on servers on the same subnet as the client, provided the server machine is running the `bootparamd(1M)` daemon. `kdmconfig` is invoked with the `-c` option when called by `sysidconfig(1M)`.
`-d filename`	Set up a `sysidcfg(4)` file. This option displays the same screens as the `-c` option but the information you specify is saved as `sysidcfg(4)` keywords (`monitor`, `keyboard`, `display`, and `pointer`). This option enables you to use a `sysidcfg (4)` file to preconfigure a system's device information and bypass `kdmconfig` during an installation.

filename specifies the sysidcfg(4) file that is created in the directory where kdmconfig is being run unless you also specify a path. If *filename* already exists in the specified directory, append the keywords to the existing file.

-f	Force screens mode. Do not probe network. This option is helpful for debugging the client's configuration environment. Note that the -s option implies the use of -f, bypassing network probing when setting up a server.
-s *hostname*	Set up the bootparams(4) database on this system for the specified client. This option presents the same screens as it does when run on a client but writes the resulting information to the /etc/bootparams file. Also, -s implies the use of the -f option. That is, the program always presents the screens when invoked this way. This option reconfigures the nsswitch.conf(4) file to look for a bootparams(4) database on a local server. Only superuser can use this option.
-t	Run the program in test mode. Use device probe information to determine whether the OWconfig file contains complete and up-to-date information about the keyboard, display, and mouse. If the information is accurate, kdmconfig exits silently. Otherwise, it prompts for the superuser password and proceeds to a normal editing session (as though it had been run without options).
-u	Unconfigure the system, returning it to an "out of the box" state. Remove the device configuration entries from the /etc/openwin/server/etc/OWconfig file, returning the configuration to the factory default keyboard, mouse, and display settings. This option can result in an unusable configuration for the display server.
-v	Display verbose output. Normally, kdmconfig does not produce any output. This option is helpful for debugging because it records the different actions taken by kdmconfig on standard error.

No Options

You can run the kdmconfig command with no options to edit the current configuration. kdmconfig uses the information from the OWconfig file in addition to information obtained from the bootparams(4) file and from device probes. In other respects, it is similar to the -c option of kdmconfig.

Files

/etc/openwin/server/etc/OWconfig

> OpenWindows configuration file.

/etc/bootparams

> Contains list of clients that diskless clients use for booting.

/etc/nsswitch.conf

> Nameservice configuration file.

IA Platform Only

`/dev/openprom`

> Installed devices and properties.

Attributes

See `attributes`(5) for descriptions of the following attributes.

Attribute Type	Attribute Value
Architecture	IA
Availability	SUNWos86r

See Also

`bootparamd(1M)`, `sys-unconfig(1M)`, `sysidconfig(1M)`, `bootparams(4)`, `nsswitch.conf(4)`, `sysidcfg(4)`, `attributes(5)`

kerbd — Generate and Validate Kerberos Tickets for Kernel RPC

Synopsis

`/usr/sbin/kerbd [-dg]`

Description

The `kerbd` user-mode daemon interfaces between kernel RPC and the Kerberos key distribution center (KDC) for generating and validating Kerberos authentication tickets. In addition, `kerbd` maps Kerberos user names into local user and group IDs. By default, all groups that the requested user belongs to are included in the `grouplist` credential. `kerbd` is automatically started when the system enters the multiuser state.

Options

-d	Run in debug mode and output information about Kerberos tickets being processed.
-g	Do not initialize the group list in the user credential when mapped from Kerberos' principal name. Include only each user's group from the `passwd` entry in mapped credentials.

Attributes

See attributes(5) for descriptions of the following attributes.

Attribute Type	Attribute Value
Availability	SUNWcsu

See Also

kdestroy(1), kerberos(1), kinit(1), krb.conf(4), attributes(5)

---

kernel — UNIX System Executable File Containing Basic Operating System Services

Synopsis

```
kernel-name [-afsrv]
```

Description

The operating system image, or kernel, is the collection of software made up of the core image files (unix and genunix) and all of the modules loaded at any instant in time. The system does not function without a kernel to control it.

The kernel is loaded by the boot(1M) command in a machine-specific way. The kernel can be loaded from disk or CD-ROM (diskfull boot) or over the network (diskless boot). In either case, the directories under /platform and /kernel must be readable and must contain executable code that is able to perform the required kernel service. If you specify the -a option, you can supply different path names for the default locations of the kernel and modules. See boot(1M) for more information on loading a specific kernel.

If the kernel name is not explicitly specified, then on systems capable of supporting the 64-bit kernel, by default the boot program tries to load the 64-bit kernel in preference to the 32-bit kernel. See boot(1M).

The moddir variable contains a colon-separated list of directories that the kernel searches for modules. You can set moddir in the /etc/system file. The minimal default is /platform/platform-name/kernel:/kernel:/usr/kernel, but this default can be overridden by a specific platform. It is common for many systems to override the default path with /platform/platform-name/kernel:/platform/hardware-classname/kernel:/kernel:/usr/kernel, where platform-name can be found with the -i option of uname(1), and hardware-class-name can be found with the -m option of uname(1).

The kernel configuration can be controlled by the /etc/system file (see system(4)). genunix is the platform-independent component of the base kernel.

Options

-a	Ask for configuration information such as where to find the system file, where to mount root, and even override the name of the kernel itself. Default responses are displayed in square brackets ([ ]) and you can simply press Return to use the default response. (Note that Return is labeled Enter on some keyboards). To help repair a damaged /etc/system file, enter /dev/null at the prompt that asks for the path name of the system configuration file. See system(4).
-f	Flush and reinitialize the client system's local cache for Autoclient systems. Ignore this option for all non-Autoclient systems.
-r	Do a reconfiguration boot by probing all attached hardware devices and assigning nodes in the file system to represent only those devices actually found. Also configure the logical namespace in /dev and the physical namespace in /devices. See add_drv(1M) and rem_drv(1M) for additional information about maintaining device drivers.
-s	Boot only to init level s. See init(1M).
-v	Boot with verbose messages enabled. If you do not specify this option, the messages are still printed but the output is directed to the system logfile. See syslogd(1M).

Examples

See boot(1M) for examples and instructions on how to boot.

Files

/kernel	Contains kernel components common to all platforms within a particular instruction set that are needed for booting the system.
/platform/*platform-name*/kernel	
	The platform-specific kernel components.
/platform/*hardware-class-name*/kernel	
	The kernel components specific to this hardware class.
/usr/kernel	Contains kernel components common to all platforms within a particular instruction set.

The /kernel, /platform/*platform-name*/kernel, /platform/*hardware-class-name*/kernel, and /usr/kernel directories can potentially contain the following subdirectories.

drv	Loadable device drivers.
exec	The modules that execute programs stored in various file formats.
fs	File-system modules.
misc	Miscellaneous system-related modules.
sched	Operating system schedulers.
strmod	System V STREAMS loadable modules.

    sys   Loadable system calls.

SPARC Platform
The subdirectories mentioned in this section can also contain sparcv9 subdirectories that contain 64-bit versions of the same module classes.

    cpu   Processor specific modules.

    tod   Time-Of-Day hardware interface modules.

IA Platform
    mach   IA hardware support.

Attributes
See attributes(5) for descriptions of the following attributes.

Attribute Type	Attribute Value
Availability	SUNWcar, SUNWcarx

See Also
isainfo(1), uname(1), add_drv(1M), boot(1M), init(1M), kadb(1M), rem_drv(1M), savecore(1M), syslogd(1M), system(4), attributes(5)

SPARC Platform Only
monitor(1M)

Diagnostics
The kernel gives various warnings and error messages. If the kernel detects an unrecoverable fault, it panics or halts.

Bugs
Bugs in the kernel often result in kernel panics.
    Reconfiguration boot does not currently remove file system entries for devices that have been physically removed from the system.

keyserv — Server for Storing Private Encryption Keys

Synopsis
/usr/sbin/keyserv [-c] [-d] [-D] [-n] [-s *sizespec*]

Description
The keyserv daemon is used for storing the private encryption keys of each user logged in to the system. These encryption keys are used for accessing secure network services such as secure NFS and NIS+.

Normally, root's key is read from the file `/etc/.rootkey` when the daemon is started. This behavior is useful during power-fail reboots when no one is around to type a password.

Options

`-c`	Do not use disk caches. This option overrides any `-s` option.
`-d`	Disable the use of default keys for `nobody`.
`-D`	Run in debugging mode and log all requests to `keyserv`.
`-n`	Do not read root's secret key from `/etc/.rootkey`. Instead, prompt for the password to decrypt root's key stored in the `publickey` database, and then store the decrypted key in `/etc/.rootkey` for future use. This option is useful if the `/etc/.rootkey` file ever gets out of date or is corrupted.
`-s` *sizespec*	Specify the size of the extended Diffie-Hellman common key disk caches. The *sizespec* can be one of the following forms.

        `mechtype=`*size*   *size* is an integer specifying the maximum number of entries in the cache, or an integer immediately followed by the letter `M`, denoting the maximum size in megabytes.

        size   This form of *sizespec* applies to all caches.

       See `nisauthconf`(1M) for mechanism types. Note that the `des` mechanism, `AUTH_DES`, does not use a disk cache.

Files

`/etc/.rootkey`

        Superuser secret key file.

Attributes

See `attributes`(5) for descriptions of the following attributes.

Attribute Type	Attribute Value
Availability	SUNWcsu

See Also

`keylogin`(1), `keylogout`(1), `nisauthconf`(1M), `publickey`(4), `attributes`(5)

killall — Kill All Active Processes

Synopsis

```
/usr/sbin/killall [signal]
```

Description

The killall command is used by shutdown(1M) to kill all active processes not directly related to the shutdown procedure. killall terminates all processes with open files so that the mounted file systems are unbusied and can be unmounted. killall sends *signal* (see kill(1)) to the active processes. If no signal is specified, a default of 15 is used.

Only superuser can run the killall command.

Attributes

See attributes(5) for descriptions of the following attributes.

Attribute Type	Attribute Value
Availability	SUNWcsu

See Also

kill(1), ps(1), fuser(1M), shutdown(1M), signal(3C), attributes(5)

New! ktkt_warnd — Kerberos Warning Daemon

Synopsis

```
/usr/lib/krb5/ktkt_warnd
```

Description

The ktkt_warnd daemon is new in the Solaris 8 release. It runs on Kerberos clients to warn users when their Kerberos tickets are about to expire. ktkt_warnd is invoked by inetd when a ticket-granting ticket (TGT) is obtained for the first time, such as after using the kinit command. You can configure ktkt_warnd on the client system with the /etc/krb5/warn.conf file.

Examples

The following example shows the default warn.conf file.

```
paperbark% more /etc/krb5/warn.conf
#
# Copyright (c) 1999, by Sun Microsystems, Inc.
# All rights reserved.
```

```
#
#pragma ident   "@(#)warn.conf  1.1     99/07/18 SMI"
#
#   <principal> <syslog|terminal> <time>
#        or
#   <principal> mail <time> <e-mail address>
#
*  terminal 30m
paperbark%
```

Files

/etc/krb5/warn.conf

        Kerberos warning configuration file.

See Also

inetd(1M), warn.conf(4), SEAM(5)

kstat — Display Kernel Statistics

Synopsis

```
/bin/kstat [-lpq][-T u | d][-c class][-m module][-i instance]
   [-n name][-s statistic][interval [count]]
/bin/kstat [-lpq][-T u | d][-c class][module:instance:name:statistic
   ...][interval [count]]
```

Description

Use the kstat command to examine the available kernel statistics—kstats—on the system and to get a report on those statistics that match the criteria specified on the command line. Each matching statistic is printed with its module, instance, and name fields, as well as its actual value.

Various subsystems such as drivers or loadable modules can publish kernel statistics. Each kstat has a *module* field that denotes its publisher. Because each module can have countable entities (such as multiple disks associated with the sd(7D) driver) for which it wants to report statistics, the kstat also has an *instance* field to index the statistics for each entity; kstat instances are numbered starting from 0. Finally, the kstat is given a name unique within its module.

Each kstat can be a special kstat type, an array of name-value pairs, or raw data. In the name-value case, each reported value is given a label, which is referred to as the statistic. Known raw and special kstats are given *statistic* labels for each of their values by kstat; thus, you can reference all published values as *module:instance:name:statistic*.

When invoked without any module operands or options, kstat matches all defined statistics on the system. Example invocations are provided below. All times are displayed as fractional seconds since system boot.

Note — If the pattern argument contains glob or Perl RE metacharacters that are also shell metacharacters, you need to enclose the pattern in appropriate shell quotes.

Options

The tests specified by the following options are logically ANDed, and all matching kstats are selected. You must protect a regular expression containing shell metacharacters from the shell by enclosing it with the appropriate quotes.

You can specify the argument for the -c, -i, -m, -n, and -s options as a shell glob pattern or a Perl regular expression enclosed in \ characters.

c *class*	Display only kstats that match the specified class.
-i *instance*	Display only kstats that match the specified instance.
-l	List matching kstat names without displaying values.
-m *module*	Display only kstats that match the specified module.
-n *name*	Display only kstats that match the specified name.
-p	Display output in parsable format. All example output in this document is given in this format. If you do not specify this option, produce output in a human-readable, table format.
-q	Display no output, but return appropriate exit status for matches against given criteria.
-s *statistic*	Display only kstats that match the specified statistic.
-T d | u	Display a timestamp before each statistics block, either in ctime(3C) format (d) or as an alphanumeric representation of the value returned by time(2) (u).

Operands

module:instance:name:statistic

Alternate method of specifying module, instance, name, and statistic as described above. Each of the module, instance, name, or statistic specifiers can be a shell glob pattern or a Perl regular expression enclosed by \ characters. You can use both specifier types within a single operand. Leaving a specifier empty is equivalent to using the * glob pattern for that specifier.

interval	The number of seconds between reports.
count	The number of reports to be printed.

Examples

In the following examples, all the command lines in a block produce the same output, as shown immediately below. The exact statistics and values, of course, vary from machine to machine.

Example 1

```
$ kstat -p -m unix -i 0 -n system_misc -s 'avenrun*'
$ kstat -p -s 'avenrun*'
$ kstat -p 'unix:0:system_misc:avenrun*'
$ kstat -p ':::avenrun*'
$ kstat -p ':::/^avenrun_+min$/'

unix:0:system_misc:avenrun_15min          3
unix:0:system_misc:avenrun_1min 4
unix:0:system_misc:avenrun_5min 2
```

Example 2

```
$ kstat -p -m cpu_stat -s 'intr*'
$ kstat -p cpu_stat:::/^intr/

cpu_stat:0:cpu_stat0:intr        29682330
cpu_stat:0:cpu_stat0:intrblk     87
cpu_stat:0:cpu_stat0:intrthread 15054222
cpu_stat:1:cpu_stat1:intr        426073
cpu_stat:1:cpu_stat1:intrblk     51
cpu_stat:1:cpu_stat1:intrthread 289668
cpu_stat:2:cpu_stat2:intr        134160
cpu_stat:2:cpu_stat2:intrblk     0
cpu_stat:2:cpu_stat2:intrthread 131
cpu_stat:3:cpu_stat3:intr        196566
cpu_stat:3:cpu_stat3:intrblk     30
cpu_stat:3:cpu_stat3:intrthread 59626
```

Example 3

```
$ kstat -p :::state ':::avenrun*'
$ kstat -p :::state :::/^avenrun/

cpu_info:0:cpu_info0:state        on-line
cpu_info:1:cpu_info1:state        on-line
cpu_info:2:cpu_info2:state        on-line
cpu_info:3:cpu_info3:state        on-line

unix:0:system_misc:avenrun_15min          4
unix:0:system_misc:avenrun_1min 10
unix:0:system_misc:avenrun_5min 3
```

Example 4

```
$ kstat -p 'unix:0:system_misc:avenrun*' 1 3
unix:0:system_misc:avenrun_15min          15
unix:0:system_misc:avenrun_1min 11
unix:0:system_misc:avenrun_5min 21
unix:0:system_misc:avenrun_15min          15
unix:0:system_misc:avenrun_1min 11
unix:0:system_misc:avenrun_5min 21
unix:0:system_misc:avenrun_15min          15
unix:0:system_misc:avenrun_1min 11
unix:0:system_misc:avenrun_5min 21
```

Example 5

```
$ kstat -p -T d 'unix:0:system_misc:avenrun*' 5 2
Thu Jul 22 19:39:50 1999
unix:0:system_misc:avenrun_15min        12
unix:0:system_misc:avenrun_1min 0
unix:0:system_misc:avenrun_5min 11

Thu Jul 22 19:39:55 1999
unix:0:system_misc:avenrun_15min        12
unix:0:system_misc:avenrun_1min 0
unix:0:system_misc:avenrun_5min 11
```

Example 6

```
$ kstat -p -T u 'unix:0:system_misc:avenrun*'
932668656
unix:0:system_misc:avenrun_15min        14
unix:0:system_misc:avenrun_1min 5
unix:0:system_misc:avenrun_5min 18
$
```

Exit Status

0	One or more statistics were matched.
1	No statistics were matched.
2	Invalid command-line options were specified.
3	A fatal error occurred.

Files

/dev/kstat   Kernel statistics driver.

Attributes

See attributes(5) for descriptions of the following attributes.

Attribute Type	Attribute Value
Availability	SUNWcsu

See Also

sh(1), time(2), ctime(3C), gmatch(3GEN), kstat(3KSTAT), attributes(5), kstat(7D), sd(7D), kstat(9S)

L

---

labelit — List or Provide Labels for File Systems

Synopsis

```
/usr/sbin/labelit [-F FSType] [-V] special [operands]
```

Description

Use the `labelit` command to write or display labels on unmounted disk file systems.

Note — This command may not be supported for all FSTypes.

Options

`-F FSType`	Specify the *FSType* on which to operate. Either specify the *FSType* here, or `labelit` should be able to determine it from `/etc/vfstab` by matching *special* with an entry in the table. If no matching entry is found, use the default file-system type specified in `/etc/default/fs`.
`-V`	Echo the complete command line. You can use this option to verify and validate the command line. Additional information obtained from an `/etc/vfstab` lookup is included in the output. The command is not executed.

Operands

If you specify no operands, `labelit` displays the value of the labels.

special	The disk partition (for example, `/dev/rdsk/c0t3d0s6`). The device may not be on a remote machine.
operands	FSType-specific operands. Consult the manual page of the FSType-specific `labelit` command for detailed descriptions.

Note — Although `labelit` accepts either the physical device name (dev/dsk/...) or the raw device name (/dev/rdsk/...) for the *special* argument, it's best to use the raw device name to write directly to the disk.

Examples

The following example uses the `labelit` command with no options to display labels for an unmounted disk. As you can see, the disk is not labeled.

```
# labelit /dev/rdsk/c0t1d0s0
fsname:
volume:
#
```

Usage

See `largefile`(5) for the description of the behavior of `labelit` when encountering files greater than or equal to 2 Gbytes (2**31 bytes).

Exit Status

0	Write or display of labels was successful.
non-zero	An error occurred.

Files

`/etc/vfstab`	List of default parameters for each file system.
`/etc/default/fs`	

Default local file system type. You can set default values for the following flag in `/etc/default/fs`. For example, `LOCAL=ufs`.

LOCAL	The default partition for a command if you specify no FSType.

Attributes

See `attributes`(5) for descriptions of the following attributes.

Attribute Type	**Attribute Value**
Availability	SUNWcsu

See Also

volcopy(1M), vfstab(4), attributes(5), largefile(5)
Manual pages for the FSType-specific modules of labelit

labelit_hsfs — Provide and Print Labels for HSFS File Systems

Synopsis

/usr/sbin/labelit-Fhsfs[*generic-options*][-o*specific-options*]*special*

Description

Use the labelit command to provide labels for unmounted CD-ROM images. You cannot label CD-ROMs themselves, because they are read-only media.

generic-options are options supported by the generic labelit command.

If you specify no *specific-options*, labelit prints the current value of all label fields.

The special name should be the physical disk section (for example, /dev/dsk/c0d0s6).

Options

-o	Use one or more of the following *name*=*value* pairs separated by commas with no intervening spaces to specify values for specific label fields. According to the ISO 9660 specification, you can use only certain sets of character to fill in these labels. Thus, d-*characters* refers to the characters A through Z, the digits 0 through 9, and the underscore (_) character. a-*characters* refers to A through Z, 0 through 9, space, and ! "%&'()*+,-./:;<=>?_.

absfile=	Abstract file identifier, d-*characters*, 37 characters maximum.
applid=	Application identifier, d-*characters*, 128 characters maximum.
bibfile=	Bibliographic file identifier, d-*characters*, 37 characters maximum.
copyfile=	Copyright file identifier, d-*characters*, 128 maximum.
prepid=	Data preparer identifier, d-*characters*, 128 maximum.
pubid=	Publisher identifier, d-*characters*, 128 characters maximum.
sysid=	System identifier, a-*characters*, 32 characters maximum.

`volid=`	Volume identifier, d-*characters*, 32 characters maximum.
`volsetid=`	Volume set identifier, d-*characters*, 128 characters maximum.

Attributes

See `attributes`(5) for descriptions of the following attributes.

Attribute Type	Attribute Value
Availability	SUNWcsu

See Also

`labelit`(1M), `volcopy`(1M), `attributes`(5)

New! **labelit_udfs** — Provide and Print Labels for UDF File System

Synopsis

`/usr/sbin/labelit -F udfs [`*generic-options*`]` *special* `[`*fsname volume*`]`

Description

The `labelit_udfs` command is new in the Solaris 8 release. Use it to write labels on an unmounted disk that contains a universal disk file (`udf`) system. These labels can be used to identify volumes.

Options

generic-options

Specify *generic-options* supported by the generic `labelit` command. See `labelit`(1M) for descriptions of supported options.

Operands

special	The physical disk slice, for example, `/dev/rdsk/c0t0d0s6`. The device cannot be on a remote machine.
fsname	The mount point (for example, `/`, `u1`, and so forth) of the file system.
volume	The physical volume name.
	If you do not specify *fsname* or *volume*, `labelit` prints the current values of these labels.

Exit Status

0	Successful completion.
non-zero	An error occurred.

Attributes

See attributes(5) for descriptions of the following attributes.

Attribute Type	Attribute Value
Availability	SUNWudf

See Also

labelit(1M), attributes(5)

labelit_ufs — Provide and Print Labels for UFS File Systems

Synopsis

/usr/sbin/labelit -F ufs [*generic-options*] *special* [*fsname volume*]

Description

Use labelit to write labels on unmounted disk file systems. You can use such labels to uniquely identify volumes, and they are used by volume-oriented programs such as volcopy(1M).

Options

generic-options

Options supported by the generic labelit command. See labelit(1M).

Operands

special	The physical disk section (for example, /dev/dsk/c0d0s6). The device cannot be on a remote machine.
fsname	The mount point (for example, /, u1, and so on) of the file system. *fsname* is limited to six or fewer characters.
volume	The physical volume name. *volume* is limited to six or fewer characters.

If you do not specify *fsname* and *volume*, labelit prints the current values of these labels.

Exit Status

0	Write or display of labels was successful.
non-zero	An error occurred.

Attributes

See attributes(5) for descriptions of the following attributes.

Attribute Type	**Attribute Value**
Availability	SUNWcsu

See Also

labelit(1M), volcopy(1M), fs_ufs(4), attributes(5)

lastlogin — Show the Last Date on Which Each Person Logged In

Synopsis

/usr/lib/acct/lastlogin

Description

See acctsh(1M).

New! ldap_cachemgr — LDAP Daemon to Cache Server and Client Information for NIS Lookups

Synopsis

/usr/lib/ldap/ldap_cachemgr [-g] [-l *log-file*] [-r *revalidate-interval*]

Description

The ldap_cachemgr command is new in the Solaris 8 release. It is a process that provides an up-to-date configuration cache for Lightweight Directory Access Protocol (LDAP) naming services. ldap_cachemgr is started during a multiuser boot.

The ldap_cachemgr command provides caching for all parameters as specified and used by the LDAP naming service clients. The ldap_cachemgr command uses the cache files as cold start files that are originally created by the ldapclient(1M) command. Updates to the cache files take place dynamically if profiles are used.

The ldap_cachemgr command helps improve the performance of the clients that are using LDAP as the naming service repository. Although it is not required that the ldap_cachemgr daemon be running for LDAP naming requests to be serviced, it is strongly recommended that it be run on all machines. It not only improves the performance on both clients and the server(s) but also improves system security by making the credential file readable by superuser only.

The cache maintained by this daemon is shared by all the processes that access LDAP naming information. All processes access this cache through a door call. On startup, ldap_cachemgr initializes the cache from the cache files (see ldapclient(1M) Thus, the cache survives machine reboots.

The ldap_cachemgr daemon is normally started from a system startup script.

The ldap_cachemgr command also acts as its own administration tool. If an instance of ldap_cachemgr is already running, commands are passed transparently to the running version.

Warning — The ldap_cachemgr command is included in the Solaris 8 release on an uncommitted basis only and is subject to change or removal in a future minor release.

Options

-g
: Print current configuration and statistics to standard output. This option is the only one that you can execute without superuser privileges.

-l log-file
: Use a log file other than the default /var/ldap/cachemgr.log.

-r *revalidate-interval*
: Override the built-in default refresh interval. When the refresh interval expires, update the cache files. The default for this value is 600 seconds. You can override this value from the server profile (see ldapclient(1M)).

Examples

The following example stops and restarts the ldap_cachemgr daemon.

```
# /etc/init.d/ldap.client stop
# /etc/init.d/ldap.client start
#
```

The following example forces ldap_cachemgr to reread the /var/ldap/ldap_client_cache and /var/ldap/ldap_client_cred files.

```
example# ps -efl | grep ldap
8 S     root 10923     1  0 71 20         ?     318
? 11:01:42 ?          0:00 ./ldap_cachemgr
   $
# kill -HUP 10923
#
```

Files

/var/ldap/ldap_client_cache

> Cold start file for the ldap_cachemgr daemon.

/var/ldap/ldap_client_cred

> Credential file as created by ldapclient(1M).

Attributes

See attributes(5) for descriptions of the following attributes.

Attribute Type	Attribute Value
Availability	SUNWnisu

See Also

ldap(1), ldapclient(1M), attributes(5)

New! ldapclient, ldap_gen_profile — Initialize LDAP Client Machine or Create an LDIF of an LDAP Client Profile

Synopsis

```
/usr/sbin/ldapclient [-v] -P profile-name [-d domainname]
   LDAP-server-addr
/usr/sbin/ldapclient -i | -m [-O][-v][-a none | simple | cram_md5]
   [-b baseDN][-B alternate-search-dn][-d domainname][-D Bind-DN]
   [-e client-TTL][-o timeout-value][-p server-preference]
   [-r follow-referrals][-w client-password] LDAP-server-addr...
/usr/sbin/ldapclient -l
/usr/sbin/ldapclient -u [-v]
/usr/sbin/ldap_gen_profile -P profile-name [-O][-a none | simple |
   cram_md5][-b baseDN][-B alternate-search-dn][-d domainname]
   [-D Bind-DN][-e client-TTL][-o timeout-value][-p server-preference]
   [-r follow-referrals][-w client-password] LDAP-server-addr...
```

Description

The ldapclient command is new in the Solaris 8 release. You can use it for the following tasks.

- To initialize Lightweight Directory Access Protocol (LDAP) client machines.
- To restore the network service environment on LDAP clients.
- To list the contents of the LDAP client cache in human-readable format.

Use the ldap_gen_profile command to create (on the standard output) an LDIF file that can be loaded into an LDAP server to be used as the client profile, which can be downloaded by ldapclient.

Use the synopsis (-P *profile-name*) to initialize an LDAP client machine, using a profile stored on an LDAP server specified by *LDAP-server-addr*. This method is the simplest and provides the default format with all the correct settings for talking to the set of servers. It also ensures that the ldap_cachemgr(1M) can automatically update the configuration file as it changes.

Use the second synopsis (-i | -m) to initialize an LDAP client machine. Use the -i option to convert machines to use LDAP or to change the machine's domain name. It assigns a default value for the required parameters if you do not specify them. You must be logged in as superuser on the machine that is to become an LDAP client. Use the m option to modify the parameters in the cache file. It updates the specified parameter.

You can use the -i option with the -a none option to initialize an unauthenticated LDAP client machine without having to specify a password.

If the authentication method such as simple or cram_md5 requires a password and you do not specify one with the -w *client-password* option, you are prompted for the password. If one is not provided, the command fails.

During the client initialization process, files that are being modified are backed up as *files*.orig. The following files are usually modified during a client initialization.

- /etc/defaultdomain.
- /etc/nsswitch.conf.
- If they exist, /var/yp/binding/`domainname` for an NIS(YP) client or /var/nis/NIS_COLD_START for an NIS+ client.
- If the machine is already an LDAP client, /var/ldap/ldap_client_cache and /var/ldap/ldap_client_cred.

Note — A file is not saved if a backup file already exists.

The -i option does not set up an LDAP client to resolve host names using DNS. Refer to the DNS documentation for information on setting up DNS. See resolv.conf(4).

Use the third synopsis (-l) to list the LDAP client cache. The output is human-readable (cache files are not guaranteed to be human readable.)

Use the fourth synopsis (-u) to uninitialize the network service environment, restoring it to the one in use before ldapclient -i was executed. You must be logged in as superuser on the machine that is to be restored. The restoration succeeds only if the machine was initialized with ldapclient -i because it uses the backup files created by the -i option.

Reboot the machine after initializing it or restoring the network service.

Options

-a none | simple | cram_md5

>   Specify the authentication method. You can specify multiple values as a comma-separated list. The default value is none. If you specify simple or cram_md5, you must provide a password (see -w).

-b *baseDN*   Specify search *baseDN* (for example, dc=eng,dc=sun,dc=com). The default is the root naming context on the first server specified.

-B *alternate-search-dn*

>   Specify alternative baseDN for LDAP searches (for example, ou=people,dc=corp,dc=sun,dc=com). You can define an alternative search *baseDN* for each database possible in the

/etc/nsswitch.conf file (see nsswitch.conf(4)). To remove a specific alternate *baseDN*, specify the database without any argument (for example, passwd:). The default value for all databases is NULL.

-d *domainname*

Specify the domain name (which becomes the default-domain for the machine). The default is the current domain name.

-D *Bind-DN*   Specify the Bind Distinguished Name (for example, cn=proxyagent,ou=profile,cd=eng,dc=sun,dc=com).

-e*client-TTL*   Specify the TTL value for the client information. This option is relevant only if the machine was initialized with a client profile. Set *client-TTL* to 0 (zero) if you do not want ldap_cachemgr to try an automatic refresh from the servers. Specify the times with either 0 (for no expiration) or a positive integer and either d for days, h for hours, m for minutes, or s for seconds. The default is 12h.

-i   Initialize client.

-l (ell)   List the contents of the LDAP client cache. The output (sent to standard output) is meant to be easily readable (the direct contents of the cache files might not be easily readable).

-m   Modify parameters in the configuration file.

-o *timeout-value*

Specify LDAP operation timeout value. The default is the TCP default (usually 3 minutes.)

-O   Inform the client to contact only the servers on the preferred list (if, for instance, they are at the wrong end of a WAN). The default is FALSE.

-p *server-preference*

Specify the server preference list (for example, 129.100.100.0:8080,129.100.200.1:386). You can define the preferred servers either by the server specific address or by the subnet in which the server resides. To remove the server preference, specify " " for the -p option. The default preference is the local subnet.

-P *profile-name*

Specify a profile that is downloaded from the server and sets all the entries automatically. This option also sets an expiration time that ldap_cachemgr can use to automatically update the file if needed. The default *profile-name* is default and is stored in the Bind Distinguished Name. The profile name is also stored in the cache file.

-r *follow-referrals*

Specify the search referral option, either followref or noref. The default is followref.

-u   Uninitialize LDAP client. This option is appropriate only if ldapclient was used to initialize the client.

-v   Specify verbose mode.

-w *client-password*

Specify the client password for `simple` and `cram_md5` authentication modes. This option is not required if the authentication mode is `none`.

Operands

LDAP-server-addr

Server address (for example, `129.100.100.1:389`, `129.100.200.1`). The port number is optional; if not specified, use the default LDAP server port number: `389`.

Examples

The following example sets up a client, using the default profile stored on the specified server. This profile should list all the correct values for talking to your domain.

```
# ldapclient -P default 129.100.100.1
```

The following example sets up a client, using only one server and with authentication mode of `none`.

```
# ldapclient -i -a none 129.100.100.1
```

The following example sets up a client using only one server and with authentication mode of `cram_md5`, with a client password of `secret`, with the domain information expiring once a week, with no search dereference, with the domain name `xyz.sun.com.`, and with the LDAP server running on port number `386` at IP address `129.100.100.1`.

```
# ldapclient -i -a cram_md5 -w secret -d xyz.sun.com.
    -r noref 129.100.100.1:386
```

The following example sets up an LDAP client, using two servers and with an authentication mode of `simple`. The user is then prompted for a client password.

```
# ldapclient -i 129.100.100.1 129.100.234.15:386
```

The following example sets up an LDAP client with authentication mode of `none` that does not try an encrypt the transport with SSL and talks to only one server.

```
# ldapclient -i -a none -a 129.140.44.1
```

The following example uses `ldap_gen_profile` to set only the Base DN and the server addresses, using all possible default values.

```
# ldap_gen_profile -D cn=proxyagent,ou=profile,cd=eng,dc=sun,dc=com
    129.100.100.1 129.100.234.15:386 > ldif_profile
```

The following example creates a profile overriding every default value.

```
# ldap_gen_profile -P eng -a cram_md5 -d ge.co.uk -w test123
    -b dc=eng,dc=ge-uk,dc=com -B ou=people,dc=lab,dc=ge-uk,dc=com
    -D cn=proxyagent,ou=profile,cd=eng,dc=ge-uk,dc=com -r noref
    -e 1h 204.34.5.6 > ldif_profile
```

Files

/var/ldap/ldap_client_cache

> Contains a list of servers, their transport addresses, and the security method used to access them.

/var/ldap/ldap_client_cred

> Contains Bind Distinguished Name (see -D) and the encrypted password.

/etc/defaultdomain

> System default domain name, matching the domain name of the "NIS data" in the LDAP servers.

/etc/nsswitch.conf

> Configuration file for the nameservice switch.

/etc/nsswitch.ldap

> Sample configuration file that uses files and ldap.

Attributes

See attributes(5) for descriptions of the following attributes.

Attribute Type	Attribute Value
Availability	SUNWnisu

See Also

ldap(1), ldapadd(1), ldapdelete(1), ldaplist(1), ldapmodify(1), ldapmodrdn(1), ldapsearch(1), ldap_cachemgr(1M), suninstall(1M), resolv.conf(4), attributes(5)

---

link, unlink — Link and Unlink Files and Directories

Synopsis

```
/usr/sbin/link existing-file new-file
/usr/xpg4/bin/link existing-file new-file
/usr/sbin/unlink file
```

Description

Use the link and unlink commands to link and unlink files and directories. Only superuser can use these commands.

Use link to create a new file that points to an existing file. The *existing-file* and *new-file* operands specify the existing file and newly-created files.

link and unlink directly invoke the link(2) and unlink(2) system calls, performing exactly what they are told to do and abandoning all error checking. This behavior differs from the ln(1) command. See ln(1).

Although you can remove linked files and directories by using unlink, it is safer to use rm(1) and rmdir(1) instead. See rm(1) and rmdir(1).

/usr/xpg4/bin/link

Now!

The /usr/xpg4/bin/link command is new in the Solaris 8 release. If the existing file being hard-linked is a symbolic link, then the newly created file (*new-file*) is a hard link to the file referenced by the symbolic link, not to the symbolic link object itself (*existing-file*).

You might prefer to use the ln command instead of link and unlink because link does little or no error checking and cannot create symbolic links, and unlink has been known to produce undesirable results.

Operands

existing-file

The name of the existing file to be linked.

file   The name of the file to be unlinked.

new-file   The name of newly created (linked) file.

Environment Variables

See environ(5) for descriptions of the following environment variables that affect the execution of link: LANG, LC_ALL LC_CTYPE, LC_MESSAGES, and NLSPATH.

Attributes

See attributes(5) for descriptions of the following attributes.

/usr/bin/link

Attribute Type	Attribute Value
Availability	SUNWcsu

/usr/xcu4/bin/link

New!

Attribute Type	Attribute Value
Availability	SUNWxcu4

See Also

ln(1), rm(1), link(2), unlink(2), attributes(5), environ(5)

list_devices — List Allocatable Devices

Synopsis

```
/usr/sbin/list_devices [-s][-U uid] -l [device]
/usr/sbin/list_devices [-s][-U uid] -n [device]
/usr/sbin/list_devices [-s][-U uid] -u [device]
```

Description

Use the list_devices command to list the allocatable devices in the system according to specified qualifications.

The device and all device special files associated with the device are listed. The *device* argument is optional and if it is not present, all relevant devices are listed.

Note — The functionality described in this manual page is available only if the Basic Security Module (BSM) has been enabled. See bsmconv(1M) for more information.

Options

-l [*device*]   List the path name(s) of the device special files associated with the device that are allocatable to the current process. If you specify *device*, list only the files associated with the specified device.

-n [*device*]   List the path name(s) of device special files associated with the device that are allocatable to the current process but are not currently allocated. If you specify *device*, list only the files associated with that device.

-s   Suppress any diagnostic output.

-u [*device*]   List the path name(s) of device special files associated with the device that are allocated to the owner of the current process. If you specify *device*, list only the files associated with that device.

-U *uid*   Use the user ID *uid* instead of the real user ID of the current process when performing the list_devices operation. Only superuser can use this option.

Examples

The following example uses the -l option to list the device special files associated with the device that are allocatable to the current process.

```
paperbark% list_devices -l
device: audio type: audio files: /dev/audio /dev/audioctl /dev/sound/0
    /dev/sound/0ctl
device: sr0 type: sr files: /dev/sr0 /dev/rsr0 /dev/dsk/c0t6d0s0
    /dev/dsk/c0t6d0s1 /dev/dsk/c0t6d0s2 /dev/dsk/c0t6d0s3
    /dev/dsk/c0t6d0s4 /dev/dsk/c0t6d0s5 /dev/dsk/c0t6d0s6
    /dev/dsk/c0t6d0s7 /dev/rdsk/c0t6d0s0 /dev/rdsk/c0t6d0s1
    /dev/rdsk/c0t6d0s2 /dev/rdsk/c0t6d0s3 /dev/rdsk/c0t6d0s4
```

        /dev/rdsk/c0t6d0s5 /dev/rdsk/c0t6d0s6 /dev/rdsk/c0t6d0s7
    paperbark%

Diagnostics

    list_devices returns a non-zero exit status in the event of an error.

Files

    /etc/security/device_allocate

            File that contains mandatory access control information about each
            physical device.

    /etc/security/device_maps

            File that contains access control information about each physical
            device.

    /etc/security/dev/*

            Security device directory.

    /usr/security/lib/*

            Security library directory.

Attributes

    See attributes(5) for descriptions of the following attributes.

Attribute Type	Attribute Value
Availability	SUNWcsu

See Also

    allocate(1M), bsmconv(1M), deallocate(1M), device_allocate(4),
    device_maps(4), attributes(5)

listdgrp — List Members of a Device Group

Synopsis

    /usr/bin/listdgrp dgroup...

Description

    Use the listdgrp command to display the members of the device groups specified by the
    dgroup list.

Examples

The following example lists the devices that belong to the group partitions.

```
castle% listdgrp partitions
root
swap
usr
castle%
```

Exit Status

0	Successful completion.
1	Command syntax was incorrect, an invalid option was used, or an internal error occurred.
2	A device group table could not be opened for reading.
3	A device group *dgroup* could not be found in the device group table.

Files

/etc/dgroup.tab

Device group table.

Attributes

See attributes(5) for descriptions of the following attributes.

Attribute Type	**Attribute Value**
Availability	SUNWcsu

See Also

putdgrp(1M), attributes(5)

listen — Network Listener Daemon

Synopsis

/usr/lib/saf/listen [-m *devstem*] *net-spec*

Description

The listen process listens to a network for service requests, accepts requests when they arrive, and invokes servers in response to those service requests. The network listener process can be used with any connection-oriented network (more precisely, with any connection-oriented transport provider) that conforms to the Transport Layer Interface (TLI) Specification.

The listener internally generates a path name for the minor device for each
connection; it is this path name that is used in the utmpx entry for a service (changed
from utmp in the Solaris 8 release) if one is created. By default, this path name is the
concatenation of the prefix /dev/netspec with the decimal representation of the minor
device number. In either case, the representation of the minor device number is at least
two digits (for example, 05 or 27) or longer when it is necessary to accommodate minor
device numbers larger than 99.

Notes

When a connection is passed to a standing server, the user and group IDs contained in
the strrecvfd structure are those for the listener (that is, they both are 0); the user
name under which the service was registered with the listener is not reflected in these
IDs.

When multiple instances of the listener are operating on a single transport provider,
there is a potential race condition in the binding of addresses during initialization of the
listeners if any of their services have dynamically assigned addresses. This condition
would appear as an inability of the listener to bind a static-address service to its
otherwise valid address, and would result from a dynamic-address service having been
bound to that address by a different instance of the listener.

Server Invocation

When a connection indication is received, the listener creates a new transport endpoint
and accepts the connection on that endpoint. Before giving the file descriptor for this
new connection to the server, any designated STREAMS modules are pushed and the
configuration script is executed (if one exists). This file descriptor is appropriate for use
with either TLI (see t_sync(3N)) or the sockets interface library.

By default, a new instance of the server is invoked for each connection. When the
server is invoked, file descriptor 0 refers to the transport endpoint, and is open for
reading and writing. File descriptors 1 and 2 are copies of file descriptor 0; no other file
descriptors are open. The service is invoked with the user and group IDs of the user
name under which the service was registered with the listener and with the current
directory set to the HOME directory of that user.

Alternatively, a service may be registered so that the listener passes connections to a
standing server process through a FIFO or a named STREAM instead of invoking the
server anew for each connection. In this case, the connection is passed in the form of a
file descriptor that refers to the new transport endpoint. Before the file descriptor is sent
to the server, the listener interprets any configuration script registered for that service
using doconfig(3N), although doconfig is invoked with both the NORUN and NOASSIGN
flags. The server receives the file descriptor for the connection in a strrecvfd structure
by using an I_RECVFD ioctl(2).

For more details about the listener and its administration, see nlsadmin(1M).

Options

    -M *devstem*   Use *devstem* as the prefix for the path name.

Files

    /etc/saf/pmtag/*

                Port monitor tags directory.

Attributes

See `attributes`(5) for descriptions of the following attributes.

Attribute Type	Attribute Value
Availability	SUNWcsu

See Also

nlsadmin(1M), pmadm(1M), sac(1M), sacadm(1M), ioctl(2), doconfig(3N),
nlsgetcall(3N), nlsprovider(3N), t_sync(3N), attributes(5), streamio(7I)
System Administration Guide, Volume I

New! llc2_loop — Loopback Diagnostics to Test the Driver, Adapter, and Network

Synopsis

```
/usr/lib/llc2/llc2_loop2 [-v] ppa
/usr/lib/llc2/llc2_loop3 ppa sap frames
/usr/lib/llc2/llc2_loop3 ppa type frames
/usr/lib/llc2/llc2_loop4 [-v] ppa
```

Description

The loopback diagnostics commands are new in the Solaris 8 release.

Loop 2

Use the `llc2_loop2` command to determine who is listening and can receive frames sent out from a node. The verbose (-v) option displays the MAC address of responding nodes. All possible responders may not be displayed because the `llc2_loop2` test waits for responses only for 2 seconds, but during this time 50-200 nodes may be displayed. The `llc2_loop` test sends a null XID frame to the broadcast (all 1's) destination MAC address. The source SAP (Service Access Point) value used is 0x04 (SNA's SAP). Therefore, if SNA is running on the system, the `llc2_loop2` test fails. The destination SAP value is the null SAP (0x00). The most likely error is

Unexpected DLPI primitive x, expected y. where x = 5 and y = 6. From
/usr/include/sys/dlpi.h, the expected return value from one of the
DLPI primitives is 6 (DL_OK_ACK), but instead a 5 (DL_ERROR_ACK)
was received.

This error can occur for two reasons.

- The `llc2_loop2` command was issued to a nonexistent PPA (Physical Point of Attachment).
- The SAP (0x04) is already in use (for example, the SNA subsystem is up).

Note — For information about how to start the service, see `llc2`(7)

Loop 3

Use the llc2_loop3 command along with data capture either on the local node or another node on the same LAN to verify the transmission of data. The llc2_loop3 command sends 1,495 byte Unnumbered Information (UI) frames to the null (all 0's) destination MAC address. The *ppa* argument specifies the adapter on which to run the test. The *ppa* is the relative physical position of the adapter; you can ascertain it by viewing the adapter configuration (see llc2_config(1)). For Token Ring or Ethernet, specify an even *sap* value from 2 through 254, or, for Ethernet only, any type value from 1519 (0x05ef) through 65535 (0xffff). It is advisable to pick a value that is easily recognized when you view the data capture output. *frames* is the decimal number of 1,495 bytes packets to transmit. The test displays a message only if a failure occurs.

Loop 4

Use the llc2_loop4 command to find out who is listening and can receive frames sent out from a node. The verbose (-v) option displays the MAC address of responding nodes. All possible responders may not be displayed because the llc2_loop4 command waits for responses only for 2 seconds, but during this time 50-200 nodes can be displayed. The llc2_loop command sends a TEST frame (no information field) to the broadcast (all 1's) destination MAC address. The source SAP value used is 0x04 (SNA's SAP). Therefore, if SNA is running on the system, the loop4 test fails. The destination SAP value is the null SAP (0x00). The loop4 test displays information similar to the following example if other nodes are listening and respond (verbose mode).

```
-Attaching
        -Binding
        -Sending TEST
        -Responders
                    1-0000c0c12449
                    2-08000e142990
                    3-08000e142a51
                    4-0000c0450044
                    5-0000c0199e46
        Unbinding
-Detaching
5 nodes responding
```

The errors displayed are the same as for llc2_loop2.

Options

-v   Display the MAC address of responding nodes.

Operands

ppa   The physical point of attachment.

sap   The service access point. Specify an even *sap* value from 2 through 254, or for Ethernet only, any type value from 1519 (0x05ef) through 65535 (0xffff).

frames   The decimal number of 1,495 bytes packets to transmit.

Attributes

See attributes(5) for descriptions of the following attributes.

Attribute Type	Attribute Value
Availability	SUNWllc

See Also

llc2_config(1), llc2(4), attributes(5), llc2(7)

lockd — Network Lock Daemon

Synopsis

/usr/lib/nfs/lockd [-g *graceperiod*][-t *timeout*][*nthreads*]

Description

The lockd daemon is part of the NFS lock manager, which supports record locking operations on NFS files. See fcntl(2) and lockf(3C). The lock manager provides two functions.

- It forwards fcntl(2) locking requests for NFS-mounted file systems to the lock manager on the NFS server.
- It generates local file locking operations in response to requests forwarded from lock managers running on NFS client machines.

State information kept by the lock manager about these locking requests can be lost if the lockd is killed or the operating system is rebooted. Some of this information can be recovered as follows. When the server lock manager restarts, it waits for a grace period for all client-side lock managers to submit reclaim requests. Client-side lock managers, on the other hand, are notified by the status monitor daemon, statd(1M), of the restart and promptly resubmit previously granted lock requests. If the lock daemon fails to secure a previously granted lock at the server site, then it sends SIGLOST to a process.

Options

-g *graceperiod*

Specify the number of seconds that clients have to reclaim locks after the server reboots. The default is 45 seconds.

-t *timeout* Specify the number of seconds to wait before retransmitting a lock request to the remote server. The default value is 15 seconds.

  nthreads   Specify the maximum number of concurrent threads that the server can handle. This concurrency is achieved by up to *nthreads* threads created as needed in the kernel. *nthreads* should be based on the load expected on this server. If you do not specify *nthreads*, the maximum number of concurrent threads defaults to 20.

Attributes

See attributes(5) for descriptions of the following attributes.

Attribute Type	Attribute Value
Availability	SUNWcsu

See Also

statd(1M), fcntl(2), lockf(3C), attributes(5)

lockfs — Change or Report File-System Locks

Synopsis

/usr/sbin/lockfs [-adefhnuw] [-c *string*] [*filesystem*...]

Description

Use the lockfs command to change and report the status of file system locks. lockfs reports the lock status and unlocks the file systems that were improperly left locked by an application such as ufsdump(1M). This condition could occur if ufsdump(1M) is killed using kill(1).

  Using lockfs to lock a file system is discouraged because it requires extensive knowledge of SunOS internals to be used effectively and correctly.

  When invoked with no arguments, lockfs lists the UFS file systems that are locked. If you do not specify *filesystem* and specify -a, lockfs is run on all mounted, UFS-type file systems.

Options

You must be superuser to use any of the following options with the exception of -a.

  -a   Apply command to all mounted, UFS-type file systems. With this option, ignore the *filesystem* operand.

  -c *string* Accept a string that is passed as the comment field. The -c option takes effect only when the lock is being set with the -d, -h, -n, -u, or -w option.

  -d   Delete-lock (dlock) the specified file system. Suspend access that could remove directory entries.

-e	Error-lock (`elock`) the specified file system. Block all local access to the locked file system and return `EWOULDBLOCK` on all remote access. UFS elocks file systems on detection of internal inconsistency. You can unlock them only after successful repair by `fsck`, which is usually done automatically (see `mount_ufs`(1M)). You can unmount elocked file systems.
-f	Flush all transactions out of the log and write the transactions to the master file system. This option is valid only if logging has been enabled on the file system.
-h	Hard-lock (`hlock`) the specified file system. Return an error on every access to the locked file system, and prohibit unlocking. You can unmount hlocked file systems.
-n	Name-lock (`nlock`) the specified file system. Suspend accesses that could change or remove existing directories entries.
-u	Unlock (`ulock`) the specified file system. Awaken suspended accesses.
-w	Write-lock (`wlock`) the specified file system. Suspend writes that would modify the file system. Do not keep access times while a file system is write-locked.

Operands

`filesystem`   A list of path names separated by white spaces.

Usage

See `largefile`(5) for the description of the behavior of `lockfs` when encountering files greater than or equal to 2 Gbytes (2**31 bytes).

Examples

In the following examples, `Filesystem` is the path name of the mount directory (mount point). `Locktype` is one of `write`, `name`, `delete`, `hard`, or `unlock`. When enclosed in parentheses, the lock is being set. `Comment` is a string set by the process that last issued a lock command.

The following example shows the output of `lockfs` when you specify only the `-a` option.

```
# lockfs -a
Filesystem    Locktype        Comment
/             unlock
/var          unlock
#
```

The following example uses the `lockfs -w` option to write-lock the `/var` file system and set the comment string with the `-c` option. It then uses the `-a` option on a separate command line to display the results of the previous command.

```
# /usr/sbin/lockfs -w -c "lockfs: write lock example" /var
# /usr/sbin/lockfs -a
Filesystem              Locktype        Comment
/                       unlock
```

```
/var                    write                lockfs: write lock example
#
```

The following example uses the `lockfs -u` option to unlock the `/var` file system and sets the comment string with the `-c` option.

```
# /usr/sbin/lockfs -uc "lockfs: unlock example" /var
# /usr/sbin/lockfs /var
Filesystem              Locktype             Comment
/var                    unlock               lockfs: unlock example
#
```

Attributes

See `attributes`(5) for descriptions of the following attributes.

Attribute Type	Attribute Value
Availability	SUNWcsu

See Also

`kill`(1), `mount_ufs`(1M), `ufsdump`(1M), `fs_ufs`(4), `attributes`(5), `largefile`(5)
System Administration Guide, Volume I

Diagnostics

`file system: Not owner`

You must be root to use this command.

`file system: Deadlock condition detected/avoided`

A file is enabled for accounting or swapping, on file system.

`file system: Device busy`

Another process is setting the lock on file system.

lockstat — Report Kernel Lock Statistics

Synopsis

```
/usr/sbin/lockstat [-ACEH][-e event-list][-b | -t | -h | -s depth]
    [-n nlocks][-l lock [, size]][-d duration][-T][-cwWRp][-D count]
    [-o filename] command [args]
```

Description

Use the `lockstat` command to gather and display statistics on kernel synchronization objects. `lockstat` enables you to specify which lock events to watch (for example, spin on adaptive mutex, block on read access to rwlock because of waiting writers, and so forth), how much data to gather for each event, and how to display that data. By default, lockstat monitors all lock contention events, gathers frequency and timing data about those events, and displays that data in order of decreasing frequency so that the most heavily contended locks appear first.

lockstat gathers kernel locking statistics until the specified command completes. For example, to gather statistics for a fixed time interval, specify sleep(1) as the command, as follows.

lockstat sleep 5

lockstat relies on the lockstat(7D) driver, an exclusive access device that modifies the running kernel's text to intercept events of interest. This driver imposes a small but measurable overhead on all system activity, so access to the lockstat(7D) driver is restricted to superuser by default. The system administrator can relax this restriction by changing the permissions on /dev/lockstat.

> **Note** — The lockstat technology is provided as is. The format and content of lockstat output reflect the current Solaris kernel implementation and are, therefore, subject to change in future releases.

Options

Event Selection Options

-C	Watch contention events [on by default].
-E	Watch error events [on by default].
-H	Watch hold events [off by default].
-A	Watch all events. -A is equivalent to -CEH.
-e *event-list*	Watch only the specified events. *event-list* is a comma-separated list of events or ranges of events, (for example, 1,4-7,35). Run lockstat with no arguments to get a brief description of all events.

Data Gathering Options (Mutually Exclusive)

-b	Gather the basic statistics for lock, caller, and number of events.
-t	Gather timing statistics for basic statistics plus timing for all events [default].
-h	Display a histogram of timing plus time distribution.
-s *depth*	Display a stack trace histogram plus stack traces of events.

Data Filtering Options

-n *nlocks*   Specify the maximum number of locks to watch.

-l *lock*[,*size*]

Watch only *lock*, which you can specify as either a symbolic name or hex address. *size* defaults to the ELF symbol size or 1 if the symbol size is not available.

-d *duration*   Watch only events longer than *duration*.

-T   Trace (instead of sample) events [off by default].

Data Reporting Options

-c   Coalesce lock data for lock arrays (for example, pse_mutex[]).

-w   Wherever: distinguish events only by lock, not by caller.

-W   Whichever: distinguish events only by caller, not by lock.

-R   Display rates (events per second) instead of counts.

-p   Display output in parsable format.

-D *count*   Display only the top *count* events of each type.

-o *filename*   Direct output to *filename*.

Examples

The fields from the output of lockstat are described below.

count | ops/s

Number of times this lock was acquired by this caller, or the rate (times per second) if you specified -R.

indv   Percentage of all events represented by this individual event.

cuml   Cumulative percentage; a running total of the individuals.

rcnt   Average reference count. Always 1 for exclusive locks (mutexes, spin locks, rwlocks held as writer) but may be greater than 1 for shared locks (rwlocks held as reader, shared pages, counting semaphores).

spin | nsec   Average number of times caller spun trying to get the lock, or average duration of the events in nanoseconds, as appropriate for the event.

lock   Address of the lock.

caller   Address of the caller.

The following example uses lockstat to gather kernel locking statistics for five seconds.

```
# lockstat sleep 5
    Adaptive mutex spin: 513 events
                    Count   indv   cuml   rcnt   spin   Lock
    Caller
                       99    19%    19%   1.00    194   0x6335e5f4
```

```
cv_timedwait+0xac
                 95     19%    38%    1.00    192    0x6335e5f4
nfs_async_start+0x7c
                 55     11%    49%    1.00    297    0x6335e5f4

        nfs_async_
      readahead+0xf4
                 24      5%    53%    1.00     12    rt_callout_state
untimeout+0x24
                 19      4%    57%    1.00
    11    0x61325e3c       nfs3_readahead+0x3c
                 16      3%    60%    1.00     26    0x61478554
nfs3_readahead+0x3c
                 15      3%    63%    1.00     28    rt_callout_state
realtime_timeout+0xc
                 15      3%
     66%    1.00    286    0x620f0280

        cv_wait_sig_
        swap+0x1d0
                 14      3%    69%    1.00      7    0x61325e3c
nfs3_getapage+0xec
                 11      2%    71%    1.00    264    pidlock
thread_exit+0x58
                 11      2%    73%    1.00     16    0x61478554
nfs_async_start+0x2d0
                 10      2%    75%    1.00     58    fpc_mutex+0x8
page_list_add+0xb8
                 10      2%    77%    1.00     13    0x61478554

        nfs_async_
      readahead+0xa8
                  9      2%    79%    1.00     42    0x61325e3c
nfs_async_start+0x2d0
                  8      2%    80%    1.00     52    fpc_mutex+0x48
page_list_add+0xb8
                  7      1%    82%    1.00      7
    0x61478554        nfs3_getapage+0xec
                  6      1%    83%    1.00      3    0x61325e3c

        nfs_async_
      readahead+0xa8
                  6      1%    84%    1.00     63    fpc_mutex+0x48

      page_get_mnode_
        freelist+0xa8
                  6      1%    85%
    1.00     13    pidlock

        cv_wait_sig_
        swap+0x1d0
                  5      1%    86%    1.00      7    0x61478554
nfs3_getapage+0x22c
                  5      1%    87%    1.00     87    fpc_mutex+0x28
page_list_add+0xb8
                  5      1%
     88%    1.00     30    0x61325e3c        nfs3_getapage+0x5a4
```

5	1%	89%	1.00	319	0x620f0500

```
        cv_wait_sig_
          swap+0x1d0
```
4	1%	90%	1.00	61	fpc_mutex+0x8

```
    page_get_mnode_
```

```
    freelist+0xa8
```

. . .*(Additional lines deleted from this example)*

Files

```
/dev/lockstat
```
>   `lockstat` driver.

Attributes

See `attributes`(5) for descriptions of the following attributes.

Attribute Type	Attribute Value
Availability	SUNWcsu (32-bit)
	SUNWcsxu (64-bit)

See Also

`attributes(5)`, `lockstat(7D)`, `mutex(9F)`, `rwlock(9F)`

---

lofiadm — Administer Files Available as Block Devices Through lofi

New!

Synopsis

```
/usr/sbin/lofiadm -a file [device]
/usr/sbin/lofiadm -d file | device
/usr/sbin/lofiadm [file | device]
```

Description

The `lofiadm` command is new in the Solaris 8 release. Use the `lofiadm` command to administer `lofi`(7D), the loopback file driver. You can use this command to create a quick file system when a spare disk slice is not available. The `lofi`(7D) file driver enables you to associate a file with a block device. That file can then be accessed through the block device, which is useful when the file contains an image of some file system (such as a floppy or CD-ROM image) because you can then use the block device with normal system commands for mounting, checking, or repairing file systems. See `fsck`(1M) and `mount`(1M).

Use lofiadm to add a file as a loopback device, remove such an association, or print information about the current associations.

Notes

Just as you would not directly access a disk device that has mounted file systems, you should not access a file associated with a block device except through the lofi file driver. It might also be appropriate to ensure that the file has appropriate permissions to prevent such access.

Associations are not persistent across reboots. You can use a script to reestablish them if required.

The abilities of lofiadm, and who can use them, are controlled by the permissions of /dev/lofictl. Read access enables query operations, such as listing all the associations. Write access is required to do any state-changing operations, such as adding an association. As shipped, /dev/lofictl is owned by root, in group sys, and has mode 0644, so all users can do query operations but only root can change anything. Permissions should probably be given only to a trusted group.

When mounting a file-system image, take care to use appropriate mount options. In particular, the nosuid mount option might be appropriate for UFS images whose origin is unknown. Also, some options might not be useful or appropriate, such as logging or forcedirectio for UFS. For compatibility, a raw device is also exported along with the block device. For example, newfs(1M) requires a raw device.

The output of lofiadm (without arguments) may change in future releases.

Options

-a *file* [*device*]

> Add *file* as a block device.
>
> If you do not specify *device*, lofiadm chooses an available device.
>
> If you specify *device*, try to assign it to *file*. *device* must be available or lofiadm fails. The ability to specify a device is provided for use in scripts that want to reestablish a particular set of associations.

-d *file* | *device*

> Remove an association by *file* or *device* name if the associated block device is not busy, and deallocate the block device.

Operands

file   Print the block device associated with file.

device   Print the file name associated with the block device *device*.

> Without arguments, print a list of the current associations. File names must be valid absolute path names.
>
> When a file is added, it is opened for reading or writing by root. Any restrictions apply (such as restricted root access over NFS). The file is held open until the association is removed. It is not actually accessed until the block device is used, so it is never written to if the block device is opened read-only.

Examples

When mounting an existing CD-ROM image, ensure that the Solaris Operating Environment understands the image before creating the CD. `lofi` enables you to mount the image and see if it works.

The following example mounts an existing CD-ROM image (`sparc.iso`), of the Red Hat 6.0 CD that was downloaded from the Internet. It was created with the `mkisofs` command from the Internet. The example uses `lofiadm` to attach a block device.

```
# lofiadm -a /home/mike_s/RH6.0/sparc.iso /dev/lofi/1
```

`lofiadm` picks the device and prints the device name to the standard output. You can run `lofiadm` again by issuing the following command.

```
# lofiadm Block Device File /dev/lofi/1
    /home/mike_s/RH6.0/sparc.iso
```

Or, you can give it one name and ask for the other by issuing the following command.

```
# lofiadm /dev/lofi/1 /home/mike_s/RH6.0/sparc.iso
```

Use the `mount` command to mount the image.

```
# mount -F hsfs -o ro /dev/lofi/1 /mnt
```

Check to ensure that the Solaris Operating Environment understands the image.

```
# df -k /mnt
Filesystem kbytes used avail capacity Mounted on
/dev/lofi/1 512418 512418 0 100% /mnt
# ls /mnt
./              RedHat/         doc/            ls-lR           rr_moved/
../             TRANS.TBL       dosutils/       ls-lR.gz        sbin@
.buildlog       bin@            etc@            misc/           tmp/
COPYING         boot/           images/         mnt/            usr@
README          boot.cat*       kernels/        modules/
RPM-PGP-KEY     dev@            lib@            proc/
#
```

The Solaris Operating Environment can mount the CD-ROM image and understand the file names. The image was created properly, and you can now create the CD-ROM with confidence.

As a final step, unmount and detach the images.

```
# umount /mnt
# lofiadm -d /dev/lofi/1
# lofiadm
Block Device File
#
```

The following example is similar to the previous one except that it mounts a diskette image.

Using `lofi` to help you mount files that contain floppy images is helpful if a diskette contains a file that you need, but the machine that you're on doesn't have a floppy drive. It is also helpful if you don't want to take the time to use the `dd` command to copy the image to a diskette.

The following example accesses an MDB diskette for the Solaris IA platform.

```
# lofiadm -a /export/s28/MDB_s28x_wos/latest/boot.3 /dev/lofi/1
# mount -F pcfs /dev/lofi/1 /mnt
# ls /mnt
./              COMMENT.BAT*   RC.D/          SOLARIS.MAP*
../             IDENT*         REPLACE.BAT*   X/
APPEND.BAT*     MAKEDIR.BAT*   SOLARIS/
# umount /mnt
# lofiadm -d /export/s28/MDB_s28x_wos/latest/boot.3
#
```

Making a UFS file system on a file can be useful, particularly if a test suite requires a scratch file system. It can be painful (or annoying) to have to repartition a disk just for the test suite. Instead, you can use newfs on a file with lofi.

First, create the file, as shown in the following example.

```
# mkfile 35m /export/home/test
#
```

Then, attach it to a block device. You also get the character device that newfs requires, so use the newfs command.

```
# lofiadm -a /export/home/test /dev/lofi/1
# newfs /dev/rlofi/1
newfs: construct a new file system /dev/rlofi/1: (y/n)? y
/dev/rlofi/1:    71638 sectors in 119 cylinders of 1 tracks, 602
sectors
35.0MB in 8 cyl groups (16 c/g, 4.70MB/g, 2240 i/g)
super-block backups (for fsck -F ufs -o b=#) at:
32, 9664, 19296, 28928, 38560, 48192, 57824, 67456,
```

Note that ufs might not be able to use the entire file. Mount and use the file system.

```
# mount /dev/lofi/1 /mnt
# df -k /mnt
Filesystem              kbytes    used   avail  capacity  Mounted on
/dev/lofi/1              33455       9   30101     1%     /mnt
# ls /mnt
./              ../            lost+found/
# umount /mnt
# lofiadm -d /dev/lofi/1
```

Environment Variables

See environ(5) for descriptions of the following environment variables that affect the execution of lofiadm: LC_CTYPE, LC_MESSAGES, and NLSPATH.

Exit Status

0	Successful completion.
>0	An error occurred.

Attributes

See `attributes`(5) for descriptions of the following attributes.

Attribute Type	Attribute Value
Availability	SUNWcsu

See Also

`fsck`(1M), `mount`(1M), `mount_ufs`(1M), `attributes`(5), `lofi`(7D)

logins — List User and System Login Information

Synopsis

`/usr/bin/logins` [-admopstux][-g *group*...][-l *login*...]

Description

Use the `logins` command to display information on user and system logins known to the system. You must be superuser to run this command. The default information displayed is login ID, user ID, primary group name, primary group ID, and the account field value. Output is sorted by user ID, system logins, followed by user logins. You can control the contents of the output with the command options. Such output can include user or system login, user ID number, `passwd` account field value (user name or other information), primary group name, primary group ID, multiple group names, multiple group IDs, home directory, login shell, and four password-aging parameters.

Options

You can combine options. If you do so, any login that matches any criterion is displayed.

-a	Add two password expiration fields to the display. The fields show how many days a password can remain unused before it automatically becomes inactive, and the date that the password expires.
-d	Display logins with duplicate UIDs.
-m	Display multiple group membership information.
-o	Format output into one line of colon-separated fields.
-p	Display logins with no passwords.
-s	Display all system logins.
-t	Sort output by login instead of by UID.
-u	Display all user logins.

-x   Print an extended set of information about each selected user. The extended information includes home directory, login shell, and password aging information, each displayed on a separate line. The password information consists of password status (PS for password, NP for no password, or LK for locked). If the login is passworded, status is followed by the date the password was last changed, the number of days required between changes, and the number of days allowed before a change is required. The password-aging information shows the time interval that the user receives a password expiration warning message (when logging on) before the password expires.

-g *group*   Display all users belonging to *group*, sorted by login. You can specify multiple groups as a comma-separated list. When you combine the -l and -g options, a user is listed only once even if the user belongs to more than one of the selected groups.

-l *login*   Display the requested login. You can specify multiple logins as a comma-separated list. Depending on the nameservice lookup types set in /etc/nsswitch.conf, the information can come from the /etc/passwd and /etc/shadow files and other nameservices. When you combine the -l and -g options, a user is listed only once even if the user belongs to more than one of the selected groups.

Examples

The following example displays the default output of the logins command with no options.

```
# logins
root         0        other        1        Super-User
daemon       1        other        1
bin          2        bin          2
sys          3        sys          3
adm          4        adm          4        Admin
uucp         5        uucp         5        uucp Admin
nuucp        9        nuucp        9        uucp Admin
listen       37       adm          4        Network Admin
lp           71       lp           8        Line Printer Admin
winsor       1001     staff        10
ray          1002     staff        10
des          1003     staff        10
rob          1004     staff        10
nobody       60001    nobody       60001    Nobody
noaccess     60002    noaccess     60002    No Access User
nobody4      65534    nogroup      65534    SunOS 4.x Nobody
#
```

Attributes

See `attributes`(5) for descriptions of the following attributes.

Attribute Type	Attribute Value
Availability	SUNWcsu

See Also

`attributes(5)`

---

lpadmin — Configure the LP Print Service

Synopsis

```
/usr/sbin/lpadmin -p printer options
/usr/sbin/lpadmin -x dest
/usr/sbin/lpadmin -d [dest]
/usr/sbin/lpadmin -S print-wheel -A alert-type [-W minutes] [-Q requests]
/usr/sbin/lpadmin -M -f form-name [-a [-o filebreak] [-t tray-number]]
```

Description

Use the `lpadmin` command to configure the LP print service by defining printers and devices. Use it to add and change printers, to remove printers from service, to set or change the system default destination, to define alerts for printer faults, and to mount print wheels.

Options

Adding or Changing a Printer

Use the first form of the `lpadmin` command (`lpadmin -p printer options`) to configure a new printer or to change the configuration of an existing printer. When creating a new printer, you must use one of the -v, -U, or -s options. In addition, you can use only one of the -e, -i, or -m options. If you use none of these three options, the model `standard` is used. The -h and -l options are mutually exclusive. Printer and class names may be no longer than 14 characters and must consist entirely of the characters A-Z, a-z, 0-9, dash (-) or underscore (_). If you specify the -s option, the -A, -e, -F, -h, -i, -l, -M, -m, -o, -U, -v, and -W options are invalid.

You can specify the following printer options in any order.

-A *alert-type* [-W *minutes*]

> Define an alert that informs the administrator when a printer fault is detected, and periodically thereafter, until the printer fault is cleared by the administrator. Values for the *alert-types* are shown below.

> mail   Send the alert message using mail (see mail(1)) to the administrator.

write
Write the message to the terminal on which the administrator is logged in. If the administrator is logged in on several terminals, choose one arbitrarily.

quiet
Do not send messages for the current condition. You can use this option to temporarily stop receiving further messages about a known problem. Once the fault has been cleared and printing resumes, messages are sent again when another fault occurs with the printer.

showfault
Try to execute a fault handler on each system that has a print job in the queue. The fault handler is `/etc/lp/alerts/printer`. You invoke this alert type with three parameters: `printer-name`, `date`, `filename`. The `filename` is the name of a file containing the fault message.

none
Do not send messages; remove any existing alert definition for the printer. Send no alert when the printer faults until a different `alert-type` (except `quiet`) is used.

`shell-command`

Run the `shell-command` each time the alert needs to be sent. The shell command should expect the message in standard input. If the command has embedded blank spaces, enclose it in quotes. Note that the `mail` and `write` values for this option are equivalent to the values `mail username` and `write username`, where `username` is the current name for the administrator. `username` is the login name of the person submitting this command unless you have used the `su` command to change to another user ID. If you have used the `su` command to change the user ID, then use the `user-name` for the new ID.

list
Display the type of the alert for the printer fault. No change is made to the alert.

The message sent appears as follows.

```
The printer printer has stopped printing for the reason
given below. Fix the problem and bring the printer back
on line. Printing has stopped, but is restarted in a few
minutes; issue an enable command if you want to restart
sooner.
```

Unless someone issues the change request

```
lp -i request-id -P...
```

to change the page list to print, the current request is reprinted from the beginning. The reason(s) it stopped (multiple reasons indicate reprinted attempts).

The LP print service can detect printer faults only through an adequate fast filter and only when the standard interface program or a suitable customized interface program is used. Furthermore, the level of recovery after a fault depends on the capabilities of the filter.

If the printer is all, the alerting defined in this command applies to all existing printers.

If you do not use the -W option to arrange fault alerting for *printer*, the default procedure is to mail one message to the administrator of *printer* per fault. This is equivalent to specifying -W once or -W 0. If *minutes* is a number greater than 0, an alert is sent at intervals specified by *minutes*.

-c *class*   Insert printer into the specified class. Create *class* if it does not already exist.

-D *comment*   Save this comment for display whenever a user asks for a full description of *printer* (see lpstat(1)). The LP print service does not interpret this comment.

-e *printer*   Copy the interface program of an existing printer to be the interface program for *printer*. (You cannot specify the -i or -m option with this option.)

-f allow:*form-list*
-f deny:*form-list*

Allow or deny the forms in *form-list* to be printed on *printer*. By default no forms are allowed on a new printer.

You must first invoke the -T option with lpadmin to identify the printer type before you can use the -f option.

For each printer, the LP print service keeps two lists of forms: an allow-list of forms that can be used with the printer and a deny-list of forms that cannot be used with the printer. With the -f allow option, the forms listed are added to the allow-list and removed from the deny-list. With the -f deny option, the forms listed are added to the deny-list and removed from the allow-list.

If the allow-list is not empty, only the forms in the list can be used on the printer, regardless of the contents of the deny-list. If the allow-list is empty but the deny-list is not, the forms in the deny-list cannot be used with the printer. You can exclude all forms from a printer by specifying -f deny:all. You can include all forms on a printer (provided the printer can handle all the characteristics of each form) by specifying -f allow:all.

The LP print service uses the information from the -f option as a set of guidelines for determining where a form can be mounted. Administrators are not restricted from mounting a form any printer. If mounting a form on a particular printer is in disagreement with the information in the allow-list or deny-list, the administrator is warned but the mount is accepted. Nonetheless, if a user tries to issue a print or change request for a form and printer combination that is in disagreement with the information, the request is accepted only if the form is currently mounted on the printer. If the form is later unmounted before the request can print, the request is cancelled and the user is notified by mail.

If the administrator tries to specify a form as acceptable for use on a printer that does not have the capabilities needed by the form, the command is rejected.

Note the other use of -f, with the -M option, below.

-F *fault-recovery*

Specify the recovery to be used for any print request that is stopped because of a printer fault, according to the value of *fault-recovery*:

continue	Continue printing on the top of the page where printing stopped. This value requires a filter to wait for the fault to clear before automatically continuing.
beginning	Start printing the request again from the beginning.
wait	Disable printing on *printer* and wait for the administrator or a user to enable printing again.
	During the wait, the administrator or the user who submitted the stopped print request can issue a change request that specifies where printing should resume. (See the -i option of the lp command.) If no change request is made before printing is enabled, printing resumes at the top of the page where stopped if the filter allows; otherwise, the request is printed from the beginning.

-h   Indicate that the device associated with the printer is hardwired. If you specify neither of the mutually exclusive options, -h and -l, -h is assumed.

-I *content-type-list*

Allow *printer* to handle print requests with the content types listed in *content-type-list*. If the list includes names of more than one type, separate the names with commas or blank spaces. (If the names are separated by blank spaces, enclose the entire list in double quotes.)

The type simple is recognized as the default content type for files in the UNIX system. A simple type of file is a data stream containing only printable ASCII characters and the following control characters.

Control Character	Octal Value	Meaning
Backspace	H	Move back one character, except at beginning of line.
Tab	I	Move to next Tab stop.
Linefeed (Newline)	J	Move to beginning of next line.
Formfeed	L	Move to beginning of next page.
Return	15	Move to beginning of current line.

To prevent the print service from considering simple a valid type for the printer, specify either an empty list or an explicit value (such as the printer type) in the content-type-list. If you do want simple included along with other types, you must include simple in the content-type-list.

Except for simple, you can freely determine each content-type name. If you specify the printer type with the -T option, then the printer type is implicitly considered to also be a valid content type.

-i interface Establish a new interface program for printer. interface is the path name of the new program. (You cannot specify the -e or -m options with this option.)

-l Indicate that the device associated with printer is a login terminal. The LP scheduler (lpsched) disables all login terminals automatically each time it is started. (You cannot specify the -h option with this option.)

-m model Select model interface program, provided with the LP print service, for the printer. (You cannot specify the -e and -i options with this option.)

-M -f form-name [-a [-o filebreak]] [-t tray-number]]

Mount the form form-name on printer. Print requests that need the preprinted form form-name on printer. If more than one printer has the form mounted and the user has specified any (with the -d option of the lp command) as the printer destination, then print the print request on the one printer that also meets the other needs of the request.

Compare the page length and width, and character and line pitches needed by the form with those allowed for the printer by checking the capabilities in the terminfo database for the type of printer. If the form requires attributes that are not available with the printer, the administrator is warned but the mount is accepted. If the form lists a print wheel as mandatory but the print wheel mounted on the printer is different, the administrator is also warned but the mount is accepted.

If you specify the -a option, print an alignment pattern preceded by the same initialization of the physical printer that precedes a normal print request, except do not print a banner page. Printing is assumed to start at the top of the first page of the form. After the pattern is printed, you can adjust the mounted form in the printer and press Return for another alignment pattern (no initialization this time), and can continue printing as many alignment patterns as needed. Quit the printing of alignment patterns by typing q.

If you specify the -o *filebreak* option, insert a formfeed between each copy of the alignment pattern. By default, the alignment pattern is assumed to correctly fill a form, so no formfeed is added.

If you specify the -t *tray-number* option, use printer tray *tray-number*.

You unmount a form either by mounting a new form in its place or by using the -f none option. By default, a new printer has no form mounted.

Note the other use of -f without the -M option.

-M -S *print-wheel*

Mount the *print-wheel* on *printer*. Print the requests that need the *print-wheel* on *printer*. If more than one printer has *print-wheel* mounted and the user has specified any (with the -d option of the lp command) as the printer destination, then print the print request on the one printer that also meets the other needs of the request.

If *print-wheel* is not listed as acceptable for the printer, the administrator is warned but the mount is accepted. If the printer does not take print wheels, the command is rejected.

You unmount a print wheel either by mounting a new print wheel in its place or by using the option -S none. By default, a new printer has no print wheel mounted.

Note the other uses of the -S option without the -M option as described below.

-o *option*   Define default printer configuration values given to an interface program. The default may be explicitly overwritten for individual requests by the user (see lp(1)) or taken from a preprinted form description (see lpforms(1M) and lp(1)).

Several options are predefined by the system. In addition, you can define any number of key-value pairs. Each of the predefined and undefined options is described.

The Predefined Options

The following options are predefined.

- Adjusting printer capabilities.
- Adjusting printer port characteristics.
- Configuring network printers.
- Controlling the use of banner.

Adjusting Printer Capabilities

```
length=scaled-decimal-number
width=scaled-decimal-number
cpi=scaled-decimal-number
lpi=scaled-decimal-number
```

The term *scaled-decimal-number* refers to a nonnegative number used to indicate a unit of size. The type of unit is shown by a trailing letter attached to the number. You can use three types of scaled decimal-numbers with the LP print service.

- Numbers that show sizes in centimeters (marked with a trailing c).
- Numbers that show sizes in inches (marked with a trailing i).
- Numbers that show sizes in units appropriate to use (without a trailing letter), that is, lines, characters, lines per inch, or characters per inch.

The option values must agree with the capabilities of the type of physical printer, as defined in the terminfo database for the printer type. If they do not, the command is rejected.

The defaults are defined in the terminfo entry for the specified printer type. You can reset the defaults with the following commands.

```
lpadmin -p printername -o length=value
lpadmin -p printername o width=value
lpadmin -p printername o cpi=value
lpadmin -p printername o lpi=value
```

Adjusting Printer Port Characteristics

```
stty="'stty-option-list'"
```

The *stty-option-list* is not checked for allowed values but is passed directly to the stty program by the standard interface program. Any error messages produced by stty when a request is processed (by the standard interface program) are mailed to the user submitting the request.

The default for stty is shown below.

```
stty="'9600 cs8 -cstopb -parenb ixon
      -ixany opost -olcuc onlcr
      -ocrnl -onocr                    .
      -onlret -ofill nl0 cr0 tab0 bs0 vt0 ff0'"
```

You can reset the default with the following syntax.

```
lpadmin -p printername -o stty=value
```

Configuring Network Printers

```
dest=string
protocol=string
bsdctrl=string
timeout=non-negative-integer-seconds
```

These four options are provided to support network printing. Each option is passed directly to the interface program; any checking for allowed values is done there.

The value of dest is the name of the destination for the network printer; the semantics for value dest are dependent on the printer and the configuration. There is no default.

The value of the protocol option sets the over-the-wire protocol to the printer. The default for protocol is bsd. The value of the bsdctrl option sets the print order of control and data files (BSD protocol only); the default for this option is control file first. The value of the timeout option sets the seed value for backoff time when the printer is busy. The default value for the timeout option is 10 seconds. You can reset the defaults with the following syntax.

```
lpadmin -p printername -o protocol=value
lpadmin -p printername -o bsdctrl=value
lpadmin -p printername -o timeout=value
```

Controlling the Use of the Banner Page

nobanner   Print no banner page.

banner   Force a banner page to be printed with every print request, even when a user asks for no banner page. This behavior is the default. Specify -o nobanner to allow users to specify -o nobanner with the lp command.

Undefined Options

In addition to predefined options, you can define any number of key-value pairs.

key=value   Each key=value is passed directly to the interface program. The interface program does any checking for allowed values.

The interface program defines any default values for a given key=value option. If a default is provided, you can reset it by typing the key without any value.

```
lpadmin -p printername -o key=value
```

-P paper-name

Specify a list of paper types that the printer supports.

-r class   Remove printer from the specified class. If printer is the last member of class, then remove class.

-S list   Allow either the print wheels or aliases for character sets named in list to be used on the printer.

You must first invoke the -T option with lpadmin to identify the printer type before you can use the -S option.

If the printer is a type that takes print wheels, then list is a comma- or space-separated list of print wheel names. (Enclose the list with quotes if it contains blank spaces.) The print wheels you specify are the only ones considered mountable on the printer. (You can, however, always force a different print wheel to be mounted.) Until you use this option to specify a list, no print wheels are considered mountable on the printer and print requests that ask for a particular print wheel with this printer are rejected.

If the printer is a type that has selectable character sets, then *list* is a comma- or blank-separated list of character set name mappings or aliases. (Enclose the list with quotes if it contains blank spaces.) Each mapping is of the form *known-name=alias*. The *known-name* is a character set number preceded by cs (such as cs3 for character set three) or a character set name from the terminfo database entry csnm. See terminfo(4). If you do not use this option to specify a list, only the names already known from the terminfo database or numbers with a prefix of cs are acceptable for the printer. If *list* is the word none, remove any existing print wheel lists or character set aliases.

Note the other uses of -S with the -M option described above.

-s *system-name*[!*printer-name*]

Make a remote printer (one that must be accessed through another system) accessible to users on your system. *system-name* is the name of the remote system on which the remote printer is located. *printer-name* is the name used on the remote system for that printer. For example, if you want to access printer1 on system1 and you want it called printer2 on your system, you would enter

-p printer2 -s system1!printer1

-T *printer-type-list*

Identify the printer as being of one or more printer types. Each printer type is used to extract data from the terminfo database; this information is used to initialize the printer before printing each user's request. Some filters may also use a printer type to convert content for the printer. If you do not use this option, the default printer-type is unknown; no information is extracted from terminfo, so each user request is printed without first initializing the printer. Also, you must use this option if the following options of the lpadmin and lp commands are to work: -o cpi, -o lpi, -o width, and -o length, and the -S and -f options of the lpadmin command.

If the *printer-type-list* contains more than one type, then you must either specify the *content-type-list* of the -I option as simple, as empty (-I ""), or not specify it at all.

-t *number-of-trays*

Specify the number of trays when creating the printer.

-u allow:*login-ID-list*

-u deny:*login-ID-list*

Allow or deny the users in *login-ID-list* access to the printer. By default, all users are allowed on a new printer. The *login-ID-list* argument can include any or all of the following constructs.

login-ID   A user on any system.

system-name!login-ID

> A user on system *system-name*.

system-name!all

> All users on system *system-name*.

all!login-ID A user on all systems.

all All users on all systems.

For each printer, the LP print service keeps two lists of users: an `allow-list` of people allowed to use the printer and a `deny-list` of people denied access to the printer. The `-u allow` option adds the listed users to the `allow-list` and removes them from the `deny-list`. The `-u deny` option adds the listed users to the `deny-list` and removes them from the `allow-list`.

If the `allow-list` is not empty, only the users in the list can use the printer, regardless of the contents of the `deny-list`. If the `allow-list` is empty but the `deny-list` is not, the users in the `deny-list` cannot use the printer. You can deny all users access to the printer by specifying `-u deny:all`. You can allow all users to use the printer by specifying `-u allow:all`.

`-U` *dial-info* The `-U` option allows your print service to access a remote printer. (It does not enable your print service to access a remote printer service.) Specifically, `-U` assigns the dialing information *dial-info* to the printer. The dial routine uses *dial-info* to call the printer. Any network connection supported by the Basic Networking Utilities works. *dial-info* can be either a phone number for a modem connection or a system name for other kinds of connections. If you specify `-U direct`, no dialing takes place because the name `direct` is reserved for a printer that is directly connected. If you specify a system name, use it to search for connection details from the file `/etc/uucp/Systems` or related files. The Basic Networking Utilities are required to support this option. `-U direct` is the default.

`-v` *device* Associate a device with printer. *device* is the path name of a file that is writeable by `lp`. Note that you can associate the same device with more than one printer.

Removing a Printer Destination

The `-x` *dest* option removes the destination *dest* (a printer or a class) from the LP print service. If *dest* is a printer and is the only member of a class, then the class is deleted, too. If *dest* is `all`, all printers and classes are removed. No other options are allowed with `-x`.

Setting/Changing the System Default Destination

The `-d` [*dest*] option makes *dest* (an existing printer or class) the new system default destination. If you do not supply *dest*, then there is no system default destination. No other options are allowed with `-d`.

Setting an Alert for a Print Wheel

```
-S print-wheel -A alert-type [-W minutes][-Q requests]
```

Use the -S *print-wheel* option with the -A *alert-type* option to define an alert to mount the print wheel when jobs are queued for it. If you do not use this command to arrange alerting for a print wheel, no alert is sent for the print wheel. Note the other use of -A, with the -p option, above.

You can specify the following *alert-types*.

mail
: Send the alert message to the administrator, using the mail command.

write
: Write the message, using the write command, to the terminal on which the administrator is logged in. If the administrator is logged in on several terminals, arbitrarily choose one.

quiet
: Do not send messages for the current condition. You can use this option to temporarily stop receiving further messages about a known problem. Once the *print-wheel* has been mounted and subsequently unmounted, messages are sent again when the number of print requests reaches the threshold specified by the -Q option.

none
: Do not send messages until you again specify the -A option with a different *alert-type* (other than quiet).

shell-command
: Run the *shell-command* each time the alert needs to be sent. The shell command expects the message from standard input. If the command has embedded blanks, enclose the command in quotes. Note that the mail and write values for this option are equivalent to the values mail *username* and write *username*, where *username* is the current name for the administrator. Unless you have used the su command to change to another user ID, the login name is the login name of the person submitting this command. If you have used the su command to change the user ID, then use the *username* for the new ID.

list
: Display the type of the alert for the print wheel on standard output. No change is made to the alert.

The message sent appears as follows.

```
The print wheel print-wheel needs to be mounted on the
printer(s): printer(integer1 requests) integer2 print
requests await this print wheel.
```

The printers listed are those that the administrator earlier specified as candidates for this print wheel. The number *integer1* listed next to each printer is the number of requests eligible for the printer. The number *integer2* shown after the printer list is the total number of requests awaiting the print wheel. *integer2* is less than the sum of the other numbers if some requests can be handled by more than one printer.

If *print-wheel* is all, the alerting defined in this command applies to all print wheels already defined to have an alert.

If you do not specify the -W option, by default only one message is sent per need to mount the print wheel. Not specifying the -W option is equivalent to specifying -W once or -W 0. If *minutes* is a number greater than 0, send an alert at intervals specified by *minutes*.

If you also specify the -Q option, send the alert when a certain number (specified by the argument requests) of print requests that need the print wheel are waiting. If you do not specify the -Q option or *requests* is 1 or any (which are both the default), send a message as soon as anyone submits a print request for the print wheel when it is not mounted.

Exit Status

0	Successful completion.
non-zero	An error occurred.

Files

/var/spool/lp/*

Print spooling directory

/etc/lp

lp commands directory.

/etc/lp/alerts/printer

Fault handler for lpadmin.

Attributes

See attributes(5) for descriptions of the following attributes.

Attribute Type	**Attribute Value**
Availability	SUNWpcu

See Also

enable(1), lp(1), lpstat(1), mail(1), stty(1), accept (1M), lpforms (1M), lpsched(1M), lpsystem(1M), dial(3N), terminfo(4), attributes(5)
System Administration Guide, Volume II

lpfilter — Administer Filters Used with the LP Print Service

Synopsis

```
/usr/sbin/lpfilter -f filter-name {- | -i | -l | -x | -F pathname}
```

Description

Use the lpfilter command to add, change, delete, or list a filter used with the LP print service. These filters convert the content of a file to have a content type acceptable to a printer.

> **Note —** If the lp command specifies more than one document, the filtering chain is determined by the first document. Other documents may have a different format, but they print correctly only if the filter chain is able to handle their format.

Options

Arguments consist of the -f *filter-name* option and exactly one of the following arguments {- | -i | -l | -x | -F *pathname*}.

-f *filter-name*

    Specify the *filter-name* of the filter to be added, changed, reset, deleted, or listed. The filter name all is a special filter name defined below. The -f option is required.

−

    Add or change a filter as specified from standard input. The format of the input is specified below. If you specify -f all with the - option, make the specified change to all existing filters, which is not useful.

-F *pathname*

    Add or change a filter as specified by the contents of the file *pathname*. The format of the file's contents is specified below. If you specify -f all with the - option, make the specified change to all existing filters, which is not useful.

-i

    Reset a filter to its default settings. Using -f all with the -i option restores all filters for which predefined settings are available to their original settings.

-x

    Delete a filter. Using -f all with the -x option deletes all filters.

-l

    List a filter description. Using -f all with the -l option lists all filters.

Usage

Adding or Changing a Filter

The filter named in the -f option is added to the filter table. If the filter already exists, its description is changed to reflect the new information in the input.

When you specify –, standard input supplies the filter description. When you specify –F, the file path name supplies the filter description. You must specify one of these two options to add or change a filter.

When you change an existing filter with the –F or – option, lines in the filter description that are not specified in the new information are not changed. When you add a new filter with this command, unspecified lines receive default values.

Filters are used to convert the content of a request from its initial type into a type acceptable to a printer. For a given print request, the LP print service knows the following information.

- The content type of the request (specified by lp –T or determined implicitly).
- The name of the printer (specified by lp –d).
- The printer type (specified by lpadmin –T).

  The printer type is intended to be a printer model, but some people specify it with a content type even though lpadmin –I is intended for this purpose.
- The content types acceptable to the printer (specified by lpadmin –I).

  The values specified by the lpadmin –T are treated as if they were specified by the –I option as well.
- The modes of printing asked for by the originator of the request (specified by various options to lp).

The system uses the above information to construct a list of one or more filters that convert the document's content type into a content type acceptable to the printer and consumes all lp arguments that invoke filters (–y and –P).

The contents of the file (specified by the –F option) and the input stream from standard input (specified by –) must consist of a series of lines each of which conforms to the syntax specified by one of the seven lines below. All lists are comma- or space-separated. Each item contains a description.

```
Input types: content-type-list
Output types: content-type-list
Printer types: printer-type-list
Printers: printer-list
Filter type: filter-type
Command: shell-command
Options: template-list
```

Input Types   The content types that can be accepted by the filter. The default is any. The document content type must be a member of this list for the initial filter in the sequence.

Output Types   The content types that the filter can produce from any of the input (content) types. The default is any. The intersection of the output types of this list and the content types acceptable to the printer (from lpadmin –I and lpadmin –T) must be non-null for the last filter in the sequence. For adjacent filters in the sequence, the intersection of output types of one and the input types of the next must be non-null.

Printer Types

               The printer types for which this printer can be used. The LP print service restricts the use of the filter to these printer types (from lpadmin –T). The default is any.

Printers   The names of the printers for which the filter can be used. The LP print service restricts the use of the filter to just the printers named. The default is `any`.

Filter Type   Mark the filter as a slow filter or a fast filter. Slow filters are generally those that take a long time to convert their input (that is, minutes or hours). They are run before the job is scheduled for a printer to keep the printers from being tied up while the filter is running. If a listed printer is on a remote system, the filter type for it must have the value `slow`. That is, if a client defines a filter, it must be a slow filter. Fast filters are generally those that convert their input quickly (that is, faster than the printer can process the data) or those that must be connected to the printer when run. Fast filters are given to the interface program to run while connected to the physical printer.

Command   Specify which program to run to invoke the filter. You must include the full program path name as well as fixed options in the shell command; additional options are constructed according to the characteristics of each print request and on the `Options` field. You must specify a command for each filter. The command must accept a data stream as standard input and produce the converted data stream on its standard output; this behavior enables filter pipelines to be constructed to convert data not handled by a single filter.

Options   A comma-separated list of templates used by the LP print service to construct options to the filter from the characteristics of each print request listed later in the table. The `-y` and `-P` arguments to the `lp` command build a filter sequence even if there is no need for a conversion of content types.

In general, each template is of the following form.

keyword pattern = replacement

keyword names the characteristic that the template tries to map into a filter-specific option; each valid keyword is listed in the table below.

pattern is a literal pattern of one of the forms listed in the table, a single asterisk (`*`), or a regular expression. If *pattern* matches the value of the characteristic, the template fits and is used to generate a filter-specific option.

replacement specifies the value used as the option.

Regular expressions are the same as those found on the `regexp(5)` manual page. This expression includes the `\(...\)` and `\n` constructions, which can be used to extract portions of the pattern for copying into the replacement, and the `&`, which can be used to copy the entire pattern into the replacement.

The replacement can also contain a `*`; it, too, is replaced with the entire pattern, just like the `&` of `regexp(5)`.

The keywords are shown in the following table.

LP Option	Characteristic	Keyword	Possible Patterns
-T	Content type (input).	INPUT	*content-type*
Not applicable.	Content type (output).	OUTPUT	*content-type*
Not applicable.	Printer type.	TERM	*printer-type*
-d	Printer name.	PRINTER	*printer-name*
-f, -o cpi=	Character pitch.	CPI	*integer*
-f, -o lpi=	Page length.	LPI	*integer*
-f, -o width=	Page width.	WIDTH	*integer*
-P	Pages to print.	PAGES	*page-list*
-S	Character set print wheel.	CHARSET CHARSET	*character-set-name* *print-wheel-name*
-f	Form name.	FORM	*form-name*
-y	Modes.	MODES	*mode*
-n	Number of copies.	COPIES	*integer*

Large File Behavior
See `largefile(5)` for the description of the behavior of `lpfilter` when encountering files greater than or equal to 2 Gbytes (2**31 bytes).

Examples
The following template shows that if a print request is submitted with the -y landscape option, the filter is given the option -l.

```
MODES landscape = -l
```

The following template shows that the filter is given the option -T *printer-type* for whichever *printer-type* is associated with a print request using the filter.

```
TERM * = -T *
```

With the following template

```
MODES prwidth\=\(.*\) = -w\1
```

suppose a user gives the following command

```
lp -y prwidth=10
```

From the table above, the LP print service determines that the -y option is handled by a MODES template. The MODES template here works because the pattern prwidth=) matches the prwidth=10 given by the user. The replacement -w1 generates the filter option -w10. If necessary, the LP print service constructs a filter pipeline by concatenating several filters to handle the user's file and all the print options. See sh(1) for a description of a pipeline. If the print service constructs a filter pipeline, the INPUT and OUTPUT values used for each filter in the pipeline are the types of input and output for that filter, not for the entire pipeline.

Resetting a Filter to Defaults

If the filter named is one originally delivered with the LP print service, the -i option restores the original filter description.

Deleting a Filter

Use the -x option to delete the filter specified in *filter-name* from the LP filter table.

Listing a Filter Description

Use the -l option to list the description of the filter named in *filter-name*. If the command is successful, the following message is sent to standard output.

```
Input types: content-type-list
Output types: content-type-list
Printer types: printer-type-list
Printers: printer-list
Filter type: filter-type
Command: shell-command
Options: template-list
```

If the command fails, an error message is sent to standard error.

Exit Status

0	Successful completion.
non-zero	An error occurred.

Attributes

See attributes(5) for descriptions of the following attributes.

Attribute Type	Attribute Value
Availability	SUNWpsu

See Also

lp(1), sh(1), lpadmin(1M), attributes(5), largefile(5), regexp(5)
System Administration Guide, Volume II

lpforms — Administer Forms Used with the LP Print Service

Synopsis

```
/usr/sbin/lpforms -f form-name option
/usr/sbin/lpforms -f form-name -A alert-type [-P paper-name [-d]]
  [-Q requests] [-W minutes]
```

Description

Use the lpforms command to administer the use of preprinted forms, such as company letterhead paper, with the LP print service. Specify a form by its *form-name*. Users can specify a form when submitting a print request (see lp(1)). You can use the all argument instead of *form-name* with either of the command lines shown above. Use the first command line to add, change, and delete forms, to list the attributes of an existing form, and to allow and deny users access to particular forms. Use the second command line to establish the method by which the administrator is alerted that the form *form-name* must be mounted on a printer.

Options

-f *form-name*   Specify a form.

The first form of lpforms requires that you use one of the -, -1, -F, or -x options.

-F *pathname*   Add or change form *form-name* as specified by the information in *pathname*.

-                Add or change form *form-name* as specified by the information from standard input.

-x   Delete form *form-name*. (You must use this option separately; it cannot be used with any other option.)

-1   List the attributes of form *form-name*.

The second form of the lpforms command requires the -A *alert-type* option. The other options are optional.

-A *alert-type*

Define an alert to mount the form when there are queued jobs that need it.

-P *paper-name* [-d]

Specify the paper name when creating the form. If you specify the -d option, this paper is the default.

-Q *requests*   Send an alert when the specified number of print requests that need the form are waiting.

-W *minutes*   Send an alert at intervals specified by *minutes*.

Usage

Adding or Changing a Form

Use the -F *pathname* option to add a new form, *form-name*, to the LP print service or to change the attributes of an existing form. The form description is taken from *pathname* if you specify the -F option or from the standard input if you use the - option. You must use one of these two options to define or change a form.

pathname is the path name of a file that contains all or any subset of the following information about the form.

```
Page length: scaled-decimal-number1
Page width: scaled-decimal-number2
Number of pages: integer
Line pitch: scaled-decimal-number3
Character pitch: scaled-decimal-number4
Character set choice: character-set/print-wheel [mandatory]
Ribbon color: ribbon-color
Comment:comment
Alignment pattern: [content-type]
content
```

The term *scaled-decimal-number* refers to a nonnegative number used to indicate a unit of size. The type of unit is shown by a trailing letter attached to the number. You can use three types of scaled decimal-numbers with the LP print service.

- Numbers that show sizes in centimeters (marked with a trailing c).
- Numbers that show sizes in inches (marked with a trailing i).
- Numbers that show sizes in units appropriate to use (without a trailing letter); lines, characters, lines per inch, or characters per inch.

Except for the last two lines, the above lines can appear in any order. The Comment: and *comment* items must appear in consecutive order but can be positioned before the other items. The Alignment pattern: and the *content* items must appear in consecutive order at the end of the file. Also, the comment item cannot contain a line that begins with any of the key phrases above unless you precede the key phrase with a > sign. Any leading > sign found in the comment is removed when the comment is displayed. No case distinction is made among the key phrases.

When you issue this command, the form specified by *form-name* is added to the list of forms. If the form already exists, its description is changed to reflect the new information. Once added, a form is available for use in a print request except where access to the form has been restricted, as described under the -u option. You can specify that a form is available to be used only on certain printers.

The following list describes each form attribute.

Page length   Before printing the content of a print request needing this form, the
Page width   generic interface program provided with the LP print service initializes the physical printer to handle pages *scaled-decimal-number1* long, and *scaled-decimal-number2* wide, using the printer type as a key into the terminfo(4) database. The page length and page width are also passed, if possible, to each filter used in a request needing this form.

Number of Pages

> Each time the alignment pattern is printed, the LP print service tries to pass the page subset of 1-integer to each filter.

Line Pitch
Character Pitch

> Before printing the content of a print request needing this form, the interface program provided with the LP print service initializes the physical printer to handle these pitches, using the printer type as a key into the terminfo(4) database. Also, the pitches are passed, if possible, to each filter used in a request needing this form. *scaled-decimal-number3* is in lines-per-centimeter if a c is appended, and lines-per-inch otherwise; similarly, *scaled-decimal-number4* is in characters-per-centimeter if a c is appended, and characters-per-inch otherwise. You can specify the character pitch as elite (12 characters-per-inch), pica (10 characters-per-inch), or compressed (as many characters-per-inch as possible).

Character Set Choice

> When the LP print service alerts an administrator to mount this form, it also mentions that the print wheel *print-wheel* should be used on those printers that take print wheels. If printing with this form is to be done on a printer that has selectable or loadable character sets instead of print wheels, the interface programs provided with the LP print service automatically select or load the correct character set. If mandatory is appended, a user is not allowed to select a different character set for use with the form; otherwise, the character set or print wheel named is a suggestion and a default only.

Ribbon Color   When the LP print service alerts an administrator to mount this form, it also mentions that the color of the ribbon should be *ribbon-color*.

Comment   The LP print service displays the comment unaltered when a user asks about this form (see lpstat(1)).

Alignment Pattern

> When mounting this form, an administrator can ask for the content to be printed repeatedly as an aid in correctly positioning the preprinted form. The optional *content-type* defines the type of printer for which content had been generated. If you do not specify *content-type*, simple is assumed. Note that the content is stored as given and is readable only by the user lp.

When an existing form is changed with this command, items missing in the new information are left as they were. When a new form is added with this command, missing items get the following defaults.

Page Length: 66
Page Width: 80
Number of Pages: 1

```
Line Pitch: 6
Character Pitch: 10
Character Set Choice: any
Ribbon Color: any
```

Deleting a Form LP Print Service
Use the -x option to delete the form *form-name* from the LP print service.

Listing Form Attributes
Use the -l option to list the attributes of the existing form *form-name*. The attributes listed are those described under "Adding or Changing a Form" on page 615. Because of the potentially sensitive nature of the alignment pattern, only the administrator can examine the form with this command. Other people can use the lpstat(1) command to examine the nonsensitive part of the form description.

Allowing and Denying Access to a Form
Use the -u option, followed by the argument allow:*login-ID-list* or deny:*login-ID-list* to specify which users are allowed to specify a particular form with a print request. You can use the -u option with the -F or - option, each of which is described in "Adding or Changing a Form" on page 615.

The *login-ID-list* argument can include any or all of the following constructs.

login-ID	A user on any system.
system-name!*login-ID*	
	A user on system *system-name*.
system-name!all	
	All users on system *system-name*.
all!*login-ID*	A user on all systems.
all	All users on all systems.

The LP print service keeps two lists of users for each form: an allow-list of people allowed to use the form and a deny-list of people that cannot use the form. With the -u allow option, the users listed are added to the allow-list and removed from the deny-list. With the -u deny option, the users listed are added to the deny-list and removed from the allow-list. (You can run both forms of the -u option together with the -F or the - option.)

If the allow-list is not empty, only the users in the list are allowed access to the form, regardless of the content of the deny-list. If the allow-list is empty but the deny-list is not, the users in the deny-list cannot use the form, (but all others can use it). You can deny all users access to a form by specifying -f deny:all. You can allow all users access to a form by specifying -f allow:all (the default).

Setting an Alert to Mount a Form
Use the -f *form-name* option with the -A *alert-type* option to define an alert to mount the form when there are queued jobs that need it. If you do not use this option to arrange alerting for a form, no alert is sent for that form.

The method by which the alert is sent depends on the value of the *alert-type* argument specified with the -A option. The *alert-type*s are described below.

mail   Send the alert message to the administrator with the `mail` command.

write   Write the message to the administrator's login terminal with the `write` command. If the administrator is logged in on several terminals, arbitrarily choose one.

quiet   Do not send messages for the current condition. You can use this option to temporarily stop receiving further messages about a known problem. Once the form `form-name` has been mounted and subsequently unmounted, messages are sent again when the number of print requests reaches the threshold specified by the `-Q` option.

showfault   Try to execute a form alert handler on each system that has a print job for that form in the queue. The fault handler is `/etc/lp/alerts/form`. It is invoked with the parameters `form-name`, `date`, and `filename`. `filename` is the name of a file containing the form alert message.

none   Do not send messages until the `-A` option is given again with a different `alert-type` (other than `quiet`).

shell-command

Run *shell-command* each time the alert needs to be sent. The shell command expects the message from standard input. If blank spaces are embedded in the command, enclose the command in quotes. Note that the `mail` and `write` values for this option are equivalent to the values `mail` *login-ID* and `write` *login-ID*, where *login-ID* is the current name for the administrator. Unless you have used the `su` command to change to another *login-ID*, this value is the current *login-ID* of the person who issued *shell-command*. If you have used the `su` command to change the user ID, then use the user name for the new ID.

list   Display the type of the alert for the form on standard output. No change is made to the alert.

The message sent appears as follows.

```
The form form-name needs to be mounted
on the printer(s):printer (integer1 requests).
integer2 print requests await this form.
Use the ribbon-color ribbon.
Use the print-wheel print wheel, if appropriate.
```

The printers listed are those that the administrator has specified as candidates for this form. The number *integer1* listed next to each printer is the number of requests eligible for the printer. The number *integer2* shown after the list of printers is the total number of requests awaiting the form. It is less than the sum of the other numbers if some requests can be handled by more than one printer.

The *ribbon-color* and *print-wheel* are those specified in the form description. The last line in the message is always sent, even if none of the printers listed use print wheels, because the administrator can choose to mount the form on a printer that does use a print wheel.

Where any color ribbon or any print wheel can be used, the statements above reads

```
Use any ribbon.
Use any print-wheel.
```

If *form-name* is any, the *alert-type* defined in this command applies to any form for which an alert has not yet been defined. If *form-name* is all, the *alert-type* defined in this command applies to all forms.

If you do not specify the -W *minutes* option, the default procedure is that only one message is sent per need to mount the form. Not specifying the -W option is equivalent to specifying -W once or -W 0. If *minutes* is a number greater than 0, an alert is sent at intervals specified by *minutes*.

If you also specify the -Q *requests* option, the alert is sent when a certain number (specified by the argument *requests*) of print requests that need the form are waiting. If you do not specify the -Q option or the value of *requests* is 1 or any (which are both the default), a message is sent as soon as anyone submits a print request for the form when it is not mounted.

Listing the Current Alert

Use the -f option, followed by the -A option and the argument list to list the *alert-type* that has been defined for the specified form *form-name*. No change is made to the alert. If *form-name* is recognized by the LP print service, one of the following lines is sent to the standard output, depending on the type of alert for the form.

```
When requests requests are queued: alert with shell-command every
    minutes minutes
When requests requests are queued: write to user-name every minutes
    minutes
When requests requests are queued: mail to username every minutes
    minutes
No alert
```

The phrase every *minutes* minutes is replaced with once if minutes (-W *minutes*) is 0.

Terminating an Active Alert

Use the -A quiet option to stop messages for the current condition. An administrator can use this option to temporarily stop receiving further messages about a known problem. Once the form has been mounted and then unmounted, messages are sent again when the number of print requests reaches the threshold *requests*.

Removing an Alert Definition

No messages are sent after the -A none option is used until the -A option is given again with a different *alert-type*. You can use the -A none option to permanently stop further messages from being sent; any existing alert definition for the form is removed.

Large File Behavior

See largefile(5) for the description of the behavior of lpforms when encountering files greater than or equal to 2 Gbytes (2**31 bytes).

Exit Status

0	Successful completion.
non-zero	An error occurred.

File

/etc/lp/alerts/form

Fault handler for lpform.

Attributes

See attributes(5) for descriptions of the following attributes.

Attribute Type	Attribute Value
Availability	SUNWpsu

See Also

lp(1), lpstat(1), lpadmin(1M), terminfo(4), attributes(5), largefile(5)
System Administration Guide, Volume II

lpget — Get Printing Configuration

Synopsis

/bin/lpget [-k *key*] [*destination...* | *list*]

Description

Use the lpget command to display printing configuration information. The lpget command reads printing configuration information from the configuration databases in /etc/printers.conf and $HOME/.printers and displays the information (called a configuration report) to the standard output. See printers(4) and printers.conf(4) for information about the printer configuration databases.

lpget displays a configuration report for all keys for the specified destination or destinations by default. Use the -k option to display a configuration report for specific keys. Use the *list* operand to display a configuration report for all configured destinations.

Options

-k *key*	Display a configuration report for *key*. See printers.conf(4) for information about specifying *key*.

Operands

destination   Display a configuration report for `destination`. Destination can be either a printer of a class of printers (see lpadmin(1M)). Specify `destination` by using atomic, POSIX-style (`server:destination`), or Federated Naming Service (FNS) (`.../service/printer/...`) names. See `printers.conf` (4) for information regarding the naming conventions for atomic and FNS names, and standards(5) for information concerning POSIX.

list   Display a configuration report for all configured destinations.

Examples

The following example uses the lpget command with no options to display configuration information about the printer seachild.

```
paperbark% lpget seachild
seachild:
        bsdaddr=seachild,seachild,Solaris
        description=LaserJet Printer
paperbark%
```

The following example displays a configuration report for the bsdaddr key for printer seachild.

```
paperbark% lpget -k bsdaddr seachild
seachild:
        bsdaddr=seachild,seachild,Solaris
paperbark%
```

The following example displays a configuration report for all keys for all configured destinations.

```
paperbark% lpget list
seachild:
        bsdaddr=seachild,seachild,Solaris
        description=LaserJet Printer
_default:
paperbark%
```

Exit Status

0   Successful completion.

non-zero   An error occurred.

Files

/etc/printers.conf

         System printer configuration database.

$HOME/.printers

         User-configurable printer database.

```
printers.conf.byname
```
> NIS version of /etc/printers.conf.

```
fns.ctx_dir.domain
```
> NIS+ version of /etc/printers.conf.

Attributes

See attributes(5) for descriptions of the following attributes.

Attribute Type	Attribute Value
Availability	SUNWpcu
Stability Level	Stable

See Also

lp(1), lpstat(1), lpc(1B), lpq(1B), lpr(1B), lpadmin(1M), lpset(1M),
printers(4), printers.conf(4), attributes(5), standards(5)

lpmove — Move Print Requests

Synopsis

```
/usr/sbin/lpmove request-ID destination
/usr/sbin/lpmove destination1 destination2
```

Description

Use the lpmove command to move requests queued by lp(1) or lpr(1B) between
destinations. Only use lpmove to move jobs on the local system.

The first form of lpmove moves specific print requests (request-ID) to a specific
destination.

The second form of the lpmove command moves all print requests from one
destination(destination1)to another(destination2).This form of lpmove also rejects
new print requests for destination1.

When moving requests, lpmove does not check the acceptance status of the
destination to which the print requests are being moved (see accept(1M)). lpmove does
not move requests that have options (for example, content type or requirement for a
special form) that cannot be handled by the new destination.

Operands

destination	The name of the printer or class of printers (see lpadmin(1M)) to which lpmove moves a specified print request. Specify *destination* using atomic, POSIX-style (*server:destination*), or Federated Naming Service (FNS) (.../service/printer/...) names. See printers.conf(4) for information regarding the naming conventions for atomic and FNS names.
destination1	The name of the destination from which lpmove moves all print requests. Specify *destination1* by using atomic, POSIX-style (*server:destination*), or Federated Naming Service (FNS) (.../service/printer/...) names. See printers.conf(4) for information regarding the naming conventions for atomic and FNS names, and standards(5) for information regarding POSIX.
destination2	The name of the destination to which lpmove moves all print requests. Specify *destination2* by using atomic, POSIX-style (*server:destination*), or Federated Naming Service (FNS) (.../service/printer/...) names. See printers.conf(4) for information regarding the naming conventions for atomic and FNS names.
request-ID	The specific print request to be moved. Specify *request-ID* as the identifier associated with a print request as reported by lpstat. See lpstat(1).

Exit Status

0	Successful completion.
non-zero	An error occurred.

Files

/var/spool/print/*

LP print queue.

Attributes

See attributes(5) for descriptions of the following attributes.

Attribute Type	**Attribute Value**
Availability	SUNWpcu

See Also

lp(1), lpstat(1), lpr(1B), accept(1M), lpadmin(1M), lpsched(1M), printers.conf(4), attributes(5), standards(5)

System Administration Guide, Volume II

lpsched — Start the LP Print Service

Synopsis

```
/usr/lib/lp/lpsched [-f num-filters][-n num-notifiers][-p fd-limit]
   [-r reserved-fds]
```

Description

Each print server must have only one LP scheduler, lpsched, running. The scheduler is started by the /etc/rc2.d/S801p run control script when a system is booted or enters run level 2. You can stop the scheduler by running the lpshut(1M) command and restart the scheduler with the lpsched command. Printers that are restarted using lpsched reprint in their entirety print requests that were stopped by lpshut. See lpshut(1M).

Options

-f *num-filters*

Specify the number of concurrent slow filters that can be run on a print server. Use a default value of 1 if none is specified. Depending on server configuration, with a value of 1, printers may remain idle while there are jobs queued to them.

-n *num-notifiers*

Specify the number of concurrent notification processes that can run on a print server. A default value of 1 is used when none is specified.

-p *fd-limit*   Specify the file descriptor resource limit for the lpsched process. A default value of 4096 is used if none is specified. On extremely large and active print servers, you may need to increase this value.

-r *reserved-fds*

Specify the number of file descriptors that the scheduler reserves for internal communications under heavy load. A default value of 2 is used when none is specified. You should not need to modify this value unless instructed to do so when troubleshooting problems under high load.

Exit Status

0   Successful completion.

non-zero   An error occurred.

Files

/var/spool/lp/*

LP print queue.

Attributes

See attributes(5) for descriptions of the following attributes.

Attribute Type	Attribute Value
Availability	SUNWpsu

See Also

lp(1), lpstat(1), lpadmin(1M), lpmove(1M), lpshut(1M), attributes(5)
System Administration Guide, Volume II

lpset — Set Printing Configuration in /etc/printers.conf or FNS

Synopsis

/bin/lpset [-n *system* | fns] [-x] [-a *key=value*] [-d *key*] *destination*

Description

Use the lpset command to create an /etc/printers.conf file or Federated Naming
System (FNS). See printers.conf(4) and fns(5).

Only superuser or a member of group 14 can execute lpset.

Options

[-n *system*| *fns*]

Create or update the configuration information for the destination
entry in /etc/printers.conf or FNS. *system* specifies that the
information is created or updated in /etc/printers.conf. *fns*
specifies that the information is written using Federated Naming
context. If you do not specify -n, *system* is the default.

-x   Remove all configuration for the destination entry in
/etc/printers.conf or FNS.

-a *key=value* Configure the specified *key=value* pair for the destination entry in
/etc/printers.cont or FNS. See printers.cont(4) for information
regarding the specification of *key=value* pairs.

-d *key*   Delete the configuration option specified by *key* for the destination
entry in /etc/printers.conf or FNS. See printers.conf(4) for
information regarding the specification of key and *key=value* pairs.

Operands

destination   Specify the entry in /etc/printers.conf or FNS in which to create or modify information. destination names a printer or class of printers (see lpadmin(1M)). Each entry in printers.conf describes one destination. Specify destination using atomic or Federated Naming Service (FNS) (.../service/printer/...) names. POSIX-style destination names are not acceptable. See printers.conf(4) for information regarding the naming conventions for atomic and FNS names, and standards(5) for information regarding POSIX.

Examples

The following example removes all existing printing configuration information for destination seachild from /etc/printers.conf.

```
# lpset -x seachild
```

The following example sets the user-equivalence=true key=value pair for destination tabloid in FNS context.

```
# lpset -n fns -a user-equivalence=true tabloid
```

Exit Status

0   Successful completion.

non-zero   An error occurred.

Files

/etc/printers.conf

     System configuration database.

$HOME/.printers

     User-configurable printer database.

printer.conf.byname

     NIS version of /etc/printers.conf.

fns.ctx_dir.domain

     NIS+ version of /etc/printers.conf.

Attributes

See attributes(5) for descriptions of the following attributes.

Attribute Type	Attribute Value
Availability	SUNWpcu
Stability Level	Stable

See Also

lp(1), lpstat(1), lpc(1B), lpq(1B), lpr(1B), lpadmin(1M), lpget(1M),
printers(4), printers.conf(4), attributes(5), fns(5), standards(5)

lpshut — Stop the LP Print Service

Synopsis

/usr/sbin/lpshut

Description

Use the lpshut command to stop the LP print service. Printers that are printing when
lpshut is invoked stop printing. Start or restart printers with lpsched(1M).

Exit Status

0	Successful completion.
non-zero	An error occurred.

Files

/var/spool/lp/*

LP print queue.

Attributes

See attributes(5) for descriptions of the following attributes.

Attribute Type	Attribute Value
Availability	SUNWpsu

See Also

lp(1), lpstat(1), lpadmin(1M), lpmove(1M), lpsched(1M), attributes(5)
System Administration Guide, Volume II

lpsystem — Register Remote Systems with the Print Service

Description

The lpsystem command is obsolete and could be removed at any time. The print system no longer uses the information generated by lpsystem. See lpadmin(1M), lpusers(1M), or printers.conf(4) for equivalent functionality.

Attributes

See attributes(5) for descriptions of the following attributes.

Attribute Type	Attribute Value
Availability	SUNWpcu
Stability Level	Obsolete

See Also

lpadmin(1M), lpusers(1M), printers.conf(4), attributes(5)

lpusers — Set Printing Queue Priorities

Synopsis

```
/usr/sbin/lpusers -d priority-level
/usr/sbin/lpusers -q priority-level -u login-ID-list
/usr/sbin/lpusers -u login-ID-list
/usr/sbin/lpusers -q priority-level
/usr/sbin/lpusers -l
```

Description

Use the lpusers command to set limits to the queue priority level that can be assigned to jobs submitted by users of the LP print service.

Use the first form of the command (with -d) to set the system-wide priority default to priority-level, where priority-level is a value of 0 to 39, with 0 being the highest priority. If a user does not specify a priority level with a print request (see lp(1)), the default priority level is used. Initially, the default priority level is 20.

Use the second form of the command (with -q and -u) to set the default highest priority-level(0-39) that the users in login-ID-list can request when submitting a print request. The login-ID-list argument can include any or all of the following constructs.

login-ID   A user on any system.

system-name!login-ID

        A user on the system system-name.

system-name!all

> All users on system *system-name*.

all!*login-ID*   A user on all systems.

all   All users on all systems.

Users that have been given a limit cannot submit a print request with a higher priority level than the one assigned, nor can they change a request that has already been submitted to have a higher priority. Any print requests submitted with priority levels higher than allowed are given the highest priority allowed.

Use the third form of the command (with -u) to remove any explicit priority level for the specified users.

Use the fourth form of the command (with -q) to set the default highest priority level for all users not explicitly covered by the use of the second form of this command.

Use the last form of the command (with -l) to list the default priority level and the priority limits assigned to users.

Options

-d *priority-level*

> Set the system-wide priority default to *priority-level*.

-q *priority-level* -u *login-ID-list*

> Set the default highest priority level that the users in *login-ID-list* can request when submitting a print request.

-u *login-ID-list*

> Remove any explicit priority level for the specified users.

-q *priority-level*

> Set the default highest priority level for all users not explicitly covered.

-l   List the default priority level and the priority limits assigned to users.

Examples

The following example lists the default priority level and the priority limits assigned to users on a system that has no priorities set.

```
paperbark% lpusers -l
Default priority: 20
Priority limit for users not listed below: 0
Priority  Users
paperbark%
```

Exit Status

0   Successful completion.

non-zero   An error occurred.

Attributes

See attributes(5) for descriptions of the following attributes.

Attribute Type	Attribute Value
Availability	SUNWpsu

See Also

lp(1), attributes(5)

luxadm — Administration Program for the Sun Enterprise Network Array (SENA), RSM, and SPARCstorage Array (SSA) Subsystems

Synopsis

```
/usr/sbin/luxadm [options...] subcommand [options...] enclosure,dev |
    pathname...
```

Description

Use the luxadm administrative command to manage the SENA, RSM, and SPARCstorage Array subsystems. luxadm performs a variety of control and query tasks such as powering down a specific disk so that you can hot-swap it or blinking an LED so you can figure out where a disk is in the storage array. You can use the luxadm command to get information about drives in the array or to download new firmware to the device.

The command line must contain a *subcommand*. The command line can also contain options, usually at least one enclosure name or path name, and other parameters depending on the subcommand. You need specify only as many characters as are required to uniquely identify a subcommand.

Specify the device that a subcommand interacts with by entering a path name. For the SENA subsystem, you can instead specify a disk device or enclosure services controller by entering the World Wide Name (WWN) for the device or a port to the device. You can also specify the device by entering the name of the SENA enclosure and an optional identifier for the particular device in the enclosure.

Path Name

Specify the device or controller by either a complete physical path name or a complete logical path name.

For SENA, two typical physical path names for a device are shown below.

```
/devices/sbus@1f,0/SUNW,socal@1,0/sf@0,0/ssd@w2200002037000f96,
    0:a,raw
/devices/io-unit@f,e0200000/sbi@0,0/SUNW,socal@2,0/sf@0,0/ssd@34,
    0:a,raw
```

For all SENA IBs (Interface Boards) on the system, a logical link to the physical paths is kept in the directory `/dev/es`. An example of a logical link is `/dev/es/ses0`.

You can use WWN in place of the path name to select an `FC_AL` device or SENA subsystem. The WWN is a unique, 16-digit, hexadecimal value that specifies either the port used to access the device or the device itself. A typical WWN value is shown below.

```
2200002037000f96
```

See "Notes" on page 632 for more information on the WWN formats.

For the SPARCstorage Array controller, a typical physical path name is shown below.

```
/devices/.../.../SUNW,soc@3,0/SUNW,pln@axxxxxxx,xxxxxxxx:ctlr
```

A typical physical path name for an RSM controller is shown below.

```
/devices/sbus@1f,0/QLGC,isp@1,10000:devctl
```

To make it easier to address the SPARCstorage Array or RSM controller, a logical path name of the form *cN* is supported, where *N* is the logical controller number. `luxadm` uses the *cN* name to find an entry in the `/dev/rdsk` directory of a disk that is attached to the SPARCstorage Array or RSM controller. The `/dev/rdsk` entry is then used to determine the physical name of the SPARCstorage Array or RSM controller.

For a SPARCstorage Array disk, a typical physical path name is shown below.

```
/devices/.../.../SUNW,soc@3,0/SUNW, pln@axxxxxxx,xxxxxxxx/ssd@0,0:c,raw
```

The logical path name that corresponds to the above physical path name for a SPARCstorage array is shown below.

```
/dev/rdsk/c1t0d0s2
```

For an RSM, a typical physical path name is shown below.

```
/devices/sbus@1f,0/QLGC,isp@1,10000/sd@8,0:c,raw
```

The logical path name that corresponds to the above physical path name for an RSM is shown below.

```
/dev/rdsk/c2t8d0s2
```

For individual `FC-AL` devices, a typical physical path name is shown below.

```
/devices/sbus@3.0/SUNW,socal@d,10000/sf@0,0/ssd@w2200002037049fc3,0:a,r,raw
```

The logical path name that corresponds to the above physical path name for an FC-AL device is shown below.

```
/dev/rdsk/c1t0d0s2
```

Enclosure

For SENA, you can identify a device by its enclosure name and slot name.

```
box-name[,fslot-number]
box-name[,rslot-number]
```

box-name is the name of the SENA enclosure, as specified by the *enclosure-name* subcommand. When used without the optional *slot-number* parameter, the *box-name* identifies the SENA subsystem IB.

f or r specifies the front or rear slots in the SENA enclosure.
slot-number specifies the slot number of the device in the SENA enclosure, 0-6 or 0-10.
See devfsadm(1M) for additional information on logical names for disks and subsystems.

Notes

See the *SENA Array Installation and Service Manual* for additional information on the SENA. Refer to *Tutorial for SCSI use of IEEE Company_ID*, R. Snively, for additional information regarding the IEEE extended WWN. Currently, only some device drivers support hot-plugging. If you try hot-plugging on a disk or bus where it is not supported, an error message of the following form is displayed.

```
luxadm: can't acquire "PATHNAME": No such file or directory
```

You must be careful not to quiesce a bus that contains the root or the /usr file systems or any swap data. If you do quiesce such a bus, a deadlock can result, requiring a system reboot.

Options

The following options are supported by all subcommands. Options that are specific to particular subcommands are described with the subcommand.

-e   Run in expert mode. This option is not recommended for the novice user.

-v   Run in verbose mode.

Subcommands

```
display enclosure[,dev]...| pathname...
display -p pathname...
display -r enclosure[,dev]...| pathname...
display -v enclosure[,dev]...| pathname...
```

Display enclosure or device specific data.

Subsystem data consists of enclosure environmental sense information and status for all subsystem devices, including disks.

Disk data consists of inquiry, capacity, and configuration information.

-p   Display performance information for the device or subsystem specified by *pathname*. This option applies only to subsystems that accumulate performance information.

-r   Display error information for the FC_AL device specified by the path name or, if the path is a SENA, for all devices on the loop. The -r option applies only to SENA subsystems and individual FC_AL devices

-v   Display in verbose mode, including mode sense data.

```
pathname...
download [-s][-w WWN][f filename-path] enclosure...|
```

> Download the PROM image pointed to by *filename-path* to the
> SENA subsystem Interface Board unit or the SPARCstorage Array
> controllers specified by *enclosure* or *pathname*. You must reset the
> SPARCstorage Array before you can use the downloaded code.
>
> When the SENA download is complete, the SENA is reset and the
> downloaded code executed. If you specify no *filename*, the default
> PROM image is used. The default PROM image for the
> SPARCstorage Array controller is in
> `/usr/lib/firmware/ssa/ssafirmware`. The default PROM image
> for the SENA is in the directory `/usr/lib/locale/C/LC_MESSAGES`
> and is named `ibfirmware`. The SENA firmware is language
> dependent so, the LANG environment variable is used to find the
> directory that contains the firmware. The default directory is C.

> | `-s` | Save the downloaded firmware in the FEPROM. If you |
> | | do not specify `-s`, the downloaded firmware is not |
> | | saved across power cycles. The `-s` option does not |
> | | apply to the SPARCstorage Array controller because |
> | | it always writes the downloaded firmware into the |
> | | FEPROM. When the `-s` option is used, the download |
> | | subcommand modifies the FEPROM on the |
> | | subsystem and so should be used with caution. |

> | `-w WWN` | Change the SPARCstorage Array controller's World |
> | | Wide Name. *WWN* is a 12-digit hex number; leading |
> | | zeros are required. The `-w` option applies only to the |
> | | SPARCstorage Array. The new SPARCstorage Array |
> | | controller's image has the least significant 6 bytes of |
> | | the 8-byte World Wide Name modified to *WWN*. |

```
enclosure-name new-name enclosure | pathname
```

> Change the enclosure name of the enclosure or enclosures specified
> by *enclosure* or *pathname*. The new name (*new-name*) must be 16 or
> fewer characters. Only alphabetic or numeric characters are
> acceptable. This subcommand applies only to the SENA.

```
fc_s_download [-F][-f fcode-file]
```

> Download the fcode contained in the file *fcode-file* into all the FC/S
> SBus cards. This command is interactive and expects user
> confirmation before downloading the fcode.
>
> Use `fc_s_download` only in single-user mode. Using `fc_s_download`
> to update a host adapter while there is I/O activity through that
> adapter resets the adapter.

-f *fcode-file*

> When invoked without the -f *fcode-file* option, print the current version of the fcode in each FC/S SBus card.

-F

> Forcibly download the fcode, but still expect user confirmation before the download. The version of the FC/S SBus card fcode that was released with this version of the operating system is kept in the directory usr/lib/firmware/fc_s and is named fc_s_fcode.

fcal_s_download [-f *fcode-file*]

> Download the fcode contained in the file *fcode-file* into all the FC100/S SBus cards. This command is interactive and expects user confirmation before downloading the fcode.

> Use fcal_s_download only in single-user mode. Using fcal_s_download to update a host adapter while there is I/O activity through that adapter resets the adapter.

-f *fcode-file*

> When invoked without the -f option, print the current version of the fcode in each FC100/S SBus. The version of the FC100/S SBus cards fcode that was released with this version of the operating system is kept in the directory usr/lib/firmware/fc_s and is named fcal_s_fcode.

inquiry *enclosure*[,*dev*]... | *pathname*...

> Display the inquiry information for the selected device specified by *enclosure* or *pathname*.

insert_device [*enclosure*,*dev*...] | *pathname*...

New!

> Assist the user in the hot insertion of a new device or a chain of new devices. See "Notes" on page 632 for limitations on hot-plug operations. This subcommand applies only to the SENA, RSM, and individual FC_AL drives. For the SENA, if you specify more than one enclosure, you can perform concurrent hot insertions on multiple buses. With no arguments to the subcommand, you can insert entire enclosures.

> For the RSM, you can specify only one controller. For the SENA, if you have specified more than one enclosure, you can perform concurrent hot insertions on multiple buses. With no arguments to the subcommand, you can insert entire enclosures or individual FC_AL drives. For the RSM, you can specify only one controller. For the SENA, this subcommand guides you interactively through the hot-insertion steps of a new device or chain of devices. If you enter a list of devices, insert_device asks you to verify that the list of

devices to be inserted is correct, at which point you can continue or quit. It then interactively asks you to insert the disk(s) or enclosure(s) and then creates and displays the logical path names for the devices.

For the RSM, the following steps are taken.

- Quiesce the bus or buses that support quiescing and unquiescing.

- Inform you that the device can be safely inserted.

- Request confirmation that the device has been inserted.

- Unquiesce the bus or buses that support quiescing and unquiescing.

- Create the logical device name for the new device.

led *enclosure,dev...| pathname...*

Display the current state of the LED associated with the disk specified by *enclosure* or *pathname*. This subcommand applies only to subsystems that support this functionality.

led_blink *enclosure,dev...| pathname...*

Start blinking the LED associated with the disk specified by *enclosure* or *pathname*. This subcommand applies only to subsystems that support this functionality.

led_off *enclosure,dev...| pathname...*

Disable (turn off) the LED associated with the disk specified by *enclosure* or *pathname*. On a SENA subsystem, this action may or may not turn the LED off or stop it blinking, depending on the state of the SENA subsystem. Refer to the SENA Array Installation and Service Manual (p/n 802-7573). This subcommand applies only to subsystems that support this functionality.

led_on *pathname...*

Enable (turn on) the LED associated with the disk specified by *enclosure* or *pathname*. This subcommand applies only to subsystems that support this functionality.

power_off [-F] *enclosure[,dev]... | pathname...*
number power_off *pathname [enclosureport]... | controller tray*

When a SENA is addressed, this subcommand puts the SENA subsystem into the power-save mode. The SENA drives are not available when in the power-save mode. When an Enclosure Services card within the SPARCstorage Array is addressed, power down the RSM tray. When a drive in a SENA is addressed, set the drive to the drive off/unmated state. In the drive off/unmated state, the drive is spun down (stopped) and in bypass mode.

-F   Applies only to the SENA. Try to force a power-off of one or more devices even if those devices are being used by this host (and are, therefore, busy).

> Warning: Powering off a device that has data that is currently being used produces unpredictable results. You should first try to power off the device normally (without -F), resorting to this option only when sure of the consequences of overriding normal checks.

power_on *enclosure*[,*dev*]... | *pathname*...

> Go out of power-save mode when this subcommand is addressed to a SENA. There is no programmatic way to power on the SPARCstorage Array RSM tray. When this subcommand is addressed to a drive, the drive is set to its normal startup state.

probe [-p]

New!

> Find and display information about all attached SENA subsystems and individual FC_AL devices, including the logical path name, the WWNs, and enclosure names. This subcommand warns you if it finds different SENAs with the same enclosure names.

> -p   Include the physical path name in the display.

release *pathname*

> Release a reservation held on the specified disk. If the path name is of the SPARCstorage Array controller, then release all of the disks in the SPARCstorage Array.

remove_device [-F] *enclosure*[,*dev*]... | *pathname*...

New!

> Assist in hot-removing a device or a chain of devices. You can also use this subcommand to remove entire enclosures. This subcommand applies to the SENA, RSM, and individual FC_AL drives. See "Notes" on page 632 for limitations on hot-plug operations. For the SENA and individual FC_AL devices, this subcommand guides you through the hot removal of a device or devices. During execution it asks you to verify that the list of devices to be removed is correct, at which point you can continue or quit. It then prepares the disk(s) or enclosure(s) for removal and interactively asks you to remove the disk(s) or enclosure(s).

> For the RSM, this option takes the following steps.

> - Take the device offline.
> - Quiesce the bus or buses that support quiescing and unquiescing.
> - Inform you that the device can be safely removed.
> - Request confirmation that the device has been removed.
> - Unquiesce the bus or buses that support quiescing and unquiescing.
> - Bring the (now removed) device back online.
> - Remove the logical device name for the removed device.

-F   Try to hot-plug one or more devices even if those devices are being used by this host (and are, therefore, busy), to force the hot-plugging operation.

Warning: Removal of a device that has data that is currently being used produces unpredictable results. You should first try to hot-plug normally (without -F), resorting to this option only when sure of the consequences of overriding normal hot-plugging checks.

replace_device [-F] *pathname*

Applies only to the RSM. See "Notes" on page 632 for limitations on hot-plug operations. Guide you interactively through the hot replacement of a device.

This option takes the following steps.

- Take the device offline.
- Quiesce the bus or buses that support quiescing and unquiescing.
- Inform you that the device can be safely replaced.
- Request confirmation that the device has been replaced.
- Unquiesce the bus or buses that support quiescing and unquiescing.
- Bring the device back online.

-F   Try to hot-plug one or more devices even if those devices are busy, (that is, to force the hot-plugging operation).

Warning: Removal of a device that has data that is currently being used produces unpredictable results. You should first try to hot-plug normally (without -F), resorting to this option only when sure of the consequences of overriding normal hot-plugging checks.

reserve *pathname*

Reserve the specified disk for exclusive use by the issuing host. If the path name is that of the SPARCstorage Array controller, then reserve all of the disks in the SPARCstorage Array.

This subcommand is included for historical and diagnostic purposes only. *New!*

set_boot_dev [-y] *pathname*

Set the boot-device variable in the system PROM to the physical device name specified by *pathname*, which can be a block special device or a mount point. The command normally runs interactively, requesting confirmation for setting the default boot-device in the PROM. You can use the -y option to run the command noninteractively, in which case no confirmation is requested or required.

```
start [-t tray-number] pathname...
```

> Spin up the specified disk(s). If *pathname* specifies the SPARCstorage Array controller, this action applies to all disks in the SPARCstorage Array.
>
> -t   Spin up all disks in the tray specified by *tray-number*. *pathname* must specify the SPARCstorage Array controller.

```
stop [-t tray-number] pathname...
```

> Spin down the specified disk(s). If *pathname* specifies the SPARCstorage Array controller, this action applies to all disks in the SPARCstorage Array.
>
> -t   Spin down all disks in the tray specified by *tray-number*. *pathname* must specify the SPARCstorage Array controller.

Operands

enclosure   The *box-name* of the SENA.

pathname   The logical or physical path of a SENA IB, SPARCstorage Array, or RSM controller (c*N* name) or disk device. *pathname* can also be the WWN of a SENA IB, SENA disk, or individual FC_AL device.

SPARCstorage Array Subcommands

```
fast_write [-s] -c pathname
fast_write [-s] -d pathname
fast_write [-s] -e pathname
```

> Enable or disable the use of the NVRAM to enhance the performance of writes in the SPARCstorage Array. *pathname* refers to the SPARCstorage Array controller or to an individual disk.
>
> -s   Save the SPARCstorage Array change so it persists across power cycles.
>
> -c   Enable fast writes for synchronous writes only.
>
> -d   Disable fast writes.
>
> -e   Enable fast writes.

```
nvram_data pathname
```

> Display the amount of fast write data in the NVRAM for the specified disk. This command can be used only for an individual disk.

```
perf_statistics -d pathname
perf_statistics -e pathname
```

> Enable or disable the accumulation of performance statistics for the specified SPARCstorage Array controller. The accumulation of performance statistics must be enabled before use of the display -p

subcommand. This subcommand can be issued only to the
SPARCstorage Array controller.

-d   Disable the accumulation of performance statistics.

-e   Enable the accumulation of performance statistics.

purge *pathname*

Purge any fast write data from NVRAM for one disk or for all disks if
you specify the controller. Use this option with caution, usually only
when a drive has failed.

sync_cache *pathname*

Flush all outstanding writes for the specified disk from NVRAM to the
media. If *pathname* specifies the controller, this action applies to all
disks in the SPARCstorage Array subsystem.

Enclosure Services Card Subcommands

The env_display and alarm* subcommands apply only to an Enclosure Services Card
(SES) in an RSM tray in a SPARCstorage Array. You address the RSM tray by using the
logical or physical path of the SES device or by specifying the controller followed by the
tray number. The controller is addressed by c*N* or the physical path to the SSA's
controller.

alarm *pathname* | *controller tray-number*

Display the current state of audible alarm.

alarm_off *pathname* | *controller tray-number*

Disable the audible alarm for this RSM tray.

alarm_on *pathname* | *controller tray-number*

Enable the audible alarm for this RSM tray.

alarm_set *controller pathname* | *controller tray-number* [*seconds*]

Set the audible alarm setting to *seconds*.

env_display *pathname* | *controller tray-number*

Display the environmental information for the specified unit.

SENA and Individual FC_AL Drive Expert Mode Subcommands

New!

The following subcommands, new in the Solaris 8 release, are for expert use only and
are applicable only to the SENA and fiber channel loops. Use them only if you are
knowledgeable about the SENA subsystem and fiber channel loops.

The following subcommands work on a bus if you specify a disk; then, the bus to
which the disk is attached is used.

-e *forcelip enclosure*[*,dev*]... | *pathname*...

Force the link to reinitialize, using the Loop Initialization Primitive
(LIP) sequence. *enclosure* or *pathname* can specify any device on the
loop.

This command is for experts only. Use it with caution. It resets all ports on the loop.

`-e rdls enclosure[,dev]... | pathname...`

Read and display the link error status information for all available devices on the loop that contains the device specified by *enclosure* or *pathname*.

Other Expert Mode Subcommands

See "Notes" on page 632 for limitations of these subcommands. Use them only if you are knowledgeable about the systems you are managing.

`-e bus_getstate pathname`

Get and display the state of the specified bus.

`-e bus_quiesce pathname`

Quiesce the specified bus.

`-e bus_reset pathname`

Reset the specified bus.

`-e bus_resetall pathname`

Reset the specified bus.

`-e bus_unquiesce pathname`

Unquiesce the specified bus.

`-e dev_getstate pathname`

Get and display the state of the specified device.

`-e dev_reset pathname`

Reset the specified device.

`-e offline pathname`

Take the specified device offline.

`-e online pathname`

Put the specified device online.

Examples

New!

The following example finds and displays all of the SENAs and individual FC_AL devices on a system.

```
castle% luxadm probe
```

The following example displays an SSA.

```
castle% luxadm display c1
```

The following example displays a SENA.

```
castle% luxadm display /dev/es/ses0
```

The following example displays two subsystems, using the enclosure names.
```
castle% luxadm display BOB system1
```

The following example displays information about the first disk in the front of the enclosure named BOB. Use f to specify the front disks. Use r to specify the rear disks.
```
castle% luxadm display BOB.f0
```

The following example displays information about a SENA disk, an enclosure, or an individual FC_AL drive with the port WWN of 2200002037001246.
```
castle% luxadm display 2200002037001246
```

The following example uses only as many characters as are required to uniquely identify a subcommand.
```
castle% luxadm disp BOB
```

The following example displays error information about the loop that the enclosure BOB is on.
```
castle% luxadm display -r BOB
```

The following example downloads new firmware into the Interface Board in the enclosure named BOB (this example is using the default path for the file to download).
```
castle% luxadm download -s BOB
```

The following example displays information from the SCSI inquiry command from all individual disks on the system, using only as many characters as necessary to uniquely identify the inquiry subcommand.
```
castle% luxadm inq /dev/rdsk/c?t?d?s2
```

The following example hot-plugs a new drive into the first slot in the front of the enclosure named BOB.
```
castle% luxadm insert_device BOB,f0
```

The following example runs an expert subcommand. The subcommand forces a loop initialization on the loop that the enclosure BOB is on.
```
castle% luxadm -e forcelip BOB
```

The following example uses the expert mode hot-plugging subcommands to hot-remove a disk on an SSA. The first step reserves the SCSI device so that it can't be accessed by way of its second SCSI bus.
```
# luxadm reserve /dev/rdsk/c1t8d0s2
```

The next two steps take the disk to be removed offline, then quiesce the bus.
```
# luxadm -e offline /dev/rdsk/c1t8d0s2
# luxadm -e bus_quiesce /dev/rdsk/c1t8d0s2
```

The user then removes the disk and continues by unquiescing the bus, putting the disk back online, then unreserving it.

```
# luxadm -e bus_unquiesce /dev/rdsk/c1t8d0s2
# luxadm -e online /dev/rdsk/c1t8d0s2
# luxadm release /dev/rdsk/c1t8d0s2
```

Environment Variables

See environ(5) for a description of the LANG environment variable that affects the execution of luxadm.

Exit Status

0   Successful completion.

-1   An error occurred.

Files

/usr/lib/firmware/fc_s/fcal_s_fcode

> The version of the FC100/S SBus cards fcode that was released with this version of the operating system.

/usr/lib/firmware/fc_s/fc_s_fcode

> The version of the FC/S SBus card fcode that was released with this version of the operating system.

/usr/lib/firmware/ssa/ssafirmware

> The default PROM image for the SPARCstorage Array controller.

/usr/lib/locale/C/LC_MESSAGES/libfirmware

> The default PROM image for the SENA.

Attributes

See attributes(5) for descriptions of the following attributes.

Attribute Type	Attribute Value
Availability	SUNWluxop

See Also

devlinks(1M), disks(1M), ssaadm(1M), attributes(5), environ(5), ses(7D)
Snively, R., *Tutorial for SCSI use of IEEE company_ID*, X3T10/97-101r2, February 25, 1996.
SENA Array Installation and Service Manual (p/n 802-7573)
RAID Manager 6.1 Installation and Support Guide AnswerBook
RAID Manager 6.1 User's Guide AnswerBook

M

m64config — Configure the M64 Graphics Accelerator

Synopsis

```
/usr/sbin/m64config [-dev device-filename] [-res video-mode [now | try]
    [noconfirm | nocheck]] [-file machine|system] [-propt] [-prconf]
    [-defaults] [-depth 8|24]
/usr/sbin/m64config [-propt] [-prconf]
/usr/sbin/m64config [-help] [-res ?]
```

Description

Use the m64config command to configure the M64 Graphics Accelerator and some of the X11 window system defaults for M64.

Note — The m64config command is not automatically installed when you do a complete install. If the m64config file is not available in the /usr/sbin directory, install the SUNWm64cf package.

Use the first form of m64config to store the specified options in the OWconfig file. These options are used to initialize the M64 device the next time the window system is run on that device. Updating options in the OWconfig file provides persistence of these options across window system sessions and system reboots.

The second and third forms, which invoke only the -prconf, -propt, -help, and -res ? options, do not update the OWconfig file. Additionally, for the third form all other options are ignored.

You can specify options for only one M64 device at a time. To specify options for multiple M64 devices, invoke m64config for each device.

You can specify only M64-specific options through m64config. The normal window system options for specifying default depth, default visual class, and so forth, are still specified as device modifiers on the openwin command line. See the *OpenWindows Desktop Reference Manual* for details.

You can also specify the OWconfig file that is to be updated. By default, the machine-specific file in the /etc/openwin directory tree is updated. You can use the -file option to update the system-global OWconfig file in the /usr/openwin directory tree instead.

Both of these standard OWconfig files can be written only by root. Consequently, the m64config program, which is owned by the root user, always runs with setuid root permission.

Options

-defaults   Reset all option values to their default values.

-depth 8|24   Set the screen depth to 8 or 24 bits per pixel. Twenty-four bits per pixel enables TrueColor graphics in the window system at the expense of screen resolution.

The maximum resolution that is available with 24 bits per pixel depends on the amount of memory installed on the PGX card. For 2-megabyte PGX cards, the maximum available resolution is 800x600. For 4 megabyte cards, it is 1152x900. If there is not enough memory for the specified combination of resolution and depth, print an error message and exit.

-dev *device-filename*

Specify the M64 special file. If not specified, m64config tries /dev/fbs/m640 through /dev/fbs/m648 until it finds one.

-file machine|system

Specify which OWconfig file to update. If machine, use the machine-specific OWconfig file in the /etc/openwin directory tree. If system, use the global OWconfig file in the /usr/openwin directory tree. If the file does not exist, create it.

-help   Print a list of the m64config command-line options, along with a brief explanation of each.

-prconf   Print the M64 hardware configuration. The following is a typical display with the -prconf option.

--- Hardware Configuration for /dev/fbs/m640

-ASIC: version 0x41004754 DAC: version 0x0 PROM: version 0x0

Card possible resolutions: 640x480x60, 800x600x75, 1024x768x60 x768x70, 1024x768x75, 1280x1024x75, 1280x1024x76 J80x1024x60, 1152x900x66, 1152x900x76, 1280x1024x67 960x680x112S, 960x680x108S, 640x480x60i, 768x575x50i, 1280x800x76 x900x76, 1600x1000x66, 1600x1000x76, vga, svga, 1152, 1280 stereo, ntsc, pal

Monitor possible resolutions: 720x400x70, 720x400x88,
640x480x60 x480x67, 640x480x72, 640x480x75, 800x600x56,
800x600x60 800x600x72, 800x600x75, 832x624x75,
1024x768x87, 1024x768x60 x768x70, 1024x768x75,
1280x1024x75, 1280x1024x76, 1152x900x66 jx900x76,
1280x1024x67, 960x680x112S, vga, svga, 1152, 1280 stereo

Possible depths: 8, 24 Current resolution setting:
1280x1024x76 Current depth: 8

-propt   Print the current values of all M64 options in the OWconfig file
specified by the -file option for the device specified by the -dev
option. Print the values of options as they are set in the OWconfig file
after the call to m64config completes. The following is a typical
display with the -propt option.

--- OpenWindows Configuration for /dev/fbs/m640 --OWcon-
fig: machine Video Mode: not set Depth: 8

-res *video-mode* [now | try [noconfirm | nocheck]]

Specify the video mode used to drive the monitor connected to the
specified M64 device. Video modes are built-in. *video-mode* has the
format of *widthxheightxrate*. *width* is the screen width in pixels,
height is the screen height in pixels, and *rate* is the vertical
frequency of the screen refresh. As a convenience, -res also accepts
formats with @ preceding the refresh rate instead of x. For example,
1280x1024@76.

The following list shows the valid video modes. You can also obtain
this list by running m64config -res '?'. Note that you must quote
the ?. Not all resolutions are supported by both the video board and by
the monitor. m64config does not permit you to set a resolution the
board does not support and requests confirmation before setting a
resolution the monitor does not support.

```
720x400x70
720x400x88
640x480x60
640x480x67
640x480x72
640x480x75
800x600x56
800x600x60
800x600x72
800x600x75
832x624x75
1024x768x87
1024x768x60
1024x768x70
1024x768x75
1280x1024x75
1280x1024x76
```

```
1152x870x75
1280x1024x60
1152x900x66
1152x900x76
1280x1024x67
1600x1280x76
1920x1080x72
1280x800x76
1440x900x76
1600x1000x66
1600x1000x76
1920x1200x70
```

For convenience, some video modes have symbolic names. Instead of the form `widthxheightxrate`, you can supply one of these names as the argument to -res. The meaning of the symbolic name none is that when the window system is run, the screen resolution is the video mode that is currently programmed in the device.

Name	Corresponding Video Mode
svga	1024x768x60
1152	1152x900x76
1280	1280x1024x76
none	Video mode currently programmed in device.

The -res option also accepts additional, optional arguments immediately following the video mode specification. You can specify any or all of these.

now   If present, update the video mode in the OWconfig file and immediately program the M64 device to display this video mode. (This option is useful for changing the video mode before starting the window system).

If you use this suboption with m64config while the configured device is being used (for example, while running the window system), you may get unpredictable results. To run m64config with the now suboption, first bring the window system down. If you use the now suboption within a window system session, the video mode is changed immediately but the width and height of the affected screen don't change until the window system is exited and reentered again. Consequently, this usage is strongly discouraged.

noconfirm

Bypass confirmation and program the requested video mode. Without this option, you can potentially put the system into an unusable state where there is no video output if there is ambiguity in the monitor sense codes for the particular code read. To reduce the chance of this, the default behavior of m64config is to print a warning message and to prompt to find out if it is okay to continue. This option is useful when m64config is being run from a shell script.

nocheck

Suspend normal error checking based on the monitor sense code. The specified video mode is accepted regardless of whether it is appropriate for the currently attached monitor. This option is useful if a different monitor is to be connected to the M64 device. Use of this option also implies noconfirm.

try

Program the specified video mode on a trial basis. You are asked to confirm the video mode by typing y within 10 seconds. You can terminate the trial before 10 seconds elapse by typing any character. Any character other than y or Return is considered a no response, the previous video mode is restored, and m64config does not change the video mode in the OWconfig file (other specified options still take effect). If you press Return, you are prompted for a yes or no answer on whether to keep the new video mode. This option implies the now suboption. (see the warning note on the now suboption).

Defaults

If you do not specify an option on the command line for a given invocation of m64config, the corresponding OWconfig option is not updated; it retains its previous value.

When the window system is run, if an M64 option has never been specified by m64config, a default value is used. The option defaults are as follows.

Option	Default
-dev	/dev/fbs/m640
-file	machine
-res	none

The default for the -res option of none means that when the window system is run, the screen resolution is the video mode that is currently programmed in the device.

This default provides compatibility for users who are accustomed to specifying the device resolution through the PROM. On some devices (for example, GX), this is the only way of specifying the video mode. The PROM ultimately determines the default M64 video mode.

Examples

The following example switches the monitor type to the maximum resolution of 1280 x 1024 at 76 Hz.

```
castle% /usr/sbin/m64config -res 1280x1024x76
```

Files

`/dev/fbs/m640`

> Device special file.

`/usr/openwin/server/etc/OWconfig`

> System configuration file.

`/etc/openwin/server/etc/OWconfig`

> System configuration file.

Attributes

See `attributes`(5) for descriptions of the following attributes.

Attribute Type	Attribute Value
Availability	SUNWm64cf

See Also

`mmap(2)`, `attributes(5)`, `fbio(7I)`, `m64(7D)`
OpenWindows Desktop Reference Manual

mail.local — Store Mail in a Mailbox

Synopsis

```
/usr/lib/mail.local [-f sender][-d] recipient
```

Description

The `mail.local` command is used by `sendmail`(1M) as a mail delivery agent for local mail. It is not a user interface. `mail.local` reads the standard input up to an end-of-file and appends it to each user's mail file (mailbox).

Messages are appended to the user's mail file in the `/var/mail` directory. The user must be a valid user name.

Each delivered mail message in the mailbox is preceded by a UNIX `From` line with the following format.

```
From sender_address time_stamp
```

The *sender_address* is extracted from the SMTP envelope address (the envelope address is specified with the `-f` option).

A trailing blank line is also added to the end of each message.
The mail files are locked with a `.lock` file while mail is appended.
The mail files are created with mode `660`, owner is set to `recipient`, and group is set to `mail`. If the `biff` service is returned by `getservbyname(3N)`, the `biff` server is notified of delivered mail. This program also computes the `Content-Length:` header that is used by the mailbox reader to mark the message boundary.

Options

`-f sender`	Specify the "envelope from address" of the message. This option is technically optional but should be used.
`-d`	Specify the recipient of the message. This option is also optional and is supported here for backward compatibility. That is, `mail.local` `recipient` is the same as `mail.local -d recipient`.

Operands

`recipient`   The recipient of the mail message.

Environment Variables

`TZ`   Set the appropriate time zone on the timestamp.

Exit Status

`0`	Successful operation.
`>0`	An error occurred.

Files

`/tmp/local.XXXXXX`

  Temporary files.

`/tmp/lochd.XXXXXX`

  Temporary files.

`/var/mail/username`

  User's mail file.

Attributes

See `attributes(5)` for descriptions of the following attributes.

Attribute Type	Attribute Value
Availability	SUNWcsu

See Also

`mail(1)`, `comsat(1M)`, `sendmail(1M)`, `getservbyname(3N)`, `attributes(5)`

makedbm — Make a dbm File or Get a Text File from a dbm File

Synopsis

`New!`

```
/usr/sbin/makedbm [-b][-l][-s][-E][-i yp-input-file]
    [-o yp-output-name][-d yp-domain-name][-m yp-master-name]
    [-S delimiter][-D number-of-delimiters] infile outfile
/usr/sbin/makedbm [-u dbmfilename]
```

Description

makedbm is mainly used to generate NIS maps from text files. You do not invoke the makedbm command directly. It is called from the /var/yp/Makefile script. It generates a special entry with the key yp_last_modified, which is the date of *infile* (or the current time if *infile* is -). The entries that have keys with the prefix yp_ are interpreted by NIS server commands.

The makedbm command converts the *infile* to a pair of files in ndbm format (see dbm_clearerr(3C)), namely, *outfile*&.pag and *outfile*&.dir. Each line of the input file is converted to a single dbm record. All characters up to the first Tab or space form the key, and the rest of the line is the data. If a line ends with a backslash (\), the data for that record is continued on the next line. makedbm does not treat the pound sign (#) as a special character.

Options

-b   Insert the YP_INTERDOMAIN into the output so that ypserv(1M) uses DNS for host name and address lookups for hosts not found in the maps.

-d *yp-domain-name*

                            Create a special entry with the key *yp-domain-name*.

`New!`   -D *number-of-delimiters*

                            Specify the number of delimiters to skip before forming the key.

`New!`   -E   Escape delimiters.

-i *yp-input-file*

                            Create a special entry with the key *yp-input-file*.

-l   Convert the keys of the given map to lower case, so that, for example, host name matches succeed independently of upper- or lowercase distinctions.

-m *yp-master-name*

                            Create a special entry with the key *yp-master-name*. If you specify no master host name, *yp-master-name* is set to the local host name.

-o *yp-output-name*

                            Create a special entry with the key *yp-output-name*.

-s	Accept connections from secure NIS networks only.
-S *delimiter*	Specify the delimiter to use instead of the default delimiter to form the key.
-u *dbmfilename*	

Undo a dbm file. Print the file in text format, one entry per line, with a single space separating keys from values.

Operands

infile	Input file for makedbm. If *infile* is a dash (-), read the standard input.
outfile	One of two output files in ndbm format: *outfile*.pag and *outfile*.dir.

Attributes

See attributes(5) for descriptions of the following attributes.

Attribute Type	**Attribute Value**
Availability	SUNWcsu

See Also

ypserv(1M), dbm_clearerr(3C), attributes(5)

makemap — Create Database Maps for sendmail

Synopsis

/usr/sbin/makemap [-N][-d][-f][-o][-r][-s][-v] *mantype mapname*

Description

Use the makemap command to create the binary form of the database maps used by the keyed map lookups in sendmail(1M). makemap reads from the standard input and outputs to the specified *mapname*.

In all cases, makemap reads lines from the standard input consisting of two words separated by white space. The first is the database key, the second is the value. The value can contain %n strings to indicated parameter substitution. Literal percents should be doubled (%%). Blank lines and lines beginning with # are ignored.

makemap handles three different database formats, which you choose by specifying the *maptype* parameter.

Options

-N	Include the null byte that terminates strings in the map. This string must match the -N option in the K line in sendmail.cf.
-d	Allow duplicate keys in the map. This option is allowed only on B-Tree format maps. If two identical keys are read, insert them both into the map.
-f	Disable folding of all uppercase letters in the key to lower case. This option is intended to mesh with the -f option in the K line in sendmail.cf. The value is never case folded.
-o	Append to an old file. This option enables you to augment an existing file.
-r	Allow replacement of existing keys. Normally, makemap complains if you repeat a key and does not do the insert.
-s	Ignore safety checks on maps being created, and check for hard or symbolic links in world-writeable directories.
-v	Verbosely print what makemap is doing.

Operands

mapname	File name of the database map being created.
maptype	Specify the database format. The following *maptype* parameters are available.

dbm	Specify DBM format maps.
btree	Specify B-Tree format maps.
hash	Specify hash format maps.

Attributes

See attributes(5) for descriptions of the following attributes.

Attribute Type	Attribute Value
Availability	SUNWsndmu

See Also

sendmail(1M), attributes(5)

mibiisa — Sun SNMP Agent

Synopsis

/usr/lib/snmp/mibiisa [-ar][-c *config-dir*][-d *debug-level*][-p *port*]

Description

The mibiisa command is an RFC 1157-compliant SNMP agent. It supports MIB-II as defined in RFC 1213, with Sun extensions under Sun's enterprise number. The MIB (Management Information Base) is both readable and writeable. The mibiisa command supports all SNMP protocol operations, including GETREQUEST, GETNEXT-REQUEST, SET-REQUEST, GET-REPLY, and TRAP.

The mibiisa command must be run with superuser privileges. It is typically run by the /etc/rc3.d/S76snmpdx script at system startup. mibiisa cannot be started with inetd(1M). When started, mibiisa detaches itself from the keyboard, disables all signals except SIGKILL, SIGILL, SIGUSR1, and SIGUSR2, and puts itself in the background. mibiisa uses the configuration in the snmpd.conf file, which you modify as appropriate. See "Configuration File" on page 654.

The mibiisa command supports the coldStart, linkUp, linkDown, and authentication traps. You can disable the authentication trap with a command-line switch, which itself can be overridden by a management station writing to a MIB variable in the standard SNMP MIB group.

The mibiisa command supports four distinct views of the MIB. The view used for any request is determined by the community string contained in that request.

To enhance security, mibiisa supports an option to block all writes to the MIB. You can also limit the set of management stations from which the agent accepts requests in the configuration file used when starting the mibiisa. See "Security" on page 655 for more information.

Unless overridden, mibiisa uses UDP port 161, the standard SNMP port. The mibiisa command issues traps through the same port on which it receives SNMP requests.

Options

-a
: Disable the generation of authentication traps. An SNMP manager can, however, write a value into snmpEnableAuthenTraps to enable or disable authentication traps.

-c config-dir
: Specify a directory for the snmpd.conf file on startup. The default directory is /etc/snmp/conf for Solaris 2.x.

-d debug-level
: Specify a level value for debugging. A value of 0 disables all debugging and is the default. Levels 1 through 3 represent increasing levels of debug output. When mibiisa receives the signal SIGUSR1, it resets the debug-level to 0. When mibiisa receives the signal SIGUSR2, it increments the debug-level by 1.

  Debug output is sent to the standard output in effect at the time mibiisa is started. No matter what debug level is in effect, certain significant events are logged in the system log.

-p port
: Define an alternative UDP port to listen for incoming requests. The default is UDP port 161.

-r
: Put the MIB into read-only mode.

Configuration File

The `snmpd.conf` file is used for configuration information. Each entry in the file consists of a keyword followed by a parameter string. The keyword must begin in the first position. Parameters are separated from the keyword and from one another by white space. Case in keywords is ignored. Each entry must be contained on a single line. All text following (and including) a pound sign (#) is ignored. The following keywords are currently supported.

sysdescr	The value to be used to answer queries for `sysDescr`.
syscontact	The value to be used to answer queries for `sysContact`.
syslocation	The value to be used to answer queries for `sysLocation`.
trap	The parameter names one or more hosts to receive traps. You can list only five hosts.

system-group-read-community

The community name to get read access to the system group and Sun's extended system group.

system-group-write-community

The community name to get write access to the system group and Sun's extended system group.

read-community

The community name to get read access to the entire MIB.

write-community

The community name to get write access to the entire MIB (implies read access).

trap-community

The community name to be used in traps.

kernel-file	The name of the file to use for kernel symbols.
managers	The names of hosts that can send SNMP queries. You can list only five hosts on any one line. You can repeat this keyword for a total of 32 hosts.
newdevice	The additional devices that are not built in SNMPD. The format is as follows: `newdevice` *type speed name* where `newdevice` is the keyword, *type* is an integer that has to match your schema file, *speed* is the new device's speed, and *name* is the new name of the device.

The beginning of the default `/etc/snmp/conf/snmpd.conf` file is shown below.

```
# Copyright 1988 - 01/28/97 Sun Microsystems, Inc. All Rights Reserved.
#pragma ident  "@(#)snmpd.conf  2.22 97/01/28 Sun Microsystems"

# See below for file format and supported keywords

sysdescr       Sun SNMP Agent, Ultra-2
syscontact     System administrator
sysLocation    System administrators office
#
```

```
system-group-read-community       public
#system-group-write-community     private
#
read-community  public
#write-community private
#
trap            localhost
trap-community  SNMP-trap
#
#kernel-file    /vmunix
#
#managers       lvs golden
#managers       swap


##############################
```

Installation

You can put the `mibiisa` command and its configuration file, `snmpd.conf`, in any directory. However, `/usr/lib/snmp` is suggested for Solaris 2.4 through Solaris 8 for `mibiisa` itself and `/etc/snmp/conf` (Solaris 2.4 through Solaris 8) for the configuration file. You should modify the configuration file as appropriate. If you make any changes to `snmpd.conf` file keyword values, you must kill and restart `mibiisa` for the changes to take effect.

Your `/etc/services` file (or NIS equivalent) should contain the following entries.

```
snmp        161/udp                  # Simple Network Mgmt Protocol
snmp-trap   162/udp    snmptrap      # SNMP trap (event) messages
```

The following is an example for Solaris 2.x.

```
#
# Start the SNMP agent
#
if [-f /etc/snmp/conf/snmpd.conf -a -x
      /usr/lib/snmp/mibiisa];
then
/opt/SUNWconn/snm/agents/snmpd
echo 'Starting SNMP-agent.'
```

Security

SNMP, as presently defined, offers relatively little security. The `mibiisa` command accepts requests from other machines, which can have the effect of disabling the network capabilities of your computer. To limit the risk, the configuration file lets you specify a list of up to 32 manager stations from which `mibiisa` accepts requests. If you do not specify any such manager stations, `mibiisa` accepts requests from anywhere.

The `mibiisa` command also enables you to mark the MIB as "read-only" by using the `-r` option.

Finally, `mibiisa` supports four different community strings. These strings, however, are visible in the configuration file and within the SNMP packets as they flow on the network.

The configuration file should be owned by and readable only by superuser. In other words, the mode should be as follows for Solaris 2.4 through Solaris 8.

```
-rw------1 root 2090 Oct 17 15:04 /etc/snmp/conf/snmpd.conf
```

MIB

This section discusses some of the differences between the mibiisa MIB and the standard MIB-II (as defined in RFC 1213).

The following variables are read-only in the mibiisa MIB. These variables are read-write in the standard MIB-II.

```
sysName
atIfIndex
ipDefaultTTL
```

The mibiisa MIB Address Translation tables support limited write access: only atPhysAddress can be written, either to change the physical address of an existing entry or to delete an entire ARP table entry.

The mibiisa MIB IP Net to Media table supports limited write access: only ipNetToMediaPhysAddress and ipNetToMediaType can be written, either to change the physical address of an existing entry or to delete an entire ARP table entry.

The following variables are read-write in the mibiisa MIB; however, these variables have fixed values. Any new values set to them are accepted but have no effect.

```
ipRoutIfIndex
ipRouteMetric1
ipRouteMetric2
ipRouteMetric3
ipRouteMetric4
ipRouteType
ipRouteAge
ipRouteMask
ipRouteMetric5
```

The following mibiisa MIB variable reflects the actual state of the related table entry. Sets are accepted but have no effect.

```
tcpConnState
```

The following mibiisa MIB variables are readable but return a fixed value.

icmpInDestUnreachs	Returns 1.
icmpInTimeExcds	Returns 1.
icmpInParmProbs	Returns 1.
icmpInSrcQuenchs	Returns 1.
icmpInRedirects	Returns 1.
icmpInEchos	Returns 1.
icmpInEchoReps	Returns 1.
icmpInTimestamps	Returns 1.
icmpInTimestampReps	Returns 1.
icmpInAddrMasks	Returns 1.
icmpInAddrMaskReps	Returns 1.
icmpOutDestUnreachs	Returns 1.
icmpOutTimeExcds	Returns 1.

icmpOutParmProbs	Returns 1.
icmpOutSrcQuenchs	Returns 1.
icmpOutRedirects	Returns 1.
icmpOutEchos	Returns 1.
icmpOutEchoReps	Returns 1.
icmpOutTimestamps	Returns 1.
icmpOutTimestampReps	Returns 1.
icmpOutAddrMasks	Returns 1.
icmpOutAddrMaskReps	Returns 1.
ifInUnknownProtos	Returns 0.
ipAdEntBcastAddr	Returns 1.
ipAdEntReasmMaxSiz	Returns 65535.
ipRouteMetric1	Returns -1.
ipRouteMetric2	Returns -1.
ipRouteMetric3	Returns -1.
ipRouteMetric4	Returns -1.
ipRouteAge	Returns 0.
ipRouteMetric5	Returns -1.
ipNetToMediaType	Returns (3) dynamic.
ipRoutingDiscards	Returns 0.

The following variables return a fixed value of 0 for drivers not conforming to the GLD framework (see gld(7D)), including the old LAN drivers on SPARC machines.

ifInOctets	Returns 0.
ifInNUcastPkts	Returns 0.
ifInDiscards	Returns 0.
ifOutOctets	Returns 0.
ifOutNUcastPkts	Returns 0.
ifOutDiscards	Returns 0.

Schema Attributes

The following sections describes the attributes in the group and table definitions in the /var/snmp/mib/sun.mib file.

system Group

The `system` group reports statistics about a particular system (for example, a workstation or a printer).

sysDescr A textual description of the entity. This value should include the full name and version identification of the system's hardware type, software operating system, and networking software. This value must contain only printable ASCII characters. (*string*[255]).

sysObjectID The vendor's authoritative identification of the network management subsystem contained in the entity. This value is allocated within the SMI enterprises subtree (1.3.6.1.4.1) and provides an easy and unambiguous means for determining what type of equipment is being managed. For example, if vendor "Flintstones, Inc." was assigned the subtree 1.3.6.1.4.1.4242, it could assign the identifier 1.3.6.1.4.1.4242.1.1 to its "Fred Router." (*objectid*).

sysUpTime Time (in hundredths of a second) since the network management portion of the system was last reinitialized. (*timeticks*).

sysContact The textual identification of the contact person for this managed node, together with information on how to contact this person. (*string*[255]).

sysName An administratively assigned name for this managed node. By convention, this is the node's fully qualified domain name. (*string*[255]).

sysLocation The physical location of this node (for example, "telephone closet, 3rd floor" (*string*[255])).

sysServices A value indicating the set of services that this entity primarily offers. (*int*). The value is a sum. This sum initially takes the value 0. Then, for each layer L in the range 1 through 7 for which this node performs transactions, 2 raised to (L− 1) is added to the sum. For example, a node that primarily performs routing functions would have a value of 4 (2**(3-1)). In contrast, a node that is a host offering application services would have a value of 72 (2**(4-1) + 2**(7-1)). Note that in the context of the Internet suite of protocols, values should be calculated accordingly.

Layer	Functionality
1	Physical (such as repeaters).
2	Data link/subnetwork (such as bridges).
3	Internet (such as IP gateways).
4	End-to-end (such as IP hosts) layer 7 applications (such as mail relays).

For systems including OSI protocols, you can also count layers 5 and 6.

interfaces Group

The interfaces group reports the number of interfaces handled by the agent.

ifNumber   The number of network interfaces, regardless of their current state, present on this system. (*int*).

ifTable

The ifTable is a table of interface entries. The number of entries is given by the value of ifNumber.

ifIndex   A unique value for each interface. Its value ranges between 1 and the value of ifNumber. The value for each interface must remain constant at least from one reinitialization of the entity's network management system to the next reinitialization. (*int*).

ifDescr   A textual string containing information about the interface. This string should include the name of the manufacturer, the product name, and the version of the hardware interface. (*string*[255]).

ifType   The type of interface, distinguished according to the physical/link protocol(s) immediately below the network layer in the protocol stack. (*enum*).

ifMtu   The size of the largest datagram that can be sent/received on the interface, specified in octets. For interfaces used for transmitting network datagrams, this is the size of the largest network datagram that can be sent on the interface. (*int*).

ifSpeed   An estimate of the interface's current bandwidth in bits per second. For interfaces that do not vary in bandwidth or for those where no accurate estimation can be made, this object should contain the nominal bandwidth. (*gauge*).

ifPhysAddress

              The interface's address at the protocol layer immediately below the network layer in the protocol stack. For interfaces without such an address (for example, a serial line), this object should contain an octet string of zero length. (*octet*[128]).

ifAdminStatus

              The desired state of the interface. The testing(3) state indicates that no operational packets can be passed. (*enum*).

ifOperStatus

              The current operational state of the interface. The testing(3) state indicates that no operational packets can be passed. (*enum*).

ifLastChange

              The value of sysUpTime at the time the interface entered its current operational state. If the current state was entered before the last reinitialization of the local network management subsystem, then this object contains a 0 value. (*timeticks*).

`ifInOctets`   The total number of octets received on the interface, including framing characters. (*counter*). Returns a fixed value of 0.

`ifInUcastPkts`

The number of subnetwork-unicast packets delivered to a higher-layer protocol. (*counter*).

`ifInNUcastPkts`

The number of non-unicast (that is, subnetwork broadcast or subnetwork-multicast) packets delivered to a higher-layer protocol. (*counter*). Returns a fixed value of 0.

`ifInDiscards`   The number of inbound packets chosen to be discarded, even though no errors had been detected to prevent their being deliverable to a higher-layer protocol. One possible reason for discarding such a packet could be to free up buffer space. (*counter*) Returns a fixed value of 0.

`ifInErrors`   The number of inbound packets that contained errors preventing them from being deliverable to a higher-layer protocol. (*counter*).

`ifInUnknownProtos`

The number of packets received via the interface that were discarded because of an unknown or unsupported protocol. (*counter*). Returns a fixed value of 0.

`ifOutOctets`   The total number of octets transmitted out of the interface, including framing characters. (*counter*). Returns a fixed value of 0.

`ifOutUcastPkts`

The total number of packets that higher-level protocols requested be transmitted to a subnetwork-unicast address, including those that were discarded or not sent. (*counter*).

`ifOutNUcastPkts`

The total number of packets that higher-level protocols requested be transmitted to a non-unicast (that is, a subnetwork-broadcast or subnetwork-multicast) address, including those that were discarded or not sent. (*counter*). Returns a fixed value of 0.

`ifOutDiscards`

The number of outbound packets that were chosen to be discarded even though no errors had been detected to prevent their being transmitted. One possible reason for discarding such a packet could be to free up buffer space. (*counter*). Returns a fixed value of 0.

`ifOutErrors`   The number of outbound packets that could not be transmitted because of errors. (*counter*).

`ifOutQLen`   The length of the output packet queue (in packets). (*gauge*).

ifSpecific   A reference to MIB definitions specific to the particular media being used to realize the interface. For example, if the interface is realized by an Ethernet, then the value of this object refers to a document defining objects specific to Ethernet. If this information is not present, its value should be set to the OBJECT IDENTIFIER { 0 0 }, that is, a syntactically valid object identifier. Any conformant implementation of ASN.1 and BER must be able to generate and recognize this value. (*objectid*).

atTable

atTable Address Translation tables contain the NetworkAddress to physical address equivalences. Some interfaces do not use translation tables for determining address equivalences (for example, DDN-X.25 has an algorithmic method). If all interfaces are of this type, then the Address Translation table is empty, that is, has zero entries.

atIfIndex   The interface on which this entry's equivalence is effective. The interface identified by a particular value of this index is the same interface as identified by the same value of ifIndex. (*int*).

atPhysAddress

The media-dependent physical address. (*octet*[128]). Setting this object to a null string (one of zero length) has the effect of invalidating the corresponding entry in the atTable object. That is, it effectively dissociates the interface identified with said entry from the mapping identified with said entry. It is implementation specific whether the agent removes an invalidated entry from the table. Accordingly, management stations must be prepared to receive tabular information from agents that corresponds to entries not currently in use. Proper interpretation of such entries requires examination of the relevant atPhysAddress object.

atNetAddress   The network address (that is, the IP address) corresponding to the media-dependent physical address. (*netaddress*).

ip

The ip group reports statistics about the Internet Protocol (IP) group.

ipForwarding   The indication of whether this entity is acting as an IP gateway for the forwarding of datagrams received by, but not addressed to, this entity. IP gateways forward datagrams. IP hosts do not, except those source-routed via the host. (*enum*).

Note that for some managed nodes, this object can take on only a subset of the values possible. Accordingly, it is appropriate for an agent to return a badValue response if a management station tries to change this object to an inappropriate value.

ipDefaultTTL   The default value inserted into the time-to-live field of the IP header of datagrams originated at this entity, whenever a TTL value is not supplied by the transport layer protocol. (*int*).

ipInReceives   The total number of input datagrams received from interfaces, including those received in error. (*counter*).

ipInHdrErrors

The number of input datagrams discarded because of errors in their IP headers, including bad checksums, version number mismatch, other format errors, time-to-live exceeded, errors discovered in processing their IP options, and so on. (*counter*).

ipInAddrErrors

The number of input datagrams discarded because the IP address in their IP header's destination field was not a valid address to be received at this entity. This count includes invalid addresses (for example, 0.0.0.0) and addresses of unsupported Classes (for example, Class E). For entities that are not IP gateways and, therefore, do not forward datagrams, this counter includes datagrams discarded because the destination address was not a local address. (*counter*).

ipForwDatagrams

The number of input datagrams for which this entity was not their final IP destination and an attempt was made to find a route to forward them to that final destination. In entities that do not act as IP gateways, this counter includes only those packets that were source-routed via this entity, and the source-route option processing was successful. (*counter*).

ipInUnknownProtos

The number of locally addressed datagrams received successfully but discarded because of an unknown or unsupported protocol. (*counter*).

ipInDiscards   The number of input IP datagrams for which no problems were encountered to prevent their continued processing but that were discarded (for example, for lack of buffer space). Note that this counter does not include any datagrams discarded while awaiting reassembly. (*counter*).

ipInDelivers   The total number of input datagrams successfully delivered to IP user-protocols (including ICMP). (*counter*).

ipOutRequests

The total number of IP datagrams that local IP user-protocols (including ICMP) supplied to IP in requests for transmission. Note that this counter does not include any datagrams counted in ipForwDatagrams. (*counter*).

ipOutDiscards

The number of output IP datagrams for which no problem was encountered to prevent their transmission to their destination but that were discarded (for example, for lack of buffer space). Note that this counter would include datagrams counted in ipForwDatagrams if any such packets met this (discretionary) discard criterion. (*counter*).

ipOutNoRoutes

The number of IP datagrams discarded because no route could be found to transmit them to their destination. Note that this counter includes any packets counted in ipForwDatagrams that meet this "no route" criterion. Note that this includes any datagrams that a host cannot route because all its default gateways are down. (*counter*).

ipReasmTimeout

The maximum number of seconds that received fragments are held while they are awaiting reassembly at this entity. (*int*).

ipReasmReqds   The number of IP fragments received that needed to be reassembled at this entity. (*counter*).

ipReasmOKs   The number of IP datagrams successfully reassembled. (*counter*).

ipReasmFails   The number of failures detected by the IP reassembly algorithm for whatever reason: timed out, errors, and the like. Note that this is not necessarily a count of discarded IP fragments because some algorithms (notably the algorithm in RFC 815) can lose track of the number of fragments by combining them as they are received. (*counter*).

ipFragOKs   The number of IP datagrams that have been successfully fragmented at this entity. (*counter*).

ipFragFails   The number of IP datagrams that have been discarded because they needed to be fragmented at this entity but could not be, for example, because their "Don't Fragment" flag was set. (*counter*).

ipFragCreates

The number of IP datagram fragments that have been generated as a result of fragmentation at this entity. (*counter*).

ipRoutingDiscards

The number of routing entries that were chosen to be discarded even though they were valid. One possible reason for discarding such an entry could be to free buffer space for other routing entries. (*counter*). Returns a fixed value of 0.

ipAddrTable

ipAddrTable is a table of addressing information relevant to this entity's IP addresses.

ipAdEntAddr   The IP address to which this entry's addressing information pertains. (*netaddress*).

ipAdEntIfIndex

The index value that uniquely identifies the interface to which this entry is applicable. The interface identified by a particular value of

this index is the same interface as identified by the same value of
`ifIndex.`(*int*).

ipAdEntNetMask

The subnet mask associated with the IP address of this entry. The
value of the mask is an IP address with all the network bits set to 1
and all the hosts bits set to 0. (*netaddress*).

ipAdEntBcastAddr

The value of the least-significant bit in the IP broadcast address used
for sending datagrams on the (logical) interface associated with the
IP address of this entry. For example, when the Internet standard
all-ones broadcast address is used, the value is 1. This value applies
to both the subnet and network broadcast addresses used by the
entity on this (logical) interface. (*int*). Returns a fixed value of 1.

ipAdEntReasmMaxSize

The size of the largest IP datagram that this entity can reassemble
from incoming IP fragmented datagrams received on this interface.
(*int*). Returns a fixed value of 65535.

ipRouteTable

The `ipRouteTable` is this entity's IP Routing table.

ipRouteDest   The destination IP address of this route. An entry with a value of
0.0.0.0 is considered a default route. Multiple routes to a single
destination can appear in the table, but access to such multiple entries
is dependent on the table-access mechanisms defined by the network
management protocol in use. (*netaddress*).

ipRouteIfIndex

The index value that uniquely identifies the local interface through
which the next hop of this route should be reached. The interface
identified by a particular value of this index is the same interface as
identified by the same value of `ifIndex.`(*int*).

ipRouteMetric1

The primary routing metric for this route. The semantics of this metric
are determined by the routing protocol specified in the route's
`ipRouteProto` value. If this metric is not used, its value should be set
to -1. (*int*). Returns a fixed value of -1.

ipRouteMetric2

An alternate routing metric for this route. The semantics of this metric
are determined by the routing protocol specified in the route's
`ipRouteProto` value. If this metric is not used, its value should be set
to -1. (*int*). Returns a fixed value of -1.

ipRouteMetric3

> An alternate routing metric for this route. The semantics of this metric are determined by the routing protocol specified in the route's `ipRouteProto` value. If this metric is not used, its value should be set to -1. (*int*). Returns a fixed value of -1.

ipRouteMetric4

> An alternate routing metric for this route. The semantics of this metric are determined by the routing protocol specified in the route's `ipRouteProto` value. If this metric is not used, its value should be set to -1. (*int*). Returns a fixed value of -1.

ipRouteNextHop

> The IP address of the next hop of this route. (In the case of a route bound to an interface that is realized via a broadcast media, the value of this field is the agent's IP address on that interface.) (*netaddress*).

ipRouteType	The type of route. Note that the values `direct` (3) and `indirect` (4) refer to the notion of direct and indirect routing in the IP architecture. (*enum*).

Setting this object to the value `invalid` (2) has the effect of invalidating the corresponding entry in the `ipRouteTable` object. That is, it effectively dissociates the destination identified with the entry from the route identified with the entry. It is implementation specific whether the agent removes an invalidated entry from the table. Accordingly, management stations must be prepared to receive tabular information from agents that corresponds to entries not currently in use. Proper interpretation of such entries requires examination of the relevant `ipRouteType` object. |
ipRouteProto	The routing mechanism through which this route was learned. Inclusion of values for gateway routing protocols is not intended to imply that hosts should support those protocols. (*enum*).
ipRouteAge	The number of seconds since this route was last updated or otherwise determined to be correct. Note that no semantics of "too old" can be implied except through knowledge of the routing protocol by which the route was learned. (*int*). Returns a fixed value of 0.
ipRouteMask	Indicate the mask to be logical-ANDed with the destination address before being compared to the value in the `ipRouteDest` field. For those systems that do not support arbitrary subnet masks, an agent constructs the value of the `ipRouteMask` by determining whether the value of the correspondent `ipRouteDest` field belongs to a Class A, B, or C network, and then using either *mask* or *network*.

255.0.0.0	Class A.
255.255.0.0	Class B.
255.255.255.0	Class C.

If the value of the `ipRouteDest` is `0.0.0.0` (a default route), then the mask value is also `0.0.0.0`. Note that all IP routing subsystems implicitly use this mechanism. (*netaddress*).

ipRouteMetric5

An alternate routing metric for this route. The semantics of this metric are determined by the routing protocol specified in the route's `ipRouteProto` value. If this metric is not used, its value should be set to `-1`. (*int*). Returns a fixed value of `-1`.

ipRouteInfo   A reference to MIB definitions specific to the particular routing protocol responsible for this route as determined by the value specified in the route's `ipRouteProto` value. If this information is not present, its value should be set to the `OBJECT IDENTIFIER { 0 0 }`, which is a syntactically valid object identifier. Any conformant implementation of ASN.1 and BER must be able to generate and recognize this value. (*objectid*).

ipNetToMediaTable

The `ipNetToMediaTable` is the IP Address Translation table used for mapping from IP addresses to physical addresses.

ipNetToMediaIfIndex

The interface on which this entry's equivalence is effective. The interface identified by a particular value of this index is the same interface as identified by the same value of `ifIndex`. (*int*).

ipNetToMediaPhysAddress

The media-dependent physical address. (*octet*[128]).

ipNetToMediaNetAddress

The `IpAddress` corresponding to the media-dependent physical address. (*netaddress*).

ipNetToMediaType

The type of mapping. (*enum*). Returns a fixed value of (3) dynamic. Setting this object to the value `invalid(2)` has the effect of invalidating the corresponding entry in the `ipNetToMediaTable`. That is, it effectively dissociates the interface identified with said entry from the mapping identified with said entry. It is implementation specific whether the agent removes an invalidated entry from the table. Accordingly, management stations must be prepared to receive tabular information from agents that corresponds to entries not currently in use. Proper interpretation of such entries requires examination of the relevant `ipNetToMediaType` object.

icmp

The icmp group reports statistics about the ICMP group.

icmpInMsgs   The total number of ICMP messages that the entity received. Note that this counter includes all those counted by icmpInErrors. (*counter*).

icmpInErrors   The number of ICMP messages that the entity received but determined as having ICMP-specific errors (bad ICMP checksums, bad length, and the like). (*counter*).

icmpInDestUnreachs

The number of ICMP Destination Unreachable messages received. (*counter*).

icmpInTimeExcds

The number of ICMP Time Exceeded messages received. (*counter*).

icmpInParmProbs

The number of ICMP Parameter Problem messages received. (*counter*).

icmpInSrcQuenchs

The number of ICMP Source Quench messages received. (*counter*).

icmpInRedirects

The number of ICMP Redirect messages received. (*counter*).

icmpInEchos   The number of ICMP Echo (request) messages received. (*counter*).

icmpInEchoReps

The number of ICMP Echo Reply messages received. (*counter*).

icmpInTimestamps

The number of ICMP Timestamp (request) messages received. (*counter*).

icmpInTimestampReps

The number of ICMP Timestamp Reply messages received. (*counter*).

icmpInAddrMasks

The number of ICMP Address Mask Request messages received. (*counter*).

icmpInAddrMaskReps

The number of ICMP Address Mask Reply messages received. (*counter*).

icmpOutMsgs   The total number of ICMP messages that this entity tried to send. Note that this counter includes all those counted by icmpOutErrors. (*counter*).

icmpOutErrors

> The number of ICMP messages that this entity did not send because of problems discovered within ICMP, such as a lack of buffers. This value should not include errors discovered outside the ICMP layer, such as the inability of IP to route the resultant datagram. In some implementations, there may be no types of errors that contribute to this counter's value. (*counter*).

icmpOutDestUnreachs

> The number of ICMP Destination Unreachable messages sent. (*counter*).

icmpOutTimeExcds

> The number of ICMP Time Exceeded messages sent. (*counter*).

icmpOutParmProbs

> The number of ICMP Parameter Problem messages sent. (*counter*).

icmpOutSrcQuenchs

> The number of ICMP Source Quench messages sent. (*counter*).

icmpOutRedirects

> The number of ICMP Redirect messages sent. For a host, this object is always 0 because hosts do not send redirects. (*counter*).

icmpOutEchos   The number of ICMP Echo (request) messages sent. (*counter*).

icmpOutEchoReps

> The number of ICMP Echo Reply messages sent. (*counter*).

icmpOutTimestamps

> The number of ICMP Timestamp (request) messages sent. (*counter*).

icmpOutTimestampReps

> The number of ICMP Timestamp Reply messages sent. (*counter*).

icmpOutAddrMasks

> The number of ICMP Address Mask Request messages sent. (*counter*).

icmpOutAddrMaskReps

> The number of ICMP Address Mask Reply messages sent. (*counter*).

tcp

The tcp group reports statistics about the TCP group.

tcpRtoAlgorithm

> The algorithm used to determine the timeout value used for retransmitting unacknowledged octets. (*enum*).

tcpRtoMin   The minimum value permitted by a TCP implementation for the retransmission timeout, measured in milliseconds. More refined semantics for objects of this type depend on the algorithm used to determine the retransmission timeout. In particular, when the timeout algorithm is rsre(3), an object of this type has the semantics of the LBOUND quantity described in RFC 793. (*int*).

tcpRtoMax   The maximum value permitted by a TCP implementation for the retransmission timeout, measured in milliseconds. More refined semantics for objects of this type depend on the algorithm used to determine the retransmission timeout. In particular, when the timeout algorithm is rsre(3), an object of this type has the semantics of the UBOUND quantity described in RFC 793. (*int*).

tcpMaxConn   The limit on the total number of TCP connections that the entity can support. In entities where the maximum number of connections is dynamic, this object should contain the value -1. (*int*).

tcpActiveOpens

    The number of times that TCP connections have made a direct transition to the SYN-SENT state from the CLOSED state. (*counter*).

tcpPassiveOpens

    The number of times that TCP connections have made a direct transition to the SYN-RCVD state from the LISTEN state. (*counter*).

tcpAttemptFails

    The number of times that TCP connections have made a direct transition to the CLOSED state from either the SYN-SENT state or the SYN-RCVD state, plus the number of times TCP connections have made a direct transition to the LISTEN state from the SYN-RCVD state. (*counter*).

tcpEstabResets

    The number of times TCP connections have made a direct transition to the CLOSED state from either the ESTABLISHED state or the CLOSE-WAIT state. (*counter*).

tcpCurrEstab   The number of TCP connections for which the current state is either ESTABLISHED or CLOSE-WAIT. (*gauge*).

tcpInSegs   The total number of segments received, including those received in error. This count includes segments received on currently established connections. (*counter*).

tcpOutSegs   The total number of segments sent, including those on current connections but excluding those containing only retransmitted octets. (*counter*).

tcpRetransSegs

    The total number of segments retransmitted, that is, the number of TCP segments transmitted containing one or more previously transmitted octets. (*counter*).

tcpInErrs   The total number of segments received in error (for example, bad TCP checksums). (*counter*).

tcpOutRsts The number of TCP segments sent containing the RST flag. (*counter*).

tcpConnTable

The tcpConnTable is a table containing TCP connection-specific information.

tcpConnState The state of this TCP connection. (*enum*).

The only value that can be set by a management station is deleteTCB(12). Accordingly, it is appropriate for an agent to return a badValue response if a management station tries to set this object to any other value.

If a management station sets this object to the value deleteTCB(12), then the TCB (as defined in RFC 793) of the corresponding connection is deleted on the managed node. This results in immediate termination of the connection.

As an implementation-specific option, an RST segment can be sent from the managed node to the other TCP endpoint. (Note, however, that RST segments are not sent reliably.)

tcpConnLocalAddress

The local IP address for this TCP connection. For a connection in the LISTEN state that is willing to accept connections for any IP interface associated with the node, the value 0.0.0.0 is used. (*netaddress*).

tcpConnLocalPort

The local port number for this TCP connection. (*int*).

tcpConnRemAddress

The remote IP address for this TCP connection. (*netaddress*).

tcpConnRemPort

The remote port number for this TCP connection. (*int*).

upd

The udp group reports statistics about the UDP group.

udpInDatagrams

The total number of UDP datagrams delivered to UDP users. (*counter*). Returns a fixed value of 0.

udpNoPorts The total number of received UDP datagrams for which there was no application at the destination port. (*counter*). Returns a fixed value of 0.

udpInErrors The number of received UDP datagrams that could not be delivered for reasons other than the lack of an application at the destination port. (*counter*).

udpOutDatagrams

>The total number of UDP datagrams sent from this entity. (`counter`)
>Returns a fixed value of `0`.

udpTable

The `udpTable` is a table containing UDP listener information.

udpLocalAddress

>The local IP address for this UDP listener. For a UDP listener that is willing to accept datagrams for any IP interface associated with the node, use the value `0.0.0.0`. (`netaddress`).

udpLocalPort The local port number for this UDP listener. (`int`).

snmp

The `snmp` group reports statistics about the SNMP group.

snmpInPkts The total number of messages delivered to the SNMP entity from the transport service. (`counter`).

snmpOutPkts The total number of SNMP messages passed from the SNMP protocol entity to the transport service. (`counter`).

snmpInBadVersions

>The total number of SNMP messages delivered to the SNMP protocol entity that were for an unsupported SNMP version. (`counter`).

snmpInBadCommunityNames

>The total number of SNMP Messages delivered to the SNMP protocol entity that used a SNMP community name not known to said entity. (`counter`).

snmpInBadCommunityUses

>The total number of SNMP messages delivered to the SNMP protocol entity, which represented an SNMP operation not allowed by the SNMP community named in the message. (`counter`).

snmpInASNParseErrs

>The total number of ASN.1 or BER errors encountered by the SNMP protocol entity when decoding received SNMP messages. (`counter`).

snmpInTooBigs

>The total number of SNMP PDUs delivered to the SNMP protocol entity for which the value of the error-status field is `tooBig`. (`counter`).

snmpInNoSuchNames

>The total number of SNMP PDUs delivered to the SNMP protocol entity for which the value of the error-status field is `noSuchName`. (`counter`).

snmpInBadValues

> The total number of SNMP PDUs delivered to the SNMP protocol entity for which the value of the error-status field is badValue. (*counter*).

snmpInReadOnlys

> The total number of valid SNMP PDUs delivered to the SNMP protocol entity for which the value of the error-status field is readOnly. Note that it is a protocol error to generate an SNMP PDU that contains the value readOnly in the error-status field. This object is provided as a means of detecting incorrect implementations of the SNMP. (*counter*).

snmpInGenErrs

> The total number of SNMP PDUs delivered to the SNMP protocol entity for which the value of the error-status field is genErr. (*counter*).

snmpInTotalReqVars

> The total number of MIB objects successfully retrieved by the SNMP protocol entity as the result of receiving valid SNMP Get-Request and Get-Next PDUs. (*counter*).

snmpInTotalSetVars

> The total number of MIB objects successfully altered by the SNMP protocol entity as the result of receiving valid SNMP Set-Request PDUs. (*counter*).

snmpInGetRequests

> The total number of SNMP Get-Request PDUs accepted and processed by the SNMP protocol entity. (*counter*).

snmpInGetNexts

> The total number of SNMP Get-Next PDUs accepted and processed by the SNMP protocol entity. (*counter*).

snmpInSetRequests

> The total number of SNMP Set-Request PDUs accepted and processed by the SNMP protocol entity. (*counter*).

snmpInGetResponses

> The total number of SNMP Get-Response PDUs accepted and processed by the SNMP protocol entity. (*counter*).

snmpInTraps   The total number of SNMP Trap PDUs accepted and processed by the SNMP protocol entity. (*counter*).

snmpOutTooBigs

> The total number of SNMP PDUs generated by the SNMP protocol entity for which the value of the error-status field is tooBig. (*counter*).

snmpOutNoSuchNames

> The total number of SNMP PDUs generated by the SNMP protocol entity for which the value of the error-status field is `noSuchName`. (*counter*).

snmpOutBadValues

> The total number of SNMP PDUs generated by the SNMP protocol entity for which the value of the error-status field is `badValue`. (*counter*).

snmpOutGenErrs

> The total number of SNMP PDUs generated by the SNMP protocol entity for which the value of the error-status field is `genErr`. (*counter*).

snmpOutGetRequests

> The total number of SNMP Get-Request PDUs that have been generated by the SNMP protocol entity. (*counter*).

snmpOutGetNexts

> The total number of SNMP Get-Next PDUs generated by the SNMP protocol entity. (*counter*).

snmpOutSetRequests

> The total number of SNMP Set-Request PDUs generated by the SNMP protocol entity. (*counter*).

snmpOutGetResponses

> The total number of SNMP Get-Response PDUs generated by the SNMP protocol entity. (*counter*).

snmpOutTraps The total number of SNMP Trap PDUs generated by the SNMP protocol entity. (*counter*).

snmpEnableAuthenTraps

> Indicates whether the SNMP agent process is permitted to generate authentication-failure traps. The value of this object overrides any configuration information. As such, it provides a means whereby all authentication-failure traps can be disabled. (*enum*).

> Note that this object must be stored in nonvolatile memory so that it remains constant between reinitializations of the network management system.

Sun-Specific Group and Table Definitions
The following are Sun-specific group and table definitions.

sunSystem   Report general system information.

agentDescr   The SNMP agent's description of itself. (*string*[255]).

hostID   The unique Sun hardware identifier. The value returned is a four-byte binary string. (*octet*[4]).

motd   The first line of /etc/motd. (*string*[255]).

unixTime   The UNIX system time. Measured in seconds since January 1, 1970, GMT. (*counter*).

sunProcessTable

         Report UNIX process table information.

psProcessID   The process identifier for this process. (*int*).

psParentProcessID

         The process identifier of the parent of this process. (*int*).

psProcessSize

         The combined size of the data and stack segments (in kilobytes.) (*int*).

psProcessCpuTime

         The CPU time (including both user and system time) consumed so far. (*int*).

psProcessState

         The run-state of the process. (*octet*[4])

R	Runnable.
T	Stopped.
P	In page wait.
D	Noninterruptible wait.
S	Sleeping (less than 20 seconds).
I	Idle (more than 20 seconds).
Z	Zombie.

psProcessWaitChannel

         Reason process is waiting. (*octet*[16]).

psProcessTTY   Terminal, if any, controlling this process. (*octet*[16]).

psProcessUserName

         Name of the user associated with this process. (*octet*[16]).

psProcessUserID

         Numeric form of the name of the user associated with this process. (*int*).

psProcessName

         Command name to invoke this process. (*octet*[64]).

psProcessStatus

         Setting this variable sends signal of the set value to the process. (*int*).

sunHostPerf   Report hostperf information.

rsUserProcessTime

    Total number of *timeticks* used by user processes since the last system boot. (*counter*).

rsNiceModeTime

    Total number of *timeticks* used by nice mode since the last system boot. (*counter*).

rsSystemProcessTime

    Total number of *timeticks* used by system processes since the last system boot. (*counter*).

rsIdleModeTime

    Total number of *timeticks* in idle mode since the last system boot. (*counter*).

rsDiskXfer1   Total number of disk transfers since the last boot for the first of four configured disks. (*counter*).

rsDiskXfer2   Total number of disk transfers since the last boot for the second of four configured disks. (*counter*).

rsDiskXfer3   Total number of disk transfers since the last boot for the third of four configured disks. (*counter*).

rsDiskXfer4   Total number of disk transfers since the last boot for the fourth of four configured disks. (*counter*).

rsVPagesIn   Number of pages read in from disk. (*counter*).

rsVPagesOut   Number of pages written to disk. (*counter*).

rsVSwapIn   Number of pages swapped in. (*counter*).

rsVSwapOut   Number of pages swapped out. (*counter*).

rsVIntr   Number of device interrupts. (*counter*).

rsIfInPackets

    Number of input packets. (*counter*).

rsIfOutPackets

    Number of output packets. (*counter*).

rsIfInErrors   Number of input errors. (*counter*).

rsIfOutErrors

    Number of output errors. (*counter*).

rsIfCollisions

    Number of output collisions. (*counter*).

Files

/etc/snmp/conf/snmpd.conf

    Configuration information.

```
/var/snmp/mib/sun.mib
```
Standard SNMP MIBII file.

Attributes

See `attributes`(5) for descriptions of the following attributes.

Attribute Type	Attribute Value
Availability	SUNWmibii

See Also

`inetd(1M)`, `select(3C)`, `recvfrom(3N)`, `sendto(3N)`, `attributes(5)`, `gld(7D)`

Diagnostics

`cannot dispatch request`

> The proxy cannot dispatch the request. The rest of the message indicates the cause of the failure.

`select(3C) failed`

> A `select`(3C) call failed. The rest of the message indicates the cause of the failure.

`sendto(3N) failed`

> A `sendto`(3N) call failed. The rest of the message indicates the cause of the failure.

`recvfrom(3N) failed`

> A `recvfrom`(3N) call failed. The rest of the message indicates the cause of the failure.

`no response from system`

> The SNMP agent on the target system does not respond to SNMP requests. This error might indicate that the SNMP agent is not running on the target system, the target system is down, or the network containing the target system is unreachable.

`response too big`

> The agent could not fit the results of an operation into a single SNMP message. Split large groups or tables into smaller entities.

`missing attribute`

> An attribute is missing from the requested group.

`bad attribute type`

> An object attribute type received from the SNMP agent does not match the attribute type specified by the proxy agent schema. The rest of the message indicates the expected type and received type.

`cannot get sysUpTime`

> The proxy agent cannot get the variable `sysUpTime` from the SNMP agent.

`sysUpTime type bad`

> The variable `sysUpTime` received from the SNMP agent has the wrong data type.

`unknown SNMP error`

> An unknown SNMP error was received.

`bad variable value`

> The request specified an incorrect syntax or value for a set operation.

`variable is read only`

> The SNMP agent did not perform the set request because a variable to set cannot be written.

`general error`

> A general error was received.

`cannot make request PDU`

> An error occurred in the building of a request PDU.

`cannot make request varbind list`

> An error occurred in the building of a request variable binding list.

`cannot parse response PDU`

> An error occurred in the parsing of a response PDU.

`request ID - response ID mismatch`

> The response ID does not match the request ID.

`string contains non-displayable characters`

> A displayable string contains nondisplayable characters.

`cannot open schema file`

> An error occurred in the opening of the proxy agent schema file.

`cannot parse schema file`

> The proxy agent couldn't parse the proxy agent schema file.

`cannot open host file`

> An error occurred in opening the file associated with the `na.snmp.hostfile` keyword in `/etc/snmp/conf/snmpd.conf` for Solaris 2.4 through Solaris 8.

`cannot parse host file.`

> The proxy agent was unable to parse the file associated with the `na.snmp.hostfile` keyword in `/etc/snmp/conf/snm.conf` for Solaris 2.4 through Solaris 8.

```
attribute unavailable for set operations
```
> The set could not be completed because the attribute was not available for set operations.

Bugs

The mibiisa command returns the wrong interface speed for the SBUS FDDI interface (for example, "bf0").

The mibiisa command does not return a MAC address for the SBUS FDDI interface (for example, "bf0").

Process names retrieved from mibiisa contain a leading blank space.

When you change attribute values in the system group with an SNMP set request, the change is effective only as long as mibiisa is running. mibiisa does not save the changes to /etc/snmp/conf/snmpd.conf for Solaris 2.4, 2.5, and 2.6.

mk — Remake the Binary System and Commands from Source Code

Description

All source code for the UNIX system is distributed in the directory /usr/src. The directory tree rooted at /usr/src includes source code for the operating system, libraries, commands, and miscellaneous data files as needed for the system and procedures to transform this source code into an executable system.

Within the /usr/src directory are the cmd, lib, uts, head, and stand directories, as well as commands to remake the parts of the system found under each of these subdirectories. These commands are named :mk and :mkdir where the *dir* argument is the name of the directory to be recreated. Each of these :mkdir commands rebuilds all or part of the directory it is responsible for. The :mk command runs each of the other commands in order and thus recreates the whole system. The :mk command is distributed only to source code licensees.

Each command, with its associated directory, is described below.

:mklib   The lib directory contains the source code for the system libraries. The most important of these is the C library. Each library is in its own subdirectory. If you specify any arguments on the :mklib command line, then rebuild only the given libraries. The argument * rebuilds all libraries found under the lib directory.

:mkhead   The head directory contains the source code versions of the headers found in the /usr/include directory. The :mkhead command installs the headers you specify as arguments. The argument * installs all headers.

:mkuts   The uts directory contains the source code for the UNIX Operating System. The :mkuts command takes no arguments and invokes a series of makefiles that recreate the operating system.

Associated with the operating system is a set of headers that describe the user interface to the operating system. The source for these headers is found in a subdirectory within the `uts` directory tree. The user-accessible versions of these headers are found in the `/usr/include/sys` directory. The `:mksyshead` command installs these headers in the `/usr/include/sys` directory.

`:mkstand`   The `stand` directory contains standalone commands and boot programs. The `:mkstand` command rebuilds and installs these programs. Note that these standalone programs are applicable only to the DEC processors and are not built for any other machine.

`:mkcmd`   The `cmd` directory contains the source code for all the commands available on the system. It contains two types of entries: commands whose source code consists of only one file with one of the following suffixes—`.l`, `.y`, `.c`, `.s`, `.sh`—or a subdirectory that contains the multiple source files that comprise a particular command or subsystem. Each subdirectory is assumed to have a makefile (see `make`(1S)) with the name command `.mk` that takes care of creating everything associated with that directory and its subdirectories.

The `:mkcmd` command transforms source code into an executable command based on a set of predefined rules. If the `:mkcmd` command encounters a subdirectory within the `cmd` directory, then it runs the makefile found in that subdirectory. If no makefile is found, then it reports an error. For single-file commands, the predefined rules are dependent on the file's suffix. C programs (`.c`) are compiled by the C compiler and loaded stripped of shared text. Assembly language programs (`.s`) are assembled and loaded stripped. Yacc programs (`.y`) and lex programs (`.l`) are processed by `yacc()` and `lex()` respectively, before C compilation. Shell programs (`.sh`) are copied to create the command. Each of these operations leaves a command in the `./cmd` directory which is then installed into a user-accessible directory by `/usr/sbin/install`.

The arguments to `:mkcmd` are either command names or subsystem names. Some subsystems distributed with the UNIX system are `acct`, `graf`, `sgs`, `sccs`, and `text`. Prefacing the `:mkcmd` command with an assignment to the shell variable `$ARGS` rebuilds the indicated components of the subsystem.

For example, you can rebuild the entire `sccs` subsystem with the following command.

```
/usr/src/:mkcmd sccs
```

You can rebuild the delta component of `sccs` with the following command.

```
ARGS="delta" /usr/src/:mkcmd sccs
```

You can rebuild the log with the `log` command, which is a part of the `stat` package, which is itself a part of the `graf` package, with the following command.

```
ARGS="stat log" /usr/src/:mkcmd graf
```

The argument * rebuilds all commands and subsystems.

Makefiles throughout the system, and particularly in the cmd directory, have a standard format. In particular, :mkcmd depends on each makefile having target entries for install and clobber. The install target should build everything over which the makefile has jurisdiction and that is installed by /usr/sbin/install. The clobber target should completely clean up all unnecessary files resulting from the previous invocation. The :mkcmd, :mklib, and :mkuts commands use the CLOBBER environment variable. These commands all check the CLOBBER variable before executing make clobber. If this variable is set to OFF, then make clobber is not performed. If the variable is not set or is set to anything other than OFF, make clobber is performed.

An effort has been made to separate the creation of a command from source and its installation on the running system. The command /usr/sbin/install is used by :mkcmd and most makefiles to install commands in standard directories on the system. The use of install enables maximum flexibility in the administration of the system. The install command makes very few assumptions about where a command is located, who owns it, and what modes are in effect. All assumptions may be overridden on invocation of the command or, more permanently, by redefining a few variables in install. The purpose of install is to install a new version of a command in the same place, with the same attributes as the previous version.

In addition, the use of a separate command to perform installation enables you to create test systems in other than standard places, easily move commands to balance load, and independently maintain makefiles.

See Also

install(1M), make(1S)

mkfifo — Make FIFO Special File

Synopsis

/usr/bin/mkfifo [-m *mode*] *path*...

Description

Use the mkfifo command, an interface to the mknod command, when you want to create a new named pipe (FIFO) or special file. The new file has the following characteristics.

- The file type is specified by the *mode* parameter.
- The owner ID of the file is set to the effective user ID of the process.
- The group ID of the file is set to the group ID of the parent directory if the *SetGroupID* attribute of the parent directory is set. Otherwise, the group ID of the file is set to the effective group ID of the calling process.
- Permission and attribute bits are set by the value of the *mode* parameter. All bits set in the file-mode creation mask of the process are cleared.

On completion, the mkfifo command updates the st_atime, st_ctime, and st_mtime fields of the file. It also updates the st_ctime and st_mtime fields of the directory that contains the new entry.

FIFOs look like regular file-system nodes but are distinguished by a p in the first column of the output from the ls -l command.

Use the mkfifo command to create the FIFO special files named by its argument list. The arguments are taken sequentially, in the order specified, and each FIFO special file is either created completely or, in the case of an error or signal, not created at all.

If errors are encountered in creating one of the special files, mkfifo writes a diagnostic message to the standard error and continues with the remaining arguments, if any.

The mkfifo command calls the library routine mkfifo(3C), with the *path* argument passed as the path argument from the command line, and *mode* set to the equivalent of a=rw, modified by the current value of the file-mode creation mask umask(1).

Options

-m *mode*   Set the file permission bits of the newly created FIFO to the specified mode value. The *mode* option-argument is the same as the mode operand defined for the chmod(1) command. In *symbolic* mode strings, the *op* characters + and - are interpreted relative to an assumed initial mode of a=rw.

Operands

file   A path name of the FIFO special file to be created.

Example

The following example creates a FIFO special file named spclfile in the current directory and shows the p in the output from the ls -l command.

```
paperbark% mkfifo spclfile
paperbark% ls -l spclfile
prw-r--r--   1 winsor    staff            0 Mar 28 15:41 spclfile
paperbark%
```

The following example creates a FIFO special file named myfifo and sets the modes to 644 with the -m option.

```
# mkfifo -m 644 myfifo
# ls -la myfifo
prw-r--r--   1 root      other            0 Apr  5 21:49 myfifo
#
```

Usage

See largefile(5) for the description of the behavior of mkfifo when encountering files greater than or equal to 2 Gbytes (2**31 bytes).

Environment Variables

See environ(5) for descriptions of the following environment variables that affect the execution of mkfifo: LC_CTYPE, LC_MESSAGES, and NLSPATH.

Exit Status

0	All the specified FIFO special files were created successfully.
>0	An error occurred.

Attributes

See attributes(5) for descriptions of the following attributes.

Attribute Type	Attribute Value
Availability	SUNWesu

See Also

mkfifo(3C), attributes(5), environ(5), largefile(5)

mkfile — Create a File

Synopsis

/usr/sbin/mkfile [-nv] *size* [k | b | m] *filename*...

Description

As system configurations change and new software packages are installed, you may need to add more swap space. The preferred way to add more swap space is to use the mkfile command to create the swap file and then activate the swap file with the swap command. You should also add an entry for the swap file to the /etc/vfstab file so that it is automatically activated when the system is booted.

Use the mkfile command to create one or more files that are suitable for use as NFS-mounted swap areas or as local swap areas. When a root user executes mkfile(), the sticky bit is set and the file is padded with zeros by default. When non-root users execute mkfile(), they must manually set the sticky bit with the chmod(1) command. The default size is in bytes, but you can set it as kilobytes, blocks, or megabytes, with the k, b, or m suffixes.

Options

-n	Create an empty file. Note the size but do not allocate disk blocks until data is written to them. Files created with this option cannot be swapped over local UFS mounts.
-v	Verbosely report the names and sizes of created files.

Example

The following example creates a 24-megabyte swap file called /files/swapfiles.

```
# mkdir /files
# mkfile 24m /files/swapfile
```

```
# swap -a /files/swapfile
# vi /etc/vfstab
```
(Add the following line to the existing /etc/vfstab *file)*
```
/files/swapfile -    -    -    swap    -    no    -
ZZ
# swap -1
swapfile              dev    swaplo    blocks    free
/dev/dsk/c0t2d0s1    32,17        8    205624    192704
/files/swapfile         -         8     40952     40952
#
```

Usage

See largefile(5) for the description of the behavior of mkfile when encountering files greater than or equal to 2 Gbytes (2**31 bytes).

Attributes

See attributes(5) for descriptions of the following attributes.

Attribute Type	Attribute Value
Availability	SUNWcsu

See Also

chmod(1), swap(1M), attributes(5), largefile(5)

mkfs — Construct a File System

Synopsis

/usr/sbin/mkfs[-FFSType][generic-options][-oFSType-specific-options]
   raw-device-file [operands]

Description

Use the mkfs command to construct a file system on the raw-device-file by calling the specific mkfs module indicated by -F FSType.

Note — You usually create UFS file systems with the newfs(1M) command, which is a friendlier version of mkfs.

generic-options are independent of file-system type. FSType-specific-options is a comma-separated list of keyword=value pairs (with no intervening spaces), that are FSType-specific. raw-device-file specifies the disk partition on which to write the file system. It is required and must be the first argument following the specific-options (if any). Operands are FSType-specific. See the FSType-specific manual page of mkfs (for example, mkfs_ufs (1M)) for a detailed description.

Note — This command may not be supported for all FSTypes.

Options

The following options are generic for mkfs.

-F   Specify the FSType to be constructed. If you do not specify -F, mkfs must be able to determine the *FSType* from /etc/vfstab by matching the *raw-device-file* with a vfstab entry or by consulting the /etc/default/fs file.

-V   Echo the complete command line, but do not execute the command. Generate the command line by using the options and arguments provided and adding to them information derived from /etc/vfstab or /etc/default/fs. You can use this option to verify and validate the command line.

-m   Return the command line that was used to create the file system. The file system must already exist. This option provides a means of determining the command used in constructing the file system.

-o   Specify FSType-specific options. See the manual page for the mkfs module specific to the file-system type.

Usage

See largefile(5) for the description of the behavior of mkfs when encountering files greater than or equal to 2 Gbytes (2**31 bytes).

Files

/etc/default/fs

       Default file-system type. Default values can be set for the following option in /etc/default/fs. For example, LOCAL=ufs.

       LOCAL   The default partition for a command if no *FSType* is specified.

/etc/vfstab   List of default parameters for each file system.

Attributes

See attributes(5) for descriptions of the following attributes.

Attribute Type	Attribute Value
Availability	SUNWcsu

See Also

mkfs_ufs(1M), newfs(1M), vfstab(4), attributes(5), largefile(5)

mkfs_pcfs — Construct a FAT File System

New!

Synopsis

```
mkfs -F pcfs [generic-options] [-o FSType-specific-options]
   raw-device-file
```

Description

The mkfs_pcfs command is new in the Solaris 8 release. The PCFS-specific module of mkfs constructs a File Allocation Table (FAT) on removable media (diskette, JAZ disk, ZIP disk, PCMCIA card) or a hard disk. FATs are the standard MS-DOS and Windows file-system format. Note that you can use fdformat(1) to construct a FAT file system only on a diskette or PCMCIA card.

mkfs for PCFS determines an appropriate FAT size for the media, then it installs an initial boot sector and an empty FAT. A sector size of 512 bytes is used. mkfs for PCFS can also install the initial file in the file system (see the pcfs-specific -o i option). This first file can optionally be marked as read-only, system, or hidden.

If you want to construct a FAT with mkfs for PCFS on media that is not formatted, you must first perform a low-level format on the media with the fdformat(1) or format(1M) commands. You must also partition nondiskette media with the fdisk(1M) command. Note that all existing data on the diskette or disk partition, if any, is destroyed when a new FAT is constructed.

generic-options are supported by the generic mkfs command. See mkfs(1M) for a description of these options.

raw-device-file indicates the device on which to write unless you have specified the -o N option or if the -V or -m generic options are passed from the generic mkfs module.

Options

See mkfs(1M) for the list of supported generic options.

-o *FSType-specific-options*

> Specify PCFS file-system-specific options in a comma-separated list with no intervening spaces. If you specify invalid options, print a warning message and ignore the invalid options.
>
> b=*label*
>
>> Label the media with volume label. The volume label is restricted to 11 uppercase characters.
>
> B=*filename*
>
>> Install *filename* as the boot loader in the file system's boot sector. If you don't specify a boot loader, install an MS-DOS boot loader. The MS-DOS boot loader requires specific MS-DOS system files to make the diskette bootable. See "Note" for more information.

Note — The default MS-DOS boot loader, which is installed by default if you do not specify -o B, requires specific MS-DOS system files to make the diskette bootable. These MS-DOS files are not installed when you format a diskette with mkfs for PCFS, which makes a diskette formatted this way not bootable. Trying to boot from the diskette on an IA-based system results in the following message.

```
Non-System disk or disk error
Replace and strike any key when ready
```

You must format a diskette with the DOS format command to install the specific MS-DOS system files required by the default boot loader.

fat=n	Specify the size of a FAT entry. Currently, 12 and 16 are the only valid values. The default is 12 for diskettes, 16 for larger media.
h	Mark the first file installed as a hidden file. You must also specify the -i option.
hidden=n	Set the number of hidden sectors to n. This value is the number of sectors on the physical disk preceding the start of the volume (which is the boot sector itself). The default is 0 for diskettes or a computed valued (based on the fdisk table) for disks. You can use this option only in conjunction with the nofdisk option.
i=*filename*	Install *filename* as the initial file in the new file system. The initial file's contents are guaranteed to occupy consecutive clusters at the start of the files area. When creating bootable media, you should specify a boot program as the initial file.
nofdisk	Do not try to find an fdisk table on the media. Instead, rely on the size option to determine the partition size. By default, the created FAT is 16 bits and begins at the first sector of the device. You can modify this origination sector with the hidden option (-h).
nsect=n	Specify the number of sectors per track on the disk. If this value is not specified, determine it by using a dkio(7I) ioctl to get the disk geometry or (for diskette) from the results of an FDIOGCHAR ioctl.
ntrack=n	Specify the number of tracks per cylinder on the disk. If this value is not specified, determine it by using a dkio(7I) ioctl to get the disk geometry or (for diskette) from the results of an FDIOGCHAR ioctl.

N	Specify no execution mode. Print normal output, but do not actually write the file system to the media. This option is most useful when combined with the verbose option.
r	Mark the first file installed as read-only. You must also specify the -i option.
reserve=n	Set the number of reserved sectors to n. This value is the number of sectors in the volume preceding the start of the first FAT, including the boot sector. The value should always be at least 1, and the default value is exactly 1.
s	Mark the first file installed as a system file. You must also specify the -i option.
size=n	Specify the number of sectors in the file system. If you do not specify the value, determine it from the size of the partition given in the fdisk table or (for diskette) by computing it from the FDIOGCHAR ioctl.
spc=n	Specify the size of the allocation unit for space within the file system, expressed as a number of sectors. The default value depends on the FAT entry size and the size of the file system.
v	Display verbose output. Describe, in detail, operations being performed.

Files

raw-device-file

The device on which to build the FAT. The device name for a diskette must be specified as /dev/rdiskette0 for the first diskette drive, or /dev/rdiskette1 for a second diskette drive. For non-diskette media, you must qualify a disk device name with a suffix to indicate the proper partition. For example, in the name /dev/rdsk/c0t0d0p0:c, the :c suffix indicates that the first partition on the disk should receive the new FAT.

Examples

The media in the following examples must be formatted before mkfs is run for PCFS. The following example creates a FAT file system on a diskette.

```
# mkfs -F pcfs /dev/rdiskette
```

The following example creates a FAT file system on the second fdisk partition of a disk attached to an IA-based system.

```
# mkfs -F pcfs /dev/rdsk/c0d0p0:d
```

The following example creates a FAT file system on a ZIP disk located on a SPARC-based system.

```
# mkfs -F pcfs /dev/rdsk/c0t4d0s2:c
```

The following example creates a FAT file system on a JAZ disk located on a SPARC-based system and overrides the sectors/track and tracks/cylinder values obtained from the device's controller.

```
# mkfs -F pcfs -o nsect=32,ntrack=64 /dev/rdsk/c0t3d0s2:c
```

Attributes

See attributes(5) for descriptions of the following attributes.

Attribute Type	Attribute Value
Availability	SUNWesu
Stability	Stable

See Also

fdformat(1), fdisk(1M), format(1M), mkfs(1M), attributes(5), fd(7D), dkio(7I), fdio(7I)

New! **mkfs_udfs** — Construct a UDFS File System

Synopsis

```
mkfs -F udfs [generic-options] [-o specific-options] raw-device-file
     [size
```

Description

The mkfs_udfs command is new in the Solaris 8 release. This command is the universal disk format file system (UDFS)-specific module of the mkfs command. mkfs constructs a UDFS file system with a root directory.

Options

See mkfs(1M) for the list of supported *generic-options*.

-o *specific-options*

Specify a UDFS-specific option. Specify UDFS file-system-specific options in a comma-separated list with no intervening spaces. If you specify invalid options, print a warning message and ignore the invalid options. The following *specific-options* are available.

N   Print the file-system parameters without actually creating the file system.

label=string	Specify the label to be written into the volume header structures. Specify *string* as the name of the label. If you do not specify *string*, generate a default string in the form of *NoLabel*.

Operands

raw-device-file	
	Specify the disk partition on which to write.
size	Specify the number of 512-byte blocks in the file system.

Attributes

See attributes(5) for descriptions of the following attributes.

Attribute Type	**Attribute Value**
Availability	SUNWudf

See Also

fsck(1M), mkfs(1M), attributes(5)

Diagnostics

not currently a valid file system

> The specified device does not contain a valid UDFS file system.

Invalid size: larger than the partition size

> Number of blocks given as the parameter to create the file system is larger than the size of the device specified.

is mounted can't mkfs

> Device is in use; cannot create file system when the device is in use.

preposterous size

> Negative size parameter provided is invalid.

sector size must be between 512, 8192 bytes

> Sector size given is not in the valid range.

Volume integrity sequence descriptors too long
File set descriptor too long.

> Not enough space to create volume integrity sequence or file set descriptor.

mkfs: argument out of range

> One of the arguments is out of range.

```
mkfs: bad numeric arg
```
    One of the arguments is potentially a bad numeric.

mkfs_ufs — Construct a UFS File System

Synopsis

```
/usr/sbin/mkfs -F ufs [generic-options] [-o FSType-specific-options]
    raw-device-file [size]
```

Description

The UFS-specific module of mkfs builds a UFS file system with a root directory and a lost+found directory (see fsck(1M)).

Note — The UFS-specific mkfs is rarely run directly; use the newfs(1M) command instead.

---

    raw-device-file indicates the disk partition to write on unless you have specified the -o *n* option or either the -V or -m generic options are passed from the generic mkfs module. *size* specifies the number of sectors in the file system. This argument must follow the *raw-device-file* argument and is required (even with -o N) unless you specify the -V or -m generic options.

    generic-options are supported by the generic mkfs command. See mkfs(1M) for a description of these options.

Options

-o	Use one or more of the following values separated by commas (with no intervening spaces) to specify UFS-specific options.

N	Print the file-system parameters without actually creating the file system.
nsect=*n*	Set the number of sectors per track on the disk. The default is 32.
ntrack=*n*	Set the number of tracks per cylinder on the disk. The default is 16.
bsize=*n*	Set the logical block size to either 4096 or 8192. The default is 8192. (Note that the sun4u architecture does not support the 4096 block size.)
fragsize=*n*	Set the smallest amount of disk space in bytes to allocate to a file. The value must be a power of 2 selected from the range 512 to the logical block size. If logical block size is 4096, legal values are 512, 1024, 2048, and 4096; if logical block size is 8192, 8192 is also a legal value. The default is 1024.

cgsize=*n*	Set the number of cylinders per cylinder group, ranging from 16 to 256. In the Solaris 8 release, the default is no longer 16. Instead, it is calculated by dividing the number of sectors in the file system by the number of sectors in a gigabyte and then multiplying the result by 32. The default value is always between 16 and 256. The per-cylinder-group metadata must fit in a space no larger than that available in one logical file-system block. If you request too large a cgsize, decrease it by the minimum amount necessary.
free=*n*	Set the minimum percentage of free space to maintain in the file system. This space is off-limits to normal users. Once the file system is filled to this threshold, only the superuser can continue writing to the file system. You can subsequently change this parameter with the tunefs(1M) command. The default is 10%.
rps=*n*	Set the rotational speed of the disk, in revolutions per second. The default is 60.
nbpi=*n*	Set the number of bytes per inode, which specifies the density of inodes in the file system. The number is divided into the total size of the file system to determine the fixed number of inodes to create. It should reflect the expected average size of files in the file system. If you want fewer inodes, specify a larger number; to create more inodes, specify a smaller number. The default is 2048.
opt=*a*	Set the space or time optimization preference; s specifies optimization for space, t specifies optimization for time. The default is t. You can subsequently change this parameter with the tunefs(1M) command.
apc=*n*	Set the number of alternates per cylinder to reserve for bad block replacement (SCSI devices only). The default is 0.
gap=*n*	Set the rotational delay, which is the expected time (in milliseconds) to service a transfer completion interrupt and initiate a new transfer on the same disk. The value determines how much rotational spacing to place between successive blocks in a file. You can subsequently change this parameter with the tunefs(1M) command. The default is disk-type dependent.
nrpos=*n*	Set the number of different rotational positions in which to divide a cylinder group. The default is 8.

maxcontig=*n*   Set the maximum number of blocks belonging to one file that is allocated contiguously before inserting a rotational delay. For a 4-kilobyte file system, the default is 14; for an 8-kilobyte file system, the default is 7. You can subsequently change this parameter with the tunefs(1M) command.

Note that the maxconfig parameter also controls clustering. Regardless of the value of gap, clustering is enabled only when maxcontig is greater than 1. Clustering allows higher I/O rates for sequential I/O and is described in tunefs(1M).

Alternatively, you can specify parameters as a list of space-separated values (without keywords) whose meaning is positional. In this case, you omit the -o option and the list follows the *size* operand. newfs passes the parameters to mkfs in this way.

Operands

raw-device-file

The disk partition on which to write.

Attributes

See attributes(5) for descriptions of the following attributes.

Attribute Type	Attribute Value
Availability	SUNWcsu

See Also

fsck(1M), mkfs(1M), newfs(1M), tunefs(1M), dir_ufs(4), fs_ufs(4), attributes(5)

Diagnostics

```
Warning: insufficient space in super block for rotational layout
tables with nsect sblock.fs_nsect and ntraksblock.fs_ntrak. (File
system performance may be impaired.)
```

Occurs typically on very high density disks. On such disks, the file-system structure cannot encode the proper disk layout information, resulting in suboptimal performance.

```
Warning: inode blocks/cyl group (grp) >= data blocks (num) in last
cylinder
```

User request for inodes per byte (with the nbpi keyword) and the disk geometry results in a situation in which the last truncated cylinder group cannot contain the correct number of data blocks; some disk space is wasted.

`Warning: num sector(s) in last cylinder group unallocated`

User parameters and disk geometry conflict; some disk space is lost. A possible cause is the specified size being smaller than the partition size.

mknod — Make a Special File

Synopsis

```
/usr/sbin/mknod name b major minor
/usr/sbin/mknod name c major minor
/usr/sbin/mknod name p
```

Description

Use the mknod command to make a directory entry for a special file.

If you use mknod(2) to create a device, the major and minor device numbers are always interpreted by the kernel running on that machine.

Note — With the advent of physical device naming, it is preferable to create a symbolic link to the physical name of the device (in the /devices subtree) instead of using the mknod command.

Options

b	Create a block-type special file.
c	Create a character-type special file.
p	Create a FIFO (named pipe).

Operands

major	The major device number.
minor	The minor device number; can be either decimal or octal. The assignment of major device numbers is specific to each system. You must be superuser to use this form of the command.
name	A special file to be created.

Usage

See largefile(5) for the description of the behavior of mknod when encountering files greater than or equal to 2 Gbytes (2**31 bytes).

Attributes

See attributes(5) for descriptions of the following attributes.

Attribute Type	Attribute Value
Availability	SUNWcsu

See Also

ftp(1), in.ftpd(1M), mknod(2), symlink(2), attributes(5), largefile(5)

New! **modify_install_server** — Script to Replace miniroot on an Existing Net Install Server

Synopsis

```
cdrom-mnt-pt/Solaris_8/Tools/modify_install_server [-p]
    install-dir-path installer-miniroot-path
```

Description

See install_scripts(1M).

modinfo — Display Information About Loaded Kernel Modules

Synopsis

New!   /usr/sbin/modinfo [-c][-w][-i *module-id*]

Description

Use the modinfo command to display information about the loaded modules. The format of the information is as follows.

```
Id Loadaddr Size Info Rev Module Name
```

where Id is the module ID, Loadaddr is the starting text address in hexadecimal, Size is the size of text, data, and bss in hexadecimal bytes, Info is module-specific information, Rev is the revision of the loadable modules system, and Module Name is the file name and description of the module.

The module-specific information is the block and character major numbers for drivers, the system call number for system calls, or, for other module types, the index into the appropriate kernel table.

fmodsw	STREAMS modules.
vfssw	File systems.
class	Scheduling classes.
execsw	Exec modules.

Options

-c   Display the number of instances of the module loaded and the current *New!*
state of the module.

-i *module-id*   Display information about this module only.

-w   Do not truncate module information at 80 characters.   *New!*

Examples

The following example shows the output of the modinfo command with no arguments.
The example is truncated to save space.

```
paperbark% modinfo
 Id Loadaddr   Size Info Rev Module Name
  6 1011e000   42b3    1   1 specfs (filesystem for specfs)
  8 10123b70   2d38    1   1 TS (time sharing sched class)
  9 10126438    894    -   1 TS_DPTBL (Time sharing dispatch table)
 10 101264bc  25a07    2   1 ufs (filesystem for ufs)
 11 1014a37f  1083c  226   1 rpcmod (RPC syscall)
 11 1014a37f  1083c    1   1 rpcmod (rpc interface str mod)
 12 10158dff  523c0    0   1 ip (IP Streams module)
 12 10158dff  523c0    3   1 ip (IP Streams device)
 13 101a42ef   16a2    1   1 rootnex (sun4u root nexus 1.84)
 14 101a56f0    1ac   57   1 options (options driver)
 16 101a5dac   1664   12   1 sad (Streams Administrative driver's)
 17 101a72c0    567    2   1 pseudo (nexus driver for 'pseudo')
 18 101a7769  11034   32   1 sd (SCSI Disk Driver 1.320)
 19 101b7a09   73e5    -   1 scsi (SCSI Bus Utility Routines)
 22 101d0091   a713    6   1 fas (FAS SCSI HBA Driver v1.171)
 23 101da008   750c   59   1 sbus (SBus (sysio) nexus driver 1.96)
...(Additional lines deleted from this example)
```

The following example shows the output of the modinfo -c command. The example
is truncated to save space.

```
paperbark% modinfo -c
 Id    Loadcnt Module Name                          State
  1          0 krtld                     UNLOADED/UNINSTALLED
  2          0 genunix                   UNLOADED/UNINSTALLED
  3          0 platmod                   UNLOADED/UNINSTALLED
  4          0 SUNW,UltraSPARC           UNLOADED/UNINSTALLED
  5          0 cl_bootstrap              UNLOADED/UNINSTALLED
  6          1 specfs                    LOADED/INSTALLED
  7          1 swapgeneric               UNLOADED/UNINSTALLED
  8          1 TS                        LOADED/INSTALLED
```

```
 9           1 TS_DPTBL                      LOADED/INSTALLED
10           1 ufs                           LOADED/INSTALLED
11           1 rpcmod                        LOADED/INSTALLED
12           1 ip                            LOADED/INSTALLED
13           1 rootnex                       LOADED/INSTALLED
14           1 options                       LOADED/INSTALLED
15           1 dma                           UNLOADED/UNINSTALLED
```
...*(Additional lines deleted from this example)*

The following example shows the status of module 10.
```
paperbark% modinfo -i 10
 Id Loadaddr   Size Info Rev Module Name
 10 101264bc  25a07   2   1  ufs (filesystem for ufs)
paperbark%
```

Attributes

See attributes(5) for descriptions of the following attributes.

Attribute Type	Attribute Value
Availability	SUNWcsu

See Also

modload(1M), modunload(1M), attributes(5)

modload — Load a Kernel Module

Synopsis

/usr/sbin/modload [-p][-e *exec-file*] *filename*

Description

Use the modload command to load the loadable module *filename* into the running system. *filename* is an object file produced by ld -r. If *filename* is an absolute path name, then the file specified by that absolute path is loaded. If *filename* does not begin with a slash (/), then the path to load *filename* is relative to the current directory unless you specify the -p option. You can set the kernel's modpath variable in the /etc/system file. The default value of the kernel's modpath variable is set to the path where the operating system was loaded. Typically, this path is /kernel /usr/kernel. For example, if you type

modload drv/foo

the kernel looks for ./drv/foo. If you type

modload -p drv/foo

the kernel look for /kernel/drv/foo and then /usr/kernel/drv/foo.

> **Note** — Use add_drv(1M) to add device drivers, not modload. See *Writing Device Drivers* for procedures on adding device drivers.

Options

-p   Use the kernel's internal modpath variable as the search path for the module.

-e *exec-file*   Specify the name of a shell script or executable image file that is executed after the module is successfully loaded. The first argument passed is the module ID (in decimal). The other argument is module specific. The module-specific information includes the block and character major numbers for drivers, the system call number for system calls, or, for other module types, the index into the appropriate kernel table. See modinfo(1M).

Attributes

See attributes(5) for descriptions of the following attributes.

Attribute Type	Attribute Value
Availability	SUNWcsu

See Also

ld(1), add_drv(1M), kernel(1M), modinfo(1M), modunload(1M), system(4), attributes(5), modldrv(9S), modlinkage(9S), modlstrmod(9S), module_info(9S)
Writing Device Drivers
Solaris 1.x to 2.x Transition Guide

modunload — Unload a Module

Synopsis

/usr/sbin/modunload -i *module-id* [-e *exec-file*]

Description

Use the modunload command to unload a loadable module from the running system. The *module-id* is the ID of the module as shown by modinfo(1M). If ID is 0, all modules that were autoloaded and that are unloadable are unloaded. Modules loaded by modload(1M) are not affected.

Options

-i *module-id*   Specify the module to be unloaded.

-e *exec-file*   Specify the name of a shell script or executable image file to be executed before the module is unloaded. The first argument passed is the module ID (in decimal). Two additional arguments are module specific. For loadable drivers, the second and third arguments are the block major and character major numbers. For loadable system calls, the second argument is the system call number. For loadable exec classes, the second argument is the index into the execsw table. For loadable file systems, the second argument is the index into the vfssw table. For loadable streams modules, the second argument is the index into the fmodsw table. For loadable scheduling classes, the second argument is the index into the class array. -1 is passed for an argument that does not apply.

Attributes

See attributes(5) for descriptions of the following attributes.

Attribute Type	Attribute Value
Availability	SUNWcsu

See Also

modinfo(1M), modload(1M), attributes(5)

New! mofcomp — Compile MOF Files into CIM Classes

Synopsis

/usr/sadm/bin/mofcomp [-h][-v][-sc][-si][-sq][-version]
    [-c *cimom-hostname*][-p *password*][-u *username*] *file*

Description

The mofcomp command is new in the Solaris 8 release. It is executed during installation to compile Managed Object Format (MOF) files that describe the Common Information Model (CIM) and Solaris Schemas into the CIM Object Manager Repository, a central storage area for management data. The CIM Schema is a collection of class definitions used to represent managed objects that occur in every management environment. The Solaris Schema is a collection of class definitions that extend the CIM Schema and represent managed objects in a typical Solaris Operating Environment.

The mofcomp command must be run as root or as a user with write access to the namespace in which you are compiling.

MOF is a language for defining CIM classes and instances. MOF files are ASCII text files that use the MOF language to describe CIM objects. A CIM object is a computer representation or model of a managed resource, such as a printer, disk drive, or CPU.

Many sites store information about managed resources in MOF files. Because MOF can be converted to the Java programming language, Java applications that can run on any system with a Java virtual machine can interpret and exchange this information. You can also use the mofcomp command to compile MOF files at any time after installation.

Options

-c *cimom-hostname*

Specify a remote system running the CIM Object Manager.

-h   List the arguments to the mofcomp command.

-p *password*   Specify a password for connecting to the CIM Object Manager. Use this option for compilations that require privileged access to the CIM Object Manager. If you specify both -p and -u, you must type the password on the command line, which can pose a security risk. A more secure way to specify a password is to specify -u but not -p, so that the compiler prompts for the password.

-sc   Run the compiler with the set class option, which updates a class if it exists and returns an error if the class does not exist. If you do not specify this option, the compiler adds a CIM class to the connected namespace or returns an error if the class already exists.

-si   Run the compiler with the set instance option, which updates an instance if it exists, and returns an error if the instance does not exist. If you do not specify this option, the compiler adds a CIM instance to the connected namespace or returns an error if the instance already exists.

-sq   Run the compiler with the set qualifier types option, which updates a qualifier type if it exists and returns an error if the qualifier type does not exist. If you do not specify this option, the compiler adds a CIM qualifier type to the connected namespace or returns an error if the qualifier type already exists.

-u *username*   Specify user name for connecting to the CIM Object Manager. Use this option for compilations that require privileged access to the CIM Object Manager. If you specify both -p and -u, you must type the password on the command line, which can pose a security risk. A more secure way to specify a password is to specify -u but not -p, so that the compiler prompts for the password.

-v   Run the compiler in verbose mode, which displays compiler messages.

-version   Display the version of the MOF compiler.

Operands

file   The path name of the file to be compiled.

Exit Status

The mofcomp command exits with 0 on success and a positive integer on failure.

Files

The MOF files that describe the CIM Version 1 and Version 2 Schema and the Solaris Schema are listed below.

/usr/sadm/mof/CIM_Application22.mof

/usr/sadm/mof/CIM_Core22.mof

/usr/sadm/mof/CIM_DAP22.mof

/usr/sadm/mof/CIM_Device22.mof

/usr/sadm/mof/CIM_Device221.mof

/usr/sadm/mof/CIM_Network22.mof

/usr/sadm/mof/CIM_Physical22.mof

/usr/sadm/mof/CIM_Schema22.mof

/usr/sadm/mof/Solaris_Acl1.0.mof

/usr/sadm/mof/Solaris_Application1.0.mof

/usr/sadm/mof/Solaris_Core1.0.mof

/usr/sadm/mof/Solaris_Device1.0.mof

/usr/sadm/mof/Solaris_Schema1.0.mof

/usr/sadm/mof/Solaris_System1.0.mof

Attributes

See attributes(5) for descriptions of the following attributes.

Attribute Type	Attribute Value
Availability	SUNWwbcor

See Also

wbemadmin(1M), wbemlogviewer(1M), init.wbem(1M), attributes(5)

monacct — Invoke Accounting Monthly

Synopsis

/usr/lib/acct/monacct *number*

Description

See acctsh(1M).

monitor — SPARC System PROM Monitor

Synopsis

```
L1-A
BREAK
initial system power-on
exit from a client program such as the Operating System
```

Description

The CPU board of a workstation contains one or more EPROMs or EEPROMs. The program that executes from the PROMs is referred to as the monitor. Among other things, the monitor performs system initialization at power-on and provides a user interface.

Monitor Prompt

The monitor of earlier workstations was known as the SunMON monitor and displayed the > as its prompt. See "SunMON PROM Usage" on page 704 for further details.

Existing workstations use a monitor that is known as the OpenBoot monitor. The OpenBoot monitor typically displays ok as its prompt, but it can display the > prompt under certain circumstances.

If the auto-boot? NVRAM parameter is set to false when the workstation is powered on, then the system does not try to boot and the monitor issues its prompt. If auto-boot is set to true, then the system initiates the boot sequence. Users can abort the boot sequence by simultaneously pressing two keys on the system's keyboard: L1 and A (on older keyboards) or Stop and A (on newer keyboards). Note that either a lowercase a or an uppercase A works for the keyboard abort sequence. If a console has been attached to one of the system's serial ports, then you can send a BREAK to abort the sequence (see the tip(1) manual page).

When the NVRAM security-mode parameter has been turned on or when the value of the sunmon-compat? parameter is true, then the OpenBoot monitor displays the following message and displays the > prompt.

```
Type b (boot), c (continue), or n (new command mode)
```

OpenBoot PROM Usage

Some of the more useful commands that can be issued from OpenBoot's ok prompt are described here. Refer to the *OpenBoot 2.x Command Reference Manual* for a complete list of commands.

Help

You can get help for various functional areas of the OpenBoot monitor by typing help. The help listing provides a number of other keywords that can then be used in the help command to provide further details.

NVRAM Parameters

Each workstation contains one or more NVRAM devices that contain unique system ID information, as well as a set of user-configurable parameters. The NVRAM parameters enable the user a certain level of flexibility in configuring the system to act in a given manner under a specific set of circumstances.

See the eeprom(1M) manual page for a description of the parameters. This manual page also describes a way of setting the parameters from the OS level.

You can use the following commands at the OpenBoot monitor to access the NVRAM parameters.

printenv   List the NVRAM parameters along with their default values and current values.

setenv *pn pv* Set or modify a parameter. The *pn* represents the parameter name, and *pv* represents the parameter value.

set-default*pn*

                Set an individual parameter back to its default value.

set-defaults   Reset all parameters to their default values. (Note that set-defaults affects only parameters that have assigned default values.)

Hardware Checks and Diagnostics

The following commands are available for testing or checking the system's hardware. If the diag-switch? NVRAM parameter is set to true when the system is powered on, then a Power-On Self-Test (POST) diagnostic is run, if present, sending its results messages to the system's serial port A. Not all of the commands shown are available on all workstations.

test-all   Run the diagnostic tests on each device that has provided a self-test.

test floppy   Run diagnostics on the system's floppy device.

test /memory   Run the main memory tests. If the NVRAM parameter diag-switch? is set to true, test all of main memory. If the parameter is false, then test only the amount of memory specified in the selftest-#megs NVRAM parameter.

test net   Test the network connection for the on-board network controller.

watch-net   Monitor the network attached to the on-board net controller.

watch-net-all

                Monitor the network attached to the on-board net controller, as well as the network controllers installed in SBus slots.

watch-clock   Test the system clock function.

System Information

The following commands are available for displaying information about the system. Not all commands are available on all workstations.

banner   Display the power-on banner.

.enet-addr   Display the system's Ethernet address.

.idprom   Display the formatted contents of the IDPROM.

module-info   Display information about the system's processor(s).

`probe-scsi`	Identify the devices attached to the on-board SCSI controller.
`probe-scsi-all`	
	Identify the devices attached to the on-board SCSI controller as well as those devices that are attached to SBus SCSI controllers.
`show-disks`	List the device paths for installed SCSI disk controllers.
`show-displays`	
	List the device paths for installed display devices.
`show-nets`	List the device paths for installed Ethernet controllers.
`show-sbus`	List installed SBus devices.
`show-tapes`	List the device paths for installed SCSI tape controllers.
`show-ttys`	List the device paths for TTY devices.
`.traps`	List the SPARC trap types.
`.version`	Display the version and date of the OpenBoot PROM.

Emergency Commands

You must type the emergency commands from the keyboard; they do not work from a console that is attached to the serial ports. With the exception of the Stop-A command, you issue these commands by pressing and holding down the indicated keys on the keyboard immediately after the system has been powered on. You must hold the keys down until the monitor has checked their status. You can issue the Stop-A command at any time after the console display begins, and you do not need to hold the keys down once you have pressed them. The Stop-D, Stop-F, and Stop-N commands are not allowed when one of the security modes has been set. Not all commands are available on all workstations.

`Stop (L1)`	Bypass the Power-On Self-Test (POST). This command is effective only if the system is in diagnostic mode.
`Stop-A (L1-A)`	Abort the current operation and return to the monitor's default prompt.
`Stop-D (L1-D)`	Set the system's `diag-switch?` NVRAM parameter to `true`, which puts the system in diagnostic mode. Run POST diagnostics if present, and display the messages via the system's serial port A.
`Stop-F (L1-F)`	Enter the OpenBoot monitor before the monitor has probed the system for devices. Issue the `fexit` command to continue with system initialization.
`Stop-N (L1-N)`	Reset the NVRAM parameters to their default values. Note that not all parameters have default values.

Line Editor Commands

You can use the following commands while the monitor is displaying the `ok` prompt. Not all of these editing commands are available on all workstations.

`CTRL-A`	Put the cursor at the start of line.
`CTRL-B`	Move the cursor backward one character.

ESC-B	Move the cursor backward one word.
CTRL-D	Erase the character that the cursor is currently highlighting.
ESC-D	Erase the portion of word from the cursor's present position to the end of the word.
CTRL-E	Put the cursor at the end of line.
CTRL-F	Move the cursor forward one character.
ESC-F	Move the cursor forward one word.
CTRL-H	Erase the character preceding the cursor (also use Delete or Backspace).
ESC-H	Erase the portion of the word before the cursor (use also CTRL-W).
CTRL-K	Erase from the cursor's present position to the end of the line.
CTRL-L	Show the command history list.
CTRL-N	Recall the next command from the command history list.
CTRL-P	Recall a previous command from the command history list.
CTRL-Q	Quote the next character (used to type a control character).
CTRL-R	Retype the current line.
CTRL-U	Erase from the cursor's present position to the beginning of the line.
CTRL-Y	Insert the contents of the memory buffer into the line, in front (to the left) of the cursor.

nvramrc

The nvramrc is an area of the system's NVRAM where users can store Forth programs. The programs that are stored in the nvramrc are executed each time the system is reset, provided that the use-nvramrc? NVRAM parameter has been set to true. Refer to the *OpenBoot 2.x Command Reference Manual* for information on how to edit and use the nvramrc.

Restricted Monitor

Use the old-mode command to move OpenBoot into a restricted monitor mode and display the > prompt. Only three commands are allowed while in the restricted monitor mode; the go command (to resume a program that was interrupted with the Stop-A command), the n command (to return to the normal OpenBoot monitor), and a boot command. The restricted monitor's boot commands approximate the older SunMON monitor's boot command syntax. If a security-mode has been turned on, then the restricted monitor becomes the default monitor environment. The restricted monitor may also become the default environment if the sunmon-compat? NVRAM parameter is set to true. (Note that not all workstations have the sunmon-compat? parameter.)

SunMON PROM Usage

The following commands are available systems with older SunMON-based PROM.

+ | -	Increment or decrement the current address and display the contents of the new location.

^C *source destination n*

> (caret-C) Copy, byte-by-byte, a block of length *n* from the source address to the destination address.

^I *program*   (caret-I) Display the compilation date and location of *program*.

^T *virtual-address*

> (caret-T) Display the physical address to which *virtual-address* is mapped.

b [!] [*device* [(c,u,p)]] [*pathname*] [*arguments-list*] b[?]

> Reset appropriate parts of the system and bootstrap a program. A ! (preceding the device argument) prevents the system from resetting. You can load programs from various devices (such as a disk, tape, or Ethernet). b with no arguments boots the default device either from a disk or from an Ethernet controller. b? displays all boot devices and their devices.
>
> *device* is one of the following values.

le	Lance Ethernet.
ie	Intel Ethernet.
sd	SCSI disk, CD-ROM.
st	SCSI 1/4" or 1/2" tape.
fd	Diskette.
id	IPI disk.
mt	Tape Master 9-track 1/2" tape.
xd	Xylogics 7053 disk.
xt	Xylogics 1/2" tape.
xy	Xylogics 440/450 disk.

c   A controller number (0 if only one controller).

u   A unit number (0 if only one driver).

p   A partition.

pathname   A path name, such as /stand/diag, for a program.

arguments-list

> A list of up to seven arguments to pass to the program being booted.

c [*virtual-address*]

> Resume execution of a program. When given, *virtual-address* is the address at which execution resumes. The default is the current PC.
>
> Restore registers to the values shown by the d and r commands.

d [*window-number*]

> Display (dump) the state of the processor. The processor state is observable only in the following conditions.
>
> - After an unexpected trap is encountered.
> - A user program dropped into the monitor (by calling `abortent`).
> - The user manually entered the monitor by typing L1-A or Break.
>
> The following information is displayed.
>
> - The special registers: `PSR`, `PC`, `nPC`, `TBR`, `WIM`, and `Y`.
> - Eight global registers.
> - Twenty-four window registers (8 in, 8 local, and 8 out), corresponding to one of the seven available windows. If a Floating-Point Unit is on board, also show its status register along with 32 floating-point registers.
>
> *window-number*
>
> > Display the indicated *window-number*, which can be any value between 0 and 6, inclusive. If you specify no window and the PSR's current window pointer contains a valid window number, display registers from the window that was active just before entry into the monitor. Otherwise, display registers from window 0.

e [*virtual-address*][*action*]...

> Open the 16-bit word at *virtual-address* (default zero). Interpret the address in the address space defined by the s command. See the a command for a description of *action*.

f *virtual-address1 virtual-address2 pattern* [*size*]

> Fill the bytes, words, or long words from *virtual-address1* (lower) to *virtual-address2* (higher) with the constant, *pattern*. The *size* argument can take one of the following values.
>
> b   Byte format (the default).
>
> w   Word format.
>
> l   Long word format.
>
> For example, the following command fills the address block from 0x1000 to 0x2000 with the word pattern 0xABCD.
>
> f 1000 2000 ABCD W

g [*vector*][*argument*]
g [*virtual-address*][*argument*]

> Go to (jump to) a predetermined or default routine (first form), or to a user-specified routine (second form). Pass the value of *argument* to the routine. If you omit the vector or *virtual-address* argument, use the value in the PC as the address to jump to.

To set up a predetermined routine to jump to, before the g command is executed, a user program must set the variable *romp>v_vector_cmd equal to the virtual address of the desired routine. Predetermined routines need not necessarily return control to the monitor.

The default routine, defined by the monitor, prints the user-supplied vector according to the format supplied in *argument*. This format can be one of the following.

%x   Hexadecimal.

%d   Decimal.

g0   Force a panic and produce a crash dump when the monitor is running as a result of the system being interrupted.

g4   (sun-4 systems only) Force a kernel stack trace when the monitor is running as a result of the system being interrupted.

h   Display the help menu for monitor commands and their descriptions. To return to the monitor's basic command level, press Escape or q before pressing Return.

i [*cache-data-offset*][*action*]...

Modify cache data RAM command. Display or modify one or more of the cache data addresses. See the a command for a description of *action*.

j [*cache-tag-offset*][*action*]...

Modify cache tag RAM command. Display or modify the contents of one or more of the cache tag addresses. See the a command for a description of *action*.

k [*reset-level*]

Reset the system, where *reset-level* is one of the following.

0   Reset VMEbus, interrupt registers, video monitor (sun-4 systems). The default.

1   Software reset.

2   Power-on reset. Reset and clear the memory. Run the EPROM-based diagnostic self-test, which can take several minutes, depending on how much memory is being tested.

kb   Display the system banner.

l [*virtual-address*][*action*]...

Open the long word (32 bit) at memory address *virtual-address* (default 0). Interpret the address in the address space defined by the s command. See the a command for a description of *action*.

m [*virtual-address*][*action*]...

> Open the segment map entry that maps *virtual-address* (default 0).
> Interpret the address in the address space defined by the s command.
> See the a command for a description of *action*.

ne

ni

> Disable, enable, or invalidate the cache.

o [*virtual-address*][*action*]...

> Open the byte location specified by *virtual-address* (default 0).
> Interpret the address in the address space defined by the s command.
> See the a command for a description of *action*.

p [*virtual-address*][*action*]...

> Open the page map entry that maps *virtual-address* (default 0) in
> the address space defined by the s command. See the a command for
> a description of *action*.

q [*eeprom-offset*][*action*]...

> Open the EEPROM *eeprom-offset* (default 0) in the EEPROM
> address space. Reference all addresses from the beginning or base of
> the EEPROM in physical address space, and perform a limit check to
> ensure that no address beyond the EEPROM physical space is
> accessed. Use this command to display or modify configuration
> parameters, such as the amount of memory to test during self-test,
> whether to display a standard or custom banner, or if a serial port (A
> or B) is to be the system console. See the a command for a description
> of *action*.

r [*register-number*]
r [*register-type*]
r [w *window-number*]

> Display or modify one or more of the IU or FPU registers. A
> hexadecimal *register-number* can be one of the following values.
>
> 0x00-0x0f window(0,i0)-window(0,i7),
>   window(0,i0)-window(0,i7)
>
> 0x16-0x1f window(1,i0)-window(1,i7),
>   window(1,i0)-window(1,i7)
>
> 0x20-0x2f window(2,i0)-window(2,i7),
>   window(2,i0)-window(2,i7)
>
> 0x30-0x3f window(3,i0)-window(3,i7),
>   window(3,i0)-window(3,i7)
>
> 0x40-0x4f window(4,i0)-window(4,i7),
>   window(4,i0)-window(4,i7)
>
> 0x50-0x5f window(5,i0)-window(5,i7),
>   window(5,i0)-window(5,i7)

```
0x60-0x6f window(6,i0)-window(6,i7),
          window(6,i0)-window(6,i7)
0x70-0x77 g0, g1, g2, g3, g4, g5, g6, g7
0x78-0x7d PSR, PC, nPC, WIM, TBR, Y.
0x7e-0x9e FSR, f0-f31
```

Register numbers can be displayed only after an unexpected trap, when a user program has entered the monitor through the abortent function, or when the user has entered the monitor by manually typing L1-A or Break.

If you specify *register-type*, display the first register of the indicated type. *register-type* can be one of the following.

f	Floating-point.
g	Global.
s	Special.

If you specify w and a *window-number* (0-6), display the first in-register within the indicated window. If you omit *window-number*, use the window that was active just before the monitor was entered. If the PSR's current window pointer is invalid, use window 0.

s [*asi*])
Set or display the Address Space Identifier. With no argument, display the current Address Space Identifier. The *asi* value can be one of the following.

0x2	Control space.
0x3	Segment table.
0x4	Page table.
0x8	User instruction.
0x9	Supervisor instruction.
0xa	User data.
0xb	Supervisor data.
0xc	Flush segment.
0xd	Flush page.
0xe	Flush context.
0xf	Cache data.

u [*echo*]
u [*port*][*options*][*baud-rate*]
u [u][*virtual-address*]

With no arguments, display the current I/O device characteristics including current input device, current output device, baud rates for serial ports A and B, an input-to-output echo indicator, and virtual addresses of mapped UART devices. With arguments, set or configure the current I/O device. With the u argument (uu...), set the I/O device to be the *virtual-address* of a UART device currently mapped.

echo   Specify e to enable input to be echoed to the output device, or ne to indicate that input is not echoed.

port   Assign the indicated port to be the current I/O device. *port* can be one of the following.

a   Serial port A.

b   Serial port B.

k   The workstation keyboard.

s   The workstation screen.

baud-rate   Any legal baud rate.

options can be any combination of the following.

i   Input.

o   Output.

u   UART.

e   Echo input to output.

ne   Do not echo input.

r   Reset indicated serial port (a and b ports only).

If you specify either a or b with no options, assign the serial port for both input and output. If you specify k with no options, assign input only. If you specify s with no options, assign output only.

v *virtual-address1 virtual-address2* [*size*]

Display the contents of *virtual-address1* (lower) *virtual-address2* (higher) in the format specified by *size*.

b   Byte format (the default).

w   Word format.

l   Long word format.

Press Return to pause for viewing; press another Return to resume the display. To terminate the display at any time, press the space bar.

For example, the following command displays the contents of virtual address space from address 0x1000 to 0x2000 in word format.

v 1000 2000 W

w [*virtual-address*] [*argument*]

Set the execution vector to a predetermined or default routine. Pass *virtual-address* and *argument* to that routine.

To set up a predetermined routine to jump to, before executing the w command, a user program must set the variable *romp>v_vector_cmd equal to the virtual address of the desired routine. Predetermined routines need not necessarily return control to the monitor.

The default routine, defined by the monitor, prints the user-supplied vector according to the format supplied in *argument*. This format can be one of the following.

%x   Hexadecimal.

%d   Decimal.

x   Display a menu of extended tests. These diagnostics permit additional testing of such things as the I/O port connectors, video memory, workstation memory and keyboard, and boot device paths.

yc *context-number*
yp|s *contextnumber virtual-address*

Flush the indicated context, context page, or context segment.

c   Flush context *context-number*.

p   Flush the page beginning at *virtual-address* within context *context-number*.

s   Flush the segment beginning at *virtual-address* within context *context-number*.

Attributes

See attributes(5) for descriptions of the following attributes.

Attribute Type	Attribute Value
Architecture	SPARC

See Also

tip(1), boot(1M), eeprom(1M), attributes(5)
OpenBoot 2.x Command Reference Manual

mount, umount — Mount or Unmount File Systems and Remote Resources

Synopsis

```
/usr/sbin/mount [-p | -v]
/usr/sbin/mount [-F FSType] [generic-options] [-o specific-options] [-O]
    special | mount-point
/usr/sbin/mount [-F FSType] [generic-options] [-o specific-options] [-O]
    special mount-point
/usr/sbin/mount-a[-FFSType] [-V] [current-options] [-o specific-options]
    [mount-point...]
/usr/sbin/umount [-f] [-V] [-o specific-options] special | mount-point
/usr/sbin/umount -a [-f] [-V] [-o specific-options] [mount-point...]
```

New!

Description

Use the mount command to attach a file system to the file-system hierarchy at the *mount-point*, which is the path name of a directory. If *mount-point* has any contents before the mount operation, they are hidden until the file system is unmounted.

Use the umount command to unmount a currently mounted file system, which you can specify either as a *mount-point* or as *special*, the device on which the file system resides.

Only superuser can mount or unmount file systems with mount and umount. However, any user can use the mount command to list mounted file systems and resources.

You can examine the table of currently mounted file systems by looking at the /etc/mnttab table of mounted file systems, which is described in mnttab(4). Mounting a file system adds an entry to the mount table; unmounting a file system removes an entry from the table.

When invoked with both the *special* and *mount-point* arguments and the -F option, mount validates all arguments except for *special* and invokes the appropriate FSType-specific mount module. When invoked with no arguments, mount lists all the mounted file systems recorded in the mount table, /etc/mnttab. When invoked with a partial argument list (with only one of *special* or *mount-point*, or with both *special* or *mount-point* specified but not *FSType*), mount searches /etc/vfstab for an entry that supplies the missing arguments. If no entry is found and the *special* argument starts with /, the default local file-system type specified in /etc/default/fs is used. Otherwise, the default remote file-system type is used. mount determines the default remote file-system type by the first entry in the /etc/dfs/fstypes file. After filling in missing arguments, mount invokes the FSType-specific mount module.

> **Note** — If the directory on which a file system is to be mounted is a symbolic link, the file system is mounted on the directory to which the symbolic link refers instead of on the symbolic link itself.

Options

-F *FSType*   Specify the *FSType* on which to operate. You must specify *FSType*, or mount must be able to determine it from /etc/vfstab or by consulting /etc/default/fs or /etc/dfs/fstypes.

-a [*mount-points...*]

Perform mount or umount operations in parallel, when possible.

If you do not specify *mount-points*, mount all file systems whose /etc/vfstab mount at boot field is yes. If you specify *mount-points*, ignore the /etc/vfstab mount at boot field value.

If you specify *mount-points*, unmount only those mount points. If you specify no *mount-points*, try to unmount all file systems in /etc/mnttab except for the required file systems /, /usr, /var, /proc, /dev/fd, and /tmp.

-f   Forcibly unmount a file system.   *New!*

Without this option, umount does not unmount a file system if a file on the file system is busy. Using this option can result in data loss for open files; programs that access files after the file system has been unmounted get an error (EIO).

-p   Print the list of mounted file systems in /etc/vfstab format. Must be the only option specified.

-v   Print the list of mounted file systems in verbose format. Must be the only option specified.

-V   Echo the complete command line but do not execute the command. Generate a command line by using the specified options and arguments and adding to them information derived from /etc/mnttab. Use this option to verify and validate the command line.

generic-options

Options that are commonly supported by most FSType-specific command modules. The following options are available.

-g   On a clustered system, globally mount the file   *New!* system on all nodes of the cluster. On a nonclustered system, this option has no effect. This option is new in the Solaris 8 release.

-m   Mount the file system without making an entry in /etc/mnttab.

-o   Specify FSType-specific options in a comma-separated (without spaces) list of suboptions and keyword-attribute pairs for interpretation by the FSType-specific module of the command. (See mount_ufs(**1M**)).

-O	Allow the file system to be mounted over an existing mount point, making the underlying file system inaccessible. If you try to mount on a preexisting mount point without using this option, the mount fails and displays a `device busy` error message.
-r	Mount the file system read-only.

Usage

See `largefile`(5) for the description of the behavior of `mount` and `umount` when encountering files greater than or equal to 2 Gbytes (2**31 bytes).

Files

`/etc/mnttab`   Mount table.

`/etc/default/fs`

Default local file-system type. Default values can be set for the following flag in `/etc/default/fs`. For example, LOCAL=ufs.

LOCAL	The default partition for a command if you specify no *FSType*.

`/etc/vfstab`   List of default parameters for each file system.

Attributes

See `attributes`(5) for descriptions of the following attributes.

Attribute Type	**Attribute Value**
Availability	SUNWcsu

See Also

`mount_cachefs`(1M), `mount_hsfs`(1M), `mount_nfs`(1M), `mount_pcfs`(1M), `mount_tmpfs`(1M), `mount_ufs`(1M), `mountall`(1M), `umountall`(1M), `mnttab`(4), `vfstab`(4), `attributes`(5), `largefile`(5), `lofs`(7FS), `pcfs`(7FS)

mountall, umountall — Mount, Unmount Multiple File Systems

Synopsis

```
/usr/sbin/mountall [-F FSType][-l | -r][file-system-table]
/usr/sbin/umountall [-k][-s][-F FSType][-l | -r]
/usr/sbin/umountall [-k][-s][-h host]
```

Description

Use the mountall command to mount file systems specified in a file-system table. The file-system table must be in vfstab(4) format. If you specify no *file-system-table*, /etc/vfstab is used. If you specify - as *file-system-table*, mountall reads the file-system table from the standard input. mountall mounts only those file systems with the mount at boot field set to yes in the *file-system-table*.

Each file system that has an fsckdev entry specified in the file system table is checked by fsck(1M) to determine if it can be mounted safely. If the file system does not appear mountable, it is fixed by means of fsck before the mount is tried. File systems with a - entry in the fsckdev field are mounted without first being checked.

umountall unmounts all mounted file systems except root, /usr, /var, /var/adm, /var/run, /proc, and /dev/fd. In releases before Solaris 8, all file systems except root, /usr, /proc, and /var were unmounted. If you specify the *FSType*, mountall and umountall limit their actions to the specified *FSType*. There is no guarantee that umountall unmounts busy file systems, even if you specify the -k option.

New!

Options

-F *FSType*	Specify the *FSType* of the file system to be mounted or unmounted.
-h *host*	Unmount all file systems listed in /etc/mnttab that are remote-mounted from *host*.
-k	Send the SIGKILL signal to each process that is using the file with the fuser -k mount-point command. See fuser(1M) for details. Because this option spawns kills for each process, the kill messages may not show up immediately. There is no guarantee that umountall can unmount busy file systems even if you specify the -k option.
-l	Limit the action to local file systems.
-r	Limit the action to remote file-system types.
-s	Do not perform the unmount operation in parallel.

Files

/etc/mnttab	Table of mounted file systems.
/etc/vfstab	List of default parameters for each file system.

Attributes

See attributes(5) for descriptions of the following attributes.

Attribute Type	Attribute Value
Availability	SUNWcsu

See Also

fsck(1M), fuser(1M), mount(1M), mnttab(4), vfstab(4), attributes(5)

Diagnostics

No messages are printed if the file systems are mountable and clean.
Error and warning messages come from fsck(1M) and mount(1M).

mount_cachefs — Mount CacheFS File Systems

Synopsis

```
/usr/sbin/mount -F cachefs [generic-options]
   -o backfstype=file-system-type [specific-options][-O] special
   mount-point
```

Description

The CacheFS-specific version of the mount command mounts a cached file system; if necessary, it NFS-mounts its backfile system. It also provides a number of CacheFS-specific options for controlling the caching process. For more information regarding backfile systems, refer to the *System Administration Guide, Volume I*.

Options

To mount a CacheFS file system, use the generic mount command with the -F option followed by the argument cachefs.

See mount(1M) for a list of supported *generic-options*.

-o *specific-options*

Specify CacheFS file-system-specific options in a comma-separated list with no intervening spaces.

acdirmax=*n*   Hold cached attributes for no more than *n* seconds after directory update. After *n* seconds, purge all directory information from the cache. The default value is 30 seconds.

acdirmin=*n*   Hold cached attributes for at least *n* seconds after directory update. After *n* seconds, check to see if the directory modification time on the backfile system has changed. If it has, purge all information about the directory from the cache and retrieve new data from the backfile system. The default value is 30 seconds.

acregmax=*n*   Hold cached attributes for no more than *n* seconds after file modification. After *n* seconds, purge all file information from the cache. The default value is 30 seconds.

acregmin=*n*	Hold cached attributes for at least *n* seconds after file modification. After *n* seconds, check to see if the file modification time on the backfile system has changed. If it has, purge all information about the file from the cache and retrieve new data from the backfile system. The default value is 30 seconds.
actimeo=*n*	Set acregmin, acregmax, acdirmin, and acdirmax to *n*.
backfstype=*filesystem-type*	
	Specify the file-system type of the backfile system (can be nfs or hsfs).
backpath=*path*	Specify where the backfile system is already mounted. If you do not supply this argument, determine a mount point for the backfile system. The backfile system must be read-only.
cachedir=*directory*	
	Specify the name of the cache directory.
cacheid=*ID*	Specify a string identifying a particular instance of a cache. If you do not specify a cache ID, construct one.
demandconst	Verify cache consistency only when explicitly requested instead of doing the default periodic checking. You request a consistency check by using the -s option of the cfsadmin(1M) command. This option is useful for backfile systems that change infrequently, for example, /usr/openwin. demandconst and noconst are mutually exclusive.
local-access	Interpret the front file-system mode bits used for access checking instead of having the backfile system verify access permissions. Do not use this argument with secure NFS.
noconst	Disable cache consistency checking. By default, periodic consistency checking is enabled. Specify noconst only when you know that the backfile systems are not modified. Trying to perform cache consistency check by using cfsadmin -s results in error. demandconst and noconst are mutually exclusive.
purge	Purge any cached information for the specified file system.
ro | rw	Read-only or read-write (default).
suid | nosuid	Allow (default) or disallow setuid execution.

write-around | non-shared

> Specify write modes for CacheFS. The write-around mode (the default) handles writes the same as NFS does; that is, writes are made to the backfile system and the affected file is purged from the cache. You can use the nonshared mode when you are sure that no one else is writing to the cached file system. In this mode, make all writes to both the front and the backfile system, and the file remains in the cache.

-o
> Allow the file system to be mounted over an existing mount point, making the underlying file system inaccessible. If you try to mount on a preexisting mount point without using this option, the mount fails and displays a device busy error message.

Examples

The following example CacheFS-mounts the file system server1:/user2, which is already NFS-mounted on /usr/abc as /xyz.

```
# mount -F cachefs -o backfstype=nfs,backpath=/usr/abc,
    cachedir=/cache1 server1:/user2 /xyz
```

After you execute the previous mount command, lines similar to the following are added to the /etc/mnttab file.

```
server1:/user2    /usr/abc     nfs
/usr/abc          /cache1/xyz cachefs    backfstype=nfs
```

Attributes

See attributes(5) for descriptions of the following attributes.

Attribute Type	Attribute Value
Availability	SUNWcsu

See Also

cfsadmin(1M), fsck_cachefs(1M), mount(1M), attributes(5)
System Administration Guide, Volume I

mountd — Server for NFS Mount Requests and NFS Access Checks

Synopsis

```
/usr/lib/nfs/mountd [-v][-r]
```

Description

The mountd daemon is an RPC server that answers requests for NFS access information and file-system mount requests. It reads the /etc/dfs/sharetab file to determine which file systems are available for mounting by which remote machines. See sharetab(4). nfsd running on the local server contacts mountd the first time an NFS client tries to access the file system to determine whether the client should get read-write, read-only, or no access. This access can be dependent on the security mode used in the remote procedure call from the client. See share_nfs(1M).

mountd also provides information about what file systems are mounted by which clients. You can print this information with the showmount(1M) command.

The mountd daemon is automatically invoked in run level 3.

Only superuser can run the mountd daemon.

Note — If nfsd is running, mountd must also be running so that the NFS server can respond to requests; otherwise, the NFS service can hang.

Some routines that compare host names use case-sensitive string comparisons; some do not. If an incoming request fails, verify that the case of the host name in the file to be parsed matches the case of the host name called for and try the request again.

Options

-v   Run the command in verbose mode. Each time mountd determines what access a client should get, it logs the result and how it got that result to the console.

-r   Reject mount requests from clients. Clients that have file systems mounted are not affected.

Files

/etc/dfs/sharetab

Shared file-system table.

Attributes

See attributes(5) for descriptions of the following attributes.

Attribute Type	Attribute Value
Availability	SUNWcsu

See Also

nfsd(1M), share_nfs(1M), showmount(1M), sharetab(4), attributes(5)

mount_hsfs — Mount HSFS File Systems

Synopsis

```
/usr/sbin/mount -F hsfs [generic-options] [-o FSType-specific-options]
   [-O] special | mount-point
mount -F hsfs [generic-options] [-o FSType-specific-options]
   [-O] special mount-point
```

Description

Use the mount -F hsfs command to attach a High Sierra file system (hsfs) to the file-system hierarchy at the *mount-point*, which is the path name of a directory. If *mount-point* has any contents before the mount operation, these are hidden until the file system is unmounted.

If you invoke mount with *special* or *mount-point* as the only arguments, mount searches /etc/vfstab to fill in the missing arguments, including the *FSType-specific-options*; see mount(1M) for more details.

If the file system being mounted contains Rock Ridge extensions, by default they are used, enabling support of special files and features, such as symbolic links, that are not normally available under High Sierra file systems.

Note — If the directory on which a file system is to be mounted is a symbolic link, the file system is mounted on the directory to which the symbolic link refers instead of on the symbolic link itself.

Options

See mount(1M) for a list of supported *generic-options*.

-o   Specify HSFS file-system-specific options. If you specify invalid options, print a warning message and ignore the invalid options. The following options are available.

             ro   Mount the file system read-only. This option is required.

             nrr   Ignore any Rock Ridge extensions present in the file system; interpret the file system as a regular High Sierra file system.

             notraildot   Make optional the normal trailing dot to access a file whose name lacks an extension. File names on High Sierra file systems consist of a proper name and an extension separated by a dot (.) character. By default, the separating dot is always considered part of the file name for all file access operations, even if no extension is present.

This option is effective only on file systems for which Rock Ridge extensions are not active, either because they are not present on the CD-ROM or because they are explicitly ignored because the nrr option was specified. If Rock Ridge extensions are active, quietly ignore this option.

nomaplcase   Turn off mapping of uppercase names to lower case. File names on High Sierra CD-ROMs with no Rock Ridge extensions present should be uppercase characters only. By default, hsfs maps file names read from a non-Rock Ridge disk to all lowercase characters. The exceptions for notraildot discussed above also apply to nomaplcase.

nosuid   Mount the file system with setuid execution disallowed. By default, the file system is mounted with setuid execution allowed.

-O   Allow the file system to be mounted over an existing mount point, making the underlying file system inaccessible. If you try to mount on a preexisting mount point without using this option, the mount fails and displays a device busy error message.

Files

/etc/mnttab   Table of mounted file systems.

/etc/vfstab   List of default parameters for each file system.

Attributes

See attributes(5) for descriptions of the following attributes.

Attribute Type	Attribute Value
Availability	SUNWcsu

See Also

mount(1M), mountall(1M), mount(2), mnttab(4), vfstab(4), attributes(5)

mount_nfs — Mount Remote NFS Resources

Synopsis

```
/usr/sbin/mount [-F nfs][generic-options][-o specific-options][-O]
   resource
/usr/sbin/mount [-F nfs][generic-options][-o specific-options][-O]
  mount-point
/usr/sbin/mount [-F nfs][generic-options][-o specific-options][-O]
   resource mount-point
```

Description

Use the mount command to attach a named resource to the file-system hierarchy at the path-name location *mount-point*, which must already exist. If *mount-point* has any contents before the mount operation, the contents remain hidden until the resource is once again unmounted.

If the resource is listed in the /etc/vfstab file, the command line can specify either resource or *mount-point*, and mount consults /etc/vfstab for more information. If you omit the -F option, mount takes the file-system type from /etc/vfstab.

If the resource is not listed in the /etc/vfstab file, then the command line must specify both the resource and the *mount-point*.

A named resource can have one of the following formats.

host:pathname

> Where *host* is the name of the NFS server host, and *pathname* is the path name of the directory on the server being mounted. The path name is interpreted according to the server's path-name parsing rules and is not necessarily slash-separated, though on most servers, this is the case.

nfs://host[:port]/pathname

> An NFS URL that follows the standard convention for NFS URLs as described in Internet RFC 2225—*NFS URL Scheme.* See the discussion of URLs and the public option in "URLs and the Public Option" on page 726 for a more detailed discussion.

nfs://host[:port]/pathname resource

> A comma-separated list of *host:pathname* or a comma-separated list of hosts followed by a :*pathname* suffix. See the discussion of Replicated file systems and failover in "Replicated File Systems and Failover" on page 727 for a more detailed discussion.

mount maintains a table of mounted file systems in /etc/mnttab, described in mnttab(4).

Notes

An NFS server should not try to mount its own file systems. See lofs(7FS).

If the directory on which a file system is to be mounted is a symbolic link, the file system is mounted on the directory to which the symbolic link refers instead of being mounted on the symbolic link itself.

SunOS 4.X used the biod maintenance procedure to perform parallel read-ahead and write-behind on NFS clients. SunOS 5.x made biod obsolete with multithreaded processing, which transparently performs parallel read-ahead and write-behind.

Because the root (/) file system is mounted read-only by the kernel during the boot process, only the remount option (and options that can be used in conjunction with remount) affect the root (/) entry in the /etc/vfstab file.

Options

See mount(1) for the list of supported *generic-options*.

-o *specific-options*

Specify file-system-specific options as a comma-separated list with no intervening spaces.

acdirmax=n | Hold cached attributes for no more than *n* seconds after directory update. The default value is 60.

acdirmin=n | Hold cached attributes for at least *n* seconds after directory update. The default value is 30.

acregmax=n | Hold cached attributes for no more than *n* seconds after file modification. The default value is 60.

acregmin=n | Hold cached attributes for at least *n* seconds after file modification. The default value is 3.

actimeo=n | Set min and max times for regular files and directories to *n* seconds.

bg | fg | If the first attempt fails, retry in the background (foreground). The default is fg.

grpid | By default, the GID associated with a newly created file obeys the System V semantics; that is, the GID is set to the effective GID of the calling process. You can override this behavior on a per-directory basis by setting the set-GID bit of the parent directory; in this case, the GID of a newly created file is set to the GID of the parent directory (see open(2) and mkdir(2)). Files created on file systems that are mounted with the grpid option obey BSD semantics independently of whether the set-GID bit of the parent directory is set; that is, the GID is unconditionally inherited from the parent directory.

hard | soft | Return an error if the server does not respond or continue the retry request until the server responds. The default value is hard.

intr | nointr

> Allow (do not allow) keyboard interrupts to kill a process that is hung while waiting for a response on a hard-mounted file system. The default is `intr`, which makes it possible for clients to interrupt applications that may be waiting for a remote mount.

kerberos
> This option has been deprecated in favor of the `sec=krb4` option.

noac
> Suppress data and attribute caching.

port=*n*
> Specify the server IP port number. The default is `NFS_PORT`. If you specify the `port` option, if the resource includes one or more NFS URLs, and if any of the URLs include a port number, then the port number in the option and in the URL must be the same.

posix
> Request POSIX.1 semantics for the file system. Requires a `mount` Version 2 `mountd`(1M) on the server. See `standards`(5) for information regarding POSIX.

proto=*netid*

> Override the default behavior and specify a *netid* different from the `network_id` field in the `/etc/netconfig` file. By default, the transport protocol used for the NFS mount is the first available connection-oriented transport supported on both the client and the server. If no connection-oriented transport is found, then use the first available connectionless transport.

public
> Force the use of the `public` file handle when connecting to the NFS sever. The resource specified may or may not have an NFS URL. See "URLs and the Public Option" on page 726 for a more detailed discussion.

quota | noquota

> Enable (prevent) `quota`(1M) from checking whether the user is over quota on this file system; if the file system has quotas enabled on the server, quotas are still checked for operations on this file system.

remount
> Remount a read-only file system as read-write (using the `rw` option). You cannot use this option with other `-o` options, and it works only on currently mounted read-only file systems.

retrans=*n*   Set the number of NFS retransmissions to *n*. The
                  default value is 5. For connection-oriented transports,
                  this option has no effect because it is assumed that the
                  transport performs retransmissions on behalf of NFS.

retry=*n*   The number of times to retry the mount operation.
                  The default is 10000.

ro | rw   Mount resource read-only (read-write). The default
                  is rw.

rsize=*n*   Set the read buffer size to *n* bytes. The default value is
                  32768 when Version 3 of the NFS protocol is used. You
                  can negotiate the default down if the server prefers a
                  smaller transfer size. With Version 2, the default
                  value is 8192.

sec=*mode*   Set the security mode for NFS transactions. If you do
                  not specify sec, the default action is to use AUTH_SYS
                  over NFS Version 2 mounts or to negotiate a mode
                  over NFS Version 3 mounts. NFS Version 3 mounts
                  negotiate a security mode when the server returns an
                  array of security modes. The client picks the first
                  mode in the array that is supported on the client. You
                  can specify only one mode with the sec option. See
                  nfssec(5) for the available mode options.

secure   This option has been deprecated in favor of the
                  sec=dh option.

suid | nosuid

                  Allow (disallow) setuid execution. The default is suid.

timeo=*n*   Set the NFS timeout to *n* tenths of a second. The
                  default value is 11 tenths of a second for
                  connectionless transports, and 600 tenths of a second
                  for connection-oriented transports.

vers=*NFS-version-number*

                  Specify the NFS version number. By default, the
                  version of NFS protocol used between the client and
                  the server is the highest one available on both
                  systems. If the NFS server does not support NFS
                  Version 3 protocol, then the NFS mount uses NFS
                  Version 2 protocol.

wsize=*n*   Set the write buffer size to *n* bytes. The default value
                  is 32768 when Version 3 of the NFS protocol is used.
                  You can negotiate the default down if the server
                  prefers a smaller transfer size. With Version 2, the
                  default value is 8192.

-O   Allow the file system to be mounted over an existing mount point, making the underlying file system inaccessible. If you try to mount on a preexisting mount point without using this option, the mount fails and displays a `device busy` error message.

NFS File Systems

Background Versus Foreground

File systems mounted with the `bg` option indicate that `mount` is to retry in the background if the server's mount daemon (`mountd`(1M)) does not respond. `mount` retries the request up to the *count* specified in the `retry=n` option. Once the file system is mounted, each NFS request made in the kernel waits `timeo=n` tenths of a second for a response. If no response arrives, the timeout is multiplied by 2 and the request is retransmitted. When the number of retransmissions has reached the number specified in the `retrans=n` option, a file-system mounted with the `soft` option returns an error on the request; one mounted with the `hard` option prints a warning message and continues to retry the request.

Hard Versus Soft

You should always use the `hard` option to mount read-write file systems and those that contain executable files. Applications using `soft` mounted file systems may incur unexpected I/O errors, file corruption, and unexpected program core dumps. The `soft` option is not recommended.

Authenticated Requests

The server may require authenticated NFS requests from the client. Either `sec=dh` or `sec=krb4` authentication may be required. See `nfssec`(5).

URLs and the Public Option

If you specify the `public` option or if the resource includes an NFS URL, `mount` tries to connect to the server by using the `public` file handle lookup protocol. See Internet RFC 2054 *WebNFS Client Specification*. If the server supports the `public` file handle, the attempt is successful; `mount` does not need to contact the server's `rpcbind`(1M) and the `mountd`(1M) daemons to get the port number of the mount server and the initial file handle of *pathname*, respectively. If the NFS client and server are separated by a firewall that permits all outbound connections through specific ports, such as NFS_PORT, then this option enables NFS operations through the firewall. You can specify the `public` option and the NFS URL independently or together. They interact as specified in the following table.

Style	Resource	Resource
	host:pathname	NFS URL
`public` option	Force `public` file handle and fail mount if not supported.	Force `public` file handle and fail mount if not supported.
	Use native paths.	Use canonical paths.

Style	Resource	Resource
default	Use mount protocol.	Try public file handle with canonical paths. Fall back to mount protocol if not supported.

A native path is a path name that is interpreted according to conventions used on the native operating system of the NFS server. A canonical path is a path name that is interpreted according to the URL rules. See Internet RFC 1738—*Uniform Resource Locators (URL)*. Also, see that RFC for uses of native and canonical paths.

Replicated File Systems and Failover

`resource` can list multiple read-only file systems to be used to provide data. These file systems should contain equivalent directory structures and identical files. It is also recommended that you create them with a command such as rdist(1). You can specify the file systems either with a comma-separated list of *host*:/*pathname* entries or NFS URL entries, or with a comma-separated list of hosts if all file system names are the same. If you name multiple file systems and the first server in the list is down, failover uses the next alternate server to access files. If you do not specify the read-only option, replication is disabled. File access blocks on the original if NFS locks are active for that file.

File Attributes

To improve NFS read performance, files and file attributes are cached. File modification times get updated whenever a write occurs. However, file access times may be temporarily out-of-date until the cache gets refreshed.

The attribute cache retains file attributes on the client. Attributes for a file are assigned a time to be flushed. If the file is modified before the flush time, then the flush time is extended by the time since the last modification (under the assumption that files that changed recently are likely to change soon). Regular files and directories have a minimum and maximum flush time extension. Setting actimeo=n sets flush time to n seconds for both regular files and directories.

Setting actimeo=0 disables attribute caching on the client; every reference to attributes is satisfied directly from the server though file data still is cached. While this approach guarantees that the client always has the latest file attributes from the server, it has an adverse effect on performance through additional latency, network load, and server load.

Setting the noac option also disables attribute caching and client write caching. While this approach guarantees that data written by an application is written directly to a server where it can be viewed immediately by other clients, it has a significant adverse effect on client write performance. Data written into memory-mapped file pages (mmap(2)) are not written directly to this server.

Examples

The following example mounts an NFS file system.

```
# mount serv:/usr/src /usr/src
```

The following example mounts an NFS file system read-only with nosuid privileges.

```
# mount -r -o nosuid serv:/usr/src /usr/src
```

The following example mounts an NFS file system over Version2 with the UDP transport.

```
# mount -o vers=2,proto=udp serv:/usr/src /usr/src
```

The following example mounts an NFS file system, using an NFS URL (a canonical path).

```
# mount nfs://serv/usr/man /usr/man
```

The following example mounts an NFS file system, forcing use of the `public` file handle. with an NFS URL (a canonical path) that has a non 7-bit ASCII escape sequence.

```
# mount -o public nfs://serv/usr/%A0abc /mnt/test
```

The following example mounts an NFS file system, using a native path—where the server uses colons (:) as the component separator—and the `public` file handle.

```
# mount -o public serv:C:doc:new /usr/doc
```

The following example mounts an NFS file system, using AUTH_KERB authentication.

```
# mount -o sec=krb4 serv:/usr/src /usr/src
```

The following example mounts a replicated set of NFS file systems with the same path names.

```
# mount serv-a,serv-b,serv-c:/usr/man /usr/man
```

The following example mounts a replicated set of NFS file systems with different path names.

```
# mount serv-x:/usr/man,serv-y:/var/man,nfs://serv-z/man /usr/man
```

Files

/etc/mnttab   Table of mounted file systems.

/etc/dfs/fstypes

         Default distributed file-system type.

/etc/vfstab   Table of automatically mounted resources.

Attributes

See attributes(5) for descriptions of the following attributes.

Attribute Type	Attribute Value
Availability	SUNWcsu

See Also

rdist(1), mountall(1M), mountd(1M), quota(1M), mkdir(2), mmap(2), mount(2), open(2), umount(2), mnttab(4), attributes(5), nfssec(5), standards(5), lofs(7FS)

Internet RFC 1738—*Uniform Resource Locators* (URL)

Internet RFC 2054—*WebNFS Client Specification*
Internet RFC 2225—*NFS URL Scheme*

mount_pcfs — Mount PCFS File Systems

Synopsis

```
/usr/sbin/mount -F pcfs [generic-options] [-o FSType-specific-options]
    special | mount-point
/usr/sbin/mount -F pcfs [generic-options] [-o FSType-specific-options]
    special mount-point
```

Description

Use the `mount` command to attach an MS-DOS file system (`pcfs`) to the file-system hierarchy at the `mount-point`, which is the path name of a directory. If `mount-point` has any contents before the mount operation, these are hidden until the file system is unmounted.

If you invoke `mount` with `special` or `mount-point` as the only arguments, `mount` searches `/etc/vfstab` to fill in the missing arguments, including the `FSType-specific-options`; see mount(1M) for more details.

The special argument can be one of two special device file types.

- A diskette, such as `/dev/diskette0` or `/dev/diskette1`.

- A DOS logical drive on a hard disk, expressed as `device-name:logical-drive`, where `device-name` specifies the special block device-file for the whole disk and `logical-drive` is either a drive letter (c through z) or a drive number (1 through 24). Examples are `/dev/dsk/c0t0d0p0:c` and `/dev/dsk/c0t0d0p0:1`.

The `special` device file type must have a formatted MS-DOS file system with either a 12-bit, 16-bit, or 32-bit File Allocation Table.

Note — If the directory on which a file system is to be mounted is a symbolic link, the file system is mounted on the directory to which the symbolic link refers instead of on the symbolic link itself.

Options

See mount(1) for the list of supported `generic-options`.

`-o specific-options`

Specify PCFS-file-system-specific options. The following options are available.

`rw|ro`   Mount the file system read/write (read-only). The default is `rw`.

```
foldcase|nofoldcase
```
> Force (do not force) uppercase characters in file
> names to lower case when reading them from the file
> system. This option is for compatibility with the
> previous behavior of `pcfs`. The default is
> `nofoldcase`.

Files

`/etc/mnttab`	Table of mounted file systems.
`/etc/vfstab`	List of default parameters for each file system.

Attributes

See `attributes`(5) for descriptions of the following attributes.

Attribute Type	Attribute Value
Availability	SUNWesu

See Also

`mount`(1M), `mountall`(1M), `mount`(2), `mnttab`(4), `vfstab`(4), `attributes`(5), `pcfs`(7FS)

---

mount_s5fs — Mount s5 File Systems

Synopsis

```
/usr/sbin/mount -F s5fs [-r][-o specific-options] special | mount-point
/usr/sbin/mount -F s5fs [-r][-o specific-options] special mount-point
```

Description

Use the `mount` command to attach an s5 file system (a System V file system used by PC
versions of UNIX) to the file-system hierarchy at the *mount-point*, which is the path
name of a directory. If *mount-point* has any contents before the mount operation, these
are hidden until the file system is unmounted.

If you invoke `mount` with *special* or *mount-point* as the only arguments, `mount`
searches `/etc/vfstab` to fill in the missing arguments, including the
specific-options. See `mount`(1M).

If you specify *special* and *mount-point* without any *specific-options*, the default
is `rw`.

Note — If the directory on which a file system is to be mounted is a
symbolic link, the file system is mounted on the directory to which the
symbolic link refers instead of on the symbolic link itself.

Options

See mount(1) for the list of supported *generic-options*.

-o *specific-options*

> Specify s5 file-system-specific options in a comma-separated list with no intervening spaces. If you specify invalid options, print a warning message and ignore the invalid options. The following options are available.
>
> remount
> > Remount a read-only file system as read-write (using the rw option). You cannot use this option with other -o options, and it works only on currently mounted, read-only file systems.
>
> ro|rw
> > Mount the file system read-only (read/write). The default is rw.
>
> suid|nosuid
> > Allow (disallow) setuid execution. The default is suid.

-r   Mount the file system read-only.

Files

/etc/mnttab   Table of mounted file systems.

/etc/vfstab   List of default parameters for each file system.

Attributes

See attributes(5) for descriptions of the following attributes.

Attribute Type	Attribute Value
Architecture	IA
Availability	SUNWs53

See Also

mount(1M), mountall(1M), mount(2), mnttab(4), vfstab(4), attributes(5)

---

mount_tmpfs — Mount tmpfs File Systems

Synopsis

/usr/sbin/mount [-F tmpfs][-o size=*sz*][-O] *special mount-point*

Description

tmpfs is a memory-based file system that uses kernel resources relating to the VM system and page cache as a file system.

Use the mount command to attach a tmpfs file system to the file-system hierarchy at the path-name location *mount-point*, which must already exist. If *mount-point* has any contents before the mount operation, these remain hidden until the file system is once again unmounted. The attributes (mode, owner, and group) of the root of the tmpfs file system are inherited from the underlying *mount-point*, provided that those attributes are determinable. If not, the root's attributes are set to their default values.

The *special* argument is usually specified as swap but is in fact disregarded and assumed to be the virtual memory resources within the system.

Note — If the directory on which a file system is to be mounted is a symbolic link, the file system is mounted on the directory to which the symbolic link refers instead of on the symbolic link itself.

Options

-o size=*sz*   Specify the size of a particular tmpfs file system. With a k suffix, interpret the value as a number of kilobytes. With an m suffix, interpret the value as a number of megabytes. Interpret no suffix as a value in bytes. In all cases, the actual size of the file system is the number of bytes specified, rounded up to the physical page size of the system.

-O   Allow the file system to be mounted over an existing mount point, making the underlying file system inaccessible. If you try to mount on a preexisting mount point without using this option, the mount fails and displays a device busy error message.

Files

/etc/mnttab   Table of mounted file systems.

Attributes

See attributes(5) for descriptions of the following attributes.

Attribute Type	Attribute Value
Availability	SUNWcsu

See Also

mount(1M), mkdir(2), mount(2), open(2), umount(2), mnttab(4), attributes(5), tmpfs(7FS)

mount_udfs — Mount a UDFS File System

New!

Synopsis

```
mount -F udfs [generic-options] [-o specific-options] [-O] special
    mount-point
mount -F udfs [generic-options] [-o specific-options] [-O] special |
    mount-point
```

Description

The mount -F udfs command is new in the Solaris 8 release. Use the mount command to attach a UDFS file system to the file-system hierarchy at the *mount-point*, which is the path name of a directory. If *mount-point* has any contents before the mount operation, these are hidden until the file system is unmounted.

If you invoke mount with either *special* or *mount-point* as the only arguments, mount searches /etc/vfstab to fill in the missing arguments, including the *specific-options*. See mount(1M).

If *special* and *mount-point* are specified without any *specific-options*, the default is rw.

If the directory on which a file system is to be mounted is a symbolic link, the file system is mounted on the directory to which the symbolic link refers, instead of on top of the symbolic link itself.

Note — Copy-protected files can be stored on DVD-ROM media by UDF. Reading these copy-protected files is not possible because an authentication process is required. Unless an authentication process between the host and the drive is completed, reading these copy-protected files after mounting and before the authentication process returns an error.

Options

See mount(1M) for the list of supported *generic-options*.

-o *specific-options*

Specify UDFS-file-system-specific options in a comma-separated list with no intervening spaces. The following *specific-options* are available.

m
: Mount the file system without making an entry in /etc/mnttab.

nosuid
: Mount the file system with setuid execution disallowed. You can also use nosuid to disallow setuid when mounting devices.

  By default, the file system is mounted with setuid execution allowed.

remount
: Remount the file system as read-write. Use this option with the rw option.

A file-system mounted read-only can be remounted
as read-write. This option fails if the file system is
not currently mounted or if the file system is
mounted as rw.

rw | ro   Mount the file system as read-write (rw) or read-only
(ro). rw is the default.

-O   Allow the file system to be mounted over an existing mount point
making the underlying file system inaccessible. If you try to mount on
a preexisting mount point without setting this option, the mount fails,
producing the device busy error message.

Files

/etc/mnttab   Table of mounted file systems.

/etc/vfstab   List of default parameters for each file system.

Attributes

See attributes(5) for descriptions of the following attributes.

Attribute Type	Attribute Value
Availability	SUNWudf

See Also

fsck(1M), fsck_udfs(1M), mount(1M), mountall(1M), mount(2), mnttab(4),
vfstab(4), attributes(5)

Diagnostics

not super user

The command is run by a non-root user. Run as root.

no such device

The specified device name does not exist.

not a directory

The specified mount point is not a directory.

is not an udfs file system

The specified device does not contain a UDF 1.50 file system or the
udfs file system module is not available.

is already mounted

The specified device is already in use.

not a block device

The specified device is not a block device. Use block device to mount.

```
write-protected
```
>   The device is read-only.

```
is corrupted. needs checking
```
>   The file system is in an inconsistent state. Run `fsck`.

---

mount_ufs — Mount UFS File Systems

Synopsis
```
/usr/sbin/mount -F ufs [generic-options][-o specific-options][-O]
    special | mount-point
/usr/sbin/mount -F ufs [generic-options][-o specific-options][-O]
    special mount-point
```

Description
Use the `mount` command to attach a UFS file system to the file-system hierarchy at the *mount-point*, which is the path name of a directory. If *mount-point* has any contents before the mount operation, these are hidden until the file system is unmounted.

If you invoke `mount` with *special* or *mount-point* as the only arguments, `mount` searches `/etc/vfstab` to fill in the missing arguments, including the *specific-options*. See mount(1M).

If you specify *special* and *mount-point* without any *specific-options*, the default is `rw`.

If the directory on which a file system is to be mounted is a symbolic link, the file system is mounted on the directory to which the symbolic link refers, instead of on top of the symbolic link itself.

Note — Because the root (`/`) file system is mounted read-only by the kernel during the boot process, only the `remount` option (and options that can be used in conjunction with `remount`) affect the root (`/`) entry in the `/etc/vfstab` file.

Options
See mount(1M) for the list of supported *generic options*.

`-o` *specific-option*

>   Specify UFS-file-system-specific options in a comma-separated list with no intervening spaces. If you specify invalid options, print a warning message and ignore the invalid options. The following options are available.

noatime   Ignore access time updates on files except when they coincide with updates to $ctime$ or $mtime$. See stat(2). By default, the file system is mounted with normal access time ($atime$) recording. This option reduces disk activity on file systems where access times are unimportant (for example, a Usenet news spool).

New!   noatime turns off access time recording regardless of dfratime or nodfratime.

New!   dfratime | nodfratime

     Defer (dfratime) or do not defer (nodfratime) writing access time updates to the disk until the disk is accessed for a reason other than updating access times. dfratime is the default.

forcedirectio | noforcedirectio

     If you specify forcedirectio and it is supported by the file system, then for the duration of the mount, use forced direct I/O. If the file system is mounted with forcedirectio, then transfer data directly between user address space and the disk. If you mount the file system with noforcedirectio, then buffer data in kernel address space when data is transferred between user address space and the disk. forcedirectio is a performance option that benefits only from large sequential data transfers. The default behavior is noforcedirectio.

New!   global | noglobal

     Make the file system globally visible (global) or not globally visible (noglobal) on all nodes of a cluster if global is specified and supported on the file system and the system in question is part of a cluster. These options are new in the Solaris 8 release.

intr|nointr   Allow (do not allow) keyboard interrupts to kill a process that is waiting for an operation on a locked file system. The default is intr.

largefiles | nolargefiles

     If you specify nolargefiles and it is supported by the file system, then for the duration of the mount, guarantee that all regular files in the file system have a size that fits in the smallest object of type off_t supported by the system performing the mount. The mount fails if there are any files in the file system not meeting this criterion. If you specify `largefiles`, there is no such guarantee. The default behavior is `largefiles`.

If you specify `nolargefiles`, `mount` fails for UFS if the file system to be mounted has contained a large file (a file whose size is greater than or equal to 2 Gbytes) since the last invocation of `fsck` on the file system. The large file need not be present in the file system at the time of the mount for the mount to fail; it could have been created previously and then destroyed. Invoking `fsck` (see `fsck_ufs(1M)`) on the file system resets the file system state if no large files are present. After invoking `fsck`, a successful mount of the file system with `nolargefiles` specified indicates the absence of large files in the file system; an unsuccessful mount attempt indicates the presence of at least one large file.

`logging | nologging`

If you specify `logging`, then enable logging for the duration of the mounted file system. Logging is the process of storing transactions (changes that make up a complete UFS operation) in a log before the transactions are applied to the file system. Once a transaction is stored, the transaction can later be applied to the file system. This option prevents file systems from becoming inconsistent, thereby eliminating the need to run `fsck`. And, because you can bypass `fsck`, logging reduces the time required to reboot a system if it crashes or after an unclean halt. The default behavior is `nologging`.

Allocate the log from free blocks on the file system and size it approximately 1 megabytes per 1 gigabyte of file system up to a maximum of 64 megabytes. You can enable logging on any UFS, including root (`/`). The log created by UFS logging is continually flushed as it fills up. The log is totally flushed when the file system is unmounted or as a result of the `lockfs -f` command.

`m`   Mount the file system without making an entry in `/etc/mnttab`.

`onerror=action`

Specify the action that UFS should take to recover from an internal inconsistency on a file system. Specify *action* as `panic`, `lock`, or `umount`. These values force a system shutdown, apply a file system lock to the file system, or forcibly unmount the file system. The default is `panic`.

quota	Turn on quotas for the file system.
remount	Remount a read-only file system as read-write (using the `rw` option). You can use this option only in conjunction with the `f`, `logging`|`nologging`, `m`, and `noatime` options. This option works only on currently mounted, read-only file systems.
rq	Specify read-write with quotas turned on. Equivalent to `rw`, `quota`.
ro | rw	Read-only (read-write). Default is `rw`.
suid | nosuid	Allow (disallow) setuid execution. The default is `suid`. You can also use this option when mounting devices.

-O   Allow the file system to be mounted over an existing mount point, making the underlying file system inaccessible. If you try to mount on a preexisting mount point without using this option, the mount fails and displays a `device busy` error message.

Files

/etc/mnttab	Table of mounted file systems.
/etc/vfstab	List of default parameters for each file system.

Attributes

See `attributes`(5) for descriptions of the following attributes.

Attribute Type	Attribute Value
Availability	SUNWcsu

See Also

`fsck(1M)`, `fsck_ufs(1M)`, `mount(1M)`, `mountall(1M)`, `mount(2)`, `stat(2)`, `mnttab(4)`, `vfstab(4)`, `attributes(5)`, `largefile(5)`

New! **mount_xmemfs** — Mount xmemfs File Systems

Synopsis

```
mount -F xmemfs [generic-options] -o [largebsize,]size=sz [-O] special
    mount-point
```

Description

The mount -F xmemfs command is new in the Solaris 8 release. xmemfs is an IA extended-memory file system that provides file-system semantics to manage and access large amounts of physical memory that can exceed 4 Gbytes in size.

Use the mount command to attach an xmemfs file system to the file-system hierarchy at the path-name location *mount-point*, which must already exist. If *mount-point* has any contents before the mount operation, these remain hidden until the file system is once again unmounted. The attributes (mode, owner, and group) of the root of the xmemfs file system are inherited from the underlying *mount-point*, provided that those attributes are determinable. If not, the root's attributes are set to their default values.

The *special* argument is not currently used by xmemfs, but you need to specify a placeholder (such as xmem) nevertheless.

Notes

If the directory on which a file system is to be mounted is a symbolic link, the file system is mounted on the directory to which the symbolic link refers, rather than on top of the symbolic link itself.

The only file types allowed on xmemfs are directories and regular files. The execution of object files resident in xmemfs is not supported. Execution is prevented by not allowing users to set execute permissions on regular files.

Options

See mount(1M) for the list of supported *generic-options*.

-o *specific-options*

> Specify xmemfs file-system-specific options in a comma-separated list with no intervening spaces. If you specify invalid options, print a warning message and ignore the invalid options.
>
> The following options are available.

size=*sz*	The *sz* argument specifies the desired size of this particular xmemfs file system. If the *sz* argument has a k suffix, the number is interpreted as kilobytes. An m suffix is interpreted as megabytes, and g is interpreted as gigabytes. An *sz* specified with no suffix is interpreted as bytes.

> In all cases, the actual size of the file system is the number of bytes specified, rounded up to the physical page size of the system or to the large page size if you specify largebsize.

> The size=*sz specific-option* is required.

largebsize	If you specify largebsize, use the large memory page size as the file-system block size. On IA32, the large memory page size with mmu36 that supports PAE (Physical Address Extension) is 2 Mbytes. The large memory page size without mmu36/PAE is 4 Mbytes. If there is no large page support, the file-system block size is PAGESIZE.

-O   Allow the file system to be mounted over an existing mount point, making the underlying file system inaccessible. If you try to mount on a preexisting mount point without setting this option, the mount fails, producing the `device busy` error message.

Files

/etc/mnttab   Table of mounted file systems.

Attributes

See `attributes`(5) for descriptions of the following attributes.

Attribute Type	Attribute Value
Availability	SUNWcsu
Architecture	i386
Interface stability	Evolving

See Also

`mount`(1M), `mount`(2), `mkdir`(2), `open`(2), `umount`(2), `mnttab`(4), `attributes`(5), `xmemfs`(7FS)

mpstat — Report Per-Processor Statistics

Synopsis

New!

```
/usr/bin/mpstat[-p | -P set][interval [count]]
```

Description

Use the `mpstat` command to report per-processor statistics in tabular form. Each row of the table represents the activity of one processor. The first table summarizes all activity since boot; each subsequent table summarizes activity for the preceding interval. All values are rates (events per second) unless otherwise noted.

During execution of this kernel status command, the state of the kernel can change. An example would be CPUs going online or offline. `mpstat` reports this change as `<<State change>>`.

`mpstat` reports the following information.

CPU   Processor ID.

minf   Minor faults.

mjf   Major faults.

xcal   Interprocessor cross-calls.

intr   Interrupts.

ithr	Interrupts as threads (not counting clock interrupt).
csw	Context switches.
icsw	Involuntary context switches.
migr	Thread migrations (to another processor).
smtx	Spins on mutexes (lock not acquired on first try).
srw	Spins on readers/writer locks (lock not acquired on first try).
syscl	System calls.
usr	Percent user time.
sys	Percent system time.
wt	Percent wait time.
idl	Percent idle time.

For the –p option, mpstat also reports the following information.   *New!*

set	Processor set membership of the CPU.

Options   *New!*

-p	Report processor set membership of each CPU. Sort the output by set. The default output is sorted by CPU number.
-P *set*	Display only those processors in the specified set.

Operands

count	Print only *count* reports.
interval	Report once each *interval* seconds.

Examples

The following example shows the output of the mpstat command with a five-second interval.

```
paperbark% mpstat 5
CPU minf mjf xcal  intr ithr  csw icsw migr smtx  srw syscl  usr sys  wt idl
  0    3   0    0   272  153   77    2    0    0    0   156    1   0    1  98
  0    1   0    0   271  152   84    1    0    0    0   182    1   0    0  99
  0    0   0    0   277  154  100    5    0    1    0   194    0   0    0 100
  0    1   0    0   241  141   72    2    0    0    0   188    1   0    0  99
  0    0   0    0   231  131   66    1    0    0    0    96    0   0    0 100
  0    0   0    0   232  132   68    2    0    0    0   101    0   0    0 100
^Cpaperbark%
```

The following example shows the output of the mpstat command with the additional set column shown by the –p option.

```
paperbark% mpstat -p 5
CPU minf mjf xcal  intr ithr  csw icsw migr smtx  srw syscl  usr sys  wt idl
  set
```

```
0    3    0    0    272  153  78   2    0    0    0    156  1    0    1  98
 0
0    1    0    0    234  134  76   1    0    0    0    135  0    0    0 100
 0
0    0    0    0    342  193  101  1    0    0    0    206  0    1    0  99
 0
0    0    0    0    309  171  99   1    0    0    0    205  0    1    0  99
 0
0    0    0    0    232  132  71   1    0    0    0    121  0    0    0 100
 0
0    0    0    0    237  135  72   1    0    0    0    125  0    0    0 100
 0
^Cpaperbark%
```

Attributes

See attributes(5) for descriptions of the following attributes.

Attribute Type	Attribute Value
Availability	SUNWcsu

See Also

sar(1), iostat(1M), sar(1M), vmstat(1M), attributes(5)

msgid — Generate Message IDs

Synopsis

/usr/sbin/msgid

Description

Use the msgid command to generate message IDs. A message ID is a numeric identifier that, with a high probability, uniquely identifies a message. The probability of two distinct messages having the same ID is about one in a million. Specifically, the message ID is a hash signature on the message's unexpanded format string, generated by STRLOG_MAKE_MSGID() as defined in <sys/strlog.h>.

syslogd(1M) is a simple filter that takes strings as input and produces those same strings, preceded by their message IDs, as output. Every message logged by syslogd(1M) includes the message ID. The message ID is intended to serve as a small, language-independent identifier.

Examples

The following example uses the msgid command to generate a message ID for the echo command.

```
# echo hello | msgid
205790 hello
#
```

The following example uses the msgid command to enumerate all of the messages in the binary ufs directory, to generate a message catalog.

```
# strings /kernel/fs/ufs | msgid
845546 alloc: %s: file system full
213553 realloccg %s: file system full
526661 mode = 0%o, inum = %d, fs = %s
666021 free inode %s/%d had size 0x%llx
682040 %s: out of inodes
337489 ufs_dirlook:fbrelse: invalid fbp=0
941273 %s: bad dir ino %d at offset %ld: %s
802296 setting ufs_ninode to max value of %ld
172994 ip %p: i_rdev too big
403174 ufs_itrunc: %s/%d new size = %lld, blocks = %d
583501 Cannot assemble drivers for %s
583501 Cannot assemble drivers for %s
614061 %s is required to be mounted onerror=%s
...(Additional lines deleted from this example)
```

Attributes

See attributes(5) for descriptions of the following attributes.

Attribute Type	Attribute Value
Availability	SUNWcsu

See Also

syslogd(1M), attributes(5), log(7d)

mvdir — Move a Directory

Synopsis

/usr/sbin/mvdir *dirname name*

Description

Use the mvdir command to move directories within a file system. *dirname* must be a directory. If *name* does not exist, it is created as a directory. If *name* does exist and is a directory, *dirname* is created as *name/dirname*. *dirname* and *name* cannot be on the same path; that is, one can not be subordinate to the other. For example, the following command is legal.

```
castle% mvdir x/y x/z
```

The following command is not legal.

```
castle% mvdir x/y x/y/z
```

Operands

dirname   The name of the directory that is to be moved to another directory in the file system.

name   The name of the directory into which dirname is to be moved. If name does not exist, create it. name cannot be on the same path as dirname.

Usage

See largefile(5) for the description of the behavior of mvdir when encountering files greater than or equal to 2 Gbytes (2**31 bytes).

Exit Status

0   Successful operation.

>0   Operation failed.

Attributes

See attributes(5) for descriptions of the following attributes.

Attribute Type	Attribute Value
Availability	SUNWcsu

See Also

mkdir(1), mv(1), attributes(5), largefile(5)

N

---

named-bootconf — Convert Configuration File to a Format
Suitable for Bind 8.1

Synopsis

```
/usr/sbin/named-bootconf [-i infile][-o outfile]
```

Description

Use the named-bootconf command to convert the named.boot configuration file used by
BIND versions 4.9.6 and older to the named.conf format used by BIND versions 8.1.1
and greater.

The named-bootconf command by default takes /etc/named.boot as the input file,
unless you specify a different file with the -i infile option. By default, it creates
/etc/named.conf as its output file unless you specify a different file with the
-o outfile option.

The command converts all the options and directives in the input file, including
comments; then, it creates an output file in a format acceptable to the BIND 8.1.1
version of in.named.

If the input file does not exist, named-bootconf writes a message on standard error
and exits. If the input file contains the include directive, named-bootconf does the
following.

- Converts the include directive to the new format.
- Renames the original (included) file with a ~ suffix.
- Converts the included file to the new format, retaining the same file name.

Only superuser can run the named-bootconf command.

> **Note —** It is possible that named-bootconf may not maintain the exact order of comments in the input file during the conversion. You can edit the newly created named.conf file to add newly supported options and directives in BIND version 8.1.1.

Options

-i *infile*   Specify an input file. The default is /etc/named.boot.

-o *outfile*   Specify an output file. The default is /etc/named.conf.

Files

/etc/named.boot

        Configuration file for BIND versions 4.9.6 and older.

/etc/named.conf

        Configuration file for BIND versions 8.1.1 and greater.

Attributes

See attributes(5) for descriptions of the following attributes.

Attribute Type	Attribute Value
Availability	SUNWcsu

See Also

in.named(1M), attributes(5)

---

named-xfer — Ancillary Agent for Inbound Zone Transfers

Synopsis

/usr/sbin/named-xfer -z *zone-to-transfer* -f *db-file* -s *serial-no*
   [-d *debuglevel*][-l *debug-log-file*][-t *trace-file*][-p *port-no*][-S]
   nameserver...

Description

The named-xfer command is an ancillary program executed by in.named to perform an inbound zone transfer. It is rarely executed directly, and only by system administrators who are trying to debug a zone transfer problem. See RFCs 1033, 1034, and 1035 for more information on the Internet name domain system.

Options

-f *db-file*   Specify the name of the file into which to dump the zone when it is received from the primary server.

-d *debug-level*

        Print debugging information. Specify a number after the -d option to determine the level of messages printed.

-l *debug-log-file*

        Specify a log file for debugging messages. The default is system dependent but is usually in /var/tmp or /usr/tmp. Note that this option applies only if you also specify the -d option.

-p *port-no*   Use a different port number. The default is the standard port number as returned by getservbyname(3N) for service domain.

-s *serial-no* Specify the serial number of the current copy of this zone. If the Start-of-Authority (SOA) RR record from the primary server does not have a serial number higher than this, abort the transfer.

-S *nameserver*

        Perform a restricted transfer of only the SOA, NS records, and glue A records for the zone. Do not load the SOA record, but use it to determine when to verify the NS records. See the stubs directive in in.named(1M) for more information.

        Additional arguments are taken as nameserver addresses in dotted-quad syntax only; no host names are allowed. You must specify at least one address. If the first one fails to transfer successfully, the additional addresses are tried in the order given.

-t *trace-file*

        Specify a trace file that contains a protocol trace of the zone transfer. This option is probably of interest only to those debugging the nameserver itself.

-z *zone-to-transfer*

        Specify the name of the zone to be transferred.

Attributes

See attributes(5) for descriptions of the following attributes.

Attribute Type	Attribute Value
Availability	SUNWcsu

See Also

in.named(1M), resolver(3N), resolv.conf(4), hostname(1)
    RFC 882
    RFC 883
    RFC 973

RFC 974
RFC 1033
RFC 1034
RFC 1035
RFC 1123
Name Server Operations Guide for BIND

named — Internet Domain Server

Synopsis

```
/usr/sbin/in.named [-d debuglevel][-q][-r][-f][-p remote |local-port]
    [-w dirname][[-b | -c] configfile]
```

Description

See in.named(1M).

ncheck — Generate a List of Path Names Versus i-Numbers

Synopsis

```
/usr/sbin/ncheck [-F FSType][-V][generic-options]
    [-o FSType-specific-options][special...]
```

Description

When fsck cannot repair a file system, you can use the ncheck command to find the path name for a specific inode. You can also use ncheck with the -s option to look for setuid programs that might be a breach of security.

Use ncheck with no options to generate a list of inode numbers and path names for all files on *special*. If you do not specify *special* on the command line, the list is generated for all specials in /etc/vfstab that have a numeric fsckpass. *special* is a block special device on which the file system exists.

Note — This command may not be supported for all FSTypes.

Options

-F *FSType* Specify the FSType on which to operate. Either specify the *FSType* here or ncheck should be able to derive it from /etc/vfstab by finding an entry in the table that has a numeric fsckpass field and an fsckdev that matches *special*.

-V   Echo the complete command line but do not execute the command. Generate the command line by using the options and arguments and adding to them information derived from /etc/vfstab. You can use this option to verify and validate the command line.

generic-options

     Options that are commonly supported by most FSType-specific command *modules*. The following options are available.

     -i *i-list* Limit the report to the files in *i-list*, a comma-separated list with no intervening spaces.

     -a   Print the names . and . . which are ordinarily suppressed.

     -s   Report only special files and files with set-user-ID mode. You can use this option to detect violations of security policy.

-o   Specify *FSType-specific-options* in a comma-separated (without spaces) list of suboptions and keyword-attribute pairs for interpretation by the FSType-specific module of the command.

Examples

The following example shows the first screen of the output of the ncheck command piped through the more command. Names of directory files are followed by a slash (/).

```
# ncheck | more
/dev/dsk/c0t0d0s0:
3          /lost+found/.
5888       /export/.
17664      /var/.
52992      /usr/.
253185     /etc/.
14         /bin
17734      /dev/.
17735      /devices/.
200209     /kernel/.
18         /lib
259102     /mnt/.
265035     /opt/.
270894     /proc/.
276762     /sbin/.
282646     /tmp/.
306208     /platform/.
36052      /net/.
200305     /home/.
218578     /xfn/.
113        /.cpr_config
71381      /vol/.
--More--
```

Usage

See largefile(5) for the description of the behavior of ncheck when encountering files greater than or equal to 2 Gbytes (2**31 bytes).

Files

/etc/vfstab   List of default parameters for each file system.

Attributes

See attributes(5) for descriptions of the following attributes.

Attribute Type	Attribute Value
Availability	SUNWcsu

See Also

vfstab(4), attributes(5), largefile(5)
   Manual pages for the FSType-specific modules of ncheck

ncheck_ufs — Generate Path Names Versus i-Numbers for UFS File Systems

Synopsis

/usr/sbin/ncheck -F ufs [generic-options][-o m][special...]

Description

Use the ncheck -F ufs command to generate a list of inodes and path names for the UFS file system residing on special. Names of directory files are followed by /.

Options

See ncheck(1M) for the list of supported generic-options.

-o   Specify UFS file-system-specific options. The available option is shown below.

   m   Print mode information.

Attributes

See attributes(5) for descriptions of the following attributes.

Attribute Type	Attribute Value
Availability	SUNWcsu

See Also

ff(1M), ncheck(1M), attributes(5)

Diagnostics

When the file-system structure is improper, ?? denotes the parent of a parentless file and a path name beginning with . . . denotes a loop.

---

ndd — Get and Set Driver Configuration Parameters

Synopsis

/usr/sbin/ndd [-set] *driver parameter* [*value*]

Description

Usually, system parameters are configured and set in shell scripts that are executed by init when the system is booted. Use the ndd command to get and set selected configuration parameters in some kernel drivers. Currently, ndd supports only the drivers that implement the TCP/IP Internet protocol family. Each driver chooses which parameters to make visible with ndd. Because these parameters are usually tightly coupled to the implementation, they are likely to change from release to release. Some parameters may be read-only.

If you specify the -set option, ndd queries the named driver, retrieves the value associated with the specified parameter, and prints it. If you specify the -set option, ndd passes *value*, which must be specified, down to the named driver that assigns it to the named parameter.

By convention, drivers that support ndd also support a special read-only parameter named ? (which you must escape with a backslash to prevent it being interpreted as a shell metacharacter) that lists the parameters supported by the driver.

Notes

The parameters supported by each driver may change from release to release. Like programs that read /dev/kmem, user programs or shell scripts that execute ndd should be prepared for parameter names to change.

The ioctl() command that ndd uses to communicate with drivers is likely to change in a future release. User programs should avoid making dependencies on it.

The meanings of many ndd parameters make sense only if you understand how the driver is implemented.

Examples

The following example displays the parameters that are supported by the TCP driver. The example is truncated to save space.

```
paperbark% ndd /dev/tcp \?
?                            (read only)
tcp_time_wait_interval       (read and write)
tcp_conn_req_max_q           (read and write)
tcp_conn_req_max_q0          (read and write)
```

```
tcp_conn_req_min            (read and write)
tcp_conn_grace_period       (read and write)
tcp_cwnd_max                (read and write)
tcp_debug                   (read and write)
tcp_smallest_nonpriv_port   (read and write)
tcp_ip_abort_cinterval      (read and write)
tcp_ip_abort_linterval      (read and write)
tcp_ip_abort_interval       (read and write)
```
. . .(Additional lines deleted from this example)
```
paperbark%
```

Note — You may need to escape the ? parameter name with a backslash to prevent its being interpreted as a shell metacharacter.

The following example disables IP packet forwarding by setting the value of the parameter ip_forwarding in the IP driver to 0.

paperbark% **ndd -set /dev/ip ip_forwarding 0**

The following example displays the current IP forwarding table.

paperbark% **ndd /dev/ip ip_ire_status**

Attributes

See attributes(5) for descriptions of the following attributes.

Attribute Type	Attribute Value
Availability	SUNWcsu

See Also

ioctl(2), attributes(5), arp(7P), ip(7P), tcp(7P), udp(7P)

---

netstat — Show Network Status

Synopsis

New!

```
/bin/netstat [-f address-family][-anv]
/bin/netstat [-f address-family][-g | -m | -p | -s][-n][-P protocol]
/bin/netstat {[-i][-I interface]}[-f address-family][interval]
/bin/netstat -r [-f address-family][-anv]
/bin/netstat -M [-f address-family][-ns]
/bin/netstat -D [-f address-family][-I interface]
```

Description

Use the netstat command to display status information about various network-related data structures in various formats.

- The first form of the command displays a list of active sockets for each protocol.
- The second form selects one from among various other network data structures.
- The third form shows the state of the interfaces.
- The fourth form displays the routing table.
- The fifth form displays the multicast routing table.
- The sixth form displays the state of DHCP on one or all interfaces.

The netstat command has been updated to handle IPv6 interfaces.   *New!*

Notes   *New!*

When printing interface information, netstat honors the DEFAULT_IP setting in /etc/default/inet_type. If set to IP_VERSION4, then netstat omits information relating to IPv6 interfaces, statistics, connections, routes, and the like.

You can, however, override the DEFAULT_IP setting in /etc/default/inet_type on the command line. For example, if you have used the command line to explicitly request IPv6 information by using the inet6 address family or one of the IPv6 protocols, the command-line address family overrides the DEFAULT_IP setting.

If you need to examine network status information following a kernel crash, use the crash(1M) command on the savecore(1M) output.

Options

-a   Show the state of all sockets and all routing table entries; normally, sockets used by server processes are not shown, and only interface, host, network, and default routes are shown.

-d   Show the state of all interfaces that are under Dynamic Host Configuration Protocol (DHCP) control.

-D   Show the status of DHCP-configured interfaces.

-f *address-family*

               Limit statistics or address control block reports to those of the specified *address-family*, which can have one of the following values.

               inet   Specify the AF_INET address family.

               inet6   Specify the AF_INET6 address family showing IPv6   *New!* information.

               unix   Specify the AF_UNIX address family.

-g   Show the multicast group memberships for all interfaces.

-I *interface*   Show the state of a particular interface. *interface* can be any valid   *New!* interface such as hme0 or le0. Normally, the status and statistics for physical interfaces are displayed. When you combine this option with the -a option, also report information for the logical interfaces.

-i   Show the state of the interfaces that are used for TCP/IP traffic. (See ifconfig(1M)).

-m   Show the STREAMS statistics.

-M   Show the multicast routing tables. When used with the -s option, show multicast routing statistics instead.

	-n	Show network addresses as numbers. netstat normally displays addresses as symbols. You can use this option with any of the display formats.
New!	-p	Show the net-to-media table. Previous versions show the address resolution (ARP) tables.
New!	-P *protocol*	Limit display of statistics or state of all sockets to those applicable to *protocol*. The protocol can be one of IP, IPv6, ICMP, ICMPv6, IGMP, UDP, TCP, or RAQIP.
	-r	Show the routing tables.
	-s	Show per-protocol statistics. When used with the -M option, show multicast routing statistics instead.
	-v	Show additional verbose information for the sockets and the routing table.

Operands

interval	Display interface information over the last *interval* seconds, repeating forever.

Displays

Active Sockets (First Form)

The display for each active socket shows the local and remote address, the send and receive queue sizes (in bytes), the send and receive windows (in bytes), and the internal state of the protocol.

The symbolic format normally used to display socket addresses is either

hostname.port

when you specify the name of the host, or

network.port

if a socket address specifies a network but no specific host.

The numeric host address or network number associated with the socket is used to look up the corresponding symbolic host name or network name in the hosts or networks database.

If the network or host name for an address is not known (or if you specify the -n option), the numerical network address is shown. Unspecified, or wildcard, addresses and ports appear as *. For more information regarding the Internet naming conventions, refer to inet(7P).

TCP Socket

The possible state values for TCP sockets are shown below.

BOUND	Bound, ready to connect or listen.
CLOSED	Closed. The socket is not being used.
CLOSING	Closed, then remote shutdown; awaiting acknowledgment.

CLOSE_WAIT	Remote shutdown; waiting for the socket to close.
ESTABLISHED	Connection has been established.
FIN_WAIT_1	Socket closed; shutting down connection.
FIN_WAIT_2	Socket closed; waiting for shutdown from remote.
IDLE	Idle, opened but not bound.
LAST_ACK	Remote shutdown, then closed; awaiting acknowledgment.
LISTEN	Listening for incoming connections.
SYN_RECEIVED	Initial synchronization of the connection under way.
SYN_SENT	Actively trying to establish connection.
TIME_WAIT	Wait after close for remote shutdown retransmission.

Network Data Structures (Second Form)

The form of the display depends on which of the -g, -m, -p, or -s options you specify.

-g	Display the list of multicast group membership.
-m	Display the memory usage, for example, STREAMS mblks.
-p	Display the net-to-media mapping table. For IPv4, display the address resolution table. See arp(1M). For IPv6, display the neighbor cache.
-s	Display the statistics for the various protocol layers.

The statistics use the MIB specified variables. The following values are defined for ipForwarding.

forwarding(1) Acting as a gateway.

not-forwarding(2)

Not acting as a gateway.

The IPv6 and ICMPv6 protocol layers maintain per-interface statistics. If you specify the -a option with the -s option, then the per-interface statistics as well as the total sums are displayed. Otherwise, just the sum of the statistics is shown.

If you specify more than one of these options, netstat displays the information for each one of them.

Interface Status (Third Form)

The interface status display lists information for all current interfaces, one interface per line. If you specify an interface with the -I option, the command displays information for only the specified interface.

The list consists of the interface name, mtu (maximum transmission unit, or maximum packet size) (see ifconfig(1M)), the network to which the interface is attached, addresses for each interface, and the counter associated with the interface. The counters show the number of input packets, input errors, output packets, output errors, and collisions. For Point-to-Point interfaces, the Net/Dest field is the name or address on the other side of the link.

If you specify the -a option with either the -i or -I options, then the output includes additional information about the physical interface(s), input packets, and output packets for each logical interface, for example, the local IP address associated with the physical interface(s).

If you specify the -n option, the list displays the IP address instead of the interface name.

If you specify an optional *interval*, the output is continuously displayed in *interval* seconds until you interrupt it.

You specify the input interface with the -I option. In this case, the list displays only traffic information in columns; the specified interface is first, the total count is second. The column list has the following format.

```
input     le0           output              input           (Total)    output
packets   errs  packets errs  colls          packets  errs  packets  errs   colls
227681    0     659471  1     502            261331   0     99597    1      502
10        0     0       0     0              10       0     0        0      0
8         0     0       0     0              8        0     0        0      0
10        0     2       0     0              10       0     2        0      0
```

If you do not specify the input interface, the first interface of address family inet or inet6 is displayed.

Routing Table (Fourth Form)

The routing table display lists the available routes and the status of each. Each route consists of a destination host or network, and a gateway to use in forwarding packets. The flags column shows the status of the route.

U   Up.

G   Gateway.

D   Route was created dynamically by a redirect.

If you specify the -a option, routing entries can have the following flags.

A   Combined routing and address resolution entries.

B   Broadcast addresses.

L   The local addresses for the host.

Interface routes are created for each interface attached to the local host; the gateway field for such entries shows the address of the outgoing interface.

The refcnt column gives the current number of routes that share the same link layer address.

The use column displays the number of packets sent with a combined routing and address resolution (A) or a broadcast (B) route. For a local (L) route, this count is the number of packets received, and for all other routes it is the number of times the routing entry has been used to create a new combined route and address resolution entry.

The interface entry indicates the network interface used for the route.

Multicast Routing Tables (Fifth Form)

The multicast routing table consists of the virtual interface table and the actual routing table.

DHCP Interface Information (Sixth Form)

New!

The DHCP interface information consists of the interface name, its current state, lease information, packet counts, and a list of flags.

The states correlate with the specifications set forth in RFC 2131.
Lease information includes the following information.

- When the lease began.
- When lease renewal begins.
- When the lease expires.

The following flags are currently defined.

BOOTP   The interface has a lease obtained through BOOTP.

BUSY   The interface is busy with a DHCP transaction.

PRIMARY   The interface is the primary interface. See dhcpinfo(1M).

FAILED   The interface is in failure state and must be manually restarted.

Examples

The following example shows the output of the netstat command with no arguments,
which displays the status of active TCP and UDP ports.

```
paperbark% netstat

TCP: IPv4
    Local Address        Remote Address       Swind Send-Q Rwind Recv-Q  State
    -------------------  -------------------  ----- ------ ----- ------  -------
    localhost.32786      localhost.32773      32768      0 32768      0  ESTABLISHED
    localhost.32773      localhost.32786      32768      0 32768      0  ESTABLISHED
    localhost.32789      localhost.32784      32768      0 32768      0  ESTABLISHED
    localhost.32784      localhost.32789      32768      0 32768      0  ESTABLISHED
    localhost.32792      localhost.32791      32768      0 32768      0  ESTABLISHED
    localhost.32791      localhost.32792      32768      0 32768      0  ESTABLISHED
    localhost.32795      localhost.32784      32768      0 32768      0  ESTABLISHED
    localhost.32784      localhost.32795      32768      0 32768      0  ESTABLISHED
    localhost.32798      localhost.32797      32768      0 32768      0  ESTABLISHED
    localhost.32797      localhost.32798      32768      0 32768      0  ESTABLISHED
    localhost.32813      localhost.32784      32768      0 32768      0  ESTABLISHED
    localhost.32784      localhost.32813      32768      0 32768      0  ESTABLISHED
    localhost.32816      localhost.32815      32767      0 32768      0  ESTABLISHED
    localhost.32815      localhost.32816      32768      0 32768      0  ESTABLISHED
    paperbark.32891      G3.ftp               17520      0 24820      0  ESTABLISHED
    paperbark.8888       paperbark.32904      32768      0 32768      0  TIME_WAIT
    paperbark.32905      paperbark.32779      32768      0 32768      0  TIME_WAIT

Active UNIX domain sockets
Address  Type        Vnode    Conn     Local Addr       Remote Addr
707f1d90 stream-ord 705b89e0 00000000 /tmp/.X11-unix/X0
707f1ea8 stream-ord 00000000 00000000
paperbark%
```

The following example uses the netstat -i command on the system paperbark to
display the status of network interfaces.

```
paperbark% netstat -i
Name  Mtu  Net/Dest    Address      Ipkts  Ierrs Opkts  Oerrs Collis Queue
lo0   8232 loopback    localhost    11787  0     11787  0     0      0
hme0  1500 paperbark   paperbark    8      0     5      0     0      0

paperbark%
```

The following example uses the netstat -r -n command to display the kernel's routing tables with the network addresses as numbers.

```
paperbark% netstat -r -n

Routing Table: IPv4
   Destination          Gateway             Flags  Ref   Use    Interface
-------------------- -------------------- ----- ----- ------ ---------
172.16.8.0           172.16.8.22          U      1     0      hme0
224.0.0.0            172.16.8.22          U      1     0      hme0
127.0.0.1            127.0.0.1            UH     16    11150  lo0
paperbark%
```

New! Files

/etc/default/inet_type

DEFAULT_IP setting.

Attributes

See attributes(5) for descriptions of the following attributes.

Attribute Type	Attribute Value
Availability	SUNWcsu

See Also

arp(1M), crash(1M), dhcpagent(1M), ifconfig(1M), iostat(1M), mibiisa(1M), savecore(1M), vmstat(1M), hosts(4), networks(4), protocols(4), services(4), attributes(5), inet(7P)

newfs — Construct a New UFS File System

Synopsis

/usr/lib/fs/newfs [-Nv][mkfs-options] raw-device

Description

The newfs command is a friendly front end to the mkfs(1M) program for making UFS file systems on disk partitions. newfs calculates the appropriate parameters to use and calls mkfs.

If run interactively (that is, standard input is a TTY), newfs prompts for confirmation before making the file system.

If you do not specify the -N option and the inodes of the device are not randomized, newfs calls fsirand(1M).

You must be superuser to use this command, except when creating a UFS file system on a diskette.

Options

-N   Print the file-system parameters that would be used in creating the file system without actually creating the file system. fsirand(1M) is not called here.

-v   Print actions, including the parameters passed to mkfs.

mkfs-options   The following options override the default parameters.

         -a apc   (SCSI devices only) The number of alternate blocks per cylinder to reserve for bad block replacement. The default is 0.

         -b bsize   The logical block size of the file system in bytes (either 4096 or 8192). The default is 8192. The sun4u architecture does not support the 4096 block size.

         -c cgsize   The number of cylinders per cylinder group (ranging from 1 to 32). The default is 16. Note that mkfs can override this value (see mkfs_ufs(1M) for details).

         -d gap   Rotational delay. The expected time (in milliseconds) to service a transfer completion interrupt and initiate a new transfer on the same disk. Use this option to specify how much rotational spacing to put between successive blocks in a file. You can subsequently change this parameter with the tunefs(1M) command. The default is disk-type dependent.

         -f fragsize   The smallest amount of disk space in bytes to allocate to a file. The values must be a power of 2 selected from the range 512 to the logical block size. If logical block size is 4096, legal values are 512, 1024, 2048, and 4096; if logical block size is 8192, 8192 is also a legal value. The default is 1024.

         -i nbpi   The number of bytes per inode, which specifies the density of inodes in the file system. The number is divided into the total size of the file system to determine the fixed number of inodes to create. It should reflect the expected average size of files in the file system. If fewer inodes are desired, specify a larger number; to create more inodes, specify a smaller number. The defaults are as follows.

Disk size	Density
−1GB	2048
−2GB	4096
−3GB	6144
3GB−	8192

-m *free* The minimum percentage of free space to maintain in the file system (between 1 and 99 percent, inclusively). This space is off-limits to normal users. Once the file system is filled to this threshold, only superuser can continue writing to the file system. You can subsequently change this parameter with the tunefs(1M) command. The default is ((64 Mbytes/partition size) * 100), rounded down to the nearest integer and limited between 1 and 10 percent, inclusively.

-n *nrpos* The number of different rotational positions in which to divide a cylinder group. The default is 8.

-o *opt* (space or time) Specify whether to minimize the time spent allocating blocks or to minimize the space fragmentation on the disk. The default is time.

-r *rpm* The speed of the disk in revolutions per minute. The default is 3600.

-s *size* The size of the file system in sectors. The default is to use the entire partition.

-t *ntrack* The number of tracks per cylinder on the disk. The default is taken from the disk label.

-C *maxcontig* The maximum number of blocks belonging to one file that is allocated contiguously before a rotational delay is inserted. For a 4-kilobyte file system, the default is 14; for an 8-kilobyte file system, the default is 7. You can subsequently change this parameter with the tunefs(1M) command.

Note that this parameter also controls clustering. Regardless of the value of *gap*, clustering is enabled only when *maxcontig* is greater than 1. Clustering allows higher I/O rates for sequential I/O and is described in tunefs(1M).

Operands

raw-device   The name of a raw special device residing in /dev/rdsk (for example, /dev/rdsk/c0t0d0s6) on which to create the file system.

Usage

See largefile(5) for the description of the behavior of newfs when encountering files greater than or equal to 2 Gbytes (2**31 bytes).

Examples

The following example verbosely displays the parameters for the raw special device, c0t1d0s0, but does not actually create a new file system.

```
# newfs -Nv /dev/rdsk/c0t1d0s0
mkfs -F ufs -o N /dev/rdsk/c0t1d0s0 4154160 80 19 8192 1024 32 3 90 4096
   t 0 -1 8 80
/dev/rdsk/c0t1d0s0:     4154160 sectors in 2733 cylinders of 19 tracks,
   80 sectors
        2028.4MB in 86 cyl groups (32 c/g, 23.75MB/g, 5888 i/g)
super-block backups (for fsck -F ufs -o b=#) at:
 32, 48752, 97472, 146192, 194912, 243632, 292352, 341072, 389792,
   438512,
 487232, 535952, 584672, 633392, 682112, 730832, 779552, 828272, 876992,
 925712, 974432, 1023152, 1071872, 1120592, 1169312, 1218032, 1266752,
   1315472,
 1364192, 1412912, 1461632, 1510352, 1556512, 1605232, 1653952, 1702672,
 1751392, 1800112, 1848832, 1897552, 1946272, 1994992, 2043712, 2092432,
 2141152, 2189872, 2238592, 2287312, 2336032, 2384752, 2433472, 2482192,
 2530912, 2579632, 2628352, 2677072, 2725792, 2774512, 2823232, 2871952,
 2920672, 2969392, 3018112, 3066832, 3112992, 3161712, 3210432, 3259152,
 3307872, 3356592, 3405312, 3454032, 3502752, 3551472, 3600192, 3648912,
 3697632, 3746352, 3795072, 3843792, 3892512, 3941232, 3989952, 4038672,
 4087392, 4136112,
#
```

The following example creates a UFS file system on a diskette that is managed by Volume Manager.

```
paperbark% newfs /vol/dev/aliases/floppy0
newfs: construct a new file system /vol/dev/aliases/floppy0: (y/n)? y
/vol/dev/aliases/floppy0:     2880 sectors in 80 cylinders of 2 tracks,
        18 sectors   1.4MB in 5 cyl groups (16 c/g, 0.28MB/g, 128 i/g)
            super-block backups (for fsck -F ufs -o b=#) at:
            32, 640, 1184, 1792, 2336, ...
```

Exit Status

0   The operation was successful.

1, 10   Usage error or internal error. A message is output to standard error explaining the error.

Other exit values may be returned by mkfs(1M), which is called by newfs.

Attributes

See attributes(5) for descriptions of the following attributes.

Attribute Type	Attribute Value
Availability	SUNWcsu

See Also

fsck(1M), fsck_ufs(1M), fsirand(1M), mkfs(1M), mkfs_ufs(1M), tunefs(1M), fs_ufs(4), attributes(5), largefile(5)

Diagnostics

newfs: No such file or directory

> The device specified does not exist or a disk partition was not specified.

special: cannot open

> You must be superuser to use this command.

newkey — Create a New Diffie-Hellman Key Pair in the publickey Database

Synopsis

```
/usr/sbin/newkey -h hostname [-s nisplus | nis | files]
/usr/sbin/newkey -u username [-s nisplus | nis | files]
```

Description

Use the newkey command to establish new public keys for users and machines on the network. These keys are needed when secure RPC or secure NFS service is used.

For NIS, superuser should run newkey on the master NIS server for that domain. For NIS+, superuser should run newkey on a machine that has permission to update the cred.org_dir table of the new user/host domain. You cannot use newkey to create keys other than 192-bit Diffie-Hellman. To add new keys for NIS+, use nisaddcred(1M).

newkey prompts for a password for the given username or hostname and then creates a new public/secret Diffie-Hellman 192-bit key pair for the user or host. The secret key is encrypted with the specified password. The key pair can be stored in the /etc/publickey file, the NIS publickey map, or the NIS+ cred.org_dir table.

newkey consults the publickey entry in the nameservice switch configuration file (see nsswitch.conf(4)) to determine which naming service is used to store the secure RPC keys. If the publickey entry specifies a unique nameservice, newkey adds the key in the specified nameservice. However, if multiple nameservices are listed, newkey cannot decide which source to update and displays an error message; you must then specify the source with the -s option.

Options

-h *hostname*	Create a new public/secret key pair for the privileged user at the given hostname. Prompt for a password for the specified host name.
-u *username*	Create a new public/secret key pair for the given user name. Prompt for a password for the specified user name.
-s nisplus -s nis -s files	Update the database in the specified source: nisplus (for NIS+), nis (for NIS), or files. Other sources may be available in the future.

Examples

The following example adds a key for the host paperbark.

```
# newkey -h paperbark
Updating files publickey database.
Adding new key for unix.paperbark@wellard.com.
#
```

Attributes

See attributes(5) for descriptions of the following attributes.

Attribute Type	Attribute Value
Availability	SUNWcsu

See Also

chkey(1), keylogin(1), nisaddcred(1M), nisclient(1M), nsswitch.conf(4), publickey(4), attributes(5)

---

nfsd — NFS Daemon

Synopsis

```
/usr/lib/nfs/nfsd [-a][-c no-conn][-l listen-backlog][-p protocol]
    [-t device][nservers]
```

Description

The nfsd daemon handles client file-system requests. Only superuser can run this daemon.

The nfsd daemon is automatically invoked in run level 3 with the -a option.

By default, nfsd starts over the tcp and udp transports.

You must stop a previously invoked nfsd daemon that was started with or without options before you invoke another nfsd command.

> **Note** — The NFS service uses kernel threads to process all of the NFS requests. Currently, system use associated with these threads is not charged to the nfsd process. Therefore, ps(1) may report 0 cpu time associated with the NFS daemon even though NFS processing is taking place on the server.
>
> Manually starting and restarting nfsd is not recommended. If you must do so, use the NFS server start/stop script (/etc/init.d/nfs.server). See *NFS Administration Guide* for more information.

Options

-a	Start an NFS daemon over all available connectionless and connection-oriented transports, including UDP and TCP.
-c *no-conn*	Set the maximum number of connections allowed to the NFS server over connection-oriented transports. By default, the number of connections is unlimited.
-l	Set connection queue length for the NFS TCP over a connection-oriented transport. The default value is 32 entries.
-p *protocol*	Start an NFS daemon over the specified protocol.
-t *device*	Start an NFS daemon for the transport specified by the given device.

Operands

nservers	Set the maximum number of concurrent NFS requests that the server can handle. This concurrency is achieved by up to *nservers* threads created as needed in the kernel. Base *nservers* on the load expected on this server. 16 is the usual number of *nservers*. If you do not specify *nservers*, the maximum number of concurrent NFS requests defaults to 1.

Usage

If the NFS_PORTMON variable is set, then clients are required to use privileged ports (ports < IPPORT_RESERVED) to get NFS services. The default value is 0. This variable has been moved from the nfs module to the nfssrv module. To set the variable, edit the /etc/system file and add the following entry.

```
set nfssrv:nfs_portmon = 1
```

Exit Status

0	Daemon started successfully.
1	Daemon failed to start.

Files

.nfs*XXX* client

> Machine pointer to an open-but-unlinked file.

/etc/init.d/nfs.server

> Shell script for starting nfsd.

/etc/system System configuration information file.

Attributes

See attributes(5) for descriptions of the following attributes.

Attribute Type	Attribute Value
Availability	SUNWcsu

See Also

ps(1), mountd(1M), sharetab(4), system(4), attributes(5)
NFS Administration Guide

---

nfslogd — NFS Logging Daemon

New!

Synopsis

/usr/lib/nfs/nfslogd

Description

The nfslogd command is new in the Solaris 8 release. The nfslogd daemon provides operational logging to the Solaris NFS server. It is the nfslogd daemon's job to generate the activity log by analyzing the RPC operations processed by the NFS server. The log is generated only for file systems exported with logging enabled. You specify logging at file-system export time by means of the share_nfs(1M) command.

Each record in the log file includes a timestamp, the IP address (or hostname if it can be resolved) of the client system, the file or directory name the operation was performed on, and the type of operation. In the basic format, the operation can either be an input (i) or output (o) operation. The basic format of the NFS server log is compatible with the log format generated by the Washington University FTPd daemon. You can extend the log format to include directory modification operations, such as mkdir, rmdir, and remove. The extended format is not compatible with the Washington University FTPd daemon format. See nfslog.conf(4) for details.

The NFS server logging mechanism is divided into two phases. The first phase is performed by the NFS kernel module, which records raw RPC requests and their results in work buffers backed by permanent storage. The /etc/nfs/nfslog.conf file specifies the location of the work buffers. Refer to nfslog.conf(4) for more information. The second phase involves the nfslogd user-level daemon, which periodically reads the work buffers, interprets the raw RPC information, groups related RPC operations into single transaction records, and generates the output log. The `nfslogd` daemon then sleeps waiting for more information to be logged to the work buffers. You can configure the amount of time that the daemon sleeps by modifying the `IDLE_TIME` parameter in `/etc/default/nfslogd`. The work buffers are intended for internal consumption of the `nfslogd` daemon.

NFS operations use file handles as arguments instead of path names. For this reason, the `nfslogd` daemon needs to maintain a database of file handle to path mappings to log the path name associated with an operation instead of the corresponding file handle. A file handle entry is added to the database when a client performs a lookup or other NFS operation that returns a file handle to the client.

Once an NFS client obtains a file handle from a server, it can hold on to it for an indefinite time and can later use it as an argument for an NFS operation on the file or directory. The NFS client can use the file handle even after the server reboots. Because the database needs to survive server reboots, it is backed by permanent storage. The location of the database is specified by the `fhtable` parameter in the `/etc/nfs/nfslog.conf` file. This database is intended for the internal use of the `nfslogd` daemon.

To keep the size of the file handle mapping database manageable, `nfslogd` prunes the database periodically. It removes file handle entries that have not been accessed in more than a specified amount of time. The `PRUNE_TIMEOUT` configurable parameter in `/etc/default/nfslogd` specifies the interval length between successive runs of the pruning process. A file handle record is removed if it has not been used since the last time the pruning process was executed. Pruning of the database can effectively be disabled by setting the `PRUNE_TIMEOUT` as high as `INT_MAX`.

When pruning is enabled, there is always a risk that a client may have held on to a file handle longer than the `PRUNE_TIMEOUT` and may perform an NFS operation on the file handle after the matching record in the mapping database had been removed. In such case, the path name for the file handle does not resolve and the log includes the file handle instead of the path name.

Various configurable parameters affect the behavior of the `nfslogd` daemon. These parameters are found in `/etc/default/nfslogd` and are described below.

UMASK   Set the file mode for the log files, work buffer files, and file handle mapping database.

MIN_PROCESSING_SIZE

                 Specify the minimum size, in bytes, that the buffer file must reach before processing the work information and writing to the log file. The value of `MIN_PROCESSING_SIZE` must be between `1` and `ulimit`.

IDLE_TIME   Specify the amount of time, in seconds, the daemon should sleep while waiting for more information to be put into the buffer file. `IDLE_TIME` also determines how often the configuration file is reread. The value of `IDLE_TIME` must be between `1` and `INT_MAX`.

MAX_LOGS_PRESERVE

                 The `nfslogd` periodically cycles its logs. Use `MAX_LOGS_PRESERVE` to specify the maximum number of log files to save. When `MAX_LOGS_PRESERVE` is reached, the oldest files are overwritten as new log files are created. These files are saved with a numbered extension, beginning with *filename*. 0. The oldest files have the highest numbered extension up to the value configured for

MAX_LOGS_PRESERVE. The value of MAX_LOGS_PRESERVE must be between 1 and INT_MAX.

CYCLE_FREQUENCY

Specify how often, in hours, the log files are cycled. Use CYCLE_FREQUENCY to ensure that the log files do not get too large. The value of CYCLE_FREQUENCY must be between 1 and INT_MAX.

MAPPING_UPDATE_INTERVAL

Specify the time interval, in seconds, between updates of the records in the file handle to path mapping tables. Instead of updating the atime of a record each time that record is accessed, atime is only updated if it has aged based on this parameter. The record access time is used by the pruning routine to determine whether the record should be removed from the database. The value of this parameter must be between 1 and INT_MAX.

PRUNE_TIMEOUT

Specify when a database record times out, in hours. If the time that elapsed since the record was last accessed is greater than PRUNE_TIMEOUT, then the record can be pruned from the database. The default value for PRUNE_TIMEOUT is 168 hours (7 days). The value of PRUNE_TIMEOUT must be between 1 and INT_MAX.

Exit Status

| 0 | Daemon started successfully. |
| 1 | Daemon failed to start. |

Files

/etc/nfs/nfslogtab

NFS log table.

/etc/nfs/nfslog.conf

NFS log configuration file for internal use by the nfslogd daemon.

/etc/default/nfslogd

Configurable parameters.

Attributes

See attributes(5) for descriptions of the following attributes.

Attribute Type	**Attribute Value**
Availability	SUNWcsu

See Also
    share_nfs(1M), nfslog.conf(4), attributes(5)

---

nis_cachemgr — NIS+ Command to Cache Location Information About NIS+ Servers

Synopsis
    /usr/sbin/nis_cachemgr [-i][-v]

Description

The nis_cachemgr daemon maintains a cache of NIS+ directory objects and active servers for domains. It is responsible for locating servers for a domain on behalf of client processes. This daemon improves performance because only one process has to search for servers. The cache contains location information necessary to contact the NIS+ servers. This information includes transport addresses, information needed to authenticate the server, and a time-to-live field that gives a hint on how long the directory object can be cached. The cache helps to improve the performance of the clients that are traversing the NIS+ namespace. nis_cachemgr should be running on all the machines that are using NIS+. However, it is not required that the nis_cachemgr program be running for NIS+ requests to be serviced.

The cache maintained by this program is shared by all the processes that access NIS+ on a machine. The cache is maintained in a file that is memory mapped (see mmap(2)) by all the processes. On startup, nis_cachemgr initializes the cache from the coldstart file (see nisinit(1M)) and preserves unexpired entries that already exist in the cache file. Thus, the cache survives machine reboots.

nis_cachemgr is normally started from a system startup script. You can use nisshowcache(1M) to look at the cached objects and active servers.

Use the nisprefadm(1M) command to control which NIS+ servers the nis_cachemgr program tries to select.

nis_cachemgr makes NIS+ requests under the NIS+ principal name of the host on which it runs. Before nis_cachemgr is run, security credentials for the host should be added to the cred.org_dir table in the host's domain using nisaddcred(1M). Credentials of type DES are needed if the NIS+ service is operating at security level 2 (see rpc.nisd(1M)). Additionally, you should do a keylogin -r on the system.

Options

-i	Ignore the previous cache file and reinitialize the cache from just the coldstart file. By default, the cache manager initializes itself from both the coldstart file and the old cache file, thereby maintaining the entries in the cache across machine reboots.
-v	Log not only errors and warnings but also additional status messages. Log the additional messages by syslog(3) with a priority of LOG_INFO.

Files

/var/nis/NIS_SHARED_DIRCACHE

The shared cache file.

/var/nis/NIS_COLD_START

The coldstart file.

/etc/init.d/rpc

Initialization scripts for NIS+.

Attributes

See attributes(5) for descriptions of the following attributes.

Attribute Type	Attribute Value
Availability	SUNWcsu

See Also

keylogin(1), nisaddcred(1M), nisinit(1M), nisprefadm(1M),
nisshowcache(1M), rpc.nisd(1M), mmap(2), rpc(3N), syslog(3), nisfiles(4),
attributes(5)

Diagnostics

The nis_cachemgr daemon logs error messages and warnings with syslog(3). Error
messages are logged to the DAEMON facility with a priority of LOG_ERR. Warning messages
are logged with a priority of LOG_WARNING. You can obtain additional status messages
with the -v option.

nfsstat — Display NFS Statistics

Synopsis

/usr/bin/nfsstat [-cmnrsz]

Description

Use the nfsstat command to display statistical information about the NFS and RPC
(Remote Procedure Call) interfaces to the kernel. You can also use it to reinitialize this
information. If you specify no options, the default is nfsstat -cnrs. That is, display
everything but reinitialize nothing.

Options

-c   Display client information. Print only the client-side NFS and RPC information. You can combine this option with the -n and -r options to print client-NFS or client-RPC information only.

-m   Display statistics for each NFS-mounted file system. This information includes the server name and address, mount flags, current read and write sizes, the retransmission count, and the timers used for dynamic retransmission. The srtt value contains the smoothed round trip time, the dev value contains the estimated deviation, and the cur value is the current backed-off retransmission value.

-n   Print NFS information for both the client and server side. You can combine this option with the -c and -s options to print client or server NFS information only.

-r   Display RPC information.

-s   Display server information.

-z   Zero (reinitialize) statistics. This option is for use only by superuser and can be combined with any of the above options to zero particular sets of statistics after printing them.

Displays

The server RPC display includes the following fields.

calls   The total number of RPC calls received.

badcalls   The total number of calls rejected by the RPC layer (the sum of badlen and xdrcall as defined below).

nullrecv   The number of times an RPC call was not available when it was thought to be received.

badlen   The number of RPC calls with a length shorter than a minimum-sized RPC call.

xdrcall   The number of RPC calls whose header could not be XDR decoded.

dupchecks   The number of RPC calls that were looked up in the duplicate request cache.

dupreqs   The number of RPC calls that were found to be duplicates.

The server NFS display shows the number of NFS calls received (calls) and rejected (badcalls), and the counts and percentages for the various calls that were made.

The client RPC display includes the following fields.

calls   The total number of RPC calls made.

badcalls   The total number of calls rejected by the RPC layer.

badxids   The number of times a reply from a server was received but did not correspond to any outstanding call.

timeouts	The number of times a call timed out while waiting for a reply from the server.
newcreds	The number of times authentication information had to be refreshed.
badverfs	The number of times the call failed because of a bad verifier in the response.
timers	The number of times the calculated timeout value was greater than or equal to the minimum specified time-out value for a call.
cantconn	The number of times the call failed because of a failure to make a connection to the server.
nomem	The number of times the call failed because of a failure to allocate memory.
interrupts	The number of times the call was interrupted by a signal before completing.
retrans	The number of times a call had to be retransmitted because of a timeout while waiting for a reply from the server. Applicable only to RPC over connectionless transports.

The client NFS display shows the number of calls sent and rejected, as well as the number of times a CLIENT handle was received (clgets), the number of times the CLIENT handle cache had no unused entries (cltoomany), as well as a count of the various calls and their respective percentages.

The -m option includes information about mount flags set by mount options, mount flags internal to the system, and other mount information. See mount_nfs(1M).

The following fields provide failover information.

noresponse	How many times servers have failed to respond.
failover	How many times a new server has been selected.
remap	How may times files have been reevaluated to the new server.
currserver	Which server is currently providing NFS service. See the *NFS Administration Guide* for additional details.

The following mount flags are set by mount options.

sec	sec has one of the following values.

none	No authentication.
unix	UNIX style authentication (UID, GID).
short	Shorthand UNIX style authentication.
des	des-style authentication (encrypted timestamps).
krb4	kerberos style authentication.
hard	Hard mount.
soft	Soft mount.
intr	Interrupts allowed on hard mount.
nointr	No interrupts allowed on hard mount.
noac	Client is not caching attributes.

`rsize`	Read buffer size in bytes.
`wsize`	Write buffer size in bytes.
`retrans`	NFS retransmissions.
`nocto`	No close-to-open consistency.
`llock`	Local locking being used (no lock manager).
`grpid`	System V group ID inheritance.
`rpctimesync`	RPC time sync.

The following mount flags are internal to the system.

`printed`	`Not responding` message printed.
`down`	Server is down.
`dynamic`	Dynamic transfer size adjustment.
`link`	Server supports links.
`symlink`	Server supports symbolic links.
`readdir`	Use `readdir` instead of `readdirplus`.
`acl`	Server supports `NFS_ACL`.

The following flags relate to additional mount information.

`vers`	NFS version.
`proto`	Protocol.

Examples

The following example shows the output of the `nfsstat` command on the system paperbark.

```
paperbark% nfsstat

Server rpc:
Connection oriented:
calls       badcalls     nullrecv     badlen      xdrcall      dupchecks
0           0            0            0           0            0
dupreqs
0
Connectionless:
calls       badcalls     nullrecv     badlen      xdrcall      dupchecks
0           0            0            0           0            0
dupreqs
0

Server nfs:
calls       badcalls
0           0
Version 2: (0 calls)
null        getattr      setattr      root        lookup       readlink
0 0%        0 0%         0 0%         0 0%        0 0%         0 0%
read        wrcache      write        create      remove       rename
```

```
0 0%          0 0%          0 0%          0 0%          0 0%          0 0%
link          symlink       mkdir         rmdir         readdir       statfs
0 0%          0 0%          0 0%          0 0%          0 0%          0 0%
Version 3: (0 calls)
null          getattr       setattr       lookup        access        readlink
0 0%          0 0%          0 0%          0 0%          0 0%          0 0%
read          write         create        mkdir         symlink       mknod
0 0%          0 0%          0 0%          0 0%          0 0%          0 0%
remove        rmdir         rename        link          readdir       readdirplus
0 0%          0 0%          0 0%          0 0%          0 0%          0 0%
fsstat        fsinfo        pathconf      commit
0 0%          0 0%          0 0%          0 0%


Server nfs_acl:
Version 2: (0 calls)
null          getacl        setacl        getattr       access
0 0%          0 0%          0 0%          0 0%          0 0%
Version 3: (0 calls)
null          getacl        setacl
0 0%          0 0%          0 0%


Client rpc:
Connection oriented:
calls         badcalls      badxids       timeouts      newcreds      badverfs
68            0             0             0             0             0
timers        cantconn      nomem         interrupts
0             0             0             0
Connectionless:
calls         badcalls      retrans       badxids       timeouts      newcreds
3             1             0             0             0             0
badverfs      timers        nomem         cantsend
0             0             0             0


Client nfs:
calls         badcalls      clgets        cltoomany
3             1             3             0
Version 2: (2 calls)
null          getattr       setattr       root          lookup        readlink
0 0%          1 50%         0 0%          0 0%          0 0%          0 0%
read          wrcache       write         create        remove        rename
0 0%          0 0%          0 0%          0 0%          0 0%          0 0%
link          symlink       mkdir         rmdir         readdir       statfs
0 0%          0 0%          0 0%          0 0%          0 0%          1 50%
Version 3: (0 calls)
null          getattr       setattr       lookup        access        readlink
0 0%          0 0%          0 0%          0 0%          0 0%          0 0%
read          write         create        mkdir         symlink       mknod
0 0%          0 0%          0 0%          0 0%          0 0%          0 0%
remove        rmdir         rename        link          readdir       readdirplus
0 0%          0 0%          0 0%          0 0%          0 0%          0 0%
fsstat        fsinfo        pathconf      commit
0 0%          0 0%          0 0%          0 0%


Client nfs_acl:
Version 2: (1 calls)
null          getacl        setacl        getattr       access
0 0%          0 0%          0 0%          1 100%        0 0%
```

```
Version 3: (0 calls)
null       getacl      setacl
0 0%       0 0%        0 0%
paperbark%
```

Exit Status

0   Successful completion.

>0   An error occurred.

Attributes

See `attributes`(5) for descriptions of the following attributes.

Attribute Type	Attribute Value
Availability	SUNWcsu

See Also

mount_nfs(1M), attributes(5)
Solaris Advanced Installation Guide
NFS Administration Guide

nisaddcred — Create NIS+ Credentials

Synopsis

```
/bin/nisaddcred [-p principal][-P nis-principal][-l login-password]
  auth-type [domain-name]
/bin/nisaddcred -r [nis-principal][domain-name]
```

Description

Use the `nisaddcred` command to create security credentials for NIS+ principals. NIS+ credentials serve two purposes. The first is to provide authentication information to various services; the second is to map the authentication service name into an NIS+ principal name.

Note — It is simpler to add credentials by means of `nisclient`(1M) because that command obtains the required information itself. You can use `nispopulate`(1M) for "bulk" updates and also to add credentials for entries in the `hosts` and the `passwd` NIS+ tables.

When you run the `nisaddcred` command, credentials are created and stored in a table named `cred.org_dir` in the default NIS+ domain. If you specify *domain-name*, the entries are stored in the `cred.org_dir` of the specified domain. The specified domain must either be the one to which you belong or one in which you are authenticated and authorized to create credentials, that is, a subdomain. The credentials of normal users must be stored in the same domain as their passwords.

Note — The `cred.org_dir` NIS+ table replaces the maps `publickey.byname` and `netid.byname` used in NIS (YP).

NIS+ principal names are used in specifying clients that have access rights to NIS+ objects. For more details, refer to the "Principal Names" subsection of the nis+(1) manual page. See `nischmod`(1), `nischown`(1), `nis_objects`(3N), and `nis_groups`(3N). Various other services can also implement access control based on these principal names.

The `cred.org_dir` table is organized in the following way.

```
cname              auth_type      auth_name          public_data    private_data
user1.foo.com.       LOCAL           2990            10,102,44
user1.foo.com.        DES        unix.2990@foo.com   098...819      3b8...ab2
user1.foo.com.      DHmmm-n      unix.2990@foo.com   248...428      a42...f32
```

The `cname` column contains a canonical representation of the NIS+ principal name. By convention, this name is the login name of a user or the host name of a machine, followed by a dot (.) followed by the fully qualified "home" domain of that principal. For users, the home domain is defined to be the domain where their DES credentials are kept. For hosts, the home domain is defined to be the domain name returned by the `domainname`(1M) command executed on that host.

The `cred.org_dir` table has two basic types of *auth-type* entries; those with authentication type LOCAL and those with authentication type DES. When you specify *auth-type* on the command line you can use either upper or lower case, and the value should be either `local` or `des`.

You can also use the `cred.org_dir` table to hold data for other values of *auth-type*. Currently, this data is limited to the mechanisms listed on the `nisauthconf`(1M) manual page, for which the `nisaddcred` *auth-type* argument is the same as the name of the mechanism. These mechanisms use a modified form of Secure RPC, and they are similar to the DES authentication type.

If the *auth-type* is des and other authentication mechanisms are configured with `nisauthconf`(1M), then credential entries are added or updated for each mechanism configured. To add or update only 1992-bit Diffie Hellman credentials, that is, those with the *auth-type* of DES, use `dh192-0` on the command line. If no authentication mechanisms are configured, using des on the command line adds or updates only 192-bit Diffie Hellman credentials.

The NIS+ service uses entries of type LOCAL to determine the correspondence between fully qualified NIS+ principal names and users identified by UIDs in the domain containing the `cred.org_dir` table. This correspondence is required when requests made using the AUTH_SYS RPC authentication flavor (see `rpc_clnt_auth`(3N)) are associated to an NIS+ principal name. It is also required for mapping a UID in one domain to its fully qualified, NIS+ principal name whose home domain may be elsewhere. The principal's credentials for any authentication flavor may then be sought for within the `cred.org_dir` table in the principal's home domain (extracted from the principal name). The same NIS+ principal can have LOCAL credential entries in more than one domain. Only users, and not machines, have LOCAL credentials. In their home domain, users of NIS+ should have both types of credentials.

The *auth-name* associated with the LOCAL type entry is a UID that is valid for the principal in the domain containing the `cred.org_dir` table. This UID may differ from that in the principal's home domain. The public information stored in `public_data` for this type contains a list of GIDs for groups in which the user is a member. The GIDs also apply to the domain in which the table resides. No private data is associated with this type. Neither a UID nor a principal name should appear more than once among the LOCAL entries in any one `cred.org_dir` table.

The DES `auth-type` is used for Secure RPC authentication (see `secure_rpc`(3N)).

The authentication name associated with the DES `auth-type` is a Secure RPC netname. A Secure RPC netname has the form `unix.id@domain`.com, where `domain` must be the same as the domain of the principal. For principals that are users, the ID must be the UID of the principal in the principal's home domain. For principals that are hosts, the ID is the host's name. In Secure RPC, processes running under effective UID 0 (root) are identified with the host principal. Unlike the case with LOCAL, one NIS+ principal can have only one DES credential entry in the NIS+ namespace.

The public information in an entry of authentication type DES is the public key for the principal. The private information in this entry is the private key of the principal encrypted by the principal's network password.

User clients of NIS+ should have credentials of both types in their home domain. In addition, a principal must have a LOCAL entry in the `cred.org_dir` table of each domain from which the principal wants to make authenticated requests. A client of NIS+ that makes a request from a domain in which it does not have a LOCAL entry is unable to acquire DES credentials. An NIS+ service running at security level 2 or higher considers such users unauthenticated and assigns them the name `nobody` for determining access rights.

Only those NIS+ principals who are authorized to add or delete the entries in the `cred` table can run the `nisaddcred` command.

If credentials are being added for the caller itself, `nisaddcred` automatically performs a `keylogin` for the caller.

You can list the `cred` entries for a particular principal with `nismatch`(1).

Options

-p *principal*   Specify the name of the principal as defined by the naming rules for that specific mechanism. For example, LOCAL credential names include a string specifying a UID. For DES credentials, specify a Secure RPC netname of the form `unix.id @domain`.com. If you do not specify the -p option, construct the `auth-name` from the effective UID of the current process and the name of the local domain.

-P *nis-principal*

Use the NIS+ principal name `nis-principal`. Use this option when creating LOCAL or DES credentials for users whose home domain is different than the local machine's default domain.

If you do not specify the -P option, construct a principal name for the entry as follows. When it is not creating an entry of type LOCAL, call `nis_local_principal`, which looks for an existing LOCAL entry for the effective UID of the current process in the `cred.org_dir` table and uses the associated principal name for the new entry. When creating an entry of authentication type LOCAL, construct a default NIS+ principal name by taking the login name of the effective UID for its own process and appending to it a dot (.) followed by the local machine's default domain. If the caller is superuser, use the machine name instead of the login name.

-l *login-password*

> Use the *login-password* specified as the password to encrypt the secret key for the credential entry. This option overrides the prompting for a password from the shell. This option is intended for administration scripts only. Prompting guarantees not only that no one using ps(1) can see your password on the command line but it also checks to make sure you have not made any mistakes. Note that *login-password* does not really have to be the user's password but if it is, logging in is simplified.

-r [*nis-principal*]

> Remove all credentials associated with the principal *nis-principal* from the cred.org_dir table. You can use this option when removing a client or user from the system. If *nis-principal* is not specified the default is to remove credentials for the current user. If *domain-name* is not specified, the operation is executed in the default NIS+ domain.

Examples

The following example illustrates how to add the LOCAL credentials for some user, user1, with a UID of 2990, who is an NIS+ user principal in the some.domain.com. NIS+ domain.

```
paperbark% nisaddcred -p 2990 -P user1.some.domain.com. local
```

Note — Credentials are always added in the cred.org_dir table in the domain where nisaddcred is run unless you specify *domain-name* as the last parameter on the command line. If credentials are being added from the domain server for its clients, then you should specify *domain-name*. The caller should have adequate permissions to create entries in the cred.org_dir table.

The following example adds a DES credential for the same user.

```
paperbark% nisaddcred -p unix.2990@some.domain.com
-P user1.some.domain.com. des
```

You can add DES credentials only after the LOCAL credentials have been added. Also, if the system is configured to use more than one authentication mechanism, credentials are made for each mechanism configured. See nisauthconf(1M).

Note — The secure RPC netname does not end with a dot (.), whereas the NIS+ principal name (specified with the -P option) does. This command should be executed from a machine in the user's domain.

The following example shows how to add a machine's DES credentials in the same domain.

```
paperbark% nisaddcred -p unix.foo@some.domain.com
-P foo.some.domain.com. des
```

Note — No LOCAL credentials are needed in this case.

The following example illustrates how to add an NIS+ workstation's principal DES credential.

```
paperbark% nisaddcred -p unix.host1@sub.some.domain.com
  -P newhost.sub.some.domain.com. des sub.some.domain.com.
```

This format is particularly useful if you are running this command from a server that is in a higher domain than `sub.some.domain.com`. Without the last option for domain name, `nisaddcred` fails because it tries to use the default domain of `some.domain.com.`.

The following example illustrates adding DES credentials without being prompted for the root login password.

```
paperbark% nisaddcred -p unix.2990@some.domain.com
  -P user1.some.domain.com. -l login-password des
```

The following example shows how to add a credential for a user by using a specific authentication mechanism that was previously configured with `nisauthconf`(1M). See `nisauthconf`(1M) for a list of the valid values of `auth-type`.

```
paperbark% nisaddcred -p unix.2990@some.domain.com
  -P user.1.some.domain.com dh640-0
```

Note — The password should be the same for all the credentials that belong to the user. Otherwise, only the credentials encrypted with the user's password are used at login, and the user has to run `chkey`(1) with the `-p` option.

The following example shows how to add a DES credential when other authentication mechanisms are configured on the system.

```
paperbark% nisaddcred -p unix.2990@some.domain.com
  -P user1.some.domain.com dh192-0
```

Exit Status

0	Successful completion.
1	An error occurred.

Attributes

See `attributes`(5) for descriptions of the following attributes.

Attribute Type	Attribute Value
Availability	SUNWnisu

See Also

`chkey`(1), `keylogin`(1), `nis+`(1), `nischmod`(1), `nischown`(1), `nismatch`(1), `nistbladm`(1), `ps`(1), `domainname`(1M), `nisclient`(1M), `nispopulate`(1M), `nis_groups`(3N),`nis_local_names`(3N),`nis_objects`(3N),`rpc_clnt_auth`(3N), `secure_rpc`(3N), `attributes`(5)

nisaddent — Create NIS+ Tables from Corresponding /etc Files or NIS Maps

Synopsis

```
/usr/lib/nis/nisaddent [-D defaults] [-Paorv] [-t table] type [nisdomain]
/usr/lib/nis/nisaddent [-D defaults] [-Paprmov] -f file [-t table] type
  [nisdomain]
/usr/lib/nis/nisaddent [-D defaults] [-Parmv] [-t table] -y ypdomain
  [-Y map] type [nisdomain]
/usr/lib/nis/nisaddent -d [-AMoq] [-t table] type [nisdomain]
```

Description

Use the `nisaddent` command to create entries in NIS+ tables from their corresponding /etc files and NIS maps. This operation is customized for each of the standard tables that are used in the administration of Solaris systems. The `type` argument specifies the type of the data being processed. Legal values for this type are one of `aliases`, `bootparams`, `ethers`, `group`, `hosts`, `netid`, `netmasks`, `networks`, `passwd`, `protocols`, `publickey`, `rpc`, `services`, `shadow`, or `timezone` for the standard tables, or `key-value` for a generic two-column (`key`, `value`) table. You can administer a site-specific table that is not of key-value type with `nistbladm(1)`.

> **Note** — It is easier to use `nispopulate(1M)` instead of `nisaddent` to populate the system tables.

Before you use `nisaddent`, the NIS+ tables should have already been created with `nistbladm(1)`, `nissetup(1M)`, or `nisserver(1M)`.

By default, `nisaddent` reads from the standard input and adds this data to the NIS+ table associated with the type specified on the command line. You can specify an alternate NIS+ table with the `-t` option. For type `key-value`, a table specification is required.

> **Note** — The data type can be different than the table name (`-t`). For example, the automounter tables have `key-value` as the table type.

Although there is a `shadow` data type, there is no corresponding shadow table. Both the `shadow` and the `passwd` data are stored in the `passwd` table itself.

You can process files with the `-f` option, and NIS version 2 (YP) maps with the `-y` option. The `merge` option is not available when reading data from standard input.

When you specify a `ypdomain`, the `nisaddent` command takes its input from the dbm files for the appropriate NIS map (`mail.aliases`, `bootparams`, `ethers.byaddr`, `group.byname`, `hosts.byaddr`, `netid.byname`, `netmasks.byaddr`, `networks.byname`, `passwd.byname`, `protocols.byname`, `publickey.byname`, `rpc.bynumber`, `services.byname`, or `timezone.byname`). You can specify an alternate NIS map with the `-Y` option. A map specification is required for type `key-value`. The map must be in the `/var/yp/ypdomain` directory on the local machine. Note that `ypdomain` is case sensitive. You can use `ypxfr(1M)` to get the NIS maps.

If you specify a `nisdomain`, `nisaddent` operates on the NIS+ table in that NIS+ domain; otherwise, the default domain is used.

In terms of performance, loading up the tables is fastest when done through the dbm files (`-y`).

To accommodate other credential entries used by other authentication mechanisms stored in the cred.org_dir table, the publickey dump output has been modified to include a special algorithm type field. This format is incompatible with older versions of nisaddent. To produce dumps that can be read by older versions of nisaddent or to load dumps created by such older versions, use the -o option.

Options

-a   Add the file or map to the NIS+ table without deleting any existing entries (the default). Note that this mode propagates only additions and modifications, not deletions.

-A   Return all the data within the table and all of the data in tables in the initial table's concatenation path.

-d   Dump the NIS+ table to the standard output in the appropriate format for the given type. For tables of type key-value, use niscat(1) instead. To dump the cred table, dump the publickey and the netid types.

-D defaults   Specify a different set of defaults to be used during this operation. The defaults string is a series of tokens separated by colons. These tokens represent the default values to be used for the generic object properties. All of the legal tokens are described below.

         ttl=time   Set the default time-to-live for objects that are created by this command. The value time is specified in the format as defined by the nischttl(1) command. The default is 12 hours.

         owner=ownername

             Specify that the NIS+ principal ownername owns the created object. The default for this value is the principal who is executing the command.

         group=groupname

             Specify groupname as the group owner for the object that is created. The default is null.

         access=rights

             Specify the set of access rights that are to be granted for the given object. Specify the value rights in the format as defined by the nischmod(1) command. The default is ----rmcdr---r---.

-f file   Use file as the source of input (instead of the standard input).

-m   Merge the file or map with the NIS+ table. This option is the most efficient way to bring an NIS+ table up-to-date with a file or NIS map when there are only a small number of changes. This option adds entries that are not already in the database, modifies entries that already exist (if changed), and deletes any entries that are not in the source. Use the -m option whenever the database is large and replicated and the map being loaded differs only in a few entries. This option reduces the number of update messages that have to be sent to the replicas. Also see the -r option.

-M   Send lookups to the master server. This option guarantees that the most up-to-date information is seen at the possible expense that the master server may be busy or that it may be made busy by this operation.

-o   Use strictly conforming `publickey` files. Dumps do not add the algorithm type field used by additional authentication mechanisms that might be configured with `nisauthconf`(1M). 192-bit keys that are dumped by this option can be read by previous versions of `nisaddent`. However, the algorithm field is lost and assumed to be 0 when read. Use the -o option when reading `publickey` files from previous versions of `nisaddent` to avoid warnings about the missing algorithm field.

-p   Process the password field when loading password information from a file. By default, the password field is ignored because it is usually not valid (the actual password appears in a `shadow` file).

-P   Follow concatenation path. Lookups follow the concatenation path of a table if the initial search is unsuccessful.

-q   Dump tables in "quick" mode. The default method for dumping tables processes each entry individually. For some tables (such as `hosts`), multiple entries must be combined into a single line, so extra requests to the server must be made. In "quick" mode, all of the entries for a table are retrieved in one call to the server, so the table can be dumped more quickly. However, for large tables, there is a chance that the process runs out of virtual memory and the table is not dumped.

-r   Replace the file or map in the existing NIS+ table by first deleting any existing entries and then adding the entries from the source (`/etc` files, or NIS+ maps). This option has the same effect as the -m option. The use of this option is strongly discouraged unless there are a large number of changes because of its adverse impact on performance.

-t *table*   Specify *table* as the NIS+ table for this operation. *table* should be a relative name compared to your default domain or the domain name if it has been specified.

-v   Display verbose output.

-y *ypdomain* Use the dbm files for the appropriate NIS map, from the NIS domain *ypdomain*, as the source of input. The files are expected to be on the local machine in the `/var/yp/ypdomain` directory. If the system is not an NIS server, use `ypxfr`(1M) to get a copy of the dbm files for the appropriate map.

-Y *map*   Use the dbm files for *map* as the source of input.

Examples

The following example adds the contents of /etc/passwd to the passwd.org_dir table.

paperbark% **cat /etc/passwd | /usr/lib/nis/nisaddent passwd**

The following example adds the shadow information. Note that the table type here is shadow, not passwd, even though the actual information is stored in the passwd table.

paperbark% **cat /etc/shadow | /usr/lib/nis/nisaddent shadow**

The following example replaces the hosts.org_dir table with the contents of /etc/hosts (in verbose mode).

paperbark% **/usr/lib/nis/nisaddent -rv -f /etc/hosts hosts**

The following example merges the passwd map from myypdomain with the passwd.org_dir.nisdomain table (in verbose mode). The example assumes that the /var/yp/myypdomain directory contains the yppasswd map.

paperbark% **/usr/lib/nis/nisaddent -mv -y myypdomain passwd nisdomain**

The following example merges the auto.master map from myypdomain with the auto_master.org_dir table.

paperbark% **/usr/lib/nis/nisaddent -m -y myypdomain -Y auto.master
-t auto_master.org_dir key-value**

The following example dumps the hosts.org_dir table.

paperbark% **/usr/lib/nis/nisaddent -d hosts**

Environment Variables

NIS_DEFAULTS	Specify a default string that overrides the NIS+ standard *defaults*. If you use the -D option, those values then override both the NIS_DEFAULTS variable and the standard *defaults*. To avoid security accidents, the access rights in the NIS_DEFAULTS variable are ignored for the passwd table (but access rights specified with -D are used).
NIS_PATH	If this variable is set and neither the *nisdomain* nor the table are fully qualified, each directory specified in NIS_PATH is searched until the table is found (see nisdefaults(1)).

Exit Status

0	Successful operation.
1	Failure caused by an error other than parsing.
2	A parsing error occurred on an entry. A parsing error does not terminate the program; the invalid entries are simply skipped.

Attributes

See attributes(5) for descriptions of the following attributes.

Attribute Type	Attribute Value
Availability	SUNWnisu

See Also

niscat(1), nischmod(1), nischttl(1), nisdefaults(1), nistbladm(1), nisauthconf(1M), nispopulate(1M), nisserver(1M), nissetup(1M), ypxfr(1M), hosts(4), passwd(4), shadow(4), attributes(5)

nisauthconf — Configure NIS+ Security

Synopsis

/usr/lib/nis/nisauthconf [-v][*mechanism*,...]

Description

Use the nisauthconf command to control which authentication flavors NIS+ should use when communicating with other NIS+ clients and servers. If the command is not executed, then NIS+ defaults to AUTH_DES when running security level 2. See rpc.nisd(1M).

nisauthconf takes a list of authentication mechanism's in order of preference. An authentication mechanism can use one or more authentication flavors listed below. If des is the only specified mechanism, then NIS+ can use AUTH_DES only with other NIS+ clients and servers. If des is the first mechanism, then other authentication mechanisms after des are ignored by NIS+, except for nisaddcred(1M). After changing the mechanism configuration, you must restart the keyserv(1M) daemon.

> **Note —** Restarting the keyserv daemon removes encryption keys stored by the running keyserv process. Rebooting is usually the safest option when you change the mechanism configuration.

The following authentication mechanisms are available.

Mechanism	Authentication Flavor
des	AUTH_DES.
dh640-0	RPCSEC_GSS using 640-bit Diffie-Hellman keys.
dh1024-0	RPCSEC_GSS using 1024-bit Diffie-Hellman keys.

If you specify no mechanisms, then a list of currently configured mechanisms is printed.

> **Note** — An NIS+ client of a server that is configured for either dh640-0 or dh1024-0 must run Solaris 7, even if the server is also configured with des.

Options

-v   Display a verbose table listing the currently configured
                        authentication mechanisms.

Examples

The following example, executed as root, configures a system to use only the RPCSEC_GSS authentication flavor with 640-bit Diffie-Hellman keys.

/usr/lib/nis/nisauthconf dh640-0

The following example configures a system to use both RPCSEC_GSS (with 640-bit Diffie-Hellman keys) and AUTH_DES authentication flavors.

/usr/lib/nis/nisauthconf dh640-0 des

You can use the following example when transitioning to other authentication flavors while adding credentials for a new mechanism and before NIS+ is authenticating with the new mechanism.

/usr/lib/nis/nisauthconf des dh640-0

> **Note** — Except for nisaddcred(1M), NIS+ does not use mechanisms that follow des.

Exit Status

0   Successful completion.

1   An error occurred.

Files

/etc/rpcsec/nisplussec.conf

                        NIS+ authentication configuration file. This file may change or be
                        removed in future versions of Solaris.

Attributes

See attributes(5) for descriptions of the following attributes.

Attribute Type	Attribute Value
Availability	SUNWnisu

See Also

nis+(1), keyserv(1M), nisaddcred(1M), rpc.nisd(1M), attributes(5)

nisbackup — Back Up NIS+ Directories

Synopsis

```
/usr/sbin/nisbackup [-v] backup-dir directory...
/usr/sbin/nisbackup [-v] -a backup-dir
```

Description

Use the nisbackup command to back up an NIS+ directory object on an NIS+ master server. Updates to the NIS+ database are temporarily disabled while nisbackup is running. The *backup-dir* is a UNIX directory that must exist before you run nisbackup. You can use the nisbackup command to back up an individual NIS+ directory object or all (-a) of the NIS+ directory objects served by a master server. The NIS+ directory objects being backed up are put into subdirectories under the *backup-dir* directory. These subdirectories are named according to the NIS+ directory object they contain. nisbackup operates on individual NIS+ directory objects (for example, org_dir.wiz.com). This naming scheme enables you to selectively back up specific directories.

The rpc.nisd(1M) process must be running on the master server with a stable NIS+ database for nisbackup to complete. nisbackup does not try to correct any corruption in the NIS+ database, so it is important that backups be done regularly as part of the NIS+ administration.

Use the first synopsis to back up a single NIS+ directory object or a list of NIS+ directory objects. The objects can be partially qualified or fully qualified. The machine on which the command is executing must be the master for the NIS+ directory objects specified.

Use the second synopsis to back up all of the NIS+ directory objects that are served by this master. The -a option is the recommended method of backing up a master server because it backs up all NIS+ directory objects that are served by this master. If this server is a master server for more than one domain, the backup includes NIS+ directories that belong to all of the domains served. You can choose individual NIS+ directory objects for restoring from a *backup-dir* created with the -a option (see nisrestore(1M)).

Notes

The -a option includes only directory objects for which this server is the master. It is possible, but not recommended, to configure a master server as a replica for other domains. The objects belonging to those replicated domains are not backed up with the -a option. The backup of replicated objects must be run on the master server for those objects.

Do not use the same *backup-dir* to back up different master servers. Each master server must have its own *backup-dir*.

nisbackup sets the rpc.nisd(1M) to read-only mode, which disables updates to the NIS+ database. This mode change is needed to ensure the consistency of the backup. Because of the mode change to rpc.nisd, you should not run nisbackup while large numbers of updates are being applied to the NIS+ database. Update commands such as nisaddent(1M) should not be run simultaneously with nisbackup.

Options

-a	Create a backup of all NIS+ directory objects for which this server is a master.
-v	Produce and send additional output to syslog(3) on execution of the command (see syslog.conf(4)).

Operands

backup-dir	Specify the directory into which the subdirectories containing the backed-up objects are placed. This directory must be created before nisbackup is run.
directory	Specify the NIS+ directory object(s) being backed up.

Examples

The following example backs up the org_dir NIS+ directory object of the domain foo.com on a master server to a directory named /backup.

```
master_server# nisbackup /backup org_dir.foo.com.
```

The following example backs up the several tables in the NIS+ domain foo.com to a directory named /backup.

```
master_server# nisbackup /backup foo.com. org_dir.foo.com.
   groups_dir.foo.com. ctx_dir.foo.com.
```

The following example backs up an entire NIS+ database to a backup directory named /backup.

```
master_server# nisbackup -a /backup
```

Exit Status

0	Successful completion.
1	An error occurred.

Files

/backup-dir/backup-list	
	ASCII file containing a list of all the objects contained in the *backup-dir* directory.
/backup-dir/directory-object	
	A subdirectory created in the *backup-dir*. Contains the NIS+ *directory-object* backup.
*/backup-dir/directory-object/*data	
	A subdirectory containing the data files that are part of the NIS+ *directory-object* backup.

*/backup-dir/directory-object/*last.upd

> A data file containing timestamp information about the
> *directory-object.*

*/backup-dir/directory-object/*data.dict

> An NIS+ data dictionary for all of the objects contained in the NIS+
> *directory-object* backup.

Attributes

See attributes(5) for descriptions of the following attributes.

Attribute Type	Attribute Value
Availability	SUNWnisu

See Also

nis+(1), nisdefaults(1), nisrm(1), nisrestore(1M), rpc.nisd(1M),
syslog(3), xfn(3N), nisfiles(4), syslog.conf(4), attributes(5)

nisclient — Initialize NIS+ Credentials for NIS+ Principals

Synopsis

```
/usr/lib/nis/nisclient -c [-x][-o][-v][-l network-passwd]
  [-d NIS+-domain] client-name...
/usr/lib/nis/nisclient -i [-x][-v] -h NIS+-server-host
  [-an NIS+-server-addr][-k key-domain][-d NIS+-domain][-S 0 | 2]
/usr/lib/nis/nisclient -u [-x][-v]
/usr/lib/nis/nisclient -r [-x]
```

Description

Use the nisclient command in the following ways.

- To create NIS+ credentials for hosts and users.
- To initialize NIS+ hosts and users.
- To restore the network service environment.

NIS+ credentials provide authentication information of NIS+ clients to NIS+ service.

Creating NIS+ Credentials for Hosts and Users

Use the first synopsis (-c) to create individual NIS+ credentials for hosts or users. You must be logged in as an NIS+ principal in the domain for which you are creating the new credentials. You must also have write permission to the local cred table. The *client-name* argument accepts any valid host or user name in the NIS+ domain (for example, the *client-name* must exist in the hosts or passwd table). nisclient verifies each *client-name* against both the host and passwd tables, then adds the proper NIS+ credentials for hosts or users.

Note — If you are creating NIS+ credentials outside of your local domain, the host or user must exist in the host or passwd tables in both the local and remote domains.

By default, nisclient does not overwrite existing entries in the credential table for the hosts and users specified. To overwrite, use the -o option. After the credentials have been created, nisclient prints the command that must be executed on the client machine to initialize the host or the user. The -c option requires a client network password, which is used to encrypt the secret key for the client. You can either specify the password on the command line with the -l option or the command prompts you for it. You can change this network password later with nispasswd(1) or chkey(1).

nisclient -c is not intended to be used to create NIS+ credentials for all users and hosts that are defined in the passwd and hosts tables. To define credentials for all users and hosts, use nispopulate(1M).

Initializing NIS+ Hosts

Use the second synopsis (-i) to initialize an NIS+ client machine. You can use the -i option to convert machines to use NIS+ or to change the machine's domain name. You must be logged in as superuser on the machine that is to become an NIS+ client. Your administrator must have already created the NIS+ credential for this host by using nisclient -c or nispopulate -C. You need the network password your administrator created. nisclient prompts you for the network password to decrypt your secret key and then for this machine's root login password to generate a new set of secret/public keys. If the NIS+ credential was created by your administrator by means of nisclient -c, then you can simply use the initialization command that was printed by the nisclient command to initialize this host instead of typing it manually.

To initialize an unauthenticated NIS+ client machine, use the -i option with -S 0. With these options, the nisclient -i option does not ask for any passwords.

During the client initialization process, files that are being modified are backed up as *files*.no_nisplus. The following files are usually modified during a client initialization:/etc/defaultdomain,/etc/nsswitch.conf,/etc/inet/hosts,and,if it exists, /var/nis/NIS_COLD_START.

Note — A file is not saved if a backup file already exists.

The -i option does not set up an NIS+ client to resolve hostnames using DNS. Please refer to the DNS documentation for information on setting up DNS. (See resolv.conf(4)).

You do not need to initialize either NIS+ root master servers or machines that were installed as NIS+ clients by suninstall(1M).

Initializing an NIS+ User

Use the third synopsis (-u) to initialize an NIS+ user. You must be logged in as the user on an NIS+ client machine in the domain where your NIS+ credentials have been created. Your administrator should have already created the NIS+ credential for your user name by using nisclient -c or nispopulate(1M). You need the network password your administrator used to create the NIS+ credential for your user name. nisclient prompts you for this network password to decrypt your secret key and then for your login password to generate a new set of secret/public keys.

Restoring the Network Service Environment

Use the fourth synopsis (-r) to restore the network service environment to whatever you were using before nisclient -i was executed. You must be logged in as superuser on the machine that is to be restored. The restore works only if the machine was initialized with nisclient -i because it uses the backup files created by the -i option.

After initializing a machine or restoring the network service, reboot the machine.

Options

-an NIS+-server-addr

> Specify the IP address for the NIS+ server. Use this option only with the -i option.

-c   Add DES credentials for NIS+ principals.

-d NIS+-domain

> Specify the NIS+ domain where the credential should be created when used in conjunction with the -c option. Specify the name for the new NIS+ domain when used in conjunction with the -i option. The default is the current domain name.

-h NIS+-server-host

> Specify the NIS+ server's host name. Use this option only with the -i option.

-i   Initialize an NIS+ client machine.

-l network-password

> Specify the network password for the clients. Use this option only with the -c option. If you do not specify this option, nisclient prompts you for the network password.

-k key-domain

> Specify the domain where root's credentials are stored. If you do not specify a domain, assume the system default domain.

-o   Overwrite existing credential entries. The default is not to overwrite. Use this option only with the -c option.

-r   Restore the network service environment.

-S 0|2   Specify the authentication level for the NIS+ client. Level 0 is for unauthenticated clients and level 2 is for authenticated (DES) clients. The default is to set up with level 2 authentication. Use this option only with the -i option. nisclient always uses level 2 authentication (DES) for both -c and -u options. You do not need to run nisclient with -u and -c for level 0 authentication. To configure authentication mechanisms other than DES at security level 2, use nisauthconf(1M) before running nisclient.

-u   Initialize an NIS+ user.

-v   Run the script in verbose mode.

-x   Turn the echo mode on and simply print the commands that would be
              executed. Note that the commands are not actually executed. The
              default is off.

Examples

The following example adds the DES credential for host `sunws` and user `fred` in the local
domain.

`paperbark% `**`/usr/lib/nis/nisclient -c sunws fred`**

The following example adds the DES credential for host `sunws` and user `fred` in
domain `xyz.sun.com.`.

`# `**`/usr/lib/nis/nisclient -c -d xyz.sun.com. sunws fred`**

The following example initializes host `sunws` as an NIS+ client in domain
`xyz.sun.com.` where `nisplus_server` is a server for the domain `xyz.sun.com.`.

`# `**`/usr/lib/nis/nisclient -i -h nisplus_server -d xyz.sun.com.`**

If the server is not found in the `/etc/hosts` file, the command prompts you for the IP
address of `nisplus_server`. The `-d` option is needed only if your current domain name
is different from the new domain name.

The following example initializes host `sunws` as an unauthenticated NIS+ client in
domain `xyz.sun.com.` where `nisplus_server` is a server for the domain
`xyz.sun.com.`.

`# `**`/usr/lib/nis/nisclient -i -S 0 -h nisplus_server -d xyz.sun.com. -a`**
`129.140.44.1`

The following example initializes user `fred` as an NIS+ principal when you are
logged in as user `fred` on an NIS+ client machine.

`# `**`/usr/lib/nis/nisclient -u`**

Files

`/var/nis/NIS_COLD_START`

              A list of servers, their transport addresses, and their Secure RPC
              public keys that serve the machines default domain.

`/etc/defaultdomain`

              The system default domain name.

`/etc/nsswitch.conf`

              Configuration file for the nameservice switch.

`/etc/inet/hosts`

              Local host name database.

Attributes

See attributes(5) for descriptions of the following attributes.

Attribute Type	Attribute Value
Availability	SUNWnisu

See Also

chkey(1), keylogin(1), nis+(1), nispasswd(1), keyserv(1M),
nisaddcred(1M), nisauthconf(1M), nisinit(1M), nispopulate(1M),
suninstall(1M), nsswitch.conf(4), resolv.conf(4), attributes(5)

nisd — NIS+ Service Daemon

Synopsis

/usr/sbin/rpc.nisd [-ACDFhlv][-Y [-B [-t *netid*]]][-d *dictionary*]
   [-L *load*][-S *level*]

Description

See rpc.nisd(1M).

nisd_resolv — NIS+ Service Daemon

Synopsis

/usr/sbin/rpc.nisd_resolv [-v | -V][-F [-C *fd*]][-t *xx*][-p *yy*]

Description

See rpc.nisd(1M).

nisinit — NIS+ Client and Server Initialization Command

Synopsis

/usr/sbin/nisinit -r
/usr/sbin/nisinit -p Y | D | N *parent-domain host*...
/usr/sbin/nisinit -c [-k *key-domain*] -H *hostname* | -B | -C *coldstart*

Description

You can use the `nisinit` command to initialize a machine to be an NIS+ client or an NIS+ root master server.

> **Note** — It may be easier to use `nisclient`(1M) or `nisserver`(1M) to accomplish this same task.

Options

`-r` Initialize the system to be an NIS+ root server. Create the file `/var/nis/data/root.object` and initialize it to contain information about this system. Use the `sysinfo`(2) system call to retrieve the name of the default domain.

To initialize the machine as an NIS+ root server, it is advisable to use the `-r` option of `nisserver`(1M) instead of using `nisinit -r`.

`-p Y | D | N` *parent-domain host...*

Use on a root server to initialize a `/var/nis/data/parent.object` to make this domain a part of the namespace above it. Only root servers can have parent objects. A parent object describes the namespace above the NIS+ root. If this domain is isolated, do not use this option. The argument to this option tells the command what type of nameserver is serving the domain above the NIS+ domain. When clients try to resolve a name that is outside of the NIS+ namespace, this object is returned with the error `NIS_FOREIGNNS` indicating that a namespace boundary has been reached. It is up to the client to continue the name resolution process.

parent-domain is the name of the parent domain in a syntax that is native to that type of domain. The list of host names that follow the domain parameter are the names of hosts that serve the parent domain. If a parent domain has more than one server, specify the master server for that domain as the first host.

`Y` Specify that the parent directory is an NIS version 2 domain.

`D` Specify that the parent directory is a DNS domain.

`N` Specify that the parent directory is another NIS+ domain. This option is useful for connecting a preexisting NIS+ subtree into the global namespace.

Note that in the current implementation, the NIS+ clients do not take advantage of the `-p` feature. Also, because the parent object is currently not replicated on root replica servers, it is recommended that you do not use this option.

-c   Initialize the system to be an NIS+ client. The three initialization options are initialize by cold start, initialize by host name, and initialize by broadcast. The most secure mechanism is to initialize from a trusted coldstart file. The second option is to initialize by using a host name that you specify as a trusted host. The third and least secure method is to initialize by broadcast.

-C *coldstart* Use the *coldstart* file as a prototype coldstart file when initializing an NIS+ client. This coldstart file can be copied from a machine that is already a client of the NIS+ namespace. For maximum security, you can encrypt (with crypt(1) and encode (with uuencode(1C)) the coldstart file and mail it to an administrator bringing up a new system. The new administrator would then decode (with uudecode), decrypt (wth crypt), and then use this file with the nisinit command to initialize the machine as an NIS+ client. If the coldstart file is from another client in the same domain, you can safely skip the nisinit command and copy the file into the /var/nis directory as /var/nis/NIS_COLD_START.

-H *hostname* Specify the host *hostname* as a trusted NIS+ server. The nisinit command iterates over each transport in the NETPATH environment variable and tries to contact rpcbind(1M) on that system. This *hostname* must be reachable from the client without the nameservice running. For IP networks, this means that there must be an entry in /etc/hosts for this host when nisinit is invoked.

-B   Use an IP broadcast to locate an NIS+ server on the local subnet. Any system that is running the NIS+ service can answer. No guarantees are made that the server that answers is a server of the organization's namespace. If you use this option, it is advisable to check that the server and domain served are valid. The binding information can be dumped to the standard output with the nisshowcache(1M) command.

Note that nisinit -c just enables navigation of the NIS+ namespace from this client. To make NIS+ your nameservice, modify the file /etc/nsswitch.conf to reflect that. See nsswitch.conf(4) for more details.

-k *key-domain*

Specify the domain where root's credentials are stored. If you do not specify the domain, assume the system default domain. This domain name is used to create the /var/nis/NIS_COLD_START file.

Exit Status

0   Success.

1   Failure.

Examples

The following example initializes the machine as an NIS+ client, using the host freddy as a trusted server.

nisinit -cH freddy

The following example sets up a client, using a trusted coldstart file.

nisinit -cC /tmp/colddata

The following example sets up a client, using an IP broadcast.

nisinit -cB

The following example sets up a root server.

nisinit -r

Environment Variables

NETPATH   You can set this environment variable to the transports to try when contacting the NIS+ server (see netconfig(4)). The client library tries to contact the server by using only connection-oriented transports.

Files

/var/nis/NIS_COLD_START

A list of servers, their transport addresses, and their Secure RPC public keys that serve the machine's default domain.

/var/nis/data/root.object

The root object of the NIS+ namespace. It is a standard XDR-encoded NIS+ directory object that can be modified by authorized clients using the nis_modify() interface.

/var/nis/data/parent.object

The namespace that is logically above the NIS+ namespace. The most common type of parent object is a DNS object. This object contains contact information for a server of that domain.

/etc/hosts   Internet host table.

Attributes

See `attributes`(5) for descriptions of the following attributes.

Attribute Type	Attribute Value
Availability	SUNWnisu

See Also

```
nis+(1), uuencode(1C), nisclient(1M), nisserver(1M), nisshowcache(1M),
sysinfo(2), hosts(4), netconfig(4), nisfiles(4), attributes(5)
```

nislog — Display the Contents of the NIS+ Transaction Log

Synopsis

```
/usr/sbin/nislog [-h num | -t num][-v][directory...]
```

Description

Use the `nislog` command to display the contents of the NIS+ server transaction log on the standard output. You can use this command to track changes in the namespace. The `/var/nis/trans.log` file contains the transaction log maintained by the NIS+ server. When updates occur, they are logged to this file and then propagated to replicas as log transactions. Each transaction consists of the particulars of the transaction and a copy of the object definition. When the log is checkpointed, updates that have been propagated to the replicas are removed.

Only superuser can run the `nislog` command on an NIS+ server. It displays the log entries for that server only.

If you do not specify `directory`, the entire log is searched. Otherwise, only those logs entries that correspond to the specified directories are displayed.

Options

-h *num*	Display *num* transactions from the head of the log. If the numeric parameter is 0, display only the log header.
-t *num*	Display *num* transactions from the tail of the log. If the numeric parameter is 0, display only the log header.
-v	Display verbose information.

Examples

The following example shows the transaction log entry that was made when the `doc.com.` directory was first created. `XID` refers to the transaction ID.

```
# /usr/sbin/nislog -h 1
NIS Log printing facility.
NIS Log dump:
 Log state : STABLE
```

```
Number of updates : 48
Current XID : 39
Size of log in bytes : 18432
***UPDATES***
@@@@@@@@@@@@@@@TRANSACTION@@@@@@@@@@@@@@@
#00000, XID : 1
Time : Fri Mar 24 11:45:32 2000
Directory : doc.com.
Entry type : ADD Name
Entry timestamp : Fri Mar 24 11:45:32 2000
Principal : rootmaster.doc.com.
Object name : org_dir.doc.com.
.................Object.....................
Object Name : org_dir
Owner : rootmaster.doc.com.
Group : admin.doc.com.
Domain : doc.com.
Access Rights : r---rmcdr---r---
Time to Live : 24:0:0
Object Type : DIRECTORY
Name : `org_dir.doc.com.'
Type: NIS
Master Server : rootmaster.doc.com.
  .
  .
.............................................
@@@@@@@@@@@@@@@TRANSACTION@@@@@@@@@@@@@@@
#00000, XID : 2
#
```

The following example clears the NIS log file.

```
# cat /dev/null > /usr/adm/nislog
#
```

Files

```
/var/nis/trans.log
```
                        Transaction log.

Attributes

See attributes(5) for descriptions of the following attributes.

Attribute Type	Attribute Value
Availability	SUNWnisu

See Also

```
nis+(1), rpc.nisd(1M), nisfiles(4), attributes(5)
```

nispasswdd — NIS+ Password Update Daemon

Synopsis
    /usr/sbin/rpc.nispasswdd [-a attempts][-c minutes][-D][-g][-v]

Description
    See rpc.nispasswdd(1M).

nisping — Send ping to NIS+ Servers

Synopsis
    /usr/lib/nis/nisping [-uf][-H hostname][-r | directory]
    /usr/lib/nis/nisping -C [-a][-H hostname][directory]

Description
Use the nisping command to send a ping to replica servers, telling them to ask the master service for immediate updates.

In the first synopsis, the nisping command sends a ping to all replicas of an NIS+ directory. Once a replica receives a ping, it checks with the master server for the directory from which to get updates. Before pinging the replicas, nisping tries to determine the last update "seen" by a replica and the last update logged by the master. If these two timestamps are the same, the ping is not sent. You can use the -f (force) option to override this feature.

Under normal circumstances, NIS+ replica servers get the new information from the master NIS+ server within a short time. Therefore, you should not need to use nisping in the first synopsis form.

In the second synopsis, the nisping -C command sends a checkpoint request to the servers. If you specify no directory, the home domain, as returned by nisdefaults(1), is checkpointed. If all directories served by a given server have to be checkpointed, then use the -a option.

On receiving a checkpoint request, the servers commit all the updates for the given directory from the table log files to the database files. When the nisping command is sent to the master server, it also sends updates to the replicas if they are out of date. The -C option is needed because the database log files for NIS+ are not automatically checkpointed. You should use nisping at frequent intervals (such as once a day) to checkpoint the NIS+ database log files. You can add this command to the crontab(1) file to automate checkpointing. If the database log files are not checkpointed, their sizes continue to grow.

> **Note** — If the server specified by the -H option does not serve the directory, then no ping is sent.
>
> Per-server and per-directory access restrictions may apply; see nisopaccess(1). nisping uses NIS_CPTIME and NIS_PING—resync (ping) of

replicas—or `NIS_CHECKPOINT` for checkpoint. Because the `NIS_PING` operation does not return a status, the `nisping` command is typically unable to indicate success or failure for resyncs.

Options

`-a`	Checkpoint all directories on the server.
`-C`	Send a request to checkpoint instead of a ping, to each server. The servers schedule to commit all the transactions to stable storage.
`-H` *hostname*	Send the ping, check for an update time, or checkpoint only the host *hostname*.
`-f`	Force a ping, even though the timestamps indicate there is no reason to do so. This option is useful for debugging.
`-r`	Update or get status about the root object from the root servers, especially when new root replicas are added or deleted from the list.
	If used without the `-u` option, `-r` sends a ping request to the servers serving the root domain. When the replicas receive a ping, they update their root object if needed.
	You can use the `-r` option with all other options except with the `-C` option; the root object need not be checkpointed.
`-u`	Display the time of the last update; send no servers a ping.

Exit Status

`-1`	No servers were contacted, or the server specified by the `-H` option could not be contacted.
`0`	Success.
`1`	Some, but not all, servers were successfully contacted.

Examples

The following example pings all replicas of the default domain.

`paperbark% `**`/usr/lib/nis/nisping`**

Note — The above example does not ping the `org_dir` and `groups_dir` subdirectories within this domain.

The following example pings the server `example`, which is a replica of the `org_dir.foo.com.` directory.

`paperbark% `**`/usr/lib/nis/nisping -H example org_dir.foo.com.`**

The following example checkpoints all servers of the `org_dir.bar.com.` directory.

`paperbark% `**`/usr/lib/nis/nisping -C org_dir.bar.com.`**

Environment Variables

NIS_PATH   If this variable is set and the NIS+ directory name is not fully qualified, search each directory specified until the directory is found.

Attributes

See attributes(5) for descriptions of the following attributes.

Attribute Type	Attribute Value
Availability	SUNWnisu

See Also

crontab(1), nisdefaults(1), nisopaccess(1), nislog(1M), nisfiles(4), *New!*
attributes(5)

---

nispopulate — Populate the NIS+ Tables in an NIS+ Domain

Synopsis

```
/usr/lib/nis/nispopulate -Y [-x][-f][-n][-u][-v][-S 0 | 2]
   [-l network-passwd][-d NIS+-domain] -h NIS-server-host
   [-an NIS-server-addr] -y NIS-domain [table]...
/usr/lib/nis/nispopulate -F [-x][-f][-u][-v][-S 0 | 2]
   [-d NIS+-domain][-l network-passwd][-p directory-path][table]...
/usr/lib/nis/nispopulate -C [-x][-f][-v][-d NIS+-domain]
   [-l network-passwd][hosts | passwd]
```

Description

Use the nispopulate command to populate NIS+ tables in a specified domain from their corresponding files or NIS maps. nispopulate assumes that the tables have been created either through nisserver(1M) or nissetup(1M).

The *table* argument accepts standard names that are used in the administration of Solaris systems and nonstandard key-value type tables. See nisaddent(1M) for more information on key-value type tables. If the table argument is not specified, nispopulate automatically populates each of the standard tables. These standard (default) tables are: aliases, auto_master, auto_home, bootparams, ethers, group, hosts, netgroup, netmasks, networks, passwd, protocols, rpc, services, and shadow. Note that the shadow table is used only when populating from files. The nonstandard tables that nispopulate accepts are those of *key-value* type. These tables must first be created manually with the nistbladm(1) command.

Use the first synopsis (-Y) to populate NIS+ tables from NIS maps. nispopulate uses ypxfr(1M) to transfer the NIS maps from the NIS servers to the /var/yp/*NIS-domain* directory on the local machine. Then, it uses these files as the input source. Note that *NIS-domain* is case sensitive. Make sure there is enough disk space for that directory.

Use the second synopsis (-F) to populate NIS+ tables from local files. nispopulate uses those files that match the table name as input sources in the current working directory or in the specified directory.

Note — When populating the hosts and passwd tables, nispopulate automatically creates the NIS+ credentials for all users and hosts that are defined in the hosts and passwd tables. A network password is required to create these credentials. This network password is used to encrypt the secret key for the new users and hosts. You can specify this password with the -l option, or nispopulate uses the default password, nisplus. nispopulate does not overwrite any existing credential entries in the credential table. Use nisclient(1M) to overwrite the entries in the cred table. nispopulate creates both LOCAL and DES credentials for users, and DES credentials only for hosts. To disable automatic credential creation, specify the -S 0 option.

Use the third synopsis (-C) to populate the NIS+ credential table with level 2 authentication (DES) from the passwd and hosts tables of the specified domain. The valid *table* arguments for this operation are passwd and hosts. If you do not specify this argument, then nispopulate uses both passwd and hosts as the input source. If other authentication mechanisms are configured by nisauthconf(1M), the NIS+ credential table is loaded with credentials for those mechanisms.

If nispopulate was earlier used with -S 0 option, then no credentials were added for the hosts or the users. If later the site decides to add credentials for all users and hosts, you can use the -C option to add credentials.

Options

-an NIS-*server-addr*

> Specify the IP address for the NIS server. Use this option only with the -Y option.

-C

> Populate the NIS+ credential table from passwd and hosts tables using DES authentication (security level 2). If other authentication mechanisms are configured with nisauthconf(1M), populate the NIS+ credential table with credentials for those mechanisms.

-d NIS+-*domain*

> Specify the NIS+ domain. The default is the local domain.

-F

> Populate NIS+ tables from files.

-f

> Force population of the NIS+ tables without prompting for confirmation.

-h NIS-*server-host*

> Specify the NIS server host name used as a source to copy the NIS maps. Use this option only with the -Y option. This host must already exist in either the NIS+ hosts table or /etc/hosts file. If the host name is not defined, prompt you for the IP address. Alternatively, you can use the -a option to specify the address.

-l *network-passwd*

Specify the network password for populating the NIS+ credential table. Use this option only when you are populating the hosts and passwd tables. The default passwd is nisplus.

-n

Do not overwrite local NIS maps in the /var/yp/*nisdomain* directory if they already exist. The default is to overwrite the existing NIS maps in the local /var/yp/*nisdomain* directory. Use this option only with the -Y option.

-p *directory-path*

Specify the directory where the files are stored. Use this option only with the -F option. The default is the current working directory.

-S 0|2

Specify the authentication level for the NIS+ clients. Level 0 is for unauthenticated clients, and no credentials are created for users and hosts in the specified domain. Level 2 is for authenticated (DES) clients, and DES credentials are created for users and hosts in the specified domain. The default is to set up with level 2 authentication (DES). You do not need to run nispopulate with -C for level 0 authentication. Also, if other authentication mechanisms are configured with nisauthconf(1M), populate credentials for those mechanisms for the NIS+ clients.

-u

Update the NIS+ tables (that is, add, delete, or modify) from either files or NIS maps. Use this option to bring an NIS+ table up-to-date when there are only a small number of changes. The default is to add to the NIS+ tables without deleting any existing entries. Also, see the -n option for updating NIS+ tables from existing maps in the /var/yp directory.

-v

Run the command in verbose mode.

-x

Turn on the echo mode. Print the commands that would have executed. Note that the commands are not actually executed. The default is off.

-Y

Populate the NIS+ tables from NIS maps.

-y *NIS-domain*

Specify the NIS domain to copy the NIS maps from. Use this option only with the -Y option. The default domain name is the same as the local domain name.

Examples

The following example populates all the NIS+ standard tables in the domain xyz.sun.com. from NIS maps of the yp.sun.COM domain as input source where host yp_host is a YP server of yp.sun.COM..

```
nis_server# /usr/lib/nis/nispopulate -Y -y yp.sun.COM -h yp_host
  -d xyz.sun.com.
```

The following example updates all of the NIS+ standard tables from the same NIS domain and hosts shown in the previous example.

```
nis_server# /usr/lib/nis/nispopulate -Y -u -y yp.sun.COM -h yp_host
  -d xyz.sun.com.
```

The following example populates the hosts table in domain xyz.sun.com. from the hosts file in the /var/nis/files directory and uses somepasswd as the network password for key encryption.

```
nis_server# /usr/lib/nis/nispopulate -F -p /var/nis/files -l somepasswd
  hosts
```

The following example populates the passwd table in domain xyz.sun.com. from the passwd file in the /var/nis/files directory without automatically creating the NIS+ credentials.

```
nis_server# /usr/lib/nis/nispopulate -F -p /var/nis/files
  -d xys.sun.com. -S 0 passwd
```

The following example populates the credential table in domain xyz.sun.com. for all users defined in the passwd table.

```
nis_server# /usr/lib/nis/nispopulate -C -d xys.sun.com. passwd
```

The following example creates and populates a nonstandard *key-value* type NIS+ table, private, from the file /var/nis/files/private. (nispopulate assumes that the private.org_dirkey-value type table has already been created).

```
nis_server# /usr/bin/nistbladm -D access=og=rmcd,nw=r -c private
  key=S,nogw= value=,nogw= private.org.dir
nis_server# /usr/lib/nis/nispopulate -F -p /var/nis/files private
```

Environment Variables

TMPDIR   Specify a directory to contain temporary files. nispopulate normally creates temporary files in the /tmp directory. If TMPDIR is not a valid directory, then use /tmp.

Files

```
/etc/hosts local
```
         Host-name database.

`/var/yp`   NIS(YP) domain directory.

`/var/nis`   NIS+ domain directory.

`/tmp`   Directory used to contain temporary files.

Attributes

See attributes(5) for descriptions of the following attributes.

Attribute Type	Attribute Value
Availability	SUNWnisu

See Also

```
nis+(1), nistbladm(1), nisaddcred(1M), nisaddent(1M), nisauthconf(1M),
nisclient(1M), nisserver(1M), nissetup(1M), rpc.nisd(1M), ypxfr(1M),
attributes(5)
```

nisprefadm — NIS+ Command to Set Server Preferences for NIS+ Clients

Synopsis

```
/usr/bin/nisprefadm -a {-L | -G} [-o opt-string][-d domain][-C client]
    server...
/usr/bin/nisprefadm -m {-L | -G} [-o opt-string][-d domain][-C client]
    oldserver=newserver...
/usr/bin/nisprefadm -r {-L | -G} [-o opt-string][-d domain][-C client]
    server...
/usr/bin/nisprefadm -u {-L | -G} [-o opt-string][-d domain][-C client]
    server...
/usr/bin/nisprefadm -x {-L | -G} [-d domain][-C client]
/usr/bin/nisprefadm -l {-L | -G} [-d domain][-C client]
/usr/bin/nisprefadm -F
```

Description

Use the nisprefadm command to define which servers are to be preferred by NIS+ clients. This information is used by nis_cachemgr(1M) to control the order in which it selects a server to use for a particular domain. On a client system, the cache manager first looks for a local preferred server list in /var/nis. If it doesn't find one, it looks for an entry with its host name in the NIS+ table. Finally, if it doesn't find the entry there, it looks for an entry for its subnet.

By default, nis_cachemgr puts all servers that are on the same subnet as the client system (that is, local servers) on the preferred server list. In some cases this default preferred server list is inadequate. For example, if all of the servers for a domain are remote but some are closer than others, the cache manager should try to select the closest one. Because the cache manager has no reliable way to determine the distance to remote servers, you use nisprefadm to provide this information.

The preferred server information is stored either globally in an NIS+ table (with the -G option) or locally in a file, /var/nis/client_info (with the -L option). It is preferable to store the information globally so that it can be used by all clients on a subnet. The nis_cachemgr process on a client machine reloads the preferred server information periodically, depending on the machine's setup. If the local file is used, the information is reloaded every 12 hours. If the global table is used, the information is reloaded, based on the TTL value of the client information table. You can change the TTL value with nischttl(1). If you want your changes to take effect immediately, use the nisprefadm -F command. When changing local information (-L), nisprefadm automatically forces nis_cachemgr to reload the information.

The cache manager assigns weights to all of the servers on the preferred list. By default, local servers (that is, servers on the same subnet) are given a weight of 0. Other servers are given the weight, infinite. You can change the weight by using the nisprefadm command and specifying a weight in parentheses after the server name. When selecting a server for a domain, the cache manager first tries to contact the servers with the lowest weight. If it doesn't get a response, it tries the servers with the next lowest weight, and so on. If it fails to get a response from any of the preferred servers, it tries to contact the nonpreferred servers.

The use of weights gives fine control over the server selection process, but you must be careful to avoid assigning too many different weights. For example, if you assign weights 0, 1, 2, and 3 but all of the servers with weight 0, 1, and 2 are unavailable, then there is a noticeable delay in selecting a server because the cache manager waits five seconds for a response at each weight level before moving on to the next one. As a general rule, one or two weight levels provides a good balance of server selection control and performance.

When specifying a server name, you do not need to fully qualify the name. When the cache manager tries to access a domain, it compares the list of servers for the domain with the list of preferred servers. It finds a match if a preferred server name is a prefix of the name of a server for the domain. If a domain is served by two servers with the same prefix, the preferred server name must include enough of the domain name to distinguish the two.

Notes

The nis_cachemgr(1M) process automatically adds local servers (same subnet as the client) to the preferred server list with a weight of 0. Thus, you do not need to specify them, although it does no harm.

If you specify a weight for a server, you probably should quote the parentheses to avoid having the shell interpret them, as shown in the following example.

```
paperbark% nisprefadm -G -a -C client1 "srv1(2)"
```

In general, nis_cachemgr does a fairly good job of selecting servers on its own. Therefore, you do not usually need to use nisprefadm. Some situations in which its use is recommended are listed below.

No local servers, many remote servers

> In this case, nis_cachemgr needs to choose one of the remote servers. Because it doesn't have information on which is closest, it sends a ping to all of them and then selects the one that responds fastest. This behavior may not always select the best server. If some of the servers are closer to the client than the others, they should be listed as preferred servers so that nis_cachemgr tries them first, reducing the amount of network traffic for selecting a server.

Very remote servers

> In some networks, NIS+ servers are reachable only through very slow network connections. It is usually best to avoid unnecessary traffic

over that connection. If the `pref_type=pref_only` option is set along with preferred servers, then only the preferred servers are contacted for domains they serve. The nonpreferred servers are not tried at all; even if all of the preferred servers are unavailable. For domains that are not served by any of the preferred servers, the `pref_only` option is ignored.

Options

When several options are surrounded by braces (that is, by { and }), you must specify one of the options.

`-a`   Add the specified servers to the preferred server list.

`-C client`   Store the preferred server information with the key `client`. The client can be either a host name or a subnet number. When you specify a host name, apply the preferred server information to that host only. When you specify a subnet, apply the preferred server information to all clients on that subnet. The cache manager searches for host-specific entries first. It searches for subnet entries only if no host entry is found. If you do not specify this option, then use the host name of the system on which the command is run.

`-d domain`   Specify the domain to which the command is to apply.

`-F`   Tell `nis_cachemgr(1M)` to refresh its preferred server information. The program periodically does this anyway, but this option forces the refresh immediately. When updating the local information, `nis_cachemgr` automatically refreshes the preferred server information. You must be superuser to use this option.

`-l`   List the current preferred server information.

`{-L | -G}`   Store the preferred server information locally in the file `/var/nis/client_info` (the -L option) or globally in an NIS+ table `client.info.orgdir.domain` (the -G option). If the information is stored locally, then it applies only to the system on which the command is run. If the information is stored globally, then it can apply to all systems on a subnet (depending on the value of the -C option). You must be superuser to use this option.

`-m`   Modify the preferred server list. Replace the server specified by *oldserver* with *newserver*. You typically use this option to change the weight for a server.

`-o opt-string`

                Specify additional options to control server selection. Currently the only valid option is *pref-type*, which can have a value of either `all` (the default) or `pref_only`. If the value is `all`, then the cache manager tries to contact nonpreferred servers if all of the preferred servers fail to respond. If you specify `pref_only`, then it won't try nonpreferred servers. The only exception to this behavior is when a domain is not served by any of the preferred servers. In this case, the cache manager ignores the option. This behavior avoids the need to have preferred servers defined for every domain.

-r   Remove the specified servers from the preferred server list.

-u   Clear the list of preferred servers, and then add the specified servers to the preferred server list.

-x   Remove the preferred server information completely.

Exit Status

0   Successful completion.

1   An error occurred.

Examples

The following example sets the preferred server list for the system on which it is run.

```
paperbark% nisprefadm -L -a srv1 srv2
```

The information is stored in a file, /var/nis/client_info, so it affects only this one system.

The following example has the same effect, but the information is stored in an NIS+ table in the default domain.

```
paperbark% nisprefadm -G -a srv1 srv2
```

You might want to set the preferred server information for a client system other than the one on which you are running the command. The following example sets the preferred server information for a client system named client1.

```
paperbark% nisprefadm -G -a -C client1 srv1 srv2
```

It is common for all client systems on a subnet to use the same set of preferred servers. The following example sets a preferred server list that applies to all clients on subnet 192.85.18.0.

```
paperbark% nisprefadm -G -a -C 192.85.18.0 srv1 srv2
```

Attributes

See attributes(5) for descriptions of the following attributes.

Attribute Type	Attribute Value
Availability	SUNWcsu

See Also

nischttl(1), nis_cachemgr(1M), attributes(5)

nisrestore — Restore NIS+ Directory Backup

Synopsis

```
/usr/sbin/nisrestore [-tv] backup-dir directory...
/usr/sbin/nisrestore [-fv] -a backup-dir
/usr/sbin/nisrestore -t backup-dir
```

Description

Use the nisrestore command to restore an existing backup of an NIS+ directory object that was created with nisbackup(1M). The *backup-dir* is the UNIX directory that contains the NIS+ backup on the server being restored. You can use the nisrestore command to restore an NIS+ directory object or a complete NIS+ database. You can also use it as an "out of band" fast replication for a new replica server being initialized.

> **Note** — You must stop the rpc.nisd(1M) daemon before running nisrestore.

Use the first synopsis to restore a single directory object or a specified list of directory objects. The directory can be partially or fully qualified. The server being restored is verified against the list of servers serving the directory. If this server is not configured to serve this object, nisrestore exits with an error. The -f option overrides this check and forces the operation.

Use the second synopsis to restore all of the directory objects contained in the *backup-dir*. Again, the server is validated against the serving list for each of the directory objects in the *backup-dir*. If one of the objects in the *backup-dir* is not served by this server, nisrestore exits with an error. The -f option overrides this check and forces the operation.

Notes

The -a option tries to restore all NIS+ objects contained in the *backup-dir*. If any of these objects are not served by the server, nisrestore exits with an error. If the *backup-dir* contains objects that are not served by the server, you must execute nisrestore without the -a option and list the specific directory objects.

The -f option disables verification of the server being configured to serve the objects being restored. Use this option with care because you could inadvertently restore data to a server that doesn't serve the restored data. This option is required when you are restoring a single server domain (master server only) or if the other NIS+ servers are unavailable for NIS+ lookups.

Use the combination of the -f and -a options with caution because no validation of the server serving the restored objects is done.

You can quickly add new replicas to a namespace with the nisrestore command. The steps are as follows.

Configure the new replica on the master server (see nisserver(1M)).

```
master# nisserver -R -h replica
```

Kill the rpc.nisd server process on the new replica server.

```
replica# kill rpc.nisd-pid
```

Create a backup of the NIS+ database on the master, which includes the new replica information (see nisbackup(1M)). You need to export /backup (see share_nfs(1M)) to the new replica.

```
master# nisbackup -a /backup
```

Restore the backup of the NIS+ database on the new replica. Use the -f option if nisrestore is unable to look up the NIS+ objects being restored. The backup should be available through NFS or similar means (see share_nfs(1M)).

```
replica# nisrestore -f -a //nfs-mnt/backup
```

Restart the rpc.nisd(1M) process on the new replica, and the server is immediately available for service

Options

-a	Restore all directory objects included in the *backup-dir* partition.
-f	Force the restoration of a directory without the validation of the server in the directory object's serving list.
-t	List all directory objects contained in *backup-dir*.
-v	Produce additional output on execution of the command.

Operands

backup-dir	Specify the UNIX directory that contains the data files for the NIS+ directory objects to be restored.
directory	Specify the NIS+ directory object(s) to be restored. *directory* can be a fully or partially qualified name.

Examples

The following example restores the org_dir directory object of the domain foo.com on a replica server from a local UFS partition named /var/backup.

```
replica_server# nisrestore /var/backup org_dir.foo.com.
```

The following example forces the restore of an entire backed-up NIS+ namespace to a replica server from the backup partition named /var/backup.

```
replica_server# nisrestore -f -a /var/backup
```

The following example restores the subdomain sub.foo.com on a master server from a backup that includes other directory objects.

```
master_server#nisrestore/var/backupsub.foo.com.org_dir.sub.foo.com.
    groups_dir.sub.foo.com.
```

Exit Status

0	Successful completion.
1	An error occurred.

Files

/*backup-dir*/*backup-list*

>   An ASCII file containing a list of all the objects contained in this
>   *backup-dir* directory. You can display this information with the -t
>   option.

/*backup-dir*/*directory-object*

>   A subdirectory, created in the *backup-dir*, that contains the
>   *directory-object* backup.

/*backup-dir*/*directory-object*/data

>   A subdirectory that contains the data files that are part of the
>   *directory-object* backup.

/*backup-dir*/*directory-object*/last.upd

>   This data file contains timestamp information about the
>   *directory-object*.

/*backup-dir*/*directory-object*/data.dict

>   An NIS+ data dictionary for all of the objects contained in this
>   *directory-object* backup.

Attributes

See attributes(5) for descriptions of the following attributes.

Attribute Type	Attribute Value
Availability	SUNWnisu

See Also

nis+(1), nisdefaults(1), nisbackup(1M), nisserver(1M), rpc.nisd(1M),
share_nfs(1M), nisfiles(4), attributes(5)

nisserver — Set Up NIS+ Servers

Synopsis

```
/usr/lib/nis/nisserver -r [-x][-f][-v][-Y][-d NIS+-domain]
   [-g NIS+-groupname][-l network-passwd]
/usr/lib/nis/nisserver -M [-x][-f][-v][-Y] -d NIS+-domain
   [-g NIS+-groupname][-h NIS+-server-host]
/usr/lib/nis/nisserver -R [-x][-f][-v][-Y][-d NIS+-domain]
   [-h NIS+-server-host]
```

Description

Use the `nisserver` command to set up a root master, non-root master, or replica NIS+ server with level 2 security (DES). If other authentication mechanisms are configured with `nisauthconf`(1M), `nisserver` sets up an NIS+ server using those mechanisms. You should use `nisauthconf`(1M) before `nisserver`.

When setting up a new domain, this command creates the NIS+ directories (including `groups_dir` and `org_dir`) and system table objects for the domain specified. It does not populate the tables. You must use `nispopulate`(1M) to populate the tables.

Options

-d *NIS+-domain*

> Specify the name for the NIS+ domain. The default is your local domain.

-f

> Force the NIS+ server setup without prompting for confirmation.

-g *NIS+-groupname*

> Specify the NIS+ group name for the new domain. This option is not valid with the -R option. The default group is `admin.`*domain*.

-h *NIS+-server-host*

> Specify the host name for the NIS+ server. It must be a valid host in the local domain. Use a fully qualified host name (for example, `hostx.xyz.sun.com.`) to specify a host outside of your local domain. Use this option to set up only non-root master or replica servers. The default for non-root master server setup is to use the same list of servers as the parent domain. The default for replica server setup is the local host name.

-l *network-passwd*

> Specify the network password with which to create the credentials for the root master server. Use this option only for master root server setup (-r option). If you do not specify this option, prompt for the login password.

-M

> Set up the specified host as a master server. Make sure that `rpc.nisd`(1M) is running on the new master server before you execute this command.

-R

> Set up the specified host as a replica server. Make sure that `rpc.nisd` is running on the new replica server.

-r

> Set up the server as a root master server. Use the -R option to set up a root replica server.

-v

> Run in verbose mode.

-x

> Turn on the echo mode. Print the commands that it would have executed. Note that the commands are not actually executed. The default is off.

-Y

> Set up an NIS+ server with NIS-compatibility mode. The default is to set up the server without NIS-compatibility mode.

Usage

Use the first synopsis of the command (-r) to set up a root master server. To run the command, you must be logged in as superuser on the server machine.

Use the second synopsis of the command (-M) to set up a non-root master server for the specified domain. To run the command, you must be logged in as an NIS+ principal on an NIS+ machine and have write permission to the parent directory of the domain that you are setting up. The new non-root master server machine must already be an NIS+ client (see nisclient(1M)) and the rpc.nisd(1M) daemon must be running.

Use the third synopsis of the command (-R) to set up a replica server for both root and non-root domains. To run the command, you must be logged in as an NIS+ principal on an NIS+ machine and have write permission to the parent directory of the domain that you are replicating. The new non-root replica server machine must already be an NIS+ client and the rpc.nisd daemon must be running.

Examples

The following example sets up a root master server for domain sun.com..

```
root_server# /usr/lib/nis/nisserver -r -d sun.com.
```

For the following examples make sure that the new servers are NIS+ clients and rpc.nisd is running on these hosts before executing nisserver. The following example sets up a replica server for domain sun.com. on host sunreplica.

```
root_server# /usr/lib/nis/nisserver -R -d sun.com. -h sunreplica
```

The following example sets up a non-root master server for domain xyz.sun.com. on host sunxyz with the NIS+ group name as adminmgr.xyz.sun.com..

```
root_server# /usr/lib/nis/nisserver -M -d xyz.sun.com. -h sunxyz \
   -g admin-mgr.xyz.sun.com.
```

The following example sets up a non-root replica server for domain xyz.sun.com. on host sunabc.

```
sunxyz# /usr/lib/nis/nisserver -R -d xyz.sun.com. -h sunabc
```

Attributes

See attributes(5) for descriptions of the following attributes.

Attribute Type	Attribute Value
Availability	SUNWcsu

See Also

nis+(1), nisgrpadm(1), nismkdir(1), nisaddcred(1M), nisauthconf(1M),
nisclient (1M), nisinit(1M), nispopulate(1M), nisprefadm(1M),
nissetup(1M), rpc.nisd(1M), attributes(5)

nissetup — Initialize an NIS+ Domain

Synopsis

/usr/lib/nis/nissetup [-Y] [*domain*]

Description

Use the nissetup shell script to set up an NIS+ domain to service clients that want to store system administration information in a domain named *domain*. This domain should already exist before you execute the nissetup command (see nismkdir(1) and nisinit(1M)).

An NIS+ domain consists of an NIS+ directory and its org_dir and groups_dir subdirectories. org_dir stores system administration information, and groups_dir stores information for group access control.

nissetup creates the subdirectories org_dir and groups_dir in *domain*. Both subdirectories are replicated on the same servers as the parent domain. After the subdirectories are created, nissetup creates the default tables that NIS+ serves. These are auto_master, auto_home, bootparams, cred, ethers, group, hosts, mail_aliases, netmasks, networks, passwd, protocols, rpc, services, and timezone. The nissetup command uses the nistbladm(1) command to create these tables. You can easily customize the script to add site-specific tables that should be created at setup time.

This script is normally executed just once per domain.

Note — Although this script creates the default tables, it does not initialize them with data. You accomplish that task with the nisaddent(1M) command.

It is easier to use the nisserver(1M) script to create subdirectories and the default tables.

Options

-Y   Specify that the domain is served as both an NIS+ domain and an NIS domain by using the backward compatibility flag. This option sets up the domain to be less secure by making all the system tables readable by unauthenticated clients.

Attributes

See attributes(5) for descriptions of the following attributes.

Attribute Type	Attribute Value
Availability	SUNWnisu

See Also

nis+(1), nismkdir(1), nistbladm(1), nisaddent(1M), nisinit(1M) nisserver(1M), attributes(5)

nisshowcache — NIS+ Command to Print the Contents of the Shared Cache File

Synopsis

```
/usr/lib/nis/nisshowcache [-v]
```

Description

Use the nisshowcache command to print the contents of the per-machine NIS+ directory cache that is shared by all processes accessing NIS+ on the machine. By default, nisshowcache prints only the directory names in the cache along with the list of active servers. The shared cache is maintained by nis_cachemgr(1M).

The root domain's NIS_COLD_START file contains the Internet address and, eventually, public keys of the root master server. Although no NIS+ command enables you to examine the contents of the /var/nis/NIS_COLD_START file, the contents of the coldstart file are loaded into the NIS_SHARED_DIRCACHE directory cache on the server. You can examine the content of the NIS_SHARED_CACHE with the nisshowcache command.

Options

-v   Print the contents of each directory object, including information on the server name and its universal addresses.

Examples

The following example shows the output from the nisshowcache command issued from the root master server.

```
# /usr/lib/nis/nisshowcache -v
Cold Start directory:
Name : doc.com.
Type : NIS
Master Server :
 Name : rootmaster.doc.com.
 Public Key : Diffie-Hellman (192 bits)
 Universal addresses (3)
  . .
Replicate:
 Name : rootreplica1.doc.com.
 Public Key : Diffie-Hellman (192 bits)
 Universal addresses (3)

 .

 .

 .
Time to live : 12:0:0
Default Access Rights :
#
```

Files

/var/nis/NIS_SHARED_DIRCACHE

The NIS+ shared directory cache.

Attributes

See attributes(5) for descriptions of the following attributes.

Attribute Type	Attribute Value
Availability	SUNWcsu

See Also

nis_cachemgr(1M), syslogd(1M), nisfiles(4), attributes(5)

Diagnostics

Error messages are sent to the syslogd(1M) daemon.

nisstat — Report NIS+ Server Statistics

Synopsis

/usr/lib/nis/nisstat [-H *host*] [*directory*]

Description

Use the nisstat command to query an NIS+ server for various statistics about its operations. These statistics can vary between implementations and from release to release. Not all statistics are available from all servers. Requesting a statistic from a server that does not support that statistic is never fatal; it simply returns unknown statistic.

By default, statistics are fetched from the server(s) of the NIS+ directory for the default domain. If you specify *directory*, servers for that directory are queried.

Supported statistics for this release are as follows.

root server   Report whether the server is a root server.

NIS compat mode

Report whether the server is running in NIS compatibility mode.

DNS forwarding in NIS mode

Report whether the server in NIS compatibility mode forwards host lookup calls to DNS.

security level

Report the security level of this server.

serves directories

> List the directories served by this server.

Operations   Returnresultsintheform OP=*opname*:C=*calls*:E=*errors*:T=*micros*
where *opname* is replaced by the RPC procedure name or operation,
calls is the number of calls to this procedure that have been made
since the server started running. *errors* is the number of errors that
have occurred during call processing, and *micros* is the average time
in microseconds to complete the last 16 calls.

Directory Cache

> Report the number of calls to the internal directory object cache, the
> number of hits on that cache, the number of misses, and the hit rate
> percentage.

Group Cache   Report the number of calls to the internal NIS+ group object cache,
the number of hits on that cache, the number of misses, and the hit
rate percentage.

Static Storage

> Report the number of bytes the server has allocated for its static
> storage buffers.

Dynamic Storage

> Report the amount of heap the server process is currently using.

Uptime   Report the time since the service has been running.

Note — Per-server and per-directory access restrictions may apply; see   *New!*
nisopaccess(1). nisstat uses NIS_STATUS.

Options

-H *host*   Specify a host to query. Normally all servers for the directory are
queried. If the named machine does not serve the directory, return no
statistics.

Environment Variables

NIS_PATH   Specify a list of directories to search if the NIS+ directory name is not
fully qualified (see nisdefaults(1)).

Attributes

See attributes(5) for descriptions of the following attributes.

Attribute Type	Attribute Value
Availability	SUNWnisu

See Also

New!
nisdefaults(1), nisopaccess(1), attributes(5)

nisupdkeys — Update the Public Keys in an NIS+ Directory Object

Synopsis

```
/usr/lib/nis/nisupdkeys [-a | -C][-H host][directory]
/usr/lib/nis/nisupdkeys -s [-a | -C] -H host
```

Description

Occasionally, you may find that, even though you have created the proper credentials and assigned the proper access rights, some principal requests still get denied. Existence of stale objects with old versions of a server's public key can cause this problem. You can usually correct the problem by running nisupdkeys on the domain you are trying to access. You can use the nisupdkeys command to perform the following actions.

- Update the key of one particular server.
- Update the keys of all the servers that support an NIS+ directory object.
- Remove a server's public key from the directory object.
- Update a changed IP address for a server.

Because some keys are stored in files or caches, nisupdkeys cannot always correct the problem. If not, you may need to update the keys manually.

The user executing nisupdkeys must have modify access to the directory object. You can display information about the existing directory object with the niscat(1) command and the -o option.

The nisupdkeys command cannot update the directory objects stored in the NIS_COLD_START file on the principal workstations. The coldstart file is a copy of a directory object, which in turn, contains copies of the public keys of its servers. To update NIS+ client copies of a server's keys, run the nisclient command on NIS+ clients. The nisclient (or nisinit) command creates a coldstart file /var/nis/NIS_COLD_START. The coldstart file contains a copy of the directory object of the client's domain. Because the directory object already contains a copy of the server's public key, when you run the nisclient command, the key is propagated into the coldstart file of the client.

Options

-a   Update the universal addresses of the NIS+ servers in the directory object. Currently, this update works only for the TCP/IP family of transports. Use this option when the IP address of the server is changed. Resolve the server's new address by using gethostbyname(3N) on this machine. For this resolution to work, the /etc/nsswitch.conf file must point to the correct source for the hosts entry.

-C	Clear instead of set the public key(s). Communication with a server that has no public key(s) does not require the use of secure RPC.
-H *host*	Limit key changes only to the server named *host*. If the host name is not a fully qualified NIS+ name, then assume it to be a host in the default domain. If the named host does not serve the directory, take no action.
-s	Update all the NIS+ directory objects served by the specified server. This option assumes that the caller has adequate access rights to change all the associated directory objects. If the NIS+ principal making this call does not have adequate permissions to update the directory objects, those particular updates fail and the caller is notified. If the rpc.nisd on *host* cannot return the list of servers it serves, print an error message. The caller would then have to invoke nisupdkeys multiple times (as in the first synopsis), once per NIS+ directory that it serves.

Before you use this option, make sure that the new address/public key has been propagated to all replicas. If multiple authentication mechanisms are configured with nisauthconf(1M), then the keys for those mechanisms also are updated or cleared. If a server is also the root master server, then you cannot use nisupdkeys -s to update the root directory.

Examples

The following example updates the keys for servers of the foo.bar. domain.

```
paperbark% nisupdkeys foo.bar.
```

The following example updates the key(s) for host fred which serves the foo.bar. domain.

```
paperbark% nisupdkeys -H fred foo.bar.
```

The following example clears the public key(s) for host wilma in the foo.bar. directory.

```
paperbark% nisupdkeys -CH wilma foo.bar.
```

The following example updates the public key(s) in all directory objects that are served by the host wilma.

```
paperbark% nisupdkeys -s -H wilma
```

Attributes

See attributes(5) for descriptions of the following attributes.

Attribute Type	Attribute Value
Availability	SUNWnisu

See Also
chkey(1), niscat(1), nisaddcred(1M), nisauthconf(1M), nisstat(1M),
gethostbyname(3N), nis_objects(3N), attributes(5)

nlsadmin — Network Listener Service Administration

Synopsis
```
/usr/sbin/nlsadmin -x
/usr/sbin/nlsadmin [options] net-spec
/usr/sbin/nlsadmin [options] -N port-monitor-tag
/usr/sbin/nlsadmin -V
/usr/sbin/nlsadmin -c cmd | -o streamname [-p modules][-A address | -D]
    [-R prognum : versnum]
```

Description

The Service Access Facility (SAF) is a group of daemons and administrative commands that provide a flexible administrative framework for managing service requests in an open-systems environment. SAF uses port monitors to monitor a set of homogeneous incoming requests on a system port, detect incoming requests, and connect them to the appropriate service process. The network port monitor daemon is named listen.

Use the nlsadmin command to administer the network listen process(es) on a machine. Each network has at least one instance of the network listener process associated with it; each instance (and thus, each network) is configured separately. The listener process listens to the network for service requests, accepts requests when they arrive, and invokes servers in response to those service requests. The network listener process may be used with any network (more precisely, with any connection-oriented transport provider) that conforms to the transport provider specification.

With nlsadmin you can perform the following tasks.

- Establish a listener process for a given network.
- Configure the specific attributes of that listener.
- Start and kill the listener process for that network.
- Report on the listener processes on a machine, either individually (per network) or collectively.

net-spec represents a particular listener process. Specifically, *net-spec* is the relative path name of the entry under /dev for a given network (that is, a transport provider). *address* is a transport address on which to listen and is interpreted by a syntax that allows for a variety of address formats. By default, *address* is interpreted as the symbolic ASCII representation of the transport address. An address preceded by \x lets you enter an address in hexadecimal notation.

Note — An address must appear as a single word to the shell; thus, you must quote it if it contains any blanks.

Changes to the list of services provided by the listener or the addresses of those services are put into effect immediately.

Note — Dynamically assigned addresses are not displayed in reports as are statically assigned addresses.

Options

```
-a service-code [-p modules] [ w name]   c cmd   y comment net spec
```

Add a new service to the list of services available through the indicated listener. *service-code* is the code for the service, *cmd* is the command to be invoked in response to that service code, comprising the full path name of the server and its arguments, and *comment* is a brief (free-form) description of the service for use in various reports. Note that *cmd* must appear as a single word to the shell; if arguments are required, enclose *cmd* and its arguments in quotation marks. The comment must also appear as a single word to the shell. When a service is added, enable it (see the -e and -d options).

Service codes are alphanumeric strings, and are administered by AT&T. The numeric service codes 0 through 100 are reserved for internal use by the listener. Service code 0 is assigned to the nlps server, which is the service invoked on the general listening address. In particular, code 1 is assigned to the remote login service, which is the service automatically invoked for connections to the terminal login address.

If you specify the -p option, then *modules* is interpreted as a list of STREAMS *modules* for the listener to push before starting the service being added. The *modules* are pushed in the order in which they are specified. *modules* should be a comma-separated list of *modules* with no white space.

If you specify the -w option, then *name* is interpreted as the user name from /etc/passwd that the listener should look up. From the user name, the listener obtains the user ID, the group ID(s), and the home directory for use by the server. If you do not specify -w, the default is to use the user name listen.

A service must explicitly be added to the listener for each network on which that service is to be available. This operation normally is performed only when the service is installed on a system or when the list of services for a new network is populated.

```
-e service-code net-spec
-d service-code net-spec
```

Enable or disable the service indicated by *service-code* for the specified network. The service must previously have been added to the listener for that network (see the -a option). Disabling a service denies subsequent service requests for that service, but the processes from any prior service requests that are still running continue unaffected.

-i *net-spec*   Initialize an instance of the listener for the network specified by *net-spec*; that is, create and initialize the files required by the listener as well as starting that instance of the listener. Note that a particular instance of the listener should be initialized only once. The listener must be initialized before addresses or services are assigned.

-l *address net-spec*

> Change or set the transport address on which the listener listens (the general listener service). Remote processes can use this address to access the servers available through this listener (see the -a option).
>
> If *address* is just a dash (-), report the address currently configured instead of changing it.
>
> A change of address takes effect immediately.

-q *net-spec*   Query the status of the listener process for the specified network, and reflect the result of that query in its exit code. If a listener process is active, exit with a status of 0; if no process is active, exit with a status of 1; the exit code is greater than 1 in case of error.

-q -z *service-code net-spec*

> Query the status of the service with service code *service-code* on network *net-spec*, and exit with a status of 0 if that service is enabled, 1 if that service is disabled, and greater than 1 in case of error.

-r *service-code net-spec*

> Remove the entry for the *service-code* from that listener's list of services. You normally take this action only in conjunction with the deinstallation of a service from a system.

-s *net-spec*   Start/kill the listener process for the indicated network. These
-k *net-spec*   operations are normally performed as part of the system startup and shutdown procedures. Before a listener can be started for a particular network, it must first have been initialized (see the -i option). When a listener is killed, processes that are still running as a result of previous service requests continue unaffected.

-t *address net-spec*

> Change or set the address on which the listener listens for requests for terminal service but otherwise perform similarly to the -l option above. A terminal service address should not be defined unless the appropriate remote login software is available; if such software is available, it must be configured as service code 1 (see the -a option).

-v *net-spec*   Print a verbose report on the servers associated with *net-spec*, giving the service code, status, command, and comment for each. Specify the UID the server runs as and the list of modules to be pushed, if any, before the server is started.

-x   Report the status of all of the listener processes installed on this machine.

```
-z service-code net-spec
```

> Print a report on the server associated with *net-spec* that has
> service code *service-code*, giving the same information as in the -v
> option.

```
-N port-monitor-tag
```

> Under the Service Access Facility, you can have multiple instances of
> the listener on a single *net-spec*. In any of the above commands, you
> can use the option -N *port-monitor-tag* in place of the *net-spec*
> argument. This argument specifies the tag by which an instance of
> the listener is identified by the Service Access Facility. If you do not
> specify the -N option (that is, the *net-spec* is specified in the
> invocation), then it is assumed that the last component of the
> *net-spec* represents the tag of the listener for which the operation is
> destined. In other words, it is assumed that there is at least one
> listener on a designated *net-spec* and that its tag is identical to the
> last component of the *net-spec*. You can think of this listener as the
> primary, or default, listener for a particular *net-spec*.

You can also use nlsadmin in conjunction with the Service Access Facility commands.
In that capacity, you can use the following combinations of options.

```
prognum : versnum] -c cmd | -o streamname [-p modules]
[-A address | -D][-R]
```

> Format the port monitor-specific information to be used as an
> argument to pmadm(1M).

> The -c option specifies the full path name of the server and its
> arguments. *cmd* must appear as a single word to the shell, and you
> must quote its arguments.

> The -o option specifies the full path name of a FIFO or named
> STREAM through which a standing server is actually receiving the
> connection.

> If you specify the -p option, interpret *modules* as a list of STREAMS
> *modules* for the listener to push before starting the service being
> added. The *modules* are pushed in the order in which they are
> specified. *modules* must be a comma-separated list with no white
> space.

> If you specify the -A option, interpret *address* as the server's private
> address. The listener monitors this address on behalf of the service
> and dispatches all calls arriving on this address directly to the
> designated service. You cannot use this option with the -D option.

> If you specify the -D option dynamically, assign the service a private
> address, that is, the listener has the transport provider select the
> address each time the listener begins listening on behalf of this
> service. For RPC services, this option is often used with the -R option
> to register the dynamically assigned address with the rpcbinder. You
> cannot use this option with the -A option.

When you specify the $-R$ option, the service is an RPC service whose address, program number, and version number should be registered with the rpcbinder for this transport provider. This registration is performed each time the listener begins listening on behalf of the service. *prognum* and *versnum* are the program number and version number, respectively, of the RPC service.

$-V$ Write the current version number of the listener's administrative file to the standard output. The version number is used as part of the sacadm command line when sacadm adds a port monitor to the system.

Any user can invoke nlsadmin to generate reports; only superuser can run all operations that affect a listener's status or configuration.

You cannot use the options specific to the Service Access Facility with any other options.

Operands

net-spec   Print the status of the listener process for *net-spec*.

Exit Status

0   Success.

>=2   Failure.

See the $-q$ option for a return status of 1.

Attributes

See attributes(5) for descriptions of the following attributes.

Attribute Type	Attribute Value
Availability	SUNWcsu

See Also

listen(1M), pmadm(1M), rpcbind(1M), sacadm(1M), attributes(5)
System Administration Guide, Volume II

nscd — Nameservice Cache Daemon

Synopsis

```
/usr/sbin/nscd [-f configuration-file][-g][e cachename, yes | no]
  [-i cachename]
```

Description

The nscd daemon provides a cache for the most common nameservice requests. It is started up during multiuser boot by the /etc/rc2.d/S76nscd run control script. The default /etc/nscd.conf determines the behavior of the cache daemon. See nscd.conf(4).

nscd provides caching for the passwd(4), group(4), and hosts(4) databases through standard libc interfaces, such as gethostbyname(3N), gethostbyaddr(3N), and others. Each cache has a separate time-to-live for its data; modifying the local database (/etc/hosts, and so forth) invalidates that cache within 10 seconds.

Note — The shadow file is specifically not cached. getspnam(3C) calls remain uncached as a result.

---

nscd also acts as its own administration tool. If an instance of nscd is already running, commands are transparently passed to the running version.

To preserve NIS+ security, the startup script for nscd (/etc/init.d/nscd) checks the permissions on the passwd, group, and host tables if NIS+ is being used. If those tables are not readable by unauthenticated users, then caching is disabled so that each process continues to authenticate itself as before.

Options

Several of the options described below require a *cachename* specification. Supported values are passwd, group, and hosts.

-f *configuration-file*

    Read configuration data from the specified file.

-g   Print current configuration and statistics to standard output. This option is the only one executable by non-root users.

-e *cachename,* yes|no

    Enable or disable the specified cache.

-i *cachename* Invalidate the specified cache.

Examples

The following examples demonstrate how to stop and restart the nscd daemon.

```
# /etc/init.d/nscd stop
# /etc/init.d/nscd start
```

Files

/etc/nscd.conf

    Determines behavior of cache daemon.

Attributes

See attributes(5) for descriptions of the following attributes.

Attribute Type	Attribute Value
Availability	SUNWcsu

See Also

getspnam(3C), gethostbyname(3N), group(4), hosts(4), nscd.conf(4), nsswitch.conf(4), passwd(4), attributes(5)

Warning — The nscd interface is included in this release on an uncommitted basis only and is subject to change or removal in a future minor release.

nslookup — Query Nameservers Interactively

Synopsis

```
/usr/sbin/nslookup [- option]... host [server]
/usr/sbin/nslookup [- option]... - [server]
/usr/sbin/nslookup
```

Description

Use the nslookup command to query Internet domain nameservers. nslookup has two modes: interactive and noninteractive. Interactive mode enables you to contact servers for information about various hosts and domains or to display a list of hosts in a domain. Use noninteractive mode to display just the name and requested information for a host or domain.

Options

-option   Set the permissible options, as shown in the following list. These are the same options that the set command supports in interactive mode (see set in "Commands" on page 826 for more complete descriptions).

        all   List the current settings.

        class=classname

                Restrict search according to the specified class.

        d2   Set exhaustive debug mode on.

        nod2   Set exhaustive debug mode off.

        debug   Set debug mode on.

        nodebug   Set debug mode off.

        defname   Set domain-appending mode on.

nodefname   Set domain-appending mode off.

domain=*string*

                 Establish the appendable domain.

ignoretc   Ignore packet truncation errors.

noignoretc   Acknowledge packet truncation errors.

Operands

host   Specify inquiries about the specified host. In this noninteractive command format, do not prompt for additional commands.

–   Prompt for more information, such as host names, before sending one or more queries.

server   Direct inquiries to the nameserver specified in the command line instead of to the one read from the `/etc/resolv.conf` file (see `resolv.conf(4)`). `server` can be either a name or an Internet address. If the specified host cannot be reached, use the nameserver specified in `/etc/resolv.conf`.

Usage

Noninteractive Mode

Noninteractive mode is selected when the first argument is the name or Internet address of the host to be looked up.

Within noninteractive mode, you can use space-separated options. They must be entered before the host name to be queried. Prefix each option with a dash.

For example, to request extensive host information and to set the timeout to 10 seconds when inquiring about castle, enter the following command.

paperbark% **nslookup-query=hinfo-timeout=10castle**

To avoid repeated entry of an option that you almost always use, you can put a corresponding set command in a `.nslookuprc` file located inside your home directory. (See "Commands" on page 826" for more information about set.) The `.nslookuprc` file can contain several set commands if each is followed by a Return.

Entering and Leaving Interactive Mode

You enter interactive mode in the following cases.

- You supply no arguments.
- You specify a dash (–) as the host argument.

To exit from an interactive nslookup session, type Control-D or type the command exit followed by Return.

Supported Command Interactions

The commands associated with interactive mode are subject to various limitations and runtime conventions.

The maximum length of a command line is 255 characters. When you press Return, command-line execution begins. While a command is running, you can interrupt its execution by typing Control-C.

The first word entered on the command line must be the name of an `nslookup` command unless you enter the name of a host to inquire about. Any unrecognized command is handled as a host name. To force a command to be treated as a host name, precede it with a backslash character.

Commands

`exit`	Exit the `nslookup` command.
`help ?`	Display a brief summary of commands.

`host` [*server*]

Look up information for *host* using the current default server or using *server* if it is specified.

If the host supplied is an Internet address and the query type is A or 1PTR, return the name of the host. If the host supplied is a name and it does not have a trailing period, append the default domain name to the name. (This behavior depends on the state of the `set` options `domain`, `srchlist`, `defname`, and `search`.)

To look up a host that is not in the current domain, append a period to the name.

`finger` [*name*] [>> *filename*]

Connect with the `finger` server on the current host, which is defined by the most recent, successful, host lookup. If you specify no name value, generate a list of login account names on the current host.

As with a shell command interpreter, you can redirect output to a file using the usual > and >> redirection symbols.

`ls` [*-options*] *domain* [>> *filename*]

List the information available for *domain*, optionally creating or appending to *filename*. The default output contains host names and their Internet addresses.

You can redirect output to *filename* with the > and >> redirection symbols. When output is directed to a file, hash marks are shown for every 50 records received from the server. You can specify the following values for *options*.

a	List aliases of hosts in the domain. A synonym for the command `lstCNAME`.
d	List all records for the domain. A synonym for the command `ls-tANY`.
h	List CPU and operating system information for the domain. A synonym for the command `ls-tHINFO`.
s	List well-known services of hosts in the domain. A synonym for the command `ls-tWKS`.

t *querytype-value*

> List all records of the specified type (see `querytype` within the discussion of the `set` command).

set token=*value*
set keyword

> Establish a preferred mode of search operation. The following token and keyword value are permissible.

all

> Display the current values of frequently used options. Also display information about the current default server and host.

cl[ass]=*classname*

> Limit the search according to the protocol group (*classname*) for which you want lookup information. You can specify the following *classname* values.
>
> ANY   A wildcard selecting all classes.
>
> IN   The Internet class (the \ default).
>
> CHAOS   The Chaos class.
>
> HESIOD   The MIT Athena Hesiod class.

d2
nod2

> Enable or disable exhaustive debugging mode. Essentially, display all fields of every packet. By default, this option is disabled.

deb[ug]
nodeb[ug]

> Enable or disable debugging mode. Produce more information about the packet sent to the server and the resulting answer. By default, this option is disabled.

def[name]
nodef[name]

> Enable or disable appending the default domain name to a single-component lookup request (one that lacks a dot). By default, this option is enabled. The default value for the domain name is the value given in /etc/resolv.conf, unless there is a value for LOCALDOMAIN when nslookup is run or a recent value has been specified with the srchlist or the set domain command.

do[main]=*string*

> Change the default domain name to be appended to all lookup requests to string. For this option to have any effect, you must also enable the defname option and set the search option in a compatible way.

The domain search list contains the parents of the default domain if it has at least two components in its name. For example, if the default domain is CC.Berkeley.EDU, the search list is CC.Berkeley.EDU and Berkeley.EDU. Use the set srchlist command to specify a different list. Use the set all command to display the list.

ignoretc   Ignore packet truncation errors. By default, this option
noignoretc   is disabled.

srch[*list*]=*name1*/*name2*/...

Change the default domain name to *name1* and the domain search list to *name1*, *name2*, and so on. You can specify a maximum of six names along with slash characters to separate them. For example,

paperbark% **set srchlist=lcs.MIT.EDU/ai.MIT.EDU/MIT.EDU**

sets the domain to lcs.MIT.EDU and the search list to all three names. This command overrides the default domain name and search list of the set domain command. Use the set all command to display the list.

search   Enable or disable appending the domain names in the domain search
nosearch   list, generating a series of lookup queries if necessary until an answer
                  is received. To take effect, the lookup request must contain at least one
                  dot (period), yet it must not contain a trailing period. By default, this
                  option is enabled.

po[rt]=*value*   Specify the default TCP/UDP nameserver port. By default, this value
                  is 53.

q[uerytype]=*value*

ty[pe]=*value*   Change the type of information returned from a query to one of the
                  following.

A	The Internet address of the host.
CNAME	The canonical name for an alias.
HINFO	The host CPU and operating system type.
MD	The mail destination.
MX	The mail exchanger.
MB	The mailbox domain name.
MG	The mail group member.
MINFO	The mailbox or mail list information.
NS	The nameserver.
PTR	The host name if the query is in the form of an Internet address; otherwise, the pointer to other information.
SOA	The domain's start-of-authority information.
TXT	The text information.

UINFO	The user information.
WKS	The supported well-known services. (Other types specified in the RFC 1035 document are valid, but they are not as useful.)

recurse
norecurse

Enable or disable having to query other nameservers before abandoning a search. By default, this feature is enabled.

ret[ry]=*count*

Set the maximum number of times to retry a request before abandoning a search. When a reply to a request is not received within a certain amount of time (changed with set timeout), double the timeout period and resend the request. The retry value controls how many times a request is re-sent before the request is aborted. The default for *count* is 4.

ro[ot]=*host*

Change the name of the root server to *host*. This setting affects the root command. The default root server is ns.internet.net.

t[timeout]=*interval*

Change the amount of time to wait for a reply to *interval* seconds. Each retry doubles the timeout period. The default interval is 5 seconds.

vc
novc

Enable or disable the use of a virtual circuit when sending requests to the server. By default, this feature is disabled.

root

Change the default server to the server for the root of the domain namespace. Currently, the host ns.internic.net is used; this command is a synonym for server ns.internic.net. You can change the name of the root server with the set root command.

server *domain*
lserver *domain*

Change the default server to *domain*. lserver uses the initial server to look up information about *domain* and server uses the current default server. If an authoritative answer cannot be found, return the names of servers that might have the answer.

view *filename*

Sort the output of previous ls command(s) and display it one text screen at a time, similar to more(1).

Examples

To effectively search the Internet domain namespace, it helps to know its structure. At present, the Internet domain namespace is tree structured, with one top-level domain for each country except the United States. The following list shows some traditional top-level domains, not explicitly tied to any particular country.

COM	Commercial establishments.
EDU	Educational institutions.

ORG	Not-for-profit organizations.
GOV	Government agencies.
MIL	MILNET hosts.

If you are looking for a specific host, you need to know something about the host's organization to determine the top-level domain that it belongs to. For instance, if you want to find the Internet address of a machine at UCLA, do the following.

- Connect with the root server by using the `root` command. The root server of the namespace has knowledge of the top-level domains.

- Because UCLA is a university, its domain name is `ucla.edu`. Connect with a server for the `ucla.edu` domain with the command `server ucla.edu`. The response produces the names of hosts that act as servers for that domain. Note that the root server does not have information about `ucla.edu` but knows the names and addresses of hosts that do. Once the UCLA nameserver is located by the root server, all future queries are sent to that nameserver.

- To request information about a particular host in the domain (for instance, `locus`), just type the host name. To request a listing of hosts in the UCLA domain, use the `ls` command. The `ls` command requires a domain name (in this case, `ucla.edu`) as an argument.

If you are connected with a nameserver that handles more than one domain, you must fully specify all lookups for host names with its domain. For instance, the domain `harvard.edu` is served by `seismo.css.gov`, which also services the `css.gov` and `cornell.edu` domains. A lookup request for the host `aiken` in the `harvard.edu` domain must be specified as `aiken.harvard.edu`. However, you can use the `set domain=name` and `set defname` commands to automatically append a domain name to each request.

After a successful lookup of a host, use the `finger(1)` command to see who is on the system or to finger a specific person. (`finger` requires the type to be A.)

To get other information about the host, use the `set querytype=value` command to change the type of information and request another lookup.

Environment Variables

HOSTALIASES	Reference the file containing host aliases.
LOCALDOMAIN	Override default domain.

Exit Status

0	Successful completion.
1	An error occurred.

Files

`/etc/resolv.conf`

> Initial domain name and nameserver addresses.

`$HOME/.nslookuprc`

> Initial option commands.

/usr/lib/nslookup.help

> Summary of commands.

Attributes

See attributes(5) for descriptions of the following attributes.

Attribute Type	Attribute Value
Availability	SUNWcsu

See Also

finger(1), more(1), in.named(1M), nstest(1M), resolver(3N), resolv.conf(4), attributes(5)

Mockapetris, Paul, *Domain Names—Concepts and Facilities*, RFC 1034, Network Information Center, SRI International, Menlo Park, Calif., November 1987.

Mockapetris, Paul, *Domain Names—Implementation and Specification*, RFC 1035, Network Information Center, SRI International, Menlo Park, Calif., November 1987.

Diagnostics

If the lookup request is unsuccessful, an error message is produced. The following errors are possible.

Timed out — The server did not respond to a request after a certain amount of time (changed with set timeout=*value*) and a certain number of retries (changed with set retry=*value*).

No response from server

> No nameserver is running on the server machine.

No records — The server does not have resource records of the current query type for the host, although the host name is valid. The query type is specified with the set querytype command.

Non-existent domain

> The host or domain name does not exist.

Connection refused
Network is unreachable

> The connection to the name or finger server cannot be made at the current time. This error commonly occurs with ls and finger requests.

Server failure

> The nameserver found an internal inconsistency in its database and could not return a valid answer.

Refused — The nameserver refused to service the request.

Format error — The nameserver found that the request packet was not in the proper format. This may indicate an error in nslookup.

nstest — DNS Test Shell

Synopsis

/usr/sbin/nstest [-d][-i][-r][-v][-p *port*][*inet-addr* [*logfile*]]

Description

Use the nstest interactive DNS test program to query DNS. You form and send user commands. Replies are printed on the standard output. *inet-addr* is the Internet address of the DNS resolver where nstest sends its queries. If you do not specify *inet-addr*, nstest first tries to contact a DNS server on the local host; if that fails, it tries the servers listed in the /etc/resolv.conf file. If you specify a *logfile*, nstest uses it to log the queries sent and replies received.

Options

-d	Create a file named ns_packet.dump (if it does not exist) and write into it a raw (binary) copy of each packet sent. If ns_packet.dump does exist, truncate it.
-i	Set the RES_IGNTC flag on the queries it makes. See resolver(3N) for a description of the RES_IGNTC flag.
-r	Turn off the RES_RECURSE flag on the queries it makes. See resolver(3N) for a description of the RES_RECURSE flag.
-v	Turn on the RES_USEVC and RES_STAYOPEN flags on the res_send() calls made. See resolver(3N) for a description of the RES_USEVC and RES_STAYOPEN flags.
-p	Use the supplied port instead of the default nameserver port.

Usage

When you start nstest, it prints a prompt (>) and waits for input. Form DNS queries by typing a key letter followed by the appropriate argument. Each key letter results in a call to res_mkquery() with *op* set to either IQUERY or QUERY and *type* set to one of the type values (defined in arpa/nameser.h). Any key letters other than those listed below print a summary of the following table.

Key Letter and Argument	Op	Type
ahost	QUERY	T_A
A*addr*	IQUERY	T_A
B*user*	QUERY	T_MG
b*user*	QUERY	T_MB

Key Letter and Argument	Op	Type
chost	QUERY	T_CNAME
fhost	QUERY	T_UINFO
Ggid	IQUERY	T_GID
ghost	QUERY	T_GID
hhost	QUERY	T_HINFO
ihost	QUERY	T_MINFO
Mhost	QUERY	T_MAILB
mhost	QUERY	T_MX
nhost	QUERY	T_NS
phost	QUERY	T_PTR
rhost	QUERY	T_MR
shost	QUERY	T_SOA
Thost	QUERY	T_TXT
Uuid	IQUERY	T_UID
uhost	QUERY	T_UID
whost	QUERY	T_WKS
xhost	QUERY	T_AXFR

After the query is successfully formed, res_send() is called to send it and wait for a reply. nstest then prints the following information on the standard output.

- A summary of the request and reply packets, including the HEADER structure (defined in arpa/nameser.h) used in the request.
- The question being asked of the nameserver.
- An enumeration of the nameserver(s) being polled.
- A summary of the HEADER structure received in the reply.
- The question the nameserver answered.
- The answer itself.

Examples

The following example fetches the address of host playground.sun.com from the Sun nameserver.

```
$ nstest 192.9.5.1
```

```
> aplayground.sun.com
     res_mkquery(0, playground.sun.com, 1, 1)
res_send()
HEADER:
        opcode = QUERY, id = 1, rcode = NOERROR
        header flags:  rd
        qdcount = 1, ancount = 0, nscount = 0, arcount = 0

QUESTIONS:
        playground.sun.com, type = A, class = IN

Querying server (# 1) address = 192.9.5.1
got answer:
HEADER:
        opcode = QUERY, id = 1, rcode = NOERROR
        header flags:  qr aa rd ra
        qdcount = 1, ancount = 1, nscount = 0, arcount = 0

QUESTIONS:
        playground.sun.com, type = A, class = IN
ANSWERS:
        playground.sun.com
        type = A, class = IN, ttl = 1 day, dlen = 4
        internet address = 192.9.5.5
```

The following example looks up a PTR record.

```
$ nstest 192.9.5.1
> p5.5.9.192.in-addr.arpa
res_mkquery(0, 5.5.9.192.in-addr.arpa, 1, 12)
res_send()
HEADER:
        opccde = QUERY, id = 2, rcode = NOERROR
        header flags:  rd
        qdcount = 1, ancount = 0, nscount = 0, arcount = 0

QUESTIONS:
        5.5.9.192.in-addr.arpa, type = PTR, class = IN

Querying server (# 1) address = 192.9.5.1
got answer:
HEADER:
        opcode = QUERY, id = 2, rcode = NOERROR
        header flags:  qr aa rd ra
        qdcount = 1, ancount = 1, nscount = 0, arcount = 0

QUESTIONS:
        5.5.9.192.in-addr.arpa, type = PTR, class = IN

ANSWERS:
        5.5.9.192.in-addr.arpa
        type = PTR, class = IN, ttl = 7 hours 47 mins 2 secs, dlen = 23
        domain name = playground.sun.com
```

Files

/usr/include/arpa/nameser.h

Include file for implementation of DNS protocol.

/usr/include/resolv.h

Include file for the resolver daemon (in.named).

Attributes

See attributes(5) for descriptions of the following attributes.

Attribute Type	Attribute Value
Availability	SUNWcsu

See Also

nslookup(1M), resolver(3N), attributes(5)

---

nsupdate — Update DNS Nameservers

Synopsis

/usr/sbin/nsupdate [-d][-v][*filename*]

Description

Use the nsupdate command to update domain nameservers. The command has interactive and noninteractive modes. The interactive mode enables you to update servers with information about various hosts and domains. The noninteractive mode enables you to batch update zones. Both modes assume that the nameserver permits updates from the host where nsupdate is being run. See in.named(1M) for a discussion of the allow-update option for configuring in.named.

Options

-d	Debug mode.
-v	Use TCP instead of UDP for updates.

Operands

filename	The name of the file containing the update requests and entries. Data in the file must contain one line per entry and should be of the form

class section name ttl type rdata

class   Any of the opcodes update, zone, or prereq.

section	One of the opcodes add, delete, nxdomain, yxdomain, nxrrset, or yxrrset.
name	The name of the entry being added.
ttl	The time-to-live (in seconds) for this entry.
type	The RR type, for example, a, cname, ns, mx, ptr, or txt.
rdata	The data appropriate for the RR type being updated.

Usage

Interactive Mode

In interactive mode, you are expected to provide the update data in the *class section name ttl type rdata* format after each prompt, with each field separated by a space. A return at with no data assumes the end of input, and all entries on the nameserver are updated in one atomic operation. A Control-D ends the interactive mode and exits the program.

Noninteractive Mode

In noninteractive mode, you are expected to provide the update data in a file. Data in the file is in the form of rows and columns. Each row must contain the following update data.

class section name ttl type rdata

Examples

The following example initializes a packet, deletes all A records for the specified host name, adds an A record for the host name to the 9.3.145.2 association, signed and valid for 300 seconds, with a default KEY pad of 3110400, transmits the packet, and quits.

```
# nsupdate
> r;d;a;*;a;a;9.3.145.2;s;300;3110400;x;q
#
```

The following example updates the nads.zn zone with a cname entry for ivy18.nads.zn as www.nads.zn.

```
paperbark% nsupdate
> res_mkupdate: packet size = 49
;; res_send()
;; ->>HEADER<<- opcode: UPDATE, status: NOERROR, id: 53349
;; flags:; ZONE: 1, PREREQUISITE: 0, UPDATE: 1, ADDITIONAL: 0
;; nads.zn, type = SOA, class = IN
www.nads.zn.   1M IN CNAME  ivy18.nads.zn.
;; Querying server (# 1) address = 192.168.1.1
;; got answer:
;; ->>HEADER<<- opcode: UPDATE, status: NOERROR, id: 53349
;; flags: qr ra; ZONE: 0, PREREQUISITE: 0, UPDATE: 0, ADDITIONAL: 0
```

The following example deletes the entry that was created in interactive mode in the previous example.

```
paperbark% nsupdate
> update delete www.nads.zn. cname
>
;; res_mkquery(0, www.nads.zn, 1, 6)
;; res_send()
;; ->>HEADER<<- opcode: QUERY, status: NOERROR, id: 53350
;; flags: rd; QUERY: 1, ANSWER: 0, AUTHORITY: 0, ADDITIONAL: 0
;; www.nads.zn, type = SOA, class = IN
;; Querying server (# 1) address = 192.168.1.1
;; got answer:
;; ->>HEADER<<- opcode: QUERY, status: NOERROR, id: 53350
;; flags: qr aa rd ra; QUERY: 1, ANSWER: 1, AUTHORITY: 1, ADDITIONAL: 0
;; www.nads.zn, type = SOA, class = IN
www.nads.zn. 1M IN CNAME ivy18.nads.zn.
nads.zn.  1D IN SOA nserver.eng.nads.com. admin.myhost.eng.nads.com. (
     1998012604 ; serial
     3H    ; refresh
     1H    ; retry
     1W    ; expiry
     1D )  ; minimum

;; res_mkquery(0, nads.zn, 1, 6)
;; res_send()
;; ->>HEADER<<- opcode: QUERY, status: NOERROR, id: 53351
;; flags: rd; QUERY: 1, ANSWER: 0, AUTHORITY: 0, ADDITIONAL: 0
;; nads.zn, type = SOA, class = IN
;; Querying server (# 1) address = 192.168.1.1
;; got answer:
;; ->>HEADER<<- opcode: QUERY, status: NOERROR, id: 53351
;; flags: qr aa rd ra; QUERY: 1, ANSWER: 1, AUTHORITY: 1, ADDITIONAL: 1
;; nads.zn, type = SOA, class = IN
nads.zn 1D IN SOA nserver.eng.nads.com. admin.myhost.eng.nads.com. (
     1998012604 ; serial
     3H    ; refresh
     1H    ; retry
     1W    ; expiry
     1D )  ; minimum

nads.zn.   1D IN NS  obelix.nads.zn.
obelix.nads.zn.  1D IN A  192.168.1.1
res_mkupdate: packet size = 41
;; res_send()
;; ->>HEADER<<- opcode: UPDATE, status: NOERROR, id: 53352
;; flags:; ZONE: 1, PREREQUISITE: 0, UPDATE: 1, ADDITIONAL: 0
;; nads.zn, type = SOA, class = IN
;; Querying server (# 1) address = 192.168.1.1
;; got answer:
;; ->>HEADER<<- opcode: UPDATE, status: NOERROR, id: 53352
;; flags: qr ra; ZONE: 0, PREREQUISITE: 0, UPDATE: 0, ADDITIONAL: 0
```

The next example uses a file named nsupd.txt that contains the following information.

```
update delete www.nads.zn.
update add www.nads.zn. 60 CNAME ivy18.nads.zn

paperbark% nsupdate nsupd.txt
paperbark%
```

Exit Status

0	Successful completion.
>0	An error occurred.

Attributes

See attributes(5) for descriptions of the following attributes.

Attribute Type	Attribute Value
Availability	SUNWcsu

See Also

in.named(1M), attributes(5)

ntpdate — Set the Local Date and Time with the Network Time Protocol (NTP)

Synopsis

```
/usr/sbin/ntpdate [-bdosu][-a key#][-e authdelay][-k keyfile][-m]
    [-o version][-p samples][-t timeout][-w] server...
```

Description

Use the ntpdate command to set the local date and time. To determine the correct time, ntpdate polls the Network Time Protocol (NTP) servers on the hosts given as arguments. You must run this command as root on the local host. The command obtains a number of samples from each of the servers and applies the standard NTP clock filter and selection algorithms to select the best of these.

The ntpdate command declines to set the date if an NTP server daemon like xntpd(1M) is running on the same host. You can run ntpdate regularly from cron(1M) as an alternative to running a daemon. Doing so once every one to two hours results in precise enough timekeeping to avoid stepping the clock.

The reliability and precision of ntpdate improve dramatically with a greater number of servers. Although you can use a single server, you get better performance and greater accuracy on the part of any one server by providing three or four servers, if not more.

The ntpdate command makes time adjustments in one of two ways. If it determines that your clock is off by more than 0.5 seconds, it simply steps the time by calling gettimeofday(3C). If the error is less than 0.5 seconds, by default, ntpdate slews the clock's time with the offset, by way of a call to adjtime(2). The latter technique is less disruptive and more accurate when the offset is small; it works quite well when ntpdate is run by cron every hour or two. The adjustment made in the latter case is actually 50% larger than the measured offset. This adjustment tends to keep a badly drifting clock more accurate, at some expense to stability. This trade-off is usually advantageous. At boot time, however, it is usually better to step the time. You can force the adjustment in all cases by specifying the -b option on the command line.

> **Note** — The technique of compensating for clock oscillator errors to improve accuracy is inadequate. However, to further improve accuracy would require the program to save state from previous runs.

Options

-a *key#*	Authenticate transactions, using the key number, *key#*.
-b	Step the time by calling gettimeofday(3C).
-d	Display what would be done without actually doing it. Also print general debugging information.
-e *authdelay*	Specify an authentication processing delay, *authdelay* in seconds. See xntpd(1M) for details. This number is usually small enough to be negligible for purposes of ntpdate. However, specifying a value can improve timekeeping on very slow CPUs.
-k *keyfile*	Read keys from the file *keyfile* instead of the default file, /etc/ntp.keys. Specify *keyfile* in the format described in xntpd(1M).
-m	Join multicast group specified in server and synchronize to multicast NTP packets. The standard NTP group is 224.0.1.1.
-o *version*	Force the program to poll as a version 1 or version 2 implementation. By default ntpdate claims to be an NTP version 3 implementation in its outgoing packets. However, some older software declines to respond to version 3 queries. You can use this option for those cases.
-p *samples*	Set the number of samples ntpdate acquires from each server. *samples* can be between 1 and 8 inclusive. The default is 4.
-s	Log actions with the syslog(3) command instead of to the standard output. This option is useful when the program is run from cron(1M).
-t *timeout*	Set the time ntpdate spends, waiting for a response. *timeout* is rounded to a multiple of 0.2 seconds. The default is 1 second, a value suitable for polling across a LAN.
-u	Use an unprivileged port to send the packets. This option is useful when you are behind a firewall that blocks incoming traffic to privileged ports and you want to synchronize with hosts beyond the firewall. Note that the -d option always uses unprivileged ports.
-w	When used together with -m, wait until able to join group and synchronize.

Files

/etc/inet/ntp.keys

Contains the encryption keys used by ntpdate.

Attributes

See attributes(5) for descriptions of the following attributes.

Attribute Type	Attribute Value
Availability	SUNWntpu

See Also

cron(1M), xntpd(1M), adjtime(2), syslog(3), gettimeofday(3C), attributes(5)

ntpq — Standard Network Time Protocol Query Program

Synopsis

/usr/sbin/ntpq [-inp][-c *command*][*host*][...]

Description

Use the ntpq command to query the current state of Network Time Protocol (NTP) servers that implement the recommended NTP mode 6 control message format. ntpq can also request changes in that state. You can run the program in interactive mode or control it by using command-line arguments. Requests to read and write arbitrary variables can be assembled, with raw and pretty-printed output options available. By sending multiple queries to the server, ntpq can also obtain and print a list of peers in a common format.

If you include one or more request options on the command line, ntpq sends each of the requests to NTP servers running on each of the hosts given as command-line arguments. By default, ntpq sends its requests to localhost if hosts are not included on the command line. If you specify no request options, ntpq tries to read commands from the standard input and execute them on the NTP server running on the first host specified on the command line. Again, ntpq defaults to localhost if you specify no other host.

ntpq uses NTP mode 6 packets to communicate with an NTP server. Thus, you can use it to query any compatible server on the network that permits queries. Because NTP is a UDP protocol, this communication is somewhat unreliable, especially over large distances. ntpq makes one try to retransmit requests; it requests timeout if the remote host is not heard from within a suitable period.

Options

Specifying a command line option other than -i or -n sends the specified query (queries) immediately to the indicated host(s). Otherwise, ntpq tries to read interactive format commands from standard input.

-c   Interpret the next argument as an interactive format command and add it to the list of commands to be executed on the specified host(s). You can specify multiple -c options.

-i   Operate in interactive mode; write prompts to standard output and read commands from standard input.

-n   Output all host addresses in dotted-quad numeric format instead of converting them to canonical host names.

-p   Print a list of the peers known to the server as well as a summary of their state. This is equivalent to the peers interactive command.

Usage

Interactive format commands consist of a keyword followed by up to four arguments. You need to type only enough characters of the full keyword to uniquely identify the command. Normally, the output of a command is sent to standard output, but you can write the output to a file by appending a > followed by a file name to the command line.

Interactive Commands

A number of interactive format commands are executed entirely within the ntpq program itself. They do not result in NTP mode 6 requests being sent to a server. If you include no request options on the command line and if the standard input is a terminal device, ntpq prompts for these commands. The interactive commands are described below:

? [*command-keyword*]

    ? prints a list of all the command keywords known to the current version of ntpq. ? followed by a command keyword prints function and usage information about the specified command.

addvars *variable-name*[=*value*][,...]
rmvars *variable-name* [,...]
clearvars

    The data carried by NTP mode 6 messages consists of a list of items of the form

    variable-name=value

    where the =*value* is ignored and can be omitted in requests to the server to read variables. ntpq maintains an internal list to assemble and send data to be included in control messages, using the readlist and writelist commands described below. The addvars command enables you to add variables and their optional values to the list. If you want to add more than one variable, the list should be comma-separated and should contain no white space. You can use the rmvars command to remove individual variables from the list; the clearlist command removes all variables from the list.

authenticate [yes|no]

> yes sends authentication with all requests it makes. Normally, ntpq does not authenticate requests unless they are write requests. Authenticated requests are handled slightly differently by some servers and can occasionally slow the response if you turn authentication on before doing a peer display.

cooked

> Cook output from query commands. The values of variables recognized by the server are reformatted so that they can be more easily read. Variables that ntpq thinks should have a decodable value, but do not, are marked with a trailing ?.

debug [more|less|off]

> Turn on/off internal query program debugging.

delay *milliseconds*

> Specify a time interval to be added to timestamps included in requests that require authentication. Use this command to enable (unreliable) server reconfiguration over long delay network paths or between machines whose clocks are unsynchronized. Currently, the server does not require timestamps in authenticated requests. Thus, this command may be obsolete.

host *hostname*

> Set the name of the host to which future queries are to be sent. *hostname* can be either a host name or a numeric address.

hostnames yes|no

> If you specify yes, print host names in information displays. If you specify no, print numeric addresses instead. The default is yes unless modified with the command line -n option.

keyid #

> Specify a key number to be used to authenticate configuration requests. This number must correspond to a key number the server has been configured to use for this purpose.

ntpversion [1|2|3]

> Set the NTP version number that ntpq claims in packets (default is 3). Note that mode 6 control messages (and modes, for that matter) did not exist in NTP version 1. There appear to be no servers left that demand version 1.

passwd

> Prompt for a password that is used to authenticate configuration requests. If an authenticating key has been specified (see keyid above), this password must correspond to this key. ntpq does not echo the password as it is typed.

quit

> Exit ntpq.

raw

> Print all output from query commands exactly as it is received from the remote server. The only formatting/filtering done on the data is to transform non-ASCII data into printable form.

```
timeout milliseconds
```

> Specify a timeout period for responses to server queries. The default
> is about 5,000 milliseconds. Because ntpq retries each query once
> after a timeout, the total waiting time for a time out is twice the
> timeout value that is set.

Control Message Commands

Each peer known to an NTP server has a 16-bit integer association identifier assigned
to it. NTP control messages that carry peer variables must identify the peer that the
values correspond to by including its association ID. An association ID of 0 is special. It
indicates the variables are system variables, whose names are drawn from a separate
namespace.

Control message commands send one or more NTP mode 6 messages to the server
and print the data returned in some format. Most commands currently implemented
send a single message and expect a single response. The current exceptions are the
peers, mreadlist, and mreadvar commands. The peers command sends a
preprogrammed series of messages to obtain the data it needs. The mreadlist and
mreadvar commands iterate over a range of associations.

Control message commands are described below.

associations   Obtain and print a list of association identifiers and peer statuses for
               in-spec peers of the server being queried. Print the list in columns.
               The first column is an index that numbers the associations from 1, for
               internal use. The second column contains the actual association
               identifier returned by the server; and the third, the status word for the
               peer. A number of columns follow containing data decoded from the
               status word. Note that the data returned by the associations
               command is cached internally in ntpq. The index is then of use when
               dealing with "dumb" servers that use association identifiers that are
               hard for humans to type. For any subsequent commands that require
               an association identifier as an argument, you can specify the
               identifier by using the form &index. Here index is taken from the
               previous list.

lassociations

               Obtain and print a list of association identifiers and peer statuses for
               all associations for which the server is maintaining state. This
               command differs from the associations command only for servers
               that retain state for out-of-spec client associations. Such associations
               are normally omitted from the display when the associations
               command is used but are included in the output of lassociations.

passociations

               Print association data concerning in-spec peers from the internally
               cached list of associations. This command performs identically to the
               associations command except that it displays the internally stored
               data instead of making a new query.

lpassociations

>   Print data for all associations, including out-of-spec client associations, from the internally cached list of associations. This command differs from `passociations` only when dealing with servers that retain state for out-of-spec client associations.

pstatus *assocID*

>   Send a read status request to the server for the given association. Print the names and values of the peer variables returned. Note that the status word from the header is displayed preceding the variables, both in hexadecimal and in pidgin English.

readvar [*assoc*][*variable-name*[=*value*][,...]]

>   Request that the values of the specified variables be returned by the server by sending a read variables request. If you omit the association ID or specify it as 0, the variables are system variables; otherwise, they are peer variables and the values returned are those of the corresponding peer. Omitting the variable list sends a request with no data that should induce the server to return a default display.

rv [*assocID*][*variable-name*[=*value*][,...]]

>   An easy-to-type short form for the `readvar` command.

writevar *assocID variable-name*=*value* [,...]

>   Like the `readvar` request, except write the specified variables instead of reading them.

readlist [*assocID*]

>   Request that the values of the variables in the internal variable list be returned by the server. If you omit the association ID or it is 0, assume the variables to be system variables. Otherwise, treat them as peer variables. If the internal variable list is empty, send a request without data, which should induce the remote server to return a default display.

rl [*assocID*]   An easy-to-type short form of the `readlist` command.

writelist [*assocID*]

>   Like the `readlist` request, except write the internal list variables instead of reading them.

mreadvar *assocID assocID* [*variable-name*[=*value*][,...]]" 10

>   Like the `readvar` command, except do the query for each of a range of (non-zero) association IDs. This range is determined from the association list cached by the most recent association's command.

mrv *assocID assocID* [*variable-name*[=*value*][,...]]

>   An easy-to-type short form of the `mreadvar` command.

`mreadlist` *assocID assocID*

> Like the `readlist` command, except do the query for each of a range of (non-zero) association IDs. This range is determined from the association list cached by the most recent associations command.

`mrl` *assocID assocID*

> An easy-to-type short form of the `mreadlist` command.

`clockvar` [*assocID*][*variable-name*[=*value*][,...]]

> Send a list of the server's clock variables. Servers that have a radio clock or other external synchronization respond positively to this command. If you omit the association identifier or it is 0, the request is for the variables of the system clock. This request generally gets a positive response from all servers with a clock. Some servers can treat clocks as quasi-peers and, hence, can possibly have more than one clock connected at once. For these servers, referencing the appropriate peer association ID shows the variables of a particular clock. Omitting the variable list returns a default variable display.

`cv` [*assocID*][*variable-name*[=*value*][,...]]

> An easy-to-type short form of the `clockvar` command.

`peers`   Obtain a list of in-spec peers of the server along with a summary of each peer's state. Summary information includes the following.

- The address of the remote peer.
- The reference ID (0.0.0.0 if the reference ID is unknown).
- The stratum of the remote peer.
- The type of the peer (`local`, `unicast`, `multicast`, or `broadcast`) when the last packet was received.
- The polling interval in seconds.
- The reachability register, in octal.
- The current estimated delay offset and dispersion of the peer, all in seconds.

> The character in the left margin indicates the fate of this peer in the clock selection process. The codes are described below.

space	Discarded because of high stratum or failed sanity checks.
x	Designated falsticker by the intersection algorithm.
.	Culled from the end of the candidate list.
–	Discarded by the clustering algorithm.
+	Included in the final selection set.
#	Selected for synchronization, but distance exceeds maximum.
∗	Selected for synchronization.

    o   Selected for synchronization, pps signal in use.

Because the peers command depends on the ability to parse the values in the responses it gets, it may fail to work from time to time with servers that poorly control the data formats.

You can specify the contents of the host field in one of four forms. It can be a host name, an IP address, a reference clock implementation name with its parameter, or REFCLK (implementation number, parameter). On hostnames no, only IP addresses are displayed.

lpeers   Like peers, except print a summary of all associations for which the server is maintaining state. This option can produce a much longer list of peers from inadequate servers.

opeers   An old form of the peers command with the reference ID replaced by the local interface address.

Attributes

See attributes(5) for descriptions of the following attributes.

Attribute Type	Attribute Value
Availability	SUNWntpu

See Also

attributes(5)

Bugs

The peers command is nonatomic. It can occasionally result in spurious error messages about invalid associations occurring that terminate the command.

    The timeout value is a fixed constant. As a result, it often waits a long time to time out because the fixed value assumes a worst case. The program should improve the timeout estimate as it sends queries to a particular host but it does not.

ntptrace — Trace a Chain of NTP Hosts Back to Their Master Time Source

Synopsis

/usr/sbin/ntptrace [-vdn][-r retries][-t timeout][server]

Description

Use the ntptrace command to determine where a given Network Time Protocol (NTP) server gets its time and to follow the chain of NTP servers back to their master time source. If given no arguments, nptrace starts with localhost.

Options

-d	Turn on some debugging output.
-n	Turn off the printing of host names; instead, display host IP addresses. This may be necessary if a nameserver is down.
-r *retries*	Set the number of retransmission attempts for each host.
-t *timeout*	Set the retransmission timeout (in seconds); default is 2.
-v	Print verbose information about the NTP servers.

Examples

The following example shows the output from ntptrace.

```
paperbark% ntptrace
localhost: stratum 4, offset 0.0019529, synch distance 0.144135
server2.bozo.com: stratum 2, offset 0.0124263, synch distance 0.11578
usndh.edu: stratum 1, offset 0.0019298, synch distance 0.011993, refid
    'WWVB'
```

The fields, left to right, on each line are described below.

- The server's host name.
- The server's stratum.
- The time offset between that server and the local host (as measured by ntptrace; which is why it is not always zero for localhost).
- The host's synchronization distance.
- The reference clock ID (only for stratum-1 servers)

All times are given in seconds. Synchronization distance is a measure of the goodness of the clock's time.

Attributes

See attributes(5) for descriptions of the following attributes.

Attribute Type	**Attribute Value**
Availability	SUNWntpu

See Also

xntpd(1M), attributes(5)

Bugs

ntptrace does not try to improve accuracy by doing multiple samples.

nulladm — Create File Name with Mode 664 and Ensure That Owner and Group Are adm

Synopsis

    /usr/lib/acct/nulladm *filename*...

Description

See acctsh(**1M**).

obpsym — OpenBoot Firmware Kernel Symbolic Debugging

Synopsis

```
modload -p misc/obpsym
```

Description

obpsym is a kernel module that installs OpenBoot callback handlers that provide kernel symbol information to OpenBoot. OpenBoot firmware user-interface commands use the callbacks to convert numeric addresses to kernel symbol names for display purposes and to convert kernel symbol names to numeric literals allowing symbolic names to be used as input arguments to user-interface commands.

Once obpsym is installed, you can use kernel symbolic names anywhere at the OpenBoot firmware's user-interface command prompt in place of a literal (numeric) string. For example, if obpsym is installed, the OpenBoot firmware commands ctrace and dis typically display symbolic names and offsets in the form *modname: symbolname + offset*. You can give user-interface commands such as dis or a kernel symbolic name such as ufs:*ufs-mount* instead of a numeric address.

Putting the following command into the system(4) file forces loading of the kernel module misc/obpsym and activates the kernel callbacks during the kernel startup sequence.

```
forceload: misc/obpsym
```

obpsym can be useful as a kernel debugger in situations where other kernel debuggers are not useful. For example, on SPARC machines, if obpsym is loaded, you may be able to use the OpenBoot firmware's `ctrace` command to display symbolic names in the stack backtrace after a watchdog reset.

Warning — Some OpenBoot firmware user-interface commands may use system resources incompatibly with the way they are used by the UNIX kernel. These commands and the use of `obpsym` as a kernel debugger may cause interactions that the UNIX kernel is not prepared to deal with. If this occurs, the UNIX kernel or the OpenBoot firmware user-interface commands can react unpredictably and may panic the system, hang it, or cause other unpredictable results. For these reasons, the use of this feature is only minimally supported and recommended to be used only as a kernel debugger of last resort.

Kernel Symbolic Name Syntax

The kernel symbolic name has the following syntax

[*module-name*:]*symbol-name*

where *module-name* is the name of the kernel module in which the symbol *symbol-name* appears. A NULL module name is taken as "all modules, in no particular order" by `obpsym`. The module name `unix` is equivalent to a NULL module name, so that conflicts with words defined in the firmware's vocabulary can be avoided.

Typically, OpenBoot firmware reads a word from the input stream and looks the word up in its internal vocabulary before checking if the word is a literal. Thus, you can give kernel symbols such as `reset` as `unix:reset` to avoid the unexpected side effect of the firmware finding and executing a matching word in its vocabulary.

Notes

`obpsym` is supported only on architectures that support OpenBoot firmware.

On some systems, OpenBoot must be completely RAM resident so the `obpsym` symbol callback support can be added to the firmware if the firmware doesn't include support for the symbol callbacks. On these systems, `obpsym` may complain that it requires that you must use `ramforth` to use this module.

See the *OpenBoot 2.x Command Reference Manual* for details on how to use the `ramforth` command, how to place the command into `nvramrc`, and how to set `use-nvramrc?` to true. On systems with version 1.x OpenBoot firmware, `nvramrc` doesn't exist, and to use this module, you must type the `ramforth` command after each reset.

Once `obpsym` is installed, you can disable the symbol table callbacks with the following OpenBoot firmware command.

```
0 0 set-symbol-lookup
```

Files

/etc/system   System configuration information file.

/platform/*platform-name*/kernel/misc/obpsym

      `obpsym` command.

Note — You can find *platform-name* with the `-i` option of uname(1)

Attributes

See attributes(5) for descriptions of the following attributes.

Attribute Type	Attribute Value
Availability	SUNWcar

See Also

kadb(1M), kernel(1M), modload(1M), modunload(1M), uname(1), system(4), attributes(5)

OpenBoot 2.x Command Reference Manual

ocfserv — OCF Server

Synopsis

```
ocfserv start
ocfserv stop
```

Description

The ocfserv per-host daemon acts as the central point of communications with all smartcards connected to the host. Any application needing to use a smartcard communicates with the smartcard through this server, which is responsible for handling all traffic to the smartcards. All APIs exposed by this project are internally implemented to communicate with the OCF server. Applications communicate with the OCRF server by using a socket-based protocol.

At startup time, the server reads the properties file to determine the terminals and cards currently registered.

Exit Status

| 0 | Successful completion. |
| >0 | An error occurred. |

Usage

Root privileges are required to execute this command.

Files

/etc/smartcard/opencard.properties

File where server stores properties.

Attributes

See attributes(5) for descriptions of the following attributes.

Attribute Type	Attribute Value
Availability	SUNWocfr

See Also

smartcard(1M), attributes(5), smartcard(5)

P

parse_dynamic_clustertoc — Parse clustertoc File Based on
Dynamic Entries

Synopsis

cdrom/cdrom0/s0/Solaris_8/Tools/Boot/usr/sbin/install.d/
    parse_dynamic_clustertoc

Description

The parse_dynamic_clustertoc script parses the clustertoc file before the
suninstall(1M) process is run. parse_dynamic_clustertoc is called by a modified
sysconfig script on the install CD. When parse_dynamic_clustertoc runs, it reads
the clustertoc and when it encounters SUNW_CSRMBRIFF lines, it either checks the
platform by using the script's built-in function or calls an external script. The script
exits with a 0 if the cluster entry is included; otherwise, it is ignored. If the cluster entry
is to be included, the SUNW_CSRMBRIFF=(test test_arg)cluster line is converted to
SUNW_CSRMEMBER=cluster.

Examples

The following example of a simple external test checks for an SX Framebuffer. The entry
in the clustertoc file is shown, and following that is the script that must be placed in
the install.d/dynamic_test directory.

SUNW_CSRMBRIFF=(smcc.dctoc sx)SUNWCsx
!/bin/sh
#

```
# Likewise, this file is expected to live under $(TESTDIR).
#
case "$1"
in
        sx) prtconf -p | grep 'SUNW,sx' 1> /dev/null;;
esac
```

Files

cdrom/cdrom0/s0/Solaris_8/Product/locale/C/.clustertoc.dynamic
> Dynamic version of the clustertoc file.

cdrom/cdrom0/s0/Solaris_8/Tools/Boot/usr/sbin/install.d/dynamic_test
> Directory that contains any additional tests.

Attributes

See attributes(5) for descriptions of the following attributes.

Attribute Type	Attribute Value
Availability	SHWPcdrom (Solaris CD)

See Also

suninstall(1M), clustertoc(4), attributes(5)

passmgmt — Password Files Management

Synopsis

```
/usr/sbin/passmgmt -a options name
/usr/sbin/passmgmt -m options name
/usr/sbin/passmgmt -d name
```

Description

Use the passmgmt command to update information in the password files. This command works with both /etc/passwd and /etc/shadow.

Note — The passmgmt command modifies password definitions only in the local /etc/passwd and /etc/shadow files. If a network nameservice such as NIS or NIS+ is being used to supplement the local files with additional entries, passmgmt cannot change information supplied by the network nameservice.

The passmgmt command will be removed in a future release. Its functionality has been replaced and enhanced by the useradd, userdel, and usermod commands, which are currently available.

---

passmgmt -a adds an entry for user *name* to the password files. This command does not create any directory for the new user and the new login remains locked (with the string *LK* in the password field) until the passwd(1) command is executed to set the password.

passmgmt -m modifies the entry for user *name* in the password files. You can modify the name field in the /etc/shadow file and all the fields (except the password field) in the /etc/passwd file with this command. Only fields entered on the command line are modified.

passmgmt -d deletes the entry for user *name* from the password files. It does not remove any files that the user owns on the system; you must remove them manually.

Only superuser can use the passmgmt command.

Do not use a colon (:) or Return as part of an argument. It is interpreted as a field separator in the password file.

Options

-c *comment*	A short description of the login, enclosed in quotes. *comment* is limited to a maximum of 128 characters and defaults to an empty field.
-g *gid*	GID of *name*. *gid* must range from 0 to the maximum nonnegative value for the system. The default is 1.
-h *homedir*	Home directory of *name*. *homedir* is limited to a maximum of 256 characters and defaults to /usr/*name*.
-l *logname*	Change the name to *logname*. Use this option only with the -m option. The total size of each login entry is limited to a maximum of 511 bytes in each of the password files.
-o	Enable a UID to be nonunique. Use this option only with the -u option.
-s *shell*	Specify the login shell for *name*. *shell* should be the full path name of the program that is executed when the user logs in. The maximum size of *shell* is 256 characters. The default is for this field to be empty and to be interpreted as /usr/bin/sh.
-u *uid*	UID of *name*. This number must range from 0 to the maximum nonnegative value for the system. *uid* defaults to the next available UID greater than 99. Without the -o option, enforce the uniqueness of a UID.

Files

/etc/passwd	File that contains a list of users recognized by the system.
/etc/shadow	File that contains encrypted password strings.
/etc/opasswd	Old copy of the passwd file generated when you run passmgmt.
/etc/oshadow	Old copy of the shadow file generated when you run passmgmt.

Exit Status

0	Success.
1	Permission denied.
2	Invalid command syntax. Usage message of the passmgmt command is displayed.
3	Invalid argument provided to option.
4	UID in use.
5	Inconsistent password files (for example, *name* is in the /etc/passwd file and not in the /etc/shadow file, or vice versa).
6	Unexpected failure. Password files unchanged.
7	Unexpected failure. Password file(s) missing.
8	Password file(s) busy. Try again later.
9	Name does not exist (if you specified −m or −d), already exists (if you specified −a), or *logname* already exists (if you specified −m −1).

Attributes

See attributes(5) for descriptions of the following attributes.

Attribute Type	Attribute Value
Availability	SUNWcsu

See Also

passwd(1), useradd(1M), userdel(1M), usermod(1M), passwd(4), shadow(4), attributes(5)

patchadd — Apply a Patch Package to a Solaris System

Synopsis

```
/usr/sbin/patchadd [-d][-u][-B backout-dir][C net-install-image |
   -R client-root-path | -S service] patch
/usr/sbin/patchadd [-d][-u][-B backout-dir][C net-install-image |
   -R client-root-path | -S service] -M patch-dir | patch-id... |
   patch-dir patch-list
/usr/sbin/patchadd [-C net-install-image | -R client-root-path |
   -S service] -p
```

Description

Use the patchadd command to apply a patch package to a Solaris 2 or compatible version system. You cannot use this patch installation command to apply Solaris 1 patches. You must run patchadd as root.

When you install a patch, the patchadd command copies files from the patch directory to a local system disk. The patchadd command does the following.

- Determines the Solaris version number of the managing host and the target host.
- Updates the pkginfo file of the patch package with information about patches that are rendered obsolete by the patch being installed, other patches required by this patch, and patches that are incompatible with this patch.

The patchadd command does not install a patch under the following conditions.

- The package is not fully installed on the host.
- The patch architecture differs from the system architecture.
- The patch version does not patch the installed package version.
- A patch is already installed with the same base code and a higher version number.
- The patch is incompatible with another, already installed patch (this information is stored in the pkginfo file for each patch).
- The patch being installed requires another patch that is not installed.

The patchadd command has three forms.

- The first form of patchadd installs one patch to a system, client, service, or the miniroot of a Net Install Image.
- The second form of patchadd installs more than one patch to a system, client, service, or the miniroot of a Net Install Image.
- The third form of patchadd displays installed patches on the client, service, or the miniroot of a Net Install Image.

Note — To successfully install a patch to a client or server when there are both /usr and root packages in the patch, you must run patchadd twice: once with the -R option and once with the -S option. This procedure guarantees that the patch is installed to both the /usr and root partitions.

Options

-B *backout-dir*

> Save backout data to a directory other than the package database. Specify *backout-dir* as an absolute path name.

-C *net-install-image*

> Patch the files located on the miniroot on a Net Install Image created by setup_install_server. Specify *net-install-image* as the absolute path name to a Solaris 2.6 or compatible version Net Install Image created by setup_install_server.

-d

> Do not back up the files to be patched. If you use this option, you cannot remove the patch with the patchrm command.

`-M` *patch-dir patch-id...* | *patch-dir patch-list*

Specify the patches to be installed. Specify patches to the `-M` option in one of the following ways.

- By directory location and patch number. To use the directory location and patch number, specify *patch-dir* as the absolute path name of the directory that contains spooled patches. Specify *patch-id* as the patch number of a given patch. Specifying multiple *patch-id*s is recommended.

- By directory location and the name of a file containing a patch list. To use the directory location and a file containing a patch list, specify *patch-dir* as the absolute path name of the directory containing the file with a list of patches to be installed. Specify *patch-list* as the name of the file containing the patches to be installed.

`-p`   Display a list of the patches currently applied.

`-u`   Install unconditionally, turn off file validation. Apply the patch even if some of the files to be patched have been modified since their original installation.

`-R` *client-root-path*

Locate all patch files generated by `patchadd` under the directory *client-root-path*. *client-root-path* is the directory that contains the bootable root of a client from the server's perspective. Specify *client-root-path* as the absolute path name to the beginning of the directory tree under which all patch files generated by `patchadd` are to be located. You cannot specify `-R` with the `-S` option.

`-S` *service*   Specify an alternate service (for example, `Solaris_2.3`). This service is part of the server and client model and can be used only from the server's console. Servers can contain shared `/usr` file systems that are created by Host Manager. You can then make these service areas available to the clients they serve. You cannot specify `-S` with the `-R` option.

Operands

patch-id   The patch number of a given patch. `104945-02` is an example of a *patch-id*.

patch-list   The name of a file that contains a list of patches to install. *patch-list* files contain one *patch-id* on each line.

patch   The absolute path name to *patch-id*. `/var/sadm/spool/patch/104945-02` is an example of a *patch*.

patch-dir   The absolute path name to the directory that contains all the spooled patches. `/var/sadm/spool/patch` is an example of a *patch-dir*.

Examples

The examples in this section are all relative to the /usr/sbin directory.
The following example installs a patch to a standalone machine.

```
# patchadd /var/spool/patch/104945-02
```

The following example installs a patch to a client from the server's console.

```
# patchadd -R /export/root/client1 /var/spool/patch/104945-02
```

The following example installs a patch to a service from the server's console.

```
# patchadd -S Solaris_2.3 /var/spool/patch/104945-02
```

The following example installs multiple patches in a single patchadd invocation.

```
# patchadd -M /var/spool/patch 104945-02 104946-02 102345-02
```

The following example installs multiple patches specifying a file named patchlist
with the list of patches to install.

```
# patchadd -M /var/spool/patch patchlist
```

The following example installs multiple patches to a client and saves the backout
data to a directory other than the default.

```
# patchadd -M /var/spool/patch -R /export/root/client1 -B
  /export/backoutrepository 104945-02 104946-02 102345-02
```

The following example installs a patch to a Solaris 2.6 or compatible version Net
Install Image.

```
#patchadd-C/export/Solaris_2.6/Tools/Boot/var/spool/patch/104945-02
```

The following example displays the patches installed on a client.

```
# patchadd -R /export/root/client1 -p
```

Exit Status

0	Successful completion.
>0	An error occurred.

Attributes

See attributes(5) for descriptions of the following attributes.

Attribute Type	Attribute Value
Availability	SUNWswmt
	SUNWcsu

See Also

cpio(1), pkginfo(1), patchrm(1M), pkgadd(1M), pkgchk(1M), pkgrm(1M),
showrev(1M), attributes(5)

patchrm — Remove a Patch Package and Restore Previously Saved Files

Synopsis

```
/usr/sbin/patchrm [-f][-B backout-dir][-C net-install-image |
   -R client-root-path | -S service] patch-id
```

Description

Use the patchrm command to remove a patch package and restore previously saved files to a Solaris 2 or Solaris 8 system. You cannot use patchrm with Solaris 1 patches. You must run patchrm as root.

When you remove or back out a patch, the patchrm command restores all files modified by that patch unless any of the following conditions are true.

- The patch was installed with patchadd -d, which instructs patchadd not to save copies of files that are updated or replaced.
- The patch has been made obsolete by a later patch.
- The patch is required by another patch.

The patchrm command calls pkgadd to restore packages that were saved from the initial patch installation.

During the patch installation, patchrm keeps a log of the patch installation in /tmp/backoutlog.*pid*. This log is removed if the patch backs out successfully.

Options

-f   Force the patch removal regardless of whether the patch was superseded by another patch.

-B *backout-dir*

                Remove a patch whose backout data has been saved to a directory other than the package database. You need this option only if the original backout directory, supplied to the patchadd command at installation time, has been moved. Specify *backout-dir* as an absolute path name.

-C *net-install-image*

                Remove the patched files located on the miniroot on a Net Install Image created by setup_install_server. Specify *net-install-image* as the absolute path name to a Solaris 2.6 or compatible version Net Install Image created by setup_install_server.

-R *client-root-path*

                Locate all patch files generated by patchrm under the directory *client-root-path*. *client-root-path* is the directory that contains the bootable root of a client from the server's perspective. Specify *client-root-path* as the absolute path name to the beginning of the directory tree under which all patch files generated from patchrm are located. You cannot specify -R with the -S option.

-S *service*   Specify an alternate service (for example, Solaris_2.3). This service is part of the server and client model and can be used only from the server's console. Servers can contain shared /usr file systems that are created by Host Manager. You can then make these service areas available to the clients they serve. You cannot specify -S with the -R option.

Operands

patch-id   The patch number of a given patch, for example, 104945-02.

Examples

The examples in this section assume that patch 104945-02 has been installed to the system. All of the examples are relative to the /usr/sbin directory.

The following example removes a patch from a standalone system.

```
# patchrm 104945-02
```

The following example removes a patch from a client's system from the server's console.

```
# patchrm -R /export/root/client1 104945-02
```

The following example removes a patch from a server's service area.

```
# patchrm -S Solaris_2.3 104945-02
```

The following example removes a patch from a Net Install Image.

```
# patchrm -C /export/Solaris_8/Tools/Boot 104945-02
```

Exit Status

0   Successful completion.

>0   An error occurred.

Attributes

See attributes(5) for descriptions of the following attributes.

Attribute Type	Attribute Value
Availability	SUNWswmt
	SUNWcsu

See Also

cpio(1), pkginfo(1), patchadd(1M), pkgadd(1M), pkgchk(1M), pkgrm(1M), showrev(1M), attributes(5)

pbind — Control and Query Bindings of Processes to Processors

Synopsis

```
/usr/sbin/pbind -b processor-id pid...
/usr/sbin/pbind -u pid...
/usr/sbin/pbind [-q][pid...]
```

Description

In a multiprocessor environment you can use the pbind command to bind all the lightweight processes (LWPs) of a process to a specific processor, to remove a binding, and to show whether a process is bound to a particular CPU. If the process is not bound, pbind doesn't show on which CPU it is executing.

> **Note —** Using pbind to bind a process cannot guarantee exclusive use of a processor by a process. It simply executes the process only on the specified CPU unless the process needs a resource owned by another CPU. Other processes can also use the processor.

Bindings are inherited, so that new LWPs and processes created by a bound LWP have the same binding. Binding an interactive shell to a processor, for example, binds all commands executed by the shell.

Superuser can bind or unbind any process, and other users can use pbind to bind or unbind any process they own.

Options

-b processor-id

Bind all the LWPs of the specified processes to the processor processor-id. Specify processor-id as the processor ID of the processor to be controlled or queried. processor-id must be present and online. Use the psrinfo command to determine whether processor-id is present and online. See psrinfo(1M).

-q

Display the bindings of the specified processes or of all processes. If a process is composed of multiple LWPs that have different bindings, display the bindings of only one of the bound LWPs.

-u

Remove the bindings of all LWPs of the specified processes, allowing them to be executed on any online processor.

Operands

pid

The process ID of the process to be controlled or queried.

Examples

The following example binds processes 204 and 223 to processor 2.

```
paperbark% pbind -b 2 204 223
process id 204: was 2, now 2
process id 223: was 3, now 2
paperbark%
```

The following example unbinds process 204.

```
paperbark% pbind -u 204
paperbark%
```

The following example demonstrates that process 1 is bound to processor 0, process 149 has at least one LWP bound to CPU3, and process 101 has no bound LWPs.

```
paperbark% pbind -q 1 149 101
process id 1: 0
process id 149: 3
process id 101: not bound
paperbark%
```

Attributes

See attributes(5) for descriptions of the following attributes.

Attribute Type	Attribute Value
Availability	SUNWcsu

Exit Status

| 0 | Successful completion. |
| >0 | An error occurred. |

See Also

psradm(1M), psrinfo(1M), psrset(1M), processor_bind(2), processor_info(2), sysconf(3C), attributes(5)

Diagnostics

pbind: cannot query pid 31: No such process

        The process specified did not exist or has exited.

pbind: cannot bind pid 31: Not owner

        The user does not have permission to bind the process.

pbind: cannot bind pid 31: Invalid argument

        The specified processor is not online.

pcmciad — PCMCIA User Daemon

Synopsis

```
/usr/lib/pcmciad
```

Description

The pcmciad user daemon provides user-level services for the PCMCIA nexus driver and PCMCIA card client drivers. This daemon has no user-configurable options.

Attributes

See attributes(5) for descriptions of the following attributes.

Attribute Type	Attribute Value
Availability	SUNWpcmcu

See Also

```
pcmcia(4), attributes(5)
```

Diagnostics

```
pcmciad: can't open /dev/pem: No such file or directory
```

The user daemon could not communicate with the PCMCIA event management driver.

pfinstall — Test Installation Profiles

Synopsis

```
/usr/sbin/install.d/pfinstall -D | -d disk-config [-c CDpath] profile
```

Description

If you are setting up custom JumpStart installations on a network, you need to create a profile server that creates a JumpStart directory for the custom JumpStart files. As part of preparing the JumpStart files, you create a *profile* text file that defines rules for how to install the Solaris software on a system.

After you create a profile, you can use the pfinstall command to test the profile and see if it does what you want before using it to install or upgrade a system. pfinstall enables you to test a profile in the following ways.

- Test against a system's disk configuration where `pfinstall` is being run.
- Test other disks by using a disk configuration file that represents a structure of a disk. See "Notes" on page 865 for information on how to create a disk configuration file.

To successfully and accurately test a profile for a particular Solaris release, you must test a profile within the Solaris environment of the same release. For example, if you want to test a profile for the Solaris 8 Operating Environment, you have to run the `pfinstall` command on a system running the Solaris 8 Operating Environment.

So, on a system running the Solaris 8 Operating Environment, you can test Solaris 8 initial installation profiles. However, if you want to test a Solaris 8 upgrade profile on a system running a previous version of the Solaris Operating Environment or if you don't have a Solaris 8 system installed yet to test the Solaris 8 initial installation profiles, you have to boot a system from a Solaris 8, 1 of 2 CD image and temporarily create a Solaris 8 install environment. Then, you can run `pfinstall` in the Solaris 8 install environment to test your profiles.

To create a temporary Solaris 8 install environment, boot a system from a Solaris 8, 1 of 2 CD image (just as you would to install), answer any system identification questions, choose the Solaris Interactive Installation program, and exit out of the first screen that is presented. Then, from the shell, you can execute the `pfinstall` command.

Notes

You must test a profile on a system with the same platform type for which the profile was created.

SPARC Platform

Use the following steps to create a disk configuration file (`-d` option) for a SPARC-based system.

1. Locate a SPARC-based system with a disk that you want to test.
2. Create a disk configuration file by redirecting the output of the `prtvtoc`(1M) command to a file.

   `# prtvtoc /dev/rdsk/c0t3d0s2 > 535_disk`

3. (Optional) Concatenate disk configuration files into a single file to test a profile against multiple disks. The target numbers in the disk device names must be unique.

   `# cat 535_disk 1G_disk > mult_disks`

IA Platform

Use the following steps to create a disk configuration file (`-d` option) for an IA-based system.

1. Locate an IA-based system with a disk that you want to test.
2. Create part of the disk configuration file by saving the output of the `fdisk`(1M) command to a file.

   `# fdisk -R -W 535_disk /dev/rdsk/c0t3d0p0`

3. Append the output of the `prtvtoc`(1M) command to the disk configuration file.

   `# prtvtoc /dev/rdsk/c0t3d0s2 >> 535_disk`

   (Optional) Concatenate disk configuration files into a single file to test a profile against multiple disks. The target numbers in the disk device names must be

unique.
cat 535_disk 1G_disk > mult_disks

To test a profile with a specific system memory size, set SYS_MEMSIZE to the specific memory size (in Mbytes) before running pfinstall.

SYS_MEMSIZE=memory_size
export SYS_MEMSIZE

Options

Warning — If you do not specify the -d or -D option, pfinstall may perform an actual installation on the system by using the specified profile, and you may overwrite the data on the system.

-D   Use the system's disk configuration to test the profile. You must specify either this option or the -d option to test the profile.

-d *disk-config*

Use the *disk-config* file to test the profile. See "Notes" on page 865 for information on how to create a disk configuration file. You must specify either this option or the -D option to test the profile. You cannot use this option with an upgrade profile (install_type upgrade). You must always test an upgrade profile against a system's disk configuration (-D option).

-c *CDpath*   Specify the path to the Solaris installation image. This option is required if the image is not mounted on /cdrom. (For example, use this option if you copied the installation image to disk or mounted the CD-ROM on a directory other than /cdrom.)

Operands

profile   The file name of the profile to test. If *profile* is not in the directory where pfinstall is being run, you must specify the path.

Examples

The following example tests an upgrade profile, upgrade.prof, on a system with a previous version of the Solaris software installed.

1. Boot the system to be upgraded from a Solaris 8 image (just as you would to install). The image can be located in the system's local CD-ROM or on an install server.

2. Answer the system configuration questions if prompted.

3. If you are presented with a choice of installation options, choose the Solaris Interactive Installation program.

4. Exit from the first screen of the Solaris Interactive Installation program. After the Solaris Interactive Installation program exits, a shell prompt is displayed.

5. Create a temporary mount point.

mkdir /tmp/mnt

6. Mount the directory that contains the profile(s) you want to test.

To mount a remote NFS file system (for systems on the network), type the following command.

mount -F nfs *server-name:path* /tmp/mnt

To mount a UFS-formatted diskette, type the following command.

mount -F ufs /dev/diskette /tmp/mnt

To mount a PCFS-formatted diskette, type the following command.

mount -F pcfs /dev/diskette /tmp/mnt

7. Change directory to /tmp/mnt where the profile resides.

cd /tmp/mnt

8. Test the upgrade.prof profile.

/usr/sbin/install.d/pfinstall -D upgrade.prof

The following example tests the basic.prof profile against the disk configuration on a Solaris 8 system where pfinstall is being run. The path to the Solaris CD image is specified because Volume Management is being used.

/usr/sbin/install.d/pfinstall -D -c /cdrom/cdrom0/s0 basic.prof

The following example tests the basic.prof profile against the 535_test disk configuration file. This example uses a Solaris CD image located in the /export/install directory, and pfinstall is being run on a Solaris 8 system.

/usr/sbin/install.d/pfinstall -d 535_test -c /export/install
  basic.prof

Exit Status

0	Successful (system rebooted).
1	Successful (system not rebooted).
2	An error occurred.

Attributes

See attributes(5) for descriptions of the following attributes.

Attribute Type	**Attribute Value**
Availability	SUNWinst

See Also

fdisk(1M), prtvtoc(1M), attributes(5)
Solaris Advanced Installation Guide

New! pgxconfig, GFXconfig — Configure the PGX32 (Raptor GFX) Graphics Accelerator

Synopsis

```
/usr/sbin/pgxconfig [-dev device-filename] [-res videomode [try |
    noconfirm | nocheck]] [-file machine | system] [-depth 8 | 24]
    [-24only] [-defaults]
/usr/sbin/pgxconfig [-propt] [-prconf]
/usr/sbin/pgxconfig [-help] [-res ?]
/usr/sbin/pgxconfig [-i]
```

Description

Use the pgxconfig command to configure the PGX32 (Raptor GFX) Graphics Accelerator and some of the X11 window system defaults for PGX32 (Raptor GFX). A previous version of this command was named GFXconfig.

> **Note** — The pgxconfig command is part of the TSIpgxw and TSIgfxOW packages, which are not installed as part of a complete system install. If you want to run the pgxconfig command, first install these two packages.

The first form of pgxconfig stores the specified options in the OWconfig file. These options initialize the PGX32 (Raptor GFX) device the next time the window system is run on that device. Updating options in the OWconfig file provides persistence of these options across window system sessions and system reboots.

The second, third, and fourth forms, which invoke only the -prconf, -propt, -help, and -res ? options, do not update the OWconfig file. For the third form, all other options are ignored.

The -i option starts pgxconfig in interactive mode.

You can specify options for only one PGX32 (Raptor GFX) device at a time. To configure multiple PGX32 (Raptor GFX) devices, invoke pgxconfig -i for each device.

You can specify only PGX32 (Raptor GFX)-specific options through pgxconfig. You still specify the normal window system options for default depth, default visual class, and so forth as device modifiers on the openwin command line. See the Xsun(1) manual page available with the SUNWxwman package.

You can also specify the OWconfig file that is to be updated. By default, the machine-specific file in the /usr/openwin directory tree is updated. You can use the -file option to update the system-global OWconfig file in the /etc/openwin directory tree instead.

Both of these standard OWconfig files can only be written by root. Consequently, the pgxconfig program, which is owned by the root user, always runs with setuid root permission.

Options

-dev *device-filename*

> Specify the PGX32 (Raptor GFX) special file. The default is
> /dev/fbs/gfxp0, or /dev/fbs/raptor0 if applicable.

-file machine | system

> Specify which OWconfig file to update. If machine, use the
> machine-specific OWconfig file in the /etc/openwin directory tree. If
> system, use the global OWconfig file in the /usr/openwin directory
> tree. If the file does not exist, create it.

-res *video-mode* [try | noconfirm | nocheck]

> Specify the built-in video mode used to drive the monitor connected to
> the specified PGX32 (Raptor GFX) device.
>
> The format for *video-mode* can be one of the following.
>
> *widthxheightxrate*
>
>> *width* is the screen width in pixels, *height* is the
>> screen height in pixels, and *rate* is the vertical
>> frequency of the screen refresh. As a convenience,
>> -res also accepts formats with @ prepended to the
>> refresh rate instead of x, for example,
>> 1280x1024@76. You can obtain the list by running
>> pgxconfig with the -res ? option. Note that not
>> all resolutions are supported by both the video
>> board and by the monitor. The pgxconfig
>> command does not permit you to set a resolution
>> not supported by the board unless you specify the
>> noconfirm or nocheck option. It also requests
>> confirmation before setting a resolution not
>> supported by the monitor if you do not specify the
>> nocheck option.
>
>> Symbolic names   For convenience, the video modes listed below have
>> symbolic names defined. You can provide the
>> symbolic name as the argument to -res instead of
>> *widthxheightxrate*. If the symbolic name is none,
>> the screen resolution is the video mode that is
>> currently programmed in the device when the
>> window system is run.

svga	1024x768x60.
1152	1152x900x76.
1280	1280x1024x76.
vga	640x480x60.
none	Default console resolution.

The -res option also accepts additional, optional arguments immediately following the video mode specification. Any or all of these may be present.

noconfirm   Bypass warning message and confirmation requests about possible ambiguities. Using the -res option could put the system into an unusable state with no video output. This state can occur if there is ambiguity in the monitor sense codes for the particular code read. To reduce the chance of ambiguities, the default behavior is to print a warning message and ask if it is okay to continue. The noconfirm option is useful when pgxconfig is being run from a shell script.

nocheck   Suspend normal error checking based on the monitor sense code. Accept the specified video mode regardless of whether it is appropriate for the currently attached monitor. (This option is useful if a different monitor is to be connected to the PGX32 (Raptor GFX) device). Use of this option implies noconfirm.

try   Test the specified resolution before committing it. Display a pattern on the screen with the specified resolution. If the test pattern appears correctly, you can answer y to the query. The other permissible answer is n.

-res ?   Print the list of possible resolutions supported by the PGX32 and the monitor.

-24only   Force the PGX32 (Raptor GFX) device to use 24-bit only when running OpenWindows.

-defaults   Reset all option values to their default values.

-propt   Print the current values of all PGX32 (Raptor GFX) options in the OWconfig file specified by the -file option for the device specified by the -dev option. Print the values of options as they would be in the OWconfig file after the call to pgxconfig completed. The following is a typical display.

```
--- OpenWindows Configuration for /dev/fbs/gfxp0 ---
OWconfig: machine
Video Mode: not set
```

-prconf   Print the PGX32 (Raptor GFX) hardware configuration. The following is a typical display.

```
--- Hardware Configuration for /dev/fbs/gfxp0 --DAC: ver-
sion 0x0 Type: Board: PROM: version 0x0 PROM Informa-
tion: RAM: EDID Data: Monitor Sense ID: Card possible
resolutions: 640x480x60, 800x600x75,
1024x768x60
```

```
                        1024x768x70, 1024x768x75

                        1280x1024x75, 1280x1024x76, 1280x1024x60,
                        1280x1024x67

                        1152x900x66, 1152x900x76,

                        960x680x112S, 960x680x108S

                        640x480x60i

                        768x575x50i

                        1280x800x76

                        1440x900x76

                        1600x1000x66, 1600x1000x76,

                        vga, svga, 1152, 1280, stereo, ntsc, pal
        Monitor possible resolutions: 720x400x70, 720x400x88
        640x480x60,
                        640x480x67, 640x480x72, 640x480x75

                        800x600x56,
                        800x600x60, 800x600x72, 800x600x75,

                        832x624x75,

                        1024x768x87, 1024x768x60, 1024x768x70,
                        1024x768x75

                        1280x1024x75, 1280x1024x76

                        1152x900x66, 1152x900x76

                        1280x1024x67

                        960x680x112S

                        vga, svga, 1152, 1280, stereo
        Current resolution setting: 1280x1024x76

        Possible depths:

        Current depth: 8
```

-help   Print a list of the pgxconfig command-line options, along with a brief explanation of each.

-i   Start pgxconfig in interactive mode.

Defaults

For a given invocation of pgxconfig, only options specified on the command line are updated in the OWconfig file. Previous unspecified values are retained except for -depth and -24only.

A default value is used if a PGX32 (Raptor GFX) option has not been specified with pgxconfig when the window system is run. The option defaults are as follows.

-dev   /dev/fbs/gfxp0

-file   system

```
-res        none
```

The default of none for the -res option indicates that when the window system is
run, the screen resolution is the video mode that is currently programmed in the device.

Examples

The following example switches the monitor type to the resolution of 1280 x 1024 at
76 Hz.

```
paperbark% /usr/sbin/pgxconfig -res 280x1024x76
```

Files

```
/dev/fbs/gfxp0
```

Device special file.

```
/usr/openwin/server/etc/OWconfig
```

System configuration file.

```
/etc/openwin/server/etc/OWconfig
```

Machine configuration file.

Attributes

See attributes(5) for descriptions of the following attributes.

Attribute Type	Attribute Value
Availability	TSIpgxw
	TSIgfxOW

See Also

PGX32 Installation Manual

---

ping — Send ICMP (ICMP6) ECHO_REQUEST Packets to Network Hosts

Synopsis

New!

```
/usr/sbin/ping host [timeout]
/usr/sbin/ping -s [-l | -U][-adlLnrRv][-A addr-family]
  [-c traffic-class][-g gateway...][-F flow-label]
  [-i interface-address][-I interval][-p port][-P tos][-t ttl] host
  [data-size][count]
```

Description

The `ping` command has been revised in the Solaris 8 release to add IPv6 functionality. *New!*
Use the `ping` command to determine whether a remote system is accessible on the
network. The `ping` command uses the ICMP (ICMP6 in IPv6) protocol's `ECHO_REQUEST`
datagram to elicit an ICMP or ICMP6 `ECHO_RESPONSE` from the specified host or
network gateway. If *host* responds, `ping` prints the following message on the standard
output and exits.

```
host is alive
```

Otherwise, after *timeout* seconds, it writes

```
no answer from host
```

The default value of *timeout* is 20 seconds.

When you specify the `-s` option, `ping` sends one datagram per second (adjustable
with `-I`) and prints one line of output for every `ECHO_RESPONSE` that it receives. No
output is produced if there is no response. In this second form, `ping` computes round trip
times and packet loss statistics; it displays a summary of this information on
termination or timeout. The default datagram packet size is 64 bytes, or you can specify
a size with the *packetsize* command-line argument. If you specify an optional *count*,
`ping` sends ping requests until it either sends *count* requests or receives *count* replies.

When using `ping` for fault isolation, first ping the local host to verify that the local
network interface is running.

Options

-a   Ping all of the addresses, both IPv4 and IPv6, of the multihomed *New!*
destination. The output looks as though `ping` has been run once for
each IP address of the destination. If you use this option with `-A`,
probe only the addresses that are of the specified address family.
When used with the `-s` option and you do not specify *count*,
continuously probe the destination addresses in a round robin
fashion. If you specify *count*, send *count* number of probes to each IP
address of the destination and then exit.

-A *addr-family* *New!*

Specify the address family of the target host. The value of
addr-family can be either `inet` or `inet6`. Address family determines
which protocol to use. For an argument of `inet`, use IPv4. For `inet6`,
use IPv6.

By default, if you provide the name of a host and not the literal IP
address and a valid IPv6 address exists in the nameservice database,
use this address. Otherwise, if the nameservice database contains an
IPv4 address, try the IPv4 address.

Specify the address family `inet` or `inet6` to override the default
behavior. If you specify `inet`, use the IPv4 address associated with
the host name. If none exists, state that the host is unknown and exit.
Do not try to determine if an IPv6 address exists in the nameservice
database.

If you specify `inet6` as the argument, use the IPv6 address that is associated with the host name. If none exists, state that the host is unknown and exit.

New! `-c traffic-class`

Specify the traffic class of probe packets. The value must be an integer in the range from `0` to `255`. Gateways along the path may route the probe packet differently depending on the value of `traffic-class` set in the probe packet. This option is valid only on IPv6.

`-d` Set the `SO_DEBUG` socket option.

New! `-F flow-label`

Specify the flow label of the probe packets. The value must be an integer in the range from `0` to `1048575`. This option is valid only on IPv6.

`-i interface-address`

Specify the outgoing interface address to use for multicast packets. The default interface address for multicast packets is determined from the (unicast) routing tables.

`-I interval` Specify the interval between successive transmissions. The default is `1` second.

`-l` Specify loose source route. Use this option in the IP header to send the packet to the given host and back again. Usually specified with the `-R` option.

`-L` Turn off loopback of multicast packets. Normally, if there are members in the host group on the outgoing interface, a copy of the multicast packets is delivered to the local machine.

`-n` Show network addresses as numbers. `ping` normally displays addresses as host names.

New! `-p port` Set the base UPD `port` number used in probes. Use this option with the `-U` option. The default base `port` number is `33434`. `ping` starts setting the destination port number of UDP packets to this base and increments it by 1 at each probe.

New! `-P tos` Set the type of service (`tos`) in probe packets to the specified value. The default is `0`. The value must be an integer in the range from `0` to `255`. Gateways also in the path may route the probe packet differently depending on the value of `tos` that is set in the probe packet. This option is valid only on IPv4

`-r` Bypass the normal routing tables and send directly to a host on an attached network. If the host is not on a directly attached network, return an error. You can use this option to ping a local host through an interface that has been dropped by the router daemon (see `in.routed(1M)`).

-R	Set the IP record route option, which stores the route of the packet inside the IP header. Print the contents of the record route only if you specify the -v option, and set it on return packets only if the target host preserves the record route option across echoes or you specify the -l option.
-v	List any ICMP packets other than ECHO_RESPONSE that are received.
-t *ttl*	Specify the IP time-to-live for unicast and multicast packets. The default time-to-live for unicast packets is set with ndd(1M) (using the icmp_def_ttl variable). The default time-to-live for multicast is one hop.

Operands

host	The network host.

Examples

The following example shows ping sending probe packets to all the IPv6 addresses of the host london, one at a time. It sends an ICMP6 ECHO_REQUEST every second until the user interrupts it.

```
istanbul% ping -s -A inet6 -a london
PING london: 56 data bytes
64 bytes from london (4::114:a00:20ff:ab3d:83ed): icmp_seq=0. time=2. ms
64 bytes from london (fec0::114:a00:20ff:ab3d:83ed): icmp_seq=1. time=1. ms
64 bytes from london (4::114:a00:20ff:ab3d:83ed): icmp_seq=2. time=1. ms
64 bytes from london (fec0::114:a00:20ff:ab3d:83ed): icmp_seq=3. time=1. ms
64 bytes from london (4::114:a00:20ff:ab3d:83ed): icmp_seq=4. time=1. ms
64 bytes from london (fec0::114:a00:20ff:ab3d:83ed): icmp_seq=5. time=1. ms
^C
----london PING Statistics----
6 packets transmitted, 6 packets received, 0% packet loss
round-trip (ms)  min/avg/max = 1/1/2
```

Exit Status

0	Successful operation; the machine is alive.
Non-zero	An error has occurred; either a malformed argument has been specified or the machine was not alive.

Attributes

See attributes(5) for descriptions of the following attributes.

Attribute Type	Attribute Value
Availability	SUNWcsu

New!

See Also

ifconfig(1M), in.routed(1M), ndd(1M), netstat(1M), rpcinfo(1M), traceroute(1M), attributes(5), icmp(7P), icmp6(7P)

pkgadd — Transfer Software Packages to the System

Synopsis

/usr/sbin/pkgadd [-nv][-a *admin*][-d *device*][[-M] -R *root-path*]
  [-r *response*][-V *fs-file*][*pkginst*...]
/usr/sbin/pkgadd -s *spool* [-d *device*][*pkginst*...]

Description

Use the pkgadd command to install the contents of a software package from the distribution medium or a directory onto a system. Used without the -d option, pkgadd looks in the default spool directory (/var/spool/pkg) for the package. Used with the -s option, it writes the package to a spool directory instead of installing it.

Certain unbundled and third-party packages are no longer entirely compatible with the latest version of pkgadd. These packages require user interaction throughout the installation and not just at the very beginning. To install these older packages (released prior to Solaris 2.4), set the following environment variable.

NONABI_SCRIPTS=TRUE

pkgadd permits keyboard interaction throughout the installation as long as this environment variable is set.

Notes

When transferring a package to a spool directory, you cannot use the -r, -n, or -a options.

You can use the -r option to specify a directory name as well as a file name. The directory can contain numerous response files, each sharing the name of the package with which it should be associated. You would use this syntax, for example, when adding multiple interactive packages with one invocation of pkgadd.

Each package would need a response file. If you create response files with the same name as the package (for example, pkinst1 and pkinst2), then name the directory in which these files reside after the -r.

The -n option halts the installation if any interaction is needed to complete it.

If the default admin file is too restrictive, the administration file may need to be modified to allow for total noninteraction during a package installation. See admin(4) for details.

Options

-a *admin*   Define an installation administration file, *admin*, to be used in place of the default administration file. The token none overrides the use of any *admin* file and thus forces interaction with the user. Unless you specify a full path name, pkgadd looks first in the current working directory for the administration file. If the specified administration file is not in the current working directory, pkgadd looks in the /var/sadm/install/admin directory for the administration file.

-d *device*   Install or copy a package from *device*. *device* can be a full path name to a directory or the identifiers for tape, diskette, or removable disk (for example, /var/tmp or /floppy/floppy_name). It can also be a device alias (for example, /floppy/floppy0).

-M   Do not use the $*root-path*/etc/vfstab file for determining the client's mount points. This option assumes the mount points are correct on the server, and it behaves consistently with Solaris 2.5 and earlier releases.

-n   Do installation in noninteractive mode. The default mode is interactive.

-r *response*   Identify a file or directory that contains output from a previous pkgask(1M) session. This file supplies the interaction responses that would be requested by the package in interactive mode. *response* must be a full path name.

-R *root-path*   Define the full path name of a directory to use as the *root-path*. Relocate all files, including package system information files, to a directory tree starting in the specified *root-path*. You can specify the *root-path* when installing to a client from a server (for example, /export/root/client1).

-s *spool*   Write the package into the directory *spool* instead of installing it.

-v   Trace all of the scripts that get executed by pkgadd, located in the *pkginst*/install directory. Use this option for debugging the procedural and nonprocedural scripts.

-V *fs-file*   Specify an alternative *fs-file* to map the client's file systems. For example, used in situations where the $*root-path*/etc/vfstab file is nonexistent or unreliable.

When executed without options or operands, pkgadd uses /var/spool/pkg (the default spool directory).

Operands

pkginst   The package instance or list of instances to be installed. You can use the token all to refer to all packages available on the source medium. You can use the format *pkginst*.* to indicate all instances of a package.

The asterisk character (*) is a special character to some shells and may need to be escaped. In the Bourne and C shells, you must surround the asterisk with single quotes (') or precede it with a backslash (\).

Examples

The following example installs a package from a Solaris CD-ROM. After the complete list is displayed, you are prompted to enter, as a space-separated list, the number of one or more packages to install.

```
# pkgadd -d /cdrom/cdrom0/s0/Solaris_8/Product
The following packages are available:
   1  NSCPcom          Netscape Communicator
                       (sparc) 20.4.70,REV=1999.08.20.17.43
   2  NSCPcpcom        Simplified Chinese (Common) Netscape Communicator
                       (sparc) 20.4.70,REV=1999.09.17.10.07
   3  NSCPhpcom        Traditional Chinese (Common) Netscape Communicator
                       (sparc) 20.4.70,REV=1999.09.17.10.08
   4  NSCPjacom        Japanese (common) Netscape Communicator
                       (sparc) 20.4.70,REV=1999.09.06.10.53
   5  NSCPkpcom        Korean (Common) Netscape Communicator
                       (sparc) 20.4.70,REV=1999.09.17.10.07
   6  PFUdfb.m         S-4/Leia LCD Dumb Frame Buffer Driver
                       (sparc.sun4m) 1.2,REV=1999.08.19.15.35
   7  PFUvplr.m        PFU/Fujitsu platform links
                       (sparc.sun4m) 5.8,REV=1999.08.19.15.59
   8  PFUvplu.m        PFU/Fujitsu usr/platform links
                       (sparc.sun4m) 5.8,REV=1999.08.19.16.02
   9  SMEvplr.u        SME platform links
                       (sparc.sun4u) 3.1,REV=1999.02.16.07.08
  10  SMEvplu.u        SME usr/platform links
                       (sparc.sun4u) 3.3,REV=1999.05.07.13.53

... 504 more menu choices to follow;
<RETURN> for more choices, <CTRL-D> to stop display:
```

Exit Status

0	Successful execution.
1	Fatal error.
2	Warning.
3	Interruption.
4	Administration.
5	Administration. Interaction is required. Do not use pkgadd -n.
10	Reboot after removal of all packages.
20	Reboot after removal of this package.

New!

Attributes

See attributes(5) for descriptions of the following attributes.

Attribute Type	Attribute Value
Availability	SUNWcsu

See Also

pkginfo(1), pkgmk(1), pkgparam(1), pkgproto(1), pkgtrans(1),
installf(1M), pkgask(1M), pkgrm(1M), removef(1M), admin(4), attributes(5)
   Application Packaging Developer's Guide

pkgask — Store Answers to a Request Script

Synopsis

/usr/sbin/pkgask [-d device] [-R root-path] -r response pkginst...

Description

Use the pkgask command to store answers to an interactive package (a user-created file that must be named request). Invoking this command generates a *response* file that is then used as input at installation time. The use of this response file prevents any interaction from occurring during installation because the file already contains all of the information the package needs.

> **Note** — If the default admin file is too restrictive, you may need to modify it to permit total noninteraction during a package installation. See admin(4) for details.

For example, some packages may have a request script as part of the package that would make unattended installation of a package impossible. By using the pkgask command to create a *response* file, pkgadd could use the *response* file instead of running the request script.

Options

-d *device*   Run the request script for a package on *device*. *device* can be a directory path name or the identifiers for tape, diskette, or removable disk (for example, /var/tmp, /dev/diskette, and /dev/dsk/c1d0s0). The default device is the installation spool directory.

-R *root-path* Define the full path name of a directory to use as the *root-path*. Relocate all files, including package system information files, to a directory tree starting in the specified *root-path*.

-r *response*   Identify a file or directory to contain the responses to interaction with the package. The name must be a full path name. You can later use the file, or directory of files, as input to the pkgadd(1M) command.

You can use the -r option to specify a directory name as well as a file name. The directory name is used to create numerous response files, each sharing the name of the package with which it should be associated. You would use this command, for example, when you are adding multiple interactive packages with one invocation of pkgadd(1M). Each package needs a *response* file. To create multiple *response* files with the same name as the package instance, name the directory where the files will be created and supply multiple instance names with the pkgask command. When installing the packages, you can identify this directory to the pkgadd(1M) command.

Operands

pkginst   Specify the package instance or list of instances for which request scripts are created. You can use the token all to refer to all packages available on the source medium.

Examples

Suppose you have a package, FOOpkg that has a request script that asks for a configuration directory and mail account. The request script requires two parameters: CONFDIR and MAIL. When the installation is run interactively, the installer is prompted for these values.

The following example runs the pkgask command to provide values for the two parameters.

```
# pkgask -r /var/spool/responses/FOOpkg FOOpkg
Where are configurations going to be kept: /usr/etc/foo
Which mail account will get notifications: foomail
#
```

The following example shows the contents of the responses file.

```
# cat /var/spool/responses/FOOpkg
CONFDIR=/usr/etc/foo
MAIL=foomail
#
```

When you specify the responses file with the pkgadd -r command, as shown in the following example, the contents of the file are used to complete the installation without requiring any operator intervention.

```
# pkgadd -n -r /var/spool/responses/FOOpkg FOOpkg
```

Exit Status

0   Successful completion.

>0   An error occurred.

Attributes

See attributes(5) for descriptions of the following attributes.

Attribute Type	Attribute Value
Availability	SUNWcsu

See Also

pkginfo(1), pkgmk(1), pkgparam(1), pkgproto(1), pkgtrans(1), installf(1M), pkgadd(1M), pkgchk(1M), pkgrm(1M), removef(1M), admin(4), attributes(5)

Application Packaging Developer's Guide

pkgchk — Check Package Installation Accuracy

Synopsis

```
/usr/sbin/pkgchk [-l | -acfnqvx][-i file][-p path...][-R root-path]
  [-m pkgmap [-e envfile] | [pkginst]...]
/usr/sbin/pkgchk -d device [-l | -fv][-i file][-M][-p path...]
  [-V fs-file][pkginst...]
```

Description

Use the pkgchk command to check the completeness, specific path name, file contents, and file attributes of an installed package. With the -l option you can check the integrity of directory structures and files. Discrepancies are written to standard error along with a detailed explanation of the problem.

Use the first synopsis to list or check the contents or attributes of objects that are currently installed on the system or in the indicated *pkgmap*. You can list package names on the command line, or by default, the entire contents of a system is checked.

Use the second synopsis to list or check the contents of a package that has been spooled on the specified device but not installed. Note that you cannot check attributes for spooled packages.

Options

-a	Audit the file attributes only and do not check file contents. Default is to check both.
-c	Audit the file contents only and do not check file attributes. Default is to check both.
-d *device*	Specify the *device* on which a spooled package resides. *device* can be a directory path name or the identifiers for tape, diskette, or removable disk (for example, /var/tmp or /dev/diskette).
-e *envfile*	Use the *envfile* package information file to resolve parameters noted in the specified *pkgmap* file.

-f	Correct file attributes if possible. If used with the -x option, remove hidden files. When you invoke pkgchk with this option, it creates directories, named pipes, links, and special devices if they do not already exist. If the -d option calls out an uninstalled package, the -f option takes effect only if the package is in directory (not stream) format. All file attributes are set to agree with the entries in the *pkgmap* file except that setuid, setgid, and sticky bits are not set in the mode.
-i *file*	Read a list of path names from *file* and compare this list against the installation software database or the indicated *pkgmap* file. Do not check path names that are not contained in file.
-l	List information on the selected files that make up a package. This option is not compatible with the -a, -c, -f, -g, and -v options.
-m *pkgmap*	Check the package against the *pkgmap* package map file.
-M	Do not use the $*root-path*/etc/vfstab file to determine the client's mount points. This option assumes the mount points are correct on the server, and it behaves consistently with Solaris 2.5 and earlier releases.
-n	Do not check the contents of volatile or editable files. Use this option for most postinstallation checking.
-p *path*	Check the accuracy of only the listed path name or path names. *path* can be one or more path names separated by commas (or by white space if the list is quoted).
-q	Do not give messages about missing files.
-R *root-path*	Define the full name of a directory to use as the *root-path*. Relocate all files, including package system information files, to a directory tree starting in the specified *root-path*. You can specify the *root-path* when installing to a client from a server (for example, /export/root/client1).
-v	List files as processed.
-V *fs-file*	Specify an alternative *fs-file* to map the client's file systems. For example, used in situations where the $*root-path*/etc/vfstab file is nonexistent or unreliable.
-x	Search exclusive directories, looking for existing files that are not in the installation software database or the indicated *pkgmap* file.

Operands

pkgins	The package instance or instances to be checked. You can use the format *pkginst*.* to check all instances of a package. The default is to display all information about all installed packages.
	The asterisk (*) is a special character to some shells and may need to be escaped. In the C shell, surround the asterisk with single quotes (') or precede it with a backslash (\).

Examples

The following example displays package installation information for /usr/sbin/vold.

```
paperbark% pkgchk -l -p /usr/sbin/vold
Pathname: /usr/sbin/vold
Type: regular file
Expected mode: 0555
Expected owner: root
Expected group: sys
Expected file size (bytes): 120644
Expected sum(1) of contents: 40017
Expected last modification: Sep 17 02:12:00 AM 1999
Referenced by the following packages:
        SUNWvolu
Current status: installed

paperbark%
```

Exit Status

0	Successful completion.
>0	An error occurred.

Attributes

See attributes(5) for descriptions of the following attributes.

Attribute Type	**Attribute Value**
Availability	SUNWcsu

See Also

pkginfo(1), pkgtrans(1), pkgadd(1M), pkgask(1M), pkgrm(1M), attributes(5)
Application Packaging Developer's Guide

---

pkgrm — Remove a Package from the System

Synopsis

```
/usr/sbin/pkgrm [-nv][-a admin][[-A | -M] -R root-path][-V fs-file]
    [pkginst...]
/usr/sbin/pkgrm -s spool [pkginst...]
```

Description

Use the pkgrm command to remove a previously installed or partially installed package from the system. A check is made to determine if any other packages depend on the one being removed. If a dependency exists, the action taken is defined in the admin file.

The default state for the command is interactive mode, meaning that prompt messages are given during processing to enable you to confirm the actions being taken. You can request noninteractive mode with the –n option.

You can use the -s option to specify the directory from which to remove spooled packages.

Certain unbundled and third-party packages are no longer entirely compatible with the latest version of pkgrm. These packages require user interaction throughout the removal and not just at the very beginning.

To remove these older packages (released prior to Solaris 2.4), set the following environment variable.

```
NONABI_SCRIPTS=TRUE
```

pkgrm permits keyboard interaction throughout the removal as long as this environment variable is set.

Options

-a *admin*	Use the *admin* installation administration file in place of the default admin file. Look first in the current working directory for the administration file. If the specified administration file is not in the current working directory, look in the /var/sadm/install/admin directory for the administration file.
–A	Remove the package files from the client's file system absolutely. If a file is shared with other packages, the default behavior is to not remove the file from the client's file system.
–M	Do not use the $*root-path*/etc/vfstab file for determining the client's mount points. This option assumes the mount points are correct on the server, and it behaves consistently with Solaris 2.5 and earlier releases.
–n	Operate in noninteractive mode. If there is a need for interaction, the command exits. Use of this option requires that you name at least one package instance when you invoke the command.
-R *root-path*	Define the full path name of a directory to use as the *root-path*. Relocate all files, including package system information files, to a directory tree starting in the specified *root-path*.
-s *spool*	Remove the specified package(s) from the directory *spool*. The default directory for spooled packages is /var/sadm/pkg.
–v	Trace all of the scripts executed by pkgrm, located in the *pkginst*/install directory. Use this option for debugging procedural and nonprocedural scripts.
-V *fs-file*	Specify an alternative *fs-file* to map the client's file systems. Used in situations where the $*root-path*/etc/vfstab file is nonexistent or unreliable.

Operands

pkginst   Specify the package to be removed. You can use the format *pkginst.**
                  to remove all instances of a package.

                  The asterisk character (*) is a special character to some shells and
                  may need to be escaped. In the Bourne and C shells, surround the
                  asterisk with single quotes (') or precede it with a backslash (\).

Examples

The following example removes the TSIpgxw package.

pkgrm TSIpgxw

```
The following package is currently installed:
   TSIpgxw           PGX32 (Raptor GFX) X Window System Support
                     (sparc) 7.0.0,REV=1999.09.20

Do you want to remove this package? y

## Removing installed package instance <TSIpgxw>

This package contains scripts which will be executed with super-user
permission during the process of removing this package.

Do you want to continue with the removal of this package [y,n,?,q] y
## Verifying package dependencies.
## Processing package information.
## Removing pathnames in class <server>
## Removing pathnames in class <none>
/usr/sbin/pgxconfig
/usr/sbin/GFXconfig
/usr/sbin <shared pathname not removed>
/usr/openwin/server/modules/ddxTSIgfx.so.1
/usr/openwin/server/modules <shared pathname not removed>
/usr/openwin/server/etc/pgxresinfo
/usr/openwin/server/etc <shared pathname not removed>
/usr/openwin/server <shared pathname not removed>
/usr/openwin/lib <shared pathname not removed>
/usr/openwin/bin/gfxres
/usr/openwin/bin <shared pathname not removed>
/usr/openwin <shared pathname not removed>
## Updating system information.

Removal of <TSIpgxw> was successful.
#
```

Exit Status

0   Successful execution.

1   Fatal error.

2   Warning.

3	Interruption.
4	Administration.
10	Reboot after removal of all packages.
20	Reboot after removal of this package.

Attributes

See `attributes(5)` for descriptions of the following attributes.

Attribute Type	Attribute Value
Availability	SUNWcsu

See Also

```
pkginfo(1), pkgmk(1), pkgparam(1), pkgproto(1), pkgtrans(1),
installf(1M), pkgadd(1M), pkgask(1M), pkgchk(1M), removef(1M),
attributes(5)
```
Application Packaging Developer's Guide

pmadm — Port Monitor Administration

Synopsis

```
/usr/sbin/pmadm -a [-p pmtag | -t type] -s svctag -i id -m pmspecific
   -v ver [-f xu][-y comment][-z script]
/usr/sbin/pmadm -r -p pmtag -s svctag
/usr/sbin/pmadm -e -p pmtag -s svctag
/usr/sbin/pmadm -d -p pmtag -s svctag
/usr/sbin/pmadm -l [-t type | -p pmtag][-s svctag]
/usr/sbin/pmadm -L [-t type | -p pmtag][-s svctag]
/usr/sbin/pmadm -g -p pmtag -s svctag [-z script]
/usr/sbin/pmadm -g -s svctag -t type -z script
```

Description

The Service Access Facility (SAF) is a group of daemons and administrative commands that provide a flexible administrative framework for managing service requests in an open-systems environment. SAF uses port monitors. The pmadm command is the administrative command for the lower level of the Service Access Facility hierarchy, that is, for service administration. Each port monitor has its own administrative file. A port may have only one service associated with it although the same service may be available through more than one port. To uniquely identify an instance of a service, the pmadm command must identify both the port monitor or port monitors through which the *service* is available (-p or -t) and the service (-s).

Use pmadm to perform the following functions.

- Add or remove a service.
- Enable or disable a service.
- Install or replace a per-service configuration script.
- Print requested service information.

Any user on the system can invoke pmadm to request service status (-l or -L) or to print per-service configuration scripts (-g without the z option). pmadm with other options can be executed only by superuser.

Options

-a   Add an entry for the new service to the port monitor's administrative file. Because of the complexity of the options and arguments that follow the -a option, you may want to use a command script or the menu system to add services.

-d   Add x to the flag field in the entry for the service svctag in the port monitor's administrative file to disable the service. This entry is used by port monitor pmtag. See the -f option for a description of the available flags.

-e   Remove x from the flag field in the entry for the service svctag in the port monitor administrative file to enable the service. This entry is used by port monitor pmtag. See the -f option for a description of the available flags.

-f xu   Specify one or both of the following two flags. which are then included in the flag field of the entry for the new service in the port monitor's administrative file. If you do not specify the -f option, set no flags and use the default conditions. By default, a new service is enabled and no utmpx entry is created for it. An -f option without a following argument is illegal.

     x   Do not enable the service svctag available through port monitor pmtag.

     u   Create a utmpx entry (changed from utmp in the Solaris 8 release) for service svctag available through port monitor pmtag.   `New!`

-g   Print, install, or replace a per-service configuration script. When you specify the -g option with a -p option and a -s option, print the per-service configuration script for service svctag available through port monitor pmtag. Specifying the -g option with a -p option, a -s option, and a -z option installs the per-service configuration script contained in the file script as the per-service configuration script for service svctag available through port monitor pmtag. The -g option with a -s option, a -t option, and a -z option installs the file script as the per-service configuration script for service svctag available through any port monitor of type type. Other combinations of options with -g are invalid.

-i id   Specify id as the identity assigned to service svctag when it is started. id must be an entry in /etc/passwd.

-l	Request service information. Used by itself and with the options described below, act as a filter for extracting information in several different groupings.

-l	List all services on the system.
-l -p *pmtag*	List all services available through port monitor *pmtag*.
-l -s *svctag*	List all services with tag *svctag*.
-l -p *pmtag* -s *svctag*	
	List service *svctag*.
-l -t *type*	List all services available through port monitors of type *type*.
-l -t *type* -s *svctag*	
	List all services with tag *svctag* available through a port monitor of type *type*.

Other combinations of options with -l are invalid.

-L	Identical to the -l option except print the output in a condensed format.
-m *pmspecific*	
	Specify the port-monitor-specific portion of the port monitor administrative file entry for the service.
-p *pmtag*	Specify the tag associated with the port monitor through which a service (specified as -s *svctag*) is available.
-r	Remove the entry for the service from the port monitor's administrative file.
-s *svctag*	Specify the service tag associated with a given service. The service tag is assigned by the system administrator and is part of the entry for the service in the port monitor's administrative file.
-t *type*	Specify the port monitor type.
-v *ver*	Specify the version number of the port monitor administrative file. You can specify the version number in the following format, where *pmspec* is the special administrative command for port monitor *pmtag*.

   -v '*pmspec* -V'

This special command is ttyadm for ttymon and nlsadmin for listen. The version stamp of the port monitor is known by the command and is returned when you invoke pmspec with a -V option.

-y *comment*	Associate *comment* with the service entry in the port monitor administrative file.

      -z script   Use with the -g option to specify the name of the file that contains the per-service configuration script. Modifying a configuration script is a three-step procedure. First, make a copy of the existing script (-g alone). Then, edit the copy. Finally, put the copy in place over the existing script (-g with -z).

Options that request information write the requested information to the standard output. The -l option prints column headers and aligns the information under the appropriate headings. In this format, a missing field is indicated by a dash. The -L option prints the information in condensed-format, colon-separated fields; missing fields are indicated by two successive colons. # is the comment character.

Examples

The following example adds a service to a port monitor with tag pmtag and gives the service the tag svctag. Port monitor-specific information is generated by specpm. The service defined by svctag is invoked with identity root.

```
# pmadm -a -p pmtag -s svctag -i root -m `specpm -a arg1 -b arg2`-v
  `specpm -V`
```

The following example adds a service with service tag svctag, identity guest, and port monitor-specific information generated by specpm to all port monitors of type type.

```
# pmadm -a -s svctag -i guest -t type -m `specpm -a arg1 -b arg2`-v
  `specpm -V`
```

The following example removes the service svctag from port monitor pmtag.

```
# pmadm -r -p pmtag -s svctag
```

The following example enables the service svctag available through port monitor pmtag.

```
# pmadm -e -p pmtag -s svctag
```

The following example disables the service svctag available through port monitor pmtag.

```
# pmadm -d -p pmtag -s svctag
```

The following example lists status information for all services.

```
paperbark% pmadm -l
PMTAG         PMTYPE         SVCTAG        FLGS ID         <PMSPECIFIC>
zsmon         ttymon         ttya          u    root       /dev/term/a I
  - /usr/bin/login - 9600 ldterm,ttcompat ttya login: - tvi925 y  #
zsmon         ttymon         ttyb          u    root       /dev/term/b I
  - /usr/bin/login - 9600 ldterm,ttcompat ttyb login: - tvi925 y  #
paperbark%
```

The following example lists status information for all services available through the port monitor with tag ports.

```
paperbark% pmadm -l -p ports
```

The following example lists status information for all services available through port monitors of type `ttymon`.

```
paperbark% pmadm -l -t ttymon
PMTAG          PMTYPE          SVCTAG          FLGS ID        <PMSPECIFIC>
zsmon          ttymon          ttya            u    root      /dev/term/a I
  - /usr/bin/login - 9600 ldterm,ttcompat ttya login: - tvi925 y  #
zsmon          ttymon          ttyb            u    root      /dev/term/b I
  - /usr/bin/login - 9600 ldterm,ttcompat ttyb login: - tvi925 y  #
paperbark%
```

The following example lists the same information in condensed format.

```
paperbark% pmadm -L -t ttymon
zsmon:ttymon:ttya:u:root:reserved:reserved:reserved:/dev/term/a:I::/usr
    /bin/login::9600:ldterm,ttcompat:ttya login\: ::tvi925:y:#
zsmon:ttymon:ttyb:u:root:reserved:reserved:reserved:/dev/term/b:I::/usr
    /bin/login::9600:ldterm,ttcompat:ttyb login\: ::tvi925:y:#
paperbark%
```

The following example prints the per-service configuration script associated with the service `svctag` available through port monitor `pmtag`.

```
# pmadm -g -p pmtag -s svctag
```

Exit Status

0	Successful operation.
>0	Operation failed.

Files

`/etc/saf/`*pmtag*`/_config`

        Port monitor tag configuration file.

`/etc/saf/`*pmtag*`/`*svctag*

        Port monitor service tag.

`/var/saf/`*pmtag*`/*`

        Directory containing SAF port monitor tags.

Attributes

See `attributes(5)` for descriptions of the following attributes.

Attribute Type	Attribute Value
Availability	SUNWcsu

See Also

sac(1M), sacadm(1M), doconfig(3N), attributes(5)

pmconfig — Configure the Power Management System

Synopsis

    /usr/sbin/pmconfig [-r]

Description

The pmconfig command reads the configuration file power.conf(4) and issues the commands that activate the power management configuration. The pmconfig command is run at system boot by the /etc/rc2.d/S85power run control script. You can also run this command from the command line after you have made manual changes to the power.conf(4) file. You must run pmconfig after editing power.conf to have editing changes to the power.conf(4) file take effect.

Options

-r	Reset all power-managed devices to unconfigured.

Files

    /etc/power.conf

System power-management configuration file.

Attributes

See attributes(5) for descriptions of the following attributes.

Attribute Type	**Attribute Value**
Availability	SUNWpmu

See Also

    powerd(1M), power.conf(4), attributes(5), pm(7D)

Diagnostics

If the pmconfig command cannot open either the pseudodriver or the configuration file, it prints an error message to standard error. If it encounters a syntax error in the configuration file, it prints an error message and the line number of the error in the configuration file. It then skips the rest of the information on that line and processes the next line. Any configuration information already processed on the line containing the error is used.

The pmconfig command generates the following error messages, all of which begin with pmconfig (line *n*).

    Can't find device name:

The first field is not a device name.

Can't find threshold value:

> The field following the device name is not an integer.

Too many threshold values:

> More idle times than the device supports were given.

Unrecognizable dependent name:

> The dependent field is not a device name.

a standard error message

> Returned from the pm driver.

pntadm — DHCP Network Table Management Command

Synopsis

```
/usr/sbin/pntadm -C [-r resource][-p path] network
/usr/sbin/pntadm -A name-IP-address [-c comment][-e mm/dd/yyyy][-f num |
    keywords][-h host name][-i [-a] client ID][-m [-y] dhcptab-macro]
    [-s server][-r resource][-p path] network
/usr/sbin/pntadm -M name-IP-address [-c comment][-e mm/dd/yyyy]
    [-f num | keywords][-h host name][-i [-a] client ID][-m [-y]
    dhcptab-macro][-s server][-r resource][-p path] network
/usr/sbin/pntadm -D name-IP-address [-y][-r resource][-p path] network
/usr/sbin/pntadm -P [-v][-r resource][-p path] network
/usr/sbin/pntadm -R [-r resource][-p path] network
/usr/sbin/pntadm -L
```

New!

Description

New!

Use the pntadm command to manage the dhcp network DHCP client tables. You can use pntadm to add and remove IP addresses and networks under DHCP management, modify the network configuration of specified IP addresses, and display information about IP addresses and networks under DHCP management. You must specify one of the -C, -A, -M, -D, -R, or -L. options.

Note also that if the networks you want to add are subnetted, you need to update the netmasks(4) table. Depending on the resource type (-r option), you must have the proper file permissions or NIS+ credentials.

For a description of the format of dhcp network tables, see dhcp_network(4).

Options

-A *name-IP-address*

> Add a client entry with host name or client IP address, *name-IP-address*, to the named dhcp network table. The following optional suboptions are available.

Option(s)	Argument	Description	Default
-c	*comment*	Comment text.	NULL
-e	*mm/dd/yyyy*	Absolute lease.	0
-f	*num* | *keywords*	Flag value.	00
-h	*hostname*	Client host name.	NULL
-i	*client-ID*	Client identifier [-a].	00
-m	dhcptab *macro* [-y]	Macro name.	UNKNOWN
-s	*server*	Server IP or name.	nodename

When you use the -h option in this mode, add the host name to the hosts table within the resource. The command fails if this host name is already present in the hosts table.

New!

You can specify the -f option either as a single number denoting the intended flag value or as a series of the following keywords, combined with the plus (+) symbol.

Keyword	Numeric	Description
DYNAMIC	00	Server manages assignment.
PERMANENT	01	Lease on entry is permanent.
MANUAL	02	Administrator manages assignment.
UNUSABLE	04	Entry is not valid.
BOOTP	08	Entry reserved for BOOTP clients.

For a more detailed description of the flag values, see dhcp_network(4).

The -i option modified with -a specifies that the client identifier is in ASCII format and thus needs to be converted to hexadecimal format before insertion into the table.

The -m option modified with -y verifies the existence of the named macro in the dhcptab table before adding the entry.

-C   Create the DHCP network table for the network specified by *network*. For details, see dhcp_network(4) and networks(4).

-D *name-IP-address*

Delete the specified client entry with host name or client IP address, *name-IP-address*, in the named dhcp network table. (See dhcp_network(4).) The following suboptions are optional.

-y   Remove associated host table entry. Request to
                                                             remove all host names associated with the IP
                                                             address in the hosts table in the resource.

-L   List the DHCP network tables presently configured, one per line, on
                                                             standard output. If none is found, print no output and return an exit
                                                             status of 0.

-M *name-IP-address*

                                                             Modify the specified client entry with host name or client IP address,
                                                             name-IP-address, in the named dhcp network table. (See
                                                             dhcp_network(4).) The following suboptions are available.

Option(s)	Argument	Description	Default
-c	*comment*	Comment text.	NULL
-e	*mm/dd/yyyy*	Absolute lease.	0
-f	*num* | *keywords*	Flag value.	00
-h	*hostname*	Client host name.	NULL
-i	*client-ID*	Client identifier [-a].	00
-m	dhcptab *macro* [-y]	Macro name.	UNKNOWN
-n	*client-IP*	New IP address.	NULL
-s	*server*	Server IP or name.	nodename

The -h option enables you to change the current host name associated
                                                             with the IP address or to add a new host name to the hosts table if an
                                                             entry associated with this IP address does not exist.

                                                             For more detailed descriptions of the suboptions and flag values, see
                                                             the information given under the -A option and dhcp_network(4).

       -P   Display the named dhcp network table. See dhcp_network(4).
                                                             Suboptions are listed below.

                                                             -v   Display lease time in verbose format.

       -p *path*   Override the /etc/default/dhcp configuration value for resource
                                                             path, *path*. The resource path for the files resource is an absolute
                                                             UNIX path name and a fully specified nisplus directory (including
                                                             the trailing dot) for the NIS+ resource. See dhcp(4) for more details.

       -R   Remove the named dhcp network table. See dhcp_network(4).

       -r *resource*   Override the /etc/default/dhcp configuration value for *resource*.
                                                             Currently supported resource types are files or nisplus. See
                                                             dhcp(4) for more details.

Operands

network
: The network address or network name that corresponds to the dhcp network table. See dhcp_network(4).

Examples

The following example creates a DHCP table.

```
# pntadm -C 10.0.0.0
Warning: Using default subnetmask: 255.0.0.0.
#
```

The following example adds an entry 10.0.0.1 to the 10.0.0.0 table.

```
# pntadm -A 10.0.0.1 10.0.0.0
#
```

The following example modifies the 10.0.0.1 entry of the 10.0.0.0 table, changes the macro name to Green, and sets the flags field to PERMANENT and MANUAL.

```
# pntadm -M 10.0.0.1 -m Green -f 'PERMANENT+MANUAL' 10.0.0.0
#
```

The following example changes the 10.0.0.1 entry to 10.0.0.2 and makes an entry in the hosts(4) table called myclient.

```
# pntadm -M 10.0.0.1 -n 10.0.0.2 -h myclient 10.0.0.0
#
```

The following example displays the contents of the 10.0.0.0 table.

```
# pntadm -P 10.0.0.0
Client ID      Flags   Client IP       Server IP       Lease Expiration
Macro          Comment

00             03      10.0.0.2        172.20.11.14    Zero
Green

#
```

The following example deletes the myclient (10.0.0.2) entry from the 10.0.0.0 table.

```
# pntadm -D 10.0.0.2 10.0.0.0
#
```

The following example removes the named DHCP network table.

```
# pntadm -R 10.0.0.0
#
```

The following example lists the configured DHCP network tables.   *New!*

```
# pntadm -L
192.168.0.0
10.0.0.0
#
```

The following example sets the BOOTP flag on address 172.21.20.33 on the
172.21.0.0 network and sets the lease to permanent.

```
# pntadm -M 172.21.20.33 -f BOOTP 172.21.0.0
#
```

The following example adds the address 172.21.20.34, assigns it to a client whose
Ethernet address is 8:0:20:89:a1:d2, sets the BOOTP flag, assigns a permanent lease
(-e -1), and uses the blue2 macro.

```
# pntadm -A 172.21.20.34 -i 0108002089A1D2 -f BOOTP -e -1 -m blue2
    172.21.0.0
#
```

The following example modifies the address 172.21.20.33, assigns it to a client
whose Ethernet hardware address is 8:0:20:89:a1:d2, and sets the BOOTP flag.

```
# pntadm -M 172.21.20.33 -i 0108002089A1D2 -f BOOTP
#
```

The following example adds the address 172.21.20.34, assigns it to a client whose
Ethernet hardware address is 8:0:20:89:a1:d2, sets the BOOTP flag, and has the client
receive the contents of the blue2 macro.

```
# pntadm -A 172.21.20.34 -i 0108002089A1D2 -f BOOTP -m blue2 172.21.0.0
#
```

Exit Status

0	Successful completion.
1	Object already exists.
2	Object does not exist.
3	Noncritical error.
4	Critical error.

Files

/var/dhcp/*XXX_XXX_XXX_XXX*

> Files or NIS+ tables where *XXX* represents octets of the dotted IP
> address.

/etc/default/dhcp

> DHCP service configuration file.

/etc/inet/hosts

> File or NIS+ table.

Attributes

See attributes(5) for descriptions of the following attributes.

Attribute Type	Attribute Value
Availability	SUNWdhcsu

See Also

dhcpconfig(1M), dhcpmgr(1M), dhcp(4), dhcp_network(4), dhcptab(4),   *New!*
hosts(4), netmasks(4), networks(4), attributes(5)

    Alexander, S., and Droms, R., *DHCP Options and BOOTP Vendor Extensions*, RFC 1533, Lachman Technology, Inc., Bucknell University, October 1993.

    Droms, R., *Interoperation Between DHCP and BOOTP*, RFC 1534, Bucknell University, October 1993.

    Droms, R., *Dynamic Host Configuration Protocol*, RFC 1541, Bucknell University, October 1993.

    Wimer, W., *Clarifications and Extensions for the Bootstrap Protocol*, RFC 1542, Carnegie Mellon University, October 1993.

ports — Create /dev and inittab Entries for Serial Lines

Synopsis

/usr/sbin/ports [-r *rootdir*]

Description

Note — devfsadm(1M) is now the preferred command for /dev and   *New!*
/devices, and you should use it instead of ports. The ports command in the Solaris 8 release is a symbolic link to the devfsadm(1M) command.

powerd — Power Manager Daemon

Synopsis

/usr/lib/power/powerd [-n]

Description

The powerd daemon manages two types of system shutdown: automatic shutdown and low power shutdown. Low power shutdown is found on systems that support battery operation.

The daemon reads the automatic shutdown information from the file
/etc/power.conf. The daemon rereads the automatic shutdown information whenever
it receives a hang-up signal, SIGHUP.
Automatic shutdown can occur only if the following two conditions are met.

- The current time is between the start and finish times.
- The system has been idle for at least the set time period. System idleness is
  determined by the inactivity of the system. See power.conf(4).

The start and finish times are specified in power.conf(4) and measured from the
start of the day (12:00 a.m.). If the finish time is less than or equal to the start time, the
active period of the daemon spans from midnight to the finish time and from the start
time to the following midnight. To specify continuous operation, you can set the finish
time equal to the start time. To disable automatic shutdown, specify noshutdown for the
behavior field.
Low power shutdown occurs if the system is running from battery and the daemon
monitors that the charge in the battery is too low to reliably continue operation.
Immediately before system shutdown, the daemon notifies syslogd(1M) of the
shutdown, which broadcasts a notification.

Note — The daemon uses shared memory IPC, which can increase the
system image size if the shared memory module has not already been
loaded.

The daemon ensures that only one daemon is running. If another daemon is
running, then the new daemon exits with an error. If the daemon dies
unexpectedly (nonmaskable signal), residual shared memory state remains.
Starting a new daemon removes this residual state.

Options

-n   No broadcast mode. Silently shut down the system without notifying
                            syslogd(1M).

Files

/etc/power.con

Power management configuration information file.

Attributes

See attributes(5) for descriptions of the following attributes.

Attribute Type	Attribute Value
Availability	SUNWpmu

See Also

pmconfig(1M), poweroff(1M), syslogd(1M), power.conf(4), attributes(5),
cpr(7), pm(7D)

poweroff — Stop the Processor

Synopsis
```
/usr/sbin/poweroff [-lnqy]
```

Description
See halt(1M).

praudit — Print Contents of an Audit Trail File

Synopsis
```
/usr/sbin/praudit [-lrs][-ddel][filename...]
```

Description
The praudit command enables you to display audit records interactively and create very basic reports. praudit displays records in one of several human-readable but otherwise noninterpreted forms. You can produce more sophisticated displays and reporting by using sed or awk to postprocess the output from praudit. Alternatively, you can write programs that interpret and process the binary audit records.

praudit reads the listed file names (or standard input, if you specify no *filename*) and interprets the data as audit trail records as defined in audit.log(4). By default, times, UIDs, and GIDs are converted to their ASCII representation. Record type and event fields are converted to their ASCII representation. You can specify a maximum of 100 audit files on the command line.

> **Note** — The functionality described in this manual page is available only if the Basic Security Module (BSM) has been enabled. See bsmconv(1M) for more information.

Options

-l	Print one line per record. Always convert the record type and event fields to their short ASCII representation, as is done for the -s option.
-r	Print records in their raw form. Display times, UIDs, GIDs, record types, and events as integers. You cannot use this option with the -s option. If you use both, print a format usage error message.
-s	Print records in their short form. Convert all numeric fields to ASCII. Use the short ASCII representations for the record type and event fields. You cannot use this option with the -r option. If you use both, print a format usage error message.

-d*del*   Use *del* as the field delimiter instead of the comma default delimiter.
                    If *del* has special meaning for the shell, you must quote it. The
                    maximum size of a delimiter is four characters.

Files

/etc/security/audit_event

Audit event database.

/etc/security/audit_class

User-level class masks.

Attributes

See attributes(5) for descriptions of the following attributes.

Attribute Type	Attribute Value
Availability	SUNWcsu

See Also

bsmconv(1M), audit(2), getauditflags(3), audit.log(4), audit_class(4),
audit_event(4), group(4), passwd(4), attributes(5)

prctmp, prdaily, prtacct — Print Various Accounting Files

Synopsis

/usr/lib/acct/prctmp *filename*
/usr/lib/acct/prdaily [-c][-l][*mmdd*]
/usr/lib/acct/prtacct *file name* ["*heading*"]

Description

See acctsh(1M).

New! printmgr — Graphical User interface for Managing Printers in a Network

Synopsis

/usr/sadm/admin/bin/printmgr

Description

The `printmgr` command is new in the Solaris 8 release. Use the `printmgr` command to start the Solaris Print Manager, which has a Java-based graphical user interface that enables you to manage local and remote printer access. You can use this tool in the following nameservice environments.

- NIS.
- NIS+.
- NIS+ with Federated Naming Service (FNS).
- `files`.

You must be logged in as superuser to use this tool.

Solaris Printer Manager is the preferred method for managing printer access instead of AdminTool: Printers because Solaris Print Manager centralizes printer information when it is used in a nameservice environment.

Adding printer information to a nameservice makes access to printers available to all systems on the network and generally makes printer administration easier because all the information about printers is centralized.

You can run Solaris Print Manager on a remote system with the display sent to the local system. See "Managing Printing Services" in *System Administration Guide, Volume II*, for instructions on setting the `DISPLAY` environment variable.

Using Solaris Print Manager to perform printer-related tasks automatically updates the appropriate printer databases. Solaris Print Manager also includes a command-line console that displays the `lp` command line for the add, modify, and delete printer operations. Errors and warnings may also be displayed when Printer Manager operations are performed.

You can get help by clicking on the Help button.

Usage

Solaris Print Manager enables you to do the following tasks.

Select a Name Service

> Select a nameservice for retrieving or changing printer information.

Add Access to a Printer

> Add printer access on a printer client.

Add an Attached Printer

> After physically attaching the printer to a system, you can install a local printer and make it available for printing.

Add a Network Printer

> After physically attaching the printer to a system, you can install a local printer and make it available for printing.

Modify Printer Properties

> After adding access to a printer or adding an attached or network printer, you can modify certain printer attributes.

Delete a Printer

> Delete access to a printer from the print client or delete a printer from the print server or from the nameservice environment.

Examples

When you type /usr/sadm/admin/bin/printmgr& to start the Solaris Print Manager, a window is displayed, as shown below, asking you to choose your naming service.

When you choose your naming service and click on the OK button, the Solaris Print Manger window is displayed, as shown in the following example.

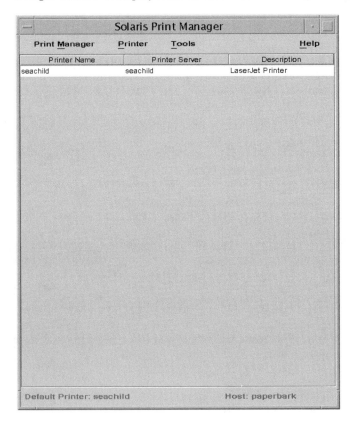

Attributes

See attributes(5) for descriptions of the following attributes.

Attribute Type	Attribute Value
Availability	SUNWppm

See Also

attributes(5)

System Administration Guide, Volume II

prstat — Report Active Process Statistics

Synopsis

```
/usr/bin/prstat [-acLmRtv][-C psrsetlist][-n nprocs[,nusers]]
[-p pidlist][-P cpulist][-s key | -S key][-u euidlist]
  [-U uidlist][interval [count]]
```

Description

The prstat command is new in the Solaris 8 release. Use it to iteratively examine all active processes on the system and to report statistics based on the selected output mode and sort order. prstat provides options to examine processes matching only specified PIDs, UIDs, CPU IDs, and processor set IDs.

The -C, -p, -P, -u, and -U options accept lists as arguments. You can separate items in a list either by commas or by separating the items with commas or spaces and enclosing the entire list in quotes.

If you do not specify an option, prstat examines all processes and reports statistics sorted by CPU usage.

Note — The snapshot of system usage displayed by prstat is true only for a split second, and it may not be accurate by the time it is displayed. When you specify the -m option, prstat tries to turn on microstate accounting for each process; the original state is restored when prstat exits. See proc(4) for additional information about the microstate accounting facility.

Options

-a   Report information about processes and users. Display separate reports about processes and users at the same time.

-c   Print new reports below previous reports instead of overprinting them.

-C *psrsetlist*

         Report only processes or lightweight processes (LWPs) that are bound to processor sets in the given list. Each processor set is identified by an integer as reported by psrset(1M).

-L   Report statistics for each LWP. By default, report only the number of LWPs for each process.

-m   Report microstate process accounting information. In addition to all fields listed in -v mode, include the percentage of time the process has spent processing system traps, text page faults, data page faults, waiting for user locks, and waiting for CPU (latency time).

`-n nproc[,nusers]`

> Restrict number of output lines. The `nproc` argument determines how many lines of process or LWP statistics are reported, and the `nusers` argument determines how many lines of user statistics are reported if you specify the `-a` or `-t` options. By default, report 15 processes and 5 users.

`-p pidlist` Report only processes whose process ID is in the given list.

`-P cpulist` Report only processes or LWPs that have most recently executed on a CPU in the given list. Each CPU is identified by an integer as reported by psrinfo(1M).

`-R` Put `prstat` in the real-time scheduling class. Give `prstat` priority over timesharing and interactive processes. This option is available only for superuser.

`-s key` Sort output lines (that is, processes, LWPs, or users) by key in descending order. You can use only one key as an argument.

> `key` has five possible values.

> | | |
> |---|---|
> | `cpu` | Sort by process CPU usage. The default. |
> | `time` | Sort by process execution time. |
> | `size` | Sort by size of process image. |
> | `rss` | Sort by resident set size. |
> | `pri` | Sort by process priority. |

`-S key` Sort output lines by key in ascending order. Possible key values are the same as for the `-s` option.

`-t` Report total usage summary for each user. The summary includes the total number of processes or LWPs owned by the user, total size of process images, total resident set size, total CPU time, and percentages of recent CPU time and system memory.

`-u euidlist` Report only processes whose effective user ID is in the given list. You can specify each user ID as either a login name or a numerical user ID.

`-U uidlist` Report only processes whose real user ID is in the given list. You can specify each user ID as either a login name or a numerical user ID.

`-v` Report verbose process usage. This output format includes the percentage of time the process has spent in user mode, in system mode, and sleeping. It also includes the number of voluntary and involuntary context switches, system calls, and the number of signals received.

Output
The following list defines the column headings and the meanings of a `prstat` report.

PID	The process ID of the process.
USERNAME	The real user (login) name or real user ID.
SIZE	The total virtual memory size of the process, including all mapped files and devices, in kilobytes (K), megabytes (M), or gigabytes (G). The resident set size of the process (RSS), in kilobytes (K), megabytes (M), or gigabytes (G).
STATE	The state of the process.

	cpu*N*	Process is running on CPU *N*.
	sleep	Sleeping: process is waiting for an event to complete.
	run	Runnable: process is on run queue.
	zombie	Zombie state: process terminated and parent not waiting.
	stop	Process is stopped.

PRI	The priority of the process. Larger numbers mean higher priority.
NICE	Nice value used in priority computation. Only processes in certain scheduling classes have a nice value.
TIME	The cumulative execution time for the process.
CPU	The percentage of recent CPU time used by the process.
PROCESS	The name of the process (name of executed file).
LWPID	The LWP ID of the LWP being reported.
NLWP	The number of LWPs in the process.

The following columns are displayed when you specify the -v or -m option.

USR	The percentage of time the process has spent in user mode.
SYS	The percentage of time the process has spent in system mode.
TRP	The percentage of time the process has spent in processing system traps.
TFL	The percentage of time the process has spent processing text page faults.
DFL	The percentage of time the process has spent processing data page faults.
LCK	The percentage of time the process has spent waiting for user locks.
SLP	The percentage of time the process has spent sleeping.
LAT	The percentage of time the process has spent in CPU latency.
VCX	The number of voluntary context switches.
ICX	The number of involuntary context switches.
SCL	The number of system calls.

SIG   The number of signals received.

Under the -1 option, one line is printed for each LWP in the process and some
reporting fields show the values for the LWP, not the process.

Operands

count   Specify the number of times that the statistics are repeated. By
               default, prstat reports statistics until a termination signal is
               received.

interval   Specify the sampling interval in seconds; the default interval is 5
               seconds.

Examples

The following example shows the output of the prstat command with no arguments.

```
paperbark% prstat
   PID USERNAME  SIZE   RSS STATE  PRI NICE      TIME  CPU PROCESS/NLWP
   398 root      133M   39M sleep   59    0   0:00.38 2.8% Xsun/1
   498 winsor   9408K 5384K sleep   59    0   0:00.06 1.4% dtwm/8
   653 winsor   1440K 1264K cpu0    48    0   0:00.00 0.4% prstat/1
   501 winsor   8192K 4456K sleep   49    0   0:00.00 0.2% dtterm/1
   204 root     2464K 1552K sleep   56    0   0:00.00 0.1% nscd/7
   627 winsor    113M   36M sleep   48    0   0:00.00 0.0% java/14
   576 winsor    22M   18M sleep   59    0   0:00.04 0.0% java/8
   513 winsor   7384K 4400K sleep   48    0   0:00.00 0.0% dtpad/1
   399 root     2408K 1520K sleep   58    0   0:00.00 0.0% mibiisa/12
   361 root     6824K 4872K sleep   58    0   0:00.01 0.0% httpd/12
   436 winsor   2360K 1216K sleep   59    0   0:00.00 0.0% fbconsole/1
   400 root     5264K 2056K sleep   43    0   0:00.00 0.0% dtlogin/4
   373 root     3616K 1432K sleep   58    0   0:00.00 0.0% snmpXdmid/5
   387 root     1776K  792K sleep   58    0   0:00.00 0.0% ttymon/1
   374 root     3096K 1896K sleep   52    0   0:00.00 0.0% dmispd/5
   362 root     2184K 1016K sleep   58    0   0:00.00 0.0% snmpdx/1
   329 root     5040K 1488K sleep   58    0   0:00.00 0.0% dtlogin/4
   393 root     1776K  968K sleep   58    0   0:00.00 0.0% ttymon/1
   347 root     1848K  992K sleep   43    0   0:00.00 0.0% nfsd/1
   279 daemon    20M 2192K sleep   59    0   0:00.00 0.0% dwhttpd/4
   345 root     2688K 1120K sleep   53    0   0:00.00 0.0% mountd/3
   278 daemon   9736K  880K sleep   51    0   0:00.00 0.0% dwhttpd/3
   291 root     1760K  680K sleep   58    0   0:00.00 0.0% auditd/1
   575 winsor   2424K 1280K sleep   33    0   0:00.00 0.0% dtexec/1
   247 root     2616K 1152K sleep   58    0   0:00.00 0.0% vold/6
   252 root     6112K 1144K sleep   48    0   0:00.00 0.0% amiserv/4
   264 root     5640K 1720K sleep   49    0   0:00.00 0.0% ocfserv/4
   231 root     1024K  560K sleep   58    0   0:00.00 0.0% utmpd/1
   242 root     1616K  696K sleep   50    0   0:00.00 0.0% cimomboot/1
   186 root     1888K  784K sleep   53    0   0:00.00 0.0% cron/1
   184 root     3360K 1432K sleep   52    0   0:00.00 0.0% syslogd/9
   166 daemon   2480K 1120K sleep   40    0   0:00.00 0.0% statd/4
   164 root     1848K  888K sleep   40    0   0:00.00 0.0% lockd/1
   171 root     2976K 1384K sleep   58    0   0:00.00 0.0% automountd/5
   165 root     1992K  648K sleep   52    0   0:00.00 0.0% slpd/3
```

```
  426 winsor   1912K  896K sleep   59    0  0:00.00 0.0% Xsession/1
  209 root     3072K  568K sleep   54    0  0:00.00 0.0% lpsched/1
  222 root     1368K  576K sleep   41    0  0:00.00 0.0% powerd/3
  127 root     2776K  816K sleep    5    0  0:00.00 0.0% keyserv/4
  107 root     1648K  544K sleep   59    0  0:00.00 0.0% in.routed/1
  161 root     2312K  912K sleep   58    0  0:00.00 0.0% inetd/1
Total: 75 processes, 207 lwps, load averages: 0.07, 0.02, 0.02
```

The following example reports the five most active superuser processes running on CPU1 and CPU2.

```
paperbark% prstat -u root -n 5 -P 1,2 1 1

PID   USERNAME SIZE   RSS STATE  PRI NICE    TIME  CPU PROCESS/LWP
   42    root  1280K  856K sleep   55    0  0:00.00 0.2% devfseventd/7
  102    root  1600K  592K sleep   59    0  0:00.00 0.1% in.rdisc/1
  250    root  1000K  552K sleep   58    0  0:00.00 0.0% utmpd/1
  288    root  1720K 1032K sleep   58    0  0:00.00 0.0% sac/1
    1    root   744K  168K sleep   58    0  0:00.00 0.0% init/1
 TOTAL:        25, load averages:  0.05, 0.08, 0.12
```

The following example displays verbose process usage information about processes with lowest resident set sizes owned by users root and winsor.

```
paperbark% prstat -S rss -n 5 -vc -u root,winsor
  PID USERNAME USR SYS TRP TFL DFL LCK SLP LAT VCX ICX SCL SIG PROCESS/NLWP
    1 root     0.0 0.0  -   -   -   -  100  -    0   0   1   0 init/1
  655 root     0.1 0.1  -   -   -   -  100  -    7   0  47   0 sh/1
  107 root     0.0 0.0  -   -   -   -  100  -    0   0   1   0 in.routed/1
  231 root     0.0 0.0  -   -   -   -  100  -    0   0   0   0 utmpd/1
  209 root     0.0 0.0  -   -   -   -  100  -    0   0   2   0 lpsched/1
Total: 73 processes, 197 lwps, load averages: 0.04, 0.03, 0.02
  PID USERNAME USR SYS TRP TFL DFL LCK SLP LAT VCX ICX SCL SIG PROCESS/NLWP
    1 root     0.0 0.0  -   -   -   -  100  -    0   0   0   0 init/1
  655 root     0.0 0.0  -   -   -   -  100  -    0   0   0   0 sh/1
  107 root     0.0 0.0  -   -   -   -  100  -    0   0   0   0 in.routed/1
  231 root     0.0 0.0  -   -   -   -  100  -    0   0   0   0 utmpd/1
  209 root     0.0 0.0  -   -   -   -  100  -    0   0   0   0 lpsched/1
Total: 73 processes, 197 lwps, load averages: 0.04, 0.03, 0.02
```

Exit Status

0   Successful completion.

1   An error occurred.

Attributes

See attributes(5) for descriptions of the following attributes.

Attribute Type	Attribute Value
Availability	SUNWcsu

See Also

proc(1), psrinfo(1M), psrset(1M), sar(1M), proc(4), attributes(5)

---

prtconf — Print System Configuration

Synopsis

SPARC Platform

/usr/sbin/prtconf -V | -F | -x | -vpPD

IA Platform

/usr/sbin/prtconf -V | -x | -vpPD

Description

Use the prtconf command to print the system configuration information. The output includes the total amount of memory and the configuration of system peripherals formatted as a device tree.

Note — The output of the prtconf command is highly dependent on the version of the PROM installed in the system. The output is affected in potentially all circumstances.

The driver not attached message means that no driver is currently attached to that instance of the device. In general, drivers are loaded and installed (and attached to hardware instances) on demand, and when needed, and may be uninstalled and unloaded when the device is not in use.

Options

-D	For each system peripheral in the device tree, display the name of the device driver used to manage the peripheral.
-F	(SPARC platform only). Return the device path name of the console frame buffer if one exists. If there is no frame buffer, return a non-zero exit code. You must use this option by itself. Return only the name of the console, frame buffer device, or a non-zero exit code. For example, if the console frame buffer on a SPARCstation 1 is cgthree in SBus slot #3, return /sbus@1, f80000000/cgthree@3, 0. You could use this option to create a symbolic link for /dev/fb to the actual console device.
-p	Display information derived from the device tree provided by the firmware (PROM) on SPARC platforms or the booting system on IA platforms.
-P	Include information about pseudodevices. By default, information regarding pseudo devices is omitted.

-v	Specify verbose mode.
-V	Display platform-dependent PROM (on SPARC platforms) or booting system (on IA platforms) version information. You must use this option by itself. The output is a string. The format of the string is arbitrary and platform dependent.
-x	Report if the firmware on this system is 64-bit ready. Some existing platforms may need a firmware upgrade to run the 64-bit kernel. If the operation is not applicable to this platform or the firmware is already 64-bit ready, exit silently with a return code of 0. If the operation is applicable to this platform and the firmware is not 64-bit ready, display a descriptive message on standard output and exit with a non-zero return code. The hardware platform documentation contains more information about the platforms that may need a firmware upgrade to run the 64-bit kernel.

This option overrides all other options, and you must use the option by itself.

Examples

The following example shows the prtconf output on a sun4/65 series machine.

```
castle% prtconf
System Configuration:  Sun Microsystems  sun4c
Memory size: 16 Megabytes
System Peripherals (Software Nodes):
Sun 4_65
    options, instance #0
    zs, instance #0
    zs, instance #1
    fd (driver not attached)
    audio (driver not attached)
    sbus, instance #0
        dma, instance #0
        esp, instance #0
            sd (driver not attached)
            st (driver not attached)
            sd, instance #0
            sd, instance #1 (driver not attached)
            sd, instance #2 (driver not attached)
            sd, instance #3
            sd, instance #4 (driver not attached)
            sd, instance #5 (driver not attached)
            sd, instance #6 (driver not attached)
        le, instance #0
        cgsix (driver not attached)
    auxiliary-io (driver not attached)
    interrupt-enable (driver not attached)
    memory-error (driver not attached)
    counter-timer (driver not attached)
    eeprom (driver not attached)
```

```
     pseudo, instance #0
castle%
```

The following example shows the prtconf output on a Sun Ultra-2 machine.

```
paperbark% prtconf
System Configuration:  Sun Microsystems   sun4u
Memory size: 128 Megabytes
System Peripherals (Software Nodes):

SUNW,Ultra-2
    packages (driver not attached)
        terminal-emulator (driver not attached)
        deblocker (driver not attached)
        obp-tftp (driver not attached)
        disk-label (driver not attached)
        sun-keyboard (driver not attached)
        ufs-file-system (driver not attached)
    chosen (driver not attached)
    openprom (driver not attached)
        client-services (driver not attached)
    options, instance #0
    aliases (driver not attached)
    memory (driver not attached)
    virtual-memory (driver not attached)
    counter-timer (driver not attached)
    sbus, instance #0
        SUNW,CS4231 (driver not attached)
        auxio (driver not attached)
        flashprom (driver not attached)
        SUNW,fdtwo (driver not attached)
        eeprom (driver not attached)
        zs, instance #0
        zs, instance #1
        sc (driver not attached)
        SUNW,pll (driver not attached)
        SUNW,fas, instance #0
            sd (driver not attached)
            st (driver not attached)
            sd, instance #0
            sd, instance #1
            sd, instance #2 (driver not attached)
            sd, instance #3 (driver not attached)
            sd, instance #4 (driver not attached)
            sd, instance #5 (driver not attached)
            sd, instance #6
            sd, instance #7 (driver not attached)
            sd, instance #8 (driver not attached)
            sd, instance #9 (driver not attached)
            sd, instance #10 (driver not attached)
            sd, instance #11 (driver not attached)
            sd, instance #12 (driver not attached)
            sd, instance #13 (driver not attached)
            sd, instance #14 (driver not attached)
```

```
        SUNW,hme, instance #0
        SUNW,bpp (driver not attached)
    SUNW,UltraSPARC (driver not attached)
    SUNW,ffb, instance #0
    pseudo, instance #0
paperbark%
```

The following example shows the version of the OpenBoot PROM on the system
paperbark.

```
paperbark% prtconf -V
OBP 3.11.2 1997/12/05 10:25
paperbark%
```

The following example shows the prtconf output on an IA machine.

```
andy% prtconf
System Configuration:  Sun Microsystems   i86pc
Memory size: 32 Megabytes
System Peripherals (Software Nodes):

i86pc
    eisa, instance #0
        kd, instance #0
        ata, instance #0
            cmdk, instance #0
        aha, instance #0
            cmdk, instance #1 (driver not attached)
            cmdk, instance #2 (driver not attached)
            cmdk, instance #3 (driver not attached)
            cmdk, instance #4 (driver not attached)
            cmdk, instance #5 (driver not attached)
            cmdk, instance #6 (driver not attached)
            cmdk, instance #7
        chanmux, instance #0
        asy, instance #0
        asy, instance #1
        elx, instance #0
        elx, instance #1 (driver not attached)
        elx, instance #2 (driver not attached)
        elx, instance #3 (driver not attached)
        fdc, instance #0
            fd, instance #0
            fd, instance #1
    options, instance #0
    objmgr, instance #0
    pseudo, instance #0
andy%
```

Exit Status

0   No error occurred.

non-zero   With the -F option (SPARC platform only), a non-zero return value means that the output device is not a frame buffer. With the -x option, a non-zero return value means that the firmware is not 64-bit ready. In all other cases, a non-zero return value means that an error occurred.

Attributes

See attributes(5) for descriptions of the following attributes.

Attribute Type	Attribute Value
Availability	SUNWesu (32 bit) SUNWesxu (64 bit)

See Also

modinfo(1M), sysdef(1M), attributes(5)
  Sun Hardware Platform Guide

SPARC Platform Only

openprom(7D)

prtdiag — Display System Diagnostic Information

Synopsis

/usr/platform/*platform-name*/sbin/prtdiag [-v] [-l]

Description

Use the prtdiag command to display system configuration and diagnostic information. The diagnostic information lists any failed Field Replaceable Units (FRUs) in the system.

The interface, output, and location in the directory hierarchy for prtdiag are uncommitted and subject to change in future releases.

platform-name is the name of the platform implementation; you can find it with the -i option of uname(1).

> **Note** — prtdiag does not display diagnostic information and environmental status when executed on the Sun Enterprise 10000 server. See the /var/opt/SUNWssp/adm/${SUNW_HOSTNAME}/messages file on the System Service Processor (SSP) to obtain such information for this server.

Options

-v   Display the time of the most recent AC power failure, the most recent hardware fatal error information, and (if applicable) environmental status. The hardware fatal error information is useful to repair and manufacturing departments for detailed diagnostics of FRUs.

-1   Log output. If failures or errors exist in the system, output this information to syslogd(1M) only.

Examples

The following example shows the prtdiag output on the system paperbark.

```
paperbark% /usr/platform/`uname -i`/sbin/prtdiag
System Configuration:  Sun Microsystems  sun4u Sun Ultra 2 UPA/SBus
   (UltraSPARC 168MHz)
System clock frequency: 84 MHz
Memory size: 128 Megabytes

======================== CPUs =========================

                     Run   Ecache   CPU    CPU
Brd   CPU   Module   MHz     MB     Impl.  Mask
---   ---   ------   -----  ------  ------ ----
 0     0      0      168    0.5     US-I   2.2


======================= IO Cards =========================

       Bus   Freq
Brd    Type  MHz    Slot  Name                             Model
---    ----  ----   ----  --------------------------------  ----------
       ----------------------
 0     SBus   25    14    SUNW,fas/sd (block)
 0     SBus   25    14    SUNW,hme
 0     SBus   25    14    SUNW,bpp
 0     UPA    84    30    FFB, Single Buffered             SUNW,501-2634

No failures found in System
===========================
paperbark%
```

Exit Status

0   No failures or errors are detected in the system.

1   Failures or errors are detected in the system.

Attributes

See attributes(5) for descriptions of the following attributes.

Attribute Type	Attribute Value
Availability	SUNWkvm

See Also

uname(1), modinfo(1M), prtconf(1M), psrinfo(1M), sysdef(1M), syslogd(1M), attributes(5), openprom(7D)

prtvtoc — Report Information About Disk Geometry and Partitioning

Synopsis

/usr/sbin/prtvtoc [-fhs][-t *vfstab*][-m *mnttab*] *device*

Description

Use the prtvtoc command to view the contents of the VTOC (volume table of contents). Only superuser can use this command.

The device name can be the file name of a raw device in the form of /dev/rdsk/c*?*t*?*d*?*s2 or can be the file name of a block device in the form of /dev/dsk/c*?*t*?*d*?*s2.

Warning — The mount command does not check the "not mountable" bit.

Options

-f	Report on the disk free space, including the starting block address of the free space, number of blocks, and unused partitions.
-h	Omit the headers from the normal output.
-s	Omit all headers but the column header from the normal output.
-t *vfstab*	Use *vfstab* as the list of file system defaults, in place of /etc/vfstab.
-m *mnttab*	Use *mnttab* as the list of mounted file systems, in place of /etc/mnttab.

Examples

The following example shows the output for a 2-gigabyte hard disk.

```
# prtvtoc /dev/dsk/c0t0d0s2
* /dev/dsk/c0t0d0s2 partition map
*
* Dimensions:
```

```
*       512 bytes/sector
*        80 sectors/track
*        19 tracks/cylinder
*      1520 sectors/cylinder
*      3500 cylinders
*      2733 accessible cylinders
*
* Flags:
*    1: unmountable
*   10: read-only
*
*                            First     Sector    Last
* Partition  Tag  Flags      Sector    Count     Sector  Mount Directory
         0    2    00      1048800   2799840   3848639  /
         1    3    01            0   1048800   1048799
         2    5    00            0   4154160   4154159
         7    8    00      3848640    305520   4154159  /export/home
#
```

The data in the Tag column above indicates the type of partition, as follows.

Name	Number
UNASSIGNED	0x00
BOOT	0x01
ROOT	0x02
SWAP	0x03
USR	0x04
BACKUP	0x05
STAND	0x06
VAR	0x07
HOME	0x08
ALTSCTR	0x09
CACHE	0x0a

The data in the Flags column above indicates how the partition is to be mounted, as follows.

Name	Number
MOUNTABLE, READ AND WRITE	0x00
NOT MOUNTABLE	0x01
MOUNTABLE, READ ONLY	0x10

The following example shows output for the -f option for the same disk as above.

```
# prtvtoc -f /dev/dsk/c0t0d0s2
FREE_START=0 FREE_SIZE=0 FREE_COUNT=0 FREE_PART=3456
#
```

Attributes

See attributes(5) for descriptions of the following attributes.

Attribute Type	Attribute Value
Availability	SUNWcsu

See Also

devinfo(1M), fmthard(1M), format(1M), mount(1M), attributes(5)

psradm — Change Processor Operational Status

Synopsis

```
/usr/sbin/psradm -f | -i | -n [-v] processor-id...
/usr/sbin/psradm -a -f | -i | -n [-v]
```

Description

Use the psradm command to change the operational status of processors. The legal states for the processor are on-line (-n), off-line (-f), and no-intr (-i).

An on-line processor processes LWPs (lightweight processes) and may be interrupted by I/O devices in the system.

An off-line processor does not process any LWPs. Usually, an off-line processor is not interruptible by I/O devices in the system. On some processors or under certain conditions, it may not be possible to disable interrupts for an off-line processor. Thus, the actual effect of being off-line can vary from machine to machine.

A no-intr processor processes LWPs but is not interruptible by I/O devices.

You cannot take a processor off-line if there are LWPs that are bound to the processor. On some architectures, it might not be possible to take certain processors off-line if, for example, the system depends on some resource provided by the processor.

At least one processor in the system must be able to process LWPs. At least one processor must also be able to be interrupted. Because an off-line processor may be interruptible, it is possible to have an operational system with one processor no-intr and all other processors off-line but with one or more accepting interrupts.

If any of the specified processors are powered off, psradm may power on one or more processors.

Only superuser can use the psradm command.

Options

-a	Perform the action on all processors or as many as possible.
-f	Take the specified processors off-line.
-i	Set the specified processors no-intr.
n	Bring the specified processors on-line.
-v	Output a message giving the results of each attempted operation.

Operands

processor-id The processor ID of the processor to be set on-line or off-line.

Examples

The following example sets processors 2 and 3 off-line.

```
# psradm -f 2 3
```

The following example sets processors 1 and 2 no-intr.

```
# psradm -i 1 2
```

The following example sets all processors on-line.

```
# psradm -a -n
```

Exit Status

0	Successful completion.
>0	An error occurred.

Files

/etc/wtmpx   Records logging processor status changes.

Attributes

See attributes(5) for descriptions of the following attributes.

Attribute Type	Attribute Value
Availability	SUNWcsu

See Also

psrinfo(1M), psrset(1M), p_online(2), attributes(5)

Diagnostics

psradm: processor 4: Invalid argument

The specified processor does not exist in the configuration.

```
psradm: processor 3: Device busy
```

> The specified processor could not be taken off-line because it either has LWPs bound to it, is the last on-line processor in the system, or is needed by the system because it provides some essential service.

```
psradm: processor 3: Device busy
```

> The specified processor could not be set no-intr because it is the last interruptible processor in the system or it is the only processor in the system that can service interrupts needed by the system.

```
psradm: processor 3: Device busy
```

> The specified processor is powered off, and it cannot be powered on because some platform-specific resource is unavailable.

```
psradm: processor 0: Not owner
```

> The user does not have permission to change processor status.

```
psradm: processor 2: Operation not supported
```

> The specified processor is powered off, and the platform does not support power-on of individual processors.

psrinfo — Display Information About Processors

Synopsis

```
/usr/sbin/psrinfo [-v][processor-id...]
/usr/sbin/psrinfo -s processor-id
```

Description

Use the psrinfo command to display information about processors.

Without the *processor-id* operand, psrinfo displays one line for each configured processor, displaying whether it is on-line, off-line, or powered off, and when that status last changed. Use the *processor-id* operand to display information about a specific processor.

Options

-s *processor-id*

> Display 1 if the specified processor is on-line, and 0 if it is off-line or powered off. Use this silent mode when using psrinfo in shell scripts.

-v

> Display additional information about the specified processors, including processor type, Floating Point Unit type, and clock speed. If any of this information cannot be determined, display unknown.

Operands

processor-id The processor ID of the processor about which information is to be
displayed.

Specify *processor-id* as an individual processor number (for   *New!*
example, 3), multiple processor numbers separated by spaces (for
example, 1 2 3), or a range of processor numbers (for example, 1-4).
You can also combine ranges and individual or multiple processor-IDs
(for example, 1-3, 5 7 8-9).

Examples

The following example displays information about all configured processors.

```
paperbark% psrinfo
0       on-line    since 12/22/99 11:35:11
paperbark%
```

The following example displays verbose information about all configured processors.

```
paperbark% psrinfo -v
Status of processor 0 as of: 12/22/99 12:50:25
  Processor has been on-line since 12/22/99 11:35:11.
  The sparcv9 processor operates at 168 MHz,
        and has a sparcv9 floating point processor.
paperbark%
```

The following example uses psrinfo in a shell script to determine if a processor is
on-line.

```
if ["`psrinfo -s 3 2> /dev/null`" -eq 1]
then
        echo "processor 3 is up"
fi
```

The following example displays information for a Sun E4000 multiCPU system.

```
# /usr/sbin/psrinfo
0       on-line    since 04/29/00 19:37:39
1       on-line    since 04/29/00 19:38:14
4       on-line    since 04/29/00 19:38:14
5       on-line    since 04/29/00 19:38:14
8       on-line    since 04/29/00 19:38:14
9       on-line    since 04/29/00 19:38:14
12      on-line    since 04/29/00 19:38:14
13      on-line    since 04/29/00 19:38:14
#
```

The following example uses the -v option to display more information for a Sun
E4000 multiCPU system.

```
# /usr/sbin/psrinfo -v
Status of processor 0 as of: 05/22/00 05:50:50
  Processor has been on-line since 04/29/00 19:37:39.
  The sparc processor operates at 248 MHz,
        and has a sparc floating point processor.
```

```
Status of processor 1 as of: 05/22/00 05:50:50
  Processor has been on-line since 04/29/00 19:38:14.
  The sparc processor operates at 248 MHz,
          and has a sparc floating point processor.
Status of processor 4 as of: 05/22/00 05:50:50
  Processor has been on-line since 04/29/00 19:38:14.
  The sparc processor operates at 248 MHz,
          and has a sparc floating point processor.
Status of processor 5 as of: 05/22/00 05:50:50
  Processor has been on-line since 04/29/00 19:38:14.
  The sparc processor operates at 248 MHz,
          and has a sparc floating point processor.
Status of processor 8 as of: 05/22/00 05:50:50
  Processor has been on-line since 04/29/00 19:38:14.
  The sparc processor operates at 248 MHz,
          and has a sparc floating point processor.
Status of processor 9 as of: 05/22/00 05:50:50
  Processor has been on-line since 04/29/00 19:38:14.
  The sparc processor operates at 248 MHz,
          and has a sparc floating point processor.
Status of processor 12 as of: 05/22/00 05:50:50
  Processor has been on-line since 04/29/00 19:38:14.
  The sparc processor operates at 248 MHz,
          and has a sparc floating point processor.
Status of processor 13 as of: 05/22/00 05:50:50
  Processor has been on-line since 04/29/00 19:38:14.
  The sparc processor operates at 248 MHz,
          and has a sparc floating point processor.
#
```

Exit Status

0	Successful completion.
>0	An error occurred.

Attributes

See `attributes`(5) for descriptions of the following attributes.

Attribute Type	**Attribute Value**
Availability	SUNWcsu

See Also

psradm(1M), p_online(2), processor_info(2), attributes(5)

Diagnostics

```
psrinfo: processor 9: Invalid argument
```
          The specified processor does not exist.

psrset — Create and Manage Processor Sets

Synopsis

```
/usr/sbin/psrset -c [processor-id...]
/usr/sbin/psrset -d processor-set-id
/usr/sbin/psrset -a processor-set-id processor-id...
/usr/sbin/psrset -r processor-id...
/usr/sbin/psrset -p [processor-id...]
/usr/sbin/psrset -b processor-set-id pid...
/usr/sbin/psrset -u pid...
/usr/sbin/psrset -e processor-set-id command [argument(s)]
/usr/sbin/psrset -f processor-set-id
/usr/sbin/psrset -n processor-set-id
/usr/sbin/psrset -q [pid...]
/usr/sbin/psrset [-i][processor-set-id...]
```

Description

Use the psrset command to control the management of processor sets. Processor sets enable the binding of processes to groups of processors, instead of just a single processor. Processor sets are of two types.

- Processors created by the user using the psrset command or the pset_create(2) system call.
- Processors automatically created by the system.

Processors assigned to user-created processor sets run only LWPs that have been bound to that processor set, but system processor sets can run other LWPs as well.

System-created processor sets do not always exist on a given machine. When they exist, they generally represent particular characteristics of the underlying machine, such as groups of processors that can communicate more quickly with each other than with other processors in the system. These processor sets cannot be modified or removed, but processes can be bound to them.

Options

-a   Assign the specified processors to the specified processor set.

     Processor sets automatically created by the system cannot have processors assigned to them. However, processors belonging to system processor sets can be assigned to user-created processor sets. This option is restricted to use by superuser.

-b   Bind all the LWPs of the specified processes to the specified processor set.

     LWPs bound to a processor set are restricted to run only on the processors in that set unless they require resources available only on another processor. Processes can be bound only to nonempty processor sets, that is, processor sets that have had processors assigned to them.

Bindings are inherited, so new LWPs and processes created by a
bound LWP have the same binding. Binding an interactive shell to a
processor, for example, binds all commands executed by the shell.

-c   Create a new processor set and display the new processor set ID.

If you specify a list of processors, also try to assign those processors to
the processor set. If this succeeds, the processors are idle until LWPs
are bound to the processor set. This option is restricted to use by
superuser.

Only a limited number of processor sets can be active (created and not
destroyed) at a given time. This limit is always greater than the
number of processors in the system. If you use the -c option when the
maximum number of processor sets is already active, the command
fails.

The following format is used for the first line of output of the -c option
when the LC_MESSAGES locale category specifies the C locale. In other
locales, the string created processor set may be replaced with
more appropriate strings corresponding to the locale.

`"created processor set %d\n"` *processor-set-ID*

-d   Remove the specified processor set, releasing all processors and
processes associated with it. Processor sets automatically created by
the system cannot be removed. This option is restricted to use by the
superuser.

-e   Execute a command with optional arguments in the specified
processor set. The command process and any child processes are
executed only by processors in the processor set.

Superuser can execute a command in any active processor set. Other
users can execute commands only in system processor sets.

-f   Disable interrupts for all processors within the specified processor
set.

See psradm(1M). If some processors in the set cannot have their
interrupts disabled, the other processors still have their interrupts
disabled and the command reports an error and returns non-zero exit
status. This option is restricted to use by superuser.

-i   Display a list of all processors within the named processor set. If you
specify no argument, display a list of all processor sets and the
processors assigned to them. This operation is also the default if the
psrset command is not given an option.

-n   Enable interrupts for all processors within the specified processor set.
See psradm(1M). This option is restricted to use by superuser.

-p   Display the processor set assignments of the specified processors or of
all processors. If you specify no argument, the processor sets
assignments for all processors in the system.

-q	Display the processor set bindings of the specified processes or of all processes. If a process is composed of multiple LWPs that have different bindings, show the bindings of only one of the bound LWPs. If you specify no argument, display the processor set bindings of all processes in the system.
-r	Remove a list of processors from their current processor sets. Processors that are removed return either to the system processor set to which they previously belonged or to the general pool of processors if they did not belong to a system processor set. This option is restricted to use by superuser. Processors with LWPs bound to them using pbind(1M) cannot be assigned to or removed from processor sets.
-u	Remove the processor set bindings of all LWPs of the specified processes, enabling them to be executed by any online processor if they are not bound to individual processors through pbind.
	Superuser can bind or unbind any process to any active processor set. Other users can bind or unbind processes only to system processor sets. Furthermore, they can bind or unbind only processes for which they have permission to signal, that is, any process that has the same effective user ID as the user.

Operands

New!

pid	A process ID number.
processor-id	An individual processor number (for example, 3), multiple processor numbers separated by spaces (for example, 1 2 3), or a range of processor numbers (for example, 1-4). You can also combine ranges and individual or multiple processor-IDs (for example, 1-3 5 7-8 9).
processor-set-id	A processor set ID number.

Exit Status

0	Successful completion.
non-zero	An error occurred.

Attributes

See attributes(5) for descriptions of the following attributes.

Attribute Type	Attribute Value
Availability	SUNWcsu
Stability level	Stable

See Also

pbind(1M),psradm(1M),psrinfo(1M),processor_bind(2),processor_info(2),
pset_bind(2), pset_create(2), pset_info(2), sysconf(3C), attributes(5)

Diagnostics

psrset: cannot query pid 31: No such process

> The process specified did not exist or has exited.

psrset: cannot bind pid 31: Not owner

> The user does not have permission to bind the process.

psrset: cannot assign processor 4: Not owner

> The user does not have permission to assign the processor.

psrset: cannot assign processor 8: Invalid argument

> The specified processor is not online, or the specified processor does
> not exist.

psrset: cannot bind pid 67: Device busy

> An LWP in the specified process is bound to a processor and cannot be
> bound to a processor set that does not include that processor.

psrset: cannot assign processor 7: Device busy

> The specified processor could not be added to the processor set. This
> may be because of bound LWPs on that processor, that processor
> cannot be combined in the same processor set with other processors in
> that set, or the processor is the last one in its current processor set.

psrset: cannot execute in processor set 8: Invalid argument

> The specified processor set does not exist.

psrset: cannot create processor set: Not enough space

> The maximum number of processor sets allowed in the system is
> already active.

putdev — Edit Device Table

Synopsis

```
/bin/putdev -a alias [attribute=value [...]]
/bin/putdev -m device attribute=value [attribute=value [...]]
/bin/putdev -d device [attribute [...]]
```

Description

Use the putdev command for the following tasks.

- To add a new device to the device table.
- To modify an existing entry by adding or changing attributes. If a specified attribute is not defined, this option adds that attribute to the device definition. If the specified attribute is already defined, the attribute definition is modified.
- To remove a device entry from the table (third synopsis). You can either delete an entire device entry or, if you use the *attribute* argument, to an attribute assignment for a device.

Options

-a	Add a device to the device table by using the specified attributes. The device must be referenced by its alias.
-m	Modify a device entry in the device table. If an entry already exists, add any specified attributes that are not defined. Also, modify any attributes that already have a value with the value specified by this command.
-d	Remove a device from the device table, when executed without the *attributes* argument. With the *attribute* argument, delete the given attribute specification for *device* from the table.

Operands

alias	Designate the alias of the device to be added.
device	Designate the path name or alias of the device whose attribute is to be added, modified, or removed.
attribute	Designate a device attribute to be added, modified, or deleted. Can be any of the device attributes described under "Device Attributes" on page 925 except alias. This restriction prevents an accidental modification or deletion of a device alias from the table.
value	Designate the value to be assigned to a device's attribute.

Device Attributes

The following list shows the standard device attributes, used by applications such as ufsdump(1M) and ufsrestore(1M), that can be defined for a device. You are not limited to this list, you can define any attribute you like.

alias	The unique name by which a device is known. No two devices in the database can share the same alias name. The name is limited in length to 14 characters and should contain only alphanumeric characters and the following special characters if they are escaped with a backslash: underscore (_), dollar sign ($), dash (-), and period (.).

bdevice   The path name to the block special device node associated with the device, if any. The associated major/minor combination should be unique within the database and should match that associated with the cdevice field, if any. (It is the administrator's responsibility to ensure that these major/minor numbers are unique in the database.)

capacity   The capacity of the device or of the typical volume, if removable.

cdevice   The path name to the character special device node associated with the device, if any. The associated major/minor combination should be unique within the database and should match that associated with the bdevice field, if any. (It is the administrator's responsibility to ensure that these major/minor numbers are unique in the database.)

cyl   Used by the command specified in the mkfscmd attribute.

desc   A description of any instance of a volume associated with this device (such as a diskette).

dpartlist The list of disk partitions associated with this device. Used only if type=disk. The list should contain device aliases, each of which must have type=dpart.

dparttype The type of disk partition represented by this device. Used only if type=dpart. The value should be either fs (for file system) or dp (for data partition).

erasecmd   The command string that, when executed, erases the device.

fmtcmd   The command string that, when executed, formats the device.

fsname   The file-system name on the file system administered on this partition, as supplied to the /usr/sbin/labelit command. This attribute is specified only if type=dpart and dparttype=fs.

gap   Used by the command specified in the mkfscmd attribute.

mkfscmd   The command string that, when executed, places a file system on a previously formatted device.

mountpt   The default mount point to use for the device. Used only if the device is mountable. For disk partitions where type=dpart and dparttype=fs, this attribute should specify the location where the partition is normally mounted.

nblocks   The number of blocks in the file system administered on this partition. Used only if type=dpart and dparttype=fs.

ninodes   The number of inodes in the file system administered on this partition. Used only if type=dpart and dparttype=fs.

norewind   The name of the character special device node that allows access to the serial device without rewinding when the device is closed.

pathname   Defines the path name to an inode describing the device (used for nonblock or character device path names such as directories).

type	A token that represents inherent qualities of the device. Standard types include `9-track`, `ctape`, `disk`, `directory`, `diskette`, `dpart`, and `qtape`.
volname	The volume name on the file system administered on this partition, as supplied to the `/usr/sbin/labelit` command. Used only if `type-dpart` and `dparttype-fs`.
volume	A text string used to describe any instance of a volume associated with this device. This attribute should not be defined for devices that are not removable.

Examples

The following example creates a device entry called `disk1` with block device `/dev/rdsk/c0t0d0s2` and character device `/dev/dsk/c0t0d0s2`.

```
# putdev -a disk1 bdevice=/dev/rdsk/c0t0d0s2 cdevice=/dev/dsk/c0t0d0s2
  desc="Disk Partition"
#
```

The following example modifies the device entry `disk1` and sets the mount point to `/mnt`, the device type to `dpart` and the type of disk partition to `fs`.

```
# putdev -m disk1 mountpt="/mnt" type=dpart dparttype=fs
#
```

The following example removes the device `disk1`.

```
# putdev -d disk1
#
```

Exit Status

0	Successful completion.
1	Command syntax was incorrect, an invalid option was used, or an internal error occurred.
2	The device table could not be opened for reading, or a new device table could not be created.
3	If executed with the `-a` option, means that an entry in the device table with the alias *alias* already exits. If executed with the `-m` or `-d` options, indicates that no entry exists for device *device*.
4	Indicates that `-d` was requested and one or more of the specified attributes were not defined for the device.

Files

`/etc/device.tab`

Device table.

Attributes

See attributes(5) for descriptions of the following attributes.

Attribute Type	Attribute Value
Availability	SUNWcsu

See Also

devattr(1M), putdgrp(1M), ufsdump(1M), ufsrestore(1M), attributes(5)
System Administration Guide, Volume I

putdgrp — Edit Device Group Table

Synopsis

/bin/putdgrp [-d] *dgroup* [*device*...]

Description

Use the putdgrp command to modify the device group table. This command performs two kinds of modification.

- It can modify the table by creating a new device group or by removing a device group.
- It can also change group definitions by adding or removing a device from the group definition.

When you invoke the command with only a *dgroup* specification, the command adds the specified group name to the device group table if it does not already exist. If you also use the -d option with only the *dgroup* specification, the command deletes the group from the table.

When you invoke the command with both a *dgroup* and a *device* specification, it adds the given device name(s) to the group definition. When invoked with both arguments and the -d option, the command deletes the device name(s) from the group definition.

When you invoke the command with both a *dgroup* and a *device* specification and the device group does not exist, it creates the group and adds the specified devices to that new group.

Options

-d	Delete the group or, if used with *device*, delete the device from a group definition.

Operands

dgroup	Specify a device group name.
device	Specify the path name or alias of the device that is to be added to, or deleted from, the *device* group.

Exit Status

0	Successful completion.
1	Command syntax was incorrect, an invalid option was used, or an internal error occurred.
2	Device group table could not be opened for reading or a new device group table could not be created.
3	If executed with the -d option, means that an entry in the device group table for the device group *dgroup* does not exist and so cannot be deleted. Otherwise, indicates that the device group *dgroup* already exists and cannot be added.
4	If executed with the -d option, means that the device group *dgroup* does not have as members one or more of the specified devices. Otherwise, means that the device group *dgroup* already has one or more of the specified devices as members.

Examples

The following example adds a new device group.

```
# putdgrp floppies
#
```

The following example adds a device to a device group.

```
# putdgrp floppies diskette2
#
```

The following example deletes a device group.

```
# putdgrp -d floppies
#
```

The following example deletes a device from a device group.

```
# putdgrp -d floppies diskette2
#
```

Files

/etc/dgroup.tab

Device group table.

Attributes

See attributes(5) for descriptions of the following attributes.

Attribute Type	Attribute Value
Availability	SUNWcsu

pwck, grpck — Password/Group File Checkers

Synopsis

```
/usr/sbin/pwck [filename]
/usr/sbin/grpck [filename]
```

Description

Use the pwck command to scan the password file and to note any inconsistencies. The checks include validation of the number of fields, login name, user ID, group ID, and whether the login directory and the program-to-use-as-shell exist. The default password file is /etc/passwd.

Use the grpck command to verify all entries in the group file. This verification includes a check of the number of fields, group name, group ID, whether any login names belong to more than NGROUPS_MAX groups, and that all login names appear in the password file. The default group file is /etc/group.

> **Note** — If you specify no *filename* argument, grpck checks the local group file, /etc/group, and also makes sure that all login names encountered in the checked group file are known to the system getpwent(3C) routine. Therefore, login names can be supplied by a network nameservice.

Examples

The following example shows that one entry in the /etc/passwd file has an incorrectly specified login shell.

```
# pwck /etc/passwd

des:x:1003:10::/export/home/des:/bin/ch
        Optional shell file not found
#
```

Files

/etc/group   File that contains a list of groups recognized by the system.

/etc/passwd   File that contains a list of users recognized by the system.

Attributes

See attributes(5) for descriptions of the following attributes.

Attribute Type	Attribute Value
Availability	SUNWcsu

See Also

getpwent(3C), group(4), passwd(4), attributes(5)

Diagnostics

Group entries in /etc/group with no login names are flagged.

Group file *filename* is empty

The /etc/passwd or /etc/group file is an empty file.

cannot open file *filename*: No such file or directory

The /etc/passwd or /etc/group file does not exist.

pwconv — Install and Update /etc/shadow with Information from /etc/passwd

Synopsis

/usr/sbin/pwconv

Description

Use the pwconv command to create and update /etc/shadow with information from /etc/passwd.

pwconv relies on a special value of x in the password field of /etc/passwd. This value indicates that the password for the user is already in /etc/shadow and should not be modified.

If the /etc/shadow file does not exist, this command creates /etc/shadow with information from /etc/passwd. The command populates /etc/shadow with the user's login name, password, and password aging information. If password aging information does not exist in /etc/passwd for a given user, none is added to /etc/shadow. However, the last changed information is always updated.

If the /etc/shadow file does exist, the following tasks are performed.

- Entries that are in the /etc/passwd file and not in the /etc/shadow file are added to the /etc/shadow file.

- Entries that are in the /etc/shadow file and not in the /etc/passwd file are removed from /etc/shadow.
- Password attributes (for example, password and aging information) that exist in an /etc/passwd entry are moved to the corresponding entry in /etc/shadow.

The pwconv command can only be used by superuser.

Examples

In the following example, the entry with the user name audit is added to the /etc/passwd file.

audit:x:0:1::/:/sbin/sh

Then the pwconv command is run to update the /etc/shadow file with the new user name. The command warns that no password has been created for user audit.

```
# pwconv
pwconv: WARNING user audit has no password
#
```

Exit Status

0	Success.
1	Permission denied.
2	Invalid command syntax.
3	Unexpected failure. Conversion not done.
4	Unexpected failure. Password file(s) missing.
5	Password file(s) busy. Try again later.
6	Bad entry in /etc/shadow file.

Files

/etc/passwd	File that contains a list of users recognized by the system.
/etc/shadow	File that contains encrypted password strings.
/etc/opasswd	Old copy of the passwd file.
/etc/oshadow	Old copy of the shadow file.

Attributes

See attributes(5) for descriptions of the following attributes.

Attribute Type	Attribute Value
Availability	SUNWcsu

See Also

passwd(1), passmgmt(1M), usermod(1M), passwd(4), attributes(5)

quot — Summarize File-System Ownership

Synopsis

```
/usr/lib/fs/ufs/quot [-acfhnv] filesystem
/usr/lib/fs/ufs/quot -a [-cfhnv]
```

Description

Use the quot command to display information about disk use. The output shows the number of blocks (1024 bytes) in the named file system currently owned by each user. There is a limit of 2048 blocks. Files larger than this are counted as a 2048-block file but the total block count is correct.

Note — Only superuser can use this command.

Options

-a	Generate a report for all mounted file systems.
-c	Display three columns giving a file size in blocks, the number of files of that size, and a cumulative total of blocks containing files of that size or a smaller size.
-f	Display count of number of files as well as space owned by each user. This option is incompatible with the -c and -v options.

-h   Estimate the number of blocks in the file. This estimate does not
                account for files with holes in them.

-n   Attach names to the list of files read from standard input. You cannot
                use quot -n alone because it expects data from standard input. For
                example, the following pipeline produces a list of all files and their
                owners.

                ncheck myfilesystem | sort +0n | quot -n myfilesystem

                This option is incompatible with all other options.

-v   In addition to the default output, display three columns containing
                the number of blocks not accessed in the last 30, 60, and 90 days.

Operands

filesystem   Mount point of the file system being checked.

Usage

See largefile(5) for the description of the behavior of quot when encountering files
greater than or equal to 2 Gbytes (2**31 bytes).

Examples

The following example shows the output of the quot -a command on the system
paperbark.

```
# quot -a
/dev/rdsk/c0t0d0s0 (/):
510021   root
231526   bin
25895    daemon
  838    uucp
  412    adm
   81    lp
   11    winsor
/dev/rdsk/c0t1d0s6 (/opt):
150347   bin
 7676    root
/dev/rdsk/c0t1d0s7 (/export/home):
  338    winsor
   41    root
    3    des
    3    ray
    3    rob
/dev/rdsk/c0t0d0s7 (/export/home0):
    9    root
#
```

Exit Status

0   Successful operation.

32   Error condition (bad or missing argument, bad path, or other error).

Files

/etc/mnttab   Mounted file systems.

/etc/passwd   File to use to get user names.

Attributes

See attributes(5) for descriptions of the following attributes.

Attribute Type	Attribute Value
Availability	SUNWcsu

See Also

du(1M), mnttab(4), passwd(4), attributes(5), largefile(5)

quota — Display a User's UFS File-System Disk Quota and Usage

Synopsis

/usr/lib/fs/ufs/quota [-v][*username*]

Description

Use the quota command to display information about quotas on a UFS file system and to search for users who have exceeded their quotas. Only superuser can use the optional *username* argument to view the limits of other users.

quota without options displays warnings about mounted file systems only when usage is over quota. Remotely mounted file systems that do not have quotas turned on are ignored.

Note — quota also displays quotas for NFS-mounted, UFS-based file systems if the rquotad daemon is running. See rquotad(1M).

Options

-v   Display user's quota on all mounted file systems where quotas exist.

Operands

username   Specify the name of users either by user name or by numeric UID.

Examples

The following example verifies the quota for user bholzgen.

```
# quota -v bholzgen
Disk quotas for bholzgen (uid 1002):
Filesystem     usage  quota  limit     timeleft  files  quota  limit     timeleft
/data          0         10    20                   0    40     50
#
```

In the following example, the /data file system is the only file system with an rq entry in the /etc/vfstab file.

```
#device                device             mount    FS     fsck    mount     mount
#to mount              to fsck            point    type   pass    at boot   options
#
/dev/dsk/c0t3d0s6 /dev/rdsk/c0t3d0s6  /work    ufs    3       yes       rq
```

The following example checks quotas for the /data file system on the /dev/rdsk/c0t0d0s6 slice.

```
# quotacheck -v /data
*** Checking quotas for /dev/rdsk/c0t3d0s6 (/data)
```

Usage

See largefile(5) for the description of the behavior of quota when encountering files greater than or equal to 2 Gbytes (2**31 bytes).

Files

/etc/mnttab   List of currently mounted file systems.

Attributes

See attributes(5) for descriptions of the following attributes.

Attribute Type	Attribute Value
Availability	SUNWcsu

See Also

edquota(1M), quotaon(1M), quotacheck(1M), repquota(1M), rquotad(1M), attributes(5), largefile(5)

quotacheck — UFS File-System Quota Consistency Checker

Synopsis

```
quotacheck [-fp][-v] filesystem...
quotacheck -a [-fpv]
```

Description

Use the quotacheck command to examine each mounted UFS file system, build a table of current disk usage, and compare this table against the information stored in the file system's disk quota file. If any inconsistencies are detected, both the quota file and the current system copy of the incorrect quotas are updated.

filesystem is either a file-system mount point or the block device on which the file system resides.

quotacheck expects each file system to be checked to have a quota file named quotas in the root directory. If none is present, quotacheck does not check the file system.

quotacheck accesses the character special device in calculating the actual disk usage for each user. Thus, the file systems that are checked should be quiescent while quotacheck is running.

Options

-a	Check the file systems that /etc/mnttab indicates are UFS file systems. These file systems must be read-write mounted with disk quotas enabled and must have an rq entry in the mntopts field in /etc/vfstab.
-f	Force check on file systems with logging enabled. Use in combination with the -p option.
-p	Check quotas of file systems in parallel. For file systems with logging enabled, perform no check unless you also specify the -f option.
-v	Indicate the calculated disk quotas for each user on a particular file system. quotacheck normally reports only those quotas modified.

Usage

See largefile(5) for the description of the behavior of quotacheck when encountering files greater than or equal to 2 Gbytes (2**31 bytes).

Files

/etc/mnttab	Mounted file systems.
/etc/vfstab	List of default parameters for each file system.

Attributes

See attributes(5) for descriptions of the following attributes.

Attribute Type	Attribute Value
Availability	SUNWcsu

See Also

edquota(1M), mount_ufs(1M), quota(1M), quotaon(1M), repquota(1M), attributes(5), largefile(5), quotactl(7I)

quotaon, quotaoff — Turn UFS File-System Quotas On and Off

Synopsis

```
/usr/lib/fs/ufs/quotaon [-v] filesystem...
/usr/lib/fs/ufs/quotaon -a [-v]
/usr/lib/fs/ufs/quotaoff [-v] filesystem...
/usr/lib/fs/ufs/quotaoff -a [-v]
```

Description

Use the quotaon command to turn on disk quotas for one or more UFS file systems.

Before a file system can have quotas enabled, a file named quotas, owned by root, must exist in the root directory of the file system. See edquota(1M) for details on how to modify the contents of this file.

Use the quotaoff command to turn off disk quotas for one or more UFS file systems. The file systems specified must already be mounted.

These commands update the mntopts field of the appropriate entries in /etc/mnttab to indicate when quotas are on or off for each file system. If quotas are on, quota is added to mntopts; if quotas are off, mntopts is marked noquota.

Options

quotaon -a	Use this option at boot time to enable quotas. It applies only to those file systems in /etc/vfstab that have rq in the mntopts field, are currently mounted rw, and have a quotas file in the root directory.
-v	Display a message for each file system after quotas are turned on.
quotaoff -a	Force all file systems in /etc/mnttab to disable their quotas.
-v	Display a message for each file system affected.

Operands

filesystem	Either the mount point of a file system or the block device on which the file system resides.

Examples

The following example turns on quotas for the file systems on the /dev/dsk/c0t3d0s6 disk.

```
# quotaon -v /dev/dsk/ c0t3d0s6
 /dev/dsk/ c0t3d0s6: quotas turned on
 #
```

Usage

See largefile(5) for the description of the behavior of quotaon and quotaoff when encountering files greater than or equal to 2 Gbytes (2**31 bytes).

Files

/etc/mnttab   Mounted file systems.

/etc/vfstab   List of default parameters for each file system.

Attributes

See attributes(5) for descriptions of the following attributes.

Attribute Type	Attribute Value
Availability	SUNWcsu

See Also

edquota(1M), quota(1M), quotacheck(1M), repquota(1M), mnttab(4), vfstab(4), attributes(5), largefile(5), quotactl(7I)

R

---

rarpd — DARPA Reverse Address Resolution Protocol Server

Synopsis
```
/usr/sbin/in.rarpd [-d] -a
/usr/sbin/in.rarpd [-d] device unit
```

Description
See in.rarpd(1M).

---

rdate — Set System Date from a Remote Host

Synopsis
```
/bin/rdate hostname
```

Description
You can use the rdate command to set the local date and time to match the local date and time of the *hostname* system. You must be superuser on the local system. Typically, you use rdate as part of a startup script.

Attributes

See attributes(5) for descriptions of the following attributes.

Attribute Type	Attribute Value
Availability	SUNWcsu

See Also

attributes(5)

---

rdisc — Network Router Discovery Daemon

Synopsis

```
/usr/sbin/in.rdisc [-a][-f][-s][send-address][receive-address]
/usr/sbin/in.rdisc -r [-p preference][-T interval][send-address]
   [receive-address]
```

Description

See in.rdisc(1M).

---

re-preinstall — Install the JumpStart Software on a System

Synopsis

```
cdrom-mnt-pt/s0/Solaris_8/Tools/Boot/usr/sbin/install.d/re-preinstall
   [-m Solaris-boot-dir][-k platform-name] target-slice
```

Description

Use the re-preinstall command to install the JumpStart software (Preinstall Boot Image) on a system so you can power-on the system and have it automatically perform a JumpStart installation on the system. When you turn on a re-preinstalled system, the system looks for the JumpStart software on the system's default boot disk. All new SPARC systems have the JumpStart software already preinstalled.

You can use the re-preinstall command in two ways.

- The most common way is to run re-preinstall on a system to install the JumpStart software on its own default boot disk. This way is useful if you want to restore a system to its original factory conditions.

- You can also run re-preinstall on a system to install JumpStart software on any attached disk (nonboot disk). Once you install the JumpStart software on a disk, you can move the disk to a different system and perform a JumpStart installation on the different system.

re-preinstall creates a standard file system on the specified *target-slice* (usually slice 0), and re-preinstall makes sure there is enough space on the *target-slice* for the JumpStart software. If sufficient space is not available, re-preinstall fails with the following message.

re-preinstall: *target-slice* too small xx Megabytes required

You can use the format(1M) command to create sufficient space on the *target-slice* for the JumpStart software.

Options

-k *platform-name*

> Platform name of the system that uses the disk with the JumpStart software. The default is the platform name of the system running re-preinstall. (Use the -i option to the uname(1) command to determine a system's platform name.)

-m *Solaris-boot-dir*

> Absolute path to the s0/Solaris_8/Tools/Boot subdirectory of a mounted Solaris CD or a Solaris CD copied to disk that re-preinstall uses to install the JumpStart software. The default is /cdrom/cdrom0/s0/Solaris_8/Tools/Boot, which is where the Solaris CD is mounted in single-user mode.

Operands

target-slice Device name of the disk slice used to install the JumpStart software (usually slice 0). For example, c0t3d0s0.

Examples

The following example installs the Jumpstart software on a system's own default boot disk.

1. From the ok prompt, type **ok boot cdrom -s** and press Return to boot the system from the Solaris CD (local or remote) in single-user mode.

2. With the re-preinstall command, install the JumpStart software on the system's default boot disk, which is the slice on the disk (usually slice 0) from which the system automatically boots. (The system's default boot disk is probably where the current root (/) file system is located, which you can determine with the format(1M) command.)

For example, the following command installs the JumpStart software on the system's default boot disk, c0t3d0s0.

```
# /cdrom/cdrom0/s0/Solaris_8/Tools/Boot/usr/sbin/install.d
    /re-preinstall c0t3d0s0
```

The following example installs the JumpStart software on a system's attached disk (nonboot disk).

1. Mount the Solaris CD if vold(1M) is not running or CD is not mounted.
2. Use the format(1M) command to determine the target slice where JumpStart is installed.
3. Use the uname -i command to determine the platform name of the system that uses the re-preinstalled disk
4. Run re-preinstall with the -m *Solaris-boot-dir* option if the Solaris CD is not mounted on /cdrom.

   For example, the following command installs the JumpStart software on the system's attached disk for a system with a sun4c kernel architecture, and it uses the Solaris CD mounted with vold(1M):

   ```
   # /cdrom/cdrom0/s0/Solaris_8/Tools/Boot/usr/bin
       /install.d/re-preinstall -m
       /cdrom/cdrom0/s0/Solaris_8/Tools/Boot -k sun4c c0t2d0s0
   ```

Exit Status

0	Successful completion.
1	An error has occurred.

Attributes

See attributes(5) for descriptions of the following attributes.

Attribute Type	Attribute Value
Availability	SUNWcdrom (Solaris CD, SPARC Platform Edition)

See Also

uname(1), eeprom(1M), format(1M), mount(1M), vold(1M), attributes(5)
Solaris Advanced Installation Guide

reboot — Restart the Operating System

Synopsis

/usr/sbin/reboot [-dlnq] [*bootarguments*]

Description

The reboot command restarts the kernel. The kernel is loaded into memory by the PROM monitor, which transfers control to the loaded kernel.

Although superuser can run reboot at any time, shutdown(1M) is normally used first to warn all users logged in of the impending loss of service. See shutdown(1M) for details.

reboot performs a sync(1M) operation on the disks and then initiates a multiuser reboot. See init(1M) for details.

reboot normally logs the reboot to the system log daemon, syslogd(1M), and puts a shutdown record in the login accounting file /var/adm/wtmpx (changed from wtmp in the **New!** Solaris 8 release). These actions are inhibited if you specify the -n or -q options. Normally, the system reboots itself at power-up or after crashes.

Options

-d	Force a system crash dump before rebooting. See dumpadm(1M) for **New!** information on configuring system crash dumps. In previous releases, this option was provided for compatibility but was not supported by the underlying reboot(3C) call.
-l	Suppress sending a message to the system log daemon, syslogd(1M), about who executed reboot.
-n	Avoid the sync(1M) operation. Use of this option can damage the file system.
-q	Reboot quickly and ungracefully, without shutting down running processes.
bootarguments	These arguments are accepted for compatibility and are passed unchanged to the uadmin(2) function.

Examples

The following example uses the two-dash delimiter (--) to separate the options of reboot from the arguments of boot(1M). The -rv options are passed to the boot command.

```
# reboot -dl -- -rv
```

Files

/var/adm/wtmpx   **New!**

                    Login accounting file. wtmpx is an extended database file that replaces the obsolete wtmp database file.

Attributes

See attributes(5) for descriptions of the following attributes.

Attribute Type	Attribute Value
Availability	SUNWcsu

See Also

boot(1M), crash(1M), dumpadm(1M), fsck(1M), halt(1M), init(1M),   **New!** shutdown(1M), sync(1M), syslogd(1M), uadmin(2), reboot(3C), attributes(5)

reject — Reject Print Requests

Synopsis
    /usr/sbin/reject [-r reason] destination...

Description
    See accept(1M).

rem_drv — Remove a Device Driver from the System

Synopsis
    /usr/sbin/rem_drv [-b basedir] device-driver

Description
Use the rem_drv command to inform the system that the device driver *device-driver* is no longer valid. If possible, rem_drv unloads *device-driver* from memory. Entries for the device in the /devices namespace are removed. rem_drv also updates the system driver configuration files.

If rem_drv has been executed, the next time the system is rebooted, it automatically performs a reconfiguration boot (see kernel(1M)).

Options
    -b basedir   Set the path to the root directory of the diskless client. Used on the
                  server to execute rem_drv for a client. The client machine must be
                  rebooted to unload the driver.

Examples
The following example removes the sd driver from use.

    paperbark% **rem_drv sd**

The next example removes the driver from the sun1 diskless client. The driver is not uninstalled or unloaded until the client machine is rebooted.

    paperbark% **rem_drv -b /export/root/sun1 sd**

Attributes
See attributes(5) for descriptions of the following attributes.

Attribute Type	Attribute Value
Availability	SUNWcsu

See Also

    add_drv(1M), drvconfig(1M), kernel(1M), attributes(5)

---

removef — Remove a File from Software Database

Synopsis

    /usr/sbin/removef [[-M] -R root-path][-V fs-file] pkginst path...
    /usr/sbin/removef [[-M] -R root-path][-V fs-file] -f pkginst

Description

Use the removef command as part of creating installation scripts to inform the system that you or the software intend to remove a path name. Output from removef is the list of input path names that can be safely removed because no other packages have a dependency on them.

Options

-f	After all files have been processed, invoke removef -f to indicate that the removal phase is complete.
-M	Do not use the $root-path/etc/vfstab file for determining the client's mount points. This option assumes the mount points are correct on the server, and it behaves consistently with Solaris 2.5 and earlier releases.
-R root-path	Define the full path name of a directory to use as the root-path. Relocate all files, including package system information files, to a directory tree starting in the specified root-path. You can specify the root-path when installing to a client from a server (for example, /export/root/client1).
-V fs-file	Specify an alternative fs-file to map the client's file systems. For example, used in situations where the $root-path/etc/vfstab file is nonexistent or unreliable.

Operands

pkginst	The package instance from which the path name is being removed.
path	The path name to be removed.

Examples

The following example shows the use of removef in an optional preinstall script.

    echo "The following files are no longer part of this package
    and are being removed."
    removef $PKGINST /dev/xt[0-9][0-9][0-9] |
    while read pathname

```
do
echo "$pathname"
rm -f $pathname
done
removef -f $PKGINST || exit 2
```

Exit Status

0	Successful completion.
>0	An error occurred.

Attributes

See attributes(5) for descriptions of the following attributes.

Attribute Type	**Attribute Value**
Availability	SUNWcsu

See Also

pkginfo(1), pkgmk(1), pkgparam(1), pkgproto(1), pkgtrans(1),
installf(1M), pkgadd(1M), pkgask(1M), pkgchk(1M), attributes(5)
Application Packaging Developer's Guide

repquota — Summarize Quotas for a UFS File System

Synopsis

```
/usr/sbin/repquota [-v] filesystem...
/usr/sbin/repquota -a [-v]
```

Description

Use the repquota command to print a summary of the disk usage and quotas for the specified UFS file systems. The current number of files and amount of space (in kilobytes), along with any quotas created with edquota(1M), are printed for each user.
The file system must have the file quotas in its root directory.
Only superusers can view quotas that are not their own.

Options

-a	Report on all mounted UFS file systems that have rq in the mntopts field of the /etc/vfstab file.
-v	Report quotas for all users, even those who do not consume resources.

Examples

The following example shows that no quotas are set for any of the mounted file systems on the system `paperbark`.

```
# repquota -a
quotactl: no quotas file on any mounted file system
#
```

The following example summarizes quotas for a UFS file system.

```
# repquota -v /data
/dev/dsk/c0t3d0s6 (/data):
                        Block  limits                    File limits
User            used    soft   hard   timeleft   used   soft   hard   timeleft
bholzgen -- 0           10     20                   0     40     50
#
```

Usage

See `largefile`(5) for the description of the behavior of `repquota` when encountering files greater than or equal to 2 Gbytes (2**31 bytes).

Attributes

See `attributes`(5) for descriptions of the following attributes.

Attribute Type	Attribute Value
Availability	SUNWcsu

See Also

`edquota`(1M), `quota`(1M), `quotacheck`(1M), `quotaon`(1M), `attributes`(5), `largefile`(5), `quotactl`(7I)

restricted_shell — Restricted Shell Command Interpreter

Synopsis

`/usr/lib/rsh` [-acefhiknprstuvx][*argument...*]

Description

See `rsh`(1M).

rexd — RPC-Based Remote Execution Server

Synopsis

```
/usr/sbin/rpc.rexd [-s]
```

Description

See rpc.rexd(1M).

rexecd — Remote Execution Server

Synopsis

```
/usr/sbin/in.rexecd
```

Description

See in.rexecd(1M).

rlogind — Remote Login Server

Synopsis

```
/usr/sbin/in.rlogind
```

Description

See in.rlogind(1M).

rm_install_client — Script to Remove Clients for Network Installation

Synopsis

```
cdrom-mnt-pt/Solaris_8/Tools/rm_install_client hostname
```

Description

See install_scripts(1M).

rmmount — Removable Media Mounter for CD-ROM and Diskette

Synopsis

`/usr/sbin/rmmount [-D]`

Description

The `rmmount` command is a removable media mounter that Volume Management executes whenever a CD-ROM or diskette is inserted. The Volume Management daemon, `vold(1M)`, manages CD-ROM and diskette devices. You can also use `rmmount` by calling `volrmmount(1)`.

On insertion, `rmmount` determines what type of file system (if any) is on the media. If a file system is present, `rmmount` mounts the file system in one of the following locations.

Mount Location	State of Media
`/floppy/floppy0`	Symbolic link to mounted diskette in local diskette drive.
`/floppy/floppy_name`	Mounted named diskette.
`/floppy/unnamed_floppy`	Mounted unnamed diskette.
`/cdrom/cdrom0`	Symbolic link to mounted CD-ROM in local CD-ROM drive.
`/cdrom/CD-ROM_name`	Mounted named CD-ROM.
`/cdrom/CD-ROM_name/partition`	Mounted named CD-ROM with partitioned file system.
`/cdrom/unnamed_cdrom`	Mounted unnamed CD-ROM.

If the media is read-only (either CD-ROM or diskette with write-protect tab set), the file system is mounted read-only.

If a file system is not identified, `rmmount` does not mount it. See the *System Administration Guide, Volume I* for more information on the location of CD-ROM and diskette media without file systems. Also see `volfs(7FS)`.

If a file-system type has been determined, it is then checked to see that it is clean. If the file system is dirty, `fsck -p` (see `fsck(1M)`) is run to try to clean it. If `fsck` fails, the file system is mounted read-only.

After the mount is complete, actions associated with the media type are executed. These actions enable other programs to be notified that new media are available. These actions are shared objects and are described in the configuration file, `/etc/rmmount.conf`.

Actions are executed in the order that they appear in the configuration file. The `action` function can return either 1 or 0. If it returns 0, no further actions are executed. This behavior enables the `action` function to control which applications are executed.

To execute an action, `rmmount` performs a `dlopen(3X)` on the shared object and calls the `action` function defined within it. The definition of the interface to actions can be found in `/usr/include/rmmount.h`.

File systems mounted by `rmmount` are always mounted with the `nosuid` flag set, thereby disabling setuid programs and access to block or character devices in that file system. On ejection, `rmmount` unmounts mounted file systems and executes actions associated with the media type. If a file system is busy (that is, it contains the current working directory of a live process), the ejection fails.

Options

    `-D`   Turn on the debugging output from the `rmmount` `dprintf` calls.

Files

    `/etc/rmmount.conf`

               Removable media mounter configuration file.

    `/usr/lib/rmmount/*.so.1`

               Shared objects used by `rmmount`.

Attributes

See `attributes(5)` for descriptions of the following attributes.

Attribute Type	Attribute Value
Availability	SUNWvolu

See Also

`volcancel(1)`, `volcheck(1)`, `volmissing(1)`, `volrmmount(1)`, `fsck(1M)`, `vold(1M)`, `dlopen(3X)`, `rmmount.conf(4)`, `vold.conf(4)`, `attributes(5)`, `volfs(7FS)`

System Administration Guide, Volume I

rmt — Remote Magtape Protocol Module

Synopsis

        /usr/sbin/rmt

Description

The rmt command is used by the remote dump and restore commands to manipulate a magnetic tape drive through an interprocess communication connection. rmt is normally started up with an rexec(3N) or rcmd(3N) call.

The rmt program accepts requests that are specific to the manipulation of magnetic tapes, performs the commands, then responds with a status indication. All responses are in ASCII and in one of two forms. Successful commands have the following response format,

        A*number*\n

where *number* is an ASCII representation of a decimal number. Unsuccessful commands have the following response format,

        E*error-number*\n*error-message*\n

where *error-number* is one of the possible error numbers described in intro(2) and *error-message* is the corresponding error string as printed from a call to perror(3C). The protocol consists of the following commands.

S\n
: Return the status of the open device, as obtained with a MTIOCGET ioctl call. If the operation was successful, send an ack with the size of the status buffer, then send the status buffer (in binary).

C*device*\n
: Close the currently open device. Ignore the specified device.

I*operation*\n*count*\n
: Perform a MTIOCOPioctl(2) command, using the specified parameters. Interpret the parameters as the ASCII representations of the decimal values to put in the mt_op and mt_count fields of the structure used in the ioctl call. When the operation is successful, the return value is the count parameter.

L*offset*\n*whence* \n
: Perform an lseek(2) operation, using the specified parameters. The response value is returned from the lseek call.

O*device*\n*mode*\n
: Open the specified device, using the indicated mode. *device* is a full path name, and mode is an ASCII representation of a decimal number suitable for passing to open(9E). If a device is already open, it is closed before a new open is performed.

R*count*\n	Read *count* bytes of data from the open device. Perform the requested read(9E) and respond with A*count*-read\n if the read was successful; otherwise, return an error in standard format. If the read was successful, send the data read.
W*count*\n	Write data onto the open device. Read *count* bytes from the connection, aborting if encountering a premature end-of-file. The response value is returned from the write(9E) call.

rmt exits with any other command.

Attributes

See attributes(5) for descriptions of the following attributes.

Attribute Type	Attribute Value
Availability	SUNWcsu

See Also

ufsdump(1M), ufsrestore(1M), intro(2), ioctl(2), lseek(2), perror(3C), rcmd(3N), rexec(3N), attributes(5), mtio(7I), open(9E), read(9E), write(9E)

Diagnostics

All responses are of the form described above.

Bugs

Do not use this command for a remote file access protocol.

New! roleadd — Administer a New Role Account

Synopsis

```
/usr/sbin/roleadd [-c comment][-d dir][-e expire][-f inactive]
    [-g group][-G group [, group...]][-m [-k skel-dir]][-u uid [-o]]
    [-s shell][-A authorization [,authorization...]] role
/usr/sbin/roleadd -D [-b base-dir][-e expire][-f inactive][-g group]
    [-A authorization [,authorization...]][-P profile [,profile...]]
```

Description

The roleadd command is new in the Solaris 8 release. Use the roleadd command to add role-based access control (RBAC). RBAC enables you to package specific superuser privileges for assignment to user accounts. In this way, you can provide certain users with the capability to solve their own problems without granting them the complete range of superuser privileges.

roleadd adds a role entry to the /etc/passwd, /etc/shadow, and /etc/user_attr files. The -A and -P options assign authorizations and profiles to the role. You cannot assign roles to other roles. roleadd also creates supplementary group memberships for the role (-G option) and creates the home directory (-m option) for the role if requested. The new role account remains locked until the passwd(1) command is executed.

Specify roleadd -D with the -g, -b, -f, or -e option (or any combination of these options) to set the default values for the respective fields. See the D option. Subsequent roleadd commands without the -D option use these arguments.

The system file entries created with this command have a limit of 512 characters per line. Specifying long arguments to several options can exceed this limit.

The *role* field accepts a string of no more than eight bytes consisting of characters from the set of alphabetic characters, numeric characters, period (.), underscore (_), and dash (-). The first character should be alphabetic, and the field should contain at least one lowercase alphabetic character. A warning message is written if these restrictions are not met. A future Solaris release may refuse to accept role fields that do not meet these requirements.

The *role* field must contain at least one character and must not contain a colon (:) or a newline (\n).

Note — If a network nameservice such as NIS or NIS+ is being used to supplement the local /etc/passwd file with additional entries, roleadd cannot change information supplied by the network nameservice.

Options

-A *authorization*

Specify one or more comma-separated authorizations as defined in auth_attr(4). Only a role with grant rights to the authorization can assign it to an account.

-b *base-dir* Specify the default base directory for the system if you do not specify -d *dir*. *base-dir* is concatenated with the account name to define the home directory. If you do not use the -m option, *base-dir* must exist.

-c *comment* Any text string, generally a short description of the role. This information is stored in the role's /etc/passwd entry.

-d *dir* Specify the home directory of the new role. The default is *base-dir*/*account-name*, where *base-dir* is the base directory for new login home directories and *account-name* is the new role name.

-D Display the default values for *group, base-dir, skel-dir, shell, inactive*, and *expire*. When used with the -g, -b, or -f options, the -D option sets the default values for the specified fields. The default values are shown below.

group	other (GID of 1)
base-dir	/home
skel-dir	/etc/skel
shell	/bin/sh
inactive	0

expire	Null
auths	Null
profiles	Null

-e *expire*   Specify the expiration date for a role. After this date, no user can access this role. The *expire* argument is a date entered in one of the date formats included in the template file /etc/datemsk. See getdate(3C). If the date format includes spaces, you must quote it. For example, you can enter 10/6/99 or "October 6, 1999". A null value (" ") defeats the status of the expired date. This option is useful for creating temporary roles

-f *inactive*   Specify the maximum number of days allowed between uses of a role ID before that ID is declared invalid. Normal values are positive integers. A value of 0 defeats the status.

-g *group*   Specify an existing group integer ID or character-string name. Without the -D option, it defines the new role's primary group membership and the default is the default group. You can reset this default value by invoking roleadd -D -g *group*.

-G *group*   Specify an existing group's integer ID or character-string name. This option defines the new role's supplementary group membership. Ignore duplicates between group with the -g and -G options. You can specify no more than NGROUPS_MAX groups.

-k *skel-dir*   Specify a directory that contains skeleton information (such as .profile) that can be copied into a new role's home directory. This directory must already exist. The system provides the /etc/skel directory that you can use for this purpose.

-m   Create the new role's home directory if it does not already exist. If the directory already exists, it must have read, write, and execute permissions by *group*, where *group* is the role's primary group.

-o   Specify a duplicate (nonunique) UID.

-P *profile*   Specify one or more comma-separated execution profiles defined in auth_attr(4).

-s *shell*   Specify the full path name of the program used as the user's shell on login. The default is an empty field so that /bin/sh is the default. The value of *shell* must be a valid executable file.

-u *uid*   Specify the UID of the new role. This UID must be a nonnegative decimal integer below MAXUID as defined in <sys/param.h>. The UID defaults to the next available (unique) number above the highest number currently assigned. For example, if UIDs 100, 105, and 200 are assigned, the next default UID number is 201. (UIDs from 0-99 are reserved for possible use in future applications.)

Operands

role   The name of the role to be created.

Examples

The following example uses the -D option to display the default settings for the roleadd command.

```
# roleadd -D
group=other,1  basedir=/home  skel=/etc/skel
shell=/bin/pfsh  inactive=0  expire=  auths=
profiles=All
#
```

You can use the -D option to change the default settings or use the options with the roleadd command to change the default settings for an individual role.

The following example creates a role named usracct that grants authorization to administer user accounts for the solaris.admin.usermgr* profiles and sets /bin/pfcsh as the default shell.

```
# roleadd -c "User Account Management" -s /bin/pfcsh  -A
  solaris.admin.usermgr.pswd,solaris.admin.usermgr.write -P "User
  Account Management" usracct
#
```

Files

/etc/datemsk	Date mask template.
/etc/passwd	A list of users known to the system.
/etc/shadow	Encrypted user passwords.
/etc/group	A list of groups known to the system.
/etc/skel	Default local.login, local.profile, and local.cshrc files. You can use this directory to store information that can be copied into a new role's home directory with the -k option.
/usr/include/limits.h	
	Limit information, such as the maximum number of characters in a login name.
/etc/user_attr	
	User attributes for roles.

Attributes

See attributes(5) for descriptions of the following attributes.

Attribute Type	Attribute Value
Availability	SUNWcsu

See Also

passwd(1), profiles(1), roles(1), users(1B), groupadd(1M), groupdel(1M), groupmod(1M), grpck(1M), logins(1M), pwck(1M), userdel(1M), usermod(1M),

getdate(3C), auth_attr(4), passwd(4), prof_attr(4), user_attr(4),
attributes(5)

Diagnostics

In case of an error, roleadd prints an error message and exits with a non-zero status.

UX: roleadd: ERROR: login is already in use. Choose another.

> The specified login is already in use.

UX: roleadd: ERROR: uid *uid* is already in use. Choose another.

> The UID specified with the -u option is not unique.

UX: roleadd: ERROR: group *group* does not exist. Choose another.

> The group specified with the -g option is already in use.

UX: roleadd: WARNING: uid *uid* is reserved.

> The UID specified with the -u option is in the range of reserved UIDs (from 0-99).

UX: roleadd: ERROR: uid *uid* is too big. Choose another.

> The UID specified with the -u option exceeds MAXUID as defined in <sys/param.h>.

UX: roleadd: ERROR: Cannot update system files - login cannot be
created.

> The /etc/passwd or /etc/shadow files do not exist.

New! roledel — Delete the Login for a Role

Synopsis

roledel [-r] *role*

Description

The roledel command is new in the Solaris 8 release. Use it to delete a role account from the system and to make the appropriate account-related changes to the system file and file system. roledel also removes the role from each user's list of assumable roles.

> **Note —** The roledel command deletes only an account definition that is in the local /etc/group, /etc/passwd, /etc/shadow, and /etc/user_attr file. If a network nameservice such as NIS or NIS+ is being used to supplement the local /etc/passwd file with additional entries, roledel cannot change information supplied by the network nameservice.

Options

    -r   Remove the role's home directory from the system. This directory must exist. The files and directories under the home directory are no longer accessible following successful execution of the command.

Operands

    role   An existing role name to be deleted.

Exit Status

0	Successful completion.
2	Invalid command syntax. A usage message for the roledel command is displayed.
6	The account to be removed does not exist.
8	The account to be removed is in use.
10	Cannot update the /etc/group or /etc/user_attr file, but the login is removed from the /etc/passwd file.
12	Cannot remove or otherwise modify the home directory.

Files

/etc/passwd	System password file.
/etc/shadow	System file containing roles' encrypted passwords and related information.
/etc/group	System file containing group definitions.
/etc/user_attr	

                System file containing additional role attributes.

Attributes

See attributes(5) for descriptions of the following attributes.

Attribute Type	Attribute Value
Availability	SUNWcsu

See Also

auths(1), passwd(1), profiles(1), roles(1), users(1B), groupadd(1M), groupdel(1M), groupmod(1M), logins(1M), roleadd(1M), rolemod(1M), useradd(1M), userdel(1M), usermod(1M), passwd(4), prof_attr(4), user_attr(4), attributes(5)

New! rolemod — Modify an Existing Role Account

Synopsis

```
/usr/sbin/rolemod [-u uid [-o]][-g group][-G group [, group...]]
   [-d dir [-m]][-s shell][-c comment][-l new-name] [-f inactive]
   [-e expire] [-A authorization [, authorization]][-P profile
   [, profile]] role
```

Description

The `rolemod` command is new in the Solaris 8 release. Use it to modify the login information for a role on the system. Use `rolemod` to change the definition of the specified login and to make the appropriate login-related system file and file-system changes.

The system file entries created with this command have a limit of 512 characters per line. Specifying long arguments to several options can exceed this limit.

Options

-A *authorization*

Specify one or more comma-separated authorizations as defined in auth_attr(4). Only a role with grant rights to the authorization can assign it to an account. This option replaces any existing authorization setting.

-c *comment*

Specify a comment string. *comment* can be any text string. It is generally a short description of the login and is currently used as the field for the user's full name. This information is stored in the user's /etc/passwd entry.

-d *dir*

Specify the new home directory of the role. The default is *base-dir*/*login*, where *base-dir* is the base directory for new login home directories, and *login* is the new login.

-e *expire*

Specify the expiration date for a role. After this date, no role can access this login. The *expire* argument is a date entered with one of the date formats included in the template file /etc/datemsk. See getdate(3C). If the date format includes spaces, you must quote it. For example, you can enter 10/6/99 or "October 6, 1999". A value of " " defeats the status of the expired date.

-f *inactive*

Specify the maximum number of days allowed between uses of a login ID before that login ID is declared invalid. Normal values are positive integers. A value of 0 defeats the status.

-g *group*

Specify an existing group's integer ID or character-string name. This option redefines the role's primary group membership.

-G *group*	Specify an existing group's integer ID or character string name. This option redefines the role's supplementary group membership. Ignore duplicates between groups with the -g and -G options. You can specify no more than NGROUPS_UMAX groups as defined in <param.h>.
-l *new-logname*	
	Specify the new login name for the role. The *new-logname* argument is a string of no more than eight bytes consisting of characters from the set of alphabetic characters, numeric characters, period (.), underline (_), and dash (-). The first character should be alphabetic and the field should contain at least one lowercase alphabetic character. Display a warning message if these restrictions are not met. A future Solaris release may refuse to accept login fields that do not meet these requirements. The *new-logname* argument must contain at least one character and must not contain a colon (:) or newline (\n).
-m	Move the role's home directory to the new directory specified with the -d option. If the directory already exists, it must have permissions read/write/execute by *group*, where *group* is the role's primary group.
-o	Duplicate the specified nonunique UID.
-P *profile*	Specify one or more comma-separated execution profiles defined in auth_attr(4). Replace any existing profile setting.
-s *shell*	Specify the full path name of the program that is used as the role's shell on login. The value of *shell* must be a valid executable file.
-u *uid*	Specify a new UID for the role. *uid* must be a nonnegative decimal integer less than MAXUID as defined in <param.h>. The UID associated with the role's home directory is not modified with this option; a role does not have access to the home directory until the UID is manually reassigned with chown(1M).

Operands

role	An existing role name to be modified.

Exit Status

In case of an error, rolemod prints an error message and exits with one of the following values.

2	The command syntax was invalid. A usage message for the rolemod command is displayed.
3	An invalid argument was provided to an option.
4	The UID given with the -u option is already in use.
5	The password files contain an error. You can use pwconv(1M) to correct possible errors. See passwd(4).

6	The login to be modified does not exist, the group does not exist, or the login shell does not exist.
8	The login to be modified is in use.
9	The *new-logname* is already in use.
10	Cannot update the /etc/group or /etc/user_attr file. Other update requests are implemented.
11	Insufficient space to move the home directory (-m option). Other update requests are implemented.
12	Unable to complete the move of the home directory to the new home directory.

Files

/etc/group	System file containing group definitions.
/etc/datemsk	System file of date formats.
/etc/passwd	System password file.
/etc/shadow	System file containing users' and roles' encrypted passwords and related information.
/etc/user_attr	

System file containing additional user and role attributes.

Attributes

See attributes(5) for descriptions of the following attributes.

Attribute Type	**Attribute Value**
Availability	SUNWcsu

See Also

passwd(1), users(1B), chown(1M), groupadd(1M), groupdel(1M), groupmod(1M), logins(1M), pwconv(1M), roleadd(1M), roledel(1M), useradd(1M), userdel(1M), usermod(1M), getdate(3C), auth_attr(4), passwd(4), attributes(5)

route — Manually Manipulate the Routing Tables

Synopsis

```
/usr/sbin/route [-inet6][-fnvq] command [[modifiers] args]
/usr/sbin/route [-inet6][-fnvq] add | change | delete | get [host | net]
  destination [gateway [args]]
/usr/sbin/route [-inet6][-n] monitor
/usr/sbin/route [-inet6][-n] flush
```

New!

Description

Use the `route` command to manually manipulate the network routing tables. These tables are normally maintained by the system routing daemon, by `routed(1M)`, or through default routes and redirect messages from routers.

This command now operates on IPv4 and IPv6 routes. By default, `route` operates on IPv4 routes. If you use the option `-inet6` on the command line immediately following the `route` command, operations are performed on IPv6 routes.

New!

This command supports a limited number of general options, but a rich command language. It enables you to specify any arbitrary request that could be delivered via the programmatic interface discussed in `route(7P)`.

`route` uses a routing socket and the new message types `RTM_ADD`, `RTM_DELETE`, `RTM_GET`, and `RTM_CHANGE`. Only superuser can modify the routing tables.

Options

`-f`	Flush the routing tables of all gateway entries. If you use this option with one of the commands described above, flush the gateways before performing the command.
`-inet6`	Operate on IPv6 routes instead of the default IPv4.
`-n`	Prevent attempts to print host and network names symbolically when reporting actions. This option is useful, for example, when all nameservers on your local net are down and you need a route before you can contact the nameserver.
`-v`	Print additional details.
`-q`	Suppress all output.

New!

Commands

`route` executes one of four commands on a route to a destination. Two additional commands operate globally on all routing information. The (six) commands are described below.

`add`	Add a route.
`change`	Change aspects of a route (such as its gateway).
`delete`	Delete a specific route.
`flush`	Remove all gateway entries from the routing table.

get   Look up and display the route for a destination.

monitor   Continuously report any changes to the routing information base, routing lookup misses, or suspected network partitioning.

The add, delete, and change commands have the following syntax.

```
route [-fnvq] command [-net | -host] destination gateway
```

where *destination* is the destination host or network, and *gateway* is the next-hop intermediary where packets should be routed.

Operands

route   Execute commands on routes to destinations.

Destinations

All symbolic names specified for a destination or gateway are looked up first as a host name, using gethostbyname(3N) If this lookup fails, getnetbyname(3N) is used to interpret the name as that of a network.

You can include an optional modifier on the command line before a destination, to force how route interprets a destination.

-host   Force the destination to be interpreted as a host.

-net   Force the destination to be interpreted as a network.

Routes to a particular host can be distinguished from those to a network by interpreting the Internet address specified as the destination. If the destination has a "local address part" of INADDR_ANY or if the destination is the symbolic name of a network, then the route is presumed to be to a network; otherwise, it is presumed to be a route to a host.

The following examples show how routes are interpreted.

Route	Interpreted as
128.32	-host 128.0.0.32
128.32.130	-host 128.32.0.130
-net 128.32	128.32.0.0
-net 128.32.130	128.32.130.0

If the destination is directly reachable by way of an interface requiring no intermediary system to act as a gateway, you can so indicate by including one of two optional modifiers after the destination. You can include the -interface modifier or specify a metric of 0. These modifiers are illustrated in the following alternative examples.

```
route add default hostname -interface
route add default hostname 0
```

hostname is the name or IP address associated with the network interface over which all packets should be sent. On a host with a single network interface, *hostname* is normally the same as the node name returned by uname -n (see uname(1)).

In the above examples, the route does not refer to a gateway but instead refers to one of the machine's interfaces. Destinations matching such a route are sent out on the interface identified by the gateway address. For interfaces using the ARP protocol, this type of route is used to specify that all destinations are local. That is, a host should use ARP for all addresses by adding a default route with one of the two commands listed above.

Use the optional -netmask qualifier to manually add subnet routes with netmasks different from that of the implied network interface. You can override the implicit network mask generated in the AF_INET by making sure the -netmask option and an ensuing address parameter (to be interpreted as a network mask) follow the destination parameter.

Routing Flags

Routes have associated flags that influence operation of the protocols when sending to destinations matched by the routes. You can set these flags (or sometimes clear them) by including the following corresponding modifiers on the command line.

Modifier	Flag	Description
-cloning	RTF_CLONING	Generate a new route on use.
-xresolve	RTF_XRESOLVE	Emit message on use (for external lookup).
-iface	~RTF_GATEWAY	Destination is directly reachable.
-static	RTF_STATIC	Manually added route.
-nostatic	~RTF_STATIC	Act as if route added by kernel or daemon.
-reject	RTF_REJECT	Emit an ICMP unreachable when matched.
-blackhole	RTF_BLACKHOLE	Silently discard packets (during updates).
-proto1	RTF_PROTO1	Set protocol-specific routing flag #1.
-proto2	RTF_PROTO2	Set protocol-specific routing flag #2.
-private	RTF_PRIVATE	Do not advertise this route.

New!

The optional modifiers are listed below.

```
-expire
-hopcount
-mtu
-recvpipe
-rtt
-rttvar
-sendpipe
-ssthresh
```
Provide initial values to quantities maintained in the routing entry by transport level protocols, such as TCP. You can lock the modifiers individually by preceding each modifier to be locked by the -lock metamodifier, or you can use the -lockrest metamodifier to specify locking of all ensuing metrics.

In a change or add command where the destination and gateway are not sufficient to specify the route (for example, when several interfaces have the same address), you can use the -ifp or -ifa modifiers to determine the interface or interface address.

Note — all destinations are local assumes that the routers implement the protocol proxy arp. Normally, using router discovery (see in.rdisc(1M)) is more reliable than using proxy arp.

Combining the all destinations are local route with subnet or network routes can lead to unpredictable results: the search order as it relates to the all destinations are local route are undefined and may vary from release to release.

Examples

The following example adds a route for network 20.5.5.0 through a router at 171.80.64.1.

```
# route add net 20.5.5.0 171.80.64.1 1
#
```

The following example deletes the default route through 172.20.11.9.

```
# route delete default 172.20.11.9
delete net default: gateway 172.20.11.9
#
```

The following example flushes the routing table.

```
# route -f
#
```

Files

/etc/hosts   List of host names and net addresses.

/etc/networks   List of network names and addresses.

Attributes

See attributes(5) for descriptions of the following attributes.

Attribute Type	Attribute Value
Availability	SUNWcsu

See Also

get(1), uname(1), in.rdisc(1M), netstat(1M), routed(1M), ioctl(2), gethostbyname(3N), getnetbyname(3N), hosts(4), networks(4), attributes(5), ARP(7P), route(7P), routing(7P)

Diagnostics

```
add [host|network] destination:gateway flags
```

> The specified route is being added to the tables. The values printed
> are from the routing table entry supplied in the ioctl(2) call. If the
> gateway address used was not the primary address of the gateway
> (the first one returned by gethostbyname(3N)), then the gateway
> address is printed numerically as well as symbolically.

```
delete [host|network] destination:gateway flags
```

> As above, but when deleting an entry.

```
destination done
```

> When you specify the -f option or the flush command, each routing
> table entry deleted is indicated with a message of this form.

```
Network is unreachable
```

> An attempt to add a route failed because the gateway listed was not
> on a directly connected network. Give the next-hop gateway instead.

```
not in table
```
A delete operation was tried for an entry that is not in the table.

```
routing table overflow
```

> An add operation was tried, but the system was unable to allocate
> memory to create the new entry.

---

routed — Network Routing Daemon

Synopsis

```
/usr/sbin/in.routed [-s][-q][-t][-g][-S][-v][logfile]
```

Description

See in.routed.(1M).

---

rpc.bootparamd, bootparamd — Boot Parameter Server

Synopsis

```
/usr/sbin/rpc.bootparamd [-d]
```

Description

The rpc.bootparamd daemon is a server process that provides information from a
bootparams database to diskless clients at boot time. See bootparams(4).

The source for the bootparams database is determined by the nsswitch.conf(4) file on the system running the rpc.bootparamd process.

The rpc.bootparamd program can be invoked either by inetd(1M) or directly from the command line.

Note — A diskless client requires service from at least one rpc.bootparamd process running on a server that is on the same IP subnetwork as the diskless client.

Some routines that compare host names use case-sensitive string comparisons; some do not. If an incoming request fails, verify that the case of the host name in the file to be parsed matches the case of the host name called for and try the request again.

Options

-d   Display debugging information.

Files

/etc/bootparams

Boot parameter database.

/etc/nsswitch.conf

Configuration file for the nameservice switch.

Attributes

See attributes(5) for descriptions of the following attributes.

Attribute Type	Attribute Value
Availability	SUNWcsu

See Also

inetd(1M), bootparams(4), nsswitch.conf(4), attributes(5)

---

rpc.nisd, nisd — NIS+ Service Daemon

Synopsis

/usr/sbin/rpc.nisd [-ACDFhv] [-Y [-B [-t netid]]] [-d dictionary]
[-L load] [-S level]

Description

The rpc.nisd daemon is an RPC service that implements the NIS+ service. This daemon must be running on all systems that serve a portion of the NIS+ namespace.

rpc.nisd is usually started from the /etc/rc2.d/S71rpc run control script at
system startup.

The -B option starts an auxiliary process, rpc.nisd_resolv, that provides ypserv
compatible DNS forwarding for NIS host requests. You can also start rpc.nisd_resolv
independently. See rpc.nisd_resolv(1M) for more information on using
rpc.nisd_resolv independently.

Options

-A	Log all the authentication-related activities to syslogd(1M) with LOG_INFO priority.
-B	Provide ypserv-compatible DNS forwarding for NIS host requests. Start and control the DNS resolving process, rpc.nisd_resolv. This option requires that the /etc/resolv.conf file be set up for communication with a DNS nameserver. You can use the nslookup command to verify communication with a DNS nameserver. See resolv.conf(4) and nslookup(1M).
-C	Open diagnostic channel on /dev/console.
-d*dictionary*	Specify an alternate dictionary for the NIS+ database. The primary use of this option is for testing. Note that the string is not interpreted; instead, it is simply passed to the db_initialize function. See nis_db(3N).
-D	Debug mode (don't fork).
-F	Force the server to do a checkpoint of the database when it starts up. Forced checkpoints may be required when the server is low on disk space. This option removes updates from the transaction log that have propagated to all of the replicas.
-h	Print list of options.
-L *load*	Specify the load the NIS+ service is allowed to place on the server as the number of child processes that the server can spawn. This number must be at least 1 for the callback functions to work correctly. The default is 128.
-S *level*	Set the authorization security level of the service. The argument is a number between 0 and 2.

	0	Use for testing and initial setup of the NIS+ namespace. Do not enforce any access controls. Any client is allowed to perform any operation, including updates and deletions.
	1	Accept both AUTH_SYS and AUTH_DES credentials for authenticating clients and authorizing them to perform NIS+ operations. This mode of operation is not secure because AUTH_SYS credentials are easily forged. You should not use it on networks in which any untrusted users can potentially have access.

<table>
<tr><td>2</td><td>Accept only authentication using the security mechanisms configured by nisauthconf(1M). The default security mechanism is AUTH_DES. Security level 2 is the default if you do not specify the -S option.</td></tr>
<tr><td>-t netid</td><td>Use netid as the transport for communication between rpc.nisd and rpc.nisd_resolv. The default transport is ticots(7D) (tcp on SunOS 4.x systems).</td></tr>
<tr><td>-v</td><td>Send a running narration of what it is doing to the syslog daemon (see syslogd(1M)) at LOG_INFO priority. This option is most useful for debugging problems with the service (see also -A option).</td></tr>
<tr><td>-Y</td><td>Put the server into NIS (YP)-compatibility mode. When operating in this mode, the NIS+ server responds to NIS Version 2 requests, using the version 2 protocol. Because the YP protocol is not authenticated, only those items that have read access to nobody (the unauthenticated request) are visible through the V2 protocol. It supports only the standard Version 2 maps in this mode (see -B option and "Notes" in ypfiles(4)).</td></tr>
</table>

Examples

The following example sets up the NIS+ service.

```
# rpc.nisd
```

The following example sets up the NIS+ service, emulating YP with DNS forwarding.

```
# rpc.nisd -YB
```

Environment Variables

NETPATH   Limit the transports that the NIS+ service uses (see netconfig(4)).

Files

/var/nis/parent.object

> An XDR-encoded NIS+ object that describes the namespace above a root server. This parent namespace can be another NIS+ namespace or a foreign namespace such as one served by the Domain Name Service. It is present only on servers that are serving the root of the namespace.

/var/nis/root.object

> An XDR-encoded NIS+ object that describes the root of the namespace. It is present only on servers that are serving the root of the namespace.

/etc/init.d/rpc

> Initialization script for NIS+.

Attributes

See attributes(5) for descriptions of the following attributes.

Attribute Type	Attribute Value
Availability	SUNWnisu

See Also

nis_cachemgr(1M), nisauthconf(1M), nisinit(1M), nissetup(1M),
nslookup(1M), rpc.nisd_resolv(1M), rpc.nispasswdd(1M), syslogd(1M),
nis_db(3N), netconfig(4), nisfiles(4), resolv.conf(4), ypfiles(4),
attributes(5), ticots(7D)

rpc.nisd_resolv, nisd_resolv — NIS+ Service Daemon

Synopsis

/usr/sbin/rpc.nisd_resolv [-v | -V][-F [-C *fd*]][-t *xx*][-p *yy*]

Description

The rpc.nisd_resolv command is an auxiliary process that provides DNS forwarding
service for NIS host requests to both ypserv and rpc.nisd that are running in the
NIS-compatibility mode. It is generally started by invocation of rpc.nisd(1M) with the
-B option or ypserv(1M) with the -d option. Although it is not recommended, you can
also start rpc.nisd_resolv independently with the following options.

> **Note —** This command requires that the /etc/resolv.conf file be set up
> for communication with a DNS nameserver. You can use the nslookup
> command to verify communication with a DNS nameserver. See
> resolv.conf(4) and nslookup(1M).

Options

-F	Run in foreground.
-C *fd*	Use *fd* for service xprt (from nisd).
-v	Send verbose output to the syslog daemon.
-V	Send verbose output to standard output.
-t *xx*	Use transport *xx*.
-p *yy*	Use transient program# *yy*.

Attributes

See attributes(5) for descriptions of the following attributes.

Attribute Type	Attribute Value
Availability	SUNWnisu

See Also

nslookup(1M), rpc.nisd(1M), resolv.conf(4), attributes(5)

rpc.nispasswdd, nispasswdd — NIS+ Password Update Daemon

Synopsis

/usr/sbin/rpc.nispasswdd [-a *attempts*] [-c *minutes*] [-D] [-g] [-v]

Description

The rpc.nispasswdd daemon is an ONC+ RPC service that services password update requests from nispasswd(1) and yppasswd(1). It updates password entries in the NIS+ passwd table.

rpc.nispasswdd is normally started from the /etc/rc2.d/S71rpc system startup script after the NIS+ server (rpc.nisd(1M)) has been started. rpc.nispasswdd determines whether it is running on a machine that is a master server for one or more NIS+ directories. If it discovers that the host is not a master server, then it promptly exits. It also determines whether rpc.nisd(1M) is running in NIS(YP)-compatibility mode (the -Y option) and registers as yppasswdd for NIS(YP) clients as well.

rpc.nispasswdd logs all failed password update attempts, which enables you to determine whether someone was trying to "crack" the passwords.

You must be superuser to run rpc.nispasswdd.

Options

-a *attempts*   Set the maximum number of attempts allowed to authenticate the caller within a password update request session. Failed attempts are logged to syslogd(1M), and the request is cached by the daemon. After the maximum number of allowed attempts, sever the connection to the client. The default is 3.

-c *minutes*   Set the number of minutes to cache a failed password update request. During this time the daemon does not respond if it receives further password update requests for the same user and authentication of the caller fails. The default is 30minutes.

-D   Run in debugging mode.

-g   Generate DES credential. If the user does not have a credential, generate one for that user and store it in the NIS+ `cred` table. By default, the DES credential is not generated for the user not having one.

-v   Send a running narration of what it is doing to the `syslog` daemon. This option is useful for debugging.

Exit Status

0   Success.

1   An error has occurred.

Files

/etc/init.d/rpc

         Initialization script for NIS+.

Attributes

See `attributes`(5) for descriptions of the following attributes.

Attribute Type	Attribute Value
Availability	SUNWnisu

See Also

nispasswd(1), passwd(1), yppasswd(1), rpc.nisd(1M), syslogd(1M), nsswitch.conf(4), attributes(5)

rpc.rexd, rexd — RPC-Based Remote Execution Server

Synopsis

/usr/sbin/rpc.rexd [-s]

Description

The `rpc.rexd` daemon is the Sun RPC server for remote program execution. This daemon is started by `inetd`(1M) whenever a remote execution request is made.

For noninteractive programs, the standard file descriptors are connected directly to TCP connections. Interactive programs use pseudoterminals in a way that is similar to the login sessions provided by `rlogin`(1). This daemon may use NFS to mount file systems specified in the remote execution request.

Security

rpc.rexd uses pam(3) for account and session management. The PAM configuration policy, listed through /etc/pam.conf, specifies the modules to be used for rpc.rexd. The following partial pam.conf file shows rpc.rexd entries for account and session management, using the UNIX module.

```
rpc.rexd account required /usr/lib/security/pam_unix.so.1
rpc.rexd session required /usr/lib/security/pam_unix.so.1
```

If the rpc.rexd service has no entries, then the entries for the other service are used. rpc.rexd uses the getpwuid() call to determine whether the given user is a legal user.

> **Note —** Root cannot execute commands by using rexd client programs such as on(1).

Options

-s   Specified requests must have valid DES credentials. If the request does not have a DES credential, reject it. Reject the default publickey credential. Only newer on(1) commands send DES credentials.

If access is denied with an authentication error, you may have to set your publickey with the chkey(1) command.

Specifying the -s option without presenting secure credentials results in the error message Unix too weak auth (DesONly)!

Files

/dev/ptsn pseudo-terminals

Used for interactive mode.

/etc/passwd   Authorized users.

/tmp_rex/rexd??????

Temporary mount points for remote file systems.

Attributes

See attributes(5) for descriptions of the following attributes.

Attribute Type	Attribute Value
Availability	SUNWnisu

See Also

chkey(1), on(1), rlogin(1), inetd(1M), pam(3), exports (4), inetd.conf(4), pam.conf(4), publickey(4), attributes(5), pam_unix(5)

Diagnostics

Diagnostic messages are normally printed on the console and returned to the requestor.

---

rpc.rstatd, rstatd — Kernel Statistics Server

Synopsis

    /usr/lib/netsvc/rstat/rpc.rstatd

Description

The `rpc.rstatd` daemon is a server that returns performance statistics obtained from the kernel. `rup(1)` uses `rpc.rstatd` to collect the uptime information that it displays. `rpc.rstatd` is an RPC service.

Attributes

See `attributes`(5) for descriptions of the following attributes.

Attribute Type	Attribute Value
Availability	SUNWcsu

See Also

`rup(1)`, `inetd(1M)`, `services(4)`, `attributes(5)`

---

rpc.rusersd, rusersd — Network User-Name Server

Synopsis

    /usr/lib/netsvc/rusers/rpc.rusersd

Description

The `rpc.rusersd` daemon is a server that returns a list of users on the host. The `rpc.rusersd` daemon can be started by `inetd`(1M) or `listen`(1M).

Attributes

See `attributes`(5) for descriptions of the following attributes.

Attribute Type	Attribute Value
Availability	SUNWcsu

See Also

inetd(1M), listen(1M), pmadm(1M), sacadm(1M), attributes(5)

rpc.rwalld, rwalld — Network rwall Server

Synopsis

/usr/lib/netsvc/rwall/rpc.rwalld

Description

The rpc.rwalld daemon is a server that handles rwall(1M) requests. You implement it by calling wall(1M) on all the appropriate network machines. Start the rpc.rwalld daemon with inetd(1M) or listen(1M).

Attributes

See attributes(5) for descriptions of the following attributes.

Attribute Type	Attribute Value
Availability	SUNWcsu

See Also

inetd(1M), listen(1M), rwall(1M), wall(1M), attributes(5)

rpc.sprayd, sprayd — Spray Server

Synopsis

/usr/lib/netsvc/spray/rpc.sprayd

Description

The rpc.sprayd daemon is a server that records the packets sent by spray(1M). Start the rpc.sprayd daemon with inetd(1M) or listen(1M).

The service provided by rpc.sprayd is not useful as a networking benchmark because it uses unreliable connectionless transports, (udp, for example). It can report a large number of packets dropped when the drops were because the program sent packets faster than they could be buffered locally (before the packets get to the network medium).

Attributes

See `attributes`(5) for descriptions of the following attributes.

Attribute Type	Attribute Value
Availability	SUNWcsu

See Also

`inetd(1M)`, `listen(1M)`, `pmadm(1M)`, `sacadm(1M)`, `spray(1M)`, `attributes(5)`

---

rpc.yppasswdd, yppasswdd — Server for Modifying NIS Password File

Synopsis

```
/usr/lib/netsvc/yp/rpc.yppasswdd [-D directory] [-nogecos] [-noshell]
    [-nopw] [-m argument1 argument2...]
/usr/lib/netsvc/yp/rpc.yppasswdd passwordfile [adjunctfile]] [-nogecos]
    [-noshell] [-nopw] [-m argument1 argument2...]
```

Description

The `rpc.yppasswdd` daemon is a server that handles password change requests from `yppasswd`(1). It changes a password entry in the `passwd`, `shadow`, `security.adjunct`, and `passwd.adjunct` files. The `passwd` and `shadow` files provide the basis for the `passwd.byname` and `passwd.byuid` maps. The `passwd.adjunct` file provides the basis for the `passwd.adjunct.byname` and `passwd.adjunct.byuid` maps. Entries in the `passwd`, `shadow` or `passwd.adjunct` files are changed only if the password presented by `yppasswd`(1) matches the encrypted password of the entry. All password files are located in the `PWDIR` directory.

If you specify the `-D` option, the `passwd`, `shadow`, or `passwd.adjunct` files are located under the directory path specified with `-D`.

If you specify the `-noshell`, `-nogecos`, or `-nopw` options, these fields cannot be changed remotely with `chfn`, `chsh`, or `passwd`(1).

If you specify the `-m` option, a `make`(1) is performed in `/var/yp` after any of the `passwd`, `shadow`, or `passwd.adjunct` files are modified. Any arguments following the option are passed to make.

The second of the listed syntaxes is provided for backward compatibility only. If you use the second syntax, `passwordfile` is the full path name of the password file and `adjunctfile` is the full path name of the optional `passwd.adjunct` file. If a shadow file is found in the same directory as `passwordfile`, the `shadow` file is used as described above. Use of this syntax and the discovery of a shadow file generates diagnostic output. The daemon, however, starts normally.

The first and second syntaxes are mutually exclusive. You cannot specify the full path name of the `passwd`, `passwd.adjunct` files and use the `-D` option at the same time.

The daemon is started automatically on the master server of the `passwd` map by the `/etc/init.d/rpc` script (see `makedbm`(1M)).

The server does not insist on the presence of a `shadow` file unless you do not specify the `-D` option or the directory named with the `-D` option is `/etc`. In addition, a `passwd.adjunct` file is not needed. If you specify the `-D` option, the server tries to find a `passwd.adjunct` file in the security subdirectory of the named directory. For example, in the presence of `-D /var/yp`, the server checks for a `/var/yp/security/passwd.adjunct` file.

If only a `passwd` file is found, then the encrypted password is expected in the second field. If a `passwd` and a `passwd.adjunct` file are found, the encrypted password is expected in the second field of the adjunct file with `##`*username* in the second field of the `passwd` file. If all three files are in use, the encrypted password is expected in the `shadow` file. Password updates fail with any deviation.

Notes

If `make` has not been installed and you specify the `-m` option, the daemon outputs a warning and proceeds, effectively ignoring the `-m` option.

When using the `-D` option, make sure that the `PWDIR` of `/var/yp/Makefile` is set accordingly.

The second listed syntax is supplied for backward compatibility only and may be removed in a future release.

The Network Information Service (NIS) was formerly known as Sun Yellow Pages (YP). The functionality of the two remains the same; only the name has changed. The name Yellow Pages is a registered trademark in the United Kingdom of British Telecommunications plc, and may not be used without permission.

Attributes

See `attributes(5)` for descriptions of the following attributes.

Attribute Type	Attribute Value
Availability	SUNWypu

See Also

`make(1)`, `passwd(1)`, `yppasswd(1)`, `inetd(1M)`, `ypmake(1M)`, `passwd(4)`, `shadow(4)`, `ypfiles(4)`, `attributes(5)`

---

rpc.ypupdated, ypupdated — Server for Changing NIS Information

Synopsis

`/usr/lib/netsvc/yp/rpc.ypupdated [-is]`

Description

The `ypupdated` daemon updates information in the Network Information Service (NIS). `ypupdated` consults the `updaters(4)` file in the `/var/yp` directory to determine which NIS maps should be updated and how to change them.

By default, the daemon requires the most secure method of authentication available to it, either DES (secure) or UNIX (insecure).

Note — The Network Information Service (NIS) was formerly known as Sun Yellow Pages (YP). The functionality of the two remains the same; only the name has changed. The name Yellow Pages is a registered trademark in the United Kingdom of British Telecommunications plc, and may not be used without permission.

Options

-i   Accept RPC calls with the insecure AUTH_UNIX credentials. This option allows programmatic updating of the NIS maps in all networks.

-s   Accept only calls authenticated with the secure RPC mechanism (AUTH_DES authentication). This option disables programmatic updating of the NIS maps unless the network supports these calls.

Files

/var/yp/updaters

Configuration file for rpc.updated command.

Attributes

See attributes(5) for descriptions of the following attributes.

Attribute Type	Attribute Value
Availability	SUNWypu

See Also

keyserv(1M), updaters(4), attributes(5)
System Administration Guide, Volume I
Network Interfaces Programmer's Guide

---

rpcbind — Universal Addresses to RPC Program Number Mapper

Synopsis

/usr/sbin/rpcbind [-d] [-w]

Description

The rpcbind daemon is a server that converts RPC program numbers into universal addresses. It must be running on the host to be able to make RPC calls on a server on that machine.

When an RPC service is started, it tells rpcbind the address at which it is listening and the RPC program numbers it is prepared to serve. When a client wants to make an RPC call to a given program number, it first contacts rpcbind on the server machine to determine the address to which RPC requests should be sent.

rpcbind should be started before any other RPC service. Normally, standard RPC servers are started by port monitors, so rpcbind must be started before port monitors are invoked.

When rpcbind is started, it checks that certain name-to-address translation-calls function correctly. If they fail, the network configuration databases may be corrupt. Because RPC services cannot function correctly in this situation, rpcbind reports the condition and terminates.

rpcbind can be started only by superuser.

> **Note —** Terminating rpcbind with SIGKILL prevents the warmstart files from being written.
>
> All RPC servers must be restarted in the following situations: rpcbind crashes (or is killed with SIGKILL) and is unable to write the warmstart files, rpcbind is started without the -w option after a graceful termination, or rpcbind does not find the warmstart files.

Options

-d   Run in debug mode. In this mode, rpcbind does not fork when it starts, prints additional information during operation, and aborts on certain errors. Show the name-to-address translation consistency checks in detail.

-w   Do a warm start. If rpcbind aborts or terminates on SIGINT or SIGTERM, write the current list of registered services to /tmp/portmap.file and /tmp/rpcbind.file. Starting rpcbind with the -w option instructs it to look for these files and start operation with the registrations found in them. This command enables rpcbind to resume operation without restarting all RPC services.

Files

/tmp/portmap.file

File that stores the current list of registered services if rpcbind aborts or terminates on SIGINT or SIGTERM.

/tmp/rpcbind.file

Temporary rcpbind file.

Attributes

See attributes(5) for descriptions of the following attributes.

Attribute Type	Attribute Value
Availability	SUNWcsu

See Also

rpcinfo(1M), rpcbind(3N), attributes(5)

rpcinfo — Report RPC Information

Synopsis

```
/bin/rpcinfo [-m | -s][host]
/bin/rpcinfo -p [host]
/bin/rpcinfo -T transport host prognum [versnum]
/bin/rpcinfo -l [-T transport] host prognum versnum
/bin/rpcinfo [-n portnum] -u host prognum [versnum]
/bin/rpcinfo [-n portnum] -t host prognum [versnum]
/bin/rpcinfo -a serv-address -T transport prognum [versnum]
/bin/rpcinfo -b [-T transport] prognum versnum
/bin/rpcinfo -d [-T transport] prognum versnum
```

Description

Use the rpcinfo command to make an RPC call to an RPC server and report what it finds.

In the first synopsis, rpcinfo lists all the RPC services registered with rpcbind on *host*. If you do not specify *host*, the local host is the default. If you specify -s, the information is displayed in a concise format.

In the second synopsis, rpcinfo lists all the RPC services registered with rpcbind, version 2. Note that the format of the information is different in the first and the second synopsis because the second synopsis is an older protocol (version 2 of the rpcbind protocol).

The third synopsis makes an RPC call to procedure 0 of *prognum* and *versnum* on the specified host and reports whether a response was received. *transport* is the transport that has to be used for contacting the given service. The remote address of the service is obtained by a call to the remote rpcbind.

The *prognum* argument is a number that represents an RPC program number (see rpc(4)).

If you specify a *versnum*, rpcinfo tries to call that version of the specified *prognum*. Otherwise, rpcinfo tries to find all the registered version numbers for the specified *prognum* by calling version 0, which is presumed not to exist; if it does exist, rpcinfo tries to get this information by calling an extremely high version number instead, and tries to call each registered version.

Note — The version number is required for the -b and -d options.

Options

-T *transport*   Specify the *transport* on which the service is required. If you do not specify this option, use the transport specified in the NETPATH environment variable, or if that is unset or null, use the transport in the netconfig(4) database. You can use this generic option with other options.

-a *serv-address*

   Use *serv-address* as the (universal) address for the service on *transport* to ping procedure 0 of the specified *prognum* and report whether a response was received. The -T option is required with the -a option.

   If you do not specify *versnum*, try to ping all available version numbers for that program number. This option avoids calls to remote rpcbind to find the address of the service. Specify the *serv-address* in universal address format of the given transport.

-b   Make an RPC broadcast to procedure 0 of the specified *prognum* and *versnum* and report all hosts that respond. If you specify *transport*, broadcast its request only on the specified transport. If broadcasting is not supported by any transport, print an error message. You should limit the use of broadcasting because of the potential for adverse effect on other systems.

-d   Delete registration for the RPC service of the specified *prognum* and *versnum*. If you specify *transport*, unregister the service on only that transport; otherwise, unregister the service on all the transports on which it was registered. Only the owner of a service can delete a registration, except for superuser, who can delete any service.

-l   Display a list of entries with a given *prognum* and *versnum* on the specified host. Return entries for all transports in the same protocol family as that used to contact the remote rpcbind.

-m   Display a table of statistics of rpcbind operations on the given host. The table shows statistics for each version of rpcbind (versions 2, 3, and 4), giving the number of times each procedure was requested and successfully serviced, the number and type of remote call requests that were made, and information about RPC address lookups that were handled. This option is useful for monitoring RPC activities on host.

-n *portnum*   Use *portnum* as the port number for the -t and -u options instead of the port number given by rpcbind. Use of this option avoids a call to the remote rpcbind to find out the address of the service. This option is made obsolete by the -a option.

-p   Probe rpcbind on *host* using version 2 of the rpcbind protocol, and display a list of all registered RPC programs. If you do not specify *host*, the default is the local host. Note that version 2 of the rpcbind protocol was previously known as the portmapper protocol.

-s	Display a concise list of all registered RPC programs on *host*. If you do not specify *host*, the default is the local host.
-t	Make an RPC call to procedure 0 of *prognum* on the specified host, using TCP, and report whether a response was received. This option is made obsolete by the -T option as shown in the third synopsis.
-u	Make an RPC call to procedure 0 of *prognum* on the specified host using UDP, and report whether a response was received. This option is made obsolete by the -T option, as shown in the third synopsis.

Examples

The following example (truncated to save space), shows all of the RPC services registered on the local machine paperbark.

```
paperbark% rpcinfo
   program version netid      address              service   owner
    100000    4     ticots    paperbark.rpc        rpcbind   superuser
    100000    3     ticots    paperbark.rpc        rpcbind   superuser
    100000    4     ticotsord paperbark.rpc        rpcbind   superuser
    100000    3     ticotsord paperbark.rpc        rpcbind   superuser
    100000    4     ticlts    paperbark.rpc        rpcbind   superuser
    100000    3     ticlts    paperbark.rpc        rpcbind   superuser
    100000    4     tcp       0.0.0.0.0.111        rpcbind   superuser
    100000    3     tcp       0.0.0.0.0.111        rpcbind   superuser
    100000    2     tcp       0.0.0.0.0.111        rpcbind   superuser
    100000    4     udp       0.0.0.0.0.111        rpcbind   superuser
    100000    3     udp       0.0.0.0.0.111        rpcbind   superuser
    100000    2     udp       0.0.0.0.0.111        rpcbind   superuser
    100024    1     udp       0.0.0.0.128.4        status    superuser
    100024    1     tcp       0.0.0.0.128.3        status    superuser
    100024    1     ticlts    \000\000\020\016     status    superuser
    100024    1     ticotsord \000\000\020\021     status    superuser
    100024    1     ticots    \000\000\020\024     status    superuser
    100133    1     udp       0.0.0.0.128.4        -         superuser
    100133    1     tcp       0.0.0.0.128.3        -         superuser
    100133    1     ticlts    \000\000\020\016     -         superuser
    100133    1     ticotsord \000\000\020\021     -         superuser
    100133    1     ticots    \000\000\020\024     -         superuser
    100232   10     udp       0.0.0.0.128.5        sadmind   superuser
```
...(*Additional lines deleted from this example*)

The following example, truncated to save space, shows all of the RPC services registered with rpcbind on the machine named castle.

```
paperbark% rpcinfo castle
   program version netid      address              service   owner
    100000    4     ticots    castle.rpc           rpcbind   superuser
    100000    3     ticots    castle.rpc           rpcbind   superuser
    100000    4     ticotsord castle.rpc           rpcbind   superuser
    100000    3     ticotsord castle.rpc           rpcbind   superuser
    100000    4     ticlts    castle.rpc           rpcbind   superuser
    100000    3     ticlts    castle.rpc           rpcbind   superuser
    100000    4     tcp       0.0.0.0.0.111        rpcbind   superuser
```

```
100000    3    tcp        0.0.0.0.0.111      rpcbind      superuser
100000    2    tcp        0.0.0.0.0.111      rpcbind      superuser
100000    4    udp        0.0.0.0.0.111      rpcbind      superuser
100000    3    udp        0.0.0.0.0.111      rpcbind      superuser
100000    2    udp        0.0.0.0.0.111      rpcbind      superuser
100029    1    ticlts     castle.keyserv     keyserv      superuser
100029    1    ticotsord  castle.keyserv     keyserv      superuser
100029    1    ticots     castle.keyserv     keyserv      superuser
100029    2    ticlts     castle.keyserv     keyserv      superuser
100029    2    ticotsord  castle.keyserv     keyserv      superuser
100029    2    ticots     castle.keyserv     keyserv      superuser
100029    3    ticlts     castle.keyserv     keyserv      superuser
100029    3    ticotsord  castle.keyserv     keyserv      superuser
100029    3    ticots     castle.keyserv     keyserv      superuser
100024    1    udp        0.0.0.0.128.4      status       superuser
100021    1    udp        0.0.0.0.15.205     nlockmgr     superuser
```
. . . (*Additional lines deleted from this example*)

The information displayed in the previous example can be quite lengthy. You can use the -s option to display a more concise list, which is shown below in its entirety for the system castle.

```
paperbark% rpcinfo -s castle
   program version(s) netid(s)                                    service   owner
   100000  2,3,4      udp,tcp,ticlts,ticotsord,ticots             rpcbind   superuser
   100029  3,2,1      ticots,ticotsord,ticlts                     keyserv   superuser
   100024  1          ticots,ticotsord,ticlts,tcp,udp             status    superuser
   100021  4,3,2,1    tcp,udp                                     nlockmgr  superuser
   100133  1          ticots,ticotsord,ticlts,tcp,udp             -         superuser
   100232  10         udp                                         sadmind   superuser
   100011  1          ticlts,udp                                  rquotad   superuser
   100002  3,2        ticots,ticotsord,tcp,ticlts,udp             rusersd   superuser
   100012  1          ticlts,udp                                  sprayd    superuser
   100008  1          ticlts,udp                                  walld     superuser
   100001  4,3,2      ticlts,udp                                  rstatd    superuser
   100083  1          tcp                                         -         superuser
   100221  1          tcp                                         -         superuser
   100235  1          tcp                                         -         superuser
   100078  4          ticlts                                      kerbd     superuser
   100099  2          ticotsord                                   -         superuser
   100234  1          ticotsord                                   -         superuser
   100068  5,4,3,2    udp                                         -         superuser
   100231  1          ticots,ticotsord,ticlts                     -         superuser
   100005  3,2,1      ticots,ticotsord,tcp,ticlts,udp             mountd    superuser
   100003  3,2        tcp,udp                                     nfs       superuser
   100227  3,2        tcp,udp                                     nfs_acl   superuser
   100249  1          ticots,ticotsord,ticlts,tcp,udp             -         superuser
   300598  1          ticots,ticotsord,ticlts,tcp,udp             -         superuser
 805306368 1          ticots,ticotsord,ticlts,tcp,udp             -         superuser
paperbark%
```

The following example shows whether the RPC service with program number 100000 and version 4 is registered on the machine named castle for the transport TCP use.

```
paperbark% rpcinfo -T tcp castle 100000 4
program 100000 version 4 ready and waiting
paperbark%
```

The following example shows all RPC services registered with version 2 of the rpcbind protocol on the local machine. The example is truncated to save space.

```
paperbark% rpcinfo -p
   program vers proto   port  service
   100000   4   tcp    111   rpcbind
   100000   3   tcp    111   rpcbind
   100000   2   tcp    111   rpcbind
   100000   4   udp    111   rpcbind
   100000   3   udp    111   rpcbind
   100000   2   udp    111   rpcbind
   100024   1   udp   32772  status
   100024   1   tcp   32771  status
   100133   1   udp   32772
   100133   1   tcp   32771
   100232  10   udp   32773  sadmind
   100011   1   udp   32774  rquotad
   100002   2   udp   32775  rusersd
   100002   3   udp   32775  rusersd
   100002   2   tcp   32772  rusersd
   100002   3   tcp   32772  rusersd
   100012   1   udp   32776  sprayd
   100008   1   udp   32777  walld
 ...(Additional lines deleted from this example)
```

Attributes

See attributes(5) for descriptions of the following attributes.

Attribute Type	Attribute Value
Availability	SUNWcsu

See Also

rpcbind(1M), rpc(3NSL), netconfig(4), rpc(4), attributes(5)

rpld — IA Network Booting RPL (Remote Program Load) Server

Synopsis

```
/usr/sbin/rpld [-fdDMblgsz] interface
/usr/sbin/rpld -a [-fdDMblgsz]
```

Description

The RPL daemon provides network booting functionality to IA clients by listening to boot requests from them according to the RPL protocol specifications. Clients can generate boot requests by using the boot diskette supplied in the IA distribution. Once the request has been received, the server validates the client and adds it to its internal service list. Subsequent requests from the client to download bootfiles results in the sending of data frames from the server to the client, specifying where to load the boot program in memory. When all the bootfiles have been downloaded, the server specifies where to start execution to initiate the boot process.

In the first synopsis, the *interface* parameter names the network interface on which rpld is to listen for requests, as shown in the following examples.

```
/usr/sbin/rpld /dev/le0
/usr/sbin/rpld /dev/smc0
```

In the second synopsis, rpld locates all of the network interfaces present on the system and starts a daemon process for each one.

The server starts by reading the default configuration file or an alternate configuration file if you specify one. If no configuration file can be found, internal default values are used. Alternatively, command-line options are available to override any of the values in the configuration file. After the configuration options are set, rpld then opens the network interface as specified in the command line and starts listening to RPL boot requests.

Network boot IA clients must have information preconfigured on a server for the RPL server to validate and serve them. This preconfiguration involves putting configuration information in both the ethers(4) and the bootparams(4) databases. The ethers database contains a translation from the physical node address to the IP address of the clients and is normally used by the RARP server. The bootparams database stores all other information needed for booting from this client, such as the number of bootfiles and the file names of the various boot components. Both databases can be looked up by the RPL server through NIS. See "Client Configuration" on page 986 for information on how to set up these databases.

To assist in the administration and maintenance of the network boot activity, the server accepts two run-time signals to change some run-time parameters and print out useful status information. See "Signals" on page 989 for details.

The RPL server is not limited to the ability to boot only IA clients. If properly configured, the server should be able to download any bootfiles to the clients.

Client Configuration

The following configuration information is specific to booting IA clients.

To enable clients to boot IA across the network, the client's information has to be preconfigured in the ethers(4) and bootparams(4) databases. Both databases can be accessed through NIS. Refer to *Solaris Advanced Installation Guide* for information on how to configure a diskless IA client. The discussion contained in the rest of this section is provided for your information only and should not be performed manually.

The ethers database contains a translation table to convert the physical node address to the IP address of the client. Therefore, an IP address must be assigned to the client (if this has not been done already), the node address of the client must be obtained, and then this information needs to be entered in the ethers database.

The bulk of the configuration is done in the bootparams database, which is a free-format database that contains a number of keyword-value string pairs. A number of keywords, like the bootparams RPC in bootparamd(1M), have been defined for specific purposes. Three additional keywords have been defined for the RPL server:

numbootfiles, bootfile, and bootaddr. All three keywords must be in lowercase letters with no spaces before or after the equals symbol following the keyword.

numbootfiles   Specify the number of files to be downloaded to the network boot client. This option has the following format.

numbootfiles=*n*

Always use numbootfiles=3 to boot IA across the network.

bootfile   Specify the path name of the bootfile to be downloaded and where in memory to start loading the bootfile. Use a complete path name. The following example assumes the client's IP address is 129.181.32.15.

bootfile=/rplboot/129.181.32.15.hw.com:45000

bootfile=/rplboot/129.181.32.15.glue.com:35000

bootfile=/rplboot/129.181.32.15.inetboot=8000

The path name following the equals symbol specifies the bootfile to be downloaded, and the hex address following the colon (:) is the absolute address of the memory location to start loading that bootfile. These addresses should be in the range of 7c00 to a0000 (that is, the base 640K range excluding the interrupt vector and BIOS data areas.) Address 45000 for this hw.com bootfile is also a suggested value and, if possible, should not be changed. The address of 35000 for glue.com is a suggested value that, if possible, should not be changed. The address of 8000 for inetboot is an absolute requirement and should never be changed.

These files, when created following the procedures in *Solaris Advanced Installation Guide* are actually symbolic links to the real file to be downloaded to the client. hw.com is linked to a special driver that corresponds to the network interface card of the client. glue.com and inetboot are generic to all network boot clients.

The order of these bootfile lines is not supposed to be significant, but because problems have been found with certain boot PROMs, it is highly recommended that the bootfile lines be ordered in descending order of the load addresses.

bootaddr   The absolute address in memory to start executing after all the bootfiles have been downloaded. This address should always correspond to the address where glue.com is being loaded. If possible, always use the following value for bootaddr.

bootaddr=35000

Options

-f config *filename*

Specify a configuration file name other than the system default /etc/rpld.conf file.

-d debug *level*

>Specify a level of 0 if you do not want any error or warning messages to be generated, or a level from 1 to 9 for increasing amounts of information. This option corresponds to the DebugLevel setting in the configuration file. The default value is 0. Note that it is best to limit the level to 8 or below; use of level 9 can generate so many debug messages that the performance of the RPL server may be impacted.

-D debug *destination*

>Specify 0 to send error or warning messages to standard output, 1 to syslogd, and 2 to the log file. This option corresponds to the DebugDest setting in the configuration file. The default value is 2.

-M maximum *clients*

>Specify the maximum number of simultaneous network boot clients to be served. This option corresponds to the MaxClients setting in the configuration file. A value of -1 means unlimited, and the actual number depends on available system resources. The default value is -1.

-b background *mode*

>Specify 1 to run the server in the background and relinquish the controlling terminal, or 0 to run in the foreground without relinquishing the controlling terminal. This option corresponds to the BackGround setting in the configuration file. If you have specified in the configuration file or by using the -D option that the error or warning messages are to be sent to standard output, you cannot run the server in background mode. If you do so, the server exits after announcing the error.

-l log *filename*

>Specify an alternate log file name to hold the error or warning messages in connection with the -D 2 option or the configuration file DebugDest = 2 setting. This option corresponds to the LogFile setting in the configuration file. The default is /var/spool/rpld.log.

-s start *delay count*

>Specify the number of delay units between outgoing data frames sent to clients to avoid retransmission requests from them. With the LLC type 1 protocol, data transfer is a one-way, best-effort delivery mechanism. The server, without any type of delay mechanism, can

overrun the client by sending data frames too quickly. Therefore, a variable delay is built into the server to limit the speed of sending data to the clients, thus avoiding the clients sending back retransmission requests. This value should be machine-environment specific. If you have a fast server machine but slow client machines, you may want to set a large start delay count. If you have comparable server and client machines, you can set the delay count to 1. The delay is only approximate and should not be taken as an accurate measure of time. There is no specific correlation between the delay unit and the actual time of delay. This option corresponds to the `StartDelay` setting in the configuration file. The default value is `20`.

`-g` *delay granularity*

If retransmission requests from clients do occur, use the delay granularity factor to adjust the delay count for this client upward or downward. If the retransmission request is because of data overrun, increment the delay count by *delay granularity* units to increase the delay between data frames. If the retransmission request is because data is being sent too slowly, use this value to adjust the delay count downward to shorten the delay. Eventually, the server settles at the delay count value that works best with the speed of the client, and no retransmission request is needed. This option corresponds to the `DelayGran` setting in the configuration file. The default value is `2`.

`-z` frame *size*

Specify the size of the data frames used to send data to the clients. Frame size is limited by the underlying physical medium. For Ethernet/802.3, the maximum physical frame size is 1500 octets. The default value is 1500. Note that the protocol overhead of LLC1 and RPL is 32 octets, resulting in a maximum data length of 1468 octets. This option corresponds to the `FrameSize` setting in the configuration file.

Signals

The RPL server accepts the following two signals to change run-time parameters and display status information.

HANGUP
The RPL server rereads the default configuration file `/etc/rpld.conf` or an alternate configuration file if one is specified when the server is started. You can use new values of certain parameters immediately, such as `DebugLevel`, `DebugDest`, `LogFile`, `DelayGran`, and `FrameSize`. For `MaxClients`, if the server is already serving more than the new value, the server does not accept additional boot requests until the number has fallen below the `MaxClients` parameter. `StartDelay` affects only new boot requests. All the existing delay counts for the various clients in service are not be affected. Finally, the `BackGround` parameter has no effect once the

server is running. You cannot change the mode of service without first killing the server and then restarting it.

USR1   Dump all the parameter values and the status of each individual boot client to the destination specified by `DebugDest`.

Files

`/usr/sbin/rpld`

> `rpld` executable.

`/etc/rpld.conf`

> Configuration file.

`/var/spool/rpld.log`

> `rpld` log file.

`/etc/ethers`   Ethernet address to host name database or domain.

`/etc/bootparams`

> Boot parameter database.

`/rplboot`   Boot file.

Attributes

See `attributes`(5) for descriptions of the following attributes.

Attribute Type	Attribute Value
Architecture	`IA`
Availability	`SUNWcsu`

See Also

`bootparamd(1M)`,`in.rarpd(1M)`,`bootparams(4)`,`ethers(4)`,`nsswitch.conf(4)`, `rpld.conf(4)`, `attributes(5)`
> *Solaris Advanced Installation Guide*

rquotad — Remote Quota Server

Synopsis

`/usr/lib/nfs/rquotad`

Description

The `rquotad` daemon is an `rpc(4)` server that returns quotas for a user of a local file system that is mounted by a remote machine over the NFS. The results are used by quota(1M) to display user quotas for remote file systems. The rquotad daemon is normally invoked by inetd(1M).

Files

quotas   Quota file at the file system root.

Attributes

See attributes(5) for descriptions of the following attributes.

Attribute Type	Attribute Value
Availability	SUNWcsu

See Also

inetd(1M), quota(1M), rpc(4), services(4), attributes(5)
Solaris Advanced Installation Guide

rsh — Restricted Shell

Synopsis

/usr/lib/rsh [-acefhiknprstuvx][*argument*...]

Description

The rsh command is a limiting version of the standard command interpreter sh. Use rsh to restrict logins to execution environments whose capabilities are more controlled than those of sh (see sh(1) for complete description and usage).

Note — Do not confuse the restricted shell, /usr/lib/rsh, with the remote shell, /usr/bin/rsh, which is documented in rsh(1).

When you invoke the shell, it scans the environment for the value of the environmental variable, SHELL. If it is found and rsh is the file-name part of its value, the shell becomes a restricted shell.

The actions of rsh are identical to those of sh, except that the following actions are not permitted.

- Changing directory (see cd(1)).
- Setting the value of $PATH.
- Specifying path or command names containing /.
- Redirecting output with > and >>.

The above restrictions are enforced after .profile is interpreted.
You can invoke a restricted shell in one of the following ways.

1. When rsh is the file-name part of the last entry in the /etc/passwd file (see passwd(4)).

2. When the environment variable SHELL exists and rsh is the file-name part of its value; the environment variable SHELL must be set in the .login file.
3. When the shell is invoked and rsh is the file-name part of argument 0.
4. When the shell is invoked with the -r option.When a command to be executed is found to be a shell procedure, rsh invokes sh to execute it. Thus, it is possible to provide the end user with shell procedures that have access to the full power of the standard shell while imposing a limited set of commands; this scheme assumes that the end user does not have write and execute permissions in the same directory.

The net effect of these rules is that the writer of the .profile (see profile(4)) has complete control over user actions by performing guaranteed setup actions and leaving the user in an appropriate directory (probably not the login directory).

The system administrator often sets up a directory of commands (that is, /usr/rbin) that can be safely invoked by a restricted shell. Some systems also provide a restricted editor, red.

Exit Status

Errors detected by the shell, such as syntax errors, return a non-zero exit status. If the shell is being used noninteractively execution of the shell file is abandoned. Otherwise, the shell returns the exit status of the last command executed.

Attributes

See attributes(5) for descriptions of the following attributes.

Attribute Type	Attribute Value
Availability	SUNWcsu

See Also

intro(1), cd(1), login(1), rsh(1), sh(1), exec(2), passwd(4), profile(4), attributes(5)

rshd — Remote Shell Server

Synopsis

/usr/sbin/in.rshd *host.port*

Description

See in.rshd(1M).

rstatd — Kernel Statistics Server

Synopsis
/usr/lib/netsvc/rstat/rpc.rstatd

Description
See rpc.rstatd(1M).

rtc — Provide All Real-Time Clock and GMT-Tag Management

Synopsis
/usr/sbin/rtc [-c][-z *zone-name*]

Description
Use the rtc command to reconcile the difference in the way time is established between UNIX and MS-DOS systems. UNIX systems use Greenwich Mean Time (GMT), whereas MS-DOS systems use local time. When used with no arguments, rtc displays the currently configured time-zone string that was recorded when rtc -z *zone-name* was last run.

The rtc command is not normally run from a shell prompt; it is generally invoked by the system. Commands such as date(1) and rdate(1M) that are used to set the time on a system invoke /usr/sbin/rtc -c to ensure that daylight saving time (DST) is corrected for properly.

Options

-c   Check for DST and make corrections if necessary. This option is normally run once a day by a cron job. If there is no RTC time zone or /etc/rtc_config file, this option does nothing.

-z *zone-name*   Specify the time zone in which the RTC is to be maintained. This option is normally run by the system at software installation time. Update the configuration file /etc/rtc_config with the name of the specified zone and the current GMT lag for that zone. If a rtc_config file exists, update it. If not, create it.

Files

/etc/rtc_config

         The data file used to record the time zone and GMT lag. This file is completely managed by /usr/sbin/rtc and is read by the kernel.

Attributes

See attributes(5) for descriptions of the following attributes.

Attribute Type	Attribute Value
Architecture	IA
Availability	SUNWcsu

See Also

date(1), rdate(1M), attributes(5)

runacct — Run Daily Accounting

Synopsis

/usr/lib/acct/runacct [*mmdd* [*state*]]

Description

The runacct command is the main daily accounting command. It is normally initiated by cron. runacct processes connect, fee, disk, and process accounting files and stores the results in /var/adm/pacct*n*, /var/adm/wtmpx (changed from wtmp in the Solaris 8 release), /var/adm/fee, and /var/adm/acct/nite/disktacct. It also prepares summary files for prdaily or billing purposes. runacct is distributed only to source code licensees.

Process Accounting

Process accounting enables you to track the following data about each process run on your system.

- User and group IDs for processes.
- Beginning and elapsed times for each process.
- CPU time for each process (user time and system time).
- Amount of memory used.
- Commands run.
- The TTY controlling the process.

Each time a process dies, the exit program collects the data and writes it to /var/adm/pacct.

Disk Accounting

Disk accounting enables you to gather and format the following data about the files each user has on disk.

- Name and ID of the user.
- Number of blocks used by the user's files.

Accounting Setup

After you set up system accounting, the commands mostly run on their own. Before you set up accounting, check to make sure the SUNWaccr and SUNWaccu packages are installed. To set up accounting, link the /etc/init.d/acct command to /etc/rc2.d/SS22acct and add accounting startup commands to crontab files so that cron starts them automatically. Once a system account is set up, it works in the following way.

- Between system startup and shutdown, the accounting commands collect raw data about system use (such as user logins, running processes, and data storage) in accounting files.
- Periodically (usually once a day), the /usr/lib/acct/runacct program (runacct(1M)) processes the various accounting files and produces both cumulative summary files and daily accounting reports. The /usr/lib/acct/prdaily (acctsh(1M)) command prints the daily reports.
- Monthly, the administrator can process and print the cumulative summary files generated by runacct(1M) by executing the monacct command. The summary reports produced by monacct (acctsh(1M)) provide an efficient means for billing users on a monthly or other fiscal basis.

See "Examples" on page 996 for a complete example of how to set up accounting.

runacct processing

runacct takes care not to damage active accounting files or summary files in the event of errors. It records its progress by writing descriptive diagnostic messages into active. When it detects an error, it writes a message to /dev/console, sends mail (see mail(1)) to root and adm, and terminates. runacct uses a series of lock files to protect against reinvocation. runacct uses the lock and lock1 files to prevent simultaneous invocation, and lastdate to prevent more than one invocation per day.

The runacct Statefile

runacct breaks its processing into separate, restartable states, using statefile to remember the last state completed. It writes the state name into statefile. runacct then looks in statefile to see what it has done and to determine what to process next. States are executed in the following order.

SETUP	Move active accounting files into working files.
WTMPFIX	Verify integrity of wtmpx file (changed from wtmp in the Solaris 8 release), correcting date changes if necessary.
CONNECT	Produce connect session records in tacct.h format.
PROCESS	Convert process accounting records into tacct.h format.
MERGE	Merge the connect and process accounting records.
FEES	Convert output of chargefee into tacct.h format, merge with connect, and process accounting records.
DISK	Merge disk accounting records with connect, process, and fee accounting records.
MERGETACCT	Merge the daily total accounting records in daytacct with the summary total accounting records in /var/adm/acct/sum/tacct.

New!

CMS	Produce command summaries.
USEREXIT	Include any installation-dependent accounting programs here.
CLEANUP	Clean up temporary files and exit. To restart runacct after a failure, first check the active file for diagnostics, then fix any corrupted data files, such as pacct or wtmpx (changed from wtmp in the Solaris 8 release). You must remove the lock, lock1, and lastdate files before you can restart runacct. You need the argument *mmdd* if you are restarting runacct. *mmdd* specifies the month and day for which runacct reruns the accounting. The entry point for processing is based on the contents of statefile; to override this default, include the desired state on the command line to designate where processing should begin.

New!

Notes

It is not recommended to restart runacct in the SETUP state. Run SETUP manually and restart by using the following command.

```
# runacct mmddWTMPFIX
```

If runacct fails in the PROCESS state, remove the last ptacct file because it is not complete.

The runacct command can process the following maxima during a single invocation.

- 6,000 distinct sessions.
- 1,000 distinct terminal lines.
- 2,000 distinct login names.

If at some point the actual number of any one of these items exceeds the maximum, the command fails.

Examples

The following examples describe how to set up system accounting.

If necessary, install the SUNWaccr and SUNWaccu packages by using either the pkgadd or admintool command.

The following example installs /etc/init.d/acct as the startup script for run level 2 and as the stop script for run level 0.

```
# ln /etc/init.d/acct /etc/rc2.d/S22acct
# ln /etc/init.d/acct /etc/rc0.d/K22acct
#
```

The following example modifies the admcrontab file to automatically start the ckpacct, runacct, and monacct programs.

```
# crontab -e adm
0 * * * * /usr/lib/acct/ckpacct
30 2 * * * /usr/lib/acct/runacct 2> /var/adm/acct/nite/fd2log
30 7 1 * * /usr/lib/acct/monacct
```

The following example modifies the root crontab file to automatically start the dodisk program.

```
# crontab -e
30 22 * * 4 /usr/lib/acct/dodisk
```

Edit /etc/acct/holidays to include national and local holidays. The following example shows the default /etc/acct/holidays file.

```
paperbark% more /etc/acct/holidays
* @(#)holidays  January 1, 1999
*
* Prime/Nonprime Table for UNIX Accounting System
*
* Curr   Prime   Non-Prime
* Year   Start   Start
*
  1999   0800    1800
*
* only the first column (month/day) is significiant.
*
* month/day      Company
*                Holiday
*
1/1             New Years Day
7/4             Indep. Day
12/25           Christmas
paperbark%
```

The following example starts accounting. You can also start accounting by rebooting the system.

```
# /etc/init.d/acct start
#
```

The following example starts runacct from the command line.

```
# nohup /usr/lib/acct/runacct 2> /var/adm/acct/nite/fd2log &
530
#
```

The following example restarts runacct from the command line.

```
# nohup /usr/lib/runacct 1019 2>> /var/adm/acct/nite/fd2log &
552
#
```

The following example restarts runacct at a specific state from the command line.

```
# nohup /usr/lib/runacct 1019 MERGE 2>> /var/adm/acct/nite/fd2log &
573
#
```

Files

/var/adm/wtmpx   *New!*

> History of user access and administration information. wtmpx is an extended database file that replaces the obsolete wtmp database file.

```
/var/adm/pacctincr

/var/adm/acct/nite/active

/var/adm/acct/nite/daytacct

/var/adm/acct/nite/lock

/var/adm/acct/nite/lock1

/var/adm/acct/nite/lastdate

/var/adm/acct/nite/statefile
```
Files that store the results of daily accounting commands.

Attributes

See attributes(5) for descriptions of the following attributes.

Attribute Type	Attribute Value
Availability	SUNWaccu

See Also

New!

acctcom(1), mail(1), acct(1M), acctcms(1M), acctcon(1M), acctmerg(1M), acctprc(1M), acctsh(1M), cron(1M), fwtmp(1M), acct(2), acct(3HEAD), utmpx(4), attributes(5)

---

rusersd — Network User Name Server

Synopsis

```
/usr/lib/netsvc/rusers/rpc.rusersd
```

Description

See rpc.rusersd(1M).

---

rwall — Write to All Users Over a Network

Synopsis

```
/usr/sbin/rwall hostname...
/usr/sbin/rwall -n netgroup...
/usr/sbin/rwall -h hostname -n netgroup
```

Description

Use the `rwall` command to broadcast a message to all users on a network. `rwall` reads a message from standard input until end-of-file. It then sends the message, preceded by the line

```
Broadcast Message...
```

to all users logged in on the specified host machines. With the `-n` option, it sends to the specified network groups.

> **Note** — The timeout is fairly short to enable transmission to a large group of machines (some of which may be down) in a reasonable amount of time. Thus, the message may not get through to a heavily loaded machine.

Options

`-n` *netgroup*   Send the broadcast message to the specified network groups.

`-h` *hostname*   Specify *hostname*, the name of the host machine.

Attributes

See `attributes`(5) for descriptions of the following attributes.

Attribute Type	Attribute Value
Availability	SUNWcsu

See Also

`inetd(1M)`, `listen(1M)`, `pmadm(1M)`, `sacadm(1M)`, `wall(1M)`, `attributes(5)`

---

rwalld — Network rwall Server

Synopsis

`/usr/lib/netsvc/rwall/rpc.rwalld`

Description

See `rpc.rwalld(1M)`.

rwhod — System Status Server

Synopsis
    /usr/sbin/in.rwhod [-m [*ttl*]]

Description
    See in.rwhod(1M).

S

---

sa1, sa2, sadc — System Activity Report Package

Synopsis

```
/usr/lib/sa/sadc [t n][ofile]
/usr/lib/sa/sa1 [t n]
/usr/lib/sa/sa2 [-aAbcdgkmpqruvwy][-e time][-f filename][-i sec]
   [-s time]
```

Description

See sar(1M).

---

sac — Service Access Controller

Synopsis

```
/usr/lib/saf/sac -t sanity-interval
/usr/lib/saf/sac
```

Description

The Service Access Controller (SAC) is the overseer of the server machine. It is started when the server machine enters multiuser mode. The SAC performs several important functions, as explained below.

Customizing the SAC Environment

When sac is invoked, it first looks for the per-system configuration script /etc/saf/_sysconfig. sac interprets _sysconfig to customize its own environment. The modifications made to the SAC environment by _sysconfig are inherited by all the children of the SAC. The children can modify this inherited environment.

Starting Port Monitors

After it has interpreted the _sysconfig file, the sac reads its administrative file /etc/saf/_sactab. _sactab specifies which port monitors are to be started. For each port monitor to be started, sac forks a child (see fork(2)) and creates a utmpx entry (changed from utmp in the Solaris 8 release) with the type field set to LOGIN_PROCESS. Each child then interprets its per-port monitor configuration script /etc/saf/pmtag/_config if the file exists. These modifications to the environment affect the port monitor and are inherited by all its children. Finally, the child process execs the port monitor, using the command found in the _sactab entry. (See sacadm; this command is used with the -c option when the port monitor is added to the system.)

Polling Port Monitors to Detect Failure

The -t option sets the frequency with which sac polls the port monitors on the system. You can also think of this time as half of the maximum latency required to detect that a port monitor has failed and that recovery action is needed.

Administrative Functions

The Service Access Controller represents the administrative point of control for port monitors. Its administrative tasks are explained below.

When queried (sacadm with either -l or -L), the Service Access Controller returns the status of the port monitors specified, which sacadm prints on the standard output. A port monitor can be in one of six states.

ENABLED	The port monitor is currently running and is accepting connections. See sacadm(1M) with the -e option.
DISABLED	The port monitor is currently running and is not accepting connections. See sacadm with the -d option, and see NOTRUNNING.
STARTING	The port monitor is in the process of starting up. STARTING is an intermediate state on the way to ENABLED or DISABLED.
FAILED	The port monitor was unable to start and remain running.
STOPPING	The port monitor has been manually terminated but has not completed its shutdown procedure. STOPPING is an intermediate state on the way to NOTRUNNING.

New!

NOTRUNNING   The port monitor is not currently running. (See sacadm with -k.) This
               state is the normal "not running" state. When a port monitor is killed,
               all ports it was monitoring are inaccessible. It is not possible for an
               external user to tell whether a port is not being monitored or the
               system is down. If the port monitor is not killed but is in the DISABLED
               state, it may be possible (depending on the port monitor being used)
               to write a message on the inaccessible port, telling the user who is
               trying to access the port that it is disabled. This capability is the
               advantage of having a DISABLED state as well as the NOTRUNNING
               state.

When a port monitor terminates, the SAC removes the utmpx entry (changed from **New!**
utmp in the Solaris 8 release) for that port monitor.

The SAC receives all requests to enable, disable, start, or stop port monitors and
takes the appropriate action.

The SAC is responsible for restarting port monitors that terminate. Whether or not
the SAC restarts a given port monitor depends on two things.

- The restart count specified for the port monitor when the port monitor was added
  by sacadm; this information is included in /etc/saf/pmtag/_sactab.
- The number of times the port monitor has already been restarted.

Security

sac uses pam(3PAM) for session management. The PAM configuration policy, listed
through /etc/pam.conf, specifies the session management module to be used for sac.
The following partial pam.conf file has entries for sac, using the UNIX session
management module.

```
sac   session   required   /usr/lib/security/pam_unix.so.1
```

If the sac service has no entries, then the entries for the other service are used.

Options

-t *sanity-interval*

               Set the frequency (*sanity-interval*) with which sac polls the port
               monitors on the system.

Files

/etc/saf/_sactab

               Administrative file that specifies which port monitors to start.

/etc/saf/_sysconfig

               Per-system configuration script.

/var/adm/utmpx   **New!**

               Extended database file (changed from utmp in the Solaris 8 release)
               used to contain user access and accounting information.

```
/var/saf/_log
```
> SAF log file.

Attributes

See `attributes(5)` for descriptions of the following attributes.

Attribute Type	Attribute Value
Availability	SUNWcsu

See Also

`pmadm(1M)`, `sacadm(1M)`, `fork(2)`, `pam(3PAM)`, `pam.conf(4)`, `attributes(5)`, `pam_unix(5)`

---

sacadm — Service Access Controller Administration

Synopsis

```
sacadm -a -p pmtag -t type -c cmd -v ver [-f dx][-n count]
  [-y comment][-z script]
sacadm -r -p pmtag
sacadm -s -p pmtag
sacadm -k -p pmtag
sacadm -e -p pmtag
sacadm -d -p pmtag
sacadm -l [-p pmtag | -t type]
sacadm -L [-p pmtag | -t type]
sacadm -g -p pmtag [-z script]
sacadm -G [-z script]
sacadm -x [-p pmtag]
```

Description

Use the `sacadm` command to administer the upper level of the Service Access Facility hierarchy (port monitor administration). `sacadm` performs the following functions.

- Adds or removes a port monitor.
- Starts or stops a port monitor.
- Enables or disables a port monitor.
- Installs or replaces a per-system configuration script.
- Installs or replaces a per-port monitor configuration script.
- Prints requested port monitor information.

Requests about the status of port monitors (-l and -L) and requests to print per-port monitor and per-system configuration scripts (-g and -G without the -z option) can be executed by any user on the system. Other `sacadm` commands can be executed only by superuser.

Options

-a	Add a port monitor. Create the supporting directory structure in /etc/saf and /var/saf and add an entry for the new port monitor to /etc/saf/_sactab. The _sactab file already exists on the delivered system. Initially, it is empty except for a single line that contains the version number of the Service Access Controller. Unless the command line that adds the new port monitor includes the -f option with the -x argument, start the new port monitor. Because of the complexity of the options and arguments that follow the -a option, it may be convenient to use a command script or the menu system to add port monitors.
-c *cmd*	Execute the command string *cmd* to start a port monitor. You can use the -c option only with -a. The -a option requires a -c.
-d	Disable the port monitor *pmtag*.
-e	Enable the port monitor *pmtag*.
-f *dx*	Specify one or both of the following two flags, which are then included in the flags field of the _sactab entry for the new port monitor. If you do not include the -f option on the command line, set no flags and use the default conditions. By default, start a port monitor. A -f option with no following argument is illegal.

	d	Do not enable the new port monitor.
	x	Do not start the new port monitor.

-g	Request output, or install or replace the per-port monitor configuration script /etc/saf/*pmtag*/_config. -g requires a -p option. The -g option with only a -p option prints the per-port monitor configuration script for port monitor *pmtag*. The -g option with a -p and a -z option installs the file *script* as the per-port monitor configuration script for port monitor *pmtag*. Other combinations of options with -g are invalid.
-G	Request output, or install or replace the per-system configuration script /etc/saf/_sysconfig. The -G option by itself prints the per-system configuration script. The -G option in combination with a -z option installs the file *script* as the per-system configuration script. Other combinations of options with a -G option are invalid.
-k	Stop port monitor *pmtag*.
-l	Request port monitor information. -l by itself lists all port monitors on the system. The -l option in combination with the -p option lists only the port monitor specified by *pmtag*. A -l in combination with the -p option lists all port monitors of type *type*. Any other combination of options with the -l option is invalid.
-L	Identical to the -l option except display the output in a condensed format.

-n *count*	Set the restart count to *count*. If you do not specify a restart count, set *count* to 0. A *count* of 0 indicates that the port monitor is not to be restarted if it fails.
-p *pmtag*	Specify the tag associated with a port monitor.
-r	Remove port monitor *pmtag*. Remove the port monitor entry from /etc/saf/_sactab. If the removed port monitor is not running, take no further action. If the removed port monitor is running, send a SIGTERM to shut it down. Note that the port monitor's directory structure remains intact.
-s	Start a port monitor *pmtag*.
-t *type*	Specify the port monitor type.
-v *ver*	Specify the version number of the port monitor. You can specify this version number as -v `pmspec -V` where *pmspec* is the special administrative command for port monitor *pmtag*. This special command is ttyadm for ttymon and nlsadmin for listen. The version stamp of the port monitor is known by the command and is returned when you invoke *pmspec* with a -V option.
-x	With no options, read the database file (_sactab). The -x option with the -p option reads the *pmtag* administrative file.
-y *comment*	Include *comment* in the _sactab entry for port monitor *pmtag*.
-z *script*	Use with the -g and -G options to specify the name of a file that contains a configuration script. With the -g option, *script* is a per-port monitor configuration script; with -G it is a per-system configuration script. Modifying a configuration script is a three-step procedure. First, make a copy of the existing script (-g or -G). Then, edit the copy. Finally, put the copy in place over the existing script (-g or -G with -z).

Output

If successful, sacadm exits with a status of 0. If sacadm fails for any reason, it exits with a non-zero status. Options that request information write the information on the standard output. In the condensed format (-L), port monitor information is printed as a sequence of colon-separated fields; empty fields are indicated by two successive colons. The standard format (-l) prints a header identifying the columns, and port monitor information is aligned under the appropriate headings. In this format, an empty field is indicated by a dash. The comment character is #.

Examples

The following example adds a port monitor. The port monitor tag is npack; its type is listen; if necessary, it restarts three times before failing; its administrative command is nlsadmin; and the configuration script to be read is in the file /etc/saf/_safconfig.

```
# sacadm -a -p npack -t listen -c /usr/lib/saf/listen -v `nlsadmin -V`
  -n 3 -z /etc/saf/_safconfig
#
```

The following example starts the npack port monitor.

```
# sacadm -s -p npack
#
```

The following example enables the npack port monitor.

```
# sacadm -e -p npack
#
```

The following example disables the npack port monitor.

```
# sacadm -d -p npack
#
```

The following example removes the npack port monitor:

```
# sacadm -r -p npack
#
```

The following example lists status information for all port monitors.

```
# sacadm -l
PMTAG          PMTYPE          FLGS RCNT STATUS     COMMAND
zsmon          ttymon       -   0    ENABLED    /usr/lib/saf/ttymon #
#
```

The following example lists status information for the port monitor whose port monitor tag is zsmon.

```
# sacadm -l -p zsmon
PMTAG          PMTYPE          FLGS RCNT STATUS     COMMAND
zsmon          ttymon       -   0    ENABLED    /usr/lib/saf/ttymon
#
```

The following example lists the same information as the previous example in condensed format.

```
# sacadm -L -p zsmon
zsmon:ttymon::0:ENABLED:/usr/lib/saf/ttymon#
#
```

The following example lists status information for all port monitors whose type is ttymon.

```
# sacadm -l -t ttymon
PMTAG          PMTYPE          FLGS RCNT STATUS     COMMAND
zsmon          ttymon       -   0    ENABLED    /usr/lib/saf/ttymon #
#
```

The following example replaces the per-port monitor configuration script associated with the port monitor whose tag is npack with the contents of the file file.config.

```
# sacadm -g -p npack -z file.config
#
```

Files

/etc/saf/_sactab

        Administrative file that specifies which port monitors to start.

/etc/saf/_sysconfig

        Per-system configuration script.

/etc/saf/*pmtag*/_config

        Per-port monitor configuration script.

Attributes

See attributes(5) for descriptions of the following attributes.

Attribute Type	Attribute Value
Availability	SUNWcsu

See Also

pmadm(1M), sac(1M), doconfig(3N), attributes(5)

sadc — System Activity Report Package

Synopsis

/usr/lib/sa/sadc [t *n*][*ofile*]

Description

See sar(1M).

sadmind — Distributed System Administration Daemon

Synopsis

sadmind [-c *keywords*][-i *secs*][-l [*logfile*]][-O *OW-path-name*]
[-S *security-level*][-v]

Description

The sadmind daemon is used by Solstice AdminSuite applications to perform distributed system administration operations.

    The sadmind daemon is started automatically by the inetd daemon whenever it receives a request to invoke an operation. The sadmind daemon process continues to run for 15 minutes after the last request is completed, unless you specify a different idle time with the -i command-line option. You can start the sadmind daemon independently from the command line, for example, at system boot time. In this case, the -i option has no effect; sadmind continues to run, even if there are no active requests.

You can configure the sadmind daemon process to write tracing information into a log file by specifying the -c and -l command-line options. The -c option specifies a comma-separated list of *keywords* indicating the types of information to be logged. The following *keywords* are useful for system administration.

System-Info   Include messages about when the sadmind daemon was started and stopped.

Requests   Include messages about which operations sadmind invoked and when.

Errors   Include messages about errors that occurred during the daemon execution.

*   Include all possible log messages.

The -l option enables logging and, optionally, specifies the path and file name of the log file. If you specify no log file, the default log file /var/adm/admin.log is used.

Notes

Whenever inetd fails to start sadmind, re-register the RPC number for sadmind, 100232, with rpcbind by sending the inetd process a SIGHUP signal

```
# kill -HUP pid
```

or

```
# kill -1
```

Sometimes inetd does not start sadmind in response to system administration requests, even though the inetd.conf file has the correct entry for the sadmind daemon. This can happen when sadmind is started manually from the command line and it takes over the previous registration of the sadmind RPC number, 100232, from inetd. When the manually started sadmind daemon is terminated, the sadmind RPC number, 100232, is de-registered with rpcbind. Subsequent system administration requests are then ignored by inetd.

Options

The following command-line options can be useful when you are starting the sadmind daemon.

-c *keywords*   Specify the types of information to be logged as a comma-separated list of *keywords*. The default is to log all types of messages.

-i *secs*   Specify the number of seconds to stay up after the last request is completed. The default is 15 minutes (900 seconds). If *secs* is 0 or over 10000000, stay up forever. -i applies only when sadmind is started by the inetd daemon. You may want sadmind to run permanently (or for extended durations) on systems that are frequently administered by applications using sadmind (for example, a server managed through Host Manager) to improve application performance.

-l [*logfile*] Enable logging and optionally define the path name to the distributed system administration log file. The default log file is /var/adm/admin.log.

-O *OW-path-name*

Define the path name to the OpenWindows home directory. If you do not specify this option, use the OpenWindows home directory defined in the OPENWINHOME environment variable if defined; use the home directory specified in the /etc/OPENWINHOME file if it exists, or the default directory /usr/openwin. When the sadmind daemon is started by the inetd daemon, the environment variable OPENWINHOME is typically not defined. If the OpenWindows home directory is not one of the path names specified (/usr/openwin or in the file /etc/OPENWINHOME), the -O option must be added to the sadmind entry in the inetd.conf(4) configuration file.

-S *security-level*

Define the level of security to be used by the sadmind daemon when checking a client's right to perform an operation on the server system. *security-level* specifies the authentication mechanism used to provide and check the client's identity. The client's identity must be authenticated by the specified mechanism for sadmind to accept the request. The system-wide authentication requirements set by the security level can take precedence over any operation-specific requirements. Consequently, the security level can be used system-wide to ensure that all operations meet minimum authentication requirements, regardless of the requirements assigned specifically to an operation. In addition, the security level determines whether sadmind performs authorization access control checking.

You can specify the following security levels.

0 Set authentication type to NONE. Set all clients' user and group identities to the nobody identity (see *Solstice AdminSuite 2.1 User's Guide*). If access is granted to nobody, execute the operation. Use this level for testing only.

1 Set authentication type to WEAK. Set clients' user and group identities from the client's authentication credentials. Accept client identities when they have satisfied either AUTH_SYS or AUTH_DES authentication mechanisms. Check the authenticated client identity for authorization to execute the operation. If an operation calls for a stronger security level, demote the user identity to

nobody and then check whether nobody is authorized to execute the operation. Because

AUTH_SYS client credentials are easily forged, use this level only in relatively secure environments. No check is done that the user ID of the client represents the same user on the server system as on the client system. It is assumed that user and group identities are set up consistently on the network. This security level is the default.

2   Set authentication type to STRONG. Set clients' user and group identities from their authentication credential mappings (effectively, user and group IDs from netid.byname for NIS, or cred table for NIS+). Accept client identities only when they have satisfied the AUTH_DES authentication mechanism. Check whether the client identity is authorized to execute the operation. This level provides the most secure environment for executing distributed administration operations. It overrides any weaker level specific to an operation. A DES credential must exist for the host running the sadmind daemon and all administration client user identities.

-v   Enable the writing of log messages to the system logger, syslogd. Messages logged include fatal errors encountered while attempting to start the sadmind daemon process and those specified by the -c trace message *keywords*.

Examples

The following example shows the default line in the /etc/inetd.conf file that starts sadmind.

```
#
# Solstice system and network administration class agent server
100232/10   tli  rpc/udp wait root /usr/sbin/sadmind    sadmind
#
```

To make a network as secure as possible, edit the /etc/inetd.conf file and change the line as shown in the following example.

```
100232/10   tli  rpc/udp wait root /usr/sbin/sadmind    sadmind -S 2
```

To minimize sadmind startup delays, you can edit the line in the /etc/inetd.conf file to include the -i option, as shown in the following example. The duration that sadmind remains up after the last operation request was completed is extended to 24 hours (86,400 seconds). Extending the timeout period can enhance performance on servers and workstations that frequently run or are administered by applications that use the sadmind daemon (for example, Solstice AdminSuite applications such as Host Manager).

```
100232/10   tli  rpc/udp wait root /usr/sbin/sadmind sadmind -i 86400
```

Files

/var/adm/admin.log

Distributed system administration default log file.

/etc/inetd.conf

Internet servers database file.

Attributes

See attributes(5) for descriptions of the following attributes.

Attribute Type	Attribute Value
Availability	SUNWadmfw

See Also

inetd(1M), rpcbind(1M), inetd.conf(4), attributes(5)
Solstice AdminSuite 2.1 User's Guide

---

saf — Service Access Facility

Description

The Service Access Facility (SAF) is a group of daemons and administrative commands that provide a flexible administrative framework for managing service requests in an open-systems environment. Use the SAF to set up and administer port monitors so that users can log in from a terminal or a modem and can use network printing resources.

Under the SAF, systems can access services through a variety of port monitors, including ttymon, the listener, and port monitors written expressly for a user's application. The way that a port monitor observes and manages access ports is specific to the port monitor and not to any component of the SAF. You can, therefore, extend systems by developing and installing your own port monitors. One of the important features of the SAF is that it can be extended in this way.

The SAF considers a service to be a process that is started. There are no restrictions on the functions a service can provide. The SAF consists of a controlling process, the service access controller (SAC), and two administrative levels corresponding to two levels in the supporting directory structure. The top administrative level is concerned with port monitor administration, the lower level with service administration. The SAC is documented in the sac(1M) manual page. The administrative levels and associated commands are documented in the *System Administration Guide, Volume II*. The requirements for writing port monitors and the functions a port monitor must perform to run under the SAF and the SAC are documented in this section.

Port Monitors

A port monitor is a process that is responsible for monitoring a set of homogeneous, incoming ports on a machine. A port monitor's major purpose is to detect incoming service requests and to dispatch them appropriately.

A port is an externally seen access point on a system. A port can be an address on a network (TSAP or PSAP), a hardwired terminal line, an incoming phone line, and so forth. The definition of what constitutes a port is strictly a function of the port monitor itself.

A port monitor performs certain basic functions. Some of these are required to conform to the SAF; others can be specified by the requirements and design of the port monitor itself. Port monitors have two main functions: managing ports and monitoring ports for indications of activity.

Port Management

The first function of a port monitor is to manage a port. The actual details of how a port is managed are specified by the person who defines the port monitor. A port monitor is not restricted to handling a single port; it can handle multiple ports simultaneously.

Some examples of port management are setting the line speed on incoming phone connections, binding an appropriate network address, reinitializing the port when the service terminates, and outputting a prompt.

Activity Monitoring

The second function of a port monitor is to monitor the port or ports for which it is responsible for indications of activity. Two types of activity can be detected.

The first is an indication to the port monitor to take some port-monitor-specific action. An example of a port monitor activity is detecting the pressing of the break key to indicate that the line speed should be cycled. Not all port monitors need to recognize and respond to the same indications. The indication used to attract the attention of the port monitor is specified by the person who defines the port monitor.

The second activity is detecting an incoming service request. When a service request is received, a port monitor must be able to determine which service is being requested from the port on which the request is received. The same service may be available on more than one port.

Restricting Access to the System

A port monitor must be able to restrict access to the system without disturbing services that are still running. To do so, a port monitor must maintain the `enabled` and `disabled` internal states. The port monitor starts in the state indicated by the `ISTATE` environment variable provided by the `sac`. See `sac`(1M) for details. Enabling or disabling a port monitor affects all ports for which the port monitor is responsible. If a port monitor is responsible for a single port, only that port is affected. If a port monitor is responsible for multiple ports, the entire collection of ports is affected.

Enabling or disabling a port monitor is a dynamic operation: it changes the internal state. The effect does not persist across new invocations of the port monitor. Enabling or disabling an individual port, however, is a static operation: it changes an administrative file. The effect of this change persists across new invocations of the port monitor.

Creating utmpx Entries

Port monitors are responsible for creating `utmpx` entries (changed from `utmp` in the Solaris 8 release) with the `type` field set to `USER_PROCESS` for services they start. If this action has been specified, by the `-fu` option in the `pmadm` command line that added the service, these `utmpx` entries can, in turn, be modified by the service. When the service terminates, the `utmpx` entry must be set to `DEAD_PROCESS`.

New!

Port Monitor Process IDs and Lock Files

When a port monitor starts, it writes its process ID into a file named _pid in the current directory and puts an advisory lock on the file.

Changing the Service Environment: Running doconfig(3N)

Before invoking the service designated in the port monitor administrative file, _pmtab, a port monitor must arrange for the per-service configuration script to be run, if one exists, by calling the library function doconfig(3N). Because the per-service configuration script can specify the execution of restricted commands, as well as for other security reasons, port monitors are invoked with root permissions. The details of how services are invoked are specified by the person who defines the port monitor.

Terminating a Port Monitor

A port monitor must terminate itself gracefully on receipt of the signal SIGTERM. The termination sequence is described below.

1. The port monitor enters the stopping state; no further service requests are accepted.

2. Any attempt to reenable the port monitor is ignored.

3. The port monitor yields control of all ports for which it is responsible. It must be possible for a new instantiation of the port monitor to start correctly while a previous instantiation is stopping.

4. The advisory lock on the process ID file is released. Once this lock is released, the contents of the process ID file are undefined and a new invocation of the port monitor can be started.

The Port Monitor Administrative File

A port monitor's current directory contains an administrative file named _pmtab; _pmtab is maintained by the pmadm command in conjunction with a port-monitor-specific administrative command.

The port monitor administrative command for a listen port monitor is nlsadmin(1M); the port monitor administrative command for ttymon is ttyadm(1M). Any port monitor written by a user must be provided with an administrative command specific to that port monitor to perform similar functions.

Per-Service Configuration Files

A port monitor's current directory also contains the per-service configuration scripts, if they exist. The names of the per-service configuration scripts correspond to the service tags in the _pmtab file.

Private Port Monitor Files

A port monitor can create private files in the directory /var/saf/tag, where tag is the name of the port monitor. Examples of private files are log files or temporary files.

The SAC/Port Monitor Interface

The SAC creates two environment variables for each port monitor it starts: PMTAG and ISTATE.

The PMTAG variable is set to a unique port monitor tag by the SAC. The port monitor uses this tag to identify itself in response to sac messages. ISTATE is used to indicate to the port monitor what its initial internal state should be. ISTATE is set to enabled or disabled to indicate the initial port monitor state.

The SAC performs a periodic sanity poll of the port monitors. The SAC communicates with port monitors through FIFOs. A port monitor should open _pmpipe, in the current directory, to receive messages from the SAC, and ../_sacpipe to send return messages to the SAC.

Message Formats

This section describes the messages that can be sent from the SAC to a port monitor (sac messages) and from a port monitor to the SAC (port monitor messages). These messages are sent through FIFOs and are in the form of C structures.

SAC Messages

The format of messages from the SAC are defined by the structure sacmsg.

```
struct sacmsg
{
        int sc_size; /* size of optional data portion */
        char sc_type; /* type of message */
};
```

The SAC can send four types of messages to port monitors. The type of message is indicated by setting the sc_type field of the sacmsg structure to one of the following values.

SC_STATUS	Status request.
SC_ENABLE	Enable message.
SC_DISABLE	Disable message.
SC_READDB	Message indicating that the port monitor's _pmtab file should be read.

The sc_size field indicates the size of the optional data part of the message. See "Message Classes" on page 1016. For the Solaris Operating Environment, sc_size should always be set to 0. A port monitor must respond to every message sent by sac.

Port Monitor Messages

The format of messages from a port monitor to the SAC is defined by the structure pmmsg.

```
struct pmmsg
{
        char pm_type; /* type of message */
        unchar_t pm_state; /* current state of port monitor */
        char pm_maxclass;  /* maximum message class this port monitor
                              understands */
        char pm_tag[PMTAGSIZE + 1]; /* port monitor's tag */
        int pm_size; /* size of optional data portion */
};
```

Port monitors can send two types of messages to the SAC. The type of message is indicated by the pm_type field of the pmmsg structure, set to one of the following values

PM_STATUS	State information.
PM_UNKNOWN	Negative acknowledgment.

For both types of messages, the `pm_tag` field is set to the port monitor's tag and the `pm_state` field is set to the port monitor's current state. The following states are valid.

PM_STARTING   Starting.

PM_ENABLED   Enabled.

PM_DISABLED   Disabled.

PM_STOPPING   Stopping.

The current state reflects any changes that result from the last message from the SAC. The status message is the normal return message. The negative acknowledgment should be sent only when the message received is not understood. `pm_size` indicates the size of the optional data part of the message. `pm_maxclass` specifies a message class. Both are discussed under "Message Classes" on page 1016. In the Solaris Operating Environment, always set `pm_maxclass` to 1 and `sc_size` to 0. Port monitors can never initiate messages; they can only respond to messages that they receive.

Message Classes

Message classes have been included to accommodate possible SAF extensions. The messages described above are all class 1 messages. None of these messages contain a variable data portion; all pertinent information is contained in the message header. If new messages are added to the protocol, they are defined as new message classes (for example, class 2). The first message the SAC sends to a port monitor is always a class 1 message. Because all port monitors, by definition, understand class 1 messages, the first message the SAC sends is guaranteed to be understood. In its response to the SAC, the port monitor sets the `pm_maxclass` field to the maximum message class number for that port monitor. The SAC does not send messages to a port monitor from a class with a larger number than the value of `pm_maxclass`. Requests that require messages of a higher class than the port monitor can understand fail. For the Solaris Operating Environment, always set `pm_maxclass` to 1.

For any given port monitor, messages of class `pm_maxclass` and messages of all classes with values lower than `pm_maxclass` are valid. Thus, if the `pm_maxclass` field is set to 3, the port monitor understands messages of classes 1, 2, and 3. Port monitors cannot generate messages; they can only respond to messages. A port monitor's response must be of the same class as that of the originating message. Because only the SAC can generate messages, this protocol functions even if the port monitor is capable of dealing with messages of a higher class than the SAC can generate. `pm_size` (an element of the `pmmsg` structure) and `sc_size` (an element of the `sacmsg` structure) indicate the size of the optional data part of the message. The format of this part of the message is undefined. Its definition is inherent in the type of message. For the Solaris Operating Environment, always set both `sc_size` and `pm_size` to 0.

Administrative Interface

This section discusses the port monitor administrative files available under the SAC.

The SAC Administrative File _sactab

The service access controller's administrative file contains information about all the port monitors for which the SAC is responsible. This file exists on the delivered system. Initially, it is empty except for a single comment line that contains the version number of the SAC. You can add port monitors to the system by making entries in the SAC's administrative file, using the administrative command `sacadm`(1M) with the `-a` option.

You also use sacadm(1M) to remove entries from the SAC's administrative file. Each entry in the SAC's administrative file contains the following information.

PMTAG   A unique tag that identifies a particular port monitor. The system administrator is responsible for naming a port monitor. This tag is then used by the SAC to identify the port monitor for all administrative purposes. PMTAG can consist of up to 14 alphanumeric characters.

PMTYPE   The type of the port monitor. In addition to its unique tag, each port monitor has a type designator. The type designator identifies a group of port monitors that are different invocations of the same entity. ttymon and listen are examples of valid port monitor types. The type designator facilitates the administration of groups of related port monitors. Without a type designator, you have no way of knowing which port monitor tags corresponds to port monitors of the same type. PMTYPE can consist of up to 14 alphanumeric characters.

FLGS   The following flags are currently defined.

    d   When started, do not enable the port monitor.

    x   Do not start the port monitor.

    If you specify no flag, take the default action. By default, a port monitor is started and enabled.

RCNT   The number of times a port monitor can fail before being placed in a failed state. Once a port monitor enters the failed state, the SAC does not try to restart it. If you do not specify a count when you create the entry, set this field to 0. A restart count of 0 does not restart the port monitor when it fails.

COMMAND   A string representing the command that starts the port monitor. The first component of the string, the command itself, must be a full path name.

The Port Monitor Administrative File _pmtab

Each port monitor has two directories for its exclusive use. The current directory contains files defined by the SAF (_pmtab, _pid) and the per-service configuration scripts, if they exist. The directory /var/saf/*pmtag*, where *pmtag* is the tag of the port monitor, is available for the port monitor's private files. Each port monitor has its own administrative file. You should use the pmadm(1M) command to add, remove, or modify service entries in this file. Each time a change is made with pmadm(1M), the corresponding port monitor rereads its administrative file. Each entry in a port monitor's administrative file defines how the port monitor treats a specific port and what service is to be invoked on that port. Some fields must be present for all types of port monitors. Each entry must include a service tag to identify the service uniquely and an identity to be assigned to the service when it is started (for example, root).

The combination of a service tag and a port monitor tag uniquely defines an instance of a service. You can use the same service tag to identify a service under a different port monitor. The record must also contain port-monitor-specific data (for example, for a ttymon port monitor, this data includes the prompt string that is meaningful to ttymon). Each type of port monitor must provide a command that takes the necessary port-monitor-specific data as arguments and outputs these data in a form suitable for storage in the file. The ttyadm(1M) command does this for ttymon, and nlsadmin(1M) does it for listen. For a user-defined port monitor, you must also supply a similar administrative command. Each service entry in the port monitor administrative file must have the following format and contain the information listed below.

```
svctag:flgs:id:reserved:reserved:reserved:pmspecific # comment
```

SVCTAG is a unique tag that identifies a service. This tag is unique only for the port monitor through which the service is available. Other port monitors may offer the same or other services with the same tag. A service requires both a port monitor tag and a service tag to identify it uniquely. SVCTAG can consist of up to 14 alphanumeric characters. The following service entries are defined.

FLGS   The following flags can currently be included in this field.

    x   Do not enable this port. By default the port is enabled.

    u   Create a utmpx entry (changed from utmp in the Solaris 8 release) for this service. By default, no utmpx entry is created for the service.

ID   The identity under which the service is to be started. The identity has the form of a login name as it appears in /etc/passwd.

PMSPECIFIC   Examples of port monitor information are addresses, the name of a process to execute, or the name of a STREAMS pipe to pass a connection through. This information varies to meet the needs of each different type of port monitor.

COMMENT   A comment associated with the service entry. Port monitors can ignore the u flag if creating a utmpx entry (changed from utmp in the Solaris 8 release) for the service is not appropriate to the way in which the service is to be invoked. Some services may not start properly unless utmpx entries have been created for them (for example, login). Each port monitor administrative file must contain one special comment of the form # VERSION=value where value is an integer that represents the port monitor's version number. The version number defines the format of the port monitor administrative file. This comment line is created automatically when a port monitor is added to the system. It appears on a line by itself, before the service entries.

Monitor-Specific Administrative Command

Previously, two pieces of information included in the _pmtab file were described: the port monitor's version number and the port monitor part of the service entries in the port monitor's _pmtab file. When a new port monitor is added, the version number must be known so that the _pmtab file can be correctly initialized. When a new service is added, the port monitor part of the _pmtab entry must be formatted correctly. Each port monitor must have an administrative command to perform these two tasks. The person who specifies the port monitor must also define such an administrative command and its input options. When the command is invoked with these options, the information required for the port monitor part of the service entry must be correctly formatted for inclusion in the port monitor's _pmtab file and must be written to the standard output. To request the version number, the command must be invoked with a -V option; when it is invoked in this way, the port monitor's current version number must be written to the standard output. If the command fails for any reason during the execution of either of these tasks, no data should be written to standard output.

The Port Monitor/Service Interface

The interface between a port monitor and a service is determined solely by the service. Two mechanisms for invoking a service are presented here as examples.

New Service Invocations

The first interface is for services that are started anew with each request. This interface requires the port monitor to first fork a child process with fork(2). The child eventually becomes the designated service by performing an exec(1). Before the exec happens, the port monitor may take some port-monitor-specific action; however, one action that must occur is the interpretation of the per-service configuration script if one is present. This action is done by a call to the library routine doconfig(3N).

Standing Service Invocations

The second interface is for invocations of services that are actively running. To use this interface, a service must have one end of a stream pipe open and be prepared to receive connections through it.

Port Monitor Requirements

For implementation of a port monitor, several generic requirements must be met. This section summarizes these requirements. An administrative command must also be supplied.

Initial Environment

When a port monitor is started, it expects the following initial execution environment conditions.

- It has no file descriptors open.
- It cannot be a process group leader.
- It has an entry in /etc/utmpx (changed from /etc/utmp in the Solaris 8 release) *New!* of type LOGIN_PROCESS.
- An environment variable, ISTATE, is set to enabled or disabled to indicate the port monitor's correct initial state.
- An environment variable, PMTAG, is set to the port monitor's assigned tag.
- The directory that contains the port monitor's administrative files is its current directory.
- The port monitor is able to create private files in the directory /var/saf/*tag*, where *tag* is the port monitor's tag.
- The port monitor is running with user ID 0 (root).

Important Files

Relative to its current directory, the following key files exist for a port monitor.

_config   The port monitor's configuration script. The port monitor
            configuration script is run by the SAC. The SAC is started by
            init(1M) as a result of an entry in /etc/inittab that calls sac(1M).

_pid   The file into which the port monitor writes its process ID.

_pmtab	The port monitor's administrative file. This file contains information about the ports and services for which the port monitor is responsible.
_pmpipe	The FIFO through which the port monitor receives messages from the SAC.
svctag	The per-service configuration script for the service with the tag *svctag*.
../_sacpipe	The FIFO through which the port monitor sends messages to sac(1M).

Port Monitor Responsibilities

A port monitor is responsible for performing the following tasks in addition to its port monitor function.

- Write its process ID into the file _pid and put an advisory lock on the file.
- Terminate gracefully on receipt of the signal SIGTERM.
- Follow the protocol for message exchange with the SAC.

A port monitor must perform the following tasks during service invocation.

New!

- Create a utmpx entry (changed from utmp in the Solaris 8 release) if the requested service has the u flag set in _pmtab.

New!

- Port monitors can ignore this flag if creating a utmpx entry for the service does not make sense because of the way the service is to be invoked. On the other hand, some services may not start properly unless utmpx entries have been created for them.
- Interpret the per-service configuration script for the requested service, if it exists, by calling the doconfig(3N) library routine.

Configuration Files and Scripts

The library routine doconfig(3N), defined in libnsl.so, interprets the configuration scripts contained in the files /etc/saf/_sysconfig (the per-system configuration file), /etc/saf/*pmtag*/_config (per-port monitor configuration files), and /etc/saf/*pmtag*/svctag (per-service configuration files). The syntax is shown below.

```
#include <sac.h>
int doconfig (int fd, char *script, long rflag);
```

script	The name of the configuration script.
fd	A file descriptor that designates the stream to which stream manipulation operations are to be applied.
rflag	A bitmask that indicates the mode in which script is to be interpreted. rflag can take two values, NORUN and NOASSIGN, which may be ORed. If rflag is zero, all commands in the configuration script are eligible to be interpreted. If rflag has the NOASSIGN bit set, the assign command is considered illegal and returns an error. If rflag has the NORUN bit set, the run and runwait commands are considered illegal and return an error. If a command in the script fails, the interpretation of the script ceases at that point and a

> positive integer is returned; this number indicates which line in the
> script failed. If a system error occurs, a value of -1 is returned. If a
> script fails, the process whose environment was being established
> should not be started.

In the following example, doconfig(3N) is used to interpret a per-service
configuration script.

```
...
if
        ((i = doconfig (fd, svctag, 0)) != 0)
        {
        error ("doconfig failed on line %d of script %s",i,svctag);
        }
```

The Per-System Configuration File

The per-system configuration file, /etc/saf/_sysconfig, is delivered empty. You can
use it to customize the environment for all services on the system by writing a command
script in the interpreted language described in "The Configuration Language" on
page 1021 and on the doconfig(3N) manual page. When the SAC is started, it calls the
doconfig(3N) function to interpret the per-system configuration script. The SAC is
started when the system enters multiuser mode.

Per-Port-Monitor Configuration Files

Per-port-monitor configuration scripts (/etc/saf/*pmtag*/_config) are optional. They
enable you to customize the environment for any given port monitor and for the services
that are available through the ports for which that port monitor is responsible.
Per-port-monitor configuration scripts are written in the same language used for
per-system configuration scripts. The per-port-monitor configuration script is
interpreted when the port monitor is started. The port monitor is started by the SAC
after the SAC has itself been started and after it has run its own configuration script,
/etc/saf/_sysconfig. The per-port-monitor configuration script may override defaults
provided by the per-system configuration script.

Per-Service Configuration Files

Per-service configuration files enable you to customize the environment for a specific
service. For example, a service may require special privileges that are not available to
the general user. Using the language described in the doconfig(3N) manual page, you
can write a script that grants or limits such special privileges to a particular service
offered through a particular port monitor. The per-service configuration can override
defaults provided by higher-level configuration scripts. For example, the per-service
configuration script can specify a set of STREAMS modules other than the default set.

The Configuration Language

The language in which configuration scripts are written consists of a sequence of
commands, each of which is interpreted separately. The following reserved keywords are
defined: assign, push, pop, runwait, and run. The comment character is #. Blank lines
are not significant. No line in a command script can exceed 1024 characters.=

assign *variable=value*

> Define environment variables; *variable* is the name of the
> environment variable, and *value* is the value to be assigned to it. The

value assigned must be a string constant; no form of parameter substitution is available. *value* can be quoted. The quoting rules are those used by the shell for defining environment variables. `assign` fails if space cannot be allocated for the new variable or if any part of the specification is invalid.

`push` *module1*[, *module2*, *module3*,...]

Push STREAMS modules onto the stream designated by `fd`; *module1* is the name of the first module to be pushed, *module2* is the name of the second module to be pushed, and so on. The command fails if any of the named modules cannot be pushed. If a module cannot be pushed, ignore the subsequent modules on the same command line and pop modules that have already been pushed.

`pop` [*module*]   Pop STREAMS modules off the designated stream. If you invoke `pop` with no arguments, pop the top module on the stream. If you specify an argument, pop modules one at a time until the named module is at the top of the stream. If the named module is not on the designated stream, leave the stream as it was; the command fails. If *module* is the special keyword `ALL`, then pop all modules on the stream. Only modules above the topmost driver are affected.

`runwait` *command*

Run a command and wait for it to complete; *command* is the path name of the command to be run. Prepend `/bin/sh -c` to the command; you can execute shell scripts from configuration scripts in this way. The `runwait` command fails if *command* cannot be found or cannot be executed or if *command* exits with a non-zero status.

`run` *command*   Identical to `runwait` except do not wait for *command* to complete; *command* is the path name of the command to be run. `run` does not fail unless it is unable to create a child process to execute the command. Although they are syntactically indistinguishable, some of the commands available to `run` and `runwait` are interpreter built-in commands. Interpreter built-ins are used when it is necessary to alter the state of a process within the context of that process. The `doconfig` interpreter built-in commands are similar to the shell special commands and, like these, they do not spawn another process for execution. See the `sh(1)` manual page. The initial set of built-in commands is `cd`, `ulimit`, `umask`.

Sample Port Monitor Code

The following example shows a "null" port monitor that simply responds to messages from the SAC.

```
# include <stdlib.h>
# include <stdio.h>
# include <unistd.h>
# include <fcntl.h>
# include <signal.h>
# include <sac.h>
```

```
char Scratch[BUFSIZ]; /* scratch buffer */
char Tag[PMTAGSIZE + 1]; /* port monitor's tag */
FILE *Fp; /* file pointer for log file */
FILE *Tfp; /* file pointer for pid file */
char State; /* portmonitor's current state*/

main(argc, argv)
     int argc;
     char *argv[];
{
     char *istate;
     strcpy(Tag, getenv("PMTAG"));
/*
 * open up a log file in port monitor's private directory
 */
     sprintf(Scratch, "/var/saf/%s/log", Tag);
     Fp = fopen(Scratch, "a+");
     if (Fp == (FILE *)NULL)
          exit(1);
     log(Fp, "starting");
/*
 * retrieve initial state (either "enabled" or "disabled") and set
 * State accordingly
 */
     istate = getenv("ISTATE");
     sprintf(Scratch, "ISTATE is %s", istate);
     log(Fp, Scratch);
     if (!strcmp(istate, "enabled"))
          State = PM_ENABLED;
     else if (!strcmp(istate, "disabled"))
          State = PM_DISABLED;
     else {
          log(Fp, "invalid initial state");
          exit(1);
     }
     sprintf(Scratch, "PMTAG is %s", Tag);
     log(Fp, Scratch);
/*
 * set up pid file and lock it to indicate that we are active
 */
     Tfp = fopen("_pid", "w");
     if (Tfp == (FILE *)NULL) {
          exit(1);
     }
     if (lockf(fileno(Tfp), F_TEST, 0) < 0) {
          log(Fp, "pid file already locked");
          exit(1);
     }

     log(Fp, "locking file");
     if (lockf(fileno(Tfp), F_LOCK, 0) < 0) {
          log(Fp, "lock failed");
          exit(1);
     }
```

```
        fprintf(Tfp, "%d", getpid());
        fflush(Tfp);

/*
 * handle poll messages from the sac ... this function never returns
 */
        handlepoll();
        pause();
        fclose(Tfp);
        fclose(Fp);
}

handlepoll()
{
        int pfd; /* file descriptor for incoming pipe */
        int sfd; /* file descriptor for outgoing pipe */
        struct sacmsg sacmsg; /* incoming message */
        struct pmmsg pmmsg; /* outgoing message */
/*
 * open pipe for incoming messages from the sac
 */
        pfd = open("_pmpipe", O_RDONLY|O_NONBLOCK);
        if (pfd < 0) {
            log(Fp, "_pmpipe open failed");
            exit(1);
        }
/*
 * open pipe for outgoing messages to the sac
 */
        sfd = open("../_sacpipe", O_WRONLY);
        if (sfd < 0) {
            log(Fp, "_sacpipe open failed");
            exit(1);
        }
/*
 * start to build a return message; we only support class 1 messages
 */
        strcpy(pmmsg.pm_tag, Tag);
        pmmsg.pm_size = 0;
        pmmsg.pm_maxclass = 1;
/*
 * keep responding to messages from the sac
 */
        for (;;) {
            if (read(pfd, &sacmsg, sizeof(sacmsg)) != sizeof(sacmsg)) {
                log(Fp, "_pmpipe read failed");
                exit(1);
            }
/*
 * determine the message type and respond appropriately
 */
                switch (sacmsg.sc_type) {
                    case SC_STATUS:
                        log(Fp, "Got SC_STATUS message");
```

```
                              pmmsg.pm_type = PM_STATUS;
                              pmmsg.pm_state = State;
                              break;
                      case SC_ENABLE:
                              /*note internal state change below*/
                              log(Fp, "Got SC_ENABLE message");
                              pmmsg.pm_type = PM_STATUS;
                              State = PM_ENABLED;
                              pmmsg.pm_state = State;
                              break;
                      case SC_DISABLE:
                              /*note internal state change below*/
                              log(Fp, "Got SC_DISABLE message");
                              pmmsg.pm_type = PM_STATUS;
                              State = PM_DISABLED;
                              pmmsg.pm_state = State;
                              break;
                      case SC_READDB:
                              /*
                               * if this were a fully functional port
                               * monitor it would read _pmtab here
                               * and take appropriate action
                               */
                              log(Fp, "Got SC_READDB message");
                              pmmsg.pm_type = PM_STATUS;
                              pmmsg.pm_state = State;
                              break;
                      default:
                              sprintf(Scratch, "Got unknown message <%d>",
                              sacmsg.sc_type);
                              log(Fp, Scratch);
                              pmmsg.pm_type = PM_UNKNOWN;
                              pmmsg.pm_state = State;
                              break;
                  }
      /*
       * send back a response to the poll
       * indicating current state
       */
              if (write(sfd, &pmmsg, sizeof(pmmsg)) != sizeof(pmmsg))
                  log(Fp, "sanity response failed");
          }
      }
      /*
       * general logging function
       */
      log(fp, msg)
          FILE *fp;
          char *msg;
      {
          fprintf(fp, "%d; %s\n", getpid(), msg);
          fflush(fp);
      }
```

The following example shows the `sac.h` header file.

```
/* length in bytes of a utmpx id */
# define IDLEN 4
/* wild character for utmpx ids */
# define SC_WILDC 0xff
/* max len in bytes for port monitor tag */
# define PMTAGSIZE 14
/*
 * values for rflag in doconfig()
 */
/* don't allow assign operations */
# define NOASSIGN 0x1
/* don't allow run or runwait operations */
# define NORUN 0x2
/*
 * message to SAC (header only). This header is forever fixed. The
 * size field (pm_size) defines the size of the data portion of the
 * message, which follows the header. The form of this optional data
 * portion is defined strictly by the message type (pm_type).
 */
struct pmmsg {
    char pm_type;                  /* type of message */
    unchar_t pm_state;              /* current state of pm */
    char pm_maxclass;            /* max message class this port monitor
                                        understands */
    char pm_tag[PMTAGSIZE + 1]; /* pm's tag */
    int pm_size;                   /* size of opt data portion */
};
/*
 * pm_type values
 */
# define PM_STATUS 1 /* status response */
# define PM_UNKNOWN 2 /* unknown message was received */
/*
 * pm_state values
 */
/*
 * Class 1 responses
 */
# define PM_STARTING 1   /* monitor in starting state */
# define PM_ENABLED 2    /* monitor in enabled state */
# define PM_DISABLED 3   /* monitor in disabled state */
# define PM_STOPPING 4   /* monitor in stopping state */
/*
 * message to port monitor
 */
struct sacmsg {
    int sc_size;         /* size of optional data portion */
    char sc_type;        /* type of message */
};
/*
 * sc_type values
 * These represent commands that the SAC sends to a port monitor.
```

```
 * These commands are divided into "classes" for extensibility. Each
 * subsequent "class" is a superset of the previous "classes" plus
 * the new commands defined within that "class". The header for all
 * commands is identical; however, a command may be defined such that
 * an optional data portion may be sent in addition to the header.
 * The format of this optional data piece is self-defining based on
 * the command. The first message sent by the SAC
 * will always be a class 1 message. The port monitor response
 * indicates the maximum class that it is able to understand. Another
 * note is that port monitors should only respond to a message with
 * an equivalent class response (i.e., a class 1 command causes a
 * class 1 response).
 */
/*
 * Class 1 commands (currently, there are only class 1 commands)
 */
# define SC_STATUS 1     /* status request *
# define SC_ENABLE 2     /* enable request */
# define SC_DISABLE 3    /* disable request */
# define SC_READDB 4     /* read pmtab request */
/*
 * `errno' values for Saferrno, note that Saferrno is used by both
 * pmadm and sacadm and these values are shared between them
 */
# define E_BADARGS 1     /* bad args/ill-formed cmd line */
# define E_NOPRIV 2      /* user not priv for operation */
# define E_SAFERR 3      /* generic SAF error */
# define E_SYSERR 4      /* system error */
# define E_NOEXIST 5     /* invalid specification */
# define E_DUP 6         /* entry already exists */
# define E_PMRUN 7       /* port monitor is running */
# define E_PMNOTRUN 8    /* port monitor is not running */
# define E_RECOVER 9
    /* in recovery */
```

Directory Structure

This section describes the SAF files and directories.

`/etc/saf/_sysconfig`

> The per-system configuration script.

`/etc/saf/_sactab`

> The SAC's administrative file. Contains information about the port monitors for which the SAC is responsible.

`/etc/saf/`*pmtag*

> The home directory for port monitor *pmtag*.

`/etc/saf/`*pmtag*`/_config`

> The per-port monitor configuration script for port monitor *pmtag*.
> `/etc/saf/`*pmtag*`/_pmtab`.

Port monitor *pmtag*'s administrative file. Contains information about the services for which *pmtag* is responsible.

`/etc/saf/`*pmtag*`/svctag`

The file in which the per-service configuration script for service `svctag` (available through port monitor *pmtag*) is placed.

`/etc/saf/`*pmtag*`/_pid`

The file in which a port monitor writes its process ID in the current directory and places an advisory lock on the file.

`/etc/saf/`*pmtag*`/_pmpipe`

The file in which the port monitor receives messages from the SAC and `../_sacpipe` and sends return messages to the SAC.

`/var/saf/_log`

The SAC's log file.

`/var/saf/`*pmtag*

The directory for files created by port monitor *pmtag*, for example, its log file.

List of Commands

The following administrative commands relate to SAF.

`sacadm(1M)`	Port monitor administrative command.
`pmadm(1M)`	Service administration command.

Attributes

See `attributes`(5) for descriptions of the following attributes.

Attribute Type	**Attribute Value**
Availability	`SUNWcsr`

See Also

`exec(1)`, `sh(1)`, `init(1M)`, `nlsadmin(1M)`, `pmadm(1M)`, `sac(1M)`, `sacadm(1M)`, `ttyadm(1M)`, `fork(2)`, `doconfig(3N)`, `attributes(5)`

sar, sa1, sa2, sadc — System Activity Report Package

Synopsis

```
/usr/lib/sa/sadc [t n][ofile]
/usr/lib/sa/sa1 [t n]
/usr/lib/sa/sa2 [-aAbcdgkmpqruvwy][-e time][-f filename][-i sec]
  [-s time]
```

Description

You can access system activity data by special request (see sar(1)) and automatically, on a routine basis, as described here. The operating system contains several counters that are incremented as various system actions occur. These include counters for the following activities.

- CPU use.
- Buffer use.
- Disk and tape I/O transfers.
- TTY device activity.
- Switching and system-call activity.
- File access.
- Queue manipulation.
- Interprocess communications.
- Paging.

For more general system statistics, use iostat(1M), sar(1), or vmstat(1M).

See *Solaris Transition Guide* for device naming conventions for disks.

You use sadc and the sa1 and sa2 shell procedures to sample, save, and process this data.

Use the sadc command, the data collector, to sample system data *n* times, with an interval of t seconds between samples, and write in binary format to *ofile* or to standard output. The sampling interval t should be greater than 5 seconds; otherwise, the activity of sadc itself can affect the sample. If you omit t and n, a special record is written. You can use this facility at system boot time, when booting to a multiuser state, to mark the time at which the counters restart from zero. You can enable system accounting by editing the entry in the /etc/init.d/perf file and removing the comments (#) from the beginning of each line, as shown in the following example.

```
# Uncomment the following lines to enable system activity data
  gathering.
# You will also need to uncomment the sa entries in the system crontab
# /var/spool/cron/crontabs/sys.  Refer to the sar(1) and sadc(1m) man
  pages
# for more information.

  if [ -z "$_INIT_RUN_LEVEL" ]; then
        set -- `/usr/bin/who -r`
        _INIT_RUN_LEVEL="$7"
        _INIT_RUN_NPREV="$8"
        _INIT_PREV_LEVEL="$9"
```

```
fi

if [ $_INIT_RUN_LEVEL -ge 2 -a $_INIT_RUN_LEVEL -le 4 -a \
    $_INIT_RUN_NPREV -eq 0 -a \( $_INIT_PREV_LEVEL = 1 -o \
    $_INIT_PREV_LEVEL = S \) ]; then

    /usr/bin/su sys -c "/usr/lib/sa/sadc /var/adm/sa/sa`date +%d`"
fi
```

Use the `sa1` shell script, a variant of `sadc`, to collect and store data in the binary file `/var/adm/sa/sa`dd`, where `dd` is the current day. The arguments `t` and `n` write records `n` times at an interval of `t` seconds, or once if omitted. Using `crontab` to add the following entries in `/var/spool/cron/crontabs/sys` produces records every 20 minutes during working hours and hourly otherwise.

```
0 * * * 0-6 /usr/lib/sa/sa1
20,40 8-17 * * 1-5 /usr/lib/sa/sa1
```

See `crontab`(1) for details.

Use the `sa2` shell script, a variant of `sar`, to write a daily report in the file `/var/adm/sa/sar`dd. See the "Options" section in `sar`(1) for an explanation of the various options. Adding the following entry in `/var/spool/cron/crontabs/sys` reports important activities hourly during the working day.

```
5 18 * * 1-5 /usr/lib/sa/sa2 -s 8:00 -e 18:01 -i 1200 -A
```

Files

/etc/init.d/perf

> Shell script used to enable system activity data gathering.

/tmp/sa.adrfl

> Address file.

/var/adm/sa/sa`dd`

> Daily data file.

/var/adm/sa/sar`dd`

> Daily report file.

/var/spool/cron/crontabs/sys

> File used to do performance collection.

Attributes

See `attributes`(5) for descriptions of the following attributes.

Attribute Type	Attribute Value
Availability	SUNWaccu

See Also

crontab(1), sag(1), sar(1), timex(1), iostat(1M), vmstat(1M),
attributes(5)
> *System Administration Guide, Volume I*
> *Solaris Transition Guide*

savecore — Save a Crash Dump of the Operating System

Synopsis

/usr/bin/savecore [-Lvd] [-f *dumpfile*] *directory*

Description

System crashes can occur because of hardware malfunctions, I/O problems, and
software errors. If the system crashes, it displays an error message on the console and
then writes a copy of its physical memory to the dump device. The system then reboots
automatically. When the system reboots, the savecore command is invoked by
/etc/init.d/savecore to retrieve the data from the dump device and write the saved
crash dump to the savecore directory. The saved crash dump files provide valuable
information to aid in diagnosing the problem. If savecore is enabled by way of
dumpadm(1M), savecore is enabled on reboot by default.

Crash dump files are saved in a predetermined directory, which by default is   *New!*
/var/crash/*hostname*. In previous Solaris releases, crash dump files were overwritten
when a system rebooted unless you manually enabled the system to save the images of
physical memory in a crash dump file. Now, the saving of crash dump files is enabled by
default.

The savecore command checks the crash dump to be certain it corresponds to the
version of the operating system currently running. If it does, savecore saves the crash
dump data in the file *directory*/vmcore.*n* and saves the kernel's namelist in
directory/unix.*n*. The trailing .*n* in the path names is replaced by a number that
grows every time savecore is run in that directory.

Before writing out a crash dump, savecore reads a number from the file
directory/minfree. This number is the minimum number of kilobytes that must
remain free on the file system containing *directory*. If after the crash dump was saved
the file system containing *directory* would have less free space than the number of
kilobytes specified in minfree, the crash dump is not saved. If the minfree file does not
exist, savecore assumes a minfree value of 1 megabyte.

The savecore command also logs a reboot message by using facility LOG_AUTH (see
syslog(3)). If the system crashed as a result of a panic, savecore also logs the panic
string.

Options

-L	Save a crash dump of the live running Solaris system without actually rebooting or altering the system in any way. This option forces savecore to save a live snapshot of the system to the dump device and then immediately to retrieve the data and to write it out to a new set of crash dump files in the specified directory. Live system crash dumps can be performed only if a system has been configured with dumpadm(1M) to have a dedicated dump device.
-v	Enable verbose error messages.
-d	Disregard dump header valid flag. Force an attempt to save a crash dump even if the header information stored on the dump device indicates the dump has already been saved.
-f *dumpfile*	Try to save a crash dump from the specified file instead of from the system's current dump device. This option can be useful if the information stored on the dump device has been copied to an on-disk file with the dd(1M) command.

Operands

directory	Save the crash dump files to the specified directory. If no directory argument is present on the command line, save the crash dump files to the default savecore directory, configured by the dumpadm(1M) command.

Files

directory/vmcore.*n*

> File used to save crash dump data.

directory/unix.*n*

> File used to store the kernel's namelist.

directory/bounds

> File that contains the next crash number for savecore to use.

directory/minfree

> File that contains a number representing the number of minimum kilobytes on a system that must remain free on the file system containing *directory*.

/dev/ksyms   The kernel namelist.

/etc/init.d/savecore

> Savecore shell script.

/var/crash/`uname -n`

> Default crash dump directory.

Attributes

See attributes(5) for descriptions of the following attributes.

Attribute Type	Attribute Value
Availability	SUNWesu (32-bit)
	SUNWesxu (64-bit)

See Also

adb(1), crash(1M), dd(1M), dumpadm(1M), syslog(3), attributes(5)

Bugs

If the dump device is also being used as a swap device, you must run savecore soon after booting, before the swap space containing the crash dump is overwritten by programs currently running.

sendmail — Send Mail Over the Internet

Synopsis

```
/usr/lib/sendmail [-ba][-bD][-bd][-bi][-bm][-bp][-bs][-bt][-bv]
    [-B type][-C file][-d X][-F fullname][-f name][-h N][-Mxvalue]
    [-N notifications][-n][-Ooption=value][-oxvalue][-p protocol]
    [-q[time]][-q Xstring][-R ret][-r name][-t][-V envid][-v]
    [-X logfile][address...]
```

Description

sendmail is the transport agent responsible for receiving and delivering e-mail messages. sendmail performs the following functions.

- Accepts messages from the user agent.
- Understands destination addresses.
- Delivers mail originating on the local system to the proper mailbox(es) if local or to a delivery agent if not local.
- Receives incoming mail from other delivery agents and delivers it to local users.

sendmail sends a message to one or more people, routing the message over whatever networks are necessary. sendmail does internetwork forwarding as needed to deliver the message to the correct place.

sendmail is not intended as a user interface routine; other programs provide user-friendly front ends. sendmail is used only to deliver preformatted messages.

With no flags, sendmail reads its standard input up to an end-of-file or a line with a single dot and sends a copy of the letter found there to all of the addresses listed. It determines the network to use based on the syntax and contents of the addresses.

Local addresses are looked up in the local aliases(4) file or in a nameservice, as defined by the nsswitch.conf(4) file, and aliased appropriately. In addition, if there is a .forward file in a recipient's home directory, sendmail forwards a copy of each message to the list of recipients that file contains. Refer to "Notes" on page 1034 for more information about `.forward` files. You can prevent aliasing by preceding the address with a backslash. Normally, the sender is not included in alias expansions. For example, if `john` sends to `group` and `group` includes `john` in the expansion, then the message is not delivered to `john`. See the `MeToo` processing option for more information.

There are several conditions under which the expected behavior is for the alias database to be either built or rebuilt. It is important to note that this cannot occur under any circumstances unless root owns and has exclusive write permission to the `/etc/mail/aliases*` files.

If a message is found to be undeliverable, it is returned to the sender with diagnostics that indicate the location and nature of the failure; or, the message is placed in a `dead.letter` file in the sender's home directory.

Notes

The `sendmail` program requires a fully qualified host name when starting. A script has been included to help verify whether the host name is defined properly (see `check-hostname(1M)`).

The permissions and the ownership of several directories have been changed to increase security. In particular, access to `/etc/mail` and `/var/spool/mqueue` have been restricted.

Security restrictions have been put on users using `.forward` files to pipe mail to a program or redirect mail to a file. The default shell (as listed in `/etc/passwd`) of these users must be listed in `/etc/shells`. This restriction does not affect mail that is being redirected to another alias.

Additional restrictions have been put in place on `.forward` and `:include:` files. These files and the directory structure that they are placed in cannot be writeable by group or world (see `check-permissions(1M)`).

Options

`-ba`	Go into ARPANET mode. End all input lines with a Return-linefeed, and generate all messages with a Return-linefeed at the end. Also examine the `From:` and `Sender:` fields for the name of the sender.
`-bd`	Run as a daemon in the background waiting for incoming SMTP connections.
`-bD`	Run as a daemon in the foreground waiting for incoming SMTP connections.
`-bi`	Initialize the `aliases(4)` database. Root must own and have exclusive write permission to the `/etc/mail/aliases*` files for successful use of this option.
`-bm`	Deliver mail in the usual way (default).
`-bp`	Print a summary of the mail queue.
`-bs`	Use the SMTP protocol as described in RFC 821. This option implies all the operations of the `-ba` flag that are compatible with SMTP.
`-bt`	Run in address test mode. This mode reads addresses and shows the steps in parsing; use it for debugging configuration tables.
`-bv`	Verify names only; do not try to collect or deliver a message. Verify mode is normally used for validating users or mailing lists.

-B *type*	Indicate body type (7BIT or 8BITMIME).
-C *file*	Use alternate configuration file.
-d *X*	Set debugging value to *X*.
-F *fullname*	Set the full name of the sender.
f *name*	Set the name of the from person (that is, the sender of the mail).
-h *N*	Set the hop count to *N*. Increment the hop count every time the mail is processed. When it reaches a limit, return the mail with an error message, the victim of an aliasing loop.
-M*xvalu*	Set macro *x* to the specified value.
-n	Do not do aliasing.
-N *notifications*	
	Tag all addresses being sent as wanting the indicated notifications, which consists of the word NEVER or a comma-separated list of SUCCESS,FAILURE,DELAY for successful delivery, failure, and a message that is stuck in a queue somewhere. The default is FAILURE,DELAY.
-o*xvalue*	Set option *x* to the specified *value*. See "Processing Options" on page 1036.
-O*option=value*	
	Set *option* to the specified *value* (for long from names). See "Processing Options" on page 1036.
-p *protocol*	Set the sending protocol. The protocol field can be in form protocol:host to set both the sending protocol and the sending host. For example: -pUUCP:uunet sets the sending protocol to UUCP and the sending host to uunet. (Some existing programs use -oM to set the r and s macros; this syntax is equivalent to using -p.)
-q[*time*]	Process saved messages in the queue at given intervals. If you omit *time*, process the queue once. Specify *time* as a tagged number, with s for seconds, m for minutes, h for hours, d for days, and w for weeks. For example, -q1h30m or -q90m both set the timeout to one hour thirty minutes.
-q *Xstring*	Run the queue once, limiting the jobs to those matching *Xstring*. The key letter *X* can be one of the following.
	I Limit based on queue identifier.
	R Limit based on recipient.
	S Limit based on sender.
	Accept a particular queued job if one of the corresponding addresses contains the indicated string.
-r *name*	An alternate and obsolete form of the -f option.
-R *ret*	Identify the information you want returned if the message bounces; *ret* can be HDRS for headers only or FULL for headers plus body.

`-t`	Read message for recipients. Scan `To:`, `Cc:`, and `Bcc:` lines for people to send to. Delete the `Bcc:` line before transmission. Suppress any addresses in the argument list. You can use the `NoRecipientAction` processing option to change the behavior when no legal recipients are included in the message.
`-v`	Go into verbose mode. Announce alias expansions, and so forth.
`-V` *envid*	Pass the indicated *envid* with the envelope of the message and return it if the message bounces.
`-X` *logfile*	Log all traffic in and out of `sendmail` in the indicated *logfile* for debugging mailer problems. This option produces a lot of data very quickly and should be used sparingly.

Processing Options

You can set a number of random options from a configuration file. Options are represented by a single character or by multiple-character names. The syntax for the single-character names sets option *x* to *value*.

`Oxvalue`

Depending on the option, *value* can be a string, an integer, a boolean (with legal values t, T, f, or F; the default is `true`), or a time interval.

The multiple-character or long names use the following syntax, which sets the option *Longname* to *argument*.

`O Longname=argument`

Long names are beneficial because they are easier to interpret than the single character names.

Not all processing options have single-character names. In the list below, the multiple-character name is presented first, followed by the single-character syntax enclosed in parentheses.

`AliasFile (Afile)`

> Specify possible alias file(s).

`AliasWait (a N)`

> Wait up to *N* minutes for an `@:@` entry to exist in the `aliases(4)` database before starting up. If it does not appear in *N* minutes, rebuild the database (if the `AutoRebuildAliases` option is also set) or issue a warning. Default is `10` minutes.

`AllowBogusHELO`

> Allow a `HELO` SMTP command that does not include a host name. By default this option is disabled.

`AutoRebuildAliases (D)`

> Rebuild the `/etc/mail/aliases` database if necessary and possible. If this option is not set, `sendmail` never rebuilds the `aliases` database unless explicitly requested with `-bi`, or by invoking `newaliases(1)`.

Note that for the database to be rebuilt, root must own and have exclusive write permission to the `/etc/mail/aliases*` files.

`BlankSub (Bc)`

Set the blank substitution character to *c*. Replace unquoted spaces in addresses with this character. Default is space (that is, no change is made).

`CheckAliases (n)`

Validate the RHS of aliases when rebuilding the `aliases(4)` database.

`CheckpointInterval (CN)`

Checkpoint the queue every *N* (default `10`) addresses sent. If your system crashes during delivery to a large list, this option prevents retransmission to any but the last *N* recipients.

`ClassFactor (zfact)`

Multiply the indicated factor *fact* by the message class (determined by the `Precedence:` field in the user header and the P lines in the configuration file) and subtract from the priority. Thus, favor messages with a higher `Priority:`. Default is `1800`.

`ColonOkInAddr`

Treat colons as a regular character in addresses. If not set, they are treated as the introducer to the RFC 822 group syntax. This option is on for version 5 and lower configuration files.

`ConnectionCacheSize (kN)`

Cache the maximum number of open connections at a time. The default is `1`. Delay closing the current connection until either this invocation of `sendmail` needs to connect to another host or it terminates. Setting this option to `0` default is the old behavior, that is, connections are closed immediately.

`ConnectionCacheTimeout (Ktimeout)`

Set the maximum amount of time a cached connection is permitted to idle without activity. If this time is exceeded, immediately close the connection. This value should be small (on the order of 10 minutes). Before `sendmail` uses a cached connection, it always sends a `NOOP` (no operation) command to check the connection; if this command fails, it reopens the connection. This behavior keeps your end from failing if the other end times out. This option enables you to be a good network neighbor and avoid using up excessive resources on the other end. The default is `5` minutes.

`ConnectionRateThrottle`

Set the maximum number of connections permitted per second. After this time, many connections are accepted, further connections are delayed. If not set or `<= 0`, there is no limit.

DaemonPortOptions (O*options*)

> Set server SMTP options. The options are *key=value* pairs. The following keys are known.

> | | |
> |---|---|
> | Addr | Address mask (default is INADDR_ANY). The address mask can be a numeric address in dot notation or a network name. |
> | Family | Address family (default is INET). |
> | Listen | Size of listen queue (default is 10). |
> | Port | Name/number of listening port (default is smtp). |
> | ReceiveSize | The size of the TCP/IP receive buffer. |
> | SendSize | The size of the TCP/IP send buffer. |

DefaultCharSet

> Set the default character set to use when converting unlabeled 8-bit input to MIME.

DefaultUser (g*gid*) or (u*uid*)

> Set the default group ID for mailers to run in to *gid*, or set the default user ID for mailers to *uid*. Default is 1. The value can also be given as a symbolic group or user name.

DeliveryMode (d*x*)

> Deliver in mode *x*. The following modes are legal.

> | | |
> |---|---|
> | i | Deliver interactively (synchronously). |
> | b | Deliver in background (asynchronously). |
> | d | Deferred mode. Defer database lookups until the actual queue run. |
> | q | Just queue the message (deliver during queue run). |

> Default is b if you specify no option, i if you specify it with no argument (that is, Od is equivalent to Odi).

DialDelay

> If a connection fails, wait this many seconds and try again. 0 means do not retry.

DontBlameSendmail

> Override the file safety checks. This option compromises system security and should not be used. See http://www.sendmail.org/tips/DontBlameSendmail.htmlfor more information.

DontExpandCnames

> Do not expand CNAME records $[... $] DNS-based lookups.

DontInitGroups

> Never invoke the initgroups(3C) routine. If you set this option, agents that are run on behalf of users have only their primary (/etc/passwd) group permissions.

DontProbeInterfaces

> Do not insert the names and addresses of any local interfaces into the $=w class. If set, you must also include support for these addresses; otherwise, mail to addresses in this list bounces with a configuration error.

DontPruneRoutes (R)

> Do not prune route-addr syntax addresses to the minimum possible.

DoubleBounceAddress

> If an error occurs when sending an error message, send that "double bounce" error message to this address.

EightBitMode (8)

> Use 8-bit data handling. This option requires one of the following keys. You can specify the key by using just the first character, but using the full word is better for clarity.

> mimify   Do any necessary conversion of 8BITMIME to 7-bit.

> pass   Pass unlabeled 8-bit input through as is.

> strict   Reject unlabeled 8-bit input.

ErrorHeader (Efile/*message*)

> Append error messages with the indicated message. If the message begins with a slash, assume it to be the path name of a file containing a message (this is the recommended setting). Otherwise, it is a literal message. The error file might contain the name, e-mail address, or phone number of a local postmaster who could provide assistance to end users. If the option is missing or null or if it names a file that does not exist or is not readable, then print no message.

ErrorMode (ex)

> Dispose of errors by using mode *x*. You can specify the following values for *x*.

> e   Mail back errors and always return 0 exit status.

> m   Mail back errors.

> p   Print error messages (default).

> q   No messages, just give exit status.

> w   Write back errors (mail if user not logged in).

FallbackMXhost (V*fallbackhost*)

> Act like a very low priority MX on every host. This option is intended for sites with poor network connectivity.

ForkEachJob (Y)

> Deliver each job that is run from the queue in a separate process. Use this option if you are short of memory because the default tends to consume considerable amounts of memory while the queue is being processed.

ForwardPath (Jpath)

> Set the path for searching for `.forward` files. The default is `$z/.forward`. Some sites that use the automounter may prefer to change this path to `/var/forward/$u` to search a file with the same name as the user in a system directory. You can also set it to a sequence of paths separated by colons; `sendmail` stops at the first file it can successfully and safely open. For example, `/var/forward/$u:$z/.forward` searches first in `/var/forward/username` and then in `~username/.forward` (but only if the first file does not exist). See "Notes" on page 1034 for more information.

HelpFile (Hfile)

> Specify the help file for SMTP.

HoldExpensive (c)

> If an outgoing mailer is marked as being expensive, don't connect immediately.

HostsFile   Set the file to use when doing "file" type access of host names.

HostStatusDirectory

> Keep host status on disk between `sendmail` runs in the named directory tree. If you do not use a full path, then interpret the path relative to the queue directory.

IgnoreDots (i)

> Ignore dots in incoming messages. This option is always disabled (that is, dots are always accepted) when reading SMTP mail.

LogLevel (L*n*)

> Set the default log level to *n*. Default is 9.

(M*xvalue*)   Set the macro *x* to value. This option is intended for use only from the command line.

MatchGECOS (G)

> Try to match recipient names using the GECOS field. This option allows mail to be delivered using names defined in the GECOS field in `/etc/passwd` as well as the login name.

MaxDaemonChildren

> Set the maximum number of children the daemon permits. After this number, reject connections. If not set or <=0, there is no limit.

MaxHopCount (h*N*)

> Set the maximum hop count. Assume that messages have been processed. Default is 25.

MaxMessageSize

> Set the maximum size of messages that are accepted (in bytes).

MaxMimeHeaderLength=*M*[/*N*]

> Set the maximum length of certain MIME header field values to *M* characters. For some of these headers that take parameters, the maximum length of each parameter is set to *N* if specified. If you do not specify /*N*, use one half of *M*. By default, these values are 0, meaning no checks are done.

MaxQueueRunSize

> Limit the maximum size of any given queue run to this number of entries. Stop reading the queue directory after this number of entries is reached; do not use job priority. If not set, there is no limit.

MeToo (M)   Send to me too, even if I am in an alias expansion.

MaxRecipientsPerMessage

> Permit no more than the specified number of recipients in an SMTP envelope. Further recipients receive a 452 error code and are deferred until the next delivery attempt.

MinFreeBlocks (b*N*/*M*)

> Insist on at least *N* blocks free on the file system that holds the queue files before accepting e-mail via SMTP. If there is insufficient space, sendmail gives a 452 response to the MAIL command. This response invites the sender to try again later. The optional *M* is a maximum message size advertised in the ESMTP EHLO response. It is currently otherwise unused.

MinQueueAge   Specify the amount of time a job must sit in the queue between queue runs. This option enables you to set the queue run interval low for better responsiveness without trying all jobs in each run. The default is 0.

MustQuoteChars

> Automatically quote characters in a full name phrase: &, ; : \ ( ) [ ].

NoRecipientAction

> Set action if there are no legal recipient files in the message. The following values are legal.
>
> add-apparently to
>
> > Add an Apparently to: header with all the known recipients (which may expose blind recipients).
>
> add-bcc   Add an empty Bcc: header.

add-to   Add a `To:` header with all the known recipients (which may expose blind recipients).

add-to-undisclosed

Add a `To: undisclosed-recipients:` header.

none   Do nothing, leave the message as it is.

OldStyleHeaders (o)

Assume that the headers may be in old format, that is, spaces delimit names. This option actually turns on an adaptive algorithm: if any recipient address contains a comma, parenthesis, or angle bracket, assume that commas already exist. If this option is not on, only commas delimit names. Headers are always output with commas between the names.

OperatorChars ($o)

Define the list of characters that can be used to separate the components of an address into tokens.

PostmasterCopy (P*postmaster*)

Send copies of error messages to the named postmaster. Send only the header of the failed message. Because most errors are user problems, it is probably not a good idea to use this option on large sites. It arguably contains all sorts of privacy violations, but it seems to be popular with certain operating systems vendors.

PrivacyOptions (p*opt*,*opt*,...)

Set privacy options. Privacy is really a misnomer; many of these options are simply a way of insisting on stricter adherence to the SMTP protocol.

The `goaway` pseudoflag sets all flags except `restrictmailq` and `restrictqrun`. If `mailq` is restricted, only people in the same group as the queue directory can print the queue. If queue runs are restricted, only root and the owner of the queue directory can run the queue. `authwarnings` adds warnings about various conditions that can indicate attempts to spoof the mail system, such as using a nonstandard queue directory.

You can specify the following options.

authwarnings Put `X-Authentication-Warning:` headers in messages.

goaway   Disallow essentially all SMTP status queries.

needexpnhelo Insist on HELO or EHLO command before EXPN.

needmailhelo Insist on HELO or EHLO command before MAIL.

needvrfyhelo Insist on HELO or EHLO command before VRFY.

noetrn   Disallow ETRN entirely.

noexpn   Disallow EXPN entirely.

noreceipts	Prevent return receipts.
novrfy	Disallow VRFY entirely.
public	Allow open access.
restrictmailq	Restrict mailq command.
restrictqrun	Restrict -q command-line flag

QueueDirectory (Qdir)

Use the named dir as the queue directory.

QueueFactor (qfactor)

Use factor as the multiplier in the map function to decide when to just queue up jobs instead of run them. This value is divided by the difference between the current load average and the load average limit (xflag) to determine the maximum message priority that is sent. Default is 600000.

QueueLA (xLA) When the system load average exceeds LA, just queue messages (that is, do not try to send them). Default is 8.

QueueSortOrder

Select the queue sort algorithm. The default value is Priority. Other values are Host or Time.

QueueTimeout (Trtime/wtime)

Set the queue timeout to rtime. After this interval, return to sender all messages that have not been successfully delivered. Default is five days (5d). The optional wtime is the time after which a warning message is sent. If it is missing or 0, then send no warning messages.

RecipientFactor (yfact)

Add the indicated factor fact to the priority (thus lowering the priority of the job) for each recipient; that is, this value penalizes jobs with large numbers of recipients. Default is 30000.

RefuseLA (XLA)

When the system load average exceeds LA, refuse incoming SMTP connections. Default is 12.

RemoteMode (>[RemoteMboxHost])

Enable remote mode by using this host. If you do not specify RemoteMboxHost and if /var/mail is remotely mounted, then enable remote mode by using the remote mount host. If you do not specify RemoteMboxHost and /var/mail is locally mounted, then disable remote mode.

When remote mode is enabled, all outgoing messages are sent through that server.

ResolverOptions (I)

Tune DNS lookups.

`RetryFactor (Zfact)`

> Add the indicated factor *fact* to the priority every time a job is processed. Thus, each time a job is processed, decrease its priority by the indicated value. In most environments, this value should be positive, because hosts that are down are all too often down for a long time. Default is `90000`.

`RunAsUser`   Become this user when reading and delivering mail. Intended for use on firewalls where users do not have accounts.

`SafeFileEnvironment`

> Do a `chroot` into this directory before writing files.

`SaveFromLine (f)`

> Save UNIX-style `From` lines at the front of headers. Normally, they are assumed redundant and are discarded.

`SendMimeErrors (j)`

> Send error messages in `MIME` format (see RFC 1341 and RFC 1344 for details).

`ServiceSwitchFile`

> Define the path to the service-switch file. Because the service-switch file is defined in the Solaris operating environment, this option is ignored.

`SevenBitInput (7)`

> Strip input to seven bits for compatibility with old systems. This option should not be needed.

`SingleLineFromHeader`

> Unwrap `From:` lines that have embedded newlines onto one line.

`SingleThreadDelivery`

> If this option and the `HostStatusDirectory` option are both set, use single-thread deliveries to other hosts.

`SmtpGreetingMessage or $e`

> Set the initial SMTP greeting message.

`StatusFile (Sfile)`

> Log statistics in the named file.

`SuperSafe(s)` Be supersafe when running things; that is, always instantiate the queue file, even if you are going to try immediate delivery. `sendmail` always instantiates the queue file before returning control to the client under any circumstances.

`TempFileMode (Fmode)`

> Set the file mode for queue files.

Timeout (r*timeouts*)

> Timeout reads after time interval. The `timeouts` argument is a list of
> `keyword=value` pairs. All but `command` apply to client SMTP. For
> backward compatibility, a timeout with no `keyword=` part sets all of
> the longer values. The following list contains recognized timeouts,
> their default values, and their minimum values specified in RFC 1123
> section 5.3.2.

command	Command read [1h, 5m].
connect	Initial connect [0, unspecified].
datablock	Data block read [1h, 3m].
datafinal	Reply to final . in data [1h, 10m].
datainit	Reply to DATA command [5m, 2m].
fileopen	File open [60sec, none].
helo	Reply to HELO or EHLO command [5m, none].
hoststatus	Host retry [30m, unspecified].
iconnect	First attempt to connect to a host [0, unspecified].
ident	IDENT protocol timeout [30s, none].
initial	Wait for initial greeting message [5m, 5m].
mail	Reply to MAIL command [10m, 5m].
misc	Reply to NOOP and VERB commands [2m, none].
queuereturn	Undeliverable message returned [5d].
queuewarn	Deferred warning [4h].
quit	Reply to QUIT command [2m, none].
rcpt	Reply to RCPT command [1h, 5m].
rset	Reply to RSET command [5m, none].

TimeZoneSpec (t*tzinfo*)

> Set the local time zone to *tzinfo*, for example, PST8PDT. Actually, if
> this option is not set, the TZ environment variable is cleared (so the
> system default is used); if set but null, use the user's TZ variable, and
> if set and non-null, set the TZ variable to this value.

TryNullMXList (w)

> If you are the "best" (that is, lowest preference) MX for a given host, you
> should normally detect this situation and treat that condition
> specially by forwarding the mail to a UUCP feed, treating it as local or
> whatever is appropriate. However, in some cases (such as Internet
> firewalls) you may want to try to connect directly to that host as
> though it had no MX records at all. Setting this option tries a direct
> connection. The downside is that errors in your configuration are
> likely to be diagnosed as "host unknown" or "message timed out"
> instead of something more meaningful. This option is deprecated.

`UnixFromLine or $l`

> Use the `From:` line when sending to files or programs.

`UnsafeGroupWrites`

> Consider group-writeable `:include:` and `.forward` files unsafe; that is, programs and files cannot be directly referenced from such files.

`UseErrorsTo (l)`

> If there is an `Errors-To:` header, send error messages to the addresses listed there. They normally go to the envelope sender. Use of this option violates RFC 1123.

`UserDatabaseSpec (U)`

> Define the name and location of the file containing User Database information.

`Verbose (v)`   Run in verbose mode. Adjust the `HoldExpensive` and `DeliveryMode` options so that all mail is delivered completely in a single job so that you can see the entire delivery process. You should never set the Verbose option in the configuration file; it is intended for command-line use only.

You can specify all options on the command line with the `-o` option, but most relinquish `sendmail` setuid permissions. The options that do not do this are b, d, e, E, i, L, m, o, p, r, s, v, C, and 7. Also considered "safe" is M (define macro) when defining the r or s macros.

If the first character of the user name is a vertical bar, use the rest of the user name as the name of a program to pipe the mail to. You may need to quote the name of the user to keep `sendmail` from suppressing the blanks between arguments.

If invoked as `newaliases`, `sendmail` rebuilds the alias database as long as the `/etc/mail/aliases*` files are owned by root and root has exclusive write permission. If invoked as `mailq`, `sendmail` prints the contents of the mail queue.

Operands

`address`   Address of an intended recipient of the message being sent.

Usage

See `largefile(5)` for the description of the behavior of `sendmail` when encountering files greater than or equal to 2 Gbytes (2**31 bytes).

Exit Status

`sendmail` returns an exit status describing what it did. The codes are defined in `/usr/include/sysexits.h`.

`EX_OK`   Successful completion on all addresses.

`EX_NOUSER`   User name not recognized.

`EX_UNAVAILABLE`

> Catchall. Necessary resources were not available.

EX_SYNTAX	Syntax error in address.
EX_SOFTWARE	Internal software error, including bad arguments.
EX_OSERR	Temporary operating system error, such as `cannot fork`.
EX_NOHOST	Host name not recognized.
EX_TEMPFAIL	Message could not be sent immediately but was queued.

Files

`dead.letter`	Unmailable text.
`/etc/mail/aliasesq`	
	Mail aliases file (ASCII).
`/etc/mail/aliases.dir`	
	Database of mail aliases (binary).
`/etc/mail/aliases.pag`	
	Database of mail aliases (binary).
`/etc/mail/sendmail.cf`	
	Defines environment for `sendmail`.
`/var/spool/mqueue/*`	
	Temp files and queued mail.
`~/.forward`	List of recipients for forwarding messages.

Attributes

See `attributes`(5) for descriptions of the following attributes.

Attribute Type	Attribute Value
Availability	SUNWsndmu

See Also

New!

`mail(1)`, `mailx(1)`, `newaliases(1)`, `biff(1B)`, `checkhostname(1M)`, `check-permissions(1M)`,`getusershell(3C)`,`resolver(3RESOLV)`,`aliases(4)`, `hosts(4)`, `attributes(5)`, `largefile(5)`

Postel, Jon, *Simple Mail Transfer Protocol*, RFC 821, Network Information Center, SRI International, Menlo Park, Calif., August 1982.

Crocker, Dave, *Standard for the Format of ARPA-Internet Text Messages,* RFC 822, Network Information Center, SRI International, Menlo Park, Calif., August 1982.

Costales, Bryan, with Allman, Eric, *sendmail, Second Edition*, O'Reilly & Associates, Inc., 1997.

server_upgrade — Upgrade Clients of a Heterogeneous OS Server

Synopsis

```
/usr/sbin/server_upgrade -d install-image-dir [-p profile]
```

Description

When performing JumpStart installations, use the server_upgrade command to upgrade clients of a heterogeneous OS server that has different platforms (for example, SPARC or IA platforms) or platform groups (for example, sun4d, sun4L) from the OS server. This command is needed because clients of an OS server are not upgraded during a standard upgrade if the installation image does not support their platform or platform group.

The following steps describe how to use the server_upgrade command to perform a standard upgrade of an OS server and clients, followed by the steps for upgrading clients with different platforms and platform groups. The steps assume you are mounting the Solaris CD locally, remotely, or otherwise making it available.

1. Using the Solaris CD that matches the platform of the OS server, boot the OS server and perform a standard upgrade. Only clients that have the same platform and platform group supported on the installation image are upgraded. For example, when you boot a SPARC-based server from a Solaris SPARC CD; all clients that are SPARC-based and share the same platform group are upgraded.

2. Reboot the OS server.

3. Insert a platform-specific CD into the CD-ROM drive. For example, if the OS server is a SPARC-based system that shares services for both SPARC- and IA-based clients, you would load the IA Solaris CD.

4. At the root prompt, type

   server_upgrade -d *install-image-dir* [-p *profile*]

   The command upgrades the platform-specific services for clients on the OS server from the installation image.

5. Reboot the OS server.

6. Repeat steps 3-5 to upgrade platforms or platform groups of other clients.

Options

-p *profile*   Specify the full path to a custom JumpStart profile (a text file that defines how to install Solaris software on a system). For information on setting up a profile, see *Installing Solaris Software*. Note that the profile must have the keyword set to upgrade.

-d *install-image-dir*

Specify the path to the installation image. For example, /cdrom/cdrom0.

Examples

The following example shows the states of a SPARC-based OS server and its clients each time the `server_upgrade` command is used to upgrade clients. The scenario uses the `server_upgrade` command once to upgrade a client with an IA platform and once to upgrade a client with a different platform group (`sun4L`).

Initial State of the Solaris Operating Environment

The OS server is a `sparc.sun4d`, running the Solaris 2.4 Operating Environment, sharing the following services.

```
> Solaris 2.4 for sparc.{sun4c, sun4d, sun4e, sun4m, and sun4L}
> Solaris 2.4 for i386.i86pc
> Solaris 2.3 for sparc.{sun4c, sun4d, sun4e, sun4m}
```

The clients are in the following initial states.

Host Name	Platform	Release Level
red	sparc.sun4c	Solaris 2.4 Operating Environment
blue	sparc.sun4e	Solaris 2.4 Operating Environment
yellow	sparc.sun4L	Solaris 2.4 Operating Environment
green	i386.i86pc	Solaris 2.4 Operating Environment
purple	sparc.sun4c	Solaris 2.3 Operating Environment
brown	sparc.sun4e	Solaris 2.3 Operating Environment

Upgrade the 2.4 OS Server to 2.5

Use the SPARC Solaris 2.5 CD to upgrade the Solaris 2.4 OS server, then reboot the OS server.

After the OS server is rebooted, it is running the Solaris 2.5 Operating Environment and sharing the following services.

```
> Solaris 2.5 for sparc.{sun4c, sun4d, sun4m}
> Solaris 2.3 for sparc.{sun4c, sun4d, sun4e, sun4m}
```

The clients are in the following states. The asterisks in the following tables indicate systems that change state after the `server_upgrade` command is run.

Host Name	Platform	Release Level	State
* red	sparc.sun4c	Solaris 2.5	Bootable.
blue	sparc.sun4e	Solaris 2.4	Not bootable.
yellow	sparc.sun4L	Solaris 2.4	Not bootable.
green	i386.i86pc	Solaris 2.4	Not bootable.
* purple	sparc.sun4c	Solaris 2.5	Bootable.
* brown	sparc.sun4e	Solaris 2.3	Bootable.

Note — Client brown can still be booted because it is running the Solaris 2.3 Operating Environment, which is supported by the OS server, and because this release supports sun4e.

Upgrade the IA Clients and Services
Insert the IA Solaris 2.5 CD and type the following command.

server_upgrade -d /cdrom/cdrom0

After the OS server is rebooted, it is running the Solaris 2.5 Operating Environment and sharing the following services.

```
> Solaris 2.5 for sparc.{sun4c, sun4d, sun4m}
> Solaris 2.5 for i386.i86pc
> Solaris 2.3 for sparc.{sun4c, sun4d, sun4e, sun4m}
```

The clients are in the following states.

Host Name	Platform	Release Level	State
red	sparc.sun4c	Solaris 2.5	Bootable.
blue	sparc.sun4e	Solaris 2.4	Not bootable.
yellow	sparc.sun4L	Solaris 2.4	Not bootable.
* green	i386.i86pc	Solaris 2.5	Bootable.
purple	sparc.sun4c	Solaris 2.5	Bootable.
brown	sparc.sun4e	Solaris 2.3	Bootable.

Upgrade the sun4L (Hardware Partner) Client
Insert the Hardware Edition Solaris 2.5 CD and type the following command.

server_upgrade -d /cdrom/cdrom0

After rebooting the OS server, it is running the Solaris 2.5 Operating Environment and sharing the following services.

```
> Solaris 2.5 for sparc.{sun4c, sun4d, sun4m, sun4L}
> Solaris 2.5 for i386.i86pc
> Solaris 2.3 for sparc.{sun4c, sun4d, sun4e, sun4m}
```

The clients are in the following states.

Host name	Platform	Release Level	State
red	sparc.sun4c	Solaris 2.5	Bootable.
blue	sparc.sun4e	Solaris 2.4	Not bootable.
* yellow	sparc.sun4L	Solaris 2.5	Bootable.
green	i386.i86pc	Solaris 2.5	Bootable.

Host name	Platform	Release Level	State
purple	sparc.sun4c	Solaris 2.5	Bootable.
brown	sparc.sun4e	Solaris 2.3	Bootable.

State of sun4e Clients

Client `blue` is not bootable because `sun4e` systems are not supported by the Solaris 2.5 Operating Environment. However, you can make it bootable again by using the Solstice Host Manager and adding the Solaris 2.4 services to the OS server.

Attributes

See `attributes`(5) for descriptions of the following attributes.

Attribute Type	Attribute Value
Availability	SUNWcsu

setmnt — Establish Mount Table

Synopsis

```
/usr/sbin/setmnt
```

Description

The `setmnt` command creates the `/etc/mnttab` table that is needed for both the `mount` and `umount` commands. `setmnt` reads standard input and creates a `mnttab` entry for each line. Input lines have the following format.

```
filesys node
```

where *filesys* is the name of the file system's special file (such as `/dev/dsk/c?d?s?`) and *node* is the root name of that file system. Thus, *filesys* and *node* become the first two strings in the mount table entry.

The setmnt command is run automatically when a system is booted; there is no reason to run the command manually.

Files

`/etc/mnttab`   Mount table.

Attributes

See `attributes`(5) for descriptions of the following attributes.

Attribute Type	Attribute Value
Availability	SUNWcsu

See Also

mount(1M), attributes(5)

Bugs

Problems may occur if *filesys* or *node* are longer than 32 characters. setmnt silently enforces an upper limit on the maximum number of mnttab entries.

setuname — Change System Information

Synopsis

setuname [-t][-n *node*][-s *name*]

Description

Use the setuname command to change the system name or the node name in real time. You must specify either or both the -s and -n options when invoking setuname.

If you omit the -t option, any change is permanent. Otherwise, only the name in the running kernel is changed.

The system architecture may put requirements on the size of the system and network node name. The command issues a fatal warning message and an error message if the name entered is incompatible with the system requirements.

Note — setuname tries to change the parameter values in two places: the running kernel and, as necessary per implementation, to cross-system reboots. A temporary change changes only the running kernel.

Options

-t	Temporary change. Do not create a permanent change.
-n *node*	Change the node name. *node* specifies the new network node name and can consist of alphanumeric characters and the special characters dash (-), underbar (_), and dollar sign ($).
-s *name*	Change the system name. *name* specifies a new system name and can consist of alphanumeric characters and the special characters dash, underbar, and dollar sign.

Examples

Once, a user made a change to a system that trashed the host name. uname -n displayed uname instead of production, which was the real host name even though /etc/hostname/.le0 had the correct entry, /etc/nodename had the correct entry, and /etc/hosts had the correct entry.

The following example used setuname to fix the problem.

```
# setuname -s production
#
```

Attributes

See attributes(5) for descriptions of the following attributes.

Attribute Type	Attribute Value
Availability	SUNWcsu (32 bit)
	SUNWcsxu (64-bit)

See Also

attributes(5)

---

setup_install_server — Script to Copy the Solaris CD to a Disk

Synopsis

cdrom-mnt-pt/Solaris_8/Tools/setup_install_server [-b] install-dir-path

Description

See install_scripts(1M).

---

share — Make Local Resource Available for Remote Mounting

Synopsis

share [-F FSType] [-o specific-options] [-d description] [pathname]

Description

Use the share command to export a resource or make it available for mounting through a remote file system of type FSType. If you omit the -F FSType option, the first file-system type listed in /etc/dfs/fstypes is used as the default. For a description of NFS-specific options, see share_nfs(1M). pathname is the path name of the directory to be shared. When invoked with no arguments, share displays all shared file systems.

Notes

File-system sharing used to be called exporting on SunOS 4.x, so the share command used to be invoked as exportfs(1B) or /usr/sbin/exportfs.

If share commands are invoked multiple times on the same file system, the last share invocation supersedes the previous; the options set by the last share command replace the old options. For example, if read-write permission was given to usera on /somefs, then the following command also gives read-write permission to userb on /somefs.

paperbark% **share -F nfs -o rw=usera:userb /somefs**

This behavior is not limited to sharing the root file system, but applies to all file systems.

Options

-F *FSType* Specify the file-system type.

-o *specific-options*

Use the *specific-options* to control access of the shared resource. (See share_nfs(1M) for the NFS-specific options.) The specific options can be any of the following.

rw Share *pathname* read/write to all clients. The default.

rw=*client*[:*client*]...

Share *pathname* read/write only to the listed clients. No other systems can access *pathname*.

ro Share *pathname* read-only to all clients.

ro=*client*[:*client*]...

Share *pathname* read-only only to the listed clients. No other systems can access *pathname*.

-d *description*

Provide a description of the resource being shared.

Examples

The following example shares the /disk file system read-only at boot time.

share -F nfs -o ro /disk

Files

/etc/dfs/dfstab

List of share commands to be executed at boot time.

/etc/dfs/fstypes

List of file-system types, NFS by default.

`/etc/dfs/sharetab`

> System record of shared file systems.

Attributes

See `attributes`(5) for descriptions of the following attributes

Attribute Type	Attribute Value
Availability	SUNWcsu

See Also

`mountd(1M)`, `nfsd(1M)`, `share_nfs(1M)`, `shareall(1M)`, `unshare(1M)`, `attributes(5)`

---

share_nfs — Make Local NFS File Systems Available for Remote Mounting

Synopsis

```
share [-d description][-F nfs][-o specific-options] pathname
```

Description

Use the `share` command to make local file systems available for mounting by remote systems.

If you specify no argument, then `share` displays all file systems currently shared, including NFS file systems and file systems shared through other distributed file-system packages.

Notes

If you specify the `sec=` option at least once, all uses of the `window=`, `rw`, `ro`, `rw=`, `ro=`, and `root=` options must come after the first `sec=` option. If you do not specify the `sec=` option, then `sec=sys` is implied.

If you specify one or more explicit `sec=` options, you must include `sys` in one of the options mode lists to allow access through use of the AUTH_SYS security mode. For example, the following commands grant read-write access to any host using AUTH_SYS.

```
share -F nfs /var
share -F nfs -o sec=sys /var
```

The following command, however, grants no access to clients that use AUTH_SYS.

```
share -F nfs -o sec=dh /var
```

Unlike previous implementations of `share_nfs`(1M), access checking for the `window=`, `rw`, `ro`, `rw=`, and `ro=` options is done per NFS request, instead of per mount request.

Combining multiple security modes can be a security hole in situations where the ro= and rw= options are used to control access to weaker security modes. In the following example, an intruder can forge the IP address for hosta (albeit on each NFS request) and side step the stronger controls of AUTH_DES.

```
share -F nfs -o sec=dh,rw,sec=sys,rw=hosta /var
```

The following example is safer because any client (intruder or legitimate) that avoids AUTH_DES gets only read-only access.

```
share -F nfs -o sec=dh,rw,sec=sys,ro /var
```

In general, you should use multiple security modes per share command only in situations where the clients using more secure modes get stronger access than clients using less secure modes.

If you specify rw= and ro= options in the same sec= clause and a client is in both lists, the order of the two options determines the access the client gets. If client hosta is in two netgroups—group1 and group2—in the following example, the client would get read-only access.

```
share -F nfs -o ro=group1,rw=group2 /var
```

In the following example, hosta would get read-write access.

```
share -F nfs -o rw=group2,ro=group1 /var
```

If within a sec= clause, you specify both the ro and rw= options, for compatibility, the order of the options rule is not enforced. All hosts would get read-only access, with the exception of those in the read-write list. Likewise, if you specify the ro= and rw options, all hosts get read-write access with the exceptions of those in the read-only list.

The ro= and rw= options are guaranteed to work over UDP and TCP but may not work over other transport providers.

The root= option with AUTH_SYS is guaranteed to work over UDP and TCP but may not work over other transport providers.

The root= option with AUTH_DES and AUTH_KERB is guaranteed to work over any transport provider.

There are no interactions between the root= option and the rw, ro, rw=, and ro= options. Putting a host in the root list does not override the semantics of the other options. The access the host gets is the same as when the root= options is absent. For example, the following share command denies access to hostb.

```
share -F nfs -o ro=hosta,root=hostb /var
```

The following command gives read-only permissions to hostb.

```
share -F nfs -o ro=hostb,root=hostb /var
```

The following command gives read-write permissions to hostb.

```
share -F nfs -o ro=hosta,rw=hostb,root=hostb /var
```

If the file system being shared is a symbolic link to a valid path name, the canonical path (the path which the symbolic link follows) is shared. For example, if /export/foo is a symbolic link to /export/bar (/export/foo -> /export/bar), the following share command uses /export/bar as the shared path name (and not /export/foo).

```
# share -F nfs /export/foo
```

Note that an NFS mount of `server:/export/foo` really mounts
`server:/export/bar`.

The following line in the `/etc/dfs/dfstab` file shares the `/disk` file system
read-only at boot time.

```
share -F nfs -o ro /disk
```

Note — The same command entered from the command line does not share
the `/disk` file system unless there is at least one file-system entry in the
`/etc/dfs/dfstab` file. The `mountd`(1M) and `nfsd`(1M) daemons run only if
there is a file-system entry in `/etc/dfs/dfstab` when starting or rebooting
the system.

Options

`-d description`

> Provide a comment that describes the file system to be shared.

`-F nfs`   Share NFS file-system type.

`-o specific-options`

> Specify `specific-options` as a comma-separated list of `keywords`
> and attribute values for interpretation by the
> file-system-type-specific command. If you do not specify
> `specific-options`, then by default, sharing is read-write to all
> clients. `specific-options` can be any combination of the following.

> `aclok`   Allow the NFS server to do access control for NFS
>   Version 2 clients (running SunOS 2.4 or earlier).
>   When `aclok` is set on the server, give maximal
>   access to all clients. For example, with `aclok` set, if
>   anyone has read permissions, then everyone does.
>   If `aclok` is not set, give minimal access to all
>   clients.

> `anon=uid`   Set `uid` to be the effective user ID of unknown
>   users. By default, unknown users are given the
>   effective user ID UID_NOBODY. If `uid` is set to -1,
>   deny access.

> `index=file`   Load `file` instead of a listing of the directory
>   containing this file when the directory is referenced
>   by an NFS URL.

> `kerberos`   This option has been deprecated in favor of the
>   `sec=krb4` option.

> `nosub`   Prevent clients from mounting subdirectories of
>   shared directories. For example, if `/export` is
>   shared with the `nosub` option on server `fooey`, then
>   an NFS client is not able to do the following.

> ```
> mount -F nfs fooey:/export/home/mnt
> ```

nosuid   Silently ignore any attempts to enable the setuid or setgid mode bits. By default, clients are allowed to create files on the shared file system with the setuid or setgid mode enabled.

public   Enable NFS browsing of the file system by a Web NFS-enabled browser. Only one file system per server can use this option. You can include the -ro=list and -rw=list options with this option.

ro   Share read-only to all clients.

ro=*access-list*

Share read-only to the clients listed in *access-list*; overrides the rw suboption for the clients specified. See *access-list* below.

root=*access-list*

Allow root access only to root users from the hosts specified in *access-list*. See *access-list* below. By default, no host has root access, so root users are mapped to an anonymous user ID (see the anon=*uid* option). Netgroups can be used if the file system shared is using UNIX authentication (AUTH_SYS).

rw   Share read-write to all clients.

rw=*access-list*

Share read-write to the clients listed in *access-list*; overrides the ro suboption for the specified clients. See *access-list* below.

sec=*mode*[:*mode*]...

Use one or more of the specified security modes. The mode in the sec=*mode* option must be a node name supported on the client. If you do not specify the sec= option, the default security mode used is AUTH_SYS. You can specify multiple sec= options on the command line, although each mode can appear only once. The security modes are defined in nfssec(5).

Each sec= option specifies modes that apply to any subsequent window=, rw, ro, rw=, ro=, and root= options that are provided before another sec= option. Each additional sec= resets the security mode context, so that more window=, rw, ro, rw=, ro= and root= options can be supplied for additional modes.

sec=*none*	If specified when the client uses AUTH_NONE or if the client uses a security mode that is not one with which the file system is shared, then treat the credential of each NFS request as unauthenticated. See the anon=*uid* option for a description of how unauthenticated requests are handled.
secure	This option has been deprecated in favor of the sec=dh option.
window=*value*	When sharing with sec=dh or sec=krb4, set the maximum lifetime (in seconds) of the RPC request's credential (in the authentication header) that the NFS server allows. If a credential arrives with a lifetime larger than that allowed, the NFS server rejects the request. The default value is 30000 seconds (8.3 hours).

Access List

The *access-list* is a colon-separated list whose components can be any number of the following.

hostname	The name of a host. With a server configured for DNS naming in the nsswitch hosts entry, any host name must be represented as a fully qualified DNS name.
netgroup	A number of host names. With a server configured for DNS naming in the nsswitch hosts entry, any host name in a netgroup must be represented as a fully qualified DNS name.
DNS suffix	To use domain membership, the server must use DNS to resolve host names to IP addresses; that is, the hosts entry in /etc/nsswitch.conf specifies dns ahead of nis or nisplus because only DNS returns the full domain name of the host. You cannot use other nameservices like NIS or NIS+ to resolve host names on the server because when mapping an IP address to a host name, they do not return domain information. For example,

NIS or NIS+ 129.144.45.9 --> myhost

DNS 129.144.45.9 --> myhost.mydomain.mycompany.com

The DNS suffix is distinguished from host names and netgroups by a prefixed dot. For example,

rw=.mydomain.mycompany.com

You can use a single dot to match a host name with no suffix. For example,

rw=.

matches mydomain but not mydomain.mycompany.com. You can use this feature to match hosts resolved through NIS and NIS+ instead of DNS.

network | The network or subnet component is preceded by an at-sign (@). It can be either a name or a dotted address. If a name, it is converted to a dotted address by getnetbyname(3N). For example,

=@mynet

is equivalent to

=@129.144 or =@129.144.0.0

The network prefix assumes an octet-aligned netmask determined from the zero octets in the low-order part of the address. In the case where network prefixes are not byte aligned, the syntax enables you to explicitly specify a mask length following a slash (/) delimiter. For example,

=@mynet/17 or rw=@129.144.132/17

where the mask is the number of leftmost contiguous significant bits in the corresponding IP address.

A prefixed minus sign (-) denies access to that component of *access-list*. The list is searched sequentially until a match is found that either grants or denies access or until the end of the list is reached. For example, if host terra is in the engineering netgroup, then

rw=-terra:engineering

denies access to terra but

rw=engineering:-terra

grants access to terra.

Operands

pathname | The path name of the file system to be shared.

Exit Status

0 | Successful completion.

>0 | An error occurred.

Files

/etc/dfs/fstypes

List of system types, NFS by default.

/etc/dfs/sharetab

System record of shared file systems.

Attributes

See attributes(5) for descriptions of the following attributes.

Attribute Type	Attribute Value
Availability	SUNWcsu

See Also

mount(1M), mountd(1M), nfsd(1M), share(1M), unshare(1M), getnetbyname(3N), netgroup(4), attributes(5), nfssec(5)

shareall, unshareall — Share, Unshare Multiple Resources

Synopsis

```
shareall [-F FSType [,FSType...]][-| file]
unshareall [-F FSType [,FSType...]]
```

Description

When used with no arguments, shareall shares all resources from *file*, which contains a list of share command lines. If the operand is a dash (-), then the share command lines are obtained from the standard input. Otherwise, if you specify neither a file nor a dash, then the file /etc/dfs/dfstab is used as the default.

Resources can be shared by specific file-system types by specification of the file systems in a comma-separated list as an argument to -F.

unshareall unshares all currently shared resources. Without a -F option, it unshares resources for all distributed file-system types.

Options

-F *FSType*   Specify file-system type. Default is the first entry in /etc/dfs/fstypes.

Files

/etc/dfs/dfstab

        File containing commands for sharing resources across a network.

Attributes

See attributes(5) for descriptions of the following attributes.

Attribute Type	Attribute Value
Availability	SUNWcsu

See Also

share(1M), unshare(1M), attributes(5)

---

showmount — Show All Remote Mounts

Synopsis

/usr/sbin/showmount [-ade] [*hostname*]

Description

Use the showmount command to list all the clients that have remotely mounted a file system from *hostname*. This information is maintained by the mountd(1M) server on *hostname* and is saved across crashes in the file /etc/rmtab. The default value for *hostname* is the value returned by hostname(1).

Options

-a	Print all remote mounts in the format
	hostname:*directory*
	where *hostname* is the name of the client and *directory* is the root of the file system that has been mounted.
-d	List directories that have been remotely mounted by clients.
-e	Print the list of shared file systems.

Examples

The following example lists all clients and the local directories that they have mounted.

```
# showmount -a bee
lilac:/export/share/man
lilac:/usr/src
rose:/usr/src
tulip:/export/share/man
#
```

The following example lists the directories that have been mounted.

```
# showmount -d bee
/export/share/man
/usr/src
#
```

The following example lists file systems that have been shared.

```
 # showmount -e bee
/usr/src        (everyone)
/export/share/man    eng
#
```

Files

/etc/rmtab   List of clients that have remotely mounted a system from *hostname*.

Attributes

See attributes(5) for descriptions of the following attributes.

Attribute Type	Attribute Value
Availability	SUNWcsu

See Also

hostname(1), mountd(1M), attributes(5)
Solaris Advanced Installation Guide

Bugs

If a client crashes, its entry is not removed from the list of remote mounts on the server.

---

showrev — Show Machine and Software Revision Information

Synopsis

/usr/bin/showrev [-a][-p][-w][-c *command*][-s *hostname*]

Description

Use the showrev command to display revision information for the current hardware and software. With no arguments, showrev shows the system revision information including host name, host ID, release, kernel architecture, application architecture, hardware provider, domain, and kernel version.

If you supply a command with the -c option, showrev shows the PATH and LD_LIBRARY_PATH and finds out all the directories within the PATH that contain it. For each file found, its file type, revision, permissions, library information, and checksum are printed as well.

Options

-a	Print all system revision information available. Add window system and patch information.
-p	Print only the revision information about patches.
-w	Print only the OpenWindows revision information.
-c *command*	Print the revision information about *command*.
-s *hostname*	Perform this operation on the specified *hostname*. The -s operation completes correctly only when *hostname* is running the Solaris 2.5 Operating Environment or compatible versions.

Examples

The following example shows the output of the showrev command with no options on the system paperbark.

```
paperbark% showrev
Hostname: paperbark
Hostid: 807d79d4
Release: 5.8
Kernel architecture: sun4u
Application architecture: sparc
Hardware provider: Sun_Microsystems
Domain: wellard.COM
Kernel version: SunOS 5.8 Generic February 2000
paperbark%
```

The following example shows the output of the showrev -a command on the system paperbark.

```
paperbark% showrev -a
Hostname: paperbark
Hostid: 807d79d4
Release: 5.8
Kernel architecture: sun4u
Application architecture: sparc
Hardware provider: Sun_Microsystems
Domain:
Kernel version: SunOS 5.8 Generic February 2000

OpenWindows version:
X11 Version 6.4.1 15 December 1999

No patches are installed
paperbark%
```

The following example shows the output of the showrev -c command for the /opt directory on the system paperbark.

```
paperbark% showrev -c /opt

PATH is:
/usr/openwin/bin:/usr/dt/bin:/export/home/opt/SUNWadm/bin:/bin:/usr/bin
  :/usr/sbin:/usr/ucb:/etc:/usr/proc/bin:/usr/ccs/bin:/opt/hpnp/bin:/op
  t/NSCPcom:/usr/local/games:.

PWD is:
/export/home/winsor

LD_LIBRARY_PATH is not set in the current environment
```

```
File: /opt
==========
File type: directory
File mode: rwxrwxr-x
User owning file: root
```

```
Group owning file: sys
Sum: 6592
```

paperbark%

Exit Status

0	Successful completion.
>0	An error occurred.

Attributes

See attributes(5) for descriptions of the following attributes.

Attribute Type	Attribute Value
Availability	SUNWadmc

See Also

arch(1), ldd(1), mcs(1), sum(1), patchadd(1M), attributes(5)   *New!*

Bugs

For the -s option to work when *hostname* is running a version of the Solaris Operating Environment before 2.5, the Solstice AdminSuite must be installed on *hostname*.

---

shutacct — Turn Process Accounting Off at Shutdown

Synopsis

/usr/lib/acct/shutacct ["*reason*"]

Description

See acctsh(1M).

---

shutdown — Shut Down System, Change System State

Synopsis

/usr/sbin/shutdown [-y][-g *grace-period*][-i *init-state*][*message*]

Description

Use the shutdown command as superuser to change the state of the machine. In most cases, you use the shutdown command to change from the multiuser state (state 2) to another state.

By default, shutdown brings the system to a state where only the console has access to the operating system. This state is called single-user.

Before starting to shut down daemons and killing processes, shutdown sends a warning message and, by default, a final message asking for confirmation. *message* is a string that is sent out following the standard warning message The system will be shut down in..." If the string contains more than one word, you should enclose it in single (') or double (") quotation marks.

The warning message and the user provided message are output when there are 7200, 3600, 1800, 1200, 600, 300, 120, 60, and 30 seconds remaining before shutdown begins.

The system state definitions are described below.

state 0   Stop the operating system.

state 1   The administrative state. Mount file systems required for multiuser operations. Logins requiring access to multiuser file systems can be used. When the system comes up from firmware mode into state 1, only the console is active and other multiuser (state 2) services are unavailable. Note that not all user processes are stopped when transitioning from multiuser state to state 1.

state s, S   The single-user state. Stop all user processes on transitions to this state. Unmount file systems required for multiuser logins. Permit access to the system only through the console. Logins requiring access to multiuser file systems cannot be used.

state 5   Shut the machine down so that it is safe to remove the power. Have the machine remove power if possible. The rc0 procedure is called to perform this task.

state 6   Stop the operating system and reboot to the state defined by the initdefault entry in /etc/inittab. The rc6 procedure is called to perform this task.

Options

-y   Pre-answer the confirmation question so the command can be run without user intervention.

-g *grace-period*

              Specify the number of seconds for the grace period. The default is 60.

-i *init-state*

              If there are warnings, *init-state* specifies the state init is to be in. By default, use system state s.

Examples

In the following example, shutdown is being executed on host paperbark and is scheduled in 120 seconds. The warning message is output 2 minutes, 1 minute, and 30 seconds before the final confirmation message.

```
# shutdown -i S -g 120 "===== disk replacement ======"

Shutdown started.   Wed Dec 29 16:43:06 WST 1999

Broadcast Message from root (pts/6) on paperbark Wed Dec 29 16:43:06...
The system paperbark will be shut down in 2 minutes
===== disk replacement ======
Broadcast Message from root (pts/6) on paperbark Wed Dec 29 16:44:07...
The system paperbark will be shut down in 1 minute
===== disk replacement ======
Broadcast Message from root (pts/6) on paperbark Wed Dec 29 16:44:37...
The system paperbark will be shut down in 30 seconds
===== disk replacement ======
Do you want to continue? (y or n):
```

If you answer **n** to the Do you want to continue? question, the following message is displayed.

```
False Alarm:  The system paperbark will not be brought down.
```

Files

/etc/inittab Controls process dispatching by init.

Attributes

See attributes(5) for descriptions of the following attributes.

Attribute Type	Attribute Value
Availability	SUNWcsu

See Also

boot(1M), halt(1M), init(1M), killall(1M), reboot(1M), ufsdump(1M), init.d(4), inittab(4), nologin(4), attributes(5)

slpd — Service Location Protocol Daemon

New!

Synopsis

/usr/lib/inet/slpd [-f configuration-file]

Description

The slpd command is new in the Solaris 8 release. The slpd daemon provides common server functionality for the Service Location Protocol (SLP) versions 1 and 2, as defined by IETF in RFC 2165 and RFC 2608. SLP provides a scalable framework for the discovery and selection of network services.

slpd provides the following framework services.

Directory Agent

> This service automatically caches service advertisements from service agents to provide them to user agents and makes directory agent advertisements of its services. This service is optional. slpd does not provide directory agent service by default. Directory agents are not databases, and they do not need to be maintained.

Service Agent Server

> All service agents on the local host register and deregister with this server. This service responds to all requests for services and forwards registrations to directory agents. By default, slpd is a service agent server.

Passive Directory Agent Discovery

> This service listens for directory agent advertisements and maintains a table of active directory agents. When a user agent wants to discover a directory agent, it can simply query slpd, obviating the need to perform discovery by means of multicast. By default, slpd performs this service.

Proxy Registration

> This service can act as a proxy service agent for services that cannot register themselves. slpd reads the proxy registration file for information on services it is to proxy. By default, no services are registered by proxy.

All configuration options are available from the configuration file. slpd reads its configuration file on startup.

Stop and start the slpd daemon by using the startup script /etc/init.d/slpd. Use the command /etc/init.d/slpd stop to stop the slpd daemon. Use the command /etc/init.d/slpd start to start it.

The /etc/inet/slp.conf file must exist before the startup script can start the daemon. Only the example file /etc/inet/slp.conf.example is present by default. To enable SLP, copy /etc/inet/slp.conf.example to /etc/inet/slp.conf.

Options

-f configuration-file

> Specify an alternate configuration file

Examples

The following example stops the `slpd` daemon.

```
# /etc/init.d/slpd stop
#
```

The following example restarts the `slpd` daemon.

```
# /etc/init.d/slpd start
#
```

Files

`/etc/inet/slp.conf`

> The default configuration file.

`slpd.reg`   The proxy registration file.

Attributes

See `attributes(5)` for descriptions of the following attributes.

Attribute Type	Attribute Value
Availability	SUNWslpr
Stability	Evolving

See Also

`slp_api(3SLP)`, `slp.conf(4)`, `slpd.reg(4)`, `attributes(5)`, `slp(7P)`
Service Location Protocol Administration Guide
Guttman, E., Perkins, C., Veizades, J., and Day, M., RFC 2608, *Service Location Protocol, Version 2*, The Internet Society, June 1999.

smartcard — Configure and Administer a Smartcard   *New!*

Synopsis

```
smartcard -c admin [-a application][propertyname...]
smartcard -c admin [-a application][-x {add|delete|modify}
    propertyname=value...]
smartcard -c admin -t service -j classname -x {add|delete|modify}
smartcard -c admin -t terminal -j classname -d device -r
    userfriendlyreadername -n readername -x {add|delete|modify} [-R]
smartcard -c admin -t debug -j classname -l level -x {add|delete|modify}
smartcard -c admin -t override -x {add|delete|modify} propertyname=value
smartcard -c admin -I -k keytype -i filename
smartcard -c admin -E -k keytype -o filename
smartcard -c load -A aid [-r userfriendlyreadername] -P pin [-s slot]
    [-i inputfile][-p propfile][-v][propertyname=value...]
```

```
smartcard -c load -u -P pin [-A aid][-r userfriendlyreadername]
   [-s slot][-v]
smartcard -c bin2capx -T cardname [-i inputfile][-o outputfile]
   [-p propfile][-I anothercapxfile][-v][propertyname=value...]
smartcard -c init -A aid [-r readername][-s slot] -L
smartcard -c init -A aid [-r readername] -P pin [-s slot]
   [propertyname=value...]
smartcard -c enable
smartcard -c disable
smartcard -D
```

Description

The smartcard command is new in the Solaris 8 release. Use it for all configurations related to a smartcard. Use the subcommands to perform the tasks described below.

1. Administering OCF properties. (-c admin).

   Use this subcommand to list and modify any of the OCF properties. With no arguments it lists all the current properties. Only root can execute this subcommand. Some OCF properties are listed below.

defaultcard	Default card for an application.
defaultreader	Default reader for an application.
authmechanism	Authentication mechanism.
validcards	List of cards valid for an application.

   You can display a complete listing of the properties and their values with the smartcard -c admin command.

2. Loading and unloading applets from the smartcard (-c load) and performing initial configuration of a non-Java card.

   Use this subcommand to administer the applets or properties on a smartcard. You can use it to load or unload applets or properties to and from a smartcard. The applet is a java class file that has been run through a converter to make the byte code Java Card compliant. You can use this command to load both an applet file in the standard format or a file converted to the capx format. If you specify no -r option, the loader tries to load to any connected reader, provided it has already been inserted with the smartcard -c admin command.

3. Converting card applets or properties to the capx format (-c bin2capx)

   Use this subcommand to convert a Java Card applet or properties into a new format called capx before downloading it onto the smartcard. Converting to this format enables the applet developer to add applet-specific information that is useful during the downloading process and that identifies the applet.

   In the following example, if you do not specify an output file, a default file with the name input_file.capx is created in the current directory. The mandatory -T option requires you to specify the card name for which the capx file is being generated.

   ```
   smartcard -c bin2capx -i cyberflex.bin -T CyberFlex
      aidto-00010203040506070809A0B0C0D0E0F fileID=2222
      instanceID=2223
   ```

The following example tells the loader eventually that the capx file contains the binary for IButton. A single capx file can hold binaries for multiple cards (1 binary per card.)

smartcard -c bin2capx -T IButton

Users can hold binary files for both CyberFlex and IButton in the same capx file, as shown in the following example.

smartcard -c bin2capx -T IButton -i IButton.jib -o file.capx

The following example uses the -l option to provide an already generated capx file. The output is directed to the same capx file, resulting in capx file holding binaries for both cards.

smartcard -c bin2capx -T CyberFlex -i cyberflex.bin -l file.capx
**   -o file.capx**

4. Personalizing the smartcard (-c init).

   Use this subcommand to set user-specific information required by an applet on a smartcard. For example, the Sun applet requires a user name to be set on the card. Also use this subcommand to personalize information for non-Java cards.

5. Enabling and disabling the host for smartcard (-c {enable | disable}).

Note — The command-line options contain only alphanumeric input.

Options

-a *application*

  Specify an application name for the configuration parameter. Parameters can differ depending on the application. If you specify no application name, then ocf is the default application.

-A *aid*

  Specify a unique alphanumeric string that identifies the applet. The *aid* argument must be a minimum of 5 characters and can be a maximum of 16 characters in length. If an applet with an identical *aid* already exists on the card, a load results in an error.

-c

  Specify subcommand name. Valid options are admin, load, bin2capx, init, enable, and disable.

-d *device*

  Specify the device on which the reader is connected (for example, /dev/cua/a).

-D

  Disable a system from using smartcards.

-E

  Export the keys to a file.

-i *filename* Specify input file name.

-I

  Import from a file.

-j *classname* Specify fully qualified class name.

-k *keytype*

  Specify type of key (for example, challenge_response, pki.)

-l

  Specify debug level (0-9), signifying level of debug information displayed.

-L

  List all properties configurable in an applet.

-n *readername*

> Specify reader name as required by the driver.

-o *filename*   Specify output file name.

-p *propfile*   Specify properties file name. This file could contain a list of property names and value pairs, in the format *propertyname=value*.

-P *pin*   Specify *pin* used to validate to the card.

-r *userfriendlyreadername*

> Specify user-defined reader name where the card to be initialized is inserted.

-R   Restart the OCF server.

-s *slot*   Specify slot number. If a reader has multiple slots, this option specifies which slot to use for initialization. If a reader has only one slot, this option is not required. If you specify no slot number, by default the first slot of the reader is used.

-t   Specify type of property being updated. The following values are valid.

service	Update a card's service-provider details.
terminal	Update a card's reader-provider details.
debug	OCF trace level.
override	Override a system property of the same name.

-T *cardname*   Specify card name.

-u   Unload the applet specified by the application ID from the card. If you specify no application ID, unload all applets from the card.

-v   Display verbose messages.

-x   Specify action to be taken. Valid values are add, delete, or modify.

Examples

The following example displays the values for all of the properties that are set.

```
# smartcard -c admin

Client Properties:

   ClientName.PropertyName        Value
   ----------------------         -----
   default.validcards           = CyberFlex IButton PayFlex
   default.authmechanism        = Pin=UserPin
   default.defaultaid           = A000000062030400

Server Properties:

   PropertyName                   Value
   ------------                   -----
   ocfserv.protocol             = rpc
   authmechanism                = Pin Password
```

```
PayFlex.ATR                = 3B6900005792020101000100A9
3B6911000000005792020101000100
authservicelocations       = com.sun.opencard.service.auth
OpenCard.services          =
com.sun.opencard.service.cyberflex.CyberFlexServiceFactory
com.sun.opencard.service.ibutton.IButtonServiceFactory
com.sun.opencard.service.payflex.PayFlexServiceFactory
initializerlocations       = com.sun.opencard.cmd.IButtonInit
IButton.ATR            = 008F0E00000000000000000000004000034909000
cardservicelocations       = com.sun.opencard.service.common
CyberFlex.ATR              = 3B169481100601810F 3B169481100601811F
country                    = US
debugging.filename         = /tmp/ocf_debugfile
language                   = en
debugging                  = 0
keys.chkey.login.user      = 3132333435363738
#
```

You can display the values for specific properties by naming them as a space-separated list on the command line following the -c admin option, as shown in the following example.

```
# smartcard -c admin language country

Server Properties:

   PropertyName                Value
   ------------                -----
   language                = en
   country                 = US
#
```

The following example adds a card-service factory property for a CyberFlex card, available in the package com.sun.services.cyberflex.

```
paperbark% smartcard -c admin -t service -j
    com.sun.services.cyberflex.CyberFlexCardServiceFactory -x add
```

The following example adds an SCM reader, available in the package com.sun.services.scm, to the properties on device /dev/cua/a and assigns it a name of SCM.

```
paperbark% smartcard -c admin -t terminal -j
    com.sun.terminal.scm.SCMstcCardTerminalFactory-xadd-d/dev/cua/a
    -r SCM -n SCM123
```

The following example deletes from the properties the SCM reader that was added in the previous example.

```
paperbark% smartcard -c admin -t terminal -r SCM -x delete
```

The following example changes the debug level for all of the com.sun package to 9.

```
paperbark% smartcard -c admin -t debug -j com.sun -l 9 -x modify
```

The following example sets the default card for an application (dtlogin) to be
CyberFlex.

```
paperbark% smartcard -c admin -a dtlogin defaultcard=CyberFlex
```

The following example exports the challenge_response keys for a user into a file.

```
paperbark% smartcard -c admin -k challenge_response -E -o /tmp/mykeys
```

The following example imports the challenge_response keys for a user from the file
/tmp/mykeys.

```
paperbark% smartcard -c admin -k challenge_response -I -i /tmp/mykeys
```

The following example downloads an applet into a Java Card or configures a PayFlex
(non-Java) card inserted into a SCM reader for the capx file supplied in the
/usr/share/lib/smartcard directory:

```
paperbark% smartcard -c load -r SCM -i
    /usr/share/lib/smartcard/SolarisAuthApplet.capx
```

The following example downloads an applet binary from some place other than the
capx file supplied with the Solaris 8 Operating Environment into an IButton (the AID
and input file are mandatory, the remaining parameters are optional.

```
paperbark% smartcard -c load -A A000000062030400 -i newapplet.jib
```

The following example on a CyberFlex Access Card downloads an applet
newapplet.bin at fileID 2222, instanceID 3333, using the specified verifyKey and a
heap size of 2000 bytes.

```
paperbark% smartcard -c load -A newAID -i newapplet.bin fileID=2222
    instanceID=3333 verifyKey=newKey MAC=newMAC heapsize=2000
```

The following example configures a PayFlex (non-Java) card with specific AID,
transport key, and initial pin.

```
paperbark% smartcard -c load -A A00000006203400 pin=242424246A617661
    transportKey=4746584932567840
```

The following example unloads the applet with ID A000000062030400 from the card
inserted into an IButton reader.

```
paperbark% smartcard -c load -r IButtonAdapter -u -A A000000062030400
```

The following example displays the usage of the smartcard -c load command.

```
paperbark% smartcard -c load
Usage:  smartcard -c load -A aid -i infile [-r readername] [-s slot number]
        [-p propfile] [-v] [property=value]*

        smartcard -c load -A aid [-i infile] [-r readername] [-s slot number]
        [-p propfile] [-v] {property=value}*

        smartcard -c load -A aid -p propfile [-i infile] [-r readername]
        [-s slot number] [-v] [property=value]*
```

```
smartcard -c load [-r readername] [-s slot number] [-A aid] -u [-v]
```

paperbark%

The following example displays all the configurable parameters for an applet with
aid 123456 residing on a card inserted into an SM reader.

paperbark% **smartcard -c init -r SM -A 123456 -L**

The following example changes the pin for the SolarisAuthApplet residing on a
card or changes the pin for a PayFlex (non-Java) card inserted into an SM reader.

paperbark% **smartcard -c init -A A000000062030400 -P oldpin pin=newpin**

The following example displays all the configurable parameters for the
SolarisAuthApplet residing on a card inserted into an SM reader.

paperbark% **smartcard -c init -A A000000062030400 -L**

The following example sets the property called user to the value james and
application to the value login on a card inserted into an SM reader that has a pin
testpin.

paperbark% **smartcard -c init -A A000000062030400 -r CyberFlex -P testpin
        application=login user=james**

The following example converts an applet for the CyberFlex card into the capx
format required for downloading the applet into the card.

paperbark% **smartcard -c bin2capx -i
        /usr/share/lib/smartcard/SolarisAuthApplet.bin -T CyberFlex
        -o /home/CorporateCard.capx -v memory=128 heapsize=12**

The following example converts an applet for the IButton card into the capx format
required for downloading the applet into the button.

paperbark% **smartcard -c bin2capx -i
        /usr/share/lib/smartcard/SolarisAuthApplet.jib -T IButton
        -o /home/CorporateCard.capx -v**

Exit Status

0	Successful completion.
1	An error occurred.

Attributes

See attributes(5) for descriptions of the following attributes.

Attribute Type	Attribute Value
Availability	SUNWocf

See Also

ocfserv(1M), attributes(5), smartcard(5)

New! **smrsh** — Restricted Shell for sendmail

Synopsis

```
/usr/lib/smrsh -c command
```

Description

The smrsh command is new in the Solaris 8 release. It is a replacement for the sh command in the prog mailer in sendmail(1M) configuration files. The smrsh command sharply limits commands that can be run using the |program syntax of sendmail. This restriction improves overall system security. smrsh limits the set of programs that a programmer can execute, even if sendmail runs a program without going through an alias or .forward file.

Briefly, smrsh limits programs to be in the directory /var/adm/sm.bin, enabling system administrators to choose the set of acceptable commands. It also rejects any commands with the characters , , <, >, |, ;, &, $, \r (Return), or \n (newline) on the command line to prevent end-run attacks.

Initial path names on programs are stripped, so forwarding to /usr/ucb/vacation, /usr/bin/vacation, /home/server/mydir/bin/vacation, and vacation all actually forward to /var/adm/sm.bin/vacation.

System administrators should be conservative about populating /var/adm/sm.bin. Reasonable additions are commands such as vacation(1) and procmail. Never include any shell or shell-like program (for example, Perl) in the sm.bin directory. The absence of perl in the sm.bin directory does not restrict the use of shell or Perl scripts in the sm.bin directory (using the #! syntax); it simply disallows the execution of arbitrary programs.

Options

-c *command*   Where *command* is a valid command, execute *command*.

Files

/var/adm/sm.bin

Directory for restricted programs.

Attributes

See attributes(5) for descriptions of the following attributes.

Attribute Type	Attribute Value
Availability	SUNWcsr, SUNWcsu

See Also

sendmail(1M), attributes(5)

snmpdx — Sun Solstice Enterprise Master Agent

Synopsis
```
/usr/lib/snmp/snmpdx [-hy][-a filename][-c config-dir]
  [-d debug-level][-i filename][-m GROUP -m SPLIT][-o filename]
  [-p port][-r filename]
```

Description
The snmpdx Master Agent is the main component of Solstice Enterprise Agent technology. It runs as a daemon process and listens to User Datagram Protocol (UDP) port 161 for SNMP requests. The Master Agent also opens another port to receive SNMP trap notifications from various subagents. These traps are forwarded to various managers, as determined by the configuration file.

On invocation, snmpdx reads its various configuration files and takes appropriate actions by activating subagents, determining the subtree Object Identifier (OID) for various subagents, populating its own Management Information Bases (MIBs), and so forth. The Master Agent invokes subagents, registers subagents, sends requests to subagents, receives responses from subagents, and traps notifications from subagents.

Options
-a *filename*   Specify the full path of the access control file used by the Master Agent. The default access control file is /etc/snmp/conf/snmpdx.acl.

-c *config-dir*

Specify the full path of the directory containing the Master Agent configuration files. The default directory is /etc/snmp/conf.

-d *debug-level*

Specify a debug level from 0 to 4. The default is 0, which means give no debug information.

-h   Print the command-line usage.

-i *filename*   Specify the full path of the enterprise-name OID map. This file contains the PID used by the Master Agent for recovery after a crash. It contains tuples of the UNIX process ID, port number, resource name, and agent name. The default file is /var/snmp/snmpdx.st.

-m GROUP | -m SPLIT

Specify the mode to use for forwarding of SNMP requests.

GROUP   Multiple variables can be included in each request from the Master Agent to the subagents. The result is, at most, one send-request per agent. The default is GROUP.

SPLIT   Each variable in the incoming request sends one send-request to each subagent.

-o *filename*	Specify the full path of the file containing the tuple (enterprise-name, OID). For example, (Sun Microsystems, 1.3.1.6.1.4.32). The Master Agent uses this file as a base for lookup in the trap filtering and forwarding process. The default file is `/etc/snmp/conf/enterprises.oid`.
-p *port*	Specify the port number. The default port number is 161.
-r *filename*	Specify the full path of the resource file to be used by the Master Agent. This file stores information about the subagents that the Master Agent invokes and manages. The default resource file is `/etc/snmp/conf/snmpdx.rsrc`.
-y	Set a recovery indicator to invoke the recovery module. The recovery process discovers which subagents in the previous session are still active; those subagents not active are respawned by the Master Agent.

Files

`/var/snmp/conf/enterprises.oid`

> Enterprise-name OID map.

`/var/snmp/conf/snmpdx.acl`

> Access control file.

`/var/snmp/conf/snmpdx.rsrc`

> Resource configuration file.

`/var/snmp/snmpdx.st`

> Master Agent status file.

`/var/snmp/mib/snmpdx.mib`

> Master Agent MIB file.

Exit Status

0	Successful completion.
non-zero	An error occurred.

Attributes

See attributes(5) for descriptions of the following attributes.

Attribute Type	Attribute Value
Availability	SUNWsasnm

See Also

snmpd(1M), snmpXdmid(1M), attributes(5)

snmpXdmid — Sun Solstice Enterprise SNMP-DMI Mapper Subagent

Synopsis

`/usr/lib/dmi/snmpXdmid -s` *hostname* `[-h] [-c` *config-dir*`] [-d` *debug-level*`]`

Description

The `snmpXdmid` command is a subagent in the Solstice Enterprise Agent Desktop Management Interface package. It maps the SNMP requests forwarded by the Master Agent (`snmpdx`(1M)) into one or more equivalent DMI requests. Further, it remaps the DMI response into SNMP response back to `snmpdx`. By default, `snmpXdmid` also forwards the DMI indications as SNMP traps to `snmpdx`. The feature is configurable; you disable it by setting `TRAP_FORWARD_TO_MAGENT=0` in the `snmpXdmid.conf` configuration file.

This subagent runs as a daemon in the system. The subagent uses a set of `.MAP` files located in `/var/dmi/map` to map the SNMP Object Identifier (OID) into a corresponding DMI component. The map files are generated with the MIF-to-MIB command, `miftomib`. They are read by `snmpXdmid` when a corresponding MIF file gets registered with the DMI Service Provider (`dmispd`(1M)).

The `snmpXdmid.conf` file is used for configuration information. Each entry in the file consists of a keyword followed by an equal sign (=), followed by a parameter string. The keyword must begin in the first position. A line beginning with a pound sign (#) is treated as a comment and the subsequent characters on that line are ignored. The following keywords are currently supported.

`WARNING_TIMESTAMP`

        Indication subscription expiration, warning time.

`EXPIRATION_TIMESTAMP`

        Indication subscription expiration timestamp.

`FAILURE_THRESHOLD`

        DMISP retries before dropping indication because of communication errors.

`TRAP_FORWARD_TO_MAGENT`

        `0`   Drop indication at the subagent level.

        non-zero   Forward indications as SNMP traps to `snmpdx`.

The default `snmpXdmid.conf` configuration file, shown below, is located in the `/etc/dmi/conf` directory.

```
/* Copyright 09/12/96 Sun Microsystems, Inc. All Rights Reserved.
*/
#pragma ident  "@(#)snmpXdmid.conf    1.5 96/09/12 Sun Microsystems"

WARNING_TIMESTAMP = 20101231110000.000000-420
EXPIRATION_TIMESTAMP = 20101231120000.000000-420
FAILURE_THRESHOLD = 1
TRAP_FORWARD_TO_MAGENT = 1
```

You can specify an alternative directory with the -c option.

Options

-c *config-dir*

> Specify the directory where the snmpXdmid.conf file is located.

-d *debug-level*

> Specify the debug level as a number from 1 to 5.

-h   Print the command-line usage.

-s *hostname*   Specify the host on which dmispd is running.

Files

/etc/dmi/conf/snmpXdmid.conf

> DMI mapper configuration file.

Attributes

See attributes(5) for descriptions of the following attributes.

Attribute Type	Attribute Value
Availability	SUNWsadmi

See Also

dmispd(1M), snmpd(1M), snmpdx(1M), attributes(5)

snoop — Capture and Inspect Network Packets

Synopsis

New!

/usr/sbin/snoop [-aCDNPqrSvV][-t [r | a | d]][-c *maxcount*][-d *device*]
[-i *filename*][-n *filename*][-o *filename*][-p *first* [, *last*]]
[-s *snaplen*][-x *offset* [, *length*]][*expression*]

Description

Use the snoop command to capture packets from the network and display their
contents. snoop uses both the network packet filter and streams buffer modules to
provide efficient capture of packets from the network. You can either display captured
packets as they are received or save them to a file for later inspection.

New!

Note — New options have been added to the snoop command in the Solaris
8 release to accommodate both the IPv4 and IPv6 protocols.

snoop can display packets in a single-line summary form or in verbose multiline forms. In summary form, only the data pertaining to the highest level protocol is displayed. For example, an NFS packet displays only NFS information. The underlying RPC, UDP, IP, and Ethernet frame information is suppressed but can be displayed if you specify either of the verbose options.

snoop requires an interactive interface.

Warnings

The processing overhead is much higher for real-time packet interpretation. Consequently, the packet drop count may be higher. For more reliable capture, output raw packets to a file by using the -o option and analyze the packets offline.

Unfiltered packet capture imposes a heavy processing load on the host computer, particularly if the captured packets are interpreted in real time. This processing load further increases if you use verbose options. Because heavy use of snoop can deny computing resources to other processes, you should not use it on production servers. Heavy use of snoop should be restricted to a dedicated computer.

snoop does not reassemble IP fragments. Interpretation of higher-level protocol halts at the end of the first IP fragment.

snoop can generate extra packets as a side effect of its use. For example, it can use a network nameservice (NIS or NIS+) to convert IP addresses to host names for display. You can postpone the address-to-name mapping until after the capture session is completed by capturing the output in a file for later display. Capturing into an NFS-mounted file can also generate extra packets.

Setting the *snaplen* (-s option) to small values can remove header information that is needed to interpret higher-level protocols. The exact cutoff value depends on the network and protocols being used. For NFS Version 2 traffic using UDP on 10 Mb/s Ethernet, do not set *snaplen* less than 150 bytes. For NFS Version 3 traffic using TCP on 100 Mb/s Ethernet, *snaplen* should be 250 bytes or more.

snoop requires information from an RPC request to fully interpret an RPC reply. If an RPC reply in a capture file or packet range does not have a request preceding it, then only the RPC reply header is displayed.

Options

-a	Listen to packets on /dev/audio (warning: can be noisy).
-c *maxcount*	Quit after capturing *maxcount* packets. Otherwise, keep capturing until no disk is left or until interrupted with Control-C.
-C	List the code generated from the filter expression for either the kernel packet filter, or snoop's own filter.
-d *device*	Receive packets from the network using the interface specified by *device*, usually le0 or ie0. The program netstat(1M), when invoked with the -i option, lists all the interfaces that a machine has. Normally, snoop automatically chooses the first non-loopback interface it finds.
-D	Display number of packets dropped during capture on the summary line.

-i *filename*   Display packets previously captured in *filename*. Without this
option, read packets from the network interface. If you specify a
filename.names file, automatically load it into snoop's IP
address-to-name mapping table (see -N option).

-n *filename*   Use *filename* as an IP address-to-name mapping table. This file
must have the same format as the /etc/hosts file (IP address
followed by the host name).

-N   Create an IP address-to-name file from a capture file. You must use
this option with the -i option that names a capture file. The
address-to-name file has the same name as the capture file with
.names appended. This file records the IP address to host-name
mapping at the capture site and increases the portability of the
capture file. Generate a .names file if the capture file is to be analyzed
elsewhere. Packets are not displayed when you use this option.

-o *filename*   Save captured packets in *filename* as they are captured. During
packet capture, display a count of the number of packets saved in the
file. If you want to just count packets without saving to a file, name
the file /dev/null.

-p *first* [, *last*]

Select one or more packets to be displayed from a capture file. The
first packet in the file is packet #1.

-P   Capture packets in nonpromiscuous mode. Only show broadcast,
multicast, or packets addressed to the host.

New!   -q   When capturing network packets into a file, do not display the packet
count. This quiet option can improve packet capturing performance.
This option is new in the Solaris 8 release.

New!   -r   Do not resolve the IP address to the symbolic name. This option
prevents snoop from generating network traffic while capturing and
displaying packets. If, however, you use the -n option and an address
is found in the mapping file, its corresponding name is displayed. This
option is new in the Solaris 8 release.

-s *snaplen*   Truncate each packet after *snaplen* bytes. Usually, the whole packet
is captured. This option is useful if you require only certain packet
header information. The packet truncation is done within the kernel,
giving better use of the streams packet buffer. There is less chance of
dropped packets because of buffer overflow during periods of high
traffic. It also saves disk space when capturing large traces to a
capture file. To capture only IP headers (no options), use a *snaplen* of
34. For UDP use 42, and for TCP use 54. You can capture RPC
headers with a *snaplen* of 80 bytes. NFS headers can be captured in
120 bytes.

-S   Display size of the entire Ethernet frame in bytes on the summary
line.

-t [r | a | d]

Use timestamp presentation. Timestamps are accurate to within 4 microseconds. The default is for times to be presented in d (delta) format (the time since receiving the previous packet). Option a (absolute) gives wall clock time. Option r (relative) gives time relative to the first packet displayed. You can use this option with the -p option to display time relative to any selected packet.

-v

Print packet headers in lots of detail. This display consumes many lines per packet and should be used only on selected packets.

-V

Print information in verbose summary mode, which is halfway between summary mode and verbose mode. Instead of displaying just the summary line for the highest-level protocol in a packet, display a summary line for each protocol layer in the packet. For example, for an NFS packet, display a line each for the ETHER, IP, UDP, RPC, and NFS layers. You can pipe verbose summary mode through grep to extract packets of interest. The following example shows only RPC summary lines.

snoop -i rpc.cap -V | grep RPC

-x offset [, length]

Display packet data in hexadecimal and ASCII format. The offset and length values select a portion of the packet to be displayed. To display the whole packet, use an offset of 0. If you do not provide a length value, display the rest of the packet.

Operands

expression

Select packets either from the network or from a capture file. Select only packets for which the expression is true. If no expression is provided, it is assumed to be true.

Given a filter expression, snoop generates code for either the kernel packet filter or for its own internal filter. If capturing packets with the network interface, code for the kernel packet filter is generated. This filter is implemented as a streams module, upstream of the buffer module. The buffer module accumulates packets until it becomes full and passes the packets on to snoop. The kernel packet filter is very efficient because it rejects unwanted packets in the kernel before they reach the packet buffer or snoop. The kernel packet filter has some limitations in its implementation—you can construct filter expressions that it cannot handle. In this event, snoop generates code for its own filter. You can use the -C option to view generated code for either the kernel's or snoop's own packet filter. If packets are read from a capture file with the -i option, only snoop's packet filter is used.

A filter expression consists of a series of one or more boolean primitives that you can combine with boolean operators (AND, OR, and NOT). Normal precedence rules for boolean operators apply. You can control the order of evaluation of these operators with parentheses. Because parentheses and other filter expression characters are known to the shell, you often need to enclose the filter expression in quotes. The expression operand recognizes the following primitives.

host *hostname*

> True if the source or destination address is that of *hostname*. You can omit the host keyword if the name does not conflict with the name of another expression primitive. For example, pinky selects packets transmitted to or received from the host pinky, whereas "pinky and dinky" selects packets exchanged between hosts pinky *and* dinky. Normally the IP address is used. With the ether qualifier, the Ethernet address is used, for instance, ether pinky.

> *New!* The type of address used depends on the primitive that precedes the host primitive. The possible qualifiers are inet, inet6, inetboth, either, or none. These four primitives are discussed below. If none of these primitives are present, snoop tries to resolve the host name to an IPv4 address. If that is not successful, it tries IPv6.

New! inet | inet6 | inetboth

> A qualifier that modifies the host primitive that follows. If you specify inet, try to resolve the host name to an IPv4 address. If you specify inet6, try to resolve it to an IPv6 address. If you specify inetboth, try both IPv4 and IPv6. When the host name can be resolved to both IPv4 and IPv6 addresses, use the first address of each type and capture both IPv4 and IPv6 packets.

ipaddr | etheraddr

> Literal addresses, recognize both IP dotted and Ethernet colon.

> 129.144.40.13 matches all packets with that IP address.

> *New!* 2::9255:a00:20ff:fe73:6e35 matches all packets with that IPv6 address as source or destination.

> 8:0:20:f:b1:51 matches all packets with the Ethernet address as source or destination.

> An Ethernet address beginning with a letter is interpreted as a host name. To avoid this, prepend a 0 when specifying the address. For example, if the Ethernet address is aa:0:45:23:52:44, then specify it by adding a leading zero to make it 0aa:0:45:23:52:44.

from | src

> A qualifier that modifies the subsequent host, net, ipaddr, etheraddr, port or rpc primitive to match just the source address, port, or RPC reply.

to | dst

> A qualifier that modifies the subsequent host, net, ipaddr, etheraddr, port or rpc primitive to match just the destination address, port, or RPC call.

ether

> A qualifier that modifies the subsequent host primitive to resolve a name to an Ethernet address. Normally, IP address matching is performed.

ethertype *number*

> True if the Ethernet type field has value number. Equivalent to
> `ether[12:2] = number`.

ip, arp, rarp

> True if the packet is of the appropriate `ethertype`.

broadcast   True if the packet is a broadcast packet. Equivalent to
                 `ether[2:4] = 0xffffffff`.

multicast   True if the packet is a multicast packet. Equivalent to
                 `ether[0] & 1 = 1`.

apple   True if the packet is an Apple EtherTalk packet. Equivalent to
                 `ethertype 0x809b` or `ethertype 0x803f`.

decnet   True if the packet is a DECNET packet.

greater *length*

> True if the packet is longer than *length*.

less *length*   True if the packet is shorter than *length*.

udp, tcp, icmp, icmp6, ah, esp   **New!**

> True if the IP or IPv6 protocol is of the appropriate type.

net *net*   True if either the IP source or destination address has a network
                 number of *net*. You can use the `from` or `to` qualifier to select packets
                 for which the network number occurs only in the source or
                 destination address.

port *port*   True if either the source or destination port is *port*. The port can be
                 either a port number or name from `/etc/services`. You can use the
                 `tcp` or `udp` primitives to select TCP or UDP ports only. You can use
                 the `from` or `to` qualifier to select packets for which the port occurs
                 only as the source or destination.

rpc *prog* [, *vers* [, *proc*]]

> True if the packet is an RPC call or reply packet for the protocol
> identified by *prog*. *prog* can be either the name of an RPC protocol
> from `/etc/rpc` or a program number. You can use *vers* and *proc* to
> further qualify the program version and procedure number, for
> example, `rpc nfs,2,0` selects all calls and replies for the NFS null
> procedure. You can use the `to` or `from` qualifier to select either call or
> reply packets only.

gateway *host*   True if the packet used *host* as a gateway, that is, the Ethernet
                 source or destination address was for *host* but not the IP address.
                 Equivalent to `ether host host` and not `host host`.

nofrag   True if the packet is unfragmented or is the first in a series of IP
                 fragments. Equivalent to `ip[6:2] & 0x1fff = 0`.

expr *relop expr*

> True if the relation holds, where *relop* is one of >, <, >=, <=, =, !=, and *expr* is an arithmetic expression composed of numbers, packet field selectors, the length primitive, and arithmetic operators +, -, *, &, |, ^, and %. The arithmetic operators within *expr* are evaluated before the relational operator, and normal precedence rules apply between the arithmetic operators, such as multiplication before addition. You can use parentheses to control the order of evaluation. To use the value of a field in the packet use the following syntax,
>
> *base[expr [: size]]*
>
> where *expr* evaluates the value of an offset into the packet from a base offset that can be ether, ip, udp, tcp, or icmp. The *size* value specifies the size of the field. If you do not specify *size*, 1 is assumed. Other legal values are 2 and 4. Examples are shown below.
>
> ether[0] & 1 = 1 is equivalent to multicast.
>
> ether[2:4] = 0xffffffff is equivalent to broadcast.
>
> ip[ip[0] & 0xf * 4 : 2] = 2049 is equivalent to udp[0:2] = 2049.
>
> ip[0] & 0xf > 5 selects IP packets with options.
>
> ip[6:2] & 0x1fff = 0 eliminates IP fragments.
>
> udp and ip[6:2]&0x1fff = 0 and udp[6:2] != 0 finds all packets with UDP checksums.
>
> You can use the length primitive to obtain the length of the packet. For instance, length > 60 is equivalent to greater 60, and ether[length - 1] obtains the value of the last byte in a packet.

and	Perform a logical AND operation between two boolean values. The AND operation is implied by the juxtaposition of two boolean expressions, for example dinky pinky is the same as dinky AND pinky.
or | ,	Perform a logical OR operation between two boolean values. You can use a comma instead. For example, dinky,pinky is the same as dinky OR pinky.
not | !	Perform a logical NOT operation on the subsequent boolean value. This operator is evaluated before AND or OR.
slp	True if the packet is an SLP packet.

Examples

The following example captures all packets and displays them as they are received.

```
# snoop
Using device /dev/hme (promiscuous mode)
   paperbark -> (broadcast)   ARP C Who is 172.16.8.21, G3 ?
         G3 -> paperbark      ARP R 172.16.8.21, G3 is 0:5:2:35:aa:1c
```

```
   paperbark -> G3          FTP C port=32841
         G3 -> paperbark    FTP R port=32841
   paperbark -> G3          FTP C port=32841
         G3 -> paperbark    FTP R port=32841 220 NetPresenz v4.0.
   paperbark -> G3          FTP C port=32841
   paperbark -> G3          FTP C port=32841 USER winsor\r\n
         G3 -> paperbark    FTP R port=32841 331 Password require
   paperbark -> G3          FTP C port=32841
   paperbark -> G3          FTP C port=32841 PASS 123ABC\r\n
         G3 -> paperbark    FTP R port=32841
         G3 -> paperbark    FTP R port=32841 230-This file must b
   paperbark -> G3          FTP C port=32841
   paperbark -> G3          FTP C port=32841 CWD Ref*\r\n
         G3 -> paperbark    FTP R port=32841 250 "/RefSysadmin" c
   paperbark -> G3          FTP C port=32841
   paperbark -> G3          FTP C port=32841 PORT 172,16,8,22,128
         G3 -> paperbark    FTP R port=32841 200 PORT command suc
   paperbark -> G3          FTP C port=32841 STOR examples\r\n
         G3 -> paperbark    FTP-DATA R port=32842
   paperbark -> G3          FTP-DATA C port=32842
         G3 -> paperbark    FTP R port=32841
         G3 -> paperbark    FTP-DATA R port=32842
         G3 -> paperbark    FTP R port=32841 150 ASCII transfer s
   paperbark -> G3          FTP-DATA C port=32842 # snoop\r\nUsing devic
   paperbark -> G3          FTP-DATA C port=32842   G3          FTP C
   paperbark -> G3          FTP-DATA C port=32842 astle -> paperbark
         G3 -> paperbark    FTP-DATA R port=32842
   paperbark -> G3          FTP-DATA C port=32842 aperbark    FTP-DATA
         G3 -> paperbark    FTP-DATA R port=32842
         G3 -> paperbark    FTP-DATA R port=32842
         G3 -> paperbark    FTP-DATA R port=32842
   paperbark -> G3          FTP-DATA C port=32842
   paperbark -> G3          ^C
#
```

The following example captures packets with host g3 as either the source or destination and displays them as they are received.

```
# snoop g3
Using device /dev/hme (promiscuous mode)
   paperbark -> G3          FTP C port=32845 PORT 172,16,8,22,128
         G3 -> paperbark    FTP R port=32845 200 PORT command suc
   paperbark -> G3          FTP C port=32845 STOR examples\r\n
         G3 -> paperbark    FTP-DATA R port=32848
   paperbark -> G3          FTP-DATA C port=32848
         G3 -> paperbark    FTP R port=32845
         G3 -> paperbark    FTP-DATA R port=32848
         G3 -> paperbark    FTP R port=32845 150 ASCII transfer s
   paperbark -> G3          FTP-DATA C port=32848 \r\n# snoop\r\nUsing dev
   paperbark -> G3          FTP-DATA C port=32848    FTP R port=32841
   paperbark -> G3          FTP-DATA C port=32848    FTP C port=32843
         G3 -> paperbark    FTP-DATA R port=32848
   paperbark -> G3          FTP-DATA C port=32848    paperbark -> castl
         G3 -> paperbark    FTP-DATA R port=32848
         G3 -> paperbark    FTP-DATA R port=32848
         G3 -> paperbark    FTP-DATA R port=32848
```

```
paperbark -> G3            FTP-DATA C port=32848
paperbark -> G3            FTP C port=32845
      G3 -> paperbark      FTP R port=32845 226 Transfer complet
paperbark -> G3            FTP C port=32845
```

The following example captures packets between `paperbark` and `castle` and saves them to a file. Then, it inspect the packets, using times (in seconds) relative to the first captured packet.

```
# snoop -o cap paperbark castle
Using device /dev/hme (promiscuous mode)
60 ^C
# snoop -i cap -t r | more
   1   0.00000    paperbark -> castle      FTP C port=32851
   2   0.00109       castle -> paperbark   FTP R port=32851
   3   0.00116    paperbark -> castle      FTP C port=32851
   4   0.11223       castle -> paperbark   FTP R port=32851 220 castle FTP ser
ve
   5   0.11231    paperbark -> castle      FTP C port=32851
   6   1.41084    paperbark -> castle      FTP C port=32851 USER winsor\r\n
   7   1.41136       castle -> paperbark   FTP R port=32851
   8   1.42538       castle -> paperbark   FTP R port=32851 331 Password requi
re
   9   1.52419    paperbark -> castle      FTP C port=32851
  10   2.71104    paperbark -> castle      FTP C port=32851 PASS 123ABC\r\n
  11   2.75072       castle -> paperbark   FTP R port=32851 230 User winsor lo
gg
  12   2.84418    paperbark -> castle      FTP C port=32851
  13   6.65304    paperbark -> castle      FTP C port=32851 PORT 172,16,8,22,1
28
  14   6.65426       castle -> paperbark   FTP R port=32851 200 PORT command s
uc
  15   6.65478    paperbark -> castle      FTP C port=32851 STOR examples\r\n
  16   6.66896       castle -> paperbark   FTP-DATA R port=32852
  17   6.66904    paperbark -> castle      FTP-DATA C port=32852
  18   6.66953       castle -> paperbark   FTP-DATA R port=32852
  19   6.67022       castle -> paperbark   FTP R port=32851 150 ASCII data con
ne
  20   6.67249    paperbark -> castle      FTP-DATA C port=32852 # snoop g3\r\
nUsing de
  21   6.67272    paperbark -> castle      FTP-DATA C port=32852
  22   6.67416       castle -> paperbark   FTP-DATA R port=32852
  23   6.67423       castle -> paperbark   FTP-DATA R port=32852
  24   6.68509       castle -> paperbark   FTP-DATA R port=32852
  25   6.68516    paperbark -> castle      FTP-DATA C port=32852
  26   6.76417    paperbark -> castle      FTP C port=32851
  27   6.76462       castle -> paperbark   FTP R port=32851 226 Transfer compl
et
  28   6.86418    paperbark -> castle      FTP C port=32851
  29  13.63151    paperbark -> castle      FTP C port=32851 PORT 172,16,8,22,1
28
  30  13.63290       castle -> paperbark   FTP R port=32851 200 PORT command s
uc
  31  13.63341    paperbark -> castle      FTP C port=32851 RETR examples\r\n
  32  13.63670       castle -> paperbark   FTP-DATA R port=32853
  33  13.63678    paperbark -> castle      FTP-DATA C port=32853
```

```
  34  13.63727       castle -> paperbark    FTP-DATA R port=32853
  35  13.63778       castle -> paperbark    FTP R port=32851 150 ASCII data con
ne
  36  13.64172       castle -> paperbark    FTP-DATA R port=32853 # snoop g3\r\
nUsing de
--More--
```

The following example looks at selected packets in the capture file named `pkts`.

```
paperbark% snoop -i pkts -p99,108
 99 0.0027 boutique -> sunroof NFS C GETATTR FH=8E6C
100 0.0046 sunroof -> boutique NFS R GETATTR OK
101 0.0080 boutique -> sunroof NFS C RENAME FH=8E6C MTra00192 to .nfs08
102 0.0102 marmot -> viper NFS C LOOKUP FH=561E screen.r.13.i386
103 0.0072 viper -> marmot NFS R LOOKUP No such file or directory
104 0.0085 bugbomb -> sunroof RLOGIN C PORT=1023 h
105 0.0005 kandinsky -> sparky RSTAT C Get Statistics
106 0.0004 beeblebrox -> sunroof NFS C GETATTR FH=0307
107 0.0021 sparky -> kandinsky RSTAT R
108 0.0073 office -> jeremiah NFS C READ FH=2584 at 40960 for 8192
```

The following example looks at packet 101 in more detail.

```
paperbark% snoop -i pkts -v -p101
ETHER: ----- Ether Header ----
ETHER:
ETHER: Packet 101 arrived at 16:09:53.59
ETHER: Packet size = 210 bytes
ETHER: Destination = 8:0:20:1:3d:94, Sun
ETHER: Source = 8:0:69:1:5f:e, Silicon Graphics
ETHER: Ethertype = 0800 (IP)
ETHER:
IP:   ----- IP Header ----
IP:
IP: Version = 4, header length = 20 bytes
IP: Type of service = 00
IP: ..0..... = routine
IP:...0.... = normal delay
IP:.... 0... = normal throughput
IP:.... .0.. = normal reliability
IP: Total length = 196 bytes
IP: Identification 19846
IP: Flags = 0X
IP: .0...... = may fragment
IP: ..0..... = more fragments
IP: Fragment offset = 0 bytes
IP: Time to live = 255 seconds/hops
IP: Protocol = 17 (UDP)
IP: Header checksum = 18DC
IP: Source address = 129.144.40.222, boutique
IP: Destination address = 129.144.40.200, sunroof
IP:
UDP: ----- UDP Header ----
UDP:
UDP: Source port = 1023
```

```
UDP: Destination port = 2049 (Sun RPC)
UDP: Length = 176
UDP: Checksum = 0
UDP:
RPC: ----- SUN RPC Header ----
RPC:
RPC: Transaction id = 665905
RPC: Type = 0 (Call)
RPC:
RPC version = 2
RPC: Program = 100003 (NFS), version = 2, procedure = 1
RPC: Credentials: Flavor = 1 (Unix), len = 32 bytes
RPC: Time = 06-Mar-90 07:26:58
RPC: Hostname = boutique
RPC: Uid = 0, Gid = 1
RPC: Groups = 1
RPC: Verifier : Flavor = 0 (None), len = 0 bytes
RPC:
NFS: ----- SUN NFS ----
NFS:
NFS: Proc = 11 (Rename)
NFS: File handle = 0000164300000000100080000305A1C47
NFS: 597A0000000800002046314AFC450000
NFS: File name = MTra00192
NFS: File handle = 0000164300000000100080000305A1C47
NFS: 597A0000000800002046314AFC450000
NFS: File name = .nfs08
NFS:
```

The following example views just the NFS packets between sunroof and boutique.

```
paperbark% snoop -i pkts rpc nfs and sunroof and boutique
1 0.0000 boutique -> sunroof NFS C GETATTR FH=8E6C
2 0.0046 sunroof -> boutique NFS R GETATTR OK
3 0.0080 boutique -> sunroof NFS C RENAME FH=8E6C MTra00192 to .nfs08
```

The following example saves these packets to a new capture file.

```
paperbark% snoop -i pkts -o pkts.nfs rpc nfs sunroof boutique
```

The following example views packets that indicate they are encapsulated.

```
# snoop ip-in-ip
sunroof -> boutique ICMP Echo request       (1 encap)
```

The following example uses the -V option on an encapsulated packet.

```
# snoop -V ip-in-ip
sunroof -> boutique  ETHER Type=0800 (IP), size = 118 bytes
sunroof -> boutique  IP  D=129.144.40.222 S=129.144.40.200 LEN=104,
  ID=27497
sunroof -> boutique  IP  D=10.1.1.2 S=10.1.1.1 LEN=84, ID=27497
sunroof -> boutique  ICMP Echo request
```

The following examples set up a more efficient filter and use the greater, less, port, rpc, nofrag, and relop filters toward the end of the expression so that the first part of the expression can be set up in the kernel. The presence of OR makes it difficult to split the filtering when these primitives that cannot be set are used in the kernel. Instead, use parentheses to enforce the primitives that should be ORed.

The following example captures packets between funky and pinky of type tcp or udp on port 80

```
# snoop funky and pinky and port 80 and tcp or udp
```

Because the primitive port cannot be handled by the kernel filter and there is also an OR in the expression, a more efficient way to filter is to move the OR to the end of the expression and to use parentheses to enforce the OR between tcp and udp.

```
# snoop funky and pinky and (tcp or udp) and port 80
```

Exit Status

0	Successful completion.
1	An error occurred.

Files

/dev/audio	Symbolic link to the system's primary audio device.
/dev/null	The null file.
/etc/hosts	Host-name database.
/etc/rpc	RPC program number database.
/etc/services	
	Internet services and aliases.

Attributes

See attributes(5) for descriptions of the following attributes.

Attribute Type	Attribute Value
Availability	SUNWcsu

See Also

netstat(1M), hosts(4), rpc(4), services(4), attributes(5), audio(7I), *New!*
bufmod(7M), dlpi(7P), ie(7D), le(7D), pfmod(7M), tun(7M)

soconfig — Configure Transport Providers for Use by Sockets

Synopsis
```
/sbin/soconfig -f file
/sbin/soconfig family type protocol [path]
```

Description
The soconfig command configures the transport provider driver for use with sockets. It specifies how the family, type, and protocol parameters in the socket(3N) call are mapped to the name of a transport provider such as /dev/tcp. This command can be used to add an additional mapping or to remove a previous mapping.

The init(1M) command uses soconfig with the sock2path(4) file during the booting sequence.

Options
-f file   Set up the soconfig configuration for each driver according to the information stored in file. A soconfig file consists of lines of at least the first three fields listed below, separated by spaces.

                    family type protocol path

Operands
family   The protocol family as listed in the /usr/include/sys/socket.h file, expressed as an integer.

type   The socket type as listed in the /usr/include/sys/socket.h file, expressed as an integer.

protocol   The protocol number as specified in the family specific include file, expressed as an integer. For example, for AF_INET this number is specified in /usr/include/netinet/in.h. Denote an unspecified protocol number with the value 0.

path   The string that specifies the path name of the device that corresponds to the transport provider. If you specify this parameter, add the configuration for the specified family, type, and protocol. If you do not specify this parameter, remove the configuration.

Examples
The following example sets up /dev/tcp for family AF_INET and type SOCK_STREAM.

soconfig 2 2 0 /dev/tcp

The following is a sample file used with the -f option. Comment lines begin with a pound sign (#).

```
#      Family  Type     Protocol  Path
       2       2        0         /dev/tcp
```

2	2	6	/dev/tcp
2	1	0	/dev/udp
2	1	17	/dev/udp
1	2	0	/dev/ticotsord
1	1	0	/dev/ticlts
2	4	0	/dev/rawip

Files

/etc/sock2path

File containing mappings from sockets to transport.

Attributes

See attributes(5) for descriptions of the following attributes.

Attribute Type	Attribute Value
Availability	SUNWcsr

See Also

init(1M), sock2path(4), attributes(5)
Network Interfaces Programmer's Guide

soladdapp — Add an Application to the Solstice Application Registry

Synopsis

/usr/snadm/bin/soladdapp [-r *registry*] -n *name* -i *icon* -e *executable*
    [*args*]

Description

Note — The Solstice Launcher is part of AdminSuite 2.3, and is no longer
supported in the Solaris 8 release.

New!

Use the soladdapp command to add an application to the Solstice application registry.
After the application is added, it is displayed in the Solstice Launcher main window (see
solstice(1M)).

Note — Globally registered applications are used by local and remote users
sharing the software in a particular /opt directory. They can be added only
with soladdapp.

Options

-r *registry*   Define the full path name of the Solstice registry file.

-n *name*   Define the name of the tool to be registered.

-i *icon*   Define the full path name of the tool icon.

-e *executable*

Define the full path name of the tool.

args   Specify any arguments to use with the tool.

When executed without options, soladdapp uses
/opt/SUNWadm/etc/.solstice_registry (the default registry path).

Exit Status

0   Success.

1   Failure.

2   The registry is locked.

3   The entry is a duplicate.

Examples

The following example adds an application called Disk Manager to the Solstice application registry for display in the Solstice Launcher main window.

```
# soladdapp -r /opt/SUNWadm/etc/.solstice_registry -n "Disk Manager"
    -i opt/SUNWdsk/etc/diskmgr.xpm -e /opt/SUNWdsk/bin/diskmgr
```

Files

/opt/SUNWadm/etc/.solstice_registry

The default registry path.

Attributes

See attributes(5) for descriptions of the following attributes.

Attribute Type	Attribute Value
Availability	SUNWsadml

See Also

soldelapp(1M), solstice(1M), attributes(5)

soldelapp — Remove an Application from the Solstice Application Registry

Synopsis

/usr/snadm/bin/soldelapp [-r *registry*] -n *name*

Description

> **Note** — The Solstice Launcher is part of AdminSuite 2.3, and is no longer
> supported in the Solaris 8 release.

New!

Use the soldelapp to remove an application from the Solstice application registry. After removal, the application is no longer displayed in the Solstice Launcher main window (see solstice(1M)).

> **Note** — Globally registered applications are used by local and remote users
> sharing the software in a particular /opt directory. They can be removed
> only with soldelapp.

Options

-r *registry*   Define the full path name of the Solstice registry file.

-n *name*   Define the name of the tool to be removed.

When executed without options, soldelapp uses /opt/SUNWadm/etc/.solstice_registry (the default registry path).

Exit Status

0	Success.
1	Failure.
2	The registry is locked.
3	The entry is a duplicate.

Examples

The following removes an application called Disk Manager from the Solstice application registry and the Solstice Launcher main window.

soldelapp -r /opt/SUNWadm/etc/.solstice_registry -n "Disk Manager"

Files

/opt/SUNWadm/etc/.solstice_registry

The default registry file.

Attributes

See attributes(5) for descriptions of the following attributes.

Attribute Type	Attribute Value
Availability	SUNWsadml

See Also

soladdapp(1M), solstice(1M), attributes(5)

---

solstice — Access System Administration Tools with a Graphical User Interface

Synopsis

/bin/solstice

Description

New!

> **Note** — The Solstice Launcher is part of AdminSuite 2.3, and is no longer supported in the Solaris 8 release.

Use the solstice command to display the Solstice Launcher, a graphical user interface that provides access to the Solstice AdminSuite product family of system administration tools. The tools that are displayed in the launcher depend on what Solstice products are installed on the system.

Help is available through the Help button.

> **Note** — The Solstice Launcher adds or removes local applications that are private to the user (not local to the system) only. The properties of globally registered applications that are used by local and remote users sharing the software from a particular /opt directory cannot be modified from the Solstice Launcher. To register global applications for use by local and remote users, use the soladdapp(1M) command. To remove globally registered applications, use the soldelapp(1M) command.

Usage

The Solstice Launcher enables you to do the following tasks.

- Launch system administration tools.
- Add and register applications locally with the launcher.
- Remove locally registered applications.
- Show, hide, or remove applications in the launcher, reorder the icons, change the launcher window width, modify applications properties, and add applications.

Files

/$HOME/.solstice_registry

> Local registry information.

Attributes

See attributes(5) for descriptions of the following attributes.

Attribute Type	Attribute Value
Availability	SUNWsadml

See Also

soladdapp(1M), soldelapp(1M), attributes(5)

---

spray — Spray Packets

Synopsis

/usr/sbin/spray [-c count][-d delay][-l length][-t nettype] host

Description

If an NFS server is hit with more packets than it can receive through its network interface, some client requests are lost and eventually retransmitted. Use the spray command to gauge network interface capacity by sending a one-way stream of packets to host, using RPC, and reporting the number received and the transfer rate. The host argument can be either a name or an Internet address.

You can use spray to exercise combinations of client and server systems with varying packet sizes to identify cases where a client can race ahead of its server.

spray is not useful as a networking benchmark because it uses unreliable connectionless transports, (upd for example). spray can report a large number of packets dropped when the drops result because spray sends packets faster than they can be buffered locally (before the packets get to the network medium).

Options

-c count   Specify how many packets to send. The default value of count is the number of packets required to make the total stream size 100,000 bytes.

-d delay   Specify how many microseconds to pause between sending each packet. The default is 0.

-1 *length*   Specify the numbers of bytes in the Ethernet packet that holds the RPC call message. Because the data is encoded with XDR and XDR deals only with 32-bit quantities, not all values of *length* are possible, and spray rounds up to the nearest possible value. When *length* is greater than 1514, then the RPC call can no longer be encapsulated in one Ethernet packet, so the *length* field no longer has a simple correspondence to Ethernet packet size. The default value of *length* is 86 bytes (the size of the RPC and UDP headers).

-t *nettype*   Specify class of transports. The default is *netpath*. See rpc(3N) for a description of supported classes.

Examples

The following example sprays castle from the system paperbark.

```
paperbark% spray castle
sending 1162 packets of length 86 to castle ...
        1052 packets (90.534%) dropped by castle
        7 packets/sec, 625 bytes/sec
paperbark%
```

The following example sends 100 (-c100) packets to sparc14 with each packet size of 2048 bytes (-12048). The packets are sent with a delay time of 20 microseconds between each burst (-d20).

```
# spray -c100 -d20 -12048 sparc14
sending 100 packets of length 2048 to sparc14 ...
        2 packets (2.000%) dropped by sparc14
        567 packets/sec, 1161394 bytes/sec
#
```

Attributes

See attributes(5) for descriptions of the following attributes.

Attribute Type	Attribute Value
Availability	SUNWcsu

See Also

rpc(3N), attributes(5)

sprayd — Spray Server

Synopsis

/usr/lib/netsvc/spray/rpc.sprayd

Description

See rpc.sprayd(1M).

---

ssaadm — Administration Program for SPARCstorage Array and SPARCstorage RSM Disk Systems

Synopsis

ssaadm [-v][-e] *subcommand subcommand-option... | pathname...*

Description

Use the ssaadm administrative command to manage the SPARCstorage Array and SPARCstorage RSM disk systems (henceforth called SPARCstorage systems). ssaadm performs a variety of control and query tasks depending on the specified command-line arguments and options.

The command line must contain a *subcommand* (listed in "Usage" on page 1100) and at least one *pathname*. Commands specific to either a SPARCstorage Array or a SPARCstorage RSM state that fact. ssaadm can also contain options and other parameters, depending on the subcommand. The subcommand is applied to each of the path names on the command line.

pathname specifies the SPARCstorage system controller or a disk in the SPARCstorage system. The controller name is specified by its physical name, for example,

/devices/.../.../SUNW,soc@3,0/SUNW, pln@axxxxxxx,xxxxxxxx:ctlr

or by a name of the form

c*N*

where *N* is the logical controller number. ssaadm uses the c*N* name to find an entry in the /dev/rdsk directory of a disk that is attached to the SPARCstorage system controller. The /dev/rdsk entry is then used to determine the physical name of the SPARCstorage system controller. A disk in the SPARCstorage system is specified by its logical or physical device name, for example,

/dev/rdsk/c1t0d0s2

or

/devices/.../.../SUNW,soc@3,0/SUNW, pln@axxxxxxx,xxxxxxxx/ssd@0,0:c,raw

Notes

Currently, only some device drivers support hot-plugging. If hot-plugging is attempted on a disk or bus where it is not supported, an error message of the following form is displayed.

ssaadm: can't acquire "PATHNAME": No such file or directory

The nonexpert-mode, hot-plugging subcommands insert_device, remove_device, and replace_device are currently supported only for the RSM SPARCstorage platform. See "Examples" on page 1104 for how to use the expert mode subcommands to hot-plug on any platform that supports hot-plugging.

To avoid possible system deadlock, do not quiesce any bus containing a disk with the root, usr, or swap partitions.

Options

-v   Verbose mode.

-e   Enter expert mode, required for the expert mode subcommands. See "Expert Mode Subcommands" on page 1103.

Operands

pathname   The SPARCstorage system controller or a disk in the SPARCstorage system.

Usage

Subcommands

display [-p] *pathname...*

Display configuration information for the specified unit(s), or display performance information for the specified SPARCstorage Array controller. If *pathname* specifies the controller, display the configuration information for all disks in the SPARCstorage Array. For each drive that has fast write enabled, display (FW) after the drive identification.

-p   Display performance information for the specified SPARCstorage Array controller. The accumulation of the performance statistics must be enabled with the perf_statistics subcommand before the performance information is displayed. If not enabled, all of the I/Os per second are displayed as zeros.

The performance display reports the following information.

BUSY   How busy the controller in the SPARCstorage Array is, expressed as a percentage.

IOPS   The total I/Os per second for the SPARCstorage Array.

entries for each disk.

The total number of I/Os per second.

```
download -f filename pathname
download -w wwn pathname
```

Download an image to the SPARCstorage Array controller.

-f
: Download the PROM image specified by *filename* to the SPARCstorage Array controller FEPROMs. When the download is complete, the SPARCstorage Array must be reset to use the downloaded code. Note that the download subcommand modifies the FEPROM on the SPARCstorage Array and should be used with caution.

-w
: Change the SPARCstorage Array controller's World Wide Name. *wwn* is a 12-digit hex number, leading zeros required. The new SPARCstorage Array controller's image have the least significant 6 bytes of the 8-byte World Wide Name modified to *wwn*.

```
fast_write [-s] -c pathname
fast_write [-s] -d pathname
fast_write [-s] -e pathname
```

Enable or disable the use of the NVRAM to enhance the performance of writes in the SPARCstorage Array. *pathname* may refer to the SPARCstorage Array controller or to an individual disk.

-s
: Save the state that is currently being requested so it persists across power cycles.

-c
: Enable fast writes for synchronous writes only.

-e
: Enable fast writes.

-d
: Disable fast writes.

```
fc_s_download [-f fcode-file]
```

Download the fcode contained in the file *fcode-file* into all the FC/S SBus cards. This command is interactive and expects user confirmation before downloading the fcode. When invoked without the [-f *fcode-file*] option, print the current version of the fcode in each FC/S SBus card. Note that you should use the fc_s_download subcommand only in single-user mode; otherwise, the FC/S card could be reset.

```
insert_device pathname
```

Guide user through hot insertion of a disk device. See "Notes" on page 1099 for hot-plugging limitations.

```
perf_statistics -e pathname
perf_statistics -d pathname
```

Enable or disable the accumulation of performance statistics for the specified SPARCstorage Array controller. You must enable the accumulation of performance statistics before using the display -p

subcommand. This subcommand can be issued only to the
SPARCstorage Array controller.

-e   Enable the accumulation of performance statistics.

-d   Disable the accumulation of performance statistics.

purge *pathname*

Purge any fast write data from NVRAM for one disk, or all disks if you
specify the controller. Use this option with caution, usually only when
a drive has failed.

reserve *pathname*

Reserve the specified controller(s) or disk(s) for exclusive use by the
issuing host. When HA (High_Availability) software is running on a
system, do not use this subcommand to reserve a disk on an SSA.
Doing so could cause problems for the HA software.

release *pathname*

Release a reservation held on the specified controller(s) or disk(s).
When HA (High_Availability) software is running on a system, do not
use this subcommand to release a disk on an SSA. Doing so could
cause problems for the HA software.

remove_device *pathname*

Guide user through hot removal of a disk device. See "Notes" on
page 1099 for hot-plugging limitations.

replace_device *pathname*

Guide user through hot replacement of a disk device. See "Notes" on
page 1099 for hot-plugging limitations.

set_boot_dev [-y] *pathname*

Set the boot-device variable in the PROM to the physical device name
specified by *pathname*, which can be a block special device or a mount
point. The command normally runs interactively and requests
confirmation for setting the default boot-device in the PROM. You can
use the -y option to run the command in noninteractive mode, in
which case no confirmation is requested or required.

start [-t *tray-number*] *pathname*

Spin up the specified disk(s). If *pathname* specifies the controller, this
action applies to all disks in the SPARCstorage Array.

-t   Spin up all disks in the tray specified by
                      tray-number. *pathname* must specify the controller.

stop [-t *tray-number*] *pathname*

Spin down the specified disk(s). If *pathname* specifies the controller,
this action applies to all disks in the SPARCstorage Array.

-t   Spin down all disks in the tray specified by
                      tray-number. *pathname* must specify the controller.

```
sync_cache pathname
```
> Flush all outstanding writes for the specified disk from NVRAM to the media. If *pathname* specifies the controller, this action applies to all disks in the SPARCstorage Array.

SCSI Enclosure Services (SES) Commands

Address the SPARCstorage RSM tray by using the logical or physical path of the SES device or specifying the controller followed by the tray number if that controller has multiple trays. The controller is addressed by c*N* or the physical path to the SPARCstorage Array's controller.

See ses(7D) for more information about environmental sensor cards and associated devices.

The following commands also work with RSM trays directly attached to wide differential SCSI controllers.

```
env_display pathname | controller tray-number
```
> Display the environmental information for the specified unit.

```
alarm pathname | controller tray-number
```
> Display the current state of the audible alarm.

```
alarm_on pathname | controller tray-number
alarm_off pathname | controller tray-number
```
> Enable or disable the audible alarm for this enclosure.

```
alarm_set pathname | controller tray-number [seconds]
```
> Set the audible alarm setting to seconds.

```
led pathname
```
Display the current state of the LED for the specified disk.

```
led_on pathname
led_off pathname
```
> Turn on or off the LED for this disk.

```
power_off pathname | controller tray-number
```
> Power down this RSM. The RSM needs to be powered back on manually. This command does not work with RSMs directly attached to wide differential SCSI controllers.

Expert Mode Subcommands

See "Notes" on page 1099 for limitations of these subcommands. Only users that are knowledgeable about the systems they are managing should use the expert mode subcommands.

For the following subcommands that work on a bus if you specify a disk, then the bus to which the disk is attached is used.

```
bus_getstate pathname
```
> Get and display the state of the specified bus.

```
bus_quiesce pathname
```
> Quiesce the specified bus.

bus_reset *pathname*

>Reset the specified bus.

bus_resetall *pathname*

>Reset the specified bus and all devices on that bus.

bus_unquiesce *pathname*

>Unquiesce the specified bus.

dev_getstate *pathname*

>Get the state (online or offline) of the specified device.

dev_reset *pathname*

>Reset the specified device.

offline *pathname*

>Turn the specified disk offline.

online *pathname*

>Turn the specified disk online.

Examples

The following example uses the expert-mode, hot-plugging subcommands to hot-remove a disk on a SSA. See "Notes" on page 1099 for hot-plugging limitations.

The first step reserves the SCSI device so that it can't be accessed via its second SCSI bus.

```
# ssaadm reserve /dev/dsk/c1t8d0s2
```

The next two steps take the disk to be removed offline, then quiesce the bus.

```
# ssaadm -e offline /dev/dsk/c1t8d0s2
# ssaadm -e bus_quiesce /dev/dsk/c1t8d0s2
```

The user then removes the disk and continues by unquiescing the bus, putting the disk back online, then releasing it.

```
# ssaadm -e bus_unquiesce /dev/dsk/c1t8d0s2
# ssaadm -e online /dev/dsk/c1t8d0s2
# ssaadm release /dev/dsk/c1t8d0s2
```

Exit Status

0   Successful completion.

non-zero   An error occurred.

Attributes

See attributes(5) for descriptions of the following attributes.

Attribute Type	Attribute Value
Availability	SUNWssaop

See Also

disks(1M), luxadm(1M), attributes(5), ses(7D)
SPARCstorage Array User's Guide
RAID Manager 6.1 Installation and Support Guide
RAID Manager 6.1 User's Guide

startup — Turn Process Accounting On at Startup

Synopsis

/usr/lib/acct/startup

Description

See acctsh(1M).

statd — Network Status Monitor

Synopsis

/usr/lib/nfs/statd

Description

The statd daemon is an intermediate version of the status monitor. It interacts with lockd(1M) to provide the crash and recovery functions for the locking services on NFS. statd keeps track of the clients with processes that hold locks on a server. When the server reboots after a crash, statd sends a message to the statd on each client, indicating that the server has rebooted. The client statd processes then inform the lockd on the client that the server has rebooted. The client lockd then tries to reclaim the lock(s) from the server.

statd on the client host also informs the statd on the server(s) holding locks for the client when the client has rebooted. In this case, the statd on the server informs its lockd to release all locks held by the rebooting client, enabling other processes to lock those files.

Note — The crash of a server is detected only on its recovery.

Files

/var/statmon/sm

Lists hosts and network addresses to be contacted after a reboot.

/var/statmon/sm.bak

>Lists hosts and network addresses that could not be contacted after last reboot.

/var/statmon/state

>Includes a number that changes during a reboot.

/usr/include/rpcsvc/sm_inter.x

>Contains the rpcgen source code for the interface services provided by the statd daemon.

Attributes

See attributes(5) for descriptions of the following attributes.

Attribute Type	Attribute Value
Availability	SUNWcsu

See Also

lockd(1M), attributes(5)
NFS Administration Guide

strace — Print STREAMS Trace Messages

Synopsis

strace [*mid sid level*...]

Description

The strace command is part of the set of error and trace loggers—log(7D), strace(1M), strclean(1M), strerr(1M), and strlog(9F)—that are provided for debugging and administering STREAMS modules and drivers.

Use the strace command without arguments to write all STREAMS event trace messages from all drivers and modules to its standard output. These messages are obtained from the STREAMS log driver (see log(7D)). If arguments are provided, they must be in triplets of the form *mid*, *sid*, *level*, where *mid* is a STREAMS module ID number, *sid* is a sub-ID number, and *level* is a tracing priority level. Each triplet indicates that tracing messages are to be received from the given module/driver, sub-ID (usually indicating minor device), and priority level equal to or less than the given level. You can use the token all for any member to indicate no restriction for that attribute.

Each trace message output has the following format.

seq time ticks level flags mid sid text

seq	Trace sequence number.
time	Time of message in *hh:mm:ss*.

`ticks`	Time of message in machine ticks since boot.	
`level`	Tracing priority level.	
`flags`	E	Message is also in the error log.
	F	Indicates a fatal error.
	N	Mail was sent to the system administrator (hardcoded as root).
`mid`	Module ID number of source.	
`sid`	Sub-ID number of source.	
`text`	Formatted text of the trace message.	

Once initiated, `strace` continues to execute until you terminate it.

Notes

- There is no restriction to the number of `strace` processes opening the STREAMS log driver at a time.
- The log-driver records the list of the triplets specified in the command invocation, and compares each potential trace message against this list to decide if it should be formatted and sent up to the `strace` process. Hence, long lists of triplets have a greater impact on overall STREAMS performance. Running `strace` has the most impact on the timing of the modules and drivers generating the trace messages that are sent to the `strace` process. If trace messages are generated faster than the `strace` process can handle them, some of the messages are lost. This last case can be determined by examination of the sequence numbers on the trace messages output.

Examples

The following example outputs all trace messages from the module or driver whose module ID is 41.

```
# strace 41 all all
```

The following example outputs those trace messages from driver or module ID 41 with sub-IDs 0, 1, or 2.

```
# strace 41 0 1 41 1 1 41 2 0
```

Messages from sub-IDs 0 and 1 must have a tracing level less than or equal to 1. Those from sub-ID 2 must have a tracing level of 0.

Attributes

See `attributes`(5) for descriptions of the following attributes.

Attribute Type	**Attribute Value**
Availability	SUNWcsu

See Also

attributes(5), log(7D)
STREAMS Programming Guide

strclean — STREAMS Error Logger Cleanup Program

Synopsis

strclean [-a *age*][-d *logdir*]

Description

Use strclean to regularly clean up the STREAMS error logger directory (for example, by using cron). By default, all files with names matching error.* in /var/adm/streams that have not been modified in the last three days are removed.

Note — strclean is typically run from cron daily or weekly.

Options

-a *age*	Specify the maximum age in days a log file can be changed.
-d *logdir*	Specify a directory other than /var/adm/streams.

Examples

The following example has the same result as running strclean with no arguments.

example% **strclean -d /var/adm/streams -a 3**

Files

/var/adm/streams/error.*

STREAMS error logger files.

Attributes

See attributes(5) for descriptions of the following attributes.

Attribute Type	Attribute Value
Availability	SUNWcsu

See Also

cron(1M), strerr(1M), attributes(5)
STREAMS Programming Guide

strerr — STREAMS Error Logger Daemon

Synopsis

```
strerr
```

Description

The `strerr` daemon receives error log messages from the STREAMS log driver (see `log`(7D)) and appends them to a log file. The resultant error log files reside in the directory `/var/adm/streams` and are named `error.`*mm-dd*, where *mm* is the month and *dd* is the day of the messages contained in each log file.

An error log message has the following format.

```
seq time ticks flags mid sid text
```

`seq`	Error sequence number.
`time`	Time of message in *hh*:*mm*:*ss*.
`ticks`	Time of message in machine ticks since boot priority level.
`flags`	T The message was also sent to a tracing process.
	F Indicates a fatal error.
	N Send mail to the system administrator (hardcoded as root).
`mid`	Module ID number of source.
`sid`	Sub-ID number of source.
`text`	Formatted text of the error message.

Messages that appear in the error log are intended to report exceptional conditions that require the attention of the system administrator. Those messages that indicate the total failure of a STREAMS driver or module should have the F flag set. Those messages requiring the immediate attention of the administrator have the N flag set, which sends the message to the system administrator using mail. The priority level usually has no meaning in the error log but has meaning if the message is also sent to a tracer process.

Once initiated, `strerr` continues to execute until terminated by the user. It is commonly executed asynchronously.

Notes

There is no restriction to the number of `strerr` processes opening the STREAMS log driver at a time.

If a module or driver is generating a large number of error messages, running the error logger degrades STREAMS performance. If a large burst of messages is generated in a short time, the log driver may not be able to deliver some of the messages. This situation is indicated by gaps in the sequence numbering of the messages in the log files.

Files

/var/adm/streams/error.*mm-dd*

Error log file.

Attributes

See attributes(5) for descriptions of the following attributes.

Attribute Type	Attribute Value
Availability	SUNWcsu

See Also

attributes(5), log(7D)

STREAMS Programming Guide

sttydefs — Maintain Line Settings and Hunt Sequences for TTY Ports

Synopsis

/usr/sbin/sttydefs -a *ttylabel* [-b] [-f *final-flags*] [-i *initial-flags*]
   [-n *nextlabel*]
/usr/sbin/sttydefs -l [*ttylabel*]
/usr/sbin/sttydefs -r *ttylabel*

Description

Use the sttydefs administrative command to maintain the line settings and hunt sequences for the system's TTY ports by making entries in, and deleting entries from, the /etc/ttydefs file.

Only superuser can invoke sttydefs with -a or -r options. Any user on the system can use sttydefs -l.

Options

-a *ttylabel*   Add a record to the ttydefs file, using *ttylabel* as its label.

-b   Enable autobaud to set the line speed of a given TTY port to the line speed of the device connected to the port without the user's intervention. Use with the -a option.

-f *final-flags*

Specify the value to be used in the *final-flags* field in /etc/ttydefs. *final-flags* must be in a format recognized by the stty command. These flags are the termio(7I) settings used by ttymon after receiving a successful connection request and immediately before invoking the service on the port. If you do not specify this option, set *final-flags* equal to the termio(7I) flags 9600 and sane. Use with the -a option.

-i *initial-flags*

Specify the value to be used in the *initial-flags* field in /etc/ttydefs. *initial-flags* must be in a format recognized by the stty command. These flags are used by ttymon when searching for the correct baud rate. They are set before the prompt is written. If you do not specify this option, set *initial-flags* equal to the termio(7I) flag 9600. Use with the -a option.

-l[*ttylabel*] Display the record from /etc/ttydefs whose TTY label matches the specified *ttylabel*. If you specify no *ttylabel*, display the entire contents of /etc/ttydefs. Verify that each entry it displays is correct and that the entry's *nextlabel* field references an existing label.

-n *nextlabel* Specify the value to be used in the *nextlabel* field in /etc/ttydefs. If you do not specify this option, set *nextlabel* equal to *ttylabel*. Use with the -a option.

-r *ttylabel* Remove any record in the ttydefs file that has *ttylabel* as its label.

Output

If successful, sttydefs exits with a status of 0. sttydefs -l generates the requested information and sends it to standard output.

Examples

The following command lists all the entries in the ttydefs file and prints an error message for each invalid entry that is detected. The example is truncated to save space.

```
paperbark% sttydefs -l

-----------------------------------------
460800:460800 hupcl:460800 hupcl::307200
-----------------------------------------

ttylabel:       460800
initial flags:  460800 hupcl
final flags:    460800 hupcl
autobaud:       no
nextlabel:      307200


-----------------------------------------
307200:307200 hupcl:307200 hupcl::230400
-----------------------------------------

ttylabel:       307200
initial flags:  307200 hupcl
final flags:    307200 hupcl
autobaud:       no
nextlabel:      230400
```

```
-------------------------------------------
230400:230400 hupcl:230400 hupcl::153600
-------------------------------------------

ttylabel:        230400
initial flags:   230400 hupcl
final flags:     230400 hupcl
autobaud:        no
nextlabel:       153600
```
. . .(*Additional lines deleted from this example*)

The following shows a command that requests information for a single label and its output.

```
paperbark% sttydefs -l 19200

-----------------------------------
19200:19200 hupcl:19200 hupcl::9600
-----------------------------------

ttylabel:        19200
initial flags:   19200 hupcl
final flags:     19200 hupcl
autobaud:        no
nextlabel:       9600
paperbark%
```

The following sequence of commands adds the labels 1200, 2400, 4800, and 9600 and puts them in a circular list.

```
# sttydefs -a 1200 -n 2400 -i 1200 -f "1200 sane"
# sttydefs -a 2400 -n 4800 -i 2400 -f "2400 sane"
# sttydefs -a 4800 -n 9600 -i 4800 -f "4800 sane"
# sttydefs -a 9600 -n 1200 -i 9600 -f "9600 sane"
```

Files

/etc/ttydefs File that contains terminal line settings information for ttymon.

Attributes

See attributes(5) for descriptions of the following attributes.

Attribute Type	Attribute Value
Availability	SUNWcsu

See Also

attributes(5), termio(7I)

su — Become Superuser or Another User

Synopsis

```
su [-] [username [arg...]]
```

Description

Use the su (switch user) command to become another user without logging off. The default user name is root (superuser).

To use su, you must supply the appropriate password unless you are already root. If the password is correct, su creates a new shell process that has the real and effective user ID, group IDs, and supplementary group list set to those of the specified *username*. The new shell is the shell specified in the shell field of *username*'s password file entry (see passwd(4)). If no shell is specified, /usr/bin/sh is used (see sh(1)). To return to normal user ID privileges, type an end-of-file character (Control-D) to exit the new shell.

Any additional arguments given on the command line are passed to the new shell. When using programs such as sh, an *arg* of the form -c *string* executes *string*, using the shell, and an *arg* of -r gives the user a restricted shell.

The following statements are true only if either /usr/bin/sh or NULL is named in the specified user's password file entry. If the first argument to su is a dash (-), the environment is passed along unchanged as if the user actually logged in as the specified user. Otherwise, the environment is passed along, with the exception of $PATH, which is controlled by PATH and SUPATH in /etc/default/su.

All attempts to become another user by use of su are logged in the log file /var/adm/sulog (see sulog(4)).

Security

su uses pam(3) for authentication, account management, and session management. The PAM configuration policy, listed through /etc/pam.conf, specifies the modules to be used for su. The following partial pam.conf file shows entries for the su command, using the UNIX authentication, account management, and session management modules.

```
su auth    required /usr/lib/security/pam_unix.so.1
su account required /usr/lib/security/pam_unix.so.1
su session required /usr/lib/security/pam_unix.so.1
```

If the su service has no entries, then the entries for the other service are used. If multiple authentication modules are listed, then the user may be prompted for multiple passwords.

Examples

The following example switches to user bin while retaining the previously exported environment.

example% **su bin**

The following example switches to user bin but changes the environment to what would be expected if bin had originally logged in.

example% **su - bin**

The following example executes *command* with the temporary environment and permissions of user bin.

```
example% su - bin -c "command args"
```

Environment Variables

If any of the LC_* variables (LC_CTYPE, LC_MESSAGES, LC_TIME, LC_COLLATE, LC_NUMERIC, and LC_MONETARY) (see environ(5)) are not set in the environment, the operational behavior of su for each corresponding locale category is determined by the value of the LANG environment variable. If LC_ALL is set, its contents are used to override both the LANG and the other LC_* variables. If none of the above variables are set in the environment, the C (U.S. style) locale determines how su behaves.

LC_CTYPE   Determine how su handles characters. When LC_CTYPE is set to a valid value, su can display and handle text and file names containing valid characters for that locale. su can display and handle Extended Unix Code (EUC) characters where any individual character can be 1, 2, or 3 bytes. su can also handle EUC characters of 1, 2, or more column widths. In the C locale, only characters from ISO 8859-1 are valid.

LC_MESSAGES   Determine how diagnostic and informative messages are presented. This presentation includes the language and style of the messages and the correct form of affirmative and negative responses. In the C locale, the messages are presented in the default form found in the program itself (in most cases, U.S. English).

Files

$HOME/.profile

     User's login commands for sh and ksh.

/etc/passwd   System password file.

/etc/profile   System-wide sh and ksh login commands.

/var/adm/sulog

     Log file.

/etc/default/su

     File containing the following default parameters.

SULOG   Log all attempts to use su to switch to another user in the indicated file.

CONSOLE   Log all attempts to use su to switch to root on the console.

PATH   Default path. (/usr/bin:)

SUPATH   Default path for a user invoking su to root. (/usr/sbin:/usr/bin)

SYSLOG	Determine whether the syslog(3) LOG_AUTH facility should be used to log all su attempts. LOG_NOTICE messages are generated when su is used to change to root, LOG_INFO messages are generated for su switches to other users, and LOG_CRIT messages are generated for failed su attempts.
SLEEPTIME	Set the number of seconds to wait before login failure is printed to the screen and another login attempt is allowed. Default is 4 seconds. Minimum is 0 seconds. Maximum is 5 seconds.

Attributes

See attributes(5) for descriptions of the following attributes.

Attribute Type	Attribute Value
Availability	SUNWcsu

See Also

csh(1), env(1), ksh(1), login(1), sh(1), syslogd(1M), pam(3), syslog(3), pam.conf(4), passwd(4), profile(4), sulog(4), attributes(5), environ(5), pam_unix(5)

sulogin — Access Single-User Mode

Synopsis

sulogin

Description

The sulogin command is automatically invoked by init when the system is first started. It prompts the user to type the root password to enter system maintenance mode (single-user mode) or to type end-of-file (typically Control-D) for normal startup (multiuser mode). You should never directly invoke sulogin.

Files

/etc/default/sulogin

Default value can be set for the following flag.

PASSREQ	Determine if login requires a password. Default is PASSREQ=YES.

```
/etc/default/login
```
Default value can be set for the following flag.

SLEEPTIME   Set the number of seconds to wait before login
failure is printed to the screen and another
login attempt is allowed. Default is 4 seconds.
Minimum is 0 seconds. Maximum is 5 seconds.

Attributes

See attributes(5) for descriptions of the following attributes.

Attribute Type	Attribute Value
Availability	SUNWcsr

See Also

init(1M), attributes(5)

suninstall — Install the Solaris Operating Environment

Synopsis

```
suninstall
```

Description

Use the suninstall forms-based command to install the operating system onto any
stand-alone system. suninstall loads the software available on the CD-ROM. Refer to
the installation manual for disk space requirements.

To abort the installation procedure, use the interrupt character (typically, Control-C).
suninstall exists only on the Solaris CD-ROM and should be invoked only from
there. Refer to the installation manual for more details.

Note — It is advisable to exit suninstall through the exit options from
the suninstall menus.

Usage

Refer to the installation manual for more information on the various menus and
selections.

Attributes

See attributes(5) for descriptions of the following attributes.

Attribute Type	Attribute Value
Availability	SUNWcdrom (Solaris CD)

See Also

pkginfo(1), install(1M), pkgadd(1M), attributes(5)
Solaris Advanced Installation Guide

---

swap — Swap Administrative Interface

Synopsis

```
/usr/sbin/swap -a swapname [swaplow][swaplen]
/usr/sbin/swap -d swapname [swaplow]
/usr/sbin/swap -l
/usr/sbin/swap -s
```

Description

Use the swap administrative interface to add, delete, and monitor the system swap areas used by the memory manager.

Warning — No check is done to see if a swap area being added overlaps with an existing file system.

Options

-a *swapname*   Add the specified swap area. Only superuser can use this option. *swapname* is the name of the swap file, for example, /dev/dsk/c0t0d0s1 or a regular file. *swaplow* is the offset in 512-byte blocks into the file where the swap area should begin. *swaplen* is the desired length of the swap area in 512-byte blocks. The value of *swaplen* cannot be less than 16. For example, if you specify n blocks, then the actual swap length is $(n-1)$ blocks. *swaplen* must be at least one page in length. One page of memory is equivalent to eight 512-byte blocks. You can determine the size of a page of memory by using the pagesize command. See pagesize(1). Because the first page of a swap file is automatically skipped and a swap file needs to be at least one page in length, the minimum size should be a factor of 2 pagesize bytes. The size of a page of memory is machine dependent.

swaplow + *swaplen* must be less than or equal to the size of the swap file. If you do not specify *swaplen*, add an area starting at *swaplow* and extending to the end of the designated file. If you specify neither *swaplow* nor *swaplen*, use the whole file except for the first page. Swap areas are normally added automatically during system startup by the /sbin/swapadd script. This script adds all swap areas that have been specified in the /etc/vfstab file; for the syntax of these specifications, see vfstab(4).

To use an NFS or local file-system *swapname*, you should first create a file by using mkfile(1M). You can add a local file-system swap file to the running system by just running the swap -a command. For NFS-mounted swap files, the server needs to export the file. Do this by performing the following steps.

1. Add the following line to /etc/dfs/dfstab.

share -F nfs -o rw=*clientname*, root=*clientname* *path-to-swap-file*

2. Run shareall(1M).

3. Have the client add the following lines to /etc/vfstab.

server: *path-to-swapfile* - *local-path-to-swapfile* nfs - - - *local-path-to-swapfile* -- swap - - -

The following example adds swap space from the server castle.
castle:/files1/swap - /files/swap nfs - - - /files/swap - - swap - no -

4. Have the client run mount.

 # mount *local-path-to-swapfile*

5. The client can then run swap -a to add the swap space.

 # swap -a *local-path-to-swapfile*

-d *swapname* Delete the specified swap area. Only superuser can use this option. *swapname* is the name of the swap file, for example, /dev/dsk/c0t0d0s1 or a regular file. *swaplow* is the offset in 512-byte blocks into the swap area to be deleted. If you do not specify *swaplow*, delete the area starting at the second page. When the command completes, swap blocks can no longer be allocated from this area and all swap blocks previously in use in this swap area have been moved to other swap areas.

-l List the status of all the swap areas. The output has five columns.

path The path name for the swap area.

dev The major/minor device number in decimal if it is a block special device; zeros otherwise.

swaplo The *swaplow* value for the area in 512-byte blocks.

blocks The *swaplen* value for the area in 512-byte blocks.

free | The number of 512-byte blocks in this area that are not currently allocated.

The list does not include swap space in the form of physical memory because this space is not associated with a particular swap area.

If you run swap -l while *swapname* is in the process of being deleted (by swap -d), the string INDEL is displayed in a sixth column of the swap statistics.

-s | Print summary information about total swap space usage and availability.

allocated | The total amount of swap space in bytes currently allocated for use as backing store.

reserved | The total amount of swap space in bytes not currently allocated but claimed by memory mappings for possible future use.

used | The total amount of swap space in bytes that is either allocated or reserved.

available | The total swap space in bytes that is currently available for future reservation and allocation.

These numbers include swap space from all configured swap areas as listed by the -l option, as well swap space in the form of physical memory.

Usage

You can use only the first 2 Gbytes of a block device larger than 2 Gbytes for swap in swapfs on a 32-bit operating system. With a 64-bit operating system, you can fully use a block device larger than 2 Gbytes for swap up to 2**63 -1 bytes.

New!

Environment Variables

New!

See environ(5) for descriptions of the following environment variables that affect the execution of swap: LC_CTYPE and LC_MESSAGE.

Attributes

See attributes(5) for descriptions of the following attributes.

Attribute Type	**Attribute Value**
Availability	SUNWcsu

See Also

pagesize(1), mkfile(1M), shareall(1M), getpagesize(3C), vfstab(4), attributes(5), largefile(5)

swmtool — Install, Upgrade, and Remove Software Packages

Synopsis

```
/usr/sbin/swmtool [-d directory]
```

Description

The swmtool command is a link to the admintool(1M) command. You can use the swmtool command to invoke the admintool(1M) application, which is preselected to display only the software portion of the AdminTool window. Using the swmtool command, you can add software from a product CD or hard disk to an installed system, or you can remove software from an installed system.

Once logged in, you can run swmtool to examine the packages on your local system.

Membership in the sysadmin group (gid 14) is used to restrict access to administrative tasks. Members of the sysadmin group can use swmtool to add or remove software packages. Nonmembers have read-only permissions (where applicable).

Help is available through the Help button.

Options

-d directory Specify the directory containing the software to be installed.

Examples

The following example starts the admintool application and tells it to look for software packages in the local directory /cdrom/cdrom0/s0 (the default directory for a CD when running Volume Manager).

```
example% /usr/sbin/swmtool -d /cdrom/cdrom0/s0
```

Attributes

See attributes(5) for descriptions of the following attributes.

Attribute Type	Attribute Value
Availability	SUNWadmap

See Also

admintool(1M), pkgadd(1M), pkgrm(1M), attributes(5)
Solaris Advanced User's Guide

sxconfig — Configure Contiguous Memory for the SX Video Subsystem

Synopsis

```
/usr/platform/platform-name/sbin/sxconfig -c
/usr/platform/platform-name/sbin/sxconfig -d
/usr/platform/platform-name/sbin/sxconfig [-f | -n] [-l limit] [-s size]
```

Description

Use the sxconfig command to configure contiguous memory parameters for exclusive use by the SX video system on the Desktop SPARC systems with graphics option. You can find *platform-name* with the -i option of uname(1).

After configuring the physically contiguous memory, using the various options described below, you must reboot the system for the changes to take effect. If you use this command to configure physically contiguous memory for the first time after the system software has been installed, then you must use the recofiguration option (-r) of boot(1M) to reboot the system.

The amount of memory to be reserved depends on the type of application. Applications that benefit from the availability of contiguous memory are those that are written to the XGL and XIL graphics and imaging foundation library APIs.

The *Platform Notes: SPARCstation 10SX System Configuration Guide* provides more detailed information regarding how much memory to reserve for various types of graphics and imaging applications.

sxconfig is supported only on Desktop SPARC systems with SX graphics option.

The interface, output, and command location are uncommitted and subject to change in future releases.

Options

-c	Display the current configuration parameters in the driver configuration file. If the system was not rebooted after the configuration parameters were changed, then the displayed values do not reflect the actual system setup.
-d	Restore all configuration parameters to the default values. By default, reserve 0 megabytes of physically contiguous memory, do not allow fragmentation, and reserve 32 megabytes of memory for system use.
-f	Allow fragmentation. If no single chunk of memory of at least the requested size is found, allow the request to span multiple chunks. This option also specifies that less than *size* megabytes of data can be reserved if not enough contiguous chunks are available. If you do not specify this option, then the memory reserved must be exactly one chunk of the requested size for the request to succeed.
-n	Fragmentation not allowed.

-l *limit*   Specify that at least *limit* megabytes of total memory must remain for system use after the contiguous memory has been reserved.

-s *size*   Reserve *size* megabytes of contiguous memory for exclusive use by the SX video subsystem.

Examples

The following example reserves 16 megabytes of contiguous memory without fragmentation and indicates 32 megabytes of memory should remain for system use after the contiguous memory is reserved.

```
# sxconfig -s 16 -l 32
```

The following example is identical to the one above except that fragmentation is allowed.

```
# sxconfig -s 16 -f -l 32
```

The following example reports current configuration parameters in the driver configuration file.

```
# sxconfig -c
```

The following example restores all configuration parameters to the default values.

```
# sxconfig -d
```

The following example disables fragmentation.

```
# sxconfig -n
```

Exit Status

sxconfig returns 0 on success, and a positive integer on failure.

1	Permission denied. Only root can run this command.
2	Configuration file sx_cmem.conf does not exist.
3	Illegal option.
4	Illegal combination of options.
5	Illegal argument for -s option. Should be an integer.
6	Illegal argument for -l option. Should be an integer.

Files

/platform/*platform-name*/kernel/drv/sx_cmem

Contiguous memory device driver.

/platform/*platform-name*/kernel/drv/sx_cmem.conf

Configuration file for contiguous memory driver.

/etc/init.d/sxcmem

Contiguous memory startup script.

Attributes

See `attributes`(5) for descriptions of the following attributes.

Attribute Type	Attribute Value
Availability	SUNWkvm

See Also

`uname(1)`, `boot(1M)`, `init(1M)`, `attributes(5)`
Platform Notes: SPARCstation 10SX System Configuration Guide

---

sync — Update the Superblock

Synopsis

`sync`

Description

The `sync` command executes the `sync` system primitive. If the system is to be stopped, `sync` must be called to ensure file system integrity. It flushes all previously unwritten system buffers out to disk, thus assuring that all file modifications up to that point are saved. See `sync(2)` for details.

Note — If you have done a write to a file on a remote machine in a Remote File Sharing environment, you cannot use `sync` to force buffers to be written out to disk on the remote machine. `sync` writes only local buffers to local disks.

Attributes

See `attributes`(5) for descriptions of the following attributes.

Attribute Type	Attribute Value
Availability	SUNWcsu

See Also

`sync(2)`, `attributes(5)`

syncinit — Set Serial Line Interface Operating Parameters

Synopsis

```
/usr/sbin/syncinit device [baud-rate | keyword=value,... | single-word
    option]
```

Description

Use the syncinit command to modify some of the hardware operating modes common to synchronous serial lines. This command can be useful in troubleshooting a link or may be required for the operation of a communications package.

If run without options, syncinit reports the options as presently set on the port. If options are specified, the new settings are reported after they have been made.

Warning — Do not use syncinit on an active serial link unless you need to resolve an error condition. It should not be run casually or if you are not sure of the consequences of its use.

Options

Options to syncinit normally take the form of a *keyword*, followed by an equal sign and a *value*. The exception is that you can specify a baud rate as a decimal integer by itself. *keywords* must begin with the value shown in the options table but can contain additional letters up to the equal sign. For example, loop= and loopback= are equivalent.

Recognized options are listed in the table below.

Keyword	Value	Effect
loop	yes	Set the port to operate in internal loopback mode. The receiver is electrically disconnected from the DCE receive data input and tied to the outgoing transmit data line. Transmit data is available to the DCE. The Digital Phase Lock Loop (DPLL) may not be used as a clock source in this mode. If no other clocking options have been specified, perform the equivalent of txc=baud and rxc=baud.
	no	Disable internal loopback mode. If no other clocking options have been specified, perform the equivalent of txc=txc and rxc=rxc.

Keyword	Value	Effect
echo	yes	Set the port to operate in auto-echo mode. The transmit data output is electrically disconnected from the transmitter and tied to the receive data input. Incoming receive data is still visible. Use of this mode in combination with local loopback mode has no value and should be rejected by the device driver. The auto-echo mode is useful to make a system become the end point of a remote loopback test.
	no	Disable auto-echo mode.
nrzi	yes	Set the port to operate with NRZI data encoding.
	no	Set the port to operate with NRZ data encoding.
txc	txc	Transmit clock source is the TxC signal (pin 15).
	rxc	Transmit clock source is the RxC signal (pin 17).
	baud	Transmit clock source is the internal baud rate generator.
	pll	Transmit clock source is the output of the DPLL circuit.
rxc	rxc	Receive clock source is the RxC signal (pin 17).
	txc	Receive clock source is the TxC signal (pin 15).
	baud	Receive clock source is the internal baud rate generator.
	pll	Receive clock source is the output of the DPLL circuit.
speed	*integer*	Set the baud rate to *integer* bits per second.

The following single-word options set one or more parameters at a time.

Keyword	Equivalent to Options
external	txc=txc rxc=rxc loop=no
sender	txc=baud rxc=rxc loop=no
internal	txc=pll rxc=pll loop=no
stop	speed=0

Examples

The following example sets the first CPU port to loop internally, use internal clocking, and operate at 38400 baud.

```
# syncinit zsh0 38400 loop=yes device: /dev/zsh ppa: 0 speed=38400,
    loopback=yes, echo=no, nrzi=no, txc=baud, rxc=baud
```

The following example sets the same port's clocking, local loopback, and baud rate settings to their default values.

```
# syncinit zsh0 stop loop=no device: /dev/zsh ppa: 0 speed=0,
    loopback=no, echo=no, nrzi=no, txc=txc, rxc=rxc
```

Attributes

See attributes(5) for descriptions of the following attributes.

Attribute Type	Attribute Value
Availability	SUNWcsu

See Also

syncloop(1M), syncstat(1M), intro(2), ioctl(2), attributes(5), zsh(7D)

Diagnostics

device missing minor device number

> The name device does not end in a decimal number that can be used as a minor device number.

bad speed: *arg*

> The string *arg* that accompanied the speed= option could not be interpreted as a decimal integer.

Bad arg: *arg*

> The string *arg* did not make sense as an option.

ioctl failure code = *errno*

> An ioctl(2) system called failed. You can find the meaning of the value of errno in intro(2).

syncloop — Synchronous Serial Loopback Test Program

Synopsis

/usr/sbin/syncloop [-cdlstv] *device*

Description

Use the `syncloop` command to perform several loopback tests that are useful in exercising the various components of a serial communications link.

Before running a test, `syncloop` opens the designated port and configures it according to command-line options and the specified test type. It announces the names of the devices being used to control the hardware channel, the channel number (ppa) corresponding to the device argument, and the parameters it has set for that channel. It then runs the loopback test in three phases.

The first phase is to listen on the port for any activity. If no activity is seen for at least four seconds, `syncloop` proceeds to the next phase. Otherwise, you are informed that the line is active and that the test cannot proceed, and the program exits.

In the second phase, called the "first packet" phase, `syncloop` tries to send and receive one packet. The program waits for up to four seconds for the returned packet. If no packets are seen after five attempts, the test fails with an excoriating message. If a packet is returned, the result is compared with the original. If the length and content do not match exactly, the test fails.

The final phase, known as the "multiple packet" phase, tries to send many packets through the loop. Because the program has verified the integrity of the link in the first-packet phase, the test does not fail after a particular number of timeouts. If a packet is not seen after four seconds, a message is displayed. Otherwise, a count of the number of packets received is updated on the display once per second. If it becomes obvious that the test is not receiving packets during this phase, you may want to stop the program manually. The number and size of the packets sent during this phase is determined by default values, or by command-line options. Each returned packet is compared with its original for length and content. If a mismatch is detected, the test fails. The test completes when the required number of packets have been sent, regardless of errors.

After the multiple-packet phase has completed, the program displays a summary of the hardware event statistics for the channel that was tested. The display takes the following form.

```
CRC errors Aborts Overruns Underruns In<-Drops-> Out
         0      0        0         0 0              0
```

These lines are followed by an estimated line speed, which is an approximation of the bit rate of the line, based on the number of bytes sent and the actual time that it took to send them.

Warning — To permit `syncloop` tests to run properly and prevent disturbance of normal operations, run the command only on a port that is not being used for any other purpose at that time.

Options

Option	Parameter	Default	Description
-c	*packet-count*	100	Specify the number of packets to be sent in the multiple-packet phase.
-d	*hex-data-byte*	random	Specify that each packet is filled with bytes with the value of *hex_data_byte*.

Option	Parameter	Default	Description
-l	*packet-length*	100	Specify the length of each packet in bytes.
-s	*line-speed*	9600	Bit rate in bits per second.
-t	*test-type*	none	A number, from 1 to 4, that specifies which test to perform. The values for *test-type* are as follows.
			1. Internal loopback test. Port loopback is on. Transmit and receive clock sources are internal (baud rate generator).
			2. External loopback test. Port loopback is off. Transmit and receive clock sources are internal. Requires a loopback plug suitable to the port under test.
			3. External loopback test. Port loopback is off. Transmit and receive clock sources are external (modem). Requires that one of the local modem, the remote modem, or the remote system be set in a loopback configuration.
			4. Test using predefined parameters. User defines hardware configuration and can select port parameters with the syncinit(1M) command.
-v			Sets verbose mode. If data errors occur, the expected and received data are displayed.

Enter all numeric options except -d as decimal numbers (for example, -s 19200). If you do not provide the -t *test-type* option, syncloop prompts for it.

Examples

In the following example, syncloop uses a packet length of 512 bytes over the first CPU port. The command asks you to choose one of four test options.

```
# syncloop -l 512 zsh0
[ Data device: /dev/zsh0 | Control device: /dev/zsh, ppa=0 ]
Enter test type:
1: Internal Test
          (internal data loop, internal clocking)
```

```
2: Test using loopback plugs
            (external data loop, internal clocking)
3: Test using local or remote modem loopback
            (external data loop, external clocking)
4: Other, previously set, special mode
> 1
speed=9600, loopback=yes, nrzi=no, txc=baud, rxc=baud
[ checking for quiet line ]
[ Trying first packet ]
[ Trying many packets ]
 100
100 packets sent, 100 received
CRC errors    Aborts   Overruns  Underruns           In <-Drops-> Out
        0          0         0          0             0               0
estimated line speed = 9464 bps
#
```

The following example performs an internal loopback test on the first CPU port, using 5000 packets and a bit rate of 56 Kbps.

```
# syncloop -t 1 -s 56000 -c 5000 zsh0
[ Data device: /dev/zsh0 | Control device: /dev/zsh, ppa=0 ]
speed=55854, loopback=yes, nrzi=no, txc=baud, rxc=baud
[ checking for quiet line ]
[ Trying first packet ]
[ Trying many packets ]
 5000
5000 packets sent, 5000 received
CRC errors    Aborts   Overruns  Underruns           In <-Drops-> Out
        0          0         0          0             0               0
estimated line speed = 55191 bps
#
```

Attributes

See attributes(5) for descriptions of the following attributes.

Attribute Type	Attribute Value
Availability	SUNWcsu

See Also

syncinit(1M), syncstat(1M), attributes(5), zsh(7D)

Diagnostics

device missing minor device number

> The name device does not end in a decimal number that can be used as a minor device number.

`invalid packet length:` *nnn*

> The packet length was specified to be less than zero or greater than 4096.

`poll: nothing to read`
`poll: nothing to read or write.`

> The `poll(2)` system call indicates that there is no input pending or that output would be blocked if attempted.

`len` *xxx* `should be` *yyy*

> The packet that was sent had a length of *yyy* but was received with a length of *xxx*.

nnn `packets lost in outbound queueing`
nnn `packets lost in inbound queueing`

> A discrepancy has been found between the number of packets sent by `syncloop` and the number of packets the driver counted as transmitted, or between the number counted as received and the number read by the program.

syncstat — Report Driver Statistics from a Synchronous Serial Link

Synopsis

`/usr/sbin/syncstat [-c]` *device* `[`*interval*`]`

Description

Use the `syncstat` command to report the event statistics maintained by a synchronous serial device driver. The report can be a single snapshot of the accumulated totals or a series of samples showing incremental changes. Before the output, `syncstat` prints the device name being used to query a particular device driver, along with a number indicating the channel number (ppa) under control of that driver.

Event statistics are maintained by a driver for each physical channel that it supports. They are initialized to zero at the time the driver module is loaded into the system, which may be either at boot time or when one of the driver's entry points is first called.

The *device* argument is the name of the serial device as it appears in the `/dev` directory. For example, `zsh0` specifies the first on-board serial device.

The fields of the `syncstat` output are described below.

speed	The line speed setting of the device. You should make this value correspond to the modem clocking speed when clocking is provided by the modem.
ipkts	The total number of input packets.
opkts	The total number of output packets.

undrun	The number of transmitter underrun errors.
ovrrun	The number of receiver overrun errors.
abort	The number of aborted received frames.
crc	The number of received frames with CRC errors.
isize	The average size (in bytes) of input packets.
osize	The average size (in bytes) of output packets.

Warnings

Underrun, overrun, frame-abort, and CRC errors have a variety of causes. Communication protocols are typically able to handle such errors and initiate recovery of the transmission in which the error occurred. Small numbers of such errors are not a significant problem for most protocols. However, because the overhead involved in recovering from a link error can be much greater than that of normal operation, high error rates can greatly degrade overall link throughput. High error rates often result because of problems in the link hardware, such as cables, connectors, interface electronics, or telephone lines. They can also be related to excessive load on the link or the supporting system.

The percentages for input and output line use reported when the interval option is reported may occasionally be reported as slightly greater than 100 percent because of inexact sampling times and differences in the accuracy between the system clock and the modem clock. If the percentage of use greatly exceeds 100 percent or never exceeds 50 percent, then the baud rate set for the device probably does not reflect the speed of the modem.

Options

-c	Clear the accumulated statistics for the device specified. This option can be useful when you do not want to unload a particular driver or when the driver is not capable of being unloaded.

Operands

interval	Sample the statistics every *interval* seconds and report incremental changes. The output reports line use for input and output in place of average packet sizes. These are the relationships between bytes transferred and the baud rate, expressed as percentages. The loop repeats indefinitely, with a column heading printed every twenty lines for convenience.

Examples

The following example shows output from the syncstat command for device zsh0.

```
# syncstat zsh0
syncstat: control device: /dev/zsh, ppa=0
   speed   ipkts   opkts   undrun   ovrrun   abort   crc   isize
   osize
   55854    5001    5001       0        0        0     0    100     100
#
```

The following example shows output from the syncstat command for device zsh0 with the -c option.

```
# syncstat -c zsh0
syncstat: control device: /dev/zsh, ppa=0
    speed   ipkts   opkts   undrun  ovrrun  abort     crc   isize
    osize
    55854      0       0       0       0      0       0       0      0
#
```

The following example shows output of the syncstat command for device zsh0 with a new line of output generated every five seconds.

```
# syncstat zsh0 5
syncstat: control device: /dev/zsh, ppa=0
   ipkts   opkts   undrun  ovrrun  abort     crc   iutil   outil
      0       0       0       0       0       0     0%      0%
      0       0       0       0       0       0     0%      0%
      0       0       0       0       0       0     0%      0%
      0       0       0       0       0       0     0%      0%
^C#
```

Attributes

See attributes(5) for descriptions of the following attributes.

Attribute Type	Attribute Value
Availability	SUNWcsu

See Also

syncinit(1M), syncloop(1M), attributes(5), zsh(7D)

Diagnostics

bad interval: *arg*

> The argument *arg* is expected to be an interval and could not be understood.

device missing minor device number

> The name device does not end in a decimal number that can be used as a minor device number.

baud rate not set

> The *interval* option is being used and the baud rate on the device is zero. A divide-by-zero error results when computing the line use statistics.

sys-unconfig — Undo a System's Configuration

Synopsis

    /usr/sbin/sys-unconfig

Description

Use the sys-unconfig command to restore a system configuration to an "as manufactured" state in preparation for configuring it again. A system's configuration consists of host name, Network Information Service (NIS) domain name, time zone, IP address, IP subnet mask, and root password. This operation is the inverse of those performed by the sysidnet(1M), sysidnis(1M), and sysidsys(1M) programs run at boot. See sysidtool(1M).

sys-unconfig performs the following tasks.

- Saves current /etc/inet/hosts file information in /etc/inet/hosts.saved.
- If the current /etc/vfstab file contains NFS mount entries, saves the /etc/vfstab file to /etc/vfstab.orig.
- Restores the default /etc/inet/hosts file.
- Removes the default host name in /etc/hostname.interface files for all interfaces configured when this command is run. To determine which interfaces are configured, run the command ifconfig -a. The /etc/hostname.interface files corresponding to all of the interfaces listed in the resulting output, with the exception of the loopback interface (lo0), are removed.
- Removes the default domainname in /etc/defaultdomain.
- Restores the time zone to PST8PDT in /etc/TIMEZONE.
- Disables the Network Information Service (NIS) and Network Information Service Plus (NIS+) if either NIS or NIS+ was configured.
- Removes the entries for this host in /etc/net/*/hosts.
- Removes the file /etc/inet/netmasks.
- Removes the password set for root in /etc/shadow.
- Removes the file /etc/.rootkey.
- Execute all system configuration applications. These applications are defined by prior executions of a sysidconfig -a application. (See sysidconfig(1M)). When sys-unconfig is run, all system configuration applications are passed one argument, -u.

When sys-unconfig is finished, it performs a system shutdown. sys-unconfig is a potentially dangerous command and can be run only by superuser.

Note — sys-unconfig is not available on diskless clients.

Files

    /etc/default/init

Process control initialization.

/etc/defaultdomain

> The default domain name for a system.

/etc/hostname.*interface*

> Interface information for a system.

/etc/inet/hosts

> Host-name database.

/etc/inet/netmasks

> Network mask database.

/etc/net/*/hosts

> List of net hosts

/etc/nodename

> Node name.

/etc/.rootkey

> Superuser's secret key.

/etc/shadow   Shadow password file.

/etc/vfstab   Virtual file-system table.

/var/nis/NIS_COLD_START

> NIS coldstart file.

/var/yp/binding/*/ypservers

> List of NIS servers.

Attributes

See attributes(5) for descriptions of the following attributes.

Attribute Type	Attribute Value
Availability	SUNWadmap

See Also

init(1M), kdmconfig(1M), sysidconfig(1M), sysidtool(1M), hosts(4),
netmasks(4), shadow(4), attributes(5)

sysdef — Output System Definition

Synopsis

```
/usr/sbin/sysdef [-n namelist]
/usr/sbin/sysdef [-h][-d][-D]
```

Description

Use the sysdef command to display the current system definition in tabular form. It lists all hardware devices, as well as pseudodevices, system devices, loadable modules, and the values of selected kernel tunable parameters.

sysdef generates the output by analyzing the named, bootable, operating system file (*namelist*) and extracting the configuration information from it.

The default system namelist is /dev/kmem.

Options

-n *namelist*	Specify a *namelist* other than the default (/dev/kmem). The *namelist* specified must be a valid, bootable operating system.
-h	Print the identifier of the current host in hexadecimal. This numeric value is unique across all Sun hosts.
-d	Display the configuration of system peripherals formatted as a device tree.
-D	For each system peripheral in the device tree, display the name of the device driver that manages the peripheral.

Examples

The following example displays the output of the sysdef -d command. The output is truncated to save space.

```
paperbark% sysdef -d
Node 'SUNW,Ultra-2', unit #-1
        Node 'packages', unit #-1 (no driver)
                Node 'terminal-emulator', unit #-1 (no driver)
                Node 'deblocker', unit #-1 (no driver)
                Node 'obp-tftp', unit #-1 (no driver)
                Node 'disk-label', unit #-1 (no driver)
                Node 'sun-keyboard', unit #-1 (no driver)
                Node 'ufs-file-system', unit #-1 (no driver)
        Node 'chosen', unit #-1 (no driver)
        Node 'openprom', unit #-1 (no driver)
                Node 'client-services', unit #-1 (no driver)
        Node 'options', unit #0
        Node 'aliases', unit #-1 (no driver)
        Node 'memory', unit #-1 (no driver)
        Node 'virtual-memory', unit #-1 (no driver)
        Node 'counter-timer', unit #-1 (no driver)
        Node 'sbus', unit #0
                Node 'SUNW,CS4231', unit #-1 (no driver)
                Node 'auxio', unit #-1 (no driver)
                Node 'flashprom', unit #-1 (no driver)
                Node 'SUNW,fdtwo', unit #-1 (no driver)
                Node 'eeprom', unit #-1 (no driver)
                Node 'zs', unit #0
                Node 'zs', unit #1
 ...(Additional lines deleted from this example)
```

Files

/dev/kmem   Default operating system image.

Attributes

See attributes(5) for descriptions of the following attributes.

Attribute Type	Attribute Value
Availability	SUNWcsu (32-bit) SUNWcsxu (64-bit)

See Also

hostid(1), prtconf(1M), nlist(3E), attributes(5)

---

sysidconfig — Execute or Define System Configuration Applications

Synopsis

sysidconfig [-lv][-a application][-b basedir][-r application]

Description

Invoked without any options, the sysidconfig program executes a list of applications. An application on this list is referred to as a "system configuration application." Every application on this list is passed one command-line argument, -c. This option performs the configuration function. Without options, sysidconfig should be invoked only by startup scripts, which are run during the initial installation and during a reconfigure reboot (boot -r).

All applications on the list are executed, if possible. All activity taken by the sysidconfig program is logged in the sysidconfig log file, /var/log/sysidconfig.log. If one or more of the applications on the list is either not present at execution time, not executable, or executes but returns a failure code on completion, then that information is logged as well. Successful completion of the program can be assumed if no error message is present in the log file. Programs are executed sequentially, with only one configuration application active at a time.

Executed with the -l, -a, or -r options, the sysidconfig program enables superuser to list the defined configuration applications and to add items to or remove items from that list. Running sysidconfig with options is the only way to view or manipulate the list. Only superuser can execute the sysidconfig program with options.

The -b and -v options change the behavior of sysidconfig and can be used with or without the list manipulation options discussed above. You can use the -b basedir option to specify a reference root directory other than the default, /. The -v option duplicates the log file output on standard output.

By default, no SPARC-based applications exist on this list. However, the IA-based systems are delivered with one application, kdmconfig(1M), on the list. kdmconfig is not delivered on SPARC-based systems.

This application is an extension of the sysidtool(1M) suite of programs. It is executed during initial installation and during a reconfigure reboot before the window system has been started. Graphical User Interface (GUI) applications do not execute successfully if they are added to the list of configuration applications with sysidconfig -a.

This program is referenced, but not fully described, in the sysidtool(1M) manual page.

Options

-a *application*

Add the named application to the list of defined applications. When next invoked without arguments, run this newly added application after all previously defined applications. *application* must be a fully qualified path name that is not currently on the list of applications to execute.

-b *basedir*
Specify an alternate base directory (/ is defined as the default base directory if you specify no other). Use the specified directory as the root directory when adding, listing, removing, or executing configuration applications. Information is recorded in /var/log, relative to the specified *basedir*. In the log file, the *basedir* is not noted. This means, for example, that if superuser on a diskless client's server executes the following command, then the diskless client would have /sbin/someapp executed on reconfigure reboot.

sysidconfig -b /export/root/client -a /sbin/someapp

The diskless client's log file would note that /sbin/someapp was added, not /export/root/client/sbin/someapp.

-l
List defined configuration applications. Execute applications one at a time, in the order shown in the list.

-r *application*

Remove the named application from the list of defined applications. *application* must be a fully qualified path name, and it must be on the existing list of applications to execute.

-v
Echo all information sent to the log file to standard output. Such information includes timestamp information about when the program was executed, the names of applications being executed, and results of those executions.

Exit Status

The sysidconfig program returns 0 if it completes successfully.

When you execute sysidconfig with the -r or -a options, error conditions or warnings are reported on standard error. If the requested action completes successfully, an exit code of 0 is returned.

Errors

EPERM   The program was executed by a user other than superuser.

EINVAL   Option -1, -a, or -r was passed and the action could not be completed
                     successfully.

Files

/var/log/sysidconfig.log

sysidconfig log file.

Attributes

See attributes(5) for descriptions of the following attributes.

Attribute Type	Attribute Value
Availability	SUNWadmap

See Also

sys-unconfig(1M), sysidtool(1M), attributes(5)

IA Platform Only
kdmconfig(1M)

Diagnostics

When you run sysidconfig without options, you can find a log of the sysidconfig
program's activity in /var/log/sysidconfig.log. This file contains a timestamp log of
each program executed, its resulting standard error output, and its exit code. If an
application in the list was not found or is not executable, that information is also noted.

sysidtool, sysidnet, sysidns, sysidsys, sysidroot, sysidp — System Configuration

Synopsis

/usr/sbin/sysidnet
/usr/sbin/sysidns
/usr/sbin/sysidsys
/usr/sbin/sysidroot
/usr/sbin/sysidpm

Description

sysidtool is a suite of five programs that configure a new system or one that has been
unconfigured with sys-unconfig(1M). The sysidtool programs run automatically at

system installation or during the first boot after a machine has been successfully unconfigured.

These programs have no effect except at such times and should never be run manually.

The `sysidtool` programs set up the appropriate information in the machine's configuration files, in the kernel, and on the machine's network interface. They may prompt for the following information

`sysidnet: Network configuration.`

- Machine's default locale.
- Machine's console type.
- Machine's host name.
- Machine's IP address.

`sysidns: Nameservice configuration` (Formerly `sysidnis`).

- Name service choice: NIS+, NIS, or none.
- Machine's IP subnet mask (if no NIS/NIS+ server can automatically be located on the machine's subnetwork).
- Domain name for chosen nameservice.
- Host name and IP address of nameserver(s).
- DNS search list (DNS nameservice only).
- Domain.

`sysidsys: Miscellaneous system configuration.`

- Machine's IP subnet mask (if an NIS/NIS+ server was automatically located on the machine's subnetwork).
- Machine's time zone.
- Date and time.

`sysidroot: Control superuser information.`

- Machine's root password.

`sysidpm: Power Management configuration.`

- Autoshutdown confirmation if the system is Energystar-V2 compliant, that is, a new system model shipped after October 1, 1995.

`sysidconfig: Host or platform-specific configuration.`

- This command controls specification and execution of custom configuration applications that can be specified for a particular host or a particular platform. (See `sysidconfig`(1M)).

The `sysidtool` commands try to get system configuration information from various nameservice databases (for example, NIS) or from the `sysidcfg`(4) file, and you are prompted to provide the information if it cannot be found. However, you can avoid one or more of the prompts by preconfiguring the appropriate configuration information in the nameservice databases or in the `sysidcfg`(4) file.

To preconfigure the information in the nameservice databases, you must use the nameservice commands or the Solstice AdminSuite tools. See *Solaris Advanced Installation Guide* for more details about how to preconfigure the system configuration information.

The machine's configuration information is set up in its `/etc` and `/var` files.

Notes

If a system has more than one network interface, you can use sysidtool to configure only the primary interface on the system. All other interfaces on the system must be configured manually.

You cannot use the nameservice databases or the sysidcfg(4) file to suppress the Power Management configuration prompt; however, you can suppress the prompt by creating either the /autoshutdown or /noautoshutdown file before installation reboot. Accordingly, the autoshutdown feature is silently configured. The /autoshutdown or /noautoshutdown files are removed by sysidpm before it exits.

Files

/etc/.UNCONFIGURED

File present on a freshly installed Solaris system that signals the system to run the setup dialog at boot time. The file is recreated when you run the sys-unconfig command.

/etc/nodename

Node name for the system.

/etc/hostname.??[0-9]

File used to match the host names in the /etc/hosts file with the network interfaces, such as le0 or hme0, at boot time.

/etc/default/init

Default init script.

/etc/defaultdomain

Default domain for the system.

/etc/passwd　Password file. See passwd(4).

/etc/shadow　Shadow password file. See shadow(4).

/etc/inet/hosts

Internet hosts table.

/etc/inet/netmasks

Internet netmasks table.

/etc/net/*/hosts

Net hosts table.

/var/nis/NIS_COLD_START

NIS coldstart file.

/var/yp/aliases

NIS aliases file.

/var/yp/binding/*/ypservers

List of NIS servers.

`/etc/.sysIDtool.state`

> State of system identification information.

`/etc/power.conf`

> Power management configuration file. See `power.conf`(4).

`/etc/.PM_RECONFIGURE`

> If this file is present during system reboot, the `sysidpm` program is
> run. This file is removed by `sysidpm`.

Attributes

See `attributes`(5) for descriptions of the following attributes.

Attribute Type	Attribute Value
Availability	SUNWadmap
	SUNWpmu

See Also

`powerd(1M)`,`sys-unconfig(1M)`,`sysidconfig(1M)`,`passwd(4)`,`power.conf(4)`,
`shadow (4)`, `sysidcfg(4)`, `attributes(5)`
> *Solaris Advanced Installation Guide*

syslogd — Log System Messages

Synopsis

`/usr/sbin/syslogd [-d][-f configfile][-m markinterval][-p path][-t]` *New!*

Description

The `syslogd` daemon reads and forwards system messages to the appropriate log files or
users, depending on the priority of a message and the system facility from which it
originates. The configuration file `/etc/syslog.conf` (see `syslog.conf`(4)) controls
where messages are forwarded. `syslogd` logs a *mark* (timestamp) message every
markinterval minutes (default 20) at priority LOG_INFO to the facility whose name is
given as *mark* in the `syslog.conf` file.

A system message consists of a single line of text that you can prefix with a priority
code number enclosed in angle brackets (<>); priorities are defined in <sys/syslog.h>.

`syslogd` reads from the STREAMS log driver, /dev/log, and from any transport
provider specified in /etc/netconfig, /etc/net/transport/hosts, and
/etc/net/transport/services.

`syslogd` reads the configuration file when it starts up, and again whenever it
receives a HUP signal (see `signal`(5), at which time it also closes all files it has open,
rereads its configuration file, and then opens only the log files that are listed in that file.
`syslogd` exits when it receives a TERM signal.

As it starts up, `syslogd` creates the file `/etc/syslog.pid`, if possible, containing its process identifier (PID).

New! If message generation is enabled (see `log(7D)`), each message is preceded by an identifier in the following format.

```
[ID msgid facility.priority]
```

msgid is the numeric identifier of the message described in `msgid(1M)`. *facility* and *priority* are described in `syslog.conf(4)`. An example of an identifier when message ID generation is enabled is `[ID 123456 kern.notice]`.

If the message originated in a loadable kernel module or driver, the name of the kernel module (for example, `ufs`) is displayed instead of `unix`. See "Examples" on page 1142 for sample output from `syslogd` with and without message ID generation enabled.

To reduce visual clutter, `syslogd` does not display message IDs when writing to the console. It writes message IDs only to the log file.

Note — The mark message is a system timestamp and so it is defined only for the system on which `syslogd` is running. It cannot be forwarded to other systems.

Options

-d   Turn on debugging. Use this option only interactively in a root shell once the system is in multiuser mode. Do not use it in system startup scripts, because the system hangs at the point where `syslogd` is started.

-f *configfile*

            Specify an alternate configuration file.

-m *markinterval*

            Specify an interval, in minutes, between mark messages.

-p *path*   Specify an alternative log device name. The default is `/dev/log`.

New! -t   Disable the `syslogd` UPD port to turn off logging of remote messages.

New! Examples

The following example shows the output from `syslogd` when message ID generation is not enabled.

```
Sep 29 21:41:18 cathy unix: alloc /: file system full
```

The following example shows the output from `syslogd` when message ID generation is enabled. Note that the message ID is displayed when `syslogd` is writing to log file `/var/adm/messages`.

```
Sep 29 21:41:18 cathy ufs: [ID 845546 kern.notice] alloc /: file system
    full
```

The following example shows the output from `syslogd` when message ID generation is enabled when the console is written to. Note that even though message ID is enabled, the message ID is not displayed at the console.

```
Sep 29 21:41:18 cathy ufs: alloc /: file system full
```

Files

`/etc/syslog.conf`

> Configuration file.

`/etc/syslog.pid`

> Process ID.

`/dev/log`   STREAMS log driver.

`/etc/netconfig`

> Transport providers available on the system.

`/etc/net/transport/hosts`

> Network hosts for each transport.

`/etc/net/transport/services`

> Network services for each transport.

Attributes

See `attributes`(5) for descriptions of the following attributes.

Attribute Type	Attribute Value
Availability	SUNWcsu

See Also

`logger(1)`, `msgid(1M)`, `syslog(3C)`, `syslog.conf(4)`, `attributes(5)`, `signal(3HEAD)`, `log(7D)`

New!

T

talkd — Server for Talk Program

Synopsis

```
/usr/sbin/in.talkd
```

Description

See in.talkd(1M).

tapes — Create /dev Entries for Tape Drives

Synopsis

```
/usr/sbin/tapes [-r rootdir]
```

Description

Note — The devfsadm(1M) command is now the preferred command for /dev and /devices, and you should use it instead of tapes. The tapes command in the Solaris 8 release is a symbolic link to the devfsadm(1M) command.

New!

taskstat — Print ASET Task Status

Synopsis

```
/usr/aset/util/taskstat [-d aset-dir]
```

Description

The `taskstat` command is part of the Automated Security Enhancement Tool (ASET) suite of commands. Because `aset` dispatches its tasks to run in the background, when it returns, these tasks may or may not have completed. You can use the `taskstat` command to print the status of ASET tasks, listing those that are completed and those that are still executing. `taskstat` is located in the `/usr/aset/util` directory. `/usr/aset` is the default ASET operating directory. Administrators can specify an alternative working directory with the `aset -d` command or the `ASETDIR` environment variable. See aset(1M).

The ASET reports, which are located in the `/usr/aset/reports` directory (see the `-d` option), are not complete until all the tasks finish executing.

Options

-d *aset-dir*   Specify the working directory for ASET. By default, this directory is `/usr/aset`.

Examples

The following example shows output from the `taskstat` command when not all tasks are done.

```
# /usr/aset/util/taskstat

Checking ASET tasks status...
Task firewall is done.
Task env is done.
Task sysconf is done.
Task usrgrp is done.

The following tasks are done:
        firewall
        env
        sysconf
        usrgrp

The following tasks are not done:
        tune
        cklist
        eeprom
#
```

Attributes

See attributes(5) for descriptions of the following attributes.

Attribute Type	Attribute Value
Availability	SUNWast

See Also

aset(1M), attributes(5)
System Administration Guide, Volume I

tcxconfig — Configure S24 (TCX) Frame Buffer

Synopsis

/usr/sbin/tcxconfig [linear | nonlinear]

Description

Use the tcxconfig command to change the default linearity of a 24-bit TrueColor
Visual for OpenWindows on a system with an S24 frame buffer. When the S24 graphics
driver for OpenWindows is installed, the default 24-bit TrueColor Visual is nonlinear.
You can run tcxconfig with an argument that specifies the setting you want.

OpenWindows should not be running when you execute the tcxconfig command
with an option. Start OpenWindows after tcxconfig has set the linearity you desire.

Options

If you specify no option, tcxconfig displays the current default setting.

You must become superuser before you can execute tcxconfig with one of the
following options.

linear   Set linear visual to be the default 24-bit TrueColor Visual. Colors are
            gamma-corrected.

nonlinear   Set nonlinear visual to be the default 24-bit TrueColor Visual.

Examples

The following example shows the current default setting on the system paperbark.

```
paperbark% tcxconfig
Current default visual for S24 is NonLinear.
usage: tcxconfig {linear | nonlinear}
paperbark%
```

Exit Status

0 — Success.

1 — An error has occurred.

Attributes

See attributes(5) for descriptions of the following attributes.

Attribute Type	Attribute Value
Availability	SUNWtcxow

See Also

attributes(5)

---

telinit — Process Control Initialization

Synopsis

```
/etc/telinit [0123456abcQqSs]
```

Description

See init(1M).

---

telnetd — DARPA TELNET Protocol Server

Synopsis

```
/usr/sbin/in.telnetd
```

Description

See in.telnetd(1M).

---

tftpd — Internet Trivial File Transfer Protocol Server

Synopsis

```
/usr/sbin/in.tftpd [-s] [homedir]
```

Description

See `in.tftpd`(1M).

---

tic — terminfo Compiler

Synopsis

`/bin/tic [-v [n]][-c] file`

Description

Use the `tic` command to translate a `terminfo` file from the source format into the compiled format. The results are placed in the directory `/usr/share/lib/terminfo`. The compiled format is needed for use with the library routines in `curses`(3X).

If the environment variable `TERMINFO` is set, the compiled results are placed there instead of `/usr/share/lib/terminfo`.

Total compiled entries cannot exceed 4096 bytes. The name field cannot exceed 128 bytes. Terminal names exceeding 14 characters are truncated to 14 characters, and a warning message is printed.

Note — When an entry, for example, *entry_name_1*, contains a `use=`*entry_name_2* field, any canceled capabilities in *entry_name_2* must also appear in *entry_name_1* before `use=` for these capabilities are canceled in *entry_name_1*.

Options

`-v[n]`   Write verbose progress output to standard error trace information. The optional integer *n* is a number from 1 to 10, indicating the desired level of detail of information. If you omit *n*, the default level is 1. Numbers greater than 1 specify increasing levels of detail.

`-c`   Check only *file* for errors. Do not detect errors in `use=` links.

Operands

file   A file containing one or more `terminfo` terminal descriptions in source format [see `terminfo`(4)]. Each description in the file describes the capabilities of a particular terminal. When a `use=`*entry-name* field is discovered in a terminal entry currently being compiled, read in the binary from `/usr/share/lib/terminfo` to complete the entry. (Entries created from *file* are used first. If the environment variable `TERMINFO` is set, search that directory instead of `/usr/share/lib/terminfo`.) Duplicate the capabilities in *entry-name* for the current entry, with the exception of those capabilities that are explicitly defined in the current entry.

Files

/usr/share/lib/terminfo/?/*

Compiled terminal description database.

Attributes

See attributes(5) for descriptions of the following attributes.

Attribute Type	Attribute Value
Availability	SUNWcsu

See Also

captoinfo(1M), infocmp(1M), curses(3X), terminfo(4), attributes(5)

---

tnamed — DARPA Trivial Name Server

Synopsis

/usr/sbin/in.tnamed [-v]

Description

See in.tnamed(1M).

---

traceroute — Print the Route Packets Take to Network Host

Synopsis

New!

/usr/sbin/traceroute [-adFIlnSvx][-A *addr-family*][-c *traffic-class*]
[-f *first-hop*][-g *gateway* [-g *gateway*...] | -r][-i *iface*]
[-L *flow-label*] [-m *max-hop*][-P *pause-sec*][-p *port*]
[-Q *max-timeout*][-q *nqueries*] [-s *src-addr*][-t *tos*][-w *wait-time*]
host [*packet-len*]

Description

New!

New options have been added to the traceroute command in the Solaris 8 release to accommodate both the IPv4 and IPv6 protocols.

The Internet is a large and complex aggregation of network hardware connected together by gateways. Tracking the route that a packet follows can be difficult. Use the traceroute command to trace the route that an IP packet follows to another Internet host.

> **Warning** — traceroute is intended for use in network testing,
> measurement, and management. Use it primarily for manual fault
> isolation. Because of the load it could impose on the network, it is unwise to
> use traceroute(1M) during normal operations or from automated scripts.

traceroute uses both the IPv4 and IPv6 protocols. Use the -A option to override the *New!*
default behavior. traceroute uses the IPv4 protocol TTL (time-to-live) field or the IPv6
field *hop-limit*. It tries to elicit an ICMP or ICMP6 TIME_EXCEEDED response from each
gateway along the path and a PORT_UNREACHABLE (or ECHO_REPLY if you specify the -I
option) response from the destination host. It starts by sending probes with a *ttl* or
hop-limit of 1 and increases by 1 until it either gets to the host or hits the maximum
max-hop. The default maximum *max-hop* is 30 hops; you can set it with the -m option.

Three probes are sent at each *ttl* or *hop-limit* setting, and a line is printed showing
the *ttl* or *hop-limit*, the host name and the address of the *gateway*, and the *rtt* (round
trip time) of each probe. You can specifically set the number of probes with the -q option.
If the probe answers come from different *gateway*s, the host name and the address of
each responding system are printed. If no response is received within a 5-second
timeout interval, an asterisk (*) is printed for that probe. You can use the -w option to
set the timeout interval. Other possible annotations that can appear after the time are
shown below.

!	The *ttl* or *hop-limit* value in the received packet is <= 1. *New!*
!H	Host unreachable.
!X	Communication administratively prohibited.
<!*N*>	ICMP (ICMP6) unreachable code *N*. If almost all the probes result in *New!* some kind of unreachable code, then traceroute gives up and exits.

The following annotations are used only for IPv4.

!F	Fragmentation needed. This annotation should never occur. If you see this annotation, the associated gateway is broken.
!N	Network unreachable.
!P	Protocol unreachable.
!S	Source route failed. This annotation should never occur. If you see this annotation, the associated gateway is broken.
!T	Unreachable for the specified *tos* (type of service). *New!*
!U	Source host isolated or precedence problem. *New!*

The following annotations are used only for IPv6.   *New!*

!A	Host unreachable for a reason other than lack of an entry in the routing table.
!B	Packet too big.
!E	Destination is not a neighbor.
!R	Unrecognized text header.

If almost all the probes result in some kind of unreachable code, then traceroute
gives up and exits.

The destination host is not supposed to process the UDP probe packets, so the destination port default is set to an unlikely value. However, if some application on the destination is using that value, you can change the value of *port* with the -p option.

The only mandatory parameter is the destination host name or IP number. The default probe datagram length is 40 bytes (60 bytes for IPv6), but you can increase this length by specifying a packet length (in bytes) after the destination host name.

You can specify all numeric arguments to traceroute in either decimal or hexadecimal notation. For example, *packetlen* can be specified either as 256 or 0x100.

Options

New! -a   Probe all of the addresses of a multihomed destination. The output looks like traceroute has been run once for each IP address of the destination. If you use this option with -A, probe only the addresses that are of the specified address family. While probing one of the addresses of the destination, you can skip to the next address by sending a SIGINT, or you can exit traceroute by sending a SIGQUIT signal. See signal(5).

New! -A *addr-family*

Specify the address family of the target host. *addr-family* can be either inet or inet6. Address family determines which protocol to use. For an argument if inet, use IPv4. For inet6, use IPv6.

By default, if you provide the name of a host, not the literal IP address, and a valid IPv6 address exists in the nameservice database, use this address. Otherwise, if the nameservice contains an IPv4 address, try the IPv4 address.

Specify the address family inet or inet6 to override the default behavior. If you specify inet, use the IPv4 address associated with the host name. If none exists, state that the host is unknown and exit. Do not try to determine if an IPv6 address exists in the nameservice database.

If you specify inet6, use the IPv6 address that is associated with the host name. If none exists, state that the host is unknown and exit.

New! -c *traffic-class*

Specify the traffic class of probe packets as an integer between 0 and 255. Gateways along the path may route the probe packet differently depending on the value of *traffic-class* set in the probe packet. This option is valid only on IPv6.

          -d   Set the SO_DEBUG socket option.

New! -f *first-hop*   To override the default value of 1, set the starting TTL (*hop-limit*) value to *first-hop*. Skip processing for those intermediate gateways that are less than *first-hop* hops away.

          -F   Set the don't fragment bit.

-g *gateway*	Specify a loose source route *gateway*. You can specify more than one *gateway* by using -g for each *gateway*. The maximum number of gateways is 8 for IPv4 and 127 for IPv6. Note that links such as MTU can further limit the number of gateways for IPv6. You cannot use this option with the -r option.
i *iface*	For IPv4, specify a network interface to obtain the source IP address for outgoing probe packets. This option is normally useful only on a multihomed host. You can achieve the same result with the -s option.
	For IPv6, specify the network interface on which probe packets are transmitted. The argument can be either an interface index such as 1 or 2 or an interface name such as le0 or hme0.
-I	Use ICMP or ICMP6 ECHO instead of UDP datagrams.
-l	Print the value of the TTL (*hop-limit*) field in each packet received.
-L *flow-label*	
	Specify the flow label of probe packets as an integer in the range from 0 to 1048575. This option is valid only on IPv6.
-m *max-hop*	Set the maximum TTL (*hop-limit*) used in outgoing probe packets. The default is 30 hops, which is the same default used for TCP connections.
-n	Print hop addresses numerically instead of symbolically and numerically. This option saves a nameserver address-to-name lookup for each gateway found on the path.
-p *port*	Set the base UDP port number used in probes. The default is 33434. traceroute hopes that nothing is listening on UDP ports (base+(nhops-1)*nqueries)to (base+(*nhops**nqueries)-1) at the destination *host*, so that an ICMP or ICMP6 PORT_UNREACHABLE message is returned to terminate the route tracing. If something is listening on a port in the default range, you can use this option to select an unused port range. *nhops* is the number of hops between the source and the destination.
-P *pause-sec*	Specify a delay, in seconds, to pause between probe packets. You may need to specify a delay if the final destination does not accept undeliverable packets in bursts.
-q *nqueries*	Set the desired number of probe queries. The default is 3.
-Q *max-timeout*	
	Stop probing this hop after *max-timeout* consecutive timeouts are detected. The default is 5. This option is useful in combination with the -q option if you have specified a large *nqueries* probe count.
-r	Bypass the normal routing tables and send directly to a host on an attached network. If the host is not on a directly attached network, return an error. You can use this option to send probes to a local host through an interface that has been dropped by the router daemon. See in.routed(1M). You cannot use this option with the -g option.

New!	-s *src-addr*	Use the following address—which usually is given as an IP address, not a host name—as the source address in outgoing probe packets. On multihomed hosts, those with more than one IP address, you can use this option to force the source address to be something other than the IP address traceroute picks by default. If the IP address is not one of this machine's interface addresses, return an error and send nothing. For IPv4, the given address, when used together with the -i option, should be configured on the specified interface. Otherwise, an error is returned. For IPv6, the interface name and the source address do not have to match.
New!	-t *tos*	Set the *tos* (type of service) in probe packets to the specified value. The default is 0. The value must be an integer in the range from 0 to 255. *gateways* along the path can route the probe packet differently depending on the *tos* value set in the probe packet. This option is valid only on IPv4.
	-v	For each hop, display the size and the destination of the response packets. Also list ICMP packets received other than TIME_EXCEEDED and UNREACHABLE.
	-w *waittime*	Set the time, in seconds, to wait for a response to a probe. The default is 5 seconds.
New!	-x	Prevent traceroute from calculating checksums. Note that checksums are usually required for the last hop when ICMP ECHO probes are used. This option is valid only on IPv4. See the -I option.

Operands

host	The network host.

Examples

The following example shows output from the traceroute command.

```
istanbul% traceroute london
traceroute: Warning: london has multiple addresses; using
   4::114:a00:20ff:ab3d:83ed
traceroute: Warning: Multiple interfaces found; using
   4::56:a00:20ff:fe93:8dde @ le0:2
traceroute to london (4::114:a00:20ff:ab3d:83ed), 30 hops max, 60 byte
   packets
1  frbldg7c-86 (4::56:a00:20ff:fe1f:65a1)  1.786 ms  1.544 ms  1.719 ms
2  frbldg7b-77 (4::255:0:0:c0a8:517)  2.587 ms 3.001 ms  2.988 ms
3  london (4::114:a00:20ff:ab3d:83ed)  3.122 ms  2.744 ms  3.356 ms
```

The target host, london, has both IPv4 and IPv6 addresses in the nameservice database. According to the default behavior, traceroute uses IPv6 address of the destination host.

In the following example, traceroute is tracking the route to host sanfrancisco, which has only IPv4 addresses in the nameservice database. Therefore, traceroute uses only IPv4 addresses. It shows the 7-hop path that a packet would follow from the host istanbul to the host sanfrancisco.

```
castle% traceroute sanfrancisco
traceroute: Warning: Multiple interfaces found; using 172.31.86.247 @
  le0 traceroute to sanfrancisco (172.29.64.39), 30 hops max, 40 byte
  packets
1 frbldg7c-86 (172.31.86.1) 1.516 ms 1.283 ms 1.362 ms
2 bldg1a-001 (172.31.1.211) 2.277 ms 1.773 ms 2.186 ms
3 bldg4-bldg1 (172.30.4.42) 1.978 ms 1.986 ms 13.996 ms
4 bldg6-bldg4 (172.30.4.49) 2.655 ms 3.042 ms 2.344 ms
5 ferbldg11a-001 (172.29.1.236) 2.636 ms 3.432 ms 3.830 ms
6 frbldg12b-153 (172.29.153.72) 3.452 ms 3.146 ms 2.962 ms
7 sanfrancisco (172.29.64.39) 3.430 ms 3.312 ms 3.451 ms
```

The following example shows the path of a packet that goes from istanbul to sanfrancisco through the hosts cairo and paris, as specified by the -g option. The -I option sends ICMP ECHO probes to the host sanfrancisco. The -i option sets the source address to the IP address configured on the interface qe0.

```
castle% traceroute -g cairo -g paris -i qe0 -q 1 -I sanfrancisco
traceroute to sanfrancisco (172.29.64.39), 30 hops max, 56 byte packets
1 frbldg7c-86 (172.31.86.1) 2.012 ms
2 flrbldg7u (172.31.17.131) 4.960 ms
3 cairo (192.168.163.175) 4.894 ms
4 flrbldg7u (172.31.17.131) 3.475 ms
5 frbldg7c-017 (172.31.17.83) 4.126 ms
6 paris (172.31.86.31) 4.086 ms
7 frbldg7b-82 (172.31.82.1) 6.454 ms
8 bldg1a-001 (172.31.1.211) 6.541 ms
9 bldg6-bldg4 (172.30.4.49) 6.518 ms
10 ferbldg11a-001 (172.29.1.236) 9.108 ms
11 frbldg12b-153 (172.29.153.72) 9.634 ms
12 sanfrancisco (172.29.64.39) 14.631 ms
```

Exit Status

0	Successful operation.
>0	An error occurred.

Attributes

See attributes(5) for descriptions of the following attributes.

Attribute Type	Attribute Value
Availability	SUNWcsu

See Also

netstat(1M), ping(1M), attributes(5)

ttyadm — Format and Output Port-Monitor-Specific Information

Synopsis

```
/usr/sbin/ttyadm [-b][-c][-h][-I][-r count][-i msg][-m modules]
  [-p prompt][-t timeout][-S y | n][-T termtype] -d device -l ttylabel
  -s service
/usr/sbin/ttyadm -V
```

Description

The ttyadm administrative command formats ttymon(1M)-specific information and writes it to standard output. The Service Access Facility (SAF) requires each port monitor to provide such a command.

Note — The port monitor administrative file is updated by the Service Access Controller's administrative commands, sacadm(1M) and pmadm(1M). ttyadm provides a way to present formatted port-monitor-specific (ttymon-specific) data to these commands.

Options

-b	Set the bidirectional port option so the line can be used in both directions. Users can connect to the service associated with the port, but if the port is free, uucico(1M), cu(1C), or ct(1C) can use it for dialing out.
-c	Set the connect-on-carrier option for the port. Invoke the port's associated service immediately when a connect indication is received (that is, print no prompt and search no baud rate).
-d *device*	Specify the full path name of the device file for the TTY port.
-h	Set the hangup option for the port. If you do not specify the -h option, force a hangup on the line by setting the speed to 0 before setting the speed to the default or specified value.
-i *message*	Specify the inactive (disabled) response message. This message is sent to the TTY port if the port is disabled or the ttymon monitoring the port is disabled.
-I	Initialize the service only once. You can use this option to configure a particular device without actually monitoring it, as with software carrier.
-l *ttylabel*	Specify which *ttylabel* in the /etc/ttydefs file to use as the starting point when searching for the proper baud rate.

-m *modules*	Specify a list of pushable STREAMS modules. The modules are pushed in the order that they are specified before the service is invoked. *modules* is a comma-separated list of modules with no white space included. Any modules currently on the stream are popped before these modules are pushed.
-p *prompt*	Specify the prompt message, for example, login:.
-r *count*	Wait to receive data from the port before displaying a prompt. If *count* is 0, wait until it receives any character. If *count* is greater than 0, wait until *count* newlines have been received.
-s *service*	Specify the full path name of the service to be invoked when a connection request is received. If arguments are required, enclose the command and its arguments in double quotes (" ").
-S y|n	Set the software carrier value. y turns software carrier on. n turns software carrier off.
-t *timeout*	Close a port if the open on the port succeeds and no input data is received in *timeout* seconds.
-T *termtype*	Set the terminal type. The TERM environment variable is set to *termtype*.
-V	Display the version number of the current /usr/lib/saf/ttymon command.

Output

If successful, ttyadm generates the requested information, writes it to standard output, and exits with a status of 0. If you invoke ttyadm with an invalid number of arguments or invalid arguments or specify an incomplete option, an error message is written to standard error and ttymon exits with a non-zero status.

Files

/etc/ttydefs File that contains terminal line settings information for ttymon.

Attributes

See attributes(5) for descriptions of the following attributes.

Attribute Type	Attribute Value
Availability	SUNWcsu

See Also

ct(1C), cu(1C), pmadm(1M), sacadm(1M), ttymon(1M), uucico(1M), attributes(5)

System Administration Guide, Volume I

ttymon — Port Monitor for Terminal Ports

Synopsis

```
/usr/lib/saf/ttymon
/usr/lib/saf/ttymon -g [-d device][-h][-t timeout][-l ttylabel]
   [-p prompt][-m modules][-T termtype]
```

Description

Use the ttymon STREAMS-based TTY port monitor to monitor ports; to set terminal modes, baud rates, and line disciplines for the ports; and to connect users or applications to services associated with the ports. Normally, ttymon is configured to run under the Service Access Controller, sac(1M), as part of the Service Access Facility (SAF). You configure it by using the sacadm(1M) command. Each instance of ttymon can monitor multiple ports. The ports monitored by an instance of ttymon are specified in the port monitor's administrative file. You configure the administrative file with the pmadm(1M) and ttyadm(1M) commands. When the sac command invokes an instance of ttymon, it starts to monitor its ports. For each port, ttymon first initializes the line disciplines, if they are specified, and the speed and terminal settings. For ports with entries in /etc/logindevperm, device owner, group, and permissions are set. (See logindevperm(4).) The values used for initialization are taken from the appropriate entry in the TTY settings file. This file is maintained by the sttydefs(1M) command. Default line disciplines on ports are usually set up by the autopush(1M) command of the Autopush Facility.

ttymon then writes the prompt and waits for user input. If the user indicates that the speed is inappropriate by pressing the BREAK key, ttymon tries the next speed and writes the prompt again. When valid input is received, ttymon interprets the per-service configuration file for the port, if one exists, creates a utmpx entry (changed from utmp in the Solaris 8 release) if required (see utmpx(4)), establishes the service environment, and then invokes the service associated with the port. Valid input consists of a string of at least one non-newline character, terminated by a Return. After the service terminates, ttymon cleans up the utmpx entry, if one exists, and returns the port to its initial state.

If autobaud is enabled for a port, ttymon tries to determine the baud rate on the port automatically. Users must press Return before ttymon can recognize the baud rate and print the prompt. Currently, the baud rates that can be determined by autobaud are 110, 1200, 2400, 4800, and 9600.

If a port is configured as a bidirectional port, ttymon enables users to connect to a service and, if the port is free, allows uucico(1M), cu(1C), or ct(1C) to use it for dialing out. If a port is bidirectional, ttymon waits to read a character before it prints a prompt.

If the connect-on-carrier flag is set for a port, ttymon immediately invokes the port's associated service when a connection request is received. The prompt message is not sent.

If a port is disabled, ttymon does not start any service on that port. If a disabled message is specified, ttymon sends out the disabled message when a connection request is received. If ttymon is disabled, all ports under that instance of ttymon are also disabled.

Note — If a port is monitored by more than one ttymon, it is possible for the ttymons to send out prompt messages so that they compete for input.

Service Invocation

The service ttymon invokes for a port is specified in the ttymon administrative file. ttymon scans the character string giving the service to be invoked for this port, looking for a %d or a %% two-character sequence. If %d is found, ttymon modifies the service command to be executed by replacing those two characters with the full path name of this port (the device name). If %% are found, they are replaced by a single %. When the service is invoked, file descriptor 0, 1, and 2 are opened to the port device for reading and writing. The service is invoked with the user ID, group ID, and current home directory set to that of the user name under which the service was registered with ttymon. ttymon adds two environment variables, HOME and TTYPROMPT, to the service's environment. HOME is set to the home directory of the user name under which the service is invoked. TTYPROMPT is set to the prompt string configured for the service on the port. TTYPROMPT is provided so that a service invoked by ttymon has a way to determine if a prompt was actually issued by ttymon and, if so, what that prompt actually was.

See ttyadm(1M) for options that can be set for ports monitored by ttymon under the Service Access Controller.

Security

ttymon uses pam(3) for session management. The PAM configuration policy, listed through /etc/pam.conf, specifies the modules to be used for ttymon. The following partial pam.conf file entries for ttymon use the UNIX session management module.

```
ttymon session required /usr/lib/security/pam_unix.so.1
```

If the ttymon service has no entries, then the entries for the other service are used.

Options

-g	A special invocation of ttymon. This form of the command should be used only by applications that cannot be preconfigured under SAC and that need to set the correct baud rate and terminal settings on a port and then connect to a login service. You can use the following combinations of options with -g.
-d *device*	Specify the full path name of the port to which ttymon is to attach. If you do not specify this option, file descriptor 0 must be set up by the invoking process to a TTY port.
-h	Use this option to override the default behavior. If you do not specify the -h option, ttymon forces a hangup on the line by setting the speed to 0 before setting the speed to the default or specified speed.
-l *ttylabel*	Specify a link to a speed and TTY definition in the ttydefs file. This definition tells ttymon at what speed to run initially, what the initial TTY settings are, and what speed to try next if the user indicates that the speed is inappropriate by pressing the Break key. The default speed is 9600 baud.
-m *modules*	When initializing the port, pop all modules on the port, and then push *modules* in the order specified. *modules* is a comma-separated list of pushable modules. Default modules on the ports are usually set up by the Autopush Facility.

-p *prompt*   Enable the user to specify a prompt string. The default prompt is
                 Login:.

-t *timeout*   Exit if no one types anything in *timeout* seconds after the prompt is
                 sent.

-T *termtype*   Set the TERM environment variable to *termtype*.

Environment Variables

If any of the LC_* variables (LC_CTYPE, LC_MESSAGES, LC_TIME, LC_COLLATE,
LC_NUMERIC, and LC_MONETARY) (see environ(5)) are not set in the environment, the
operational behavior of ttymon for each corresponding locale category is determined by
the value of the LANG environment variable. If LC_ALL is set, its contents are used to
override both the LANG and the other LC_* variables. If none of the above variables is set
in the environment, the C (U.S. style) locale determines how ttymon behaves.

LC_CTYPE   Determine how ttymon handles characters. When LC_CTYPE is set to
                a valid value, ttymon can display and handle text and file names
                containing valid characters for that locale. ttymon can display and
                handle Extended Unix Code (EUC) characters where any individual
                character can be 1, 2, or 3 bytes wide. ttymon can also handle EUC
                characters of 1, 2, or more column widths. In the C locale, only
                characters from ISO 8859-1 are valid.

Files

/etc/logindevperm

                 Login-based device permissions.

Attributes

See attributes(5) for descriptions of the following attributes.

Attribute Type	Attribute Value
Availability	SUNWcsu

See Also

ct(1C), cu(1C), autopush(1M), pmadm(1M), sac(1M), sacadm(1M),
sttydefs(1M), ttyadm(1M), uucico(1M), pam(3), logindevperm(4),
pam.conf(4), utmp(4), attributes(5), environ(5), pam_unix(5)
  System Administration Guide, Volume I

tunefs — Tune an Existing File System

Synopsis

    /usr/sbin/tunefs [-a maxcontig] [-d rotdelay] [-e maxbpg] [-m minfree]
       [-o [space | time]] special | filesystem

Description

Use the tunefs command to change a file system's dynamic parameters that affect the layout policies. The file system must be unmounted before you use tunefs. When you use tunefs with *filesystem*, *filesystem* must be in /etc/vfstab. Use the options listed below to specify the parameters that are to be changed.

Generally, you should optimize for time unless the file system is over 90 percent full.

Options

-a *maxcontig*   Specify the maximum number of contiguous blocks that are laid out   *New!*
                 before forcing a rotational delay (see -d). In the Solaris 8 release, the
                 default value is determined from the disk drive's maximum transfer
                 rate. The maximum *maxconfig* that UFS supports is 1048576. In
                 previous releases, the default value was 1 because most device drivers
                 require an interrupt per disk transfer.

-d *rotdelay*   Specify the expected time (in milliseconds) to service a transfer
                 completion interrupt and initiate a new transfer on the same disk.
                 Use this option to decide how much rotational spacing to place
                 between successive blocks in a file.

-e *maxbpg*   Indicate the maximum number of blocks any single file can allocate
                 out of a cylinder group before it is forced to begin allocating blocks
                 from another cylinder group. Typically, this value is set to
                 approximately one-quarter of the total blocks in a cylinder group. The
                 intent is to prevent any single file from using up all the blocks in a
                 single cylinder group, thus degrading access times for all files
                 subsequently allocated in that cylinder group. The effect of this limit
                 is that big files do long seeks more frequently than if they were
                 allowed to allocate all the blocks in a cylinder group before seeking
                 elsewhere. For file systems with exclusively large files, set this
                 parameter higher.

-m *minfree*   Specify the percentage of space held back from normal users—the
                 minimum free space threshold. This value can be set to 0; however, up
                 to a factor of three in throughput is lost over the performance
                 obtained at a 10 percent threshold. Note that if you raise the value
                 above the current usage level, users cannot allocate files until enough
                 files have been deleted to get under the higher threshold.

-o [space|time]

                 Change optimization strategy for the file system.

space	Conserve space.
time	Try to organize file layout to minimize access time.

Usage

See largefile(5) for the description of the behavior of tunefs when encountering files greater than or equal to 2 Gbytes (2**31 bytes).

Attributes

See attributes(5) for descriptions of the following attributes.

Attribute Type	Attribute Value
Availability	SUNWcsu

See Also

mkfs(1M), fork(2), terminfo(4), attributes(5), largefile(5)

turnacct — Turn Process Accounting On or Off

Synopsis

/usr/lib/acct/turnacct on | off | switch

Description

See acctsh(1M).

U

uadmin — Administrative Control

Synopsis

```
/sbin/uadmin cmd fcn
```

Description

Use the `uadmin` command to provide control for basic administrative functions. This command is tightly coupled to the System Administration procedures and is not intended for general use. Only superuser can use this command.

Both `cmd` (command) and `fcn` (function) are converted to integers and passed to the `uadmin` system call.

Attributes

See `attributes`(5) for descriptions of the following attributes.

Attribute Type	Attribute Value
Availability	SUNWcsu

See Also

`uadmin(2)`, `attributes(5)`

ufsdump — Incremental File System Dump

Synopsis

```
/usr/sbin/ufsdump [options][arguments] files-to-dump
```

Description

New!

The Solaris 8 release adds -L and -T options to the ufsdump command. Use the ufsdump command to back up all files specified by *files-to-dump* (normally either a whole file system or files within a file system changed after a certain date) to magnetic tape, diskette, or disk file. When ufsdump is running, the file system must be inactive; otherwise, the output of ufsdump may be inconsistent and restoring files correctly may be impossible. A file system is inactive when it is unmounted or the system is in single user mode. A file system is not considered inactive if one tree of the file system is quiescent while another tree has files or directories being modified.

options is a single string of one-letter ufsdump options.

arguments can be multiple strings whose association with the options is determined by order. That is, the first argument goes with the first option that takes an argument; the second argument goes with the second option that takes an argument, and so on.

files-to-dump is required and must be the last argument on the command line. See "Operands" on page 1167 for more information.

With most devices, ufsdump can automatically detect end-of-media. Consequently, the d, s, and t options are not needed for multivolume dumps unless ufsdump does not understand the way the device detects end-of-media, or the files are to be restored on a system with an older version of the restore command.

Note — Read errors fewer than 32 read errors on the file system are ignored.

Options

0-9	Specify the dump level. All files specified by *files-to-dump* that have been modified since the last ufsdump at a lower dump level are copied to the *dump-file* destination (normally a magnetic tape device). For instance, if a level 2 dump was done on Monday, followed by a level 4 dump on Tuesday, a subsequent level 3 dump on Wednesday would contain all files modified or added since the level 2 (Monday) backup. A level 0 dump copies the entire file system to the *dump-file*.

a *archive-file*

Archive a dump table-of-contents in the specified *archive-file* to be used by ufsrestore(1M) to determine whether a file is in the dump file that is being restored.

b *factor*	Specify the blocking factor for tape writes. The default is 20 blocks per write for tapes of density less than 6250BPI (bytes-per-inch). The default blocking factor for tapes of density 6250BPI and greater is 64. The default blocking factor for cartridge tapes (c option) is 126. The highest blocking factor available with most tape drives is 126. Note that you specify the blocking factor in terms of 512-byte blocks, for compatibility with tar(1).
c	Set the defaults for cartridge instead of the standard half-inch reel. This option sets the density to 1000BPI and the blocking factor to 126. Because ufsdump can automatically detect end-of-media, only the blocking parameter normally has an effect. When you use cartridge tapes and do not specify this option, ufsdump slightly miscomputes the size of the tape. If you specify the b, d, s, or t options with this option, use these values to override the defaults set by this option.
d *bpi*	Specify tape density. This option is not normally required because ufsdump can detect end-of-media. You can use this parameter to keep a running tab on the amount of tape used per reel. The default density is 6250BPI except when you use the c option for cartridge tape, in which case it is assumed to be 1000BPI per track. The following values are typical for tape devices.

1/2-inch tape   6250 BPI.

1/4-inch cartridge

> 1000 BPI. The tape densities and other options are documented in the st(7D) manual page.

D	Dump to diskette.
f *dump-file*	Use *dump-file* as the file to dump to instead of /dev/rmt/0. If you specify *dump-file* as -, dump to standard output.
	If the name of the file is of the form *machine*:*device*, do the dump from the specified machine over the network, using rmt(1M). Because root normally runs ufsdump, the name of the local machine must be in the /.rhosts file of the remote machine. If you specify the file as *user@machine*:*device*, try to execute as the specified user on the remote machine. The specified user must have a .rhosts file on the remote machine to allow the user invoking the command from the local machine to access the remote machine.
l	Autoload by taking the drive offline when the end-of-tape is reached before the dump is complete and wait up to two minutes for the tape drive to be ready again. This option gives autoloading (stackloader) tape drives a chance to load a new tape. If the drive is ready within two minutes, continue. If it is not, prompt for another tape and wait.
-L *string*	Set the tape label to *string* instead of the default none. *string* can be no more than 16 characters long. If it is longer, truncate the string and print a warning message. The dump is still done. The tape label is specific to the ufsdump tape format and bears no resemblance to IBM or ANSI-standard tape labels.

New!

n   Notify all operators in the sys group that ufsdump requires attention
             by sending messages to their terminals in a manner similar to that
             used by the wall(1M) command. Otherwise, send such messages only
             to the terminals (such as the console) on which the user running
             ufsdump is logged in.

o   Take the drive offline when the dump is complete or end-of-media is
             reached and rewind the tape or eject the diskette. In the case of some
             autoloading 8mm drives, the tape is removed from the drive
             automatically. This option prevents another process that rushes in to
             use the drive from inadvertently overwriting the media.

s size   Specify the size of the volume being dumped to. This option is not
             normally required because ufsdump can detect end-of-media. When
             the specified size is reached, wait for you to change the volume.
             Interpret the specified size as the length in feet for tapes and
             cartridges and as the number of 1024-byte blocks for diskettes. The
             values should be a little smaller than the actual physical size of the
             media (for example, 425 for a 450-foot cartridge). Typical values for
             tape devices depend on the c option for cartridge devices and the D
             option for diskettes.

             1/2-inch tape   2300 feet.

             60-Mbyte 1/4-inch cartridge

                                425 feet.

             150-Mbyte 1/4-inch cartridge

                                700 feet.

             diskette   1422 blocks. (Corresponds to a 1.44-Mbyte diskette,
                                with one cylinder reserved for bad block
                                information.)

S   Determine the amount of space that is needed to perform the dump
             without actually doing it, and display the estimated number of bytes
             it takes. This option is useful with incremental dumps to determine
             how many volumes of media are needed.

t tracks   Specify the number of tracks for a cartridge tape. This option is not
             normally required because ufsdump can detect end-of-media. The
             default is 9 tracks. The t option is not compatible with the D option.
             The following values are available for Sun-supported tape devices.

             60-Mbyte 1/4-inch cartridge

                                9 tracks.

             150-Mbyte 1/4-inch cartridge

                                18 tracks.

u   Update the dump record. For each file system successfully dumped,
             add an entry to the file /etc/dumpdates that includes the file-system
             name, date, and dump level.

-T *time-wait* [h | m | s]   `New!`

> Specify the amount of time to wait for an autoload to complete. Ignore
> this option unless you have also specified the l option. The default
> time to wait is 2 minutes. Specify time units with a trailing h for
> hours, m for minutes, or s for seconds. The default unit is minutes.

v

> After each tape or diskette is written, verify the contents of the media
> against the source file system. If any discrepancies occur, prompt for
> new media, then repeat the dump/verification process. The file system
> must be unmounted. You cannot use this option to verify a dump to
> standard output.

w

> Warn by providing a list of the file systems that have not been backed
> up within a day. This information is gleaned from the files
> /etc/dumpdates and /etc/vfstab. When you use the w option, ignore
> all other options. After reporting, exit immediately.

W

> Warn with highlight. Similar to the w option, except that the W option
> includes all file systems that appear in /etc/dumpdates along with
> information about their most recent dump dates and levels. File
> systems that have not been backed up within a day are highlighted.

Operands

files-to-dump

> Specify the files to dump. Usually, identify a whole file system by its
> raw device name (for example, /dev/rdsk/c0t3d0s6). Incremental
> dumps (levels 1 to 9) of files changed after a certain date apply only to
> a whole file system. Alternatively, *files-to-dump* can identify
> individual files or directories. All files or directories are dumped,
> which is equivalent to a level 0 dump; however, /etc/dumpdates is
> not updated even when you specify the u option. In all cases, the files
> must be contained in the same file system and the file system must be
> local to the system where ufsdump is being run.
>
> *files-to-dump* is required and must be the last argument on the
> command line.
>
> If you specify no options, the default is 9uf /dev/rmt/0
> *files-to-dump*.

Usage

See largefile(5) for the description of the behavior of ufsdump when encountering files
greater than or equal to 2 Gbytes (2**31 bytes).

Examples

The following example makes a full dump of a root file system on c0t3d0, on a
150-Mbyte cartridge tape unit.

```
# ufsdump 0cfu /dev/rmt/0 /dev/rdsk/c0t3d0s0
```

The following example makes and verifies an incremental dump at level 5 of the usr partition of c0t3d0, on a 1/2-inch reel tape unit 1.

```
# ufsdump 5fuv /dev/rmt/1 /dev/rdsk/c0t3d0s6
```

Process Per Reel
Because each reel requires a new process, parent processes for reels that are already written hang around until the entire tape is written.

Operator Intervention
ufsdump requires operator intervention on the following conditions.

- End of volume.
- End of dump.
- Volume write error.
- Volume-open error or disk read error (if there are more than a threshold of 32).

In addition to alerting all operators, as implied by the n option, ufsdump interacts with the operator on ufsdump's control terminal at times when ufsdump can no longer proceed or if something is grossly wrong. All questions ufsdump poses must be answered by typing yes or no, as appropriate.

Because backing up a disk can involve a lot of time and effort, ufsdump checkpoints at the start of each volume. If writing that volume fails for some reason, ufsdump, with operator permission, restarts itself from the checkpoint after a defective volume has been replaced.

Suggested Dump Schedule
It is vital to perform full, level 0, dumps at regular intervals. When performing a full dump, bring the machine down to single-user mode by using shutdown(1M). While preparing for a full dump, it is a good idea to clean the tape drive and heads. Perform incremental dumps with the system running in single-user mode.

Incremental dumps allow for convenient backup and recovery of active files on a more frequent basis with a minimum of media and time. However, there are some trade-offs. First, keep the interval between backups to a minimum (once a day at least). To guard against data loss as a result of a media failure (a rare, but possible occurrence), capture active files on (at least) two sets of dump volumes. Another consideration is to keep unnecessary duplication of files to a minimum to save both operator time and media storage. A third consideration is the ease with which a particular backed-up version of a file can be located and restored. The following four-week schedule offers a reasonable trade-off between these goals.

	Sun	Mon	Tue	Wed	Thu	Fri
Week 1:	Full	5	5	5	5	3
Week 2:		5	5	5	5	3
Week 3:		5	5	5	5	3
Week 4:		5	5	5	5	3

Although the Tuesday-through-Friday incrementals contain extra copies of files from Monday, this scheme assures that any file modified during the week can be recovered from the previous day's incremental dump.

Process Priority of ufsdump

ufsdump uses multiple processes to enable it to read from the disk and write to the media concurrently. Because of the way it synchronizes between these processes, any attempt to run dump with a nice (process priority) of -5 or better is likely to make ufsdump run slower instead of faster.

Overlapping Partitions

Most disks contain one or more overlapping slices because slice 2 covers the entire disk. The other slices are of various sizes and usually do not overlap. For example, a common configuration places root on slice 0, swap on slice 1, /opt on slice 5 and /usr on slice 6.

It should be emphasized that ufsdump dumps one UFS file system at a time. Given the above scenario where slice 0 and slice 2 have the same starting offset, executing ufsdump on slice 2 with the intent of dumping the entire disk instead dumps only the root file system on slice 0. To dump the entire disk, you must dump the file systems on each slice separately.

Exit Status

While running, ufsdump emits many verbose messages.

0	Normal exit.
1	Startup errors encountered.
3	Abort. No checkpoint attempted.

Files

/dev/rmt/0	Default unit to dump to.
/etc/dumpdates	
	Dump date record.
/etc/group	To find group sys.
/etc/hosts	To gain access to remote system with drive.
/etc/vfstab	List of file systems.

Attributes

See attributes(5) for descriptions of the following attributes.

Attribute Type	**Attribute Value**
Availability	SUNWcsu

See Also

cpio(1), tar(1), dd(1M), devnm(1M), prtvtoc(1M), rmt(1M), shutdown(1M), ufsrestore(1M), volcopy(1M), wall(1M), attributes(5), largefile(5), st(7D)

Bugs

The /etc/vfstab file does not allow the desired frequency of backup for file systems to be specified (as did /etc/fstab). Consequently, the w and W options assume file systems should be backed up daily, which limits the usefulness of these options.

ufsrestore — Incremental File System Restore

Synopsis

New!

/usr/sbin/ufsrestore i | r | R | t | x [abcdfhlLmstTvy] [*archive-file*]
[*factor*] [*dumpfile*] [n] [*filename...*]

Description

Use the ufsrestore command to restore files from backup media created with the ufsdump command. Control the actions of ufsrestore with the key argument. The key is exactly one function letter (i, r, R, t, or x) and zero or more function modifiers (letters). The key string contains no space characters. List the function modifier arguments on the command line in the same order as their corresponding function modifiers appear in the key string.

New!

filename arguments that appear on the command line or as arguments to an interactive command are treated as shell glob patterns by the x and t functions; any files or directories matching the patterns are selected. You must protect the metacharacters *, ?, and [ ] from the shell if you use them on the command line. There is no way to quote these metacharacters to explicitly match them in a file name.

The temporary files rstdir* and rstmode* are put in /tmp by default. If the TMPDIR environment variable is defined with a nonempty value, that location is used instead of /tmp.

Note — ufsrestore can get confused when doing incremental restores from dump tapes that were made on active file systems.

You must do a level 0 dump after a full restore. Because ufsrestore runs in user mode, it has no control over inode allocation. ufsrestore repositions the files, although it does not change their contents. Thus, you must do a full dump to get a new set of directories reflecting the new file positions so that later incremental dumps are correct.

Options

Function Letters

One (and only one) of the following function letters is required.

i   After reading in the directory information from the media, invoke an interactive interface that enables you to browse through the dump file's directory hierarchy and select individual files to be extracted. See "Interactive Commands" on page 1173 for a description of available commands.

r   Recursively restore the entire contents of the media into the current directory (which should be the top level of the file system). To completely restore a file system, use this function letter to restore the level 0 dump and again for each incremental dump. Although this function letter is intended for a complete restore onto a clear file system, if the file system contains files not on the media, they are preserved.

R   Resume restoring. Request a particular volume of a multivolume set from which to resume a full restore (see the r function letter). This option enables ufsrestore to start from a checkpoint when it is interrupted in the middle of a full restore.

t   List a table of contents with each file name that appears on the media. If you specify no *filename* argument, list the root directory, which provides a list of all files on the media unless you specify the h function modifier. When you use a function modifier, the table of contents is taken from the media or from the specified archive file. This function modifier is mutually exclusive with the x and r function letters.

x   Extract the named files from the media. If a named file matches a directory whose contents were written onto the media and you did not specify the h modifier, recursively extract the directory. If possible, restore the owner, modification time, and mode. Overwrite existing files and give a warning. If you specify no *filename* argument, extract the root directory, which extracts the entire tape unless you specify that the h modifier is in effect. Use the x option to restore partial file-system dumps because they are (by definition) not entire file systems.

Function Modifiers

a *archive-file*

     Read the table of contents from *archive-file* instead of the media. You can use this function modifier in combination with the t, i, or x function letters, making it possible to check whether files are on the media without having to mount the media. When used with the x and interactive (i) function letters, prompt for the volume containing the file(s) before extracting them.

b *factor*   Specify the blocking factor for tape reads. For variable length SCSI tape devices, unless the data was written with the default blocking factor, you must use a blocking factor at least as great as that used to write the tape; otherwise, an error is generated. Note that a tape block is 512 bytes. Refer to the manual page for your specific tape driver for the maximum blocking factor.

c   Convert the contents of the media in 4.1 BSD format to the new UFS file-system format.

d   Turn on debugging output.

f *dump-file* Use *dump-file* instead of /dev/rmt/0 as the file to restore from. Typically *dump-file* specifies a tape or diskette drive. If you specify *dump-file* as -, read from the standard input. This feature enables ufsdump(1M) and ufsrestore to be used in a pipeline to copy a file system.

> # **ufsdump 0f - /dev/rdsk/c0t0d0s7|**
> **(cd /home;ufsrestore xf -)**

If the name of the file is of the form *machine:device*, do the restore from the specified machine over the network by using rmt(1M). Because root normally runs ufsrestore, the name of the local machine must appear in the /.rhosts file of the remote machine. If you specify the file as *user@machine:device*, try to execute as the specified user on the remote machine. The specified user must have a .rhosts file on the remote machine that allows the user invoking the command from the local machine to access the remote machine.

h Extract or list the actual directory instead of the files that it references. This option prevents hierarchical restoration of complete subtrees from the tape.

New! l Specify autoload. When the end-of-tape is reached before the restore is complete, take the drive offline and wait up to two minutes (the default, see the T function modifier) for the tape drive to be ready again. This delay gives autoloading (stackloader) tape drives a chance to load a new tape. If the drive is ready within two minutes, continue. If it is not, prompt for another tape and wait.

New! L *label* Specify the label to appear in the header of the dump file. If the labels do not match, issue a diagnostic and exit. The tape label is specific to the ufsdump tape format and bears no resemblance to IBM or ANSI-standard tape labels.

m Extract by inode numbers instead of by file name to avoid regenerating complete path names. Regardless of where the files are located in the dump hierarchy, restore them into the current directory and rename them with their inode number. This option is useful if only a few files are being extracted.

s *n* Skip to the *n*th file when there are multiple dump files on the same tape. For example, the following command positions you to the fifth file on the tape when reading volume 1 of the dump.

> # **ufsrestore xfs /dev/rmt/0hn 5**

If a dump extends over more than one volume, assume all volumes except the first start at position 0, no matter what s *n* value is specified.

If you specify s *n*, the backup media must be at BOT (beginning of tape). Otherwise, the initial positioning to read the table of contents fails because it is performed by skipping the tape forward *n-1* files instead of by using absolute positioning. On some devices, absolute positioning is very time consuming.

T *timeout* [h | m | s]   *New!*

Specify the amount of time to wait for an autoload command to
complete. Ignore this function modifier unless you have also specified
the l function modifier. The default timeout period is two minutes.
You can specify the time units as a trailing h for hours, m for minutes,
or s for seconds. The default unit is seconds.

v   Display the name and inode number of each file restored, preceded by
its file type.

y   Do not ask whether to abort the restore in the event of tape errors. Try
to skip over the bad tape block(s) and continue.

Interactive Commands

ufsrestore enters interactive mode when invoked with the i function letters.
Interactive commands are reminiscent of the shell. For those commands that accept an
argument, the default is the current directory. The interactive options are described
below.

add [*filename*]

Add the named file or directory to the list of files to extract. If you
specify a directory, add that directory and its files (recursively) to the
extraction list (unless you specify the h modifier).

cd *directory* Change to *directory* within the dump file.

delete [*filename*]

Delete the current directory or the named file or directory from the list
of files to extract. If you specify a directory, delete that directory and
all its descendants from the extraction list (unless you specify the h
modifier). The most expedient way to extract a majority of files from
a directory is to add that directory to the extraction list and then
delete specific files.

extract   Extract all files on the extraction list from the dump media. Ask which
volume you want to mount. The fastest way to extract a small number
of files is to start with the last volume and work toward the first. If you
specify s *n* on the command line, automatically position volume 1 to
file *n* when it is read.

help   Display a summary of the available commands.

ls [*directory*]

List files in *directory* or the current directory, represented by a dot
(.). Append directories with a slash (/). Prefix entries marked for
extraction with an asterisk (*). If you specify the verbose option, also
list inode numbers.

marked [*directory*]   *New!*

Like ls except list only files marked for extraction.

New!	pager	Toggle the pagination of output from the ls and marked commands. The pager used is that defined by the PAGER environment variable or more(1) if PAGER is not defined. PAGER can include white-space-separated arguments for the pagination program.
	pwd	Print the full path name of the current working directory.
	quit	Exit immediately, even if the extraction list is not empty.
	setmodes	Prompt set owner/mode for '.' (period). Type y for yes to set the mode (permissions, owner, times) of the current directory dot (.) into which files are being restored equal to the mode of the root directory of the file system from which they were dumped. Normally, you want to set modes when you are restoring a whole file system or when restoring individual files into the same locations from which they were dumped. Type n for no to leave the mode of the current directory unchanged. Normally, you want to leave modes unchanged when restoring part of a dump to a directory other than the one from which the files were dumped.
New!	setpager command	
		Set the command to use for paginating output instead of the default or that inherited from the environment. You can include arguments in the command string in addition to the command itself.
	verbose	Toggle the status of the v modifier. While v is in effect, the ls command lists the inode numbers of all entries, and ufsrestore displays information about each file as it is extracted.
	what	Display the dump header on the media.

Operands

filename	Specify the path name of files (or directories) to be restored to disk. Unless you also use the h function modifier, a directory name refers to the files it contains and (recursively) its subdirectories and the files they contain. filename is associated with either the x or t function letters and must come last.

Usage

See largefile(5) for the description of the behavior of ufsrestore when encountering files greater than or equal to 2 Gbytes (2**31 bytes).

Exit Status

0	Successful completion.
1	An error occurred. Verbose messages are displayed.

Environment Variables

New!

PAGER	Specify the command to use as a filter for paginating output. You can also use this variable to specify the options to be used. Default is more(1).
TMPDIR	Specify the directory for temporary files. The default is /tmp if this environment variable is not defined.

Files

/dev/rmt/0	The default tape drive.
/tmp/rstdir*	File containing directories on the tape.
/tmp/rstmode*	Owner, mode, and timestamps for directories.
./restoresymtable	
	Information passed between incremental restores.

Attributes

See attributes(5) for descriptions of the following attributes.

Attribute Type	**Attribute Value**
Availability	SUNWcsu

See Also

mkfs(1M), mount(1M), rmt(1M), ufsdump(1M), attributes(5), largefile(5)

Diagnostics

ufsrestore complains about bad option characters.

Read errors result in complaints. If you specify y on the command line or respond y, ufsrestore tries to continue.

If the dump extends over more than one tape, ufsrestore asks you to change tapes. If you specify the x or i function letter, ufsrestore also asks which volume you want to mount. If you specify the s modifier and volume 1 is mounted, it is automatically positioned to the indicated file.

ufsrestore can list numerous consistency checks. Most checks are self-explanatory or can never happen. Common errors are listed below.

Converting to new file-system format

A dump tape created from the old file system has been loaded. It is automatically converted to the new file-system format.

filename: not found on tape

The specified file name was listed in the tape directory, but it was not found on the tape because of tape read errors while looking for the file or from using a dump tape created on an active file system.

expected next file *inumber*, got *inumber*

> A file that was not listed in the directory showed up. This error can occur when a dump tape created on an active file system is used.

Incorrect tape label. Expected 'foo', got 'bar'.

> The L option was specified and its value did not match what was recorded in the header of the dump file.

Incremental tape too low

> When an incremental restore is being done, a tape that was written before the previous incremental tape, or that has too low an incremental level has been loaded.

Incremental tape too high

> When an incremental restore is being done, a tape that does not begin its coverage where the previous incremental tape left off or one that has too high an incremental level has been loaded.

media read error: invalid argument

> Blocking factor specified for read is smaller than the blocking factor used to write data.

Tape read error while restoring *filename*
Tape read error while skipping over inode *inumber*
Tape read error while trying to resynchronize 10
A tape read error has occurred

> If a file name is specified, then its contents are probably partially wrong. If an inode is being skipped or the tape is trying to resynchronize, then no extracted files have been corrupted, though files may not be found on the tape.

resync ufsrestore, skipped num

> After a tape read error, ufsrestore may have to resynchronize itself. This message lists the number of blocks that were skipped over.

umount — Unmount File Systems and Remote Resources

Synopsis

```
/usr/sbin/umount [-V][-o specific-options] special | mount-point
/usr/sbin/umount -a [-V][-o specific-options][mount-point...]
```

Description

See mount(1M).

umountall — Unmount Multiple File Systems

Synopsis
```
/usr/sbin/umountall [-k][-s][-F FSType][-l | -r]
/usr/sbin/umountall [-k][-s][-h host]
```

Description
See mountall(1M).

unlink — Unlink Files and Directories

Synopsis
```
/usr/sbin/unlink file
```

Description
See link(1M).

unshare — Make Local Resource Unavailable for Mounting by Remote Systems

Synopsis
```
/usr/sbin/unshare [-F FSType][-o specific-options][pathname |
  resourcename]
```

Description
Use the unshare command to make a shared local resource unavailable as file-system type *FSType*. If you omit the option -F *FSType*, then the first file-system type listed in the /etc/dfs/fstypes file is used as the default. *specific-options*, as well as the semantics of *resourcename*, are specific to particular distributed file systems.

> **Note** — If *pathname* or *resourcename* is not found in the shared information, an error message is sent to standard error.

Options

-F *FSType*   Specify the file-system type.

-o *specific-options*

Specify options specific to the file system provided by the -F option.

Files

/etc/dfs/fstypes

File that registers distributed file-system packages.

/etc/dfs/sharetab

Shared file system table.

Attributes

See attributes(5) for descriptions of the following attributes.

Attribute Type	Attribute Value
Availability	SUNWcsu

See Also

share(1M), shareall(1M), attributes(5)

---

unshare_nfs — Make Local NFS File Systems Unavailable for Mounting by Remote Systems

Synopsis

/usr/sbin/unshare [-F nfs] *pathname*

Description

Use the unshare command to make local file systems unavailable for mounting by remote systems. The shared file system must correspond to a line with NFS as the *FSType* in the file /etc/dfs/sharetab.

Notes

If the file system being unshared is a symbolic link to a valid path name, the canonical path (the path which the symbolic link follows) is unshared.

For example, if /export/foo is a symbolic link to /export/bar (/export/foo -> /export/bar), the following unshare command uses /export/bar as the unshared path name, not /export/foo.

unshare -F nfs /export/foo

Options

-F   You can omit this option if NFS is the first file-system type listed in the `/etc/dfs/fstypes` file.

Files

`/etc/dfs/fstypes`

File that registers distributed file-system packages.

`/etc/dfs/sharetab`

Shared file system table.

Attributes

See `attributes`(5) for descriptions of the following attributes.

Attribute Type	Attribute Value
Availability	SUNWcsu

See Also

`share(1M)`, `attributes(5)`

---

unshareall — Unshare Multiple Resources

Synopsis

`/usr/sbin/unshareall [-F FSType [,FSType...]]`

Description

See `shareall`(1M).

---

useradd — Administer a New User Login or Role on a System

Synopsis

```
/usr/sbin/useradd [-c comment][-d dir][-e expire][-f inactive]
    [-g group][-G group [, group...]][-m [-k skel-dir]][-u uid [-o]]
    [-s shell][-A authorization [,authorization...]][-P profile
    [,profile...]][-R role [,role...]] login
/usr/sbin/useradd -D [-b base-dir][-e expire][-f inactive][-g group]
```

New!

Description

New!

Note — useradd adds a user definition only to the local /etc/group, /etc/passwd, /etc/shadow, and /etc/user_attr files. If you are using a network nameservice such as NIS or NIS+ to supplement the local /etc/passwd file with additional entries, you cannot use the useradd command to change information supplied by the network nameservice. However, useradd does verify the uniqueness of the user name (or role) and user ID and the existence of any group names specified against the external nameservice.

Use the useradd command to add a new user entry to the /etc/passwd and /etc/shadow files. You can also create supplementary group memberships for the user (-G option) and create the home directory (-m option) for the user. The new login remains locked until the passwd(1) command is executed.

Specifying useradd -D with the -g, -b, -f, or -e options (or any combination of these) sets the default values for the respective fields. Subsequent useradd commands without the -D option use these arguments.

New!

The -A *authorization*, -P *profile*, and -R *role* options have been added to the useradd command in the Solaris 8 release for administering the new role-based access control (RBAC).

The system file entries created with this command have a limit of 512 characters per line. Specifying long arguments to several options can exceed this limit.

Specify the login (*login*) and role (*role*) fields as a string of no more than eight bytes consisting of characters from the set of alphabetic characters, numeric characters, period (.), underscore (_), and dash (-). The first character should be alphabetic, and the argument should contain at least one lowercase alphabetic character. A warning message is written if these restrictions are not met. A future Solaris release may refuse to accept login and role fields that do not meet these requirements. The login and role fields must contain at least one character and must not contain a colon (:) or a newline (\n).

Options

New!

-A *authorization*

Specify one or more comma-separated authorizations as defined in auth_attr(4). Only a user or role that has grant rights to the authorization can assign it to an account.

-b *base-dir*   Specify the default base directory for the system. If you do not specify -d *dir*, concatenate *base-dir* with the user's login to define the home directory. If you do not use the -m option, *base-dir* must exist.

-c *comment*   Specify the text string of a comment, which is usually a short description of the login. *comment* is currently used as the field for the user's full name. This information is stored in the user's /etc/passwd entry.

-d *dir*   Specify the home directory of the new user. *dir* defaults to *base-dir*/*login*, where *base-dir* is the base directory for new login home directories and *login* is the new login name.

-D	Display the default values for group, *base-dir*, *skel-dir*, *shell*, *inactive*, and *expire*. When used with the -g, -b, -f, or -e options, -D sets the following default values for the specified fields.

group	other (GID of 1).
base-dir	/home
skel-dir	/etc/skel
shell	/bin/sh
inactive	0
expire	Null (unset).

-e *expire*　Specify the expiration date for a login. After this date, no user can access this login. Enter *expire*, using one of the formats included in the template file /etc/datemsk. See getdate(3C). In the Solaris 8 release, the /etc/datemsk file defines acceptable date formats.

If the date format that you choose includes spaces, you must quote it. For example, you can enter 10/6/99 or "October 6, 1999". A null value (" ") defeats the status of the expired date. This option is useful for creating temporary logins.

-f *inactive*　Specify the maximum number of days allowed between uses of a login ID before that login ID is declared invalid. Normal values are positive integers. A value of 0 defeats the status.

-g *group*　Specify either an integer or name for an existing group. Without the -D option, define the new user's primary group membership and default to the default group. You can reset this default value by invoking useradd -D -g *group*.

-G *group*　Define supplementary group membership as either an integer or name for an existing group. Ignore duplicates between *group* with the -g and -G options. You can specify no more than NGROUPS_MAX groups.

-k *skel-dir*　Specify a directory that contains skeleton information (such as .profile) that can be copied into a new user's home directory. This directory must already exist. The system provides the /etc/skel directory that you can use for this purpose.

-m　Create the new user's home directory if it does not already exist. If the directory already exists, it must have read, write, and execute permissions for the user's primary group.

-o　Create a duplicate (nonunique) UID.

-P *profile*　Specify one or more comma-separated execution profiles as defined in prof_attr(4).

-R *role*　Specify one or more comma-separated execution profiles as defined in user_attr(4). You cannot assign roles to other roles.

-s *shell*　Specify the full path name of the user's login shell. The default is an empty field that uses /bin/sh. The value of *shell* must be a valid executable file.

-u *uid*   Specify the UID of the new user as a nonnegative decimal integer below MAXUID as defined in <sys/param.h>. The default is the next available (unique) number above the highest number currently assigned. For example, if UIDs 100, 105, and 200 are assigned, the next default UID number is 201. (UIDs from 0-99 are reserved by SunOS for future applications.)

Files

New!   /etc/datemsk File that contains a list of format specifiers and characters that provide a set of allowable date formats.

/etc/passwd   User account information.

/etc/shadow   Password file.

/etc/group   Group file.

/etc/skel   File that contains default local.profile, local.login, and local.cshrc files.

/usr/include/limits.h

               File that contains limit specifications, including the maximum length of a line and maximum characters allowed for a user name.

New!   /etc/user_attr

               Extended user attributes database.

Attributes

See attributes(5) for descriptions of the following attributes.

Attribute Type	Attribute Value
Availability	SUNWcsu

See Also

New!   passwd(1), profiles(1), roles(1), users(1B), groupadd(1M), groupdel(1M), groupmod(1M), grpck(1M), logins(1M), pwck(1M), userdel(1M), usermod(1M), getdate(3C), auth_attr(4), passwd(4), prof_attr(4), user_attr(4), attributes(5)

Diagnostics

In case of an error, useradd prints an error message and exits with a non-zero status.

UX: useradd: ERROR: *login* is already in use.

               Choose another. The login specified is already in use.

UX: useradd: ERROR: uid *uid* is already in use.

               Choose another. The UID specified with the -u option is not unique.

UX: useradd: ERROR: group *group* does not exist.

> Choose another. The group specified with the -g option does not exist.

UX: useradd: WARNING: uid *uid* is reserved.

> The UID specified with the -u option is in the range of reserved UIDs (from 0-99).

UX: useradd: ERROR: uid *uid* is too big.

> Choose another. The UID specified with the -u option exceeds MAXUID as defined in <sys/param.h>.

created. UX: useradd: ERROR: Cannot update system files login cannot be determined.

> The /etc/passwd or /etc/shadow files do not exist.

userdel — Delete a User Login from a System

Synopsis

```
/usr/sbin/userdel [-r] login
```

Description

> **Note** — The userdel command deletes only a user definition that is in the local /etc/group, /etc/passwd, /etc/shadow, and /etc/user_attr file. If you are using a network nameservice such as NIS or NIS+ to supplement the local /etc/passwd file with additional entries, userdel cannot change information supplied by the network nameservice.   *New!*

Use the userdel command to delete a user's login from the system and make the appropriate login-related changes to the system file and file system. The userdel command has been modified in the Solaris 8 release as part of role-based access control (RBAC) to remove the user from any roles.   *New!*

Options

-r
> Remove the user's home directory from the system. This directory must exist. The files and directories under the home directory are no longer accessible after successful execution of the command.

Operands

login
> An existing login name to be deleted.

Exit Status

0	Success.
2	Invalid command syntax. A usage message for the usimerdel command is displayed.
6	The login to be removed does not exist.
8	The login to be removed is in use.
10	Cannot update the /etc/group or /etc/user_attr file, but the login is removed from the /etc/passwd file.
12	Cannot remove or otherwise modify the home directory.

New! appears beside exit status 10.

Files

/etc/passwd	System password file.
/etc/shadow	System file contain users' encrypted passwords and related information.
/etc/group	System file containing group definitions.
/etc/user_attr	System file containing additional user attributes.

New! appears beside /etc/user_attr.

Attributes

See attributes(5) for descriptions of the following attributes.

Attribute Type	Attribute Value
Availability	SUNWcsu

See Also

New!

auths(1), passwd(1), profiles(1), roles(1), users(1B), groupadd(1M), groupdel(1M), groupmod(1M), logins(1M), roleadd(1M), roledel(1M), rolemod(1M), useradd(1M), usermod(1M), passwd(4), prof_attr(4), user_attr(4), attributes(5)

usermod — Modify User Login or Role Information on a System

Synopsis

New!

```
/usr/sbin/usermod [-u uid [-o]][-g group][-G group [, group...]]
    [-d dir [-m]][-s shell][-c comment][-l new-logname][-f inactive]
    [-e expire][-A authorization [,authorization...]][-P profile
    [,profile...]][-R role [,role...]] login
```

Description

> **Note** — The `usermod` command modifies password definitions only in the
> local `/etc/passwd`, `/etc/shadow`, and `/etc/user_attr` files. If you are using
> a network nameservice such as NIS or NIS+ to supplement the local files
> with additional entries, `usermod` cannot change information supplied by the
> network nameservice. However, `usermod` does verify the uniqueness of user
> name and user ID against the external nameservice.

> The `usermod` command uses the `/etc/datemsk` file, available with `SUNWaccr`,
> for date formatting.

Use the `usermod` command to modify a user's login definition on the system. It
changes the definition of the specified login and makes the appropriate login-related
system-file and file-system changes.

The `-A authorization`, `-P profile`, and `-R role` options have been added to the
`usermod` command in the Solaris 8 release for administering the new role-based access
control (RBAC).

The system-file entries created with this command have a limit of 512 characters per
line. Specifying long arguments to several options can exceed this limit.

Options

`-A authorization`

Specify one or more comma-separated authorizations as defined in
`auth_attr(4)`. Only a user or role who has `grant` rights to the
authorization can assign it to an account. The new authorization
value replaces any existing authorization setting.

`-c comment`
Specify a comment string, which is generally a short description of
the login. `comment` is currently used as the field for the user's full
name. This information is stored in the user's `/etc/passwd` entry.

`-d dir`
Specify the new home directory of the user. The default is
`base-dir/login`, where `base-dir` is the base directory for new login
home directories and `login` is the new login.

`-e expire`
Specify the expiration date for a login. After this date, no user can
access this login. You can type the value of the `expire` argument by
using one of the date formats included in the template file
`/etc/datemsk`. See `getdate(3C)`. In the Solaris 8 release, the
`/etc/datemsk` file defines acceptable date formats.

For example, you can enter `10/6/99` or `"October 6, 1999"`. A value
of `" "` defeats the status of the expired date.

`-f inactive`
Specify the maximum number of days allowed between uses of a login
ID before that login ID is declared invalid. Normal values are positive
integers. A value of `0` defeats the status.

`-g group`
Redefine the user's primary group membership by specifying an
integer or name for an existing group.

	-G *group*	Redefine the user's supplementary group membership by specifying an integer or name for an existing group. Ignore duplicates between groups with the -g and -G options. You can specify no more than NGROUPS_UMAX groups as defined in <param.h>.
	-l *new-logname*	
		Specify the new login name for the user as a string of no more than eight bytes and consisting of characters from the set of alphabetic characters, numeric characters, period (.), underline (_), and dash (-). The first character should be alphabetic, and the field should contain at least one lowercase alphabetic character. A warning message is displayed if these restrictions are not met. A future Solaris release may refuse to accept login fields that do not meet these requirements. The *new-logname* argument must contain at least one character and must not contain a colon (:) or newline (\n).
	-m	Move the user's home directory to the new directory specified with the -d option. If the directory already exists, it must have permissions read/write/execute by *group*, where *group* is the user's primary group.
	-o	Allow the specified UID to be duplicated (nonunique).
New!	-P *profile*	Specify one or more comma-separated execution profiles as defined in prof_attr(4). The new profile replaces any existing profile setting.
New!	-R *role*	Specify one or more comma-separated execution profiles as defined in user_attr(4). You cannot assign roles to other roles. The new role replaces any existing profile setting.
	-s *shell*	Specify the full path name of user's login shell. The value of *shell* must be a valid executable file.
	-u *uid*	Specify a new UID for the user as a nonnegative decimal integer less than MAXUID as defined in <param.h>. Note that the UID associated with the user's home directory is not modified with this option; users do not have access to their home directory until the UID is manually reassigned with chown(1M).

Operands

login	An existing login name to be modified.

Exit Status

In case of an error, usermod prints an error message and exits with one of the following values.

2	The command syntax was invalid. A usage message is displayed.
3	An invalid argument was provided to an option.
4	The UID given with the -u option is already in use.

5	The password files contain an error. You can use pwconv(1M) to correct possible errors. See passwd(4).
6	The login to be modified does not exist, the group does not exist, or the login shell does not exist.
8	The login to be modified is in use.
9	The *new-logname* is already in use.
10	Cannot update the /etc/group or /etc/user_attr file. Other update requests are implemented.
11	Insufficient space to move the home directory (-m option). Other update requests are implemented.
12	Unable to complete the move of the home directory to the new home directory.

Files

/etc/datemsk	System file of date formats.
/etc/group	System file containing group definitions.
/etc/passwd	System password file.
/etc/shadow	System file containing users' encrypted passwords and related information.
/etc/user_attr	
	System file containing additional user attributes.

Attributes

See attributes(5) for descriptions of the following attributes.

Attribute Type	**Attribute Value**
Availability	SUNWcsu

See Also

passwd(1), users(1B), chown(1M), groupadd(1M), groupdel(1M), groupmod(1M), logins(1M), pwconv(1M), roleadd(1m), roledel(1M), rolemod(1M), useradd(1M), userdel(1M), getdate(3C), auth_attr(4), passwd(4), prof_attr(4), user_attr(4), attributes(5)

utmp2wtmp — Create an Entry in /var/adm/wtmpx Created by runacct

Synopsis
/usr/lib/acct/utmp2wtmp

Description
See acct(1M).

utmpd — utmpx Monitoring Daemon

Synopsis
/etc/init.d/utmpd [-debug]

Description
The utmpd daemon monitors /var/adm/utmpx files. See utmpx(4).

New!

> **Note** — /var/adm/utmp is obsolete in the Solaris 8 release and is no longer present on the system. Third-party applications may recreate utmp if they find it missing from the system. You should not permit utmp files to remain on the system and should investigate to determine which application is recreating the file.

utmpd receives requests from pututline(3C) and pututxline(3C) by way of a named pipe. It maintains a table of processes and uses poll(2) on /proc files to detect process termination. When utmpd detects that a process has terminated, it checks that the process has removed its utmpx entry from /var/adm/utmpx. If the utmpx entry for the process has not been removed, utmpd removes the entry. By periodically scanning the /var/adm/utmpx file, utmpd also monitors processes that are not in its table.

Options

-debug	Run in debug mode, leaving the process connected to the controlling terminal. Write debugging information to standard output.

Exit Status

0	Successful completion.
>0	An error occurred.

Files

/var/adm/utmpx

File containing user and accounting information. utmpx is an
extended database file that replaces the obsolete utmp database file.

/proc

Directory containing files for processes whose utmpx entries are being
monitored.

Attributes

See attributes(5) for descriptions of the following attributes.

Attribute Type	Attribute Value
Availability	SUNWcsu

See Also

poll(2),pututline(3C),pututxline(3C),proc(4),utmpx(4),attributes(5)

---

uucheck — Check the UUCP Directories and Permissions File

Synopsis

/usr/lib/uucp/uucheck [-v][-x *debug-level*]

Description

The uucheck command checks for the presence of the uucp system-required files and
directories. uucheck also does error checking of the Permissions file
(/etc/uucp/Permissions).

uucheck is executed during package installation. uucheck can be used only by
superuser or uucp.

Options

-v

Explain in detail how the uucp programs interpret the Permissions
file.

-x *debug-level*

Produce debugging output on the standard output. *debug-level* is a
number from 0 to 9. Higher numbers give more detailed debugging
information.

Files

/etc/uucp/Devices

> Equipment that can be used to connect to other computers.

/etc/uucp/Limits

> UUCP limits file that specifies the maximum number of simultaneous connections with uucico, uuqts, and uuscheds.

/etc/uucp/Permissions

> Per-machine and per-login permissions file.

/etc/uucp/Systems

> Names, phone numbers, and passwords of systems with which you can communicate.

/var/spool/locks/*

> Lock files directory.

/var/spool/uucp/*

> UUCP spooling directory.

/var/spool/uucppublic/*

> World-writeable directory.

Attributes

See attributes(5) for descriptions of the following attributes.

Attribute Type	Attribute Value
Availability	SUNWbnuu

See Also

uucp(1C), uustat(1C), uux(1C), uucico(1M), uusched(1M), attributes(5)

Bugs

The program does not check file/directory modes or some errors in the Permissions file such as duplicate login or machine name.

uucico — File Transport Program for the UUCP System

Synopsis

```
/usr/lib/uucp/uucico [-f][-c type][-d spooldirectory][-i interface]
   [-r role-number][-s system-name][-x debug-level]
```

Description

The uucico command is the file transport program for uucp work file transfers.

Options

-f   Force execution by ignoring the limit on the maximum number of
                      uucicos defined in the /etc/uucp/Limits file.

-c *type*   Force use of only entries in Devices file with a Type field that
                      matches the specified *type*. *type* is usually the name of a local area
                      network.

-d *spool-directory*

                      Specify the directory *spool-directory* that contains the UUCP work
                      files to be transferred. The default spool directory is
                      /var/spool/uucp.

-i *interface*   Define the interface. The interface affects only slave mode. Known
                      interfaces are UNIX (default), TLI (basic Transport Layer Interface),
                      and TLSI (Transport Layer Interface with Streams modules,
                      read/write).

-r *role-number*

                      Specify the *role-number*. Values are 1 for master mode and 0 for slave
                      mode (the default). When uucico is started by a program or cron, you
                      should use *role-number* 1.

-s *system-name*

                      Specify the remote system to contact. This option is required when
                      the role is master; *system-name* must be defined in the Systems file.

-x *debug-level*

                      Transfer both uux and uucp queue jobs by uucico. These jobs are
                      normally started by the uusched scheduler for debugging purposes
                      and can be started manually. For example, the shell Uutry starts
                      uucico with debugging turned on. The *debug-level* is a number
                      between 0 and 9. Higher numbers give more detailed debugging
                      information.

Files

/etc/uucp/Devconfig

                      File that enables you to configure devices by service.

/etc/uucp/Devices

                      Equipment that can be used to connect to other computers.

/etc/uucp/Limits

                      UUCP limits file that specifies the maximum number of
                      simultaneous connections with uucico, uuqts, and uuscheds.

`/etc/uucp/Permissions`

> Per-machine and per-login permissions file.

`/etc/uucp/Sysfiles`

> File that enables you to specify different `Systems`, `Devices`, and `Dialers` files for `uucico` and `cu`.

`/etc/uucp/Systems`

> Names, phone numbers, and passwords of systems with which you can communicate.

`/var/spool/locks/*`

> Lock files directory.

`/var/spool/uucp/*`

> UUCP spooling directory.

`/var/spool/uucppublic/*`

> World-writeable directory.

Attributes

See `attributes`(5) for descriptions of the following attributes.

Attribute Type	Attribute Value
Availability	SUNWbnuu

See Also

`uucp`(1C), `uustat`(1C), `uux`(1C), `cron`(1M), `uusched`(1M), `Uutry`(1M), `attributes`(5)

uucleanup — UUCP Spool Directory Cleanup

Synopsis

`/usr/lib/uucp/uucleanup[-Ctime][-Dtime][-mstring][-otime][-ssystem]`
`[-Wtime][-xdebug-level][-Xtime]`

Description

The `uucleanup` command scans the spool directories for old files and takes appropriate action to remove them in a useful way.

- Inform the requester of send/receive requests for systems that cannot be reached.
- Return undeliverable mail to the sender.
- Deliver `rnews` files addressed to the local system.
- Remove all other files.

In addition, users can be warned of requests that have been waiting for a given number of days (default 1 day).

Note — uucleanup processes as if all option times were specified to the default values unless time is specifically set.

This program is typically started by the shell uudemon.cleanup, which should be started by cron(1M).

Options

-Ctime	Remove any C. files greater than or equal to *time* days old and send appropriate information to the requester (default 7 days).
-Dtime	Remove any D. files greater than or equal to *time* days old, try to deliver mail messages, and execute rnews when appropriate (default 7 days).
-mstring	Include *string* in the warning message generated by the -W option. The default string is See your local administrator to locate the problem.
-otime	Delete other files whose age is more than *time* days (default 2 days).
-ssystem	Execute for *system* spool directory only.
-Wtime	Send a mail message to the requester about any C. files equal to *time* days old, warning about the delay in contacting the remote system. The message includes the job ID, and in the case of mail, the mail message. The administrator can include a message line telling whom to call to check the problem (-m option) (default 1 day).
-xdebug-level	
	Produce debugging output on standard output. Specify debug-*level* as a single digit between 0 and 9; higher numbers give more detailed debugging information. (This option may not be available on all systems.)
-Xtime	Remove any X. files greater than or equal to *time* days old. The D. files are probably not present (if they were, the X. could be executed). But if there are D. files, they are taken care of by D. processing (default 2 days).

Files

/usr/lib/uucp

Directory with commands used internally by uucleanup.

/var/spool/uucp

Spool directory.

Attributes

See attributes(5) for descriptions of the following attributes.

Attribute Type	Attribute Value
Availability	SUNWbnuu

See Also

uucp(1C), uux(1C), cron(1M), attributes(5)

uucpd — UUCP Server

Synopsis

/usr/sbin/in.uucpd [-n]

Description

See in.uucpd(1M).

uusched — UUCP File Transport Program Scheduler

Synopsis

/usr/lib/uucp/uusched [-u *debug-level*][-x *debug-level*]

Description

The uusched command is the uucp(1C) file transport scheduler. It is usually started by the daemon uudemon.hour that is started by the following cron(1M) entry in the user uucp crontab file.

11,41 * * * * /etc/uucp/uucp/uudemon.hour

Options

The options are for debugging purposes only. *debug-level* is a number between 0 and 9. Higher numbers give more detailed debugging information.

-u *debug-level*

Pass the -u *debug-level* option to uucico(1M) as -x *debug-level*.

-x *debug-level*

Output debugging messages from uusched.

Files

/etc/uucp/Devices

>   Equipment that can be used to connect to other computers.

/etc/uucp/Permissions

>   Per machine and per login permissions file.

/etc/uucp/Systems

>   Names, phone numbers, and passwords of systems with which you can communicate.

/var/spool/locks/*

>   Lock files directory.

/var/spool/uucp/*

>   UUCP spooling directory.

/var/spool/uucppublic/*

>   World-writeable directory.

Attributes

See attributes(5) for descriptions of the following attributes.

Attribute Type	Attribute Value
Availability	SUNWbnuu

See Also

uucp(1C), uustat(1C), uux(1C), cron(1M), uucico(1M), attributes(5)

Uutry, uutry — Try to Contact Remote System with Debugging On

Synopsis

/usr/lib/uucp/Uutry [-r][-c type][-x *debug-level*] system-name

Description

The Uutry shell script invokes uucico(1M) to call a remote site. Debugging is initially turned on and is set to the default value of 5. The debugging output is put in the /tmp/*system-name* file.

Options

-r   Override the retry time that is set in file
                     /var/uucp/.Status/*system-name*.

-c *type*   Force uucico to use only entries in the Devices file Type field that
                     match *type*. *type* is usually the name of a local area network.

-x *debug-level*

                     Specify a debug level number from 0 to 9. Higher numbers give more
                     detailed debugging information.

Files

/etc/uucp/Devices

                     Equipment that can be used to connect to other computers.

/etc/uucp/Limits

                     UUCP limits file that specifies the maximum number of
                     simultaneous connections with uucico, uuqts, and uuscheds.

/etc/uucp/Permissions

                     Per-machine and per-login permissions file.

/etc/uucp/Systems

                     Names, phone numbers, and passwords of systems with which you
                     can communicate.

/var/spool/locks/*

                     Lock files directory.

/var/spool/uucp/*

                     UUCP spooling directory.

/var/spool/uucppublic/*

                     World-writeable directory.

Attributes
See attributes(5) for descriptions of the following attributes.

Attribute Type	Attribute Value
Availability	SUNWbnuu

See Also
uucp(1C), uux(1C), uucico(1M), attributes(5)

uuxqt — Execute Remote Command Requests

Synopsis

```
/usr/lib/uucp/uuxqt [-s system][-x debug-level]
```

Description

The uuxqt command executes remote job requests from remote systems generated by the use of the uux command. (mail uses uux for remote mail requests). uuxqt searches the spool directories looking for execution requests. For each request, uuxqt checks to see if all the required data files are available, accessible, and the requested commands are permitted for the requesting system. The Permissions file is used to validate file accessibility and command execution permission.

You must set two environment variables before you execute the uuxqt command.

UU_MACHINE   The system that sent the previous job.

UU_USER   The user that sent the job.

These environment variables are used in writing commands that remote systems can execute to provide information, auditing, or restrictions.

Options

-s system   Specify the remote system name.

-x debug-level

                Specify debug-level as a number from 0 to 9. Higher numbers give more detailed debugging information.

Files

/etc/uucp/Limits

                UUCP limits file that specifies the maximum number of simultaneous connections with uucico, uuqts, and uuscheds.

/etc/uucp/Permissions

                Per-machine and per-login permissions file.

/var/spool/locks/*

                Lock files directory.

/var/spool/uucp/*

                UUCP spooling directory.

Attributes

See attributes(5) for descriptions of the following attributes.

Attribute Type	Attribute Value
Availability	SUNWbnuu

See Also

mail(1), uucp(1C), uustat(1C), uux(1C), uucico(1M), attributes(5)

V

vmstat — Report Virtual Memory Statistics

Synopsis

```
/bin/vmstat [-cisS][disks][interval [count]]
```

Description

Use the vmstat command to report virtual memory statistics for process, virtual memory, disk, trap, and CPU activity.

On MP systems, vmstat averages the number of CPUs into the output. For per-process statistics, see mpstat(1).

vmstat supports statistics only for certain devices. For more general system statistics, use sar(1), iostat(1M), or sar(1M).

Without options, vmstat displays a one-line summary of the virtual memory activity since the system was booted.

During execution of this kernel status command, the state of the kernel can change. An example would be CPUs going online or offline. vmstat reports this change as <<State change>>.

See *Solaris 1.x to 2.x Transition Guide* for device naming conventions for disks.

Options

-c	Report cache-flushing statistics. By default, report the total number of each kind of cache flushed since boot time. The types are user, context, region, segment, page, and partial-page.

-i   Report the number of interrupts per device. *count* and *interval* do not apply to the -i option.

-s   Display the total number of various system events since boot. *count* and *interval* do not apply to the -s option.

-S   Report on swapping instead of paging activity. This option changes two fields in the vmstat paging display instead of the re and mf fields. Report si (swap-ins) and so (swap-outs).

Operands

count   Specify the number of times that the statistics are repeated. *count* does not apply to the -i and -s options.

disks   Specify which disks are to be given priority in the output (only four disks fit on a line). Common disk names are id, sd, xd, or xy followed by a number, such as sd2 and xd0.

interval   Specify the last number of seconds over which vmstat summarizes activity. This number of seconds repeats forever. *interval* does not apply to the -i and -s options.

Examples

The following example displays a summary of what the system is doing every five seconds.

```
paperbark% vmstat 5
 procs     memory            page            disk          faults      cpu
 r b w   swap  free  re  mf pi po fr de sr s0 s1 -- --   in   sy   cs us sy id
 0 0 0 217352 60448   0   5  6  0  0  0  0  1  0  0  0  115  144   55  0  0 99
 0 0 0 212592 51392   0   1  0  0  0  0  0  0  0  0  0  114  117   57  0  0 100
 0 0 0 212592 51392   0   0  0  0  0  0  0  0  0  0  0  113  113   54  0  0 100
 0 0 0 212592 51392   0   0  0  0  0  0  0  0  0  0  0  162  197   74  0  0 100
 0 0 0 212576 51104   0  51 182 0  0  0  0 15  0  0  0  187  689  207  4  3 93
 0 0 0 212096 50112   0   7  0  0  0  0  0  0  0  0  0  248 5151  933  5  6 89
 0 0 0 212096 50104   0   5  0  0  0  0  0  0  0  0  0  223  212   80  1  0 99
 0 0 0 211888 49896   0   0  0  0  0  0  0  5  0  0  0  146  226  117  0  0 100
 0 0 0 211680 49408   0   7 280 0  0  0  0 44  0  0  0  282  867  205  1  4 95
 0 1 0 211152 45744   0   0 768 0  0  0  0 110 0  0  0  494 1199  276  1  6 93
 0 1 0 210816 41792   0   0 712 0  0  0  0 105 0  0  0  492 1142  276  1  9 90
 0 1 0 210392 37800   0   0 734 0  0  0  0 103 0  0  0  605 1508  299  1  9 90
 0 0 0 210008 33544   0   0 688 0  0  0  0 104 0  0  0  530 1992  274  2 14 84
 0 1 0 209344 29744   0   0 675 0  0  0  0 103 0  0  0  525 1813  274  1 15 84
 0 1 0 209136 30128   0   0 238 0  0  0  0 90  0  0  0  530 2490  243  2 27 71
 0 2 0 209048 32064   0   0 104 0  0  0  0 97  0  0  0  603  661  156  0  8 91
 0 1 0 209024 32720   0   0 92  0  0  0  0 106 0  0  0  606  898  141  1  9 90
 0 0 0 208992 33344   0   0 571 0  0  0  0 94  0  0  0  547 2175  276  1 20 79
 0 0 0 208704 31688   0  26 273 0  0  0  0 41  0  0  0  358 3004  483 10 17 73
 procs     memory            page            disk          faults      cpu
 r b w   swap  free  re  mf pi po fr de sr s0 s1 -- --   in   sy   cs us sy id
 0 0 0 208392 31168   0  10  0  0  0  0  0  0  0  0  0  215  196   79  1  1 99
^Cpaperbark%
```

The fields of the vmstat display are described below.

procs	Report the number of processes in each of the three following states.	
	r	In run queue.
	b	Blocked for resources I/O, paging, and so forth.
	w	Runnable but swapped.
memory	Report on usage of virtual and real memory.	
	swap	Amount of swap space currently available (kilobytes).
	free	Size of the free list (kilobytes).
page	Report information about page faults and paging activity. The information on each of the following activities is given in units per second.	
	re	Page reclaims. See the -s option for how this field is modified.
	mf	Minor faults. See the -s option for how this field is modified.
	pi	Kilobytes paged in.
	po	Kilobytes paged out.
	fr	Kilobytes freed.
	de	Anticipated short-term memory shortfall (kilobytes).
	sr	Pages scanned by clock algorithm.
disk	Report the number of disk operations per second. There are slots for up to four disks, labeled with a single letter and number. The letter indicates the type of disk (s = SCSI, i = IPI, and so forth); the number is the logical unit number.	
faults	Report the trap/interrupt rates (per second).	
	in	(Nonclock) device interrupts.
	sy	System calls.
	cs	CPU context switches.
cpu	Give a breakdown of percentage usage of CPU time. On MP systems, this is an average across all processors.	
	us	User time.
	sy	System time.
	id	Idle time.

Attributes

See `attributes`(5) for descriptions of the following attributes.

Attribute Type	Attribute Value
Availability	SUNWcsu

See Also

`sar(1)`, `iostat(1M)`, `mpstat(1M)`, `sar(1M)`, `attributes(5)`
Solaris 1.x to 2.x Transition Guide
System Administration Guide, Volume I

volcopy — Make an Image Copy of File System

Synopsis

```
/usr/sbin/volcopy [-F FSType] [-V] [generic-options]
   [-o FSType-specific-options] operands
```

Description

Use the `volcopy` command to make a literal copy of a file system. This command may not be supported for all *FSType*s.

Options

-F *FSType*   Specify the *FSType* on which to operate. You should either specify the *FSType* here, or `volcopy` should be able to derive it from `/etc/vfstab` by matching the operands with an entry in the table. Otherwise, use the default file-system type specified in `/etc/default/fs`.

-V   Echo the complete command line, but do not execute the command. Generate the command line by using the options and arguments provided and adding to them information derived from `/etc/vfstab`. Use this option to verify and validate the command line.

generic-options

    Options that are commonly supported by most FSType-specific command modules. The following options are available.

      -a   Require the operator to respond `yes` or `no` instead of simply waiting 10 seconds before making the copy.

      -s   (Default) Invoke the `DEL if wrong` verification sequence.

-o *FSType-specific-options*

>   Specify FSType-specific options in a comma-separated (without
>   spaces) list of suboptions and keyword-attribute pairs for
>   interpretation by the FSType-specific module of the command.

Operands

Operands generally include the device and volume names and are file-system specific.
You can find a detailed description of the operands in "Operands" on page 1204.

Exit Status

0	Successful file system copy.
1	An error has occurred.

Files

/etc/vfstab List of default parameters for each file system.

/etc/default/fs

>   Default local file-system type. Default values can be set for the
>   following flag in /etc/default/fs. For example, LOCAL=ufs.

>   LOCAL The default partition for a command if you specify
>   no *FSType*.

Attributes

See attributes(5) for descriptions of the following attributes.

Attribute Type	**Attribute Value**
Availability	SUNWcsu

See Also

labelit(1M), vfstab(4), attributes(5)
    Manual pages for the FSType-specific modules of volcopy.

volcopy_ufs — Make an Image Copy of a UFS File System

Synopsis

/usr/sbin/volcopy [-F ufs] [*generic-options*] *fsname srcdevice volname1*
    destdevice volname2

Description

Use the `volcopy` command to make a literal copy of the UFS file system, using a block size matched to the device.

> **Note** — `volcopy` does not support copying to tape devices. Use dd(1M) for copying to and from tape devices.

Options

generic-options options supported by the generic `volcopy` command. See volcopy(1M).

Operands

fsname	The mount point (for example, `root` and `u1`) of the file system being copied.
srcdevice, *destdevice*	The specified disk partition that is using the raw device (for example, `/dev/rdsk/c1d0s8` and `/dev/rdsk/c1d1s8`).
srcdevice, *volname1*	The device and physical volume from which the copy of the file system is being extracted.
destdevice, *volname2*	The target device and physical volume.
fsname, *volname*	File system and volume name, limited to six or fewer characters and recorded in the superblock. You can specify *volname* as - to use the existing volume name.

Exit Status

0	Successful file-system copy.
non-zero	An error has occurred.

Files

`/var/adm/filesave.log`

A record of file systems/volumes copied.

Attributes

See attributes(5) for descriptions of the following attributes.

Attribute Type	Attribute Value
Availability	SUNWcsu

See Also

cpio(1), dd(1M), labelit(1M), volcopy(1M), fs_ufs(4), attributes(5)

vold — Volume Management Daemon to Manage CD-ROM and Diskette Devices

Synopsis

```
/usr/sbin/vold [-n] [-t] [-v] [-f config-file] [-l log-file] [-d root-dir]
   [-L debug-level]
```

Description

The vold volume management daemon creates and maintains a file-system image rooted at *root-dir* that contains symbolic names for diskettes and CD-ROMs. The default *root-dir* is set to /vol if you specify no directory with the -d option.

vold reads the /etc/vold.conf configuration file on startup. If the configuration file is modified later, you must tell vold to reread the /etc/vold.conf file with the following command.

```
# kill -HUP vold-pid
```

To tell vold to clean up and exit, use the SIGTERM signal.

```
# kill -TERM vold-pid
```

where *vold-pid* is the process ID of vold.

Options

-d *root-dir*   Specify an alternate root directory. The default location is /vol. Setting this option enables other volume management commands to use this directory as the default root directory.

-f *config-file*

Specify an alternate configuration file. The default file is /etc/vold.conf.

-l *log-file*   Specify an alternate log file. The default log file is /var/adm/vold.log.

-L *debug-level*

Change the level (verbosity) of debug messages sent to the log file. The range is 0 to 99 where 0 is nothing and 99 is everything. The default level is 0.

-n   Never write back. Volume management updates media labels with unique information if labels are not unique. This option keeps volume management from changing your media. The default setting is false.

-t   Dump NFS trace information to the log file. The default setting is false.

-v   Provide lots of status information to the log file. The default setting is false (do not provide status information to log file).

Environment Variables

vold sets the following environment variables to aid programs that are called when events such as insert, notify, and eject occur.

VOLUME_ACTION

> Event that executed this program.

VOLUME_PATH Path name of the matched regular expression from the vold.conf file.

VOLUME_DEVICE

> Device (in /vol/dev) that applies to the media.

VOLUME_NAME Name of the volume in question.

VOLUME_USER User ID of the user initiating the event.

VOLUME_SYMNAME

> Symbolic name of a device containing the volume.

VOLUME_MEDIATYPE

> Name of the type of media (CD-ROM or diskette)

Files

/etc/vold.conf

> Volume management daemon configuration file. Directs the volume management daemon to control certain devices and initiates events when specific criteria are met.

/usr/lib/vold/*.so.

> Shared objects called by volume management daemon when certain actions occur.

/var/adm/vold.log

> The default log file location (see the -l option for a description).

/vol   The default volume management root directory.

Attributes

See attributes(5) for descriptions of the following attributes.

Attribute Type	Attribute Value
Availability	SUNWvolu

See Also

volcancel(1), volcheck(1), volmissing(1) rmmount(1M), rmmount.conf(4), vold.conf(4), attributes(5), volfs(7FS)

> *System Administration Guide, Volume I*

W

---

wall — Write to All Users

Synopsis

`/usr/sbin/wall [-a][-g grpname][filename]`

Description

Use the `wall` (write all) command to broadcast a message to all users on a local system. You typically use `wall` to warn all users before shutting down a system. To send a message to all users on a system, type `wall` and press Return, then type the message you want to send. When the message is complete, press Control-D. `wall` sends

`Broadcast Message from...`

followed by the message.

You can send a message from a file by specifying `filename`. Then, the message is read in from that file.

Normally, pseudoterminals that do not correspond to `rlogin` sessions are ignored. Thus, when a window system is used, the message appears only on the console window. However, you can use the `-a` option to send the message even to such pseudoterminals.

The sender must be superuser to override any protections the users may have invoked See `mesg`(1).

`wall` runs `setgid()` to the group ID `tty` to get write permissions on other user's terminals. See `setuid`(2).

`wall` detects nonprintable characters before sending them to the user's terminal. Control characters are displayed as a ^ followed by the appropriate ASCII character;

1207

characters with the high-order bit set are displayed in metanotation. For example, \003 is displayed as ^C and \372 as M-z.

> **Note** — wall displays Cannot send to... when the open on a user's TTY file fails.

Options

-a   Broadcast message to the console and pseudoterminals.

-g *grpname*   Broadcast to a specified group only.

Examples

The following example sends a message to the console and all pseudoterminals on a system.

```
# wall -a
System will be rebooted at 12:00 Noon.
^D
#
```

The following message is displayed in all user's windows on the system.

```
Broadcast Message from root (pts/6) on paperbark Wed Jan  5 08:32:30
...
System will be rebooted at 12:00 Noon.
```

Environment Variables

If the LC_* variables (LC_CTYPE, LC_TIME, LC_COLLATE, LC_NUMERIC, and LC_MONETARY) are not set in the environment, the operational behavior of wall for each corresponding locale category is determined by the value of the LANG environment variable. See environ(5). If LC_ALL is set, its contents are used to override both the LANG and the other LC_* variables. If none of the above variables is set in the environment, the C (U.S. style) locale determines how wall behaves.

Files

/dev/tty*   TTY character special device files.

Attributes

See attributes(5) for descriptions of the following attributes.

Attribute Type	Attribute Value
Availability	SUNWcsu

See Also

mesg(1), write(1), setuid(2), attributes(5), environ(5)

wbemadmin — Start Sun WBEM User Manager

New!

Synopsis

```
/usr/sadm/bin/wbemadmin
```

Description

The wbemadmin command is new in the Solaris 8 release. Use wbemadmin to start the Sun Web-based enterprise management (WBEM) User Manager, a graphical user interface that enables you to add and delete authorized WBEM users and to set their access privileges. Use this application to manage access to groups of managed resources, such as disks and installed software, in the Solaris operating environment.

The wbemadmin command enables you to perform the following tasks.

- Manage user access rights. Add, delete, or modify an individual user's access rights to a namespace on a WBEM-enabled system.

- Manage namespace access rights. Add, delete, or modify access rights for all users to a namespace.

The Sun WBEM User Manager displays the following Login dialog box.

You must log in as root or a user with write access to the root\security namespace to grant access rights to users. By default, Solaris users have guest privileges, which grants them read access to the default namespaces, as shown below.

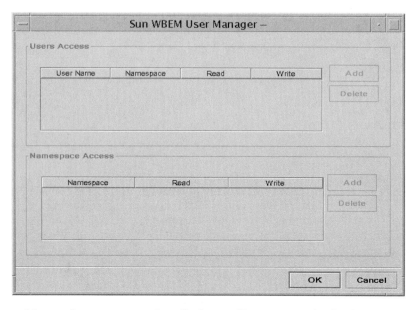

Managed resources are described according to a standard information model called Common Information Model (CIM). A CIM object is a computer representation, or model, of a managed resource, such as a printer, disk drive, or CPU. CIM objects can be shared by any WBEM-enabled system, device, or application. CIM objects are grouped into meaningful collections called schema. One or more schemas can be stored in directory-like structures called namespaces.

All programming operations are performed within a namespace. The following two namespaces are created by default during installation.

- `root\cimv2`—Contains the default classes that represent objects on your system.
- `root\security`—Contains the security classes used by the CIM Object Manager to represent access rights for users and namespaces.

Warning — The `root\security` namespace stores access privileges. If you grant other users access to the `root\security` namespace, those users can grant themselves or other users rights to all other namespaces.

When a WBEM client application connects to the CIM Object Manager in a particular namespace, all subsequent operations occur within that namespace. When you connect to a namespace, you can access the classes and instances in that namespace (if they exist) and in any namespaces contained in that namespace.

When a WBEM client application accesses CIM data, the WBEM system validates the user's login information on the current host. By default, a validated WBEM user is granted read access to the Common Information Model (CIM) Schema. The CIM Schema describes managed objects on your system in a standard format that all WBEM-enabled systems and applications can interpret.

You can set access privileges on individual namespaces or for a user-namespace combination. When you add a user and select a namespace, by default the user is granted read access to CIM objects in the selected namespace. An effective way to combine user and namespace access rights is to first restrict access to a namespace. Then, grant individual users read, read and write, or write access to that namespace.

You cannot set access rights on individual managed objects. However, you can set access rights for all managed objects in a namespace as well as on a per-user basis. Root can set the following types of access to CIM objects.

- Read Only—Enable read-only access to CIM Schema objects. Users with this privilege can retrieve instances and classes but cannot create, delete, or modify CIM objects.
- Read/Write—Enable full read, write, and delete access to all CIM classes and instances.
- Write—Enable write and delete, but not read access, to all CIM classes and instances.
- None—Enable no access to CIM classes and instances.

Context help is displayed in the left side of the wbemadmin dialog boxes. When you click on a field, the help content changes to describe the selected field. No context help is available on the main User Manager window.

The wbemadmin security administration tool updates the following Java classes in the root\security namespace.

- Solaris_UserAc—Updated when access rights are granted or changed for a user.
- Solaris_namespaceAcl—Updated when access rights are granted or changed for a namespace.

Usage

The wbemadmin command is not the tool for a distributed environment. Use it for local administration on the system on which the CIM Object Manager is running.

Exit Status

The wbemadmin command terminates with exit status 0.

Attributes

See attributes(5) for descriptions of the following attributes.

Attribute Type	Attribute Value
Availability	SUNWwbcor

See Also

init.wbem(1M), mofcomp(1M), wbemlogviewer(1M), attributes(5)

wbemlogviewer — Start WBEM Log Viewer

Synopsis

/usr/sadm/bin/wbemlogviewer

Description

Use the `wbemlogviewer` command to start the Web-based enterprise management
(WBEM) Log Viewer graphical user interface, which enables you to view and maintain
log records created by WBEM clients and providers. The WBEM Log Viewer displays a
Login dialog box. You must log in as root or a user with write access to the `root\cimv2`
namespace to view and maintain log files. Namespaces are described in `wbemadmin(1M)`.

Log events can have three severity levels.

- Errors.
- Warnings.
- Informational.

The WBEM log file is created in the `/var/sadm/wbem/log` directory, with the name
`wbem_log`. The first time the log file is backed up, it is renamed `wbem_log.1` and a new
`wbem_log` file is created. Each succeeding time the `wbem_log` file is backed up, the file
extension number of each backup log file is increased by 1, and the oldest backup log file
is removed. Older backup files have higher file extension numbers than more recent
backup files.

The log file is renamed with a `.1` file extension and saved when one of the following
two conditions occurs.

- The current file reaches the file size limit specified in the WBEM Services
  properties file, `/var/sadm/wbem/WbemServices.properties`.
- A WBEM client application uses the `clearLog()` method in the
  `Solaris_LogService` class to clear the current log file.

The WBEM Services properties file `/var/sadm/wbem/WbemServices.properties` is
modified when you change the properties of log files.

Help is displayed in the left panel of each dialog box. Context help is not displayed in
the main Log Viewer window.

Usage

The WBEM Log Viewer is not the tool for a distributed environment. It is used for local
administration.

The WBEM Log Viewer enables you to perform the following tasks.

- View the logs.
- Set properties of log files. Click Action->Log File Settings to specify log file
  parameters and the log file directory.
- Back up a log file. Click Action->Back Up Now to back up and close the current log
  file and start a new log file.
- Delete an old log file. Click Action->Open Log File to open a backed-up log file. To
  delete a backed-up log file, open it and then click Action->Delete Log File. You can
  delete only backed-up log files.
- View log record details. Double-click a log entry to display its details.
- Sort the logs. Click View->Sort By to sort displayed entries. You can also click any
  column heading to sort the list. By default, the log entries are displayed in reverse
  chronological order (new logs first).

Examples

The Sun WBEM Log Viewer displays the following Login dialog box. You must log in as root or a user with write access to the `root\cimv2` namespace to view and maintain log files.

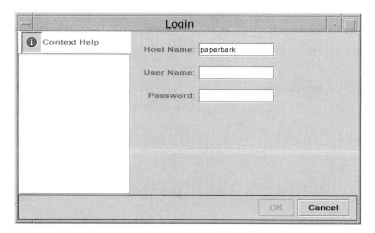

After you log in, the Log Viewer window is displayed, as shown in the following example.

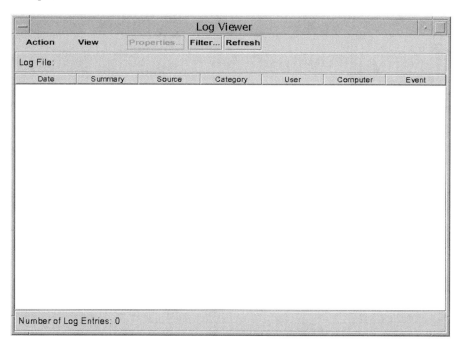

Exit Status

The `wbemlogviewer` command terminates with exit status 0.

Files

/var/sadm/wbem/log/wbem_log

> WBEM log file.

/var/sadm/wbem/WbemServices.properties

> WBEM Services properties file.

Attributes

See attributes(5) for descriptions of the following attributes.

Attribute Type	Attribute Value
Availability	SUNWwbcor

See Also

init.wbem(1M), mofcomp(1M), wbemadmin(1M), attributes(5)

---

whodo — Report Who Is Doing What

Synopsis

/usr/sbin/whodo [-h][-l][user]

Description

New!

Use the whodo command to find out what users on a system are doing. whodo produces formatted and dated output, using information from the /var/adm/utmpx (changed from utmp in the Solaris 8 release), /tmp/ps_data, and /proc/pid files.

The display is headed by the date, time, and machine name. For each user logged in, device name, user ID, and login time is shown, followed by a list of active processes associated with the user-ID. The list includes the device name, process ID, CPU minutes and seconds used, and process name.

If you specify *user*, output is restricted to all sessions pertaining to that user.

Options

-h   Suppress the heading.

-l   Produce a long form of output. The fields displayed are the user's login name, the name of the user's TTY, the time of day the user logged in (in *hours:minutes*), the idle time (the time since the user last typed anything in *hours:minutes*), the CPU time used by all processes and their children on that terminal (in *minutes:seconds*), the CPU time used by the currently active processes (in *minutes:seconds*), and the name and arguments of the current process.

Examples

The following example shows a sample of output from the whodo command.

```
paperbark% whodo
Wed Jan  5 15:46:25 WST 2000
paperbark

console        winsor     7:28
       ?            430     0:00 Xsession
    pts/2           476     0:00 sdt_shell
    pts/2           479     0:00 csh
    pts/2           495     0:00 dtsession
       ?            507     0:00 sdtperfmeter
       ?            506     0:00 netscape
       ?            516     0:00 netscape
       ?            515     0:27 .netscape.bin
       ?            532     0:00 .netscape.bin
       ?            502     0:06 dtwm
       ?            578     0:00 dtexec
       ?            579     0:00 dtterm
    pts/7           581     0:00 csh
       ?            504     0:00 dtterm
    pts/5           527     0:00 csh
    pts/4           524     0:00 csh
    pts/3           521     0:00 csh
    pts/3           657     0:03 snapshot
    pts/6           530     0:00 csh
    pts/6           980     0:00 whodo
       ?            503     0:00 dtfile
       ?            541     0:00 dtfile
    pts/2           518     0:00 dtpad
    pts/2           517     0:00 sh
    pts/2           494     0:00 ttsession
       ?            440     0:00 fbconsole
       ?            478     0:00 dsdm

  pts/3        winsor     7:28

  pts/4        winsor     7:28

  pts/5        winsor     7:28

  pts/6        winsor     7:28

  pts/7        winsor     8:31
paperbark%
```

Environment Variables

If any of the LC_* variables (LC_CTYPE, LC_MESSAGES, LC_TIME, LC_COLLATE, LC_NUMERIC, and LC_MONETARY) (see environ(5)) are not set in the environment, the operational behavior of whodo for each corresponding locale category is determined by the value of the LANG environment variable. If LC_ALL is set, its contents are used to override both the LANG and the other LC_* variables. If none of the above variables is set in the environment, the C (U.S. style) locale determines how whodo behaves.

LC_CTYPE	Determine how whodo handles characters. When LC_CTYPE is set to a valid value, whodo can display and handle text and file names containing valid characters for that locale. whodo can display and handle Extended Unix code (EUC) characters where any individual character can be 1, 2, or 3 bytes wide. tar can also handle EUC characters of 1, 2, or more column widths. In the C locale, only characters from ISO 8859-1 are valid.
LC_MESSAGES	Determine how diagnostic and informative messages are presented. This presentation includes the language and style of the messages, and the correct form of affirmative and negative responses. In the C locale, the messages are presented in the default form found in the program itself (in most cases, U.S. English).
LC_TIME	Determine how whodo handles date and time formats. In the C locale, date and time handling follow the U.S. rules.

Files

/etc/passwd	System password file.
/tmp/ps_data	Internal data structure
/var/adm/utmpx	
	User access and administration information. utmpx replaces the obsolete utmp database file.
/proc/pid	Directory for process information and control files.

Attributes

See attributes(5) for descriptions of the following attributes.

Attribute Type	Attribute Value
Availability	SUNWcsu

Exit Status

0	Success.
non-zero	Failure.

See Also

ps(1), tar(1), who(1), attributes(5), environ(5)

Diagnostics

If the PROC driver is not installed or configured or if /proc is not mounted, a message to that effect is issued and whodo fails.

wtmpfix — Manipulate Connect Accounting Records

Synopsis

/usr/lib/acct/wtmpfix [*file*...]

Description

See fwtmp(1M).

X

xntpd — Network Time Protocol Daemon

Synopsis

```
/usr/lib/inet/xntpd [-aAbdm] [-c conffile] [-e authdelay] [-f driftfile]
    [-k keyfile] [-l logfile] [-p pidfile] [-r broadcastdelay]
    [-s statsdir] [-t trustedkey] [-v variable] [-V variable]
```

Description

The xntpd daemon sets and maintains a UNIX system time-of-day in agreement with Internet standard time servers. xntpd is a complete implementation of the Network Time Protocol (NTP) version 3 standard, as defined by RFC 1305. It also retains compatibility with version 1 and 2 servers as defined by RFC 1059 and RFC 1119. The computations done in the protocol and clock adjustment code are carried out with high precision and with attention to the details that might introduce systematic bias into the computations. This procedure tries to maintain an accuracy suitable for synchronizing with even the most precise external time source.

Ordinarily, xntpd reads its configuration from a configuration file at startup. The default configuration file name is /etc/inet/ntp.conf, although you can override this configuration file from the command line. You can also specify a working, although limited, xntpd configuration entirely on the command line, obviating the need for a configuration file. Specifying the configuration on the command line can be particularly appropriate when xntpd is to be configured as a broadcast or multicast client, with all peers being determined by listening to broadcasts at runtime. Through the use of the ntpq(1M) program, you can display various internal xntpd variables and alter configuration options while the daemon is running.

> **Note** — The daemon can operate in any of several modes, including symmetric active/passive, client/server, and broadcast/multicast. A broadcast/multicast client can automatically discover remote servers, compute one-way delay correction factors and configure itself automatically. This feature makes it possible to deploy a fleet of workstations without specifying a configuration file or configuration details specific to its environment.

Options

	-a	Run in authentication mode.
New!	-A	Disable authentication mode.
	-b	Listen for broadcast NTP and synchronize to this if available.
	-c *conffile*	Specify an alternate configuration file.
	-d	Specify debugging mode. You can specify this option multiple times, with each occurrence indicating greater detail of display.
New!	-e *authdelay*	Specify the time (in seconds) it takes to compute the NTP encryption field on this computer.
	-f *driftfile*	Specify the location of the drift file.
New!	-k *keyfile*	Specify the location of the file that contains the NTP authentication keys.
	-l *logfile*	Specify a log file instead of logging to `syslog`.
	-m	Listen for multicast messages and synchronize to them if available (requires multicast kernel).
New!	-p *pidfile*	Specify the name of the file to record the daemon's process ID.
New!	-r *broadcast*	If the network delay calibration procedure fails, use the specified default delay (in seconds). Ordinarily, the daemon automatically compensates for the network delay between the broadcast/multicast server and the client.
New!	-s *statsdir*	Specify the directory to be used for creating statistics files.
	-t *trustedkey*	Add a key number to the trusted key list.
New!	-v *variable*	Add a system variable.
New!	-V *variable*	Add a system variable listed by default.

See "Configuration Commands" on page 1221 for a more complete functional description.

Usage

`xntpd`'s configuration file format is similar to that of other UNIX configuration files. Comments begin with a # character and extend to the end of the line. Blank lines are ignored. Configuration commands consist of an initial keyword followed by a list of arguments, separated by white space. Some arguments may be optional. Commands cannot be continued over multiple lines. Arguments can be host names, host addresses written in dotted-decimal, integers, floating-point numbers (when specifying times in seconds) and text strings.

Configuration Commands

In the following descriptions, optional arguments are delimited by [ ] and alternatives are separated by |. The first three commands specify various time servers to be used and time services to be provided.

`peer` *host-address* [*key*] [*version*] [*prefer*]

> Specify that the local server is to operate in "symmetric active" mode with the remote server *host-address* named in the command. In this mode, the local server can be synchronized to the remote server. In addition, you can synchronize the remote server by the local server. This feature is useful in a network of servers where, depending on various failure scenarios, either the local or remote server host may be the better source of time. The `peer` command, and the server and broadcast commands that follow, can take the following arguments.

> | | |
> |---|---|
> | *key* | Indicate that all packets sent to the address are to include authentication fields, encrypted using the specified key number. The range of this number is that of an unsigned 32-bit integer. By default, an encryption field is not included. |
> | *version* | Specify the version number to be used for outgoing NTP packets. Versions 1, 2, and 3 are the choices; version 3 is the default. |
> | *prefer* | Mark the host as a preferred host. This host is preferred for synchronization over other comparable hosts. |

`server` *host-address* [*key*] [*version f1*] [*prefer*] [*mode f1*] `server`

> Specify that the local server is to operate in client mode with the remote server named in the command. In this mode, the local server can be synchronized to the remote server but the remote server can never be synchronized to the local server.

`broadcast` *host-address* [*key*] [*version*] [*ttl*]

> Specify that the local server is to operate in broadcast mode where the local server sends periodic broadcast messages to a client population at the broadcast/multicast address named in the command. Ordinarily, this specification applies only to the local server operating as a transmitter. For operation as a broadcast client, see `broadcastclient` or `multicastclient` commands. In broadcast mode, the *host-address* is usually the broadcast address on a local network or a multicast address assigned to NTP. The IANA has assigned the network 224.0.1.1 to NTP. This network is presently the only one that should be used. The following option is used only with the broadcast mode.

ttl   Specify the time-to-live (TTL) to use on multicast
                         packets. Selection of the proper value, which defaults
                         to 127, is something of a black art and must be
                         coordinated with the network administrator(s).

broadcastclient

Direct the local server to listen for broadcast messages on the local
network, to discover other servers on the same subnet. On hearing a
broadcast message for the first time, the local server measures the
nominal network delay, using a brief client/server exchange with the
remote server. Then, the server enters the broadcastclient mode, in
which it listens for and synchronizes to succeeding broadcast
messages. To avoid accidental or malicious disruption in this mode,
both the local and remote servers must operate using authentication,
with the same trusted key and key identifier.

multicastclient [*IP-address*...]

Operate in the same way as the broadcastclient command except
use IP multicasting. Support for this command requires the use of
authentication. If you specify one or more IP addresses, the server
joins the respective multicast group(s). If you specify none, assume
the IP address assigned to NTP (224.0.1.1).

driftfile *filename*

Specify the name of the file used to record the frequency offset of the
local clock oscillator. If the file exists, read it at startup to set the
initial frequency offset. Then, update the file once per hour with the
current offset computed by the daemon. If the file does not exist or you
do not specify this command, assume the initial frequency offset is 0.
In this case, it may take some hours for the frequency to stabilize and
the residual timing errors to subside. The file contains a single
floating point value equal to the offset in parts-per-million (ppm).
xntpd updates the file by first writing the current drift value into a
temporary file and then using rename(2) to replace the old version.
This behavior implies that xntpd must have write permission for the
directory the drift file is located in, and that you should probably avoid
file-system links, symbolic or otherwise.

enable auth | bclient | pll | monitor | stats [...]
disable auth | bclient | pll | monitor | stats [...]

Provide a way to enable or disable various server options. To do so,
execute a two-word command, where the first word is enable or
disable and the second is the flag. Flags not mentioned are
unaffected. Flags that can be changed are described below, along with
their default values.

Flag	Default	Description
auth	disable	Synchronize the server with unconfigured peers only if the peer has been correctly authenticated with a trusted key and key identifier.
bclient	disable	Listen for a message from a broadcast or multicast server. After this occurs, an association is automatically instantiated for that server. Default for this flag is disable (off).
pll	enable	Enable the server to adjust its local clock. If not set, the local clock free-runs at its intrinsic time and frequency offset. This flag is useful in case the local clock is controlled by some other device or protocol and NTP is used only to provide synchronization to other clients.
monitor	disable	Enable the monitoring facility. See "Monitoring Commands" on page 1226 for more information.
stats	enable	Enable statistics facility filegen. See "Monitoring Commands" on page 1226 for more information.

Authentication Commands

keys *filename*

Specify the name of a file that contains the encryption keys and key identifiers used by xntpd when operating in authenticated mode. The format of this file is described in "Authentication Key File Format" on page 1231.

trustedkey # [#...]

Specify the encryption key identifiers that are trusted for the purposes of authenticating peers suitable for synchronization. The authentication procedures require that both the local and remote servers share the same key and key identifier defined to be used for this purpose. However, you can use different keys with different servers. The arguments are 32-bit unsigned integers. Note, however, that key 0 is fixed and globally known. If meaningful authentication is to be performed, you should not trust the 0 key.

controlkey # Specify the key identifier to use with the ntpq(1M) program, which is useful to diagnose and repair problems that affect xntpd operation. The operation of the ntpq program and xntpd conform to those specified in RFC 1305. Requests from a remote ntpq program that affect the state of the local server must be authenticated. Authentication requires that both the remote program and local server share a common key and key identifier. The argument to this command is a 32-bit unsigned integer. If no `controlkey` command is included in the configuration file or if the keys don't match, ignore these requests.

`authdelay` *seconds*

Indicate the amount of time it takes to encrypt an NTP authentication field on the local computer. Use this value to correct transmit timestamps when the authentication is used on outgoing packets. The value usually lies somewhere in the range 0.0001 seconds to 0.003 seconds, though it is very dependent on the CPU speed of the host computer.

Access Control Commands

`restrict` *address* [mask *numeric-mask*][*flag*][...]

xntpd implements a general purpose address-and-mask-based restriction list. The list is sorted by IP address and mask, and the list is searched in this order for matches, with the last match found defining the restriction flags associated with the incoming packets. The source address of incoming packets is used for the match, with the 32-bit address being logically ANDed with the mask associated with the restriction entry and then compared with the entry's address (which has also been ANDed with the mask) to look for a match. The `mask` argument defaults to `255.255.255.255`, meaning that the address is treated as the address of an individual host. A default entry (`address 0.0.0.0, mask 0.0.0.0`) is always included and, given the sort algorithm, is always the first entry in the list. Note that while you normally specify `address` in dotted-quad format, you can use the text string `default` with no `mask` option to indicate the default entry.

In the current implementation, flags always restrict access; that is, an entry with no flags gives free access to the server. The flags are not orthogonal, in that more restrictive flags often make less restrictive ones redundant. You can generally class the flags into two categories, those that restrict time service and those that restrict informational queries and attempts to do runtime reconfiguration of the server.

You can specify one or more of the following flags.

`ignore`   Ignore all packets from hosts that match this entry. If you specify this flag, respond to neither queries nor time server polls.

`noquery`   Ignore all NTP mode 7 packets, that is, information queries and configuration requests) from the source. Time service is not affected.

`nomodify`   Ignore all NTP mode 7 packets that try to modify the state of the server (that is, runtime reconfiguration). Permit queries that return information.

notrap   Decline to provide mode 6 control-message trap service to matching hosts. The trap service is a subsystem of the mode 6 control message protocol that is intended for use by remote event logging programs.

lowpriotrap   Declare traps set by matching hosts to be low priority. The number of traps a server can maintain is limited to 3. Traps are usually assigned on a first come, first served basis, with later trap requestors being denied service. This flag modifies the assignment algorithm by allowing low-priority traps to be overridden by later requests for normal-priority traps.

noserve   Ignore NTP packets whose mode is other than 7. In effect, deny time service, although queries may still be permitted.

nopeer   Provide stateless time service to polling hosts but do not allocate peer memory resources to these hosts even if they otherwise might be considered useful as future synchronization partners.

notrust   Treat these hosts normally in other respects but never use them as synchronization sources.

limited   Limit the number of clients from the same net that are accepted. Net in this context refers to the IP notion of net (Class A, Class B, Class C, and so on). Accept only the first *client-limit* hosts that have shown up at the server and that have been active during the last *client-limit-period* seconds. Reject requests from other clients from the same net. Take only time request packets into account. Private, control, and broadcast packets are not subject to client limitation and therefore do not contribute to client count. Keep a history of clients, using the monitoring capability of xntpd. Thus, monitoring is active as long as there is a restriction entry with the limited flag. The default value for *client-limit* is 3. The default value for *client-limit-period* is 3600 seconds. Currently, both variables are not runtime configurable.

ntpport

A match algorithm modifier instead of a restriction flag. Match the restriction entry only if the source port in the packet is the standard NTP UDP port (123). You can specify both `ntpport` and `non-ntpport`. The `ntpport` is considered more specific and is sorted later in the list. Default restriction list entries, with the flags `ignore` and `ntpport`, for each of the local host's interface addresses are inserted into the table at startup to prevent the server from trying to synchronize to its own time.

A default entry is also always present, though if it is otherwise unconfigured, no flags are associated with the default entry (that is, everything besides your own NTP server is unrestricted). The restriction facility was added to allow the current access policies of the time servers running on the NSF net backbone to be implemented with `xntpd` as well. This facility can be useful for keeping unwanted or broken remote time servers from affecting your own. However, you should not consider it an alternative to the standard NTP authentication facility.

clientlimit *limit*

Set `clientlimit` to *limit*; allow configuration of client limitation policy. This variable defines the number of clients from the same network that are allowed to use the server.

clientperiod *period*

Set *client-limit-period*; allow configuration of client limitation policy. This variable specifies the number of seconds after which a client is considered inactive and thus is no longer counted for client limit restriction.

Monitoring Commands

statsdir /*directory path*/

Indicate the full path of a directory to create statistics files (see below). This keyword enables you to modify the (otherwise constant) `filegen` file-name prefix for file generation sets used for handling statistics logs (see `filegen` statement below).

statistics *name*...

Enable writing of statistics records. Currently, three kinds of statistics are supported. Each type is described below by giving its name, a sample line of data, and an explanation of each field.

loopstats   Enable recording of loop filter statistics information.
                 Each update of the local clock outputs a line of the
                 following form to the file generation set named
                 loopstats.

48773 10847.650 0.0001307 17.3478 2

Field No.	Description
1	The date (Modified Julian day).
2	The time (seconds and fraction past UTC midnight).
3	Time offset in seconds.
4	Frequency offset in parts-per-million.
5	Time constant of the clock-discipline algorithm at each update of the clock.

peerstats   Enable recording of peer statistics information,
                 including statistics records of all peers of an NTP
                 server and of the 1-pps signal, where present and
                 configured. Each valid update appends a line similar
                 to the one below, to the current element of a
                 file-generation set named peerstats.

48773 10847.650 127.127.4.1 9714 -0.001605 0.00000 0.00142

Field No.	Description
1	The date (Modified Julian day).
2	The time (seconds and fraction past UTC midnight).
3	The peer address in dotted-quad notation.
4	Peer status. The status field is encoded in hex in the format described in Appendix A of the NTP specification, RFC 1305.
5	Offset in seconds.
6	Delay in seconds.
7	Dispersion in seconds.

clockstats   Enable recording of clock driver statistics
                 information. Each update received from a clock
                 driver outputs a line of the following form to the file
                 generation set named clockstats.

49213 525.624 127.127.4.1 93 226 00:08:29.606 D

Field No.	Description
1	The date (Modified Julian day).
2	The time (seconds and fraction past UTC midnight).
3	The clock address in dotted-quad notation.

4   The last timecode received from the clock in decoded
ASCII format, where meaningful. In some clock
drivers a good deal of additional information can be
gathered and displayed as well. Statistic files are
managed by file generation sets (see `filegen` below).
The information obtained by enabling statistics
recording enables you to analyze the temporal
properties of an `xntpd` server. It is usually only
useful to primary servers or perhaps main campus
servers.

`filegen` *name* [file *filename*][type *typename*] [flag *flagval*]
[link|nolink] [enable|disable]

Configure setting of file generation set *name*. File generation sets
provide a way to handle files that are continuously growing during the
lifetime of a server. A typical example of such files is server statistics.
File generation sets provide access to a set of files used to store the
actual data. At any time, at most one element of the set is being
written to. `type` specifies when and how data is directed to a new
element of the set. This way, information stored in elements of a file
set that are currently unused are available for administrative
operations without the risk of disturbing the operation of `xntpd`.
(Most important, you can remove them to free space for new data.)

File names of set members are built from three elements.

prefix   A constant file-name path not subject to
modifications with the `filegen` statement. The
prefix is defined by the server, usually specified as a
compile-time constant. It can, however, be
configurable for individual file-generation sets with
other commands. For example, the prefix used with
`loopstats` and `peerstats` `filegens` can be
configured with the `statsdir` statement explained
above.

filename   Directly concatenate this string to the prefix
mentioned above with no intervening slash (`/`). You
can modify this file name by using the *file*
argument to the `filegen` statement. No `..` elements
are allowed in this component to prevent file names
referring to parts outside the file-system hierarchy
denoted by *prefix*.

suffix   Individual elements of a file set. *suffix* is generated
according to the type of a file set as explained below.

A file-generation set is characterized by its type. The following types are supported.

none   The file set is actually a single plain file.

pid   Use one element of file set per incarnation of an xntpd server. This type does not perform any changes to file-set members during runtime. However, it provides an easy way of separating files belonging to different xntpd server incarnations. The file-set-member name is built by appending a dot (.) to concatenated prefix and file-name strings and appending the decimal representation of the process ID of the xntpd server process.

day   Create one file-generation-set element per day. The term day is based on UTC. A day is defined as the period between 00:00 and 24:00 Universal Coordinated Time (UTC). The file-set member suffix consists of a dot (.) and a day specification in the form, *YYYYMMDD*. *YYYY* is a four-digit year number (such as 2000). *MM* is a two-digit month number. *DD* is a two-digit day number. Thus, all information written on December 10, 2000 would end up in a file named PrefixFilename.20001210.

week   Any file-set member contains data related to a certain week of a year. The term week is defined by computing "day of year" modulo 7. Distinguish elements of such a file-generation set by appending the following suffix to the file-set file-name base: a dot, a four-digit year number, the letter W, and a two-digit week number. For example, information from January 5, 2000 would end up in a file with suffix .2000W1.

month   Generate one file-generation-set element per month. The file-name suffix consists of a dot, a four-digit year number, and a two-digit month.

year   Generate one file-generation-set element per year. The file-name suffix consists of a dot and a four-digit year number.

age   Change to a new element of the file set every 24 hours of server operation. The file-name suffix consists of a dot, the letter a, and an eight-digit number. This number is taken to be the number of seconds the server is running at the start of the corresponding 24-hour period.

Write information to a file-generation set only when this set is enabled. Output is prevented if disabled is specified.

It is convenient to be able to access the current element of a file-generation set by a fixed name. Enable this feature by specifying link and disable with nolink. If you specify link, create a hard link from the current file-set element to a file without suffix. When there is already a file with this name and the number of links of this file is 1, rename it, appending a dot, the letter C, and the PID of the xntpd server process. When the number of links is greater than 1, unlink the file. This option enables you to access the current file by a constant name.

Miscellaneous Commands

precision #   Specify the nominal precision of the local clock. The value of # is an integer approximately equal to the base 2 logarithm of the local timekeeping precision in seconds. Normally, the daemon automatically determines the precision at startup, so you need this command only in special cases when the precision cannot be determined automatically.

broadcastdelay *seconds*

The broadcast and multicast modes require a special calibration to determine the network delay between the local and remote servers. Ordinarily, this calibration is done automatically by the initial protocol exchanges between the local and remote servers. In some cases, the calibration procedure may fail, for example, because of network or server access controls. With this command you specify the default delay to be used under these circumstances. Typically (for Ethernet), a number between 0.003 and 0.007 is appropriate for *seconds*. The default is 0.004 seconds.

trap *host-address* [port *port-number*] [interface *interface-address*]

Configure a trap receiver at the given *host-address* and *port-number* for sending messages with the specified local *interface-address*. If you do not specify the port number, use the default value of 18447. If you do not specify the interface address, send the message with the source address of the local interface the message is sent through. On a multihomed host, the interface used may change with routing changes.

Store information from the server in a log file. Although such monitor programs may also request their own trap dynamically, configuring a trap receiver ensures that no messages are lost when the server is started.

setvar *variable* [default]

Add an additional system variable. You can use variables like this to distribute additional information such as the access policy. If you follow the variable of the form, *variable-name=value* followed by the default keyword, list the variable as one of the default system variables (see the ntpq(1M) command). Additional variables serve informational purposes only. They can be listed but they are not related to the protocol. The known protocol variables always override any variables defined with the setvar mechanism.

Three special variables contain the names of all variable of the same group. sys_var_list holds the names of all system variables. peer_var_list holds the names of all peer variables. And clock_var_list hold the names of the reference clock variables.

```
authenticate [yes|no]
monitor [yes|no]
```

These commands have been superseded by the `enable` and `disable` commands. They are listed here for historical purposes.

`logconfig` *configkeyword*

Control the amount of output written to `syslog` or the log file. By default, turn on all output. Form *configkeyword* by concatenating the message class with the event class. It is permissible to use the prefix `all` instead of a message class. A message class can also be followed by the keyword `all`, meaning to enable/disable all of the respective message class. You can prefix all *configkeywords* with the symbols =, +, and -. Here, = sets the `syslog` mask, + adds messages, and – removes messages. You can control `syslog` messages in the `sys`, `peer`, `clock`, and `sync` classes. Within these classes, you can control four types of messages. Each is described below, along with its *configkeyword*.

configkeyword **Message Type**

`info`	Informational messages control configuration information.
`events`	Event messages control logging of events (reachability, synchronization, alarm conditions).
`statistics`	Statistical messages control statistical output.
`status`	Status messages describe mainly the synchronization status.

A minimal log configuration might look like the following.

```
logconfig=syncstatus + sysevents
```

A configuration like this lists just the synchronization state of `xntp` and the major system events. For a simple reference server, the following minimum message configuration could be useful.

```
logconfig=syncall + clockall
```

This configuration lists all clock information and synchronization information. All other events and messages about peers, system events and so on, are suppressed.

Authentication Key File Format

The NTP standard specifies an extension to enable verification of the authenticity of received NTP packets and to provide an indication of authenticity in outgoing packets. This extension is implemented in `xntpd` by use of the DES or MD5 algorithms to compute a digital signature, or message-digest. The specification allows any one of possibly 4 billion keys, numbered with 32-bit key identifiers, to be used to authenticate an association. The servers involved in an association must agree on the key and key identifier used to authenticate their data. However, they must each learn the key and key identifier independently. In the case of DES, the keys are 56 bits with, depending on type, a parity check on each byte. In the case of MD5, the keys are 64 bits (8 bytes).

xntpd reads its keys from a file specified by the -k command-line option or the keys statement in the configuration file. While key number 0 is fixed by the NTP standard (as 56 zero bits) and cannot be changed, you can arbitrarily set one or more of the keys numbered 1 through 15 in the keys file.

The key file uses the same comment conventions as the configuration file. Key entries use a fixed format of the form, *keyno type key*. Here, *keyno* is a positive integer, *type* is a single character that defines the format the key is given in, and *key* is the key itself.

You can specify the key in one of the following different formats, controlled by the *type* character.

Key	S
Format	A 64-bit hexadecimal number in DES format.
	Use the high-order 7 bits of each octet to form the 56-bit key while giving the low-order bit of each octet a value so that odd parity is maintained for the octet. You must specify leading zeros (that is, the key must be exactly 16 hex digits long), and you must maintain odd parity. For example, you would specify a zero key, in standard format, as 0101010101010101.
Key	N
Format	A 64-bit hexadecimal number in NTP format.
	Use the DES format, except rotate the bits in each octet one bit right so that the parity bit is now the high-order bit of the octet. You must specify leading zeros and maintain odd parity. You would specify a zero key in NTP format as 8080808080808080.
Key	A
Format	A 1- to 8-character ASCII string.
	Form a key by using the lower-order 7 bits of the ASCII representation of each character in the string. Add zeros on the right when necessary to form a full-width, 56-bit key.
Key	S
Format	A 1- to 8-character ASCII string, using the MD5 authentication scheme.
	Note that both the keys and the authentication schemes (DES or MD5) must be identical between a set of peers sharing the same key number.

Primary Clock Support

xntpd is compatible with all supported types of reference clocks. A reference clock is generally (though not always) a radio timecode receiver that is synchronized to a source of standard time such as the services offered by the NRC in Canada and NIST in the United States. The interface between the computer and the timecode receiver is device dependent and varies, but it is often a serial port.

For the purposes of configuration, xntpd treats reference clocks as much as possible in a way analogous to normal NTP peers. Reference clocks are referred to by address, much as a normal peer is. However, an invalid IP address is used to distinguish them from normal peers. Reference clock addresses are of the form 127.127.*t*.*u*, where *t* is an integer denoting the clock type and *u* indicates the type-specific unit number.

Reference clocks are configured by a server statement in the configuration file where the *host-address* is the clock address. The `key`, `version`, and `ttl` options are not used for reference clock support. Some reference clocks require a `mode` option to further specify their operation. The `prefer` option can be useful to persuade the server to cherish a reference clock with somewhat more enthusiasm than other reference clocks or peers. You can generally use clock addresses anywhere in the configuration file that a normal IP address can be used. For example, you can use clock addresses in `restrict` statements, although such use would normally be considered strange.

Reference clock support provides the `fudge` command, which you can use to configure reference clocks in special ways. The generic format that applies to this command is

```
fudge 127.127.t.u [time1 secs] [time2 secs] [stratum int] [refid int]
     [flag1 0|1] [flag2 0|1] [flag3 0|1] [flag4 0|1]
```

with options described as follows.

`time1`	Specify in fixed-point seconds. These options are used in some clock drivers as calibration constants. By convention and unless indicated otherwise, `time1` is used as a calibration constant to adjust the nominal time offset of a particular clock to agree with an external standard, such as a precision PPS signal. The specified offset is in addition to the propagation delay provided by other means, such as internal DIP switches.
`stratum`	Specify a number in the range 0 to 15 to assign a nonstandard operating stratum to the clock.
`refid`	Specify an ASCII string in the range one to four characters to assign a nonstandard reference identifier to the clock.
`flag1` `flag2` `flag3` `flag4`	Specify binary flags to customize the clock driver. The interpretation of these values and whether they are used at all is a function of the needs of the particular clock driver. However, by convention, and unless indicated otherwise, use `flag3` to attach the `ppsclock` streams module to the configured driver, and use `flag4` to enable recording verbose monitoring data to the `clockstats` file configured with the `filegen` command. Further information on the `ppsclock` streams module is in the README file in the `./kernel` directory in the current `xntp3` program distribution. Further information on this feature is available in the `./scripts/stats` directory in the same distribution.

Ordinarily, the stratum of a reference clock is 0, by default. Because the `xntpd` daemon adds 1 to the stratum of each peer, a primary server ordinarily displays stratum 1. To provide engineered backups, it is often useful to specify the reference clock stratum as greater than 0. Use the `stratum` option for this purpose.

Also, in cases involving both a reference clock and a 1-pps discipline signal, it is useful to specify the reference clock identifier as other than the default, depending on the driver. Use the `refid` option for this purpose. Except where noted, these options apply to all clock drivers.

`xntpd` on UNIX machines currently supports several different types of clock hardware. It also supports a special pseudoclock used for backup or when no other clock source is available. In the case of most of the clock drivers, support for a 1-pps precision timing signal is available as described in the README file in the `./doc` directory of the `xntp3` program distribution. The clock drivers and the addresses used to configure them are described in the file, README.refclocks in the doc directory of the current program distribution.

Variables

You can examine most variables used by the NTP protocol with ntpq (mode 6 messages). Currently, you can modify very few variables with mode 6 messages. These variables are either created with the setvar directive or the leap warning variables. The leap warning bits can be set in the leapwarning variable (up to one month ahead). Both the leapwarning and in the leapindication variable have a slightly different encoding than the usual leap bits interpretation.

00	The daemon passes the leap bits of its synchronization source (usual mode of operation).
01/10	A leap second is added/deleted (operator forced leap second).
11	Leap information from the synchronization source is ignored (thus LEAP_NOWARNING is passed on).

Files

/etc/inet/ntp.conf

The default configuration file.

/etc/inet/ntp.drift

The conventional name of the drift file

/etc/inet/ntp.keys

The conventional name of the key file.

New! /etc/inet/ntp.server

Sample server configuration file.

Attributes

See attributes(5) for descriptions of the following attributes.

Attribute Type	Attribute Value
Availability	SUNWntpu

See Also

New!   ntpdate(1M), ntpq(1M), ntptrace(1M), xntpdc(1M), rename(2), attributes(5)

xntpdc — Special NTP Query Program

Synopsis

    xntpdc [-ilnps][-c command][host][...]

Description

Use the xntpdc command to query the xntpd daemon about its current state and to request changes in that state. You can run xntpdc in interactive mode or control it by using command-line arguments.

Extensive state and statistics information is available through the xntpdc interface. In addition, by using xntpdc, you can specify nearly all the configuration options that can be specified at startup through the xntpd runtime configuration file.

If you include one or more request options on the command line when xntpdc is executed, each of the requests is sent to the Network Time Protocol (NTP) servers running on each of the hosts given as command-line arguments, or on the local host by default. If you specify no request options, xntpdc tries to read commands from the standard input and execute these on the NTP server running on the first host specified on the command line, again defaulting to the local host when you specify no other host. xntpdc prompts for commands if the standard input is a terminal device.

xntpdc uses NTP mode 7 packets to communicate with the NTP server and can be used to query any compatible server on the network that permits it. Because NTP is a UDP protocol, this communication is somewhat unreliable, especially over large distances. xntpdc does not try to retransmit requests, and requests time out if the remote host is not heard from within a suitable timeout time.

The operation of xntpdc is specific to the particular implementation of the xntpd daemon. You can expect xntpdc to work only with this and maybe some previous versions of the daemon. Requests from a remote xntpdc program that affect the state of the local server must be authenticated. This authentication requires that both the remote program and local server share a common key and key identifier.

Options

xntpdc reads interactive format commands from the standard input. If you specify the -c, -l, -p, or -s option, the specified queries are sent to the hosts immediately.

The following command-line options are supported.

-c command... Add command to the list of commands to execute on the specified hosts. command is interpreted as an interactive format command. You can specify multiple -c options.

-i   Force xntpdc to operate in interactive mode. Prompts are written to the standard output. Commands are read from the standard input.

-l   Obtain a list of peers that are known to the servers. This option is equivalent to -c listpeers. See listpeers in "Control Message Commands" on page 1237.

-n   Output all host addresses in dotted-quad numeric format instead of converting to the canonical host names.

-p   Print a list of the peers known to the server as well as a summary of their state. This option is equivalent to `-c peers`. See `peers` in "Control Message Commands" on page 1237.

-s   Print a list of the peers known to the server as well as a summary of their state, but in a slightly different format than with the -p option. This option is equivalent to `-c dmpeers`. See `dmpeers` in "Control Message Commands" on page 1237.

Usage

Interactive Commands

The interactive commands consist of a keyword (`command-keyword`) followed by zero to four arguments. You need to enter only enough characters of the `command-keyword` to uniquely identify it. The output of an interactive command is sent to the standard output by default. You can send the output of an interactive command to a file by appending a <, followed by a file name, to the command line.

A number of interactive format commands are executed entirely within the `xntpdc` program itself and do not result in NTP mode.

The following interactive commands are supported.

? [`command-keyword`]

         Without an argument, print a list of `ntpq` command keywords. If you specify `command-keyword`, print function and usage information about the `command-keyword`.

delay `milliseconds`

         Specify a time interval to add to timestamps included in requests that require authentication. This interval enables (unreliable) server reconfiguration over long delay network paths or between machines whose clocks are unsynchronized. Because the server no longer requires timestamps in authenticated requests, this command may be obsolete.

help [`command-keyword`]

         Without an argument, print a list of `ntpq` command keywords. If you specify `command-keyword`, print function and usage information about the `command-keyword`.

host `hostname`

         Set the host (`hostname`) to which future queries are sent. Specify `hostname` as a host name or a numeric address.

hostnames [yes | no]

         Print host names or numeric addresses in information displays. Specify `yes` to print host names. Specify `no` to print numeric addresses. The default is `yes`, unless you specify the -n command-line option.

keyid *keyid*   Enable specification of a key number (*keyid*) to authenticate
                 configuration requests. *keyid* must correspond to a key number the
                 server has been configured to use for this purpose.

passwd   Prompt user to enter a password to authenticate configuration
                 requests. The password is not displayed and must correspond to the
                 key configured for use by the NTP server for this purpose. If the
                 password does not correspond to the key configured for use by the
                 NTP server, requests are not successful.

quit   Exit xntpdc.

timeout *milliseconds*

                 Specify a timeout period for responses to server queries. The default is
                 approximately 8000 milliseconds. Because xntpdc retries each query
                 once after a timeout, the total waiting time for a timeout is twice the
                 timeout value set.

Control Message Commands

Query commands send NTP mode 7 packets containing requests for information to the
server. These control message commands are read-only commands in that they make no
modification of the server configuration state.

The following control message commands are supported.

clkbug   Obtain debugging information for a reference clock driver. This
                 information is provided only by some clock drivers.

clock *infoclock peer-address* [...]

                 Obtain and print information concerning a peer clock. The values
                 obtained provide information on the setting of fudge factors and
                 other clock performance information.

dmpeers   Obtain a list of peers for which the server is maintaining state, along
                 with a summary of that state. The peer summary list is identical to the
                 output of the peers command, except for the character in the leftmost
                 column. Characters appear only beside peers that were included in
                 the final stage of the clock selection algorithm. A . indicates that this
                 peer was cast off in the false ticker detection, and a + indicates that
                 the peer made it through. A * denotes the peer with which the server
                 is currently synchronizing.

iostats   Print statistics counters maintained in the input-output module.

kerninfo   Obtain and print kernel phase lock loop operating parameters. This
                 information is available only if the kernel has been specially modified
                 for a precision timekeeping function.

listpeers   Obtain and print a brief list of the peers for which the server is
                 maintaining state. These should include all configured peer
                 associations as well as those peers whose stratum is such that they
                 are considered by the server to be possible future synchronization
                 candidates.

loopinfo [oneline | multiline]

> Print the values of selected loop filter variables. The loop filter is the part of NTP that deals with adjusting the local system clock. The oneline and multiline options specify the format in which this information is printed. multiline is the default. The offset is the last offset given to the loop filter by the packet processing code. The frequency is the frequency error of the local clock in parts-per-million (ppm). The time_const controls the stiffness of the phase lock loop and thus the speed at which it can adapt to oscillator drift. The watchdog timer value is the number of seconds that have elapsed since the last sample offset was given to the loop filter.

memstats   Print statistics counters related to memory allocation code.

monlist [version]

> Obtain and print traffic counts collected and maintained by the monitor facility. You should not normally need to specify the version number.

peers   Obtain a list of peers for which the server is maintaining state, along with a summary of that state.

> The following summary information is included.
>
> - Address of the remote peer.
>
> - Local interface address. If a local address has yet to be determined, it is 0.0.0.0.
>
> - Stratum of the remote peer. A stratum of 16 indicates the remote peer is unsynchronized.
>
> - Polling interval, in seconds.
>
> - Reachability register, in octal.
>
> - Current estimated delay, offset, and dispersion of the peer, in seconds.
>
> - Mode in which the peer entry is operating. The mode is represented by the character in the left margin. A + denotes symmetric active, a – indicates symmetric passive, an = means the remote server is being polled in client mode, a ^ indicates that the server is broadcasting to this address, a ~ denotes that the remote peer is sending broadcasts, and a * marks the peer the server is currently synchronizing to.
>
> - Host. This field can contain a host name, an IP address, a reference clock implementation name with its parameter or REFCLK (implementation number, parameter). On host names no only IP-addresses are displayed.

pstats peer-address [...]

> Show the per-peer statistic counters associated with the specified peers.

reslist   Obtain and print the server's restriction list. Generally, this list is printed in sorted order.

showpeer *peer-address* [...]

       Show a detailed display of the current peer variables for one or more peers. Most of these values are described in the NTP Version 2 specification.

sysinfo   Print a variety of system state variables that are related to the local server. The output from sysinfo is described in NTP Version 3 specification, RFC-1305. All except the last four lines are described in the NTP Version 3 specification, RFC-1305.

       You can set and clear some system flags by the enable and disable configuration commands. These are the auth, bclient, monitor, pll, pps, and stats flags. See the xntpd documentation for the meaning of these flags. The additional kernel_pll and kernel_pps flags are read-only. These flags indicate the synchronization status when the precision time kernel modifications are in use. kernel_pll indicates that the local clock is being disciplined by the kernel; kernel_pps indicates the kernel discipline is provided by the PPS signal. The stability is the residual frequency error remaining after the system frequency correction is applied and is intended for maintenance and debugging. In most architectures, this value initially decreases from as high as 500 ppm to a nominal value in the range .01 to 0.1 ppm. If it remains high for some time after the daemon is started, something may be wrong with the local clock, or the value of the kernel variable tick may be incorrect. The broadcast delay shows the default broadcast delay, as set by the broadcastdelay configuration command. The authdelay shows the default authentication delay, as set by the authdelay configuration command.

sysstats   Print statistics counters maintained in the protocol module.

timerstats   Print statistics counters maintained in the timer/event queue support code.

Runtime Configuration Requests

The server authenticates all requests that change states in the server. The server uses a configured NTP key to accomplish this. The server can also disable this facility by not configuring a key.

You must use the keyid or passwd commands to make the key number and the corresponding key known to xntpdc.

The passwd command prompts users for a password to use as the encryption key. It also prompts automatically for both the key number and password the first time a command is given that would result in an authenticated request to the server. Authentication provides verification that the requester has permission to make such changes. It also gives an extra degree of protection against transmission errors.

Authenticated requests always include a timestamp in the packet data. The timestamp is included in the computation of the authentication code. This timestamp is compared by the server to its receive timestamp. If the timestamps differ by more than a small amount, the request is rejected.

Timestamps are rejected for two reasons. First, simple replay attacks on the server by someone who might be able to overhear traffic on your LAN are much more difficult. Second, it is more difficult to request configuration changes to your server from topologically remote hosts.

While the reconfiguration facility works well with a server on the local host and may work adequately between time-synchronized hosts on the same LAN, it works very poorly for more distant hosts. If you choose reasonable passwords, take care in the distribution and protection of keys, and apply appropriate source address restrictions; the runtime reconfiguration facility should provide an adequate level of security.

The following commands make authenticated requests.

addpeer *peer-address* [*keyid*] [*version*] [*prefer*]

> Add a configured peer association at the given address and operating in symmetric active mode. An existing association with the same peer may be deleted when this command is executed or may simply be converted to conform to the new configuration, as appropriate.
>
> If the optional *keyid* is a non-zero integer, all outgoing packets to the remote server attach an authentication field encrypted with this key. If the *keyid* is 0 or omitted, no authentication is done.
>
> Specify *version* as 1, 2, or 3. The default is 3.
>
> The *prefer* keyword indicates a preferred peer. This keyword is used primarily for clock synchronization, if possible. The preferred peer also determines the validity of the PPS signal. If the preferred peer is suitable for synchronization, so is the PPS signal.

addserver *peer-address* [*keyid*] [*version*] [prefer]

> Identical to the addpeer command, except that the operating mode is client.

addtrap [address [port] [interface]

> Set a trap for asynchronous messages.

authinfo   Return information concerning the authentication module, including known keys and counts of encryptions and decryptions that have been done.

broadcast *peer-address* [*keyid*] [*version*] [*prefer*]

> Identical to the addpeer command, except that the operating mode is broadcast. In this case, a valid key identifier and key are required. The *peer-address* parameter can be the broadcast address of the local network or a multicast group address assigned to NTP. If a multicast address, a multicast-capable kernel is required.

clrtrap [*address* [*port*] [*interface*]

> Clear a trap for asynchronous messages.

delrestrict *address mask* [*ntpport*]

> Delete the matching entry from the restrict list.

fudge *peer-address* [*time1*] [*time2*] [*stratum*] [*refid*]

> Provide a way to set certain data for a reference clock.

readkeys   Purge the current set of authentication keys and obtain a new set by
                  rereading the keys file. The keys file must have been specified in the
                  xntpd configuration file. This option enables you to change
                  encryption keys without restarting the server.

restrict *address mask flag* [*flag*]

                  This command operates in the same way as the restrict
                  configuration file commands of xntpd.

reset   Clear the statistics counters in various modules of the server.

traps   Display the traps set in the server.

trustkey *keyid* [...]
untrustkey *keyid* [...]

                  These commands operate in the same way as the trustedkey and
                  untrustkey configuration file commands of xntpd.

unconfig *peer-address* [...]

                  Remove the configured bit from the specified peers. In many cases
                  this command deletes the peer association. When appropriate,
                  however, the association may persist in an unconfigured mode if the
                  remote peer is willing to continue in this fashion.

unrestrict *address mask flag* [*flag*]

                  Unrestrict the matching entry from the restrict list.

Attributes

See attributes(5) for descriptions of the following attributes.

Attribute Type	Attribute Value
Availability	SUNWntpu

See Also

ntpdate(1M), ntpq(1M), ntptrace(1M), xntpd(1M), rename(2), attributes(5)

Y

---

ypbind — NIS Binder Process

Synopsis

```
/usr/lib/netsvc/yp/ypbind [-broadcast | -ypset | -ypsetme]
```

Description

NIS provides a simple network lookup service consisting of databases and processes. The databases are stored on the system that runs an NIS server process. The programmatic interface to NIS is described in ypclnt(3N). Administrative tools are described in ypinit(1M), ypwhich(1), and ypset(1M). Tools to see the contents of NIS maps are described in ypcat(1), and ypmatch(1).

The ypbind daemon is activated at system startup time from the /etc/init.d/rpc startup script. By default, it is invoked as ypbind -broadcast. ypbind runs on all client machines that are set up to use NIS; see sysidtool(1M).

ypbind remembers information that lets all NIS client processes on a node communicate with some NIS server process. The information ypbind remembers is called a binding—the association of a domain name with an NIS server.

ypbind must run on every machine that has NIS client processes. The NIS server may or may not be running on the same node but must be running somewhere on the network. The NIS server is not supported in SunOS releases any more, but ypbind can communicate with an NIS server, ypserv, on an earlier SunOS release or an NIS+ server in YP-compatibility mode; see rpc.nisd(1M). Refer to the "NOTES" section in ypfiles(4) for implications of being served by such an NIS+ server.

The process of binding is driven by client requests. As a request for an unbound domain comes in, if started with the -broadcast option, ypbind broadcasts on the net, trying to find an NIS server, either a `ypserv` process serving the domain or an `rpc.nisd` process in "YP-compatibility mode" serving an NIS+ directory with the same name as (case sensitive) the domain in the client request. Because the binding is established by broadcasting, there must be at least one NIS server on the net.

If started without the `-broadcast` option, `ypbind` steps through the list of NIS servers that was created by `ypinit -c` for the requested domain. At least one of the hosts in the NIS servers file must contain an NIS server process. All the hosts in the NIS servers file must be listed in `/etc/hosts` along with their IP addresses. Once a domain is bound by `ypbind`, that same binding is given to every client process on the node. You can query `ypbind` on a local or remote node for the binding of a particular domain by using the `ypwhich(1)` command.

If `ypbind` is unable to speak to the NIS server process it is bound to, it marks the domain as unbound, tells the client process that the domain is unbound, and tries to bind the domain once again. Requests received for an unbound domain wait until the requested domain is bound. In general, a bound domain is marked as unbound when the node running the NIS server crashes or becomes overloaded. In such a case, `ypbind` tries to bind to another NIS server by using the process described above.

`ypbind` also accepts requests to set its binding for a particular domain. The request is usually generated by the `ypset(1M)` command. For `ypset` to work, `ypbind` must have been invoked with either the `-ypset` or `-ypsetme` option.

Note — `ypbind` supports multiple domains. The `ypbind` process can maintain bindings to several domains and their servers; the default domain is the one specified by the `domainname(1M)` command at startup time.

The `-broadcast` option works only on the UDP transport. It is insecure because it trusts any machine on the net that responds to the broadcast request and poses itself as an NIS server.

The Network Information Service (NIS) was formerly known as Sun Yellow Pages (YP). The functionality of the two remains the same; only the name has changed. The name Yellow Pages is a registered trademark in the United Kingdom of British Telecommunications plc, and may not be used without permission.

Options

`-broadcast`	Send a broadcast datagram, using UDP/IP, that requests the information needed to bind to a specific NIS server. This option is analogous to `ypbind` with no options in earlier Sun releases and is recommended for ease of use.
`-ypset`	Enable users from any remote machine to change the binding with the `ypset` command. By default, no one can change the binding. This option is insecure.
`-ypsetme`	Enable only root on the local machine to change the binding to a desired server with the `ypset` command. `ypbind` can verify the caller is indeed a root user by accepting such requests only on the loopback transport. By default, no external process can change the binding.

Files

/var/yp/binding/*ypdomain*/ypservers
> List of NIS servers for the domain.

/etc/hosts   Hosts database.

Attributes

See attributes(5) for descriptions of the following attributes.

Attribute Type	Attribute Value
Availability	SUNWnisu

See Also

ypcat(1),ypmatch(1),ypwhich(1),ifconfig(1M),rpc.nisd(1M),ypinit(1M),
ypset(1M), ypclnt(3N), hosts(4), ypfiles(4), attributes(5)

---

ypinit — Set Up NIS Client

Synopsis

/usr/sbin/ypinit [-c][-m][-s *master-server*]

Description

You can use ypinit to set up an NIS client system. You must be superuser to run this command. You do not need to use ypinit at all if ypbind(1M) is started with the -broadcast option (ypbind is, by default, invoked with this option from the startup script /etc/init.d/rpc).

Normally, ypinit is run only once after the system is installed. You can run it whenever a new NIS server is added to the network or an existing one is decommissioned.

ypinit prompts for a list of NIS servers to bind the client to; this list should be ordered from the closest to the farthest server. Each of these NIS servers must be listed in /etc/hosts along with its IP address. ypinit stores the list in file /var/yp/binding/domain/ypservers. This file is used by ypbind when run without the -broadcast option.

> **Note** — The Network Information Service (NIS) was formerly known as Sun Yellow Pages (YP). The functionality of the two remains the same; only the name has changed. The name Yellow Pages is a registered trademark in the United Kingdom of British Telecommunications plc, and may not be used without permission.

Options

`-c`	Set up a `ypclient` system.
`-m`	Build a master `ypserver` database.

`-s master-server`

Slave database. `master-server` must be the same master configured in the YP maps and returned by the `ypwhich -m` command.

Files

`/var/yp/binding/ypdomain/ypservers`

List of NIS servers for the domain.

`/etc/hosts`   Hosts database.

Attributes

See `attributes`(5) for descriptions of the following attributes.

Attribute Type	Attribute Value
Availability	SUNWnisu

See Also

`ypbind(1M)`, `sysinfo(2)`, `hosts(4)`, `attributes(5)`

Bugs

`ypinit` sets up the list of NIS servers only for the current domain on the system when it is run, that is, the domain returned by the `SI_SRPC_DOMAIN` command to `sysinfo`(2). Care should be taken to ensure that this is the same as the desired domain for NIS client processes.

---

ypmake — Rebuild NIS Database

Synopsis

`cd /var/yp ; make [map]`

Description

The file called `Makefile` in `/var/yp` is used by `make`(1) to build the Network Information Service (NIS) database. With no arguments, `make` creates dbm databases for any NIS maps that are out-of-date and then executes `yppush`(1M) to notify slave databases that there has been a change.

If you supply `map` on the command line, `make` updates only that map. Typing `make passwd` creates and runs `yppush` on the password database (assuming it is out-of-date). Likewise, make hosts and make networks create and run yppush on the host and network files, /etc/hosts and /etc/networks.

make uses three special variables.

- DIR specifies the directory of the source files. The default is /etc.
- NOPUSH, when non-null inhibits doing a yppush of the new database files. The default is the null string.
- DOM constructs a domain other than the master's default domain.

Refer to ypfiles(4) and ypserv(1M) for an overview of the NIS service.

Note — The NIS makefile is used only when the ypserv(1M) server is run to provide NIS services. If these are being provided by the NIS+ server running in NIS compatibility mode (see rpc.nisd(1M)), this makefile is not relevant. See ypfiles(4) for more details.

The Network Information Service (NIS) was formerly known as Sun Yellow Pages (YP). The functionality of the two remains the same; only the name has changed. The name Yellow Pages is a registered trademark in the United Kingdom of British Telecommunications plc, and may not be used without permission.

Files

/var/yp	Directory containing NIS configuration files.
/etc/hosts	System hosts file.
/etc/networks	

System networks file.

See Also

make(1), nis+(1), makedbm(1M), rpc.nisd(1M), ypbind(1M), yppush(1M), ypserv(1M), ypclnt(3N), ypfiles(4)

---

yppasswdd — Server for Modifying NIS Password File

Synopsis

/usr/lib/netsvc/yp/rpc.yppasswdd [-D *directory*] [-nogecos] [-noshell]
   [-nopw] [-m *argument1 argument2...*]
/usr/lib/netsvc/yp/rpc.yppasswdd [*passwordfile* [adjunctfile]]
   -nogecos] [-noshell] [-nopw] [-m *argument1 argument2...*]

Description

See rpc.yppasswdd(1M).

yppoll — Return Current Version of an NIS Map at an NIS Server Host

Synopsis

/usr/sbin/yppoll [-d *ypdomain*] [-h *host*] *mapname*

Description

The yppoll command asks a ypserv() process what the order number is and which host is the master NIS server for the named map.

> **Note —** The Network Information Service (NIS) was formerly known as Sun Yellow Pages (YP). The functionality of the two remains the same; only the name has changed. The name Yellow Pages is a registered trademark in the United Kingdom of British Telecommunications plc, and may not be used without permission.

Options

-d *ypdomain*   Use *ypdomain* instead of the default domain.

-h *host*   Ask the ypserv process at *host* about the map parameters. If you do not specify *host*, use the NIS server for the local host. That is, the default host is the one returned by ypwhich(1).

Attributes

See attributes(5) for descriptions of the following attributes.

Attribute Type	Attribute Value
Availability	SUNWnisu

See Also

ypwhich(1), ypfiles(4), attributes(5)

yppush — Force Propagation of a Changed NIS Map

Synopsis

New!

/usr/lib/netsvc/yp/yppush [-v] [-h *host*] [-d *domain*] [-p #*parallel-xfrs*] *mapname*

Description

The yppush command forces propagation of an NIS map that has changed. yppush copies a new version of a Network Information Service (NIS) map from the master NIS server to the slave NIS servers. yppush is normally run only on the master NIS server by the Makefile in /var/yp after the master databases are changed. It first constructs a list of NIS server hosts by reading the NIS ypservers map within the domain. Keys within the ypservers map are the ASCII names of the machines on which the NIS servers run.

A "transfer map" request is sent to the NIS server at each host, along with the information needed by the transfer agent (the program that actually moves the map) to call back the yppush. When the attempt has completed (successfully or not) and the transfer agent has sent yppush a status message, the results may be printed to standard output. Messages are also printed when a transfer is not possible; for instance, when the request message is undeliverable or when the timeout period on responses has expired.

Refer to ypfiles(4) and ypserv(1M) for an overview of the NIS service.

Note — In the Solaris 8 release, the path to the yppush command has changed from /usr/etc/yp to /usr/lib/netsvc/yp.

New!

The Network Information Service (NIS) was formerly known as Sun Yellow Pages (YP). The functionality of the two remains the same; only the name has changed. The name Yellow Pages is a registered trademark in the United Kingdom of British Telecommunications plc, and may not be used without permission.

Options

-d domain   Specify a domain.

-h host   Propagate only to the named host.

-p #parallel-xfrs

               Allow the specified number of map transfers to occur in parallel.

-v   Prints messages when each server is called and for each response. If you omit this option, print only error messages.

Files

/var/yp   Directory where NIS configuration files reside.

/var/yp/ypdomain/ypservers.{dir, pag}

               Map containing list of NIS servers to bind to when running in server mode.

Attributes

See attributes(5) for descriptions of the following attributes.

Attribute Type	Attribute Value
Availability	SUNWypu

See Also

ypserv(1M), ypxfr(1M), ypfiles(4), attributes(5)

Bugs

In the current implementation (version 2 NIS protocol), the transfer agent is ypxfr(1M), which is started by the ypserv program. If yppush detects that it is speaking to a version 1 NIS protocol server, it uses the older protocol, sending a version 1 YPPROC_GET request, and issues a message to that effect. Unfortunately, there is no way of knowing if or when the map transfer is performed for version 1 servers. yppush prints a message saying that an "old style" message has been sent. The system administrator should later check to see that the transfer has actually taken place.

ypserv, ypxfrd — NIS Server and Binder Processes

Synopsis

/usr/lib/netsvc/yp/ypserv [-dv]
/usr/lib/netsvc/yp/ypxfrd

Description

The Network Information Service (NIS) provides a simple network lookup service consisting of databases and processes. The databases are ndbm files in a directory tree rooted at /var/yp. See dbm_clearerr(3). These files are described in ypfiles(4). The processes are /usr/lib/netsvc/yp/ypserv, the NIS database lookup server, and /usr/lib/netsvc/yp/ypbind, the NIS binder. The programmatic interface to the NIS service is described in ypclnt(3N). Administrative tools are described in yppoll(1M), yppush(1M), ypset(1M), ypxfr(1M), and ypwhich(1). Tools to see the contents of NIS maps are described in ypcat(1) and ypmatch(1). Database generation and maintenance tools are described in ypinit(1M), ypmake(1M), and makedbm(1M).

The ypserv daemon is typically activated at system startup from /etc/init.d/rpc. Alternatively, you can start NIS services from the command line as root by using ypstart(1M). ypserv runs only on NIS server machines with a complete NIS database. You can halt all NIS services with the ypstop(1M) command.

The ypxfrd daemon transfers entire NIS maps in an efficient manner. For systems that use this daemon, map transfers are 10 to 100 times faster, depending on the map. To use this daemon, run ypxfrd on the master server. See /usr/lib/netsvc/yp/ypstart. ypxfr tries to use ypxfrd first; if that fails, it prints a warning and then uses the older transfer method.

The ypserv daemon's primary function is to look up information in its local database of NIS maps.

The operations performed by ypserv are defined for the implementor by the YP Protocol Specification, and for the programmer by the header file rpcsvc/yp_prot.h.

Communication to and from ypserv is by means of RPC calls. Lookup functions are described in ypclnt(3N) and are supplied as C-callable functions in the libnsl(4) library. Four lookup functions are performed on a specified map within some NIS domain: yp_match(3N), yp_first(3N), yp_next(3N), and yp_all(3N). The yp_match operation takes a key and returns the associated value.

The yp_first operation returns the first key-value pair from the map, and yp_next can be used to enumerate the remainder. yp_all ships the entire map to the requester as the response to a single RPC request.

A number of special keys in the DBM files can alter the way ypserv operates. The following keys are of interest.

YP_INTERDOMAIN

>Forward host lookups that cannot be satisfied by the DBM files to a DNS server.

YP_SECURE   Answer only questions coming from clients on reserved ports.

YP_MULTI_HOSTNAME

>Return the closest client host name in the form YP_MULTI_HOSTNAME addr1,...,addrN.

Two other functions, yporder(3N) and yp_master(3N), supply information about the map instead of map entries. In fact, both order number and master name exist in the map as key-value pairs, but the server does not return either of them through the normal lookup functions. If you examine the map with makedbm(1M), however, they are visible. Other functions are used within the NIS service subsystem itself and are not of general interest to NIS clients. They include do_you_serve_this_domain?, transfer_map, and reinitialize_internal_state.

>**Note** — ypserv supports multiple domains. The ypserv process determines the domains it serves by looking for directories of the same name in the directory /var/yp. It replies to all broadcasts requesting yp service for that domain.
>
>The Network Information Service (NIS) was formerly known as Sun Yellow Pages (YP). The functionality of the two remains the same; only the name has changed. The name Yellow Pages is a registered trademark in the United Kingdom of British Telecommunications plc, and may not be used without permission.

Options

ypserv -d   Instruct the NIS service to go to the DNS (Domain Name Service) for more host information. This action requires the existence of a correct /etc/resolv.conf file pointing at a machine running in.named(1M). This option turns on DNS forwarding regardless of whether the YP_INTERDOMAIN flag is set in the hosts maps. See makedbm(1M). In the absence of an /etc/resolv.conf file, complain but ignore the -d option.

-v   Print diagnostic messages to standard error.

Files

/var/yp/securenets

> Define the hosts and networks that are granted access to information in the served domain; both ypserv and ypxfrd read this file at startup.

/etc/init.d/rpc

> Startup file that starts up basic RPC services and NIS by calling ypstart(1M). If the /var/yp/ypserv.log file exists when ypserv starts up, write log information to it when error conditions arise. Use the file /var/yp/binding/domainname/ypservers to list the NIS server hosts that ypbind binds to.

Attributes

See attributes(5) for descriptions of the following attributes.

Attribute Type	Attribute Value
Availability	SUNWypu

See Also

ypcat(1), ypmatch(1), ypwhich(1), domainname(1M), in.named(1M), makedbm(1M), ypbind(1M), ypinit(1M), ypmake(1M), yppoll(1M), yppush(1M), ypset(1M), ypstart(1M), ypstop(1M), ypxfr(1M), dbm_clearerr(3), ypclnt(3N), libnsl(4), securenets(4), ypfiles(4), attributes(5)
Network Interfaces Programmer's Guide
System Administration Guide, Volume I

ypset — Point ypbind at a Particular Server

Synopsis

/usr/sbin/ypset [-d *ypdomain*] [-h *host*] *server*

Description

Use the ypset command to bind a client node that is not on a broadcast net or that is on a broadcast net that is not running an NIS server host. ypset also is useful for debugging NIS client applications, for example, where an NIS map exists only at a single NIS server host.

To run ypset, you must initiate ypbind with the -ypset or -ypsetme options. See ypbind(1M). ypset tells ypbind to get NIS services for the specified ypdomain from the ypserv process running on a server. An NIS client may not discover that the server is down or is not running ypserv until it tries to get a binding for the domain. At this point, the binding set by ypset is tested by ypbind. If the binding is invalid, ypbind tries to rebind for the same domain.

In cases where several hosts on the local net are supplying NIS services, it is possible for ypbind to rebind to another host even while you try to find out if the ypset operation succeeded. For example, you can type the following two commands, which can be confusing.

```
example% ypset host1
example% ypwhich host2
```

The NIS subsystems try to load-balance among the available NIS servers. When host1 does not respond to ypbind because it is not running ypserv (or is overloaded), host2, running ypserv, gets the binding.

ypset tries to bind over a connectionless transport. The NIS library call, yp_all(), uses connection-oriented transport and derives the NIS server's address based on the connectionless address supplied by ypset.

Refer to ypfiles(4) for an overview of the NIS nameservice.

Note — The Network Information Service (NIS) was formerly known as Sun Yellow Pages (YP). The functionality of the two remains the same; only the name has changed. The name Yellow Pages is a registered trademark in the United Kingdom of British Telecommunications plc, and may not be used without permission.

Options

-d *ypdomain*   Use *ypdomain*, instead of the default domain.

-h *host*   Set ypbind's binding on *host* instead of locally. You must specify *host* as a name.

Operands

server   The NIS server to bind to. Specify *server* as a name or an IP address. *server* works only if the node has a current valid binding for the domain in question and ypbind has been set to enable the use of ypset. In most cases, you should specify *server* as an IP address.

Attributes

See attributes(5) for descriptions of the following attributes.

Attribute Type	Attribute Value
Availability	SUNWnisu

See Also

ypwhich(1), ypfiles(4), attributes(5)

ypstart, ypstop — Start and Stop NIS Services

Synopsis

```
/usr/lib/netsvc/yp/ypstart
/usr/lib/netsvc/yp/ypstop
```

Description

Use the ypstart command to start the Network Information Service (NIS). Once the host has been configured with the ypinit(1M) command, ypstart automatically determines the NIS status of the machine and starts the appropriate daemons.

Use the ypstop command to stop the Network Information Service (NIS).

Note — The Network Information Service (NIS) was formerly known as Sun Yellow Pages (YP). The functionality of the two remains the same; only the name has changed. The name Yellow Pages is a registered trademark in the United Kingdom of British Telecommunications plc, and may not be used without permission.

Attributes

See attributes(5) for descriptions of the following attributes.

Attribute Type	Attribute Value
Availability	SUNWypu

See Also

```
ypinit(1M), attributes(5)
```
System Administration Guide, Volume I
Network Interfaces Programmer's Guide

ypupdated — Server for Changing NIS Information

Synopsis

```
/usr/lib/netsvc/yp/rpc.ypupdated [-is]
```

Description

See rpc.yupdated(1M).

ypxfr, ypxfr_1perday, ypxfr_1perhour, ypxfr_2perday —
Transfer NIS Map from an NIS Server to Host

Synopsis

```
/usr/lib/netsvc/yp/ypxfr [-c][-f][-C tid prog server][-d ypdomain]
    [-h host][-s ypdomain] mapname
```

Description

Use the `ypxfr` command to move an NIS map in the default domain for the local host to the local host by making use of normal NIS services. `ypxfr` creates a temporary map in the directory `/var/yp/ypdomain` (this directory must already exist; `ypdomain` is the default domain for the local host), fills it by enumerating the map's entries, fetches the map parameters (master and order number), and loads them. It then deletes any old versions of the map and moves the temporary map to the real name.

If run interactively, `ypxfr` writes its output to the terminal. However, if you start it without a controlling terminal and if the log file `/var/yp/ypxfr.log` exists, then `ypxfr` appends all its output to that file. Because `ypxfr` is most often run from the privileged user's `crontab` file or by `ypserv`, you can use the log file to retain a record of what was tried and what resulted.

For consistency between servers, `ypxfr` should be run periodically for every map in the NIS database. Different maps change at different rates: a map may not change for months at a time and may, therefore, be checked only once a day. Some maps can change several times per day. In such a case, you may want to check hourly for updates. You can use a `crontab`(1) entry to perform periodic updates automatically. Instead of having a separate `crontab` entry for each map, you can group commands to update several maps in a shell script. Examples (mnemonically named) `ypxfr_1perday`, `ypxfr_2perday`, and `ypxfr_1perhour`. are provided in the `/usr/sbin/yp` directory. You can use them as reasonable first cuts.

Refer to `ypfiles`(4) for an overview of the NIS nameservice.

> **Note** — The Network Information Service (NIS) was formerly known as Sun Yellow Pages (YP). The functionality of the two remains the same; only the name has changed. The name Yellow Pages is a registered trademark in the United Kingdom of British Telecommunications plc, and may not be used without permission.

Options

`-c`   Do not send a `Clear current map` request to the local `ypserv` process. Use this option if `ypserv` is not running locally at the time you are running `ypxfr`. Otherwise, `ypxfr` complains that it cannot talk to the local `ypserv` and the transfer fails.

`-f`   Force the transfer even if the version at the master is not more recent than the local version.

-C *tid prog server*

> Use this option only for ypserv to specify that ypxfr should call back a yppush process at the host server, registered as program number *prog* and waiting for a response to transaction *tid*.

-d *ypdomain*   Specify a domain other than the default domain.

-h *host*   Get the map from *host* regardless of what the map says the master is. If you do not specify *host*, ask the NIS service for the name of the master and try to get the map from there. You must specify *host* as a name.

-s *ypdomain*   Specify a source domain from which to transfer a map that should be the same across domains.

Files

/var/yp/ypxfr.log

> Log file.

/usr/lib/netsvc/yp/ypxfr_1perday

> Script to run one transfer per day, for use with cron(1M).

/usr/lib/netsvc/yp/ypxfr_2perday

> Script to run two transfers per day, for use with cron(1M).

/usr/lib/netsvc/yp/ypxfr_1perhour

> Script for hourly transfers of volatile maps.

/var/yp/*ypdomain*

> NIS domain.

/usr/spool/cron/crontabs/root

> Privileged user's crontab file.

Attributes

See attributes(5) for descriptions of the following attributes.

ypxfr

Attribute Type	Attribute Value
Availability	SUNWnisu

ypxfr_1perday, ypxfr_1perhour, yxpfr_2perday

Attribute Type	Attribute Value
Availability	SUNWypu

See Also

crontab(1), cron(1M), yppush(1M), ypserv(1M), ypfiles(4), attributes(5)

ypxfrd — NIS Server and Binder Processes

Synopsis

/usr/lib/netsvc/yp/ypxfrd

Description

See ypserv(1M).

Z

zdump — Time-Zone Dumper

Synopsis

```
/usr/sbin/zdump [-v][-c cutoffyear][zonename...]
```

Description

Use the zdump command to print the current time for each time zone (*zonename*) listed on the command line.

Specifying an invalid time zone (*zonename*) to zdump does not return an error; instead, zdump uses GMT. This behavior is consistent with the behavior of the library calls; zdump reflects the same behavior of the time routines in libc. See ctime(3C) and mktime(3C).

Options

-v   Display the entire contents of the time-zone database file for *zonename*. Print the time at the lowest possible time value, the time one day after the lowest possible time value, the times both one second before and exactly at each time at which the rules for computing local time change, the time at the highest possible time value, and the time at one day less than the highest possible time value. See mktime(3C) and ctime(3C) for information regarding time value (*time_t*). Each line of output ends with isdst=1 if the given time is Daylight Saving Time or isdst=0, otherwise.

-c *cutoffyear*

Cut off the verbose output near the start of the year *cutoffyear*.

Operands

zonename   Specify the name of the time-zone database file as it is listed in the
/usr/share/lib/zoneinfo directory.

Examples

The following example shows the time-zone value for the Australia time zone.

```
paperbark% zdump Australia
Australia  Thu Jan  6 01:27:36 2000 Australia
paperbark% zdump -v Australia
Australia  Thu Jan  6 01:27:45 2000 UTC = Thu Jan  6 01:27:45 2000
   Australia isdst=0
Australia  Fri Dec 13 20:45:52 1901 UTC = Fri Dec 13 20:45:52 1901
   Australia isdst=0
Australia  Sat Dec 14 20:45:52 1901 UTC = Sat Dec 14 20:45:52 1901
   Australia isdst=0
Australia  Tue Jan 19 03:14:07 2038 UTC = Tue Jan 19 03:14:07 2038
   Australia isdst=0
Australia  Mon Jan 18 03:14:07 2038 UTC = Mon Jan 18 03:14:07 2038
   Australia isdst=0
paperbark%
```

The following example shows all of the values for the Australia time zone by use of
the -v option.

```
paperbark% zdump -v Australia
paperbark% zdump -v Australia
Australia  Thu Jan  6 01:27:45 2000 UTC = Thu Jan  6 01:27:45 2000
   Australia isdst=0
Australia  Fri Dec 13 20:45:52 1901 UTC = Fri Dec 13 20:45:52 1901
   Australia isdst=0
Australia  Sat Dec 14 20:45:52 1901 UTC = Sat Dec 14 20:45:52 1901
   Australia isdst=0
Australia  Tue Jan 19 03:14:07 2038 UTC = Tue Jan 19 03:14:07 2038
   Australia isdst=0
Australia  Mon Jan 18 03:14:07 2038 UTC = Mon Jan 18 03:14:07 2038
   Australia isdst=0
paperbark%
```

Note — The zdump command takes a few seconds to calculate the complete
list of values.

Exit Status

0   Successful completion.

1   An error occurred.

Files

/usr/share/lib/zoneinfo

> Standard zone information directory.

Attributes

See attributes(5) for descriptions of the following attributes.

Attribute Type	Attribute Value
Availability	SUNWcsu

See Also

zic(1M), ctime(3C), mktime(3C), attributes(5), environ(5)

zic — Time-Zone Compiler

Synopsis

/usr/sbin/zic [-s][-v][-1 *localtime*][-p *posixrules*][-d *directory*]
[-y *yearistype*][*filename*...]

Description

Use the zic command to add a new time zone to a system. zic reads text from the file(s) named on the command line and creates the time-conversion information files specified in this input. If a file name is -, the standard input is read.

Input lines are made up of fields. Fields are separated by any number of white-space characters. Leading and trailing white-space on input lines is ignored. A pound sign (#) indicates a comment and extends to the end of the line. If you use white-space characters and pound signs as part of a file, you can enclose them within double quotes (" "). Any line that is blank (after comment stripping) is ignored. Nonblank lines are expected to be a rule, zone, or link line.

Note — For areas with more than two types of local time, you may need to use local standard time in the *at* field of the earliest transition time's rule to ensure that the earliest transition time recorded in the compiled file is correct.

Rules

A rule line has the following form.

```
Rule name from to type in on at save letter/s
```

For example,

```
Rule USA 1969 1973 - Apr lastSun 2:00 1:00 D
```

name	The (arbitrary) name of the set of rules this rule is part of.
from	The first year in which the rule applies. The word `minimum` (or an abbreviation) means the minimum year with a representable time value. The word `maximum` (or an abbreviation) means the maximum year with a representable time value.
to	The final year in which the rule applies. In addition to `minimum` and `maximum` (as above), you can use the word `only` (or an abbreviation) to repeat the value of the *from* field.
type	The type of year in which the rule applies. *type* can have the following values.

-	The rule applies in all years between *from* and *to* inclusive.
`uspres`	The rule applies in U.S. presidential election years.
`nonpres`	The rule applies in years other than U.S. presidential election years.
`even`	The rule applies to even-numbered years.
`odd`	The rule applies to odd-numbered years.

If *type* is something else, then `zic` tries to execute the command `yearistype year type` to check the type of a year: an exit status of 0 means that the year is of the given type; an exit status of 1 means that the year is not of the given type. The `yearistype` command is not currently provided in the Solaris environment.

in	The month in which the rule takes effect. You can abbreviate month names.
on	The day on which the rule takes effect. The following forms are recognized.

`5`	The fifth day of the month.
`lastSun`	The last Sunday in the month.
`lastMon`	The last Monday in the month.
`Sun>=8`	First Sunday on or after the eighth.
`Sun<=25`	Last Sunday on or before the 25th.

You can abbreviate or spell out in full names of days of the week. Note that you cannot include spaces within the *on* field.

at
: The time of day at which the rule takes effect. The following forms are recognized.

2	Time in hours.
2:00	Time in hours and minutes.
15:00	24-hour format time (for times after noon).
1:28:14	Time in hours, minutes, and seconds.

You can follow any of these forms by the letter w for local time to indicate wall clock time, s for local standard time, or u, g, or z for universal time. In the absence of an indicator, assume wall clock time.

save
: The amount of time to be added to local standard time when the rule is in effect. This field has the same format as the at field without the w and s suffixes.

letter/S
: The "variable part" (for example, the S or D in EST or EDT of time-zone abbreviations to be used when this rule is in effect. If this field is -, the variable part is null.

Zone

A zone line has the following form.

```
Zone name gmtoff rules/save format [until]
```

For example,

```
Zone Australia/SouthWest 9:30 CST 1992 Mar 15 12:00 8:30 Aus CST
```

name
: The name of the time zone. This is the name used in creating the time-conversion information file for the zone.

gmtoff
: The amount of time to add to GMT to get standard time in this zone. This field has the same format as the at and save fields of rule lines; begin the field with a minus sign if time must be subtracted from GMT.

rules/save
: The name of the rule(s) that apply in the time zone or, alternately, an amount of time to add to local standard time. If this field is -, then standard time always applies in the time zone.

format
: The format for time-zone abbreviations in this time zone. The pair of characters %s is used to show where the variable part of the time-zone abbreviation goes.

until
: The time at which the GMT offset or the rule(s) change for a location. It is specified as a year, a month, a day, and a time of day. The time of day has the same format as the at field of rule lines. If you specify this value, generate the time-zone information from the given GMT offset and rule change until the time specified.

The next line must be a continuation line; this line has the same form as a zone line, except omit the Zone string and the name because the continuation line puts information starting at the time specified as the *until* field in the previous line in the file used by the previous line. Continuation lines can contain an *until* field, just as zone lines do, indicating that the next line is a further continuation.

Link

A link line has the following form.

```
Link link-from link-to
```

For example,

```
Link US/Eastern EST5EDT
```

The *link-from* field should appear as the *name* field in some zone line; the *link-to* field is used as an alternate name for that zone.

Except for continuation lines, you can put lines in any order in the input.

Options

-d *directory*   Create time-conversion information files in the *directory* directory instead of in the standard /usr/share/lib/zoneinfo directory.

-l *localtime*   Use the specified time zone as local time *localtime*. zic acts as if the file contains a link line of the form Link *localtime* localtime.

-p *posixrules*

Use the rules of the *posixrules* time zone when handling POSIX-format time-zone environment variables. zic acts as if the input contained a link line of the form Link *posixrules* posixrules.

ctime(3C) and mktime(3C) do not use this option in the Solaris environment.

-s   Limit time values stored in output files to values that are the same whether they are taken to be signed or unsigned. You can use this option to generate System V Verification Suite-compatible files.

-v   Complain if a year that appears in a data file is outside the range of years representable by system time values (0:00:00 a.m. GMT, January 1, 1970, to 3:14:07 a.m. GMT, January 19, 2038).

-y *yearistype*

Use the command *yearistype* instead of yearistype when checking year types (see "Rules" on page 1262).

Operands

filename   A file containing input lines that specify the time-conversion information files to be created. If you specify *filename* as -, read the standard input.

Examples

To add a new time-zone file to a system, choose an existing time-zone file for the country that does not have the correct time representation. For example, the `northamerica` file (as of this writing) does not reflect that British Columbia does not change time. The following example creates a new time-zone file called `canada_bc` and adds the British Columbia time to it.

1. Copy the `/usr/share/lib/src/northamerica` file to `canada_bc`.
2. As root, edit the `canada_bc` file, putting the following information pertinent to Canada with the addition of the time in British Columbia, where `Canada/Pacific-bc` specifies the zone name, `-8:00` specifies the time from GMT time, `-` specifies that the zone does not follow any time rule, and `PST` specifies the zone format.

```
Zone     Canada/Pacific-bc     8:00     -     PST
```

If an existing Rules definition exists that will serve the purpose, use it. If not, create a new rule line as documented in "Rules" on page 1262. Compile the file with the `zic` compiler, as shown in the following example. It's best to use the `-d` *directory* option to create the new data file in a separate directory instead of overwriting the current time-zone files.

```
# zic -d /tmp/zonefiles canada_bc
#
```

Solaris has a strange naming convention for some of its time-zone files. For example, if you lived in China and wanted to use an offset time-zone file, you would use `GMT-8`, when, in fact, China is always 8 hours ahead of GMT. The following example creates a time-zone file named `CHINA` that is always 8 hours ahead of GMT and is referred to as `CHST` (or China standard time).

```
# echo `Zone CHINA 8:00 - CHST` | zic -
#
```

This command creates a `/usr/share/lib/zoneinfo/CHINA` file. You could then use it by setting the `TZ` environment variable to `CHST` in your `/etc/TIMEZONE` file.

Note — CHINA is used only as an example. This example does not imply that China needs a time-zone file.

Files

`/usr/share/lib/zoneinfo`

Standard directory used for created files.

Attributes

See `attributes`(5) for descriptions of the following attributes.

Attribute Type	Attribute Value
Availability	SUNWcsu

See Also

time(1), ctime(3C), mktime(3C), attributes(5)

SUBJECT INDEX